Al 863 1686
Tio MAR

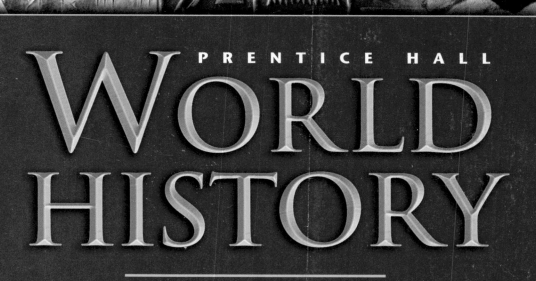

PRENTICE HALL

WORLD HISTORY

CONNECTIONS TO TODAY
VOLUME ONE

Elisabeth Gaynor Ellis
Anthony Esler

With Senior Consultant
Burton F. Beers

PEARSON

Prentice
Hall

Upper Saddle River, New Jersey
Glenview, Illinois
Needham, Massachusetts

Acknowledgments and Illustration Credits begin on page 625.

ISBN 0-13-062805-0

2 3 4 5 6 7 8 9 10   07 06 05 04 03

Authors

Elisabeth Gaynor Ellis

Elisabeth Gaynor Ellis is a historian and writer. She is a co-author of *World Cultures: A Global Mosaic*. Ms. Ellis, a former social studies teacher and school administrator, has taught world cultures, Russian studies, and European history. She holds a B.A. from Smith College and an M.A. and M.S. from Columbia University.

Anthony Esler

Anthony Esler is Professor of History at the College of William and Mary. He received his Ph.D. from Duke University and received Fulbright Fellowships to study at the University of London and to travel to Ivory Coast and Tanzania. Dr. Esler's books include *The Human Venture: A World History* and *The Western World: A History*, as well as several historical novels.

Senior Consultant

Burton F. Beers

Burton F. Beers is a retired Professor of History from North Carolina State University. He taught European history, Asian history, and American history. Dr. Beers has published numerous articles in historical journals and several books, including *The Far East: A History of Western Impacts and Eastern Responses*, with Paul H. Clyde, and *World History: Patterns of Civilization*.

PROGRAM REVIEWERS

Stone Age cave painting

Coffin of an Egyptian king

Start Smart

Before you start your study of World History, check out these special pages.

Chinese soldier

Greek vase

Olmec stone head

Viking ship carving

Byzantine Emperor Justinian

Islamic law court

Benin bronze

Japanese shrine

Italian artist
Leonardo da Vinci

Ocean-going ship

Catherine the Great,
empress of Russia

American statesman Benjamin Franklin

Early steam engine

South American liberator Simón Bolívar

A LOOK AHEAD/REFERENCE SECTION

A Look Ahead: The Modern Era

Fall of the Berlin Wall

Armistice celebration

Assessing Your Skills

Synthesizing Information

Gather clues from different sources to understand key ideas.

Port of Marseille, 1700s

Comparing Viewpoints

Explore issues by analyzing opinions across time and place.

Puritan punishment

Analyzing Primary Sources

Gain insights by examining documents and photographs.

West African griot

Exploring the Human Drama

Humanities Link

Experience great literature and arts from around the world.

Hagia Sophia

Disaster!

See how major disasters affected people's lives.

Black Death

You Are There . . .

Travel back in time to become an eye- witness to history.

Stone god

Virtual Field Trip

Start an Internet activity by visiting sites around the world.

San Martín and O'Higgins cross the Andes, 1817

Why Study History?

See how history is relevant to your life today.

King Sejong (Korea)

Compass and astrolabe

SPECIAL FEATURES

Genghiz Khan

Dodo

Replica of an ancient ship

Connections to Today

Explore links between historical events and your world today.

Kente cloth

Global Connections

See connections between events in different parts of the world.

Lighthouse at Alexandria

Spanish coin

PRIMARY SOURCES

Primary Source

Relive history through eyewitness accounts, literature, and documents.

The Adventures of Roland

This passage, located near the end of the epic the Song of Roland, *describes Roland's final moments:*

"The Count Roland, beneath a pine
   he sits . . .
 Remembering so many [different]
   things:
 So many lands where he went
   conquering,
 And France the [sweet], the
   heroes of his kin,
 And Charlemagne, his lord who
   nourished him.
 Nor can we help but weep and
   sigh at this. . . .
 His right-hand glove, to God he
   offers it
 Saint Gabriel from's hand hath
   taken it . . .
 He joins his hand: and so is life
   finish'd
 God sent him down His angel
   cherubim . . .
 So the count's soul they bear to
   Paradis[e]."

—*Song of Roland*

The Spirits Are Good

The poems in the Book of Songs *offer a rare look into the everyday lives of average people in ancient China:*

"The spirits are good,
 They will give you many blessings.
 The common people are contented,
 For daily they have their drink and food.
 The thronging herd, the many clans.
 All side with you in deeds of power.

 To be like the moon advancing to its full,
 Like the sun climbing the sky,
 Like the everlastingness of the southern
   hills,
 Without failing or falling,
 Like the pine-tree, the cypress in their
   [foliage]
 All these blessings may you receive!"

—*Shih Ching (Book of Songs)*

▶ Primary Sources and Literature

Sumerian sculpture

Aztec gold ornament

PRIMARY SOURCES: In Text

(continued)

PRIMARY SOURCES

(continued)

"Go, wondrous creature! mount where Science guides;
Go, measure earth, weigh air, and state the tides;
Instruct the planets in what orbs to run,
Correct old Time, and regulate the sun."
—Alexander Pope, *Essay on Man*

Middle Eastern market

MAPS

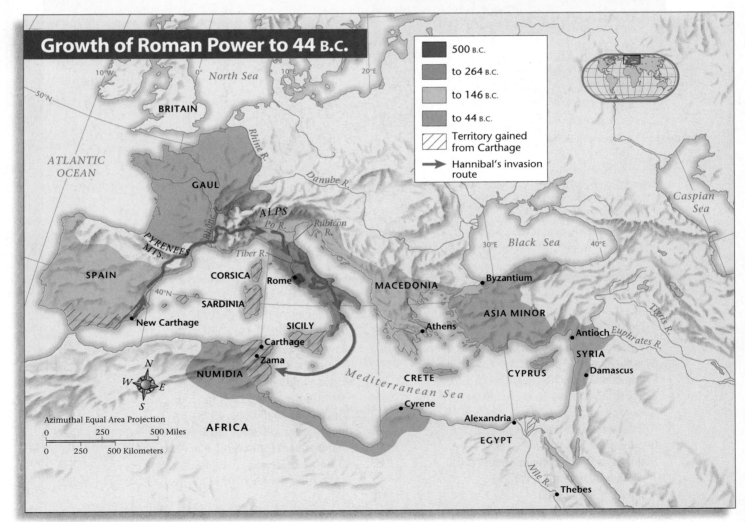

Growth of Roman Power to 44 B.C.

MAPS

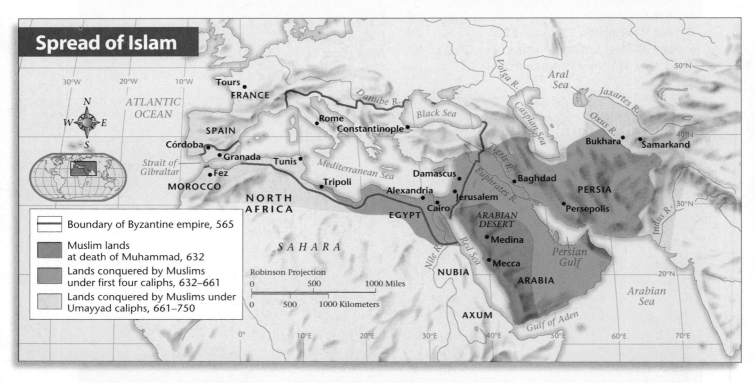

REFERENCE SECTION MAPS

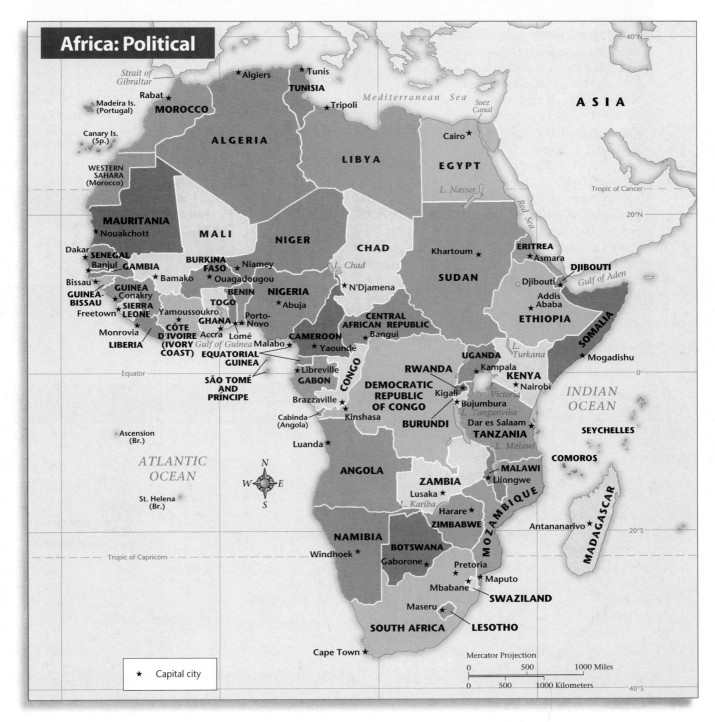

Africa: Political

★ Capital city

xxiii

CHARTS AND GRAPHS

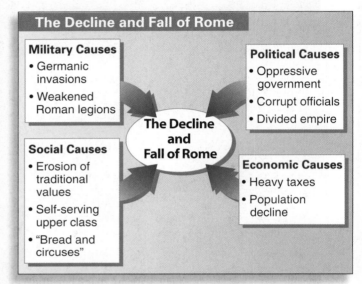

The Decline and Fall of Rome

Military Causes
- Germanic invasions
- Weakened Roman legions

Political Causes
- Oppressive government
- Corrupt officials
- Divided empire

The Decline and Fall of Rome

Social Causes
- Erosion of traditional values
- Self-serving upper class
- "Bread and circuses"

Economic Causes
- Heavy taxes
- Population decline

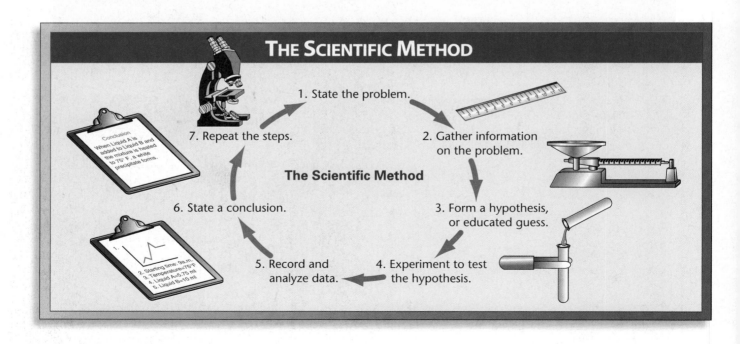

THE SCIENTIFIC METHOD

The Scientific Method

1. State the problem.
2. Gather information on the problem.
3. Form a hypothesis, or educated guess.
4. Experiment to test the hypothesis.
5. Record and analyze data.
6. State a conclusion.
7. Repeat the steps.

CHARTS AND GRAPHS/SKILLS HANDBOOK

CAUSE AND EFFECT

FACT FINDER

UNIT TIME LINES

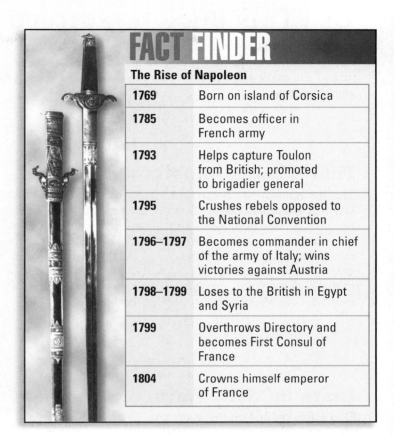

FACT FINDER

The Rise of Napoleon

1769	Born on island of Corsica
1785	Becomes officer in French army
1793	Helps capture Toulon from British; promoted to brigadier general
1795	Crushes rebels opposed to the National Convention
1796–1797	Becomes commander in chief of the army of Italy; wins victories against Austria
1798–1799	Loses to the British in Egypt and Syria
1799	Overthrows Directory and becomes First Consul of France
1804	Crowns himself emperor of France

SKILLS HANDBOOK

Latin American family

Use This Book to Succeed in World History

You can use this book as a tool to master world history. Spend a few minutes to become familiar with the structure of the book and see how you can unlock the secrets of world history.

Find What Is Important

This book makes it easy to figure out what you really need to know about world history. Each section starts with Reading Focus questions that point out the most important ideas in that section. As you read, notice that the content is organized into several parts with red headings. As you read the paragraphs under the red headings, you can learn the answers to the Reading Focus questions. Later, you will find that the Section Assessment reviews each of these important ideas.

Reading Focus

■ How did Napoleon rise to power?

■ How were revolutionary reforms changed under Napoleon?

■ How did Napoleon build an empire in Europe?

Vocabul

plebiscite
annex
blockade

Napoleon's Rise to Power

Napoleon Bonaparte was born in Corsica, a French-ruled island in the Mediterranean. His family were minor nobles, but had little money. At age nine, he was sent to France to be trained for a military career. When the revolution broke out, he was an ambitious 20-year-old lieutenant, eager to make a name for himself.

Napoleon favored the Jacobins and republican rule. However, he found the conflicting ideas and personalities of the revolution confusing. He wrote his brother in 1793: "Since one must take sides, one might as well choose the side that is victorious, the side which devastates, loots, and

Learn in Many Ways

Don't depend just on the main text. Discover world history through all parts of this book—from primary sources to pictures, from charts to activities. Preview each chapter by looking at photographs, a map, and a time line. See connections between main ideas and illustrations. Be transported back through time by reading primary sources. Read stories about real people who have changed the world. Witness grave disasters and relive great moments. Research exciting topics. Act out human dramas. Use all of your senses to explore world history.

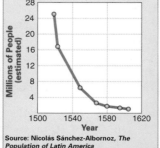

Primary Source

The Genius of Leonardo
Italian artist and architect Giorgio Vasari is best known for his engaging book of biographies of Italian artists including Leonardo da Vinci (pictured above):

"Leonardo practiced not one art but all of those that are dependent upon design, and he had great talent for geometry besides being very musical, playing the lute with great ability and being excellent in the art of improvisation. . . . In entertaining, Leonardo was so pleasant that he won everyone's ... ough he may well be ... e owned nothing and to ... ed little, he always kept ... s well as horses."

Giorgio Vasari, *Lives of the ... t Eminent Italian Painters, ... Sculptors, and Architects*

Assessment

Source What ...etails did Vasari include ...ardo da Vinci?

EXPLORING HUMAN DRAMA **Disaster!**

CYCLONE RIPS THROUGH CALCUTTA

The storm surge—walls of water pushed by powerful winds—is the deadliest part of a cyclone. Waves start small, but as the ...

Violent winds and rain struck Calcutta. Breaking waves caused a deafening roar. Then, a monstrous 40-foot wave crashed down on the shore. According to some reports, as many as 300,000 people died and 20,000 boats sank.

Native American Population of Central Mexico

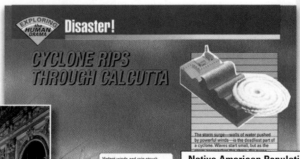

Source: Nicolás Sánchez-Albornoz, *The Population of Latin America*

Palace of Versailles

Portfolio Assessment

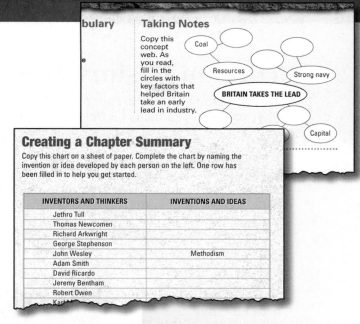

Organize Your Reading

Does so much world history content seem overwhelming? This book has ways to help you organize it. Use the Taking Notes exercise at the beginning of each section to help you take notes as you read. Then, at the end of the chapter, complete the Creating a Chapter Summary graphic organizer. This will help you capture the main ideas of the chapter in a visual way.

Develop Your Skills

Success in world history requires you to master social studies skills. Learn these skills in the Skills Handbook. Practice them by answering questions on maps, pictures, primary sources, charts, and graphs. In each chapter, you can also find an Assessing Your Skills feature, which focuses on analyzing primary sources, synthesizing information, or comparing viewpoints. Then, review your skills by completing the Skills Assessment activities at the end of every chapter.

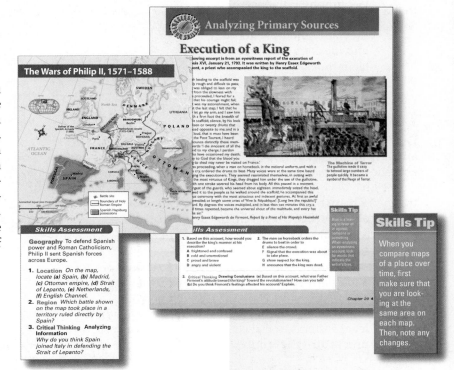

Prepare for Tests

This book will also help you prepare to take tests. To practice for standardized tests, answer the questions at the end of every section and chapter. Pay special attention to the critical-thinking questions. For portfolio assessment, complete activities in each Section Assessment and the portfolio assessment activities in Exploring the Human Drama features. Go to the **phschool.com** Web site to take a practice test for each chapter.

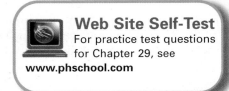

Web Site Self-Test
For practice test questions for Chapter 29, see
www.phschool.com

Human History Is Fascinating and Complex

To make world history easier for you to grasp, this textbook emphasizes nine themes. They can help you focus on the key features of each society and event you read about.

Theme: Continuity and Change

History is the story of change. Some changes can be as quick as a revolution. Others, such as the spread of democratic ideas or the shifting roles of men and women in many nations, may take decades or even centuries. Although change is always taking place, enduring traditions and concerns link people across time and space.

Theme: Geography and History

Geography influences where people settle, how they live, and how goods and ideas travel. Since ancient times, people have dug irrigation canals to water farmlands, and control of waterways or mountain passes has determined the outcome of wars. Today, environmental issues often stir heated debate.

Theme: Political and Social Systems

Monarchs, presidents, dictators, tribal councils—each society has a form of government to ensure order and guard against outside threats. Societies around the world have also developed other important institutions to ensure order, including legal systems, social classes, and the most basic unit of all—the family.

Theme: Religions and Value Systems

Today, as in the past, religion exerts a powerful impact on the world. Belief in one God guided the histories of Jews, Christians, and Muslims. Buddhism and Hinduism shaped many Asian cultures. Nonreligious values, such as Greek ideals of beauty and individuality, have also had a wide influence.

The first moon landing, 1969

Theme: Economics and Technology

Who controls vital resources? How are goods exchanged? What work do people do and how are they paid for that work? Economic questions such as these are often closely linked to technology. From Stone Age farming tools to the printing press to the steam engine to the computer, technology has transformed the world again and again.

Theme: Diversity

The vast diversity of the world's cultures is reflected in many ways, including language, ethnic background, customs, beliefs, and clothing. Such diversity has enriched the human experience. Yet, at the same time, cultural or ethnic differences often lead to bitter conflict.

Theme: Global Interaction

Different parts of the world may interact in many ways—through migration, trade, warfare, or the exchange of ideas. When people traveled by oxcart or sailing ship, interaction was a slow process. Today, communications networks can link all parts of the globe instantly.

Theme: Impact of the Individual

Everyone who ever lived is part of the human story. Yet some people have such an impact on events that we remember them long after they die. For good or ill, individuals such as Confucius, Christopher Columbus, Marie Curie, Stalin, and Mohandas Gandhi have had a lasting influence on our world.

Theme: Art and Literature

Since the days of Stone Age cave paintings, people have created art and literature to express their lives and values. In the Middle Ages, Europeans built soaring cathedrals to the glory of God. Today, novelists and filmmakers from Nigeria to Brazil vividly depict the challenges of modern life.

Are you ready to think thematically? On the next three pages, you will see pictures relating to different themes in world history. Look at the pictures and read the captions. Then, choose *three* of the nine book themes. For each of these themes, skim through the textbook and find a picture or feature that you think reflects that theme. Write a sentence explaining each of your choices.

Theme: Continuity and Change The Chinese system of writing began taking shape nearly 4,000 years ago, when priests used animal bones and tortoise shells to predict the future. Although it has changed greatly over time, this common language continues to link Chinese people across a vast area.

Theme: Geography and History Scarcity of fresh water has influenced settlement patterns, economic activities, and even political events in much of the Middle East. Here, crews assemble pipelines to carry water supplies through the Arabian Desert.

Theme: Political and Social Systems Our modern system of democracy developed largely in England. This painting by William Hogarth shows campaigners trying to win votes for their candidates outside a British tavern in the 1700s.

Theme: Religions and Value Systems According to the Bible, Moses brought the Ten Commandments from God to the Israelites. The Commandments—including "Honor your father and mother" and "You shall not murder"—have provided moral guidance to billions of people.

Theme: Economics and Technology In 1913, American automaker Henry Ford introduced the assembly line. This system allowed Ford to produce automobiles faster and more cheaply and to sell them at a lower price.

Theme: Diversity South Asia has long been home to a wide mix of people, as this ancient Indian painting shows. Today, India has 16 official languages and hundreds of regional languages.

Theme: Global Interaction For more than 200 years, Japan isolated itself from the rest of the world. Then, in 1853, an American expedition demanded that Japan open its ports to foreign trade. Japan quickly became a major world power.

Theme: Impact of the Individual Each country honors its own national heroes. Joan of Arc (left) led a French army to victory against the English. Simón Bolívar (far right) helped liberate several South American nations from Spanish rule. Nelson Mandela (near right) led a long fight against apartheid in South Africa.

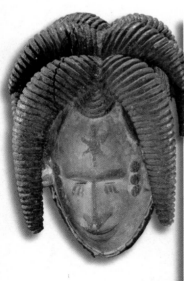

Theme: Art and Literature Throughout Africa, skilled craft-workers created elaborate masks like the one shown here (far left) for use in religious and social ceremonies. In the early 1900s, the style of African masks influenced the works of Spanish painter Pablo Picasso (near left).

Explore World History Through the Internet

As you read this book, you will notice many opportunities to make world history come alive by using the Internet. By accessing a Web site designed specifically for Prentice Hall's *World History: Connections to Today* program, you can visit amazing places, develop exciting projects, and even review for tests.

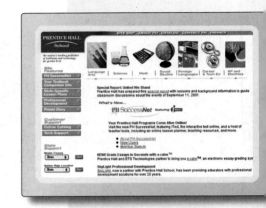

Visit the Prentice Hall World History Web Site

Follow these easy steps to find the Web site that accompanies your book:
- Go to **www.phschool.com.**
- Click on the button that says **"Social Studies."**
- Under **"PH@School,"** open "Program" and click on **"World History: Connections to Today."** Find the edition of the book you use, and select the student version.
- Select a specific chapter.

Take Virtual Field Trips

Now you can take field trips around the world and across the ages through cyberspace. In every chapter, you will find a Virtual Field Trip feature that highlights a specially selected site on the Internet. Link there via the **www.phschool.com** Web site to begin your exploration.

> **Virtual Field Trip**
> www.phschool.com
>
> **Dunaskin Open Air Museum**
> **Ayrshire, Scotland**
>
> To find more information about iron production during the Industrial Revolution, use the Internet address above to link to the Dunaskin Open Air Museum.
>
> **Ironworks**
> This painting, *Forging the Anchor*, is by William James Muler. It shows workers laboring to make an anchor of iron.
>
> **Theme: Art and Literature**
> **How would you describe the artist's opinion of factories?**

Learn Through Internet Activities

Throughout the entire program, you will find activities that are designed to use the strength of the Internet to supplement this textbook. Look for the Internet icon on Take It to the Net section and chapter review activities and Exploring the Human Drama portfolio activities.

Stay Up-to-Date With Current Events Online

For the latest developments in world history, go to the **www.phschool.com** Web site. Use the daily current events and content updates there to keep your learning up-to-date.

> **Take It to the NET**
> To learn about recent developments in Africa, visit the World History section of **www.phschool.com.**

Prepare for Tests With Web Site Self-Tests

For each chapter, you can take a practice test online at the **www.phschool.com** Web site. Completing this test will give you a quick review of the material and help you identify which areas you need to study further. You can also use the self-tests to prepare for unit tests, midterms, and finals.

CONTENTS

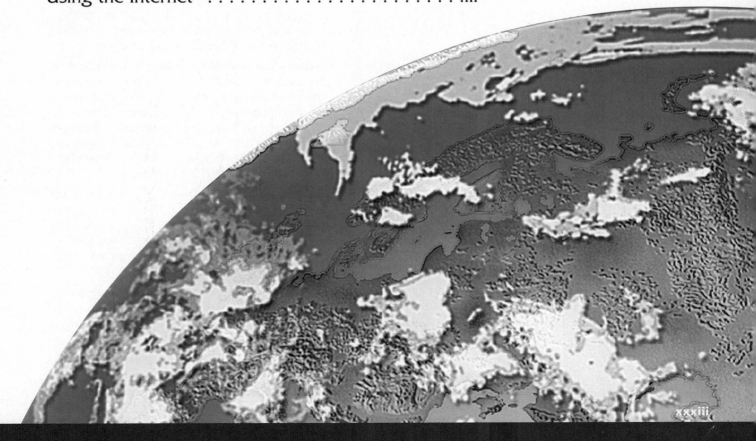

Learning From Maps

How Will I Use This Skill? Maps are not just for textbooks. They can help you find your way on a bus or in a car. They can help you understand about events in other parts of the world. You can even use them to learn about tomorrow's weather.

Learning the Skill

To learn from a map, you have to look closely at the map's features. Use the map and the information below to learn about the various parts of a map.

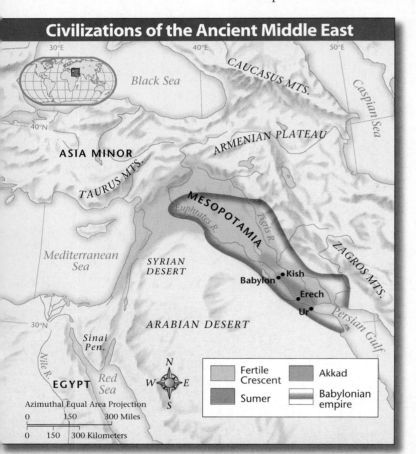

Civilizations of the Ancient Middle East

Azimuthal Equal Area Projection

| Fertile Crescent | Akkad |
| Sumer | Babylonian empire |

1. **Read the title** The title gives a clue to the main topic of the map. **What is the title of this map?**

2. **Use the scale** You can use the scale of miles and kilometers to calculate the distance between two points. A short distance on a map represents a larger distance on the Earth. For example, one inch may represent 100 miles. **How far is it from Ur to Kish?**

3. **Observe the locator map** The locator map shows which part of the whole Earth is shown on this map. **How does the locator indicate the area shown on the main map?**

4. **Check the compass** The compass shows which direction is north on the map. You can also find the other directions—south, east, and west. Some compasses also show intermediate directions, for example northeast, which is the direction between north and east. **In which direction would you travel to get from the Sinai Peninsula to the Caspian Sea?**

5. **Notice the latitude and longitude lines and numbers** Latitude lines indicate the distance north or south of the equator. Longitude lines show distance east or west from the Prime Meridian, an imaginary line that runs through Greenwich, England. Latitude and longitude are measured in degrees (°). **What desert is located around 30° N latitude?**

6. **Identify bodies of water and other physical features** Maps often show oceans, rivers, mountains, and other physical features. Sometimes, color or shading is used to identify different features. Water, for example, is usually blue. Mountains are indicated by gray shading called relief. **Name three bodies of water shown on this map. Which mountain range is farther north—the Taurus Mountains or the Zagros Mountains?**

7. **Use the key** The key explains colors or symbols used on the map. Here, purple shows Sumer. **How is the Babylonian empire shown?**

8. **Identify political areas** Political areas, such as countries, empires, or cities, can be shown with borders, colors, or other symbols. They may be labeled on the map or in the key. **Describe the location of Mesopotamia.**

Practicing the Skill

Practice learning from maps by recalling the steps you just learned and by answering the following questions based on the map below.

1. What is the title of the map?
2. About how far would you travel to get from Beirut to Riyadh?
3. Study the locator map. What region of Africa is part of the Middle East? What region of Asia is part of the Middle East?
4. In what direction would you travel to get from Ankara to Tehran?
5. Use latitude and longitude to tell the location of the Strait of Hormuz.
6. **(a)** What are three important rivers in the Middle East? **(b)** What body of water separates Egypt from Saudi Arabia?
7. **(a)** A desalinization plant removes the salt from salt water to make it suitable for drinking and watering crops. How are desalinization plants shown on the map? **(b)** Where are most of them located?
8. **(a)** Through what countries does the Tigris River flow? **(b)** Through what countries does the Euphrates River flow? **(c)** Why do you think leaders from these countries meet to discuss water resources?

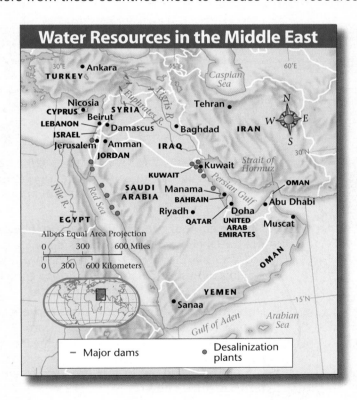

Water Resources in the Middle East

Applying the Skill

Choose a map in your textbook. Based on the skill lesson on these pages, write a series of questions that test understanding of how to read and use the map. Trade with a partner and answer each other's questions. Then, check your partner's answers.

Understanding Charts and Graphs

How Will I Use This Skill? A graph shows numerical facts in picture form. Bar graphs and line graphs allow you to compare things at different times or in different places. You often see this type of graph in newspapers, where it might show a change such as the increase in student enrollment at your school or the average temperature over the last month. Circle graphs, or pie charts, show how a whole thing is divided into parts. The segments in a circle graph represent percentages of the whole, helping you better compare the parts.

Learning the Skill

To interpret a graph, you have to look closely at its features. Use the graphs and the information below to learn how to use various types of graphs.

Bar graph

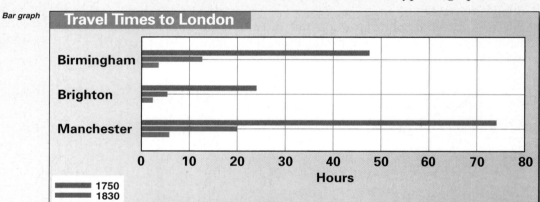

Travel Times to London

Source: E. J. Hobsbaum, *Industry and Empire*

1750
1830
1850

Circle graph

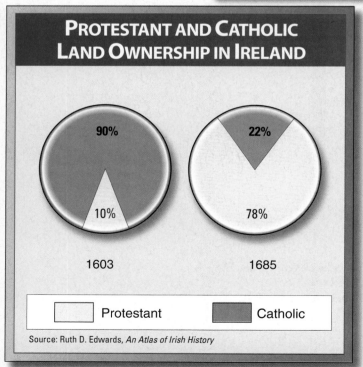

PROTESTANT AND CATHOLIC LAND OWNERSHIP IN IRELAND

Source: Ruth D. Edwards, *An Atlas of Irish History*

1. **Read the title** The title of any kind of graph tells you the main topic of the graph. **What is the title of the bar graph?**

2. **On line and bar graphs, identify the labels** Notice the labels on the bottom and side of the graph. For example, on the bar graph, the bottom, or horizontal axis, refers to hours. **What does the side, or vertical axis, of the bar graph refer to?**

3. **Determine what the bars or lines represent** Graphs use labels or a key to make clearer what the graph is about. On the line graph, for example, the red line represents the amount of steel produced in Germany. **On the bar graph, how are travel times in 1830 shown?**

4. **On circle graphs, identify the parts into which the circle is divided** A circle graph may have labels on the parts to tell you how the circle is divided. Sometimes, however, the graph includes a key to explain the use of color on the graph. For example, on the circle graph, Protestant land ownership in Ireland is shown in beige. **What color is used to show Catholic land ownership?**

5. **Read the graph** Use the title, labels, and colors to understand the meaning of the graph. You can learn from the circle graph that in 1603 Protestants owned 10 percent of the land in Ireland. **What percentage did Protestants own in 1685?**

6. **Interpret the graph** Often, graphs show trends, or tendencies in a given direction. The line graph shows steel production from 1880 to 1910 in three different countries. **(a) Which country had the greatest rise in steel production during this time? (b) Do you think this rise benefited other segments of the nation's economy? Why or why not?**

Line graph

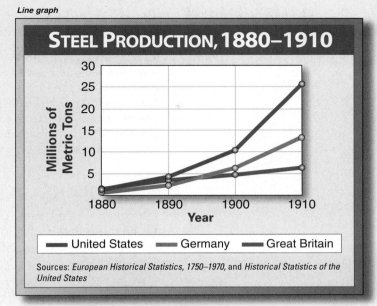

STEEL PRODUCTION, 1880–1910

Sources: *European Historical Statistics, 1750–1970*, and *Historical Statistics of the United States*

Practicing the Skill

Interpret the graph at right by recalling the steps you just learned and by answering the questions that follow.

1. What is the topic of the graph? How can you tell?
2. What percentage of enslaved Africans was shipped to Portuguese Brazil? To Europe and Asia?
3. To what other parts of the world were enslaved Africans shipped?
4. Can you learn from this graph how many slaves were shipped to North America in 1875? Why or why not?
5. Can you tell from this graph what percentage of enslaved Africans was shipped to the Caribbean? Why or why not?
6. Could this information be presented on a line graph instead of a circle graph? Explain.

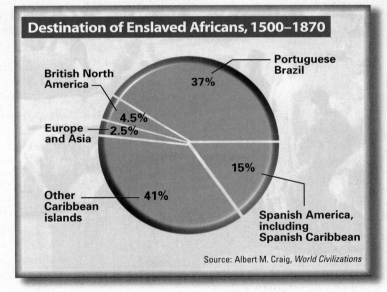

Source: Albert M. Craig, *World Civilizations*

Applying the Skill

Conduct a simple poll among your classmates about a topic related to school, such as the number of hours per day each student spends doing homework or the material used by each student to cover his or her textbooks. Then, create an appropriate graph to display the results of your poll. Be prepared to explain your graph to the class.

Interpreting Visuals

How Will I Use This Skill? **In today's fast-paced "information age," we are bombarded with visuals of all kinds. Television, film, the Internet, and print media all carry images that are designed to convey information or influence attitudes. People use drawings, art, photographs, and computer graphics to communicate facts and ideas. Today, literacy means not only the ability to read and write but also the ability to understand and interpret visuals.**

Learning the Skill

Use this black-and-white photograph and the following steps to learn some of the methods involved in interpreting visuals.

In the 1950s, children in Europe and other parts of the world were taught they could survive a nuclear attack. This 1954 image was used to advertise a bogus "radiation-resistant" blanket.

1. **Identify the content of the visual** The content of a visual includes all the individual images that make up the larger visual. Be careful to look at both the foreground and background. Note which images seem to have the main importance in the visual. **What are the three main images in this photograph?**

2. **Note the emotional elements** An artist or photographer often tries to convey attitudes and emotions in a visual. **What feelings are conveyed by the boy's position and facial expression?**

3. **Read any text that accompanies the visual** A visual often has a title, caption, or other accompanying text that helps you to interpret it. **When was this photograph produced?**

4. **Determine the purpose of the visual** A visual may be intended to provide information, to persuade, or to entertain. A good starting point for determining the purpose of a visual is to consider the individual or group that produced it. **Who produced this visual? What do you think was its purpose?**

5. **Learn more about the visual or its creator** Sometimes, it is helpful to do some research to better understand the visual or its creator. If you did research on this photograph, you would learn that in the 1950s, the United States and the Soviet Union were engaged in a dangerous rivalry, including a race to build weapons. This rivalry was called the Cold War. Many people feared that a terrible nuclear conflict might erupt at any time. **Does this information refute or confirm your understanding of the picture? Explain.**

6. **React to the visual** React to the visual based on its apparent or intended purpose. If the visual was meant to inform, decide how well it conveys information to you. If it was meant to persuade, consider how effective it might be at influencing the attitudes of those who view it. If it was meant to be entertaining, react to it in those terms. **Do you think this photograph was an effective commercial advertisement that had an influence on people in the 1950s? Why or why not?**

Practicing the Skill

Interpret the visual below by recalling the steps you have just learned and by answering the questions that follow.

Honduran Street Scene
In this colorful folk art painting by Jorge Ferman, one can learn much about the culture of the Central American country of Honduras.

1. **(a)** What are some of the main images in the painting? **(b)** What images provide the background?
2. Do you think the painter portrays village life in Honduras in a favorable or unfavorable way? Explain.
3. How does the painting suggest that Honduras has a tropical climate?
4. What do you think is the purpose of this painting?
5. If you did some research about rural life in Honduras, you would learn that more than 50 percent of the population works in agriculture. Common crops among small farmers are corn, beans, and squash. On large plantations, people grow such cash crops as coffee and cotton. Based on this information, does the painting seem to convey an accurate or inaccurate vision of life in a Honduran village? Explain.
6. **(a)** What emotions does the painting cause you to feel? **(b)** Based on the painting, would you like to visit Honduras? Why or why not?

Applying the Skill

Select a visual in a current newspaper or magazine that appears in print or online. Print out, cut out, or reproduce a copy of the visual and any accompanying text. Use the steps that you have learned in this skill lesson to write an interpretation of the visual.

Analyzing Primary Sources

How Will I Use This Skill? Primary sources include official documents, as well as firsthand accounts of events. They may also include visual evidence, such as a news photograph, a painting by an eyewitness, or a political cartoon. They are a valuable source of information about the past. Historians often use primary sources to prepare their narratives, which are secondary sources. You use primary sources when you watch an interview on television or listen to a friend tell you about something that happened at school.

Learning the Skill

Use the excerpt, the cartoon, and the steps that follow to learn about analyzing primary sources.

The following excerpt comes from *The Satires,* a series of poems written by Juvenal about life in Rome in the first century A.D. In this excerpt, Juvenal recounts a friend's reasons for moving away from Rome.

66 Since at Rome there is no place for honest pursuits, no profit to be got by honest toil—my fortune is less today than it was yesterday. . . .

What shall I do at Rome? I cannot lie; if a book is bad, I cannot praise it and beg a copy. I know not the motions of the stars . . . no one shall be a thief by my cooperation. . . .

Who, nowadays, is beloved except the confidant of crime? 99
—Juvenal, *The Satires* (tr. Lewis Evans)

This cartoon by Arcadio Esquivel from Costa Rica shows the world being bulldozed. Costa Rica has been more successful than many other countries in balancing the need for development with the need to preserve the environment.

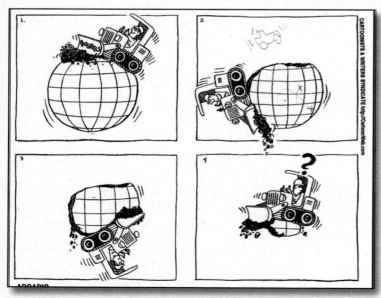

CARTOONISTS & WRITERS SYNDICATE http://CartoonWeb.com

1. **Read the headnote or caption** Often, primary sources are presented with a short introduction about the writer or the document. The headnote with the excerpt above, for example, explains that the excerpt was written by Juvenal. **According to the headnote, when was this primary source written? Why was it written?**

2. **Read the primary source** As you read the primary source, identify unfamiliar words and try to gather the general meaning of the source. **In this excerpt, what is the writer's main point?**

3. **Identify facts and opinions in the written source** A fact can be proved true. An opinion, on the other hand, cannot be proved. Often, you can identify opinion statements by introductory words like "I think" or by strongly positive or negative words like "gorgeous" or "despicable." Another clue is a statement that exaggerates. **Identify an opinion statement in the excerpt.**

4. **Read the source line** You can often get additional information about an excerpt by reading the source line. In this case, for example, you can learn that the excerpt is a translation. **Who translated Juvenal's words?**

5. **Identify bias and evaluate reliability** You have seen that primary sources include both facts and opinions. They may also reveal the bias of the author. These factors affect the reliability of the source. Other factors that affect reliability are the time that may have passed between an event and the author's writing about it and the author's own earlier experiences. Suppose you knew that Juvenal had served in the army, hoping to make his way into government service, but in the end, had not received the promotion he hoped for. **How might that fact affect Juvenal's reliability as a commentator on Roman society?**

6. **Learn from political cartoons** Political cartoons can also be primary sources. They reflect the observations of one artist about events of the time. They often use symbols to represent other things. **(a) In the cartoon on the opposite page, what does the bulldozer represent?** Cartoons also use exaggeration to make their point. **(b) What is exaggerated in this cartoon? (c) Explain the point of view expressed in the cartoon.**

Practicing the Skill

Analyze the primary source below by recalling the steps you have just learned and by answering the questions that follow.

In 1947, India gained independence after hundreds of years as a colony of Great Britain. India's new leader, Jawaharlal Nehru, had worked to bring about independence. He addressed the nation on its first independence day.

> 66 We are a free and sovereign people today, and we have rid ourselves of the burden of the past. We look at the world with clear and friendly eyes, and at the future with faith and confidence. . . .
>
> Our first and immediate objective must be to put an end to all internal strife and violence, which disfigure and degrade us and injure the cause of freedom. They come in the way of consideration of the great economic problems of the masses of the people which so urgently demand attention.
>
> . . . Production today is the first priority, and every attempt to hamper or lessen production is injuring the nation, and more especially harmful to our laboring masses. . . . 99
> —Jawaharlal Nehru, Independence Day speech, August 15, 1947

1. **(a)** Who wrote this document? **(b)** Under what circumstances?
2. **(a)** Identify one fact in Nehru's speech. **(b)** Identify one opinion statement.
3. **(a)** What was Nehru's purpose in giving this speech? **(b)** Do you think his purpose affected the words he spoke? **(c)** Do you think he achieved his purpose?
4. **(a)** Is the speech a reliable source for understanding Nehru's goal for his country? **(b)** Why or why not?

Applying the Skill

Use Internet or library sources to find a primary source that interests you. Remember that it can be either written or visual. Follow the steps outlined on these pages and then write a paragraph analyzing the primary source.

Comparing Viewpoints

How Will I Use This Skill? When people describe an idea or event, they usually provide some facts and their own personal viewpoints. A person's viewpoint is shaped by subjective influences such as feelings, prejudices, and past experiences. You often encounter divergent viewpoints, as when two of your friends describe the same event differently, when two politicians recommend different policies, or when two newspapers analyze a news event in different ways. By analyzing and comparing viewpoints, you will be able to better understand issues and form your own viewpoint.

Learning the Skill

Throughout history, people have tried to educate their children. But they have not always agreed on the goals of education. Read the excerpts below and compare the two viewpoints by using the steps that follow.

Henri Christophe, king of Haiti, set up schools for outstanding students of his nation. He believed these schools would help Haiti maintain the freedom it had won fewer than 15 years earlier. In 1817, he wrote:

❝ To form good citizens we must educate our children. From our national institutions will proceed a race of men capable of defending by their knowledge and talents those rights so long denied by tyrants. It is from these sources that light will be diffused among the whole mass of the population. ❞

—King Henri Christophe, 1817

Leo Tolstoy, a Russian aristocrat of the late 1800s, became a famous novelist as a young man. Later, he turned his attention to social issues. In 1902, he wrote:

❝ You can take a puppy and feed him, and teach him to carry something, and enjoy the sight of him; but it is not enough to rear and bring up a man, and teach him Greek; he has to be taught to live, that is, to take less from others, and give more. ❞

—Leo Tolstoy, 1902

---

1. **Identify the authors** It is important always to identify the writer or speaker. **Who are the authors of these two documents, and where and when did they live?**

2. **Make sure that you understand the arguments being made.** Try to identify the main idea and supporting arguments made by each author. **(a) According to Christophe, what is the goal of education? (b) Why does Tolstoy compare raising a puppy to teaching a person Greek?**

3. **Consider the authors' backgrounds** A person's attitudes, beliefs, and past experiences affect that person's viewpoint. By knowing the author's background, you can make judgments about the viewpoint. **How might the backgrounds of Christophe and Tolstoy affect their viewpoints?**

4. **Find common information** If two viewpoints are on the same topic, there should be some points that they agree on. Often, these will be basic facts. **According to both viewpoints, what is true about education?**

5. **Find opinions** Differentiate the opinions from the facts. The opinions represent the author's viewpoint. **Name two words used by Christophe that signal opinions.**

6. **Evaluate the validity of each viewpoint** Evaluate viewpoints by recalling the authors' background and determining if their opinions are based on facts or reasonable arguments. **Are the viewpoints of Christophe and Tolstoy based on reasonable arguments? Explain.**

7. **Draw conclusions** After following the above steps, you are ready to draw conclusions about the viewpoints and the topic that they deal with. **(a) Do you think Tolstoy's view was typical of Russian aristocrats? (b) Why might the king of Haiti have been so concerned about maintaining the freedom of his nation?**

Practicing the Skill

The document and poster below reflect different viewpoints on industry and labor in the Soviet Union during the early 1900s. Compare the two viewpoints by answering the following questions:

1. Who are the authors of the letter?
2. Based on both documents, what was one goal of the Soviet Union?
3. **(a)** According to the poster, what was the general attitude of Soviet workers? **(b)** According to the letter, were most people in the camp treated justly? Explain.
4. Which viewpoint seems more trustworthy to you? Explain.
5. What methods did the Soviet Union use to increase economic production?

This letter protesting prison conditions was written to government leaders of the Soviet Union by former prisoners.

66 We are prisoners who are returning from the Solovetsky concentration camp because of our poor health. We went there full of energy and good health, and now we are returning as invalids, broken and crippled emotionally and physically. . . . It is difficult for a human being even to imagine such terror, tyranny, violence, and lawlessness. . . . The Unified State Political Directorate [OGPU] without oversight and due process sends workers and peasants there who are by and large innocent. . . .

They die a slow and painful death . . . from hunger, cold, and backbreaking 14–16 hour days. . . . We . . . are asking you to improve the pathetic, tortured existence of those who are there who languish under the yoke of the OGPU's tyranny. . . . To this we subscribe: G. Zheleznov, Vinogradov, F. Belinskii. 99

—Letter to the Presidium of the Central Executive Committee of the Communist Party, December 14, 1926

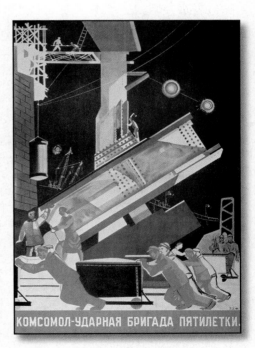

КОМСОМОЛ-УДАРНАЯ БРИГАДА ПЯТИЛЕТКИ.

Poster produced by the Soviet government, 1930s.

Applying the Skill

Use the Internet or library resources to find two documents expressing different viewpoints on a major turning point in world history. Some examples are the fall of the Roman empire, the Crusades, the Reformation, and World War I. Make copies of the documents. Then, use the steps that you have learned to write a paragraph comparing the viewpoints.

Synthesizing Information

How Will I Use This Skill? If you want to know whether a movie is worth seeing, you can read a review, watch a television commercial, view a film clip on the Internet, and talk to people who have seen the movie. You can combine the different pieces of evidence to develop a more complete impression of the movie. This process of combining pieces of evidence is called synthesizing. Today and in the future, synthesizing information will help you to become better informed and to make better decisions.

Learning the Skill

Study the three different pieces of information on this page about some developments in the 1400s and early 1500s. Then, follow the steps to learn how to synthesize information.

> **Improved Technology** Several improvements in technology helped Europeans conquer the vast oceans of the world. **Cartographers**, or mapmakers, created more accurate maps and sea charts. European sailors also learned to use the **astrolabe**, an instrument developed by the ancient Greeks and perfected by the Arabs, to determine their latitude at sea.
>
> Along with more reliable navigational tools, Europeans designed larger and better ships. The Portuguese developed the **caravel**, which combined the square sails of European ships with Arab lateen, or triangular, sails. Caravels also adapted the sternpost rudder and numerous masts of Chinese ships. The new rigging made it easier to sail across or even into the wind. Finally, European ships added more weaponry, including sturdier cannons.

The caravel, shown above, helped Europeans sail across and into the wind.

Hardships on the Uncharted Sea
In his journal, Italian sailor Antonio Pigafetta detailed the desperate conditions Magellan's sailors faced as they crossed the Pacific Ocean:

"We remained 3 months and 20 days without taking in provisions or other refreshments and ate only old biscuit reduced to powder, full of grubs and stinking from the dirt which rats had made on it. We drank water that was yellow and stinking. We also ate the ox hides from under the mainyard which we softened by soaking in seawater for several days."

—Journal of Antonio Pigafetta

1. **Focus on a topic** It is usually not very fruitful to synthesize bits of information that have little or nothing in common. The different pieces of information should be on some common topic. **To what common topic do all three bits of information relate?**

2. **Analyze each piece of information** The purpose of synthesizing is to gather evidence on a topic from more than one source. Before you can synthesize, you need to make sure that you understand the main idea and supporting details found in each source. **(a) What is the main idea of the Improved Technology paragraphs? (b) What was the benefit of the caravel? (c) What is the main idea of Pigafetta's firsthand account?**

3. **Look for similarities** Information is more complete and reliable if more than one source provides the same or similar information. Noting and analyzing the similarities will help you reach a more complete understanding of the topic. **Which two sources support the idea that European sailors became better equipped to sail the seas?**

4. **Look for differences** It is also important to look for inconsistent information or other perspectives. **Which sources convey the idea that European sailors still faced hardships at sea?**

5. **Draw conclusions** Our knowledge of a topic becomes more complete when we draw conclusions based on information synthesized from a variety of sources. **Was ocean travel easy or difficult for Europeans in the early 1500s? Explain.**

Practicing the Skill

Study the different pieces of information on this page about developments that occurred between the 1500s and 1700s. Then, answer the following questions:

1. With what general topic do all three pieces of evidence deal?
2. (a) What does Las Casas complain about? (b) How does the painting show social change in the Americas? (c) What is the main idea of the graph?
3. Which two sources emphasize negative effects on Native Americans?
4. Do you think all Europeans were cruel to Native Americans? Explain.
5. Based on the evidence, were the early encounters between Native Americans and Europeans generally harmful or beneficial to the Native Americans? Explain.

Portrait of a Spanish man in the Americas, his wife of Native American ancestry, and their daughter.

A Brutal System

Bartolomé de las Casas, a conquistador turned priest, spoke out against the encomienda system and the treatment of Native Americans:

"It is impossible to recount the burdens with which their owners loaded them [75 to 100 pounds], making them walk [hundreds of miles]. . . . They had wounds on their shoulders and backs, like animals. . . . To tell likewise of the whip-lashings, the beatings, the cuffs, the blows, the curses, and a thousand other kinds of torments to which their masters treated them, while in truth they were working hard, would take much time and much paper; and would be something to amaze mankind."

—Bartolomé de las Casas, *Short Description of the Destruction of the Indies*

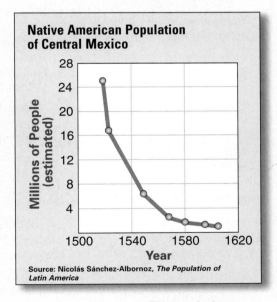

Native American Population of Central Mexico

Source: Nicolás Sánchez-Albornoz, *The Population of Latin America*

This graph shows the impact of diseases from Europe and of fighting against Europeans.

Applying the Skill

Select a current economics topic, such as e-commerce, international trade, or stock market trends. Find three different pieces of information on the topic, including at least one visual. Write questions to analyze and synthesize the information. Trade papers with a partner and answer each other's questions.

Analyzing Cause and Effect

How Will I Use This Skill? People often try to figure out the causes and effects of things. For example, government officials always conduct an investigation after an airplane accident. Their goals are to identify the causes of the mishap and to then use that knowledge to prevent future accidents. By analyzing causes and effects and by taking appropriate action based on what is learned, you can gain greater control over events and conditions that affect your life.

Learning the Skill

Read the passage below about a school soccer team. Then, follow the steps to learn how to analyze causes and effects.

A high school soccer team has won the division championship. The team's coach was named coach of the year. The team's colors were blue and gold. All the team members attended practice regularly. Because they passed all their classes, no team members were dropped from the team. As a result of winning the division title, the soccer team competed in the state tournament. The championship game was seen by college coaches on cable television. Several weeks later, a few of those coaches invited some of the players to apply for admission to their colleges and play soccer for them.

---

1. **Identify the central event** Identify the central condition or event whose causes or effects you wish to study. In the introductory paragraph at the top of this page, for example, the central event was airplane accidents. **What is the central event in the soccer story?**

2. **Disregard irrelevant information** Disregard information that has little or nothing to do with the central event. **What information in the story is neither a cause nor an effect of the team's performance?**

3. **Identify possible causes** Causes precede the central event. They are the reasons that the central event or development occurred. In a reading passage, key words that can help you identify causes include *because* and *due to*. **What are the causes of the central event in the soccer story?**

4. **Identify possible effects** Effects come after the central event. They occur as a result of the central event. In a reading passage, key words that indicate effects include *therefore* and *as a result*. **What are the effects of the central event in the soccer story?**

5. **Make generalizations** After investigators find the causes of an accident, they do not think about one plane only. They generalize and consider how the same conditions might cause an accident for other planes. For example, faulty electrical wiring can cause a fire in all planes, not just the one under investigation. **Make a generalization based on the soccer story.**

6. **Make recommendations** By understanding causes and effects, you can recommend actions or make predictions based on what you have learned. **How can any school sports team improve its chances for success?**

Practicing the Skill

By A.D. 1000, East African port cities, such as Mogadishu, Kilwa, and Sofala, were thriving centers of trade. Study the facts below, which are listed in random order, and copy the blank cause-and-effect chart at right. Then, answer the questions below and fill in the chart. (As you work, you may want to consult the world map in the Atlas at the back of this book.)

- Muslim merchants from Arabia and other lands settled in East Africa.
- Africa had gold, ivory, and other valuable resources.
- East African trading cities thrived.
- Mansa Musa ruled an empire in West Africa.
- Favorable winds aided travel between Asia and Africa.
- There were natural harbors along the East African coast.
- Arabic words became part of the Swahili language in East Africa.
- Muslim merchants introduced their religion to East Africa.

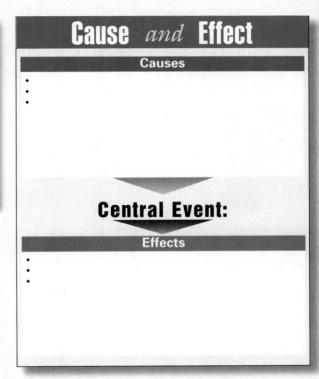

Cause *and* **Effect**

Causes
-
-
-

Central Event:

Effects
-
-
-

1. Which of the facts above is the central event whose causes and effects can be determined? Write the central event in the appropriate place on the chart.
2. Which one fact is most probably neither a cause nor an effect of the central event?
3. What three facts were most probably causes of the central event? Write them in the appropriate place on the chart.
4. What three facts about Africa were most probably effects of the central event? Write the three facts in the appropriate place on the chart.
5. In general, what is often a common effect of thriving trade between different lands?
6. In general, if a government wanted to build a profitable center for overseas trade, what do you think would be a good geographic location for the trade center?

Applying the Skill

Suppose that your dentist tells you that you have two cavities. Create a chart identifying probable causes and effects of the cavities. Then, based on the chart, write two generalizations and two recommendations.

Asking Questions

How Will I Use This Skill? Asking questions is a key part of the critical thinking process. By asking questions, you become an active thinker and learner rather than a passive observer. Using this skill will help you get the most out of any information that is presented to you.

Learning the Skill

Study the chart below and the biography on the left. Then, follow the steps to learn some of the techniques involved in asking useful questions.

Biography

Elizabeth I 1533–1603

"She takes great pleasure in dancing and music," noted an English observer of Queen Elizabeth I. The normally thrifty queen employed some 50 singers, 40 musicians, and several songwriters to stage concerts for her.

Elizabeth I also loved plays. She especially enjoyed the works of William Shakespeare, whom she helped to promote. The queen provided financial support and prestige for major acting groups, which led to a flowering of English theater.

The 45-year reign of Elizabeth I inspired other writers of the day. Poet Edmund Spenser dedicated *The Faerie Queene* to her.

Four Categories of Questions

Comprehension	Analysis	Evaluation	Prediction
Who?	How?	Is it beneficial or harmful?	If this occurs, then what might happen?
What?	Why?	Is it ethical or unethical?	If this does not occur, then what might happen?
Where?	What are the different points of view?	Is it logical or illogical?	If this had or had not happened, then what might be different?
When?	What are the causes and effects?	Is it relevant or irrelevant?	If this solution is implemented, how might the problem be affected?
How much?	What is the similarity or difference between this and that?	What are some advantages and disadvantages?	
What are the examples?	What is the problem?	What is the best solution?	
	What are some possible solutions?	What is my opinion?	
	What evidence supports the ideas?	What evidence supports my opinion?	

1. **Ask basic comprehension questions** Comprehension questions will help you to summarize or define the basic contents of what you are reading, seeing, or hearing. You might ask, "Who is discussed in the biography?" or "Where did she live?" **Ask and answer two more comprehension questions.**

2. **Ask analytical questions** Sample analytical questions are in the second column of the chart. Unlike comprehension questions, these questions involve some higher level critical thinking. You might ask, "How do the accomplishments of Elizabeth I have an impact on our lives today?" **What other analytical question could you ask?**

3. **Ask questions that evaluate** Examples of these questions are in the third column of the chart. In this step, you make judgments and form opinions based on evidence. An evaluation question might be "Based on the biography, do you think Elizabeth's spending habits were beneficial or harmful to the English people?" **Ask another evaluation question.**

4. **Ask hypothetical questions** These questions usually involve the word *if,* as do the questions in the fourth column of the chart. At this stage of critical thinking, you ask yourself questions that lead to a hypothesis or theory about what *might happen* or what *might have happened.* **Ask and answer a hypothetical question.**

Practicing the Skill

Review the chart on the preceding page once again and study the three maps at right. Then, follow the steps below to practice the skill of asking questions.

1. Write a basic comprehension question about the main idea of the three maps.
2. Write an analytical question about what happened to Poland. (Clue: Note how the borders of the countries around Poland changed over the years.)
3. Write a question that evaluates some aspect of what happened to Poland.
4. Based on what the maps show about international relations in Europe in the 1700s, write a question that leads one to make a prediction about Europe in the 1800s.

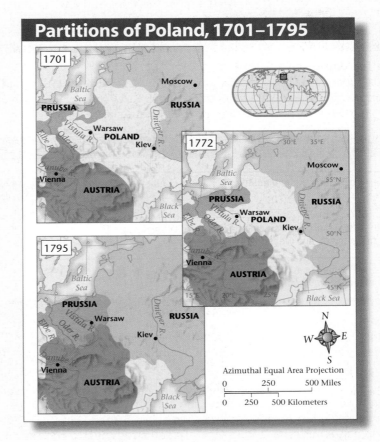

Partitions of Poland, 1701–1795

Applying the Skill

Videotape a short segment from a national news report on television or cut out an article from the national news section of a newspaper. Write a series of questions on the news story. Include one or more questions for each of the following four categories: **(a)** comprehension, **(b)** analysis, **(c)** evaluation, **(d)** prediction. Write an answer to each of the questions.

Problem Solving and Decision Making

How Will I Use This Skill? **Throughout your life, problems will arise. Today, a problem may be a dispute with a friend or a tough math test. Later, as a citizen and voter, you will be asked to make decisions about problems affecting the community, nation, or world. If you handle problems fearfully or haphazardly, they may overwhelm you. You will be more likely to find solutions if you make decisions in a logical, systematic way.**

Learning the Skill

We will use a case study to learn the skills of problem solving and decision making. Study the situation described below and copy the incomplete chart. Then, follow the steps and answer the questions.

A Problem for Japan and China

In the 1800s, Japan and China faced a problem. Industrialized nations had developed machinery and weapons that were superior to what the Japanese and Chinese had. Some industrialized nations used their new power to demand special trading privileges in Asia.

Options for Japan and China

Option	Advantages	Disadvantages
1. Give in to demands of the industrialized powers.	• Avoid conflict. •	• Native merchants lose profits to foreigners. •
2. Give in to demands, but also build modern machines and weapons.	• •	• •
3. Refuse the demands and reject much of the new technology.	• •	• •

The Decisions
- The Japanese government decided to follow option 2.
- The Chinese government decided to follow option 3.

Effects of the Decisions
- Japan quickly became a modern industrial and military power. After suffering defeat in World War II, Japan demilitarized. Today, it remains one of the world's leading industrial powers.
- China was defeated in several wars, first by Great Britain, and then by Japan. Foreign nations gained special privileges in China. Today, China is still struggling to become a leading industrial power.

1. **Identify the problem** It is almost impossible to solve a problem without examining it and having a clear understanding of its roots. **Why were foreign powers able to make demands on Japan and China?**
2. **Gather information and identify options** There is always more than one way to cope with a problem. Never follow the first option you think of. Instead, identify as many options as possible. **Describe an option, other than those in the chart, that Japan or China could have chosen.**

3. **Consider advantages and disadvantages** Analyze each option by predicting the benefits and drawbacks of choosing that option. **On the chart that you copied, fill in advantages and disadvantages for each of the options that Japan and China had.**

4. **Make a decision and implement the solution** Choose the option that seems to offer the best advantages and the least significant disadvantages. **Why do you think China decided on option 3?**

5. **Evaluate the decision** After a while, study the effects of the option that was implemented. If the problem has been solved, then stay with the decision. If the problem persists, has worsened, or has given rise to new problems, then start the process again and choose another option. **Do you think China should have chosen another option after evaluating its decision? Explain.**

Practicing the Skill

Consider this situation. A friend of yours works at a restaurant. Each month, your friend spends more than he or she earns. The money is spent on food, clothing, movies, computer software, video games, and other items. To pay for all the expenses, your friend borrows money from other friends. The result is that your friend owes more and more money each month.

1. (a) What problem does your friend have? (b) What are the underlying causes of the problem?
2. What options does your friend have? List and describe as many options as you can think of. Do not weigh the advantages and disadvantages yet. Do not reject any options yet.
3. Make a chart similar to the one on the preceding page. In the chart, describe possible advantages and disadvantages for each option.
4. Study your finished chart. Which option seems to provide the most valuable advantages and the least harmful disadvantages? Write a paragraph identifying the decision that you think would be best for your friend. Include a brief explanation as to why you think that decision is best.
5. Ask a classmate to study the options, advantages, and disadvantages on your chart and to evaluate your decision. Does your classmate agree or disagree with your decision? Explain.

Applying the Skill

Think of a problem that is affecting your school or community today. Work with several of your classmates to try to solve the problem. Remember to follow each of the problem-solving and decision-making steps that you have learned in this lesson. When you have finished your work, consider submitting a proposal to a leader in your school or community.

Using the Internet

How Will I Use This Skill? By "surfing the Net," you can link to millions of computer sites sponsored by businesses, governments, schools, museums, and individuals all over the world. The Internet provides many services, including information, e-mail, and online shopping. As a student, you may often use the Internet as a valuable research tool.

Learning the Skill

Use the steps below and the computer screen images to help you learn how to use the Internet. For this lesson, assume that you are searching for information on the Crusades, which were a series of holy wars between Christians and Muslims that began in the late 1000s.

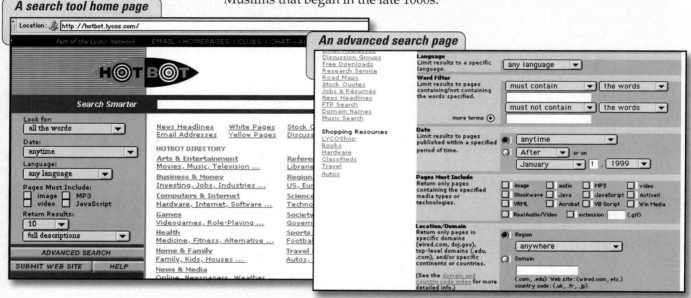

1. **Begin a search** Sometimes you know the Internet site you want and its URL, or Uniform Resource Locator. At other times, you must use search tools, such as AltaVista, HotBot, and NorthernLight, which are Internet sites that help you find other Internet sites. Some search tools are directories that list sites by category. For example, see the category called "Health" on the home page above. Other search tools are search engines that look for sites based on keywords that you choose and input yourself. Still others provide both a directory and an engine. **What does the search tool shown above provide?**

2. **Click on a help button** Search tools provide instructions on how to conduct a search. **Where is the help button on the above home page?**

3. **When you use a search engine, type in keywords** The keywords should briefly summarize your topic of choice. Usually, you should not input entire phrases or sentences like "When did the Crusades begin?" Instead, type in the word "Crusades" only. Then, click the search button. **Where is the box in the samples for typing keywords?**

4. **Use Boolean language** Two common Boolean terms are *AND* and *OR*. Use *AND* between two words when you want documents that contain both words. Use *OR* when you want documents that contain either of the words. **If you typed in "Crusades" and "Holy Wars," should you use *AND* or *OR* between them?**

5. **Try an advanced search** After clicking on the advanced search button, you can refine and limit your search. For example, you can specify documents produced only after a certain date or documents only from the **.edu** domain. Limiting the domain in this way will provide sites produced only by schools or other educational sites. The **.org** domain contains only sites produced by organizations. Another common domain is **.gov** which is used by government sites. **To what other domain could you limit your search?**

6. **Evaluate the quality of sites** When the search results page comes up, read the summaries and open those sites that seem to best match your topic. Note when each site was last updated. Note the sponsor or author, too. Universities, museums, libraries, and government agencies are usually the most useful and reliable for social studies research. **Who is the sponsor of the first site on the Crusades in the sample results page?**

7. **Explore, revise, and ask for help** Explore a variety of sites and compare them so you can select the one best suited to your needs. If the results are unsatisfactory, revise your search by typing in new keywords or by using another search tool. Seek guidance from teachers, librarians, and your parents. **What are two other keywords you could try in your search about the Crusades?**

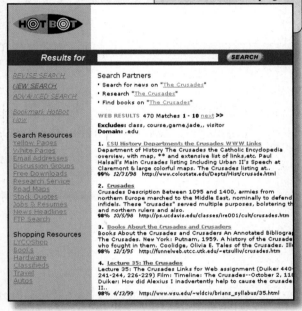

A search results page

Practicing the Skill

Use the Internet to do research on the Mongol empire, especially the Yuan dynasty that the Mongols established in China in 1279. Answer the following questions as you conduct your search:

1. What search tool do you choose? Why?
2. Describe one useful instruction that this search tool provides to users who click on the help button.
3. What keywords and/or Boolean language do you use in your search? Why?
4. How can an advanced search help you?
5. Which site provides the most useful and complete information about the Mongols and the Yuan dynasty? Explain.
6. Revise your search by inputting "Kublai Khan." How are your search results different from those of your earlier search?

Applying the Skill

Use the Internet to search for museum sites that have Native American art and artifacts. You may wish to limit your search to a particular Native American people. You could also limit your search to a particular type of art such as pottery or weaving. Print out your search result pages and circle the descriptions of those sites that you would recommend because they are the most appropriate. For each recommended site, identify the author or sponsor and explain why you recommend it.

UNIT 1

Early Civilizations

Prehistory–256 B.C.

OUTLINE

Chapter 1 **Toward Civilization** (Prehistory–3000 B.C.)

Chapter 2 **First Civilizations: Africa and Asia** (3200 B.C.–500 B.C.)

Chapter 3 **Early Civilizations in India and China** (2500 B.C.–256 B.C.)

THEMES

As you read about early human civilization, you will encounter the following unit themes.

Continuity and Change Using artifacts and written evidence, archaeologists and historians help us understand the ancient human past.

Economics and Technology During early human history, people gradually changed from the life of hunters and gatherers to the life of farmers. As civilizations developed, people began to specialize. They traded more, built large-scale public projects, and used mathematics and astronomy to better understand the world around them.

Geography and History Early people depended on their physical surroundings, using natural resources to provide food, shelter, and tools for survival. Gradually, people living in the river valleys of Egypt, the Middle East, India, and China developed complex civilizations.

Art and Literature The development of writing preserved some of the world's oldest literature, from the Egyptian *Tale of Sinuhe* and the Sumerian *Epic of Gilgamesh* to India's *Mahabharata* and ancient China's *Book of Songs.*

Unit Theme Activity

For Your Portfolio The chapters in this unit illustrate various connections between geography and history. As you read the chapters, prepare a portfolio project highlighting developments that show these connections. Your project might take one of the following forms:
- **PowerPoint presentation**
- **Museum exhibit**
- **Essay**

Abu Simbel is a temple built along the Nile River in Egypt to honor the ruler Ramses II. Its huge size reflects the pharaoh's power and godlike status.

WHY STUDY HISTORY?

Because History Is a Fascinating Story!

Why would a man devote years to studying the letters of a long-dead king? Why would a woman spend thousands of hours digging in the mud and ruins of an ancient city? The answer is simple. These people are caught up in the fascinating time machine called human history. History is a story about people—how they lived, where they traveled, how they felt about their lives. Uncovering these stories is like unraveling a mystery. The more you search, the more you can discover about the world of the past.

Who was this man?

Today, he looks so fragile he might crumble at a touch. Once, though, this withered hand held incredible power. Pharaoh Ramses II ruled Egypt for 66 years, building scores of temples and monuments. Now, more than 3,000 years later, you can see the pharaoh's mummified remains at the Egyptian Museum in Cairo, Egypt. (Exactly how the Egyptians mummified their dead was itself a mystery for a long time.)

Why did someone write on this shell?

You may wonder why anyone would write on a tortoise shell or a deer bone. But to a priest in Shang China, oracle bones were an excellent way of predicting the future. The writing on this shell was actually a request for advice from a departed ancestor. Today, objects like oracle bones give us a window, not to the future, but to the past. They show us how past peoples differed from us—and how we are alike.

Where did the people go?

Suppose you walked into New York or Los Angeles today, only to find that everyone had vanished without a trace. That was how archaeologists felt when they uncovered the ruins of Mohenjo-Daro. About 3,500 years ago, these streets bustled with activity. Then, the people abandoned the city. What happened? A flood, an invasion—no one knows for certain. But you can be sure that historians will keep looking for clues.

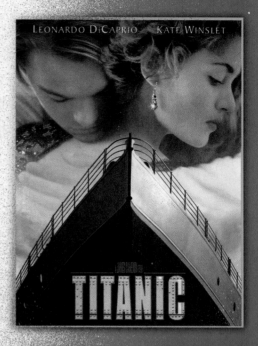

How was this pyramid built?

The Great Pyramid has stood in the Egyptian desert for nearly 5,000 years. Without machinery, workers fitted together huge hand-cut stones weighing an average of more than two tons each. The pyramid is so solidly built that it would survive a direct hit by an atomic bomb! Looking at this ancient monument, we come face to face with the awe and wonder of the human past.

Maybe you know someone who participates in Revolutionary War reenactments. Maybe you've joined in at a Renaissance Fair. Perhaps you've mused over dinosaur bones at a museum. Or maybe you've just watched a popular movie about a ship disaster of the past. The enormous popularity of such entertainments demonstrates the continuing fascination we have with history.

Portfolio Assessment

Connecting to Today Interview an older neighbor or family member. Ask the person to recount the most memorable or interesting event from his or her lifetime. Share the results of your interview with the class. What can you conclude from the collected memories of the class?

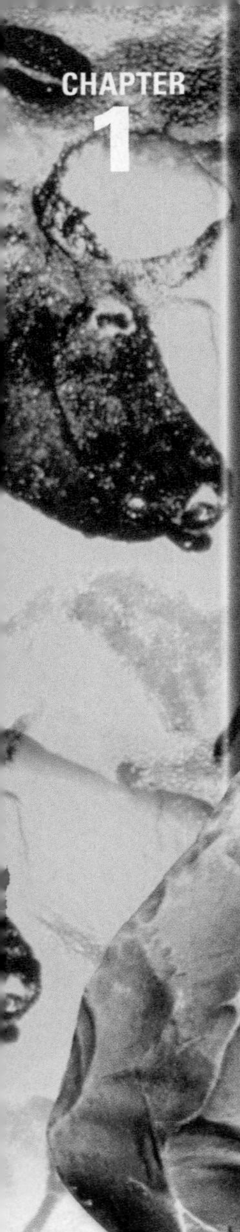

Toward Civilization

Prehistory–3000 B.C.

Chapter Preview

1 **Understanding Our Past**
2 **The Dawn of History**
3 **Beginnings of Civilization**

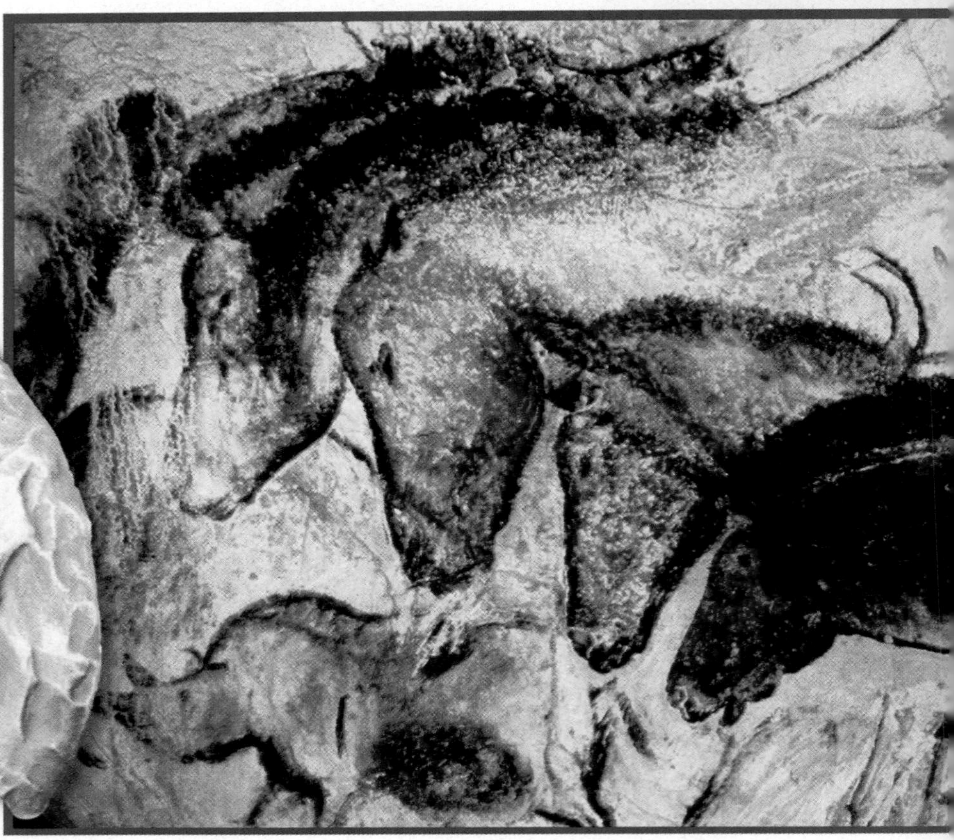

2 million B.C.

Early people first begin using stone tools, similar to this scraper and arrowhead.

30,000 B.C.

Stone Age people create cave paintings that show the animals they hunt. The Chauvet cave paintings in France, above, are the oldest ever found.

CHAPTER EVENTS

| 2 million B.C. | 35,000 B.C. | 27,000 B.C. |

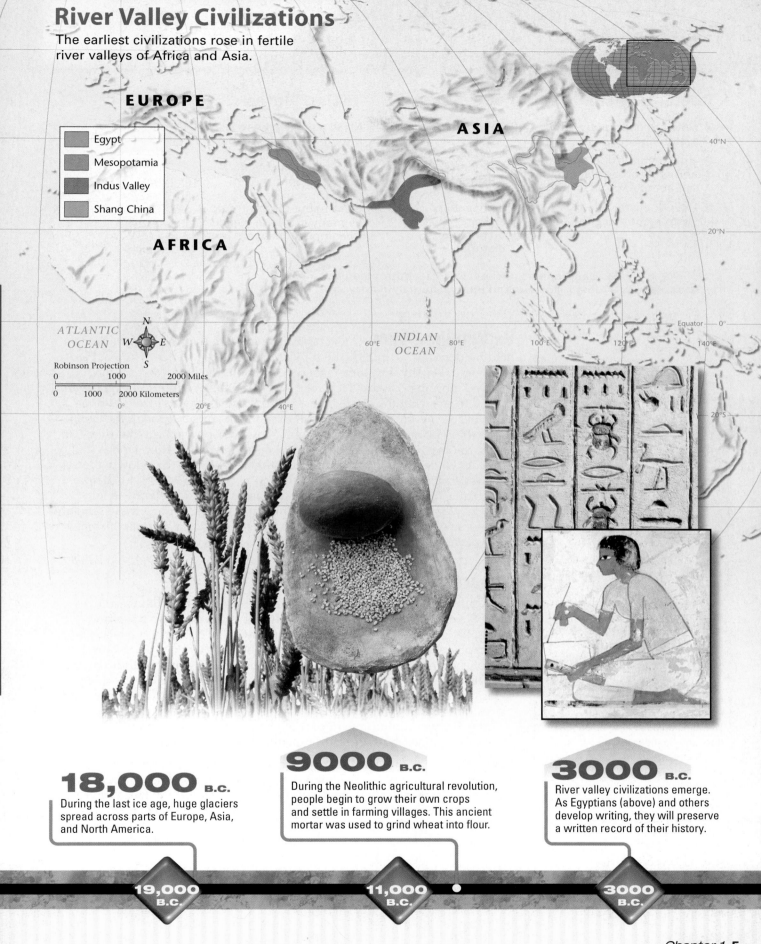

River Valley Civilizations

The earliest civilizations rose in fertile river valleys of Africa and Asia.

EUROPE

ASIA

AFRICA

Legend
- Egypt
- Mesopotamia
- Indus Valley
- Shang China

ATLANTIC OCEAN

INDIAN OCEAN

Robinson Projection

0   1000   2000 Miles

0   1000   2000 Kilometers

40°N

20°N

Equator 0°

20°S

60°E   80°E   100°E   120°E   140°E

20°E   40°E   0°

18,000 B.C.
During the last ice age, huge glaciers spread across parts of Europe, Asia, and North America.

9000 B.C.
During the Neolithic agricultural revolution, people begin to grow their own crops and settle in farming villages. This ancient mortar was used to grind wheat into flour.

3000 B.C.
River valley civilizations emerge. As Egyptians (above) and others develop writing, they will preserve a written record of their history.

19,000 B.C.

11,000 B.C.

3000 B.C.

Understanding Our Past

Reading Focus

- How are geography and history linked?
- How do anthropologists and archaeologists find out about early peoples?
- How do historians try to reconstruct the past?

Vocabulary

geography
latitude
longitude
prehistory
anthropology
culture
archaeology
artifact
technology
historian

Taking Notes

Make a concept web like the one at right. As you read the section, fill in each blank circle with important information about how experts learn about the past. Add as many circles as needed to complete the web.

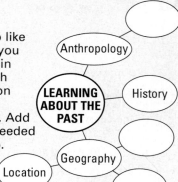

Main Idea | Geographers, archaeologists, anthropologists, and historians work to unravel human history.

Primary Source

A View of the Earth

An astronaut describes how world geography looks from space:

"As you eat breakfast you look out the window . . . and there's the Mediterranean area, Greece and Rome. . . . And you go down across North Africa, and out over the Indian Ocean and look up at that great subcontinent of India . . . out over the Philippines and up across that monstrous Pacific Ocean, that vast body of water—you've never realized how big that is before.

You finally come up across the coast of California, and you look for those friendly things, Los Angeles and Phoenix and on across to El Paso. . . . You look down there and you can't imagine how many borders and boundaries you cross, again and again and again, and you don't even see them."

—Russell L. Schweickart, quoted in *The Overview Effect* (White)

Skills Assessment

Primary Source **Based on this reading, how is looking at the world from space different from looking at a world map?**

Setting the Scene

Austen Layard was sure that the large mounds held hidden secrets. In 1845, he hired workers to dig trenches in what is today Iraq. Day by day, they inched deeper into the hot desert sands.

One morning, Layard's foreman Awad ran toward him, yelling. Layard rushed to see what the diggers had found. He was amazed to see a huge stone head emerging from the sand. Excitement spread through the camp as the diggers unearthed a giant statue. Layard soon realized that they had begun to uncover remains of the Assyrians, known only from stories in the Bible. As Layard and others found additional evidence, they slowly pieced together a picture of these people who had lived some 3,000 years before.

Thanks to the work of scholars like Austen Layard, we know a lot about how people lived in different times and places. Among these scholars are people who study geography—the stage on which all human history takes place.

Geography and History

Geography is the study of people, their environments, and the resources available to them. By showing how people lived in different times and places, geographers have added to our knowledge of human history. Often, geographers must draw conclusions from limited evidence. For example, tons of river mud found in the ruins of an ancient city may indicate that the city was wiped out by a flood. Similarities in language and art in widely separated regions may suggest that there was once contact between the two places.

Five themes sum up the impact of geography on the human story. They are location, place, human-environment interaction, movement, and region.

Location Location tells where a place is on the surface of the Earth. You can locate any place on a map using latitude and longitude. **Latitude** measures distance north or south of the Equator. **Longitude** measures distance east or west of the Prime Meridian, an imaginary line that runs north to south through Greenwich, England. For example, you can locate the city of Seoul, South Korea, at 37° N latitude and 127° E longitude. These numbers give its exact location.

Relative location—where one place is located in relation to another—is sometimes more important than exact location. For example, ancient Athens was located on the eastern Mediterranean Sea, near much older civilizations in Egypt and the Middle East. This relative location influenced the Athenians' way of life because they acquired valuable skills and ideas from their neighbors.

Place Geographers describe places in terms of their physical features and human characteristics. Physical features of a place include landforms, bodies of water, climate, soil quality, resources, and plant and animal life. Human characteristics include where most people live and their economic activities, religious beliefs, and languages.

Human-Environment Interaction Since the earliest times, people have interacted with their environment. That is, they have shaped and been shaped by the places in which they lived. Early farmers used water from rivers to irrigate their crops. Much later, European settlers in the Americas cut down trees to clear land for farms. As technology has advanced, we have changed the environment in more complex ways. Today, roads slice through deserts, and canals link distant bodies of water.

Movement The movement of people, goods, and ideas is another key link between geography and history. In early times, people followed herds of deer or buffalo on which they depended for food. In more recent times, people have migrated, or moved, from farms and villages to cities in search of jobs. Others have fled from war or religious persecution.

In ancient times, as today, traders have carried goods from one part of the Earth to another. Ideas also move, carried by people like missionaries or settlers. Today, communications satellites and television cables carry ideas faster and farther than ever before.

Region Geographers divide the world into many types of regions. Some regions are based on physical characteristics, such as location. The Gulf States, for example, are those countries bordering the Persian Gulf. They are part of a larger region of southwestern Asia, which we often call the Middle East. Regions may also be defined by political, economic, or cultural features. Culturally, the Gulf States are part of two larger regions, the Arabic-speaking world and the Muslim world.

Geography Makes a Difference
Geographic features such as landforms, climate, and natural resources have helped to shape a wide variety of human cultures. This reindeer herder in Siberia (below) lives a far different life from that of these rice farmers in Vietnam (left).

Theme: Geography and History Identify two cultural differences shown in these photographs. How might geography contribute to these differences?

How Do We Know?

The search for the human past has led all over the globe and far back to prehistoric times. Prehistory refers to the long period of time before people invented systems of writing. Prehistoric people had no cities, countries, organized central governments, or complex inventions.

Anthropology   About 200 years ago, scholars began studying the origins and development of people and their societies. Today we call this field of study anthropology. Modern anthropologists specialize. Some examine the origins of human life. Others focus on the variety of human cultures. In anthropology, culture refers to the way of life of a society that is handed down from one generation to the next by learning and experience.

Archaeology   A specialized branch of anthropology is called archaeology (ahr kee AHL uh jee), the study of past people and cultures. Archaeologists find and analyze the material remains of human cultures to learn about prehistoric people and to add to the written records of historical times.

Archaeologists study artifacts, objects made by human beings. Artifacts include tools, weapons, pottery, clothing, and jewelry. By analyzing artifacts and other items, archaeologists draw conclusions about the beliefs, values, and activities of our ancestors. Writer Agatha Christie, who was married to an archaeologist, described how people of the past speak to us through artifacts:

> "'With these bone needles we sewed our clothes.' 'These were our houses, this our bathroom, here our system of sanitation!' . . . 'Here, in this little jar, is my make-up.' 'All these cook-pots are of a very common type. You'll find them by the hundred. We get them from the potter at the corner.'"
> —Agatha Christie, *Come, Tell Me How You Live*

Archaeologists at Work   Analyzing ancient artifacts is difficult, but archaeologists have devised many useful techniques. In the 1800s and early 1900s, archaeologists picked a likely site, or place, and began digging. The farther down they dug, the older the artifacts they found. Some long-buried objects crumbled as soon as they were exposed to light and air. Today, scientists have ways to preserve such fragile artifacts.

By studying thousands of items, archaeologists have traced how early people developed new technologies. Technology refers to the skills and tools people use to meet their basic needs. The first stone tools, for example, were crudely made with jagged edges and rough surfaces. Stone tools from later times are smooth and polished, showing improved skills.

Archaeologists today also make detailed maps locating every artifact they find. By analyzing this evidence, they can tell what went on at different locations within a site. Flint chips, for example, might suggest the workplace of a toolmaker.

Technology and the Past   Archaeologists use modern technology to study and interpret their findings. Computers can be used to store and sort data or to develop accurate site maps. Aerial photography can reveal patterns of how people used the land. Techniques for measuring radioactivity help chemists and physicists determine the age of objects.

Geologists, or experts on earth science, help archaeologists date artifacts by determining the age of nearby rocks. Botanists and zoologists, experts on plants and animals, examine seeds and animal bones to learn about the diet of early people. Experts on climate determine what conditions early people faced on the plains of Africa or in ice-covered parts of Europe. Biologists analyze human bones as well as bloodstains found on old stone tools and weapons.

You Are There . . .

UNEARTHING THE PAST

Sweat runs down your forehead and into your eyes. It stings. Slowly, you stand up from where you've been kneeling in the dirt and wipe your face. You volunteered to spend your first summer after high school helping archaeologists at a dig in Mexico. Squinting against the bright sun, you wait for your eyes to adjust. . . .

You turn and you see a serene face on an urn that you helped excavate this morning. You feel a sense of pride as you realize that you have helped unearth a piece of the past.

You hear distant murmurs in English and Spanish, and you can pick out an occasional word. Louder are the clink of metal hammers on rock and the crunch of shovels in soft earth. These are the sounds of an archaeological dig.

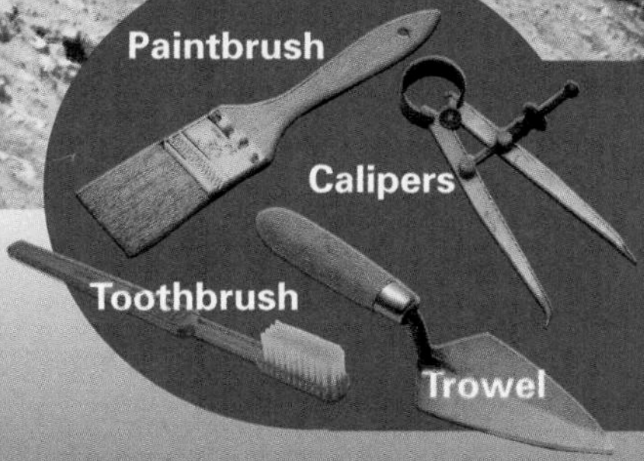

Paintbrush

Calipers

Toothbrush

Trowel

You gather your tools, lying scattered about you. You use the trowel to dig up an artifact, brushes to gently brush away dirt, and then calipers to measure it. You take great care, because you are unearthing ancient treasure.

Your eyes focus on a pit just in front of you. Archaeologists are examining a burial chamber. They are sketching and mapping the find. Precise records are needed for later analysis.

Portfolio Assessment

The sun dips below the horizon, and you are through for the day. Alone in your tent, you pick up paper and pen and start a letter home. You explain how you have reached your decision about whether to volunteer at another dig next summer.

Historians Reconstruct the Past

While archaeologists have uncovered useful information about the past, most of what goes into a textbook like this one comes from the work of historians. **Historians** study how people lived in the past. Like archaeologists, historians study artifacts, from clothing and coins to artwork and tombstones. However, they rely even more on written evidence.

About 5,000 years ago, some people in different parts of the world began to keep written records. That event marked the beginning of recorded history. Although these early records are often scanty, they do give us a narrative of events, as well as a number of names and dates. Historians carefully study written evidence, such as letters or tax records. Historians of the recent past also use such evidence as photographs or films.

Historical Detection Like a detective, the historian must evaluate the evidence to determine if it is reliable. Do records of a meeting between two officials tell us exactly what was said? Who was taking notes? Was a letter writer really giving an eyewitness report or just passing on rumors? Could the letter even be a forgery? The historian tries to find the answers.

Historians then must interpret the evidence, explaining what it means. Often, the historian's goal is to determine the causes of a certain development or event, such as a war or an economic collapse. By explaining why things happened in the past, the historian can help us understand what is going on today and what may happen tomorrow.

Generally, historians try to give a straightforward account of events. Sometimes, though, their personal experiences, cultural backgrounds, or political opinions may affect their interpretations. At times, historians disagree about what the evidence proves. Such differences can lead to lively debates.

The "Great" and the "Small" The first historians began writing thousands of years ago. These early historians wrote mostly about the deeds of well-known and powerful people such as monarchs, religious leaders, politicians, and generals.

Today, historians still write about famous people whose actions have had wide influence. Yet other historians are studying the lives of ordinary people. How did farmers or workers earn a living? What holidays did they celebrate? What was family life like? The answers to such questions have increased our understanding of the past.

What Year Is It?

Most nations today use a standard calendar that dates events from the birth of Christ. This calendar, sometimes called the Christian Era calendar, uses B.C. to stand for dates before the birth of Christ and A.D. for dates after the birth of Christ. Some modern books use C.E., or "common era," instead of A.D.

The Christian Era calendar, however, is not the only calendar used in the world. The year 2000 on the Christian Era calendar overlapped the Muslim year 1371, the Chinese year 4637, and the Jewish year 5761. In some cultures, people use the standard dates for everyday use and traditional dates for holidays and religious ceremonies.

Theme: Diversity What are the advantages of all nations using the same dating system?

SECTION 1 Assessment

Recall
1. **Define:** (a) geography, (b) latitude, (c) longitude, (d) prehistory, (e) anthropology, (f) culture (g) archaeology, (h) artifact, (i) technology, (j) historian.

Comprehension
2. (a) What are the five themes of geography? (b) Give two examples of how people interact with their environment.
3. How do anthropologists and archaeologists learn about the lives of prehistoric people?
4. What kinds of evidence do historians use to study the past?

Critical Thinking and Writing
5. **Linking Past and Present** Historians and archaeologists have worked to piece together the human story from prehistory up to today. Why do you think it is important for us to understand our past?
6. **Connecting to Geography** How can bodies of water play an important role in shaping human society and economy?

Activity

Learning From Artifacts Make a list of four or five artifacts that are in your classroom right now. Then, describe what these artifacts might tell archaeologists of the future about education in our time.

The Dawn of History

Reading Focus

■ What advances did people make during the Old Stone Age?

■ How can we learn about the religious beliefs of early people?

■ Why was the Neolithic agricultural revolution a turning point in history?

Vocabulary

nomad

glacier

animism

domesticate

Taking Notes

Copy the before-and-after chart shown below. As you read the section, add information about human history under each heading. Save the completed chart to help you recall what you learn in this section.

PEOPLE LEARN TO FARM	
Before	**After**
• Lived in small groups	• Populations grew
•	•

Main Idea The change from nomadic to farming life led to the emergence of civilizations.

Setting the Scene

A small band of hunters and food gatherers was camped on the shore of Lake Turkana in East Africa. One member of the group picked up a stone and chipped it with another stone to make a sharp, jagged edge. The toolmaker may have used this simple tool to cut meat from a dead animal or to sharpen a stick for digging up edible roots.

The toolmaker left the chipped stone near the lake. Some three million years later, anthropologist Richard Leakey picked it up. "It is a heart-quickening thought," Leakey later said, "that we share the same . . . heritage with the hand that shaped the tool that we can now hold in our own hands."

Very slowly, early people learned to make better tools and weapons from stone, bone, and wood. They also developed new skills. Technological advances like these helped more people to survive.

The Old Stone Age

Historians call the earliest period of human history the Old Stone Age, or Paleolithic age. This long period dates from about 2 million B.C., the time of the first stone toolmakers, to about 10,000 B.C.

African Beginnings Anthropologists have found startling evidence of early human life in East Africa. In 1959, Mary and Louis Leakey found pieces of bone embedded in ancient rock at Olduvai (OHL duh way) Gorge in Tanzania. After careful testing, they concluded that the bone belonged to early hominids, or humanlike primates. In 1974, Donald Johanson found part of a hominid skeleton in Ethiopia. Johanson named his find "Lucy" after a Beatles' song.

Because of such evidence, many scientists think that the earliest people lived in East Africa. Later, their descendants may have migrated north and east into Europe and Asia. In time, people reached the Americas, Australia, and the islands of the Pacific.

Hunters and Food Gatherers Paleolithic people lived in small hunting and food-gathering bands numbering about 20 or 30 people. Everyone contributed to feeding the group. In general, men hunted or fished. Women, with their small children, gathered berries, fruit, nuts, wild grain, roots, or even shellfish. This food kept the band alive when game was scarce. Paleolithic people were nomads, moving from place to place as they followed game animals and ripening fruit.

Biography

Louis Leakey 1903–1972

No one who heard Louis Leakey talk about Africa ever forgot it. "He cast a spell," recalled Donald Johanson, "making each listener believe he was speaking only to him or her." Leakey's enthusiasm inspired a whole generation of anthropologists.

Born in Kenya, Leakey began looking for early human remains in East Africa. He and his wife, Mary, found many tools, bones, and other artifacts. Even while working as a spy during World War II, Leakey continued digging in his free time. In later life, he traveled all over the world, lecturing and raising funds for new research projects.

Theme: Impact of the Individual Why might someone devote his or her life to studying human origins?

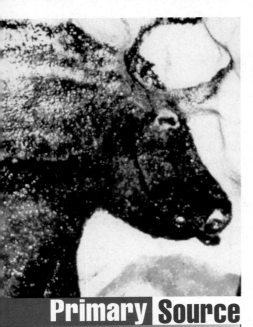

People depended wholly on their environment for survival. At the same time, they found ways to adapt to their surroundings. They made simple tools and weapons out of the materials at hand—stone, bone, or wood. At some point, Stone Age people developed spoken language, which let them cooperate during the hunt and perhaps discuss plans for the future.

Still, prehistoric people faced severe challenges from the environment. During several ice ages, the Earth cooled. Thick **glaciers,** or sheets of ice, spread across parts of Asia, Europe, and North America. To endure the cold, Paleolithic people invented clothing. Wrapped in animal skins, they took refuge in caves or under rocky overhangs during the long winters. They also learned to build fires for warmth and cooking. In this harsh life, only the hardy survived.

Early Religious Beliefs

About 30,000 years ago, people began to leave evidence of their belief in a spiritual world. To them, the world was full of spirits and forces that might reside in animals, objects, or dreams. Such beliefs are known as **animism.**

In France, Spain, and northern Africa, cave or rock paintings vividly portray animals such as deer, horses, and buffaloes. Some cave paintings show stick-figure people, too. The paintings often lie deep in the caves, far from a band's living quarters. Cave paintings may have been part of animist religious rituals in which hunters sought help from the spirit world for success in an upcoming hunt.

Archaeologists have also found small stone statues that probably had religious meaning. Statues of pregnant women, for example, may have been symbols meant to ensure survival of the band. They suggest that early people worshiped earth-mother goddesses, givers of food and life.

Toward the end of the Old Stone Age, some people began burying their dead with great care. This practice suggests a belief in life after death. They probably believed the afterlife would be similar to life in this world, so they provided the dead with tools, weapons, and other needed goods. Burial customs like these survived in many places into modern times.

The Neolithic Agricultural Revolution

About 11,000 years ago, nomadic bands made a breakthrough that had far-reaching effects. They learned to farm. By producing their own food, they could remain in one place. Farmers thus settled into permanent villages and developed a new range of skills and tools. This change from nomadic to settled farming life ushered in the New Stone Age, or Neolithic age.

The First Farmers No one knows when and how people began to plant seeds for food. Some scholars think that, in the Eastern Hemisphere, farming started in the Middle East and then spread. Others argue that farming developed independently in different regions. No matter which way it occurred, the change had such dramatic effects that historians call it the Neolithic agricultural revolution.

Food-gathering women may have been the first to notice that if seeds were scattered on the ground, new plants would grow the next year. They may also have seen that removing some plants enabled nearby ones to grow stronger. If game animals were scarce, a band might camp at a place where plants grew and begin cultivating them season after season.

The Neolithic revolution included a second feature. People learned to **domesticate,** or tame, some of the animals they had once hunted. Rather than wait for migrating animals to return each year, hunters rounded them up. Then they herded the animals to good grasslands or penned them in rough enclosures. The animals provided people with a source of protein.

Analyzing Primary Sources

Clues to the Iceman Mystery

In 1991, hikers in the Alps stumbled upon a gruesome sight: a man's head and shoulders sticking out of the ice. Investigators discovered that the man had not died recently. In fact, the Iceman, as newspapers called him, had been shot with an arrow more than 5,000 years earlier. Fascinated, scientists studied the Iceman and his belongings.

The Iceman and his possessions were preserved in a pocket of snow (right). The 4½-inch stone-and-wood dagger (below) was found near his body.

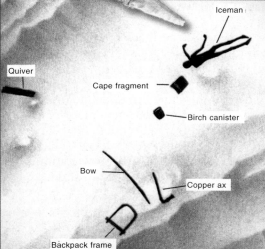

Iceman

Quiver

Cape fragment

Birch canister

Bow

Copper ax

Backpack frame

The Iceman's possessions, such as the bow and quiver shown on this diagram (left), give clues to his occupation. According to researcher Konrad Spindler, "In the high mountains, a shepherd would have to be armed with bow and arrow to defend himself from wild animals and human enemies, and also to secure food for himself."

Scientists were impressed by the complexity of the Iceman's ax. Its copper blade was bound onto a wooden handle with birch gum and leather.

Skills Assessment

1. Based on its size and shape, the dagger that was found with the Iceman might have been used to
   A chop wood for fires.
   B cut up meat or vegetables.
   C kill large animals.
   D carve through solid rock.

2. What conclusion can be made based on the discovery of the copper ax?
   E The Iceman used copper because stone was unavailable in the Alps.
   F People in the Alps knew how to mine and work with copper.
   G The early peoples of the Alps used copper for ornamental purposes.
   H Iron tools replaced copper tools.

3. **Critical Thinking Making Inferences (a)** Based on these artifacts, what can you infer about the Iceman's day-to-day life? **(b)** Consider the quality of workmanship of these artifacts. What does this tell you about the Iceman and the culture in which he lived?

Skills Tip

When using an artifact as a primary source, try to determine how that item might have been used at the time it was made.

Early Calendars

From the Stone Age on, different cultures developed calendars based on the cycles of the sun and the moon. These calendars were created by the Aztecs of Mexico (top) and the Babylonians of the Middle East (bottom).

Theme: Economics and Technology Why was it important for farming societies to create calendars?

Changing Ways of Life The Neolithic agricultural revolution enabled people to become food producers for the first time. It led to a growth in population, which in turn led to more interaction among human communities. No greater change in the way people lived took place until the Industrial Revolution of the late 1700s.

Like their Paleolithic ancestors, early farmers still divided up the work by gender and age. Still, important differences began to emerge. In settled farming communities, the status of women declined as men came to dominate family, economic, and political life. Heads of families, probably older men, formed a council of elders and made decisions about when to plant and harvest.

When food was scarce, warfare increased, and some men gained prestige as warriors. These elite warriors asserted power over both women and other men. These changes did not mean that women lost all their influence or rights. Rather, they show that village life was reshaping the roles of both women and men.

Settled people had more personal property than their nomadic ancestors. Some people accumulated more possessions than their neighbors, so differences in wealth appeared. Yet big differences among social classes did not exist at this time.

New Technologies To farm successfully, people had to develop new technologies. Like farmers today, they had to find ways to protect their crops and measure out enough seed for the next year's harvest. They also needed to measure time accurately so that they would know when to plant and harvest. Gradually, they created the first calendars. In some places, farmers learned to use animals such as oxen or water buffalo to plow the fields.

Archaeological evidence shows that some villages had separate workshops where villagers made tools, including smooth, polished ax heads and chipped arrowheads. In some parts of the world, Neolithic people learned to weave cloth from animal hair or vegetable fibers.

Inventions did not appear everywhere at the same time. Technologies might travel slowly from one area to another, taking thousands of years to spread across continents. Other technologies may have been invented separately in different parts of the world.

By about 5,000 years ago, the advances made by early farming communities led to a new stage of development—the emergence of civilizations.

SECTION 2 Assessment

Recall

1. **Identify:** (a) Paleolithic age, (b) Mary and Louis Leakey, (c) Neolithic age.
2. **Define:** (a) nomad, (b) glacier, (c) animism, (d) domesticate.

Comprehension

3. How did Paleolithic people learn to adapt to their environment?
4. What do burial customs suggest about the beliefs of early peoples?
5. (a) What were the key features of the Neolithic agricultural revolution? (b) How did it change people's lives?

Critical Thinking and Writing

6. **Recognizing Causes and Effects** (a) Why would economic scarcity often lead to increased warfare between farming communities? (b) How do you think economic scarcity and warfare changed the status of women in Stone Age societies?
7. **Connecting to Geography** Why would geography probably have played a more important role in the lives of people during the Old Stone Age than it plays in your life today?

Activity
Take It to the NET

Use Internet sources to find out more about prehistoric cave paintings. Then, use the information to write a talk that a tour guide might give to visitors. Include the location of the caves, interesting features about the paintings, and information about the people who made them.

Reading Focus

- How did the first cities emerge?
- What are the basic features of civilizations?
- How do cultures spread and change?

Vocabulary

civilization
surplus
polytheistic
artisan
pictogram
scribe
city-state
empire
steppe
cultural diffusion

Taking Notes

As you read, prepare an outline of this section. Use Roman numerals to indicate the major headings of the section, capital letters for the subheadings, and numbers for the supporting details. The sample at right will help you get started.

I. The rise of cities
  A. River valley civilizations
    1.
    2.
II. Features of civilization
  A.
    1.
    2.

Main Idea The rise of cities was a central feature in the development and spread of civilizations.

Setting the Scene Perhaps the best-known monuments of the ancient world are the great pyramids of Egypt. More than 100,000 workers labored for years under the hot North African sun to build these giant tombs. Without modern machinery, they fit into place more than two million stone blocks weighing an average of 2 ½ tons each!

Pyramid building required a society more highly organized and technologically advanced than Neolithic farming villages. In Egypt, as elsewhere, people were taking a giant step from prehistory into history.

The Rise of Cities

The rise of cities was the main feature of civilization. A civilization is a complex, highly organized social order. The first cities emerged after farmers began cultivating fertile lands along river valleys and producing surplus, or extra, food. These surpluses in turn helped populations to expand. As populations grew, some villages swelled into cities.

River Valley Civilizations Cities rose independently in the valleys of the Tigris and Euphrates rivers in the Middle East, the Nile River in Egypt, the Indus River in India, and the Yellow River, or Huang He, in China. Conditions in these river valleys favored farming. Flood waters spread silt across the valleys, renewing the soil and keeping it fertile. The animals that flocked to the rivers to drink were another source of food. In addition, rivers provided a regular water supply and a means of transportation.

Rivers also posed challenges. Farmers had to control flooding and channel waters to the fields. To meet these challenges, cooperation was needed. Early farmers worked together to build dikes, dig canals, and carve out irrigation ditches. Such large-scale projects required leadership and a well-organized government.

Ancient cities were frequently surrounded by high walls. The walls of Babylon were so wide that a chariot could turn around on top of the wall without falling off. Early cities also boasted large temples and palaces and broad avenues used for public ceremonies. Still, most city streets were narrow and tangled, with houses as small as village huts.

Cities in the Americas Unlike the civilizations in Asia, Africa, and Europe, civilizations in the Americas often did not rise in river valleys. Two major civilizations, the Aztecs and Incas, eventually emerged in the highlands of Mexico and Peru.

Did You Know?

The Walls of Jericho

The city of Jericho was tiny—just about the size of eight football fields—but it was home to several thousand people. Jericho, in present-day Jordan, is the oldest city yet found. Archaeologists believe it was first settled a stunning 10,000 years ago. Even more striking is the fact that archaeologists have uncovered a huge wall, 12 feet high and 6 feet thick, that once surrounded the city.

What can we conclude from this great wall? Jericho must have had a powerful government to oversee the building of the wall. We can also conclude that there must have been a very good reason to undertake such a difficult task. One historian put it this way: "The citizens of Jericho felt they had wealth worth defending, and they lived in a world where others would try to take it from them by force."

Theme: Economics and Technology What might be the strategic advantages of a wall 12 feet high and 6 feet thick?

In the Americas, the first cities may have begun as religious centers. There, powerful priests inspired people from nearby villages to build temples to their gods. Villagers would gather at the temples for regular worship. In time, many may have remained permanently, creating cities like those elsewhere.

Features of Civilization

How did civilizations differ from smaller farming societies? What did the early civilizations that rose in different parts of the globe have in common? Historians distinguish eight basic features found in most early civilizations. These eight features are (1) cities, (2) well-organized central governments, (3) complex religions, (4) job specialization, (5) social classes, (6) arts and architecture, (7) public works, and (8) writing.

Organized Governments As cities grew, they needed a steady food supply. To produce large amounts of food and oversee irrigation projects, new forms of government arose. City governments were far more powerful than the councils of elders and local chiefs of farming villages.

At first, priests probably had the greatest power. In time, warrior kings emerged as the chief political leaders. They took over the powers of the old councils of elders and set themselves up as hereditary rulers who passed power from father to son. Almost always, rulers claimed that their right to rule came from the gods. Early Chinese kings took the title "Son of Heaven," and Incan emperors declared that they were sons of the sun itself. Thus, political rulers gained religious power as well.

Government became more complex as rulers issued laws, collected taxes, and organized systems of defense. To enforce order, rulers relied on royal officials. Over time, separate government departments evolved that oversaw functions such as tax collection, irrigation projects, or the military.

Complex Religions Like their Stone Age ancestors, most ancient people were polytheistic, that is, they believed in many gods. People appealed to sun gods, river goddesses, and other spirits that they believed controlled natural forces. Other gods were thought to control human activities such as birth, trade, or war.

In ancient religions, priests and worshipers sought to gain the favor of the gods through complex rituals such as ceremonies, dances, prayers, and hymns. To ensure divine help, people built temples and sacrificed animals, crops, or sometimes other humans to the gods. Sacrifices and other ceremonies required the full-time attention of priests, who had special training and knowledge.

Job Specialization The lives of city dwellers differed from those of their Stone Age ancestors. Urban people developed so many new crafts that a single individual could no longer master all the skills needed to make tools, weapons, or other goods. For the first time, individuals began to specialize in certain jobs. Some became artisans, or skilled craftworkers, who made pottery or finely carved or woven goods. Among the crafts that developed in cities, metalworking was particularly important. People learned to make tools and weapons, first out of copper, then later out of bronze, a more durable mixture of copper and tin.

Cities had other specialists, too. Bricklayers built city walls. Soldiers defended them. Merchants sold goods in the marketplace. Singers, dancers, and storytellers entertained on public occasions. Such specialization made people dependent on others for their various needs.

Social Classes In cities, social organization became more complex. People were ranked according to their jobs. Such ranking led to the growth of social classes. Priests and nobles usually occupied the top level of an

Virtual Field Trip

www.phschool.com
Harappa and Mohenjo-Daro Pakistan

To see other views and artifacts from these ancient cities, use the Internet address above to link to an ancient Indus Valley site.

Remains of an Ancient Civilization

One early civilization emerged in the Indus River valley. The Indus city of Mohenjo-Daro included a huge public water tank (left). Indus Valley artifacts (below) include stone seals with writing and a small statue of a priest-king.

Theme: Diversity Describe how these pictures reflect some of the eight features of civilization.

ancient society. Next came a small class of wealthy merchants, followed by humbler artisans. Below them stood the vast majority of people, peasant farmers who lived in the surrounding villages and produced food for the city.

Slaves occupied the lowest social level. Slaves sometimes came from poor families who sold themselves into slavery to pay their debts. Others were prisoners captured in war. Because male captives were often killed, women and children made up the largest number of these slaves.

Arts and Architecture The arts and architecture of ancient civilizations expressed the beliefs and values of the people who created them. Temples and palaces dominated the city scenery. Such buildings reassured people of the strength and power of their government and religion.

Skilled workers built and decorated massive buildings. In museums today, you can see statues of gods and goddesses, temple or palace wall paintings, and furniture and jewelry found in ancient tombs from around the world. They give ample evidence of the artistic genius of the first civilizations.

Public Works Closely linked to temples and palaces were vast public works that strong rulers ordered to be built. Such projects included irrigation systems, roads, bridges, and defensive walls. Although they were costly in human labor and even lives, such projects were meant to benefit the city, protecting it from attack and ensuring its food supply.

Writing A critical new skill developed by the earliest civilizations was the art of writing. It may have begun in temples, where priests needed to record amounts of grain collected, accurate information about the seasons, and precise rituals and prayers.

Archaeologists have found masses of ancient writings, ranging from treaties and tax rolls to business and marriage contracts. The earliest writing was made up of **pictograms,** or simple drawings that looked like the objects they represented. In time, symbols were added. They might stand for sounds of words or for ideas that could not be expressed easily in pictures.

As writing grew more complex, only specially trained people called scribes learned to read and write. Scribes were educated in temple schools and kept records for priests, rulers, and merchants. In only a few societies were women permitted to attend temple schools. As a result, women were generally excluded from becoming scribes, an occupation that could lead to political power.

Spread of Civilization

As ancient rulers gained more power, they conquered territories beyond the boundaries of their cities. This expansion led to the rise of the city-state, a political unit that included a city and its surrounding lands and villages. Rulers, nobles, and priests often controlled the land outside the city and forced peasants to grow crops on it. A large portion of each harvest went to support the government and temples.

The First Empires Rival leaders often battled for power. Sometimes, ambitious rulers conquered many cities and villages, creating the first empires. An empire is a group of states or territories controlled by one ruler. For the conquered people, defeat was painful and often cruel. At the same time, empire building also brought benefits. It helped end war between neighboring communities and created common bonds among people.

Interactions With Nomadic Peoples The first cities were scattered islands in a sea of older, simpler ways of life. Most peoples lived as their Stone Age ancestors had. They hunted, gathered food, or lived in simple farming villages. On some less-fertile lands or on sparse, dry grasslands, called steppes, nomadic herders tended cattle, sheep, goats, or other animals. Because the lands were poor in water and grass, these nomads had to keep moving to find new pasture.

Nomadic cultures were not "civilized," in the sense that they did not exhibit the characteristics of civilization. They built no cities and their governments were simpler than those of settled city-states or empires. However, many nomadic peoples developed sophisticated traditions in oral poetry, music, weaving, jewelry making, animal raising, and other areas of the arts and sciences.

Throughout history, relations between nomads and city dwellers have been complex. At times, the two groups cooperated in political, economic, or military matters. At other times, they have been in conflict, with cities subduing nomadic peoples or nomads overrunning cities. You will read about such encounters in later chapters.

Civilizations and Change

All societies and civilizations change. In fact, history itself might be defined as the story of these changes. Ancient civilizations changed in many ways over the centuries. Among the chief causes of change were shifts in the physical environment and interactions among people.

Environmental Changes Like their Stone Age ancestors, people of early civilizations depended heavily on the physical environment. They needed rain and fertile soil to produce crops. Resources such as stone, timber, or metals were also essential. Changes in the environment could have an immediate impact on people's lives.

At times, sudden, drastic events devastated a community. A tremendous volcano may have wiped out Minoan civilization on the island of Crete in the Mediterranean Sea. Overfarming could destroy soil fertility, or rivers might become too salty. Cities would then suffer famine, and survivors would be forced to move away.

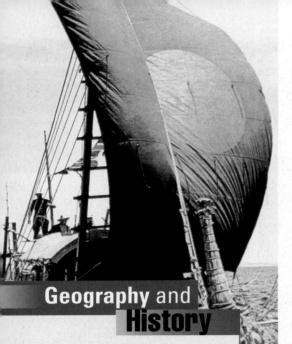

Geography and History

Ancient Travelers

Scientists long thought that ancient peoples tended to stay close to home. But startling new evidence from around the world has cast doubt on this idea.

In Europe, archaeologists found the remains of a sophisticated canoe that is 8,500 years old. In Oceania, we have learned that early people sailed small boats across hundreds, and perhaps thousands, of miles of open ocean. In Asia, scientists have mapped out ancient trade routes that crossed hundreds of miles of some of the most rugged terrain on the planet. These discoveries show that early peoples were much more mobile than anyone had ever imagined.

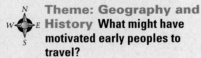

Theme: Geography and History What might have motivated early peoples to travel?

If people used up nearby timber or ran out of other building resources, they would have to adapt to this scarcity. They might, for example, trade with areas where such resources were available. Or they might use alternate building materials such as reeds.

Interactions Among People An even more important source of change was cultural diffusion, the spread of ideas, customs, and technologies from one people to another. Cultural diffusion occurred through migration, trade, and warfare.

As famine, drought, or other disasters led people to migrate, they interacted with others whose lives differed from their own. As a result, people often shared and adapted customs. Trade, too, introduced people to new goods or better methods of producing them. In ancient times, skills such as working bronze and writing, as well as religious beliefs, passed from one people to another.

Warfare also brought change. Often, victorious armies forced their way of life upon the people they defeated. On other occasions, the victors adopted the ways of a conquered people. Sometimes, nomadic rulers would become absorbed in city life.

Looking Ahead

In the next two chapters, you will read about the earliest civilizations that developed in the river valleys of Africa and Asia. They differed from one another in significant ways, each developing its own culture and traditions. At the same time, the civilizations of Egypt, Mesopotamia, India, and China all fit our definition of a civilization.

Cause *and* Effect

Long-Term Causes	Immediate Causes
• Silt deposits create fertile soil in river valleys • Neolithic people learn to farm • Hunters and gatherers settle into farming communities	• New technologies improve farming • Food surpluses support rising populations • First cities built in fertile valleys • Farmers cooperate to control flooding and channel water

Rise of River Valley Civilizations

Immediate Effects	Long-Term Effects
• Complex forms of government develop • Arts become more elaborate • Job specialization leads to social classes • Writing is invented	• Government bureaucracies emerge • Early civilizations conquer neighboring lands • Civilizations clash with nomadic peoples

Connections to Today

• Archaeologists mine rich stores of information in Egypt, Middle East, India, and China
• Large cities such as Cairo and Baghdad still flourish in river valley regions

Skills Assessment **Chart** Although river valley civilizations rose in different places, they shared many important features. **How did the rise of civilizations lead to the development of more complex governments?**

Recall
1. **Define: (a)** civilization, **(b)** surplus, **(c)** polytheistic, **(d)** artisan, **(e)** pictogram, **(f)** scribe, **(g)** city-state, **(h)** empire, **(i)** steppe, **(j)** cultural diffusion.

Comprehension
2. How did conditions in some river valleys favor the rise of early civilizations?
3. How were government and religion closely linked in early civilizations?

4. What are three causes of cultural change?

Critical Thinking and Writing
5. **Recognizing Causes and Effects** How did job specialization lead to the emergence of social classes in early civilizations?
6. **Linking Past and Present** **(a)** Give three examples that show cultural diffusion in today's world. **(b)** Why do you think that cultural changes occur more quickly today than in the past?

Activity
Take It to the NET

Use Internet sources to find out more about how early people learned to measure time. Then, use the information to create a time line about the evolution of time measurement.

Review and Assessment

Creating a Chapter Summary

Copy this Venn diagram on a sheet of paper. Use it to compare human life before and after the first civilizations began. Write information about life in both periods in the overlapping section of the circles. A few entries have been made to help you get started.

For additional review and enrichment activities, see the interactive version of *World History* available on the Web and on CD-ROM.

Before First Civilizations
- People lived in villages
- Not great difference among social classes
-

- Depended heavily on environment
-

Early Civilizations (from 5,000 years ago)
- Built cities
- Written language
-

Web Site Self-Test
For practice test questions for Chapter 1, see **www.phschool.com**.

Building Vocabulary

For each of the ten terms below, write a sentence using the term.

1. geography
2. anthropology
3. prehistory
4. artifact
5. animism
6. domesticate
7. surplus
8. polytheistic
9. scribe
10. cultural diffusion

Recalling Key Facts

11. Name five types of scientists who help archaeologists learn about the past.
12. What are the five themes of geography?
13. **(a)** How did Paleolithic people survive? **(b)** What technological advances did they make?
14. What change marked the beginning of the New Stone Age?
15. Why did early farmers need to create calendars?
16. List the eight features found in most early civilizations.
17. In which four river valleys did early civilizations emerge?

Critical Thinking and Writing

18. **Identifying Main Ideas** Reread the Global Connections feature in Section 1. Then, write a sentence stating the main idea of the feature.

19. **Recognizing Points of View** Thomas Carlyle, a Scottish writer, said that history was "the biography of great men." Ibn Khaldun, an Arab historian, defined history as "information about human social organizations." **(a)** What is the main difference between these two views of history? **(b)** How might each man's viewpoint have affected the way he wrote about history?

20. **Connecting to Geography** **(a)** Describe the community where you live in terms of each of the five themes of geography. **(b)** Explain two ways that geography affects your community and way of life.

21. **Recognizing Causes and Effects** Make a list of five major social or technological developments of the Old Stone Age and the New Stone Age. Then, for each development, identify one short-term and one long-term effect.

The excerpt below was written by an American historian. Read the passage, then answer the questions that follow.

How Historians Find Evidence

"Precisely because the historian must turn to all possible witnesses, he is the most bookish of men. For him, no printed statement is without its interest. For him, the destruction of old cookbooks, gazetteers, road maps, Sears Roebuck catalogues, children's books, railway timetables, or drafts of printed manuscripts, is the loss of potential evidence. Does one wish to know how the mail-order business was operated or how a Nebraska farmer might have dressed in 1930? Look to those catalogues. Does one wish to know whether a man from Washington just might have been in New York on a day in 1861 when it can be proved that he was in the capital on the day before and the day after? The timetables will help tell us of the opportunity."

—Robin Winks, *The Historian as Detective*

22. **(a)** Who is the author? **(b)** How does the author describe historians?
23. Why must the historian "turn to all possible witnesses"?
24. **(a)** According to the author, what could a historian learn from an old catalogue? **(b)** What might two other things be?
25. Based on this excerpt, do you think Winks considers the work of historians important?
26. Name three kinds of printed material a historian might consult that Winks does not name.

"Good effort, Sam, but it was a water jug!"

The cartoon above appeared in the British humor magazine *Punch* in May 1971. At that time, amateur archaeologists from many parts of the world were flocking to England to search for ancient artifacts and remains of early humans. Study the cartoon and then answer the following questions:

27. What kind of work are the three people in the cartoon doing?
28. **(a)** What has Sam pieced together? **(b)** Why do you think he is eager to show off his find?
29. How do the other archaeologists respond to what Sam has done?
30. What do you think is the cartoonist's view of amateur archaeologists?
31. **(a)** Based on the cartoon and on what you have read, what problems could a careless archaeologist cause? **(b)** How do professional archaeologists try to avoid such errors?

Skills Tip

Keep in mind that the cartoonist is presenting a point of view. Examine both the words and the pictures to understand what the subject matter is and how the cartoonist feels about it.

Skills Assessment
Take It to the NET

Use the Internet to research archaeological discoveries of early remains, such as "Lucy" or discoveries at Olduvai Gorge, in Africa. Then, imagine that you were present when a site was first discovered. Write an archaeological log describing what you found.

First Civilizations: Africa and Asia

3200 B.C.–500 B.C.

Chapter Preview

1 Ancient Kingdoms of the Nile
2 Egyptian Civilization
3 City-States of Ancient Sumer
4 Invaders, Traders, and Empire Builders
5 The Roots of Judaism

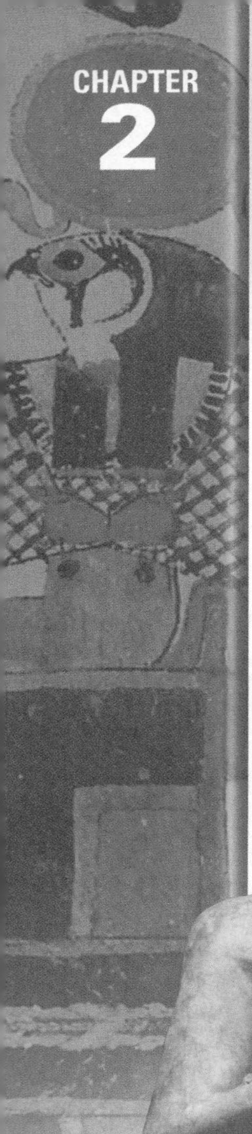

3200 B.C.

City-states flourish in Sumer. Sumerians will develop an early form of writing and produce artworks like this statue.

2700 B.C.

Egypt's Old Kingdom begins. Rulers of the Old Kingdom build huge pyramids like these to serve as their tombs.

2300 B.C.

Sargon of Akkad conquers Sumer and builds the world's first known empire.

CHAPTER
EVENTS

3500 B.C.

2900 B.C.

2300 B.C.

GLOBAL
EVENTS

2500 B.C.
Cities are built in the Indus Valley of South Asia.

Geography of Ancient Egypt and Mesopotamia

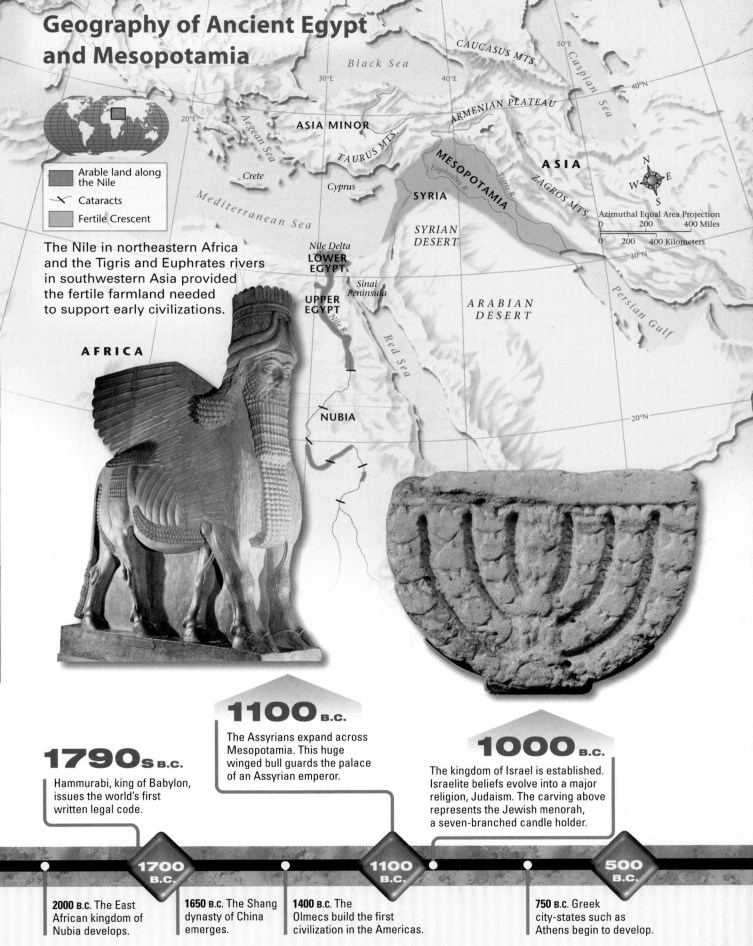

The Nile in northeastern Africa and the Tigris and Euphrates rivers in southwestern Asia provided the fertile farmland needed to support early civilizations.

Legend:
- Arable land along the Nile
- Cataracts
- Fertile Crescent

Azimuthal Equal Area Projection
0   200   400 Miles
0   200   400 Kilometers

Map labels: Black Sea, CAUCASUS MTS., Caspian Sea, 30°E, 40°E, 50°E, 40°N, ARMENIAN PLATEAU, ASIA MINOR, TAURUS MTS., MESOPOTAMIA, Euphrates R., Tigris R., ZAGROS MTS., ASIA, 20°E, Aegean Sea, Crete, Cyprus, SYRIA, SYRIAN DESERT, Mediterranean Sea, Nile Delta, LOWER EGYPT, Sinai Peninsula, UPPER EGYPT, Nile R., AFRICA, ARABIAN DESERT, Red Sea, Persian Gulf, 30°N, NUBIA, 20°N

1790s B.C.
Hammurabi, king of Babylon, issues the world's first written legal code.

1100 B.C.
The Assyrians expand across Mesopotamia. This huge winged bull guards the palace of an Assyrian emperor.

1000 B.C.
The kingdom of Israel is established. Israelite beliefs evolve into a major religion, Judaism. The carving above represents the Jewish menorah, a seven-branched candle holder.

Timeline: 1700 B.C. — 1100 B.C. — 500 B.C.

2000 B.C. The East African kingdom of Nubia develops.

1650 B.C. The Shang dynasty of China emerges.

1400 B.C. The Olmecs build the first civilization in the Americas.

750 B.C. Greek city-states such as Athens begin to develop.

Ancient Kingdoms of the Nile

Reading Focus

How did geography influence ancient Egypt?

What were the main features and achievements of Egypt's three kingdoms?

How did trade and warfare affect Egypt and Nubia?

Vocabulary

silt

cataract

delta

dynasty

pharaoh

vizier

Taking Notes

Copy the chart below. As you read, fill in the characteristics that distinguish each period in ancient Egyptian history.

	OLD KINGDOM	MIDDLE KINGDOM	NEW KINGDOM
GOVERNMENT	Pharaohs organize centralized state		
ACHIEVEMENTS		Land drained for farming	
DECLINE			

Main Idea The history of ancient Egypt is divided into three periods: Old Kingdom, Middle Kingdom, and New Kingdom.

Setting the Scene Every year, as the Nile River flooded its banks, the people of ancient Egypt sang a hymn of praise. They honored the river for nourishing the land and filling their storehouses with food:

"If the Nile smiles, the Earth is joyous
Every stomach is full of rejoicing
Every spine is happy,
Every jawbone crushes its food."
    —"Hymn to the Nile," quoted in *The Literature of the Ancient Egyptians* (Erman)

The fertile lands of the Nile Valley attracted Stone Age farmers. People migrated from the Mediterranean area, from hills and deserts along the Nile, and from other parts of Africa. In time, a powerful civilization emerged that depended on the control of river waters.

Geography of the Nile Valley

"Egypt," said the ancient Greek historian Herodotus, "is wholly the gift of the Nile." Without the Nile, Egypt would be swallowed up by the barren deserts that surround it. While the desert protected Egypt from invasion, it also limited where people could settle.

In ancient times, as today, farming villages dotted the narrow band of land watered by the Nile. Beyond the rich, irrigated "Black Land," generally no more than 10 miles wide, lay the "Red Land," a sun-baked desert that stretches across North Africa. Farmers took advantage of the fertile soil of the Nile Valley to grow wheat and flax, a plant whose fibers were used for clothing.

Yearly Floods The Nile rises in the highlands of Ethiopia and the lakes of central Africa. Every spring, rains in this interior region send water racing down streams that feed the Nile River. In ancient times, Egyptians eagerly awaited the annual flood. It soaked the land with life-giving water and deposited a layer of rich silt, or soil.

People had to cooperate to control the Nile floods. They built dikes, reservoirs, and irrigation ditches to channel the rising river and store water for the dry season.

Uniting the Land Ancient Egypt had two distinct regions, Upper Egypt in the south and Lower Egypt in the north. Upper Egypt stretched from the

first cataract, or waterfall, of the Nile northward to within 100 miles of the Mediterranean. Lower Egypt covered the delta region where the Nile empties into the Mediterranean. A delta is a triangular area of marshland formed by deposits of silt at the mouth of some rivers.

About 3100 B.C., Menes, the king of Upper Egypt, united the two regions. He and his successors used the Nile as a highway linking north and south. They could send officials or armies to towns along the river. The Nile thus helped make Egypt the world's first unified state.

The river also served as a trade route. Egyptian merchants traveled up and down the Nile in sailboats and barges, exchanging the products of Africa, the Middle East, and the Mediterranean world.

The Old Kingdom

The history of ancient Egypt is divided into three main periods: the Old Kingdom (about 2700 B.C.–2200 B.C.), the Middle Kingdom (about 2050 B.C.–1800 B.C.), and the New Kingdom (about 1550 B.C.–1100 B.C.). Although power passed from one dynasty, or ruling family, to another, the land generally remained united.

A Strong Government During the Old Kingdom, Egyptian rulers called pharaohs (FAIR ohz) organized a strong, centralized state. Pharaohs claimed divine support for their rule. Egyptians believed the pharaoh was a god. The pharaoh thus had absolute power, owning and ruling all the land in the kingdom.

Pharaohs of the Old Kingdom took pride in preserving justice and order. A pharaoh depended on a vizier, or chief minister, to supervise the business of government. Under the vizier, various departments looked after such matters as tax collection, farming, and the all-important irrigation system. Thousands of scribes carried out the vizier's instructions.

One wise vizier, Ptah-hotep (tah HOH tehp), took an interest in training young officials. Based on his vast experience of government, he wrote a

Farming the Nile Valley
This tomb painting shows the importance of agriculture to ancient Egyptian life. The man guides an ox-drawn plow. Then, the woman plants seeds in the newly turned soil.

Theme: Geography and History What does this painting show about the crops that were grown in the Nile Valley?

► **Primary Sources and Literature**

See "Instruction of Ptah-hotep" in the Reference Section at the back of this book.

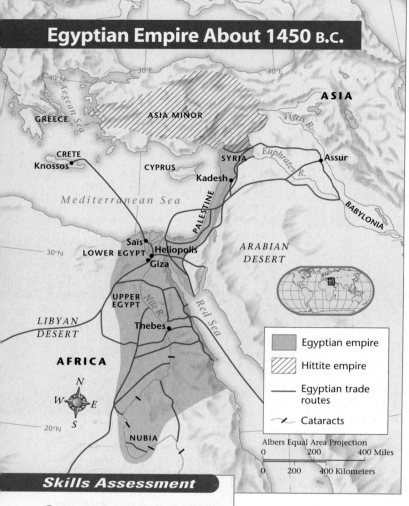

Egyptian Empire About 1450 B.C.

Skills Assessment

Geography During the New Kingdom, Egyptian influence spread throughout the eastern Mediterranean region.

1. **Location** On the map, locate **(a)** *Nile River,* **(b)** *Upper Egypt,* **(c)** *Lower Egypt,* **(d)** *Giza,* **(e)** *Hittite empire,* **(f)** *Nubia.*
2. **Movement** *What were the northernmost areas reached by Egyptian traders?*
3. **Critical Thinking**
Applying Information *What sources of information might a mapmaker today use to draw Egyptian trade routes?*

book, *Instruction of Ptah-hotep.* In it, he advised his son on how to avoid the errors he had seen in other officials:

> "If you are sitting at the table of one greater than you, take what he may give when it is set before you. Let your face be cast down until he addresses you, and you should speak only when he addresses you."
>
> —*Instruction of Ptah-hotep*

The Pyramids During the Old Kingdom, the Egyptians built the majestic pyramids that still stand at Giza. The pyramids were tombs for eternity. Because Egyptians believed in an afterlife, they preserved the bodies of their dead rulers and provided them with everything they would need in their new lives.

To complete the pyramids, workers hauled and lifted millions of limestone blocks, some weighing two tons or more. The builders had no iron tools or wheeled vehicles. Workers quarried the stones by hand, pulled them on sleds to the site, and hoisted them up earthen ramps. Building a pyramid took so long that often a pharaoh would begin to build his tomb as soon as he inherited the throne.

The pyramids suggest the strength of ancient Egyptian civilization. These costly projects required enormous planning and organization. Thousands of farmers, who had to be fed each day, worked on the pyramids when not planting or harvesting crops.

The Middle Kingdom

Power struggles, crop failures, and the cost of the pyramids contributed to the collapse of the Old Kingdom. After more than a century of disunity, new pharaohs reunited the land, ushering in the Middle Kingdom.

The Middle Kingdom was a turbulent period. The Nile did not rise as regularly as it had. Corruption and rebellions were common. Still, strong rulers did organize a large drainage project, creating vast new stretches of arable, or farmable, land. Egyptian armies occupied part of Nubia, the gold-rich land to the south. Traders also had greater contacts with the peoples of the Middle East and the Mediterranean island of Crete.

Catastrophe struck about 1700 B.C. when foreign invaders, the Hyksos (HIHK sohs), occupied the delta region. They awed the Egyptians with their horse-drawn war chariots. In time, the Egyptians mastered this new military technology. The Hyksos, in turn, were impressed by Egyptian civilization. They soon adopted Egyptian customs, beliefs, and even names. Finally, after more than 100 years, new Egyptian leaders arose. They drove out the Hyksos and set up the New Kingdom.

The New Kingdom

During the New Kingdom, powerful and ambitious pharaohs created a large empire. At its height, the Egyptian empire reached the Euphrates River. This age of conquest brought Egypt into greater contact with southwestern Asia as well as with other parts of Africa.

Powerful Rulers   One monarch of the New Kingdom, Hatshepsut (hat SHEHP soot), was a woman who exercised all the rights of a pharaoh. From 1503 B.C. to 1482 B.C., she encouraged trade with eastern Mediterranean lands and along the Red Sea coast of Africa.

The most powerful pharaoh of the New Kingdom was Ramses II. Between 1290 B.C. and 1224 B.C., Ramses pushed Egyptian rule northward as far as Syria. On temples and monuments, he boasted of his conquests, though his greatest reported victory may not actually have taken place. In a battle against the Hittites of Asia Minor, only the desperate bravery of Ramses himself prevented a crushing defeat. Back home, however, Ramses had inscriptions carved on a monument that made the near defeat sound like a stunning victory.

After years of fighting, the Egyptians and Hittites signed a peace treaty, the first such document known to have survived in history. It declared that Egypt and the Hittites "shall be at peace and in brotherhood forever."

Decline   After Ramses II, Egyptian power slowly declined. Invaders, such as the Assyrians and Persians, conquered the Nile region. Later, Greek and Roman armies came from the north. Each new conqueror was eager to add the fertile Nile Valley to a growing empire.

Egypt and Nubia

The Nile kingdom of Nubia (also known as Kush) developed to the south of Egypt. You will read more about Nubian civilization in a later chapter. Here, we will look at the relationship between the two kingdoms.

For centuries, Egyptians traded or fought with their southern neighbor. From Nubia, they acquired ivory, cattle, and slaves. During the New Kingdom, Egypt conquered Nubia. Ramses II used gold from Nubia to pay charioteers in his army. Nubians served in Egyptian armies and left their mark on Egyptian culture. Much Egyptian art of this period shows Nubian soldiers, musicians, or prisoners.

As Egypt declined, Nubia regained its independence. In 750 B.C., Nubian kings marched north, adding Egypt to their own lands. For 100 years, the Nubian empire stretched from what is today Sudan to the Mediterranean.

The Nubians saw themselves not as foreign conquerors but as restorers of Egyptian glory. They ruled Egypt like earlier pharaohs, respecting ancient Egyptian traditions. About 650 B.C., Assyrians, armed with iron weapons, descended on Egypt. They pushed the Nubians back into their original homeland, where Nubian monarchs ruled for 1,000 years more.

Biography

Hatshepsut
c. 1540 B.C.–1482 B.C.

Hatshepsut was the daughter of one pharaoh and the widow of another. Like some earlier Egyptian queens, she began ruling in the name of a male heir who was too young to take the throne. However, she then took the bold step of declaring herself pharaoh and won the support of key officials. Because Egyptians thought of their rulers as male, she wore a false beard as a sign of authority.

On the walls of her funeral temple, Hatshepsut left behind a record of her 20-year reign. Carvings depict an expedition she sent down the Red Sea coast of Africa, which brought back ivory, spices, and incense.

Theme: Impact of the Individual Why do you think Hatshepsut wanted to leave a record of her accomplishments?

Recall

1. **Identify:** **(a)** Menes, **(b)** Ptah-hotep, **(c)** Giza, **(d)** Hatshepsut, **(e)** Ramses II.
2. **Define:** **(a)** silt, **(b)** cataract, **(c)** delta, **(d)** dynasty, **(e)** pharaoh, **(f)** vizier.

Comprehension

3. Give two examples of how the Nile shaped ancient Egypt.
4. Describe one major achievement of each of Egypt's three ancient kingdoms.

5. Explain how Egypt was affected by its contacts with the Nubians.

Critical Thinking and Writing

6. **Drawing Conclusions** How are colossal monuments, such as the pyramids, a source of information about ancient Egypt?
7. **Making Inferences** Why do you think Ramses ordered misleading information about his battles to be inscribed on a public monument?

Activity

Writing Instructions Write an instruction of your own that the Vizier Ptah-hotep might have written to advise a political leader of today. The topic might be how to work with other people or how to govern fairly.

Egyptian Civilization

Reading Focus

■ How did religious beliefs shape the lives of Egyptians?

■ How was Egyptian society organized?

■ What advances did Egyptians make in learning and the arts?

Vocabulary

mummification
hieroglyphics
ideogram
demotic
papyrus
decipher

Taking Notes

Copy this concept web. As you read the section, fill in each blank circle with important facts to remember about Egyptian civilization. Part of the web has been filled in to help you get started.

Main Idea Religion and learning played an important role in ancient Egyptian civilization.

Honoring an Egyptian God
The ancient Egyptians were polytheistic, worshiping many gods and goddesses. In this painting, a musician plays for a falcon-headed god.

Theme: Religions and Value Systems What does this painting suggest about the relationship between the ancient Egyptian people and their gods?

Setting the Scene From an early age, Egyptian children heard stories about their gods and goddesses. A popular tale concerned the goddess Isis (ī sihs) and the god Osiris (oh sī rihs). Osiris ruled Egypt until he was killed by his jealous brother, Set. The wicked Set then cut Osiris into pieces, which he tossed all over Egypt.

Osiris was saved by his faithful wife, Isis. She reassembled her husband's body and brought him back to life. Because Osiris could no longer rule over the living, he became god of the dead and judge of the souls seeking admission to the afterlife.

The symbol of the divine Isis was the ankh, a cross with a loop above the bar. To Egyptians, an ankh placed on a dead person assured the soul of eternal life. "The blood of Isis," they prayed, "the charms of Isis, the power of Isis are a protection unto me." The Egyptians' belief in eternal life had a profound effect on their civilization.

Egyptian Religion

Egyptians inherited from their earliest ancestors a variety of religious beliefs and practices. Inscriptions on monuments and wall paintings in tombs reveal how Egyptians appealed to the divine forces that they believed ruled this world and the afterlife.

Chief Gods and Goddesses In the sun-drenched land of Egypt, the chief god was the sun god, Amon-Re (AH muhn RAY). The pharaoh, whom Egyptians viewed as a god as well as a monarch, was closely linked to Amon-Re. Only the pharaoh could conduct certain ceremonies for the sun god.

Most Egyptians identified more easily with Osiris and Isis, whose story touched human emotions such as love, jealousy, and fear of death. According to the myth of Osiris and Isis, their son, Horus, later took revenge on the wicked god Set, killing his uncle.

To Egyptians, Osiris was especially important. Not only did he rule over the underworld, but he was also god of the Nile. In that role, he controlled the annual flood that made the land fertile. Isis had special appeal for women, who believed that she had first taught women to grind corn, spin flax, weave cloth, and care for children. Like Osiris, Isis promised the faithful that they would have life after death.

A Religious Rebel   About 1380 B.C., a young pharaoh challenged the powerful priests of Amon-Re. He devoted his life to the worship of Aton, a minor god whose symbol was the sun's disk. The pharaoh took the name Akhenaton (ah kuh NAH tuhn), meaning "he who serves Aton." With the support of his wife, Queen Nefertiti, Akhenaton tried to sweep away all other gods in favor of Aton. He ordered priests to stop worshiping other gods and to remove the names of these gods from their temples.

Scholars disagree about Akhenaton's goals. Some think the pharaoh was trying to introduce a new religion based on worship of a single god. Others argue that he just wanted to raise Aton to the highest place among the gods.

Akhenaton's radical ideas had little success. Priests of Amon-Re and of other gods resisted the revolutionary changes. The common people, too, were afraid to abandon their old gods in favor of Aton. Nobles also deserted the pharaoh because he neglected his duty of defending the empire. After Akhenaton's death, the priests of the old gods reasserted their power.

Belief in an Afterlife

As you read, Egyptians believed that Osiris and Isis had promised them eternal life after death. Belief in the afterlife affected all Egyptians, from the highest noble to the lowest peasant.

A Fateful Test   The Egyptians believed that each soul had to pass a test in order to win eternal life. According to Egyptian belief, the dead soul would be ferried across a lake of fire to the hall of Osiris. There, Osiris would weigh the dead person's heart against the feather of truth. Those he judged to be sinners would be fed to the crocodile-shaped Eater of the Dead. Worthy souls would enter the Happy Field of Food, where they would live forever in bliss.

To survive the dangerous journey through the underworld, Egyptians relied on the Book of the Dead. It contained spells, charms, and formulas for the dead to use in the afterlife. The Book of the Dead includes a Negative Confession, which the dead soul could use to prove his or her worthiness to Osiris:

> "I have made no man to suffer hunger. I have made no one to weep. I have done no murder. . . . I have not encroached upon the fields of another. I have not added to the weights of the scales to cheat the seller. . . . I have not turned back water when it should flow. . . . I am pure. I am pure. I am pure."
> —Book of the Dead

The Book of the Dead was written on scrolls and placed in tombs. Today, these scrolls have given modern scholars a wealth of information about Egyptian beliefs and practices.

Mummification   Egyptians believed that the afterlife would be much like life on Earth. As a result, they buried the dead with everything they would need for eternity.

To give a soul use of its body in the afterlife, Egyptians perfected skills in mummification (muhm mih fih KAY shuhn), the preservation of the dead. Skilled embalmers extracted the brain of the dead person through the nostrils and removed most of the internal organs. They filled the body cavity with spices, then later dried and wrapped the body in strips of linen. This costly process took months to complete. At first, mummification was a privilege reserved for rulers and nobles. Eventually, ordinary Egyptians also won the right to mummify their dead.

Did You Know?

Mummified Cats

When archaeologists unearthed a cemetery in Bubastis, Egypt, they found something unexpected—thousands of cat mummies! Why did the Egyptians mummify these animals? Archaeologists have discovered that Bubastis was a center for the worship of Bastet, a cat goddess. Some Egyptians prayed to Bastet for protection against diseases and demons. To honor her, worshipers made gifts of cat mummies to her shrines. Many of these mummies were topped with tiny death masks in the shape of a cat's face.

Theme: Continuity and Change   Can you think of interesting beliefs that some people have about cats today?

EGYPTIAN TOMB ART

Holding a candle, archaeologist Howard Carter allowed a ray of light to penetrate the blackness of Tutankhamen's tomb. When his eyes adjusted to the gloom, Carter was astonished by what he saw—exquisite artifacts, gold, and jewels. He knew he had found some of the finest examples of Egyptian art ever uncovered.

This coffin (left) held the dead man's vital organs. The realistic features of the face and the intricate inlays of precious stones show that the goldsmiths were masters of their craft.

In the wall painting below, Anubis—the jackal-headed god of the dead—prepares the body of the pharaoh for the afterlife.

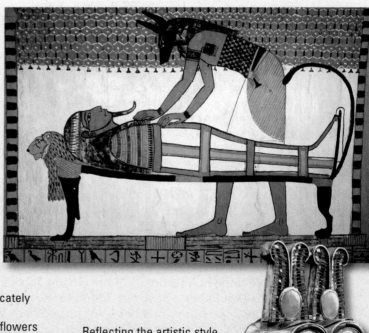

Alabaster was delicately carved into a cup representing lotus flowers (below). To the Egyptians, the lotus symbolized immortality because the blossoms filled the Nile year after year.

Reflecting the artistic style developed in the New Kingdom, this small container (right) shows Tutankhamen looking more like a man than a god. He is shown in a natural sitting position.

Portfolio Assessment

INTERNET Use the Internet or library resources to find other examples of Egyptian art. Create your own exhibit of five or more artifacts. Write a caption to describe each object, explaining why you included it in the exhibit.

Evidence of the Tomb of Tutankhamen   Many pharaohs were buried in the desolate Valley of the Kings. Their tombs, filled with fantastic riches, were a temptation to robbers in ancient times. As a result, most royal tombs were stripped of their treasures long ago. Then, in 1922, the British archaeologist Howard Carter unearthed the tomb of the pharaoh Tutankhamen (too tahng KAH muhn), the son-in-law of Akhenaton. It had remained almost untouched for more than 3,000 years. The tomb and its treasures have provided a wealth of evidence about Egyptian civilization.

The body of the 18-year-old "King Tut" had been placed in a solid-gold coffin, nested within richly decorated outer coffins. Today, the dazzling array of objects found in the tomb fills several rooms in the Egyptian Museum in Cairo. They include chariots, weapons, furniture, jewelry, toys, games, and food.

Tutankhamen was only a minor king. We can only imagine what treasures must have filled the tombs of great pharaohs like Ramses II.

Egyptian Society

Like other early civilizations, Egypt had its own class system. As both a god and an earthly leader, the pharaoh stood at the top of society, along with the royal family. Directly under the pharaoh were the high priests and priestesses, who served the gods and goddesses. Next came the nobles, who fought the pharaoh's wars. A tiny class of merchants, scribes, and artisans developed slowly. They provided for the needs of the rich and powerful.

The Life of the Farmer   Most Egyptians were peasant farmers. Many were slaves. Men and women spent their days working the soil and repairing the dikes. One ancient record describes the life of a typical Egyptian peasant. "When the water is full he irrigates [the fields] and repairs his equipment. He spends the day cutting tools for cultivating barley, and the night twisting ropes."

In the off-season, peasant men were expected to serve the pharaoh, laboring to build palaces, temples, and tombs. Besides working in the fields, women also spent much time raising children, collecting water, and preparing food—tasks similar to those of peasant women today.

Social Change   During the New Kingdom, society grew more fluid as trade and warfare increased. Trade offered new opportunities to the growing merchant class. Foreign conquests brought riches to Egypt, which in turn meant more business for artisans. These skilled craftworkers made fine jewelry, furniture, and fabrics for the palaces and tombs of pharaohs and nobles.

Women   Egyptian women generally enjoyed a higher status and greater independence than women elsewhere in the ancient world. Ramses II declared, "The foot of an Egyptian woman may walk where it pleases her and no one may deny her." Under Egyptian law, women could inherit property, enter business deals, buy and sell goods, go to court, and obtain a divorce.

Although there were often clear distinctions between the occupations of women and men, women's work was not confined to the home. They manufactured perfume and textiles, managed farming estates, and served as doctors. Women could also enter the priesthood, especially in the service of goddesses. Despite their many rights and opportunities, few women learned to read and write. Even if they did, they were excluded from becoming scribes or holding other government jobs.

Egyptian Learning

Learned scribes played a central role in Egyptian society. Temple scribes kept records of ceremonies, taxes, and gifts. Other scribes served nobles or the pharaoh. With skill and luck, a scribe from a poor family might become rich and powerful. Besides learning to read and write, scribes also acquired skills in mathematics, medicine, and engineering.

Written Records   Like other early civilizations, the ancient Egyptians developed a form of picture writing. Hieroglyphics (hi er oh GLIHF ihks) were used to keep important records. Early on, priests and scribes carved hieroglyphics on stone. Inscriptions on temples and other monuments preserved records of Egyptian culture that have endured for thousands of years.

The earliest hieroglyphics were pictograms that depicted objects. Later, written language became more complex. The Egyptians added ideograms, pictures that symbolized an idea or action. For example, a picture of a reclining figure meant sleep.

Over time, scribes developed demotic, a simpler form of writing for everyday use. They also learned to make a paperlike writing material from papyrus (puh PĪ ruhs), a plant that grows along the banks of the Nile. (Paper would not be invented until about A.D. 100, in China.) Writing with reed pens and ink on the smooth surface of papyrus strips was much easier than chiseling words onto stone. When writing official histories, however, scribes continued to carve hieroglyphics.

The Rosetta Stone   After the New Kingdom declined, Egyptians forgot the meanings of ancient hieroglyphics. Not until the early 1800s did a French scholar, Jean Champollion (ZHAHN shahm poh LYOHN), unravel the mysterious writings on Egypt's great monuments.

Champollion managed to decipher, or decode, the Rosetta Stone. This flat, black stone has the same message carved in three different forms of script—hieroglyphics, demotic, and Greek. By comparing the three versions, Champollion patiently worked out the meanings of many hieroglyphic symbols. As a result of that breakthrough, scholars could begin to read the thousands of surviving records from ancient Egypt.

Advances in Medicine and Science   The ancient Egyptians accumulated a vast store of knowledge in fields such as medicine, astronomy, and mathematics. They were a practical people. When they had a problem, they used trial and error to find a solution.

Like most doctors until recent times, Egyptian physicians believed in various kinds of magic. Yet, through their knowledge of mummification, they learned a lot about the human body. They also became skilled at observing symptoms, diagnosing illnesses, and finding cures. Doctors performed complex surgical operations, which they described on papyrus scrolls. Many medicines that Egyptian doctors prescribed are still used, including anise, castor beans, and saffron.

Egyptian priest-astronomers studied the heavens, mapping constellations and charting the movements of the planets. With this knowledge, they developed a calendar that had 12 months of 30 days each and 5 days added at the end of each year. With a few changes, this ancient Egyptian calendar became the basis for our modern calendar.

Nile floods forced Egyptians to redraw the boundaries of fields each year. To do this, they developed practical geometry to survey the land. Egyptian engineers also used geometry to calculate the exact size and location of each block of stone to be placed in a pyramid or temple. Huge building projects such as pyramids and irrigation systems required considerable skills in design and engineering.

Arts and Literature

The Egyptians left a rich legacy of art and literature. Statues, paintings, poems, and tales have given us a wealth of information about ancient Egyptian attitudes and values.

Portrait of Queen Nefertiti
Most early Egyptian art focused on scenes of death and the afterlife. During the New Kingdom, many artists turned to likenesses of living people. This famous statue presents Nefertiti, wife of the pharaoh Akhenaton, as the image of perfect beauty.

Theme: Art and Literature
How did the artist use exaggeration to emphasize the beauty of Nefertiti?

Painting and Sculpture The arts of ancient Egypt included statues, wall paintings in tombs, and carvings on temples. Some show everyday scenes of trade, farming, family life, or religious ceremonies. Others boast of victories in battles.

Painting styles remained almost unchanged for thousands of years. The pharaohs and gods were always much larger than any other human figures. Artists usually drew people with their heads and limbs in profile but their eyes and shoulders facing the viewer.

Statues often depicted people in stiff, standard poses. Some human figures have animal heads that represent special qualities. The Great Sphinx that crouches near the pyramids at Giza portrays an early pharaoh as a powerful lion.

Besides the pyramids, Egyptians erected other great buildings. The magnificent temple of Ramses II at Karnak contains a vast hall with towering 80-foot columns. Much later, the Romans would adopt building techniques like those used at Karnak.

Egyptian Literature The oldest literature of ancient Egypt includes hymns and prayers to the gods, proverbs, and love poems. Other writings tell of royal victories in battle or, like *Instruction of Ptah-hotep*, give practical advice.

In Egypt, as in other early societies, folk tales were popular, especially *The Tale of Sinuhe.* It relates the wanderings of Sinuhe (sihn oo HAY), an Egyptian official forced to flee into what is now Syria. He fights his way to fame among the desert people, whom the Egyptians consider uncivilized. As he gets older, Sinuhe longs to return home. The story ends happily when the pharaoh welcomes him back to court. (See the Primary Source, right.) *The Tale of Sinuhe* helps us see how Egyptians viewed both themselves and the people of the surrounding desert.

Looking Ahead

Long after its power declined, Egypt remained a center of learning and culture in the African and Mediterranean worlds. It also retained economic importance as a source of grain and other riches.

In later ages, new Egyptian cities like Alexandria and Cairo would attract scholars, traders, and other visitors. Yet, from ancient times to today, foreigners have gazed in awe at the monuments of a culture that flourished for 3,000 years.

Primary Source

An Egyptian Folk Tale
As Sinuhe concludes his story, he describes how he sheds the life of a nomad to live his remaining years in comfort in Egypt:

"His majesty said: 'Behold, thou art come. Thou hast trodden the foreign countries and made a flight. [But now] elderliness has attacked thee; thou hast reached old age.... Do not [live in exile] any longer.'... I answered it with the answer of one afraid: 'What is it that my lord says to me?... Behold, I am before thee.... May thy majesty do as he pleases....'

I was put into the house of a royal son, in which were splendid things.... Years were made to pass away from my body. I was shaved, my hair was combed.... And I was dressed in the finest linen and anointed with the best oil. I slept on a bed, and gave up the sand to them who live [in the desert]."

—*The Tale of Sinuhe*

Skills Assessment

Primary Source **What did the pharaoh propose to Sinuhe, and what was Sinuhe's response?**

SECTION 2 Assessment

Recall
1. **Identify: (a)** Osiris, **(b)** Isis, **(c)** Amon-Re, **(d)** Akhenaton, **(e)** Tutankhamen, **(f)** Jean Champollion, **(g)** Rosetta Stone, **(h)** *The Tale of Sinuhe.*
2. **Define: (a)** mummification, **(b)** hieroglyphics, **(c)** ideogram, **(d)** demotic, **(e)** papyrus, **(f)** decipher.

Comprehension
3. **(a)** Which gods and goddesses were especially important to the ancient Egyptians? **(b)** What role did they play in Egyptian life?

4. **(a)** What social classes existed in ancient Egypt? **(b)** What rights did women have?
5. Describe three achievements of ancient Egyptians in the arts or learning.

Critical Thinking and Writing
6. **Synthesizing Information** How were religion, government, and the arts linked in ancient Egypt?
7. **Connecting to Geography** Describe two ways that Egyptian inventions or scientific advances were linked to geography.

Activity
Take It to the NET

Use the Internet to research the Rosetta Stone. Then, write a headline and a brief news account about the decoding of the Rosetta Stone. Include quotations from historians or archaeologists explaining why this discovery is so valuable.

City-States of Ancient Sumer

Reading Focus

- How did geographic features influence the civilizations of the Fertile Crescent?
- What were the main features of Sumerian civilization?
- What advances in learning did Sumerians make?

Vocabulary

hierarchy
ziggurat
cuneiform

Taking Notes

As you read, prepare an outline of this section. Use Roman numerals to indicate the major headings of the section, capital letters for the subheadings, and numbers for the supporting details. The sample at right will help you get started.

I. Geography: The Fertile Crescent
  A. The land between the rivers
    1.
    2.
    3.
  B. Floods and irrigation
    1.
    2.
    3.

Main Idea The fertile land between the Tigris and Euphrates rivers supported the development of Sumerian civilization.

Setting the Scene "Why do you idle about? Go to school and recite your assignment. . . . After you have finished, come to me. Do not wander about in the street. Now, do you know what I said?" Almost 4,000 years ago, a father wrote those words to his son, who was studying to become a scribe. He then made his son copy the instructions so he would not forget them.

The father and son lived in Sumer, a region located between the Tigris and Euphrates rivers. The cities of Sumer lay to the northeast of the Nile in what we today call the Middle East. As builders of the earliest known civilization, the Sumerians made a lasting contribution to the world.

Geography of the Fertile Crescent

If you look at the map on the next page, you will notice an arc of land that curves from the Persian Gulf to the eastern Mediterranean coast. The dark, rich soils and golden wheat fields earned it the name Fertile Crescent.

Nomadic herders, ambitious invaders, and traders easily overcame the few natural barriers across the Fertile Crescent. As a result, the region became a crossroads where people and ideas met and mingled. Each new group that arrived made its own contributions to the turbulent history of the region.

The Land Between the Rivers The first known civilization in the Fertile Crescent was uncovered in the 1800s in Mesopotamia. The Tigris and Euphrates rivers define Mesopotamia, which means "between the rivers" in Greek. The two rivers flow from the highlands of modern-day Turkey through Iraq into the Persian Gulf.

In Sumer, as in Egypt, the fertile land of a river valley attracted Stone Age farmers from neighboring regions. In time, their descendants produced the surplus food needed to support growing populations.

Floods and Irrigation Just as control of the Nile was vital to Egypt, control of the Tigris and Euphrates was key to developments in Mesopotamia. The rivers frequently rose in terrifying floods that washed away topsoil and destroyed mud-brick villages. One story in the long Sumerian narrative poem *The Epic of Gilgamesh*, tells of a great flood that destroys the world. Archaeologists have indeed found evidence that a catastrophic flood devastated the Fertile Crescent some 4,900 years ago.

To survive and protect their farmland, villages along the riverbanks had to work together. Even during the dry season, the rivers had to be controlled

Global Connections

Flood Stories Around the World

The flood story in *The Epic of Gilgamesh* begins when the gods decide to destroy the world and its wickedness. They instruct Utnapishtim to build a boat to save his family and every species of animal. He sends out birds from his boat to search for dry land.

Stories involving floods that destroy the world can also be found in other cultures. In a tale from East Africa, a curious daughter-in-law ignores a warning not to touch a magical water pot. It breaks and a huge flood drowns everyone. In ancient China, Tse-gu-dzih sends a flood to destroy wicked humankind. Only the favored Du-mu, his family, and a few animals are saved in a hollowed-out log.

Theme: Religions and Value Systems What common theme exists in the flood stories of ancient China and Sumer?

to channel water to the fields. Temple priests or royal officials provided the leadership that was necessary to ensure cooperation. They organized villagers to build dikes to hold back flood waters and irrigation ditches to carry water to their fields.

The First Cities   Around 3200 B.C., the first Sumerian cities emerged in the southern part of Mesopotamia. The Sumerians had few natural resources, but they made the most of what they had. They lacked building materials, such as timber or stone, so they built with earth and water. They made bricks of clay, shaped in wooden molds and dried in the sun. These bricks were the building blocks for great cities like Ur and Erech.

Trade brought riches to Sumerian cities. Traders sailed along the rivers or risked the dangers of desert travel to carry goods to distant regions. (Although the wheel had been invented by some earlier unknown people, the Sumerians made the first wheeled vehicles.) Archaeologists have found goods from as far away as Egypt and India in the rubble of Sumerian cities.

Sumerian Civilization

Rival Sumerian city-states often battled for control of land and water. For protection, people turned to courageous and resourceful war leaders. Over time, these war leaders evolved into hereditary rulers.

Government and Society   In each city-state, the ruler was responsible for maintaining the city walls and the irrigation systems. He led its armies in war and enforced the laws. As government grew more complex, he employed scribes to carry out functions such as collecting taxes and keeping records. The ruler was seen as the chief servant of the gods and led ceremonies designed to please them.

Each Sumerian city-state had a distinct social hierarchy (HĪ uh rahr kee), or system of ranks. The highest class included the ruling family, leading officials, and high priests. A small middle class was made up of lesser priests and scribes. The middle class also included merchants and artisans. Artisans who practiced the same trade, such as weavers or carpenters, lived and worked in the same street.

At the base of society were the majority of people, peasant farmers. Some had their own land, but most worked land belonging to the king or temples. Sumerians also owned slaves. Most slaves had been captured in war. Some, though, had sold themselves into slavery to pay their debts.

The role of women in Sumerian society changed over time. In the earliest Sumerian myths, a mother-goddess reflected the honored role of mothers in farming communities. As large city-states emerged with warrior-leaders at their heads, male gods replaced the mother-goddess. Still, in the early city-states, wives of rulers enjoyed special powers and duties. Some supervised palace workshops and ruled for the king when he was absent. Over time, as men gained more power and wealth, women became more dependent on men. Yet women continued to have legal rights. Well-to-do women engaged in trade and owned property.

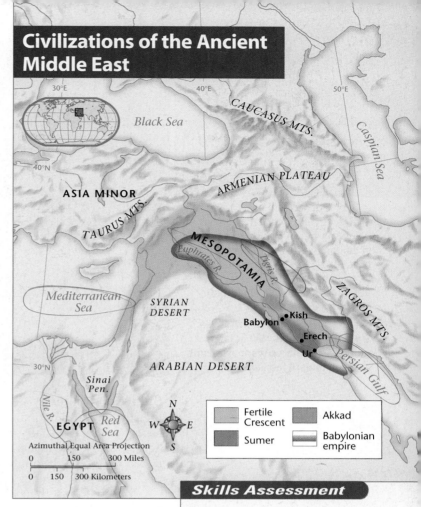

Civilizations of the Ancient Middle East

Skills Assessment

Geography   A series of early civilizations rose in the land between the Tigris and Euphrates rivers.

1. **Location**   On the map, locate (a) Tigris River, (b) Euphrates River, (c) Fertile Crescent, (d) Sumer, (e) Akkad, (f) Babylonian empire.
2. **Place**   What features may have limited the expansion of these early civilizations?
3. **Critical Thinking Comparing**   Review the map of the Egyptian empire in Section 1. Compare the location, physical features, and extent of the Egyptian and Babylonian empires.

Virtual Field Trip

www.phschool.com

**Ziggurat of Ur-Namma
Haifa, Israel**

To see other detailed views of this
ziggurat, use the Internet address
above to link to the University
of Haifa.

A Sumerian Ziggurat
Using sun-baked bricks, workers
in the Sumerian city-state of Ur
built this ziggurat around 2100 B.C.
Its wide steps were designed to
allow the gods to descend from
heaven to earth.

**Theme: Religions and
Value Systems** What later
religious structures were also built
to reach toward the heavens?

▶ **Primary Sources
and Literature**

**See "The Epic of
Gilgamesh" in the
Reference Section at
the back of this book.**

Sumerian Religion Like most ancient peoples, the Sumerians were polytheistic, worshiping many gods. These gods were thought to control every
aspect of life, especially the forces of nature. Sumerians believed that gods
and goddesses behaved like ordinary people. They ate, drank, married, and
raised families. Although the gods favored truth and justice, they were also
responsible for violence and suffering.

To Sumerians, their highest duty was to keep these divine beings
happy and thereby ensure the safety of their city-state. Each city built a
ziggurat (ZIHG uh rat), a pyramid-temple that soared toward the heavens.
At its top stood a shrine to the chief god or goddess of that city. To win the
favor of the gods, the people prayed and offered sacrifices of animals,
grain, and wine. They also celebrated holy days with ceremonies
and processions. In one ritual, the king went through a symbolic wedding
to Inanna, the life-giving goddess of love. This rite was meant to ensure
a prosperous new year.

Like the Egyptians, the Sumerians believed in an afterlife. However,
they saw the underworld as a grim place from which there was no release.
One character in *The Epic of Gilgamesh* describes the underworld as

"the place where they live on dust, their food is mud,
. . . and they see no light, living in blackness
on the door and door-bolt, deeply settled dust."
—*The Epic of Gilgamesh*

This view of the afterlife contrasts with the Egyptian vision of the Happy
Field of Food. Differences in geography may explain this contrast. The
floods of the Tigris and Euphrates were less regular and more destructive
than those of the Nile. As a result, Sumerians may have developed
a pessimistic view of the world.

Advances in Learning

By 3200 B.C., the Sumerians had invented what may be the earliest known
form of writing. This type of writing was later called cuneiform (kyoo NEE
uh form), from the Latin word *cuneus* for "wedge," because it involved
using a reed pen to make wedge-shaped marks on clay tablets.

Cuneiform grew out of a system of pictographs that priests used to record goods brought to temple storehouses. Later, priests developed symbols to represent more complicated thoughts. As their writing evolved, the Sumerians were able to use it to record not only grain harvests but also myths, prayers, laws, treaties, and business contracts.

Sumerian scribes had to go through years of difficult schooling to acquire their skills. Discipline was strict. Untidy copying or talking in class could be punished by "caning." Gifted students went on to gain a wide range of knowledge about religion, medicine, mathematics, geography, astronomy, and literature.

Over the centuries, Sumerian scholars made advances in mathematics. To measure and solve problems of calculation, they developed basic algebra and geometry. They based their number system on six, dividing the hour into 60 minutes and the circle into 360 degrees, as we still do today. Priests studied the skies, recording the movement of heavenly bodies. This knowledge enabled them to make accurate calendars, which are so essential to a farming society.

Looking Ahead

Armies of conquering peoples swept across Mesopotamia and overwhelmed the Sumerian city-states. Often the newcomers settled in the region and adopted ideas from the Sumerians. The myths and gods of these people became mingled with those of Sumer. Later peoples also elaborated on Sumerian literature, including *The Epic of Gilgamesh.*

The newcomers adapted cuneiform to their own languages and helped spread Sumerian learning across the Middle East. Building on Sumerian knowledge of the constellations and planets, later Mesopotamian astronomers developed ways to predict eclipses of the sun and moon.

By means of the various peoples who conquered the Middle East, Sumerian knowledge passed on to the Greeks and Romans. They, in turn, had a powerful impact on the development of the western world.

CUNEIFORM WRITING

Meaning	Outline character about 3000 B.C.	Sumerian about 2000 B.C.	Babylonian about 500 B.C.
Sun			
God or heaven			
Mountain			
Ox			
Fish			

SECTION 3 Assessment

Recall
1. Identify: **(a)** Fertile Crescent, **(b)** *The Epic of Gilgamesh.*
2. Define: **(a)** hierarchy, **(b)** ziggurat, **(c)** cuneiform.

Comprehension
3. How did geography influence the city-states of Sumer?
4. How was Sumerian society organized?
5. Describe how two Sumerian accomplishments influenced later peoples.

Critical Thinking and Writing
6. **Comparing** Compare the duties of Sumerian rulers to those of rulers of countries today. How are they similar? How are they different?
7. **Analyzing Information** **(a)** What are some of the benefits and drawbacks of keeping records in cuneiform on clay tablets? **(b)** What later inventions made it easier to preserve and pass on information?

Activity

Creating Symbols Review the cuneiform chart in this section. Then, create cuneiform symbols for three objects or concepts that are important in your own life.

Invaders, Traders, and Empire Builders

Reading Focus

- How did early empires arise in Mesopotamia?

- How did ideas and technology spread?

- How did the Persians unite a huge empire?

- What contributions did the Phoenicians make?

Vocabulary

codify
criminal law
civil law
tolerance
satrap
barter economy
money economy
colony
alphabet

Taking Notes

Copy the chart below. As you read, fill in the left-hand column with the names of ancient empires in the Middle East. Fill in the right-hand column with a major contribution of each empire.

EMPIRE	CONTRIBUTION
Babylon	Hammurabi's Code

Main Idea A series of strong rulers united the lands of the Fertile Crescent into well-organized empires.

Primary Source

The Code of Hammurabi
To establish respect for his laws, Hammurabi began his code with a statement of his authority and principles:

"Then [the gods] Anu and Bel called by name me, Hammurabi, the exalted prince, who feared God, to bring about the rule of righteousness in the land, to destroy the wicked and the evil-doers; so that the strong should not harm the weak; so that I should rule over the [people] and enlighten the land, to further the well-being of mankind. Hammurabi, the prince, called of Bel am I, making riches and increase . . . who conquered the four corners of the world [and] made great the name of Babylon. . . . When [the god] Marduk sent me to rule over men, to give the protection of right to the land, I did right and righteousness. . . ."

Skills Assessment

Primary Source By what authority does Hammurabi claim to issue his legal code?

Setting the Scene

If you had visited the palace of the ancient Assyrian king Assurbanipal (ah soor BAH nuh pahl), you would have found the walls decorated with magnificent carvings. One scene shows Assurbanipal and his queen enjoying a picnic in their lush palace garden. Nearby, musicians entertain the royal couple.

The scene is relaxed and elegant. Look carefully, though, and you will see something startling. Hanging from a tree branch, just behind a harp player, is the head of a defeated king.

In the ancient Middle East, as elsewhere, bloody warfare and advanced culture often went hand in hand. In this section, we will look at the accomplishments of a series of Middle Eastern civilizations across 3,000 years of war and peace.

Ruling a Large Empire

Invasion and conquest were prominent features in the history of the ancient Middle East. Again and again, nomadic peoples or ambitious warriors descended on the rich cities of the Fertile Crescent. While many invaders simply looted and burned, some stayed to rule. Powerful leaders created large, well-organized empires, bringing peace and prosperity to the region.

The First Empire Builder About 2300 B.C., Sargon, the ruler of neighboring Akkad, invaded and conquered the city-states of Sumer. He built the first empire known to history. His astonishing achievement did not last long, however. Soon after his death, other invaders swept into the wide valley between the rivers, tumbling his empire into ruin.

In time, the Sumerian city-states revived, and their power struggles resumed. Eventually, however, new conquerors followed in the footsteps of Sargon and imposed unity over the Fertile Crescent.

Hammurabi the Lawgiver About 1790 B.C., Hammurabi (hah moo RAH bee), king of Babylon, brought much of Mesopotamia under his control. He took steps to unite the Babylonian empire. His most ambitious and lasting contribution was his publication of a remarkable set of laws known as the Code of Hammurabi.

Hammurabi was not the author of the code. Most of the laws had been around since Sumerian times. Hammurabi, however, wanted everyone in his empire to know the legal principles his government would follow. He had artisans carve nearly 300 laws on a stone pillar for all to see. On it, he

How Should Society Deal With Lawbreakers?

The question of how to deal fairly and effectively with lawbreakers is as old as society itself. To begin your own investigation, examine the following viewpoints.

Babylon 1790s B.C.

The Code of Hammurabi calls for strict justice:

❝ If a son strike his father, his hands shall be cut off. If a man put out the eye of another man, his eye shall be put out. If he break another man's bone, his bone shall be broken. . . . If a man knock out the teeth of his equal, his teeth shall be knocked out.**❞**

Italy 1764

Cesare Beccaria was one of the first reformers to argue against torture, capital punishment, and harsh treatment of criminals:

❝ The purpose [of punishment] can only be to prevent the criminal from inflicting new injuries on its citizens and to deter others from similar acts. . . . Such punishments and such methods of inflicting them ought to be chosen, therefore, which will make the strongest and most lasting impression on the minds of men, and inflict the least torment on the body of the criminal.**❞**

New England 1600

Puritans in colonial New England enforced their laws with stocks, which were both painful and humiliating.

Singapore 1994

In 1994, an American teenager living in Singapore was sentenced to a painful flogging for acts of vandalism. An official defended his country's harsh penalties:

❝ Unlike some other societies which tolerate acts of vandalism, Singapore has its own standards of social order as reflected in our laws. We are able to keep Singapore relatively crime-free. We do not have a situation where acts of vandalism are commonplace, as in cities like New York, where even police cars are not spared.**❞**

Skills Assessment

1. Which of the following statements summarizes a Puritan view on punishment?
   - **A** Harsh penalties should be avoided.
   - **B** Punishments should not damage a criminal's body.
   - **C** Vandals should get the death penalty.
   - **D** Public humiliation is an effective way to prevent crime.

2. On what point would Beccaria agree with the official from Singapore?
   - **E** Criminals should be put in stocks.
   - **F** Punishments should stop people from committing future crimes.
   - **G** Capital punishment is an acceptable penalty for most crimes.
   - **H** Punishment should be as painful as possible.

3. **Critical Thinking** **Making Decisions** With which of the viewpoints above do you most strongly agree? Explain.

Skills Tip

When expressing a viewpoint, start with a statement of your opinion, and then give strong reasons to support your argument.

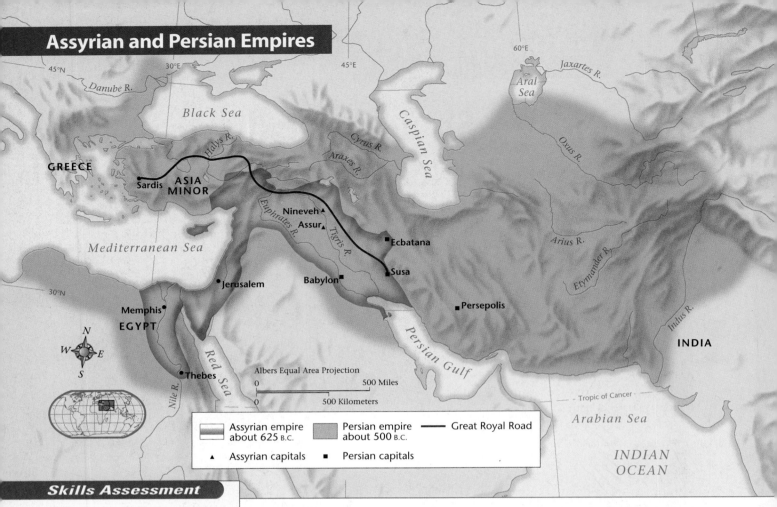

Assyrian and Persian Empires

Geography The Assyrians and Persians built huge empires in the ancient Middle East.

1. **Location** *On the map, locate* **(a)** *Assyrian empire,* **(b)** *Nineveh,* **(c)** *Persian empire,* **(d)** *Asia Minor.*
2. **Movement** *What land and water routes might a trader have taken to travel from Memphis to Nineveh?*
3. **Critical Thinking** **Making Inferences** **(a)** *How many capital cities did the Persian empire have?* **(b)** *Why do you think the Persians set up so many capitals?*

proclaimed that his goals were to "cause justice to prevail in the land / To destroy the wicked and evil / That the strong may not oppress the weak." Hammurabi's Code was the first important attempt by a ruler to codify, or arrange and set down in writing, all of the laws that would govern a state.

Crime and Punishment One section of Hammurabi's Code codified criminal law. This branch of law deals with offenses against others such as robbery, assault, or murder. Earlier traditions often permitted victims of crimes or their families to take the law into their own hands. By setting out specific punishments for specific offenses, Hammurabi's Code limited personal vengeance and encouraged social order.

By today's standards, the punishments in Hammurabi's Code often seem cruel, following the principle of "an eye for an eye and a life for a life." For example, if a house collapsed because of poor construction and the homeowner was killed, the builder of the house could be put to death. Still, such a legal code was more orderly than unrestricted personal vengeance.

Civil Law Another part of Hammurabi's Code involved civil law. This branch of law deals with private rights and matters, such as business contracts, property inheritance, taxes, marriage, and divorce.

Much of Hammurabi's civil code was designed to protect the powerless, such as slaves or women. Some laws, for example, allowed a woman to own property and pass it on to her children. Another law spelled out the rights of a married woman:

"If a woman so hated her husband that she has declared, `You may not have me,' her record shall be investigated at her city council, and if she . . . was not at fault, that woman, without incurring any blame at all, may take her dowry and go off to her father's house."

— Code of Hammurabi

If the woman were not found blameless, however, the law instructed that she be thrown in the river.

In general, Babylonian civil law gave a husband both legal authority over his wife and a legal duty to support her. The code also gave a father nearly unlimited authority over his children. The Babylonians believed that an orderly household was necessary for a stable empire.

Other Accomplishments   Although most famous for his law code, Hammurabi took other steps to unite his empire. He improved irrigation, organized a well-trained army, and had temples repaired. To encourage religious unity across his empire, he promoted the chief Babylonian god, Marduk, over older Sumerian gods.

Warfare and the Spread of Ideas

Later empires shaped the Middle East in different ways. Often, conquerors uprooted the peoples they defeated. By forcing people to move elsewhere, these invaders helped spread ideas. Other conquerors, like the Hittites, brought new skills to the region.

The Secret of Ironworking   The Hittites pushed out of Asia Minor into Mesopotamia about 1400 B.C. Although they were less advanced than the peoples of Mesopotamia, they had learned to extract iron from ore. The Hittites heated iron ore and pounded out impurities before plunging it into cold water. The tools and weapons they made with iron were harder and had sharper edges than those made out of bronze or copper. Because iron was plentiful, the Hittites were able to arm more people at less expense.

The Hittites tried to keep this valuable technology secret. But as their empire collapsed about 1200 B.C., Hittite ironsmiths migrated to serve customers elsewhere. The new knowledge thus spread across Asia, Africa, and Europe, ushering in the Iron Age.

Assyrian Warriors   The Assyrians, who lived on the upper Tigris, learned to forge iron weapons. By 1100 B.C., they began expanding across Mesopotamia. For 500 years, they earned a reputation for being among the most feared warriors in history.

Historians are unsure why warfare was so central to Assyrian culture. Was it to keep others from attacking or to please their god Assur by bringing peace and order to the region? Whatever the reason, Assyrian rulers boasted of their conquests. One told of capturing Babylon. He proclaimed, "The city and its houses, from top to bottom, I destroyed and burned with fire."

Despite their fierce reputation, Assyrian rulers encouraged a well-ordered society. They were the first rulers to develop extensive laws regulating life within

Contributions of the Fertile Crescent

Wheeled vehicles

Sumerians first used wheeled vehicles to transport goods in trade.

Alphabet

The Phoenician alphabet contained 22 symbols standing for consonant sounds, written in vertical columns from right to left. Later peoples adapted the Phoenician alphabet to produce our 26-letter alphabet.

Ironworking

Hittites learned to extract iron from ore and fashion tools and weapons that were harder than bronze or copper ones. They helped spread their knowledge of iron.

Connections to Today

Ancient civilizations of the Fertile Crescent made breakthroughs in writing, science, and technology. In some form or another, all three of the developments shown are still in use today.

Skills Assessment   **Chart** Which technological advance shown on this chart do you think was the most important? Give reasons for your answer.

the royal household. For example, women of the palace were confined in secluded quarters and had to be veiled when they appeared in public. Riches from trade and war loot paid for the splendid palaces in well-planned cities.

At Nineveh (NIHN uh vuh), King Assurbanipal founded one of the first libraries. He ordered his scribes to collect cuneiform tablets from all over the Fertile Crescent. Those tablets have given modern scholars a wealth of information about the ancient Middle East.

Babylon Revived   In 612 B.C., shortly after Assurbanipal's death, neighboring people joined forces to crush the once-dreaded Assyrian armies. An aggressive and ruthless king, Nebuchadnezzar (neh buh kuhd NEHZ uhr), revived the power of Babylon. His new Babylonian empire stretched from the Persian Gulf to the Mediterranean Sea.

Nebuchadnezzar rebuilt the canals, temples, walls, and palaces of Babylon. Near his chief palace were the famous Hanging Gardens, known as one of the wonders of the ancient world. The gardens were probably made by planting trees and flowering plants on the steps of a huge ziggurat. According to legend, Nebuchadnezzar had the gardens built to please his wife, who was homesick for the hills where she had grown up.

Under Nebuchadnezzar, the Babylonians pushed the frontiers of learning into new areas. Priest-astrologers were especially eager to understand the stars and planets, which they believed had a great influence on all events on Earth. Their observations of the heavens contributed to the growing knowledge of astronomy.

The Persian Empire

The thick walls built by Nebuchadnezzar failed to hold back new conquerors. In 539 B.C., Babylon fell to the Persian armies of Cyrus the Great. Cyrus and his successors went on to conquer the largest empire yet seen. The Persians eventually controlled a wide sweep of territory from Asia Minor to India, including present-day Turkey, Iran, Egypt, Afghanistan, and Pakistan.

In general, Persian kings pursued a policy of tolerance, or acceptance, of the people they conquered. The Persians respected the customs and religious traditions of the diverse groups in their empire.

Uniting Many Peoples   The real unification of the Persian empire was accomplished under the Persian emperor Darius, who ruled from 522 B.C. to 486 B.C. A skilled organizer, Darius set up a government that became a model for later rulers. He divided the Persian empire into provinces, each headed by a governor called a satrap. Each satrapy, or province, had to pay taxes based on its resources and wealth. Special officials, "the Eyes and Ears of the King," visited each province to check on the satraps.

Like Hammurabi, Darius adapted laws from the people he conquered and drew up a single code of laws for the empire. To encourage unity, he had hundreds of miles of roads built or repaired. Roads made it easier to communicate with different parts of the empire. Darius himself kept moving from one royal capital to another. In each, he celebrated important festivals and was seen by the people.

Economic Life   To improve trade, Darius set up a common set of weights and measures. He also encouraged the use of coins, which the Lydians of Asia Minor had first introduced. Most

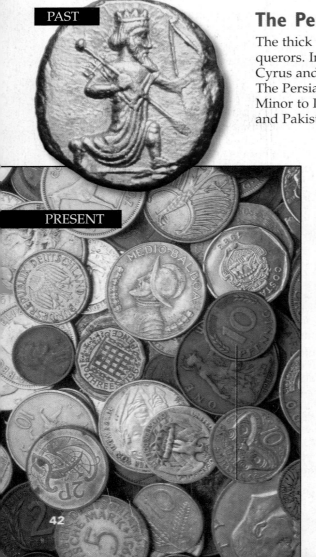

A Money Economy
Persia was the first large empire to create a uniform system of coinage. The Persian coin here depicts the emperor Darius. Today, every country in the world has its own system of coinage.

Theme: Economics and Technology What advantage does a money economy have over a barter economy?

PAST

PRESENT

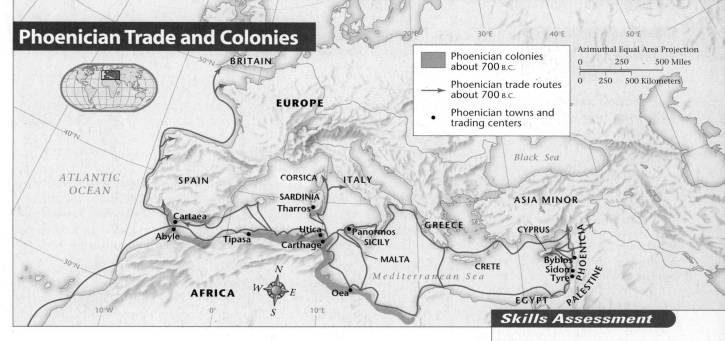

Phoenician Trade and Colonies

Phoenician colonies about 700 B.C.

→ **Phoenician trade routes** about 700 B.C.

• **Phoenician towns and trading centers**

Azimuthal Equal Area Projection
0 250 500 Miles
0 250 500 Kilometers

BRITAIN
EUROPE
ATLANTIC OCEAN
SPAIN
Cartaea
Abyle
Tipasa
AFRICA
CORSICA
ITALY
SARDINIA
Tharros
Utica
Carthage
Panormos
SICILY
MALTA
Oea
GREECE
Mediterranean Sea
CRETE
Black Sea
ASIA MINOR
CYPRUS
Byblos
Sidon
Tyre
PHOENICIA
PALESTINE
EGYPT

people continued to be part of the barter economy, exchanging one set of goods or services for another. Coins, however, brought merchants and traders into an early form of a money economy. In this system, goods and services are paid for through the exchange of some token of an agreed value, such as a coin or a bill. By setting up a single Persian coinage, Darius created economic links among his far-flung subjects.

A New Religion Religious beliefs put forward by the Persian thinker Zoroaster (zoh roh AS tuhr) also helped to unite the empire. Zoroaster lived about 600 B.C. He rejected the old Persian gods. Instead, he taught that a single wise god, Ahura Mazda (ah HOO ruh MAHZ duh), ruled the world. Ahura Mazda, however, was in constant battle against Ahriman (AH rih muhn), the prince of lies and evil. Each individual, said Zoroaster, had to choose which side to support.

Zoroaster's teachings were collected in a sacred book, the *Zend-Avesta*. It taught that in the end Ahura Mazda would triumph over the forces of evil:

> "There will come a day, the Judgment Day, when Ahura Mazda will conquer and banish Ahriman . . . when man allies himself with Ahura Mazda and helps him to banish all that is evil, all that is darkness, and all that is death."
> —Zoroaster, *Zend-Avesta*

On the Judgment Day, taught Zoroaster, all individuals would be judged for their actions. Those who had done good would enter paradise. Evildoers would be condemned to eternal suffering. Two later religions that emerged in the Middle East, Christianity and Islam, stressed similar ideas about heaven, hell, and a final judgment day.*

Phoenician Sea Traders

While powerful rulers subdued large empires, many small states of the ancient Middle East made their own contributions to civilization. The Phoenicians (fuh NEE shuhns), for example, gained fame as sailors and

---

*Today, Zoroastrianism is still practiced by tens of thousands of people, mostly in India. They are known as Parsees, from the word for *Persian*.

Skills Assessment

Geography Although their homeland was small, the Phoenicians established trade and set up colonies throughout the Mediterranean world.

1. **Location** On the map, locate **(a)** Phoenicia, **(b)** Byblos, **(c)** Tyre, **(d)** Cyprus, **(e)** Greece, **(f)** Britain.
2. **Movement** What information on the map supports the claim that the Phoenicians were skilled sailors?
3. **Critical Thinking Drawing Conclusions** How did geography influence the type of economy that the Phoenicians developed?

Geography and History

Phoenician Explorers

Did daring Phoenicians sail around Africa? No one knows for sure, but some historians believe that a Phoenician expedition rounded Africa's southern tip about 600 B.C. The only account of this expedition was written by the Greek historian Herodotus, close to 200 years later.

Herodotus gave no description of anything the Phoenicians saw in their travels—with one fascinating exception. The sailors reported that as they rounded Africa, the sun both rose and set on the right side of the ship. Because this unusual phenomenon would occur deep in the Southern Hemisphere, this statement suggests that the Phoenicians did indeed sail completely around Africa.

Theme: Geography and History Plot a course the expedition could have taken, starting in the Red Sea and ending in the Mediterranean.

---

traders. They occupied a string of cities along the eastern Mediterranean coast, in the area that is today Lebanon and Syria.

Manufacturing and Trade   The coastal land, though narrow, was fertile and supported farming. Still, the resourceful Phoenicians became best known for manufacturing and trade. They made glass from coastal sand. From a tiny sea snail, they produced a widely admired purple dye, called "Tyrian purple" after the city of Tyre. Phoenicians also used papyrus from Egypt to make scrolls, or rolls of paper, for books. The words *Bible* and *bibliography* come from the Phoenician city of Byblos.

Phoenicians traded with people all around the Mediterranean Sea. To promote trade, they set up colonies from North Africa to Sicily and Spain. A colony is a territory settled and ruled by people from another land. A few Phoenician traders braved the stormy Atlantic and sailed as far as England. There, they exchanged goods from the Mediterranean for tin.

The Alphabet   Historians have called the Phoenicians "carriers of civilization" because they spread Middle Eastern civilization around the Mediterranean. Yet the Phoenicians made their own contribution to our world, giving us our alphabet. Unlike cuneiform or hieroglyphics, in which each symbol represents a word or concept, an alphabet contains letters that represent spoken sounds.

Phoenician traders needed a quick, flexible form of writing to record business deals. The wedges of cuneiform were too clumsy, so they developed a system of 22 symbols for consonant sounds. Later, the Greeks adapted the Phoenician alphabet and added symbols for the vowel sounds. From this Greek alphabet came the letters in which this book is written.

Looking Ahead

The Middle East continued to be a vital crossroads, where warriors and traders met, clashed, and mingled. Under Persian rule, scholars drew on 3,000 years of Mesopotamian learning and added their own advances to this rich heritage. In time, the achievements of this culture filtered eastward into India and westward into Europe.

Other conquerors would overwhelm the Persian empire, although different leaders revived Persian power at various times down to the present. The Middle East remained a region where diverse peoples came into close contact. Though these people lived thousands of years ago, some of their beliefs and ideas survived to shape our modern world.

SECTION 4 Assessment

Recall

1. Identify: **(a)** Sargon, **(b)** Hammurabi, **(c)** Assurbanipal, **(d)** Nebuchadnezzar, **(e)** Cyrus the Great, **(f)** Darius, **(g)** Zoroaster.

2. Define: **(a)** codify, **(b)** criminal law **(c)** civil law, **(d)** tolerance, **(e)** satrap, **(f)** barter economy, **(g)** money economy, **(h)** colony, **(i)** alphabet.

Comprehension

3. How did Hammurabi build and strengthen an empire?

4. How did the Hittites introduce a new age of technology?

5. Describe two steps Darius took to unite the Persian empire.

6. Why were the Phoenicians called "carriers of civilization"?

Critical Thinking and Writing

7. **Connecting to Geography** How did the geography of the Fertile Crescent help a series of leaders both to conquer and to unify Mesopotamia?

8. **Making Inferences** Why do you think Darius supported the spread of Zoroastrianism throughout the Persian empire?

Activity

Take It to the NET

Use the Internet to research the Seven Wonders of the Ancient World. Then, research a list of possible Wonders of the Modern World. How are these structures similar? How are they different? What do these structures tell you about the cultures that built them?

Reading Focus

- What were the main events in the early history of the Israelites?
- How did the Jews view their relationship with God?
- What moral and ethical ideas did the prophets teach?

Vocabulary

monotheistic
covenant
patriarchal
sabbath
prophet
ethics
diaspora

Taking Notes

Copy this concept web. As you read, fill in the circles with the major beliefs of Judaism. Two circles have been filled in to help you get started.

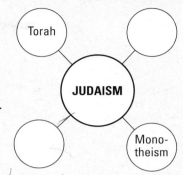

Torah

JUDAISM

Mono-theism

Main Idea The religion of the Israelites was unique in the ancient world because it was monotheistic.

Setting the Scene

"I am the Lord your God, who brought you out of the land of Egypt, out of the house of bondage. You shall have no other gods beside Me." These words—the first of the Ten Commandments—set the Israelites apart from all other people of the Fertile Crescent. Instead of worshiping many gods, the Israelites prayed to one God for guidance and protection. This promise of a unique relationship with God helped shape the history of the Israelites, later known as the Jews. Their early religion evolved into Judaism, one of the world's main faiths.

Early History of the Israelites

Early in their history, the Israelites, or Hebrews, came to believe that God was taking a hand in their lives. As a result, they recorded events and laws in the Torah, their most sacred text.

A Nomadic People According to the Torah, a man named Abraham lived near Ur in Mesopotamia. About 2000 B.C., he and his family migrated, herding their sheep and goats into a region called Canaan.* Abraham is considered the founder of the Israelite nation.

The Book of Genesis tells that a famine later forced many Israelites to migrate to Egypt. There, they were eventually enslaved. In time, Moses led the Israelites in their escape, or exodus, from Egypt. After Moses died, they entered Canaan, the land they believed God had promised them.

The Kingdom of Israel By 1000 B.C., the Israelites had set up a kingdom called Israel. David, a strong and shrewd king, united the feuding Israelite tribes into a single nation.

David's son Solomon turned Jerusalem into an impressive capital, with a splendid temple dedicated to God. Solomon won fame for his wisdom and understanding. He also tried to increase Israel's influence by negotiating with powerful empires in Egypt and Mesopotamia.

Division and Conquest Israel paid a heavy price for Solomon's ambitions. His building projects required such high taxes and so much forced labor that revolts erupted soon after his death about 922 B.C. The kingdom then split into Israel in the north and Judah in the south.

Weakened by this division, the Israelites could not fight off invading armies. In 722 B.C., Israel fell to the Assyrians. In 586 B.C., Babylonian

*Centuries later, under Roman rule, this land became known as Palestine.

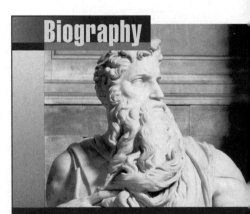

Biography

Moses
c. 1300s B.C.–1200s B.C.

According to the Bible, Moses was a reluctant hero. When God commanded him to free the Israelites from slavery in Egypt, Moses said fearfully, "Who am I that I should go to Pharaoh, and bring the sons of Israel out of Egypt?" When God insisted, Moses protested, "But I am slow of speech and of tongue." Because Moses' brother Aaron was a better public speaker, Moses asked for his help. When they saw the pharaoh, Moses told Aaron what to say, and Aaron did the talking.

Despite Moses' doubts about his abilities as a leader, he accomplished his goal. He finally freed his people from bondage in Egypt.

Theme: Impact of the Individual How did Moses conquer his fears?

armies captured Judah. Nebuchadnezzar destroyed the great temple and forced many Israelites into exile in Babylon. During this period, called the Babylonian Captivity, the Israelites became known as the Jews.

Years later, when the Persian ruler Cyrus conquered Babylon, he freed the Jews from captivity. Many returned to their homeland, where they rebuilt a smaller version of Solomon's temple. Yet, like other small groups in the region, they continued to live under Persian rule.

A Covenant With God

What you have just read is an outline of Israelite history. To the Israelites, history and faith were interconnected. Each event reflected God's plan for them. In time, their beliefs evolved into the religion we know today as Judaism.

One True God   The beliefs of the Israelites differed in basic ways from those of nearby peoples. The Israelites were monotheistic, believing in one true God. At the time, most other people worshiped many gods. A few religious leaders, such as the Egyptian pharaoh Akhenaton, spoke of a single powerful god. However, such ideas did not have the lasting impact that Israelite beliefs did.

The ancient Israelites prayed to God to save them from their enemies. Many other ancient people had also turned to particular gods as special protectors. But they thought of such gods as tied to certain places or people. The Israelites believed in an all-knowing, all-powerful God who was present everywhere.

The Chosen People   The Israelites believed that God had made a covenant, or binding agreement, with Abraham:

> "I will make nations of you, and kings shall come forth from you. . . . And I will establish my covenant between me and you and your descendants after you throughout their generations for an everlasting covenant, to be God to you."
> —Book of Genesis

Moses later renewed this covenant. In return for faithful obedience, he said, God would lead the Israelites out of bondage and into the "promised land" of Canaan. Thus, the Israelites and, later, the Jews saw themselves as God's "chosen people."

Jews Praying to God
After the Babylonian Captivity, the Jews rebuilt their temple in Jerusalem. Today, the Western Wall is all that remains of the great temple. Here, Jewish men gather at the wall to pray. Above is a morning prayer book.
Theme: Religions and Value Systems Why do you think the Western Wall is sacred to Jews around the world?

Primary Sources and Literature

See "Psalm 23" in the Reference Section at the back of this book.

Teachings on Law and Morality

From early times, the concept of law was central to the Israelites. The Torah set out many laws. Some dealt with everyday matters such as cleanliness and food preparation. Others were criminal laws.

Israelite society was patriarchal, that is, fathers and husbands held great legal and moral authority. The father or oldest male relative was head of the household and arranged marriages for his daughters. Women had few legal rights, although some laws protected them. In early times, a few outstanding women, such as the judge Deborah, won great honor.

The Ten Commandments At the heart of Judaism are the Ten Commandments, a set of laws that Jews believe God gave them through Moses. The first four Commandments stress religious duties toward God, such as keeping the sabbath, a holy day for rest and worship. The rest set out rules for conduct toward other people. They include "Honor your father and mother," "You shall not murder," and "You shall not steal."

An Ethical Worldview Often in Jewish history, spiritual leaders emerged to interpret God's will. These prophets, such as Isaiah and Jeremiah, warned that failure to obey God's law would lead their people to disaster.

The prophets also preached a strong code of ethics, or moral standards of behavior. They urged both personal morality and social justice, calling on the rich and powerful to protect the poor and weak. All people, they said, were equal before God. Unlike many ancient societies in which the ruler was seen as a god, Jews saw their leaders as fully human and bound to obey God's law.

Looking Ahead

More than 2,000 years ago, many Jews left their homeland. This diaspora (dī AS puhr uh), or scattering of people, sent Jews to different parts of the world. Wherever they settled, Jews maintained their identity as a people by living in close-knit communities and obeying their religious laws and traditions. These traditions helped them survive centuries of persecution.

Judaism is considered a major world religion for its unique contribution to religious thought. It also influenced Christianity and Islam, two other monotheistic faiths that rose in the Middle East. Today, Jews, Christians, and Muslims all honor Abraham, Moses, and the prophets, and they all teach the ethical worldview developed by the Israelites. In the west, this shared heritage of Jews and Christians is known as the Judeo-Christian tradition.

Connections to Today

Remembering the Exodus

Every year during the holiday of Passover, Jews retell the story of the Exodus from Egypt as part of an important family celebration called a seder. The storyteller, who is usually one of the adults in the family, explains the key events and symbols of the holiday to the children. The adult identifies with the Israelites who took part in the Exodus by beginning with the words "It is because of what the Lord did for me when I went free out of Egypt."

Special foods eaten during the seder also help Jews feel that they are taking part in the Exodus. A flat bread called matzo recalls how the Jews had to leave Egypt quickly and did not have time to wait for their bread to rise. Grated pieces of horseradish are eaten to symbolize the bitterness of slavery in Egypt.

Theme: Connections to Today Why is it important that the story of the Exodus be told to children as a first-person narrative?

SECTION 5 Assessment

Recall

1. **Identify:** (a) Torah, (b) Abraham, (c) Moses, (d) David, (e) Solomon, (f) Ten Commandments, (g) Judeo-Christian tradition.

2. **Define:** (a) monotheistic, (b) covenant, (c) patriarchal, (d) sabbath, (e) prophet, (f) ethics, (g) diaspora.

Comprehension

3. Why did Israel become divided?
4. How did the beliefs of the Israelites differ from those of other people of Mesopotamia?

5. Describe one Israelite teaching about each of the following: (a) family life, (b) ethics.

Critical Thinking and Writing

6. **Applying Information** Review what you have read about the Babylonian and Persian empires. Why do you think Nebuchadnezzar and Cyrus the Great treated the Jews differently?

7. **Linking Past and Present** How are the ethical beliefs of the Israelites similar to those commonly accepted in our society?

Activity

Playing a Role
With a partner, act out a conversation between an Israelite parent and child in Egypt or Babylon. The parent should try to explain why, even though they are in exile, the Israelites believe they are the "chosen people."

Review and Assessment

Creating a Chapter Summary

Copy this graphic organizer on a sheet of paper. For each category on the chart, include from one to three facts that describe the characteristics of each civilization. To help you get started, the first row has been partly filled in.

CIVILIZATION	LOCATION	GOVERNMENT	RELIGION	CONTRIBUTIONS
EGYPTIAN	• Nile River valley in North Africa	• Strong centralized state • Pharaoh believed to be divine	• Polytheistic • •	• Knowledge of human body from mummification
SUMERIAN				
BABYLONIAN				
PERSIAN				
PHOENICIAN				
ISRAELITE				

For additional review and enrich-ment activities, see the interactive version of *World History* available on the Web and on CD-ROM.

Web Site Self-Test
For practice test questions for Chapter 2, see
www. phschool.com.

Building Vocabulary

Review the chapter vocabulary words list-ed below. Then, use the words and their definitions to create a matching quiz. Exchange quizzes with another student. Check each other's answers when you are finished.

1. dynasty
2. pharaoh
3. hieroglyphics
4. papyrus
5. hierarchy
6. cuneiform
7. civil law
8. barter economy
9. monotheistic
10. ethics

Recalling Key Facts

11. Why was the Nile River important to ancient Egyptian civilization?
12. Why did the people of ancient Egypt mummify their dead?
13. How did Egyptians record events?
14. Where did Sumerian civilization develop?
15. Explain the importance of Hammurabi's Code.
16. Why did the Israelites consider them-selves to be God's "chosen people"?

Critical Thinking and Writing

17. **Comparing** Compare the view of the afterlife in the Sumerian and Egyptian religions. **(a)** What differences do you see between the two views? **(b)** Why do you think they might have been so different?

18. **Drawing Conclusions** One of Hammurabi's laws states, "If outlaws collect in the house of a wine-seller, and she does not arrest these outlaws and bring them to the palace, that wine-seller shall be put to death." **(a)** What was the purpose of this law? **(b)** Would you consider this a harsh law? **(c)** What similar laws do we have today?

19. **Connecting to Geography** Rivers played a major role in the develop-ment of ancient civilizations. Do rivers still play a major role in the world today? Why or why not?

20. **Analyzing Information** **(a)** What rights did women have in Egyptian, Sumer-ian, and Israelite civilizations? **(b)** How were these rights restricted? **(c)** What do these facts suggest about the sta-tus of women in ancient civilizations?

In this essay, found on an ancient Sumerian tablet, a young student at a school for scribes describes his school day. Read the essay and answer the questions that follow.

A School for Scribes

"I recited my tablet, ate my lunch, prepared my new tablet, wrote it, finished it. Then they assigned me my oral work, and in the afternoon they assigned me my written work. When school was dismissed, I went home, entered the house, and found my father sitting there. I told my father of my written work, then recited my tablet to him, and my father was delighted. . . . When I awoke early in the morning, I faced my mother and said to her: 'Give me my lunch, I want to go to school.' My mother gave me two rolls and I set out. . . . In school, the monitor in charge of punctuality said to me, 'Why are you late?' Afraid and with pounding heart, I entered before my teacher and made a respectful curtsey."

—quoted in *History Begins at Sumer* (Kramer)

21. What invention of the Sumerians allowed this account to be preserved?
22. What type of schoolwork was assigned to Sumerian students?
23. What seems to be the attitude of the Sumerian student toward **(a)** his father, **(b)** his mother?
24. **(a)** How does the student approach his teacher? **(b)** Why do you think he behaves this way?
25. Would you consider this account a reliable source of information about Sumerian education and family life? Explain.
26. **(a)** Based on what you have read, what role did scribes play in Sumerian society? **(b)** How might this explain the strict discipline of the school described here?
27. Based on this account, compare life at a Sumerian school to life at a modern American high school.

Skills Tip

In evaluating a primary source, you should know whether the writer had firsthand knowledge of the events being described. This will help you determine whether the source is reliable.

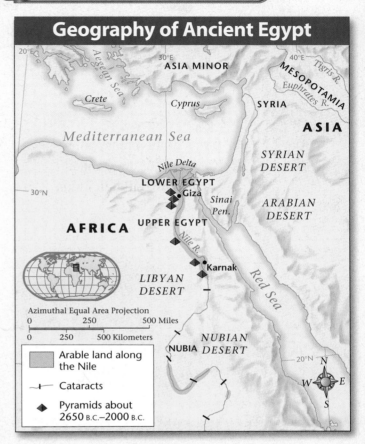

Geography of Ancient Egypt

Azimuthal Equal Area Projection
0   250   500 Miles
0   250   500 Kilometers

■ Arable land along the Nile

⊢ Cataracts

◆ Pyramids about 2650 B.C.–2000 B.C.

Look at the map above and answer the following questions:

28. Describe the location of Lower Egypt.
29. About how far was it from Karnak to Giza?
30. Why did most people in ancient Egypt live near the Nile?
31. Why was travel toward the Nile Delta easier from the northernmost cataract?
32. Based on this map, do you think Egyptian traders would be more likely to travel by the Red Sea or the Mediterranean Sea? Explain.

Skills Assessment
Take It to the NET

Use the Internet to research hieroglyphics. Then, create a cartouche (kar TOOSH) of your name. A cartouche is a hieroglyphic spelling of a name, set within a formal, oval shape. What do the images used in hieroglyphics tell you about the society and environment of ancient Egypt?

CHAPTER 3

Early Civilizations in India and China

2500 B.C.–256 B.C.

Chapter Preview

1 Cities of the Indus Valley
2 Kingdoms of the Ganges
3 Early Civilization in China

1650 B.C.
The Shang dynasty, known for fine bronzeworks such as this cauldron, gains control of territory along the Huang He.

2500 B.C.
The first Indian civilization arises in the Indus River valley. Mohenjo-Daro, a principal city, is shown here.

2000 B.C.
Chinese civilization emerges along river valleys and the east coast of Asia.

CHAPTER EVENTS

| 3000 B.C. | | 2500 B.C. | 2000 B.C. |

GLOBAL EVENTS

3000 B.C. River valley civilizations begin to emerge.

2700 B.C. The pyramid age begins in Egypt.

Geography of India and China

Geographic barriers helped shape early civilizations in India and China.

Map labels:

MANCHURIA

Sea of Japan

MONGOLIA

ALTAI MTS.

KOREA JAPAN

GOBI DESERT

TIEN SHAN

XINJIANG

ASIA

CHINA

Yellow Sea

Huang He

Wei R.

HINDU KUSH

Khyber Pass

KUNLUN MTS.

XIZANG (TIBET)

East China Sea

Persian Gulf

Bolan Pass

Indus R.

HIMALAYA MTS.

Brahmaputra R.

NORTHERN PLAIN

Yangzi R.

Si R.

PACIFIC OCEAN

VINDHYA MTS.

Ganges R.

Narmada R.

INDIA

Irrawaddy R.

South China Sea

Arabian Sea

DECCAN PLATEAU

WESTERN GHATS

EASTERN GHATS

Mekong R.

Bay of Bengal

Azimuthal Equal Area Projection

0   300   600 Miles

0   300   600 Kilometers

INDIAN OCEAN

1500 B.C.
The Aryans cross into India from the north and overrun existing cities and towns.

1027 B.C.
The Zhou overthrow the Shang. Richly adorned artworks reflect Zhou power and wealth.

500 B.C.
In India, people begin to write down Hindu sacred texts, called Vedas. The Vedas reflect Aryan belief in many deities, including Lakshmi, shown here.

1500 B.C.

1000 B.C.

500 B.C.

1400 B.C. The Olmecs develop the first civilization in the Americas.

750 B.C. Nubia conquers Egypt and gains control of the Nile Valley.

509 B.C. The Roman republic is established.

Cities of the Indus Valley

Reading Focus

■ How has geography influenced India?

■ How has archaeology provided clues about Indus Valley civilization?

■ What theories do scholars hold about the decline of Indus Valley civilization?

Vocabulary

subcontinent

plateau

monsoon

veneration

Taking Notes

As you read this section, create an outline of the main ideas. Use Roman numerals to indicate the major headings of the section, capital letters for the subheadings, and numbers for the supporting details. The sample at right has been started for you.

I. Geography of the Indian subcontinent
  A. Three regions
    1.
    2.
    3.
  B.
    1.
    2.
II. Indus Valley civilization

Main Idea Archaeologists uncovered the remains of India's first civilization in the Indus River valley.

Setting the Scene In 1922, archaeologists made a startling discovery in northwestern India. While digging in the Indus River valley, they unearthed bricks, small statues, and other artifacts unlike any they had seen before. The archaeologists soon realized that they had uncovered a "lost civilization"—one that had been forgotten for some 3,500 years. Though later discoveries have added to our knowledge of the cities of the Indus Valley, many mysteries remain.

Geography of the Indian Subcontinent

The Indus Valley is located in the region known as South Asia or the subcontinent of India. A subcontinent is a large landmass that juts out from a continent. The Indian subcontinent is a huge, wedge-shaped peninsula extending into the Indian Ocean. Today, it includes 3 of the world's 10 most populous countries—India, Pakistan, and Bangladesh—as well as the island nation of Sri Lanka (sree LAHNG kah) and the mountain nations of Nepal and Bhutan.

Towering, snow-covered mountain ranges mark the northern border of the subcontinent, including the Hindu Kush and the Himalayas. These mountains limited contacts with other lands and helped India develop a distinct culture, yet the mountains were not a complete barrier. Steep passes through the Hindu Kush served as gateways to migrating and invading peoples for thousands of years.

Regions The Indian subcontinent is divided into three major zones: the well-watered northern plain, the dry triangular Deccan, and the coastal plains on either side of the Deccan.

The northern plain lies just south of the mountains. This fertile region is watered by mighty rivers: the Indus, which gives India its name, the Ganges (GAN jeez), and the Brahmaputra (brahm uh POO truh). These rivers and their tributaries carry melting snow from the mountains to the plains, making agriculture possible. To the people of the Indian subcontinent, rivers are sacred, especially the Ganges. This great importance is reflected in one Indian name for "river": *lok-mata,* or "mother of the people."

The most recognizable feature on any map of India is the Deccan. This triangular plateau, or raised area of level land, juts into the Indian Ocean. The Deccan lacks the melting snows that feed the rivers of the north and provide water for irrigation. As a result, much of the region is arid, unproductive, and sparsely populated.

Geography and History

River of Life

Beginning in an ice cave high in the Himalayas, the Ganges River flows through one of the most heavily cultivated and densely populated regions of the world. By the time it empties into the Bay of Bengal, it has touched the lives of 10 percent of the world's population.

For more than 3,500 years, Indians have drunk from the river, bathed in it, used it for irrigation, and honored it as a giver of life. Considered the most sacred of rivers, the Ganges is central to Hinduism, which teaches that the gods brought the river's water from heaven to purify the ashes of the dead.

Theme: Religions and Value Systems How does the Ganges satisfy the material and spiritual needs of Indians today?

The coastal plains, India's third region, are separated from the Deccan by low-lying mountain ranges, the Eastern and Western Ghats. Rivers and heavy seasonal rains provide water for farmers. From very early times, people used the seas for fishing and as highways for trade.

The Monsoons Today, as in the past, a defining feature of Indian life is the monsoon, a seasonal wind. In October, the winter monsoons blow from the northeast, bringing a flow of hot, dry air that withers crops. In late May or early June, the wet summer monsoons blow from the southwest. These winds pick up moisture over the Indian Ocean and then drench the land with daily downpours.

The monsoon has shaped Indian life. Each year, people welcome the rains that are desperately needed to water the crops. If the rains are late, famine and starvation may occur. Yet, if the rains are too heavy, rushing rivers unleash deadly floods.

Cultural Diversity India's great size and diverse languages made it hard to unite. Many groups of people, with differing languages and traditions, settled in different parts of India. At times, ambitious rulers conquered much of the subcontinent, creating great empires, yet the diversity of customs and traditions remained.

Indus Valley Civilization

The earliest Indian civilization is cloaked in mystery. It emerged in the Indus River valley, in present-day Pakistan, about 2500 B.C. This civilization flourished for about 1,000 years, then vanished without a trace. Only in this century have its once prosperous cities emerged beneath the archaeologists' picks and shovels.

Archaeologists have not fully uncovered many Indus Valley sites. We have no names of kings or queens, no tax records, no literature, no accounts of famous victories. Still, we do know that the Indus Valley civilization covered the largest area of any civilization until the rise of Persia more than 1,000 years later. We know, too, that its cities rivaled those of Sumer.

Well-Planned Cities The two main cities, Harappa and Mohenjo-Daro (moh HEHN joh DAH roh), may have been twin capitals. Both were large, some three miles in circumference. Each was dominated by a massive hilltop structure, probably a fortress or temple. Both cities had huge warehouses to store grain brought in from outlying villages.

The most striking feature of Harappa and Mohenjo-Daro is that they were so carefully planned. Each city was laid out in a grid pattern, with rectangular blocks larger than modern city blocks. All houses were built of uniform oven-fired clay bricks. Houses had surprisingly modern plumbing systems, with baths, drains, and water chutes that led into sewers beneath the streets. Merchants used a uniform system of weights and measures.

From such evidence, archaeologists have concluded that the Indus Valley cities had a well-organized government. Powerful leaders, perhaps priest-kings, made sure that the tens of thousands of city-dwellers had a steady supply of grain from the villages. The rigid pattern of building and

Indus Valley Civilization

Indus Valley civilization, 2500 B.C.–1500 B.C.

Skills Assessment

Geography The earliest civilization in India developed in the Indus Valley.

1. **Location** On the map, locate **(a)** Himalaya Mountains, **(b)** Deccan Plateau, **(c)** Indus River, **(d)** Ganges River, **(e)** Harappa.
2. **Place** How has India's geography helped to protect the people living in the Deccan Plateau?
3. **Critical Thinking Making Inferences** Why do you think the Indus River valley was a more inviting location for the development of a civilization than was the Narmada River valley?

the uniform brick sizes suggest government planners. These experts must also have developed skills in mathematics and surveying to lay out the cities so precisely.

Farming and Trade As in other early civilizations, most Indus Valley people were farmers. They grew a wide variety of crops, including wheat, barley, melons, and dates. They were also the first people to cultivate cotton and weave its fibers into cloth.

Some people were merchants and traders. Their ships carried cargoes of cotton cloth, grain, copper, pearls, and ivory combs to distant lands. By hugging the Arabian Sea coast and sailing up the Persian Gulf, Indian vessels reached the cities of Sumer. Contact with Sumer may have stimulated Indus Valley people to develop their own system of writing.

Religious Beliefs From clues such as statues, archaeologists have speculated about the religious beliefs of Indus Valley people. Like other ancient people, they were polytheistic. A mother goddess, the source of creation, seems to have been widely honored. Indus people also apparently worshiped sacred animals, including the bull. Some scholars think these early practices influenced later Indian beliefs, especially the veneration of, or special regard for, cattle.

Decline and Disappearance

By 1750 B.C., the quality of life in Indus Valley cities was declining. The once orderly cities no longer kept up the old standards. Crude pottery replaced the finer works of earlier days.

We do not know for sure what happened, but scholars have offered several explanations. Damage to the local environment may have contributed to the decline. Possibly too many trees were cut down to fuel the ovens of brick makers. Tons of river mud found in the streets of Mohenjo-Daro suggest that a volcanic eruption blocked the Indus, which flooded the city. Other evidence points to a devastating earthquake.

Scholars think that the deathblow fell about 1500 B.C., when nomadic people arrived in ever larger numbers from the north. The newcomers were the Aryans, whose ancestors had slowly migrated with their herds of cattle, sheep, and goats from what is now southern Russia. With their horse-drawn chariots and superior weapons, the Aryans overran the Indus region. The cities were soon abandoned and eventually forgotten.

SECTION 1 Assessment

Recall
1. **Define: (a)** subcontinent, **(b)** plateau, **(c)** monsoon, **(d)** veneration.

Comprehension
2. Describe two ways in which geography has influenced the people of South Asia.
3. What evidence shows that Indus Valley civilization had a well-organized government?
4. Why do we know so little about Indus Valley civilization?

Critical Thinking and Writing
5. **Linking Past and Present (a)** How could natural disasters have contributed to the decline of Indus Valley civilization? **(b)** What environmental problems does the world face today?
6. **Connecting to Geography** What characteristics of rivers might explain why many people in India still consider them sacred?

Kingdoms of the Ganges

Reading Focus

- What were the main characteristics of Aryan civilization in India?
- How did expansion lead to changes in Aryan civilization?
- What do ancient Indian epics reveal about Aryan life?

Vocabulary

caste
brahman
mystic
rajah

Taking Notes

Make a concept web like the one below. As you read this section, fill in each blank circle with important information about Aryan civilization. Use the completed web to help you focus on what you learned in this section.

From Europe and Asia — ARYANS

Main Idea Aryan warriors invaded India and developed a new civilization.

Setting the Scene

The Aryans were warlike people. Their hymns praised their warriors as brave heroes and successful looters. In the *Satarudriya,* a poet lauded these warriors with the words:

> "Hail to the lord of thieves . . . hail to the destructive ones
> armed with spears, hail to the lord of plunderers.
> Hail to the archers, to those who stretch the bowstring,
> and to those who take aim."
>
> —*Yajur Veda*

Over the centuries, the Aryans who destroyed and looted the cities of the Indus Valley became the builders of a new Indian civilization. It rose in the northeast along the Ganges River, rather than in the northwest along the Indus.

Aryan Civilization

The Aryans were among many groups of Indo-European people who migrated across Europe and Asia seeking water and pasture for their horses and cattle. The early Aryans built no cities and left no statues or stone seals. Most of what we know about them comes from the Vedas, a collection of prayers, hymns, and other religious teachings. Aryan priests memorized and recited the Vedas for a thousand years before they were written down. As a result, the period from 1500 B.C. to 500 B.C. is often called the Vedic age.*

In the Vedas, the Aryans appear as warriors who fought in chariots with bows and arrows. They loved eating, drinking, music, chariot races, and dice games. These nomadic herders valued cattle, which provided them with food and clothing. Later, when they became settled farmers, families continued to measure their wealth in cows and bulls.

Aryan Society From the Vedas, we learn that the Aryans divided people by occupation. The three basic groups were the Brahmins, or priests; the Kshatriyas (kuh SHAT ree yuhz), or warriors; and the Vaisyas (vīs yuhz), or herders, farmers, artisans, and merchants. At first, warriors enjoyed the highest prestige, but priests eventually gained the most respect. Their power grew because Brahmins claimed that they alone could conduct the ceremonies needed to win the favor of the gods.

*Our knowledge about the Aryans is very limited. Historians have re-created a picture of Aryan life from studying their language, but many conclusions are still open to debate.

Primary Source

Hymn to Indra

The Rig Veda *contains this hymn to the war god Indra:*

"The one who made firm the quaking earth; the one who made fast the shaken mountains; the one who measured out wide the atmosphere; the one who propped up heaven: he, O people, is Indra. . . .

The one in whose control are horses, cows, villages, all chariots; the one who has caused to be born the sun, the dawn; the one who is the waters' leader: he, O people, is Indra. . . .

The one without whom people do not conquer; the one to whom, when fighting, they call for help; the one who is a match for everyone; the one who shakes the unshakable: he, O people, is Indra."

—*Rig Veda*

Skills Assessment

Primary Source How can you tell from this source that the Aryans admired military prowess?

Synthesizing Information

Tracing Migration Through Language

By studying the Indo-European language family, historians have learned about the migration of many peoples, including the Aryans. A *language family* is a group of related languages that developed from the same original, or parent, language. Use the map and chart below to draw conclusions about these Indo-European peoples.

Speakers of the parent Indo-European languages may have originated in north-central Europe. Over thousands of years, these people migrated across Europe and into Asia in search of good pastureland.

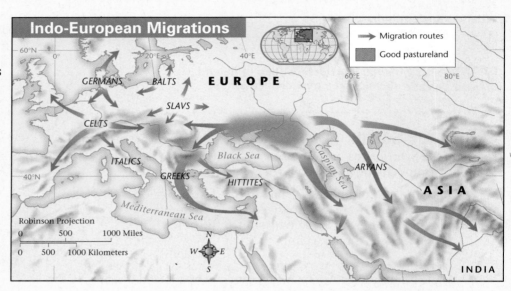

Indo-European Migrations

Comparing Languages

English	month	mother	new	night	nose	three
German	Monat	Mutter	neu	Nacht	Nase	drei
Persian	māh	mādar	nau	shab	bini	se
Sanskrit	mās	matar	nava	nakt	nās	trayas
Spanish	mes	madre	nuevo	noche	nariz	tres
Swedish	månad	moder	ny	natt	näsa	tre

The languages on the chart are all in the Indo-European language family. Similarities in words offer one clue that the languages share a common parent language. The similarities become even more apparent when the words are spoken out loud.

Skills Assessment

1. Which statement about Indo-European migrations can you base on the map?

   A Indo-European peoples migrated to the east coast of Asia.

   B Indo-European peoples migrated primarily along river and sea routes.

   C Indo-European peoples migrated across plains, mountains, and bodies of water.

   D Indo-European peoples migrated primarily to coastal areas.

2. Which statement best expresses the main idea of the chart?

   E There are six Indo-European languages.

   F There are similarities among words in Indo-European languages.

   G Indo-European languages are spoken in India and Europe.

   H Persian is unlike most other Indo-European languages.

3. **Critical Thinking Drawing Conclusions** What conclusions can you draw about Indo-European peoples, based solely on the information on this page? Explain how you arrived at each conclusion.

Skills Tip

Maps that show migrations use arrows to indicate movement. Trace routes by moving from the beginning of each arrow to its tip.

The Vedas also show that the Aryans felt vastly superior to the Dravidians, the people they conquered. Many scholars think that the Dravidians may have been descended from the original inhabitants of the Indus Valley. The Aryans separated Dravidians and non-Aryans into a fourth group, the Sudras (soo druhz). This group included farmworkers, servants, and other laborers who occupied the lowest level of society.

During the Vedic age, class divisions came to reflect social and economic roles more than ethnic differences between Aryans and non-Aryans. As these changes occurred, they gave rise to a more complex system of **castes**,* or social groups into which people are born and which they cannot change.

Aryan Religious Beliefs The Vedas show that the Aryans were polytheistic. They worshiped gods and goddesses that embodied natural forces such as sky and sun, storm and fire. Fierce Indra, the god of war, was the chief Aryan deity. Indra's weapon was the thunderbolt, which he used not only to destroy demons but also to announce the arrival of rain, so vital to Indian life. Other major gods included Varuna, the god of order and creation, and Agni, the god of fire. Agni also served as the messenger who communicated human wishes to the gods. The Aryans also honored animals, such as monkey gods and snake gods.

Brahmins offered sacrifices of food and drink to the gods. Through the correct rituals and prayers, the Aryans believed, they could call on the gods for health, wealth, and victory in war.

As the lives of the Aryans changed, so, too, did their beliefs. Some religious thinkers were moving toward the notion of a single spiritual power beyond the many gods of the Vedas, called **brahman,** that resided in all things. There was also a move toward mysticism. **Mystics** are people who devote their lives to seeking spiritual truth. Through meditation and yoga, or spiritual and bodily discipline, Aryan mystics sought direct communion with divine forces. The religions that emerged in India after the Vedic age reflected the impact of mysticism as well as the notion of brahman.

Expansion and Change

Over many centuries, waves of Aryans went through the mountain passes into northwestern India. Aryan tribes were led by chiefs called **rajahs.** A rajah was often the most skilled war leader, elected to his position by an assembly of warriors. He ruled with the advice of a council of elders made up of heads of families.

From Nomads to Farmers Aryans mingled with the people they conquered. Gradually, they gave up their nomadic ways and settled into villages to grow crops and breed cattle. From the local people, they learned farming and other skills and developed new crafts of their own.

In time, Aryans spread eastward to colonize the heavily forested Ganges basin. By about 800 B.C., they had learned to make tools out of iron. Equipped with iron axes and weapons, restless pioneers carved farms and villages out of the rain forests of the northeast. Tribal leaders fought to control trade and territory across the northern plain. Some rajahs became powerful hereditary rulers, extending their influence over many villages. Walled cities filled with multistory houses rose above the jungle.

By 500 B.C., a new Indian civilization had emerged. It consisted of many rival kingdoms. However, due to acculturation, or the blending of two or more cultures, the people shared a common culture rooted in both Aryan and Dravidian traditions. By this time, too, the Indian people had developed a written language, Sanskrit. Priests now began writing down the sacred texts.

Social Organization
Aryan society was divided into four distinct classes. One Vedic hymn explains how these classes corresponded to the human body: the Brahmins were the mouth, the Kshatriyas made up the arms, the legs were the Vaisyas, and the feet could be compared to the Sudras.

Theme: Political and Social Systems Which class does the hymn suggest was most important in Aryan society?

---

*Indians use the word *jati* to describe their social system. The Portuguese, who reached India in the late 1400s, used the word *caste,* which other Europeans adopted.

Epic Literature

Despite the new written language, the Aryans preserved a strong oral tradition. They continued to memorize and recite ancient hymns, as well as two long epic poems, the *Mahabharata* (muh HAH bah rah tuh) and the *Ramayana* (rah MAH yuh nuh). Like the Sumerian *Epic of Gilgamesh*, the *Mahabharata* and *Ramayana* mix history, mythology, adventure, and religion.

Mahabharata The *Mahabharata* is India's greatest epic. Through the tale's nearly 100,000 verses, we hear echoes of the battles that rival Aryan tribes fought to gain control of the Ganges region. Five royal brothers, the Pandavas, lose their kingdom to their cousins. After a great battle that lasts for 18 days, the Pandavas regain their kingdom and restore peace to India. One episode, known as the *Bhagavad-Gita* (BUHG uh vuhd GEE tuh), reflects important Indian religious beliefs about the immortality of the soul and the importance of duty.

Ramayana The *Ramayana* is much shorter but equally memorable. It recounts the fantastic deeds of the daring hero Rama and his beautiful bride Sita. Sita is kidnapped by the demon-king Ravana. The rest of the story tells how Rama finally rescues Sita with the aid of the monkey general Hanuman.

   Like Aryan religion, these epics evolved over thousands of years. Priest-poets added new morals to the tales to teach different lessons. For example, they pointed to Rama as a model of virtue or as an ideal king. Likewise, Sita came to be honored as an ideal woman who remained loyal and obedient to her husband through many hardships.

Looking Ahead

The Aryans were the first of many people to filter into India through passes in the Hindu Kush. Even though scholars recognize that our knowledge of the Aryan migrations is very limited, most accept that Aryan traditions and beliefs formed a framework for later Indian civilization.

   Aryan religious beliefs would evolve into major world religions. Just as the Middle East gave rise to three world religions—Judaism, Christianity, and Islam—South Asia was the birthplace of two influential faiths, Hinduism and Buddhism.

> ► **Primary Sources and Literature**
>
> **See "The Mahabharata" in the Reference Section at the back of this book.**

SECTION 2 Assessment

Recall
1. **Identify:** (a) Vedas, (b) Brahmins, (c) Kshatriyas, (d) Vaisyas, (e) Sudras, (f) Indra.
2. **Define:** (a) caste, (b) brahman, (c) mystic, (d) rajah.

Comprehension
3. What do the Vedas tell us about Aryan society and religion?
4. How did Aryan life change as a result of expansion in India?
5. What kinds of lessons do Rama and Sita teach in the epics of the *Ramayana*?

Critical Thinking and Writing
6. **Analyzing Information** Why might epic poems like the *Mahabharata* and *Ramayana* be good vehicles for teaching moral lessons?
7. **Making Generalizations** Based on what you have read about the shift in power from the Aryan warriors to the Brahmins, what generalization could you make about people and their relationship with their gods in Aryan civilization and society?

Activity

Take It to the NET

Use Internet sources to find out more about the moral dilemmas faced by characters in the *Ramayana*. Consider how these dilemmas stem from conflicting obligations. What types of dilemmas might be faced by characters in a modern-day epic?

Reading Focus

- How did geography influence early Chinese civilization?
- How did Chinese culture take shape under the Shang and the Zhou?
- What were key cultural achievements in early China?

Vocabulary

loess
clan
oracle bone
calligraphy
dynastic cycle
feudalism

Taking Notes

Make a chart like this one. As you read the section, add information about China under the Shang to the first column and information about the Zhou under the second column.

SHANG	ZHOU
• Clans controlled most of land	• Mandate of Heaven
•	•

Main Idea Early Chinese people developed a complex civilization and made many advances in learning and the arts.

Setting the Scene In very ancient times, relates a Chinese legend, flood waters rose to the top of the highest hills. Yu, a hard-working official, labored for 13 years to drain the waters:

> "I opened passages for the streams throughout the nine provinces, and conducted them to the sea. I deepened channels and canals, and conducted them to the streams."
> — *Shujing (Book of History)*

While taming the rivers, Yu did not once go home to see his wife and children. As a reward for his selfless efforts, he later became ruler of China.

The legend of Yu offers insights into early China. The ancient Chinese valued the ability to control flood waters and to develop irrigation systems for farming. The legend also shows how highly the Chinese prized devotion to duty. Both of these values played a key role in the development of Chinese civilization.

The Geography of China

The ancient Chinese called their land Zhongguo (JONG goo AW), the Middle Kingdom. China was the most isolated of the civilizations you have studied so far. Long distances and physical barriers separated it from Egypt, the Middle East, and India. This isolation contributed to the Chinese belief that China was the center of the Earth and the sole source of civilization.

Geographic Barriers To the west and southwest of China, high mountain ranges—the Tien Shan and the Himalayas—and brutal deserts blocked the easy movement of people. To the southeast, thick jungles divided China from Southeast Asia. To the north lay the forbidding desert, the Gobi. To the east, the vast Pacific Ocean rolled endlessly.

Despite formidable barriers, the Chinese did have contact with the outside world. They traded with neighboring people and, in time, Chinese goods reached the Middle East and beyond. More often, though, the outsiders whom the Chinese encountered were nomadic invaders. To the Chinese, these nomads were barbarians who did not speak Chinese and lacked the skills and achievements of a settled society. Nomads conquered China from time to time, but they were usually absorbed into the advanced Chinese civilization.

Mt. Everest
In the ancient world, the Himalayas served as one geographic barrier between China and the rest of the world. The range includes the world's highest peak, Mt. Everest, shown here.

Theme: Geography and History Why might a geographic barrier make it easier for a civilization to develop?

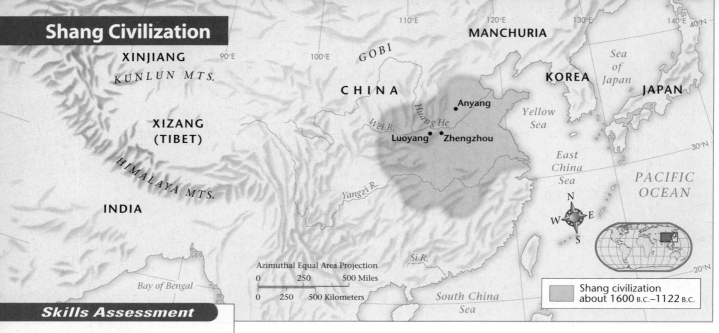

Shang Civilization

XINJIANG
KUNLUN MTS.
XIZANG (TIBET)
HIMALAYA MTS.
INDIA
Bay of Bengal

GOBI
CHINA
Wei R.
Huang He
Anyang
Luoyang Zhengzhou
Yangzi R.
Si R.
South China Sea

MANCHURIA
KOREA
Sea of Japan
JAPAN
Yellow Sea
East China Sea
PACIFIC OCEAN

Azimuthal Equal Area Projection
0   250   500 Miles
0   250   500 Kilometers

Shang civilization
about 1600 B.C.–1122 B.C.

Skills Assessment

Geography The huge landmass of China extends west from the Pacific Ocean deep into central Asia. More than two thirds of the land is made up of plateaus and mountains.

1. **Location** On the map, locate (a) Huang He, (b) Gobi, (c) Pacific Ocean.
2. **Region** What physical features acted as obstacles to contact with lands outside China?
3. **Critical Thinking Synthesizing Information** (a) Between which latitudes does most of China fall? (b) Use a map of the United States to find the latitude of your community. What part of China is at the same latitude?

Main Regions As the Chinese expanded over an enormous area, their empire came to include many regions with a variety of climates and land-forms. The Chinese heartland lay along the east coast and the valleys of the Huang He (HWAHNG HAY), or Yellow River, and the Yangzi (yahng DZEE). In ancient times, as today, these fertile farming regions supported the largest populations. Then, as now, the rivers provided water for irrigation and served as transportation routes.

Beyond the heartland are the outlying regions of Xinjiang (sheen jee AHNG), Mongolia, and Manchuria. The first two regions have harsh climates and rugged terrain. Until recent times, they were mostly occupied by nomads and subsistence farmers. All three outlying regions played a key role in China's history. Nomads repeatedly attacked and plundered Chinese cities. At other times, powerful Chinese rulers conquered or made alliances with the people of these regions. China also extended its influence over the Himalayan region of Tibet, which the Chinese called Xizang (shee DZAHNG).

"River of Sorrows" Chinese history began in the Huang He valley, where Neolithic people learned to farm. As in other places, the need to control the flow of the river through large water projects probably led to the rise of a strong central government.

The Huang He got its name from the loess, or fine windblown yellow soil, that it carries eastward from Siberia and Mongolia. Long ago, the Huang He earned a bitter nickname, "River of Sorrows." As loess settles to the river bottom, it raises the water level. Chinese peasants labored constantly to build and repair dikes that kept the river from overflowing.

If the dikes broke, flood waters burst over the land. Such disasters destroyed crops and brought mass starvation. Fear of floods is reflected in Chinese writing. The character, or written symbol, for misfortune, 巛, represents a river with a blockage that causes flooding.

China Under the Shang

About 1650 B.C., a Chinese people called the Shang gained control of a corner of northern China, along the Huang He. The Shang dynasty dominated this region until 1027 B.C. During the Shang period, Chinese civilization first took shape.

Disaster!

The Huang He Floods

For at least 4,000 years, farmers living along the Huang He in China have depended on the fertile yellow loess soil deposited along the river's banks. But they have also feared the devastating floods that the river brings every third or fourth year. In 2297 B.C., the Huang He burst its banks, destroying fields and drowning villagers.

After days of severe rains, the Huang He began to overflow its banks, spilling into the millet fields. Without the technology to dam the breach, the villagers could only flee or watch in horror as their crops and homes became completely submerged in the swirling, muddy, yellow water.

No one knows exactly how many people perished in this great flood. Worse yet, after the waters receded, many more people died as a result of a great famine that spread throughout the region. Despite this catastrophe, many villagers returned to the same spot to rebuild and plant, taking advantage of the fertile soil deposited by the flood waters.

The villagers' huts were quickly swept away in the flood. Unable to escape their pens, domestic animals reacted in fear as the waters surged toward them.

Portfolio Assessment

INTERNET Use the Internet or other research sources to learn more about a recent flood. You can start your search at **www.phschool.com**. Use the information you find to write front-page newspaper articles about the flood. You may want to use pictures or diagrams to illustrate the articles.

Virtual Field Trip

www.phschool.com

**The Tsui Museum of Art
Hong Kong, China**

To see other artworks and artifacts relating to Shang bronzes, use the Internet address above to link to the Tsui Museum of Art.

Shang Bronzes
Bronzework was a high art during the Shang period. These bronze containers were crafted to resemble a snail (left) and a pair of owls (right).

Theme: Art and Literature
What features of the bronzes suggest that the Shang were skilled metalworkers?

Government Archaeologists have uncovered large palaces and rich tombs of Shang rulers. Shang kings led other noble warriors in battle. From their walled capital city at Anyang, they emerged to drive off nomads from the northern steppes and deserts.

In one Shang tomb, archaeologists discovered the burial place of Fu Hao (FOO HOW), wife of the Shang king Wu Ding. Artifacts show that she owned land and helped to lead a large army against invaders. This evidence suggests that noblewomen had considerable status during the Shang period.

Shang kings probably controlled only a small area. Loyal princes and nobles governed most of the land. They were likely the heads of important clans, or groups of families who claimed a common (often mythical) ancestor. Thus, Shang China probably more closely resembled the city-states of Sumer than the centralized government ruled by the Egyptian pharaohs.

Social Classes Shang society mirrored that in other early civilizations. Alongside the royal family was a class of noble warriors. Shang warriors used leather armor, bronze weapons, and horse-drawn chariots. The chariots may have come from other Asian peoples.

Early Chinese cities supported a class of artisans and merchants. Artisans produced goods for nobles, including bronze weapons, silk robes, and jade jewelry. Merchants exchanged food and crafts made by local artisans for salt, cowrie shells, and other goods not found in northeastern China.

Peasant Life Most people in Shang China were peasants. They clustered together in farming villages. Many lived in thatch-roofed pit houses whose earthen floors were dug several feet below the surrounding ground.

Peasants led grueling lives. All family members worked in the fields, using stone tools to prepare the ground for planting or to harvest grain. When they were not in the fields, peasants had to repair the dikes. If war broke out between noble families, men had to fight alongside their lords.

Religious Beliefs

By Shang times, the Chinese had developed complex religious beliefs, many of which continued to be practiced for thousands of years. They prayed to many gods and nature spirits. Chief among them were Shang Di

(SHAHNG DEE) and a mother goddess who brought plants and animals to Earth. The king was seen as the link between the people and Shang Di.

Gods as great as Shang Di, the Chinese believed, would not respond to the pleas of mere mortals. Only the spirits of the greatest mortals, such as the ancestors of the king, could get the ear of the gods. Thus, the prayers of rulers and nobles to their ancestors were thought to serve the community as a whole, ensuring good harvests or victory in war.

At first, only the royal family and other nobles had ancestors important enough to influence the gods. Gradually, other classes shared in these rituals. The Chinese called on the spirits of their ancestors to bring good fortune to the family. To honor their ancestors' spirits, they offered them sacrifices of food and other necessities. When westerners reached China, they mistakenly called this practice "ancestor worship."

The Chinese believed the universe reflected a delicate balance between two forces, yin and yang. Yin was linked to Earth, darkness, and female forces, while yang stood for Heaven, light, and male forces. To the Chinese, these forces were not in opposition. Rather, the well-being of the universe depended on maintaining balance between yin and yang. For example, the king had to make the proper sacrifices to Heaven while at the same time taking practical steps to rule well.

System of Writing

The ancient Chinese also developed a system of writing. Writing, like religious beliefs, was an early development that continued to influence cultures in China throughout history. This system used both pictographs and ideographs, signs that expressed thoughts or ideas.

Consulting the Ancestors Some of the oldest examples of Chinese writing are on oracle bones. On animal bones or turtle shells, Shang priests wrote questions addressed to the gods or the spirit of an ancestor. Priests then heated the bone or shell until it cracked. By interpreting the pattern of cracks, they provided answers or advice from the ancestors.

A Difficult Study Written Chinese took shape almost 4,000 years ago. Over time, it evolved to include tens of thousands of characters. Each character represented a word or idea and was made up of a number of different strokes. In recent years, the Chinese have simplified their characters, but Chinese remains one of the most difficult languages to learn. Students must still memorize up to 10,000 characters to read a newspaper. By contrast, languages based on an alphabet, such as English or Arabic, contain only two dozen or so symbols representing basic sounds.

Not surprisingly, in earlier times, only the well-to-do could afford the years of study needed to master the skills of reading and writing. Working with brush and ink, Chinese scholars turned calligraphy, or fine handwriting, into an elegant art form.

A Force for Unity Despite its complexity, the written language fostered unity. People in different parts of China often could not understand one another's spoken language, but they all used the same system of writing.

The Zhou Dynasty

In 1027 B.C., the battle-hardened Zhou (JOH) people marched out of their kingdom on the western frontier to overthrow the Shang. They set up the Zhou dynasty, which lasted until 256 B.C.

The Mandate of Heaven To justify their rebellion against the Shang, the Zhou promoted the idea of the Mandate of Heaven, or the divine right to rule. The cruelty of the last Shang king, they declared, had so outraged the

Connections to Today

Digital Chinese

The writing systems in China, Japan, Korea, Vietnam, and Taiwan are all based on a common set of thousands of characters developed in China centuries ago. Over time, each country has modified this system in a different way. These differences have made it difficult for writers in the various countries to communicate clearly with one another.

The computer age has added new communication problems. Since the 1970s, each East Asian country has developed its own code of Chinese characters to input and transmit computer data. The codes are not always compatible, and their differences can corrupt information sent from a computer in one country to that in another. To solve this problem, an international task force is attempting to develop a standard software set of digital Chinese characters.

Theme: Continuity and Change Why might there be so much interest in developing a common Chinese character code for computer communication?

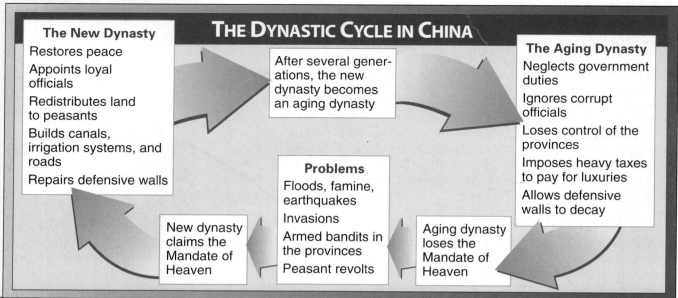

THE DYNASTIC CYCLE IN CHINA

The New Dynasty
Restores peace

Appoints loyal officials

Redistributes land to peasants

Builds canals, irrigation systems, and roads

Repairs defensive walls

After several generations, the new dynasty becomes an aging dynasty

The Aging Dynasty
Neglects government duties

Ignores corrupt officials

Loses control of the provinces

Imposes heavy taxes to pay for luxuries

Allows defensive walls to decay

Problems
Floods, famine, earthquakes

Invasions

Armed bandits in the provinces

Peasant revolts

New dynasty claims the Mandate of Heaven

Aging dynasty loses the Mandate of Heaven

Chart The Chinese believed that dynasties could gain or lose the Mandate of Heaven, depending on how wisely the emperor ruled. **According to this flowchart, how did a new dynasty try to repair the problems left by an aging dynasty?**

gods that they had sent ruin on him. The gods then passed the Mandate of Heaven to the Zhou, who "treated the multitudes of the people well." The Chinese later expanded the idea of the Mandate of Heaven to explain the dynastic cycle, or the rise and fall of dynasties. As long as a dynasty provided good government, it enjoyed the Mandate of Heaven. If the rulers became weak or corrupt, the Chinese believed that Heaven would withdraw its support.

Floods, famine, or other catastrophes were signs that a dynasty had lost the favor of Heaven. In the resulting chaos, an ambitious leader might seize power and set up a new dynasty. His success and strong government showed the people that the new dynasty had won the Mandate of Heaven. The dynastic cycle would then begin again.

A Feudal State The Zhou rewarded their supporters by granting them control over different regions. Thus, under the Zhou, China developed into a feudal state. Feudalism (FYOO duhl ihz uhm) was a system of government in which local lords governed their own lands but owed military service and other forms of support to the ruler. (In later centuries, feudal societies also developed in Europe and Japan.)

In theory, Zhou kings ruled China, and for about 250 years, they actually did enjoy great power and prestige. After about 771 B.C., though, feudal lords exercised the real power and profited from the lands worked by peasants within their domains.

Economic Growth During the Zhou period, China's economy grew. Knowledge of ironworking reached China about 500 B.C. As iron axes and ox-drawn iron plows replaced stone, wood, and bronze tools, farmers produced more food. Peasants also began to grow new crops, such as soybeans. Some feudal lords organized large-scale irrigation works, making farming even more productive.

Commerce expanded, too. The Chinese began to use money for the first time. Chinese copper coins had holes in the center so they could be strung on cords. This early form of a cash, or money, economy made trade easier. Merchants also benefited from new roads and canals constructed by feudal lords.

Economic expansion led to an increase in population. People from the Huang He heartland overflowed into central China and began to farm the immense Yangzi basin. Feudal nobles expanded their territories and encouraged peasants to settle in the conquered territories. Toward the end of the Zhou era, China was increasing in area and population, as well as in prosperity.

Chinese Achievements

The Chinese made progress in many areas during the Shang and Zhou periods. For example, astronomers studied the movement of planets and recorded eclipses of the sun. Their findings helped them develop an accurate calendar with 365 ¼ days. The Chinese also made remarkable achievements in the art and technology of bronzemaking.

Silkmaking By 1000 B.C., the Chinese had discovered how to make silk thread from the cocoons of silkworms. Soon, the Chinese were cultivating both silkworms and the mulberry trees on which they fed. Women did the laborious work of tending the silkworms and processing the cocoons into thread. They then wove silk threads into a smooth cloth that was colored with brilliant dyes. Only royalty and nobles could afford robes made from this luxurious silk.

Silk became China's most valuable export. The trade route that eventually linked China and the Middle East became known as the Silk Road. To protect their control of this profitable trade, the Chinese kept the process of silkmaking a secret.

The First Books Under the Zhou, the Chinese made the first books. They bound thin strips of wood or bamboo together and then carefully drew characters on the flat surface with a brush and ink.

Among the greatest Zhou works is the lovely *Book of Songs.* Many of its poems describe such events in the lives of farming people as planting and harvesting. Others praise kings or describe court ceremonies. The book also includes tender or sad love songs.

Looking Ahead

By 256 B.C., China was a large, wealthy, and highly developed center of civilization. Chinese culture was already dominant in East Asia. Yet the Zhou dynasty was too weak to control feudal lords who ignored the emperor and battled one another in savage wars. Out of these wars rose a ruthless leader who was determined to impose political unity. His triumphs would leave a lasting imprint on Chinese civilization.

Primary Source

The Spirits Are Good
The poems in the Book of Songs *offer a rare look into the everyday lives of average people in ancient China:*

"The spirits are good,
They will give you many blessings.
The common people are contented,
For daily they have their drink and food.
The thronging herd, the many clans
All side with you in deeds of power.

To be like the moon advancing to its full,
Like the sun climbing the sky,
Like the everlastingness of the southern hills,
Without failing or falling,
Like the pine-tree, the cypress in their [foliage]
All these blessings may you receive!"

    —Shih Ching (Book of Songs)

Skills Assessment

Primary Source Why might there be so many nature images in this poem?

SECTION 3 Assessment

Recall

1. **Identify:** **(a)** Zhongguo, **(b)** Shang, **(c)** yin and yang, **(d)** Zhou, **(e)** Mandate of Heaven, **(f)** *Book of Songs.*
2. **Define:** **(a)** loess, **(b)** clan, **(c)** oracle bone, **(d)** calligraphy, **(e)** dynastic cycle, **(f)** feudalism.

Comprehension

3. How did people in China adapt to the environment?
4. What were the characteristics of Shang and Zhou government and social structure?
5. Identify major cultural achievements in early China.

Critical Thinking and Writing

6. **Predicting Consequences** Suppose that you had to learn a language written in unfamiliar characters, rather than in a language using an alphabet you know. Give three examples of how your life and schooling might be different.
7. **Connecting to Geography** How did environmental catastrophes affect Chinese government?

Activity

Take It to the NET

Use Internet sources to learn more about the silkworm. Then, use your information to create a fact sheet about this ancient source of silk. Post your fact sheet on a classroom bulletin board for others to read.

Creating a Chapter Summary

Copy this table onto a sheet of paper. Use it to compare features of the Aryan, Shang, and Zhou civilizations. A few entries have been made to help you get started.

For additional review and enrich-ment activities, see the interactive version of *World History* available on the Web and on CD-ROM.

	ARYAN CIVILIZATION	SHANG CIVILIZATION	ZHOU CIVILIZATION
RELIGION	Polytheism		
CLASS STRUCTURE			
GOVERNMENT	Elected rajahs		Feudal state; Mandate of Heaven
CULTURAL ACHIEVEMENTS		System of writing; bronzemaking	Silk; books; calendar

Web Site Self-Test
For practice test questions for Chapter 3, see **www. phschool.com.**

Building Vocabulary

For each of the ten terms below, write a sentence using the term.

1. **subcontinent**
2. **monsoon**
3. **caste**
4. **brahman**
5. **rajah**
6. **loess**
7. **oracle bone**
8. **calligraphy**
9. **dynastic cycle**
10. **feudalism**

Recalling Key Facts

11. How has climate shaped life in the Indian subcontinent?
12. What signs of an advanced civilization can be seen in Harappa and Mohenjo-Daro?
13. Why did the Aryans migrate to India? From where did they come?
14. How did the caste system develop in early India?
15. Why was the area between the Huang He and the Yangzi the heartland of early China?
16. Describe Chinese accomplishments in writing, astronomy, and bookmaking.

Critical Thinking and Writing

17. **Connecting to Geography** In what ways might each of the following geographic features have influenced the development of civilization in ancient India and China: **(a)** rivers, **(b)** physical barriers?
18. **Linking Past and Present** Based on evidence uncovered by archaeologists, how were the cities of the ancient Indus Valley similar to and different from cities that exist around the world today?
19. **Applying Information** In the Vedas, "breaker of cities" is one of the titles of honor given to the god Indra. How might this title have linked Indra to actual events in the history of the Aryans?
20. **Making Generalizations** Based on what you have read about the ancient societies that existed in Egypt, Sumer, China, and the Indus Valley, make three generalizations about the role of religion and priests in early river valley civilizations.

In the epic *Ramayana,* Rama is the oldest of four princes. His stepmother persuades the king to name her son heir instead of Rama, and to exile Rama from the kingdom for 14 years. Rama's wife, Sita, announces that she will join him in exile. In this excerpt, Sita persuades Rama to share his exile with her.

> "*Sita's beautiful face was streaked with tears which fell continuously from her large, dark eyes as drops of water from blue lotus flowers. Rama embraced her and gently wiped away her tears. He was still apprehensive about taking her, but he could not see her endure the pain of his separation. Making up his mind to take her with him, he spoke reassuringly.*
> '*I would find no pleasure . . . if I obtained it at the cause of your suffering, O most pious lady! Not knowing your real feelings and being afraid that forest life would cause you pain, I discouraged you from following me. I see now that destiny has decreed you should dwell with me in the forest. Follow me then, O princess, and I will protect you in strict accord with the moral laws always followed by the virtuous.*'
> *Rama made clear his firm intention to go into the deep forest and remain there for the full duration. . . . He was fixed in his determination to obey the command of his parents. . . . Earth, heaven, and the kingdom of God can all be achieved by one who serves his mother, father, and teacher. Explaining all of this to his devoted wife, Rama said, 'Not even truthfulness, charity, or sacrifice are comparable to serving one's mother and father. . . . Pious men, devoted to serving their parents, reach the regions of the gods and beyond.'*"
>
> —*Ramayana* (trans. Dharma)

21. Why does Rama decide to take Sita with him?
22. How does Rama say he will treat Sita during their exile?
23. What is Rama's attitude toward his parents?
24. What does this passage suggest about the importance of family in ancient India?

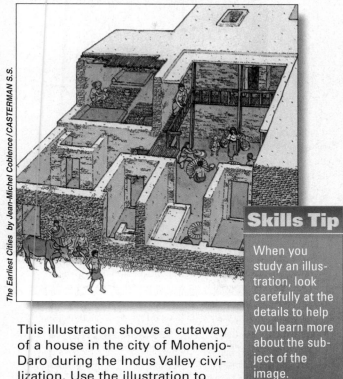

The Earliest Cities by Jean-Michel Coblence/CASTERMAN S.S.

Skills Tip

When you study an illustration, look carefully at the details to help you learn more about the subject of the image.

This illustration shows a cutaway of a house in the city of Mohenjo-Daro during the Indus Valley civilization. Use the illustration to answer the following questions:

25. How many stories are there in this house?
26. What area of the house seems to have been used for the greatest variety of activities?
27. What skills did people need to build a house like this?
28. What does the number of people in and around the house suggest?

Use the Internet to research population density in India and China today. Then, compare the information you find on the Internet with the information shown in the maps of the Indus Valley Civilization (in Section 1) and Shang Civilization (in Section 3). How do the settlement patterns of ancient India and China compare with the settlement patterns of these countries today?

Chapter 1

Toward Civilization
(Prehistory–3000 B.C.)

Archaeologists, historians, and other scholars are learning about our ancient human past through careful research. When the evidence they find is gathered, pieced together, and interpreted, a fascinating story of the emergence of civilization unfolds.

- Archaeologists analyze artifacts to trace how early people developed new technologies and ways of life.
- Historians also study how people lived in the past, but they rely more heavily on written evidence to interpret past events.
- Geographers use the themes of location, place, human-environment interaction, movement, and region to explain the impact of geography on the human story.
- People made tools, learned to build fires, and developed spoken languages during the Paleolithic period, or Old Stone Age.
- During the Neolithic period, or New Stone Age, people learned to farm, dramatically transforming the way they lived.
- By about 5,000 years ago, the advances made by early farming communities led to the rise of civilizations.
- Historians define eight basic features common to most early civilizations: (1) cities, (2) well-organized central governments, (3) complex religions, (4) job specialization, (5) social classes, (6) arts and architecture, (7) public works, and (8) writing.
- Cities first rose in river valleys where conditions favored farming and a surplus of food could be grown.

Chapter 2

First Civilizations: Africa and Asia
(3200 B.C.–500 B.C.)

The first civilizations to develop emerged in river valleys in Egypt and the Middle East more than 5,000 years ago. In these places, people developed a complex way of life and beliefs that continue to affect our world today.

- The three periods of ancient Egyptian history were the Old Kingdom, the Middle Kingdom, and the New Kingdom.
- Egyptian pharaohs organized a strong, centralized state and built majestic pyramids.
- Egyptians worshipped many deities and believed in an afterlife.
- Egyptian society was organized into a hierarchy of classes, with the pharaoh at the top and farmers and slaves at the bottom.
- Independent Sumerian city-states developed in Mesopotamia, an area of fertile land between the Tigris and Euphrates rivers.
- Sumerians invented the earliest form of writing, known as cuneiform, and made great strides in mathematics and astronomy.
- Many groups—including the Babylonians, the Assyrians, and the Persians—invaded Mesopotamia and built great empires.
- Warfare and trade in Mesopotamia helped to spread ideas and technology around the Mediterranean.
- The Hebrews developed Judaism, a monotheistic religion based on the worship of one God, whose laws are set out in the Torah and the Ten Commandments.

	3000 B.C.	2500 B.C.	2000 B.C.
AFRICA	3100 B.C. Menes unites Egypt	2550 B.C. Great Pyramid and Sphinx at Giza	2050 B.C. Middle Kingdom of Egypt begins
THE AMERICAS	3200 B.C. Cultivation of maize and cotton	2400 B.C. Temple platforms in Peru	2000 B.C. Permanent towns in Valley of Mexico
ASIA AND OCEANIA	3200 B.C. Sumerian city-states thrive	2500 B.C. Indus Valley civilization	2000 B.C. Development of Chinese writing
EUROPE	3100 B.C. Small farming communities develop		2000 B.C. Bronze Age in Europe

Chapter 3

Early Civilizations in India and China
(2500 B.C.–256 B.C.)

As civilizations took shape in the Nile Valley and the Fertile Crescent, people in India and China carved out their own civilizations. These two remarkable civilizations evolved distinct ways of life and thought that would exert a powerful influence on other civilizations.

- India's first civilization emerged in the Indus River valley.
- Excavations show that the Indus Valley covered the largest area of any ancient civilization and that its two main cities, Mohenjo-Daro and Harappa, were carefully planned.
- Aryan warriors invaded India and developed a new civilization.
- The Vedas and the great Aryan epic poems, the *Mahabharata* and the *Ramayana* reveal much about the lives and religious beliefs of the early Aryans.
- Long distances and physical barriers separated China from the other ancient civilizations and contributed to the Chinese belief that it was the sole source of civilization.
- The dynastic cycle explained the rise and fall of the many dynasties that came to rule China.
- Chinese religion centered around the veneration of ancestors and the balance of two opposing forces, yin and yang.
- During the Shang and Zhou periods, the Chinese made great strides in astronomy and bronzework, discovered how to make silk and books, and developed a complex system of writing.

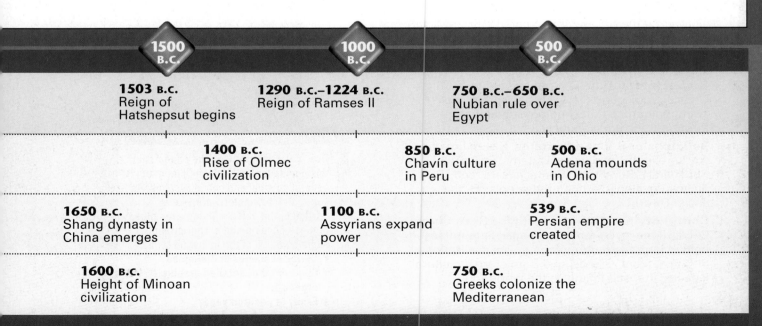

1500 B.C. **1000 B.C.** **500 B.C.**

1503 B.C.
Reign of
Hatshepsut begins

1290 B.C.–1224 B.C.
Reign of Ramses II

750 B.C.–650 B.C.
Nubian rule over
Egypt

1400 B.C.
Rise of Olmec
civilization

850 B.C.
Chavín culture
in Peru

500 B.C.
Adena mounds
in Ohio

1650 B.C.
Shang dynasty in
China emerges

1100 B.C.
Assyrians expand
power

539 B.C.
Persian empire
created

1600 B.C.
Height of Minoan
civilization

750 B.C.
Greeks colonize the
Mediterranean

UNIT 2

Empires of the Ancient World

1750 B.C.–A.D. 1570

OUTLINE

THEMES

As you read about the development of early empires in India, China, Europe, and the Americas, you will encounter the following unit themes.

Political and Social Systems Strong leaders centralized their power and created efficient government systems. These developments enabled the leaders to impose unity on diverse peoples and to strengthen their empires.

Global Interaction Civilizations in India, China, Greece, Rome, and the Americas spread ideas about government, technology, and religion through trade and conquest.

Religions and Value Systems Several major world religions and value systems, including Christianity, Buddhism, Confucianism, and Hinduism, developed among the peoples of the ancient world.

Continuity and Change From the Great Wall of China to the Incan royal road, ancient empires left behind impressive monuments. The civilizations of China, India, Greece, and Rome forged cultural legacies that still influence the world.

Unit Theme Activity

For Your Portfolio The chapters in this unit describe the development of several political and social systems. As you read the chapters, prepare a portfolio project highlighting examples of these developments. Your project might take one of the following forms:
- **Series of scenes or dialogues**
- **Chart or other detailed graphic organizer**
- **Essay or position paper**

The Colosseum was one of the great architectural achievements of the Roman empire. Completed about A.D. 82, the Colosseum was the site of spectacular competitions and other entertainments.

WHY STUDY HISTORY?

Because History Is the Story of Real People

Did you know that history is the story of *you*? True, history books often focus on kings and queens, presidents and generals, great writers and inventors. And, of course, these people are an important part of history. But the study of history is not complete unless it includes the lives of average people—their work, their play, their role in the events of their time. Historians must weave together the many strands of history to create a meaningful story of the world.

Children's toys and games tell us a lot about past cultures.

Aztec children enjoyed the board game *patolli* (left). A careful historian might note that they used beans for dice, a clue that food may have been plentiful in the Aztec empire. The ancient Greek toys (right) include a doll, a spinning top, and a baby's rattle in the shape of a pig. Toys like these are found in almost every culture. The materials used to make them or their shapes may provide important information about the past.

What jobs did people do?

In the past, women and men generally performed different jobs. In ancient Rome, young men, like these building a fort (above), were often required to serve in the army. Women, on the other hand, usually worked in jobs related to the home. Japanese women, like these shown at right, made an important contribution to the household economy.

Even clothing can offer clues to history.

The Indians of Peru in South America wove fine ponchos of wool, such as this one decorated with an intricate bird design. You may admire the artistry displayed by the poncho. The historian, however, will use this artifact of everyday life to seek answers about the past: What tools did the Peruvians use? What materials were available to them? What kind of climate did they live in? See if you can use the poncho to answer some of these questions.

We are part of history.

History is not over. It is happening all the time—and we are part of it. You and the other young people of today are helping to create the story that will become the history of tomorrow.

Portfolio Assessment

Connecting to Today Like all people, you are participating in events that will become part of history. Select one event from the recent past. Write a paragraph describing the event and how it affected your life. Explain why you think the event will be important to future students of history.

Empires of India and China 600 B.C.–A.D. 550

Chapter Preview

1 Hinduism and Buddhism
2 Powerful Empires of India
3 Pillars of Indian Life
4 Philosophy and Religion in China
5 Strong Rulers Unite China

221 B.C.
Shi Huangdi unites much of China and has the Great Wall built to keep out invaders.

268 B.C.
Asoka, whose authority was represented by regal sculptures such as this, becomes emperor of Maurya empire in India.

CHAPTER EVENTS

| 600 B.C. | | 350 B.C. | | | 100 B.C. |

GLOBAL EVENTS

460 B.C. Age of Pericles begins in Greece.

326 B.C. Invading Greeks under Alexander the Great wage battle in northern India.

Empires of India and China

Map Legend:
- Maurya empire about 250 B.C.
- Gupta empire about A.D. 400
- Qin empire, 221 B.C.–210 B.C.
- Han empire, 206 B.C.–A.D. 220
- Han protectorate

Strong rulers established empires in India and China and encouraged cultural achievements.

Map labels: CENTRAL ASIA, MONGOLIA, MANCHURIA, GOBI DESERT, TAKLA MAKAN DESERT, KUNLUN MTS., BACTRIA, HINDU KUSH, Kabul, GANDHARA, XIZANG (TIBET), Handan, Huang He, Xianyang, YELLOW SEA, KOREA, CHINA, HIMALAYA MTS., Chengdu, Yangzi R., EAST CHINA SEA, Indus R., Ganges R., Pataliputra, Nalanda, MAGADHA, Si R., Tropic of Cancer, Ajanta, DECCAN PLATEAU, KALINGA, BAY OF BENGAL, VIETNAM, SOUTH CHINA SEA, ARABIAN SEA, TAMIL KINGDOMS, SRI LANKA, INDIAN OCEAN

Mercator Projection
0   250   500 Miles
0   250   500 Kilometers

Timeline:

A.D. **100s**
Buddhism spreads from India to China.

A.D. **320**
Gupta golden age in India begins. The temple above is adorned with sculptures of Hindu gods and heroes.

A.D. 150

A.D. 400

A.D. 650

A.D. **300s** Mayan city-states flourish in Central America and Mexico.

A.D. **476** The western Roman empire collapses.

Reading Focus

- In what ways is Hinduism a complex religion?

- What are the major teachings of the Buddha?

- How did Buddhism spread beyond India to become a major world religion?

Vocabulary

atman
moksha
reincarnation
karma
dharma
ahimsa
nirvana
sect

Taking Notes

Copy the partially completed Venn diagram below. As you read about Hinduism and Buddhism, finish the diagram by writing key facts and ideas about the religions under the appropriate headings.

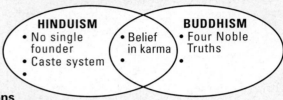

HINDUISM
- No single founder
- Caste system

• Belief in karma

BUDDHISM
- Four Noble Truths

Main Idea   Hinduism and Buddhism, two major religions with a wide variety of beliefs, emerged in ancient India.

Setting the Scene   Thousands of years ago, religious teachers in India tried to answer questions about the nature of the universe. Their ideas were later collected into the Upanishads (oo PAN ih shadz). These sacred texts use vivid images to examine complex ideas about the human soul and the connectedness of all life. In one story, a man tries to show his son that the essence of life cannot be seen. He orders the boy to break open the fruit of the banyan, or fig, tree:

> "'What do you see?'
> 'Very tiny seeds, sir.'
> 'Break one.'
> 'I have broken it, sir.'
> 'Now, what do you see?'
> 'Nothing, sir.'
> 'My son,' the father said, 'what you do not perceive is the essence, and in that essence the mighty banyan tree exists. Believe me, my son, in that essence is the soul of all that is.'"
>
> —Upanishads

Stories like this one helped people understand the teachings of Hinduism. Hinduism and Buddhism were two major religions that emerged in ancient India. The ethical and spiritual messages of both religions profoundly shaped the civilization of India.

The Beliefs of Hinduism

Unlike most major religions, Hinduism has no single founder and no single sacred text. Instead, it grew out of the overlapping beliefs of the diverse groups who settled India. The process probably began when the Aryans added the gods of the Indus Valley people to their own. Later people brought other gods, beliefs, and practices. As a result, Hinduism became one of the world's most complex religions, with countless gods and goddesses and many forms of worship existing side by side. Despite this diversity, all Hindus share certain basic beliefs.

Many Gods—or One?   "God is one, but wise people know it by many names." This ancient proverb reflects a key feature of Hinduism—the belief that all the universe is part of the unchanging, all-powerful spiritual force called brahman. To Hindus, brahman is too complex a concept for most

Shiva
This bronze sculpture portrays the god Shiva crushing a demon into submission. The circle of fire represents the Hindu belief in a cycle of creation, death, and rebirth.

Theme: Diversity   **Why do you think various cultures use the circle to symbolize continuity?**

Virtual Field Trip

www.phschool.com

Prince of Wales Museum of Western India Mumbai, India

To view other artworks relating to Hinduism and Indian history, use the Internet address above to link to the Prince of Wales Museum of Western India.

Bhagavad-Gita
This painting depicts a scene from the sacred Hindu text *Bhagavad-Gita*. The furious battle involves people, gods, goddesses, and demons.

Theme: Religions and Value Systems Why are sacred texts central to many religions?

people to understand, so they worship a variety of gods that give a concrete form to brahman.

The most important Hindu gods are Brahma, the Creator; Vishnu, the Preserver; and Shiva, the Destroyer. Each represents aspects of brahman. Each of these gods can take many forms, human or animal, and each also has his own family. Some Hindus, for example, worship Shakti, the powerful wife of Shiva. She is both kind and cruel, a creator and destroyer.

Sacred Texts Over several thousand years, Hindu teachings were recorded in sacred texts such as the Vedas and Upanishads. The *Bhagavad-Gita,* for example, spells out many ethical ideas central to Hinduism. In that poem, the god Krishna instructs Prince Arjuna on the importance of duty over personal desires and ambitions.

The Goal of Life To Hindus, every person has an essential self, or atman (AHT muhn). But atman is really just another name for brahman. The ultimate goal of existence, Hindus believe, is achieving moksha (MAHK shuh), or union with brahman. To do that, individuals must free themselves from selfish desires that separate them from brahman. Most people cannot achieve moksha in one lifetime, but Hindus believe in reincarnation, or the rebirth of the soul in another bodily form. Reincarnation allows people to continue working toward moksha through several lifetimes.

Karma and Dharma In each existence, Hindus believe, a person can come closer to achieving moksha by obeying the law of karma. Karma refers to all the actions of a person's life that affect his or her fate in the next life. To Hindus, all existence is ranked. Humans are closest to brahman. Then come animals, plants, and objects like rocks or water. People who live virtuously earn good karma and are reborn at a higher level of existence. Those who do evil acquire bad karma and are reborn into suffering. In Indian art, this endless cycle of death and rebirth is symbolized by the image of the wheel.

To escape the wheel of fate, Hinduism stresses the importance of dharma (DAHR muh), the religious and moral duties of an individual. These duties vary according to class, occupation, gender, or age. By obeying one's dharma, a person acquires merit for the next life. The concepts of karma and dharma helped ensure the social order by supporting the caste system.

Another key moral principle of Hinduism is ahimsa (uh HIM sah), or nonviolence. To Hindus, all people and things are aspects of brahman and should therefore be respected. Many holy people have tried to follow the path of nonviolence.

Opposition to the Brahmins About 500 B.C., the teacher Mahavira (muh hah VEE ruh) founded Jainism (JĪN ihz um), a new religion that grew out of Hindu traditions. Mahavira rejected the idea that Brahmin priests alone could perform certain sacred rites. Jain teachings emphasized meditation, self-denial, and an extreme form of ahimsa. To avoid accidentally killing a living thing, even an insect, Jains carried brooms to sweep the ground in front of their feet.

Gautama Buddha: The Enlightened One

In the foothills of the Himalayas, another reformer, Siddhartha Gautama (sihd DAHR tuh go TUH muh), also founded a new religion, Buddhism. His teachings eventually spread across Asia to become the core beliefs of one of the world's most influential religions.

Early Life Gautama's early life is buried in legend. We know that he was born about 566 B.C. to a high-caste family. According to tradition, his mother dreamed that a radiant white elephant descended to her from heaven. Signs such as this led a prophet to predict that the boy would someday become a wandering holy man. To stop that from happening, Gautama's father kept him in the palace, surrounded by comfort and luxury. Prince Gautama married a beautiful woman, had a son, and enjoyed a happy life.

The Search One day, as Gautama rode beyond the palace gardens, he saw a sick person, an old person, and a dead body. For the first time, he became aware of human suffering. Deeply disturbed, he bade farewell to his wife and child and left the palace, never to return. He set out to discover "the realm of life where there is neither suffering nor death."

Gautama wandered for years, vainly seeking answers from Hindu scholars and holy men. He fasted and he meditated. One day, he sat under a giant tree, determined to stay there until he understood the mystery of life. For 48 days, evil spirits tempted him to give up his meditations. Then, he suddenly believed that he understood the cause and cure for suffering and sorrow. When he rose, he was Gautama no longer, but the Buddha, the "Enlightened One."

The Buddha
This image of the Buddha in Sri Lanka is carved out of granite. Traditionally, images of the Buddha lying down represent his achievement of nirvana.

Theme: Religions and Value Systems According to Buddhism, how does one achieve nirvana?

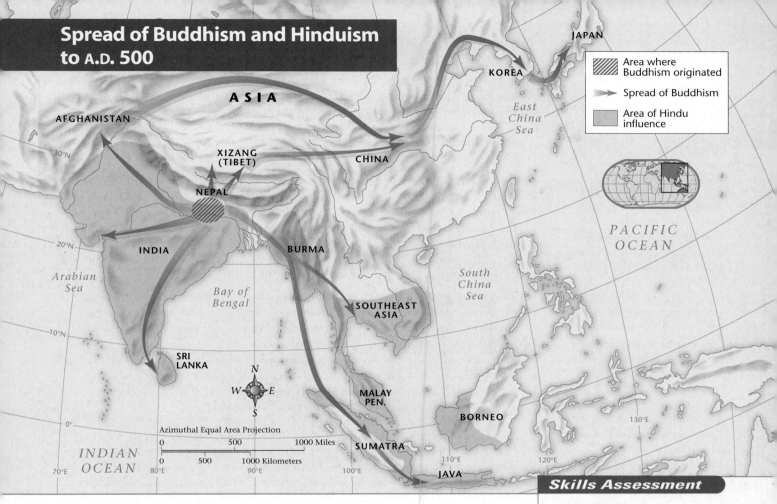

Spread of Buddhism and Hinduism to A.D. 500

ASIA

AFGHANISTAN

XIZANG (TIBET)

NEPAL

CHINA

KOREA

JAPAN

East China Sea

PACIFIC OCEAN

INDIA

BURMA

Arabian Sea

Bay of Bengal

South China Sea

SOUTHEAST ASIA

SRI LANKA

MALAY PEN.

BORNEO

INDIAN OCEAN

SUMATRA

JAVA

Azimuthal Equal Area Projection

0   500   1000 Miles
0   500   1000 Kilometers

Legend:
- Area where Buddhism originated
- Spread of Buddhism
- Area of Hindu influence

Four Noble Truths The Buddha spent the rest of his life teaching others what he had learned. In his first sermon after reaching enlightenment, he explained the Four Noble Truths that stand at the heart of Buddhism:

1. All life is full of suffering, pain, and sorrow.
2. The cause of suffering is the desire for things that are really illusions, such as riches, power, and long life.
3. The only cure for suffering is to overcome desire.
4. The way to overcome desire is to follow the Eightfold Path.

The Buddha described the Eightfold Path as "right views, right aspirations, right speech, right conduct, right livelihood, right effort, right mindfulness, and right contemplation." The first two steps involved understanding the Four Noble Truths and committing oneself to the Eightfold Path. Next, a person had to live a moral life, avoiding evil words and actions. Through meditation, a person might at last achieve enlightenment. For the Buddhist, the final goal is nirvana, union with the universe and release from the cycle of rebirth.

The Buddha saw the Eightfold Path as a middle way between a life devoted to pleasure and one based on harsh self-denial. He stressed moral principles such as honesty, charity, and kindness to all living creatures.

Buddhism and Hinduism Compared Buddhism grew from the same traditions as Hinduism. Both Hindus and Buddhists stressed nonviolence and believed in karma, dharma, moksha, and a cycle of rebirth.

Yet, the two religions differed in several ways. The Buddha rejected the priests, formal rituals, and many gods of Hinduism. Instead, he urged each person to seek enlightenment through meditation. Buddhists also rejected the caste system, offering the hope of nirvana to all regardless of birth.

Skills Assessment

Geography Missionaries and merchants spread Buddhism and Hinduism to many lands of Asia.

1. **Location** On the map, locate (a) India, (b) China, (c) Sri Lanka, (d) Japan.
2. **Movement** How did Buddhism spread to Japan?
3. **Critical Thinking Synthesizing Information** Based on the map and what you have read in this section, which arrows represent the spread of Theravada Buddhism?

Spread of Buddhism

The Buddha attracted many disciples, or followers, who accompanied him as he preached across northern India. Many men and women who accepted the Buddha's teachings set up monasteries and convents for meditation and study. Some Buddhist monasteries grew into major centers of learning.

The Buddha's death is clouded in legend. At age 80, he is said to have eaten spoiled food. As he lay dying, he told his disciples, "Decay is inherent in all things. Work out your own salvation with diligence."

Sacred Texts   After the Buddha's death, some of his followers collected his teachings into a sacred text called the *Tripitaka*, or "Three Baskets of Wisdom." One of the "baskets" includes sayings like this one, which echoes the Hindu emphasis on duty: "Let a man, after he has discerned his own duty, be always attentive to his duty." Other sayings give the Buddha's version of the golden rule: "Overcome anger by not growing angry. Overcome evil with good. Overcome the liar by truth."

Two Sects   Missionaries and traders spread Buddhism across India to many parts of Asia. Gradually, Buddhism split into two major sects, or smaller groups. These were Theravada (ther uh VAH duh) Buddhism and Mahayana (mah huh YAH nuh) Buddhism.

Theravada Buddhism closely followed the Buddha's original teachings. It required a life devoted to hard spiritual work. Only the most dedicated seekers, such as monks and nuns, could hope to reach nirvana. The Theravada sect spread to Sri Lanka and Southeast Asia.

The Mahayana sect made Buddhism easier for ordinary people to follow. Even though the Buddha had forbidden followers to worship him, Mahayana Buddhists pictured him and other holy beings as compassionate gods. People turned to these gods for help in solving daily problems as well as in achieving salvation. While the Buddha had said little about the nature of nirvana, Mahayana Buddhists described an afterlife filled with many heavens and hells. Mahayana Buddhism spread to China, Tibet, Korea, and Japan.

Decline in India   Although Buddhism took firm root across Asia, it slowly declined in India. Hinduism eventually absorbed some Buddhist ideas and made room for Buddha as another Hindu god. A few Buddhist centers survived until the 1100s, when they fell to Muslim armies that invaded India.

Buddha on Anger
This excerpt from the Tripitaka *describes how a person should deal with anger:*

"He who curbs his anger is like a charioteer controlling an unruly horse. Others merely hold the reins.

Overcome anger with kindness, evil with goodness, meanness with generosity and lying with truth.

Let a man be truthful and calm, and give to those who are in want. By these three means he will perfect himself.

The wise are free from hatred and are the controllers of their minds. They will approach Nirvana and go beyond sorrow. . . .

The wise man has control of body, tongue, and mind. He is the true master."
—*Tripitaka*

Skills Assessment

Primary Source According to this excerpt, what are the benefits of controlling one's anger?

SECTION 1 Assessment

Recall
1. **Identify:** (a) Shiva, (b) Jainism, (c) Siddhartha Gautama, (d) Four Noble Truths, (e) Theravada, (f) Mahayana.
2. **Define:** (a) atman, (b) moksha, (c) reincarnation, (d) karma, (e) dharma, (f) ahimsa, (g) nirvana, (h) sect.

Comprehension
3. What are three basic teachings of Hinduism?
4. According to Buddha, what actions would allow people to escape worldly suffering?

5. (a) How did Buddhism spread beyond India? (b) Name three of the lands in Asia to which Buddhism spread.

Critical Thinking and Writing
6. **Drawing Conclusions** How do you think Mahayana teachings increased the appeal of Buddhism?
7. **Comparing** (a) How were Hinduism and Buddhism similar? (b) How were the two religions different?

Activity
Take It to the NET

Use reliable Internet sources, such as university or museum sites, to find out more about the life story and legend of Buddha. Then, use the information that you find to write a biographical sketch of the founder of Buddhism.

Reading Focus

- How did Maurya rulers create a strong central government?
- What were some major achievements of the king-doms of the Deccan?
- Why is the period of Gupta rule in India considered a golden age?

Vocabulary

dissent
missionary
golden age
decimal system
stupa
mural

Taking Notes

As you read, prepare an outline of this section. Use Roman numerals to indicate major headings of the section, capital letters for subheadings, and numbers for supporting details. The model at right will help you begin.

I. The Maurya empire
  A. Chandragupta
    1.
    2.
  B. Asoka
    1.
    2.
  C. Division and disunity
II. Kingdoms of the Deccan

Main Idea Two great empires, the Maurya and the Gupta, flourished in ancient India.

Setting the Scene "The king's good is not that which pleases him, but that which pleases his subjects," insisted the author of an ancient Indian handbook for rulers. According to Hindu teachings, a ruler's duties included maintaining peace and order by enforcing laws, resisting invaders, and encouraging economic growth.

Achieving those goals was difficult. Northern India was often a battle-ground where rival rajahs fought for control of the rich Ganges Valley. Then, in 321 B.C., a young adventurer, Chandragupta Maurya (chun druh GUP tuh MOW uhr yuh), forged the first great Indian empire.

The Maurya Empire

We know about Chandragupta largely from reports writ-ten by Megasthenes (meh GAS thuh neez), a Greek ambas-sador to the Maurya court. He described the great Maurya capital at Pataliputra. It boasted schools and a library as well as splendid palaces and temples. An awed Megasthenes reported that the wall around the city "was crowned with 530 towers and had 64 gates."

Chandragupta Chandragupta first gained power in the Ganges Valley. He then conquered northern India. His son and grandson later pushed south, adding much of the Deccan to their empire. From 321 B.C. to 185 B.C., the Maurya dynasty ruled over a vast, united empire.

Chandragupta maintained order through a well-organized bureaucracy. Royal officials supervised the building of roads and harbors to benefit trade. Other offi-cials collected taxes and managed state-owned factories and shipyards. People sought justice in royal courts.

Chandragupta's rule was effective but harsh. A brutal secret police reported on corruption, crime, and dissent, that is, any differing or oppos-ing ideas. Fearful of his many enemies, Chandragupta had specially trained women warriors guard his palace.

Asoka The most honored Maurya emperor was Chandragupta's grand-son, Asoka (uh SOH kuh). A few years after becoming emperor in 268 B.C., Asoka fought a long, bloody war to conquer the Deccan region of Kalinga. Then, horrified at the slaughter—over 100,000 dead—Asoka turned his

Pillar of Asoka
Asoka ordered that tall stone pillars be erected throughout India. Buddhist teachings were inscribed on each pillar.

Theme: Religions and Value Systems How did Asoka help Buddhism to spread?

See "Asoka: Edicts" in the Reference Section at the back of this book.

back on further conquests. He converted to Buddhism, rejected violence, and resolved to rule by moral example.

True to the Buddhist principle of respect for all life, Asoka became a vegetarian and limited Hindu animal sacrifices. He sent **missionaries,** or people sent on a religious mission, to spread Buddhism across India and to Sri Lanka. He thus paved the way for the later spread of Buddhism throughout Asia. Although Asoka promoted Buddhism, he preached tolerance for other religions.

Asoka had stone pillars set up across India, announcing laws and promising righteous government. On one, he proclaimed: "All people are my children, and just as I desire for my children that they should obtain welfare and happiness, both in this world and the next, so do I desire the same for all people."

Asoka's rule brought peace and prosperity, and helped unite the diverse people within his empire. Asoka helped his "children" by building hospitals and Buddhist shrines. To aid transportation, he built roads and rest houses for travelers. "I have had banyan trees planted on the roads to give shade to people and animals," he noted. "I have planted mango groves, and I have had [wells] dug and shelters erected along the roads."

Division and Disunity After Asoka's death, Maurya power declined. By 185 B.C., the unity of the Maurya empire was shattered as rival princes again battled for power across the northern plain. In fact, during its long history, India has seldom been united. In ancient times, as today, the subcontinent was home to many peoples and cultures. Although the Aryan north shared a common civilization, fierce local rivalries kept it divided. Meanwhile, distance and cultural differences separated the peoples of the north and the peoples of the Deccan Plateau in the south.

Adding to the turmoil, foreign invaders frequently pushed through mountain passes into northern India. The divided northern kingdoms could not often resist such conquerors.

Kingdoms of the Deccan

Like the northern plain, the Deccan was divided into many kingdoms. Each had its own capital with magnificent temples and bustling workshops. Unlike the peoples of the Aryan north, the peoples of the Deccan were Dravidians with very different languages and traditions. Women, for example, enjoyed a high status and economic power. The Tamil kingdoms, which occupied much of the southernmost part of India, were sometimes ruled by queens.

Over the centuries, Hindu and Buddhist traditions and Sanskrit writings drifted south and blended with local cultures. Deccan rulers generally tolerated all religions as well as the many foreigners who settled in their busy ports.

Trade was important to the Tamil kingdoms. Tamil rulers improved harbors to support overseas trade. Indian merchants sent spices, fine textiles, and other luxuries westward to eager buyers in the Roman empire. As the Roman empire declined, Tamil trade with China increased.

The Tamil kingdoms have left a rich and diverse literature. Tamil poets described fierce wars, heroic deeds, and festive occasions, along with the ordinary routines of peasant and city life.

Golden Age of the Guptas

Although many kingdoms flourished in the Deccan, the most powerful Indian states rose in the north. About 500 years after the Mauryas, the Gupta dynasty again united much of India. Gupta emperors organized a strong central government that promoted peace and prosperity. Under the Guptas, who ruled from A.D. 320 to about 550, India enjoyed a golden age, or period of great cultural achievements.

Peace and Prosperity Gupta rule was probably looser than that of the Mauryas. Much power was left in the hands of individual villages and of city governments elected by merchants and artisans. Faxian (FAH shee EHN), a Chinese Buddhist monk who visited India in the 400s, reported on the mild nature of Gupta rule:

> "The people are very well off, without poll tax or official restrictions. Only those who till the royal lands return a portion of the profit of the land as tax. . . . The kings govern without corporal punishment. Criminals are fined, according to circumstances, lightly or heavily."
> —Faxian, *A Record of Buddhist Kingdoms*

Trade and farming flourished across the Gupta empire. Farmers harvested crops of wheat, rice, and sugar cane. In cities, artisans produced cotton cloth, pottery, and metalware for local markets and for export to East Africa, the Middle East, and Southeast Asia. The prosperity of Gupta India contributed to a flowering in the arts and learning.

Advances in Learning In India, as elsewhere during this period, students were educated in religious schools. However, in Hindu and Buddhist centers, learning was not limited to religion and philosophy. The large Buddhist monastery-university at Nalanda, which attracted students from other parts of Asia, taught mathematics, medicine, physics, languages, literature, and other subjects.

Indian advances in mathematics had a wide impact on the world. Gupta mathematicians devised the simple system of writing numbers that is used today. These numerals are now called "Arabic" numerals because it was Arabs who carried them from India to the Middle East and Europe. Indian mathematicians originated the concept of zero and developed the decimal system of numbers based on 10, which we still use today.

By Gupta times, Indian physicians were using herbs and other remedies to treat illness. Surgeons were skilled in setting bones and in simple surgery to repair facial injuries. Doctors also began vaccinating people against smallpox about 1,000 years before this practice was used in Europe.

Architecture Rajahs sponsored the building of magnificent stone temples. Sometimes, cities grew up around the temples to house the thousands of laborers working there. Hindu temples were designed to reflect cosmic patterns. The ideal shape was a square inscribed in a circle to symbolize eternity.

Buddhists built splendid stupas, large dome-shaped shrines that housed the sacred remains of the Buddha or other holy people. The stupas were ringed with enclosed walkways where Buddhist monks slowly walked, chanting their prayers.

Magnificent Carvings While stupas were quite plain, their gateways featured elaborate carvings that told stories of the life of the Buddha. He

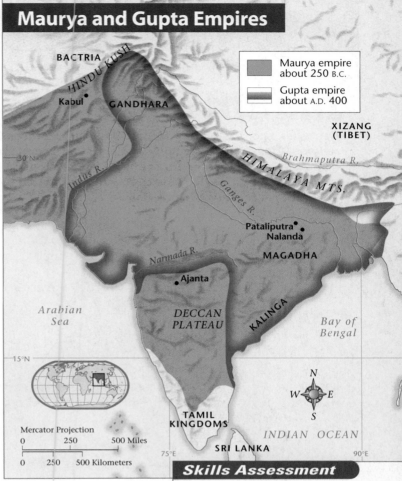

Maurya and Gupta Empires

Maurya empire about 250 B.C.

Gupta empire about A.D. 400

Mercator Projection

0   250   500 Miles

0   250   500 Kilometers

Skills Assessment

Geography Maurya and Gupta emperors were able to unite much of India under their rule.

1. **Location** On the map, locate **(a)** Ganges River, **(b)** Indus River, **(c)** Deccan Plateau.
2. **Region** What region of the Indian subcontinent remained separate from both the Maurya and the Gupta empires?
3. **Critical Thinking Connecting to Geography** How did geography limit the northward expansion of both empires?

Indian Classical Dance

Centuries ago, the Hindus of India developed dances to express their religion. Classical Indian dance is elegant and complex. Dancers use elaborate body movements and facial expressions to tell religious stories. These unique dances captivate the interest of Indians today, as they have for hundreds of years.

Much of a dance's story is told through *mudras*. Mudras are complex hand gestures whose meanings the audience recognizes. Some mudras are designed to look like the items they represent. Others are purely symbolic.

Lion face

Fish

Opening in a bracelet

This woman is performing in the Bharata Natyam dance form. She is wearing radiant, flowing clothes and elaborate gold and silver jewelry typical of this form.

Bharata Natyam dancing is named for the sage Bharat, with whom an Indian god is said to have shared the secrets of dance. His name is a combination of the abbreviations for *Bhava* (expressions), *Raga* (melody), and *Tala* (rhythm)—the three basic parts of the dance.

It takes years to learn the 120 basic positions of Bharata Natyam. Thousands of variations on the basic moves can tell an infinite number of stories.

Most of the dance takes place in one spot, as the dancer constantly bends her knees and moves her feet to complicated rhythms. The bells on her ankles emphasize these movements and accompany the music to which she is dancing.

Portfolio Assessment

INTERNET   Use the Internet or library resources to research other cultures that use dance as a form of storytelling. Using this information, illustrate and write captions for your own Humanities Link.

was portrayed with a gentle smile, symbolizing the inner peace of someone who has reached nirvana. Hindu temples, too, were covered with carvings of gods and goddesses, elephants, monkeys, and ordinary people. A familiar figure is the four-armed god Shiva, who dances the world out of existence and then creates it again. (See the sculpture in Section 1.)

Paintings at Ajanta In the cave temples at Ajanta in western India, Buddhist artists painted rich **murals**, or wall paintings, recalling Buddhist stories and legends. The murals also reveal scenes of life in Gupta India, from beggars with bowls to sailors at sea to princes courting princesses in lovely flowered gardens. (See the mural on the following page.)

Literature During Gupta times, many fine writers added to the rich heritage of Indian literature. They collected and recorded fables and folk tales in the Sanskrit language. In time, Indian fables were carried west to Persia, Egypt, and Greece.

The greatest Gupta poet and playwright was Kalidasa. His most famous play, *Shakuntala*, tells the story of a king who marries the lovely orphan Shakuntala. Under an evil spell, the king forgets his bride. After many plot twists, he finally recovers his memory and is reunited with her. At the end of the play, the king's wise adviser blesses the royal couple:

"For countless ages may the god of gods,
Lord of the atmosphere, by plentiful showers
Secure abundant harvest to your subjects;
And you by frequent offerings preserve
The Thunderer's friendship!"
—Kalidasa, *Shakuntala*

Looking Ahead

The Gupta empire reached its height just as the Roman empire in the west collapsed. Before long, Gupta India declined under the pressure of weak rulers, civil war, and foreign invaders. From central Asia came the White Huns, a nomadic people who overran the weakened Gupta empire, destroying its cities and trade.

Once again, India split into many kingdoms. It would see no great empire like those of the Mauryas or Guptas for almost 1,000 years. Then, as you will read in a later chapter, another wave of invaders pushed into India and created a powerful new empire.

SECTION 2 Assessment

Recall
1. **Identify:** (a) Chandragupta Maurya, (b) Asoka, (c) Faxian, (d) Kalidasa.
2. **Define:** (a) dissent, (b) missionary, (c) golden age, (d) decimal system, (e) stupa, (f) mural.

Comprehension
3. How did Asoka bring peace and prosperity to India?
4. What were some achievements of the kingdoms of the Deccan?
5. Why is the Gupta period considered a golden age of India?

Give examples to support your answer.

Critical Thinking and Writing
6. **Defending a Position** "All faiths deserve to be honored for one reason or another," proclaimed Asoka. How do you think Asoka's policy of toleration helped him unite his empire?
7. **Drawing Conclusions** How did the promotion of peace and prosperity contribute to cultural advancements in the age of the Guptas?

Activity
Writing a Handbook on Government
Imagine that you are either Chandragupta, Asoka, or one of the Gupta emperors. Create a brief handbook listing ways in which an emperor can bring about peace, justice, and prosperity.

Reading Focus

- How did the caste system affect Indian life?
- What values influenced family life?
- How did the traditional Indian village function economically and politically?

Vocabulary

joint family
dowry

Taking Notes

Copy the graphic organizer below. As you read the section, look for more characteristics and effects of the caste system. Add as many boxes to the organizer as you need.

COMPLEX CASTE SYSTEM

| Stable social order | | | |

Main Idea The three important parts of Indian life were the caste system, the family, and the village.

Setting the Scene In the *Bhagavad-Gita,* the god Krishna proclaims: "It is better to do one's own duty badly than to do another's duty well." This advice from Krishna underlines an essential element of Indian life— devotion to one's duty.

Most Indians knew nothing of the dazzling courts of the Mauryas or Guptas. The vast majority were peasants who lived in the countless villages that dotted the Indian landscape. In Gupta times, as today, the caste system ensured stability and order. Two other pillars of Indian life were the family and the village. In Indian society, everyday life revolved around the rules and duties associated with caste, family, and village.

The Complex Caste System

In the previous chapter, you read how the Aryans had divided society into four occupational classes. Non-Aryans were considered outcastes and held the lowest jobs.

Many Castes By Gupta times, many additional castes and subcastes had evolved. As invaders were absorbed into Indian society, they formed new castes. Other castes grew out of new occupations and religions. By modern times, there were hundreds of major castes and thousands of subcastes.

Complex Rules Caste was closely linked to Hindu beliefs. To Hindus, people in different castes were different species of beings. A high-caste Brahmin, for example, was purer and therefore closer to moksha than someone from a lower caste.

To ensure spiritual purity, a web of complex caste rules governed every aspect of life—where people lived, what they ate, how they dressed, and how they earned a living. Rules forbade marrying outside one's caste or eating with members of another caste. High-caste people had the strictest rules to protect them from the spiritually polluted, or impure, lower castes.

For the lowest-ranked outcastes, or "Untouchables," life was harsh and restricted. To them fell "impure" jobs such as digging graves, cleaning streets, or turning animal hides into leather. Other castes feared that contact with an Untouchable could spread pollution. Untouchables had to live apart. They even had to sound a wooden clapper to warn of their approach.

Many Castes
Buddhist artists painted this mural in the Ajanta caves of western India. The painting depicts people of different castes and ethnic groups.

Theme: Diversity How does this mural reflect the Buddha's rejection of the caste system?

Effects   Despite its inequalities, caste ensured a stable social order. People believed that the law of karma determined their caste. While they could not change their status in this life, they could reach a higher state in a future life by faithfully fulfilling the duties of their present caste.

The caste system gave people a sense of identity and interdependence. Each caste had its own occupation and its own leaders. Caste members cooperated to help one another. Further, each caste had its own special role in Indian society as a whole. Although strictly separated, different castes depended on one another for their basic needs. A lower-caste carpenter, for example, built the home of a higher-caste scholar.

The caste system also adapted to changing conditions, absorbing foreigners and new occupations into their own castes. This flexibility allowed people with diverse customs to live side by side in relative harmony.

Family Life

The family performed the essential function of training children in the traditions and duties of their castes. The family taught children their duties at home and in the village.

Structure   The ideal family was the joint family, in which parents, children, grandchildren, uncles, and their offspring shared a common dwelling. The joint family was usually achieved only by the wealthy. In poor families, people often died young, so several generations seldom survived long enough to live together. Still, even when relatives did not share the same house, close ties linked brothers, uncles, cousins, and nephews.

The Indian family was patriarchal. The father or oldest male in the family headed the household. Because he was thought to have wisdom and experience, the head of the family enjoyed great authority. Still, his power was limited by sacred laws and tradition. Usually, he made decisions after consulting his wife and other family members. Property belonged to the whole family.

Children and Parents   From an early age, children learned their family duties, which included obeying caste rules. Family interests came before individual wishes. Children worked with older relatives in the fields or at a family trade. While still young, a daughter learned that as a wife she would be expected to serve and obey her husband and his family. A son learned the rituals to honor the family's ancestors. Such rites linked the living and the dead, deepening family bonds across the generations.

For parents, an important duty was arranging good marriages for their children, based on caste and family interests. Marriage customs varied. In northern India, a bride's family commonly provided a dowry, or payment to the bridegroom, and financed the costly wedding festivities. After marriage, the daughter left her home and became part of her husband's family.

Women's Lives   In early Aryan society, women seem to have enjoyed a higher status than in later times. Women even composed a few Vedic hymns. By early Gupta times, upper-caste Hindu women could still move freely in society and some were well educated.

Attitudes and customs affecting women varied across India and changed over time. By late Gupta times, upper-class women were increasingly restricted to the home. When they went outside the home, they were supposed to cover themselves from head to foot. Lower-class women, however, labored in the fields or worked at spinning and weaving.

Women were thought to have shakti, a creative energy, that men lacked. In marriage, a woman's shakti helped to make the husband complete. Still, shakti might also be a destructive force. A husband's duty was to channel his wife's energy in the proper direction.

Hindu Women
Hindu society valued the creative power of women. The women in this sculpture may be offering a ritual gift of wine to help increase the fruitfulness of their garden.

Theme: Continuity and Change   How did the status of women in Hindu society change over time?

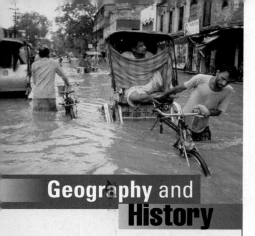

Geography and History

Monsoons and Village Life

"With the monsoon, the tempo of life and death increases," writes one Indian author. "Almost overnight grass begins to grow and leafless trees turn green. . . . Showers start and stop without warning. . . . Lightning and thunder never cease."

Villagers count on monsoons to provide much of the water that they need to live. Since ancient times, the people of India have built dams and canals to capture and control the rainwater. But when they are not successful, the water comes down in driving torrents, flooding the land. Entire villages can be washed away, and thousands of people may die.

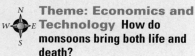

Theme: Economics and Technology How do monsoons bring both life and death?

A woman's primary duties were to marry, show devotion to her husband, and raise children. Beyond these responsibilities, women had few rights within the family and society. For a woman, rebirth into a higher existence was gained through devotion to her husband.

As customs changed, a high-caste widow was forbidden to remarry. Often, a widow was expected to join her dead husband on his funeral fire. In this way, a widow became a sati, or "virtuous woman." Some widows accepted this painful death as a noble duty that wiped out their own and their husband's sins. However, other women bitterly resisted the custom.

Village Life

Throughout India's history, the village was at the heart of life. The size of villages varied, from a handful of people to hundreds of families. A typical village included a cluster of homes made of earth or stone. Beyond these dwellings stretched the fields, where farmers grew wheat, rice, cotton, sugar cane, or other crops according to region.

Each village included people of different castes who performed the tasks needed for daily life. Castes might include priests, landowners, herders, farmers, metalworkers, and carpenters, as well as such low castes as leather workers and sweepers.

In most of India, farming depended on the rains brought by the summer monsoons. Too much or too little rain meant famine. Landlords owned much of the land. Farmers who worked the land had to give the owner part of the harvest. Often, what remained was hardly enough to feed the farmers and their families.

Villages were usually self-sufficient. They produced most of the food and goods that they needed. Occasionally, however, people from different villages met and traded at regional markets.

Each village ran its own affairs based on caste rules and traditions. It faced little outside interference as long as it paid its share of taxes. A village headman and council made decisions. The council included the most respected people of the village. In early times, women served on the village council, but as Hindu law began to place greater restrictions on women, they were later excluded. The headman and council organized villagers to cooperate on vital local projects such as building or maintaining vital irrigation systems, as well as roads and temples.

SECTION 3 Assessment

Recall
1. **Identify:** (a) Untouchable, (b) shakti, (c) sati.
2. **Define:** (a) joint family, (b) dowry.

Comprehension
3. (a) Describe the development of the caste system after Aryan times. (b) How did the caste system provide a sense of order?
4. (a) Describe the structure of the traditional Indian family. (b) What were a woman's responsibilities in the family?

5. Describe the government of an Indian village.

Critical Thinking and Writing
6. **Analyzing Information** How did the traditional Hindu doctrines of karma and dharma support the caste system?
7. **Synthesizing Information** How did each of the three pillars of Indian life—caste, family, and village—place the needs of the community or group above the needs of the individual?

Activity

Role-Playing
With a partner, act out a conversation between a father and son or a mother and daughter about the duties of parents and children in the traditional Indian family. Your discussion should touch upon the influence of caste on family life.

Philosophy and Religion in China

Reading Focus

- What were the major teachings of Confucius?
- How did Legalism and Daoism differ in their views on government?
- Why did many Chinese people accept Buddhist ideas?

Vocabulary

philosophy
filial piety

Taking Notes

Make a table like the one below to compare the philosophies and religions of China. Add information about each under the appropriate headings.

	CONFUCIANISM	LEGALISM	DAOISM	BUDDHISM
BELIEFS				
EFFECTS ON CHINESE LIFE				

Main Idea Confucianism, Legalism, Daoism, and Buddhism had a strong influence on China.

Setting the Scene

"Lead the people by laws and regulate them by punishments, and the people will simply try to keep out of jail, but will have no sense of shame. Lead the people by virtue . . . and they will have a sense of shame and moreover will become good."

The great philosopher Confucius* offered this advice to China's rulers. Confucius lived in late Zhou times, when war and social changes were disrupting old ways of life. In response to such chaos, thinkers like Confucius put forward ideas on how to restore social order.

The Wisdom of Confucius

Confucius was born in 551 B.C. to a noble but poor family. A brilliant scholar, Confucius hoped to become an adviser to a local ruler. For years, he wandered from court to court talking to rulers about how to govern. Unable to find a permanent government position, he turned to teaching. As his reputation for wisdom grew, he attracted many students.

Like two other influential thinkers who lived about the same time, Gautama Buddha in India and Socrates in Greece, Confucius never wrote down his ideas. After his death, students collected many of his sayings in the *Analects*.

Unlike the Buddha, Confucius took little interest in religious matters such as salvation. Instead, he developed a philosophy, or system of ideas, that was concerned with worldly goals, especially how to ensure social order and good government. Confucius studied ancient texts to learn the rules of conduct that had guided the ancestors.

Five Relationships Confucius taught that harmony resulted when people accepted their place in society. He stressed five key relationships: father to son, elder brother to younger brother, husband to wife, ruler to subject, friend to friend. Confucius believed that, except for friendship, none of these relationships was equal. For example, older people were superior to younger ones and men were superior to women.

According to Confucius, everyone had duties and responsibilities. Superiors should care for their inferiors and set a good example, while inferiors owed loyalty and obedience to their superiors. A woman's duty was to ensure the stability of the family and promote harmony in the home. Correct behavior, Confucius believed, would bring order and stability.

▶ **Primary Sources and Literature**

See "Confucius: Analects" in the Reference Section at the back of this book.

*The name Confucius is the western version of the name Kong Fuzi, or Master Kong.

Confucius 551 B.C.–479 B.C.

Confucius decided at an early age to dedicate himself to education and public service. He felt that educated people had a responsibility to serve in government so they could translate their good ideas into action.

As a teacher, Confucius spread education to both rich and poor. He inspired thousands of followers with his guidelines about the proper way to live.

As a public servant, he did not fare so well, however. His high standards of conduct often brought him into conflict with corrupt officials. According to Confucius, "The superior man understands righteousness. The inferior man understands profit." Because some did not agree with his values, Confucius had to move from one part of China to another in search of a permanent government position.

Theme: Impact of the Individual How did Confucius try to improve government in China?

Confucius put filial piety, or respect for parents, above all other duties. Other Confucian values included honesty, hard work, and concern for others. "Do not do to others," he declared, "what you do not wish yourself."

Government According to Confucius, a ruler had the responsibility to provide good government. In return, the people would be respectful and loyal subjects. Confucius said the best ruler was a virtuous one who led people by good example.

Confucius believed that government leaders and officials should be well educated. "By nature, men are pretty much alike," he said. "It is learning and practice that set them apart." He urged rulers to take the advice of wise, educated men.

Spread of Confucianism In the centuries after Confucius died, his ideas influenced every area of Chinese life. Chinese rulers relied on Confucian ideas and chose Confucian scholars as officials. The Confucian emphasis on filial piety bolstered traditional customs such as reverence for ancestors.

As Chinese civilization spread, hundreds of millions of people in Korea, Japan, and Vietnam accepted Confucian beliefs. Close to a third of the world's population came under the influence of these ideas.

The Harsh Ideas of Legalism

A very different philosophy grew out of the teachings of Hanfeizi (HAHN fay DZEE), who died in 233 B.C. According to Hanfeizi, "the nature of man is evil. His goodness is acquired." Greed, he declared, was the motive for most actions and the cause of most conflicts.

Hanfeizi insisted that the only way to achieve order was to pass strict laws and impose harsh punishments. Because of this emphasis on law, Hanfeizi's teachings became known as Legalism. To Legalists, strength, not goodness, was a ruler's greatest virtue. "The ruler alone possesses power," declared Hanfeizi, "wielding it like lightning or like thunder."

Many feudal rulers chose Legalism as the most effective way to keep order. It was the official policy of the Qin (CHEENG) emperor who united China in 221 B.C. His laws were so cruel that later generations despised Legalism. Yet Legalist ideas survived in laws that forced people to work on government projects and punished those who shirked their duties.

Daoism: The Unspoken Way

The founder of Daoism was known as Laozi (LOW DZEE), or "Old Master." He is said to have lived at the time of Confucius. Although we know little about him, he is credited with writing *The Way of Virtue,* a book that had enormous influence on Chinese life. Unlike Confucianism and Legalism, Daoism was not concerned with bringing order to human affairs. Instead, Daoists sought to live in harmony with nature.

Seeking "the Way" Laozi looked beyond everyday cares to focus on the *Dao,* or "the way" of the universe. How does one find the Dao? "Those who know the Dao do not speak of it," replied Laozi. "Those who speak of it do not know it."

Daoists rejected conflict and strife. They wanted to end conflict between human desires and the simple ways of nature. They stressed the virtue of yielding. Water, they pointed out, does not resist, but yields to outside pressure. Yet it is an unstoppable force. Many Daoists turned from the "unnatural" ways of society. Some became hermits, artists, or poets.

Government Daoists viewed government as unnatural and, therefore, the cause of many problems. "If the people are difficult to govern," Laozi declared, "it is because those in authority are too fond of action." To

Legalism

Hanfeizi developed a philosophy, called Legalism because of its emphasis on strict laws. Legalism stood in stark contrast to Confucianism. In the following excerpt, Hanfeizi explains why he thinks his system is superior.

"When the [wise man] rules the state, he does not count on people doing good of themselves, but employs such measures as will keep them from doing any evil. If he counts on people doing good of themselves, there will not be enough such people to be numbered by the tens in the whole country. But if he employs such measures as will keep them from doing evil, then the entire state can be brought up to a uniform standard. [The ruler] does not busy himself with morals, but with laws. . . .

[The Confucianists] neither study affairs [of] law and government, nor observe the realities of vice and wickedness, but all exalt the supposed glories of remote antiquity and the achievements of the ancient kings. Sugar-coating their speech, the Confucianists say: 'If you listen to our words, you will be able to become the leader of all feudal lords.' . . . The intelligent ruler upholds solid facts and discards [such] useless frills. He does not speak about deeds of humanity and righteousness, and he does not listen to the words of [Confucianists].

Those who are ignorant about government insistently say: 'Win the hearts of the people.' . . . As if all that the ruler would need to do would be just to listen to the people. Actually, the intelligence of people is not to be relied upon any more than the mind of a baby. . . . The baby does not understand that suffering a small pain is the way to obtain a great benefit. . . .

The [ruler] regulates penalties and increases punishments for the purpose of repressing the wicked, but the people think the [ruler] is severe. . . . [This is a method] for attaining order and maintaining peace, but the people are too ignorant to appreciate [it]."

—Hanfeizi

Symbol of Rule
The dragon was the symbol of the Chinese emperor. Under the Legalistic emperors, the fierce appearance of the dragon may have seemed especially appropriate.

Skills Tip

Excerpts from documents often include brackets [ ]. The words within brackets are not direct quotations. They are added to clarify the quoted material.

Skills Assessment

1. According to Hanfeizi, a good ruler must be sure to
   A treat the people under his control with great respect.
   B pass and enforce laws to make his people behave properly.
   C obey the wishes of his people.
   D teach his people about the achievements of ancient kings.

2. Which statement best summarizes Hanfeizi's view of Confucianism?
   E Confucianism is unrealistic and therefore useless as a system of rule.
   F Confucianism was effective in the past but is now obsolete.
   G Confucianist rulers rely too much on the law and facts.
   H Rulers who follow Confucianism are too strict.

3. **Critical Thinking** **Analyzing Information** (a) Identify the specific criticisms of the Confucianists that Hanfeizi makes. (b) Why do you think Legalist ideas were attractive to many rulers?

Daoists, the best government was one that governed the least.

A Blend of Ideas Although scholars kept to Laozi's teachings, Daoism evolved into a popular religion with gods, goddesses, and magical practices. Chinese peasants turned to Daoist priests for charms to protect them from unseen forces. Instead of accepting nature as it was, some Daoist priests searched for a substance to bring immortality. To achieve this goal, they conducted experiments. Sometimes, their work contributed to science and medicine.

Gradually, people blended Confucian and Daoist teachings. Although the two philosophies differed, people took beliefs and practices from each. Confucianism showed them how to behave. Daoism influenced their view of the natural world.

Buddhism in China

Buddhist missionaries built temples, monasteries, and rest houses along their routes between India and China. The golden images of the Buddha (above) are in the Temple of General Peace in China.

Theme: Global Interaction
How did trade aid the spread of Buddhism?

Buddhism in China

By A.D. 100, missionaries and merchants had spread Mahayana Buddhism from India into China. At first, the Chinese had trouble with the new faith. For example, Chinese tradition valued family loyalty, while Buddhism honored monks and nuns who gave up the benefits of family life for a life of solitary meditation.

Despite obstacles such as this, Buddhism became more popular, especially in times of crisis. Its great appeal was the promise of escape from suffering. Mahayana Buddhism offered the hope of eternal happiness and presented Buddha as a compassionate, merciful god. Through prayer, good works, and devotion, anyone could hope to gain salvation. Neither Daoism nor Confucianism emphasized this idea of personal salvation.

By A.D. 400, Buddhism had spread throughout China. Buddhist monasteries became important centers of learning and the arts. Buddhism absorbed many Confucian and Daoist traditions. Chinese Buddhist monks stressed filial piety and honored Confucius.

SECTION 4 Assessment

Recall
1. **Identify:** (a) *Analects*, (b) Legalism, (c) Daoism.
2. **Define:** (a) philosophy, (b) filial piety.

Comprehension
3. Describe the ethical code of conduct that Confucius promoted.
4. (a) What kind of government did Legalists favor? (b) Why did Daoists disagree with Legalist ideas on government?
5. Why did Buddhism appeal to many people in China?

Critical Thinking and Writing
6. **Recognizing Points of View** "Rewards should be rich and certain so that the people will be attracted by them. Punishments should be severe and definite so that the people will fear them." Which of the philosophers discussed in this section expressed these ideas? Explain.
7. **Comparing** Explain how each of these thinkers believed an orderly society could be achieved: (a) Confucius, (b) Hanfeizi, (c) Laozi.

Activity

Writing a Dialogue
Write a dialogue in which Confucius, Hanfeizi, and Laozi debate their ideas on the nature of the best kind of government and the role that government should play in Chinese society.

Strong Rulers Unite China

Reading Focus

- How did Shi Huangdi unite China?

- How did Han rulers strengthen the economy and government of China?

- Why is the Han period considered a golden age of Chinese civilization?

Vocabulary

monopoly

expansionism

warlord

acupuncture

Taking Notes

Copy this partially completed concept web. As you read the section, add important events and developments to provide examples of how strong rulers united China. Add as many circles as you need to the web.

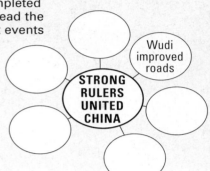

STRONG RULERS UNITED CHINA

Wudi improved roads

Main Idea Powerful emperors united much of China and encouraged cultural achievements.

Setting the Scene From his base in western China, the powerful ruler of the state of Qin rose to unify all of China. An ancient Chinese poet and historian described how Zheng (JUHNG) crushed all his rivals: "Cracking his long whip, he drove the universe before him, swallowing up the eastern and the western Zhou and overthrowing the feudal lords."

In 221 B.C., Zheng proclaimed himself Shi Huangdi (SHEE hoo ahng DEE), or "First Emperor." Though his methods were brutal, he ushered in China's classical age. Historians call it a classical civilization because it set patterns in government, philosophy, religion, science, and the arts that served as the framework for later cultures.

Shi Huangdi

Shi Huangdi was determined to end the divisions that had splintered Zhou China. He spent 20 years conquering most of the warring states. Then, he centralized power with the help of Legalist advisers. Using rewards for merit and punishments for failure, he built the strong, authoritarian government of the Qin dynasty.

Sima Qian, who served later Chinese emperors as Grand Historian of the court, described a monument that Shi Huangdi had built atop a mountain, with an inscription praising the emperor's accomplishments:

"A new age is inaugurated by the Emperor;
Rules and measures are rectified,
The myriad things set in order, . . .
And there is harmony between fathers and sons.
The Emperor in his sagacity, benevolence and justice
Has made all laws and principles manifest."
—Sima Qian, quoted in *Records of the Historian*
(Yang Hsien-yi and Gladys Yang)

Unity Imposed Emperor Shi Huangdi abolished feudalism in China, whereby many local rulers had owed little allegiance to any central government. He replaced the feudal states with 36 military districts and appointed loyal officials to administer them. He then sent inspectors to spy on the local officials and report back to him. Shi Huangdi forced noble families to live in his capital at Xianyang, where he could monitor them. He distributed the lands of the displaced nobles to peasants. Still, peasants had to pay high taxes to support Shi Huangdi's armies and building projects.

Soldier of Shi Huangdi
This terra-cotta soldier is one of more than 8,000 that stand guard inside the tomb of Emperor Shi Huangdi. A farmer uncovered the tomb in 1974 while digging a well.

Theme: Impact of the Individual How does the figure symbolize the power and authority of Shi Huangdi?

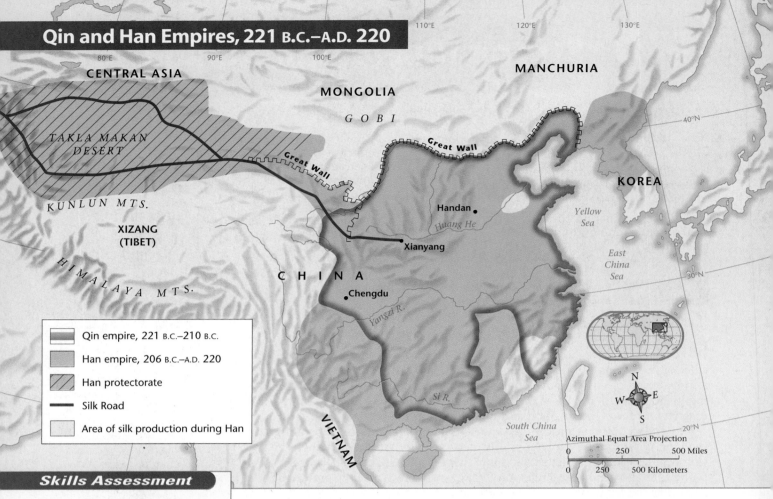

Qin and Han Empires, 221 B.C.–A.D. 220

CENTRAL ASIA

MONGOLIA

MANCHURIA

G O B I

TAKLA MAKAN DESERT

Great Wall

Great Wall

KOREA

KUNLUN MTS.

Handan •

Huang He

Yellow Sea

XIZANG (TIBET)

• Xianyang

East China Sea

HIMALAYA MTS.

C H I N A

• Chengdu

Yangzi R.

Qin empire, 221 B.C.–210 B.C.

Han empire, 206 B.C.–A.D. 220

Han protectorate

Silk Road

Area of silk production during Han

Si R.

South China Sea

VIETNAM

Azimuthal Equal Area Projection

0 — 250 — 500 Miles

0 — 250 — 500 Kilometers

Skills Assessment

Geography Under the Qin and Han dynasties, Chinese rule expanded.

1. **Location** On the map, locate (a) Silk Road, (b) Great Wall, (c) Qin empire, (d) Han empire.
2. **Place** What natural barriers helped to protect China from invaders?
3. **Critical Thinking**
Drawing Conclusions Based on the map, what Chinese town probably grew rich from the silk trade? Explain.

To promote unity, the First Emperor standardized weights and measures and replaced the diverse coins of the Zhou states with Qin coins. He also had scholars create uniformity in Chinese writing. Workers repaired and extended roads and canals to strengthen the transportation system. A new law even required cart axles to be the same width so that wheels could run in the same ruts on all Chinese roads.

Crackdown on Dissent Shi Huangdi moved harshly against critics. He jailed, tortured, and killed many who opposed his rule. Hardest hit were the feudal nobles and Confucian scholars who despised his laws. To end dissent, Shi Huangdi approved a ruthless campaign of book burning, ordering the destruction of all works of literature and philosophy. Only books on medicine and agriculture were spared.

The Great Wall Shi Huangdi's most remarkable and costly achievement was the Great Wall. In the past, individual feudal states had built walls to defend their lands against raiders. Shi Huangdi ordered the walls to be joined. Hundreds of thousands of laborers worked for years through bitter cold and burning heat. They pounded earth and stone into a mountainous wall almost 25 feet high topped with a wide brick road. Many workers died in the harsh conditions.

Over the centuries, the wall was extended and rebuilt many times. Eventually, it snaked for thousands of miles across northern China.

While the wall did not keep invaders out of China, it did demonstrate the emperor's ability to mobilize the vast resources of China. In the long run, the Great Wall became an important symbol to the Chinese people, dividing and protecting their civilized world from the nomadic, or wandering, bands north of the wall.

Collapse Shi Huangdi thought his empire would last forever. But when he died in 210 B.C., anger over heavy taxes, forced labor, and cruel policies exploded into revolts. As Qin power collapsed, Liu Bang (LEE oo BAHNG), an illiterate peasant leader, defeated rival armies and founded the new Han dynasty. Like earlier Chinese rulers, Liu Bang claimed that his power was based on the Mandate of Heaven.

The Han Dynasty

As emperor, Liu Bang took the title Gao Zu (GOW DZOO) and set about restoring order and justice to his empire. Although he continued earlier efforts to unify China, he lowered taxes and eased the Qin emperor's harsh Legalist policies. In a key move, he appointed Confucian scholars as advisers. His policies created strong foundations for the Han dynasty, which lasted from 206 B.C. to A.D. 220.

Emperor Wudi The most famous Han emperor, Wudi, took China to new heights. During his long reign from 141 B.C. to 87 B.C., he strengthened the government and economy. Like Gao Zu, he chose officials from Confucian "men of wisdom and virtue." To train scholars, he set up an imperial university at Xian.

Wudi furthered economic growth by improving canals and roads. He had granaries set up across the empire so the government could buy grain when it was abundant and sell it at stable prices when it was scarce. He reorganized finances and imposed a government monopoly on iron and salt. A **monopoly** is the complete control of a product or business by one person or group. The sale of iron and salt gave the government a source of income other than taxes on peasants.

Wudi followed a policy of expansionism by increasing the amount of territory under Chinese rule. He fought many battles to expand China's borders and to drive nomadic peoples beyond the Great Wall. Chinese armies added outposts in Manchuria, Korea, northern Vietnam, Tibet, and Central Asia. Soldiers, traders, and settlers slowly spread Chinese influence across these areas.

Silk Road to the West The emperor Wudi opened up a trade route, later called the Silk Road, that would link China and the west for centuries. During the Han period, new foods such as grapes, figs, cucumbers, and walnuts flowed to China from western Asia. Lucky traders might return to China bearing furs from Central Asia, muslin from India, or glass from Rome. At the same time, the Chinese sent tons of silk westward to fill a growing demand for the prized fabric.

Eventually, the Silk Road stretched for 4,000 miles, linking China to the Fertile Crescent in southwestern Asia. Still, few traders covered the entire distance; instead, goods were relayed in stages from one set of traders to another. At the western end, trade was controlled by various people, including the Persians.

Scholar-Officials Han emperors made Confucianism the official belief system of the state. They relied on well-educated scholars to run the bureaucratic government. A scholar-official was expected to match the Confucian ideal of a gentleman. He would be courteous and dignified and possess a thorough knowledge of history, music, poetry, and Confucian teachings.

Civil Service Examination Han emperors adopted the idea that government officials should win positions by merit rather than through family background. To find the most qualified officials, they set up a system of exams. In time, these civil service exams were given at the local, provincial, and national levels. To pass, candidates studied the Confucian classics, a

Primary Source

Travels on the Silk Road
Faxian, a Chinese Buddhist monk, described a journey crossing the Gobi on the Silk Road in A.D. 399:

"Le Hao, the [chief official] of T'un-hwang, had supplied them with the means of crossing the desert before them, in which there were many evil demons and hot winds. Travelers who encounter them perish all to a man. There is not a bird to be seen in the air above, nor an animal on the ground below. Though you look all round most earnestly to find where you can cross, you know not where to make your choice, the only mark and indication being the dry bones of the dead left upon the sand."

—Faxian, *A Record of Buddhist Kingdoms*

Skills Assessment

Primary Source According to Faxian, what landmarks did travelers use to follow the Silk Road across the Gobi?

collection of histories, poems, and handbooks on customs that Confucius was said to have compiled.

In theory, any man could take the exams. In practice, only those who could afford years of study, such as the sons of wealthy landowners or officials, could hope to succeed. Occasionally, a village or wealthy family might pay for the education of a brilliant peasant boy. If he passed the exams and obtained a government job, he, his family, and his clan all enjoyed immense prestige and moved up in society.

Confucian teachings about filial piety and the superiority of men kept women from taking the civil service exam. As a result, women were closed out of government jobs.

The civil service system had an enormous impact on China for almost 2,000 years. It put men trained in Confucian thought at every level of government and created an enduring system of values. Dynasties rose and fell, but Confucian influence survived.

Collapse of the Han Empire As the Han dynasty aged, signs of decay appeared. Court intrigues undermined emperors who could no longer control powerful warlords, or local military rulers. Weak emperors let canals and roads fall into disrepair. Burdened by heavy taxes and crushing debt, many peasants revolted. Thousands of rebellious peasants abandoned their villages and fled to the mountains. There they joined secret groups of bandits known by colorful names such as the "Red Eyebrows" and the "Green Woodsmen."

In A.D. 220, ambitious warlords overthrew the last Han emperor. After 400 years of unity, China broke up into several kingdoms. Adding to the disorder, invaders poured over the Great Wall and set up their own states. In time, many of these newcomers were absorbed into Chinese civilization.

Achievements of the Han Golden Age

The Han period was one of the golden ages of Chinese civilization. Han China made such tremendous advances in so many fields that the Chinese later called themselves "the people of Han."

Science Han scientists wrote texts on chemistry, zoology, botany, and other subjects. Han astronomers carefully observed and measured movements of the stars and planets, which enabled them to improve earlier calendars and invent better timekeeping devices. One scientist invented a simple seismograph to detect and measure earthquakes.

The scientist Wang Chong disagreed with the widely held belief that comets and eclipses showed Heaven's anger. "On the average, there is one moon eclipse about every 180 days," he wrote, "and a solar eclipse about every 41 or 42 months. Eclipses . . . are not caused by political action." Wang Chong argued that no scientific theories should be accepted unless they were supported by proof.

Medicine Chinese physicians diagnosed diseases, experimented with herbal remedies and other drugs, and developed anesthetics. Some doctors explored the uses of acupuncture. In this medical treatment, the doctor inserts needles under the skin at specific points to relieve pain or treat various illnesses.

Technology In its time, Han China was the most technologically advanced civilization in the world. Cai Lun, an official of the Han court, invented a method for making durable paper out of wood pulp. His basic method is still used to manufacture paper today. The Chinese also pioneered advanced methods of shipbuilding and invented the rudder to steer. Other practical inventions included bronze and iron stirrups, fishing reels, wheelbarrows, suspension bridges, and chain pumps. Some of these ideas

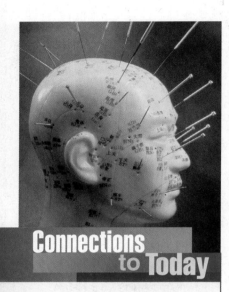

Connections to Today

How Acupuncture Works

For more than 2,500 years, Chinese physicians have used acupuncture to ease patients' suffering. There are several ways to explain how acupuncture works.

Traditional Chinese doctors believe that pain and illness are sometimes due to an imbalance of natural energy flow through the body. Equilibrium and good health can be restored by the insertion of needles at the proper points.

Other explanations involve the nervous system. Some doctors think that acupuncture works because the needles block nerves that carry pain. Another possibility is that the needles promote the release of endorphins in the brain. Endorphins are naturally produced substances that inhibit pain.

Theme: Connections to Today Why do you think some patients today are reluctant to undergo acupuncture?

moved west slowly, reaching Europe hundreds of years later.

The Arts The walled cities of Han China boasted splendid temples and palaces amid elegant parks. Although these wooden buildings have not survived, Han poets and historians have described their grandeur. Artisans produced delicate jade and ivory carvings and fine ceramic figures. Bronzeworkers and silkmakers improved on earlier techniques and set high standards for future generations.

In *Lessons for a Woman*, a handbook of behavior written by Ban Zhao (BAHN JOW) around A.D. 100, the proper behavior for women and men was carefully spelled out. Ban Zhao favored equal education for boys and girls. However, she stressed that women should be obedient, respectful, and submissive. "Let a woman modestly yield to others," she advised. "Let her respect others."

Looking Ahead

Shi Huangdi, Gao Zu, Wudi, and later Han rulers forged a vast and varied land into a united China. Han rulers created an empire roughly the size of the continental United States. During this period, Chinese officials established the pattern of government that would survive until 1912. China would undergo great changes. It would break up and be painfully reassembled over and over. On the whole, however, Chinese civilization flourished in a united land. After periods of disunity, a new dynasty would turn to Confucian scholars to revive the days of Han greatness.

Cause *and* Effect

Long-Term Causes	Immediate Causes
• Confucian ideas dominate education • China's isolation permits development without much outside interference • Common system of writing evolves	• Zheng conquers eastern and western Zhou and overthrows feudal lords • Zheng proclaims himself Shi Huangdi ("First Emperor")

Unification of China

Immediate Effects	Long-Term Effects
• Shi Huangdi standardizes weights and measures and money • Roads and canals unify distant provinces • Government cracks down on dissenters • Shi Huangdi supervises work on the Great Wall	• Han dynasty is founded by Liu Bang • China makes advances in government, trade, and transportation • Confucian-educated officials hold most government jobs • Common culture helps China survive upheavals

Connections to Today

• Mainland China remains a large, politically united country
• Chinese still share a common written language

Skills Assessment **Chart** Under Shi Huangdi, most of China united under a single ruler. **How did political unification benefit the Chinese economy?**

SECTION 5 Assessment

Recall

1. **Identify:** **(a)** Shi Huangdi, **(b)** Great Wall, **(c)** Gao Zu, **(d)** Wudi, **(e)** Silk Road, **(f)** Wang Chong, **(g)** Ban Zhao.
2. **Define:** **(a)** monopoly, **(b)** expansionism, **(c)** warlord, **(d)** acupuncture.

Comprehension

3. What were three steps Shi Huangdi took to unify China?
4. How did Han emperors further economic growth in China?
5. Describe several of the achievements that helped make the Han period a golden age in Chinese civilization.

Critical Thinking and Writing

6. **Drawing Conclusions** Based on what you know about Confucianism, how do you think the civil service examination system affected the nature of Chinese government?
7. **Comparing** Describe one major difference between Qin government and Han government.

Activity

Take It to the NET

Use Internet sources to find out more about Chinese art during the Qin and Han dynasties. In a scrapbook, collect photocopies of art objects that you find. Write a brief description of each image so that others can learn about Chinese art during these periods.

Creating a Chapter Summary

Copy this table on a sheet of paper. Fill in key facts about government, society, religions and value systems, and arts and sciences. To help you get started, some examples have been filled in already.

For additional review and enrichment activities, see the interactive version of *World History* available on the Web and on CD-ROM.

	GOVERNMENT	SOCIETY	RELIGIONS AND VALUE SYSTEMS	ARTS AND SCIENCES
INDIA	• Maurya emperors conquered northern India. •			
CHINA				• Doctors used acupuncture •

Web Site Self-Test
For practice test questions for Chapter 4, see **www. phschool.com**.

Building Vocabulary

Use the words below to make a crossword puzzle. Then, exchange puzzles with a classmate and complete the puzzles.

1. **reincarnation**
2. **dharma**
3. **nirvana**
4. **missionary**
5. **stupa**
6. **patriarchal**
7. **philosophy**
8. **expansionism**

Recalling Key Facts

9. According to Hinduism, what is the ultimate goal of existence?
10. What are the Four Noble Truths of Buddhism?
11. Describe three cultural advances made by Indian scholars and artists in the Gupta empire.
12. How did caste rules affect the daily lives of Indians?
13. How did the primary goal of Daoism differ from the primary goal of Confucianism?
14. How did the Silk Road benefit the Chinese economy?
15. What was the purpose of the Great Wall?
16. Describe three advances of Han civilization in science and technology.

Critical Thinking and Writing

17. **Comparing** Both Indian and Chinese rulers faced difficult challenges in uniting their lands. **(a)** How were these challenges similar? **(b)** How were they different?
18. **Defending a Position** Confucius said that people are basically good and can be led by example. Hanfeizi felt that people are basically evil and have to be controlled by laws. Select one of these positions and write several arguments to defend it.
19. **Connecting to Geography** Review the map of India on the following page. **(a)** How did geography help protect India from invasion? **(b)** What land route might invaders have used to successfully enter India?
20. **Linking Past and Present** In Han China, government officials were required to be schooled in Confucian values. In the United States today, why is it important for government officials to be well educated?
21. **Drawing Conclusions** In China, Shi Huangdi used a policy of book burning to increase his power. Why is book burning so often a policy of authoritarian governments?

Read the excerpt below from *Lessons for a Woman,* written around A.D. 100 by Ban Zhao. Then, answer the questions that follow.

> "Let a woman retire late to bed, but rise early to duties; let her not dread tasks by day or by night. Let her not refuse to perform domestic duties whether easy or difficult. That which must be done, let her finish completely, tidily, and systematically. When a woman follows such rules as these, then she may be said to be industrious.
>
> Let a woman be correct in manner and upright in character in order to serve her husband. Let her live in purity and quietness of spirit, and attend to her own affairs. Let her love not gossip and silly laughter. Let her cleanse and purify and arrange in order the wine and the food for the offerings to ancestors. When a woman observes such principles as these, then she may be said to continue ancestor worship."
>
> —Ban Zhao, *Lessons for a Woman*

22. According to Ban Zhao, what daily routines should an industrious woman follow?
23. (a) Whom should a woman serve? (b) How does a woman show proper worship of her ancestors?
24. How does a woman's role, as described by Ban Zhao, fulfill the Confucian ideas of order and harmony?
25. Do you think it was easy or difficult for Chinese women to follow the advice of Ban Zhao? Explain.
26. Do you agree or disagree with the teachings of Ban Zhao? Explain.

Skills Assessment
Take It to the NET

Use reliable Internet sources, such as university sites and online encyclopedias to learn more about one of the dynasties of ancient China. Then, use the information that you find to create a time line listing major events and achievements that occurred during that dynasty's reign.

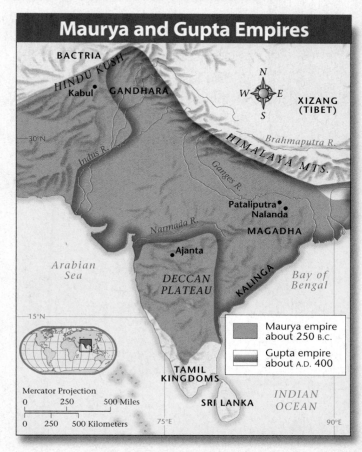

Maurya and Gupta Empires

The map above shows the Maurya and Gupta empires in India. Use the map to answer the following questions:

27. The city of Kabul was part of which of the two empires shown?
28. What physical features marked the northern boundary of the Maurya empire?
29. Which lands included in the Maurya empire were not part of the Gupta empire?
30. How does the map help explain the differences in culture between the people of northern India and those in the south?
31. What part of India was not controlled by either the Gupta or the Maurya empire?

Skills Tip

To get the most information from a map, take careful note of the symbols in the map key.

CHAPTER 5

Ancient Greece

1750 B.C.–133 B.C.

Chapter Preview

1600 B.C.

Minoan civilization on the island of Crete is at its height. The palace at Knossos (above) was the center of Minoan civilization.

460 B.C.

The Age of Pericles marks the height of democracy in Athens.

431 B.C.

The Peloponnesian War begins, pitting Athens against its rival city-state, Sparta. This painting shows soldiers in the Peloponnesian War.

CHAPTER EVENTS

1750 B.C.	500 B.C.	400 B.C.

GLOBAL EVENTS

539 B.C. Cyrus the Great founds the Persian empire.

450 B.C. The Roman Republic publishes its legal code.

Centers of Greek Civilization About 500 B.C.

A common language and civilization linked the many Greek city-states. Although Greek civilization arose in a small corner of southeastern Europe, it had a worldwide impact.

Mt. Olympus ▲

PINDUS MTS.

Peneus R.

Axios R.

Aegean Sea

ASIA MINOR

Delphi

GREECE

Corinth

Athens

Olympia

Mycenae

PELOPONNESUS

Sparta

Milos

Crete

Mediterranean Sea

Albers Equal Area Projection

0   50   100 Miles

0   50   100 Kilometers

331 B.C.

Alexander the Great conquers the Persian empire. The young Macedonian general already rules all of Greece.

323 B.C.

The Hellenistic Age begins, spreading Greek culture through the lands conquered by Alexander. This statue, called *Nike* or Winged Victory, is a masterpiece of Hellenistic art.

133 B.C.

Greek dominance of the Mediterranean world ends.

300 B.C.

200 B.C.

100 B.C.

321 B.C.
The Maurya dynasty begins in India.

221 B.C.
Shi Huangdi unites China.

Early People of the Aegean

Reading Focus

- What civilizations influenced the Minoans?
- How did Mycenaean civilization affect the later Greeks?
- What do the epics of Homer reveal about the Greeks?

Vocabulary

shrine

fresco

strait

Taking Notes

Copy this time line. As you read, fill in the major civilizations and events that occurred.

Trojan War
1250 B.C.

1800 B.C. 1600 B.C. 1400 B.C. 1200 B.C. 1000 B.C. 800 B.C.

1750 B.C.–1500 B.C.
Minoan civilization
at its height

Main Idea The Minoans and Mycenaeans shaped the first Greek civilizations.

Setting the Scene

Europa, the beautiful daughter of the king of Phoenicia, was gathering flowers when she saw a bull quietly grazing with her father's herds. The bull was actually Zeus, king of the gods, who had fallen in love with her. When Europa reached to place flowers on his horns, he suddenly bounded into the air and carried the weeping princess far across the Mediterranean Sea to the island of Crete. Eventually, Europa married the king of Crete and gave her name to a new continent—Europe.

This Greek legend carries seeds of truth. Crete was the cradle of an early civilization that later influenced Greeks on the European mainland. The people of Crete, however, had absorbed many ideas from the older civilizations of Egypt and Mesopotamia. Europa's journey from Phoenicia to Crete thus suggests the movement of ideas from east to west.

Minoan Civilization

Washed by the warm waters of the Aegean (uh JEE uhn) Sea, Crete was home to a brilliant early civilization. We do not know what the people who built this civilization called themselves. However, the British archaeologist who unearthed its ruins called them Minoans after Minos, a legendary king of Crete. Minoan civilization reached its height, or greatest success, between 1750 B.C. and 1500 B.C.

The success of the Minoans was based on trade, not conquest. Minoan traders set up outposts throughout the Aegean world. From their island home in the eastern Mediterranean, they crossed the seas to the Nile Valley and the Middle East. Through contact with Egypt and Mesopotamia, they acquired ideas and technology that they adapted to their own culture.

The Palace at Knossos The rulers of this trading empire lived in a vast palace at Knossos (NAHS uhs). It housed rooms for the royal family, banquet halls, and working areas for artisans. It also included religious shrines, areas dedicated to the honor of gods and goddesses.

The walls of the palace at Knossos are covered with colorful frescoes, watercolor paintings done on wet plaster. These frescoes tell us much about Minoan society. Leaping dolphins reflect the importance of the sea to the Minoan people. Religious images indicate that the Minoans worshiped the bull and a mother goddess. Other paintings show young men and women strolling through gardens or jumping through the horns of a charging bull. They suggest that women appeared freely in public and may have enjoyed more rights than women in most other ancient civilizations.

Geography and History

From Egypt to Crete

When Minoan traders sailed the Mediterranean, they often headed for Egypt. Some Egyptian tomb paintings even show Minoan traders offering gifts to the pharaoh. In return, the traders brought valuable items such as linen home to Crete.

Trading goods led to cultural borrowing. Early Greek painting, with its stiff, formal poses, resembles Egyptian art styles. In addition, Egyptian notions of life after death—including a ferry ride across a river to the underworld—may have influenced Greek religious ideas.

Theme: Geography and History How does Egyptian influence on Minoan culture reflect the geographic themes of location and movement?

A Civilization Disappears By about 1400 B.C., Minoan civilization had vanished. Archaeologists are not sure of the reasons for its disappearance. A sudden volcanic eruption on a nearby island may have rained flaming death on Knossos. An earthquake may have destroyed the palace, followed by a tidal wave that drowned the inhabitants of the island.

However, invaders certainly played a role in the destruction of Minoan civilization. These intruders were the Mycenaeans (mī suh NEE uhnz), the first Greek-speaking people of whom we have a written record.

Rulers of Mycenae

Like the Aryans who swept into India, the Mycenaeans were an Indo-European people. They conquered the Greek mainland before overrunning Crete.

Successful Sea Traders Mycenaean civilization dominated the Aegean world from about 1400 B.C. to 1200 B.C. Like the Minoans, the Mycenaeans were sea traders. They reached out beyond the Aegean to Sicily, Italy, Egypt, and Mesopotamia. The newcomers learned many skills from the Minoans, including the art of writing. They, too, absorbed Egyptian and Mesopotamian influences, which they passed on to later Greeks.

The Mycenaeans lived in separate city-states on the mainland. In each, a warrior-king built a thick-walled fortress from which he ruled the surrounding villages. Wealthy rulers amassed hoards of treasure, including fine gold ornaments that archaeologists have unearthed from their tombs.

The Trojan War The Mycenaeans are best remembered for their part in the Trojan War, which took place around 1250 B.C. The conflict may have had its origins in economic rivalry between Mycenae and Troy, a rich trading city in present-day Turkey. Troy controlled the vital straits, or narrow water passages, that connect the Mediterranean and Black seas. However, Greek legend attributes the war to a more romantic cause. After the Trojan prince Paris kidnapped Helen, the beautiful wife of a Greek king, the Mycenaeans sailed to Troy to rescue her. For the next 10 years, the two sides battled until the Greeks finally seized Troy and burned the city to the ground.

For centuries, most people regarded the Trojan War as purely a legend. Then, in the 1870s, a wealthy German businessman, Heinrich Schliemann (HĪN rihk SHLEE mahn), set out to prove that the legend was rooted in fact. As he excavated the site of ancient Troy, Schliemann found evidence of fire and war dating to about 1250 B.C. Though most of the details remain lost in legend, modern scholars agree that the Trojan War was an actual event.

The Age of Homer

Not long after the fall of Troy, Mycenaean civilization crumbled under the attack of sea raiders. About the same time, another wave of Greek-speaking people, the Dorians, invaded from the north. As Mycenaean power faded, people abandoned the cities, and trade declined. From 1100 B.C. to 800 B.C., Greek civilization seemed to step backward. People forgot many skills, including the art of writing.

We get hints about life during this period from two great epic poems, the *Iliad* and the *Odyssey*. These epics may have been the work of many

A Minoan Fresco
These dolphins from the palace at Knossos show the lightness and sense of movement of Minoan frescoes.

Theme: Geography and History Why do you think Minoan artists chose dolphins as a subject?

Hero of the *Odyssey*
Odysseus was admired for cleverness. Here, he outwits the siren, whose song lures sailors to their doom. He fills his crew's ears with beeswax. Then, he has himself tied to the ship's mast so he can hear the siren's song without endangering the ship.

Theme: Art and Literature Name some fictional heroes of the past and present. What admirable qualities do they possess?

people, but they are credited to the poet Homer, who probably lived about 750 B.C. According to tradition, Homer was a blind poet who wandered from village to village, singing of heroic deeds. Like the great Indian epics, Homer's tales were passed on orally for generations before they were finally written down.

The *Iliad* is our chief source of information about the Trojan War, although the story involves gods, goddesses, and even a talking horse. At the start of the poem, Achilles (uh KIHL eez), the mightiest Greek warrior, is sulking in his tent because of a dispute with his commander. Although the war soon turns against the Greeks, Achilles stubbornly refuses to listen to pleas that he rejoin the fighting. Only after his best friend is killed does Achilles return to battle.

The *Odyssey* tells of the struggles of the Greek hero Odysseus (oh DIHS ee uhs) to return home to his faithful wife, Penelope, after the fall of Troy. On his long voyage, Odysseus encounters a sea monster, a race of one-eyed giants, and a beautiful sorceress who turns men into swine.

The *Iliad* and *Odyssey* reveal much about the values of the ancient Greeks. The heroes display honor, courage, and eloquence, as when Achilles rallies his troops:

> "Every man make up his mind to fight
>   And move on his enemy! Strong as I am,
>   It's hard for me to face so many men
>   And fight with all at once. . . .
>   And yet I will!"
>
> —Homer, *Iliad*

For almost 3,000 years, the epics of Homer have inspired European writers and artists.

Looking Ahead

For centuries after the Dorian invasions, the Greeks lived in small, isolated villages. They had no writing and few contacts with the outside world. From this unpromising start, they would develop a civilization that influenced many parts of the world. As they emerged from obscurity, they benefited from the legacy of earlier civilizations. Over time, the stories they heard about Crete and Mycenae underwent changes and became part of the Greek heritage.

SECTION 1 Assessment

Recall
1. **Identify: (a)** Trojan War, **(b)** Heinrich Schliemann, **(c)** Homer.
2. **Define: (a)** shrine, **(b)** fresco, **(c)** strait.

Comprehension
3. How did trade contribute to the development of Minoan and Mycenaean civilizations?
4. What impact did Mycenaean civilization have on later Greeks?
5. What values of the ancient Greeks are found in the poems of Homer?

Critical Thinking and Writing
6. **Connecting to Geography** In addition to location near water, what other geographic features or natural resources would have been important to an early people who made their living as sea traders?
7. **Drawing Conclusions** Do you think the epics of Homer are probably a reliable source of information about the history of the ancient Greeks? Why or why not?

Activity
Take It to the NET

Use the Internet to research ancient Greek myths such as the story of Europa. Then, make a list of five words, like *Europe,* that are derived from these myths. For each word, include an explanation of the connection between the English word and its Greek origin.

The Rise of Greek City-States

Reading Focus

- How did geography influence the Greek city-states?

- What kinds of government did the Greek city-states develop?

- How did Athens and Sparta differ?

- What forces unified the Greek city-states?

Vocabulary

polis
acropolis
monarchy
aristocracy
oligarchy
phalanx
helot
democracy
tyrant
legislature

Taking Notes

Copy this diagram. As you read, fill in both similarities and differences between Athens and Sparta. Parts of these circles have been completed to help you get started.

ATHENS
- Limited democracy
-

• Common language
•

SPARTA
- Monarchy with two kings

Main Idea > As Greek city-states grew, they developed different types of government, including an early form of democracy.

Setting the Scene

"We live around the sea like frogs around a pond," noted the Greek thinker Plato. Indeed, the Mediterranean and Aegean seas were as central to the development of Greek civilization as the Nile was to the Egyptians. The ancient Greeks absorbed many ideas and beliefs from the older civilizations of Mesopotamia and Egypt. At the same time, they evolved their own unique ways. In particular, the Greeks developed new ideas about how best to govern a society.

Geography of the Greek Homeland

As you have read, the earliest civilizations rose in fertile river valleys. There, strong rulers organized irrigation works that helped farmers produce food surpluses needed to support large cities. A very different set of geographic conditions influenced the rise of Greek civilization.

Mountains and Valleys Greece is part of the Balkan peninsula, which extends southward into the eastern Mediterranean Sea. Mountains divide the peninsula into isolated valleys. Beyond the rugged coast, hundreds of rocky islands spread toward the horizon.

The Greeks who farmed the valleys or settled on the scattered islands did not create a large empire such as that of the Egyptians or Persians. Instead, they built many small city-states, cut off from one another by mountains or water. Each included a city and its surrounding countryside. Greeks fiercely defended the independence of their tiny city-states. Endless rivalry led to frequent wars.

The Seas While mountains divided Greeks, the seas were a vital link to the world outside. With its hundreds of bays, the Greek coastline provided safe harbors for ships. The Greeks became skilled sailors, carrying cargoes of olive oil, wine, and marble around the eastern Mediterranean. They returned not only with grains and metals but also with ideas, which they adapted to their own needs. For example, the Greeks expanded the Phoenician alphabet. The resulting Greek alphabet became the basis for all western alphabets.

By 750 B.C., rapid population growth was forcing many Greeks to leave their own overcrowded valleys. With fertile land limited, the Greeks expanded overseas. Gradually, a scattering of Greek colonies took root all around the Mediterranean from Spain to Egypt. Wherever they traveled, Greek settlers and traders carried their ideas and culture.

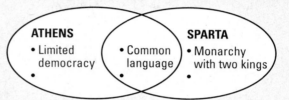

DEVELOPMENT OF THE ALPHABET

Phoenician	Greek	Roman
K	A	A
4	B	B
⊿	△	D
Ψ	K	K
L	Λ	L
7	N	N

Skills Assessment

Chart Our alphabet comes to us from the Phoenicians by way of the Greeks. The word *alphabet* itself comes from the first two Greek letters, *alpha* and *beta*. **Describe how the modern letter A changed over time.**

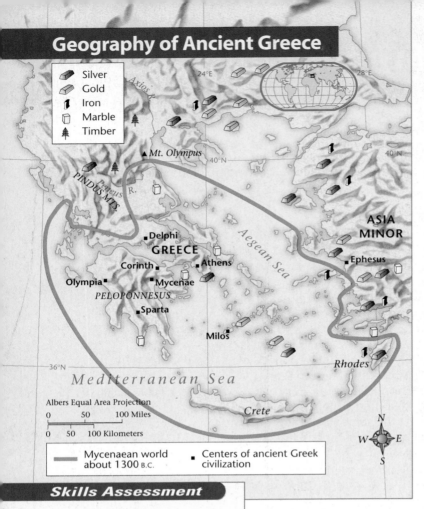

Geography of Ancient Greece

Legend:
- Silver
- Gold
- Iron
- Marble
- Timber

Mt. Olympus
PINDUS MTS.
Peneus R.
Axios R.
Delphi
GREECE
Corinth
Olympia
Mycenae
PELOPONNESUS
Sparta
Athens
Milos
ASIA MINOR
Ephesus
Aegean Sea
Rhodes
Mediterranean Sea
Crete

Albers Equal Area Projection
0   50   100 Miles
0   50   100 Kilometers

— Mycenaean world about 1300 B.C.
■ Centers of ancient Greek civilization

Skills Assessment

Geography Greek civilization was shaped by both rugged mountains and the surrounding seas.

1. **Location** On the map, locate (a) Aegean Sea, (b) Mediterranean Sea, (c) Greece, (d) Crete, (e) Mycenae, (f) Athens, (g) Sparta, (h) Mt. Olympus.
2. **Region** How did the geography of Greece present obstacles to unity?
3. **Critical Thinking Comparing** How did the geography of Greece differ from that of other ancient civilizations?

Governing the City-States

As their world expanded after 750 B.C., the Greeks evolved a unique version of the city-state, which they called the polis. Typically, the city itself was built on two levels. On a hilltop stood the acropolis (uh KRAHP uh lihs), or high city, with its great marble temples dedicated to different gods and goddesses. On flatter ground below lay the walled main city with its marketplace, theater, public buildings, and homes.

The population of each city-state was fairly small, which helped citizens share a sense of responsibility for its triumphs and defeats. In the warm climate of Greece, free men spent much time outdoors in the marketplace, debating issues that affected their lives. The whole community joined in festivals honoring the city's special god or goddess.

Early Governments Between 750 B.C. and 500 B.C., Greeks evolved different forms of government. At first, the ruler of the polis, like those in the river valley empires, was a king. A government in which a king or queen exercises central power is a monarchy. Slowly, though, power shifted to a class of noble landowners. They were also the military defenders of the city-states, because only they could afford bronze weapons and chariots. At first these nobles defended the king. In time, they won power for themselves. The result was an aristocracy, or rule by a landholding elite.

As trade expanded, a new middle class of wealthy merchants, farmers, and artisans emerged in some cities. They challenged the landowning nobles for power and came to dominate some city-states. The result was a form of government called an oligarchy. In an oligarchy, power is in the hands of a small, powerful elite, usually from the business class.

Changes in Warfare Changes in military technology increased the power of the middle class. By about 650 B.C., iron weapons replaced bronze ones. Since iron was cheaper, ordinary citizens could afford iron helmets, shields, and swords. Meanwhile, a new method of fighting emerged. The phalanx was a massive formation of heavily armed foot soldiers. It required long hours of drill. Shared training created a strong sense of unity among citizen-soldiers.

By putting the defense of the city-state in the hands of ordinary citizens, the phalanx reduced class differences. The new type of warfare, however, led the two most influential city-states to develop very different ways of life. While Sparta stressed military virtues and stern discipline, Athens glorified the individual and extended political rights to more citizens.

Sparta: A Nation of Soldiers

The Spartans were Dorians who conquered Laconia. This region lies in the Peloponnesus (pehl uh puh NEE suhs), the southern part of Greece. The invaders turned the conquered people into state-owned slaves, called helots, and made them work the land. Because the helots greatly outnumbered their rulers, the Spartans set up a brutal system of strict control.

The Spartan government included two kings and a council of elders who advised the monarchs. An assembly made up of all citizens approved major decisions. Citizens were male, native-born Spartans over the age of 30. The assembly also elected five ephors, officials who held the real power and ran day-to-day affairs.

The Rigors of Citizenship   From childhood, a Spartan prepared to be part of a military state. Officials examined every newborn, and sickly children were abandoned to die. Spartans wanted future soldiers or mothers of soldiers to be healthy.

At the age of seven, boys began training for a lifetime in the military. They moved into barracks, where they endured a brutal existence. Toughened by a coarse diet, hard exercise, and rigid discipline, Spartan youths became excellent soldiers. To develop cunning and supplement their diet, boys were even encouraged to steal food. If caught, though, they were beaten severely.

At the age of 20, a man could marry, but he continued to live in the barracks for another 10 years and to eat there for another 40 years. At the age of 30, after further specialized training, he took his place in the assembly.

Women   Girls, too, had a rigorous upbringing. As part of a warrior society, they were expected to produce healthy sons for the army. They therefore were told to exercise and strengthen their bodies—something no other Greek women did.

Like other Greek women, Spartan women had to obey their fathers or husbands. Under Spartan law, though, they had the right to inherit property. Because men were occupied with war, some women took on responsibilities such as running the family's estates.

Sparta and Its Neighbors   The Spartans isolated themselves from other Greeks. They looked down on trade and wealth, forbade their own citizens to travel, and had little use for new ideas or the arts. While other Greeks admired the Spartans' military skills, no other city-state imitated their rigorous way of life. "Spartans are willing to die for their city," some suggested, "because they have no reason to live."

Athens: A Limited Democracy

Athens was located in Attica, just north of the Peloponnesus. As in many Greek city-states, Athenian government evolved from a monarchy into an aristocracy. Around 700 B.C., noble landowners held power and chose the chief officials. Nobles judged major cases in court and dominated the assembly.

Demands for Change   Under the aristocracy, Athenian wealth and power grew. Yet discontent spread among ordinary people. Merchants and soldiers resented the power of the nobles. They argued that their service to Athens entitled them to more rights. Foreign artisans, who produced many goods that Athens traded abroad, were resentful that foreigners were barred from becoming citizens. Farmers, too, demanded change. During hard times, many farmers were forced to sell their land to nobles. A growing number even sold themselves and their families into slavery to pay their debts.

As discontent spread, Athens moved slowly toward democracy, or government by the people. As you will see, the term had a different meaning for the ancient Greeks than it has for us today.

Solon's Reforms   Solon, a wise and trusted leader, was appointed archon (AHR kahn), or chief official, in 594 B.C. Athenians gave Solon a free hand to make needed reforms. He outlawed debt slavery and freed those who had already been sold into slavery for debt. He opened high offices to more citizens, granted citizenship to some foreigners, and gave the Athenian assembly more say in important decisions.

Primary Source

A Spartan Education
An Athenian historian explains the system of education set up by Lycurgus, the Spartan lawgiver:

"Instead of softening the boys' feet with sandals he required them to harden their feet by going without shoes. He believed that if this habit were cultivated it would enable them to climb hills more easily and descend steep inclines with less danger, and that a youth who had accustomed himself to go barefoot would leap and jump and run more nimbly than a boy in sandals. And instead of letting them be pampered in the matter of clothing, he introduced the custom of wearing one garment throughout the year, believing that they would thus be better prepared to face changes of heat and cold."

—Xenophon, *Constitution of the Lacedaemonians*

Skills Assessment

Primary Source Describe the Spartan student dress code. What was its purpose?

Solon introduced economic reforms as well. He encouraged the export of wine and olive oil. This policy helped merchants and farmers by increasing demand for their products.

Although Solon's reforms ensured greater fairness and justice to some groups, citizenship remained limited, and many positions were open only to wealthy landowners. Widespread and continued unrest led to the rise of tyrants, or people who gained power by force. Tyrants often won support of the merchant class and the poor by imposing reforms to help these groups. (Although Greek tyrants often governed well, the word *tyrant* has come to mean a vicious and brutal ruler.)

Later Reforms   The Athenian tyrant Pisistratus (pi SIHS truh tuhs) seized power in 546 B.C. He helped farmers by giving them loans and land taken from nobles. New building projects gave jobs to the poor. By giving poor citizens a greater voice, he further weakened the aristocracy.

In 507 B.C., another reformer, Cleisthenes (KLĪS thuh neez), broadened the role of ordinary citizens in government. He set up the Council of 500, whose members were chosen by lot from among all citizens. The council prepared laws for the assembly and supervised the day-to-day work of government. Cleisthenes made the assembly a genuine legislature, or law-making body, that debated laws before deciding to approve or reject them. All male citizens over the age of 30 were members of the assembly.

Limited Rights   By modern standards, Athenian democracy was quite limited. Only male citizens could participate in government, and citizenship was severely restricted. Also, tens of thousands of Athenians were slaves without political rights or personal freedom. In fact, it was the labor of slaves that gave citizens the time to participate in government. Still, Athens gave more people a say in decision making than did the other ancient civilizations we have studied.

Women   In Athens, as in other Greek city-states, women had no share in public life. The respected thinker Aristotle saw women as imperfect beings who lacked the ability to reason as well as men. "The man is by nature fitter for command than the female," he wrote, "just as an older person is superior to a younger, more immature person."

In well-to-do Athenian homes, women lived a secluded existence. There, they managed the entire household. They spun and wove, cared for their children, and prepared food. Their slaves or children were sent to buy

Athenian Education
Athenians believed that education should teach all arts for the development of well-rounded citizens. This vase painting shows young men learning music and grammar at an Athenian school.

Theme: Continuity and Change How is the ideal of education shown in this painting reflected in American schools today?

food and to fetch water from the public well. Poorer women worked outside the home, tending sheep or working as spinners, weavers, or potters.

Education for Democracy Unlike girls, who received little or no formal education, boys attended school if their families could afford it. Besides learning to read and write, they studied music and memorized poetry. They studied to become skilled public speakers because, as citizens in a democracy, they would have to voice their views. Young men received military training and, to keep their bodies healthy, participated in athletic contests. Unlike Sparta, which put military training above all else, Athens encouraged young men to explore many areas of knowledge.

Forces for Unity

Strong local ties, an independent spirit, and economic rivalry led to fighting among the Greek city-states. Despite these divisions, Greeks shared a common culture. They spoke the same language, honored the same ancient heroes, participated in common festivals, and prayed to the same gods.

Religious Beliefs Like most other ancient people, the Greeks were polytheistic. They believed that the gods lived on Mount Olympus in northern Greece. The most powerful Olympian was Zeus, who presided over the affairs of gods and humans. His children included Aphrodite (af ruh DĪ tee), goddess of love, and Ares, god of war. His daughter Athena, goddess of wisdom, gave her name to Athens.

Greeks honored their gods with temples and festivals. To discover the will of the gods, Greeks consulted the oracles, priests or priestesses through whom the gods were thought to speak. Although religion was important, some Greek thinkers came to believe that the universe was regulated, not by the will of gods, but by natural laws.

View of Non-Greeks As trade and colonies expanded, the Greeks came in contact with people with different languages and customs. Greeks felt superior to non-Greeks and called them *barbaroi*, people who did not speak Greek. The English word *barbarian* comes from this Greek root. These "barbarians" included such people as the Phoenicians and Egyptians, from whom the Greeks borrowed important ideas and inventions. Still, this sense of uniqueness would help the Greeks face a threat from the mightiest power in the Mediterranean world—the Persian empire.

Connections to Today

The Olympic Games

Every four years, in the city-state of Olympia, the Greeks held athletic contests to honor Zeus. Winning athletes, such as wrestlers or discus throwers, would be crowned with a wreath. The Olympic games helped unify the Greek world. Warring city-states would even call a truce so that people could attend the games.

Today, thousands of athletes from around the world compete in the summer and winter Olympics. To honor the Greek origins of the games, relay runners carry a torch from Greece to the host city.

Theme: Global Interaction
Do you think the Olympic games are a force for unity in the world? Why or why not?

SECTION 2 Assessment

Recall

1. **Identify:** **(a)** Peloponnesus, **(b)** Solon, **(c)** Cleisthenes, **(d)** Zeus.
2. **Define:** **(a)** polis, **(b)** acropolis, **(c)** monarchy, **(d)** aristocracy, **(e)** oligarchy, **(f)** phalanx, **(g)** helot, **(h)** democracy, **(i)** tyrant, **(j)** legislature.

Comprehension

3. Identify two ways that geography influenced Greece.
4. **(a)** How did noble landowners gain power in Greek city-states? **(b)** How did the phalanx affect Greek society and government?
5. Describe the system of education in **(a)** Sparta and **(b)** Athens.
6. What cultural ties united the Greek world?

Critical Thinking and Writing

7. **Drawing Conclusions** **(a)** In what ways was Athenian democracy limited? **(b)** Despite such limits, Athens is still admired as an early model of democracy. Why do you think this is so?
8. **Analyzing Ideas** Like the early Chinese, the Greeks felt superior to people outside their own land. How might such an attitude be both a strength and a weakness?

Activity

Creating a Dialogue
Create a dialogue between an Athenian and a Spartan in which they discuss the best form of government and the responsibilities of citizenship.

Victory and Defeat in the Greek World

Reading Focus

- What impact did the Persian Wars have on Greece?

- How did Athens enjoy a golden age under Pericles?

- What were the causes and effects of the Peloponnesian War?

Vocabulary

alliance

direct democracy

stipend

jury

ostracism

Taking Notes

Copy this flowchart. As you read, fill in the boxes with the major events of the many wars in the Greek world. The first box has been completed to help you get started.

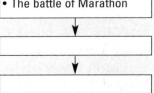

THE WARS OF THE GREEK WORLD

- Athens fights Persia
- Other city-states fight on the side of Athens
- The battle of Marathon

Main Idea Competition among the Greek city-states led to conflict.

Setting the Scene In 492 B.C., King Darius I of Persia cast an angry eye across the Aegean to the proud Greek city-states. Seeking revenge for a Greek insult, he sent messengers throughout Greece. The messengers demanded gifts of "earth and water"—symbols of submission to Darius I.

Many of the city-states obeyed Darius' demand. After all, the Persian empire was the most powerful in the Mediterranean world. But Athens and Sparta were not so quick to submit. Instead, the Athenians threw Darius' messengers into a well, while the Spartans tossed them into a pit. The Persians, they said, could collect their own earth and water.

The Greek historian Herodotus (hih RAHD uh tuhs) told this story of Greek defiance and pride. Despite their cultural ties, the Greek city-states were often bitterly divided. Yet, when the Persians threatened, the Greeks briefly put aside their differences to defend their freedom.

The Persian Wars

By 500 B.C., Athens had emerged as the wealthiest Greek city-state. But Athens and the entire Greek world soon faced a fearsome threat from outside. The Persians, you will recall, conquered a huge empire stretching from Asia Minor to the border of India. Their subjects included the Greek city-states of Ionia in Asia Minor.

Though under Persian rule, these Ionian city-states were largely self-governing. Still, they resented their situation. In 499 B.C., Ionian Greeks rebelled against Persian rule. Athens sent ships to help them. As Herodotus wrote some years later, "These ships were the beginning of mischief both to the Greeks and to the barbarians."

Victory at Marathon The Persians soon crushed the rebel cities. However, Darius I was furious at Athens' role in the uprising. To keep his anger hot, reported Herodotus, he had a servant whisper to him at every meal, "Master, remember the Athenians."

In time, Darius I sent a huge force across the Aegean to punish Athens for its interference. The mighty Persian army landed near Marathon, a plain north of Athens, in 490 B.C. The Athenians asked for help from neighboring city-states, but received little support.

The Persians greatly outnumbered Athenian forces. Yet the invaders were amazed to see "a mere handful of men coming on at a run without either horsemen or archers." The Persians responded with a rain of arrows, but the Greeks rushed onward. They broke through the Persian line and

Did You Know?

The First Marathon

After the battle of Marathon, the Greeks sent Pheidippides, their fastest runner, to carry home news of the stunning victory. Though exhausted, he sprinted 26.2 miles to Athens. "Rejoice, we conquer," he gasped—then dropped dead. Today, in honor of Pheidippides, marathon runners still cover the same distance that he ran 2,500 years ago.

Theme: Continuity and Change Today, many American communities hold annual marathons. Why do you think such races are popular?

engaged the enemy in fierce hand-to-hand combat. Overwhelmed by the fury of the Athenian assault, the Persians hastily retreated to their ships.

The Athenians celebrated their triumph. Still, the Athenian leader, Themistocles (thuh MIHS tuh kleez), knew the victory at Marathon had bought only a temporary lull in the fighting. He urged Athenians to build a fleet of warships and prepare other defenses.

Renewed Attacks Darius died before he could mass his troops for another attack. But in 480 B.C., his son Xerxes (ZERK seez) sent a much larger force to conquer Greece. By this time, Athens had persuaded Sparta and other city-states to join in the fight against Persia.

Once again, the Persians landed an army in northern Greece. A small Spartan force guarded the narrow mountain pass at Thermopylae (thuhr MAHP uh lee). Led by the great warrior-king Leonidas, the Spartans held out heroically against the enormous Persian force. Herodotus described the heroic stand of the Spartans:

> "Here they defended themselves to the last, such as still had swords using them, and the others resisting with their hands and teeth; till the barbarians who . . . now encircled them upon every side, overwhelmed and buried the remnant that was left beneath showers of missile weapons."
> —Herodotus, *The Persian Wars*

After defeating the Spartans, the Persians marched south and burned Athens. The city was empty, however. The Athenians had withdrawn to safety.

The Greeks now put their faith in the fleet of ships that Themistocles had urged them to build. The Athenians lured the Persian navy into the narrow strait of Salamis. Athenian warships, powered by rowers, drove into the Persian boats with underwater battering rams. On the shore, Xerxes watched helplessly as his mighty fleet sank.

The following year, the Greeks defeated the Persians on land in Asia Minor. This victory marked the end of the Persian invasions. Although fighting continued for years, Greek raiders were on the offensive from this time on. In a brief moment of unity, the Greek city-states had saved themselves from the Persian threat.

Results Victory in the Persian Wars increased the Greeks' sense of their own uniqueness. The gods, they felt, had protected their superior form of government—the city-state—against invaders from Asia.

Athens emerged from the war as the most powerful city-state in Greece. To continue the struggle against Persia, it organized the Delian League, an alliance with other Greek city-states. An **alliance** is a formal agreement between two or more nations or powers to cooperate and come to one another's defense.

From the start, Athens dominated the Delian League. It slowly used its position of leadership to create an Athenian empire. It moved the league treasury from the island of Delos to Athens, using money contributed by other city-states to rebuild its own city. When its allies protested and tried

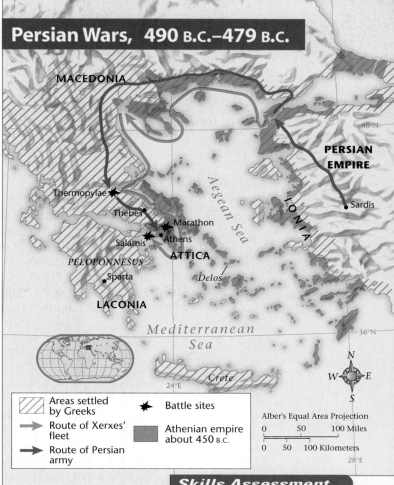

Persian Wars, 490 B.C.–479 B.C.

MACEDONIA

PERSIAN EMPIRE

Thermopylae

Thebes

Marathon

Salamis · Athens

ATTICA

PELOPONNESUS

Sparta

Delos

LACONIA

Aegean Sea

IONIA

Sardis

Mediterranean Sea

Crete

Areas settled by Greeks

Route of Xerxes' fleet

Route of Persian army

Battle sites

Athenian empire about 450 B.C.

Alber's Equal Area Projection

0   50   100 Miles

0   50   100 Kilometers

N W E S

Skills Assessment

Geography When the Persian empire attacked Greece, the Greek city-states briefly joined forces to defend their independence.

1. **Location** On the map, locate **(a)** Athens, **(b)** Sparta, **(c)** Marathon, **(d)** Thermopylae, **(e)** Salamis.
2. **Movement** Describe the route of the Persian army toward Athens.
3. **Critical Thinking**
   Making Inferences Why do you think Xerxes' fleet hugged the coastline instead of sailing directly across the Aegean?

to withdraw from the league, Athens used force to make them remain. Yet, while Athens was enforcing its will abroad, Athenian leaders were championing political freedom at home.

Athens in the Age of Pericles

The years after the Persian Wars were a golden age for Athens. Under the able statesman Pericles (PEHR uh kleez), the economy thrived and the government became more democratic. Because of his wise and skillful leadership, the period from 460 B.C. to 429 B.C. is often called the Age of Pericles.

Political Life Periclean Athens was a direct democracy. Under this system, a large number of citizens take direct part in the day-to-day affairs of government. By contrast, in most democratic countries today, citizens participate in government indirectly through elected representatives.

By the time of Pericles, the Athenian assembly met several times a month. At least 6,000 members had to be present in order to decide important issues. Pericles believed that all male citizens, regardless of wealth or social class, should take part in government. Athens therefore began to pay a stipend, or fixed salary, to men who held public office. This reform enabled poor men to serve in government.

In addition to serving in the assembly, Athenians served on juries. A jury is a panel of citizens who have the authority to make the final judgment in a trial. Unlike a modern American trial jury, which is usually made up of 12 members, an Athenian jury might include hundreds or even thousands of jurors. Male citizens over 30 years of age were chosen by lot to serve on the jury for a year. Like members of the assembly, jurors received a stipend.

Athenian citizens could also vote to banish, or send away, a public figure whom they saw as a threat to their democracy. This process was called ostracism (AHS trah sihzm). To ostracize someone, a citizen wrote that person's name on a piece of pottery. Depending on the number of votes cast, an ostracized individual would have to live outside the city, usually for a period of 10 years.

Primary Sources and Literature

See "Thucydides: A History of the Peloponnesian War" in the Reference Section at the back of this book.

The Funeral Oration Thucydides (thoo SIHD uh deez), a historian who lived in the Age of Pericles, recorded a speech given by Pericles at the funeral of Athenians slain in battle. In this famous Funeral Oration, Pericles praised the Athenian form of government. He pointed out that, in Athens, power rested in the hands "not of a minority but of the whole people."

In the Funeral Oration, Pericles stressed not only the rights but also the duties of citizenship. As citizens of a democracy, he said, Athenians bore a special responsibility. "We alone," he stated, "regard a man who takes no interest in public affairs, not as a harmless but as a useless character." Today, Pericles' Funeral Oration is considered one of the earliest and greatest expressions of democratic ideals.

Economic and Cultural Life Athens prospered during the Age of Pericles. With the riches of the Athenian empire, Pericles hired the best architects and sculptors to rebuild the Acropolis, which the Persians had destroyed. Magnificent new temples and colossal statues rose from the ruins of the Acropolis. Such building projects increased Athenians' prosperity by creating jobs for artisans and workers. They also served as a further reminder to both citizens and visitors that the gods had favored the Athenians.

With the help of an educated foreign-born woman named Aspasia, Pericles turned Athens into the cultural center of Greece. Pericles and Aspasia surrounded themselves with thinkers, writers, and artists. Through building programs and public festivals, they supported the arts. In the next section, you will read about Greek contributions to architecture, art, literature, history, and philosophy.

How Should a Society's Leaders Be Chosen?

In his Gettysburg Address, Abraham Lincoln expressed his abiding belief in democracy, which he described as "government of the people, by the people, and for the people." But through the years, not everyone has agreed that democracy is the best form of government. Consider the following viewpoints.

Algeria 1990s

The Arabic writing on this poster says "Your election equals the restoration of the country's glory."

Greece 400s B.C.

In a famous Funeral Oration, Pericles praised the Athenian form of government:

❝ Our constitution is called a democracy because power is in the hands not of a minority but of the whole people. . . . When it is a question of putting one person before another in positions of public responsibility, what counts is not membership of a particular class, but the ability the man possesses. ❞

United States 1787

Alexander Hamilton, a Caribbean-born statesman who helped shape the Constitution, distrusted ordinary citizens:

❝ All communities divide themselves into the few and the many. The first are rich and well-born, the other the mass of the people. . . . The people are turbulent and changing; they seldom judge or determine right. Give therefore to the first class a distinct, permanent share in the government. ❞

Chile 1986

Santiago Sinclair, an aide to Chilean military dictator Augusto Pinochet, defended the right of strong leaders to take power into their own hands:

❝ Command is voice, conscience, justice. . . . Command guides spirits and unites wills, carrying them to success. . . . ❞

Skills Assessment

1. Which writer seems most opposed to choosing leaders in a democratic way?
   A Pericles
   B Hamilton
   C Sinclair
   D the creator of the voting poster

2. With which statement would Pericles agree?
   E Class is more important than ability.
   F The minority should rule.
   G Leaders know best.
   H Power should be shared by all.

3. **Critical Thinking** **Making Decisions** For more than 200 years, people in the United States have been concerned with the way elections are run. If you could change one thing about the American elections, what would it be? Why?

Skills Tip

Someone may express an opinion that is not necessarily what you would expect. A person's background, as well as the time and place in which he or she lived, may have influenced his or her way of thinking.

The Peloponnesian War

The power of Athens contained the seeds of disaster. Many Greeks outside of Athens resented Athenian domination. Before long, the Greek world split into rival camps. To counter the Delian League, Sparta and other enemies of Athens formed the Peloponnesian League. Sparta encouraged oligarchy in the cities of the Peloponnesian League, while Athens supported democracy among its allies.

In 431 B.C., warfare broke out in earnest between Athens and Sparta. The Peloponnesian War soon engulfed all of Greece. The fighting would drag on for 27 years.

Greek Against Greek   Despite its riches and powerful navy, Athens faced a serious geographic disadvantage. Sparta was located inland, so it could not be attacked from the sea. Yet Sparta had only to march north to attack Athens by land.

When Sparta invaded Athens, Pericles allowed people from the surrounding countryside to move inside the city walls. The overcrowded conditions soon led to disaster. A terrible plague broke out, killing at least a third of the population, including Pericles himself. His successors were much less able leaders. Their power struggles quickly undermined the city's democratic government.

As the war dragged on, each side committed savage acts against the other. Sparta even allied itself with Persia, the longtime enemy of the Greeks. Finally, in 404 B.C., with the help of the Persian navy, the Spartans captured Athens. The victors stripped Athenians of their fleet and empire. However, Sparta rejected calls from its allies to destroy Athens, possibly out of respect for the city's role in the Persian Wars.

The Aftermath of War   The Peloponnesian War ended Athenian domination of the Greek world. The Athenian economy eventually revived and Athens remained the cultural center of Greece. However, its spirit and vitality declined. In Athens, as elsewhere in the Greek world, democratic government suffered. Corruption and selfish interests replaced older ideals such as service to the city-state.

For the next century, fighting continued to disrupt the Greek world. Sparta itself soon suffered defeat at the hands of Thebes, another Greek city-state. As Greeks battled among themselves, a new power rose in Macedonia (mas uh DOHN ee yuh), a kingdom to the north. By 359 B.C., its ambitious ruler stood poised to conquer the quarrelsome Greek city-states.

Primary Source

The Plague in Athens

The Greek historian Thucydides describes the unknown plague that struck Athens in 430 B.C.:

"Bodies of dying men lay one upon another, and half-dead people rolled about in the streets and, in their longing for water, near all the fountains. The temples, too, in which they had quartered themselves were full of the corpses of them who had died in them; for the calamity which weighed upon them was so overpowering that men, not knowing what was to become of them, became careless of all law, sacred as well as profane [worldly]. And the customs which they had hitherto observed regarding burial were all thrown into confusion, and they buried their dead each one as he could."

—Thucydides, *A History of the Peloponnesian War*

Skills Assessment

Primary Source What strains would a plague such as this put on a society?

SECTION 3 Assessment

Recall
1. **Identify:** (a) Marathon, (b) Themistocles, (c) Delian League, (d) Pericles, (e) Aspasia.
2. **Define:** (a) alliance, (b) direct democracy, (c) stipend, (d) jury, (e) ostracism.

Comprehension
3. Describe two effects of the Persian Wars.
4. How did Pericles contribute to Athenian greatness?
5. How did the growth of Athenian power lead to war?

Critical Thinking and Writing
6. **Linking Past and Present** Compare Athenian democracy during the Age of Pericles to American democracy today. (a) How are they similar? (b) How are they different?
7. **Recognizing Causes and Effects** (a) What were the reasons that the Athenians and the Spartans formed their rival alliances? (b) Do nations today form alliances with one another for the same reasons? Explain.

Activity

Drawing a Political Cartoon Draw a political cartoon commenting on the causes or effects of the Peloponnesian War. Take the viewpoint of either an Athenian or a Spartan.

The Glory That Was Greece

Reading Focus

- What political and ethical ideas did Greek philosophers develop?
- What were the goals of Greek architects and artists?
- What themes did Greek writers and historians explore?

Vocabulary

logic
rhetoric
tragedy
comedy

Taking Notes

Copy the concept web at right. Include three or four blank circles. As you read, fill in each blank circle with important facts to remember about Greek civilization. Two circles have been completed to help you get started.

Philosophy

GREEK CIVILIZATION

Plato describes ideal government

Main Idea Greek thinkers, artists, and writers explored the nature of the universe and the place of people in it.

Setting the Scene Despite wars and political turmoil, Greeks had confidence in the power of the human mind. "We cultivate the mind," boasted Pericles. "We are lovers of the beautiful, yet simple in our tastes." Driven by curiosity and a belief in reason, Greek thinkers, artists, and writers explored the nature of the universe and the place of people in it.

To later admirers, Greek achievements in the arts represented the height of human development in the western world. They looked back with deep respect on what one poet called "the glory that was Greece."

Greek Philosophers

As you read, some Greek thinkers challenged the belief that events were caused by the whims of gods. Instead, they used observation and reason to find causes for what happened. The Greeks called these thinkers philosophers, meaning "lovers of wisdom."

Greek philosophers explored many subjects, from mathematics and music to logic, or rational thinking. Through reason and observation, they believed, they could discover laws that governed the universe. Much modern science traces its roots to the Greek search for such principles.

Ethical Issues Other Greek philosophers were more interested in ethics and morality. They debated such questions as what was the best kind of government and what standards should rule human behavior.

In Athens, the Sophists questioned accepted ideas. To them, success was more important than moral truth. They developed skills in rhetoric, the art of skillful speaking. Ambitious men could use clever rhetoric to advance their careers. The turmoil of the Peloponnesian War led many young Athenians to follow the Sophists. Older citizens, however, accused the Sophists of undermining traditional values.

Socrates One outspoken critic of the Sophists was Socrates, an Athenian stonemason and philosopher. Most of what we know about Socrates comes from his student Plato. Socrates himself wrote no books. Instead, he lounged around the marketplace, asking his fellow citizens about their beliefs. Using a process we now call the Socratic method, he would pose a series of questions to his students and challenge them to examine the implications of their answers. To Socrates, this patient examination was a way to help others seek truth and self-knowledge. To many Athenians, however, such questioning was a threat to accepted traditions.

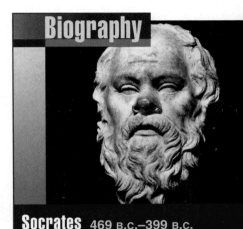

Biography

Socrates 469 B.C.–399 B.C.

To most Athenians, Socrates was not an impressive figure. Tradition tells us that his clothes were untidy and he made a poor living. But young men loved to watch him as he questioned citizens, leading them to contradict themselves.

Many Athenians found Socrates annoying—and he knew it. When he was put on trial, he told the jury, "All day long and in all places I am always fastening upon you, stirring you and persuading you and reproaching you. You will not easily find another like me." But Plato had a different view of his teacher. He called Socrates "the wisest, justest, and best of all I have ever known."

Theme: Impact of the Individual Socrates said, "The unexamined life is not worth living." How did his actions support this idea?

When he was about 70 years old, Socrates was put on trial. His enemies accused him of corrupting the city's youth and failing to respect the gods. Standing before a jury of 501 citizens, Socrates offered a calm defense. But the jurors condemned him to death. Loyal to the laws of Athens, Socrates accepted the death penalty. He drank a cup of hemlock, a deadly poison.

Plato The execution of Socrates left Plato with a lifelong distrust of democracy. He fled Athens for 10 years. When he returned, he set up a school called the Academy. There, he taught and wrote about his own ideas. Like Socrates, Plato emphasized the importance of reason. Through rational thought, he argued, people could discover unchanging ethical values, recognize perfect beauty, and learn how best to organize society.

In *The Republic*, Plato described his vision of an ideal state. He rejected Athenian democracy because it had condemned Socrates. Instead, Plato argued that the state should regulate every aspect of its citizens' lives in order to provide for their best interests. He divided his ideal society into three classes: workers to produce the necessities of life, soldiers to defend the state, and philosophers to rule. This elite class of leaders would be specially trained to ensure order and justice. The wisest of them, a philosopher-king, would have the ultimate authority.

Plato thought that, in general, men surpassed women in mental and physical tasks, but that some women were superior to some men. Talented women, he said, should be educated to serve the state. The ruling elite, both men and women, would take military training together and raise their children in communal centers for the good of the republic.

Aristotle Plato's most famous student, Aristotle, developed his own ideas about government. He analyzed all forms of government, from monarchy to democracy, and found good and bad examples of each. Like Plato, he was suspicious of democracy, which he thought could lead to mob rule. In the end, he favored rule by a single strong and virtuous leader.

Aristotle also addressed the question of how people ought to live. In his view, good conduct meant pursuing the "golden mean," a moderate course between extremes. He promoted reason as the guiding force for learning.

Aristotle set up a school, the Lyceum, for the study of all branches of knowledge. He left writings on politics, ethics, logic, biology, literature, and many other subjects. When the first European universities evolved some 1,500 years later, their courses were largely based on the works of Aristotle.

Architecture and Art

Plato argued that every object on Earth had an ideal form. The work of Greek artists and architects reflected a similar concern with balance, order, and beauty.

Architecture Greek architects sought to convey a sense of perfect balance to reflect the harmony and order of the universe. The most famous example of Greek architecture is the Parthenon, a temple dedicated to the goddess Athena. The basic plan of the Parthenon is a simple rectangle, with tall columns supporting a gently sloping roof. The delicate curves add dignity and grace.

Greek architecture has been widely admired for centuries. Today, you can see many public buildings that have adopted various kinds of Greek columns.

Sculpture and Painting Early Greek sculptors carved figures in rigid poses, perhaps imitating Egyptian styles. By 450 B.C., Greek sculptors had developed a new style that emphasized natural poses. While their work was lifelike, it was also idealistic. That is, sculptors carved gods, goddesses,

▶ **Primary Sources and Literature**

See "Aristotle: The Politics" in the Reference Section at the back of this book.

Connections to Today

The Parthenon in Danger

The Parthenon has survived nearly 2,500 years. It even withstood being blown up. In 1687, the temple was used to store gunpowder. An explosion damaged the roof and many of the columns.

Today, the Parthenon faces an even greater danger. Air pollution is slowly eating away the ancient marble. Scientists say the temple could be destroyed in a century. International teams are now working to shore up the building. Restorers are using a different-colored stone, so visitors can tell which parts are original.

Theme: Global Interaction
Why do you think people from many different countries are interested in saving the Parthenon?

Virtual Field Trip

www.phschool.com

The Acropolis
Athens, Greece

To see other images of the ancient buildings on the Acropolis, use the Internet address above to link to the Ancient City of Athens.

The Acropolis
The buildings on the Acropolis stand as proud monuments of classical Greek architecture. The most revered temple on the Acropolis is the Parthenon, with its balanced rows of majestic columns.

Theme: Art and Literature
Based on this picture, what kinds of modern buildings were influenced by the style of the Parthenon?

athletes, and famous men in a way that showed individuals in their most perfect, graceful form.

The only Greek paintings to survive are on vases and other pottery. They offer intriguing views of Greek life. Women carry water from wells, warriors race into battle, and athletes compete in javelin contests. Each scene is designed to fit the shape of the pottery.

Poetry and Drama

In literature, as in art, the ancient Greeks developed their own style. To later Europeans, Greek styles were a model of perfection. They admired what they called the "classical style," referring to the elegant, balanced forms of traditional Greek works.

Greek literature began with the epics of Homer, whose stirring tales inspired later writers. In later times, Sappho sang of love and of the beauty of her island home, and Pindar celebrated the victors in athletic contests.

Beginnings of Greek Drama   Perhaps the most important Greek contribution to literature was in the field of drama. The first Greek plays evolved out of religious festivals, especially those held in Athens to honor Dionysus (di uh NĪ suhs), god of fertility and wine. Plays were performed in large outdoor theaters with little or no scenery. Actors wore elaborate costumes and stylized masks. A chorus sang or chanted comments on the action.

Greek dramas were often based on popular myths and legends. Through these familiar stories, playwrights discussed moral and social issues or explored the relationship between people and the gods.

Tragedy   The greatest Athenian playwrights were Aeschylus (EHS kuh luhs), Sophocles (SAHF uh kleez), and Euripides (yu RIHP uh deez). All three wrote tragedies, plays that told stories of human suffering that usually ended in disaster. The purpose of tragedy, the Greeks felt, was to stir emotions of pity and fear. In *The Oresteia* (ohr eh STEE uh), for example, Aeschylus showed a powerful family torn apart by betrayal, murder, and revenge. Audiences saw how pride could cause horrifying misfortune and how the gods could bring down even the greatest heroes.

In *Antigone* (an TIHG uh nee), Sophocles explored what happens when an individual's moral duty conflicts with the laws of the state. Antigone

GREEK DRAMA

Ancient Greek drama reached the height of its popularity in the 400s B.C. In every Greek city, enthusiastic audiences attended festivals in which playwrights competed to win prizes for their work. Though changed in form, today's theater arts still use many techniques perfected over 2,000 years ago.

Aristotle Describes a Tragedy

A philosopher of wide-ranging interests, Aristotle turned his attention to Greek drama in his book *Poetics,* written in the 300s B.C. He defined characteristics of a tragedy:

> ❝In the finest kind of tragedy . . . it is evident that good men ought not to be shown passing from prosperity to misfortune, for this does not inspire either pity or fear, but only disgust; nor evil men rising from ill fortune to prosperity, for this is the most untragic plot of all—it lacks every requirement, in that it neither appeals to human sympathy nor stirs pity or fear. And again, neither should an extremely wicked man be seen falling from prosperity into misfortune, for a plot so constructed might indeed call forth human sympathy, but would not excite pity or fear. . . . We are left with the man who on the one hand does not excel in virtue or justice, and yet on the other hand does not fall into misfortune through vice or corruption, but falls because of some mistake.❞

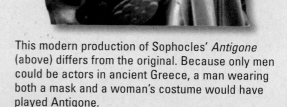

This modern production of Sophocles' *Antigone* (above) differs from the original. Because only men could be actors in ancient Greece, a man wearing both a mask and a woman's costume would have played Antigone.

Fast Facts

- At the government's request, wealthy Athenian citizens paid part of the production costs.

- Actors held high social status because of their speaking skills, and some served as diplomats.

- Greek judges awarded garlands of ivy leaves to recognize superior Greek playwrights and actors.

This carved marble relief (left) shows the playwright Menander, who wrote some of the most popular comedies in ancient Greece. He holds a mask that would be worn by an actor in a comedy. In both tragedies and comedies, actors wore leather masks with exaggerated features to help define the different characters.

Portfolio Assessment

Find a character in a play, novel, or movie who matches Aristotle's definition of a tragic character. Identify the character's strengths and weaknesses and describe the mistake that leads to his or her downfall.

is a young woman whose brother has been killed leading a rebellion. King Creon forbids anyone to bury the traitor's body. When Antigone buries her brother anyway, she is sentenced to death. She defiantly tells Creon that duty to the gods is greater than human law:

> "For me, it was not Zeus who made that order. Nor did I think your orders were so strong that you, a mortal man, could overrule the gods' unwritten and unfailing laws."
> —Sophocles, *Antigone*

Like Sophocles, Euripides survived the horrors of the Peloponnesian War. That experience probably led him to question accepted ideas. His plays suggested that people, not the gods, were the cause of human misfortune. In *The Trojan Women*, he stripped war of its glamour by showing the suffering of women who were victims of the war.

Comedy Some Greek playwrights wrote comedies, humorous plays that mocked people or customs. Almost all surviving Greek comedies were written by Aristophanes (ar ihs TAHF uh neez). In *Lysistrata,* he shows the women of Athens banding together to force their husbands to end a war against Sparta. Through ridicule, comic playwrights sharply criticized society, much as political cartoonists do today.

The Writing of History

The Greeks applied observation, reason, and logic to the study of history. Herodotus is often called the "Father of History" in the western world because he went beyond listing names of rulers or retelling ancient legends. Before writing *The Persian Wars,* Herodotus visited many lands, collecting information from people who remembered the events he chronicled.

Herodotus cast a critical eye on his sources, noting bias and conflicting accounts. Yet, his writings reflected his own view that the war was a clear moral victory of Greek love of freedom over Persian tyranny. He also invented conversations and speeches for historical figures.

Thucydides wrote about the Peloponnesian War, a much less happy subject for the Greeks. He had lived through the war and vividly described its savagery and its corrupting influence on all those involved. Although he was an Athenian, he tried to be fair to both sides.

Both writers set standards for future historians. Herodotus stressed the importance of research. Thucydides showed the need to avoid bias.

SECTION 4 Assessment

Recall

1. **Identify:** (a) Socrates, (b) Aristotle, (c) Parthenon, (d) Sophocles, (e) Euripides, (f) Herodotus, (g) Thucydides.
2. **Define:** (a) logic, (b) rhetoric, (c) tragedy, (d) comedy.

Comprehension

3. (a) Why did Plato reject democracy as a form of government? (b) Describe the ideal form of government as set forth in Plato's *Republic.*

4. What standards of beauty did Greek artists follow?
5. (a) How were Greek plays performed? (b) What were the topics of Greek poetry and plays?

Critical Thinking and Writing

6. **Making Inferences** Why do you think many Greeks condemned the ideas of the Sophists?
7. **Recognizing Bias** Do you think it is ever possible for a historian to be completely free of bias? Why or why not?

Activity

Writing a Paragraph
Thucydides wrote about an event he had lived through because he believed it would have a lasting impact. Choose a recent event that you think historians will write about 100 years from now. Write a paragraph explaining the importance of this event.

Alexander and the Hellenistic Age

Reading Focus

■ How did Alexander the Great build a huge empire?

■ What were the results of Alexander's conquests?

■ How did individuals contribute to Hellenistic civilization?

Vocabulary

assassination
assimilate
heliocentric

Taking Notes

Copy this chart. As you read, fill in the chart with examples of contributions made during the Hellenistic period. Parts of the chart have been filled in to help you get started.

ACHIEVEMENTS OF THE HELLENISTIC AGE

| • Art and architecture • | • Philosophy • | • Mathematics and science • | • Medicine • |

Main Idea Alexander the Great created a large empire and spread Greek culture throughout the region.

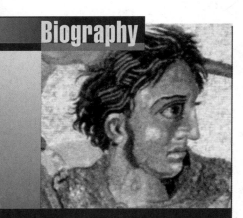

Biography

Alexander the Great
356 B.C.–323 B.C.

As a boy, Alexander had heard tales of Achilles, hero of the *Iliad*. The legendary Greek warrior was all a soldier should be—brave, daring, strong, and almost unbeatable. Alexander saw himself as a second Achilles.

From his tutor, Aristotle, young Alexander acquired a love of learning and the arts, but he was first and foremost a warrior. When Thebes rebelled, he ordered the city to be burned and its inhabitants to be killed or sold into slavery. But he told his soldiers to spare one house—the house where the Greek poet Pindar had once lived.

Theme: Impact of the Individual Why do you think Alexander refused to burn Pindar's house?

Setting the Scene "He is always taking in more, everywhere casting his net around us, while we sit idle and do nothing!" Demosthenes (dih MAHS thuh neez) was warning his fellow Athenians about Philip II, the king of Macedonia. Bit by bit, Philip was bringing Greece under his rule. "When," asked Demosthenes, "will you Athenians take the necessary action?"

When Athenians finally did take action against Philip, it was too late. Athens and the other Greek city-states lost their independence. Yet the disaster ushered in a new age in which Greek influence spread from the Mediterranean to the borders of India. The architect of this new era was Philip's son, known to history as Alexander the Great.

Alexander the Great

To the Greeks, the rugged, mountainous kingdom of Macedonia was a backward, half-civilized land. The rulers of this frontier land, in fact, were of Greek origin and kept ties to their Greek neighbors. As a youth, Philip had lived in Thebes and had come to admire Greek culture. Later, he hired Aristotle as a tutor to his young son Alexander.

Philip's Dream When Philip gained the throne in 359 B.C., he dreamed of conquering the prosperous city-states to the south. He built a superb army. Through threats, bribery, and diplomacy, he formed alliances with many Greek city-states. Others he conquered. In 338 B.C., when Athens and Thebes joined forces against him, he defeated them at the battle of Chaeronea (kehr uh NEE uh). Philip then brought all of Greece under his control.

Philip had a still grander dream—to conquer the Persian empire. Before he could achieve that plan, though, he was assassinated at his daughter's wedding. **Assassination** is the murder of a public figure, usually for political reasons. Philip's determined wife, Olympias, then outmaneuvered his other wives and children to put her own son, Alexander, on the throne.

Conquest of Persia Alexander was only 20 years old. Yet he was already an experienced soldier who shared his father's ambitions. With Greece subdued, he began organizing the forces needed to conquer Persia. By 334 B.C., he had enough ships to cross the Dardanelles, the strait separating Europe from Asia Minor.

Persia was no longer the great power it had once been. The emperor Darius III was weak, and the provinces were often in rebellion against him. Still, the Persian empire stretched more than 2,000 miles from Egypt to India.

Empire of Alexander the Great

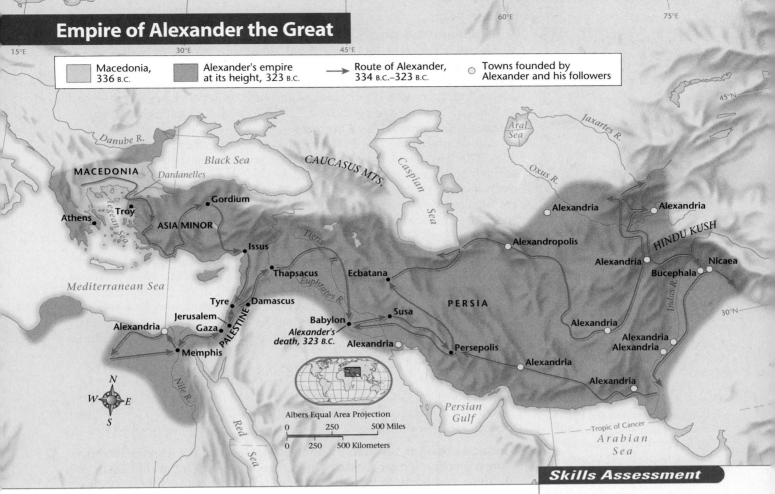

Macedonia, 336 B.C.	Alexander's empire at its height, 323 B.C.	→ Route of Alexander, 334 B.C.–323 B.C.	○ Towns founded by Alexander and his followers

Albers Equal Area Projection

0   250   500 Miles

0   250   500 Kilometers

Alexander won his first victory against the Persians at the Granicus River. He then moved from victory to victory, marching through Asia Minor into Palestine and south to Egypt. In 331 B.C., he took Babylon, then seized the other Persian capitals. But before Alexander could capture Darius, the Persian emperor was murdered.

Onward to India With much of the Persian empire under his control, the restless Alexander headed farther east. He crossed the Hindu Kush into northern India. There, in 326 B.C., his troops for the first time faced soldiers mounted on war elephants. Although Alexander never lost a battle, his soldiers were tired of the long campaign and refused to go farther east. Reluctantly, Alexander agreed to turn back. After a long, hard march, they reached Babylon, where Alexander began planning a new campaign.

Sudden Death Before he could set out again, Alexander fell victim to a sudden fever. As he lay dying, his commanders asked to whom he left his immense empire. "To the strongest," he is said to have whispered.

In fact, no one leader proved strong enough to succeed Alexander. Instead, after years of disorder, three generals divided up the empire. Macedonia and Greece went to one general, Egypt to another, and most of Persia to a third. For 300 years, their descendants competed for power over the lands Alexander had conquered.

The Legacy of Alexander

Although Alexander's empire soon crumbled, he had unleashed changes that would ripple across the Mediterranean world and the Middle East for centuries. His most lasting achievement was the spread of Greek culture.

Skills Assessment

Geography Alexander's ambitions led him to conquer lands across a wide area.

1. **Location** On the map, locate **(a)** Aegean Sea, **(b)** Arabian Sea, **(c)** Euphrates River, **(d)** Indus River, **(e)** Macedonia, **(f)** Persia.
2. **Region** Locate the map Assyrian and Persian Empires, *which appears in an earlier chapter. Which parts of Alexander's empire had not been part of the Persian empire?*
3. **Critical Thinking Predicting Consequences** *Judging from this map, do you think Alexander's empire would be difficult to keep united? Explain.*

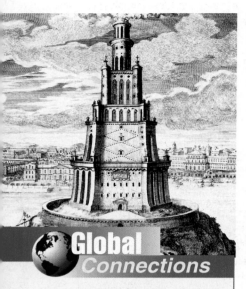

The Seven Wonders of the Ancient World

Around 100 B.C., a Hellenistic traveler named the lighthouse at Alexandria as one of the Seven Wonders of the World. This famous list of awesome structures also included the Hanging Gardens of Babylon and the Colossus, a 100-foot bronze statue on the Aegean island of Rhodes.

Since then, six of the Seven Wonders of the Ancient World have been destroyed, including the Pharos. Only the pyramids of ancient Egypt—the oldest structures on the list—are still standing.

Theme: Arts and Literature
What structures would you include on a list of Seven Wonders of the Modern World?

A Blending of Cultures   Across his far-flung empire, Alexander founded many new cities, most of them named after him. The generals who succeeded him founded still more. Greek soldiers, traders, and artisans settled these new cities. From Egypt to the borders of India, they built Greek temples, filled them with Greek statues, and held athletic contests as they had in Greece. Local people assimilated, or absorbed, Greek ideas. In turn, Greek settlers adopted local customs.

Gradually, a blending of eastern and western cultures occurred. Alexander had encouraged this blending when he married a Persian woman and urged his soldiers to follow his example. He had also adopted many Persian customs, including Persian dress. After his death, a vital new culture emerged which blended Greek, Persian, Egyptian, and Indian influences. This Hellenistic civilization would flourish for centuries.

Alexandria   At the very heart of the Hellenistic world stood the city of Alexandria, Egypt. Located on the sea lanes between Europe and Asia, its markets boasted a wide range of goods, from Greek marble to Arabian spices to East African ivory. A Greek architect had drawn up plans for the city, which would become home to almost a million people. Greeks, Egyptians, Persians, Hebrews, and many others crowded its busy streets. Among the city's marvelous sights was the Pharos, an enormous lighthouse that soared 440 feet into the air.

Alexander and his successors encouraged the work of scholars. The rulers of Alexandria built the great Museum as a center of learning.* The Museum boasted laboratories, lecture halls, and a zoo. Its well-stocked library had thousands of scrolls representing the accumulated knowledge of the ancient world. Unfortunately, the library was later destroyed in a fire.

Opportunities for Women   Paintings, statues, and legal codes show that women were no longer restricted to their homes during the Hellenistic period. More women learned to read and write. Some became philosophers or poets. Royal women held considerable power, working alongside husbands and sons who were the actual rulers. In Egypt, the able and clever queen Cleopatra came to rule in her own right.

Hellenistic Civilization

The cities of the Hellenistic world employed armies of architects and artists. Temples, palaces, and other public buildings were much larger and grander than the buildings of classical Greece. The elaborate new style reflected the desire of Hellenistic rulers to glorify themselves as godlike monarchs.

New Schools of Thought   Political turmoil during the Hellenistic age contributed to the rise of new schools of philosophy. The most influential was Stoicism. Its founder, Zeno, urged people to avoid desires and disappointments by accepting calmly whatever life brought. Stoics preached high moral standards, such as the idea of protecting the rights of fellow humans. They taught that all people, including women and slaves, though unequal in society, were morally equal because all had the power of reason. Stoicism later influenced many Roman and Christian thinkers.

Advances in Learning   During the Hellenistic age, thinkers built on earlier Greek, Babylonian, and Egyptian knowledge. In mathematics, Pythagoras (pih THAG uhr uhs) derived a formula ($a^2 + b^2 = c^2$) to calculate the relationship between the sides of a right triangle. Euclid wrote *The Elements*, a textbook that became the basis for modern geometry.

Using mathematics and careful observation, the astronomer Aristarchus (ar ihs TAHR kuhs) argued that the Earth rotated on its axis and orbited

---

* *Museum* means "house of the Muses." The Muses were nine Greek goddesses who presided over the arts and sciences.

around the sun. This theory of a **heliocentric**, or sun-centered, solar system was not accepted by most scientists until almost 2,000 years later. Another Hellenistic astronomer, Eratosthenes, (air uh TAHS thu neez), showed that the Earth was round and accurately calculated its circumference.

The most famous Hellenistic scientist, Archimedes (ahr kuh MEE deez), applied principles of physics to make practical inventions. He mastered the use of the lever and pulley. He boasted, "Give me a lever long enough and a place to stand on, and I will move the world." An awed audience watched as he used his invention to draw a ship onto shore.

Medicine   About 400 B.C., the Greek physician Hippocrates (hih PAHK ruh teez) studied the causes of illnesses and looked for cures. His Hippocratic oath set ethical standards for doctors. Physicians swore to "help the sick according to my ability and judgment but never with a view to injury and wrong" and to protect the privacy of patients. Doctors today take a similar oath.

Looking Ahead

During the Hellenistic period, Rome emerged as a powerful new state. After its conquest of Asia Minor in 133 B.C., it replaced Greece as the dominant power in the Mediterranean world. Still, by then, the Greeks had already made their greatest contributions.

Greek ideas about law, freedom, justice, and government have influenced political thinking to the present day. In the arts and sciences, Greek works set a standard for later people of Europe. These achievements were especially remarkable because they were produced by a scattering of tiny city-states whose rivalries cost them their freedom. In later chapters, you will see how the Greek legacy influenced the civilizations of Rome and of Western Europe.

Cause *and* Effect

Causes

- Rise of civilizations in Persia, Egypt, and Greece
- Macedonian conquest of Greece
- Growth of Alexander's empire from Greece to northern India
- Growing contacts among kingdoms of eastern Mediterranean and Middle East

Rise of Hellenistic Civilization

Effects

- Learning and arts encouraged by Alexander and his successors
- Alexandria, Egypt, becomes center of trade and learning
- Spread of Greek, Middle Eastern, and Persian religions
- Spread of Christianity

Connections to Today

- Continued practice of Christianity and Judaism in the region
- Alexandria, Egypt, still a center of learning
- Greek architecture still visible in ruins across Middle East

Skills Assessment   **Chart** Although Alexander's empire split apart soon after his death, his conquests had an impact that endured for centuries. **How did the conquests of Alexander the Great encourage contact among different Mediterranean civilizations?**

SECTION 5 Assessment

Recall

1. **Identify:** **(a)** Philip of Macedonia, **(b)** Stoicism, **(c)** Pythagoras, **(d)** Euclid, **(e)** Archimedes, **(f)** Hippocrates.
2. **Define:** **(a)** assassination, **(b)** assimilate, **(c)** heliocentric.

Comprehension

3. What was the extent of Alexander's vast empire?
4. How did Alexander's conquests lead to a new civilization?

5. What new ideas did the Stoics introduce?

Critical Thinking and Writing

6. **Defending a Position** Would you agree that Alexander deserved to be called "the Great"? Why or why not?
7. **Ranking** What do you think were the three most important contributions made by Hellenistic scientists and mathematicians? Explain.

Activity

Take It to the NET

Use the Internet to research the lasting effects of Alexander and his ideas on the areas he conquered. Then, create a poster entitled "The Lasting Legacy of Alexander the Great."

Creating a Chapter Summary

Copy this graphic organizer on a sheet of paper. For each period of ancient Greek history, identify the time period and list three or four characteristics and achievements.

MINOAN CIVILIZATION 1750 B.C.–1500 B.C.
1. Traded with other Mediterranean people.
2.

MYCENAEAN CIVILIZATION
1.
2.

GREEK CITY-STATES
1.
2.

HELLENISTIC CIVILIZATION
1.
2.

iTEXT

For additional review and enrichment activities, see the interactive version of *World History* available on the Web and on CD-ROM.

Web Site Self-Test
For practice test questions for Chapter 5, see **www.phschool.com**.

Building Vocabulary

Write sentences using the chapter vocabulary words listed below; leave blanks where the vocabulary words should go. Exchange your sentences with another student and fill in the blanks in each other's sentences.

1. fresco
2. strait
3. aristocracy
4. tyrant
5. alliance
6. direct democracy
7. jury
8. logic
9. tragedy
10. assimilate

Recalling Key Facts

11. What were the *Iliad* and the *Odyssey?*
12. How did mountains help shape the development of Greek civilization?
13. (a) What was the social status of women in Sparta and in Athens? (b) How did the status of women change during the Hellenistic period?
14. What were the results of the Persian Wars?
15. What is the Socratic method?
16. What cultures blended to form Hellenistic civilization?

Critical Thinking and Writing

17. **Connecting to Geography** How did the geography and climate of Greece and the Aegean influence the development of Greek civilization?
18. **Analyzing Information** (a) How did Athenian culture stress the importance of the individual? Give two examples. (b) Do you think there is a relationship between the importance placed on the individual and the development of democracy? Explain.
19. **Recognizing Causes and Effects** (a) Identify two immediate and two long-range causes of the Peloponnesian War. (b) Why might it be said that all Greeks were losers in this war?
20. **Synthesizing Information** (a) How was the form of government outlined in Plato's *Republic* similar to the government of Sparta? (b) How was it different?
21. **Linking Past and Present** Reread the description of the Hippocratic oath. (a) How did Hippocrates address the question of medical ethics? (b) What ethical issues do doctors face today?

The excerpt below is from a pamphlet written by an anonymous Greek calling himself the Old Oligarch. Read the excerpt and answer the questions that follow.

> "[The Athenians] have chosen to let the worst people be better off than the good. Therefore, on this account I do not think well of their constitution. But since they have decided to have it so, I intend to point out how well they preserve their constitution and accomplish those other things for which the rest of the Greeks criticize them.
>
> First I want to say this: There the poor and the people generally are right to have more than the highborn and wealthy for the reason that it is the people who man the ships and impart strength to the city. . . .
>
> Everywhere on earth the best element is opposed to democracy. For among the best people there is minimal wantonness [undisciplined behavior] and injustice but a maximum of care for what is good, whereas among the people there is a maximum of ignorance, disorder, and wickedness."

—Old Oligarch, *The Constitution of the Athenians*

22. According to the Old Oligarch, what do the other Greek city-states think about the Athenian political system?

23. According to the Old Oligarch, why is it proper that Athens have a democracy?

24. **(a)** According to the Old Oligarch, who would support democracy in Athens? **(b)** Who would oppose it?

25. This anonymous author chose to call himself the Old Oligarch. **(a)** What was an oligarchy? **(b)** What does the writer's choice of a name indicate about his own social and economic status?

26. What do you think the Old Oligarch means when he refers to the "best" and the "worst" people?

27. Would you consider the Old Oligarch's view of Athenian democracy to be biased? Explain.

> **Skills Tip**
>
> When you analyze a primary source, keep in mind the author's own background. Factors such as age, education, social class, or economic status often influence a person's point of view.

The scene below is from a Greek painting that was created in the 400s B.C. It shows a group of Athenian women preparing a young bride for her wedding. Look at the painting, and then answer the questions that follow.

28. **(a)** What is the subject of this picture? **(b)** Who are the central figures?

29. To what social class would you say these women belonged?

30. What kinds of information about the lives of these women can you get from this painting? Identify at least three details.

31. Based on what you have read about surviving Greek artworks, where would you find this painting?

32. Compare the representations of the human form in Greek painting and Egyptian painting. **(a)** How are the two styles similar? **(b)** How are they different? **(c)** Why might there be some similarities between these two styles of painting?

Use the Internet to research information about the city-states in ancient Greece other than Athens and Sparta. Locate five of these city-states on a blank map of Greece. Then, make a fact sheet that includes two or three facts about each of these five city-states.

Ancient Rome and the Rise of Christianity

509 B.C.–A.D. 476

Chapter Preview

1 The Roman World Takes Shape
2 From Republic to Empire
3 The Roman Achievement
4 The Rise of Christianity
5 The Long Decline

509 B.C.
Romans set up a republic.

218 B.C.
The Carthaginian general Hannibal invades Italy during the Punic Wars between Rome and Carthage.

27 B.C.
The Roman republic ends, and the Roman empire begins under Emperor Augustus.

CHAPTER EVENTS

500 B.C. **300** B.C. **100** B.C.

GLOBAL EVENTS

321 B.C. Chandragupta begins the Maurya dynasty in India.

221 B.C. Shi Huangdi unites much of China.

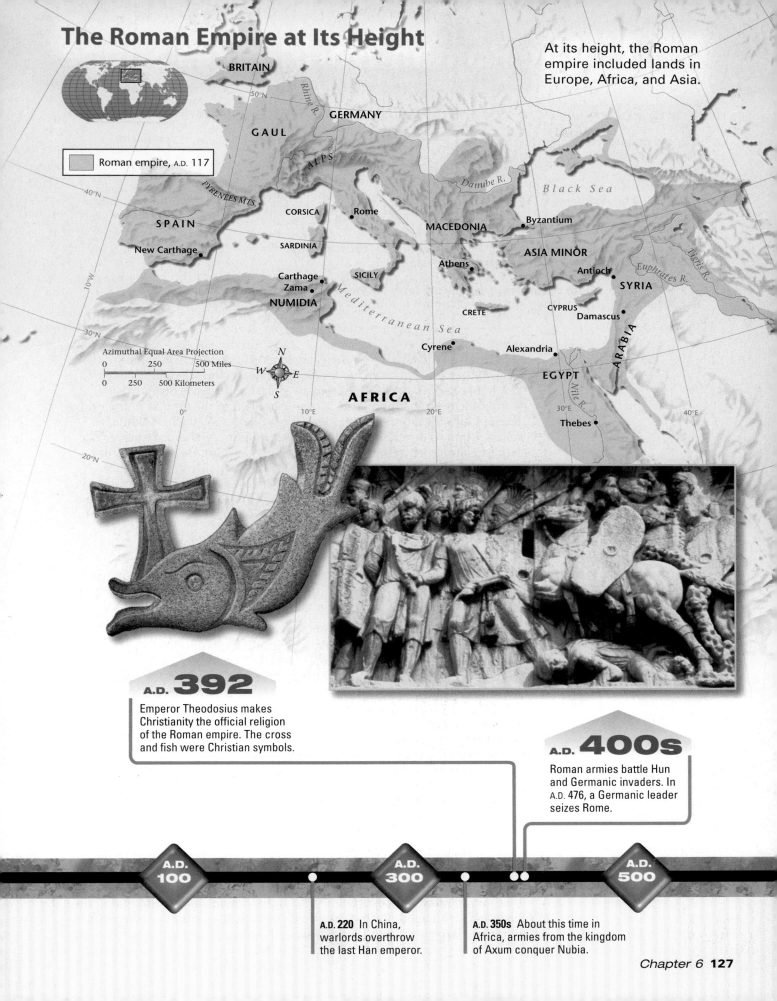

The Roman Empire at Its Height

At its height, the Roman empire included lands in Europe, Africa, and Asia.

Roman empire, A.D. 117

BRITAIN

GERMANY

GAUL

ALPS

Rhine R.

Danube R.

Black Sea

SPAIN

PYRENEES MTS.

CORSICA

Rome

MACEDONIA

Byzantium

New Carthage

SARDINIA

ASIA MINOR

Antioch

Euphrates R.

Tigris R.

Carthage

SICILY

Athens

SYRIA

Zama

CYPRUS

Damascus

NUMIDIA

Mediterranean Sea

CRETE

ARABIA

Cyrene

Alexandria

Azimuthal Equal Area Projection

0   250   500 Miles

0   250   500 Kilometers

EGYPT

Nile R.

AFRICA

Thebes

A.D. 392

Emperor Theodosius makes Christianity the official religion of the Roman empire. The cross and fish were Christian symbols.

A.D. 400s

Roman armies battle Hun and Germanic invaders. In A.D. 476, a Germanic leader seizes Rome.

A.D. 100   A.D. 300   A.D. 500

A.D. 220 In China, warlords overthrow the last Han emperor.

A.D. 350s About this time in Africa, armies from the kingdom of Axum conquer Nubia.

The Roman World Takes Shape

Reading Focus

- How did geography shape the early development of Rome?

- What were the major characteristics of government and society in the Roman republic?

- Why was Rome's expansion in Italy successful?

Vocabulary

republic
patrician
consul
dictator
plebeian
tribune
veto
legion

Taking Notes

At right is a partially completed outline of this section. As you read, finish the outline. Use Roman numerals for major headings, capital letters for subheadings, and numbers for supporting details.

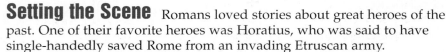

I. Geography and peoples of Italy
   A. Geography
      1. Peninsula
      2.
   B.
II. The Roman republic
   A. The government takes shape
      1.
      2.
   B.

Main Idea Rome developed a republican form of government based on strong civic virtues and gained control over much of the Italian peninsula.

Setting the Scene Romans loved stories about great heroes of the past. One of their favorite heroes was Horatius, who was said to have single-handedly saved Rome from an invading Etruscan army.

As the enemy approached, Horatius rushed to the far end of the bridge that led into the city. Standing alone, he held off the attackers while his fellow Romans tore down the bridge behind him. As the last timber fell, Horatius flung himself into the river below. Dodging the spears raining down all around him, he swam safely to the other side.

The story of Horatius is more legend than it is history. Still, it helps us to understand the virtues that the Romans admired. Courage, loyalty, and devotion to duty were the pillars on which Romans would build an empire.

Geography and Peoples of Italy

Rome began as a small city-state in Italy but ended up ruling the entire Mediterranean world. The story of the Romans and how they built a world empire starts with the land where they lived.

Geography The Italian peninsula looks like a boot, jutting into the Mediterranean Sea. The peninsula is centrally located in the Mediterranean, and the city of Rome is in the center of Italy. That location helped the Romans as they expanded, first in Italy, and then into lands around the Mediterranean.

Because of its geography, Italy was much easier to unify than Greece. Unlike Greece, Italy is not broken up into small, isolated valleys. In addition, the Apennine Mountains, which run like a backbone down the length of the Italian peninsula, are less rugged than the mountains of Greece. Finally, Italy has the advantage of broad, fertile plains, both in the north under the shadow of the Alps, and in the west, where the Romans settled. These plains supported a growing population.

Peoples The ancestors of the Romans, the Latins, migrated into Italy by about 800 B.C. The Latins settled along the Tiber River in small villages scattered over seven low-lying hills where they herded and farmed. Those villages would in time grow into Rome, the city on seven hills.

The Romans shared the Italian peninsula with other peoples. Among them were Greek colonists whose city-states dotted southern Italy and the Etruscans who lived north of Rome. For a time, the Etruscans ruled much of central Italy, including Rome itself.

Etruscan Helmet
The Etruscans were skilled in metalworking, as is shown by the bronze helmet above. Romans learned much from the other peoples in Italy.

Theme: Diversity What other peoples lived in the Italian peninsula?

The Romans learned much from Etruscan civilization. They adapted the alphabet that the Etruscans had earlier acquired from the Greeks. They also learned to use the arch in building and adapted Etruscan engineering techniques to drain the marshy lands along the Tiber. Etruscan gods and goddesses merged with Roman deities.

The Roman Republic

The Romans drove out their Etruscan ruler in 509 B.C. This date is traditionally considered to mark the founding of the Roman state.

The Romans set up a new government in which some officials were chosen by the people. They called it a republic, or "thing of the people." A republic, Romans thought, would keep any individual from gaining too much power.

The Government Takes Shape In the early republic, the most powerful governing body was the senate. Its 300 members were all patricians, members of the landholding upper class. Senators, who served for life, made the laws.

Each year, the senators elected from the patrician class two consuls. Their job was to supervise the business of government and command the armies. Consuls, however, could serve only one term. They were also expected to consult with the senate. By limiting their time in office and making them responsible to the senate, Rome had a system of checks on the power of government.

In the event of war, the senate might choose a dictator, or ruler who has complete control over a government. Each Roman dictator was granted power to rule for six months. Then, he had to give up power. Romans admired Cincinnatus as a model dictator. Cincinnatus organized an army, led the Romans to victory over the attacking enemy, attended victory celebrations, and returned to his farmlands—all within 16 days.

Plebeians Demand Equality At first, all government officials were patricians. Plebeians (plih BEE uhnz), the farmers, merchants, artisans, and traders who made up the bulk of the population, had little influence. The efforts of the plebeians to gain power shaped politics in the early republic.

The plebeians' first breakthrough came in 450 B.C., when the government had the laws of Rome inscribed on 12 tablets and set up in the Forum, or marketplace. Plebeians had protested that citizens could not know what the laws were, because they were not written down. The Laws of the Twelve Tables made it possible for the first time for plebeians to appeal a judgment handed down by a patrician judge.

In time, the plebeians gained the right to elect their own officials, called tribunes, to protect their interests. The tribunes could veto, or block, those laws that they felt were harmful to plebeians. Little by little, plebeians forced the senate to choose plebeians as consuls, appoint plebeians to other high offices, and finally to open the senate itself to plebeians.

A Lasting Legacy Although the senate still dominated the government, the common people had gained access to power and won safeguards for their rights without having to resort to war or revolution. More than 2,000 years later, the framers of the United States Constitution would adapt such Roman ideas as the senate, the veto, and checks on political power.

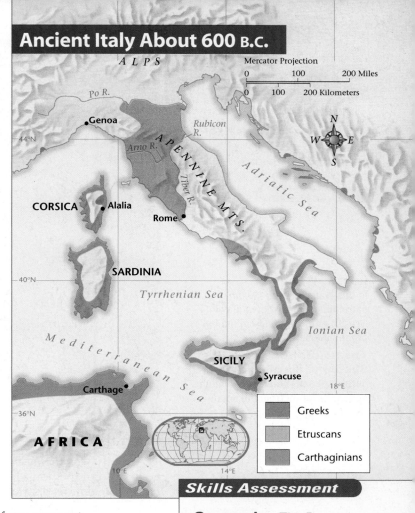

Ancient Italy About 600 B.C.

Mercator Projection

Greeks
Etruscans
Carthaginians

Skills Assessment

Geography The Romans shared the Italian peninsula with other peoples, many of whose ideas they adapted for their own use.
1. **Location** On the map, locate (a) Rome, (b) Alps, (c) Mediterranean Sea, (d) Carthage, (e) Sicily.
2. **Region** Based on this map, which group do you think had the most influence on the Romans? Explain.
3. **Critical Thinking Comparing** Why was Italy easier to unite than Greece?

Virtual Field Trip

www.phschool.com

**Metropolitan Museum of Art
New York, New York**

To see other artworks and artifacts relating to ancient Rome, use the Internet address above to link to the Metropolitan Museum of Art.

Roman Women
In this wall painting, a woman of the patrician class is shown playing a lyre. The girl standing behind her is probably a servant or slave.

Theme: Political and Social Systems Describe how a portrait of a plebeian scene might appear different from the scene shown here.

Roman Society

The family was the basic unit of Roman society. Under Roman law, the male head of the household, usually the father, had absolute power in the family. He enforced strict discipline and demanded total respect for his authority. His wife was subject to his authority and was not allowed to administer her own affairs. The ideal Roman woman was loving, dutiful, dignified, and strong.

Changing Role of Women Roman women played a larger role in society than did Greek women. In later Roman times, women from all classes ran a variety of businesses, from small shops to major shipyards. Those who made their fortunes earned respect by supporting the arts or paying for public festivals. Most women, though, worked at home, raising their families, spinning, and weaving.

Over the centuries, Roman women gained greater freedom and influence. Patrician women went to the public baths, dined out, and attended the theater or other public entertainments with their husbands. Some women, such as Livia and Agrippina the Younger, had highly visible public roles and exercised significant political influence.

Education Girls and boys alike learned to read and write. Even lower-class Romans were taught to write, as can be seen from the jokes and other graffiti that archaeologists found scrawled on walls around the city.

By the late republic, many wealthy Romans were hiring private tutors, often Greeks, to supervise the education of their children. Under their guidance, children memorized major events and developments in Roman history. Rhetoric was an important subject for boys who wanted to pursue political careers.

Religion Roman gods and goddesses resembled those of the Etruscans and Greeks. Like the Greek god Zeus, the Roman god Jupiter ruled over the sky and the other gods. Juno, his wife, like the Greek goddess Hera, protected marriage. Romans also prayed to Neptune, god of the sea, whose powers were the same as those of the Greek god Poseidon. On the battle-field, they turned to Mars, the god of war.

The Roman calendar was full of feasts and other celebrations to honor the gods and to ensure divine favor for the city. As loyal citizens, Romans joined in these festivals, which inspired a sense of community. Throughout Rome were dozens of temples where statues of the gods were housed. Inside these temples, Romans worshiped and asked for divine assistance.

Expansion in Italy

As Rome's political and social systems evolved at home, its armies expanded Roman power across Italy. Roman armies conquered first the Etruscans and then the Greek city-states in the south. By about 270 B.C., Rome controlled most of the Italian peninsula.

Citizen-Soldiers Rome's success was due to skillful diplomacy and to its loyal, well-trained army. The basic military unit was the legion, made up of about 5,000 men. As in Greece, Roman armies consisted of citizen-soldiers who fought without pay and supplied their own weapons. Roman citizens often made good soldiers because they were brought up to value loyalty, courage, and respect for authority.

To ensure success, Roman commanders mixed rewards with harsh punishment. Young soldiers who showed courage in action won praise and gifts. If a unit fled from battle, however, 1 out of every 10 men from the disgraced unit was put to death.

Conquered Lands Rome generally treated its defeated enemies with justice. Conquered peoples had to acknowledge Roman leadership, pay taxes, and supply soldiers for the Roman army. In return, Rome let them keep their own customs, money, and local government.

To a few privileged groups among the conquered people, Rome gave the highly prized right of full citizenship. Others became partial citizens, who were allowed to marry Romans and carry on trade in Rome. As a result of such generous policies, most conquered lands remained loyal to Rome even in troubled times.

Protection and Unification To protect its conquests, Rome posted soldiers throughout the land. It also built a network of all-weather military roads to link distant territories to Rome. As trade and travel increased, local peoples incorporated Latin into their languages and adopted many Roman customs and beliefs. Slowly, Italy began to unite under Roman rule.

SECTION **1** **Assessment**

Recall
1. **Identify:** (a) Latins, (b) Etruscans, (c) Laws of the Twelve Tables, (d) Jupiter.
2. **Define:** (a) republic, (b) patrician, (c) consul, (d) dictator, (e) plebeian, (f) tribune, (g) veto, (h) legion.

Comprehension
3. Describe two ways that the geography of Italy influenced the rise of Rome.
4. (a) What reforms did plebeians win during the early republic?
(b) How did male and female roles differ in the Roman family?
5. What were two reasons for Rome's success in expanding its power across Italy?

Critical Thinking and Writing
6. **Linking Past and Present** Roman heroes were admired for their courage, loyalty, and devotion to duty. What qualities do American heroes display?
7. **Analyzing Information** Did the Roman republic have a democratic government? Why or why not?

Activity
Writing News Headlines Write a series of newspaper headlines announcing major events in the rise of the Roman republic. Remember that news headlines are usually clear and concise.

From Republic to Empire

Reading Focus

- How did Rome win an empire?
- Why did the Roman republic decline?
- How did Roman emperors promote peace and stability in the empire?

Vocabulary

imperialism
province
latifundia
census

Taking Notes

Copy this concept web. As you read the section, fill in the blank circles with important facts about the decline of the Roman republic. Add more circles if you need them.

THE REPUBLIC DECLINES

Gracchus brothers are killed

Main Idea As Roman power spread around the Mediterranean, the republic ended and the age of the Roman empire began.

Setting the Scene

After gaining control of the Italian peninsula, Rome began to build an empire around the Mediterranean Sea. Expansion created strains and conflicts in Roman society. Addressing plebeians, the Roman tribune Tiberius Gracchus described one of the injustices that he saw in Roman society:

> "The beasts of the field and the birds of the air have their holes and their hiding places, but the men who fight and die for Italy enjoy only the light and the air. . . . You fight and die to give wealth and luxury to others. You are called the masters of the world, but there is not a foot of ground that you can call your own."
>
> —Plutarch, *Parallel Lives*

The effects of territorial expansion gradually weakened and finally crushed the republic. Out of the rubble, though, rose the Roman empire and a new chapter in Rome's long history.

Winning an Empire

Rome's conquest of the Italian peninsula brought it into contact with Carthage, a city-state on the northern coast of Africa. Settled by North Africans and Phoenician traders, Carthage ruled over an empire that stretched across North Africa and the western Mediterranean. As Rome expanded westward, conflict between these two powers became inevitable.

Wars With Carthage Between 264 B.C. and 146 B.C., Rome fought three wars against Carthage. They are called the Punic Wars, from *Punicus*, the Latin word for Phoenician. In the First Punic War, Rome defeated Carthage and won Sicily, Corsica, and Sardinia.

The Carthaginians sought revenge in the Second Punic War. In 218 B.C., the Carthaginian general Hannibal led his army, including dozens of war elephants, on an epic march across the Pyrenees, through France, and over the Alps into Italy. The trek cost Hannibal nearly half his army. However, the Carthaginian general had surprised the Romans who had expected an invasion from the south. For 15 years, Hannibal and his army moved across Italy, winning battle after battle.

The Carthaginians, however, failed to capture Rome itself. In the end, the Romans outflanked Hannibal by sending an army to attack Carthage.

Wars With Carthage
Hannibal crossed the Alps into Italy with an invasion force that included thousands of troops and more than three dozen elephants. From towers on the elephants' backs, soldiers rained arrows and spears on their Roman enemies.

Theme: Impact of the Individual How did Hannibal's invasion route surprise the Romans?

Hannibal returned to defend his homeland, where the Romans defeated him at last. Carthage gave up all its lands except those in Africa.

Nevertheless, many Romans still saw Carthage as a rival and wanted revenge for the terrible destruction that Hannibal's army had brought to Italy. For years, Cato, a wealthy senator, ended every speech he made with the words "Carthage must be destroyed."

Finally, in the Third Punic War, Rome completely destroyed Carthage. Survivors were killed or sold into slavery. The Romans poured salt over the earth so that nothing would grow there again. The Romans were now masters of the western Mediterranean.

Other Conquests "The Carthaginians fought for their own preservation and the sovereignty of Africa," observed a Greek witness to the fall of Carthage; "the Romans, for supremacy and world domination." The Romans were committed to a policy of imperialism, or establishing control over foreign lands and peoples. While Rome fought Carthage in the west, it was also expanding into the eastern Mediterranean. There, Romans confronted the Hellenistic rulers who had divided up the empire of Alexander the Great.

Sometimes to defend Roman interests, sometimes simply for plunder, Rome launched a series of wars in the area. One by one, Macedonia, Greece, and parts of Asia Minor surrendered and became Roman provinces, that is, lands under Roman rule. Other regions, like Egypt, allied with Rome. By 133 B.C., Roman power extended from Spain to Egypt. Truly, the Romans were justified in calling the Mediterranean *Mare Nostrum*, or "Our Sea."

Social and Economic Effects Conquests and control of busy trade routes brought incredible riches into Rome. Generals, officials, and traders amassed fortunes from loot, taxes, and commerce. A new class of wealthy Romans emerged. They built lavish mansions and filled them with luxuries imported from the east. Wealthy families bought up huge estates, called latifundia. As the Romans conquered more and more lands, they forced people captured in war to work as slaves on the latifundia.

The widespread use of slave labor hurt small farmers, who were unable to produce food as cheaply as the latifundia could. The farmers' problems were compounded when huge quantities of grain pouring in from the conquered lands drove down grain prices. Many farmers fell into debt and had to sell their land.

In despair, landless farmers flocked to Rome and other cities looking for jobs. There, they joined a restless class of unemployed people. As the gap between rich and poor widened, angry mobs began to riot.

The new wealth also increased corruption. Greed and self-interest replaced virtues such as simplicity, hard work, and devotion to duty so prized in the early republic.

Attempts at Reform Two young patricians, brothers named Tiberius and Gaius Gracchus (GAY uhs GRAK uhs), were among the first to attempt reform. Tiberius, who was elected a tribune in 133 B.C., called on the state to distribute land to poor farmers. Gaius, elected tribune 10 years later, sought a wider range of reforms, including the use of public funds to buy grain to feed the poor.

The reforms of the Gracchus brothers angered the senate, which saw them as a threat to its power. The brothers, along with thousands of their followers, were killed in waves of street violence set off by senators and their hired thugs.

Connections to Today

Ancient Ruins Under the Sea

Swimming among brightly colored fish, archaeologists are exploring an underwater treasure off the coast of Egypt. In a rare find, they have uncovered remains of the ancient city of Alexandria beneath the waters of the Mediterranean. Divers can swim among sphinxes, columns, and temples—a rich mix of Egyptian, Greek, and Roman artifacts.

Mingled among the ruins created long ago by earthquakes are the wrecks of Roman ships that failed to navigate the dangerous harbor. Cargoes of olive oil and wine are still intact after resting on the sea floor for some 2,000 years.

Theme: Geography and History How did geography contribute to the creation of this archaeological site?

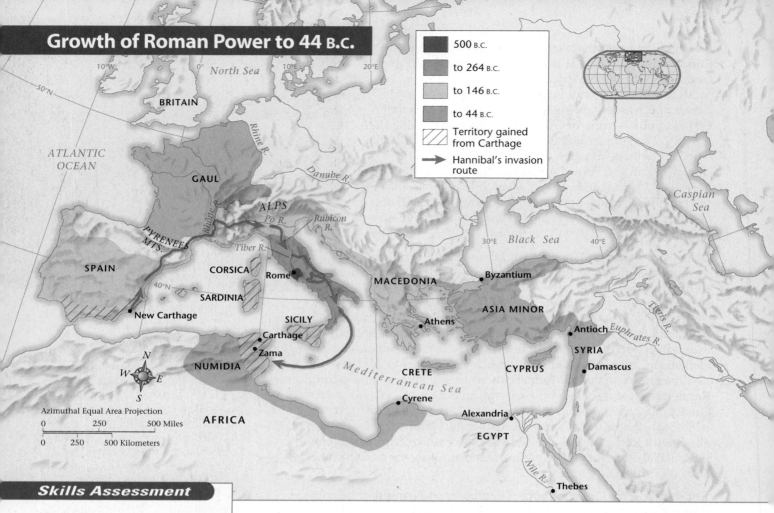

Growth of Roman Power to 44 B.C.

■	500 B.C.
■	to 264 B.C.
■	to 146 B.C.
■	to 44 B.C.
▨	Territory gained from Carthage
→	Hannibal's invasion route

Azimuthal Equal Area Projection

0   250   500 Miles
0   250   500 Kilometers

Decline of the Republic

Unable to resolve its problems peacefully, Rome was plunged into a series of civil wars. At issue was who should hold power—the senate, which wanted to govern as it had in the past, or popular political leaders, who wanted to weaken the senate and enact reforms.

The turmoil sparked slave uprisings and revolts among Rome's allies. Meanwhile, the old legions of Roman citizen-soldiers became professional armies whose first loyalty was to their commanders. Rival generals marched their armies into Rome to advance their ambitions.

Julius Caesar's Rise to Power Out of this chaos emerged Julius Caesar, an ambitious military commander. For a time, Caesar dominated Roman politics with Pompey, another brilliant general. Then, in 59 B.C., Caesar set out with his army to make new conquests. After nine years of fighting, he completed the conquest of Gaul—the area that is now France.

Fearful of Caesar's rising fame, Pompey persuaded the senate to order Caesar to disband his army and return to Rome. Caesar defied the order. Swiftly and secretly, he led his army across the Rubicon River into northern Italy and then headed toward Rome. Once again, civil war erupted across the Roman world.

Caesar crushed Pompey and his supporters. He then swept around the Mediterranean, suppressing rebellions. *"Veni, vidi, vici"*—"I came, I saw, I conquered"—he announced after one victory. Later, returning to Rome, he forced the senate to make him dictator. Although he kept the senate and other features of the republic, he was in fact the absolute ruler of Rome.

Caesar's Reforms Between 48 B.C. and 44 B.C., Caesar pushed through a number of reforms intended to deal with Rome's many problems. He launched a program of public works to employ the jobless and gave public land to the poor. He also reorganized the government of the provinces and granted Roman citizenship to more people. Caesar's most lasting reform was the introduction of a new calendar based on Egyptian knowledge. The Julian calendar, as it was later called, was used in western Europe for over 1,600 years. With minor changes, it is still our calendar today.

Assassination and Civil Wars Caesar's enemies worried that he planned to make himself king of Rome. In order to save the republic, they plotted against him. In March 44 B.C., as Caesar arrived in the senate, his enemies stabbed him to death.

The death of Julius Caesar plunged Rome into a new round of civil wars. Mark Antony, Caesar's chief general, and Octavian, Caesar's grand-nephew, joined forces to hunt down the murderers. The two men soon quarreled, however, setting off a bitter struggle for power. In 31 B.C., Octavian finally defeated Antony and his powerful ally Queen Cleopatra of Egypt.

Roman Empire and Roman Peace

The senate gave the triumphant Octavian the title of *Augustus,* or Exalted One, and declared him *princeps,* or first citizen. Although he was careful not to call himself king, a title that Romans had hated since Etruscan times, Augustus exercised absolute power and named his successor, just as a king would do.

Under Augustus, who ruled from 31 B.C. to A.D. 14, the 500-year-old republic came to an end. Romans did not know it at the time, but a new age had dawned—the age of the Roman empire.

A Stable Government Through firm but moderate policies, Augustus laid the foundation for a stable government. Although he left the senate in place, Augustus created an efficient, well-trained civil service to enforce the laws. High-level jobs were open to men of talent, regardless of their class. In addition, he cemented the allegiance of cities and provinces to Rome by allowing them a large measure of self-government.

Augustus undertook economic reforms, too. To make the tax system more fair, he ordered a census, or population count, to be taken in the empire. He set up a postal service and issued new coins to make trade easier. He put the jobless to work building roads and temples and sent others to farm the land.

The government that Augustus organized functioned well for 200 years. Still, a serious problem kept arising: Who would rule after an emperor died? Romans did not accept the idea of power passing automatically from father to son. As a result, the death of an emperor often led to intrigue and violence.

Bad Emperors and Good Emperors Not all of Augustus' successors were great rulers. Indeed, some were weak and incompetent. Two early emperors, Caligula and Nero, were downright evil and perhaps insane. Caligula, for example, appointed his favorite horse as consul. Nero viciously persecuted Christians and was even blamed for setting a great fire that destroyed much of Rome.

Between A.D. 96 and A.D. 180, the empire benefited from the rule of a series of "good emperors." The emperor Hadrian, for example, codified Roman law, making it the same for all provinces. He also had soldiers build a wall across Britain to hold back attackers from the non-Roman north.

The emperor Marcus Aurelius, who read philosophy while on military campaigns, was close to Plato's ideal of a philosopher-king. His *Meditations* show his Stoic philosophy and commitment to duty: "Hour by hour resolve firmly . . . to do what comes to hand with correct and natural dignity."

Biography

Julius Caesar
100 B.C.(?)—44 B.C.

Julius Caesar's bold rise to power echoed his boldness on the battle-field. His brilliant conquest of Gaul made him enormously popular. Romans were thrilled by reports of his many victories, which added great riches and huge territories to the empire. In nine years of cam-paigning, Caesar lost only two bat-tles. His tactics in Gaul are still studied at military academies today.

When Caesar crossed the Rubicon from Gaul back into Italy, he said, *"alea iacta est,"* or "the die is cast," meaning there was no turning back. Today, people use the phrase "crossing the Rubicon" to mean making a decision from which there is no turning back. In this way, Caesar's legendary bold-ness lives on.

Theme: Impact of the Individual How might the history of Rome be different if Caesar had been defeated in Gaul?

The Pax Romana The 200-year span that began with Augustus and ended with Marcus Aurelius is known as the period of the *Pax Romana,* or "Roman Peace." During that time, Roman rule brought peace, order, unity, and prosperity to lands stretching from the Euphrates River in the east to Britain in the west, an area approximately equal in size to the continental United States.

During the Pax Romana, Roman legions maintained and protected the roads, and Roman fleets chased pirates from the seas. Trade flowed freely to and from distant lands in Africa and Asia. Egyptian farmers in the Nile Valley supplied Romans with grain. From other parts of Africa came ivory and gold, as well as lions and other wild animals that were used in public entertainments. From India came spices, cotton, and precious stones. Trade caravans traveled along the great Silk Road, bringing silk and other goods from China.

People too, moved easily within the Roman empire, spreading ideas and knowledge, especially the advances of the Hellenistic east. As you will read, ideas from Greece and Judea would have tremendous impact on Rome and the western world.

Bread and Circuses Throughout the empire, rich and poor alike loved spectacular entertainments. At the Circus Maximus, Rome's largest racecourse, chariots thundered around an oval course, making dangerously tight turns at either end. Fans bet feverishly on their favorite teams—the Reds, Greens, Blues, or Whites—and successful charioteers were hailed as heroes.

Gladiator contests were even more popular. Many gladiators were slaves who had been trained to fight. In the arena, they battled one another, either singly or in groups. Crowds cheered a skilled gladiator, and a good fighter might even win his freedom. But if a gladiator made a poor showing, the crowd turned thumbs down, a signal that he should be killed.

To the emperors who paid for them with the taxes they collected from the empire, these amusements were a way to pacify the city's restless mobs. In much the same spirit, the government provided free grain to feed the poor. Critics warned against this policy of "bread and circuses," but few listened.

During the Pax Romana, the general prosperity hid underlying social and economic problems. Later Roman emperors, however, would face problems that could not be solved with "bread and circuses."

The Colosseum

Romans marveled at the shows put on at the Colosseum, ancient Rome's largest stadium. Spectators watched the slaughter of exotic animals, gladiators battling to the death, and mock naval battles, like the one shown above.

The Colosseum was an architectural marvel. Its floor was about the size of a modern football field. As many as 50,000 spectators could crowd onto the Colosseum's marble and wooden benches. There, they were protected from the hot Roman sun by a giant canvas roof.

Theme: Political and Social Systems How does the architectural accomplishment of the Colosseum contrast with what took place there?

SECTION 2 Assessment

Recall
1. **Identify:** **(a)** Punic Wars, **(b)** Hannibal, **(c)** Tiberius and Gaius Gracchus, **(d)** Julius Caesar, **(e)** Augustus, **(f)** Hadrian, **(g)** Pax Romana, **(h)** Circus Maximus.
2. **Define:** **(a)** imperialism, **(b)** province, **(c)** latifundia, **(d)** census.

Comprehension
3. How did Rome build an empire around the Mediterranean Sea?
4. What problems contributed to the decline of the Roman republic?

5. How did Augustus lay the foundation for stable government in the Roman empire?

Critical Thinking and Writing
6. **Analyzing Information** How do you think the founders of the Roman republic would have viewed the government of the Roman empire? Explain.
7. **Predicting Consequences** What were some possible negative consequences of following the policy of "bread and circuses"?

Activity

Creating a Political Cartoon Imagine that you are one of the senators who oppose Julius Caesar. Create a political cartoon that criticizes one of Caesar's policies and shows why you oppose him.

The Roman Achievement

Reading Focus

- How was Greco–Roman civilization formed?
- What were some Roman contributions to literature, the arts, and technology?
- What principles of law did Romans develop?

Vocabulary

satirize
mosaic
engineering
aqueduct

Taking Notes

Make a table like the one below to focus on the cultural achievements of the Romans. Add more information and more rows as you read the section.

LAW	Civil law, law of nations
LITERATURE	Virgil's *Aeneid*
HISTORY	

Main Idea Romans absorbed ideas from other cultures and made great advances in law, literature, engineering, and other areas.

Setting the Scene Marcus Tullius Cicero was a philosopher, politician, and passionate defender of law. As the republic declined, he attacked ambitious men such as Julius Caesar. When Caesar came to power, however, he forgave Cicero, noting that it was "more glorious to have enlarged the limits of the Roman mind than the boundaries of Roman rule."

Romans such as Cicero and Caesar both had a lasting impact. Through war and conquest, Roman generals carried the achievements of Roman civilization to distant lands. Yet the civilization that developed was not simply Roman. Rather, it blended Greek, Hellenistic, and Roman achievements.

Greco-Roman Civilization

In its early days, Rome absorbed ideas from Greek colonists in southern Italy, and it continued to borrow heavily from Greek culture after it conquered Greece. To the Romans emerging from their villages, Greek art, literature, philosophy, and scientific genius represented the height of cultural achievement. Their admiration never wavered, leading the Roman poet Horace to note, "Greece has conquered her rude conqueror."

The Romans adapted Greek and Hellenistic achievements, just as the Greeks had once absorbed ideas from Egypt and the Fertile Crescent. The blending of Greek, Hellenistic, and Roman traditions produced what is known as Greco-Roman civilization. Trade and travel during the Pax Romana helped spread this vital new civilization.

Literature, Philosophy, and History

In the field of literature, the Romans owed a great debt to the Greeks. Many Romans spoke Greek and imitated Greek styles in prose and poetry. Still, the greatest Roman writers used Latin to create their own literature.

Poetry In his epic poem, the *Aeneid,* Virgil tried to show that Rome's past was as heroic as that of Greece. He linked his epic to Homer's work by telling how Aeneas escaped from Troy to found Rome. Virgil wrote the *Aeneid* soon after Augustus came to power. He hoped it would arouse patriotism and help unite Rome after years of civil wars.

Other poets used verse to satirize, or make fun of, Roman society. Horace's satires were gentle, using playful wit to attack human folly. Juvenal and Martial were more biting. Martial's poems were so harsh that he had to use fictitious names to protect himself from retribution.

Primary Source

A Roman Epic

In the opening lines of the Aeneid, *Virgil introduces "the hero" Aeneas and hints at his daring and destiny:*

"I tell about war and the hero who first from Troy's frontier,
Displaced by destiny, came . . .
To Italy—a man much travailed on sea and land
By the powers above, because of the brooding anger of [the goddess] Juno,
Suffering much in war until he could found a city
And march his gods into Latium, whence rose the Latin race,
. . . and the high walls of Rome."

—Virgil, *Aeneid*

Skills Assessment

Primary Source What forces caused Aeneas' suffering and led to his founding of Rome?

History Roman historians pursued their own theme—the rise and fall of Roman power. Like the poet Virgil, the historian Livy sought to rouse patriotic feeling and restore traditional Roman virtues by recalling images of Rome's heroic past. In his history of Rome, Livy recounted tales of great heroes such as Horatius and Cincinnatus.

Another historian, Tacitus, wrote bitterly about Augustus and his successors, who, he felt, had destroyed Roman liberty. He admired the simple culture of the Germans who lived on Rome's northern frontier and would later invade the empire.

Philosophy Romans borrowed much of their philosophy from the Greeks. The Hellenistic philosophy of Stoicism impressed Roman thinkers like the emperor Marcus Aurelius. Stoics stressed the importance of duty and acceptance of one's fate. They also showed concern for the well-being of all people, an idea that would be reflected in Christian teachings. (See Section 4 of this chapter.)

A Roman Aqueduct
Roman engineers built this aqueduct across the Gardon River in present-day France.

Theme: Economics and Technology Why were aqueducts important to Roman towns?

Art and Architecture

To a large degree, Roman art and architecture were based on Greek and Etruscan models. However, as with literature, the Romans made adaptations to develop their own style.

Art Like the Greeks before them, Roman sculptors stressed realism, portraying their subjects with every wart and vein in place. The Romans also broke new ground, however, by revealing an individual's character. A statue of a soldier, a writer, or an emperor might capture an expression of smugness, discontent, or haughty pride.

Some Roman sculpture was more idealistic. For example, sculptors transformed Augustus, who was neither handsome nor imposing, into a symbol of power and leadership.

Romans beautified their homes with works of art. Examples of these works were preserved in Pompeii, a city buried by the volcanic eruption of Mount Vesuvius in A.D. 79. Artists depicted scenes from Roman literature and daily life in splendid frescoes and mosaics. A mosaic is a picture made from chips of colored stone or glass.

Architecture While the Greeks aimed for simple elegance in architecture, the Romans emphasized grandeur. Immense palaces, temples, and stadiums stood as mighty monuments to Roman power and dignity. The Romans improved on devices such as the column and the arch. Using concrete as a building material, they developed the rounded dome to roof large spaces. The most famous domed structure is the Pantheon, a temple to all the Roman gods, which still stands in Rome.

Technology and Science

The Romans excelled in engineering, which is the application of science and mathematics to develop useful structures and machines. Roman engineers built roads, bridges, and harbors throughout the empire. Roman roads were so solidly built that many of them were still used long after the fall of the empire.

Roman engineers also built many immense aqueducts, or bridgelike stone structures that brought water from the hills into Roman cities. The wealthy had water piped in, and almost every city boasted public baths. Here, people gathered not only to wash themselves but to hear the latest news and exchange gossip.

The Romans generally left scientific research to the Greeks who were by that time citizens of the empire. In Alexandria, Egypt, Hellenistic scientists

Vesuvius Erupts!

One summer day in A.D. 79, the townspeople of Pompeii, a wealthy Roman resort town, felt tremors and heard a low rumble but were not alarmed. Though they lived in the shadow of a huge volcano, no one could remember the last time it had erupted. Within hours, a giant explosion had ripped off the mountaintop. Within two days, the town of Pompeii had disappeared.

Before the eruption, Pompeii was a busy town. Its fanciest homes boasted beautiful mosaic floors and colorful murals.

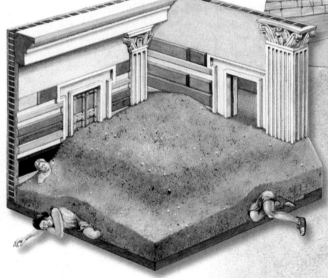

As ash started to fall, many people tried to flee while others sought safety in their cellars. Still, most people suffocated and were buried in the ash. Rain hardened the ash, forming perfect molds of people and preserving articles of everyday living.

With little warning, Mt. Vesuvius exploded. Gas and hot, liquid rock burst through the cone, shooting ash and whole rocks into the air. Spectacular lightning bolts and clouds of ash filled the sky.

This is a cast of the body of a child who was entombed in the hardened ash.

Portfolio Assessment

INTERNET Use the Internet or other research sources to learn about a recent volcanic eruption. Use the information you find to write articles about the event for the front page of a newspaper. You may want to use pictures or diagrams to illustrate the articles.

exchanged ideas freely. It was there that astronomer-mathematician Ptolemy (TAHL uh mee) proposed his theory that the Earth was the center of the universe, a mistaken idea that was accepted in the western world for nearly 1,500 years.

The Greek doctor Galen advanced the frontiers of medical science by insisting on experiments to prove a conclusion. Galen compiled a medical encyclopedia summarizing what was known at the time. It remained a standard text for more than 1,000 years.

Although the Romans did little original research, they did put science to practical use. They applied geography to make maps, and medical knowledge to help doctors improve public health. Like Galen, they collected knowledge into encyclopedias. Pliny the Elder, a Roman scientist, compiled volumes on geography, zoology, botany, and other topics, all based on other people's works.

Roman Law

"Let justice be done," proclaimed a Roman saying, "though the heavens fall!" Probably the greatest legacy of Rome was its commitment to the rule of law and to justice. During the Roman empire, the rule of law fostered unity and stability. Many centuries later, the principles of Roman law would become the basis for legal systems in Europe and Latin America.

Two Systems During the republic, Rome developed a system of law, known as the civil law, that applied to its citizens. As Rome expanded, however, it ruled many foreigners who were not covered under the civil law. Gradually, a second system of law, known as the law of nations, emerged. It applied to all people under Roman rule, citizens and noncitizens. Later, when Rome extended citizenship across the empire, the two systems merged.

Common Principles As Roman law developed, certain basic principles evolved. Many of these principles are familiar to Americans today. An accused person was presumed innocent until proven guilty. The accused was allowed to face the accuser and offer a defense against the charge. Guilt had to be established "clearer than daylight" through evidence. Judges were allowed to interpret the laws and were expected to make fair decisions.

Law and Government
Knowledge of the laws and legal procedures of Rome was helpful in pursuing a career in government. Many Roman officials, such as the senator depicted in this sculpture, had argued cases in court and served as judges.

Theme: Continuity and Change Today, many American government officials are lawyers. How do you think this affects the quality of government?

SECTION 3 Assessment

Recall

1. **Identify:** (a) Greco-Roman civilization, (b) Virgil, (c) Livy, (d) Pantheon, (e) Galen, (f) civil law, (g) law of nations.
2. **Define:** (a) satirize, (b) mosaic, (c) engineering, (d) aqueduct.

Comprehension

3. How did Greek culture influence the development of Roman civilization?
4. How did Romans use technology to improve life in the empire?
5. What principles of law did Romans develop?

Critical Thinking and Writing

6. **Linking Past and Present** Give two examples of how the principles of law developed by Rome affect life in the United States today.
7. **Analyzing Primary Sources** The Roman poet Horace said of Roman civilization: "Greece has conquered her rude conqueror." (a) What did he mean by this? (b) Give three examples that support his statement.

The Rise of Christianity

Reading Focus

- What was Rome's policy toward different religions in the early empire?

- What were the major teachings of Jesus, and how were they spread?

- How did the early Christian Church develop?

Vocabulary

messiah
apostle
martyr
bishop
diocese
patriarch
pope
heresy

Taking Notes

Copy the partially completed flowchart at right. As you read, finish the flowchart by writing in the main events in the rise of Christianity. Add more boxes as needed.

Romans tolerate various religions
↓
Jesus preaches his ideas
↓
Followers of Jesus spread Christianity
↓
↓

Main Idea A new religion, Christianity, emerged in the Roman empire. It gradually spread and became the official religion of the empire.

Setting the Scene

Early in the Pax Romana, a new religion, Christianity, sprang up in a distant corner of the Roman empire. At first, Christianity was just one of many religions practiced in the empire. But despite many obstacles, the new faith grew rapidly, and by A.D. 395, it had been declared the official religion of the Roman empire.

As it gained strength and spread through the empire, Christianity reshaped Roman beliefs. And when the Roman empire fell, the Christian Church took over much of its role, becoming the central institution of western civilization for nearly 1,000 years.

Religious Diversity in the Early Empire

Within the culturally diverse Roman empire, a variety of religious beliefs and practices coexisted. Jupiter, Mars, Juno, and other traditional Roman gods remained important to some people. However, a growing number of people were looking elsewhere for spiritual fulfillment.

Mystery Religions Some turned to mystery religions that emphasized secret rituals and promised special rewards. One of the most popular of these was the cult of Isis, which originated in Egypt and offered women equal status with men. Others worshiped the Persian god Mithras, who championed good over evil and offered life after death. Mithraism was especially favored by Roman soldiers.

Religious Toleration Generally, Rome tolerated the varied religious traditions. As long as citizens showed loyalty by honoring Roman gods and acknowledging the divine spirit of the emperor, they were allowed to worship other gods as they pleased. Because most people at the time were polytheistic, they were content to worship the Roman gods along with their own.

Divisions in Judea By 63 B.C., the Romans had conquered Judea, where most Jews of the time lived. As you have learned, the Jews were devoted to their monotheistic traditions. To avoid violating the Jewish belief in one god, the Romans excused Jews from worshiping Roman gods.

Among the Jews themselves, however, religious ferment was creating deep divisions. During the Hellenistic age, many Jews absorbed Greek customs and ideas. Concerned about the weakening of their religion, Jewish conservatives rejected these influences and called for strict obedience to Jewish laws and traditions.

Global Connections

A Jewish-Greek Connection

During Roman times and before, many Jews left their homeland in Judea. They settled in lands around the Mediterranean and elsewhere.

Many of those who migrated began to speak Greek instead of Hebrew, and two Greek words became an important part of Jewish history. The Greek word *diaspora,* which means "scattering," refers to the fact that some Jews migrated and settled in various parts of the world. The Greek word *synagogue,* "a bringing together," was used for the places where Jews gathered to read the sacred Torah. Meeting in synagogues helped Jews share ideas, hold their community together, and preserve traditions. Today, synagogues can be found in most major cities throughout the world.

Theme: Global Interaction
How did synagogues help Jewish culture survive the diaspora?

Jesus Healing a Woman
Jesus promised everlasting life to all who followed his teachings. This Roman mural depicts Jesus miraculously healing an afflicted woman.

Theme: Religions and Value Systems Which social classes were most attracted to Christianity? Why?

While most Jews were reluctantly willing to live under Roman rule, others, called Zealots, were not. They called on Jews to revolt against Rome and reestablish an independent state. Some Jews believed that a messiah, or anointed king sent by God, would soon appear to lead the Jewish people to freedom.

Jewish Revolt In A.D. 66, discontent flared into rebellion. Roman forces crushed the rebels, captured Jerusalem, and destroyed the Jewish temple. When revolts broke out again in the next century, Roman armies leveled Jerusalem. Thousands of Jews were killed in the fighting, and many others were enslaved and transported to various parts of the empire. Faced with the destruction that resulted from the rebellions, growing numbers of Jews decided to leave Judea.

Although they were defeated in their efforts to regain political independence, Jews survived in scattered communities around the Mediterranean. Over the centuries, Jewish rabbis, or scholars, extended and preserved the religious law, as set forth in the Talmud. Commitment to learning Jewish law and traditions enabled the Jews to survive over the centuries.

Jesus and His Message

As turmoil engulfed the Jews in Palestine, a new religion, Christianity, rose among them. Its founder was a Jew named Jesus.

Almost all that we know about the life of Jesus comes from the Gospels, the first four books of the New Testament of the Bible. These accounts were attributed by early Christians to Matthew, Mark, Luke, and John, four followers of Jesus. *Gospel* comes from the Old English word for "good news."

Life of Jesus Jesus was born about 4 B.C. in Bethlehem, near Jerusalem. According to the Gospels, he was a descendant of King David of Israel. An angel, the Gospels say, told Jesus' mother, Mary, that she would give birth to the messiah. "He will be great," said the angel, "and will be called the Son of the Most High God."

Growing up in the small town of Nazareth, Jesus worshiped God and followed Jewish law. As a young man, he may have worked as a carpenter, the occupation of Mary's husband Joseph. At the age of 30, the Gospels relate, he began preaching to villagers near the Sea of Galilee. To help him in his mission, he recruited twelve close followers, known as the apostles, from the Greek word meaning "a person sent forth." Chief among these was one called Peter.

Large crowds gathered to hear Jesus' teachings, especially when word spread that he had performed miracles of healing. Jesus often used parables, or short stories with simple moral lessons, to communicate his ideas. After three years, he and his disciples, or loyal followers, went to Jerusalem to spread his message there.

The Message Jesus' teachings were firmly rooted in Jewish tradition. Jesus believed in one God and accepted the Ten Commandments. He preached obedience to the laws of Moses and defended the teachings of the Jewish prophets.

At the same time, Jesus preached new beliefs. According to his followers, he called himself the Son of God. Many people believed he was the messiah whose appearance Jews had long predicted. Jesus proclaimed that his mission was to bring spiritual salvation and eternal life to anyone who would believe in him.

In the Sermon on the Mount, Jesus summed up his ethical message, which echoed Jewish ideas of mercy and sympathy for the poor and helpless:

> "Blessed are the meek, for they shall inherit the earth.
> Blessed are those who hunger and thirst for righteousness,
>   for they shall be satisfied.
> Blessed are the merciful, for they shall obtain mercy.
> Blessed are the pure in heart, for they shall see God.
> Blessed are the peacemakers, for they will be called sons of God."
> —Gospel According to Matthew

Jesus emphasized God's love and taught the need for justice, morality, and service to others. According to Jesus, a person's major responsibilities were to "love the Lord your God with all your heart" and to "love your neighbor as yourself." Jesus emphasized the importance of forgiveness. "Love your enemies," he told his followers. "If anyone hits you on one cheek, let him hit the other one, too."

Death on the Cross Some Jews welcomed Jesus to Jerusalem. Others, however, regarded him as a dangerous troublemaker. Jewish priests, in particular, felt that he was challenging their leadership. To the Roman authorities, Jesus was a revolutionary who might lead the Jews in a rebellion against Roman rule.

Jesus was betrayed by one of his disciples, the Gospels state. Arrested by the Romans, he was tried and condemned to be crucified. In crucifixion, a Roman method of execution, a person was nailed to or hung on a cross and left to die.

Jesus' disciples were thrown into confusion. But then rumors spread through Jerusalem that Jesus was not dead at all. His disciples, the Gospels say, saw and talked with Jesus, who had risen from the dead. They say Jesus commanded them to spread his teachings, and that he then ascended into heaven.

Spread of Christianity

Following Jesus' death, the apostles and other disciples spread Jesus' message and helped establish Christian communities. First, they preached only among the Jews of Judea. Slowly, some Jews accepted the teaching that Jesus was the messiah, or the Christ, from the Greek for "the anointed one." These people became the first Christians. For a time, Christianity remained a sect within Judaism.

Gradually, disciples of Jesus began to preach in Jewish communities throughout the Roman world. According to tradition, Peter established Christianity in the city of Rome itself. However, it was Paul, a Jew from Asia Minor, who played the most influential role in the spread of Christianity.

Work of Paul Paul had never seen Jesus. In fact, he had been among those who persecuted Jesus' followers. Then one day, Paul had a vision in which Jesus spoke to him. Immediately converting to the new faith, Paul made an important decision. He would spread the teachings of Jesus beyond Jewish communities to gentiles, or non-Jews.

Paul's missionary work set Christianity on the road to becoming a world religion. A tireless traveler, Paul journeyed around the Mediterranean and set up churches from Mesopotamia to Rome. In long letters to the Christian communities, he explained difficult doctrines, judged disputes, and expanded Christian teachings. These letters are part of the New Testament. In his writings, Paul emphasized the idea that Jesus had sacrificed his life out of love for humankind. Paul promised that those

 Primary Sources and Literature

See "St. Paul: First Letter to the Corinthians" in the Reference Section at the back of this book.

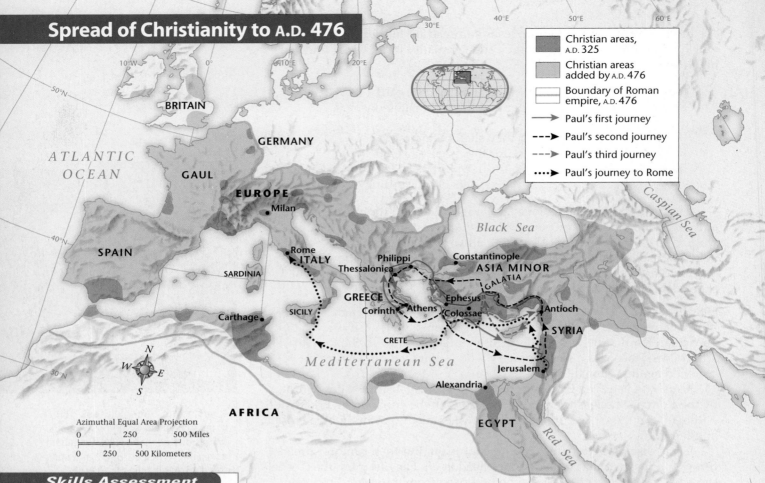

Spread of Christianity to A.D. 476

Legend:
- Christian areas, A.D. 325
- Christian areas added by A.D. 476
- Boundary of Roman empire, A.D. 476
- Paul's first journey
- Paul's second journey
- Paul's third journey
- Paul's journey to Rome

ATLANTIC OCEAN

BRITAIN

GERMANY

GAUL

EUROPE
Milan

SPAIN

Black Sea

Caspian Sea

Rome
ITALY

SARDINIA

Philippi
Thessalonica

Constantinople
ASIA MINOR
GALATIA

GREECE
Corinth Athens
Ephesus
Colossae
Antioch

Carthage

SICILY

CRETE

SYRIA

Mediterranean Sea

Jerusalem

Alexandria

AFRICA

EGYPT

Red Sea

Azimuthal Equal Area Projection

0   250   500 Miles

0   250   500 Kilometers

N W E S

Skills Assessment

Geography Aided by the work of Paul and other missionaries, Christianity gradually spread across the Roman empire.

1. **Location** On the map, locate **(a)** Jerusalem, **(b)** Asia Minor, **(c)** Antioch, **(d)** Constantinople, **(e)** Alexandria.
2. **Movement** In what areas did Paul travel on his first journey?
3. **Critical Thinking** **Connecting to Geography** How was the Mediterranean Sea important in the spread of Christianity?

who believed Jesus was the son of God and followed his teachings would achieve salvation, or eternal life.

Persecution Rome's tolerant attitude toward religion did not extend to Christianity. Roman officials suspected Christians of disloyalty to Rome because they refused to make sacrifices to the emperor or to honor the Roman gods. When Christians met in secret to avoid persecution, rumors spread that they were engaged in evil practices.

In times of trouble, persecution increased. Roman rulers like Nero used Christians as scapegoats, blaming them for social or economic ills. Over the centuries, thousands of Christians became martyrs, people who suffer or die for their beliefs. According to tradition, both Peter and Paul were killed in Rome during the reign of Nero.

Reasons for Christianity's Appeal Despite the attacks, Christianity continued to spread. The reasons were many. Jesus had welcomed all people, especially the humble, poor, and oppressed. They found comfort in his message of love. Equality, human dignity, and the promise of a better life beyond the grave were very attractive teachings.

As they did their work, Christian missionaries like Paul added ideas from Plato, the Stoics, and other Greek thinkers to Jesus' message. Educated Romans, in particular, were attracted to a religion that incorporated the discipline and moderation of Greek philosophy.

The work of missionaries such as Paul was made easier by the unity of the Roman empire. Christians traveled along Roman roads and across the Mediterranean Sea, which was protected by Roman fleets. Early Christian documents were usually written in Greek or Latin, languages that many people in the empire understood.

Even persecution brought new converts. Observing the willingness of Christians to die for their religion, people were impressed by the strength of Christians' belief. "The blood of the martyr is the seed of the [Christian] Church," noted one Roman.

Triumph The persecution of Christians finally ended in A.D. 313, when the emperor Constantine issued the Edict of Milan. It granted freedom of worship to all citizens of the Roman empire. In making his decision, Constantine was influenced by his mother, who was a devout Christian. Some 80 years later, the emperor Theodosius (thee uh DOH shuhs) made Christianity the official religion of the Roman empire.

The Early Christian Church

Early Christian communities shared a common faith in the teachings of Jesus and a common way of worship. Only gradually did the scattered communities organize a structured Church.

Patterns of Life and Worship A person fully joined the Christian community by renouncing evil in the rite of baptism. Christians believed that through baptism their sins were forgiven by the grace of God. Members of the community were considered equals, and they addressed each other as "brother" or "sister." Each Sunday, Christians gathered for a ceremony of thanksgiving to God. The baptized ate bread and drank wine in a sacred meal called the Eucharist. They did this in memory of Jesus, whose last supper was described in the Gospels. Justin, an early Christian philosopher and martyr, tried to explain the Eucharist in a letter to the Roman emperor and senate:

> "And this food is called among us the Eucharist. . . . For not as common bread and common drink do we receive these; but in like manner as Jesus Christ our Savior, having been made flesh by the Word of God . . . so likewise we have been taught that the food which is blessed by the prayer of his word, and from which our blood and flesh by transformation are nourished, is the flesh and blood of that Jesus who was made flesh."
>
> —*First Apology of Justin*

A Sacred Meal
Christians gathered frequently to celebrate the sacred meal of the Eucharist. The gilded plate and chalice shown here held the bread and wine of the Eucharist.

Theme: Religions and Value Systems Why did Christians consider the Eucharist so important?

Role of Women Women often led the way to Christianity. Many welcomed its promise that in the Church "there is neither Jew nor Greek . . . neither slave nor free . . . neither male nor female." In early Christian communities, women served as teachers and administrators. Even when they were later barred from any official role in the Church, they still worked to win converts across the Roman world.

Structure of the Church Each Christian community had its own priest. Only men were allowed to become members of the Christian clergy. Priests came under the authority of a bishop, a Church official who was responsible for all Christians in an area called a diocese (dī uh sihs). Bishops traced their spiritual authority to the apostles, and through the apostles, to Jesus himself. In the early Christian Church, all bishops were considered equal successors of the apostles.

Gradually, the bishops of the most important cities in the Roman empire gained greater authority. The bishops of Rome, Antioch, Alexandria, Jerusalem, and Constantinople gained the honorary title of patriarch, and exercised authority over other bishops in their area. Except for Rome, the cities in which patriarchs resided were all in the eastern empire. The Christian Church thus developed into a hierarchy, or organization in which officials are arranged according to rank.

Divisions in the Church   As the rituals and structure of the Church became more defined, divisions began to arise. A major divisive force was rivalry among the patriarchs. In the Latin-speaking west, bishops of Rome, who came to be called popes, began to claim greater authority over all other bishops. In the Greek-speaking east, the patriarchs felt that the five patriarchs should share spiritual authority as equals.

Another source of disunity was the emergence of heresies, or beliefs said to be contrary to official Church teachings. To end disputes over questions of faith, councils of Church leaders met to decide official Christian teachings. The Church also sent out missionaries both within the Roman empire and beyond to convert people to Christianity.

Theology and Scholarship   Early Christians produced an abundance of works on Judeo-Christian theology. The word *theology* was borrowed from Greek philosophy and literally means "talk or discourse about God."

Two leading scholars of the early Christian Church were Clement and Origen. Both lived and worked as teachers in the Egyptian city of Alexandria, a major center of learning in the Roman world. And, like most Christian scholars of their time, they both wrote in Greek.

Origen was most respected for his intellectual achievements. Though he fully accepted the traditions of the Gospels, he also believed that he and other Christians could reach a deeper understanding of Jesus' teachings through reflection. Several of his works, such as *On Prayer* and *On First Principles,* exerted a lasting influence on Christianity.

Perhaps the greatest of the early Church scholars was Augustine, who was bishop of Hippo in North Africa. He combined Greco-Roman learning, especially the philosophy of Plato, with Christian doctrine. Shocked by the sack of Rome in 410, Augustine wrote *The City of God*. In this work, Augustine said the City of God was the community of those who loved God and would one day live with him in heaven. Those whose minds and hearts were set only on worldly things lived outside the City of God.

Looking Ahead

While the Christian Church was growing in strength and influence, Roman power was fading. When the western Roman empire finally collapsed, the Church inherited many of its functions. The Church preserved and spread not only Christian teachings but also the achievements of Greco-Roman civilization. In this way, the foundation was laid for the future development of western civilization.

SECTION 4 Assessment

Recall
1. **Identify: (a)** Jesus, **(b)** Gospels, **(c)** Paul, **(d)** Edict of Milan.
2. **Define: (a)** messiah, **(b)** apostle, **(c)** martyr, **(d)** bishop, **(e)** diocese, **(f)** patriarch, **(g)** pope, **(h)** heresy.

Comprehension
3. What was Rome's policy toward most of the religions in the empire?
4. **(a)** Describe three basic teachings of Jesus. **(b)** Why did many people find Jesus' ideas attractive?
5. What beliefs and practices did early Christians have in common?

Critical Thinking and Writing
6. **Synthesizing Information** How do you think the geography of the Roman empire and Rome's extensive road system helped Christianity to spread?
7. **Making Inferences** Some emperors persecuted Christians for their refusal to make sacrifices to the emperor or to honor Roman gods. Why do you think emperors considered this refusal a threat to the empire?

Activity
Take It to the NET

Use Internet sources to find information about the life and career of Origen or Augustine. Use the information to write a brief biographical sketch of the person you have chosen.

Reading Focus

How did Roman emperors try to end the crisis in the empire?

How did Hun invasions contribute to the decline of Rome?

How did economic and social problems lead to the fall of Rome?

Vocabulary

inflation

mercenary

Taking Notes

Copy the partially completed cause-and-effect chart below. As you read, fill in two more categories of causes. Then, add individual causes under the appropriate categories.

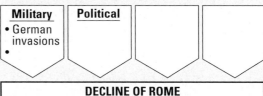

Military	Political		
• German invasions			
•			

DECLINE OF ROME

Main Idea Foreign invasions, along with political, social, and economic problems, led to the fall of the Roman empire.

Setting the Scene More than 1,500 years ago, the western half of the Roman empire stumbled into ruin. At the time, the spectacle of decline and defeat left Romans stunned. Some looked for reasons for the decay. The Roman historian Ammianus Marcellinus pointed to declining values. "Centers of learning," he wrote, "are now filled with ridiculous amusements . . . and the libraries are closed forever like so many graves." Marcellinus witnessed moral decay among Romans of all classes. Of the powerful, he complained that they "fall away into error and vice." Of the lower classes, he reported that "some spend the whole night in the wine shops . . . or else they play at dice." He was also alarmed about external threats to the empire, such as the invading Huns, who he feared could "force their way through all obstacles."

The end of Roman greatness did not occur overnight. Decay had set in centuries before the final fall. In the late 200s, for example, the empire was divided into two parts, each ruled by a co-emperor. A complex combination of problems led to the decline and fall of the western Roman empire.

Crisis and Reforms

After the death of the emperor Marcus Aurelius in 180, the golden age of the Pax Romana ended. For the next 100 years, political and economic turmoil rocked the Roman empire.

Struggles for Power During this period, a disruptive political pattern emerged. Again and again, emperors were overthrown by political intriguers or ambitious generals who seized power with the support of their troops. Those who rose to the imperial throne in this way ruled for just a few months or years until they, too, were overthrown or assassinated. In one 50-year period, at least 26 emperors reigned. Only one died of natural causes. Political violence and instability, rather than order and efficiency, thus became the rule.

Economic and Social Problems At the same time, the empire was shaken by disturbing social and economic trends. High taxes to support the army and the bureaucracy placed heavy burdens on business people and small farmers. Farmland that had been overcultivated for too many years lost its productivity.

Many poor farmers left their land and sought protection from wealthy landowners. Living on large estates, they worked for the landowners and

Sharing Power
Co-emperors Diocletian and Maximian shared the responsibility of ruling and defending the empire. Both established mobile imperial courts so that they could move swiftly to wherever a crisis broke out.

Theme: Political and Social Systems How do you think the division of the empire might have hastened Rome's decline?

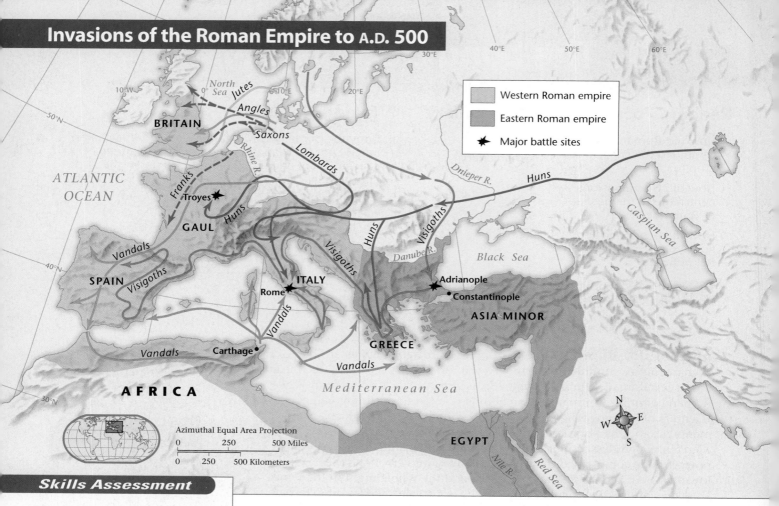

Invasions of the Roman Empire to A.D. 500

Western Roman empire

Eastern Roman empire

★ Major battle sites

Azimuthal Equal Area Projection

0 — 250 — 500 Miles

0 — 250 — 500 Kilometers

farmed small plots for themselves. Although technically free, they were not allowed to leave the land.

Emperor Diocletian   In 284, the emperor Diocletian (DĪ uh KLEE shuhn) set out to restore order. To make the empire easier to govern, he divided it into two parts. He kept control of the wealthier eastern part himself but appointed a co-emperor to rule the western provinces. The co-emperor was responsible to Diocletian, who retained absolute power.

Diocletian tried to increase the prestige of the emperor by surrounding himself with elaborate ceremonies. He wore purple robes embroidered with gold and a crown encrusted with jewels. Anyone who approached the throne had to kneel and kiss the hem of the emperor's robe.

Diocletian also took steps to end the empire's economic decay. To slow inflation, or the rapid rise of prices, he fixed prices for goods and services. Other laws forced farmers to remain on the land. In cities, sons were required to follow their fathers' occupations. These rules were meant to ensure steady production of food and other goods.

Emperor Constantine   In 312, the talented general Constantine gained the throne. As emperor, Constantine continued Diocletian's reforms. More important, he took two steps that changed the course of European history.

First, as you have read, Constantine granted toleration to Christians. By doing so, he encouraged the rapid growth of Christianity within the empire and guaranteed its future success.

Second, he built a new capital, Constantinople, on the Bosporus, the strait that connects the Black and Mediterranean seas. By making his capital there, Constantine made the eastern portion of the empire the center of power. The western Roman empire was in decline, but the eastern Roman empire, which had more people and greater resources, would prosper for centuries to come.

Mixed Results The reforms of Diocletian and Constantine had mixed results. They revived the economy. And by increasing the power of government, they helped hold the empire together for another century. Still, the reforms failed to stop the long-term decline. In the end, internal problems combined with attacks from outside to bring the empire down.

Foreign Invasions

For centuries, Rome had faced attacks from the Germanic peoples who lived east of the Rhine and north of the Danube rivers. When Rome was powerful, the legions on the frontiers were successful in holding back the invaders. Some of the Germanic peoples who lived along the borders learned Roman ways and became allies of the Romans.

Impact of the Huns As early as A.D. 200, wars in East Asia set off a chain of events that would eventually overwhelm Rome, thousands of miles to the west. Those wars sent the Huns, a nomadic people, migrating across Central Asia. By 350, the Huns reached eastern Europe. These skilled riders fought fierce battles to dislodge the Germanic peoples in their path. The Visigoths, Ostrogoths, and other Germanic peoples crossed into Roman territory seeking safety.

Men armed with spears moved in bands along with women and children, carts and herds, hoping to settle on Roman land. With the empire in decline, Roman legions were hard pressed to halt the invading peoples. Under pressure from attacks, the Roman empire surrendered first Britain, then France and Spain. It was only a matter of time before foreign invaders marched into Italy and took over Rome itself.

Rome Defeated In 378, when a Roman army tried to turn back the Visigoths at Adrianople, it suffered a stunning defeat. Roman power was fading. New waves of invaders were soon hammering at Rome's borders, especially in the west. In 410, the Visigoth general Alaric overran Italy and plundered Rome. Meanwhile, the Vandals moved through Gaul and Spain into North Africa. Gradually, other Germanic peoples occupied more and more of the western Roman empire.

For Rome, the worst was yet to come. Starting in 434, the Hun leader Attila embarked on a savage campaign of conquest across much of Europe. Christians called Attila the "scourge of God" because they believed his attacks were a punishment for the sins of humankind. Attila died in 453. Although his empire collapsed soon after, the Hun invasion sent still more Germanic peoples fleeing into the Roman empire.

Finally, in 476, Odoacer (oh doh AY suhr), a Germanic leader, ousted the emperor in Rome. Later, historians referred to that event as the "fall" of Rome. By then, however, Rome had already lost many of its territories, and Roman power in the west had ended.

Causes of the Fall of Rome

The passing of Rome's power and greatness was a major turning point in the history of western civilization. Why did Rome "fall"? Modern historians identify a number of interrelated causes.

Military Causes Perhaps the most obvious cause of Rome's fall was the Germanic invasions. Still, these attacks were successful in part because Roman legions of the late empire lacked the discipline and training of past Roman armies. To meet its need for soldiers, Rome hired mercenaries, or foreign soldiers serving for pay, to defend its borders. Many were German warriors who, according to some historians, felt little loyalty to Rome.

Why Did Rome Fall?

Although historians often cite 476 as the official date of the fall of Rome, the Roman empire had been in trouble for centuries. The illustration, the quotation, and the graphic organizer on this page all give clues to why Rome declined.

Hun Warrior

Hun warriors struck fear in the hearts of their enemies. Swooping down on horseback, they shot arrows great distances with deadly accuracy. The Huns were among the many groups of invaders who defeated weakened Roman legions.

Corruption in Rome

"Rome is still looked upon as the queen of the earth, and the name of the Roman people is respected and venerated. But the magnificence of Rome is defaced by the [stupidity] of a few, who never recollect where they are born, but fall away into error and [corruption]. . . . The Romans have even sunk so far, that not long ago, when [there was a famine] and the foreigners were driven from the city, [scholars] were expelled instantly, yet the followers of actresses and all their ilk were [allowed] to stay. . . . "

—Ammianus Marcellinus,
The Luxury of the Rich in Rome

The Decline and Fall of Rome

Military Causes
- Germanic invasions
- Weakened Roman legions

Political Causes
- Oppressive government
- Corrupt officials
- Divided empire

The Decline and Fall of Rome

Social Causes
- Erosion of traditional values
- Self-serving upper class
- "Bread and circuses"

Economic Causes
- Heavy taxes
- Population decline

Skills Tip

Graphic organizers show information in an easy-to-read format. Read the information in the boxes and trace the arrows to determine the main idea of the graphic organizer.

Skills Assessment

1. What type of cause shown in the graphic organizer does the Hun warrior illustrate?
   A social cause
   B political cause
   C economic cause
   D military cause

2. According to Ammianus Marcellinus, Rome's greatness was threatened by
   E Romans who wanted only amusements.
   F an increase in interest in liberal studies.
   G invasion by the Huns.
   H a shrinking population of foreigners.

3. **Critical Thinking** **Synthesizing Information** According to one historian, Rome's decline and fall were a result of its prosperity and power. He said that we should not concern ourselves with why the Roman empire fell, but with why it lasted as long as it did. Using the information above, explain why you agree or disagree with this idea.

Political Causes Political problems also contributed to Rome's decline. First, as the government became more oppressive and authoritarian, it lost the support of the people. Growing numbers of corrupt officials undermined loyalty, too. So did frequent civil wars over succession to the imperial throne. Again and again, rival armies battled to have their commanders chosen as emperor. Perhaps most important, dividing the empire at a time when it was under attack may have weakened it beyond repair. The richer eastern Roman empire did little to help the west.

Economic Causes Economic problems were widespread in the empire. Heavier and heavier taxes were required to support the vast government bureaucracy and huge military establishment. At the same time, reliance on slave labor discouraged Romans from exploring new technology. The wealth of the empire dwindled as farmers abandoned their land and the middle classes sank into poverty. Some scholars have suggested that climatic change was yet another reason for reduced agricultural productivity. In addition, the population itself declined as war and epidemic diseases swept the empire.

Social Causes For centuries, worried Romans pointed to the decline in values such as patriotism, discipline, and devotion to duty on which the empire was built. The need to replace citizen soldiers with mercenaries testified to the decline of patriotism. The upper class, which had once provided leaders, devoted itself to luxury and self-interest. Besides being costly, providing "bread and circuses" may also have undermined the self-reliance of the masses.

Did Rome Fall? Although we talk of the "fall" of Rome, the Roman empire did not disappear from the map in 476. An emperor still ruled the eastern Roman empire, which later became known as the Byzantine empire and lasted for another 1,000 years.

The phrase "the fall of Rome" is, in fact, shorthand for a long, slow change from one way of life to another. Roman civilization survived the events of 476. In Italy, people continued to live much as they had before, though under new rulers. Many still spoke Latin and obeyed Roman laws.

Over the next centuries, however, German customs and languages replaced much of Roman culture. Old Roman cities crumbled, and Roman roads disappeared. Still, the Christian Church preserved elements of Roman civilization. In later chapters, you will read how Roman and Christian traditions gave rise to medieval civilization in western Europe.

SECTION 5 Assessment

Recall
1. **Identify: (a)** Diocletian, **(b)** Constantine, **(c)** Huns, **(d)** Visigoths, **(e)** Alaric, **(f)** Attila, **(g)** Odoacer.
2. **Define: (a)** inflation, **(b)** mercenary.

Comprehension
3. **(a)** Describe the crisis that afflicted the Roman empire after the Pax Romana ended. **(b)** List two ways in which Diocletian tried to ease the crisis.
4. How did the invasion of the Huns weaken the Roman empire?

5. What social problems contributed to the decline of the Roman empire?

Critical Thinking and Writing
6. **Linking Past and Present** Imagine that the United States government in Washington no longer existed. What would be the effects on **(a)** your life, **(b)** your state, **(c)** the United States?
7. **Recognizing Causes and Effects** What were the causes and effects of the division of the Roman empire into two parts?

Activity
Creating a Booklet
Create an illustrated booklet explaining why the Roman empire fell. You may wish to use pictures, maps, cartoons, and graphic organizers to illustrate your booklet.

Creating a Chapter Summary

On a sheet of paper create a time line like the one started here. Add other important dates and events. Use the time line to review the events and developments that you have learned about in this chapter.

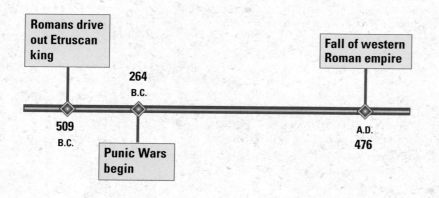

Romans drive out Etruscan king

509 B.C.

Punic Wars begin

264 B.C.

Fall of western Roman empire

A.D. 476

*i*TEXT

For additional review and enrichment activities, see the interactive version of *World History* available on the Web and on CD-ROM.

Web Site Self-Test
For practice test questions for Chapter 6, see **www.phschool.com**.

Building Vocabulary

Review the chapter vocabulary words listed below. Then, use the words and their definitions to create a matching quiz. Exchange quizzes with another student. Check each other's answers when you are finished.

1. **republic**
2. **dictator**
3. **plebeian**
4. **imperialism**
5. **census**
6. **satirize**
7. **aqueduct**
8. **messiah**
9. **heresy**
10. **mercenary**

Recalling Key Facts

11. How did tribunes protect plebeian interests in the Roman republic?
12. What were the results of the wars between Rome and Carthage?
13. How did Augustus' rise to power mark a significant change in Rome's form of government?
14. What were the major characteristics of the Pax Romana?
15. What were the important principles of Roman law?
16. How did Christianity spread through the Roman empire?

17. Describe three reasons for the fall of the Roman empire.

Critical Thinking and Writing

18. **Connecting to Geography** **(a)** How did geographic conditions make it easier to unite Italy than to unite Greece? **(b)** How did both Greece and Rome benefit from their location on the Mediterranean Sea?
19. **Making Decisions** Imagine that you were a Roman senator living at the time of Cato. Would you have supported his call to destroy Carthage? Why or why not?
20. **Linking Past and Present** "History," said Cicero, "illuminates reality, vitalizes memory, provides guidance in daily life, and brings us tidings of antiquity."
    (a) How did the work of Roman historians like Livy and Tacitus illustrate Cicero's idea? **(b)** Do you think Cicero's views on the value of history are still valid today? Why or why not?
21. **Solving Problems** **(a)** Describe two policies that Rome might have followed to restore its strength in the later years of the empire. **(b)** Do you think it would have been possible for the Romans to follow such policies? Why or why not?

The excerpt below is from a letter sent by Emperor Trajan to Pliny the Younger, one of his governors. After reading the excerpt, answer the questions that follow.

> "The method you have pursued, my dear Pliny, in sifting the cases of those denounced to you as Christians is extremely proper. . . . No search should be made for these people; when they are denounced and found guilty they must be punished, with the restriction, however, that when the party denies himself to be a Christian and shall give proof that he is not (that is, by adoring our gods), he shall be pardoned on the ground of repentance, even though he may have formerly incurred suspicion. Information without the accuser's name subscribed [affixed] must not be admitted in evidence against anyone, as it is introducing a very danger-ous precedent and by no means agreeable to the spirit of the age."
>
> —quoted in Pliny the Younger, *Letters*

22. Based on this letter, why do you think Trajan supported the persecution of Christians?
23. Why do you think Trajan felt the need to write this letter to Pliny?
24. **(a)** How could a person accused of being a Christian be pardoned? **(b)** Do you think many Christians avoided punishment in this way? Explain.
25. What kind of evidence does Trajan declare to be inadmissible evidence?
26. Based on this letter, do you think Trajan was strongly committed to the policy of persecution? Why or why not?

Use the Internet to research the territorial expansion of the Roman empire. Then, create a map of the empire at its height. Draw present-day national boundaries on the map to show which nations were once part of the Roman empire.

INFLUENTIAL ROMAN EMPERORS

Leader Years in Office	Major Policies
Augustus 31 B.C.–A.D. 14	Ended civil war; reformed government; established empire
Nero A.D. 54–A.D. 68	Persecuted Christians after fire destroyed much of Rome
Vespasian A.D. 69–A.D. 79	Authorized building projects in Rome; reorganized government finance
Hadrian A.D. 117–A.D. 138	Built Hadrian's Wall in Britain; codified Roman law
Marcus Aurelius A.D. 161–A.D. 180	Helped unify empire economically; made legal reforms
Constantine A.D. 306–A.D. 337	Ended persecution of Christians; called Nicaea council to settle Church disputes; built new capital of Constantinople

Study the table above and then answer the following questions:

27. Which emperor's reign was the longest? Which was the shortest?
28. How did the religious policies of Nero and Constantine differ?
29. Which emperor built a structure to help keep invaders out of Britain?
30. How did Constantine reduce the importance and power of the city of Rome?
31. Which emperor made legal reforms?

Skills Tip

When you use a table, be sure to read the title and the headings first.

Civilizations of the Americas 1400 B.C.–A.D. 1570

Chapter Preview

1 Civilizations of Middle America
2 The World of the Incas
3 Peoples of North America

1400 B.C.

The Olmecs establish the first American civilization. Remains of their culture include giant heads carved in stone.

850 B.C.

Construction takes place on a huge temple in Chavín de Huantar.

A.D. 300

The Mayas begin to build elaborate cities, which include enormous pyramids such as the Temple of the Magician, shown here.

CHAPTER EVENTS

1400 B.C. — 1000 B.C. — A.D. 400

GLOBAL EVENTS

1027 B.C. The Zhou dynasty is founded in China.

A.D. 392 Christianity becomes the official religion of the Roman empire.

Trade Routes in the Americas

Early civilizations throughout the Americas traded a wide variety of goods.

SIBERIA

Bering Strait

NORTH AMERICA

ROCKY MTS.

GREAT PLAINS

MISSISSIPPI R.

APPALACHIAN MTS.

ATLANTIC OCEAN

W. SIERRA MADRE

E. SIERRA MADRE

Gulf of Mexico

Yucatán Peninsula

CENTRAL AMERICA

Caribbean Sea

PACIFIC OCEAN

Robinson Projection

0   1000   2000 Miles

0   1000   2000 Kilometers

N W E S

0° Equator

Amazon R.

ANDES MTS.

SOUTH AMERICA

Brazilian Highlands

Atacama Desert

— Trade routes

A.D. 900s
The Anasazi build pueblo towns and create elaborately decorated pottery, such as these clay mugs.

A.D. 1200
The Mississippian center of Cahokia thrives.

A.D. 1400s
The Aztec empire expands across Mexico, from the Gulf of Mexico to the Pacific Ocean.

A.D. 800

A.D. 1200

A.D. 1600

A.D. 800 Pope Leo III crowns Charlemagne emperor of the Romans.

A.D. 1556 Akbar begins his rule of Mughal India.

Civilizations of Middle America

Reading Focus

- How did geography affect the development of cultures in the Americas?
- What were the main features of Olmec and Mayan civilizations?
- How did the Aztec culture develop?

Vocabulary

global warming
plains
chinampas
tribute

Taking Notes

As you read this section, prepare an outline of the contents. Use Roman numerals to indicate major headings. Use capital letters for the sub-headings and numbers for the supporting details. The sample at right will help you get started.

I. Civilizations of
   Middle America
   A. Geography of
      the Americas
      1. Earth grows
         warmer
      2. Agricultural
         revolution
   B. Olmecs develop
      first American
      civilization

Main Idea Climate and geography contributed to the rise of several powerful civilizations in Middle America.

Setting the Scene

The Aztecs of Middle America evolved a complex system of religious beliefs. Their religions, like those of many other people, included a belief that the world and all of its inhabitants would someday come to a fiery end.

According to the Aztec Legend of the Suns, the universe had been created and destroyed four times in the past. People living under the First Sun had been destroyed by jaguars. Next, people living under the Second Sun were swept away by wind. People living under the Third Sun perished in the fire and ash of volcanoes, while those people who lived under the Fourth Sun had been swallowed by water. The Fifth Sun represented the time of the Aztec empire:

> "This is our Sun, the one in which we now live. And here is its sign, how the Sun fell into the fire, into the divine hearth . . . . And as the elders continue to say, under the Sun there will be earthquakes and hunger, and then our end shall come."
> —quoted in *Seeds of Change* (Viola)

The Legend of the Suns reflects the important role of the sun in Aztec religion. It also suggests a feeling of helplessness in the face of the harsh forces of nature. Despite this sense of impending doom, the Aztecs were able to create a remarkable civilization. In order to do so, they built on the achievements of earlier peoples. To understand more about these early American civilizations, we must go far back in time to the arrival of the first people in the Americas.

Geography of the Americas

Perhaps as early as 30,000 years ago,* according to some scholars, small family groups of Paleolithic hunters and food gatherers reached North America from Asia. This great migration took place during the last ice age. At that time, so much water froze into thick ice sheets that the sea level dropped, exposing a land bridge between Siberia and Alaska, in the area now known as the Bering Strait. Many historians believe that hunters followed herds of bison and mammoths across this land bridge. Other migrating people may have paddled small boats and fished along the coasts.

Geography and History

When Were the Americas First Settled?

For many years, scientists believed that human migration to the Americas from Siberia began about 11,500 years ago. But recent finds challenge that view.

In New Mexico, fingerprints were found preserved in clay at least 13,000 years old. In Virginia, stone tools more than 15,000 years old were found.

Based on such finds, archaeologists are beginning to question when the first people migrated to the Americas from Asia, and even if they may have come from other places as well.

Theme: Geography and History A skeleton found in Brazil is believed to be 11,500 years old. How would this information contradict the theory that people first migrated from Siberia to Alaska 11,500 years ago?

---

*Scholars disagree about exactly when the first people reached the Americas. They have proposed dates ranging from 70,000 to 10,000 years ago.

Global Warming About 10,000 B.C., the Earth's climate grew warmer. As the ice melted, water levels rose, covering the land bridge under the Bering Strait. The global warming—or worldwide temperature increase—along with the hunting skills of the first Americans, may have killed off large game animals like the mammoth. People adapted by hunting smaller animals, fishing, and gathering fruit, roots, and shellfish. These nomadic hunter-gatherers slowly migrated eastward and southward across the Americas.

Regions What lands did the first Americans explore and settle? The Americas are made up of the two continents of North America and South America. Within these two geographic regions is a cultural region that historians call Middle America. Middle America includes Mexico and Central America and was home to several early civilizations.

Great mountain chains form a spiny backbone down the western Americas. In North America, the Rocky Mountains split into the East and West Sierra Madre of Mexico. The towering Andes run down the length of South America. The continents are drained by two of the world's three longest rivers, the Amazon of South America and the Mississippi of North America.

The first Americans adapted to a variety of climates and resources. Far to the north and the south, people learned to survive in icy, treeless lands. Closer to the Equator, people settled in the hot, wet climate and thick vegetation of the Amazon rain forests. Elsewhere, hunters adapted to deserts like the Atacama of Chile, woodlands like those in eastern North America, and the fertile plains, or rolling flatlands, of both continents.

The Agricultural Revolution In the Americas, as elsewhere, the greatest adaptation occurred when some people learned to cultivate plants and domesticate animals. Archaeologists think that farming was partly a response to the disappearance of the large mammals. With fewer animals to hunt, people came to depend more on other food sources. In Mexico, or perhaps farther south, Neolithic people began cultivating a range of crops, from corn and beans to sweet potatoes, peppers, tomatoes, and squash. These changes took place slowly between about 8500 B.C. and 2000 B.C.

Early American farmers learned to domesticate animals. In South America, domesticated animals include the llama and other creatures valued for their wool. However, the Americas had no large animals such as oxen or horses that were capable of bearing heavy loads or pulling wagons. This lack of draft animals would limit development in some areas.

In the Americas, as in Africa and Eurasia, the agricultural revolution helped to cause other changes. Farming people settled into villages. Populations expanded. Some villages grew into large religious centers and then into the great cities of the first American civilizations.

Legacy of the Olmecs

The earliest American civilization emerged in the tropical forests along the Mexican Gulf Coast. The Olmec civilization lasted from about 1400 B.C. to 500 B.C.

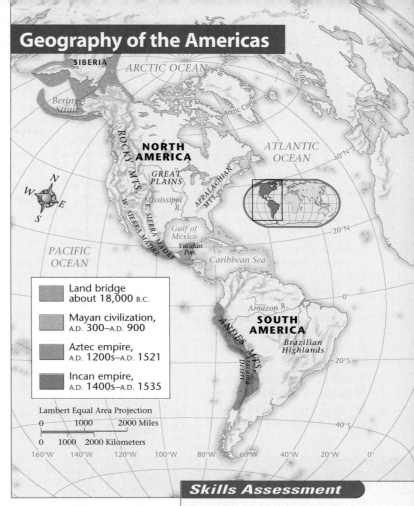

Geography of the Americas

Land bridge about 18,000 B.C.

Mayan civilization, A.D. 300–A.D. 900

Aztec empire, A.D. 1200s–A.D. 1521

Incan empire, A.D. 1400s–A.D. 1535

Lambert Equal Area Projection

Skills Assessment

Geography The descendants of the first Americans spread throughout the Americas, adapting to varied landforms and environments.

1. **Location** On the map, locate **(a)** Bering Strait, **(b)** Gulf of Mexico, **(c)** Amazon River, **(d)** Rocky Mountains.
2. **Place** Which culture flourished in the Yucatán Peninsula?
3. **Critical Thinking**
   Linking Past and Present Using a modern map of the Americas, identify the present-day countries located on lands where the Aztecs and Incas lived.

Archaeologists know very little about the Olmecs. However, rich tombs and temples suggest that a powerful class of priests and aristocrats stood at the top of Olmec society. The Olmecs did not build true cities. Rather, they built ceremonial centers made up of pyramid-shaped temples and other buildings. People came from nearby farming villages to work on the temples or attend religious ceremonies.

The most dramatic remains of the Olmec civilization are the giant carved stone heads found in the ruins of a religious center at La Venta. No one knows how the Olmecs moved these colossal 40-ton stones from distant quarries without wheeled vehicles or draft animals.

Through trade, Olmec influence spread over a wide area. The grinning jaguars and serpents that decorate many Olmec carvings appear in the arts of later peoples. The Olmecs also invented a calendar and used carved inscriptions as a form of writing. But their most important legacy may have been the tradition of priestly leadership and religious devotion that became a basic part of later Middle American civilizations.

The World of the Mayas

Among the peoples influenced by the Olmecs were the Mayas. Between A.D. 300 and 900, Mayan city-states flourished from the Yucatán in southern Mexico through much of Central America.

Scientists have recently determined how Mayan farming methods allowed them to thrive in the tropical environment. Mayan farmers cleared the dense rain forests and then built raised fields that caught and held rainwater. They also built channels that could be opened to drain excess water. This complex system produced enough native corn, called maize, and other crops to support rapidly growing cities.

Temples and Palaces Towering pyramid temples dominated the largest Mayan city of Tikal (tee KAHL), in present-day Guatemala. Priests climbed steep temple stairs to perform sacrifices on high platforms, while ordinary people watched from the plazas far below. Some temples also served as burial places for nobles and priests. The Mayan pyramids remained the tallest structures in the Americas until 1903, when the Flatiron Building, a skyscraper, was built in New York City.

Tikal also boasted large palaces and huge stone pillars covered with elaborate carvings. The carvings, which usually record events in Mayan history, preserve striking images of haughty aristocrats, warriors in plumed headdresses, and captives about to be sacrificed to the gods.

Much of the wealth of Tikal and the other Mayan cities came from trade. Along roads made of packed earth, traders carried valuable cargoes of honey, cocoa, cotton cloth, and feathers to exchange with other people across Middle America.

Social Classes Each Mayan city had its own ruling chief. He was surrounded by nobles who served as military leaders and officials who managed public works, collected taxes, and enforced laws. Rulers were usually men, but Mayan records and carvings show that women occasionally governed on their own or in the name of young sons. Priests held great power because only they could conduct the elaborate ceremonies needed to ensure good harvests and success in war.

Mayan Ball Games
Ball courts (PAST) were a key feature of Mayan cities. Spectators watched as two teams competed to drive a solid rubber ball through a stone ring that hung from a wall. Opposing players moved the ball across the court by using their bodies, but not their hands and feet. Players wore protective helmets and padding, but injuries were still common. Today, ball games such as soccer (PRESENT) continue to be popular with players and spectators alike.

Theme: Continuity and Change What modern games are similar to the Mayan ball game? Describe the similarities.

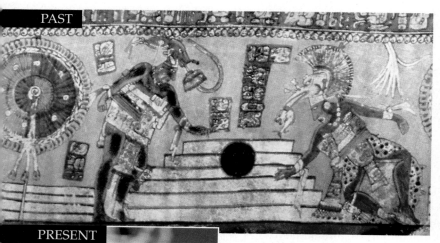

PAST

PRESENT

Most Mayas were farmers. They grew corn, beans, and squash—the basic food crops of Middle America—as well as fruit trees, cotton, and brilliant tropical flowers. Men usually cultivated the crops, while women turned them into food. To support the cities, farmers paid taxes in food and helped build the temples.

Advances in Learning   Along with their magnificent buildings and carvings, the Mayas made impressive advances in learning. They developed a hieroglyphic writing system, which has only recently been deciphered. Mayan scribes kept their sacred knowledge in books made of bark. Though Spanish conquerors later burned most of these books, a handful were taken to Europe and survive in European museums.

Mayan priests needed to measure time accurately in order to hold ceremonies at the correct moment. As a result, many priests became expert mathematicians and astronomers. They developed an accurate 365-day solar calendar, as well as a 260-day calendar based on the orbit of the planet Venus. Mayan priests also invented a numbering system and understood the concept of zero.

Decline   About A.D. 900, the Mayas abandoned their cities, leaving their great stone palaces and temples to be swallowed up by the jungle. Not until modern times were these "lost cities" rediscovered.

No one knows for sure why Mayan civilization declined. Possibly, frequent warfare forced the Mayas to abandon their traditional agricultural methods. Or overpopulation may have led to overfarming, which in turn exhausted the soil. Heavy taxes to finance wars and temple building may have sparked peasant revolts. Still, remnants of Mayan culture have survived. Today, millions of people in Guatemala and southern Mexico speak Mayan languages and are descended from the builders of this early American civilization.

Roots of Aztec Culture

Long before Mayan cities rose to the south, the city of Teotihuacán (tay oh tee wah KAHN) had emerged in the Valley of Mexico. The Valley of Mexico is a huge oval basin ringed by snowcapped volcanoes, located in the high plateau of central Mexico. From A.D. 100 to A.D. 750, Teotihuacán dominated a large area.

Teotihuacán   The city of Teotihuacán was well planned, with wide roads, massive temples, and large apartment buildings. Along the main avenue, the Pyramid of the Sun and the Pyramid of the Moon rose majestically toward the sky. Citizens of Teotihuacán worshiped a powerful nature goddess and rain god, whose images often appear on public buildings and on everyday objects. Teotihuacán eventually fell to invaders, but its culture influenced later peoples, especially the Aztecs.

Arrival of the Aztecs   In the late 1200s, bands of nomadic people, the ancestors of the Aztecs, migrated into the Valley of Mexico from the north. According to Aztec legend, the gods had told them to search for an eagle perched atop a cactus holding a snake in its beak. They finally saw the sign on a swampy island in Lake Texcoco. Once settled, the Aztecs shifted from hunting to farming. Slowly, they built the city of Tenochtitlán (tay nawch tee TLAHN), on the site of present-day Mexico City.

As their population grew, the Aztecs found ingenious ways to create more farmland. They built chinampas, artificial islands made of earth piled on reed mats that were anchored to the shallow lake bed. On these "floating gardens," they raised corn, squash, and beans. They gradually filled in parts of the lake and created canals for transportation. Wide stone causeways linked Tenochtitlán to the mainland.

Mayan Society in Art
Mayan potters fashioned clay figurines depicting people at all levels of society. Here, an aristocrat (top) poses in his robes, while a peasant woman (bottom) holds tortillas.

Theme: Art and Literature
How do these figurines suggest that these two people were from different social classes?

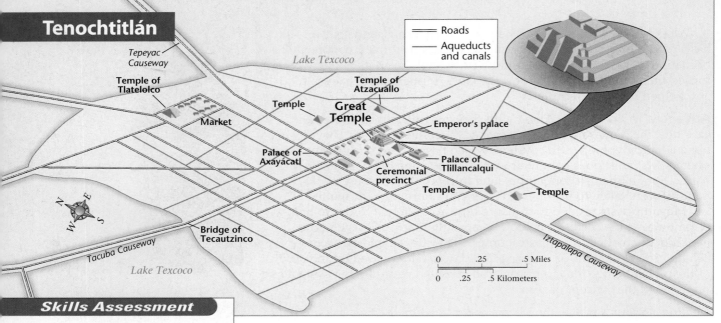

Tenochtitlán

Tepeyac Causeway
Lake Texcoco
Temple of Tlatelolco
Market
Temple
Temple of Atzacuallo
Great Temple
Emperor's palace
Palace of Axayácatl
Ceremonial precinct
Palace of Tlillancalqui
Temple
Temple
Bridge of Tecautzinco
Tacuba Causeway
Lake Texcoco
Iztapalapa Causeway

Roads
Aqueducts and canals

N W E S

0   .25   .5 Miles
0   .25   .5 Kilometers

Skills Assessment

Geography The Aztec capital, Tenochtitlán, was located in Lake Texcoco and connected to the mainland by causeways. In the center of the city, people gathered at the Great Temple, the emperor's palace, the market, or other public centers.

1. **Location** On the map, locate **(a)** Great Temple, **(b)** market, **(c)** emperor's palace, **(d)** Lake Texcoco.
2. **Interaction** Give two examples of ways the Aztecs adapted their environment to meet their needs in Tenochtitlán.
3. **Critical Thinking** **Analyzing Information** How does the map suggest that religion played an important role in Aztec life?

Conquering an Empire In the 1400s, the Aztecs greatly expanded their territory. Through a combination of fierce conquests and shrewd alliances, they spread their rule across most of Mexico, from the Gulf of Mexico on the east to the Pacific Ocean on the west. By 1500, the Aztec empire numbered an estimated 30 million people.

War brought immense wealth as well as power. Tribute, or payment from conquered peoples, helped the Aztecs turn their capital into a magnificent city.

The World of the Aztecs

When the Spanish reached Tenochtitlán in 1519, they were awestruck at its magnificence. The Spanish conqueror Hernán Cortés described the city as it looked then:

> "The city has many squares where markets are held and trading is carried on. There is one square . . . where there are daily more than 60,000 souls, buying and selling, and where are found all the kinds of merchandise produced in these countries, including food products, jewels of gold and silver, lead, brass, copper, zinc, bones, shells, and feathers."
>
> —Hernán Cortés, quoted in
> *Latin American Civilization* (Keen)

From its temples and royal palaces to its zoos and floating gardens, Tenochtitlán was a city of wonders. It was also the center of a complex, well-ordered empire.

Government and Society Unlike the Mayan city-states, each of which had its own king, the Aztecs had a single ruler. The emperor was chosen by a council of nobles and priests to lead in war. Below him, nobles served as officials, judges, and governors of conquered provinces. They enjoyed special privileges such as wearing luxurious feathered cloaks and gold jewelry. Next came the warriors, who could rise to noble status by killing or capturing enemy soldiers. The majority of people were commoners who farmed the land.

At the bottom of society were the slaves, mostly criminals or prisoners of war. Despite their low status, slaves' rights were clearly spelled out by law. For example, slaves could own land and buy their freedom.

You Are There . . .

Buying Treasures in an Aztec Market

Thoughts of shopping fill you with excitement. Although Tenochtitlán's market is packed with eager buyers and sellers today, the crowd doesn't bother you. You are a wealthy Aztec noble, and your servants carry you above it all. Carefully, you clutch your bag of cocoa beans; they are very valuable and you will use them to buy what you want.

Thousands of different goods spill out over the vendors' tables. Some are ordinary—food products like tomatoes, chili peppers, or turkeys. Others dazzle you—turquoise masks and fine gold and silver jewelry.

First, you buy a fan made of brilliantly colored feathers. You will give it to your brother, an important government official. It will show his high rank in society.

After shopping for hours, you are ready to go home. Then, a cup carved like a rabbit catches your eye. You could use it to drink chocolate. Only the wealthy can drink this brew made from cocoa beans, so chocolate deserves a special cup. You decide to buy it.

Portfolio Assessment

Write a shopping list for your next trip to the market. Briefly explain why you need each item on the list. Refer to the mural above for ideas.

Protected by Aztec power, a class of long-distance traders ferried goods across the empire and beyond. From the highlands, they took goods such as weapons, tools, and rope to barter for tropical products such as jaguar skins and cocoa beans. They also served as spies, finding new areas for trade and conquest.

Religious Beliefs The priests were a class apart. They performed rituals they believed pleased the Aztec gods and prevented droughts or other disasters. The chief Aztec god was Huitzilopochtli (wee tsee loh POHKT lee), the sun god. His pyramid-temple towered above central Tenochtitlán.

Huitzilopochtli, the Aztecs believed, battled the forces of darkness each night and was reborn each morning. As the Legend of the Suns shows, there was no guarantee that the sun would always win. To give the sun strength to rise each day, the Aztecs offered human sacrifices. Priests offered the hearts of tens of thousands of victims to Huitzilopochtli and other Aztec gods. Most of the victims were prisoners of war, but sometimes a noble family gave up one of its own members to appease the gods.

Other cultures, such as the Olmecs and the Mayas, had practiced human sacrifice, but not on the massive scale of the Aztecs. The Aztecs carried on almost continuous warfare, using the captured enemy soldiers for a regular source of sacrificial victims. Among the conquered peoples, discontent festered and rebellion often flared up. When the armies from Spain later arrived, they found ready allies among peoples who were ruled by the Aztec empire.

Education and Learning Priests were the keepers of Aztec knowledge. They recorded laws and historical events. Some ran schools for the sons of nobles. Others used their knowledge of astronomy and mathematics to foretell the future. The Aztecs, like the Mayas, had an accurate calendar.

Like many other ancient peoples, the Aztecs believed that illness was a punishment from the gods. Still, Aztec priests used herbs and other medicines to treat fevers and wounds. Aztec physicians could set broken bones and treat dental cavities. They also prescribed steam baths as cures for various ills, a therapy still in use today.

Looking Ahead

The Aztecs developed a sophisticated and complex culture, but their world would not last forever. At the height of Aztec power, word reached Tenochtitlán that pale-skinned, bearded men had landed on the east coast. Later, you will read about the results of the encounter between the Aztecs and the newcomers from far-off Spain.

SECTION 1 Assessment

Recall

1. **Identify:** **(a)** Olmecs, **(b)** Tikal, **(c)** Teotihuacán, **(d)** Tenochtitlán.
2. **Define:** **(a)** global warming, **(b)** plains, **(c)** chinampas, **(d)** tribute.

Comprehension

3. How did early people adapt to different environments in the Americas?
4. **(a)** What role did religion play in Olmec and Mayan culture? **(b)** How did religion influence Mayan ideas and technology?

5. How did the Aztecs build and control a powerful empire in Mexico?

Critical Thinking and Writing

6. **Connecting to Geography** Explain why a lack of large draft animals might limit agricultural development in some regions.
7. **Analyzing Information** How would archaeologists use evidence such as artwork and public buildings to trace the influence of the Olmecs or similar civilizations on later Middle American people?

Activity
Take It to the NET

Use the Internet to research the migration of people across the land bridge. Then, write a series of diary entries describing the crossing from Siberia into the Americas. Include descriptions of the animal and plant life encountered along the way.

The World of the Incas

Reading Focus

■ What were the main achievements of the early peoples of Peru?

■ How did Incan emperors extend and maintain their empire?

■ How did the Incas live?

Vocabulary

glyph

quipu

alloy

Taking Notes

Copy this flowchart, adding information about each of the successive cultures that inhabited Peru. When possible, indicate how cultures influenced later peoples. Add more boxes as necessary.

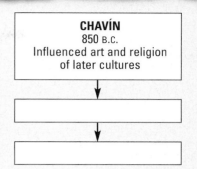

```
┌─────────────────────────┐
│         CHAVÍN           │
│        850 B.C.          │
│ Influenced art and       │
│ religion of later        │
│ cultures                 │
└─────────────────────────┘
            │
            ▼
┌─────────────────────────┐
│                         │
└─────────────────────────┘
            │
            ▼
┌─────────────────────────┐
│                         │
└─────────────────────────┘
```

Main Idea The Incas built a complex civilization that relied on order and absolute authority.

Setting the Scene

The Sapa Inca lifted a golden cup to the rising sun, a gesture to honor his divine ancestor. He then entered the temple, where sunlight glinted off the golden statues along the walls. A priest placed a bundle of fibers on the altar. With a copper mirror, he directed the magical power of the sun's rays to explode the fibers into flame.

Other rituals followed. Priests sacrificed a llama and prayed for success in the coming year. When the ceremonies ended, horns blared the news to the crowds outside the temple. A shout rose: *"Hailli!"*—"Victory!" Reed pipes and flutes echoed the joy as people prepared for a day of feasting and dancing.

This ceremony honoring the sun god took place each year in Cuzco, capital of the Incan empire of Peru. By the early 1500s, the Incas, like the Aztecs, ruled a mighty empire.

Early Peoples of Peru

Western South America includes a wide variety of climates and terrains. The narrow coastal plain is a dry, lifeless desert crossed by occasional river valleys. Further inland, the snow-capped Andes Mountains rise steeply, leveling off into high plateaus that bake by day and freeze at night. East of the Andes lie dense jungles that stretch from Peru into Brazil.

Native American peoples developed many different styles of life across South America. Hunters and gatherers thrived in some regions, while farmers grew root crops in the Amazon rain forests. Thousands of years ago, people settled in fishing villages along the desert coast of Peru. Gradually they expanded inland, farming the river valleys that run up into the highland plateaus. Using careful irrigation, they grew corn, cotton, squash, and beans. On mountain slopes, they cultivated potatoes, eventually producing 700 varieties. In high plateaus, they domesticated the llama and the alpaca. Like the Mayas, they built large ceremonial centers and developed skills in pottery and weaving.

Chavín Through painstaking work at many sites, archaeologists have pieced together a chronology of various cultures that left their mark on the region. The earliest of these was the Chavín (chah VEEN) culture, named for ruins at Chavín de Huantar in the Andes. There, about 850 B.C., people built a huge temple complex. Stone carvings and pottery show that the Chavín people worshiped a ferocious-looking god, part jaguar and part human with grinning catlike features. The arts and religion of the Chavín culture influenced later peoples of Peru.

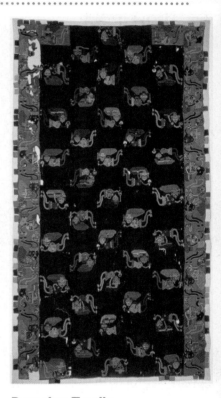

Peruvian Textile
Artisans among the Paracas, an early people of Peru, produced this cloak around the 500s B.C. Spinners, weavers, and skillful dyers worked together to create this fabric adorned with complex and imaginative designs.

Theme: Art and Literature
What does this fabric suggest about cultural development among the Paracas?

Mochica Between about A.D. 100 and 700, the Mochica people forged an empire along the arid north coast of Peru. The Mochicas were skilled farmers, developing methods of terracing, irrigation, and fertilization of the soil. Their leaders built roads and organized networks of relay runners to carry messages, ideas that the Incas would later adopt.

Remains of Mochica cities and temples dot the land. To build one temple, workers had to produce 130 million sun-dried adobe bricks. The people perfected skills in textile production, goldwork, and woodcarving. They produced remarkable pots decorated with realistic scenes of daily life. On these painted vases, helmeted warriors go into battle, musicians play pipes and drums, and women weave textiles on small portable looms.

Nazca Many other cultures left tantalizing clues to their lives and beliefs. In southern Peru, the Nazca people etched glyphs in the desert. A **glyph** is a pictograph or other symbol carved into a surface. Nazca glyphs include straight lines that run for miles, as well as giant figures of birds, whales, and other creatures. These figures may have been family symbols or part of an ancient calendar.

For more than 2,000 years, diverse civilizations rose and fell in Peru. Then, in the mid-1400s, the Incas emerged from high in the Andes. Incan armies rapidly conquered an empire that stretched 2,500 miles down the Andes and along the Pacific coast. Like the Romans, who also ruled a diverse empire, the Incas drew heavily on the ideas and skills of the peoples they conquered.

The Incan Empire

Pachacuti, a skilled warrior and leader, was the founder of the Incan empire. In 1438, he proclaimed himself Sapa Inca, or emperor, and set out on a policy of conquest. From a small kingdom in the high mountain valley of Cuzco, he came to dominate an immense empire. Once he had subdued neighboring peoples, he enlisted them in his armies for future campaigns. In this way, he and his son extended Incan rule from Ecuador in the north to Chile in the south.

Government The Sapa Inca exercised absolute power over the empire. Claiming that he was divine, the son of the sun itself, he was also the chief religious leader. Like the pharaohs of ancient Egypt, the Incan god-king owned all the land, herds, mines, and people. Gold, the "sweat of the sun," was his symbol. He lived in splendor, eating from golden plates and dressing in richly embroidered clothes. In fact, the Sapa Inca never wore the same royal garments twice. His queen, the Coya, carried out important religious duties and sometimes governed when the Sapa Inca was absent.

From Cuzco, the Incas ran an efficient government with a chain of command reaching into every village. Nobles ruled the provinces along with local chieftains whom the Incas had conquered. Below them, officials carried out the day-to-day business of collecting taxes and enforcing laws. Specially trained officials kept records on a **quipu,** a collection of knotted, colored strings. Modern scholars think that quipus noted dates and events as well as statistics on population and crops.

Roads and Runners To unite their empire, the Incas imposed their own language, Quechua (KEHCH wuh), and religion on the people. They also created one of the great road systems of history. It wound more than 12,000 miles through mountains and deserts. Hundreds of bridges spanned rivers and deep gorges. Steps were cut into steep slopes and tunnels dug through hillsides. Even more impressive than the roads that united the Roman empire, the Incan road system was unmatched until modern times.

The roads allowed armies and news to move rapidly throughout the empire. At regular stations, runners waited to carry messages. Relays of

Synthesizing Information

Incan Government

People of the Incan empire lived in one of the most highly ordered societies in history. Use the quotation, chart, and diagram below to draw conclusions about the government that created this order.

Incan System of Rule

Leader	Responsibility
The Inca	• Ruled the entire Incan empire
Suyuyuq Apu	• Controlled one of four regions of the empire
Hunu Kamayoq	• Governed a province containing 10,000 families
Waranq Kamayoq	• Acted as head of 1,000 families
Pichqa Pachaq Kamayoq	• Acted as head of 500 families
Pachaq Kamayoq	• Acted as head of 100 families
Pichqa Chunka Kamayoq	• Acted as head of 50 families
Chunka Kamayoq	• Acted as head of 10 families
Pichqa Kamayoq	• Acted as head of 5 families
Pureq	• Acted as head of 1 family

The Incan bureaucracy controlled life, even at the individual family level.

Incan Farming System

Field of the sun god, used for priests

Field of the sick, orphans, widows, and those away on government service

Field of the Inca, used for the state and the community

Field assigned for the needs of the individual familes

All land belonged to the community. Farmers grew crops in different fields.

A Sapa Inca's Purpose

In the following quotation, the Inca explains what he believes the sun has ordered Incan rulers to do.

"'Each day that passes,' said our father, the sun, 'I go around the world in order to have a better knowledge of men's needs and to satisfy those needs. Follow my example: Do unto all of them as a merciful father would do to his well-beloved children; for I have sent you on earth for the good of men, that they might cease to live like wild animals. You shall be the kings and lords of all the peoples who accept our law and our rule.'"
—Garcilaso de la Vega, *The Royal Commentaries of the Inca*

Skills Tip

Start by reading the title of the activity to identify its general topic. Then, when you examine each source, ask yourself how the specific information presented relates to the general topic.

Skills Assessment

1. Like the sun god, the Inca was supposed to
   A satisfy his people's needs.
   B act like a favorite child.
   C prevent the division of land by the community.
   D accept the rule of the high priests.

2. How were orphans provided for by Incan society?
   E They became priests of the sun god.
   F They went to live with the Hunu Kamayoq.
   G They received crops from land assigned to them.
   H They were adopted by Incan nobles.

3. **Critical Thinking** **Drawing Conclusions** How might an Incan ruler explain the need to have such an extensive bureaucracy?

Virtual Field Trip

www.phschool.com

Machu Picchu, Peru

To learn more about Machu Picchu, use the Internet address above to link to the Web site of Machu Picchu, Peru.

Machu Picchu

Machu Picchu lies some 7,000 feet above sea level. The sturdy walls have withstood centuries of earthquakes. Incan workers cut and fitted the stones together without the aid of mortar. Abandoned for some 300 years, the ruins of Machu Picchu were rediscovered in 1911.

Theme: Economics and Technology How do the ruins of Machu Picchu show that the Incan empire was well organized and technologically advanced?

Global Connections

Finding a Way Across

Like the Romans, the Incas were inventive road builders. But the deep gorges of the Andes presented a formidable obstacle: How can a road cross from one steep canyon wall to another, often high above a rushing river? The Incans built massive stone piers on either side and slung five cables of twisted fiber between them. They attached wooden crosspieces to three cables and made the other two handrails.

When Europeans first saw these flimsy-looking suspension bridges swaying in the wind, they were terrified of them. But they marveled too, knowing no way to improve upon their design.

Theme: Economics and Technology How did the environment affect Incan construction methods?

runners could carry news of a revolt swiftly from a distant province to the capital. The Incas kept soldiers at outposts throughout the empire. Within days of an uprising, they would be on the move to crush the rebels. Ordinary people, though, were restricted from using the roads at all.

Cuzco All roads led through Cuzco. The population was made up of representatives of all the peoples of the empire, each living in a particular part of the city. They wore regional costumes and practiced traditional crafts. In the heart of the city stood the great Temple of the Sun, its interior walls lined with gold. Like Incan palaces and forts, the temple was made of enormous stone blocks, each polished and carved to fit exactly in place. The engineering was so precise that, although no mortar was used to hold the stones together, Incan buildings have survived severe earthquakes.

Daily Life

The Incas strictly regulated the lives of millions of people within their empire. People lived in close-knit communities, called ayllus (Ī LOOZ). Leaders of each ayllu carried out government orders, assigning jobs to each family and organizing the community to work the land. Government officials arranged marriages to ensure that men and women were settled at a certain age.

Farming Farmers expanded the step terraces built by earlier peoples. On steep hillsides, they carved out strips of land to be held in place by stone walls. These terraces kept rains from washing away the soil and made farming possible in places where flat land was scarce.

Farmers had to spend part of each year working land for the emperor and the temples as well as for their own communities. All land belonged to the Inca, but cultivation and crops were allotted to specific groups of people or for particular purposes. The government took possession of each harvest, dividing it among the people and storing part of it in case of famine.

Metalworking The Incas were the best metalworkers in the Americas. They learned to work and alloy, or blend, copper, tin, bronze, silver, and gold. While they employed copper and bronze for useful objects, they used precious metals for statues of gods and goddesses, eating utensils for the aristocracy, and decorations.

Medical Advances The Incas developed some important medical practices, including surgery on the human skull. In such operations, they first cleaned the operating area and then made the patient unconscious with a drug—procedures much closer to the use of modern antiseptics and anesthesia than anything practiced in Europe at that time.

Religion Like other early peoples, the Incas were polytheistic, worshiping many gods linked to the forces of nature. People offered food, clothing, and drink to the guardian spirits of the home and the village. Religion was tied to the routines of life. Each month had its own festival, from the great ripening and the dance of the young maize to the festival of the water. Festivals were celebrated with ceremonies, sports, and games. A powerful class of priests served the gods, celebrating their special festivals and tending to their needs.

Chief among the gods was Inti, the sun god. His special attendants, the "Chosen Women," were selected from each region of the empire. During years of training, they studied the mysteries of the religion, learned to prepare ritual food and drink, and made the elaborate wool garments worn by the Sapa Inca and the Coya. At the end of their training, most of the Chosen Women continued to serve the sun god. Others, however, joined the Inca's court or married nobles.

Looking Ahead

At its height, the Incan civilization, like those of Middle America, was a center of learning and political power. Then, in 1525, the emperor Huayna Capac (wī nah KAH pahk) died suddenly of an unknown plague that swept across the land. As he had not named a successor, civil war broke out between two of his sons. The fighting weakened the empire at a crucial moment. Like the Aztecs to the north, the Incas soon faced an even greater threat from Spanish invaders.

SECTION 2 Assessment

Recall
1. **Identify: (a)** Pachacuti, **(b)** Quechua.
2. **Define: (a)** glyph, **(b)** quipu, **(c)** alloy.

Comprehension
3. Describe one achievement of each of the following early peoples of Peru: **(a)** Chavín, **(b)** Mochica.
4. Describe two ways in which the Incas united their empire.
5. What were some elements of daily life for the Incas?

Critical Thinking and Writing
6. **Connecting to Geography** **(a)** How did geography pose a challenge to the Incas as they built their empire? **(b)** How did they meet this challenge? **(c)** What does this suggest about the level of government and learning among the Incas?
7. **Recognizing Points of View** For the average Inca, what might be the benefits of the absolute rule of the Sapa Inca? What might be the disadvantages?

Activity

Take It to the NET

Use the Internet to research the ancient Incan city of Machu Picchu. Then, create a museum exhibit describing the discovery of this "lost city" in 1911, as well as the buildings and artifacts found there.

Reading Focus

■ How did people in the desert southwest adapt to their environment?

■ How did the culture of the Mound Builders reflect their contact with other regions?

■ How did the diverse regional cultures in the Americas differ from one another?

Vocabulary

pueblo

kiva

potlatch

Taking Notes

Create a table that compares three culture areas in North America. This sample will help you get started.

CULTURE AREA	GEOGRAPHY	WAY OF LIFE	OTHER
ARCTIC	Harsh climate		
NORTHWEST COAST			Shared wealth
EASTERN WOODLANDS		Built villages in forests	

Main Idea Geographic diversity contributed to the growth of a great variety of cultures in North America.

Setting the Scene Climate and natural resources had profound effects on daily life for the first people in North America. A traditional southwest song reflects how the natural world provided beauty as well as the necessities of life:

> "The whole Southwest was a House Made of Dawn. It was made of pollen and of rain. The land was old and everlasting. There were many colors on the hills and on the plain, and there was a dark wilderness on the mountains beyond. The land was tilled and strong and it was beautiful all around."
> —quoted in *The Native Americans: An Illustrated History* (Ballantine)

The impact of the environment stretched far beyond the southwest. Hundreds of cultural groups emerged in the present-day United States and Canada. For centuries, they lived by hunting, fishing, and gathering wild plants. As farming spread north from Middle America, many people raised corn and other food crops. Some people farmed so successfully that they built large permanent settlements. Here, we will look at the earliest of these farming cultures, in the desert southwest and in the Mississippi Valley.

The Desert Southwest

More than 1,000 years ago, fields of corn, beans, and squash bloomed in the desert southwest. The farmers who planted these fields were called the Hohokams, or "Vanished Ones," by their later descendants, the Pimas and Papagos. To farm the desert, they built a complex irrigation system.

The Hohokams lived near the Gila River in present-day Arizona. They may have acquired skills such as irrigation from the civilizations of Middle America. They built temple mounds and ball courts, as the Mayas did. The Hohokams survived until about A.D. 1500, when drought seems to have forced them to leave their settlements.

Anasazi The best-known society of the southwest was that of the Anasazi. They lived in what is today the Four Corners region of Arizona, New Mexico, Colorado, and Utah. Between about A.D. 900 and 1300, the Anasazi built large villages, later called pueblos by the Spanish.

Remains of Pueblo Bonito still stand in New Mexico. The village consisted of a huge complex with 800 rooms that housed about 6,000 people.

Connections to Today

Apartment Living

"Cliff dwellers"—today that term could describe people who live in tall apartment buildings. But it was first used to describe the Anasazi.

Named because it backed up against a sheer cliff, the Cliff Palace was one of the Anasazi's major "apartment buildings." With 217 rooms and 250 residents, it was larger than many modern apartment buildings. In place of brick, its walls were made of carefully cut slabs of stone, fitted tightly together. Rather than flat boards, great logs formed its floors and roofs. There were no elevators, though—its residents reached their rooms by either climbing ladders or mounting steps carved in the stone.

Theme: Continuity and Change Why do you think that the Anasazi and modern city dwellers developed similar types of housing?

Builders used stone and adobe bricks to erect a crescent-shaped compound rising five stories high.

At the center of the great complex was a plaza. There, the Anasazi dug their kiva, a large underground chamber used for religious ceremonies. Paintings on the walls show their concern with weather, including storms that might damage crops.

Cliff Dwellings In the late 1100s, the Anasazi began building housing complexes in the shadow of canyon walls, where the cliffs offered protection from raiders. The largest of these cliff dwellings at Mesa Verde, in present-day Colorado, had over 200 rooms. People had to climb ladders to reach their fields on the flatlands above or the canyon floor below.

In the late 1200s, a long drought forced the Anasazi to abandon their cliff dwellings. Without rain, they could no longer live in large settlements. Attacks by Navajos and Apaches may have contributed further to their decline. Anasazi traditions survived, however, among the Hopis and other Pueblo Indians of the present-day southwestern United States.

The Mound Builders

Far to the east of the Anasazi, in the Mississippi and Ohio valleys, other farming cultures emerged as early as 700 B.C. The Adena and Hopewell people left behind giant earthen mounds. Some mounds were cone-shaped, while others were made in the shape of animals. The Great Serpent Mound in Ohio wriggles and twists for almost a quarter of a mile.

Objects found in Hopewell mounds show that traders extended their influence over a wide area. They brought back shells and shark teeth from the Gulf of Mexico and copper from the Great Lakes region. Skilled artisans hammered and shaped the copper into fine ornaments.

Cahokia By A.D. 800, these early cultures had disappeared, but a new people, the Mississippians, gained influence. As their culture spread, the Mississippians built clusters of earthen mounds and ever larger towns and ceremonial centers.

Their greatest center, Cahokia in present-day Illinois, housed as many as 40,000 people by about A.D. 1200. Cahokia boasted at least 60 mounds. On top of some mounds stood the homes of rulers and nobles. The largest mound probably had a temple on its summit, where priests and rulers offered prayers and sacrifices to the sun. Archaeologists think that this temple mound shows the influence of Middle American civilizations.

Heirs of the Mound Builders The Mississippians left no written records, and their cities had disappeared by the time Europeans reached the area. Still, their traditions survived among the Natchez people, whose ruler, the Great Sun, had absolute power. He and his family lived on the top of pyramid mounds.

Diverse Regional Cultures

Many other groups of Native Americans emerged in North America prior to 1500. Modern scholars have identified 10 culture areas based on the environments in which people lived: the Arctic, Subarctic, Northwest Coast, California, Great Basin, Plateau, Southwest, Great Plains, Eastern Woodlands, and Southeast. In each area, people adapted to geographic conditions that influenced their ways of life.

Legacy of the Mound Builders
The Great Serpent Mound (center) in Ohio shows careful planning in its even curves. Archaeologists have discovered artifacts such as this mica bird's claw (top) and carved frog (bottom) in mounds built by the Adena, Hopewell, and Mississippian peoples.

Theme: Global Interaction
Why do scholars think that Mississippian mounds may show the influence of Middle American civilizations?

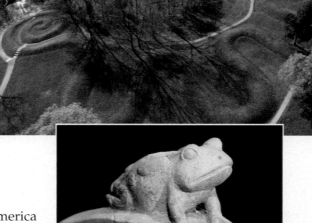

North American Culture Areas About 1450

Skills Assessment

Geography As Native Americans spread out to populate North America, they developed a wide variety of cultures. The map shows culture areas in which tribes shared similar environments and ways of life.

1. **Location** On the map, locate (a) Northwest Coast culture area, (b) Eastern Woodlands culture area, (c) Great Basin culture area.

2. **Place** (a) Name two tribes in the Great Plains culture area. (b) With which culture area are the Cherokees associated?

3. **Critical Thinking Making Inferences** The Navajos lived in the Southwest culture area but spoke a Subarctic language. (a) How might this be explained? (b) What were some other characteristics of peoples in the Southwest culture area?

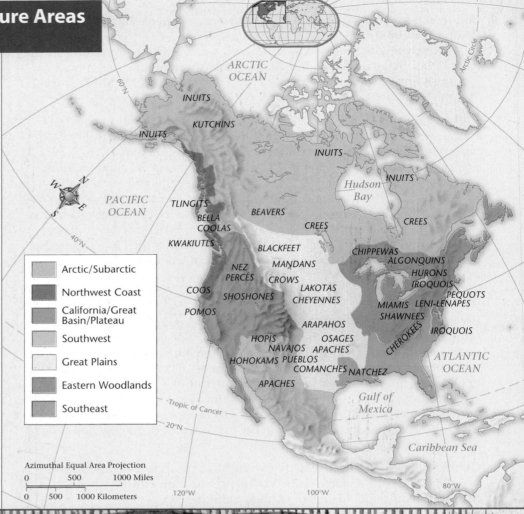

Legend:
- Arctic/Subarctic
- Northwest Coast
- California/Great Basin/Plateau
- Southwest
- Great Plains
- Eastern Woodlands
- Southeast

Azimuthal Equal Area Projection

0   500   1000 Miles

0   500   1000 Kilometers

Native American Culture Groups of North America

Arctic/Subarctic

Beavers, Crees, Inuits, Kutchins

Lived as nomadic hunters and food gatherers in cold climate; honored ocean, weather, and animal spirits

California/Great Basin/Plateau

Nez Percés, Pomos, Shoshones

Lived as hunters and gatherers in small family groups; ate mainly fish, berries, acorns

Southwest

Apaches, Hohokams, Hopis, Navajos, Pueblos

Lived in villages in homes made of adobe; built irrigation systems to grow corn and other crops; honored earth, sky, and water spirits

Southeast

Cherokees, Natchez

Grew corn, squash, beans, and other crops; held yearly Green Corn Ceremony to mark end of year and celebrate harvest

Northwest Coast

Bella Coolas, Coos, Kwakiutls, Tlingits

Lived in villages; benefited from rich natural resources in forests, rivers, and ocean; held potlatches, or ceremonial dinners, where host families gave gifts to guests to show wealth and gain status

Great Plains

Apaches, Arapahos, Blackfeet, Cheyennes, Comanches, Crows, Lakotas, Mandans, Osages

Lived in tepees; animals hunted by men; crops grown by women; relied on buffalo to meet basic needs of food, shelter, and clothing

Eastern Woodlands

Algonquins, Chippewas, Hurons, Iroquois, Leni-Lenapes, Miamis, Pequots, Shawnees

Lived in farming villages, but also hunted for food; long houses shared by several families; women held social and political power

Here, we will look in greater detail at the distinct ways of life that developed in three regions—the Arctic, the Northwest Coast, and the Eastern Woodlands.

A Frozen World In the far north, the Inuits* adapted to a harsh climate, using the resources of the frozen land to survive. Small bands lived by hunting and fishing. Seals and other sea mammals provided them with food, skins for clothing, bones for needles and tools, and oil for cooking. They paddled kayaks in open waters or used dog sleds to transport goods across the ice. In some areas, Inuits constructed igloos, or dome-shaped homes made from snow and ice. In others, they built sod dwellings that were partly underground.

A Land of Plenty The people of the Northwest Coast lived in a far richer environment than the Inuits. Rivers teemed with salmon, and the Pacific Ocean offered other fish and sea mammals. Hunters tracked deer, wolves, and bears in the forests. In this land of plenty, people built large permanent villages with homes made of wood. They traded their surplus goods, gaining wealth that was shared in ceremonies like the potlatch. At this ceremony, which continues in Canada today, a person of rank and wealth distributes lavish gifts to large numbers of guests. By accepting the gifts, the guests acknowledge the host's high status.

The Iroquois League The Eastern Woodlands, stretching from the Atlantic Coast to the Great Lakes, was home to a number of groups, including the Iroquois. They cleared land and built villages in the forests. While women farmed, men hunted and frequently warred against rival nations.

According to Iroquois tradition, the prophet Dekanawidah (deh kan ah WEE dah) urged rival Iroquois nations to stop their constant wars. In the late 1500s, he became one of the founders of the unique political system known as the Iroquois League. This was an alliance of five nations who spoke the same language and shared similar traditions.

The Iroquois League did not always succeed in keeping the peace. Still, it was the best-organized political group north of Mexico. Member nations governed their own villages but met jointly in a council when they needed to address larger issues. Only men sat on the council, but each clan had a "clan mother" who could name or depose members of the council.

The Iroquois League emerged just at the time when Europeans arrived in the Americas. Encounters with Europeans would take a fearful toll on the peoples of North America and topple the Aztec and Incan empires.

* The Inuits were late immigrants from Siberia. Other Native Americans called them Eskimos, "eaters of raw flesh," but they called themselves the Inuits, the "people."

Primary Source

A Plea for Peace
In about 1570, the prophet Dekanawidah persuaded warring Iroquois nations to form a confederacy:

"I, Dekanawidah, and the confederate lords now uproot the tallest tree and into the cavity thereby made we cast all weapons of war. Into the depths of the earth we cast all weapons of strife. We bury them from sight forever and plant again the tree. Thus shall all Great Peace be established and hostilities shall no longer be known between the Five Nations but only peace to a united people."

—Iroquois Constitution

Skills Assessment

Primary Source What does Dekanawidah believe the Iroquois must do to achieve the Great Peace?

SECTION 3 Assessment

Recall
1. **Identify: (a)** Hohokams, **(b)** Anasazi, **(c)** Mound Builders, **(d)** Inuits, **(e)** Iroquois League.
2. **Define: (a)** pueblo, **(b)** kiva, **(c)** potlatch.

Comprehension
3. How did the Hohokams farm the desert southwest?
4. How do we know about the lives of the Mound Builders and their contacts with other peoples?

5. Give examples of how the environment influenced three early cultures of North America.

Critical Thinking and Writing
6. **Asking Questions** If you were an archaeologist studying the Adena and Hopewell people, what three questions might you ask about the giant mounds they built?
7. **Linking Past and Present** How does environment affect your community?

Activity

Creating a Poster
With a partner, create a poster that expresses the ideas behind the formation of the Iroquois League. Use symbols to represent the five Iroquois nations.

Review and Assessment

Creating a Chapter Summary

Fill in the missing events and dates on the following time line. Add more events and dates to create a time line that includes the major cultures discussed in this chapter.

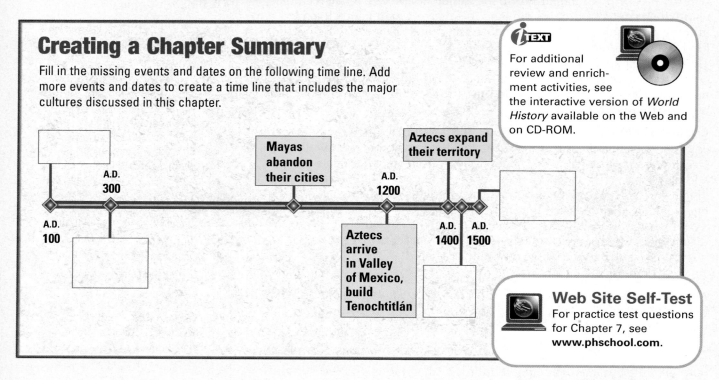

iTEXT

For additional review and enrichment activities, see the interactive version of *World History* available on the Web and on CD-ROM.

Web Site Self-Test
For practice test questions for Chapter 7, see **www.phschool.com.**

Building Vocabulary

Review the vocabulary words listed below. Then, use the words and their definitions to create a matching quiz. Exchange quizzes with another student. Check each other's answers when you are finished.

1. global warming
2. plains
3. chinampas
4. tribute
5. glyph
6. quipu
7. alloy
8. pueblo
9. kiva
10. potlatch

Recalling Key Facts

11. How and when do historians think that people first migrated to the Americas?
12. Name three advances in learning made by the Mayas.
13. Describe the social structure of the Aztec empire.
14. Why did the Incas build an extensive road system?
15. Why did the Anasazi abandon their cliff dwellings?
16. What was the main goal of the Iroquois League?

Critical Thinking and Writing

17. **Analyzing Information** (a) What advances in agriculture did the Mayas, Aztecs, and Incas make? (b) Why were these farming methods critical to the development of each of these civilizations?
18. **Predicting Consequences** How do you think the people conquered by the Aztecs might respond to an invasion by a foreign power? Explain.
19. **Synthesizing Information** (a) How were religion and government linked in the Incan empire? (b) Identify two other ancient civilizations you have read about in which rulers claimed divine powers.
20. **Comparing** Review the information on the Roman empire in the previous chapter. Then, compare the methods used by the Incas and the Romans to unite and control their diverse, far-flung empires.
21. **Connecting to Geography** (a) Describe the environment of the Northwest Coast. (b) How did people adapt to this environment?

Father Bernabe Cobo was a seventeenth-century Spanish missionary who worked with the Indians of Peru. Over the years, Cobo closely observed the Incas. In the excerpt below, Cobo describes the great majesty and splendor of the Sapa Inca. Read the excerpt and answer the questions that follow.

> *"The multitude of servants that they had in their palace was incredible. They were served all the exquisite, precious, and rare things that the land produced. . . . Serving women brought him all of his food. . . . When he pointed out the dish that he wanted, . . . one of these serving women would take it to him and hold it in her hand while he ate. . . . All leftovers from the meal and whatever the Inca touched with his hands were kept by the Indians in chests; thus, in one chest they placed the little [mats] that they placed before him when he ate; in another, the bones of the poultry and meat left over from his meals; in another, the clothes that he discarded. Finally, everything that the Inca had touched was kept in a hut, . . . and on a certain day each year it was all burned. They said that since the Incas were children of the Sun, whatever they touched had to be burned, . . . and no one was to touch it."*

—Bernabe Cobo, *History of the Inca Empire*

22. What is the source of the excerpt?
23. According to Cobo, how was the Inca treated by his subjects?
24. **(a)** What happened to things that the Inca touched? **(b)** Why?
25. Do you think this is a reliable source of information about the Incas? Explain.

Take It to the NET

Use the Internet to research Aztec, Incan, or Mayan art. Then, create a sketch, sculpture, or textile in the artistic style of the civilization you have researched. If you prefer, write a description of a piece of art you have researched, focusing on special features of that civilization's style.

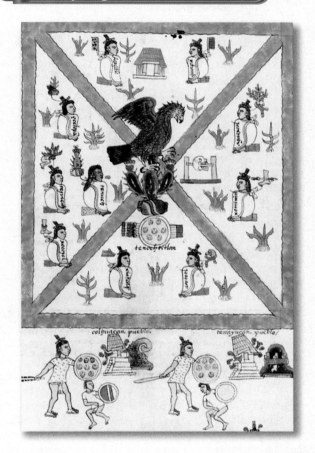

This picture is from an Aztec codex, or book. It is a symbolic representation of the rise of Tenochtitlán, the Aztec capital. Study the picture and review what you have learned about the Aztec empire to answer the following questions:

26. **(a)** Identify two symbols in the top portion of the picture. **(b)** What might they represent?
27. **(a)** What is the bird in the center of the picture? **(b)** What is the bird perched on? **(c)** Why do you think the Aztec artist placed it there?
28. Canals divided Tenochtitlán into four quarters. How did the artist represent the canals?
29. **(a)** What might the symbols at the bottom of the panel represent? **(b)** What do the symbols suggest about Aztec culture?

Skills Tip

Artists often use symbols to represent ideas. Study the symbols and compare them with your own knowledge to identify their meaning.

Chapter 4

Empires of India and China
(600 B.C.–A.D. 550)

Between 600 B.C. and A.D. 550, strong, unified empires with complex belief systems emerged in India and China. These civilizations set patterns in government, religion, and philosophy that influenced later cultures.

- Hindu beliefs, including the concepts of reincarnation, karma, and dharma, profoundly influenced Indian civilization.
- The Buddha, an Indian religious reformer, sought spiritual enlightenment. His teachings gave rise to a new religion, Buddhism, that spread through Southeast and East Asia.
- Under the Maurya and Gupta dynasties, India developed into a center of trade and had contacts with civilizations in Africa, the Middle East, and Central and Southeast Asia.
- The caste system, the village, and the family influenced many aspects of Indian life.
- The teachings of Confucius, based on ideals of duty and social good, influenced Chinese government and society.
- Legalism and Daoism were two other important philosophies that arose in China.
- Shi Huangdi united China and built a strong authoritarian government, which laid the groundwork for China's classical age.
- Under Han rulers, the Chinese made huge advances in trade, government, technology, and the arts.

Chapter 5

Ancient Greece
(1750 B.C.–133 B.C.)

Despite bitter rivalry, Greek city-states gave rise to a civilization that set a standard of excellence for later civilizations. Greek ideas about the universe, the individual, and government still live on in the world today.

- Through trading contacts, Minoan and Mycenaean culture acquired many ideas from older civilizations of Egypt and Mesopotamia.
- Separated by mountains, the Greek city-states often warred with one another but united to defeat the Persians.
- After the Persian Wars, democracy flourished and culture thrived in Athens under the leadership of Pericles.
- Guided by a belief in reason, Greek artists, writers, and philosophers used their genius to seek order in the universe.
- The conquests of Alexander the Great spread Greek civilization throughout the Mediterranean world and across the Middle East to the outskirts of India.
- Greek culture blended with Persian, Egyptian, and Indian cultures to create the Hellenistic civilization, in which art, science, mathematics, and philosophy flourished.

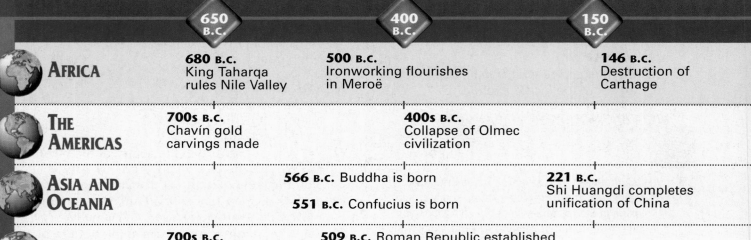

	650 B.C.	400 B.C.	150 B.C.
AFRICA	**680 B.C.** King Taharqa rules Nile Valley	**500 B.C.** Ironworking flourishes in Meroë	**146 B.C.** Destruction of Carthage
THE AMERICAS	**700s B.C.** Chavín gold carvings made	**400s B.C.** Collapse of Olmec civilization	
ASIA AND OCEANIA	**566 B.C.** Buddha is born / **551 B.C.** Confucius is born		**221 B.C.** Shi Huangdi completes unification of China
EUROPE	**700s B.C.** Rise of Greek city-states	**509 B.C.** Roman Republic established / **460 B.C.** Age of Pericles begins / **323 B.C.** Hellenistic age begins	

Chapter 6

Ancient Rome and the Rise of Christianity
(509 B.C.–A.D. 476)

Rome expanded across the Mediterranean to build a huge, diverse empire. In the process, it spread the civilizations of Greece, Egypt, and the Fertile Crescent westward into Europe.

- After the Romans threw out their Etruscan king, they set up a republic. Eventually, commoners were allowed to be elected to the Roman senate.

- Conquest and diplomacy helped the Romans to extend their rule from Spain to Egypt. However, expansion created social and economic problems that led to the decline of the republic and the rule of an emperor.

- During the Pax Romana, Roman emperors brought peace, order, unity, and prosperity to the lands under their control.

- Rome acted as a bridge between the east and the west by borrowing and transforming Greek and Hellenistic achievements to produce Greco-Roman civilization.

- Christianity, which emerged in Roman-held lands in the Middle East, spread quickly throughout the Roman empire. The new faith reshaped Roman beliefs.

- Foreign invasions, the division of the empire, a corrupt government, poverty and unemployment, and declining moral values finally contributed to the downfall of the Roman empire.

Chapter 7

Civilizations of the Americas
(1400 B.C.–A.D. 1570)

Four advanced civilizations—those of the Olmecs, the Mayas, the Aztecs, and the Incas—developed in Middle and South America. In North America, diverse culture groups emerged.

- The first settlers in the Americas were nomadic hunters who migrated across a land bridge between Siberia and Alaska and gradually populated two vast continents.

- From about 1400 B.C to 500 B.C., the Olmec civilization flourished along the Mexican Gulf Coast. Their religious, scientific, and architectural contributions influenced later civilizations in Mexico.

- Mayan civilization flourished from southern Mexico through Central America between A.D. 300 and A.D. 900. Its system of city-states supported a complex religious structure.

- In the 1400s, the Aztecs conquered most of Mexico and built a highly developed civilization led by a single ruler.

- By the 1500s, the Incas established a centralized government in Peru, ruled by a god-king and a powerful class of priests.

- Ten culture groups developed in the Arctic, Subarctic, Northwest Coast, California, Great Basin, Plateau, Southwest, Great Plains, Southeast, and Eastern Woodlands. Their diverse ways of life were strongly influenced by geography.

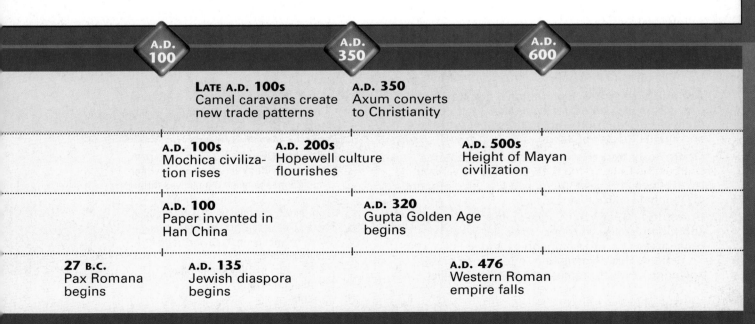

A.D. 100

A.D. 350

A.D. 600

LATE A.D. 100s
Camel caravans create new trade patterns

A.D. 350
Axum converts to Christianity

A.D. 100s
Mochica civilization rises

A.D. 200s
Hopewell culture flourishes

A.D. 500s
Height of Mayan civilization

A.D. 100
Paper invented in Han China

A.D. 320
Gupta Golden Age begins

27 B.C.
Pax Romana begins

A.D. 135
Jewish diaspora begins

A.D. 476
Western Roman empire falls

UNIT 3

Regional Civilizations

750 B.C.–A.D. 1650

OUTLINE

THEMES

As you read about the rise of regional civilizations around the world, you will encounter the following themes.

Religions and Value Systems Religions and value systems such as Christianity, Islam, and Confucianism united people across wide areas.

Art and Literature Rich regional cultures found expression in such art forms as the Gothic cathedrals of Europe, bronze sculptures of West Africa, and kabuki theater of Japan.

Geography and History Geographic features such as the Sahara, the Mediterranean Sea, and the steppes of Russia influenced the development of regional civilizations.

Diversity As regional civilizations learned more about one another through trade and war, they became lands of diverse peoples and ideas. Sometimes this diversity led to tolerance and a flowering of ideas; sometimes it led to conflict.

Unit Theme Activity

For Your Portfolio The chapters in this unit discuss various ways in which societies expressed themselves through the arts. As you read the chapters, prepare a portfolio project highlighting examples of this artistic expression. Your project might take one of the following forms:
- **Museum exhibit and catalog**
- **Annotated map**
- **Collage**

Built during the Ming dynasty, the Forbidden City was home to the emperors of China for nearly five centuries. All but a chosen few were forbidden to enter the imperial palace.

WHY STUDY HISTORY?

Because Past Heroes Can Be Today's Role Models

We are all capable of heroism. And we can learn from the heroes of the past. Throughout history, exceptional men and women have acted boldly to change the world. Some were great leaders. Others revolutionized the way we think. Many were simply people who refused to accept injustice and unfairness as a condition of everyday life. Whoever they were, these past heroes can serve as role models for us today. By studying their lives, we may discover new ways to make our own world a better place.

Heroes strive to reach their potential.

In the Middle Ages, Europeans looked on educated women as oddities. Women, they believed, belonged in the home, managing the household and raising children. Christine de Pizan refused to accept this role. After her husband's death, she dared to support herself as a writer, an occupation usually reserved for men. In her many works, she celebrated the achievements of women and defended them against unfair attacks.

Heroes promote new ideas.

It takes great courage for a leader to promote unpopular ideas. In Korea, in the 1400s, King Sejong instituted a bold reform. Ignoring the objections of scholars, Sejong introduced a new alphabet to simplify the system of writing that Koreans had used for centuries. Sejong's policy paid off. With the help of the new alphabet, Korea became one of the most literate nations in the world.

Heroes expand our knowledge of the universe.

Scientists have always challenged accepted ideas about the nature of the world. In the early 1900s, physicist Albert Einstein advanced a series of theories that suggested entirely new ways of thinking about space, time, and gravitation. Einstein's theories of relativity and gravitation revolutionized the fields of science and philosophy.

Heroes lead the fight for freedom.

Mohandas Gandhi (above left) was a new kind of leader. Although he organized India's struggle for independence from British rule, he renounced the use of force. Instead, he called on his followers to adopt the weapon of nonviolent resistance. His campaigns of civil disobedience eroded British power and won wide support for India's cause. Gandhi's teachings continue to inspire people throughout the world today.

Who are today's heroes?

Study the daily newspaper or watch TV—you are certain to find people who qualify as heroes. For example, Colin Powell (right) was the first African American to serve as chairman of the Joint Chiefs of Staff, the highest military post in the United States. General Powell has chosen to use his celebrity to run America's Promise—The Alliance for Youth, an organization devoted to helping children at risk.

Portfolio Assessment

Connecting to Today Select either a person you know or a public figure whom you would consider a role model. Write a paragraph explaining why you think this person is a hero.

CHAPTER 8

The Rise of Europe

500–1300

Chapter Preview

1 The Early Middle Ages
2 Feudalism and the Manor Economy
3 The Medieval Church
4 Economic Expansion and Change

500s

Germanic tribes such as the Franks dominate Western Europe. This bronze brooch depicts a Frankish warrior.

732

Frankish forces defeat Muslim armies at the battle of Tours.

800

Frankish King Charlemagne is crowned emperor by the pope. Under Charlemagne, much of Western Europe is briefly united.

**CHAPTER
EVENTS**

400   600   800

**GLOBAL
EVENTS**

527 Justinian rules Byzantine empire.

622 The Muslim prophet Muhammad leaves Mecca.

Geography and Resources of Europe

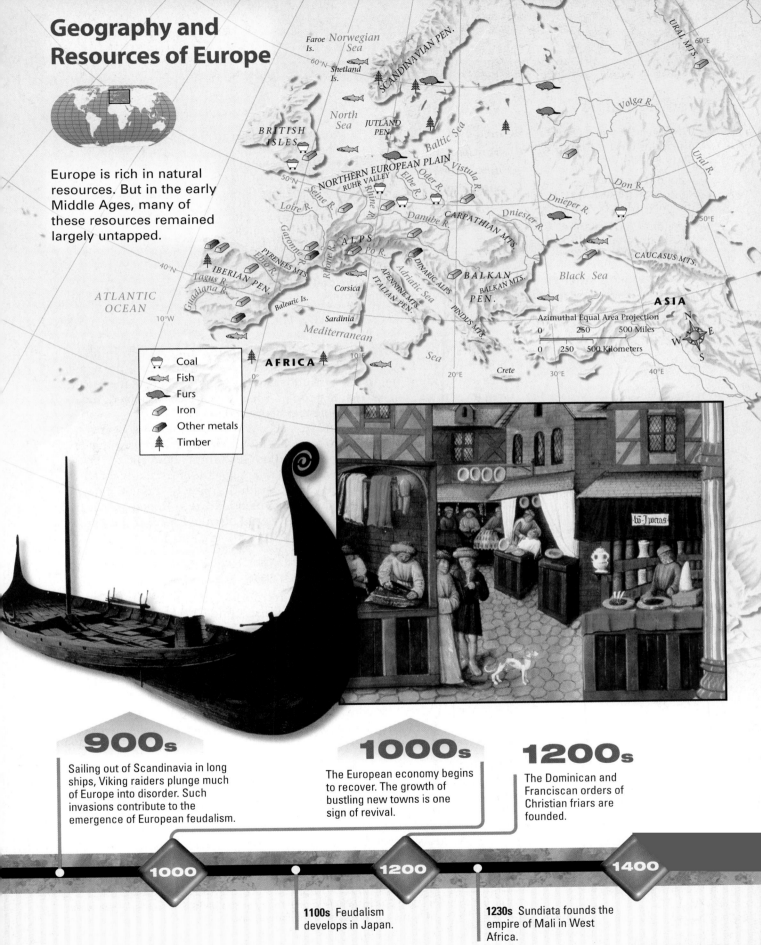

Europe is rich in natural resources. But in the early Middle Ages, many of these resources remained largely untapped.

Legend:
- Coal
- Fish
- Furs
- Iron
- Other metals
- Timber

Azimuthal Equal Area Projection
0 — 250 — 500 Miles
0 — 250 — 500 Kilometers

900s
Sailing out of Scandinavia in long ships, Viking raiders plunge much of Europe into disorder. Such invasions contribute to the emergence of European feudalism.

1000s
The European economy begins to recover. The growth of bustling new towns is one sign of revival.

1200s
The Dominican and Franciscan orders of Christian friars are founded.

1000

1100s Feudalism develops in Japan.

1200

1230s Sundiata founds the empire of Mali in West Africa.

1400

The Early Middle Ages

Reading Focus

- Why was Western Europe a frontier land during the early Middle Ages?

- How did Germanic kingdoms gain power in the early Middle Ages?

- How did Charlemagne briefly reunite much of Western Europe?

Vocabulary

medieval

frontier

missi dominici

curriculum

Taking Notes

As you read, prepare an outline of this section. Use Roman numerals to indicate the major headings of the section, letters for the subheadings, and numbers for the supporting details. The sample at right will help you get started.

I. **Geography of Western Europe**
   A. Location
      1.
      2.
   B.
II. **The Germanic kingdoms**
   A. The Franks
      1.
      2.
   B.

Main Idea After the fall of Rome, Germanic tribes divided Western Europe into many small kingdoms.

Setting the Scene Pope Gregory the Great sat at his desk, thinking about the perils facing Italy. The Lombards were attacking from the north. Once again, Rome might fall to plundering invaders. "Where is the senate?" Gregory wrote. "Where are the people? The bones are all dissolved, the flesh is consumed. . . . The whole mass is boiled away."

Gregory was writing around A.D. 600, as waves of invaders swept across Europe. Trade slowed to a trickle, towns emptied, and learning virtually ceased. During the early Middle Ages,* from about 500 to 1000, Europe was a relatively backward region largely cut off from advanced civilizations in the Middle East, China, and India. Slowly, though, a new European civilization would emerge that blended Greco-Roman, Germanic, and Christian traditions. Much later, it would be called medieval civilization, from the Latin for "middle age."

Geography of Western Europe

Rome had linked its distant European territories with miles of roads and had spread classical ideas, the Latin language, and Christianity to the tribal peoples of Western Europe. But Rome was a Mediterranean power. The Germanic peoples who ended Roman rule in the West shifted the focus of European history to the north.

Location Europe is relatively small—the second smallest in land area of the seven continents. It lies on the western end of Eurasia, the giant landmass that stretches from present-day Portugal in the west all the way to China in the east. Despite Europe's size, its impact on the modern world has been enormous.

Resources From about 500 to 1000, this region was a frontier land—a sparsely populated, undeveloped area on the outskirts of a civilization. Still, it had great untapped potential. Dense forests flourished in the north. The region's rich earth was better suited to raising crops than were the dry soils of the Mediterranean. Underground lay mineral resources. Nearby seas provided fish for food and served as transportation routes. Europe's large rivers were ideal for trade, and its mountain streams could turn water wheels.

---

* The period from about 500 to 1450 is known today as the Middle Ages because it came between the fall of Rome and the start of the modern era.

The Germanic Kingdoms

The Germanic tribes who migrated across Europe were farmers and herders. Their culture differed greatly from that of the Romans. They had no cities or written laws. Instead, they lived in small communities governed by unwritten customs. They elected kings to lead them in war. Warrior nobles swore loyalty to the king in exchange for weapons and loot.

The Franks Between 400 and 700, Germanic tribes carved Western Europe into small kingdoms. The strongest kingdom to emerge was that of the Franks. In 486, Clovis, king of the Franks, conquered the former Roman province of Gaul. He ruled his new lands according to Frankish custom but did preserve much of the Roman legacy in Gaul.

Clovis took an important step when he converted to Christianity, the religion of the people in Gaul. Not only did he earn their support, but he also gained a powerful ally in the Christian Church of Rome.

Europe and the Muslim World As the Franks and other Germanic peoples carved up Europe, a new power was emerging across the Mediterranean. The religion of Islam appeared in Arabia in 622. From there, Muslims, or believers in Islam, built a huge empire and created a new civilization, as you will read in Chapter 11.

European Christians were stunned when Muslim armies overran Christian lands from Palestine to North Africa to Spain. When a Muslim army crossed into France, Charles Martel rallied Frankish warriors. At the battle of Tours in 732, Christian warriors triumphed. To them, the victory was a sign that God was on their side. Muslims advanced no farther into Western Europe, although they continued to rule most of Spain.

To European Christians, the Muslim presence was a source of anxiety. Even when Islam was no longer a threat, Christians viewed the Muslim world with hostility. In time, though, medieval Europeans would learn much from Muslims, whose learning in many areas exceeded their own.

The Age of Charlemagne

Around 800, Western Europe had a moment of unity when the grandson of Charles Martel built an empire reaching across France, Germany, and part of Italy. This emperor is known to history as Charlemagne (SHAHR luh mayn), or Charles the Great. Charlemagne towered over most people of his time. He loved battle and spent much of his 46-year reign fighting Muslims in Spain, Saxons in the north, Avars and Slavs in the east, and Lombards in Italy. His conquests reunited much of the old Roman empire.

A Christian Emperor In 800, Pope Leo III called on Charlemagne for help against rebellious nobles in Rome. Frankish armies marched south and crushed the rebellion. On Christmas Day, the pope showed his gratitude by placing a crown on Charlemagne's head and proclaiming him Emperor of the Romans.

The ceremony would have enormous significance. A Christian pope had crowned a German king successor to the Roman emperors. In doing so,

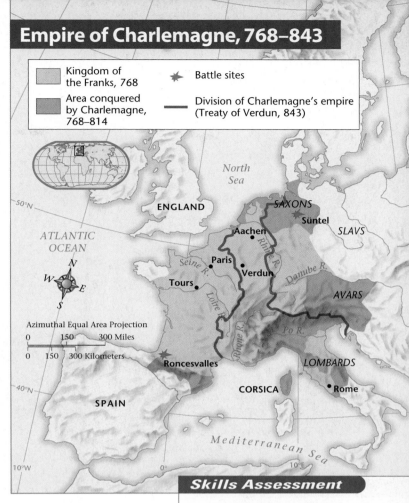

Empire of Charlemagne, 768–843

▨ Kingdom of the Franks, 768	✦	Battle sites
▨ Area conquered by Charlemagne, 768–814	—	Division of Charlemagne's empire (Treaty of Verdun, 843)

North Sea

ENGLAND

SAXONS

Süntel

SLAVS

Aachen

ATLANTIC OCEAN

Seine R.

Paris

Verdun

Rhine R.

Danube R.

Tours

Loire

AVARS

Azimuthal Equal Area Projection

0   150   300 Miles

0   150   300 Kilometers

Rhône R.

Po R.

Roncesvalles

LOMBARDS

CORSICA

Rome

SPAIN

Mediterranean Sea

50°N

40°N

10°W

0°

10°E

Skills Assessment

Geography Charlemagne built an empire in Europe, but his descendants were unable to hold it together.

1. **Location** On the map, locate *(a)* the Frankish kingdom in 768, *(b)* Charlemagne's empire in 814, *(c)* Tours, *(d)* Aachen.
2. **Region** Look at a map of the Roman empire in Chapter 6. Compare the location and extent of Charlemagne's empire with that of Rome.
3. **Critical Thinking Predicting Consequences** What might be one result of the division of Charlemagne's empire?

Invasions of Europe, 700–1000

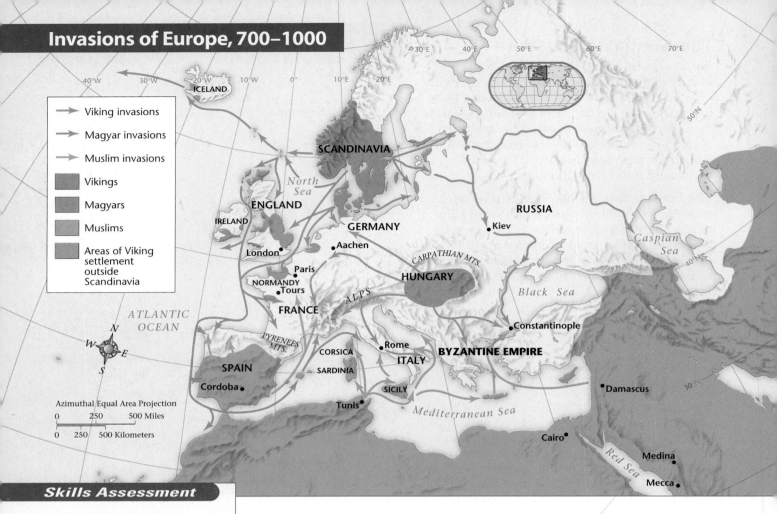

Map legend:
- → Viking invasions
- → Magyar invasions
- → Muslim invasions
- ■ Vikings
- ■ Magyars
- ■ Muslims
- ■ Areas of Viking settlement outside Scandinavia

Azimuthal Equal Area Projection

0   250   500 Miles
0   250   500 Kilometers

Map labels: ICELAND, SCANDINAVIA, North Sea, ENGLAND, IRELAND, GERMANY, RUSSIA, Kiev, Caspian Sea, Aachen, London, Paris, CARPATHIAN MTS., HUNGARY, NORMANDY, Tours, ALPS, FRANCE, Black Sea, Constantinople, ATLANTIC OCEAN, PYRENEES MTS., CORSICA, Rome, ITALY, BYZANTINE EMPIRE, SPAIN, SARDINIA, Cordoba, SICILY, Damascus, Tunis, Mediterranean Sea, Cairo, Red Sea, Medina, Mecca

Skills Assessment

Geography Between 700 and 1000, Western Europe was battered by invaders.

1. **Location** On the map, locate **(a)** Byzantine empire, **(b)** Scandinavia, **(c)** Ireland, **(d)** England, **(e)** Cordoba.
2. **Place** **(a)** From where did the Magyars set out? **(b)** Where did the Vikings and Muslims build settlements?
3. **Critical Thinking** **Comparing** How did the Viking invasions differ from those of the Magyars and the Muslims?

he revived the ideal of a united Christian community. He also laid the ground for desperate power struggles between future Roman Catholic popes and German emperors.

The pope's action outraged the emperor of the eastern Roman empire in Constantinople. The eastern emperor saw himself, and not some backward Frankish king, as the sole Roman ruler. In the long run, the crowning of Charlemagne helped widen the split between the eastern and western Christian worlds.

Government Charlemagne tried to exercise control over his many lands and create a united Christian Europe. Working closely with the Church, he helped spread Christianity to the conquered peoples on the fringes of his empire. Missionaries converted many Saxons and Slavs.

Like other Germanic kings, Charlemagne appointed powerful nobles to rule local regions. He gave them land so that they could offer support and supply soldiers for his armies. To keep control of these provincial rulers, he sent out officials called *missi dominici* (MIH see dohm in NEE kee) to check on roads, listen to grievances, and see that justice was done. Charlemagne instructed the *missi* to "administer the law fully and justly in the case of the holy churches of God and of the poor, of wards and of widows, and of the whole people."

Revival of Learning Charlemagne wanted to make his court at Aachen (AH kuhn) a "second Rome." To do so, he set out to revive Latin learning in his empire. Education had declined so much that even supposedly educated clergy were often sadly ignorant. Charlemagne himself could read but not write. Still, as a ruler, he saw the need for officials to keep accurate records and write clear reports.

Charlemagne founded a school at Aachen under the direction of a respected scholar, Alcuin (AL kwihn) of York. Alcuin created a curriculum, or formal course of study, based on Latin learning. It included grammar, rhetoric, logic, arithmetic, geometry, music, and astronomy. Alcuin also hired scholars to copy ancient manuscripts, including the Bible and Latin works of history and science. Alcuin's system would become the educational model for medieval Europe.

After Charlemagne

After Charlemagne died in 814, his empire soon fell apart. His heirs battled for power for nearly 30 years. Finally, in 843, Charlemagne's grandsons drew up the Treaty of Verdun, which split the empire into three regions.

Legacy of Charlemagne Still, Charlemagne left a lasting legacy. He extended Christian civilization into northern Europe and furthered the blending of German, Roman, and Christian traditions. He also set up strong, efficient governments. Later medieval rulers looked to his example when they tried to strengthen their own kingdoms.

A New Wave of Invasions Charlemagne's heirs faced new waves of invasions. Despite the Christian victory at Tours, Muslim forces still posed a threat to Europe. In the late 800s, they conquered Sicily, which became a thriving center of Islamic culture. Not until the 900s, when power struggles erupted in the Middle East, did Muslim attacks finally subside.

About 896, a new wave of nomadic people, the Magyars, settled in what is today Hungary. From there, they overran eastern Europe and moved on to plunder Germany, parts of France, and Italy. Finally, after about 50 years, they were pushed back into Hungary.

The Vikings snapped the last threads of unity in Charlemagne's empire. These expert sailors burst out of Scandinavia, a northern region that now includes Norway, Sweden, and Denmark. Starting in the 900s, they looted and burned communities along the coasts and rivers of Europe.

The Vikings were not just destructive raiders. They were also traders and explorers who sailed around the Mediterranean Sea and across the Atlantic Ocean. Vikings opened trade routes that linked northern Europe to Mediterranean lands. Vikings also settled in England, Ireland, northern France, and parts of Russia. Around the year 1000, Leif Erikson set up a short-lived Viking colony on North America.

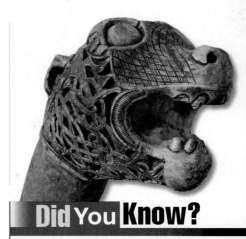

Did You Know?

The Voyage to Valhalla
According to Viking mythology, Valhalla was a great hall in the grandest palace of Odin, king of the gods. The walls of Valhalla were gold, and its roof was made of battle shields. Vikings believed that if they died heroically in battle, they would spend eternity fighting and then feasting in Valhalla with Odin.

To make the voyage to Valhalla, a Viking hero needed a proper funeral. This included being buried with his weapons, his clothing, and a ship. The servants of Viking warriors were buried with them to serve their masters on the journey and beyond. Sometimes, instead of being buried, the fully stocked ship was cast adrift and burned.

Theme: Religions and Value Systems How might a Viking's beliefs have affected his behavior in battle?

SECTION 1 Assessment

Recall
1. **Identify:** (a) Clovis, (b) Islam, (c) Charlemagne, (d) Alcuin, (e) Treaty of Verdun, (f) Vikings.
2. **Define:** (a) medieval, (b) frontier, (c) *missi dominici*, (d) curriculum.

Comprehension
3. What untapped resources did Western Europe possess in the early Middle Ages?
4. How did Clovis increase the power of the Frankish kingdoms?
5. (a) What steps did Charlemagne take to improve government and unify his empire? (b) What happened to his empire after he died?

Critical Thinking and Writing
6. **Recognizing Points of View** The term *Middle Ages* was coined by Europeans to describe the period from 500 to 1450. Do you think that other civilizations use the same term for that period? Why or why not?
7. **Ranking** List the accomplishments of Charlemagne. Which do you think had the most lasting importance? Why?

Activity
Take It to the NET

The Vikings did not produce much art, but they did decorate many of their possessions with elaborate designs. Use the Internet to find out about Viking ornamentation. Then, draw an example to share with the class. Explain how or where the Vikings might have used the design.

Feudalism and the Manor Economy

Reading Focus

- How did feudalism shape medieval society?

- What was feudal life like for nobles and peasants?

- What was the basis of the manor economy?

Vocabulary

feudalism
vassal
feudal contract
fief
knight
tournament
chivalry
troubadour
manor
serf

Taking Notes

Copy the table below. Then, fill it in as you read. Part of the table has been filled in to help you get started.

	NOBLES	PEASANTS
OBLIGATIONS	• Military service to lord •	
RIGHTS AND BENEFITS		• Protection from lord •
LIVES		

Main Idea A new political and social system, called feudalism, shaped medieval life.

Connections to Today

The Middle Ages Are Alive and Well!

The town is abuzz: Soon the king and queen will be passing by! Peasants crowd the muddy street. Shopkeepers loudly peddle food and drink. Minstrels wander through the crowd, singing and playing instruments. On the outskirts of town, knights in armor prepare to joust.

Scenes like this are common today all over this country at medieval festivals. Professional actors and others dress up in period costumes, pretend to have European accents, and play people from all levels of medieval society. The results are very romanticized and not always accurate. Still, the fairs give thousands of visitors a small taste of medieval life.

Theme: Continuity and Change Do you think a medieval festival would be a good place to learn about the Middle Ages? Why or why not?

Setting the Scene

Setting the Scene Count William had just inherited the rich lands of Flanders. The local nobles gathered to pledge loyalty to their new lord. One by one, they knelt before him and took a solemn oath. "I promise on my faith," pledged each lord, "that I will in future be faithful to Count William and will observe my [loyalty] to him completely against all persons in good faith and without deceit."

The count then touched the noble with a small rod. With that gesture, he granted the noble a parcel of land, which included any towns, castles, or people on it.

Although the words might vary, ceremonies like this one took place across Europe during the Middle Ages. In public, before witnesses, great nobles and lesser lords exchanged vows of loyalty and service. Those vows were part of a new political and social system that governed medieval life.

The Emergence of Feudalism

In the face of invasions by Vikings, Muslims, and Magyars, kings and emperors were too weak to maintain law and order. People needed protection for themselves, their homes, and their lands. In response to this basic need for protection, a new system evolved, known as feudalism. **Feudalism** was a loosely organized system of rule in which powerful local lords divided their landholdings among lesser lords. In exchange, these lesser lords, or **vassals,** pledged service and loyalty to the greater lord.

Mutual Obligations The relationship between lords and vassals was established by custom and tradition and by an exchange of pledges known as the **feudal contract.** A lord granted his vassal a **fief** (FEEF), or estate. Fiefs ranged from a few acres to hundreds of square miles. In addition to the land itself, the fief included peasants to work the land, as well as any towns or buildings on the land.

As part of the feudal contract, the lord promised to protect his vassal. In return, the vassal pledged loyalty to his lord. He also agreed to provide the lord with 40 days of military service each year, certain money payments, and advice.

A Structured Society Everyone had a place in feudal society. Below the monarch were powerful lords, such as dukes and counts, who held the largest fiefs. Each of these lords had vassals, and these vassals in turn had their own vassals. In many cases, the same man was both vassal and lord—vassal to a more powerful lord above him and lord to a less powerful vassal below him.

Because vassals often held fiefs from more than one lord, feudal relationships grew very complex. A vassal who had pledged loyalty to several lords could have serious problems if his overlords quarreled with each other. What was he to do if both demanded his aid? To solve this problem, a vassal usually had a liege lord to whom he owed his first loyalty.

The World of Nobles

For feudal nobles, warfare was a way of life. Rival lords battled constantly for power. Many nobles trained from boyhood for a future occupation as a knight, or mounted warrior.

Achieving Knighthood At the age of seven, a boy slated to become a knight was sent away to the castle of his father's lord. There, he learned to ride and fight. He also learned to keep his armor and weapons in good condition. Training was difficult and discipline was strict. Any laziness was punished with an angry blow or even a severe beating.

With his training finished, the youth was ready to become a knight. Kneeling before an older knight, he bowed his head. The knight struck the young man with his hand or the flat side of his sword and declared something like the following: "In the name of God, Saint Michael, and Saint George, I dub thee knight. Be valiant." After this "dubbing," the young knight took his place beside other warriors.

As feudal warfare decreased in the 1100s, tournaments, or mock battles, came into fashion. A lord would invite knights from the surrounding area to enter contests of fighting skill. Early tournaments were as dangerous as real battles, and captured knights were held for ransom. In time, tournaments acquired more ceremony and ritual.

Castles During the early Middle Ages, powerful lords fortified their homes to withstand attack. Their strongholds included a keep, or wooden tower, ringed by a fence. The keep was separated from the surrounding area by a moat, or water-filled ditch.

The strongholds gradually became larger and grander. By the 1100s, monarchs and nobles owned sprawling stone castles with high walls, towers, and drawbridges over wide moats. Wars often centered on seizing

A Medieval Castle
By the late Middle Ages, some feudal castles had become vast fortresses. This castle at Carcassonne in France, which people still visit today, had a double outer wall to protect it from attack.

Theme: Economics and Technology What do you think was the function of the high turrets, or towers, that surround this castle?

Feudalism

For centuries, feudalism was the way of life in Western Europe. Everyone, from the poorest peasant to the richest king, was touched in some way by feudal relationships. The painting, the chart, and the quotation on this page all provide information about these relationships.

Feudal Society

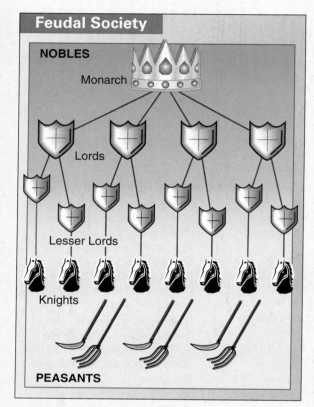

Under the feudal system, everyone had a well-defined place in society. At the head of society was the monarch. Peasants, who made up the bulk of the population, were at the bottom.

A King Grants Land

In exchange for a pledge of loyalty, a king grants a fief of land.

A Vassal Pledges Loyalty

"I John of Toul, make it known that I am the faithful man of the lady Beatrice, Countess of Troyes, and of my most dear lord, Theobald, Count of Champagne, her son, against all persons living or dead, except for my allegiance to lord Enjorand of Coucy, lord John of Arcis and the count of Grandpré. If it should happen that the count of Grandpré should be at war with the countess and count of Champagne on his own quarrel, I will aid the count of Grandpré in my own person and will send to the count and countess of Champagne the knights whose service I owe them for the fief which I hold of them."

—quoted in *Institutions in European History* (Esler)

Skills Tip

In a chart showing hierarchy, the lines show relationships between those of lesser and greater positions.

Skills Assessment

1. According to the chart of feudal society, the person kneeling in the picture is a
   A lord.
   B lesser lord.
   C knight.
   D peasant.

2. In a battle between the Count of Champagne and the Count of Grandpré, John of Toul would
   E remain neutral.
   F fight for Grandpré.
   G fight for Champagne.
   H send knights to each.

3. **Critical Thinking Drawing Conclusions (a)** Lords provided for their vassals. In return, what did a lord gain from his vassals? **(b)** Feudalism was based partly on the assumption that only the powerful could maintain peace and provide protection. What conclusions about life in medieval Europe can you draw from this?

castles that commanded strategic river crossings, harbors, or mountain passes. Castle dwellers stored up food and water so that they could withstand a long siege. If attackers failed to starve the defender into submission, they might try to tunnel under the castle walls.

Noblewomen Noblewomen played active roles in this warrior society. While her husband or father was off fighting, the "lady of the manor" took over his duties. She supervised vassals, managed the household, and performed necessary agricultural and medical tasks. Sometimes she might even have to go to war to defend her estate.

A few medieval noblewomen took a hand in politics. For example, Eleanor of Aquitaine inherited lands in southwestern France. Through two marriages, she became, first, queen of France and, later, queen of England. Eleanor was a leading force in European politics for more than 50 years.

Women's rights to inheritance were severely restricted under the feudal system. Land usually passed to the eldest son in a family. A woman did, however, receive land as part of her dowry, and fierce negotiations swirled around an unmarried or widowed heiress. If her husband died before her, a woman regained rights to her land.

Like their brothers, the daughters of nobles were sent to friends or relatives for training. Before her parents arranged her marriage, a young woman was expected to know how to spin and weave and how to supervise servants. A few learned to read and write. As a wife, she was expected to bear many children and be dutiful to her husband.

Chivalry In the later Middle Ages, knights adopted a code of conduct called chivalry. Chivalry required knights to be brave, loyal, and true to their word. In warfare, they had to fight fairly. A knight, for example, agreed not to attack another knight before the opponent had a chance to put on his armor. Chivalry also dictated that warriors treat a captured knight well or even release him if he promised to pay his ransom. Chivalry had limits, though. It applied to nobles only, not to commoners.

In theory, if not always in practice, chivalry placed women on a pedestal. The code of chivalry called for women to be protected and cherished. Troubadours, or wandering poets, adopted this view. Their love songs praised the perfection, beauty, and wit of women. Much later, ideas of chivalry would shape western ideas of romantic love.

Peasants and Manor Life

The heart of the medieval economy was the manor, or lord's estate. Most manors included one or more villages and the surrounding lands. Peasants, who made up the majority of the population in medieval society, lived and worked on the manor.

Most peasants on a manor were serfs, bound to the land. Serfs were not slaves who could be bought and sold. Still, they were not free. They could not leave the manor without the lord's permission. If the manor was granted to a new lord, the serfs went along with it.

Mutual Obligations Peasants and their lords were tied together by mutual rights and obligations. Peasants had to work several days a week farming the lord's lands. They also repaired his roads, bridges, and fences. Peasants paid the lord a fee when they married, when they inherited their father's acres, or when they used the local mill to grind grain. Other payments fell due at Christmas and Easter. Because money had largely disappeared from medieval Europe, they paid with products such as grain, honey, eggs, or chickens.

In return for a lifetime of labor, peasants had the right to farm several acres for themselves. They were also entitled to their lord's protection from Viking raids or feudal warfare. Although they could not leave the manor

Biography

Eleanor of Aquitaine
1122–1204

Eleanor of Aquitaine married King Louis VII of France when she was 15. Not content just to enjoy her wealth and status, Eleanor joined in the Second Crusade, wearing armor and riding on horseback alongside male crusaders.

Soon afterward, she ended her marriage to Louis. She then wed another king, Henry II of England, with whom she had eight children. Later, Eleanor spurred several of her sons in an attempt to overthrow Henry. The revolt failed, and Eleanor landed in prison, where she spent 15 years. After Henry died, her son Richard (known as "the Lion-Hearted") became king of England. Richard freed his mother, and she later ruled in his place while he went on a crusade to the Holy Land.

Theme: Impact of the Individual Eleanor has been called the "Grandmother of Europe." Why do you think she was given this title?

A View of Peasant Life
This French painting from the late Middle Ages presents an idealized picture of farm life in winter. While a peasant takes cattle to market, his family members warm themselves by the fire in their hut.

Theme: Art and Literature
Illustrations like these were created for nobles. Why do you think they might have idealized peasant life?

freely, they also could not be forced off it. In theory, at least, they were guaranteed food, housing, and land.

A Self-Sufficient World The manor was generally self-sufficient. That is, peasants produced almost everything they needed, from food and clothing to simple furniture and tools. Most peasants never ventured more than a few miles from their village. They had no schooling and no knowledge of a larger world outside.

A typical manor included a few dozen one-room huts clustered close together in a village. Nearby stood a water mill to grind grain, a tiny church, and the manor house. The fields surrounding the village were divided into narrow strips. Each family had strips of land in different fields so that good land and bad land were shared evenly.

Peasant Life For most peasants, life was harsh. Men, women, and children worked long hours, from sunup to sundown. During planting season, a man might guide an ox-drawn plow through the fields while his wife walked alongside, goading the ox into motion with a pointed stick. Children helped plant seeds, weeded, and took care of pigs or sheep.

The peasant family ate a simple diet of black bread with vegetables such as peas, cabbage, turnips, or onions. They seldom had meat unless they poached wild game on their lord's manor, at the risk of harsh punishment. If they lived near a river, a meal might include fish. At night, the family and any cows, chickens, pigs, or sheep slept together in their one-room hut.

Like farmers everywhere, European peasants worked according to the season. In spring and autumn, they plowed and harvested. In summer, they hayed. At other times, they weeded, repaired fences, and performed chores. In late winter, when the harvest was exhausted and new crops had not yet ripened, hunger was common. Disease took a heavy toll, and few peasants lived beyond the age of 35.

Still, peasants found occasions to celebrate, such as marriages and births. Welcome breaks came at Christmas and Easter, when peasants had a week off from work. Dozens of other festivals in the Christian calendar brought days off. At these times, people might butcher an animal so that they could feast on meat. There would also be dancing and rough sports, from wrestling to ball games.

SECTION 2 Assessment

Recall

1. **Define: (a)** feudalism, **(b)** vassal, **(c)** feudal contract, **(d)** fief, **(e)** knight, **(f)** tournament, **(g)** chivalry, **(h)** troubadour, **(i)** manor, **(j)** serf.

Comprehension

2. Describe three features of feudal society.

3. **(a)** What obligations did lords and vassals have under the feudal system? **(b)** How did the code of chivalry affect medieval ideas about women?

4. **(a)** What responsibilities did the peasant have toward the lord of a manor? **(b)** What responsibilities did the lord of the manor have toward the peasants?

Critical Thinking and Writing

5. **Recognizing Causes and Effects** How did the breakdown of central authority in Europe lead to the development of feudalism?

6. **Linking Past and Present** Compare the code of chivalry to ideas about "good sportsmanship" today.

Activity
Take It to the NET

Use the Internet to learn more about the way knights in the early Middle Ages dressed. Make a diagram showing the various items in a knight's armor and add labels to identify them. Display your diagram on a bulletin board.

The Medieval Church

Reading Focus

- How did the Church and its monks and nuns shape medieval life?
- How did the power of the Church grow?
- How did reformers work for change in the Church?
- What problems did Jewish communities face?

Vocabulary

sacrament
tithe
secular
papal supremacy
canon law
excommunication
interdict
simony
friar
antisemitism

Taking Notes

Copy this concept web. As you read, add information about the role of the Church in medieval times. Add as many circles as you need to complete the web.

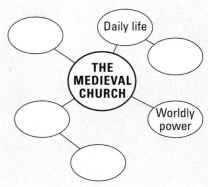

Main Idea — The Church played a vital role in medieval life and in time grew into a secular power as well.

Setting the Scene

Charlemagne waged battle in the name of Christianity. "It is our task," he said, "with the aid of divine goodness, to defend the holy church of Christ everywhere . . . and to strengthen it within through the knowledge of the Catholic faith."

It took centuries for Christian missionaries to spread their faith across Europe. But in time, the medieval Church emerged as the most powerful force in Europe. The Church's teachings and practices shaped the lives of Christian Europeans.

The Church and Medieval Life

During the early Middle Ages, the Church's most important achievement was to Christianize the diverse peoples of Western Europe. In 597, Pope Gregory I sent Augustine to convert the Anglo-Saxons in England. From Britain, later missionaries went back to the continent to spread their faith among Germanic tribes.

Women also spread the faith even at the risk of their own lives. Some women married pagan kings and brought their husbands into the Church. Clothilde, for example, persuaded her husband Clovis, who was king of the Franks, to accept Christianity.

The Parish Priest In manor villages, the priest of the parish, or local region, was usually the only contact people had with the Church. The priest cared for the souls of his parishioners by celebrating the mass and by administering the sacraments, the sacred rites of the Church. Christians believed that faith in Christ and participation in the sacraments would lead them to salvation, or everlasting life with God.

In addition to administering the sacraments, priests preached the Gospels and the teachings of the Church. They guided people on issues regarding values and morality. They offered assistance to the sick and needy.

Christian rituals and faith were part of the fabric of everyday life. Priests married peasants and nobles, baptized their children, and buried the dead in sacred ground.

The Village Church The church was a social center as well as a place of worship. After services, peasants gossiped or danced, although the priest might condemn their rowdy songs or behavior. In the later Middle Ages, some parish priests ran schools.

Primary Source

The Role of the Parish Priest

The English poet Geoffrey Chaucer describes an ideal parish priest:

"Wide was his parish, with houses far asunder,
But he would not be kept by rain or thunder,
If any had suffered a sickness or a blow
From visiting the farthest, high or low,
Plodding his way on foot, his staff in hand,
He was a model his flock could understand,
For first he did and afterward he taught."

—Geoffrey Chaucer,
The Canterbury Tales

Skills Assessment

Primary Source What were some of the duties of this fictional parish priest?

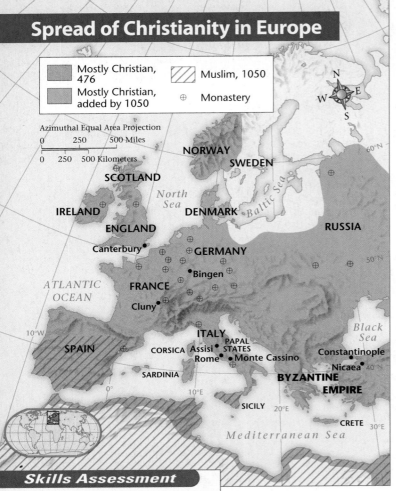

Spread of Christianity in Europe

Mostly Christian, 476

Mostly Christian, added by 1050

Muslim, 1050

⊕ Monastery

Azimuthal Equal Area Projection

0   250   500 Miles

0   250   500 Kilometers

NORWAY

SWEDEN

SCOTLAND

North Sea

IRELAND

DENMARK

Baltic Sea

ENGLAND

RUSSIA

Canterbury

GERMANY

Bingen

ATLANTIC OCEAN

FRANCE

Cluny

Black Sea

SPAIN

ITALY

PAPAL STATES

CORSICA   Assisi

Rome   Monte Cassino

Constantinople

Nicaea

SARDINIA

BYZANTINE EMPIRE

SICILY

CRETE

Mediterranean Sea

Skills Assessment

Geography Missionaries helped spread Christianity throughout medieval Europe.

1. **Location** *On the map, locate (a) Papal States, (b) Rome, (c) Cluny, (d) Bingen, (e) Assisi.*

2. **Region** *(a) Name three areas of Europe that became Christian between 476 and 1050. (b) Which areas of Europe remained under Muslim control?*

3. **Critical Thinking Understanding Sequence** *What device is used on this map to demonstrate a sequence of events? Explain.*

Villages took pride in their church buildings and decorated them with care. In later medieval times, prosperous communities built stone churches rather than wooden ones. Some churches housed relics, or remains of martyrs or other holy figures. Local people, as well as visitors, might make pilgrimages, or journeys, to pray before the relics.

To support itself and its parishes, the Church required Christians to pay a tithe, or tax equal to a tenth of their income. The tithe had its origins in the Bible. Tithing is still common in many Christian churches today.

Daily life revolved around the Christian calendar, which marked "holy days" such as Easter in addition to changes in the seasons. In medieval times, many holidays were added to the calendar to honor saints.

Views of Women The Church taught that men and women were equal before God. But on Earth, women were viewed as "daughters of Eve," weak and easily led into sin. Thus, they needed the guidance of men. At the same time, the Church offered a view of the ideal woman, as modest and pure as Mary, the mother of Jesus. Many churches were dedicated to the "mother of God" and "queen of heaven." Men and women asked Mary to pray to God on their behalf.

The Church tried to protect women. It set a minimum age for marriage. Church courts could fine men who seriously injured their wives. Yet they often punished women more harshly than men for the same offense.

Monks and Nuns

During the early Middle Ages, both women and men withdrew from worldly life to become nuns and monks. Behind the walls of monasteries and convents, they devoted their lives to spiritual goals.

The Benedictine Rule About 530, a monk named Benedict organized the monastery of Monte Cassino in southern Italy. He drew up a set of rules to regulate monastic life. In time, the Benedictine Rule was used by monasteries and convents across Europe.

Under the Benedictine Rule, monks and nuns took three vows. The first was obedience to the abbot or abbess, who headed the monastery or convent. The second was poverty, and the third was chastity, or purity. Each day was divided into periods for worship, work, and study. Benedict believed in the spiritual value of manual labor, so he required monks to work in the fields or at other physical tasks. As part of their labor, monks and nuns cleared and drained land and experimented with crops.

A Life of Service In a world without hospitals or schools, monasteries and convents often provided basic services. Monks and nuns looked after the poor and sick and sometimes set up schools for children. They gave food and lodging to travelers, especially to Christian pilgrims traveling to holy shrines. Some monks and nuns became missionaries. St. Patrick, for example, was a monk who set up the Irish Church. Later, the Church honored many missionaries by declaring them saints.

 **Virtual Field Trip**

www.phschool.com

**Trinity College Library
Dublin, Ireland**

To see other pages from this illuminated manuscript, use the Internet address above to link to the *Book of Kells*, Trinity College, Dublin.

The Book of Kells
As monks and nuns copied books, they illuminated, or illustrated, each page. They decorated the letters and framed the text with intricate designs or scenes. This page is from the *Book of Kells*, illuminated by Irish monks on the island of Iona in the 800s.

Theme: Religions and Value Systems Why do you think copiers wanted to make this book so beautiful?

Centers of Learning Monasteries and convents also performed a vital role in preserving the writings of the ancient world. Often, monks and nuns copied ancient works as a form of labor. Once copied, the work might remain unread for centuries. Still, it would be there when later scholars took an interest in ancient learning.

Educated monks and nuns kept learning alive. In Italy, Abbot Cassiodorus wrote useful summaries of Greek and Latin works and taught the classics to other monks. In Britain, the Venerable Bede wrote the earliest known history of England. Bede introduced the use of B.C. and A.D. to date historical events.

Convents Although women could not become priests, many did enter convents. There, capable, strong-minded women could escape the limits of society. In the 1100s, Abbess Hildegard of Bingen composed religious music and wrote books on many subjects. Because of her mystical visions, popes and rulers sought her advice. She spoke her mind freely. "Take care that the Highest King does not strike you down because of the blindness that prevents you from governing justly," she warned one ruler.

In the later Middle Ages, the Church put more restrictions on nuns. It withdrew rights that nuns had once enjoyed, such as preaching the Gospel, and placed most independent convents under the control of Church officials. It frowned on too much learning for women, preferring them to accept Church authority. Although women's role within the Church was limited, they made valuable contributions to their faith.

The Power of the Church Grows

In the centuries after the fall of Rome, the Church carved out a unique position in Western Europe. It not only controlled the spiritual life of Christians but gradually became the most powerful secular, or worldly, force in medieval Europe.

The Church and Feudal Society During the Middle Ages, the pope was the spiritual leader of the Roman Catholic Church. As representatives of Christ on Earth, medieval popes eventually claimed papal supremacy, or authority over all secular rulers.

You Are There . . .

Seeking Shelter in a Medieval Monastery

You've been walking since dawn, and the sun is now setting. You and another knight are on a long journey. After many days of travel, you look forward to a day of rest at a Benedictine monastery along the way. A monk welcomes you at the gate. You are curious about what life is like in the monastery.

After a simple meal of oatmeal, you spend the night on a straw mattress. A bell wakes you before dawn. The monks begin the day with prayers and household chores. They pray together seven times a day, including once in the middle of the night.

The bell rings again—it is time for study. Many of the monks are copying books. You see one monk spend hours illuminating, or illustrating, just one page.

Another bell sounds, and the monks head for the fields. You watch them hard at work farming. According to St. Benedict, "Idleness is the enemy of the soul!"

In the evening, you share a light supper with the monks. The day ends with the monks praying and singing hymns. The next day's routine will be the same.

Portfolio Assessment

When you get home, you decide to create an illuminated manuscript similar to the ones you saw at the monastery. In it, you include pictures and text detailing the lives and accomplishments of the monks you met.

The pope headed an army of churchmen who supervised Church activities. High clergy, such as bishops and archbishops, were usually nobles. Like other feudal lords, some had their own territories. The pope himself held vast lands in central Italy, later called the Papal States.

Church officials were closely linked to secular rulers. Because churchmen were often the only educated people, feudal rulers appointed them to high government positions.

Religious Authority The medieval Christian Church was dedicated to the worship of God. At the same time, Christians believed that all people were sinners and that many were doomed to eternal suffering. The only way to avoid the tortures of hell was to believe in Christ and participate in the sacraments. Because the medieval Church administered the sacraments, it had absolute power in religious matters.

The medieval Church developed its own body of laws, known as **canon law,** as well as its own courts. Canon law applied to religious teachings, the clergy, marriages, and morals. Anyone who disobeyed Church law faced a range of penalties. The most severe and terrifying was **excommunication.** If excommunicated, people could not receive the sacraments or a Christian burial. A powerful noble who opposed the Church could face the **interdict,** an order excluding an entire town, region, or kingdom from receiving most sacraments and Christian burial. Even the strongest ruler gave in rather than face the interdict.

A Force for Peace The Church tried to use its great authority to end feudal warfare. It declared periods of truce, or temporary peace, known as the Peace of God. It demanded that fighting stop between Friday and Sunday each week and on religious holidays. Such efforts may have contributed to the decline of feudal warfare in the 1100s.

Reform Movements

The very success of the medieval Church brought problems. As its wealth and power grew, discipline weakened. Pious Christians left their wealth and lands to monasteries and convents, leading some monks and nuns to ignore their vows of poverty. Some clergy lived in luxury. Priests could marry, but some spent more time on family matters than on Church duties, and some even treated the priesthood as a family inheritance. Throughout the Middle Ages, voices called for reform in the Church.

Cluniac Reforms One reform movement swept across Western Europe in the early 900s. Abbot Berno of Cluny, a monastery in eastern France, set out to end abuses. First, he revived the Benedictine Rule, which had been allowed to lapse. Then, he declared that he would no longer allow nobles to interfere in monastery affairs. Finally, he filled the monastery at Cluny with men devoted to religious pursuits. In time, many monasteries and convents copied the Cluniac reforms.

In 1073, Pope Gregory VII, a former monk, extended the Cluniac reforms to the entire Church. He outlawed marriage for priests and prohibited **simony,** the selling of Church offices. He then called on Christians to renew their faith. To end secular influence, Gregory insisted that the Church, not kings or nobles, choose Church officials. That policy, as you will read, would spark a bitter battle of wills with the German emperor.

Preaching Orders Over the centuries, other reform movements battled corruption and worldliness. In the early 1200s, Francis of Assisi and Dominic took a new approach. They set up orders of **friars,** monks who did not live in isolated monasteries but traveled around Europe's growing towns preaching to the poor.

Francis left a comfortable home in the Italian town of Assisi to preach the Gospel and teach by example. The Franciscan order he set up preached

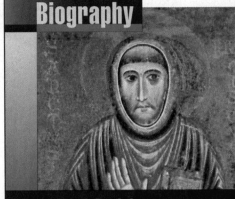

poverty, humility, and love of God. Soon after, Dominic, a Spanish priest, set up the Dominican order. Its chief goal was to combat heresy by teaching official Roman Catholic beliefs.

Women joined this reform movement by creating new religious groups. One such group was the Beguines (BEHG eenz). Most convents accepted only well-born women whose families gave a dowry, or gift, to the Church. The Beguines welcomed women without the wealth to enter a regular convent. Using funds from selling their weavings and embroidery, they helped the poor and set up hospitals and shelters.

Jews in Europe

Jewish communities existed across Europe. In their homes, Jews preserved the oral and written laws that were central to their faith.

Jews flourished in Spain, where they became known as Sephardim, from the Hebrew word for Spain. The Muslims who conquered Spain in 711 were tolerant of both Jews and Christians. Muslim Spain became a center of Jewish culture and scholarship. There, Sephardic Jews served as officials in Muslim royal courts.

During the Middle Ages, Jewish farmers migrated to other parts of Western Europe. Later, they became known as Ashkenazim, or "German" Jews. For centuries, Christians and Jews lived side by side in relative peace. Early German kings gave educated Jews positions at court. Many rulers in northern Europe valued and protected Jewish communities, although they taxed them heavily.

In the late 1000s, Christian persecution of Jews increased. Many Church leaders charged that Jews were responsible for the death of Jesus. As the Church grew in power, it issued orders forbidding Jews to own land or practice most occupations. Yet popes and rulers still turned to educated Jews as financial advisers and physicians.

In bad times, antisemitism, or prejudice against Jews, worsened. Faced with disasters they could not understand, such as illness or famine, many Christians blamed Jews. People also blamed their economic woes on Jews, as many Jews barred from other professions had become moneylenders. In response to growing persecution, thousands of Jews migrated to Eastern Europe. There, rulers welcomed the newcomers' skills and knowledge. Jewish communities thrived in Eastern Europe until modern times.

Preserving a Jewish Tradition
Jewish communities in medieval Europe observed their unique customs. This plate belonged to a Jewish family in Spain. On Passover, it was filled with the traditional foods of the Seder, or Passover meal.

Theme: Diversity In what way is this Seder plate similar to the illuminated manuscript on page 193?

SECTION 3 Assessment

Recall
1. **Identify:** (a) Benedictine Rule, (b) Cluny, (c) Francis of Assisi, (d) Dominicans, (e) Beguines.
2. **Define:** (a) sacrament, (b) tithe, (c) secular, (d) papal supremacy, (e) canon law, (f) excommunication, (g) interdict, (h) simony, (i) friar, (j) antisemitism.

Comprehension
3. (a) Describe three ways in which the Church shaped medieval life. (b) How did monks and nuns help build Christian civilization in Europe?
4. How did the Church increase its secular power?

5. What reforms did Francis and Dominic promote?
6. Why were Jewish communities able to flourish in Spain?

Critical Thinking and Writing
7. **Analyzing Information** (a) What views did the Church put forth about women? (b) Why do you think important leaders were willing to accept the advice of Hildegard of Bingen?
8. **Identifying Main Ideas** Choose one of the main headings from this section. Write a sentence describing the main idea of the material in that subsection.

Activity

Writing a Letter
Write a letter that Benedict might have sent to a neighboring monastery in the 500s. Explain why you have drawn up a set of rules for the monks at Monte Cassino and why you think it would be worthwhile for other monasteries to follow the Benedictine Rule.

Economic Expansion and Change

Reading Focus

- How did new technologies spark an agricultural revolution?
- How did the revival of trade revolutionize commerce?
- How were guilds linked to the rise of towns and cities?

Vocabulary

charter
capital
partnership
bill of exchange
tenant farmer
middle class
usury
guild
apprentice
journeyman

Taking Notes

Create a diagram like the one shown below. As you read the section, fill in the main causes for the economic recovery in Europe. The first one has been partially filled in for you.

New Technology
- Iron plows
- Windmills

ECONOMIC RECOVERY IN EUROPE

Main Idea During the High Middle Ages, Europe's economy grew, cities and towns expanded, and a middle class arose.

Setting the Scene The castle of Count William of Flanders was a bustling place. Hundreds of people lived and worked there, from nobles to servants. Such a large castle had many needs, and people came from near and far to supply them. "There began to throng before the gate near the castle bridge, traders and merchants selling costly goods," wrote one medieval chronicler. After that, other merchants came and built inns where visitors could eat and sleep, "and the houses so increased that there grew up a town."

The appearance of new towns was a symbol of Europe's economic recovery. This revival, which lasted from about 1000 to 1300, is called the High Middle Ages.

An Agricultural Revolution

By 1000, Europe's economic recovery was well underway. It had begun in the countryside, where peasants adapted new farming technologies that made their fields more productive. The result was an agricultural revolution that transformed Europe.

New Technologies By the 800s, peasants were using new iron plows that carved deep into the heavy soil of northern Europe. These plows were a big improvement over the old wooden plows, which had been designed for the light soils of the Mediterranean region. Also, a new kind of harness allowed peasants to use horses rather than oxen to pull the plows. Because faster-moving horses could plow more land in a day than could oxen, peasants were able to enlarge their fields and plant more crops.

A peasant might look up and see another new device, a windmill, turning slowly against the sky. Where there were no fast-moving streams to turn a water mill, the power of the wind had been harnessed to grind the peasants' grain into flour.

Expanding Production Other changes brought still more land into use. Feudal lords who wanted to boost their incomes pushed peasants to clear forests, drain swamps, and reclaim wasteland for farming and grazing.

Peasants also adopted the three-field system. They planted one field with grain, a second with legumes, such as peas and beans, and they left the third fallow, or unplanted. The legumes restored soil fertility while adding variety to the peasant diet. Unlike the old two-field system, the new method left only a third of the land unplanted.

Geography and History

Roadblock

The roads to places like Count William's castle in Flanders bustled with travelers. Among them were peasants, carrying farm products to the marketplace.

In those days, wealthy travelers might ride horses, but the farmers walked. Neither riders nor walkers were comfortable on the road, however, because of the ruts, cracks, and potholes. The roads built by the Romans were still in use but had been poorly maintained. Other minor roads had been added since Roman times, but these were little more than narrow tracks. Worse, peasants would dig up the roads for clay to repair their houses. The story goes that one miller dug a deep hole in the middle of a nearby road. When it rained, the hole filled with water and a traveling glovemaker fell in, drowning both himself and his horse!

Theme: Economics and Technology What conditions or developments might lead to the improvement of medieval roads?

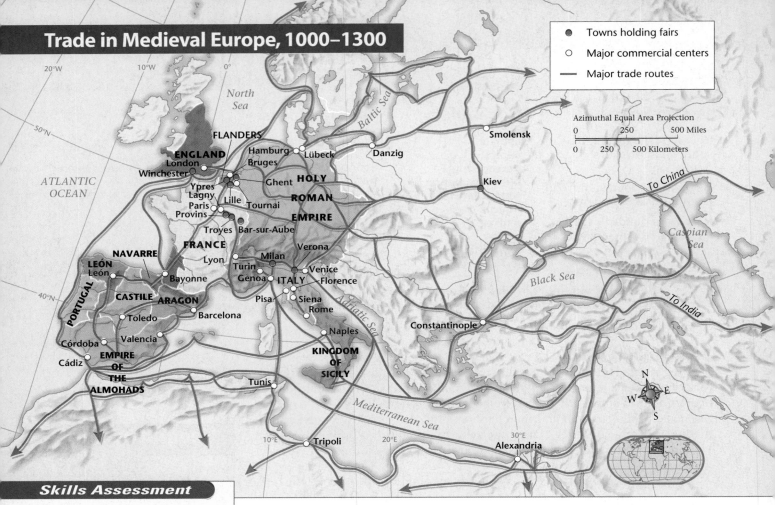

Trade in Medieval Europe, 1000–1300

Legend:
- ● Towns holding fairs
- ○ Major commercial centers
- — Major trade routes

Azimuthal Equal Area Projection
0 250 500 Miles
0 250 500 Kilometers

Skills Assessment

Geography As trade revived in medieval Europe, trade routes multiplied and many towns hosted trade fairs.

1. **Location** On the map, locate **(a)** Constantinople, **(b)** Adriatic Sea, **(c)** Venice, **(d)** Flanders, **(e)** London, **(f)** Baltic Sea.
2. **Region** In which two areas were most of the principal commercial centers located?
3. **Critical Thinking**
   Linking Past and Present
   (a) Identify two medieval towns that held trade fairs.
   (b) What might be today's equivalent of a medieval trade fair? Explain.

All these improvements let farmers produce more food. With more food available, the population grew. Between about 1000 and 1300, the population of Europe doubled.

Trade Revives

Europe's growing population needed goods that were not available on the manor. Peasants needed iron for farm tools. Wealthy nobles wanted fine wool, furs, and spices from Asia. As foreign invasions and feudal warfare declined, traders crisscrossed Europe to meet the growing demand for goods.

New Trade Routes Enterprising traders formed merchant companies that traveled in armed caravans for safety. They followed regular trade routes. Along these routes, merchants exchanged local goods for those from remote markets in the Middle East and further east into Asia.

In Constantinople, merchants bought Chinese silks, Byzantine gold jewelry, and Asian spices. They shipped these goods to Venice on the Adriatic Sea. In Venice, traders loaded their wares onto pack mules and headed north over the Alps and up the Rhine River to Flanders. In Flanders, other traders bought the goods to send on to England and the lands along the Baltic Sea. Northern Europeans paid for the goods with products such as honey, furs, cloth, tin, and lead.

Trade Fairs At first, traders and their customers did business at local trade fairs. These fairs took place each year near navigable rivers or where busy trade routes met.

People from the surrounding villages, towns, and castles flocked to the fairs. Peasants traded farm goods and animals. As they ate and drank, they enjoyed the antics of jugglers, acrobats, or even dancing bears. Still, peasants had no money to buy fine swords, sugar, and silks. The customers for these luxuries were the feudal rulers, nobles, and wealthy churchmen.

New Towns Trade fairs closed in the autumn when the weather made roads impassable. Merchants might wait out the winter months near a castle or in a town with a bishop's palace. These settlements attracted artisans who made goods that the merchants could sell.

Slowly, these small centers of trade and handicraft developed into the first real medieval cities. Some boasted populations of 10,000, and a few topped 100,000. Europe had not seen towns of this size since Roman times. The richest cities grew up in northern Italy and Flanders—the two ends of the profitable north-south trade route. Both areas were centers of the wool trade and had prosperous textile industries.

To protect their interests, the merchants who set up a new town would ask the local lord, or if possible the king himself, for a charter. This written document set out the rights and privileges of the town. In return, merchants paid the lord or the king a large sum of money, a yearly fee, or both.

Although charters varied from place to place, they almost always granted townspeople the right to choose their own leaders and control their own affairs. Most charters also had a clause, popular with runaway serfs, that declared that anyone who lived in the town for a year and a day was free. "Town air makes free," was a common medieval saying.

A Commercial Revolution

As trade revived, money reappeared, which in turn led to more changes. Merchants, for example, needed money to buy goods so they borrowed from moneylenders. In time, their need for capital, or money for investment, spurred the growth of banking houses.

New Business Practices To meet the needs of the changing economy, Europeans developed new ways of doing business. For example, many merchants joined together in an organization known as a partnership. Under this setup, a group of merchants pooled their funds to finance a large-scale venture that would have been too costly for any individual trader. This practice made capital available more easily. It also reduced the risk for any one partner in the venture because no one had to invest all his or her capital in the company.

Merchants also developed a system of insurance to help reduce business risks. For a small fee, an underwriter would insure the merchant's shipment. If the shipment was lost or destroyed, the underwriter paid the merchant most of its value. If the goods arrived safely, the merchant lost only the insurance payment.

Europeans adopted other practices from Middle Eastern merchants. Among the most important was the bill of exchange. A merchant deposited money with a banker in his home city. The banker issued a bill of exchange, which the merchant exchanged for cash in a distant city. A merchant could thus travel without carrying gold coins, which were easily stolen.

Social Changes These new ways of doing business were part of a commercial revolution that transformed the medieval economy. Slowly, they also reshaped medieval society.

For example, the use of money undermined serfdom. Feudal lords needed money to buy fine goods. As a result, many peasants began selling farm products to townspeople and fulfilling their obligations to their lords by paying their rent in cash rather than in labor. By 1300, most peasants in Western Europe were either tenant farmers, who paid rent for their land, or hired farm laborers.

Guild Members at Work
All over Europe, artisans in many fields organized craft guilds. These Italian pictures show medieval artisans weaving tapestries (top) and building cabinets (bottom).

Theme: Economics and Technology How do modern factories differ from these medieval workshops?

In towns, the old social order of nobles, clergy, and peasants gradually changed. By 1000, a new class appeared that included merchants, traders, and artisans. They formed a middle class, standing between nobles and peasants.

Nobles and the clergy despised the new middle class. To nobles, towns were a disruptive influence beyond their control. To the clergy, the profits that merchants and bankers made from usury (YOO zhuh ree), or lending money at interest, were immoral.*

During the Middle Ages, the Church forbade Christians to lend money at interest. As a result, many Jews who were barred from other professions became moneylenders. Although money-lenders played an essential role in the growing medieval economy, the need to pay them back led to much resentment and a rise in antisemitism, as you have read.

Role of Guilds

In medieval towns, merchants and artisans formed associations known as guilds. Merchant guilds appeared first. They dominated town life, passing laws and levying taxes. They also decided whether to spend funds to pave the streets with cobblestones, build protective walls, or raise a new town hall.

In time, artisans came to resent the powerful merchants. They organized craft guilds. Each guild represented workers in one occupation, such as weavers, bakers, brewers, or goldsmiths. In some towns, struggles between craft guilds and the wealthier mer-chant guilds led to riots.

Guild members cooperated to protect their own economic interests. To prevent competition, they limited membership in the guild. No one except guild members could work in any trade. Guilds made rules to protect the quality of their goods, regulate hours of labor, and set prices. Guilds also provided social services. Besides operating schools and hospitals, they looked after the needs of their members. For example, the regulations of a craft guild in the leather-making trade stated:

> "If by chance any of the said trade shall fall into poverty, whether through old age or because he cannot labor or work, and have nothing with which to keep himself, he shall have every week from the said box 7d for his support, if he be a man of good repute."
> —*Ordinances of the White-Tawyers*

Guilds also pledged to provide support for the widows and orphans of their members.

Becoming a Guild Member To become a guild member meant many years of hard work. At the age of seven or eight, a child might become an apprentice, or trainee, to a guild master. The apprentice usually spent seven years learning the trade. The guild master paid no wages, but was required to give the apprentice bed and board.

Few apprentices ever became guild masters unless they were related to one. Most worked for guild members as journeymen, or salaried workers. Journeymen often accused masters of keeping their wages low so that they could not save enough to open a competing shop.

Women and the Guilds Women worked in dozens of crafts. A woman often engaged in the same trade as her father or husband and might inherit his workshop if he died. Because she knew the craft well, she kept the shop

---

*Today, the term *usury* refers to charging excessive interest.

going and sometimes might become a guild master herself. Young girls became apprentices in trades ranging from ribbonmaking to papermaking to surgery.

Women dominated some trades and even had their own guilds. In Paris, they far outnumbered men in the profitable silk and woolen guilds. A third of the guilds in Frankfurt were composed entirely of women.

Town and City Life

Medieval towns and cities were surrounded by high, protective walls. As the city grew, space within the walls filled to overflowing, and newcomers had to settle in the fields outside the walls. To keep up with this constant growth, every few years the city might rebuild its walls farther and farther out.

A typical medieval city was a jumble of narrow streets lined with tall houses. Upper floors hung out over the streets, making those below dim even in daytime. In the largest cities, a great cathedral, where a bishop presided, or a splendid guild hall might tower above humbler residences.

During the day, streets echoed with the cries of hawkers selling their wares and porters grumbling under heavy loads. A wealthy merchant might pass, followed by a procession of servants. At night, the unlit streets were deserted.

Even a rich town had no garbage collection or sewer system. Residents simply flung their wastes into the street. Larger cities might pass laws, such as one requiring butchers to dump their garbage on the edge of town. But towns remained filthy, smelly, noisy, and crowded.

Looking Ahead

By 1300, Western Europe was a different place from what it had been in the early Middle Ages. Although most people had no way of knowing it, slow but momentous changes were sending shock waves through medieval life. Trade, for example, put ideas as well as money into circulation. New riches revised the social structure. In politics, too, new forces were at work.

In the global sphere, the economic revival of the High Middle Ages was bringing Europeans into contact with civilizations much more advanced than their own. From these lands to the east came products, ideas, and technologies that would spark an even greater transformation in how Europeans thought and lived.

Primary Source

City Fun and Games
A Londoner describes some of the sports and pastimes enjoyed by young city dwellers in the 1100s:

"In the holidays, all the summer the youths are exercised in leaping, dancing, shooting, wrestling, casting the stone, and practicing their shields. The maidens . . . dance as long as they can well see. . . .

When the great [swamp] which watereth the walls of the city on the north side, is frozen, many young men play upon the ice . . . some tie bones to their feet and under their heels; and shoving themselves by a little picked staff, do slide as swift as a bird flieth in the air."

—William Fitz-Stephen, quoted in *Source-Book of English History* (Kendall)

Skills Assessment

Primary Source How are the sports described above similar to those enjoyed by young people today? How are they different?

SECTION 4 Assessment

Recall

1. **Identify:** High Middle Ages.
2. **Define: (a)** charter, **(b)** capital, **(c)** partnership, **(d)** bill of exchange, **(e)** tenant farmer, **(f)** middle class, **(g)** usury, **(h)** guild, **(i)** apprentice, **(j)** journeyman.

Comprehension

3. What were two effects of the agricultural revolution that took place during the Middle Ages?
4. What new ways of doing business evolved in the Middle Ages?

5. **(a)** How did a merchant guild differ from a craft guild? **(b)** How did guilds improve life for townspeople?

Critical Thinking and Writing

6. **Synthesizing Information** Give three pieces of evidence to support the idea that the High Middle Ages were a time of economic growth.
7. **Comparing** Compare economic life in the early Middle Ages to economic life in the High Middle Ages.

Activity

Creating an Advertisement Imagine that a growing medieval city has hired you to attract people to move there. Create an ad that describes opportunities the city provides for merchants, artisans, and peasants.

Creating a Chapter Summary

On a sheet of paper start a table like the one shown here. Add important facts under each heading to help you review the events you have learned about in this chapter. Part of the table has been filled in to help you get started.

For additional review and enrichment activities, see the interactive version of *World History* available on the Web and on CD-ROM.

EARLY MIDDLE AGES	HIGH MIDDLE AGES
Feudal society	Rise of middle class
Life centered on manors	Cities develop

Web Site Self-Test
For practice test questions for Chapter 8, see **www.phschool.com.**

Building Vocabulary

Write sentences using the chapter vocabulary words listed below, leaving blanks where the vocabulary words would go. Exchange your sentences with another student and fill in the blanks in each other's sentences.

1. **medieval**
2. **feudalism**
3. **vassal**
4. **fief**
5. **tithe**
6. **secular**
7. **interdict**
8. **charter**
9. **guild**
10. **journeyman**

Recalling Key Facts

11. How did the culture of the Germanic tribes differ from that of the Romans?
12. What happened to Charlemagne's empire after his death?
13. Why was the pope a powerful figure in medieval Europe?
14. What role did monasteries and convents play in the preservation of ancient culture?
15. What social changes were caused by the commercial revolution of the Middle Ages?
16. Describe the typical medieval city.

Critical Thinking and Writing

17. **Connecting to Geography** Compare life on a medieval manor with life on an American farm today. Which do you think would be more self-sufficient? Why?
18. **Predicting Consequences** How do you think the weakening of the feudal system affected the Church? Explain your answer.
19. **Recognizing Causes and Effects** As you have read, antisemitism increased during economic bad times. Why do you think this was so?
20. **Understanding Sequences** Arrange the following developments in the order in which they occurred: new technologies, growth of towns, agricultural revolution, population growth, revival of trade. Then, explain why they occurred in that order.
21. **Making Decisions** If you had been a European peasant during the High Middle Ages, do you think you would have chosen to stay in the countryside or move to a town? Give reasons to support your decision.

Einhard, a medieval monk at the court of Charlemagne, wrote a life of the king. In this letter, quoted by Einhard, Charlemagne instructs one of his lords, Abbot Fulrad, about what to bring to a meeting of nobles. Read the passage and answer the questions that follow.

> "[Arrive] so prepared with your men that you may be able to go thence well equipped in any direction which our command shall order, that is with arms and accoutrements [equipment] and other provisions for war in the way of food and clothing. Each horseman is expected to have a shield, lance, sword, dagger, bow, quiver with arrows, and in your cart shall be . . . axes, planes, augers, boards, spades, iron shovels and other utensils which are necessary in any army. In the wagons shall be supplies for three months, together with arms and clothing for six months."

—Einhard, *Life of Charlemagne*

22. What is each horseman expected to bring to the meeting?
23. Why do you think Charlemagne wants the men prepared in the way that he describes?
24. How long might these men be engaged in the king's service?
25. **(a)** Based on what you have learned about feudalism, what does the lord abbot owe Charlemagne? **(b)** What do the lord's men owe the lord?
26. Fulrad was both an abbot and a lord. What does this fact suggest about the role of the Church at this time?

Use the Internet to research daily life in early medieval Europe. Then, write a diary entry from the point of view of a medieval European. You might choose to take the role of a lord, noblewoman, knight, monk, nun, serf, or town merchant. Include information about how your status in medieval society affects your tasks, beliefs, and expectations of life.

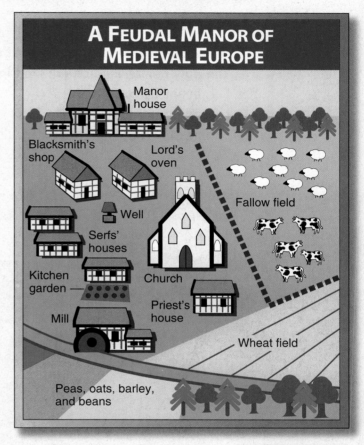

A FEUDAL MANOR OF MEDIEVAL EUROPE

Manor house
Blacksmith's shop
Lord's oven
Well
Fallow field
Serfs' houses
Kitchen garden
Church
Priest's house
Mill
Wheat field
Peas, oats, barley, and beans

The diagram above represents a medieval manor. Study the diagram and answer the following questions:

27. **(a)** What kinds of buildings does the diagram show? **(b)** How many fields are shown?
28. Describe the purpose of: **(a)** the kitchen garden, **(b)** the blacksmith's shop, **(c)** the lord's oven, **(d)** the mill.
29. How does the diagram show that religion played an important role in manor life?
30. Does this diagram represent a manor before or after the agricultural revolution of the High Middle Ages? How can you tell?
31. How does the diagram support the statement that the medieval manor was self-sufficient?
32. Do you think this diagram represents an actual manor? Give reasons for your answer.

Skills Tip

Some diagrams represent an actual place or object, such as the blueprint of a house. Others give a more general picture of a typical place or object.

CHAPTER 9

The High Middle Ages
1050–1450

Chapter Preview

1 Growth of Royal Power in England and France
2 The Holy Roman Empire and the Church
3 Europeans Look Outward
4 Learning, Literature, and the Arts
5 A Time of Crisis

1215
King John, shown above, signs the Magna Carta limiting royal power in England.

1096
Christians launch the First Crusade. The siege of Antioch is shown above.

CHAPTER EVENTS

1000   1100   1200

GLOBAL EVENTS

1000s Kilwa, Sofala, and other East African port cities thrive on trade.

1192 Minamoto Yoritomo establishes the Kamakura shogunate in Japan.

Europe About 1300

By the 1300s, monarchs in Western Europe were increasing their power and building strong united kingdoms.

Boundary of the Holy Roman Empire

NORWAY
SWEDEN
NOVGOROD
SCOTLAND
North Sea
DENMARK
Baltic Sea
ORDER
LITHUANIA
IRELAND
TEUTONIC
ENGLAND
BRANDENBURG
POLAND
RUSSIAN PRINCIPALITIES
GOLDEN HORDE
LUXEMBOURG
BRANDENBURG (SMALL STATES)
BOHEMIA (Lux.)
PALATINATE (Brandenburg)
MORAVIA (Lux.)
FRANCE
BAVARIA (Brandenburg)
HAPSBURG STATES (Austria)
AUSTRIA
HUNGARY
GASCONY (Eng.)
ALPS
Black Sea
GEORGIA
NAVARRE
PYRENEES MTS.
VENETIAN REP.
REP. OF GENOA
PAPAL STATES
TREBIZOND
PORTUGAL
CASTILE
ARAGON
SARDINIA (Aragon)
SERBIA
BULGARIA
BYZANTINE EMPIRE
OSMAN
ILKHAN EMPIRE
MALLORCA
NAPLES
SELJUK STATES
GRANADA
SICILY (Aragon)
ACHAIA
ATHENS
VENETIAN REPUBLIC
CYPRUS
ATLANTIC OCEAN
Mediterranean Sea
MARINID CALIPHATE
ZAYYANID CALIPHATE
HAFSID CALIPHATE
MAMLUKE SULTANATE

Azimuthal Equal Area Projection
0   250   500 Miles
0   250   500 Kilometers

1347
Black Death breaks out in Italy.

1429
After leading French troops to victory over the English, Joan of Arc marches triumphantly into Orléans.

1492
Spanish complete the Reconquista.

1300   1400   1500

1368 Ming dynasty is established in China.

1453 Ottoman Turks capture Constantinople.

Growth of Royal Power in England and France

Reading Focus

- How did monarchs gain power over nobles and the Church?
- What traditions of government developed under John and later English monarchs?
- How did strong monarchs succeed in unifying France?

Vocabulary

exchequer
common law
jury

Taking Notes

Copy this incomplete Venn diagram. As you read, write key facts about royal power in England and France in the appropriate sections. Write common characteristics in the overlapping section.

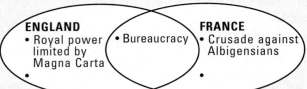

ENGLAND
- Royal power limited by Magna Carta
-

Bureaucracy

FRANCE
- Crusade against Albigensians
-

Main Idea — In England and France, monarchs expanded royal authority and laid the foundations for united nation-states.

Biography

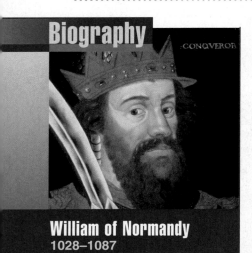

William of Normandy
1028–1087

From the time he became Duke of Normandy at age seven, William's life and position were in constant danger, mostly from jealous relatives. Four of his guardians were murdered—one in the very room in which William lay sleeping.

As an adult, William did all that he could to get and keep power. At age 20, he led an army to defeat a rebellious cousin. When an abbot condemned his marriage to Matilda of Flanders because they were too closely related, an enraged William burned down a monastery. But when the pope validated the marriage, William had a new abbey built.

Theme: Impact of the Individual How did William's experience as duke prepare him to be king of England?

Setting the Scene A monarch could not always count on the loyalty of powerful nobles and Church officials. A medieval chronicle tells of the difficulties faced by one English king in the 1100s:

> "King Stephen . . . seized . . . Alexander, bishop of Lincoln, and Roger, the chancellor, his nephew, and he kept them all in prison. . . . They had done homage to him, and sworn oaths, but they . . . broke their allegiance, for every rich man built his castles, and defended them against him."
> —Anglo-Saxon Chronicle

During the Middle Ages, monarchs struggled to exert royal authority over nobles and churchmen. Bit by bit over many centuries, they built the framework for what would become the European nation-states of today.

Monarchs, Nobles, and the Church

Feudal monarchs in Europe stood at the head of society, but had limited power. While they ruled their own domains, they relied on vassals for military support. Nobles and the Church had as much—or more—power as the monarch. Both nobles and the Church had their own courts, collected their own taxes, and fielded their own armies. They jealously guarded their rights and privileges against any effort by rulers to increase royal authority.

Monarchs used various means to centralize power. They expanded the royal domain and set up a system of royal justice that undermined feudal or Church courts. They organized a government bureaucracy, developed a system of taxes, and built a standing army. Monarchs strengthened ties with the middle class. Townspeople, in turn, supported royal rulers, who could impose the peace and unity that were needed for trade.

Strong Monarchs in England

During the early Middle Ages, Angles, Saxons, and Vikings invaded and settled in England. Although feudalism developed, English rulers generally kept their kingdoms united.

In 1066, the Anglo-Saxon king Edward died without an heir. A council of nobles chose Edward's brother-in-law Harold to rule. But Duke William of Normandy, a tough, ruthless descendant of the Vikings, also claimed the English throne. The answer to the rival claims lay on the battlefield.

Norman Conquest Duke William raised an army and won the backing of the pope. He then sailed across the English Channel. At the Battle of Hastings, William and his Norman knights triumphed over Harold. On Christmas Day 1066, William the Conqueror, as he was now called, assumed the crown of England.

Although William's French-speaking nobles dominated England, the country's Anglo-Saxon population survived. Over the next 300 years, a gradual blending occurred of Norman French and Anglo-Saxon customs, languages, and traditions.

Growth of Royal Power William exerted firm control over his new lands. Like other feudal monarchs, he granted fiefs to the Church and his Norman lords, or barons, but he kept a large amount of land for himself. He monitored who built castles and where. He required every vassal to swear first allegiance to him rather than to any other feudal lord.

To learn about his kingdom, William had a complete census taken in 1086. The result was the *Domesday Book* (pronounced "doomsday"), which listed every castle, field, and pigpen in England. As the title suggests, the survey was as thorough and inevitable as doomsday, believed to be God's final day of judgment that no one could escape. Information in the *Domesday Book* helped William and later English monarchs build an efficient system of tax collecting.

William's successors continued to increase royal authority. In the area of finance, they created the royal exchequer, or treasury, to collect taxes. Into the exchequer flowed fees, fines, and other dues.

A Unified Legal System In 1154, an energetic, well-educated king, Henry II, inherited the throne. He broadened the system of royal justice. As a ruler, he could not simply write new laws but had to follow accepted customs. Henry found ways to expand customs into law. He then sent out traveling justices to enforce royal laws. The decisions of the royal courts became the foundation of English common law, a legal system based on custom and court rulings. Unlike local feudal laws, common law applied to all of England. In time, people chose royal courts over those of nobles or the Church. Because royal courts charged fees, the exchequer benefited from the growth of royal justice.

Under Henry II, England also developed an early jury system. When traveling justices visited an area, local officials collected a jury, or group of men sworn to speak the truth. (The word *jury* is derived from the French *juré*, meaning "sworn on oath.") These early juries determined which cases should be brought to trial and were the ancestors of today's grand jury. Later, another jury evolved that was composed of 12 neighbors of an accused. It was the ancestor of today's trial jury.

Conflict With the Church Henry's efforts to extend royal power led to a bitter dispute with the Church. Henry claimed the right to try clergy in royal courts. Thomas Becket, the archbishop of Canterbury and once a close friend of Henry's, fiercely opposed the king's move. The conflict simmered for years.

At last, Henry's fury exploded. "What a pack of fools and cowards I have nourished," he cried, "that not one of them will avenge me of this turbulent priest." Four hotheaded knights took Henry at his word. In 1170, they murdered the archbishop in his own cathedral. Henry denied any part in the attack. Still, to make peace with the Church,

FACT FINDER

Evolution of English Government

1066	**Norman Conquest** William of Normandy defeats Anglo-Saxons at Hastings.
1086	***Domesday Book*** William I uses this survey as a basis for taxation.
1160s–1180s	**Common Law** Henry II lays foundation for English legal system.
1215	**Magna Carta** John signs this document limiting royal power and extending rights.
1295	**Model Parliament** Edward I summons Parliament, which includes representatives of common people.

Skills Assessment

Chart Traditions of English government and law evolved during the Middle Ages. **How did the *Domesday Book* benefit William I? How did the Magna Carta affect English government?**

he eased his attempts to regulate the clergy. Becket, meantime, was honored as a martyr and declared a saint. Pilgrims flocked to his tomb at Canterbury, where miracles were said to happen.

Evolving Traditions of English Government

Later English rulers repeatedly clashed with nobles and the Church. Most battles developed as a result of efforts by the monarch to raise taxes or to impose royal authority over traditional feudal rights. Out of those struggles evolved traditions of government that would influence the modern world.

John's Troubles Henry's son John was a clever, greedy, cruel, and untrustworthy ruler. During his reign, he faced three powerful enemies: King Philip II of France, Pope Innocent III, and his own English nobles. He lost his struggles with each.

Ever since William the Conqueror, Norman rulers of England had held vast lands in France. In 1205, John suffered a major setback when he lost a war with Philip II and had to give up English-held lands in Anjou and Normandy.

Next, John battled with Innocent III over selecting a new archbishop of Canterbury. When John rejected the pope's nominee, the pope responded by excommunicating him. He also placed England under the interdict—as you recall, a papal order that forbade Church services in an entire kingdom. Even the strongest ruler was likely to give in to that pressure. To save himself and his crown, John had to accept England as a fief of the papacy and pay a yearly fee to Rome.

The Magna Carta Finally, John angered his own nobles with oppressive taxes and other abuses of power. In 1215, a group of rebellious barons cornered John and forced him to sign the Magna Carta, or great charter. In this document, the king affirmed a long list of feudal rights.

Besides protecting their own privileges, the barons included a few clauses recognizing the legal rights of townspeople and the Church. Among the most significant of these was a clause protecting every freeman from arbitrary arrest, imprisonment, and other legal actions, except "by legal judgment of his peers or by the law of the land." This famous clause formed the basis of the right now known as "due process of law."

The king also agreed not to raise new taxes without first consulting his Great Council of lords and clergy. Many centuries later, American colonists would claim that those words meant that any taxation without representation was unjust. In 1215, though, neither the king nor his lords could have imagined such an idea.

The Magna Carta contained two very important ideas that in the long run would shape government traditions in England. First, it asserted that the nobles had certain rights. Over time, the rights that had been granted to nobles were extended to all English citizens. Second, the Magna Carta made it clear that the monarch must obey the law.

Development of Parliament In keeping with the Magna Carta, English rulers often called on the Great Council for advice. During the 1200s, this body evolved into Parliament. Its name comes from the French word *parler*, meaning "to talk." As Parliament acquired a larger role in government, it helped unify England.

In 1295, Edward I summoned Parliament to approve money for his wars in France. "What touches all," he declared, "should be approved by all." He had representatives of the "common people" join with the lords and clergy. The

Edward I and Parliament
In this scene, King Edward I presides over what was later called the Model Parliament. On both sides of him are his vassals, the rulers of Scotland and Wales. Clergy sit on the left, and lords sit on the right.

Theme: Political and Social Systems What other social class was represented in the Model Parliament?

Magna Carta

King John of England was forced to sign the Magna Carta, which means "Great Charter," in 1215. Ideas from the Magna Carta still influence the systems of government in many countries around the world. Below are excerpts from 5 of the 63 articles of this important document.

A group of nobles forced King John to sign the Magna Carta at Runnymede.

1. We also have granted to all the freemen of our kingdom, for us and for our heirs forever, all the underwritten liberties, to be had and holden by them and their heirs, of us and our heirs forever. . . .

12. No scutage [tax] or aid shall be imposed in our kingdom, unless by the general council of our kingdom; except for ransoming our person, making our eldest son a knight and once for marrying our eldest daughter; and for these there shall be paid no more than a reasonable aid.

14. And for holding the general council of the kingdom concerning the assessment of aids, except in the three cases aforesaid, and for assessing of scutage, we shall cause to be summoned the archbishops, bishops, abbots, earls, and greater barons of the realm, singly by our letters. And furthermore, we shall cause to be summoned generally, by our sheriffs and bailiffs all others who hold of us in chief, for a certain day, that is to say, forty days before the meeting at least, and to a certain place. And in all letters of such summons we will declare the cause of such summons. And summons being thus made, the business shall proceed on the day appointed, according to the advice of such as shall be present, although all that were summoned come not.

39. No freeman shall be taken or imprisoned, or diseised [deprived], or outlawed, or banished, or in any way destroyed . . . unless by the lawful judgment of his peers, or by the law of the land.

40. We will sell to no man, we will not deny to any man, either justice or right.

—Magna Carta

Skills Tip

Very old documents often contain unfamiliar words. Sometimes they are explained in brackets. Others, however, require the reader to consult a dictionary. This helps the reader both to understand the words themselves and to understand the full meaning of the document.

Skills Assessment

1. In Article 1, who is granted the rights described elsewhere in the Magna Carta?
   A only the king and his heirs
   B only the general council
   C all freemen and their heirs
   D only nobles assembled at the signing

2. Approval by the general council was not required for any tax that would
   E fund the building of roadways.
   F pay for schools.
   G support the general council.
   H ransom the king.

3. **Critical Thinking** **Making Inferences** (a) What do Articles 14 and 40 suggest about royal abuse of power during this period of English history? (b) Think about the membership of the general council, as described in Article 14. Who is *not* included? What can you infer from this?

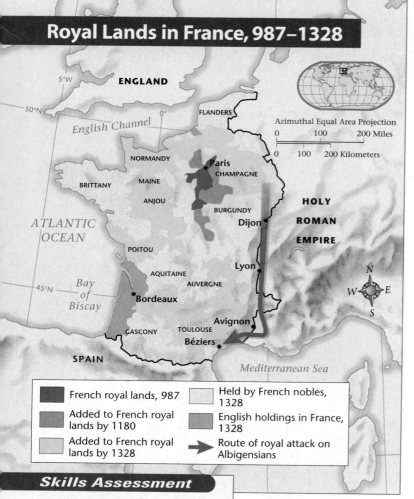

Royal Lands in France, 987–1328

ENGLAND

English Channel

FLANDERS

NORMANDY

Paris
CHAMPAGNE

BRITTANY

MAINE

ANJOU

BURGUNDY

HOLY

BURGUNDY
Dijon

ROMAN

ATLANTIC OCEAN

EMPIRE

POITOU

Lyon

AQUITAINE

AUVERGNE

Bay of Biscay

Bordeaux

Avignon

GASCONY

TOULOUSE

Béziers

SPAIN

Mediterranean Sea

Azimuthal Equal Area Projection
0   100   200 Miles
0   100   200 Kilometers

Legend:
- French royal lands, 987
- Added to French royal lands by 1180
- Added to French royal lands by 1328
- Held by French nobles, 1328
- English holdings in France, 1328
- Route of royal attack on Albigensians

Skills Assessment

Geography From a small area around the city of Paris, Capetian monarchs gradually extended royal control over almost all of France.

1. **Location** On the map, locate (a) Paris, (b) Normandy, (c) Avignon.
2. **Place** What territories were held by the English in 1328?
3. **Critical Thinking Identifying Main Ideas** What main idea does the map show about royal lands in France between 987 and 1328?

"commons" included two knights from each county and representatives of the towns.

Much later, this assembly became known as the Model Parliament because it set up the framework for England's legislature. In time, Parliament developed into a two-house body: the House of Lords with nobles and high clergy and the House of Commons with knights and middle-class citizens.

Looking Ahead Like King Edward I, later English monarchs summoned Parliament for their own purposes. Over the centuries, though, Parliament gained the crucial "power of the purse." That is, it won the right to approve any new taxes. With that power, Parliament could insist that the monarch meet its demands before voting for taxes. In this way, it could check, or limit, the power of the monarch.

Successful Monarchs in France

Unlike William the Conqueror in England, monarchs in France did not rule over a unified kingdom. The successors to Charlemagne had little power over a patchwork of French territories ruled by great feudal nobles.

The Capetians In 987, these feudal nobles elected Hugh Capet, the count of Paris, to fill the vacant throne. They probably chose him because he was too weak to pose a threat to them. Hugh's own lands around Paris were smaller than those of many of his vassals.

Hugh and his heirs slowly increased royal power. First, they made the throne hereditary, passing it from father to son. Fortunately, the Capetians enjoyed an unbroken succession for 300 years. Next, they added to their lands by playing rival nobles against each other. They also won the support of the Church.

Perhaps most important, the Capetians built an effective bureaucracy. Government officials collected taxes and imposed royal law over the king's domain. By establishing order, they added to their prestige and gained the backing of the new middle class of townspeople.

Philip Augustus An outstanding French king of this period was Philip II, often called Philip Augustus. A bald, red-faced man who ate and drank too much, Philip was a shrewd and able ruler. He strengthened royal government in many ways. Instead of appointing nobles to fill government positions, he used paid middle-class officials who would owe their loyalty to him. He granted charters to many new towns, organized a standing army, and introduced a new national tax.

Philip also quadrupled royal land holdings. Through trickery, diplomacy, and war, he brought English-ruled lands in Normandy, Anjou, and elsewhere under his control. He then began to take over southern France. Informed by the pope that the Albigensian (al buh JEHN see uhn) heresy had sprung up in the south, he sent his knights to suppress it and add this vast area to his domain. Before his death in 1223, Philip had become the most powerful ruler in Europe.

Louis IX, King and Saint Perhaps the most admired French ruler of this time was Louis IX. Louis, who ascended to the throne in 1226, embodied the ideal of the perfect medieval monarch—generous, noble, and devoted to justice and chivalry. Within 30 years of his death, he was declared a saint. A knight at Louis's court praised the king's charity:

> "The king daily gave countless generous alms, to poor religious, to poor hospitals, to poor sick people, to other poor convents, to poor gentlemen and gentlewomen and girls . . . and to poor minstrels who from old age or sickness were unable to work."
>
> —John of Joinville, *The Life of St. Louis*

Saint Louis was a deeply religious man, and he pursued religious goals that were acceptable to Christians in his day. He persecuted heretics and Jews and led thousands of French knights in two wars against Muslims.

Louis did much to improve royal government. Like Charlemagne, he sent out roving officials to check on local officials. He expanded the royal courts, outlawed private wars, and ended serfdom in his lands. To ensure justice, he even heard cases himself under a tree in the royal park of Vincennes. His enormous personal prestige helped create a strong national feeling among his subjects. By the time of his death in 1270, France was an efficient centralized monarchy.

Philip IV Clashes With the Pope Louis's grandson, Philip IV, ruthlessly extended royal power. To raise cash, he tried to collect new taxes from the clergy. These efforts led to a clash with Pope Boniface VIII.

Declaring that "God has set popes over kings and kingdoms," Pope Boniface VIII forbade Philip to tax the clergy without papal consent. Philip countered by threatening to arrest any clergy who did not pay up. As their quarrel escalated, Philip sent troops to seize Boniface. The pope escaped, but he was badly beaten and died soon afterward.

Shortly after, a Frenchman was elected pope. He moved the papal court to Avignon (ah veen YOHN) on the border of southern France, ensuring that future French rulers would control religion within their own kingdoms.

The Estates General During this struggle with the pope, Philip rallied French support by setting up the Estates General in 1302. This body had representatives from all three estates, or classes: clergy, nobles, and towns-people. Although later French kings consulted the Estates General, it did not develop the same role that the English Parliament did. It never gained the power of the purse or otherwise served as a balance to royal power.

SECTION 1 Assessment

Recall
1. **Identify: (a)** *Domesday Book,* **(b)** Henry II, **(c)** Thomas Becket, **(d)** Parliament, **(e)** Louis IX, **(f)** Philip IV, **(g)** Estates General.
2. **Define: (a)** exchequer, **(b)** common law, **(c)** jury.

Comprehension
3. **(a)** How were nobles and the Church obstacles for monarchs who wanted more power? **(b)** How did William increase royal power in England?
4. What principles were established by the Magna Carta?
5. How did the Capetians increase royal power in France?

Critical Thinking and Writing
6. **Analyzing Information (a)** Based on the map in this section, identify three groups of people who stood in the way of expanding royal power in France. **(b)** Which of the three do you think was the most difficult challenge for French kings? Explain.
7. **Linking Past and Present** How is the jury system important to us today?

The Holy Roman Empire and the Church

Reading Focus

- Why did Holy Roman emperors fail to build a unified state in Germany?
- How did power struggles and rivalry in Italy affect popes and emperors?
- What powers did the Church have at its height?

Vocabulary

lay investiture

annul

crusade

Taking Notes

As you read, complete this table listing the actions of Holy Roman emperors and popes. Add as many rows as needed to finish the table.

POPE OR EMPEROR	ACTIONS	EFFECTS
OTTO I	• Cooperated with Church • Helped pope defeat Roman nobles	• Pope crowned Otto emperor •
GREGORY VII		
HENRY IV		

Main Idea With secular and religious rulers advancing rival claims to power, explosive conflicts erupted between monarchs and popes.

Setting the Scene The Church, you will recall, spread its influence across Europe during the early Middle Ages. By the High Middle Ages, both popes and monarchs were extending their authority. In the early 1200s, Pope Innocent III claimed broad powers:

> "Just as the moon gets her light from the sun, and is inferior to the sun in quality, quantity, position, and effect, so the royal power gets the splendor of its dignity from the papal authority."
>
> —Letter of Innocent III to Nobles of Tuscany, 1198

With secular rulers advancing their own claims to power, explosive conflicts erupted between monarchs and Church officials. The longest and most destructive struggle pitted popes against Holy Roman emperors who ruled vast lands from Germany to Italy.

The Holy Roman Empire

In the early Middle Ages, as you have learned, the emperor Charlemagne had brought much of present-day France and Germany under his rule. After Charlemagne's death, his empire dissolved into a number of separate states. In time, the dukes of Saxony extended their power over neighboring German lands. In 936, Duke Otto I of Saxony took the title King of Germany.

Like Charlemagne, Otto I worked closely with the Church. He appointed bishops to top government jobs. He also took an army into Italy to help the pope defeat rebellious Roman nobles. In 962, a grateful pope crowned Otto emperor. Later, Otto's successors took the title Holy Roman emperor—"holy" because they were crowned by the pope, "Roman" because they saw themselves as heirs to the emperors of ancient Rome.

German emperors claimed authority over much of central and eastern Europe as well as parts of France and Italy. In fact, the real rulers of these lands were the emperor's vassals—hundreds of nobles and Church officials. For German emperors, the challenge was to control their vassals. In the end, as you will see, it was a challenge they never met.

Another problem for the emperors was conflict with the popes over the appointment of Church officials. Like other monarchs, the Holy Roman emperors often decided who would become bishops and abbots within their realm. As the Cluny reforms strengthened the Church, popes tried to end such outside interference from secular rulers.

Imperial Crown
Holy Roman emperors first wore this crown around the 900s. Some, however, claimed that Charlemagne had worn it almost two centuries earlier.

Theme: Continuity and Change Why do you think emperors wanted people to believe that Charlemagne had worn the crown?

Conflict Between Popes and Emperors

Under the reforming pope Gregory VII, the conflict between emperors and the Church burst into flames. Gregory was one of the greatest medieval popes. He was also among the most controversial.

Pope Gregory VII Few Europeans of the time had a neutral view of Pope Gregory VII. Many admired and revered him. Among his enemies, however, he probably aroused more hatred and contempt than did any other pope of this time period.

Gregory was determined to make the Church independent of secular rulers. To do so, he banned the practice of **lay investiture.** Under this practice, the emperor or another lay person (a person who is not a member of the clergy) "invested," or presented, bishops with the ring and staff that symbolized their office. Only the pope, said Gregory, had the right to appoint and install bishops in office.

Emperor Henry IV Pope Gregory's ban brought an angry response from the Holy Roman emperor Henry IV. He argued that bishops held their lands as royal fiefs. Since he was their overlord, Henry felt entitled to give them the symbols of office. The feud heated up as the two men exchanged insulting notes. Meanwhile, rebellious German princes saw a chance to undermine Henry by supporting the pope.

The Struggle Intensifies In 1076, Gregory excommunicated Henry, freeing his subjects from their allegiance to the emperor. The pope then headed north to crown a new emperor. Faced with revolts at home, Henry was forced to make peace with the pope. In January 1077, Henry crossed the icy Alps to Canossa. There, "with bare feet and clad only in a wretched woolen garment," he presented himself to the pope as a repentant sinner.

Gregory knew that Henry was just trying to save his throne. Still, as a priest, Gregory had no choice but to forgive a confessed sinner. He lifted the order of excommunication, and Henry quickly returned to Germany to subdue his rebellious nobles. In later years, he took revenge on Gregory when he led an army to Rome and forced the pope into exile.

Concordat of Worms The struggle over investiture dragged on for almost 50 years. Finally, in 1122, both sides accepted a treaty known as the Concordat of Worms (VOHRMS). In it, they agreed that the Church had the sole power to elect and invest bishops with spiritual authority. The emperor, however, had the right to invest them with fiefs.

The Struggle for Italy

Although the investiture struggle was over, new battles were soon raging between popes and emperors. During the 1100s and 1200s, ambitious German emperors sought to master Italy. As they did so, they came into conflict with popes and with the wealthy towns of northern Italy.

Frederick Barbarossa The emperor Frederick I, called Barbarossa, or "Red Beard," dreamed of building an empire from the Baltic to the Adriatic. For years, he fought to bring the wealthy cities of northern Italy under his control. With equal energy, they resisted. By joining forces with the pope in the Lombard League, they managed to defeat Barbarossa's armies.

Barbarossa did succeed, however, in arranging a marriage between his son Henry and Constance, heiress to Sicily and southern Italy. That move entangled German emperors even more deeply in Italian affairs.

Frederick II The child of Henry and Constance, Frederick II, was raised in southern Italy. He was an able, arrogant leader, willing to use any means to achieve his ends.

Primary Source

A Pope Deposes a King
On February 22, 1076, Pope Gregory VII issued this decree against Henry IV:

"O St. Peter, chief of the apostles . . . I withdraw, through thy power and authority, from Henry the king, . . . who has risen against thy church with unheard of insolence, the rule over the whole kingdom of the Germans and over Italy. And I absolve all Christians from the bonds of the oath which they have made . . . to him; and I forbid anyone to serve him as king. For it is fitting that he who strives to lessen the honour of thy church should himself lose the honour which belongs to him. And since he has scorned to obey . . . my commands which . . . I issued to him for his own salvation . . . I bind him in thy stead with the chain of [excommunication]."

—Gregory VII, First Deposition and Banning of Henry IV

Skills Assessment

Primary Source What reasons does Gregory give for excommunicating Henry?

Biography

Innocent III 1160(?)–1216

Lotario de' Conti grew up in an influential Roman family. Several of his uncles were leading Church figures, including one pope. Lotario attended the finest schools of Europe, studying theology in Paris and law in Bologna. He became a leading expert on canon law and rose quickly through Church ranks. In 1198, he was elected pope, just one month before he was ordained a priest.

One of Innocent's most lasting achievements was to convene an important Church council in Rome. There, more than 1,000 Church officials established several practices that are still followed by Catholics today, such as regular confession of sins.

Theme: Impact of the Individual How did Innocent's background prepare him to assume the role of pope?

As Holy Roman emperor, Frederick spent little time in Germany. Instead, he pursued his ambitions in Italy. There, he clashed repeatedly and unsuccessfully with several popes. Like his grandfather, Frederick also tried but failed to subdue the cities of northern Italy.

Effects on Germany and Italy While Frederick was embroiled in Italy, German nobles grew more independent. The Holy Roman Empire survived, but it remained fragmented into many feudal states. The German people paid a high price for their emperors' ambitions. Unlike France and England, Germany would not achieve unity for another 600 years.

Southern Italy and Sicily also faced centuries of upheaval. There, popes turned to the French to overthrow Frederick's heirs. A local uprising against French rule in Sicily led to 200 years of chaos as French and Spanish rivals battled for power. The region that had once been a thriving center of culture was left in ruins.

The Height of Church Power

Pope Innocent III, who took office in 1198, embodied the triumph of the Church. As head of the Church, he claimed supremacy over all other rulers. The pope, he said, stands "between God and man, lower than God but higher than men, who judges all and is judged by no one."

Innocent clashed with all the powerful rulers of his day. More often than not, the pope came out ahead. As you have read, when King John of England dared to appoint an archbishop of Canterbury without the pope's approval, Innocent excommunicated the king and placed his kingdom under interdict. Innocent ordered the same punishment for France when Philip II tried unlawfully to **annul,** or invalidate, his marriage. The Holy Roman emperor Frederick II also felt the wrath of the powerful pope.

In 1209, Innocent, aided by Philip II, launched a brutal **crusade,** or holy war, against the Albigensians in southern France. The Albigensians wanted to purify the Church and return to the simple ways of early Christianity. Tens of thousands of people were slaughtered in the Albigensian Crusade.

After Innocent's death, popes continued to press their claim to supremacy. During this period, though, the French and English monarchies were growing stronger. In 1296, Philip IV of France successfully challenged Pope Boniface VIII on the issue of taxing the clergy. After Philip engineered the election of a French pope, the papacy entered a period of decline.

SECTION 2 Assessment

Recall
1. **Identify: (a)** Holy Roman Empire, **(b)** Gregory VII, **(c)** Henry IV, **(d)** Concordat of Worms, **(e)** Frederick II, **(f)** Innocent III, **(g)** Albigensian Crusade.
2. **Define: (a)** lay investiture, **(b)** annul, **(c)** crusade.

Comprehension
3. Why was the power of German emperors limited?
4. How did conflicts between popes and emperors affect **(a)** the Holy Roman Empire, and **(b)** Italy?

5. How did Pope Innocent III assert the power of the Church?

Critical Thinking and Writing
6. **Comparing (a)** How did the political development of the Holy Roman Empire differ from that of England and France? **(b)** What were the causes of these differences?
7. **Analyzing Primary Sources** Review the words of Innocent III at the beginning of this section. **(a)** To what does Innocent compare a monarch? **(b)** What point was he trying to make?

Activity

Making a Map
On an outline map of Europe, label the places that you have read about in this section. Illustrate your map to show what happened in each location.

Reading Focus

- What advanced civilizations flourished around the world in 1050?

- What were the causes and effects of the Crusades?

- How did Christians in Spain carry out the Reconquista?

Vocabulary

schism

levy

religious toleration

Taking Notes

As you read, complete the following chart showing the effects that the Crusades had on life in Europe.

THE CRUSADES

Economy	Monarch	Church	Worldview
• Encouraged trade	•	•	•

Main Idea The Crusades stimulated economic and political change in Europe and broadened Europeans' view of the world.

Setting the Scene
Nearly 23 weeks after departing France, Count Stephen of Blois reached the city of Antioch in Syria. There, in March 1098, he composed a letter to his wife, Adele. He described the battles he had fought and the riches he had won. Stephen proudly told Adele that he and his fellow knights were "full of fury" and "prepared to die for Christ."

Stephen of Blois was one of thousands of Europeans who took part in a series of wars known as the Crusades. In these wars, which began in 1096, Christians battled Muslims for control of lands in the Middle East. As they streamed eastward over the next 200 years, Western Europeans learned that the world was much larger than they had ever dreamed. Their encounters outside Europe would serve to stimulate the pace of change.

The World in 1050

In 1050, as Western Europe was just emerging from a period of isolation, civilizations were thriving elsewhere. These civilizations are described in detail in other chapters. What follows here is an overview of the world at the time that medieval Europe was first beginning to test its strength.

During Europe's Middle Ages, Islam had given rise to a brilliant new civilization that stretched from Spain to India. Muslim traders and scholars spread goods and ideas even further. Trading caravans regularly crossed the Sahara to West Africa. Arab ships visited East African ports and sailed to India and East Asia.

Although India was politically divided, it was a land of thriving cities. Hindu and Buddhist traditions flourished, and wealthy princes built stunning temples and palaces. Indian mathematicians invented a number system, which Arabs adapted and eventually passed to Europeans.

China had a strong central government. Under the Tang and Song dynasties, China's culture flourished and influenced neighboring peoples. The Chinese made amazing advances in technology, inventing paper, printing, and gunpowder. In dozens of cities, traders used coins and paper money, unknown to medieval Europeans.

In West Africa, the Soninke people were building the great trading empire of Ghana. Its merchants traded goods, especially gold, across the Sahara to North Africa, the Middle East, and even Europe.

Across the Atlantic, in the Americas, the Mayas had cleared rain forests and built cities dominated by towering temples. In Peru, Native Americans were building empires and creating great works of art, including elegant

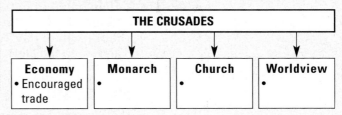

A Mongol Alliance?

Later during the Crusades, Pope Innocent IV sent a diplomatic mission to the Mongols in Central Asia. The pope hoped that the Mongol khan would halt his invasions of Christian lands, convert to Christianity, and join European Christians in their struggle against the Muslims. In a letter written in Mongol, Arabic, and Latin, the khan rejected the pope's proposal.

The pope's mission failed to win an alliance, but it did bring the Europeans new knowledge about the world. Giovanni da Pian del Carpini, the monk who had led the mission, wrote a text based on his extensive travels. His book on the Mongol empire consisted of chapters on climate, customs, religion, character, history, policy, and tactics.

Theme: Global Interaction
How can increased knowledge of other cultures improve international relations?

pottery, textiles, and jewelry. The civilizations of the Americas, however, remained outside the contacts that were taking place among Africans, Europeans, and Asians.

Closer to Western Europe, the Byzantine empire was generally prosperous and united. Byzantine scholars still studied ancient Greek and Roman writings. In Constantinople, Byzantine and Muslim merchants mingled with traders from Venice and other Italian cities.

In the 1050s, the Seljuk Turks invaded the Byzantine empire. The Turks had migrated from Central Asia into the Middle East, where they converted to Islam. By 1071, the Seljuks had overrun most Byzantine lands in Asia Minor (present-day Turkey). The Seljuks also extended their power over Palestine to the Holy Land* and attacked Christian pilgrims.

The Crusades

The Byzantine emperor Alexius I urgently asked Pope Urban II for Christian knights to help him fight the Turks. Although Roman popes and Byzantine emperors were longtime rivals, Urban agreed.

At the Council of Clermont in 1095, Urban incited bishops and nobles to action. "From Jerusalem and the city of Constantinople comes a grievous report," he began. "An accursed race . . . has violently invaded the lands of those Christians and has depopulated them by pillage and fire." Urban then called for a crusade to free the Holy Land:

> "Both knights and footmen, both rich and poor . . . strive to help expel [the Seljuks] from our Christian lands before it is too late. . . . Christ commands it. Remission of sins will be granted for those going thither."
> —Fulcher of Chartres, *Chronicle of the First Crusade*

Motives "God wills it!" roared the assembly. By 1096, thousands of knights were on their way to the Holy Land. As the crusading spirit swept through Western Europe, armies of ordinary men and women inspired by fiery preachers left for the Holy Land, too. Few returned.

Religious zeal and other factors motivated the crusaders. Many knights hoped to win wealth and land. Some crusaders sought to escape troubles at home. Others yearned for adventure.

The pope, too, had mixed motives. Urban hoped to increase his power in Europe and perhaps heal the schism, or split, between the Roman and Byzantine churches. (See the next chapter.) He also hoped that the Crusades would set Christian knights to fighting Muslims instead of one another.

Victories and Defeats Only the First Crusade came close to achieving its goals. After a long, bloody campaign, Christian knights captured Jerusalem in 1099. They capped their victory with a massacre of Muslim and Jewish residents of the city.

The Crusades continued, off and on, for over 200 years. The crusaders divided their captured lands into four small states. The Muslims repeatedly sought to destroy these Christian kingdoms, prompting Europeans to launch new crusades. By 1187, Jerusalem had fallen to the able Muslim leader Salah al-Din, known to Europeans as Saladin. On the Third Crusade, Europeans tried but failed to retake Jerusalem. After negotiations, though, Saladin did reopen the holy city to Christian pilgrims.

Europeans also mounted crusades against other Muslim lands, especially in North Africa. All ended in defeat. During the Fourth Crusade, the crusaders were diverted from fighting Muslims to fighting Christians. After

Connections to Today

A Holy City

Today, Jews, Christians, and Muslims still consider Jerusalem sacred. Each year, the city's population is swelled by thousands of pilgrims who arrive to visit places that are holy to their faiths. Christian pilgrims make certain to visit the Church of the Holy Sepulcher, believed to be the site of Jesus' resurrection. Equally sacred to Muslims is the Dome of the Rock, from which the Prophet Muhammad is believed to have ascended to heaven. Jewish pilgrims join in prayer at the Old City's western wall, all that remains of the city's ancient temple.

Theme: Religions and Value Systems Why do Muslims consider Jerusalem a holy city?

---

*Christians called Jerusalem and other places in Palestine where Jesus had lived and taught the Holy Land. Jerusalem was also a holy place for Jews and Muslims.

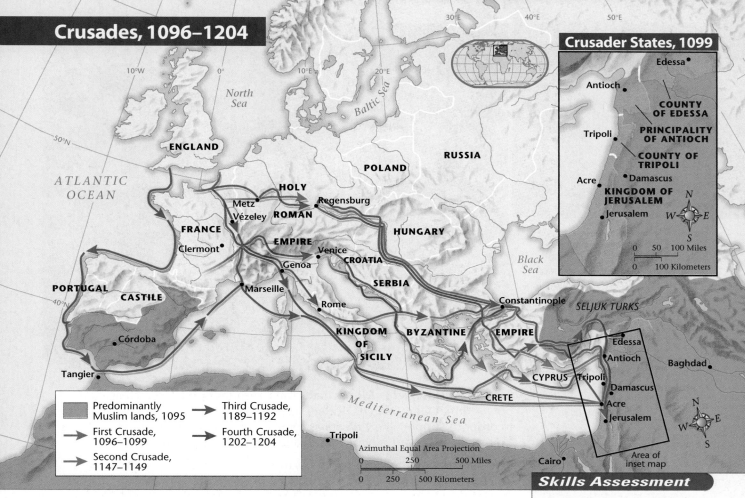

Crusades, 1096–1204

Crusader States, 1099

Legend:
- Predominantly Muslim lands, 1095
- First Crusade, 1096–1099
- Second Crusade, 1147–1149
- Third Crusade, 1189–1192
- Fourth Crusade, 1202–1204

Azimuthal Equal Area Projection

0 250 500 Miles
0 250 500 Kilometers

helping Venetian merchants defeat their Byzantine trade rivals in 1204, crusaders captured and looted Constantinople, the Byzantine capital.

Muslim armies, meanwhile, overran the crusader states. By 1291, they captured the last Christian outpost, the port city of Acre. As in Jerusalem 200 years earlier, the victors massacred their defeated enemies. This time, the victims were Christians.

Effects of the Crusades on Europe

The Crusades left a bitter legacy of religious hatred behind them. In the Middle East, both Christians and Muslims committed appalling atrocities in the name of religion. In Europe, crusaders sometimes turned their religious fury against Jews, massacring entire communities.

Though the Crusades failed to conquer the Holy Land, they did have significant effects on life in Europe. The wars helped to quicken the pace of changes already underway.

Economic Expansion Even before the Crusades, Europeans had a taste for luxuries from the Byzantine empire. The Crusades increased trade. Crusaders introduced fabrics, spices, and perfumes from the Middle East to Europe.

Merchants in Venice and other northern Italian cities built large fleets to carry crusaders to the Holy Land. They later used those fleets to carry on trade with the Middle East. Our words *sugar, cotton,* and *rice,* borrowed from Arabic, show the range of trade goods involved.

The Crusades further encouraged the growth of a money economy. To finance a journey to the Holy Land, nobles needed money. They allowed peasants to pay rents in money rather than in grain or labor, which helped undermine serfdom.

Skills Assessment

Geography Urged on by Pope Urban II, thousands of Europeans joined the Crusades to expel the Muslims from the Holy Land.

1. **Location** On the map, locate (a) Holy Roman Empire, (b) Kingdom of Jerusalem, (c) Acre, (d) Constantinople.
2. **Movement** What route did English crusaders take to the Holy Land?
3. **Critical Thinking Drawing Conclusions** Based on the map, why was it difficult for Europeans to defend the Crusader states?

The Reconquista
In 1492, the fall of the Muslim city of Granada completed the Christian reconquest of Spain. This Spanish woodcarving shows Granada surrendering to Queen Isabella and King Ferdinand.

Theme: Economics and Technology How were Granada and other medieval towns designed to provide defense?

Increased Power for Monarchs The Crusades helped to increase the power of feudal monarchs. Rulers won new rights to levy, or collect, taxes in order to support the Crusades. Some rulers, including the French king Louis IX, led crusades, which added greatly to their prestige.

The Church Enthusiasm for the Crusades brought papal power to its greatest height. This period of enhanced prestige was short-lived, however. As we have seen, popes were soon involved in bitter clashes with feudal monarchs. Also, the Crusades did not end the split between the Roman and Byzantine churches. In fact, Byzantine resentment against the West hardened as a result of the Fourth Crusade.

A Wider Worldview Contacts with the Muslim world led Christians to realize that millions of people lived in regions they had never known existed. Soon, a few curious Europeans visited far-off places like India and China.

In 1271, a young Venetian, Marco Polo, set out for China with his merchant father and uncle. After many years in China, he returned to Venice full of stories about the wonders of Chinese civilization. Doubting Europeans called Marco Polo the "prince of liars." To them, his tales of a government-run mail service and black stones (coal) that were burned to heat homes were totally untrue.

The experiences of crusaders and of travelers like Marco Polo expanded European horizons. They brought Europe into a wider world from which it had been cut off since the fall of Rome. By the 1400s, a desire to trade directly with India and China led Europeans to a new age of exploration.

The Reconquista in Spain

The crusading spirit continued long after the European defeat at Acre. It flourished especially in Spain, where Christian warriors had been battling Muslims for centuries. Muslims had conquered most of Spain in the 700s. Several tiny Christian kingdoms survived in the north, however. As they slowly expanded their borders, they sought to take over Muslim lands. Their campaign to drive the Muslims from Spain became known as the Reconquista, or "reconquest."

Christian Advances Efforts by Christian warriors to expel the Muslims began in the 700s. Their first real success did not come, however, until 1085, when they recaptured the city of Toledo. During the next 200 years, Christian forces pushed slowly and steadily southward. By 1300, Christians controlled the entire Iberian Peninsula except for Granada. Muslim influences remained strong, though, and helped shape the arts and literature of Christian Spain.

Ferdinand and Isabella In 1469, Isabella of Castile married Ferdinand of Aragon. This marriage between the rulers of two powerful kingdoms opened the way for a unified state. Using their combined forces, the two monarchs made a final push against the Muslim stronghold of Granada. In 1492, Granada fell. The Reconquista was complete.

Isabella and Ferdinand tried to impose unity on their diverse peoples. They joined forces with townspeople against powerful nobles. Isabella was determined to bring religious as well as political unity to Spain.

Under Muslim rule, Spain had enjoyed a tradition of religious toleration, that is, a policy of allowing people to worship as they choose. Christians, Jews, and Muslims lived there in relative peace. Isabella ended that policy of toleration. With the support of the Inquisition, a Church court set up to try people accused of heresy, Isabella launched a brutal crusade against Jews and Muslims. Often, those who refused to convert to Christianity were burned at the stake.

The queen achieved religious unity but at a high price. More than 150,000 people fled Spain. Many of these exiles were skilled, educated people who had contributed much to Spain's economy and culture.

Cause *and* Effect

Long-Term Causes	Immediate Causes
• Growth of strong monarchs • Growth of towns and cities • Growth of representative bodies • Crusades • Increased trade • Population decline	• Economic revival • New technology and agricultural productivity • Development of universities • Wider worldview

Western European Emergence From Isolation

Immediate Effects	Long-Term Effects
• Population growth • End of feudalism • Centralized monarchies • Growth of Italian trading centers • Increased productivity	• Renaissance • Age of Exploration • Scientific Revolution • Western European colonies in Asia, Africa, and the Americas

Connections to Today

• Growth of strong central governments
• Spread of representative government
• Capitalism and powerful business classes
• Influence of Western European culture around the world
• Influence of technology on everyday life

Skills Assessment **Chart** During the late Middle Ages, Europe was emerging from a period of isolation. **How did the Crusades contribute to economic revival?**

SECTION 3 Assessment

Recall
1. **Identify: (a)** Crusades, **(b)** Council of Clermont, **(c)** Saladin, **(d)** Reconquista, **(e)** Ferdinand and Isabella.
2. **Define: (a)** schism, **(b)** levy, **(c)** religious toleration.

Comprehension
3. What advanced civilizations existed around the world at the time of the First Crusade?
4. **(a)** Why did Europeans join the Crusades? **(b)** What were three results of the Crusades?

5. How did Spain achieve political and religious unity?

Critical Thinking and Writing
6. **Analyzing Information** How did the Crusades reflect the growing strength of medieval Europe?
7. **Making Generalizations (a)** How was the Reconquista part of the crusading spirit that appealed to many Europeans? **(b)** How were the goals of Ferdinand and Isabella similar to the goals of other monarchs in Europe?

Activity

Expressing Different Points of View
Write two articles reporting on the First Crusade: one from the point of view of a Christian knight, and another from the point of view of a Muslim living in Jerusalem.

Learning, Literature, and the Arts

Reading Focus

- How did medieval universities advance learning?

- How did "new" learning affect medieval thought?

- What styles of literature, architecture, and art developed in the High Middle Ages?

Vocabulary

scholasticism

vernacular

epic

flying buttress

illumination

Taking Notes

Copy this concept web. As you read, complete the web. Add circles as needed.

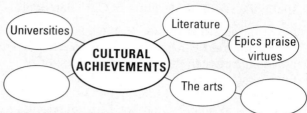

Main Idea **As economic and political conditions improved, Europeans made notable achievements in learning, literature, and the arts.**

Setting the Scene By the 1100s, Europe was experiencing dynamic changes. No longer was everyone preoccupied with the daily struggle to survive. Improvements in agriculture were creating a steadier food supply. The revival of trade and the growth of towns were signs of increased prosperity. Within the towns and cities of medieval Europe, a few people were acquiring wealth. In time, towns contributed a vital spark that ignited the cultural flowering of the High Middle Ages.

Medieval Universities

As economic and political conditions improved in the High Middle Ages, the need for education expanded. The Church wanted better-educated clergy. Royal rulers also needed literate men for their growing bureaucracies. By getting an education, the sons of wealthy townspeople might hope to qualify for high jobs in the Church or royal governments.

Academic Guilds By the 1100s, schools had sprung up around the great cathedrals to train the clergy. Some of these cathedral schools evolved into the first universities. They were organized like guilds with charters to protect the rights of members and set standards for training.

Salerno and Bologna in Italy boasted the first universities. Paris and Oxford soon had theirs. In the 1200s, other cities rushed to organize universities. Students often traveled from one university to another. They might study law in Bologna, medicine in Montpellier, and theology, or religion, in Paris.

Student Life University life offered few comforts. A bell wakened students at about 5 A.M. for prayers. Students then attended classes until 10 A.M., when they had their first meal of the day—perhaps a bit of beef and soup mixed with oatmeal. Afternoon classes continued until 5 P.M. Students usually ate a light supper and then studied until it was time for bed.

Because medieval universities did not have permanent buildings, classes were held in rented rooms or in the choir loft of a church. Students sat for hours on hard benches as the teacher dictated and then explained Latin texts. Students were expected to memorize what they heard.

University of Paris
Students listened as teachers read aloud five logic books and two grammar books, as part of the course of study for a bachelor of arts.

Theme: Economics and Technology Why do you think there was not a book for each student?

A program of study covered the seven liberal arts: arithmetic, geometry, astronomy, music, grammar, rhetoric, and logic. To show that they had mastered a subject, students took an oral exam. Earning a degree as a bachelor of arts took between three and six years. Only after several more years of study could a man qualify to become a master of arts and a teacher.

Women and Education Women were not allowed to attend the universities. This exclusion seriously affected their lives. Without a university education, they could not become doctors, lawyers, administrators, church officials, or professors. They were also deprived of the mental stimulation that was an important part of university life.

An exception was Christine de Pizan (duh pee ZAHN), an Italian-born woman who came to live in the French court. De Pizan was married at 15, but her husband died before she was 25. Left with three children to raise, De Pizan earned her living as a writer, an unusual occupation for a woman of that time.

De Pizan used her pen to examine the achievements of women. In *The City of Ladies,* she questions several imaginary characters about men's negative views of women. She asks Lady Reason, for example, whether women are less capable of learning and understanding, as men insist. Lady Reason replies: "If it were customary to send daughters to school like sons, and if they were then taught the same subjects, they would learn as thoroughly and understand the subtleties of all arts and sciences as well as sons."

Still, men continued to look on educated women as oddities. Women, they felt, should pursue their "natural" gifts at home, raising children, managing the household, and doing needlework, and leave books and writing to men.

Europeans Acquire "New" Learning

Universities received a further boost from an explosion of knowledge that reached Europe in the High Middle Ages. Many of the "new" ideas had originated in ancient Greece but had been lost to Western Europeans after the fall of Rome.

Spread of Learning In the Middle East, Muslim scholars had translated the works of Aristotle and other Greek thinkers into Arabic, and their texts had spread across the Muslim world. In Muslim Spain, Jewish scholars translated these works into Latin, the language of Christian European scholars. By the 1100s, these new translations were seeping into Western Europe. There they set off a revolution in the world of learning.

Philosophy The writings of the ancient Greeks posed a challenge to Christian scholars. Aristotle taught that people should use reason to discover basic truths. Christians, however, accepted many ideas on faith. They believed that the Church was the final authority on all questions. How could they use the logic of Aristotle without undermining their Christian faith?

Christian scholars, known as scholastics, tried to resolve the conflict between faith and reason. Their method, known as scholasticism, used reason to support Christian beliefs. Scholastics studied the works of the Muslim philosopher Averroës (ah VEHR oh eez) and the Jewish rabbi Maimonides (mī MAHN uh deez). These thinkers, too, used logic to resolve the conflict between faith and reason.

The writings of these thinkers influenced the scholastic Thomas Aquinas (uh KWĪ nuhs). In a monumental work, *Summa Theologica,* Aquinas examined Christian teachings in the light of reason. Faith and reason, he concluded, existed in harmony. Both led to the same truth, that God ruled over an orderly universe. He thus brought together Christian faith and classical Greek philosophy.

Biography

Christine de Pizan
1364(?)–1430(?)

Christine de Pizan was more educated than most men of her time. Her father, a physician and astronomer in the French court of Charles V, had seen that she received an excellent education. She spoke French, Italian, and possibly Latin as well.

To support her family, De Pizan wrote poems, songs, and ballads. Her work was supported by lords and ladies, by King Charles VI of France, and by his wife, Queen Isabella. Because of her desire to comment on social issues, De Pizan gradually switched her focus to prose. In much of her work, she promoted women's rights and accomplishments. Shortly before her death, she wrote the poem "Hymn to Joan of Arc" to honor a young Frenchwoman who was leading French soldiers to victory over the English.

Theme: Impact of the Individual What was a major theme of De Pizan's writing?

"The Count Roland, beneath a pine
    he sits . . .
  Remembering so many [different]
    things:
  So many lands where he went
    conquering,
  And France the [sweet], the
    heroes of his kin,
  And Charlemagne, his lord who
    nourished him.
  Nor can we help but weep and
    sigh at this. . . .
  His right-hand glove, to God he
    offers it
  Saint Gabriel from's hand hath
    taken it . . .
  He joins his hand: and so is life
    finish'd
  God sent him down His angel
    cherubim . . .
  So the count's soul they bear to
    Paradis[e]."

—*Song of Roland*

Skills Assessment

Primary Source Why would
the *Song of Roland* be considered
an epic poem?

Science and Mathematics Works of science, translated from Arabic and Greek, also reached Europe from Spain and the Byzantine empire. Christian scholars studied Hippocrates on medicine and Euclid on geometry, along with works by Arab scientists. They saw, too, how Aristotle had used observation and experimentation to study the physical world.

Yet science made little real progress in the Middle Ages because most scholars still believed that all true knowledge must fit with Church teachings. It would take many centuries before Christian thinkers changed the way they viewed the physical world.

In mathematics, as we have seen, Europeans adopted Hindu-Arabic numerals. This system was much easier to use than the cumbersome system of Roman numerals that had been traditional throughout Europe for centuries. In time, Arabic numerals allowed both scientists and mathematicians to make extraordinary advances in their fields.

Medieval Literature

While Latin was the language of scholars and churchmen, new writings began to appear in the vernacular, or the everyday languages of ordinary people, such as French, German, and Italian. These writings captured the spirit of the High Middle Ages. Medieval literature included epics, or long narrative poems, about feudal warriors and tales of the common people.

Heroic Epics Across Europe, people began writing down oral traditions in the vernacular. French pilgrims traveling to holy sites loved to hear the *chansons de geste,* or "songs of heroic deeds." The most popular was the *Song of Roland,* which praises the courage of one of Charlemagne's knights who died while on a military campaign in Muslim Spain. A true feudal hero, Roland loyally sacrifices his life out of a sense of honor.

Spain's great epic, *Poem of the Cid,* also involves battle against Muslim forces. The Cid was Rodrigo Díaz, a bold and fiery Christian lord who battled Muslims in Spain. Calling to his warriors, he surges into battle full of zeal:

"There are three hundred lances that each a pennant bears.
  At one blow every man of them his Moor has slaughtered
    there,
  And when they wheeled to charge anew as many more
    were slain,
  You might see great clumps of lances lowered and raised
    again. . . .
  Cried the Moor "Muhammed!" The Christians shouted
    on St. James of Grace,
  On the field Moors thirteen hundred were slain in
    little space."

—*Poem of the Cid*

Dante's *Divine Comedy* "In the middle of the journey of life, I found myself in a dark wood, where the straight way was lost." So begins the *Divine Comedy* by the famed Italian poet Dante Alighieri (DAHN tay al lee GYEH ree). The poem takes the reader on an imaginary journey into hell and purgatory, where souls await forgiveness. Finally, Dante describes a vision of heaven.

"Abandon all hope, ye that enter here" is the warning Dante receives as he approaches hell. There, he talks with people from history who tell how they earned a place in hell. Humor, tragedy, and the endless medieval quest for religious understanding are all ingredients in Dante's poem. His journey summarizes Christian ethics. It also highlights in vivid detail a key idea of Christianity—that people's actions in life will determine their fate in the afterlife.

Chaucer's *Canterbury Tales* In *The Canterbury Tales*, Geoffrey Chaucer follows a band of English pilgrims traveling to Thomas Becket's tomb. In brilliant word portraits, he sketches a range of characters, including a knight, a plowman, a merchant, a miller, a monk, a nun, and the five-times-widowed "wife of Bath." Each character tells a story. Whether funny, romantic, or bawdy, each tale adds to our picture of medieval life.

Architecture and Art

"In the Middle Ages," wrote French author Victor Hugo, "men had no great thought that they did not write down in stone." With riches from trade and commerce, townspeople, nobles, and monarchs indulged in a flurry of building. Their greatest achievements were the towering stone cathedrals that served as symbols of their wealth and religious devotion.

Romanesque Strength About 1000, monasteries and towns built solid stone churches that reflected Roman influences. These Romanesque churches looked like fortresses with thick walls and towers. Typically, the roof of a Romanesque church was a barrel vault, a long tunnel of stone that covered the main part of the structure. It was so heavy that it had to be supported by massive thick walls. Builders provided no windows or only tiny slits of windows for fear of weakening the walls that supported the roof. As a result, the interior of a Romanesque church was dark and gloomy.

Gothic Grace About 1140, Abbot Suger wanted to build a new abbey church at St. Denis near Paris. He hoped that it "would shine with wonderful and uninterrupted light." Urged on by the abbot, builders developed what became known as the Gothic style of architecture. A key feature of this style was the flying buttresses, or stone supports that stood outside the church. These supports allowed builders to construct higher walls and leave space for huge stained-glass windows.

▶ **Primary Sources and Literature**

See "Geoffrey Chaucer: The Canterbury Tales" in the Reference Section at the back of this book.

Gothic Style
The Cathedral of Notre Dame in Paris is a fine example of the Gothic style. Medieval artists adorned Gothic cathedrals with brilliant stained-glass windows and a variety of sculptures, such as the mythical beast shown here.
Theme: Art and Literature
How did Gothic style differ from Romanesque style?

The new Gothic churches soared to incredible heights. Their graceful spires, lofty ceilings, and enormous windows carried the eye upward to the heavens. "Since their brilliance lets the splendor of the True Light pass into the church," declared a medieval visitor, "they enlighten those inside."

Cities all over Europe competed to build grander, taller cathedrals. The faithful contributed money, labor, and skills to help build these monuments "to the greater glory of God."

Art in Stone and Glass As churches rose, stonemasons carved sculptures to decorate them inside and out. The sculptors portrayed scenes from the Bible and other religious themes. They also carved images of everyday life that included lifelike forms of plants and animals. Among the most interesting of their creations were whimsical or frightening images of mythical creatures such as dragons, griffins, and unicorns.

At the same time, other skilled craftworkers created stained-glass windows that added to the brilliant splendor of Gothic churches. The artisans stained small pieces of glass in glowing colors. They then set the pieces in thin lead frames to create pictures depicting the life of Jesus, a biblical event, or other religious themes. Stained glass and carvings served as a religious education for the people, most of whom were illiterate.

Art and Religion
Stained-glass windows depicted biblical or other religious scenes. In the 1100s, a monk wrote that his church was filled with "the most radiant windows" to "illuminate men's minds so that they may travel through it [light] to an apprehension of God's light."

Theme: Art and Literature
How did medieval art help illiterate Christians learn about the Bible?

Illuminated Manuscripts In the 1300s and 1400s, the Gothic style was applied to paintings and illumination, that is, the artistic decoration of books. Since the early Middle Ages, monks, nuns, and other skilled artisans had illuminated books with intricate designs and miniature paintings of biblical scenes and daily life. Characteristics of the new Gothic style included bold, brilliant colors and decorative detail. Some fine examples of Gothic painting appeared in prayer books known as Books of Hours. Artists decorated these prayer books with depictions of towns and castles, knights and ladies in gardens or at banquet, and peasants working in the fields.

SECTION 4 Assessment

Recall
1. **Identify:** **(a)** Christine de Pizan, **(b)** Thomas Aquinas, **(c)** *Song of Roland,* **(d)** *Poem of the Cid,* **(e)** Dante Alighieri, **(f)** Geoffrey Chaucer.
2. **Define:** **(a)** scholasticism, **(b)** vernacular, **(c)** epic, **(d)** flying buttress, **(e)** illumination.

Comprehension
3. What subjects were included in the course of study in medieval universities?
4. How did new knowledge pose a challenge to Christian scholars?

5. What were the characteristics of Gothic architecture?

Critical Thinking and Writing
6. **Making Inferences** Why do you think Gothic churches are sometimes referred to as "Bibles in stone"?
7. **Solving Problems** Solve this problem using Roman numerals: MCMLXXX + MMCCCLX. Then, translate and solve the problem using Arabic numerals. How do you think the introduction of Arabic numerals might have affected mathematics in Western Europe?

Activity
Take It to the NET

Use the Internet to learn more about the literature and views of Dante or Chaucer. Then, with a small group of classmates, stage a TV program in which you interview one of the writers. Develop your questions and answers by referring to what you learned in your research.

Reading Focus

■ How did the Black Death cause social and economic decline?

■ What problems afflicted the Church in the late Middle Ages?

■ What were the causes, turning points, and effects of the Hundred Years' War?

Vocabulary

epidemic

inflation

longbow

Taking Notes

Copy the chart at right on conditions before and after the Hundred Years' War. As you read, fill in each column with appropriate information.

HUNDRED YEARS' WAR	
Before	**After**
• Castles offered adequate protection	• English hold only Calais in France
•	•

Main Idea Plague, upheaval in the Church, and war made the 1300s and early 1400s a time of crisis for Europeans.

Setting the Scene In the autumn of 1347, a fleet of Genoese trading ships, loaded with grain, left the Black Sea port of Caffa and set sail for Messina, Sicily. By midvoyage, sailors were falling sick and dying. Soon after the ships tied up at Messina, townspeople, too, fell sick and died. A medieval chronicler described how the people of Messina "drove (the Genoese) in all haste from their city and port." Nevertheless, "the sickness remained and a terrible mortality ensued." Within months, the disease that Europeans called the Black Death was raging through Italy.

To Europeans in the mid-1300s, the end of the world seemed to have come. First, widespread crop failures brought famine and starvation. Then, plague and war deepened the crisis. Europe eventually recovered from these disasters. Still, the upheavals of the 1300s and 1400s marked the end of the Middle Ages and the beginning of the early modern age.

The Black Death

By 1348, the Black Death had reached beyond Italy to Spain and France. From there, it ravaged the rest of Europe. One in three people died—worse than in any war in history.

A Global Epidemic The sickness was bubonic plague, a disease spread by fleas on rats. Bubonic plague had broken out before in Europe, Asia, and North Africa but had subsided. One strain, though, had survived in Mongolia. In the 1200s, Mongol armies conquered much of Asia, probably setting off the new epidemic, or outbreak of rapid-spreading disease.

In the premodern world, rats infested ships, towns, and even the homes of the rich and powerful, so no one took any notice of them. In the early 1300s, rats scurrying through crowded Chinese cities spread the plague, which killed about 35 million people there.

Fleas jumped from those rats to infest the clothes and packs of traders traveling west. As a result, the disease spread from Asia to the Middle East. Terrible reports reached Europe: "India was depopulated," wrote a chronicler. "Mesopotamia, Syria, and Armenia were covered with dead bodies." In Cairo, one of the world's largest cities, the plague at its peak killed about 7,000 people a day.

Social Upheaval In Europe, the plague brought terror and bewilderment, as people had no way to stop the disease. Some people turned to magic and witchcraft for cures. Others plunged into wild pleasures, believing they would soon die anyway. Still others saw the plague as God's punishment. They beat themselves with whips to show that they repented their sins. Christians blamed Jews for the plague, charging that they had poisoned the wells. "The whole world," a French friar noted, "rose up against [the Jews] cruelly on this account." In the resulting hysteria, thousands of Jews were slaughtered.

Normal life broke down. The Italian poet Boccaccio described the social decay that he witnessed in Florence as people tried to avoid contracting the plague from neighbors and relatives:

> "In the horror thereof brother was forsaken by brother . . .
> and oftentimes husband by wife; nay, what is more, and
> scarcely to be believed, fathers and mothers were found to
> abandon their own children, untended, unvisited, to their
> fate, as if they had been strangers."
> —Boccaccio, *The Decameron*

Economic Effects As the plague kept recurring in the late 1300s, the European economy plunged to a low ebb. As workers and employers died, production declined. Survivors demanded higher wages. As the cost of labor soared, inflation, or rising prices, broke out too.

Landowners and merchants pushed for laws to limit wages. To stop rising costs, landowners converted croplands to sheep raising, which required less labor. Villagers forced off the land sought work in towns. There, guilds limited apprenticeships, refused to accept new members, and denied journeymen the chance to become masters.

Coupled with the fear of the plague, these restrictions sparked explosive revolts. Bitter, angry peasants rampaged in England, France, Germany, and elsewhere. In cities, too, artisans fought, usually without success, for more power. The plague had spread both death and social unrest. Western Europe would not fully recover from its effects for more than 100 years.

Upheaval in the Church

The late Middle Ages brought spiritual crisis, scandal, and division to the Roman Catholic Church. Many priests and monks died during the plague. Their replacements faced challenging questions. "Why did God spare some and kill others?" asked survivors.

Divisions Within the Catholic Church The Church was unable to provide the strong leadership needed in this desperate time. In 1309, Pope Clement V had moved the papal court to Avignon on the border of southern France. There it remained for about 70 years under French domination. This period is often called the Babylonian Captivity of the Church, referring to the time when the ancient Israelites were held captive in Babylon.

In Avignon, popes reigned over a lavish court. Critics lashed out against the worldly, pleasure-loving papacy, and anticlergy sentiment grew. Within the Church itself, reformers tried to end the "captivity."

In 1378, reformers elected their own pope to rule from Rome. French cardinals responded by choosing a rival pope. For decades, there was a schism, or split, in the Church as two and sometimes even three popes claimed to be the true "vicar of Christ." Not until 1417 did a Church council at Constance finally end the crisis.

New Heresies With its moral authority weakened, the Church faced still more problems. Popular preachers challenged its power. In England, John Wycliffe, an Oxford professor, attacked Church corruption.

Wycliffe insisted that the Bible, not the Church, was the source of all Christian truth. His followers began translating the Bible into English so

Disaster!

The Black Death Strikes

Between 1347 and 1353, the Black Death, or bubonic plague, killed one person out of every three in Europe. In this short time, over 25 million people died.

The Black Death struck with stunning speed. Within hours, victims developed egg-sized lumps under their arms. Then, horrible black spots appeared on their skin. Once they started spitting blood, death was certain. The sickness seemed all the more terrifying because it could strike anyone. The image above shows Death dancing (left to right) with a woman, a noble, a priest, a peasant, and a monk.

Spread of the Black Death

ATLANTIC OCEAN
RUSSIA
DENMARK
ENGLAND
HOLY ROMAN EMPIRE
POLAND
LITHUANIA
FRANCE
HUNGARY
PORTUGAL
SPAIN
ITALY
Black Sea
OTTOMAN EMPIRE
Mediterranean Sea

0   500 Miles
0   500 Kilometers

Extent of plague in:
1347   1353

By 1347, the bubonic plague had arrived in Europe. Spreading outward in waves of terror, it soon ravaged most of the continent.

Unsanitary conditions spread disease. During the Middle Ages, people threw garbage and human waste into the streets.

"Bring out your dead!" This gruesome call sounded through deserted streets. The death toll was so high that gravediggers used carts to collect corpses. Piles of bodies were buried in vast pits.

Flea-covered rats thrived in the filthy streets. One bite from an infected flea could bring an agonizing death.

Portfolio Assessment

INTERNET Use the Internet or other research sources to learn about a recent epidemic. Create a chart tracing the spread of the disease. Describe how people are trying to prevent or cure this modern plague.

Turning Points of the Hundred Years' War

Longbow

During the early years of the war, English armies equipped with the longbow overpowered their French counterparts equipped with the crossbow. An English archer could shoot three arrows in the time it took a French archer to shoot one.

Joan of Arc

From 1429 to 1431, Joan's successes in battle rallied the French forces to victory. French armies continued to win even after she was executed by the English.

Cannon

The cannon helped the French to capture English-held castles and defeat England's armies. French cannons were instrumental in defeating English forces in Normandy.

Connections to Today

England, which is now part of the United Kingdom, and France have friendly relations today. Their economies are closely linked in that both nations are members of the European Union. The two cooperate militarily as members of the North Atlantic Treaty Organization.

Skills Assessment **Chart** Changes in leadership and new technology marked some of the major turning points in the Hundred Years' War. **How did technology benefit the English in the early years of the war?**

that people could read it themselves rather than rely on the clergy to read it. Czech students at Oxford carried Wycliffe's ideas to Bohemia—what is today the Czech Republic. There, Jan Hus led the call for reforms.

The Church responded by persecuting Wycliffe and his followers and suppressing the Hussites. Hus was tried for preaching heresy—ideas contrary to Church teachings. Found guilty, he was burned at the stake in 1415. The ideas of Wycliffe and Hus survived, however. A century later, other reformers took up the same demands.

The Hundred Years' War

On top of the disasters of famine, plague, and economic decline came a long, destructive war. Between 1337 and 1453, England and France fought a series of conflicts, known as the Hundred Years' War.

Causes As you have read, English rulers had battled for centuries to hold onto the French lands of their Norman ancestors. French kings, for their part, were intent on extending their own power in France. When Edward III of England claimed the French crown in 1337, war erupted anew between these rival powers. Once fighting started, economic rivalry and a growing sense of national pride made it hard for either side to give up the struggle.

English Victories At first, the English won a string of victories—at Crécy in 1346, Poitiers 10 years later, and Agincourt in 1415. They owed much of their success to the longbow wielded by English archers. This powerful new weapon was six feet long and took years to master. But it could discharge three arrows in the time a French archer with his crossbow fired just one, and its arrows pierced all but the heaviest armor.

The English victories took a heavy toll on French morale. England, it seemed, was likely to bring all of France under its control. Then, in what seemed to the French a miracle, their fortunes were reversed.

Joan of Arc and French Victory In 1429, a 17-year-old peasant woman, Joan of Arc, appeared at the court of Charles VII, the uncrowned king of France. She told Charles that God had sent her to save France. She persuaded the desperate French king to let her lead his army against the English.

To Charles's amazement, Joan inspired the battered and despairing French troops to fight anew. In an astonishing year of campaigning, she led the French to several victories and planted the seeds for future triumphs.

Joan paid for success with her life. She was taken captive by allies of the English and turned over to her enemies for trial. The English wanted to discredit her, and they had her tried for witchcraft. She was convicted and burned at the stake. Much later, however, the Church declared her a saint.

The execution of Joan rallied the French, who saw her as a martyr. After Joan's death, the French took the offensive. With a powerful new weapon, the cannon, they attacked English-held castles. By 1453, the English held only the port of Calais in north-western France.

Effects The Hundred Years' War set France and England on different paths. The war created a growing sense of national feeling in France and allowed French kings to expand their power. During the war, English rulers turned repeatedly to Parliament for funds, which helped that body win the "power of the purse." The loss of French lands shattered English dreams of a continental empire, but English rulers soon began looking at new trading ventures overseas.

The Hundred Years' War brought many changes to the late medieval world. The long-bow and cannon gave common soldiers a new importance on the battlefield and undermined the value of armored knights. Castles and knights were doomed to disappear because their defenses could not stand up to the more deadly firepower. Feudal society was changing. Monarchs needed large armies, not feudal vassals, to fight their wars.

Looking Ahead

In the 1400s, as Europe recovered from the Black Death, other changes occurred. The population expanded and manufacturing grew. These changes, in turn, led to increased trade. Italian cities flourished as centers of shipping. They sent European cloth to the Middle East in exchange for spices, sugar, and cotton. Europeans developed new technologies. German miners, for example, used water power to crush ore and built blast furnaces to make cast iron.

The recovery of the late Middle Ages set the stage for further changes during the Renaissance, Reformation, and Age of Exploration. As Europe grew stronger over the next few centuries, it would take a more prominent role on the global stage.

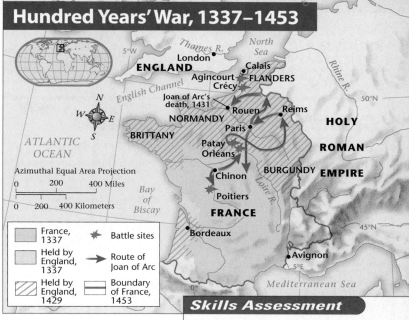

Hundred Years' War, 1337–1453

France, 1337
Held by England, 1337
Held by England, 1429
Battle sites
Route of Joan of Arc
Boundary of France, 1453

Skills Assessment

Geography The English and French fought for control of France in the Hundred Years' War.

1. **Location** On the map, locate **(a)** Normandy, **(b)** Poitiers, **(c)** Calais.
2. **Place** What city in northern France was still under English control in 1453?
3. **Critical Thinking Analyzing Information** What regions of France did England gain between 1337 and 1429?

SECTION 5 Assessment

Recall

1. **Identify: (a)** Black Death, **(b)** Babylonian Captivity, **(c)** John Wycliffe, **(d)** Jan Hus, **(e)** Hundred Years' War, **(f)** Joan of Arc.
2. **Define: (a)** epidemic, **(b)** inflation, **(c)** longbow.

Comprehension

3. What were three effects of the bubonic plague on late medieval Europe?
4. **(a)** Why did reformers criticize the Church? **(b)** How did the Church respond to this criticism?

5. **(a)** How did new technologies affect fighting during the Hundred Years' War? **(b)** What were the results of the war?

Critical Thinking and Writing

6. **Understanding Sequence** Make a step-by-step list showing how the bubonic plague spread from Asia to Europe and resulted in the deaths of millions of Europeans.
7. **Comparing** Compare the effects of the Hundred Years' War on France and on England.

Activity
Take It to the NET

Use the Internet to research the Black Death in Europe, especially its effects on population and the economy. Then, use the information you have found to create graphs showing the decline of Europe's population and economy during the plague years. You might download pictures from the Net to illustrate your graphs.

Review and Assessment

Creating a Chapter Summary

On a separate sheet of paper, copy and complete the following chart showing the major political, economic, cultural, and religious developments of the High Middle Ages.

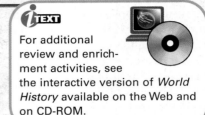

TEXT

For additional review and enrichment activities, see the interactive version of *World History* available on the Web and on CD-ROM.

POLITICAL	ECONOMIC	CULTURAL	RELIGIOUS
Monarchs expanded royal power.	Crusades spurred growth of a money economy.	Universities were established.	Church reached height of its power.

Web Site Self-Test
For practice test questions for Chapter 9, see **www.phschool.com**.

Building Vocabulary

Review the meaning of the chapter vocabulary words listed below. Then, write a sentence for each word, describing its significance in medieval Europe.

1. **common law**
2. **jury**
3. **lay investiture**
4. **crusade**
5. **schism**
6. **scholasticism**
7. **vernacular**
8. **epidemic**
9. **inflation**
10. **longbow**

Recalling Key Facts

11. List two ways English and French monarchs increased royal power.
12. Why did Holy Roman emperors come into conflict with the Church?
13. (a) What was the goal of the Crusades? (b) Did they achieve their goal? Explain.
14. (a) What steps did Isabella take to bring religious unity to Spain? (b) What were the results of her policy?
15. What new knowledge reached Europe in the High Middle Ages?
16. (a) What steps did reformers take to end the Babylonian Captivity of the Church? (b) What were the results?

Critical Thinking and Writing

17. **Analyzing Information** (a) List four goals of medieval monarchs. (b) Explain how one ruler furthered these goals.
18. **Defending a Position** Review the conflict between Gregory VII and Henry IV. Cite two arguments each man might have given to defend his position.
19. **Ranking** List four effects of the Crusades. Then, rank them in order of their importance. Give reasons for your ranking.
20. **Connecting to Geography** Review the map titled "Trade in Medieval Europe" in the last chapter and the map titled "Spread of the Black Death" in this chapter. How might trade routes and the spread of the disease be linked?

21. **Making Inferences** How might the rise of medieval literature written in the vernacular reflect a change in education and literacy rates?
22. **Recognizing Causes and Effects** (a) How did the creation of the Magna Carta affect government in England? (b) How do you think the lack of a similar document in France affected the development of government there?

Roger of Wendover, an English monk, describes how King John came to sign the Magna Carta. Read the excerpt and answer the questions that follow.

> "In Easter week of [1215], the . . . nobles assembled . . . with horses and arms; for they had now induced almost all the nobility of the whole kingdom to join them . . . and when the king learned this, he sent . . . to them to inquire [what] they demanded. The barons then delivered to the messengers a paper, containing in great measure the laws and ancient customs of the kingdom, and declared that, unless the king immediately granted them . . . they would, by taking possession of his fortresses, force him to give them sufficient satisfaction. . . .
>
> King John, when he saw that he was deserted by almost all, . . . deceitfully pretended to make peace with the aforesaid barons, and . . . told them that . . . he would willingly grant them the laws and liberties they required."
>
> —Roger of Wendover, quoted in *Source Book of English History* (Kendall)

23. **(a)** What demands did the nobles make? **(b)** What did they threaten to do if King John did not agree?
24. Do you think Roger of Wendover expected King John to keep his word and honor the Magna Carta? Explain.
25. What was contained in the Magna Carta?
26. What does this excerpt suggest about English royal power in 1215? Explain.

Skills Assessment
Take It to the NET

Use the Internet to research medieval Gothic cathedrals. Based on information that you find on the Internet, draw a simple diagram of part of a cathedral. With your diagram, include a description of the technology used to build that section of the cathedral, or an explanation of that section's significance to medieval architects, clergy, and citizens.

Skills Assessment
Analyzing Maps

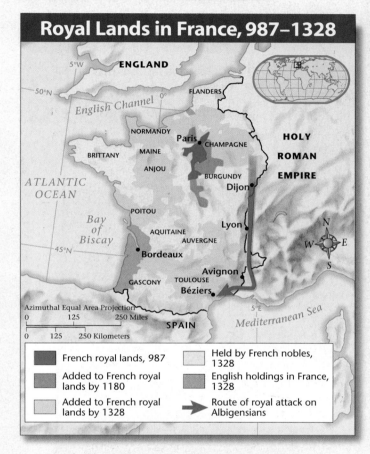

Royal Lands in France, 987–1328

ENGLAND
5°W
50°N
FLANDERS
English Channel 0°
NORMANDY
Paris CHAMPAGNE
BRITTANY MAINE
ANJOU
ATLANTIC OCEAN
BURGUNDY
Dijon
HOLY ROMAN EMPIRE
POITOU
Bay of Biscay
AQUITAINE
AUVERGNE
Lyon
45°N
Bordeaux
GASCONY
TOULOUSE
Béziers
Avignon
N W E S
5°E
Mediterranean Sea
Azimuthal Equal Area Projection
0   125   250 Miles
0   125   250 Kilometers
SPAIN

French royal lands, 987		Held by French nobles, 1328	
Added to French royal lands by 1180		English holdings in France, 1328	
Added to French royal lands by 1328		Route of royal attack on Albigensians	

The map above shows the growth of royal lands over a period of several hundred years. Use the map to answer the following questions:

27. Describe the extent of French royal lands in 987.
28. **(a)** Between what years did Anjou become part of French royal lands? **(b)** Between what years did royal lands increase the most?
29. **(a)** Describe the route used by Philip Augustus's army to attack the Albigensians. **(b)** About how many miles did the army travel?
30. In 1328, who controlled **(a)** Normandy? **(b)** Brittany? **(c)** Bordeaux?

Skills Tip

To understand a map, compare the information on the map with what you have read in your textbook.

The Byzantine Empire and Russia 330–1613

Chapter Preview

1 **The Byzantine Empire**
2 **The Rise of Russia**
3 **Shaping Eastern Europe**

527
Justinian (above) begins his rule of the Byzantine empire.

330
Constantinople becomes capital of the eastern Roman empire.

CHAPTER EVENTS

1019
The reign of Yaroslav the Wise begins in Kiev. Soon, the golden-domed Cathedral of St. Sophia (above) is built to show Kiev's ties to the Byzantine empire.

300   600   900

GLOBAL EVENTS

622 Muhammad makes a journey, known as the hijra, from Mecca to Yathrib.

800 Pope Leo III crowns Charlemagne emperor of the Romans.

Major Religions About 1300

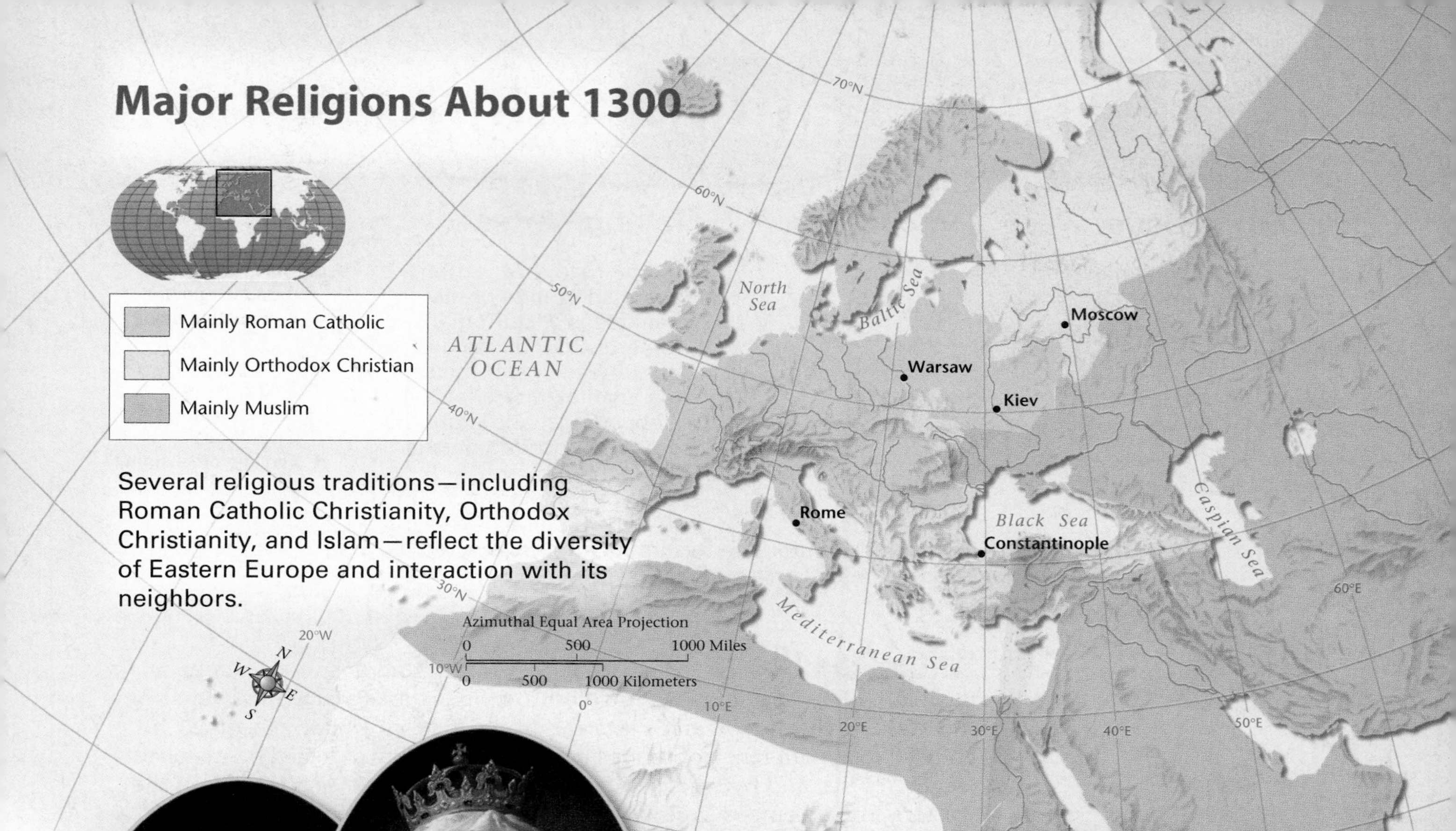

Mainly Roman Catholic
Mainly Orthodox Christian
Mainly Muslim
ATLANTIC OCEAN
North Sea
Baltic Sea
Moscow
Warsaw
Kiev
Rome
Black Sea
Constantinople
Caspian Sea
Mediterranean Sea
Azimuthal Equal Area Projection
0 500 1000 Miles
0 500 1000 Kilometers
70°N
60°N
50°N
40°N
30°N
20°W
10°W
0°
10°E
20°E
30°E
40°E
50°E
60°E
N
S
E
W

Several religious traditions—including Roman Catholic Christianity, Orthodox Christianity, and Islam—reflect the diversity of Eastern Europe and interaction with its neighbors.

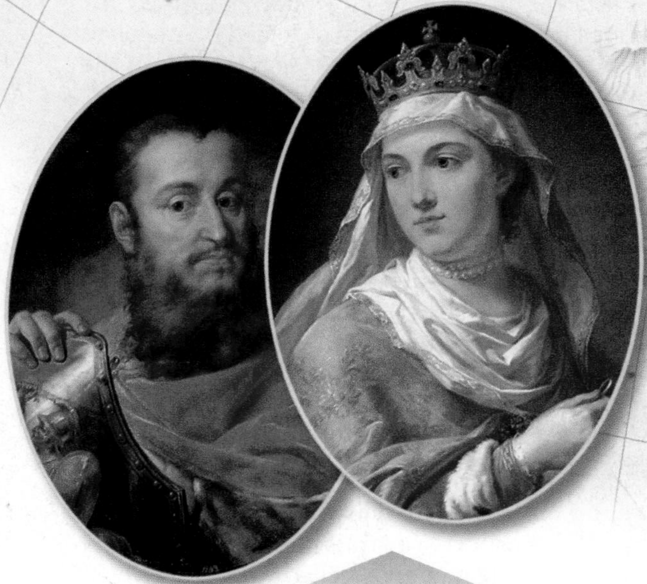

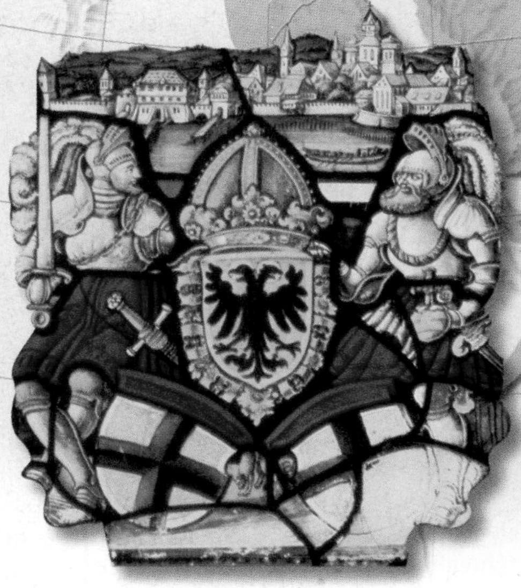

1386

Duke Wladyslav Jagiello of Lithuania marries Queen Jadwiga of Poland, making Poland-Lithuania the largest state in Europe.

1462

Ivan the Great begins his reign in Russia. He uses the double-headed eagle, shown above, to show his connections to the Byzantine empire.

1613

The Romanov dynasty begins its 304-year reign in Russia.

1200 | 1500 | 1800

1076 Pope Gregory VII excommunicates Henry IV, the Holy Roman emperor.

1324 Mansa Musa, ruler of Mali, makes a pilgrimage to Mecca.

1556 Akbar becomes ruler of the Mughal empire in India.

The Byzantine Empire

Reading Focus

- How did Justinian extend Byzantine power?
- What were the key elements of Byzantine Christianity?
- Why did the Byzantine empire collapse?
- What was the heritage of the Byzantine empire?

Vocabulary

autocrat
patriarch
icon

Taking Notes

As you read this section, create an outline of the main ideas. Use Roman numerals to indicate the major headings of the section, capital letters for the subheadings, and numbers for the supporting details. The sample at right will help you get started.

I. The growth of Byzantine power
  A. Constantinople
    1.
    2.
    3.
  B. A blending of cultures
II. The age of Justinian

Main Idea The emperor Justinian expanded the Byzantine empire, erected grand buildings, and established a code of laws.

Global Connections

The Quest for Silk

It is nearly impossible for us today to imagine how rare and costly silk was in the Byzantine empire. Wars made the supply unreliable. Persia, which controlled the silk trade with China, levied high taxes that made silk outrageously expensive.

The Byzantine emperor Justinian wanted a reliable supply of silk at a reasonable price. He tried to set up other trade routes, but with little success. In the end, smugglers changed the picture. According to one legend, monks sneaked silkworm eggs out of China in their walking sticks. Although the details are unclear, the results are not. By the 700s, state-owned silk factories in the Byzantine empire fed a growing and profitable silk industry.

Theme: Economics and Technology Why did the Persians want to keep control over the silk trade with China?

Setting the Scene The bazaars of Constantinople awed visitors. Benjamin of Tudela, a Jewish traveler from Spain, saw merchants there from the Middle East, Egypt, and Eastern Europe. "The city's daily income," he noted, "what with rent from shops and markets and taxes levied on merchants coming by sea and by land, reaches 20,000 gold pieces." As the cities of the western Roman empire crumbled, Constantinople prospered. With its high walls and golden domes, it stood as the proud capital of the Byzantine empire.

The Growth of Byzantine Power

You will recall that, as German invaders pounded the Roman empire in the west, emperors shifted their base to the eastern Mediterranean. The emperor Constantine rebuilt the Greek city of Byzantium and gave it the name Constantinople. In 330, he made Constantinople the new capital of the empire. From this "New Rome," roads fanned out to the Balkans, to the Middle East, and to North Africa. In time, the eastern Roman empire became known as the Byzantine empire.

Constantinople The vital center of the empire was Constantinople. The city was located on the shores of the Bosporus, a strait that linked the Mediterranean and Black seas. Constantinople had an excellent harbor and was guarded on three sides by water. Later emperors built an elaborate system of land and sea walls to bolster its defenses. Equally important, Constantinople commanded key trade routes linking Europe and Asia. For centuries, the city's favorable location made it Europe's busiest marketplace. There, merchants sold silks from China, wheat from Egypt, gems from India, spices from Southeast Asia, and furs from Viking lands in the north.

At the center of the city, Byzantine emperors and empresses lived in glittering splendor. Dressed in luxurious silk, they attended chariot races at the Hippodrome, an arena built in the 200s. Crowds cheered wildly as rival charioteers careened their vehicles around and around. The spectacle was another reminder of the city's glorious Roman heritage.

A Blending of Cultures After rising to spectacular heights, the Byzantine empire eventually declined to a small area around Constantinople itself. Yet it was still in existence nearly 1,000 years after the fall of the western Roman empire. As the heir to Rome, it promoted a brilliant civilization that blended ancient Greek, Roman, and Christian influences with other traditions of the Mediterranean world.

Humanities Link

The Church of Hagia Sophia

The Church of Hagia Sophia survives as an important legacy of the Byzantine empire. During a revolt in 532, the original Hagia Sophia was destroyed. Emperor Justinian quickly began the task of rebuilding the church as Constantinople's brightest jewel. He divided 10,000 workers into two crews and had them compete to finish opposite sides of the church.

Sunlight filters through the windows and highlights the interior of the Hagia Sophia. In its early days, gold glittered from the ceiling, and marble gleamed from the walls.

Inside the church, dazzling mosaics adorn the walls. This mosaic shows Christ Pantocrator, center, flanked by Emperor Constantine IX Monamachus and the Empress Zoë.

Completed in less than six years, Justinian's Church of Hagia Sophia stood as the largest religious building of its day. A huge dome dominated the church. Four minarets, or narrow towers, were added later. After the empire's fall in 1453, the Hagia Sophia served as a mosque and, in recent years, as a museum.

Portfolio Assessment

INTERNET Use the Internet or library resources to find out more about Byzantine art or architecture. Then, choose one example of Byzantine art or architecture. Create a model, diagram, or drawing that points out important features of the work. Prepare a presentation to summarize your research.

The Age of Justinian

The Byzantine empire reached its greatest size under the emperor Justinian, who ruled from 527 to 565. Justinian was determined to revive ancient Rome by recovering the provinces that had been overrun by invaders. Led by the brilliant general Belisarius, Byzantine armies reconquered North Africa, Italy, and southern Spain. The fighting exhausted Justinian's treasury and weakened his defenses in the east. In the end, the victories were temporary. Justinian's successors lost the bitterly contested lands.

Hagia Sophia Justinian left a more lasting monument in his buildings. To restore Roman glory, he launched a program to beautify Constantinople. His great triumph was the church of Hagia Sophia ("Holy Wisdom"). Its immense, arching dome improved on earlier Roman buildings. The interior glowed with colored marble and embroidered silk curtains. Seeing this church, the emperor recalled King Solomon's temple in Jerusalem. "Glory to God who has judged me worthy of accomplishing such a work as this!" Justinian exclaimed. "O Solomon, I have surpassed you!"

Code of Laws Justinian is best remembered for his reform of the law. Early in his reign, he set up a commission to collect, revise, and organize all the laws of ancient Rome. The result was the *Corpus Juris Civilis,* or "Body of Civil Law," popularly known as Justinian's Code. This massive collection included laws passed by Roman assemblies or decreed by Roman emperors, as well as the legal writings of Roman judges and a handbook for students.

Justinian's Code had an impact far beyond the Byzantine empire. By the 1100s, it had reached Western Europe. There, both the Roman Catholic Church and medieval monarchs modeled their laws on its principles. Centuries later, the code also guided legal thinkers who began to put together the international law in use today.

Absolute Power Justinian used the law to unite the empire under his control. He ruled as an autocrat, or sole ruler with complete authority. The emperor also had power over the Church. He was deemed Christ's co-ruler on Earth. As a Byzantine official wrote, "The emperor is equal to all men in the nature of his body, but in the authority of his rank he is similar to God, who rules all." Unlike feudal monarchs in Western Europe, he combined both political power and spiritual authority. His control was aided by his wife, Theodora. A shrewd politician, she served as adviser and co-ruler to Justinian and even pursued her own policies.

Changing Fortunes In the centuries after Justinian, the fortunes of the empire rose and fell. Attacks by Persians, Slavs, Vikings, Mongols, and Turks were largely unsuccessful. The empire thus served as a buffer for Western Europe. Beginning in the 600s and 700s, however, Arab armies gained control of much of the Mediterranean world. Constantinople itself withstood their attack, and the Byzantines held onto their heartland in the Balkans and Asia Minor. The empire's greatest strengths came from a strong central government and a prosperous economy.

Peasants formed the backbone of the empire, working the land, paying taxes, and providing soldiers for the military. In the cities of the empire, trade and industry flourished. While Western Europe was reduced to a barter economy, the Byzantine empire preserved a healthy money economy. The bezant, the Byzantine gold coin stamped with the emperor's image, circulated from England to China.

Byzantine Christianity

Christianity was as influential in the Byzantine empire as it was in Western Europe. But religious divisions grew between the two regions.

Biography

Theodora 500–548

From humble beginnings as the daughter of a bearkeeper, Theodora rose to become Justinian's adviser and co-ruler. A shrewd, tough, and sometimes ruthless politician, Theodora did not hesitate to challenge the emperor and pursue her own policies.

Her most dramatic act came during a revolt in 532. "Emperor, if you wish to flee, well and good, you have the money, the ships are ready, the sea is clear," calmly spoke Theodora. "But I shall stay," she concluded. "I accept the ancient proverb: Royal purple is the best burial sheet." Theodora's courageous words inspired Justinian to remain in Constantinople and crush the revolt that threatened his power.

Theme: Impact of the Individual How did Theodora affect the outcome of the revolt?

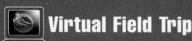

Virtual Field Trip

www.phschool.com

**Byzantine Museum
Athens, Greece**

To see other examples of Orthodox
Christian icons, use the Internet
address above to link to the
Byzantine Museum.

Icons

In this early Byzantine icon, the
figures of Christ (right) and a saint
stare directly outward, inviting the
viewer into a personal relationship.
The figures and their golden halos
seem to glow because the artist
painted on a background of reflecting gold paint. Over the centuries,
Byzantine artists tended to use similar styles and techniques.

Theme: Art and Literature
**What do you think the artist was
trying to accomplish with this icon?**

Differences East and West   Since early Christian times, differences had
emerged over Church leadership. Although the Byzantine emperor was not
a priest, he controlled Church affairs and appointed the **patriarch,** or highest Church official, in Constantinople. Byzantine Christians rejected the
pope's claim to authority over all Christians.

Further differences developed. Unlike priests in Western Europe, the
Byzantine clergy kept their right to marry. Greek, not Latin, was the language of the Byzantine Church. The chief Byzantine holy day was Easter,
celebrated as the day Jesus rose from the dead. In contrast, western
Christians placed greater emphasis on Christmas, the birthday of Jesus.

Schism   During the Middle Ages, the two branches of Christianity drew
farther apart. A dispute over the use of **icons,** or holy images, contributed
to the split. Many Byzantine Christians prayed to images of Christ, the
Virgin Mary, and the saints. In the 700s, however, a Byzantine emperor
outlawed the veneration of icons, saying it violated God's commandment
against worshiping "graven images."

The ban set off violent battles within the empire. From the west, the
pope took a hand in the dispute, excommunicating the emperor. Although
a later empress eventually restored the use of icons, the conflict left great
resentment against the pope.

In 1054, other controversies provoked a schism, or permanent split,
between the Byzantine, or Eastern (Greek) Orthodox, and the Roman
Catholic churches. The pope and the patriarch excommunicated each other.
Thereafter, contacts between the two churches were guarded and distant.
They treated each other as rivals rather than as branches of the same faith.

Crisis and Collapse

By the time of the schism, the Byzantine empire was declining. Struggles
over succession, court intrigues, and constant wars undermined its strength.
As in Western Europe, powerful local lords gained control of large areas. As
the empire faltered, its enemies advanced. The Normans conquered southern
Italy. Even more serious, the Seljuk Turks advanced across Asia Minor.

A nomadic people out of central Asia, the Seljuks had converted to Islam in their migrations westward.

The Crusades   In the 1090s, the Byzantine emperor called for western help to fight the Seljuks, who had closed the pilgrimage routes to Jerusalem. The result was the First Crusade. During later crusades, however, trade rivalry sparked violence between the Byzantine empire and Venice. Venetian merchants persuaded knights on the Fourth Crusade to attack Constantinople in 1204. For three days, crusaders burned and plundered the city, sending much treasure westward. Western Christians ruled Constantinople for 50 years. Although a Byzantine emperor reclaimed the capital in the 1260s, the empire never recovered. Venetian merchants gained control of Byzantine trade, draining the wealth of the empire. More threatening, the Ottoman Turks overran most of Asia Minor and the Balkans.

Constantinople Falls   In 1453, Ottoman forces surrounded the city of Constantinople. After a siege lasting two months, they stormed the broken walls. When the last Byzantine emperor was offered safe passage, he replied, "God forbid that I should live an emperor without an empire." He chose instead to die fighting.

Forces led by Ottoman ruler Muhammad II entered the city in triumph. The ancient Christian city was renamed Istanbul and became the capital of the Ottoman

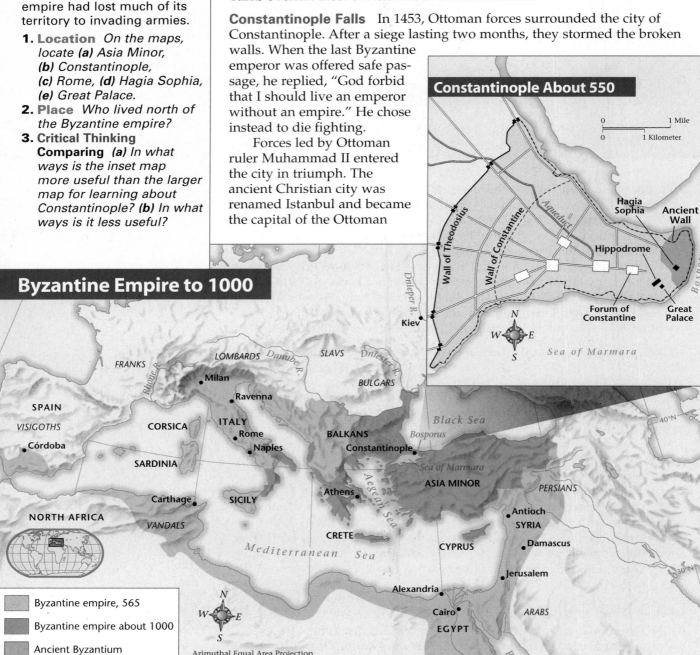

Constantinople About 550

Wall of Theodosius · Wall of Constantine · Aqueduct · Hagia Sophia · Ancient Wall · Hippodrome · Bosporus · Forum of Constantine · Great Palace · Sea of Marmara

Byzantine Empire to 1000

FRANKS · LOMBARDS · Danube R. · SLAVS · Dniester R. · BULGARS · Milan · Ravenna · Rhone R. · SPAIN · VISIGOTHS · Córdoba · CORSICA · ITALY · Rome · Naples · SARDINIA · BALKANS · Bosporus · Black Sea · Kiev · Dnieper R. · Constantinople · Sea of Marmara · Carthage · SICILY · Athens · Aegean Sea · ASIA MINOR · PERSIANS · NORTH AFRICA · VANDALS · CRETE · CYPRUS · Antioch · SYRIA · Damascus · Mediterranean Sea · Alexandria · Jerusalem · Cairo · ARABS · EGYPT · Nile R. · Red Sea · Medina · Mecca

Legend:
- Byzantine empire, 565
- Byzantine empire about 1000
- Ancient Byzantium
- City under Constantine and later rulers

Azimuthal Equal Area Projection
0   250   500 Miles
0   250   500 Kilometers

empire. Hagia Sophia was turned into an Islamic house of worship, and Istanbul soon emerged as a great center of Muslim culture.

The Byzantine Heritage

Although Byzantine power had faded long before, the fall of Constantinople marked the end of an era. To Europeans, the empire had stood for centuries as the enduring symbol of Roman civilization. Throughout the Middle Ages, Byzantine influence radiated across Europe. Even the Ottoman conquerors adapted features of Byzantine government, social life, and architecture.

What was the Byzantine heritage? For 1,000 years, the Byzantines built on the culture of the Hellenistic world. Byzantine civilization blended Christian religious beliefs with Greek science, philosophy, arts, and literature. The Byzantines also extended Roman achievements in engineering and law.

The Arts Byzantine artists made unique contributions, especially in religious art and architecture, that influenced western styles from the Middle Ages to the present. Icons, designed to evoke the presence of God, gave viewers a sense of personal contact with the sacred. Mosaics brought scenes from the Bible to glowing life. In architecture, Byzantine palaces and churches blended Greek, Roman, Persian, and other Middle Eastern styles.

The World of Learning Byzantine scholars preserved the classic works of ancient Greece. In addition, they produced their own great books, especially in the field of history.

Like the Greek historians Herodotus and Thucydides, Byzantine historians were mostly concerned with writing about their own times. Procopius, an adviser to the general Belisarius, chronicled the Byzantine campaign against Persia. In his *Secret History*, Procopius savagely criticized Justinian and Theodora. He called the emperor "both an evil-doer and easily led into evil . . . never of his own accord speaking the truth." Anna Comnena is considered by many scholars to be the western world's first important female historian. In the *Alexiad*, she analyzed the reign of her father, Emperor Alexius I. Comnena's book portrayed Latin crusaders as greedy barbarians.

As the empire tottered in the 1400s, many Greek scholars left Constantinople to teach at Italian universities. They took valuable Greek manuscripts to the West, along with their knowledge of Greek and Byzantine culture. The work of these scholars contributed to the European cultural flowering that became known as the Renaissance.

SECTION 1 Assessment

Recall
1. **Identify: (a)** Hagia Sophia, **(b)** *Corpus Juris Civilis*, **(c)** Theodora, **(d)** Procopius, **(e)** Anna Comnena.
2. **Define: (a)** autocrat, **(b)** patriarch, **(c)** icon.

Comprehension
3. Describe three of Justinian's major accomplishments.
4. What were some differences between Byzantine Christianity and Roman Catholic Christianity?
5. **(a)** How did the Crusades affect the Byzantine empire? **(b)** Why did the empire finally fall?
6. Describe the legacy of Byzantine civilization.

Critical Thinking and Writing
7. **Defending a Position** The Byzantine empire preserved part of the heritage of the Roman empire. What, in your opinion, was the most important result of this legacy? Why do you think so?
8. **Drawing Conclusions** As emperor, Justinian made many contributions to the strength and prosperity of the Byzantine empire. Which contribution do you think had the most lasting impact? Explain your answer.

Activity
Take It to the NET

Use the Internet to research the history of Hagia Sophia in Istanbul. Then, use your information to create a time line showing important events in the building's history. If possible, include illustrations of the interior and exterior.

The Rise of Russia

Reading Focus

- How did geography help shape early Russia and the growth of Kiev?

- How did the Mongol conquest affect Russia?

- Why did Moscow emerge as the chief power in Russia?

Vocabulary

steppe

boyar

czar

Taking Notes

Create a time line that shows events in the rise of Russia between the 700s and 1613. The sample on this page will help you get started.

700s	900	1100	1300	1500	1613

Varangians
appear

Main Idea In its early years, Russia was influenced by the Slavs, Vikings, Byzantines, and Mongols.

Setting the Scene In Russia, a patriotic monk saw a special meaning in the fall of Constantinople. Moscow, he declared, was a "third Rome," the successor to the Roman and Byzantine empires:

> "The third Rome . . . shines like the sun . . . throughout the whole universe. . . . Two Romes have fallen, and the third one stands, and a fourth one there shall not be."
> —Philotheos, quoted in *Tsar and People* (Cherniavsky)

Moscow had reason to claim itself heir to the Byzantine empire. Over many centuries, Byzantine culture greatly influenced the development of Russian society.

The Geography of Russia

Russia lies on the vast Eurasian plain that reaches from Europe to the borders of China. Although mapmakers use the Ural Mountains to mark the boundary between Europe and Asia, these ancient mountains were long ago worn away to wooded hills. They posed no obstacle to migration.

Three broad zones with different climates and resources helped shape early Russian life. The northern forests supplied lumber for building and fuel. Fur-bearing animals attracted hunters, but poor soil and a cold, snowy climate hindered farming. Farther south, a band of fertile land attracted early farmers. This region—today the country of Ukraine—was home to Russia's first civilization.

A third region, the southern steppe, is an open, treeless grassland. It offered splendid pasture for the herds and horses of nomadic peoples. With no natural barriers, the steppe was a great highway, along which streams of nomads migrated from Asia into Europe.

Russia's network of rivers provided transportation for both people and goods. The Dnieper (NEE puhr) and Volga rivers became productive trade routes. Major rivers ran from north to south, linking the Russians early on to the advanced Byzantine world in the south.

Growth of Kiev

During Roman times, the Slavs expanded into southern Russia. Like the Germanic peoples who pushed into Western Europe, the Slavs had a simple political organization and were organized into clans. They lived in small

Primary Source

The Russians Become Christians

Prince Vladimir of Kiev sent representatives to visit the churches of many lands:

"The envoys reported, 'When we journeyed among the Bulgars, we beheld how they worship in their temple. . . . Their religion is not good. Then we went among the Germans, . . . but we beheld no glory there. Then we went on to Greece, and the Greeks led us to the edifices [buildings] where they worship their God, and we knew not whether we were in heaven or on earth. For on earth there is no such splendor or such beauty, and we are at a loss how to describe it. We know only that God dwells there among men, and their service is fairer than the ceremonies of other nations. For we cannot forget that beauty.'"

—*The Primary Chronicle*

Skills Assessment

Primary Source What impressed the Russians about the Greek Orthodox Church?

villages, farmed, and traded along the rivers that ran between the Baltic and the Black seas.

The Varangians   In the 700s and 800s, the Vikings steered their long ships out of Scandinavia. These expert sailors were as much at home on Russian rivers as on the stormy Atlantic. The Vikings, called Varangians by later Russians, worked their way south along the rivers, trading with and collecting tribute from the Slavs. They also conducted a thriving trade with Constantinople.

Located at the heart of this vital trade network was the city of Kiev. In time, it would become the center of the first Russian state. Within a few generations, the Varangians who had settled among the Slavs were absorbed into the local culture. Viking names like *Helga* and *Waldemar* became the Slavic names *Olga* and *Vladimir*.

Byzantine Influences   Early on, trade had brought Kiev into the Byzantine orbit. Constantinople later sent Christian missionaries to convert the Slavs. About 863, two Greek monks, Cyril and Methodius, adapted the Greek alphabet so they could translate the Bible into Slavic languages. This Cyrillic (suh RIHL ihk) alphabet became the written script used in Russia and Ukraine to the present.

In 957, Princess Olga of Kiev converted to Byzantine Christianity. But it was not until the reign of her grandson Vladimir that the new religion spread widely. After his own conversion, Vladimir married the sister of a Byzantine emperor. Soon, Greek priests arrived in Kiev to preside over the mass baptisms organized by the prince.

As Byzantine Christianity gained strength in Russia, princes began to see themselves as heirs to many cultural and political aspects of the Byzantine empire. The Russians acquired a written language, and a class of educated Russian priests emerged. Russians adapted Byzantine religious art, music, and architecture. Byzantine domes capped with colorful, carved "helmets" became the onion domes of Russian churches.

Byzantine Christianity set the pattern for close ties between Church and state. Russian rulers, like the Byzantine emperor, eventually controlled the Church, making it dependent on them for support. The Russian Orthodox Church would long remain a pillar of state power.

Yaroslav   Kiev enjoyed a golden age under Yaroslav the Wise, who ruled from 1019 to 1054. Like Justinian, he issued a written law code to improve justice. A scholar, he translated Greek works into his language. Yaroslav arranged marriages between his children and some of the royal families of Western Europe.

Kiev declined in the 1100s as rival families battled for the throne. Also, Russian trading cities were hurt because Byzantine prosperity faded. As Russian princes squabbled among themselves, Mongol invaders from central Asia struck the final blow.

Mongol Conquest

In the early 1200s, a young leader united the nomadic Mongols of central Asia. As his mounted bowmen overran lands from China to Eastern Europe, he took the title Genghiz Khan (GEHNG gihz KAHN), "World Emperor."

The Golden Horde   Between 1236 and 1241, Batu, the grandson of Genghiz, led Mongol armies into Russia. Known as the Golden Horde, from

Constantinople and Russia
Cyril and Methodius became saints in both the Orthodox and Roman Catholic churches. Modern Russian script is based on the Cyrillic alphabet developed by the two Greek monks.

Theme: Impact of the Individual How does this image, from a church fresco, reflect the contributions of Cyril and Methodius?

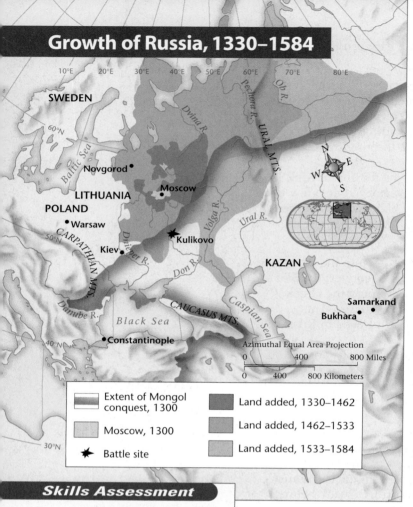

Growth of Russia, 1330–1584

SWEDEN

Novgorod

Moscow

LITHUANIA
POLAND

Warsaw

Kiev

Kulikovo

KAZAN

Samarkand

Bukhara

Black Sea

Constantinople

Azimuthal Equal Area Projection

0   400   800 Miles

0   400   800 Kilometers

Extent of Mongol conquest, 1300

Moscow, 1300

★ Battle site

Land added, 1330–1462

Land added, 1462–1533

Land added, 1533–1584

Skills Assessment

Geography Between 1300 and 1584, Russian lands grew from a small area around Moscow to a large territory.

1. **Location** On the map, locate (a) Black Sea, (b) Volga River, (c) Danube River, (d) Caspian Sea, (e) Kulikovo.

2. **Place** During what years did Novgorod come under Russian rule?

3. **Critical Thinking Synthesizing Information** Locate the natural feature many mapmakers consider the boundary between Europe and Asia. In 1584, were Russian lands mostly in Europe or in Asia?

the color of their tents, they looted and burned Kiev and other Russian towns. So many inhabitants were killed, declared a Russian historian, that "no eye remained to weep for the dead." From their capital on the Volga, the Golden Horde ruled Russia for the next 240 years.

The Mongols, although fierce conquerors, were generally tolerant rulers. They demanded regular payments of heavy tribute, and Russian princes had to acknowledge the Mongols as their overlords. But as long as the tribute was paid, the Mongols left Russian princes to rule without much interference.

Mongol Influences Historians have long debated how Mongol rule affected Russia. Peasants felt the burden of heavy taxes. Some fled to remote regions, and others sought protection from Mongol raids by becoming serfs of Russian nobles. Even though the Golden Horde converted to Islam, the Mongols tolerated the Russian Orthodox Church, which grew more powerful during this period. The Mongol conquest brought peace to the huge swath of land between China and Eastern Europe, and Russian merchants benefited from new trade routes across this region.

During the period of Mongol rule, Russians adopted the practice of isolating upper-class women in separate quarters. Beginning in the 1200s, women became totally subject to male authority in the household. Husbands could even sell their wives into slavery to pay family debts.

The absolute power of the Mongols served as a model for later Russian rulers. Russian princes developed a strong desire to centralize their own power without interference from nobles, the clergy, or wealthy merchants. Perhaps most important, Mongol rule cut Russia off from contacts with Western Europe at a time when Europeans were making rapid advances in the arts and sciences.

Moscow Takes the Lead

During the Mongol period, the princes of Moscow steadily increased their power. Their success was due in part to the city's location near important river trade routes. They also used their positions as tribute collectors for the Mongols to subdue neighboring towns. When the head of the Russian Orthodox Church made Moscow his capital, the city became not just Russia's political center, but its spiritual center as well.

As Mongol power declined, the princes of Moscow took on a new role as patriotic defenders of Russia against foreign rule. In 1380, they rallied other Russians and defeated the Golden Horde at the battle of Kulikovo. Although the Mongols continued their terrifying raids, their strength was much reduced.

Ivan the Great A driving force behind Moscow's successes was Ivan III, known as Ivan the Great. Between 1462 and 1505, he brought much of northern Russia under his rule. He also recovered Russian territories that had fallen into the hands of neighboring Slavic states.

Ivan built the framework for absolute rule. He tried to limit the power of the **boyars**, or great landowning nobles. After he married Sophia-Zoë

Paleologus, niece of the last Byzantine emperor, he adopted Byzantine court rituals to emphasize Russia's role as the heir to Byzantine power. Like the Byzantine emperors, he used a double-headed eagle as his symbol. Ivan and his successors took the title **czar,** the Russian word for Caesar. "The czar," claimed Ivan, "is in nature like all men, but in authority he is like the highest God."

Ivan the Terrible Ivan IV, grandson of Ivan the Great, further centralized royal power. He limited the privileges of the old boyar families and granted land to nobles in exchange for military or other service. At a time when the manor system was fading in Western Europe, Ivan IV introduced new laws that tied Russian serfs to the land.

About 1560, Ivan IV became increasingly unstable. He trusted no one and became subject to violent fits of rage. In a moment of madness, he even killed his own son. He organized the *oprichniki* (aw PREECH nee kee), agents of terror who enforced the czar's will. Dressed in black robes and mounted on black horses, they slaughtered rebellious boyars and sacked towns where people were suspected of disloyalty. Their saddles were decorated with a dog's head and a broom, symbols of their constant watchfulness to sweep away their master's enemies.

The czar's awesome power, and the ways he used it, earned him the title "Ivan the Terrible." When he died in 1584, he left a land seething with rebellion. But he had introduced Russia to a tradition of extreme absolute power.

Looking Ahead

Disputes over succession, peasant uprisings, and foreign invasions soon plunged Russia into a period of disorder. This "Time of Troubles" lasted from 1604 to 1613. Finally, the zemsky sobor (ZEHM skee suh BAWR), an assembly of clergy, nobles, and townsmen, chose a new czar, 17-year-old Michael Romanov. His reign established the Romanov dynasty, which would rule Russia until 1917.

In the 1600s, Russia was an emerging power. Like monarchs in France or Spain, the czars expanded national borders and centralized royal control. But Russia developed along far different lines. Byzantine influences had helped establish a strong tradition of autocratic rule. Later Russian rulers were generally more autocratic than western kings and queens. Authoritarian leaders, from Peter the Great and Catherine the Great to Joseph Stalin, would shape Russian history down to this century.

Biography

Ivan the Terrible 1530–1584

"I grew up on the throne," explained Ivan of his unhappy childhood. His father, Vasily, died when Ivan was only three years old. Intelligent, well read, and religious, young Ivan was crowned czar at age 17.

Though Ivan had long been a harsh ruler, his behavior became increasingly unstable after his wife died. Prone to violence, he crushed any opposition, real or imagined. He had thousands of people killed in the city of Novgorod because he feared a plot. Almost every noble family was affected by his murders. "From Adam to this day I have surpassed all sinners," he confessed in his will.

Theme: Impact of the Individual How did Ivan's reign affect Russia?

SECTION 2 Assessment

Recall

1. **Identify:** **(a)** Cyril and Methodius, **(b)** Vladimir, **(c)** Yaroslav, **(d)** Genghiz Khan, **(e)** Golden Horde, **(f)** "Time of Troubles," **(g)** Michael Romanov.
2. **Define:** **(a)** steppe, **(b)** boyar, **(c)** czar.

Comprehension

3. Describe how Russia's geography affected the rise of Kiev.
4. How did Mongol rule influence the economy and political structure of Russia?

5. How did Ivan III and Ivan IV establish royal power in Russia?

Critical Thinking and Writing

6. **Recognizing Points of View** Supporters of Ivan III called Moscow "the third Rome." **(a)** Why do you think they wanted to compare Moscow to Rome? **(b)** Do you agree that Moscow was truly the heir to Rome? Why or why not?
7. **Connecting to Geography** How did geography aid the princes of Moscow in gaining power?

Activity

Creating a Chart
Create a chart that summarizes the various cultural, religious, and political influences of the following groups on Russia: Varangians, Byzantines, Mongols.

Shaping Eastern Europe

Reading Focus

- How did geography influence developments in Eastern Europe?
- Why did Eastern Europe become a cultural crossroads with a diverse mix of peoples?
- What threats did the early kingdoms of Europe face?

Main Idea Ethnic diversity contributed to the varied cultural traditions of Eastern Europe.

Vocabulary

ethnic group
diet

Taking Notes

On a sheet of paper begin a concept web like this one. As you read the section, fill in the blank circles with relevant information about Eastern Europe. Add more circles if needed.

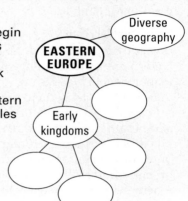

Geography and History

The Blue Danube

"The Danube is Eastern Europe's great throbbing artery," wrote one journalist. "No other river in Europe . . . flows through as many nations . . . or echoes to as many languages." For more than 2,500 years, the Danube River has been a pathway for armies, goods, and ideas. Greek traders sailed along the lower part of the river as early as 600 B.C. Roman and, later, Ottoman armies built forts along its banks. Some of those fortresses grew into major cities, including Budapest and Belgrade. Today, dams on the 1,800 mile-long "Blue Danube" are a vital source of electric power.

Theme: Geography and History What resources has the Danube provided over the centuries?

Setting the Scene Many times in the past hundred years, people have opened their newspapers to find news about turbulent events in Eastern Europe. In 1914, a political assassination by Serbian nationalists triggered World War I. In 1938 and 1939, German aggression in Czechoslovakia and Poland sparked World War II. In 1989, revolts in Eastern European nations helped topple the Soviet empire. In the 1990s, war again erupted in the Balkans as rival national groups clashed in Bosnia and Kosovo.

The roots of such conflicts lie deep in the history of Eastern Europe. As you will see, it has been a history often marked by war, revolution, and foreign conquest. At the same time, its diverse mix of peoples has enriched the culture of the region.

The Geography of Eastern Europe

The region known as Eastern Europe is a wide swath of territory lying between German-speaking Central Europe to the west and the largest Slavic nation, Russia, to the east. Many peoples and many nations have flourished in the area over the centuries.

Eastern Europe reaches from the chilly waters of the Baltic Sea, down across the plains of Poland, then through the mountainous Balkans. The Balkan Peninsula, a roughly triangular arm of land, juts southward into the warm Mediterranean. Several geographic features contributed to developments in Eastern Europe. Much of the region lies on the great European plain that links up with the steppes of southern Russia.

The main rivers of Eastern Europe, like the Danube and the Vistula, flow either south into the Black Sea or north into the Baltic Sea. Goods and cultural influences traveled along these river routes. As a result, the Balkans in the south felt the impact of the Byzantine empire and, later, the Muslim Ottoman empire. In contrast, the northern regions bordering Germany and the Baltic Sea forged closer links to Western Europe.

A Diverse Mix of Peoples

Eastern Europe's geography has made it a cultural crossroads. The ease of migration encouraged many different peoples to seek new homes, as well as increased power, in the region. As a result, Eastern Europe now includes a wealth of languages and cultures.

The Balkans In the early Middle Ages, the Slavs spread out from a central heartland in Russia. The West Slavs filtered into present-day Poland and the Czech and Slovak republics. The South Slavs descended into the Balkans and became the ancestors of the Serbs, Croats, and Slovenes.

The Balkans were peopled by other ethnic groups as well. An **ethnic group** is a large group of people who share the same language and cultural heritage. Waves of Asian peoples migrated into Eastern Europe, among them the Huns, Avars, Bulgars, Khazars, and Magyars. Vikings and other Germanic peoples added to the mix.

Powerful neighboring states exercised strong cultural influences on Eastern Europe. Byzantine missionaries carried Eastern Orthodox Christianity and Byzantine culture throughout the Balkans. German knights and missionaries from the West spread Roman Catholic Christianity to Poland, Hungary, the Czech area, and the western Balkans. In the 1300s, the Ottomans invaded the Balkans, spreading Islam into pockets of that area.

Jewish Settlements In the late Middle Ages, Eastern Europe was a refuge for many Jewish settlers. Western European Christians launched brutal attacks on Jewish communities, particularly during the Crusades and the Black Death. To escape persecution, many Jews fled east. Monarchs in England, France, and Spain also expelled Jews from their lands. (See "Synthesizing Information" on the next page.)

In the 1300s, Polish kings followed a policy of toleration toward Jews. As a result, Jewish villages sprang up in Poland and other sparsely populated areas of Eastern Europe. Jewish merchants and scholars contributed to the economic and cultural development of Poland during this period.

Early Kingdoms

During the Middle Ages, Eastern Europe included many kingdoms and small states. Sometimes, empires absorbed national groups. Alliances or royal marriages might bind others together for a time. To get a sense of these shifting fortunes, we will look at the kingdoms of Poland, Hungary, and Serbia.

Poland Missionaries brought Roman Catholicism to the West Slavs of Poland in the 900s. A century later, the first Polish king was crowned. To survive, Poland often had to battle Germans, Russians, and Mongols.

Poland's greatest age came after Queen Jadwiga (yahd VEE gah) married Duke Wladyslav Jagiello (vwah DIHS wahv yahg YEH loh) of Lithuania in 1386. Poland-Lithuania controlled the largest state in Europe, stretching from the Baltic to the Black Sea. Jadwiga supported a university in Cracow, which became a major center of science and the arts.

Byzantine Cavalry
Although Byzantine civilization influenced many people in Eastern Europe, conflict often erupted. In this illustration from the 1300s, Byzantine knights defeat Bulgar soldiers.

Theme: Political and Social Systems What reasons might the Bulgars have had for fighting the Byzantine empire?

Jewish Migrations in Europe

The late Middle Ages were a time of troubles for the Jews of Europe. Though masters of trade, finance, and learning, Jews were expelled from several of the Christian nations of Western Europe. The map and the time line below show events related to their migrations.

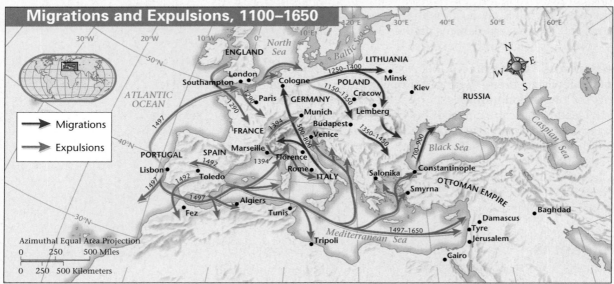

Migrations and Expulsions, 1100–1650

During the early Middle Ages, Jews created economically and intellectually vital communities in Western Europe. Beginning in the 1200s, however, the rulers of several nations formally expelled the Jews from their lands. Many migrated to Poland and other parts of Eastern Europe, where they were allowed to build their own communities.

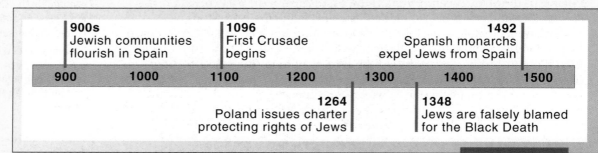

| **900s**
Jewish communities
flourish in Spain | **1096**
First Crusade
begins | | **1492**
Spanish monarchs
expel Jews from Spain |

| 900 | 1000 | 1100 | 1200 | 1300 | 1400 | 1500 |

1264
Poland issues charter
protecting rights of Jews

1348
Jews are falsely blamed
for the Black Death

Skills Assessment

1. When expelled from France in 1394, Jews migrated to
   A England.
   B Italy and Germany.
   C Spain and Portugal.
   D Poland and Eastern Europe.

2. Which event resulted in a widespread scattering of the Jewish population outside Europe?
   E expulsion from Spain
   F Polish charter
   G Black Death
   H First Crusade

3. **Critical Thinking** **Drawing Conclusions** Based on the evidence provided, where were Jews more likely to settle after 1350? Why?

Unlike Russia or Western Europe, Poland gradually increased the power of its nobles at the expense of the monarch. They met in a **diet,** or assembly, where the vote of a single noble was enough to block the passage of a law. This liberum veto, or "free veto," made it hard for the government to take decisive action.

Without a strong central government, Poland declined. It enjoyed a final moment of glory in 1683 when the Polish king Jan Sobieski (YAHN SAW BYEH skee) broke the Ottoman siege of Vienna. In the next century, however, Poland was gobbled up by ambitious neighbors and disappeared from the map entirely.

Hungary The Magyars raided Europe from the Asian steppes and settled in Hungary. Like the West Slavs of Poland, they adopted Roman Catholic Christianity. During the Middle Ages, the country was much larger than it is today. Hungarian rulers controlled present-day Slovakia, Croatia, and parts of Romania.

Like King John of England, the Hungarian king was forced to sign a charter recognizing the rights of his nobles. Known as the Golden Bull of 1222, it strictly limited royal power.

The Mongols overran Hungary in 1241, killing perhaps as much as half its population. They soon withdrew, so their invasion did not have the same impact it had on Russia. The expansion of the Ottoman Turks, though, ended Hungarian independence in 1526.

Serbia During the 600s, South Slavs settled the mountainous Balkans. Serbs, Croats, Slovenes, and other Slavic peoples in the Balkans had different histories during the Middle Ages. The Serbs accepted Orthodox Christianity. By the late 1100s, they had set up their own state, which reached its height under Stefan Dušan (STEH fahn DOO shahn). Stefan also encouraged Byzantine culture, even modeling his law code on that of Justinian.

Dušan's successors lacked his political gifts, however, and Serbia could not withstand the advance of Ottoman Turks. At the battle of Kosovo in 1389, Serbs fought to the death, a memory still honored by their descendants more than 600 years later.

Looking Ahead

Migration, conquest, dynastic marriages, and missionary activity helped produce a tangle of overlapping claims to territories in Eastern Europe. During the 1600s and 1700s, large empires to the east and west swallowed up much of the region. Yet whenever they had a chance, the peoples of Eastern Europe tried to recover their independence. In later chapters, we will see how the desire to rebuild separate states repeatedly ignited new turmoils.

Connections to Today

Balkan Boiling Pot

Throughout the 1990s, violence exploded in the Balkans. In 1992, Eastern Orthodox Serbs, Bosnian Muslims, and Catholic Croats fought a bloody civil war in Bosnia. In 1998, Christian Serbs and Muslims of Albanian heritage clashed in Kosovo.

The modern-day wars echo ethnic struggles that have gone on for more than 600 years in the Balkans. In 1389, Turkish soldiers from the Ottoman empire defeated Serbs at the Battle of Kosovo and took over the region. Different ethnic groups practicing different religions dispersed throughout the area. Even though they were forced to live together, the different groups have remained fiercely independent. Instead of being a melting pot of cultures, the Balkan region has continued to simmer and occasionally boil over.

Theme: Religions and Value Systems How have religions and ethnic groups affected life in the Balkans?

SECTION 3 Assessment

Recall

1. **Identify: (a)** Jadwiga and Wladyslaw Jagiello, **(b)** Jan Sobieski, **(c)** Golden Bull of 1222, **(d)** Stefan Dušan.
2. **Define: (a)** ethnic group, **(b)** diet.

Comprehension

3. What role did rivers play in Eastern Europe?
4. How did Eastern Europe become home to many ethnic groups?

5. What relationship did the Ottoman Turks have with the early kingdoms of Eastern Europe?

Critical Thinking and Writing

6. **Comparing (a)** How were the histories of Poland, Hungary, and Serbia similar? **(b)** How were their histories different?
7. **Linking Past and Present** Why is Kosovo so important to modern-day Serbs?

Activity
Take It to the NET

Use the Internet to research old Cracow in Poland. Use your information to create a guide to the old part of the city. Then, take your classmates on a virtual tour.

Creating a Chapter Summary

Copy the table shown below. Fill in the spaces under each heading to help you review key facts about the chapter.

For additional review and enrichment activities, see the interactive version of *World History* available on the Web and on CD-ROM.

	BYZANTINE EMPIRE	RUSSIA	EASTERN EUROPE
IMPORTANT CITIES	Constantinople	Kiev, Moscow	Cracow (Poland), Kosovo (Serbia)
RULERS			
RELIGION			
OTHER CONTRIBUTIONS			

Web Site Self-Test
For practice test questions for Chapter 10, see **www.phschool.com**.

Building Vocabulary

Use the chapter vocabulary words listed below to create a crossword puzzle. Exchange puzzles with a classmate. Complete the puzzles and then check each other's answers.

1. **autocrat**
2. **patriarch**
3. **icon**
4. **steppe**
5. **boyar**
6. **czar**
7. **ethnic group**
8. **diet**

Recalling Key Facts

9. How was the Byzantine empire an outgrowth of the Roman empire?
10. What important split in Christianity occurred in 1054?
11. What was the Golden Horde?
12. What were the accomplishments of Ivan the Great?
13. What peoples and religions are represented in Eastern Europe?
14. Why did many Jews migrate to Eastern Europe?
15. Why did the kingdom of Poland decline?

Critical Thinking and Writing

16. **Drawing Conclusions** How might European history have been different if the Byzantine empire had fallen after the death of Justinian?
17. **Defending a Position** Autocratic rule helped leaders of Moscow and Russia create a strong central state. Do you think that there is any justification for autocratic rule? Explain.
18. **Linking Past and Present** **(a)** How have long-standing ethnic differences in Eastern Europe influenced events in modern times? **(b)** Do you think that ethnic differences have played a similar role in the growth of American society? Explain.
19. **Synthesizing Information** **(a)** Construct a time line showing events in the Byzantine empire, Russia, and Eastern Europe. **(b)** Identify influences that had a significant impact on the history of all three regions.
20. **Connecting to Geography** Describe the role that bodies of water played in linking the Byzantine empire with Russia and Eastern Europe.

During the reign of Czar Ivan IV, a book called the *Domostroi* was published. The title means "house order." The *Domostroi* contains instructions on all aspects of a noble's home life, including the preparation and serving of food; the treatment of children, guests, merchants, and servants; and the celebration of religious holidays. The author may have been a priest who served at the Kremlin Cathedral of the Annunciation in Moscow. Read the excerpt below and answer the questions that follow.

> *"If God send any disease or ailment down upon a person let him cure himself through the grace of God, through tears, prayer, fasting, charity to the poor, and true repentance. Let him thank the Lord and beg His forgiveness, and show mercy and undisguised charity to everybody. . . .*
>
> *When a sick person is in the house, let the homeowner invite seven or more priests and as many deacons as he can find. They will pray over commemorative beer for health and over frumenty [a kind of pudding] to bring peace of mind.*
>
> *After someone departs this life, the priest or deacon will cense [perfume with incense] every room, sprinkling it with holy water and making the sign of the cross. Then those in the house, praising God according to the divine liturgy, should at once set up a table so that the priests and monks, along with the rest of the guests and the neighborhood poor, may eat and drink. Then all, contented and replete [full], will go to their homes praising God."*
>
> —*Domostroi*

21. **(a)** According to the writer, what should a person do if he or she becomes ill? **(b)** What does this suggest about the author's view of sickness?
22. What does the author say a homeowner should do when someone in the home is ill?
23. What actions should follow the death of a sick person?
24. What does this passage suggest about the role of religious figures in everyday Russian life?
25. Based on this passage, would you say that rituals were important in the Russian Orthodox religion? Explain.

DECLINE OF THE BYZANTINE EMPIRE

EXTERNAL FACTORS	OUTCOMES
Invasions	Normans conquer southern Italy.
	Seljuk Turks advance through Asia Minor.
Crusades	Trade rivalries lead to conflict with Venice.
	Knights capture Constantinople during Fourth Crusade.
Ottoman Attack	Constantinople is captured by Turks.
	Constantinople is transformed into Muslim Istanbul.

This chart summarizes information about the decline of the Byzantine empire. Study the chart and answer the following questions:

26. What was the result of the invasion in southern Italy?
27. Name two results of the Crusades that contributed to the decline of the Byzantine empire.
28. Why did Constantinople become Istanbul?
29. What do the three events listed on the chart have in common?

Skills Tip

When conducting research on the Internet, try to determine if the information seems inaccurate or presents only one point of view. Check facts against sites provided by governments or universities.

Skills Assessment
Take It to the NET

Use the Internet to research a period of Byzantine history—for example, the age of Justinian, the schism, the Crusades, or the fall of Constantinople. Then, write a brief explanation of how the events of that period affected life in the Byzantine empire.

The Muslim World
622–1629

Chapter Preview

1 **Rise of Islam**
2 **Islam Spreads**
3 **Golden Age of Muslim Civilization**
4 **Muslims in India**
5 **The Ottoman and Safavid Empires**

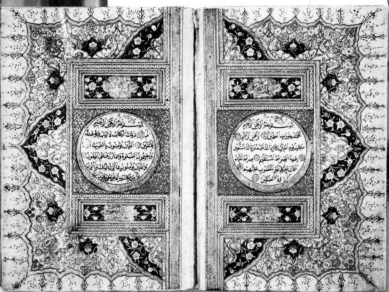

750

Abu al-Abbas establishes the Abbassid dynasty. Over the next several centuries, Muslim merchant ships travel around the Abbassid empire and beyond.

622

Muhammad journeys from Mecca to Yathrib, an event that marks the rise of Islam. The Quran, shown above, is the sacred book of Islam.

1099

Christian crusaders from Europe capture Jerusalem from the Muslims.

CHAPTER EVENTS

600 · · 800 · 1000 ·

GLOBAL EVENTS

732 At the battle of Tours, the Muslim advance into Europe is stopped.

843 In Europe, the Frankish empire is split in three by the Treaty of Verdun.

1000s East African port cities flourish.

The Muslim World, 1150

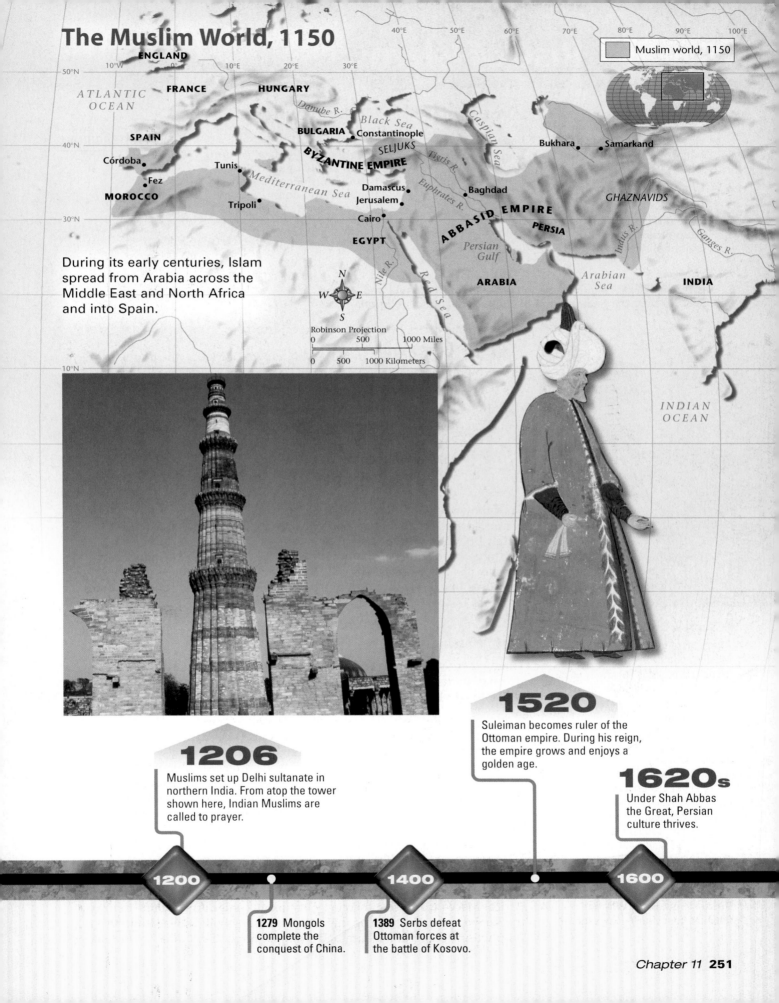

Muslim world, 1150

ENGLAND
ATLANTIC OCEAN
FRANCE
HUNGARY
Danube R.
SPAIN
BULGARIA
Constantinople
Black Sea
SELJUKS
BYZANTINE EMPIRE
Córdoba
Tunis
Mediterranean Sea
Tigris R.
Caspian Sea
Bukhara
Samarkand
Fez
Damascus
Baghdad
MOROCCO
Tripoli
Jerusalem
Euphrates R.
ABBASID EMPIRE
PERSIA
GHAZNAVIDS
Cairo
EGYPT
Nile R.
Red Sea
Persian Gulf
ARABIA
Arabian Sea
Indus R.
Ganges R.
INDIA

INDIAN OCEAN

During its early centuries, Islam spread from Arabia across the Middle East and North Africa and into Spain.

Robinson Projection
0   500   1000 Miles
0   500   1000 Kilometers

1206
Muslims set up Delhi sultanate in northern India. From atop the tower shown here, Indian Muslims are called to prayer.

1520
Suleiman becomes ruler of the Ottoman empire. During his reign, the empire grows and enjoys a golden age.

1620s
Under Shah Abbas the Great, Persian culture thrives.

1200

1400

1600

1279 Mongols complete the conquest of China.

1389 Serbs defeat Ottoman forces at the battle of Kosovo.

Reading Focus

■ How did Muhammad become the prophet of Islam?

■ What are the teachings of Islam?

■ How did Islam help shape the way of life of its believers?

Vocabulary

oasis

hijra

monotheistic

mosque

hajj

jihad

Taking Notes

Copy this chart. As you read, fill in the first column with key events concerning the emergence of Islam. In the second column, write down some of the basic teachings of Islam.

KEY EVENTS	TEACHINGS

Main Idea Islam arose in the Arabian Peninsula and became one of the world's major religions.

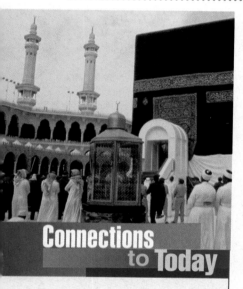

Connections to Today

A Sacred Duty

Today, more than two million Muslims gather each year in Mecca. Every Muslim who is physically and financially able must make a journey there at least once. Muslims believe that Abraham built the Kaaba in Mecca as the first house of worship for God. Today, it is adorned with a black cloth containing religious verses embroidered in gold. Pilgrims wear special clothes: simple garments that erase cultural and class differences so that all stand equal before God. The simple attire also symbolizes the abandonment of the material world for the sake of God.

Theme: Religions and Value Systems Why do Muslims consider Mecca sacred?

Setting the Scene In the Arabian town of Mecca, the marketplace echoed with the bustle of bargaining. One corner, though, was hushed. There, a husky, black-bearded man spoke to a handful of followers:

"In the name of God, the Compassionate, the Merciful,
Praise be to God, Lord of the Universe,
The Compassionate, the Merciful,
Sovereign of the Day of Judgment!
You alone we worship, and to You alone we turn for help."
—Quran

Some bowed their heads, moved by Muhammad's words. But many merchants scoffed. Muhammad had once been a good merchant himself. Surely, they thought, he had gone mad.

In years to come, Muhammad would be recognized by millions of Muslims as the Prophet. His followers would carry the message of Islam to people on three continents and set off one of the most powerful forces in world history.

The Prophet Muhammad

Islam emerged in the Arabian Peninsula, part of southwestern Asia. (See the map in Section 2 of this chapter.) Its deserts and trade centers helped shape the early life of Muhammad.

Geographic Setting The Arabian Peninsula is mostly desert, but farming is possible through irrigation or in scattered oases. An oasis is a fertile area in a desert, watered by a natural well or spring.

Many Arab clans occupied Arabia at the time of Muhammad. Nomadic herders, called Bedouins (BEHD oo ihnz), used camels to cross the scorching desert in search of seasonal pasturelands. Raids for scarce grazing land led to frequent warfare. The Bedouins would form the backbone of the armies that conquered a huge empire in the 600s and 700s. Bedouins traded with other Arabs who had settled in oasis towns. One of these was Mecca.

Mecca was a bustling market town at the crossroads of two main caravan routes. One route linked southern Arabia to Syria and Palestine on the Mediterranean coast. The other route crossed from Mesopotamia to eastern Africa. Mecca was also a thriving pilgrimage center. Arabs came to pray at the Kaaba, an ancient shrine that Muslims today believe was built by the prophet Abraham. In Muhammad's time, though, the Kaaba housed statues of many local gods and goddesses. The pilgrim traffic brought good profits to the local merchants.

Muhammad's Vision   Muhammad was born in Mecca about 570. In his youth, he worked as a shepherd among the Bedouins. Later, he led caravans across the desert and became a successful merchant. When he was about 25, Muhammad married Khadija (kah DEE jah), a wealthy widow who ran a prosperous caravan business. By all accounts, he was a devoted husband and a loving father to his daughters.

Muhammad was troubled by the idol worship and moral ills of society. When he was about 40, he went to a desert cave to meditate. According to Muslim belief, he heard a voice saying, "Recite!" Muhammad replied, "What shall I recite?" The voice explained: "Recite in the name of your God, the Creator, who created man from clots of blood."

Muhammad understood that it was the voice of the angel Gabriel calling him to be the messenger of God. But Muhammad was terrified and puzzled. How could he, an illiterate merchant, become the messenger of God? But Khadija encouraged him to accept the call. She became the first convert to the faith called Islam, from the Arabic word for "submission." Muhammad devoted the rest of his life to spreading Islam. He urged Arabs to give up their false gods and submit to the one true God. In Arabic, the word for god is *Allah.*

The Hijra: A Turning Point   At first, few people listened to the teachings of Muhammad. His rejection of the traditional Arab gods angered Meccan merchants who feared neglecting their idols and disrupting the pilgrim trade. In 622, faced with the threat of murder, Muhammad and his followers left Mecca for Yathrib, a journey known as the hijra. Later, Yathrib was renamed Medina, or "city of the Prophet," and 622 became the first year of the Muslim calendar.*

The hijra was a turning point for Islam. In Medina, Muhammad was welcomed by Muslim converts, not only as God's prophet, but also as ruler and lawgiver. As his reputation grew, thousands of Arabs adopted Islam. From Medina, Muslims launched attacks on Meccan caravans and defeated the Meccans in battle.

Finally, in 630, Muhammad returned in triumph to Mecca, where he destroyed the idols in the Kaaba. In the next two years, Muhammad worked to unite the Arabs under Islam. Muhammad died in 632, but the faith that he proclaimed continued to spread. Today, Islam is one of the world's major religions.

Teachings of Islam

Like Judaism and Christianity, Islam is monotheistic, based on belief in one God. The Quran (ku RAHN), the sacred text of Islam, teaches that God is all-powerful and compassionate. It also states that people are responsible for their own actions: "Whoever strays bears the full responsibility for straying." According to the Quran, each individual will stand before God on the final judgment day to face either eternal punishment in hell or eternal bliss in paradise. Muslims recognize no official priests who mediate between the people and God.

---

* The Muslim calendar uses A.H. for dates after the hijra. However, this chapter, like the rest of the book, will continue to use dates based on the Christian Era calendar.

Messenger of God
On several occasions Muhammad heard the angel Gabriel calling him to be the messenger of God. In this miniature painting, an angel's announcement is symbolized by the blowing of a horn.

Theme Religions and Value Systems   How did Muhammad respond to God's calling?

A Revered Islamic Site

One of the holiest sites in the Muslim world is the Dome of the Rock in Jerusalem. It was built in the 690s above a rock from which Muslims believed Muhammad had risen into heaven.

Theme: Religions and Value Systems Why is the city of Jerusalem also sacred to Christians and Jews?

▶ **Primary Sources and Literature**

See "The Quran" in the Reference Section at the back of this book.

Five Pillars All Muslims accept five basic duties, known as the Five Pillars of Islam. The first is a declaration of faith. "There is no god but God, Muhammad is the messenger of God." Muslims believe that God had sent other prophets, including Abraham, Moses, and Jesus, but that Muhammad was the last and greatest prophet. The second pillar is daily prayer. After a ritual washing, Muslims face the holy city of Mecca to pray. Although Muslims may pray anywhere, they often gather in houses of worship called *masjids* or **mosques.** The third pillar is giving charity to the poor. The fourth is fasting from sunrise to sunset during the holy month of Ramadan. The fifth pillar is the **hajj,** or pilgrimage to Mecca. All Muslims who are able are expected to visit the Kaaba at least once in their lives.

Some Muslims look on **jihad** (jee HAHD), or effort in God's service, as another duty. Jihad has often been mistakenly translated simply as "holy war." In fact, it may include acts of charity or an inner struggle to achieve spiritual peace, as well as any battle in defense of Islam.

The Quran To Muslims, the Quran contains the sacred word of God as revealed to Muhammad. It is the final authority on all matters. The Quran not only teaches about God but also provides a complete guide to life. Its ethical standards emphasize honesty, generosity, and social justice. It sets harsh penalties for crimes such as stealing or murder.

Muslims believe that, in its original Arabic form, the Quran is the direct, unchangeable word of God. Because the meaning and beauty of the Quran reside in its original language, converts to Islam learn Arabic. This shared language has helped unite Muslims from many regions.

"People of the Book" Muslims profess faith in the same God as that worshiped by Jews and Christians. The Quran teaches that Islam is God's final and complete revelation, and that the Torah and Bible contain partial revelation from God. To Muslims, Jews and Christians are "People of the Book," spiritually superior to polytheistic idol worshipers. Although some later Muslims overlooked Muhammad's principle of tolerance, in general, the People of the Book enjoyed religious freedom in early Muslim societies.

A Way of Life

Islam is both a religion and a way of life. Its teachings help shape the lives of Muslims around the world. Islamic law governs many aspects of daily life, and Islamic traditions determine ethical behavior and influence family relations.

Sharia Over time, Muslim scholars developed an immense body of law interpreting the Quran and applying its teachings to daily life. This Islamic system of law, called the Sharia, regulates moral conduct, family life, business practices, government, and other aspects of a Muslim community. Like the Quran, the Sharia helped unite the many peoples who converted to Islam.

Unlike the law codes that evolved in the west, the Sharia does not separate religious matters from criminal or civil law. The Sharia applies the Quran to all legal situations.

Impact of Islam on Women Before Islam, the position of women in Arab society varied. In some communities, women took a hand in religion, trade, or warfare. Most women, however, were under the control of a male guardian and could not inherit property. Furthermore, among a few tribes, unwanted daughters were sometimes killed at birth.

Islam affirmed the spiritual equality of women and men. "Whoever does right, whether male or female," states the Quran, "and is a believer, all such will enter the Garden." Women therefore won greater protection under the law. The Quran prohibited the killing of daughters. Inheritance laws guaranteed a woman a share of her parents' or husband's property. Muslim women had to consent freely to marriage and had the right to an education. In the early days of Islam, some Arab women participated actively in public life.

Though spiritually equal, men and women had different roles and rights. For example, the amount of an inheritance given to a daughter was less than that given to a son. A woman could seek a divorce, but it was harder for her to get one than for a man.

As Islam spread, Arabs sometimes absorbed attitudes from the peoples they conquered. In Persian and Byzantine lands, Arabs adopted the practice of veiling upper-class women and secluding them in a separate part of the home. There, they managed the affairs of the household but seldom ventured out. Still, as in other cultures, women's lives varied according to region and class. Veiling and seclusion were not so strictly followed among lower-class city women. In rural areas, peasant women continued to contribute to the economy in many ways.

Islamic Law Court
The Sharia applies Islamic teachings to legal issues. In this Persian painting, a man and woman seek a decision before a judge.

Theme: Political and Social Systems What does this picture suggest about the rights of Muslim women?

SECTION 1 Assessment

Recall
1. **Identify:** (a) Mecca, (b) Bedouins, (c) Kaaba, (d) Khadija, (e) Quran, (f) People of the Book, (g) Sharia.
2. **Define:** (a) oasis, (b) hijra, (c) monotheistic, (d) mosque, (e) hajj, (f) jihad.

Comprehension
3. How did Muhammad become the prophet of Islam?
4. (a) What are the Five Pillars of Islam? (b) How do they help unite Muslims?

5. How do the Quran and Sharia guide the lives of Muslims?

Critical Thinking and Writing
6. **Comparing** In what ways are the religious teachings of Islam similar to those of Judaism and Christianity?
7. **Identifying Main Ideas** Review the three paragraphs that appear in this section under the heading "The Hijra: A Turning Point." For each paragraph, identify the main idea and two details that support the main idea.

Activity

Take It to the NET

Use the Internet to learn more about the hajj, or pilgrimage to Mecca, today. Then, assume the role of a news reporter in Mecca. Write a news article describing the special customs and rites associated with the hajj.

Reading Focus

■ How did Muslims conquer many lands?

■ What movements emerged within Islam?

■ Why did the empire of the caliphs decline?

Vocabulary

caliph

minaret

muezzin

sultan

Taking Notes

On a piece of paper, make a time line like the model below. As you read, fill in the time line with major events concerning the spread of Islam and the rise and fall of Muslim empires.

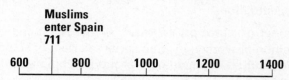

Muslims
enter Spain
711

600   800   1000   1200   1400

Main Idea Inspired by Muhammad's teachings, Arab armies spread Islam through parts of three continents.

Setting the Scene

The death of Muhammad plunged his followers into grief. The Prophet had been a pious man and a powerful leader. No one else had ever been able to unify the Bedouin tribes. Could his legacy survive without him?

Abu Bakr, an early convert to Islam, was determined to continue the Prophet's work. He sternly told the faithful, "If you worship Muhammad, Muhammad is dead. If you worship God, God is alive."

Despite some bitter struggles, Arab unity did not collapse. Inspired by the teachings of the Prophet, Arab armies surged across the Byzantine and Persian empires. In a stunningly short time, an Arabic empire reached from the Atlantic to the borders of India.

An Age of Conquests

As the first caliph, or successor to Muhammad, Abu Bakr faced an immediate crisis. The loyalty of some Arab tribal leaders had been dependent on Muhammad's personal command. They now refused to follow Abu Bakr and withdrew their loyalty to Islam. Abu Bakr succeeded in reuniting the Arabs, based first and foremost on their allegiance to Islam. Once reunited, the Arabs set out on a remarkable series of military conquests.

From Victory to Victory Under the first four caliphs, Arab armies marched from victory to victory. They conquered great chunks of the Byzantine empire, including the provinces of Syria and Palestine, with the cities of Damascus and Jerusalem. Next, they rapidly demolished the Persian empire. The Arabs then swept into Egypt.

Later Muslim armies conquered even more lands. From Egypt, Muslims dashed west, defeating Byzantine forces across North Africa. In 711, they crossed the Strait of Gibraltar into Spain and pushed north into France. There, in 732, they were defeated at the battle of Tours. The Muslim advance into Western Europe was halted. Even so, Muslims would rule parts of Spain for centuries. Elsewhere, Muslims besieged the Byzantine capital of Constantinople, but failed to take the well-defended city. Later waves of conquests would expand Muslim rule farther into the continents of Asia and Africa.

Reasons for Success Why did the Arabs have such an astonishing series of victories? One reason was the weakness of the Byzantine and Persian empires. These longtime rivals had fought each other to exhaustion. Many people in the Fertile Crescent welcomed the Arabs as liberators from harsh

Geography and History

Desert Warfare

"Fight the enemy in the desert," said one wounded Muslim leader. "There you will be victorious . . . you will have the friendly and familiar desert at your backs. The enemy cannot follow you there."

In response to the geographic conditions of the Arabian Peninsula, Arab soldiers became skilled in the special tactics of desert warfare. They knew how to use horses and camels to cross broad areas quickly and then sweep down to catch their enemies by surprise. The sudden charge of an Arab cavalry overwhelmed unprepared defenders. The elements of surprise and speed, as well as maneuverability, helped the Arabs conquer much of the Byzantine and Persian empires.

Theme: Geography and History Why were Arab soldiers skilled in the tactics of desert warfare?

Byzantine or Persian rule. Bold, efficient fighting methods also contributed to the Arab success. The Bedouin camel and horse cavalry mounted aggressive and mobile offensives that overwhelmed more traditional armies.

Perhaps the key reason for Arab success, however, was the common faith Muhammad had given his people. Islam knitted a patchwork of tribes into a determined, unified state. Belief in Islam and the certainty of paradise for those who fell in battle spurred the Arab armies to victory.

Treatment of Conquered People The advancing Arabs brought many people under their rule. Muslim leaders imposed a special tax on non-Muslims, but allowed Christians, Jews, and Zoroastrians to practice their own faiths and follow their own laws. As Muslim civilization developed, many Jews and Christians played key roles as officials, doctors, and translators. In time, many non-Muslims converted to Islam.

Many nomadic peoples in North Africa and Central Asia chose Islam immediately. Its message was simple and direct, and they saw its triumph as a sign of God's favor. Moreover, Islam had no religious hierarchy or class of priests. In principle, it emphasized the equality of all believers, regardless of race, sex, class, or wealth. In later centuries, Turkish and Mongol converts helped spread Islam far across Asia.

Muslims in Europe For centuries after the battle of Tours, Christian forces fought to reconquer Spain. Only in 1492 did they seize the last Muslim stronghold. In the meantime, Spain flourished as a center of Muslim civilization.

Muslim rulers in Spain presided over brilliant courts, where the arts and learning thrived. In general, they were more tolerant of other religions than Christian rulers of the time. At centers of learning such as the city of Córdoba, rulers employed Jewish officials and welcomed Christian scholars to study science and philosophy. Architects built grand buildings, such as the Alhambra, a fortified palace in Granada. Its lovely gardens, reflecting pools, and finely decorated marble columns mark a high point of Muslim civilization in Spain.

Muslim civilization also thrived in Sicily and other Mediterranean islands seized by Arab forces in the late 800s. Muslim rule lasted briefly. But even after knights from Normandy gained control of Sicily, it remained strongly Arabic in culture. Muslim officials governed the island well, and merchants and farmers helped the economy prosper. Muslim poets, philosophers, and scientists enriched the courts of Norman kings.

Great Mosque of Córdoba Córdoba was the cultural center of Muslim Spain. The columns and arches of this mosque in Córdoba show the elaborate nature of Muslim architecture.

Theme: Continuity and Change What earlier civilizations pioneered the use of columns and arches?

Movements Within Islam

Not long after Muhammad's death, divisions arose within Islam over his successor. The split between Sunni (SOO nee) and Shiite (SHEE ite) Muslims had a profound impact on later Islamic history.

Sunni and Shiites The Sunni felt that the caliph should be chosen by leaders of the Muslim community. Although the Sunni agreed that the caliph should be a pious Muslim, they viewed him simply as a leader, not as a religious authority.

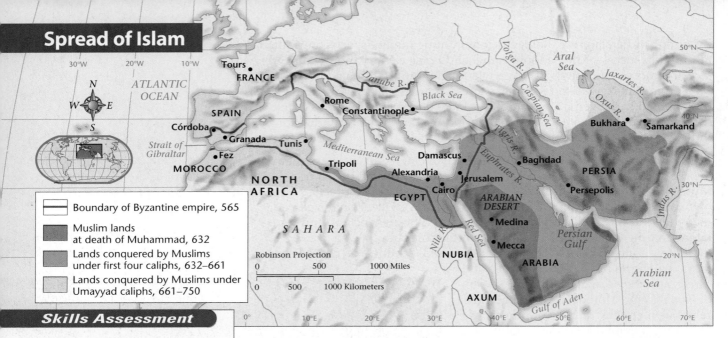

Spread of Islam

Tours
FRANCE
ATLANTIC OCEAN
Danube R.
Rome
Constantinople
Black Sea
SPAIN
Córdoba
Granada
Tunis
Strait of Gibraltar
Fez
MOROCCO
Tripoli
Mediterranean Sea
Damascus
Baghdad
Alexandria
Jerusalem
Cairo
NORTH AFRICA
EGYPT
ARABIAN DESERT
Medina
PERSIA
Persepolis
Bukhara
Samarkand
SAHARA
NUBIA
Mecca
Persian Gulf
ARABIA
Arabian Sea
AXUM
Gulf of Aden

Legend:
- Boundary of Byzantine empire, 565
- Muslim lands at death of Muhammad, 632
- Lands conquered by Muslims under first four caliphs, 632–661
- Lands conquered by Muslims under Umayyad caliphs, 661–750

Robinson Projection
0   500   1000 Miles
0   500   1000 Kilometers

Skills Assessment

Geography In less than 150 years, Islam spread from Arabia across southwest Asia and North Africa and into Europe.

1. **Location** On the map, locate (a) Arabian Desert, (b) Mecca, (c) Medina, (d) Persia, (e) Cairo, (f) Constantinople, (g) Córdoba.
2. **Region** During what period did Spain come under Muslim rule?
3. **Critical Thinking Applying Information** How might the spread of Islam have contributed to Muslim success in trade?

The Shiites, on the other hand, argued that the only true successors to the Prophet were descendants of Muhammad's daughter and son-in-law, Fatima and Ali. The Shiites believed that the descendants of the Prophet were divinely inspired. The Sunni believed that inspiration came from the example of Muhammad as recorded by his early followers.

Ali became the fourth caliph, but he was assassinated in 661 in a struggle for leadership. Later, his son, too, was killed. Many other Shiites died in battle against Sunni, trying to install their candidates for caliph. Shiites grew to admire martyrdom as a demonstration of their faith.

Like the schism between Roman Catholic and Eastern Orthodox Christians, the division between Sunni and Shiite Muslims has survived to the present day. Members of both branches of Islam believe in the same one God, look to the Quran for guidance, and make the hajj. But numerous differences have emerged in such areas as religious practice, law, and daily life. Today, about 90 percent of Muslims are Sunni. Most Shiites live in Iran, Lebanon, Iraq, and Yemen. The Shiite movement itself has split into several different factions.

Sufi A third tradition in Islam emerged with the Sufis, Muslim mystics who sought communion with God through meditation, fasting, and other rituals. Sufis were respected for their piety and miraculous powers.

Like Christian monks and nuns, some Sufis helped spread Islam through missionary work. They carried the faith to remote villages, where they blended local traditions and beliefs into Muslim culture.

Empire of the Caliphs

After the death of Ali, the Umayyad (oh MĪ ad) family set up a dynasty that ruled the Islamic world until 750. From their capital at Damascus in Syria, they directed the spectacular conquests that carried Islam from the Atlantic to the Indus Valley.

Umayyads Even as victories expanded the Arab empire, the Umayyads faced numerous problems. First, they had to adapt from desert life to ruling large cities and huge territories. To govern their empire, the Umayyads often relied on local officials, including educated Jews, Greeks, and Persians. As a result, Byzantine and Persian traditions of government influenced Arab rulers.

While conquests continued, vast wealth flowed into Umayyad hands. When conquests slowed in the 700s, economic tensions increased between wealthy Arabs and those who had less. Many Muslims criticized the court at Damascus for abandoning the simple ways of the early caliphs. Shiites hated the Umayyads because they had defeated Ali and killed his son, dishonoring the Prophet's family. Unrest also festered among non-Arab converts to Islam, who under the Umayyads had fewer rights than Arabs.

Abbassids Discontented Muslims found a leader in Abu al-Abbas, who captured Damascus in 750. Soon after, one of his generals invited members of the defeated Umayyad family to a banquet—and killed them all. Abu al-Abbas then founded the Abbassid dynasty, which lasted until 1258.

The Abbassid dynasty ended Arab dominance and helped make Islam a truly universal religion. Under the early Abbassids, the empire of the caliphs reached its greatest wealth and power, and Muslim civilization enjoyed a golden age.

Splendors of Baghdad The Abbassid caliph al-Mansur chose as the site of his new capital Baghdad, a small market town in present-day Iraq. "It is an excellent military camp," he wrote. "Besides here is the Tigris to put us in touch with lands as far as China and bring us all that the seas yield." Under the Abbassids, Baghdad exceeded Constantinople in size and wealth.

In Baghdad, Persian traditions strongly influenced Arab life, but Islam remained the religion and Arabic the language of the empire. Poets, scholars, philosophers, and entertainers from all over the Muslim world flocked to the Abbassid court. Visitors no doubt felt that Baghdad deserved its title "City of Peace, Gift of God, Paradise on Earth."

Many gardens, dotted with fabulous fountains, gleamed in the sunlight. Above the streets loomed domes and **minarets**, the slender towers of mosques. Each day, a mosque official called a **muezzin** climbed to the top of the minaret and called the faithful to prayer. In busy market courtyards, merchants sold goods from Africa, Asia, and Europe. The palace of the caliph echoed with the music of flutes, cymbals, and tambourines, along with the voices of female singers.

The city of Baghdad reached its peak under the reign of caliph Harun al-Rashid, who ruled from 786 to 809. For centuries, in both Europe and the Muslim world, Harun was admired as a model ruler. He was viewed as a symbol of wealth and splendor.

Decline of the Caliphate

Starting about 850, Abbassid control over the Arab empire fragmented. In Spain, Egypt, and elsewhere, independent dynasties ruled separate Muslim states. As the caliph's power faded, civil wars erupted, and Shiite rulers took over parts of the empire. Between 900 and 1400, a series of invasions added to the chaos.

Seljuks In the 900s, the Seljuk Turks migrated into the Middle East from Central Asia. They adopted Islam and built a large empire across the Fertile Crescent. By 1055, a Seljuk **sultan**, or authority, controlled Baghdad, but he left the Abbassid caliph as a figurehead. As the Seljuks pushed into Asia Minor, they threatened the Byzantine empire. Reports of Seljuk interference with Christian pilgrims traveling to Jerusalem led Pope Urban II, in 1095, to call for the First Crusade.

Crusaders In 1099, after a long and bloody siege, Christian crusaders captured Jerusalem. For 150 years, the city passed back and forth between Muslims and Christians. The Muslim general Salah al-Din, or Saladin, ousted Christians from Jerusalem in 1187. They regained it after his death, holding it until 1244.

Christians also ruled a few tiny states in Palestine, but they were eventually expelled. In the long term, as you read, the Crusades had a much greater impact on Europe than on the Muslim world.

Biography

Harun al-Rashid
763(?)–809

Many stories and legends recall Caliph Harun al-Rashid's wealth, generosity, and support of learning. Poets, physicians, philosophers, and artists all gathered at his court in Baghdad. One story tells how Harun rewarded a favorite poet with a robe of honor, a splendid horse, and 5,000 dirhams—a vast sum of money.

Harun used his generosity to create closer ties with other rulers. He sent the Frankish king Charlemagne several gifts, including a mechanical clock and an elephant. Harun hoped that the Franks would join him in an alliance against the rival Umayyad caliphate in Spain.

Despite his lavishness and generosity, Harun amassed a great fortune. At his death, he had millions of dirhams, plus huge stores of jewels and gold.

Theme: Impact of the Individual How did Harun help make Baghdad a major center of Muslim culture?

Cause and Effect

Long-Term Causes	Immediate Causes
• Weakness of Byzantine and Persian empires • Economic and social changes in Arabia	• Tribes of Arabia unified by Islam around a central message • Wide acceptance of religious message of Islam • Easy acceptance of social ideas of Islam, such as equality among believers

Spread of Islam

Immediate Effects	Long-Term Effects
• Islam spreads from the Atlantic coast to the Indus Valley • Centers of learning flourish in Cairo, Córdoba, and elsewhere	• Muslim civilization emerges • Linking of Europe, Asia, and Africa through Muslim trade network • Arabic becomes shared language of Muslims • Split between Sunni and Shiites

Connections to Today

• Islam is religion of nearly one fifth of world population
• Millions of Muslims make pilgrimages to Mecca
• Arabic is among the most widely spoken languages in the world

Skills Assessment **Chart** Religion, politics, and culture all played a significant role in the rapid spread of Islam. **How does the spread of Islam help explain the wide knowledge of Arabic in today's world?**

Mongols In 1216, Genghiz Khan led the Mongols out of Central Asia across Persia and Mesopotamia. Mongol armies returned again and again. In 1258, Hulagu, grandson of Genghiz, burned and looted Baghdad, killing the last Abbassid caliph. Later, the Mongols adopted Islam.

In the late 1300s, another Mongol leader, Timur the Lame, or Tamerlane, led his armies into the Middle East. Though he himself was a Muslim, Tamerlane's ambitions led him to conquer Muslim as well as non-Muslim lands. His victorious armies overran Persia and Mesopotamia before invading Russia and India.

Looking Ahead

As the 1200s drew to a close, the Arab empire had fragmented and fallen. Independent Muslim caliphates and states were scattered across North Africa and Spain, while a Mongol khan ruled the Middle East. After five centuries of relative unity, the Muslim world was as politically divided as Christian Europe.

Even though the empire crumbled, Islam continued to link diverse people across an enormous area that Muslims called the *Dar al-Islam,* or "Abode of Islam." In the future, other great Muslim empires would arise in the Middle East and India. Muslims also benefited from an advanced civilization that had taken root under the Abbassids. In the next section, you will read about the achievements of their Muslim civilization in art, literature, and other fields of endeavor.

SECTION 2 Assessment

Recall

1. **Identify:** **(a)** Abu Bakr, **(b)** battle of Tours, **(c)** Fatima and Ali, **(d)** Sufi, **(e)** Umayyads, **(f)** Abbassids, **(g)** Harun al-Rashid, **(h)** Seljuks, **(i)** Tamerlane.
2. **Define:** **(a)** caliph, **(b)** minaret, **(c)** muezzin, **(d)** sultan.

Comprehension

3. **(a)** What areas did Arab armies conquer? **(b)** Give three reasons for the rapid success of the Arab conquests.
4. What issues divided Sunni Muslims and Shiite Muslims?

5. Why did the empire of the Abbassid caliphs decline and eventually break up?

Critical Thinking and Writing

6. **Connecting to Geography** How did the migration of the Turks lead to conflict in the Middle East?
7. **Drawing Conclusions** Muhammad said, "Know ye that every Muslim is a brother to every other Muslim and that ye are now one brotherhood." How might this idea have increased the appeal of Islam to conquered peoples?

Activity

Writing a Diary
Imagine that you are a Bedouin who is visiting Baghdad for the first time during the reign of Harun al-Rashid. Record in your diary how city life differs from nomadic life in the desert.

Golden Age of Muslim Civilization

Reading Focus

- How were the Muslim society and economy organized?
- What traditions influenced Muslim art and literature?
- What advances did Muslims make in centers of learning?

Vocabulary

social mobility
arabesque
calligraphy

Taking Notes

Copy this partially completed concept web. As you read, finish the diagram by adding advances made during the golden age of Muslim civilization. Draw as many circles as you need to complete the web.

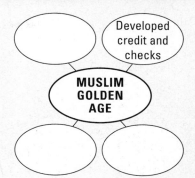

Main Idea During the Abbassid golden age, Muslims made advances in economics, art, literature, and science.

Setting the Scene

One night, Caliph al-Mamun had a vivid dream. There in his chambers he came upon a balding, blue-eyed stranger sitting on the low couch.

"Who are you?" the caliph demanded.

"Aristotle," the man replied. The caliph was delighted. He plied the great Greek philosopher with questions about ethics, reason, and religion.

Although al-Mamun soon awoke, his dream inspired him to action. He had scholars collect the great works of the classical world and translate them into Arabic. By 830, the caliph had set up the "House of Wisdom," a library and university in Baghdad.

Under the Abbassids, Islam absorbed traditions from many cultures. In the process, a vital new civilization rose that flourished in cities from Damascus to Cairo to Córdoba and later to Delhi in India. The great works produced by scholars of the Abbassid golden age shaped the Muslim world just as Greek and Roman classics shaped western culture.

Society and the Economy

Muslim rulers united people from diverse cultures, including Arabs, Persians, Egyptians and other Africans, and Europeans. Later, Mongols, Turks, Indians, and people in Southeast Asia declared their faith in Islam. In time, Muslim civilization absorbed and blended many traditions.

Social Classes Muslim society was more open than that of medieval Christian Europe. Although Arabs had held themselves apart from non-Arab Muslims at first, that distinction faded under the Abbassids. People enjoyed a certain degree of social mobility, the ability to move up in social class. People could improve their social rank through religious, scholarly, or military achievements.

As in Greece and Rome, slavery was a common institution in the cities of the Muslim world. Slaves were brought from conquered lands in Spain, Greece, Africa, India, and Central Asia. Muslims could not be enslaved. If non-Muslim slaves converted to Islam, they did not automatically gain their freedom, but their children did. A female slave who married her owner also gained freedom.

Most slaves worked as household servants. Some were skilled artisans. The Abbassids used slave-soldiers who fought loyally for the caliph. Slaves of rulers sometimes rose to high positions in government, and a number of caliphs were the sons of slave mothers. Islamic law encouraged the freeing

Muslim Scholars
During the golden age of Muslim civilization, scholars made advances in a variety of fields. Here, some learned men gather in an observatory for studying the heavens.

Theme: Global Interaction
How did Muslim conquests contribute to advances in the arts and sciences?

In the Marketplace
In the painting (top), Muslim merchants sell their wares. In cities like Baghdad, merchants sold goods in roofed bazaars containing miles of streets. Today's multilevel shopping mall (bottom) is a modern version of the bazaar.

Theme: Economics and Technology In what businesses are the four bazaar merchants engaged?

of slaves. Many slaves bought their freedom, often with the help of charitable donations or even state funds.

An International Trade Network Merchants were honored in the Muslim world, in part because Muhammad had been a merchant. A traditional collection of deeds and sayings stated:

> "The honest, truthful Muslim merchant will stand with the martyrs on the Day of Judgment. I commend the merchants to you, for they are the couriers of the horizon and God's trusted servants on Earth."
> —Sayings of the Prophet

Between 750 and 1350, merchants built a vast trading network across the Muslim world and beyond, spreading Islam peacefully in their wake. Camel caravans—the "ships of the desert"—crossed the Sahara into West Africa. Muslim traders traveled the Silk Road from China. Monsoon winds carried Arab ships from East Africa to India. Everywhere Muslim traders bought and exchanged goods, creating great fortunes for the most successful.

Trade spread both products and technologies. As you have read, Muslim merchants brought Arabic numerals from India to the western world. Arabs also carried sugar from India and papermaking from China. A common language and a common religion helped this global exchange to grow and thrive.

Extensive trade and a prosperous money economy led Muslims to pioneer new business practices. They set up partnerships, bought and sold on credit, and formed banks to change currency. To transfer money more easily, Muslims invented the ancestors of today's bank checks. We get our word *check* from the Arabic word *sakk*. Bankers developed a sophisticated system of accounting. They opened branch banks in all major cities, so that a check written in Baghdad might be cashed in Cairo.

Manufacturing As in medieval Europe, handicraft manufacturing in Muslim cities was typically organized by guilds. The heads of the guilds, chosen by their members, often had the authority to regulate prices, weights and measures, methods of production, and the quality of the product. Most labor was done by wage workers.

Across the Muslim world, artisans produced a wealth of fine goods. Steel swords from Damascus, leather goods from Córdoba, cotton textiles from Egypt, and carpets from Persia were highly valued. Workshops also turned out fine glassware, furniture, and tapestries.

Agriculture Outside the cities, agriculture flourished across a wide variety of climates and landforms. Muslim farmers cultivated sugar cane, cotton, dyes, medicinal herbs, fruits, vegetables, and flowers that were bought and sold in world markets.

The more arid regions of the Muslim world were basically divided into two kinds of land, "the desert and the sown." Small farming communities faced a constant scarcity of water. To improve farm output, the Abbassids organized massive irrigation projects and drained swamplands between the Tigris and Euphrates. Farmers in Mesopotamia, Egypt, and the Mediterranean coast produced grain, olives, dates, and other crops.

The deserts continued to support independent nomads who lived by herding. Still, nomads and farmers shared economic ties. Nomads bought dates and grain from settled peoples, while farming populations acquired meat, wool, and hides from the nomads.

Art and Literature

As in Christian Europe and Hindu India, religion shaped the arts and literature of the Islamic world. The great work of Islamic literature was the poetic Quran itself. Scholars studied the sacred words of the Quran in Arabic and then produced their own works interpreting its meaning.

Muslim art and literature reflected the diverse traditions of the various peoples who lived under Muslim rule. Muslim artists and writers were also influenced by the skills and styles of the many peoples with whom they came in contact, including Greeks, Romans, Persians, and Indians.

Design and Decoration Because the Quran strictly banned the worship of idols, Muslim religious leaders forbade artists to portray God or human figures in religious art. The walls and ceilings of mosques were decorated with elaborate abstract and geometric patterns. The arabesque, an intricate design composed of curved lines that suggest floral shapes, appeared in rugs, textiles, and glassware. Muslim artists also perfected skills in calligraphy, the art of beautiful handwriting. They worked the flowing Arabic script, especially verses from the Quran, into decorations on buildings and objects of art.

In nonreligious art, some Muslim artists did paint human and animal figures. Arabic scientific works were often lavishly illustrated. Literary works and luxury objects sometimes showed stylized figures. In later periods, Persian, Turkish, and Indian artists excelled at painting miniatures to illustrate books of poems and fables.

Architecture Muslim architects adapted the domes and arches of Byzantine buildings to new uses. In Jerusalem, they built the Dome of the Rock, a great shrine capped with a magnificent dome. Domed mosques and high minarets dominated Muslim cities in the same way that cathedral spires dominated medieval Christian cities.

Poetry Long before Muhammad, Arabs had a rich tradition of oral poetry. In musical verses, Bedouin poets chanted the dangers of desert journeys, the joys of battle, or the glories of their clans. Their most important themes, chivalry and the romance of nomadic life, recurred in Arab poetry throughout the centuries. Through Muslim Spain, these traditions came to influence medieval European literature and music.

Later Arab poets developed elaborate formal rules for writing poetry and explored both religious and worldly themes. The poems of Rabiah al-Adawiyya expressed Sufi mysticism and encouraged the faithful to worship God selflessly without hope of reward. "If I worship Thee in hope of Paradise / Exclude me from Paradise," she wrote in one prayer poem. Other poets praised important leaders, described the lavish lives of the wealthy, sang of the joys and sorrows of love, or conveyed nuggets of wisdom.

Persian Muslims also had a fine poetic tradition. Firdawsi (fihr DOW see) wrote in Persian using Arabic script. His masterpiece, the *Shah Namah,* or *Book of Kings,* tells the history of Persia. Omar Khayyám (kī YAHM),

Primary Source

A Hero's Super Powers

Firdawsi's Shah Namah *tells the story of many Persian heroes—among them, Rustam:*

"The tale is told that Rustam had at first
Such strength bestowed by Him who giveth all
That if he walked upon a rock his feet
Would sink therein. Such [power] as that
Proved an abiding trouble, and he prayed
To God in bitterness of soul to [diminish]
His strength that he might walk like other men."

—Firdawsi, *Shah Namah*

Skills Assessment

Primary Source Why was Rustam's strength both an advantage and a disadvantage?

Art of the Muslim World

Throughout the Middle Ages, Muslim artists from Spain to India created paintings, sculptures, and mosaics in many different forms and styles, often borrowing ideas from the local cultures. Some of the artwork reflected religious themes, while other pieces focused on more worldly concerns, such as war, nature, and wealth.

This sixteenth-century painting was created by a Muslim artist from India. As a rule, representations of humans and animals were prohibited in Muslim art. But some people considered images of living creatures harmless if they were small, appeared on everyday objects, or did not cast a shadow.

Muslim artists showed their praise for Allah by decorating mosques with intricate mosaics. This sixteenth-century niche is created from ceramic tiles fitted together in geometric designs and decorated with floral patterns and calligraphy.

Fast Facts

- Calligraphy became a major Muslim art form because it reflected the holiness of the written Quran.

- As a sign of respect, Muhammad's face is never depicted in Muslim art.

- In the Middle Ages, Europeans prized Persian carpets so highly that they used them to cover tables instead of floors.

Portfolio Assessment

INTERNET   Use the Internet or library resources to discover other examples of Muslim art. Choose two pieces from different time periods and geographic regions. Using what you have learned here, prepare a presentation comparing the two pieces.

This large sculpture, created by Muslim metalworkers around the year 1000, portrays an ancient mythological figure called a griffin. Arabic inscriptions on the figure wish its owner health and good fortune.

famous in the Muslim world as a scholar and astronomer, is best known to westerners for *The Rubáiyát* (ROO bī yaht). In this collection of four-line poems, Khayyám meditates on fate and the fleeting nature of life:

"The Moving Finger writes; and having writ,
Moves on; nor all your Piety nor Wit
Shall lure it back to cancel half a line,
Nor all your Tears wash out a word of it."

—Omar Khayyám, *The Rubáiyát*

Tales Arab writers prized the art of storytelling. Across their empire, they gathered and adapted stories from Indian, Persian, Greek, Jewish, Egyptian, and Turkish sources. The best-known collection is *The Thousand and One Nights*, a group of tales narrated by the fictional princess Scheherezade (shu hehr uh ZAH duh). They include romances, fables, adventures, and humorous anecdotes, many set in the Baghdad of Harun al-Rashid. Later versions filtered into Europe, where millions of children thrilled to "Aladdin and His Magic Lamp" or "Ali Baba and the Forty Thieves."

The World of Learning

"Seek knowledge even as far as China," said Muhammad. Although he could not read or write, his respect for learning inspired Muslims to make great advances in learning.

Centers of Learning Both boys and girls were provided with elementary education. This training emphasized reading and writing, especially study of the Quran. Institutions of higher learning included schools for religious instruction and for the study of Islamic law.

Al-Mamun and later caliphs made Baghdad into the greatest Muslim center of learning. Its vast libraries attracted a galaxy of scholars, who were well paid and highly respected. Other cities, like Cairo, Bukhara, Timbuktu, and Córdoba, had their own centers of learning. In all these places, Muslim scholars made advances in philosophy, mathematics, medicine, and other fields. They preserved the learning of earlier civilizations by translating ancient Persian, Sanskrit, and Greek texts into Arabic.

Philosophy Muslim scholars translated the works of the Greek philosophers, as well as many Hindu and Buddhist texts. Like later Christian thinkers in Europe, Muslim scholars tried to harmonize Greek ideas about reason with religious beliefs based on divine revelation. In Córdoba, the philosopher Ibn Rushd—known in Europe as Averroës—put all knowledge except the Quran to the test of reason. His writings on Aristotle were translated into Latin and influenced Christian scholastics in medieval Europe.

Another Arab thinker, Ibn Khaldun, set standards for the scientific study of history. He stressed the importance of economics and social structure as causes of historical events. He also warned about common sources of error in historical writing. These included bias, exaggeration, and overconfidence in the accuracy of one's sources. Khaldun urged historians to trust sources only after a thorough investigation.

Mathematics Muslim scholars studied both Indian and Greek mathematics before making their original contributions. The greatest Muslim mathematician was al-Khwarizmi (ahl kwah REEZ mee). His work pioneered the study of algebra (from the Arabic word *al-jabr*). In the 800s, he wrote a book that was later translated into Latin and became a standard mathematics textbook in Europe.

Astronomy Like many scholars of the time, al-Khwarizmi made contributions in other fields. He developed a set of astronomical tables based on Greek and Indian discoveries. At observatories from Baghdad to Central

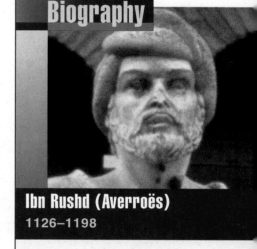

Biography

Ibn Rushd (Averroës)
1126–1198

While growing up in Spain, Muslim scholar Ibn Rushd (known to Europeans as Averroës) was interested in almost every subject and profession. He first focused on medicine and became chief physician to the Muslim ruler in Spain. Later, he studied astronomy and wrote several important books on the subject. Ibn Rushd also studied law, became a famous judge, and wrote a digest of Islamic law.

Ibn Rushd is best known as a philosopher—both Muslims and Christians have studied his commentaries on Aristotle for centuries. For part of his life, however, Ibn Rushd was forced to live in exile outside Spain because some Muslim religious leaders felt that his writings contradicted the teachings of Islam.

Theme: Impact of the Individual **What role did Ibn Rushd play in increasing the knowledge of people during the Middle Ages?**

An Arabic Medical Text
At hospitals in Baghdad, Cairo, and Damascus, libraries were well stocked with medical textbooks. This page is from an Arabic textbook on anatomy.

Theme: Economics and Technology Identify three details that suggest that this drawing was based on the study of actual human skeletons.

Asia, Muslim astronomers studied eclipses, observed the Earth's rotation, and calculated the circumference of the Earth to within a few thousand feet. The work of Muslim astronomers and navigators helped pave the way for later explorers like Christopher Columbus.

Medicine Building on the knowledge of the ancient Greeks, Muslims made remarkable advances in medicine and public health. Under the caliphs, physicians and pharmacists had to pass a test before they could practice their profession. The government set up hospitals, with separate wards for women. Injured people could get quick treatment at a facility similar to today's emergency room. Physicians traveled to rural areas to provide health care to those who could not get to a city, while others regularly visited jails.

One of the most original medical thinkers was Muhammad al-Razi, head physician at Baghdad's chief hospital. He wrote many books on medicine, including a pioneering study of measles and smallpox. He also challenged accepted medical practices. Treat the mind as well as the body, he advised young doctors. If a doctor made hopeful comments, he taught, patients would recover faster.

Equally famous was the Persian physician Ibn Sina, known in Europe as Avicenna. By the age of 16, he was already a doctor to the Persian nobility. His great work was the *Canon on Medicine,* a huge encyclopedia of what the Greeks, the Arabs, and he himself had learned about the diagnosis and treatment of disease. The book includes a list of more than 4,000 prescriptions, made with such ingredients as mercury from Spain, myrrh from East Africa, and camphor from India.

Behind these two great names stood dozens of others. Muslim surgeons developed a way to treat cataracts, drawing fluid out of the lenses with a hollow needle. For centuries, surgeons around the world used this method to save patients' eyesight. Arab pharmacists were the first to mix bitter medicines into sweet-tasting syrups and gums.

Knowledge Moves West Over time, Muslim scholars helped knowledge move into Christian Europe. The two main routes of entry were through Spain and through Sicily. Christian European scholars were reintroduced to achievements of Greco-Roman civilization. They studied Muslim philosophy, art, and science. Eventually, European physicians began to attend Muslim universities in Spain and to translate Arabic medical texts. For 500 years, the works of Avicenna and al-Razi were the standard medical textbooks at European schools.

SECTION 3 Assessment

Recall

1. **Identify:** (a) Omar Khayyám, (b) Averroës, (c) Muhammad al-Razi, (d) Avicenna.
2. **Define:** (a) social mobility, (b) arabesque, (c) calligraphy.

Comprehension

3. How did new business methods encourage trade and industry?
4. How did the teachings of Islam influence the arts?
5. Describe one advance made by Muslim civilization in each of the following areas: (a) mathematics, (b) astronomy, (c) medicine.

Critical Thinking and Writing

6. **Analyzing Primary Sources** Muhammad taught that "the ink of the scholar is holier than the blood of the martyr." (a) What do you think he meant? (b) How might this attitude have contributed to the development of Muslim civilization?
7. **Comparing** What were the similarities and differences between Muslim society under the Abbassids and European society in the early Middle Ages?

Activity

Take It to the NET

Visit some Internet museum sites that contain descriptions and examples of Muslim art and architecture. Then, make a poster that shows the major characteristics of Muslim art during the Abbassid golden age.

Muslims in India

Reading Focus

- What impact did the Delhi sultanate have on India?
- How did Muslim and Hindu traditions clash and blend?
- How did Akbar strengthen Mughal India?

Vocabulary

sultanate

caste

rajah

Taking Notes

Copy the partially completed outline at right. As you read this section, finish the outline. Use Roman numerals to indicate the major headings of the section, capital letters for the subheadings, and numbers for the supporting details.

I. The Delhi sultanate
  A. Origins of the sultanate
    1.
    2.
  B. Effects of Muslim rule
    1.
    2.
II. Muslims and Hindus

Main Idea   Muslim invasions and rule over India led to cultural diffusion as well as bloody clashes between Muslims and Hindus.

Setting the Scene

"The whole of India is full of gold and jewels," advisers told Sultan Mahmud of Ghazni. "And since the inhabitants are chiefly infidels and idolaters, by the order of God and his Prophet, it is right for us to conquer them." In 1001, Mahmud led his armies into northern India. Smashing and looting Hindu temples, Mahmud used the fabulous riches of India to turn his capital into a great Muslim center. Later Muslim invaders did more than loot and destroy. They built a dazzling new Muslim empire in India.

The arrival of Islam brought changes to India as great as those caused by the Aryan migrations 2,000 years earlier. As Muslims mingled with Indians, each civilization absorbed elements from the other.

The Delhi Sultanate

After the Gupta empire fell in about 550, India again fragmented into many local kingdoms. Rival princes battled for control of the northern plain. Despite power struggles, Indian culture flourished. Hindu and Buddhist rulers spent huge sums to build and decorate magnificent temples. Trade networks linked India to the Middle East, Southeast Asia, and China.

Origins of the Sultanate Although Arabs conquered the Indus Valley in 711, they advanced no farther into the subcontinent. Then about 1000, Muslim Turks and Afghans pushed into India. At first, they were adventurers like Mahmud, who pillaged much of the north. However, in the late 1100s, the sultan of Ghur defeated Hindu armies across the northern plain. He made Delhi his capital. From there, his successors organized a sultanate, or land ruled by a sultan. The Delhi sultanate, which lasted from 1206 to 1526, marked the start of Muslim rule in northern India.

Why did the Muslim invaders triumph? They won on the battlefield in part because Muslim mounted archers had far greater mobility than Hindu forces, who rode slow-moving war elephants. Also, Hindu princes wasted resources battling one another instead of uniting against a common enemy. In some places, large numbers of Hindus, especially from low castes, converted to Islam. In the Hindu social system, you will recall, people were born into castes, or social groups from which they could not change.

Effects of Muslim Rule Muslim rule brought changes to Indian government and society. Sultans introduced Muslim traditions of government. Many Turks, Persians, and Arabs migrated to India to serve as soldiers

Global Connections

Ibn Battuta: World Traveler

In 1333, the sultan of Delhi was seeking the services of educated foreigners. To fill the position of judge, he hired a scholarly traveler from Morocco. The name of the traveler was Ibn Battuta.

Ibn Battuta was no ordinary traveler. By the time he reached India, he had already visited Egypt, the eastern coast of Africa, Asia Minor, and Central Asia. After eight years in India, he sailed on to Southeast Asia and China. Still later, he trekked across the Sahara to tour West Africa. In all, he logged an estimated 75,000 miles. After finally returning to Morocco, Ibn Battutta dictated an account of his extraordinary travels that has survived to this day.

Theme: Global Interaction
Why was it so rare for people of the time to travel as widely as Ibn Battuta had?

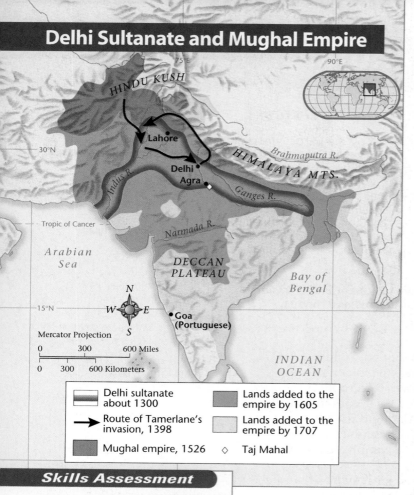

Delhi Sultanate and Mughal Empire

HINDU KUSH

Lahore

Delhi
Agra

HIMALAYA MTS.

Brahmaputra R.

Indus R.

Ganges R.

Tropic of Cancer

Narmada R.

Arabian
Sea

DECCAN
PLATEAU

Bay of
Bengal

N
W   E
S

Goa
(Portuguese)

Mercator Projection

0   300   600 Miles

0   300   600 Kilometers

INDIAN
OCEAN

Delhi sultanate about 1300	Lands added to the empire by 1605
→ Route of Tamerlane's invasion, 1398	Lands added to the empire by 1707
Mughal empire, 1526	◇ Taj Mahal

Skills Assessment

Geography Two Muslim dynasties ruled much of the Indian subcontinent. The Delhi sultanate lasted more than 300 years before the Mughal dynasty replaced it.

1. **Location** On the map, locate *(a)* Delhi, *(b)* Hindu Kush, *(c)* Ganges River, *(d)* Taj Mahal.
2. **Movement** Describe Tamerlane's invasion route into India.
3. **Critical Thinking Linking Past and Present** Use the map of Asia in the Reference Section to identify the present-day countries that now occupy the lands of the Mughal empire.

or officials. Trade between India and the Muslim world increased. During the Mongol raids of the 1200s, many scholars and adventurers fled from Baghdad to India, bringing Persian and Greek learning. The newcomers helped create a brilliant civilization at Delhi, where Persian art and architecture flourished.

Decline In 1398, Tamerlane invaded India. He plundered the northern plain and smashed into Delhi. "Not a bird on the wing moved," reported stunned survivors. Thousands of artisans were enslaved to build Tamerlane's capital at Samarkand. Delhi, an empty shell, slowly recovered. But the sultans no longer controlled a large empire, and northern India again fragmented, this time into rival Hindu and Muslim states.

Muslims and Hindus

At its worst, the Muslim conquest of northern India inflicted disaster on Hindus and Buddhists. The widespread destruction of Buddhist monasteries contributed to the drastic decline of Buddhism as a major religion in India. During the most violent onslaughts, many Hindus were killed. Others may have converted to escape death. In time, though, relations became more peaceful.

Hindu-Muslim Differences The Muslim advance brought two utterly different religions and cultures face to face. Hinduism was an ancient religion that had evolved over thousands of years. Hindus recognized many sacred texts and prayed before statues representing many gods and goddesses. Islam, by contrast, was a newer faith with a single sacred text. Muslims were devout monotheists who saw the statues and carvings in Hindu temples as an offense to the one true god.

Hindus accepted differences in caste status and honored Brahmans as a priestly caste. Muslims taught the equality of all believers before God and had no religious hierarchy. Hindus celebrated religious occasions with music and dance, a practice that many strict Muslims condemned.

Interactions Eventually, the Delhi sultans grew more tolerant of their subject population. Some Muslim scholars argued that behind the many Hindu gods and goddesses was a single god. Hinduism was thus accepted as a monotheistic religion. Although Hindus remained second-class citizens, as long as they paid the non-Muslim tax, they could practice their religion. Some sultans even left rajahs, or local Hindu rulers, in place.

During the Delhi sultanate, a growing number of Hindus converted to Islam. Some lower-caste Hindus preferred Islam because it rejected the caste system. Other converts came from higher castes. They chose to adopt Islam either because they accepted its beliefs or because they served in the Muslim government. Indian merchants were attracted to Islam in part because of the strong trade network across Muslim lands.

Cultural Blending During this period, too, Indian Muslims absorbed elements of Hindu culture, such as marriage customs and caste ideas. A new language, Urdu, evolved as a marriage of Persian, Arabic, and Hindi. Local artisans applied Persian art styles to Indian subjects. Indian music and dance reappeared at the courts of the sultan.

Virtual Field Trip

www.phschool.com
**Prince of Wales Museum of Western India
Mumbai, India**

To see more artworks from the Mughal period, as well as other periods in Indian history, use the Internet address above to link to the Prince of Wales Museum of Western India.

Akbar the Great
As ruler of the Mughal empire, Akbar tried to promote harmony among the diverse peoples of India. Here, Akbar enjoys a performance of traditional Hindu dance.

Theme: Diversity How does this picture reflect Akbar's policy of toleration?

An Indian holy man, Nanak, sought to blend Islamic and Hindu beliefs. He preached "the unity of God, the brotherhood of man, the rejection of caste, and the futility of idol worship." His teachings led to the rise of a new religion, Sikhism, in northern India. (See the chart in the Chapter Review and Assessment.) The Sikhs later organized into military forces that clashed with the powerful Mughal rulers of India.

Mughal India

In 1526, Turkish and Mongol invaders again poured through the mountain passes in India. At their head rode Babur (BAH buhr), who claimed descent from Genghiz Khan and Tamerlane. Babur was a military genius, poet, and author of a fascinating book of memoirs.

Babur Founds a Dynasty Just north of Delhi, Babur met a huge army led by the sultan Ibrahim. "I placed my foot in the stirrup of resolution and my hands on the reins of confidence in God," recalled Babur. His force was small but had cannons, which he put to good use:

> "The sun had mounted spear-high when the onset began, and the battle lasted till midday, when the enemy was completely broken and routed. By the grace and mercy of Almighty God, this difficult affair was made easy to me, and that mighty army . . . was crushed in the dust."
> —Babur, *Memoirs*

In no time, Babur swept away the remnants of the Delhi sultanate and set up the Mughal dynasty, which ruled from 1526 to 1857. (*Mughal* is the Persian word for "Mongol.") Babur and his heirs conquered an empire that stretched from the Himalayas to the Deccan Plateau.

Akbar the Great The chief builder of the Mughal empire was Babur's grandson Akbar. During his long reign, from 1556 to 1605, he created a strong central government, earning the title Akbar the Great.

Akbar was a leader of unusual abilities. Although a Muslim, he won the support of Hindu subjects through his policy of toleration. He opened

Comparing Viewpoints

Does Diversity Strengthen or Weaken a Society?

"India has not ever been an easy country to understand," commented Indian prime minister Indira Gandhi in the 1970s. "Perhaps it is too deep, contradictory, and diverse." Should a nation encourage diversity? Or can lack of unity weaken the fabric of a society? Keep these questions in mind as you examine the following viewpoints.

India Late 1500s

Akbar the Great spoke eloquently about the diversity he found in his land:

66 O God, in every temple I see people that seek You. In every language I hear spoken, people praise You. If it be a mosque, people murmur the holy prayer. If it be a Christian church, they ring the bell for love of You. . . . It is You whom I seek from temple to temple. 99

Italy 1835

Giuseppe Mazzini, who led a movement to unite Italy into a single state, defined the ties that bind a nation:

66 A nation is an association of those who are brought together by language, by given geographical locations, or by the role assigned them by history, who acknowledge the same principles and who march together to the conquest of a single definite goal under the rule of a common body of law. . . . It is necessary that [a nation's] ideas be shown to other lands in their beauty and purity, free from any alien mixture. 99

Egypt 1933

Taha Husayn, a respected scholar, pointed out that his nation's culture was a blend of three distinct traditions. The first came from ancient Egypt, the second from Arabian Muslims:

66 As for the third element, it is the foreign element which has always influenced Egyptian life, and will always do so. It is what has come to Egypt from its contacts with the civilized peoples in the east and west. . . . I should like Egyptian education to be firmly based on a certain harmony between these three elements. 99

Canada 1980s

This cartoon comments on long-standing tensions between French-speaking Canadians and those who speak English. René Levesque was a leader who called for French Quebec to break away from the rest of Canada.

"CANADA IS MADE UP OF TWO DISTINCT NATIONS. JUST LIKE TWO TRAINS ON PARALLEL TRACKS THAT WILL NEVER MEET" *PREMIER RENE LEVESQUE*

Skills Assessment

1. Whose points of view least favor diversity?
   A Akbar and Mazzini
   B Mazzini and Husayn
   C Husayn and Levesque
   D Mazzini and Levesque

2. Akbar and Husayn would probably agree that
   E diversity weakens a society.
   F members of a society must share the same religion.
   G diversity can enhance a society.
   H a society should try to repel diversity.

3. **Critical Thinking** **Recognizing Points of View** As an American, you live in a highly diverse society. Write a statement in which you identify and explain two advantages and two disadvantages this diversity brings to American society.

Skills Tip

To help you understand the context in which a point of view developed, try to identify the place and time in which it arose.

government jobs to Hindus of all castes and treated Hindu princes as his partners in ruling the vast empire. He ended the tax on non-Muslims and himself married a Hindu princess.

Akbar could not read or write, but he consulted leaders of many faiths, including Muslims, Hindus, Buddhists, and Christians. Like the early Indian leader Asoka, he hoped to promote religious harmony through toleration. By recognizing India's diversity, Akbar placed Mughal power on a firm footing.

Akbar strengthened his empire in other ways as well. To improve government, he used paid officials in place of hereditary officeholders. He modernized the army, encouraged international trade, standardized weights and measures, and introduced land reforms.

Akbar's Successors Akbar's son Jahangir (juh hahn GIR) was a weaker ruler than his father. He left most details of government in the hands of his wife, Nur Jahan. Fortunately, she was an able leader whose shrewd political judgment was matched only by her love of poetry and royal sports. She was the most powerful woman in Indian history up until the twentieth century.

The high point of Mughal literature, art, and architecture came with the reign of Shah Jahan, Akbar's grandson. When his wife, Mumtaz Mahal, died at age 39, Shah Jahan was distraught. "Empire has no sweetness," he cried, "life itself has no relish left for me now." He then had a stunning tomb built for her, the Taj Mahal (TAHZH muh HAHL). It was designed in Persian style, with spectacular white domes and graceful minarets mirrored in clear blue reflecting pools. Verses from the Quran adorn its walls. The Taj Mahal stands as perhaps the greatest monument of the Mughal empire.

Shah Jahan planned to build a twin structure to the Taj Mahal as a tomb for himself. However, before he could do so, his son Aurangzeb usurped the throne in 1658. Shah Jahan was kept imprisoned until he died several years later.

Looking Ahead

In the late 1600s, the emperor Aurangzeb rejected Akbar's tolerant policies and resumed persecution of Hindus. Economic hardships increased under heavy taxes, and discontent sparked revolts against Mughal rule. As you will read, this climate of discontent helped European traders gain a foothold in the once powerful Mughal empire.

SECTION 4 **Assessment**

Recall

1. **Identify:** **(a)** Sikhism, **(b)** Babur, **(c)** Mughal, **(d)** Nur Jahan, **(e)** Taj Mahal.
2. **Define:** **(a)** sultanate, **(b)** caste, **(c)** rajah.

Comprehension

3. **(a)** Why were the founders of the Delhi sultanate able to conquer India? **(b)** How did Delhi sultans affect life in northern India?
4. How did relations between Hindus and Muslims evolve over time?
5. What policies did Akbar follow to strengthen his empire?

Critical Thinking and Writing

6. **Applying Information** How does the history of Muslims in India illustrate the process of cultural diffusion?
7. **Predicting Consequences** Rulers after Akbar rejected the policy of toleration of other religious beliefs. How do you think this rejection of toleration affected relations between Hindus and Muslims? Explain.

Activity

Creating a Chart
Using information from this chapter and other chapters in this book, create a chart showing differences between Islam and Hinduism. Include information such as when each emerged, where they spread, and their major beliefs. Consult the table of contents and index to find the information you need.

The Ottoman and Safavid Empires

Reading Focus

- How did the Ottoman empire expand?
- What were the characteristics of Ottoman culture?
- How did Abbas the Great strengthen the Safavid empire?

Vocabulary

millet

janizary

shah

Taking Notes

Copy this Venn diagram. As you read, fill in key characteristics of the Ottoman and Safavid empires in the appropriate sections of the diagram. The diagram has been partially completed to help you get started.

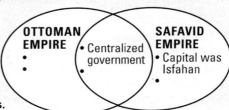

OTTOMAN EMPIRE
-
-
- Centralized government

SAFAVID EMPIRE
- Capital was Isfahan
-

Main Idea Ottoman and Safavid rulers governed large empires and encouraged cultural achievements.

Setting the Scene While the Mughals ruled India, two other dynasties, the Ottomans and Safavids, dominated the Middle East and parts of Eastern Europe. All three empires owed much of their success to new weapons. In 1453, Ottoman cannons blasted gaps in the great defensive walls of Constantinople. Later, muskets gave greater firepower to ordinary foot soldiers, thus reducing the importance of mounted warriors.

The new military technology helped the Ottomans and Safavids create strong central governments. As a result, this period from about 1450 to 1650 is sometimes called "the age of gunpowder empires."

Expanding the Ottoman Empire

The Ottomans were yet another Turkish-speaking nomadic people who had migrated from Central Asia into northwestern Asia Minor. In the 1300s, they expanded across Asia Minor and into southeastern Europe. They established a capital in the Balkan Peninsula.

Fall of Constantinople Ottoman expansion threatened the crumbling Byzantine empire. After several failed attempts to capture Constantinople, Muhammad II finally succeeded in 1453. In the next 200 years, the Ottoman empire continued to expand.

Suleiman The Ottoman empire enjoyed its golden age under the sultan Suleiman (soo lay mahn), who ruled from 1520 to 1566. Called Suleiman the Magnificent by westerners, he was known to his own people as the "Lawgiver." A brilliant general, Suleiman modernized the army and conquered many new lands. He extended Ottoman rule eastward into Mesopotamia, and also into Kurdistan and Georgia in the Caucasus Mountain region. In the west, Suleiman advanced deeper into Europe. He was able to gain control of nearly all of Hungary through diplomacy and warfare. In 1529, his armies besieged the Austrian city of Vienna, sending waves of fear through Western Europe.

Although they failed to take Vienna, the Ottomans ruled the largest, most powerful empire in both Europe and the Middle East for centuries. At its height, the empire stretched from Hungary to Arabia and Mesopotamia and across North Africa.

Suleiman felt justified in claiming to be the rightful heir of the Abbassids and caliph of all Muslims. To the title of "Emperor," he added the symbolic name of "Protector of the Sacred Places" (Mecca and Medina).

Ottoman Culture

Suleiman was a wise and capable ruler. He strengthened the government of the rapidly growing empire and improved its system of justice. As sultan, Suleiman had absolute power, but he ruled with the help of a grand vizier and a council. A huge bureaucracy supervised the business of government, and the powerful military kept the peace. As in other Muslim states, Ottoman law was based on the Sharia, supplemented by royal edicts. Government officials worked closely with religious scholars who interpreted the law.

Social Organization The Ottomans divided their subjects into four classes, each with its appointed role. At the top were "men of the pen"—such as scientists, lawyers, judges, and poets—and "men of the sword," soldiers who guarded the sultan and defended the state. Below them were "men of negotiation"—such as merchants, tax collectors, and artisans, who carried out trade and production—and "men of husbandry," farmers and herders who produced food for the community.

The Ottomans ruled diverse peoples who had many religions. The men of the sword and men of the pen were almost all Muslims, while the other classes included non-Muslims as well. Non-Muslims were organized into **millets,** or religious communities. These included Greek Christians, Armenian Christians, and Jews. Each millet had its own religious leaders who were responsible for education and some legal matters.

Janizaries Like earlier Muslim empires, the Ottomans recruited officers for the army and government from among the huge populations of conquered peoples in their empire. The Ottomans levied a "tax" on Christian families in the Balkans, requiring them to turn over young sons to the government.

The boys were converted to Islam and put into rigorous military training at the palace school. The best soldiers won a prized place in the janizaries, the elite force of the Ottoman army. The brightest students received special education to become government officials. They might serve as judges, poets, or even grand vizier.

Like the boys, non-Muslim girls from Eastern Europe were brought to serve as slaves in wealthy Muslim households. There, they might be accepted as members of the household. Some of the enslaved girls were freed after the death of their masters.

Literature and the Arts The arts blossomed under Suleiman. Ottoman poets adapted Persian and Arab models to produce works in their own Turkish language. Influenced by Persian artistic styles, Ottoman painters produced magnificently detailed miniatures and illuminated manuscripts.

The royal architect Sinan, a janizary military engineer, designed hundreds of mosques and palaces. He compared his most famous building, the Selimiye Mosque at Edirne, to the greatest church of the Byzantine empire. "With God's help and the Sultan's mercy," Sinan wrote, "I have succeeded in building a dome for the mosque which is greater in diameter and higher than that of Hagia Sophia."

The Ottomans Take Constantinople
In this French painting, Turkish land and sea forces lay siege to the fortified city of Constantinople in 1453. In a surprise move, the Ottomans hauled ships overland and launched them into the harbor outside the city.

Theme: Geography
Compare this picture to the map of Constantinople in the previous chapter. In what ways does the picture accurately reflect the geography of the city?

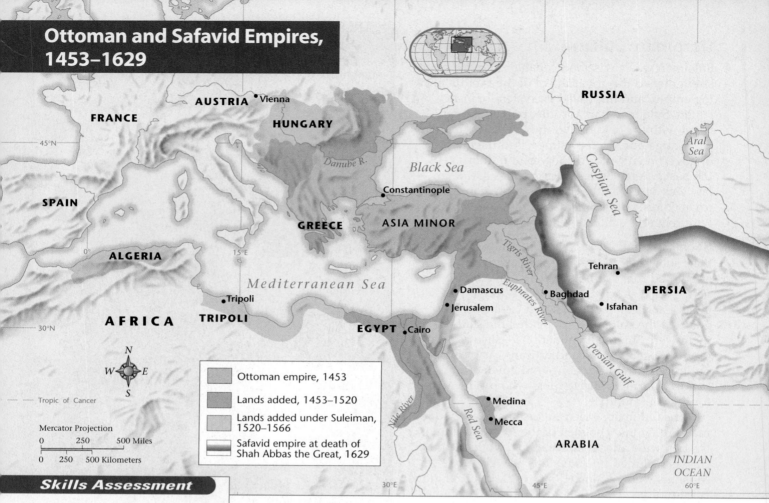

Ottoman and Safavid Empires, 1453–1629

RUSSIA

AUSTRIA • Vienna

FRANCE

HUNGARY

Danube R.

Black Sea

Aral Sea

SPAIN

GREECE

• Constantinople

ASIA MINOR

Caspian Sea

ALGERIA

Mediterranean Sea

Tigris River

• Tehran

• Damascus

Euphrates River

• Baghdad

PERSIA

• Tripoli

• Jerusalem

• Isfahan

AFRICA

TRIPOLI

EGYPT • Cairo

Tropic of Cancer

N W E S

Mercator Projection

0   250   500 Miles

0   250   500 Kilometers

Persian Gulf

• Medina

Red Sea

Nile River

• Mecca

ARABIA

INDIAN OCEAN

Ottoman empire, 1453

Lands added, 1453–1520

Lands added under Suleiman, 1520–1566

Safavid empire at death of Shah Abbas the Great, 1629

Skills Assessment

Geography At its greatest extent, the Ottoman empire stretched across three continents. During the same period, the Safavid empire controlled most of present-day Iran.

1. **Location** On the map, locate (a) Constantinople, (b) Black Sea, (c) Isfahan, (d) Hungary.

2. **Region** Into what regions did the Ottoman empire expand under Suleiman?

3. **Critical Thinking Recognizing Points of View** How do you think Russians probably felt about the expansion of the Ottoman and Safavid empires? Explain.

Decline By the 1700s, European advances in both commerce and military technology were leaving the Ottomans behind. While European industry and trade pressed ahead, the aging Ottoman empire remained dependent on agriculture. Russia and other European powers chipped away at Ottoman lands, while local rulers in North Africa and elsewhere broke away from Ottoman control. From time to time, able sultans tried to revive Ottoman power, but with limited success.

The Safavid Empire

By the early 1500s, the Safavid (sah FAH weed) dynasty had united a strong empire in Persia, present-day Iran. Sandwiched between two other expansionist powers, Mughal India and the Ottoman empire, the Safavids engaged in frequent warfare. Religion played a major role in the conflict. The Safavids were Shiite Muslims who enforced their beliefs throughout their empire. The Ottomans were Sunni Muslims who despised the Shiites as heretics.

Abbas the Great The outstanding Safavid shah, or king, was Abbas the Great. Shah Abbas revived the glory of ancient Persia. From 1588 to 1629, he centralized the government and created a powerful military force modeled on the Ottoman janizaries. Abbas used a mixture of force and diplomacy against the Ottomans. He also sought alliances with European states that had reason to fear Ottoman power.

To strengthen the economy, Abbas reduced taxes on farmers and herders and encouraged the growth of industry. While earlier Safavids had imposed their faith on the empire, Abbas tolerated non-Muslims and valued their economic contributions. He built a magnificent new capital at Isfahan (is fuh HAHN), a center of the international silk trade. Because the trade was controlled by Armenians, Abbas had thousands of Armenians brought to Isfahan. Even though they were Christians, he had a settlement built for them just outside the capital, where they could govern themselves.

Under Abbas, Isfahan flourished as a center of Persian culture. The shah welcomed artists, poets, and scholars to the court. Palace workshops produced magnificent porcelains, clothes, and rugs. Women and men wove intricately designed flowers and animals into marvelous garden scenes.

Abbas liked to walk the streets of Isfahan in disguise, mingling with the crowds in bazaars. Amid the cries of street vendors and swarms of traders and customers, he asked people about their problems. If he heard stories of corruption, he punished the guilty.

Decline Safavid glory slowly faded after the death of Shah Abbas. One cause of the decline was continuing pressure from Ottoman armies. Another factor was that conservative Shiite scholars challenged the authority of the shah by stressing their own authority to interpret law. They also encouraged persecution of religious minorities. In the end, Sunni Afghans rebelled. They defeated imperial armies, captured Isfahan, and forced the last Safavid ruler to abdicate in 1722.

In the late 1700s, a new dynasty, the Qajars (kah JAHRZ), won control of Iran. They made Tehran their capital and ruled until 1925. Still, the Safavids had left a lasting legacy. They planted Shiite traditions firmly in Iran and gave Persians a strong sense of their own identity.

Looking Ahead

By 1500, Islam had become the dominant faith across a large part of the world from West Africa to Southeast Asia. An extraordinary diversity of peoples—Arabs, Berbers, Turks, Persians, Slavs, Mongols, Indians, and many others—answered the muezzin's call to prayer each day. This vast world was not politically united, but the Quran, the Sharia, and a network of cultural and economic ties linked Muslims across the *Dar al-Islam.*

Three large states dominated the Muslim world in the 1500s. The Ottomans, the Safavids, and the Mughals were reaching their peak of power. At the same time, however, the nations of Europe were undergoing a period of dynamic growth. Several of these nations would soon challenge Muslim power.

Primary Source

Shah Abbas the Great
In 1604, a Carmelite missionary visited the Persian court. The monk recorded his observations of Shah Abbas the Great:

"He is sagacious in mind, likes fame and to be esteemed: he is courteous in dealing with everyone and at the same time very serious. For he will go through the public streets, eat from what they are selling there and . . . speak at ease freely with the lower classes . . . or will sit down beside this man or that. He says that is how to be a king, and that the king of Spain and other Christians do not get any pleasure out of ruling, because they are obliged to comport themselves with so much pomp and majesty as they do."
—*A Chronicle of the Carmelites in Persia*

Skills Assessment

Primary Source According to Abbas, how does his style of leadership differ from that of Christian rulers?

SECTION 5 Assessment

Recall
1. **Identify:** (a) Sinan, (b) Isfahan.
2. **Define:** (a) millet, (b) janizary, (c) shah.

Comprehension
3. Describe the geographic extent of the Ottoman empire at its height.
4. (a) How was the Ottoman empire governed under Suleiman? (b) How did the arts flourish under Suleiman?
5. What policies did Abbas the Great use to strengthen the Safavid empire?

Critical Thinking and Writing
6. **Drawing Conclusions** Why do you think Ottoman and Safavid rulers allowed some religious toleration in their empires?
7. **Linking Past and Present** (a) How did new military technology benefit the Ottoman and Safavid empires? (b) Explain how new military technology affects international relations today.

Activity
Take It to the NET

Use the Internet to research the Ottoman sultan Suleiman the Magnificent. Then, write a brief essay explaining why Suleiman earned the title "magnificent." Discuss military, political, and cultural achievements.

Creating a Chapter Summary

Copy this partially completed graphic organizer on a piece of paper. For each item in the left column, provide two or more main ideas in the right column.

Rise of Islam	• •
Teaching of Islam	• •
Umayyads	• •
Abbassids	• •
Mughals	• •
Ottomans	• •
Safavids	• •

 TEXT

For additional review and enrichment activities, see the interactive version of *World History* available on the Web and on CD-ROM.

 Web Site Self-Test
For practice test questions for Chapter 11, see **www.phschool.com**.

Building Vocabulary

Using the chapter vocabulary words listed below, write sentences, leaving blanks where the words would go. Exchange your sentences with another student and fill in the blanks in each other's sentences.

1. **mosque**
2. **caliph**
3. **social mobility**
4. **arabesque**
5. **janizary**
6. **shah**

Recalling Key Facts

7. What are the Five Pillars of Islam?
8. How did Muslims treat conquered peoples?
9. Describe some of the cultural achievements made by Muslim scholars.
10. **(a)** How did Akbar's rule affect life in India? **(b)** Why did the Mughal empire decline after the reign of Akbar?
11. From the highest to the lowest, what were the four social classes in the Ottoman empire?

Critical Thinking and Writing

12. **Comparing** How does the Christian belief about Jesus differ from the Muslim belief about Muhammad?
13. **Analyzing Information** In what ways was traditional Bedouin society different from the society that was formed under Islam?
14. **Recognizing Causes and Effects** Do you think there would have been a split between Sunni and Shiites if Muhammad had designated a successor before he died? Explain.
15. **Connecting to Geography** How do you think the geography of the Middle East might have helped Muslims spread the teachings of Islam throughout the region?

16. **Making Inferences** Do you think Ottoman policies encouraged Christians in the empire to be loyal or disloyal to their Muslim rulers? Explain the reasons for your answer.
17. **Solving Problems** How do you think Safavid shahs might have been able to halt or slow the decline of their empire after the reign of Abbas the Great?

Skills Assessment
Analyzing Primary Sources

The excerpt below describes the capture of the Turkish city of Antioch by the crusaders during the First Crusade. Read the description and answer the questions that follow.

> *"After the siege had been going on for a long time, the Franks made a deal with one of the men who were responsible for the towers. He was an armor-maker called Ruzbih whom they bribed. . . . The Franks sealed their pact with the armor-maker, God curse him! And made their way to the water gate. They opened it and entered the city. Another gang of them climbed the tower with ropes. At dawn, when more than 500 of them were in the city, and the defenders were worn out after the night watch, they sounded their trumpets. . . . This happened in 491."*
>
> —Ibn al-Athir, *Account of the First Crusade*

18. **(a)** Were the Franks Christian or Muslim? **(b)** Was the armor-maker Christian or Muslim?

19. According to this account, how were the crusaders able to capture Antioch?

20. Why does the author curse Ruzbih?

21. According to Christian historians, the Franks captured Antioch in 1098. Why did al-Athir give the date of the event as 491?

22. Do you consider this account a reliable source of information about the Crusades? Why or why not?

Skills Assessment
Take It to the NET

Use the Internet to learn more about one of the Muslim scholars described in the text. Based on your research, write a brief biography. Try to explain how the person's early life helped lead to a life of significant achievement. Focus especially on the contributions that the scholar made. Describe in some detail a few of the scholar's most influential works.

Skills Assessment
Analyzing Charts

SIKHISM: A BLEND OF RELIGIOUS BELIEFS
Hinduism
• Belief in many gods, all part of brahman
• Religious and moral duties, or dharma, stressed
• Belief in cycle of birth, death, and rebirth
• Priests are part of the social caste system
Islam
• Belief in one God
• Religious and moral duties defined in Five Pillars
• Belief in Heaven and Hell, and a Day of Judgment
• No priests; all believers are religious equals
Sikhism
• Belief in the "unity of God"
• Belief in reincarnation
• Rejection of caste

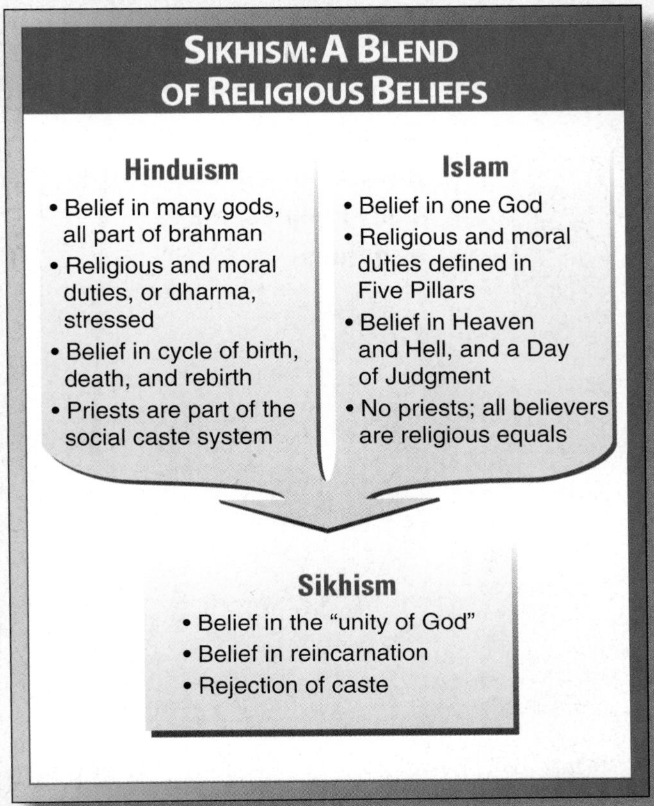

The chart above shows some teachings of Hinduism, Islam, and Sikhism. Use the chart to answer the following questions:

23. **(a)** Which teachings of Sikhism are similar to those of Hinduism? **(b)** Which are different?

24. Which teachings of Sikhism are similar to those of Islam?

25. According to the chart, what is the relationship of Sikhism to both Hinduism and Islam?

26. Based on what you have read, do you think Sikhism would attract followers in India? Explain.

Skills Tip

As you analyze a chart with arrows, note the directions of the arrows. They indicate relationships between items on the chart.

CHAPTER 12

Kingdoms and Trading States of Africa 750 B.C.–A.D. 1586

Chapter Preview

1 Early Civilizations of Africa
2 Kingdoms of West Africa
3 Trade Routes of East Africa
4 Many Peoples, Many Traditions

CHAPTER EVENTS

750 B.C.
Nubia conquers Egypt. Nubians adopt many aspects of Egyptian culture but worship their own gods. Here, King Taharqa is shown as the lion-headed warrior god, Apedemak.

200 B.C.
Axum gains control of an extensive trade network. The Axumites carve granite pillars such as the Great Stela, pictured above, to show their power.

800 B.C.		400 B.C.		B.C. A.D.

GLOBAL EVENTS

500 B.C. In India, the sacred Hindu texts are recorded.

460 B.C. The Age of Pericles begins in Athens.

218 B.C. Hannibal crosses the Alps to attack Rome during the Second Punic War.

Geography and Climates of Africa

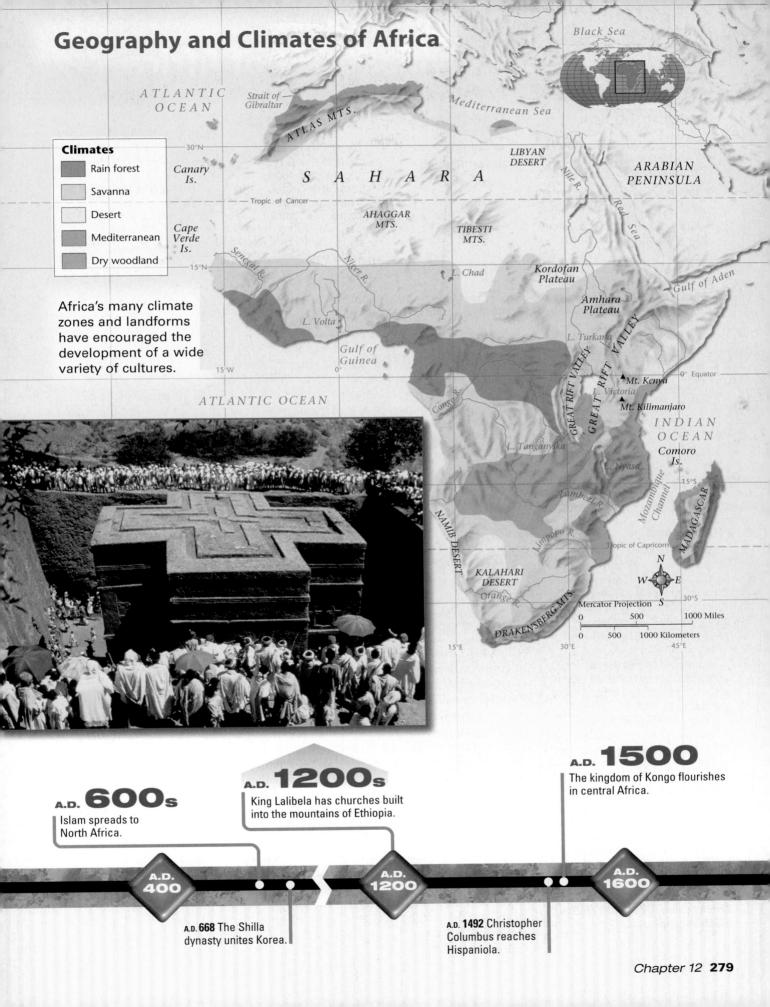

Climates
- Rain forest
- Savanna
- Desert
- Mediterranean
- Dry woodland

Africa's many climate zones and landforms have encouraged the development of a wide variety of cultures.

ATLANTIC OCEAN

Strait of Gibraltar

ATLAS MTS.

Mediterranean Sea

Black Sea

LIBYAN DESERT

ARABIAN PENINSULA

SAHARA

Canary Is.

Cape Verde Is.

Tropic of Cancer

AHAGGAR MTS.

TIBESTI MTS.

Nile R.

Red Sea

Gulf of Aden

Senegal R.

Niger R.

L. Chad

Kordofan Plateau

Amhara Plateau

L. Turkana

Gulf of Guinea

L. Volta

Congo R.

GREAT RIFT VALLEY

GREAT RIFT VALLEY

Mt. Kenya

L. Victoria

Equator

Mt. Kilimanjaro

INDIAN OCEAN

ATLANTIC OCEAN

L. Tanganyika

Nyasa

Comoro Is.

Zambezi R.

Mozambique Channel

MADAGASCAR

NAMIB DESERT

Limpopo R.

Tropic of Capricorn

KALAHARI DESERT

Orange R.

DRAKENSBERG MTS.

N W E S

Mercator Projection

0 500 1000 Miles

0 500 1000 Kilometers

A.D. 600s
Islam spreads to North Africa.

A.D. 1200s
King Lalibela has churches built into the mountains of Ethiopia.

A.D. 1500
The kingdom of Kongo flourishes in central Africa.

A.D. 400

A.D. 1200

A.D. 1600

A.D. 668 The Shilla dynasty unites Korea.

A.D. 1492 Christopher Columbus reaches Hispaniola.

Early Civilizations of Africa

Reading Focus

- How did geography affect cultural development and the migration of peoples?
- What were the achievements of the kingdom of Nubia?
- How did outside influences lead to change in North Africa?

Vocabulary

savanna
desertification
outpost

Taking Notes

Copy this concept web. As you read the section, complete the circles with important facts to remember about desertification. Add as many circles as you need.

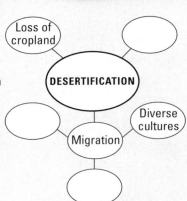

Main Idea Africa's geographic features had a major impact on the development of societies.

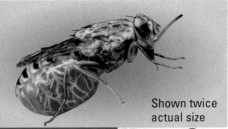

Shown twice actual size

Did You Know?

The Tsetse Fly

The tsetse fly carries one of Africa's most troublesome diseases—sleeping sickness. Flies pass on the deadly disease by biting humans and large animals. Some people have abandoned their villages in heavily infested areas. In other regions, people have stopped raising horses and cattle because of the pests. Many tourists arrange their trips to avoid the tsetse fly.

How can Africans overcome this menace? Tsetse flies are attracted to moving vehicles, dark colors, and perfume and after-shave. Using this knowledge, scientists have built traps. A dark blue cloth, treated to smell like ox breath—irresistible to the tsetse fly—acts as a lure. The cloth is also treated with insecticide, to kill the flies.

Theme: Economics and Technology How might African economies be affected by eliminating the tsetse fly?

Setting the Scene As the sun rose above the east bank of the Nile, workers hurried to the construction site. They had only a few hours to work in comfort before the sun turned the desert into a furnace. Still, as long as King Taharqa (tuh HAHR kuh) was determined to turn the old mud-brick temple into a magnificent monument, their work would continue. An ancient inscription explains how the monument was "built of good white sandstone, excellent, hard, . . . the house being of gold, the columns of gold, the inlays thereof being of silver."

About 680 B.C., Taharqa commanded the Nile Valley from Nubia to the Mediterranean. By that time, Nubia was already 3,000 years old. Along with Egypt, it stood as one of the world's early civilizations.

The Geography of Africa

After Asia, Africa is the second largest continent, covering one fifth of all the Earth's land surface. Its geography is immensely varied. However, certain geographic features, such as distinct climate zones, have had a major impact on its development.

Climate Zones Many outsiders, misled by movies, imagine Africa as a continent covered with thick jungles. In fact, tropical rain forests cover less than five percent of the land, mostly along the Equator. Thick trees and roots make this region unsuitable for farming.

Africa's largest and most populated climate zone is the savanna, or grassy plain, which stretches north and south of the forest zone. Although the savanna has good soil, irregular patterns of rainfall sometimes cause long, deadly droughts. In parts of the savanna, the tsetse fly infects people and cattle with sleeping sickness. But in other parts, cattle herding is a common occupation.

The savanna belts trail off into increasingly dry steppe zones and then into two major deserts. The blistering Sahara in the north is the world's largest desert. Although the Sahara did become a highway for migration and trade, its size and harsh terrain limited movement. The Kalahari and Namib in the south are smaller but equally forbidding. Finally, along the Mediterranean coast of North Africa and at the tip of southern Africa lie areas of fertile farmland. These varied regions also offer a variety of mineral resources, such as salt, gold, iron, copper, diamonds, and oil, all of which have spurred trade.

Movement In addition to deserts and rain forests, other geographic features have acted as barriers to easy movement of people and goods. Africa has an enormous coastline, but few good natural harbors. In addition, much of the interior is a high plateau. As rivers approach the coast, they cascade through a series of rapids and cataracts that hinder travel between the coast and the interior.

Despite geographic barriers, people did migrate within Africa and to neighboring lands. The Great Rift Valley of East Africa served as one interior corridor. Many rivers were navigable in the interior of the continent. The Red Sea and Indian Ocean linked East Africa to the Middle East and other Asian lands, while North Africa was a part of the Mediterranean world.

Resources Mineral resources spurred trade among various African regions. Salt, gold, iron, and copper were particularly valuable to early trade. In later centuries, diamonds and oil would also gain importance.

Migration of Peoples

Archaeologists have uncovered evidence that the Great Rift Valley of East Africa was the home of the earliest people. Gradually, their descendants spread to almost every corner of the Earth.

The Changing Sahara In Africa, as elsewhere, Paleolithic people developed skills as hunters and food gatherers. By 5500 B.C., Neolithic farmers had learned to cultivate the Nile Valley and to domesticate animals. As farming spread across North Africa, Neolithic villages even appeared in the Sahara, which was then a well-watered zone. Ancient rock paintings show a Sahara full of forests and rivers.

About 2500 B.C., a climate change slowly dried out the Sahara. As the land became parched, the desert spread. This process of desertification has continued to the present, devouring thousands of acres of cropland and pastureland each year. Desertification has also encouraged migration, as people are forced to seek new areas to maintain their ways of life.

The Bantu Migrations Over thousands of years, migrations contributed to the rich diversity of peoples and cultures. Scholars have traced these migrations by studying language patterns. They have learned that West African farmers and herders migrated to the south and east between about 1000 B.C. and A.D. 1000. Like the Indo-European peoples of Europe and Asia, these West African peoples spoke a variety of languages that derived from a common root language. We call this root language Bantu.

As people migrated across Africa, they adapted to its many climates and developed a diversity of cultures. While some were nomadic cattle herders, others cultivated grain or root crops. In several regions, farming people built great empires.

The Nile Kingdom of Nubia

While Egyptian civilization was developing, another African civilization took shape on a wide band of fertile land among the cataracts of the upper Nile. The ancient kingdom of Nubia, also called Kush, was located in present-day Sudan.

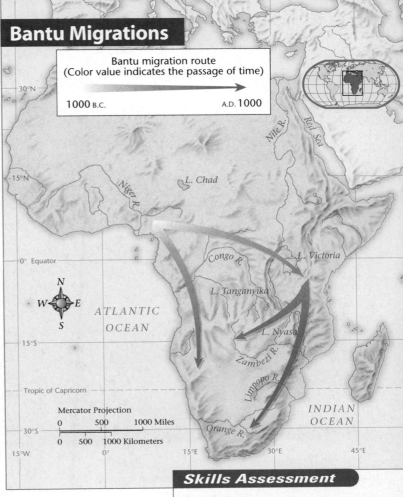

Bantu Migrations

Bantu migration route
(Color value indicates the passage of time)

1000 B.C.   A.D. 1000

ATLANTIC OCEAN

INDIAN OCEAN

Mercator Projection
0   500   1000 Miles
0   500   1000 Kilometers

Skills Assessment

Geography Over a period of 2,000 years, Bantu peoples migrated to southern Africa. Today, as many as one third of Africans speak a Bantu language.

1. **Location** *On the map, locate (a) Lake Victoria, (b) Orange River, (c) Lake Nyasa.*
2. **Movement** *(a) Where did Bantu peoples originate? (b) About when did Bantu-speaking peoples reach the Orange River?*
3. **Critical Thinking** **Solving Problems** *How have scientists learned about the Bantu migrations?*

Nubian Carvings
Conquest and trade provided Nubia with opportunities to learn about Egyptian culture. Many traditions and beliefs were adapted to become part of Nubian civilization.

Theme: Art and Literature
How do these Nubian carvings reflect the influence of Egyptian art?

From time to time, ambitious Egyptian pharaohs subdued Nubia, but the Nubians always regained their independence. As a result of conquest and trade, Nubian rulers adapted many Egyptian traditions. They modeled palaces and pyramids on Egyptian styles. About 750 B.C., the Nubian king Piankhi (pee AHNG kee) conquered Egypt. For a century, Nubian kings ruled Egypt. But their armies could not match the iron weapons of the invading Assyrians. The Nubians retreated south from Egypt.

The Furnaces of Meroë By 500 B.C., Nubian rulers moved their capital to Meroë (MEHR uh wee). Meroë commanded both the north-south Nile route and the east-west route from the Red Sea into the savanna and North Africa. Along this wide trade network, Nubia sent gold, ivory, animal skins, perfumes, and slaves to the Mediterranean world and the Middle East.

Equally important, Meroë was rich in iron ore. Its furnaces, fueled by large quantities of timber, produced iron. Today, giant heaps of iron waste remain as evidence of ancient Meroë's industry.

Splendor and Decline Although Nubia absorbed much from Egypt, it later followed an independent course. Nubians worshiped their own gods including Apedemak, a lion-headed warrior god. At Meroë, artistic styles reflected a greater sense of freedom than did Egyptian styles. Nubians also created their own system of writing, using an alphabet instead of hieroglyphics. Unfortunately, the Nubian alphabet has yet to be deciphered.

After the joint reign of King Natakamani and Queen Amanitere in the first century A.D., Nubia's golden age dimmed. Finally, about A.D. 350, armies from the kingdom of Axum on the Red Sea overwhelmed Nubia. King Ezana of Axum boasted, "I burnt their towns, both those built of brick and those built of reeds, and my army carried off their food and copper and iron . . . and destroyed the statues in their temples." As you will read later, Axum would make its own mark on this region beyond the Nile.

North Africa

Early African civilizations had strong ties to the Mediterranean world. At the opposite end of the Mediterranean from Nubia and Axum, Carthage rose as a great North African power. Like Nubia, its wealth came from trade. Founded by Phoenician traders, Carthage came to dominate trade in the western Mediterranean and North Africa. Between 800 B.C. and 146 B.C., it forged an empire that stretched from the Maghreb (present-day Tunisia, Algeria, and Morocco) to southern Spain and Sicily. Carthage also established outposts, or distant military stations, in England and France.

As Rome expanded, territorial and trade rivalries erupted between the two powers, resulting in the Punic Wars. Despite the efforts of Hannibal, Rome eventually crushed Carthage. Trade, however, continued.

Roman Rule The Romans built roads, dams, aqueducts, and cities across North Africa. They developed its farmlands and imported lions and other fierce animals to do battle with gladiators. North Africa also provided soldiers for the Roman army. One of them, Septimius Severus, later became emperor of Rome.

Under Roman rule, Christianity spread to the cities of North Africa. St. Augustine, the most influential Christian thinker of the late Roman empire, was born in present-day Algeria. From A.D. 395 to A.D. 430, Augustine was bishop of Hippo, a city near the ruins of ancient Carthage.

Camels and Trade By A.D. 200, camels had been brought to North Africa from Asia. These hardy "ships of the desert" revolutionized trade across the Sahara. Camels could carry loads of up to 500 pounds and could plod 20 or 30 miles a day, often without water. Although daring traders had earlier made the difficult desert crossing in horse-drawn chariots, camel caravans created new trade networks.

Spread of Islam Further changes came in the 600s, when Arab armies carried Islam into North Africa. At first, the Arabs occupied the cities and battled the Berbers in the desert. Later, Berbers and Arabs joined forces to conquer Spain. Islam replaced Christianity as the dominant religion of North Africa, and Arabic replaced Latin as its language.

North Africa benefited from the blossoming of Muslim civilization. Cities like Cairo, Fez, and Marrakesh were famed for their mosques and libraries. Linked into a global trade network, North African ports did a busy trade in grain, wine, fruit, ivory, and gold. Along with their goods, Muslim traders from North Africa carried Islam into West Africa.

SECTION 1 Assessment

Recall
1. **Identify:** (a) Taharqa, (b) Bantu, (c) Piankhi, (d) Meroë, (e) St. Augustine.
2. **Define:** (a) savanna, (b) desertification, (c) outpost.

Comprehension
3. (a) What geographic barriers hindered movement in Africa? (b) Describe two examples of migration in Africa.
4. How did Nubia prosper?
5. Describe one way each of the following influenced North Africa: (a) the growth of the Roman empire, (b) the spread of Islam.

Critical Thinking and Writing
6. **Linking Past and Present** (a) What effects did desertification have on African peoples? (b) How might life in the United States today be affected if well-watered areas began to turn into desert?
7. **Connecting to Geography** Explain the link between geography and the introduction of camel caravans.

Activity
Take It to the NET

Search on the Internet for Lepcis Magna, an archaeological site on the Mediterranean coast of North Africa. Write a paragraph about the city's history and its link to Septimius Severus.

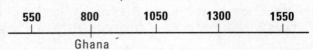
Reading Focus

- Why were gold and salt important in early Africa?
- How did the rulers of Ghana, Mali, and Songhai build strong kingdoms?
- How did other West African kingdoms develop?

Vocabulary

surplus
commodity
mansa
oba

Taking Notes

Copy and complete the time line below. As you read, add entries for the establishment of kingdoms mentioned in this section. One has been included as an example.

550	800	1050	1300	1550
	Ghana			

Main Idea Between about A.D. 800 and A.D. 1600, several powerful kingdoms won control of the Sahara trade and built prosperous cities in West Africa.

Geography and History

The Salt Trade

The camel changed the Saharan salt trade. For centuries, trade was limited because the horses that transported the salt were not suited to desert travel. However, about A.D. 300, the Berbers, an Arabic people of North Africa, began using camels to carry their goods. When the caravans reached Ghana, merchants would pay one pound of gold dust for one pound of salt. The salt trade began to thrive.

Now, more than 1,000 years later, the salt trade still exists. As late as 1975, workers in Taghaza (now called Taoudenni) were living in salt huts and mining several thousand tons of salt per year. Small caravans of camels carrying salt still arrive in Timbuktu today.

Theme: Continuity and Change Why are camels still used in the salt trade in today's technological age?

Setting the Scene

In the early 1500s, the scholar Hassan ibn Muhammad—known in the West as Leo Africanus—described the commercial wealth and bustling markets of the West African city of Timbuktu:

> "Here are many shops of . . . merchants, and especially such as weave linen and cotton cloth. And here do the Barbary (North African) merchants bring the cloth of Europe. All the women of this region, except maidservants, go with their faces covered and sell all the necessary foods."
>
> —Hassan ibn Muhammad, quoted in *Ancient African Kingdoms* (Shinnie)

Timbuktu stood at one end of a trade network that reached north to Cairo and then across the Mediterranean Sea to Italy. Between about 800 and 1600, several powerful kingdoms in turn won control of the prosperous Sahara trade. Among the richest of these West African states were Ghana, Mali, and Songhai.

Trading Gold and Salt

As the Sahara dried out, you will recall, some Neolithic people migrated southward into the savanna. There, farmers grew beans, melons, and cereal grains. By A.D. 100, settled farming villages were expanding, especially along the Senegal and Niger rivers and around Lake Chad.

Villagers traded any surplus, or excess, food they produced. Gradually, a trade network linked the savanna to forest lands in the south and then funneled goods across the Sahara to civilizations along the Mediterranean and in the Middle East.

Two products, gold and salt, dominated the Sahara trade. Gold was plentiful in present-day Ghana, Nigeria, and Senegal. Men dug the gold-bearing soil from pits. Women then washed the soil to extract the gold dust. The precious metal was stuffed into hollow feather quills for safe travel to the markets of North Africa and Europe.

In return, West Africans received an equally important commodity, or valuable product, salt. People need salt in their diet to prevent dehydration, especially in hot, tropical areas. The Sahara had an abundance of salt. At Taghaza, in the central Sahara, people even built homes of salt blocks. But in the savanna, several hundred miles south, salt was scarce. A block of salt was easily worth its weight in gold.

As farming and trade prospered, cities developed on the northern edges of the savanna. Strong monarchs gained control of the most profitable trade routes and built powerful kingdoms.

Gold Wealth of Ghana

By A.D. 800, the rulers of the Soninke people had united many farming villages to create the kingdom of Ghana.* Ghana was located in the broad "V" made by the Niger and Senegal rivers. From there, the king controlled gold-salt trade routes across West Africa. The two streams of trade met in the marketplaces of Ghana, where the king collected tolls on all goods entering or leaving his land. So great was the flow of gold that Arab writers called Ghana "land of gold."

Capital and King The capital of Ghana was Kumbi Saleh, made up of two separate, walled towns, some six miles apart. The first town was dominated by the royal palace, surrounded by a complex of domed buildings. Here, in a court noted for its wealth and splendor, the king of Ghana presided over elaborate ceremonies. To the people, he was a semidivine figure who dispensed justice and kept order.

In the second town of Kumbi Saleh, prosperous Muslim merchants from north of the Sahara lived in luxurious stone buildings. Lured by the gold wealth of Ghana, these merchants helped make Kumbi Saleh a bustling center of trade.

Influence of Islam Muslim merchants, settled in their own communities throughout the kingdom, brought their Islamic faith to Ghana. Islam spread slowly at first. The king employed Muslims as counselors and officials, gradually absorbing Muslim military technology and ideas about government. Muslims also introduced their written language, coinage, business methods, and styles of architecture. In time, a few city dwellers adopted Islam, but most of the Soninke people continued to follow their own traditional beliefs.

About 1050, the Almoravids (al MOR uh veedz), pious Muslims of North Africa, launched a campaign to spread their form of Islam. They eventually overwhelmed Ghana, but were unable to maintain control over such a distant land. In time, Ghana was swallowed up by a rising new power, the West African kingdom of Mali.

The Kingdom of Mali

Amid the turmoil of Ghana's collapse, the Mandinka people on the upper Niger suffered a bitter defeat by a rival leader. Their king and all but one of his sons were executed. According to tradition, the survivor was Sundiata. By 1235, he had crushed his enemies, won control of the gold trade routes, and founded the empire of Mali.

Mali is an Arab version of the Mandinka word meaning "where the king dwells." The mansas, or kings, expanded their influence over both the gold-mining regions to the south and the salt supplies of Taghaza. Where caravan routes crossed, towns like Timbuktu mushroomed into great trading cities.

The greatest emperor of Mali was Mansa Musa (MAHN sah MOO sah), who came to the throne in about 1312. He expanded Mali's borders westward to the Atlantic Ocean and pushed northward to conquer many cities. During Mansa Musa's 25-year reign, he worked to ensure peace and order in his empire. "There is complete and general safety throughout the land,"

---

*Ghana, meaning ruler, was the name used for the kingdom by Arab traders. The modern nation of Ghana is not located on the site of the ancient kingdom, but lies several hundred miles to the south.

The Gold Trade
This gold scorpion was probably used as a weight by West African merchants. Along with salt, gold dominated the Sahara trade and was a mainstay of the West African economy.

Theme: Economics and Technology Why might someone choose to make a weight from so valuable a material as gold?

Biography

Sundiata (?)–1255

During the early 1200s, a tyrant named Sumanguru ruled in western Africa. According to legend, Sumanguru feared a royal Mandinka family. He killed 11 brothers in the family. But he spared the life of one brother, Sundiata, who appeared to be sickly and already near death. Sundiata survived and recruited an army. In 1235, Sundiata defeated Sumanguru and quickly persuaded other Mandinka chiefs to surrender to his rule.

History tells us that over the next two decades, Sundiata expanded his power. He founded the empire of Mali, which lasted for 200 years. Sundiata became a great hero, and West Africans have told stories about his exploits for hundreds of years.

Theme: Impact of the Individual Why did West Africans tell stories about Sundiata long after his death?

Traveling With Mansa Musa

Despite the blistering heat of the Sahara, your heart is light. As a minor official, you feel honored to be a part of the *hajj*—or pilgrimage—of your emperor, Mansa Musa. Although there are still many miles between you and the holy city of Mecca, you know that the people of Mali will sing songs about this trip for generations to come.

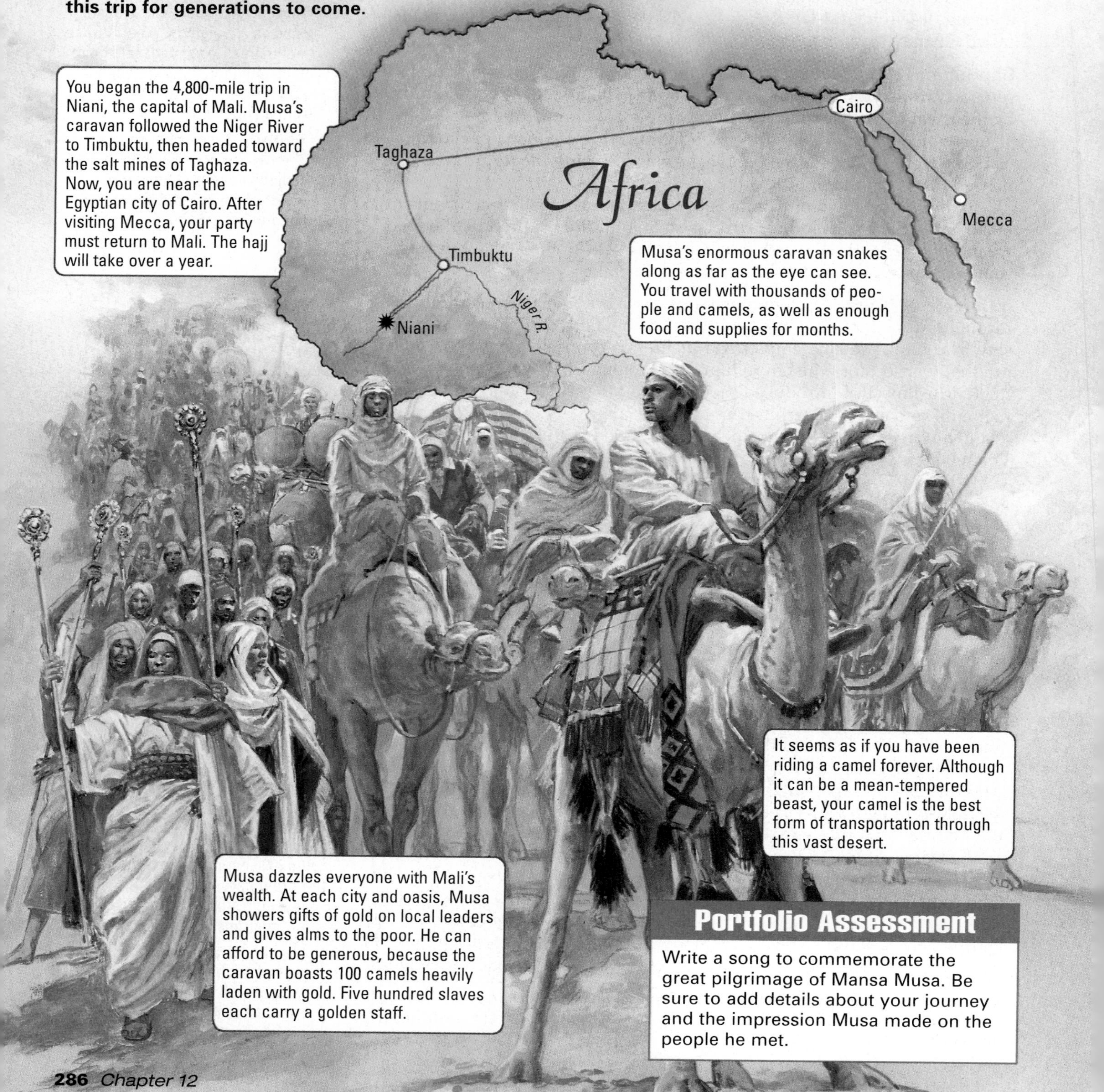

You began the 4,800-mile trip in Niani, the capital of Mali. Musa's caravan followed the Niger River to Timbuktu, then headed toward the salt mines of Taghaza. Now, you are near the Egyptian city of Cairo. After visiting Mecca, your party must return to Mali. The hajj will take over a year.

Africa

Cairo

Taghaza

Mecca

Timbuktu

Niger R.

Niani

Musa's enormous caravan snakes along as far as the eye can see. You travel with thousands of people and camels, as well as enough food and supplies for months.

It seems as if you have been riding a camel forever. Although it can be a mean-tempered beast, your camel is the best form of transportation through this vast desert.

Musa dazzles everyone with Mali's wealth. At each city and oasis, Musa showers gifts of gold on local leaders and gives alms to the poor. He can afford to be generous, because the caravan boasts 100 camels heavily laden with gold. Five hundred slaves each carry a golden staff.

Portfolio Assessment

Write a song to commemorate the great pilgrimage of Mansa Musa. Be sure to add details about your journey and the impression Musa made on the people he met.

commented Ibn Battuta when he visited Mali. "The traveler here has no more reason to fear thieves than the man who stays at home."

Mansa Musa converted to Islam and based his system of justice on the Quran. At the same time, he did not adopt all customs associated with some nearby Muslim societies. For example, women in Mali wore no veils and were not secluded within the home.

In 1324, Mansa Musa fulfilled one of the Five Pillars of Islam by making the hajj, or pilgrimage to Mecca. Through his pilgrimage, Mansa Musa showed his devotion to Islam. He also forged new diplomatic and economic ties with other Muslim states. The movement of wealth, people, and ideas increased Mali's renown. By the 1400s, Timbuktu had become a leading center of learning. The city drew some of the best scholars from all over the Muslim world.

A New Empire in Songhai

In the 1400s, disputes over succession weakened Mali. Subject peoples broke away, and the empire shriveled. By 1450, the wealthy trading city of Gao (GOW) had emerged as the capital of a new West African kingdom, Songhai (SAWNG hī).

Two Great Leaders Songhai grew up on the bend of the Niger River in present-day Niger and Burkina Faso. Between 1464 and 1492, the soldier-king Sonni Ali used his powerful army to forge the largest state that had ever existed in West Africa. Sonni Ali brought trade routes and wealthy cities like Timbuktu under his control. Unlike the rulers of Mali, he did not adopt the practices of Islam. Instead, he followed traditional religious beliefs.

Soon after Sonni Ali's death, though, the emperor Askia Muhammad set up a Muslim dynasty. He further expanded the territory of Songhai and improved the government. Askia Muhammad set up a bureaucracy with separate departments for farming, the army, and the treasury.

Like Mansa Musa, Askia Muhammad made a pilgrimage to Mecca that led to increased ties with the Muslim world. Scholars and poets from Muslim lands flocked to his court at Gao. In towns and cities across Songhai, Askia Muhammad built mosques and opened schools for the study of the Quran.

Invaders From the North Songhai prospered until about 1586, when disputes over succession led to civil war. Soon after, the ruler of Morocco sent his armies south to seize the West African gold mines. The invaders used gunpowder weapons to defeat the disunited forces of Songhai.

Like the Almoravids in Ghana, however, the Moroccans were not able to rule an empire across the Sahara. With the downfall of Songhai, this part of West Africa splintered into many small kingdoms.

Other Kingdoms of West Africa

In the period from 500 to 1500, other kingdoms flourished in various parts of West Africa. The fertile northern lands of modern-day Nigeria were home to the Hausa people, who had probably migrated there when the Sahara dried out. They were successful at both farming and trading.

Walled City-States of the Hausa By the 1300s, the Hausa had built a number of clay-walled cities. While these city-states remained independent of one another, in time they expanded into thriving commercial centers. In the cities, cotton weavers and dyers, leatherworkers, and other artisans produced goods for sale. Merchants traded with Arab and Berber caravans from north of the Sahara. Hausa goods were sold as far away as North Africa and southern Europe.

Kano was the most prosperous Hausa city-state. Its walls, 14 miles in circumference, protected a population of more than 30,000. Kano's greatest

Benin Bronzes

The forest kingdom of Benin was famous for its sculptures, such as this depiction of a queen mother. Benin artisans used a lost-wax process to create sculptures of bronze and brass. In this process, the sculptor formed a wax model inside a clay shell and then poured molten metal into the shell. The melting wax ran out, leaving behind a finished metal sculpture.

Theme: Political and Social Systems How does this casting suggest that the subject was an important person in Benin?

king, Muhammad Rumfa, was a Muslim, as were many merchants and officials. The Hausa developed a written language based on Arabic.

Many Hausa rulers were women, such as Amina of the city-state of Zaria. In the 1500s, she conquered Kano and expanded the boundary of Zaria as far as the Niger River. Under Amina, the Hausa came to dominate many Saharan trade routes.

The Forest Kingdom of Benin South of the savanna, Benin (beh NIN) rose in the rain forests of the Guinea coast. The forest peoples carved out farming villages and traded pepper, ivory, and, later, slaves to their neighbors in the savanna.

The rulers of Benin organized their kingdom in the 1300s, probably building on the achievements of earlier forest cultures. An **oba,** or king, was both a political and a religious leader. Still, much power was spread among other figures, including the queen mother and a council of hereditary chiefs. A three-mile-long wall surrounded the capital, Benin City. Its broad avenues were dotted with tidy homes and a great palace.

The palace, in particular, was decorated with elaborate brass plaques and sculptures. According to tradition, artisans from Ife (EE fay), an earlier forest society, had taught the people of Benin how to cast bronze and brass. Benin sculptors developed their own unique style for representing the human face and form. Their works depicted warriors armed for battle, queen mothers with upswept hairstyles, and the oba himself.

Looking Ahead

Later Benin bronzeworks showed helmeted and bearded Portuguese merchants. These newcomers began to arrive in growing numbers in the 1500s. At first, Benin benefited from the new trade with European countries. However, increasing contacts with Europe opened the door to a booming slave trade that would have far-reaching consequences for all of West Africa.

SECTION 2 Assessment

Recall

1. **Identify: (a)** Almoravids, **(b)** Sundiata, **(c)** Sonni Ali, **(d)** Askia Muhammad, **(e)** Amina.
2. **Define: (a)** surplus, **(b)** commodity, **(c)** mansa, **(d)** oba.

Comprehension

3. How did the gold-salt trade develop between West Africa and North Africa?
4. How did Mansa Musa, Sonni Ali, and Askia Muhammad change their kingdoms?

5. What were the achievements of the **(a)** Hausa city-states, **(b)** kingdom of Benin?

Critical Thinking and Writing

6. **Recognizing Causes and Effects (a)** Describe two short-term effects of Mansa Musa's hajj. **(b)** What do you think was the most important long-term effect?
7. **Drawing Conclusions** What might historians learn about the kingdom of Benin by studying its sculpture?

Activity

Creating a Map
Research the pilgrimages of Mansa Musa and Askia Muhammad. On a map, trace the routes of the pilgrimages. What regions and kingdoms did each ruler visit during his pilgrimage? Label each of these regions.

Trade Routes of East Africa

Reading Focus

- How did religion influence the development of Axum and Ethiopia?

- What effects did trade have on city-states in East Africa?

- What have archaeologists discovered about Great Zimbabwe?

Taking Notes

Copy this table. As you read, fill in the columns with trade goods from Africa, Asia, and Europe and the Mediterranean that passed through the markets of Axum and the East African coast.

AFRICA	ASIA	EUROPE AND THE MEDITERRANEAN
		Linen cloth
Hides, skins, and animal products		
		Copper
	Cotton cloth and silk	
	Porcelain, china, and glassware	

Main Idea Religion and trade played an important role in Ethiopia and East African city-states.

Setting the Scene According to Ethiopian tradition, the first emperor of Ethiopia was the son of the Israelite king Solomon and Makeda, the queen of Sheba. An ancient chronicle described how Makeda decided to journey to Jerusalem after hearing of Solomon's wisdom. "Learning is better than treasures of silver and gold," she said. The queen spent six months at Solomon's court, gathering knowledge to bring back to her people.

According to the chronicle, when Makeda was about to return to Sheba, Solomon gave her a ring and a blessing:

"May the peace of God be with thee. While I was sleeping . . . I had a vision. The sun which before my eyes was shining upon Israel, moved away. It went and soared above Ethiopia. It remained there. Who knows but that thy country may be blessed because of thee? Above all keep the truth which I have brought thee. Worship God."

—*The Glory of Kings*

The kingdom of Ethiopia was proud of its ancient Jewish roots and Christian traditions of Byzantine origin. In later centuries, other areas in Africa were joining the Islamic world. Ethiopia, however, remained mainly Christian and established the Coptic church.

Axum and Its Successors

About A.D. 350, as you will recall, King Ezana of Axum conquered and absorbed the ancient Nile kingdom of Nubia. Located to the southeast of Nubia, Axum extended from the mountains of present-day Ethiopia to the sun-bleached shores of the Red Sea. The peoples of Axum were descended from African farmers and from traders who brought Jewish religious traditions through Arabia. This merging of cultures introduced another religion to Axum. It also gave rise to a unique written and spoken language, Geez.

A Trade Network The kingdom of Axum profited from the strategic location of its two main cities, the port of Adulis on the Red Sea and the upland capital city of Axum. From about 200 B.C. to A.D. 400, Axum commanded a triangular trade network that connected Africa to India by way of the Arabian Sea and to the Mediterranean world.

From the interior of Africa, traders brought ivory, animal hides, rhinoceros horns, and gold to the markets of Axum. Goods from farther south along the African coast came to the harbor of Adulis. There, too, markets offered iron, spices, precious stones, and cotton cloth from India and other lands beyond the Indian Ocean. Ships bore these goods up the Red Sea, where they collected linen cloth, brass, copper, iron tools, wine, and olive oil from Europe and countries along the Mediterranean.

The Spread of Christianity In these great centers of international trade, Greek, Egyptian, Arab, and Jewish merchants mingled with traders from Africa, India, and other regions. As elsewhere, ideas spread along with goods. In the 300s, Axum's great king, Ezana, converted to Christianity. As the new religion took hold among the people, Christian churches replaced older temples.

At first, Christianity strengthened the ties between Axum, North Africa, and the Mediterranean world. Axum's other African neighbors, however, were not Christian. In the 600s, Islam began spreading across Africa. Many African rulers embraced this new faith, creating strong cultural ties across much of the continent. Axum was now isolated from its own trade network—by distance from Europe and by religion from many former trading partners. Civil war and economic decline combined to weaken Axum, and the kingdom slowly declined.

Ethiopia, a Christian Outpost Though Axum's political and economic power faded, its cultural and religious influence did not vanish. This legacy survived among the peoples of the interior uplands, in what today is Ethiopia. Protected by rugged mountains, descendants of the Axumites were able to maintain their independence for centuries. Their success was due in part to the unifying power of their Coptic Christian faith, which gave them a unique sense of identity and helped establish a culture distinct from that of neighboring peoples.

During the reign of King Lalibela in the early 1200s, Christian monks built a number of remarkable churches. They were carved into the solid rock of the mountains. According to Ethiopian chronicles, the builders had divine help:

> "Angels joined the workers, the quarry men, the stone cutters, and the laborers. The angels worked with them by day and by themselves at night. The men . . . doubted whether the angels were doing this work because they could not see them, but Lalibela knew, because the angels, who understood his virtue, did not hide from him."
> —*The Ethiopian Royal Chronicles*

Despite their isolation, Ethiopian Christians kept ties with the Holy Land. Some made pilgrimages to Jerusalem. Ethiopians also were in touch with Christian communities in Egypt. Still, Ethiopians saw their country as a Christian outpost. Over time, Ethiopian Christians absorbed many local customs. They adapted traditional East African drum music and dances that are still used in church services today.

The kings of Ethiopia claimed descent from the Israelite king Solomon and the queen of Sheba. This belief was recorded in an ancient Ethiopian book called *The Glory of Kings* and reinforced by observing Jewish holidays and dietary laws. One group of Ethiopians practiced Judaism rather than Christianity. These Ethiopian Jews, known as the Falasha, survived in the mountains of Ethiopia until recent years, when they were evacuated to Israel during a famine.

East African City-States

While Axum declined, a string of commercial cities—including Kilwa, Mogadishu, Mombasa, and Sofala—gradually rose along the East African coast. Since ancient times, Phoenician, Greek, Roman, and Indian traders had visited this coast. Under the protection of local African rulers, Arab and

Persian merchants set up Muslim communities beginning in the A.D. 600s. Later, Bantu-speaking peoples migrated into the region and adopted Islam. Port cities, as well as offshore islands like Lamu and Zanzibar, were ideally located for trade with Asia. As a result, Asian traders and immigrants from as far away as Indonesia soon added to the rich cultural mix.

Growing Trade Early mariners learned that the annual monsoon winds could carry sailing ships northeast to India in summer and back to Africa in winter. On the East African coast, rulers saw the advantages of trade. They welcomed ships from Arabia, Persia, and China. Traders acquired ivory, leopard skins, iron, copper, and gold from the interior of Africa, as well as from coastal regions. From India, Southeast Asia, and China came cotton cloth, silk, spices, porcelain, glassware, and swords. A thriving slave trade also developed, sending captured people from the African interior to the Middle East and beyond.

Trade helped local rulers build strong city-states. A Muslim visitor described Kilwa as "one of the most beautiful and well-constructed towns in the world." Its royal palace stands on cliffs that today overlook the modern city. The complex of courtyards and large rooms runs for two acres. Built of coral and cut stone, the structure is evidence of the city's splendor.

A Blend of Cultures International trade created a rich and varied mix of cultures in the East African city-states. Bantu-speaking Africans, Arabs, and other Middle Easterners mingled in the streets with people from Southeast Asia, India, and China. With the spread of Islam, Middle Eastern influences grew stronger. Marriages between African women and non-African Muslim men furthered the spread of Muslim culture. An African wife's traditional property rights allowed her husband to settle and own land, creating opportunities for these non-African men. Their children often gained positions of leadership.

Both private houses and palaces show strong Arab and Middle Eastern influences in the East African cities. Additionally, the blend of cultures gave rise to a new language. Known as Swahili, it fused many Arabic words onto a Bantu base and was written in Arabic script.

Great Zimbabwe

To the south and inland from the coastal city-states, massive stone ruins sprawl across rocky hilltops near the great bend in the Limpopo River. The looming walls, great palace, and cone-shaped towers testify that these structures were part of the powerful and prosperous capital of a great inland empire. Today, these impressive ruins are known as Great Zimbabwe, which means "great stone buildings."

Europeans who came upon these ruins in the 1800s thought they were the work of the ancient Phoenicians. In fact, the builders were a succession of Bantu-speaking peoples who settled in the region between 900 and 1500. The newcomers brought improved farming skills, iron, and mining methods. On the relatively fertile land, they produced enough food to support a growing population.

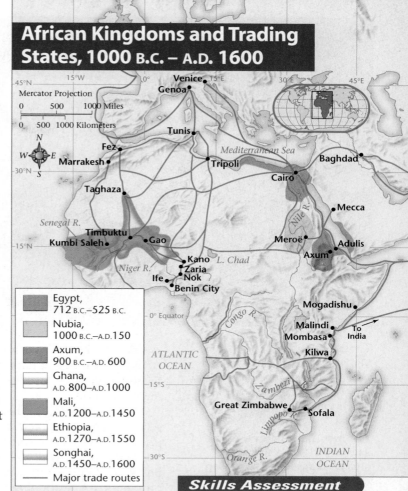

African Kingdoms and Trading States, 1000 B.C. – A.D. 1600

Mercator Projection

0   500   1000 Miles
0   500   1000 Kilometers

Egypt, 712 B.C.–525 B.C.
Nubia, 1000 B.C.–A.D. 150
Axum, 900 B.C.–A.D. 600
Ghana, A.D. 800–A.D. 1000
Mali, A.D. 1200–A.D. 1450
Ethiopia, A.D. 1270–A.D. 1550
Songhai, A.D. 1450–A.D. 1600
— Major trade routes

Skills Assessment

Geography From 1000 B.C. in Nubia to the A.D. 1400s and 1500s in Songhai, Africans built strong trading kingdoms in East Africa and West Africa. Many of the kingdoms developed because of profitable trade with other lands.

1. **Location** On the map, locate **(a)** Indian Ocean, **(b)** Nile River, **(c)** Axum, **(d)** Ghana, **(e)** Malindi.
2. **Region (a)** What was the major hub of West Africa? **(b)** Which cities were most likely to trade directly with India?
3. **Critical Thinking Drawing Conclusions** Explain why West and East Africa saw a series of kingdoms develop within the same general areas, rather than in different places.

Economy and Government

We know little about how this civilization developed. Early settlers raised cattle. They built stone enclosures to protect their livestock. In time, they improved their building methods and erected large walls and palaces. The capital probably reached its height about 1300. By then, it had tapped nearby gold resources and created profitable commercial links with coastal cities like Sofala. Archaeologists have found beads from India and porcelain from China, showing that Great Zimbabwe was part of a trade network that reached across the Indian Ocean.

Besides controlling trade, Zimbabwe was a center for manufacturing. Artisans turned gold and copper into beautiful jewelry and made iron tools for everyday use. Weaving cotton into cloth seems to have been an important craft.

Very little is known about the government in Great Zimbabwe. Some scholars have suggested, however, that the ruler was a god-king who presided over a large court. He may have shared authority with a powerful queen mother as well as nine queens, each of whom had her own court. Below the king, a central bureaucracy may have ruled an inner ring of provinces, while appointed governors had authority in more distant villages.

Decline By 1500, Zimbabwe was in decline. Some scholars suggest that overfarming had exhausted the soil. In addition, civil war and dwindling trade probably contributed to the breakup of Zimbabwe. By then, Portuguese traders were pushing inland to find the source of gold that they were able to buy in cities along the coast. They failed to discover the gold mines, and their intrusion helped undermine later small states that formed in the region.

Great Zimbabwe

The ruins of Great Zimbabwe suggest a rich and varied society. This aerial view of the stone structures shows the extent of the empire's capital.

Theme: Economics and Technology Which of the structures appears to have been most significant in the capital? Explain your answer.

SECTION 3 Assessment

Recall

1. **Identify:** **(a)** queen of Sheba, **(b)** Ezana, **(c)** Geez, **(d)** Lalibela, **(e)** Falasha, **(f)** Swahili, **(g)** Great Zimbabwe.

Comprehension

2. What religious traditions came together in Ethiopia?
3. **(a)** Why did Axum become a key trading center for three continents? **(b)** How did trade encourage a blending of cultures in East African city-states such as Kilwa, Mombasa, and Mogadishu?

4. **(a)** What evidence suggests that Great Zimbabwe was a center of trade? **(b)** What do historians think were the reasons that Great Zimbabwe declined?

Critical Thinking and Writing

5. **Analyzing Information** Why did Ethiopia become increasingly isolated from its neighbors over the centuries?
6. **Making Inferences** Why might the language of Swahili have emerged in the East African city-states?

Activity
Take It to the NET

Research African beadmaking between 10,000 B.C. and A.D. 1200. Write a paragraph about the impact of shell, stone, clay, metal, and glass beads on Africa's trade networks and cultures.

Many Peoples, Many Traditions

Reading Focus

■ How did the interaction of people and the environment lead to diverse societies?

■ How did government, family, and religion hold African societies together?

■ How did artistic and literary traditions reflect the values of African societies?

Vocabulary

slash-and-burn agriculture

nuclear family

patrilineal

matrilineal

lineage

griot

Taking Notes

As you read, prepare an outline of this section. Use Roman numerals to indicate the major headings of the section, capital letters for the subheadings, and numbers for the supporting details. The sample at right has been started for you.

I. People and the environment
   A. Hunting and food gathering
      1. Lived in Africa's fringe areas
      2.
   B. Herding and fishing

Main Idea   The process of adapting to the land contributed to the development of many different cultures in Africa.

Setting the Scene   At harvest time, the Kikuyu (kee koo yoo) people of East Africa offered prayers of thanksgiving to their traditional gods. A modern writer recorded one ancient prayer:

> "Mwene-Nyaga, you who have brought us rain and have given us good harvest, let people eat grain of this harvest calmly and peacefully. . . . Guard us against illness of people or our herds and flocks so that we may enjoy this season's harvest in tranquility."
>
> —Jomo Kenyatta, *Facing Mount Kenya*

In West African mosques, Muslims recited a different prayer: "Praise be to God, Lord of the Universe, the Compassionate, the Merciful."

Differing religious traditions contributed to the diversity of the vast continent of Africa. At the same time, religious beliefs formed deep bonds that united individual societies.

People and the Environment

Over thousands of years, Bantu-speaking peoples migrated across Africa. With them, they carried farming skills and knowledge of ironworking to its many regions. Wherever these people settled, they adapted to local environments and absorbed ideas from the peoples they encountered. Trade or other contacts brought additional changes. As a result, the ways of life of African societies varied greatly from place to place.

Hunting and Food Gathering   Bantu migrations pushed many hunting and food-gathering peoples of Africa to fringe areas. The Khoisan people, for example, adapted to the harsh conditions of the Kalahari Desert by gathering roots and herbs and hunting small game.

Because food was scarce, hunting-gathering people lived in small bands numbering only about 20 or 30. Their knowledge of the natural world, however, was unmatched by city dwellers or farming villagers. They could track animals across long distances and identify the food and healing properties of many different plants.

Herding and Fishing   In parts of the savanna free from the tsetse fly, some peoples raised herds of cattle. Because grazing areas were limited, these societies were often nomadic. To protect their herds against raiders, these peoples perfected skills in warfare.

Along the coasts and rivers, fish was the basic food for some people. Most fishing peoples used nets. They traded any surplus fish for grain, animal skins, and other products made by people who lived inland. Some fishing areas had enough food resources to support large populations.

Settled Farming Societies Farming communities raised a variety of crops from grains to root crops like yams or tree crops like bananas. Most farming peoples practiced a method that is today called slash-and-burn agriculture. They cleared forest and brush land with iron axes and hoes, then burned the remains, using the ash for fertilizer. Because the land lost its fertility within a few years, villagers would move on to clear other land. Eventually, after giving the soil time to renew its fertility, they might return to the abandoned fields.

Forms of Village Government

Farming peoples generally lived in tightknit communities and helped one another in tasks such as clearing the land, planting, and harvesting. Both men and women planted, but they usually were responsible for different crops. Political patterns varied, depending in part on the size of the communities. However, village governments often had similar features.

Sharing Power In these pre-urban societies, power was usually shared among a number of people rather than centralized in the hands of a single leader. In some villages, a chief had a good deal of authority, but in many others, elders made the major decisions. In some places, especially in parts of West Africa, women took the dominant role in the marketplace or acted as official peacemakers in the village.

Villages often made decisions by a process known as consensus. In open discussions, people whose opinions were valued voiced their views before

African Masks
Many societies in Africa used masks in political, religious, and social rituals. Carved masks might be elaborately decorated with paint or items such as shells to show the authority of the wearer or to represent a particular spiritual force.

Theme: Art and Literature
What kinds of artistic skills would be needed to create these masks?

a general agreement was reached. The opinions of older women and men usually held the greatest weight.

Villages within a large kingdom like that of Songhai had to obey decisions made at a distant court. These villagers had to pay taxes and provide soldiers to the central government.

The Kingdom of Kongo The kingdom of Kongo, which flourished about 1500 in central Africa, illustrates one of the many forms of government organization in Africa. It consisted of many villages grouped into districts and provinces and governed by officials appointed by the king. Each village had its own chief, a man chosen on the basis of the descent of his mother's family.

The king of Kongo might seem to have absolute power, but actually that power was limited. The king was chosen by a board of electors and had to govern according to traditional laws. Unlike rulers of West African states, who maintained strong standing armies, kings of Kongo could only call upon men to fight in times of need. Through local governors, the king collected taxes either in goods or in cowrie shells, a common African currency.

Family Patterns

In Africa, as elsewhere, the family was the basic unit of society. Patterns of family life varied greatly. In hunting-and-gathering societies, for example, the nuclear family was typical, with parents and children living and working together as a unit. In other African communities, people lived in joint families. Several generations shared the same complex of houses.

Lines of Descent Family organization varied in other ways. Some families were patrilineal. In these families, important kinship ties and inheritance were passed through the father's side. Other families were matrilineal, with inheritance traced through the mother's side. In a patrilineal culture, a bride would move to her husband's village to become part of his family. In a matrilineal culture, the husband joined his wife's family.

Matrilineal cultures also forged strong ties between brothers and sisters. Brothers were expected to protect their sisters, and sisters made their sons available to help their brothers whenever needed.

Wider Ties Each family belonged to a lineage, or group of households who claimed a common ancestor. Several lineages formed a clan that traced its descent to an even more remote and often legendary ancestor. Belonging to a particular family, lineage, or clan gave people a sense of community.

An individual's place in society was also determined by a system of age grades. An age grade included all girls or boys born in the same year. Each age grade had particular responsibilities and privileges. In the older age grades, children began to take part in village activities, which created social ties beyond the family.

Religious Beliefs

Across Africa, religious beliefs were varied and complex. Like Hindus or ancient Greeks and Romans, village Africans worshiped many gods and goddesses. They identified the forces of nature with divine spirits and tried to influence those forces through rituals and ceremonies.

Many African peoples believed that a single, unknowable supreme being stood above all the other gods and goddesses. This supreme being was the creator and ruler of the universe and was helped by the lesser spirits, who were closer to the people. Like the Chinese, many African peoples believed that the spirits of their ancestors could help, warn, or punish their descendants on Earth. Just as Christians in medieval Europe called on the saints, people in Africa turned to the spirits of their departed ancestors.

The Griots of Africa

As historians, poets, and musicians, the griots of West Africa have captivated their audiences for centuries. They are greatly respected for their knowledge, wisdom, and honesty. Becoming a griot takes years of training. Here is part of a speech by a modern griot from Guinea.

"I am a griot. It is I, Djeli Mamoudou Kouyate, son of Bintou Kouyate and Djeli Kedian Kouyate, master in the art of eloquence. Since time immemorial the Kouyates have been in the service of the Keita princes of Mali; we are vessels of speech, we are the repositories which harbor secrets many centuries old. The art of eloquence has no secrets for us; without us the names of kings vanish into oblivion, we are the memory of mankind; by the spoken word we bring to life the deeds and exploits of kings for younger generations.

I derive my knowledge from my father, Djeli Kedian, who also got it from his father; history holds no mystery for us. . . .

I know the list of all the sovereigns who succeeded to the throne of Mali. I know how the black people divided into tribes, for my father bequeathed to me all his learning; I know why such and such is called Kamara, another Keita, and yet another Sibibe or Traore; every name has a meaning, a secret import.

From Generation to Generation History—and the lessons to be learned from it—becomes lively stories in the mouth of the griot. Here, children listen to the stories of their people.

I teach kings the history of their ancestors so that the lives of the ancients might serve them as an example, for the world is old, but the future springs from the past.

My word is pure and free of all untruth; it is the word of my father; it is the word of my father's father. I will give you my father's words just as I received them; royal griots do not know what lying is. When a quarrel breaks out between tribes it is we who settle the difference, for we are the depositories of oaths which the ancestors swore.

Listen to my word, you who want to know . . . . To acquire my knowledge I have journeyed all round Mali. . . . Everywhere I was able to see and understand what my masters were teaching me, but between their hands I took an oath to teach only what is to be taught and to conceal what is to be kept concealed."

—Djeli Mamoudou Kouyate, *Through African Eyes* (Clark)

Skills Assessment

1. From whom did Kouyate learn to be a griot?
   A the ruler of Mali
   B his mother
   C his father
   D his grandfather

2. Kamara, Keita, Sibibe, and Traore are
   E griots.
   F Kouyate's ancestors.
   G tribes of Mali.
   H rulers of Mali.

3. **Critical Thinking** **Analyzing Information** **(a)** According to Kouyate, for what two special tasks besides relating history are griots responsible? What purposes do these tasks serve? Why might griots be especially well equipped to handle these tasks? **(b)** Does Kouyate relate everything he knows to everyone who hears him? How do you know? What might be the reason for this?

Skills Tip

In an excerpt, dots indicate where something has been left out. Three spaced dots (. . .) usually indicate that part of a sentence has been omitted. A period followed by three spaced dots (. . . .) usually indicates the omission of the last part of a sentence.

Christianity and Islam, as you have seen, influenced peoples in some parts of Africa. Converts often associated the God of Christians and Muslims with their traditional supreme being. In this way, Christianity and Islam absorbed many local practices and beliefs.

Artistic and Literary Traditions

In art and architecture, African traditions extend far back in time to the ancient rock paintings of the Sahara. The pyramids of Egypt and Nubia, the rock churches of Ethiopia, and the palace of Great Zimbabwe bear lasting witness to the creative power of these early civilizations. Sadly, many wooden buildings and works of art have not survived.

Arts African artists created works in ivory, wood, and bronze. Sometimes, their work was decorative. Artisans wove and dyed cloth, inscribed jugs and bowls, and shaped bracelets and neck ornaments simply for beauty. Much art, though, served social and religious purposes.

Art strengthened bonds within the community and linked both the makers and the users of the work. Patterns used to decorate textiles, baskets, swords, and other objects had important meanings. Often, they identified an object as the work of a particular clan or the possession of royalty.

In Africa, as elsewhere, much art was closely tied to religion. Statues and other objects were used in religious ceremonies. In many rituals, leaders wore impressively carved wooden masks decorated with cowrie shells or grass. Once the mask was in place, both the wearer and the viewers could feel the presence of the spiritual force it represented.

Literature African societies preserved their histories and values through both oral and written literature. Ancient Egypt, Nubia, and Axum left written records of their past. Later, Arabic provided a common written language in parts of Africa influenced by Islam. African Muslim scholars gathered in cities like Timbuktu and Kilwa as well as in North African cities. Documents in Arabic offer invaluable evidence about law, religion, and history.

Oral traditions date back many centuries. In West Africa, griots (GREE ohs), or professional poets, recited ancient stories. They preserved both histories and traditional folk tales in the same way that the epics of Homer or Aryan India were passed orally from generation to generation.

Histories praised the heroic deeds of famous ancestors or kings. Folk tales, which blended fanciful stories with humor and sophisticated word play, taught important moral lessons. Oral literature, like religion and art, thus encouraged a sense of community and common values.

Connections to Today

Kente Cloth

Centuries ago, the Asante people of Ghana developed a colorful, intricately designed cloth called kente. Once the apparel of Asante royalty, today kente designs represent the philosophy, moral values, and code of conduct in Ghanaian culture. Some designs symbolize good omens and spiritual rebirth, while others may represent family unity, cooperation, or sharing.

In recent years, many Americans have begun wearing kente cloth as a celebration of their African heritage. Traditionally the garb of joyous occasions, imported kente is used in a wide variety of items, from shirts to neckties to backpacks.

Theme: Religions and Value Systems Why might the people in this picture have chosen to wear kente cloth?

SECTION 4 Assessment

Recall
1. **Identify:** (a) Khoisan people, (b) Kongo.
2. **Define:** (a) slash-and-burn agriculture, (b) nuclear family, (c) patrilineal, (d) matrilineal, (e) lineage, (f) griot.

Comprehension
3. List three examples of how the environment influenced African societies.
4. What types of institutions and traditions held African societies together?

5. How was art connected to religion in African cultures?

Critical Thinking and Writing
6. **Analyzing Information** How might a matrilineal line of descent allow women to exercise greater authority in village affairs?
7. **Predicting Consequences** (a) Describe the process of slash-and-burn agriculture. (b) What might be some dangers of the extensive use of slash-and-burn agriculture?

Activity

Retelling a Tale
Find an African folk tale and read it. Then, retell it without using the book. Based on this experience, write two or three sentences describing the challenges that a griot faces.

Creating a Chapter Summary

Copy this chart on a sheet of paper. For each kingdom listed, fill in the row by naming the kingdom's characteristics. To help you get started, one row has been filled in.

For additional review and enrichment activities, see the interactive version of *World History* available on the Web and on CD-ROM.

KINGDOM	ERA	RULER	RELIGION	ECONOMIC BASE
NUBIA				
AXUM				
GHANA				
MALI				
HAUSA				
BENIN	1300s	Oba, queen mother, and council	Unknown	Farming, pepper, ivory
GREAT ZIMBABWE				
SONGHAI				

Web Site Self-Test
For practice test questions for Chapter 12, see **www.phschool.com**.

Building Vocabulary

Write sentences using the vocabulary words listed below, leaving blanks for the vocabulary words. Exchange your sentences with another student, and complete each other's sentences.

1. **savanna**
2. **desertification**
3. **outpost**
4. **commodity**
5. **oba**
6. **nuclear family**
7. **patrilineal**
8. **matrilineal**
9. **lineage**
10. **griot**

Recalling Key Facts

11. How do ancient rock paintings help scholars determine that the Sahara was a well-watered zone during the Neolithic age?
12. Into what present-day countries did the empire of Carthage extend?
13. How did the Hausa come to dominate Saharan trade routes under Amina's rule?
14. Why did Ethiopia's roots embrace both Jewish and Christian traditions?
15. How did the Khoisan people adapt to their environment?

Critical Thinking and Writing

16. **Drawing Conclusions** From what you have learned about African religions, why do you think many Africans found it easy to accept the monotheism of Christianity or Islam?

17. **Linking Past and Present** **(a)** Describe three traditions that created social bonds in African communities. **(b)** How are these traditions similar to the traditions that create bonds in your community? How are they different?

18. **Analyzing Information** Reread Setting the Scene, including the selection from *The Glory of Kings* in Section 3. **(a)** What reason does Makeda give for going to Jerusalem? **(b)** According to Solomon, what is the great lesson he has taught Makeda? **(c)** Would you consider *The Glory of Kings* a reliable source of historical information? Explain.

19. **Connecting to Geography** Look at the maps in this chapter. **(a)** Into which areas did Bantu-speaking peoples migrate? **(b)** Why might certain climate zones act as barriers?

In the 1000s, the Spanish Arab geographer al-Bakri wrote an encyclopedia of the entire world he knew about. Here, he describes the ceremonies when the king of ancient Ghana held court. Read the passage and answer the questions that follow.

> "The king adorns himself . . . with neck-laces and bracelets, and when he sits before the people he puts on a high cap decorated with gold and wrapped in turbans of fine cotton. The court of appeal is held in a domed pavilion around which stand ten horses with gold embroidered trappings. Behind the king stand ten pages holding shields and swords decorated with gold, and on his right are the sons of the secondary kings of his country, all wearing splendid garments and with their hair mixed with gold. On the ground around him are seated his ministers, whilst the governor of the city sits before him. . . . The royal audience is announced by the beating of a drum which they call 'deba' made out of a long piece of hollowed-out wood. When the people have gathered, those who profess the same religion as the king draw near upon their knees, sprinkling dust upon their heads as a sign of respect, whilst the Muslims clap hands as their form of greeting."

—al-Bakri, *Book of Roads and Kingdoms*

20. How does this passage reflect the image of Ghana as a "land of gold"?
21. What details show the importance of the king's audience?
22. How does al-Bakri's description illustrate the people's view of their king as a semidivine figure?
23. How do the Muslims at court differ from the followers of the king's own religion?
24. Would you consider this a reliable source of information about the ancient kingdom of Ghana? Why or why not?

Skills Tip

Secondary sources are accounts by people who did not directly witness the events they are describing. In reading a secondary source, be aware of what sources of information the writer used.

The sculpted panel above depicts a family at work in an African agricultural village. Look at the panel and answer the following questions:

25. What economic and social activities are depicted in this sculpture?
26. How does the sculpture depict a nuclear family?
27. How does the picture reflect the importance of family in African societies?
28. What seems to be the principal source of food for this family?
29. What does this picture suggest about the family's living conditions?

Skills Assessment

Take It to the NET

Use the Internet to research the history of Swahili and the countries in which it is commonly spoken today. Then, create a simple map that indicates concentrations of Swahili-speaking peoples. Compare your map to the Bantu Migrations map in this chapter. Using both maps, prepare a brief oral report that explains the development of the Swahili language.

CHAPTER 13

Spread of Civilizations in East Asia 500–1650

Chapter Preview

1 **Two Golden Ages of China**
2 **The Mongol and Ming Empires**
3 **Korea and Its Traditions**
4 **The Emergence of Japan**
5 **Japan's Feudal Age**

618

The Tang dynasty begins in China. The achievements of the Tang included fine porcelain figures, such as this soldier.

668

Shilla rulers unite Korea.

794

The Japanese royal court moves to Heian. The shrine above is a duplicate of one in the Heian imperial palace.

CHAPTER EVENTS

450   700   950

GLOBAL EVENTS

527 Justinian becomes ruler of the Byzantine empire.

800 Charlemagne is crowned emperor by the pope.

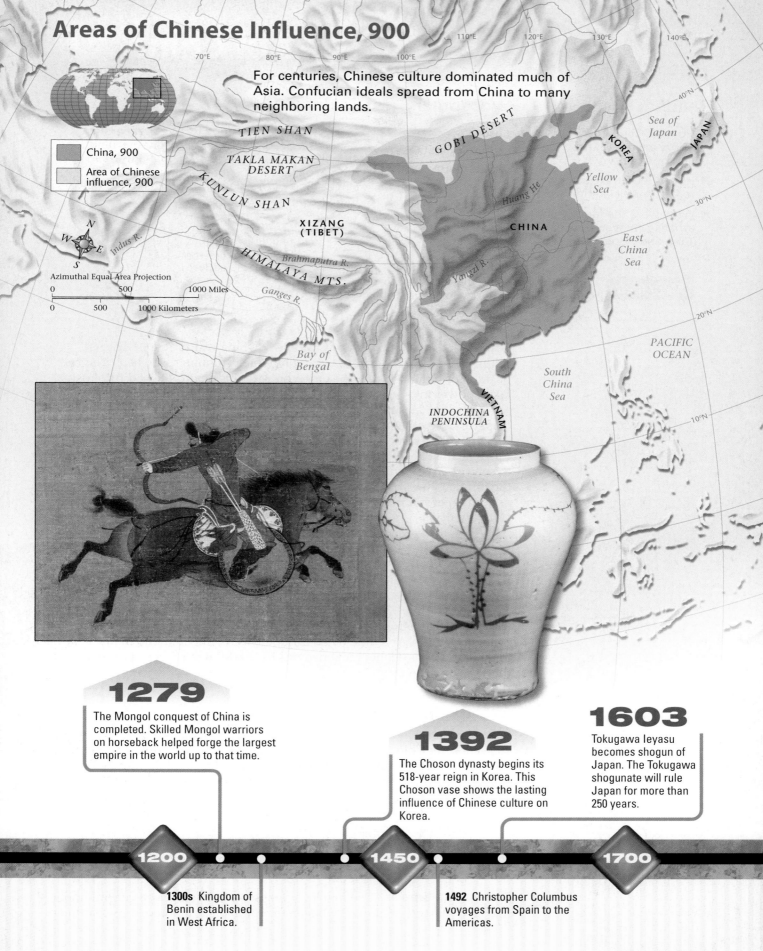

Areas of Chinese Influence, 900

For centuries, Chinese culture dominated much of Asia. Confucian ideals spread from China to many neighboring lands.

China, 900

Area of Chinese influence, 900

Azimuthal Equal Area Projection

0   500   1000 Miles

0   500   1000 Kilometers

TIEN SHAN

TAKLA MAKAN DESERT

KUNLUN SHAN

XIZANG (TIBET)

HIMALAYA MTS.

Brahmaputra R.

Ganges R.

Indus R.

Bay of Bengal

GOBI DESERT

Huang He

Yangzi R.

CHINA

KOREA

Sea of Japan

JAPAN

Yellow Sea

East China Sea

PACIFIC OCEAN

South China Sea

INDOCHINA PENINSULA

VIETNAM

1279
The Mongol conquest of China is completed. Skilled Mongol warriors on horseback helped forge the largest empire in the world up to that time.

1392
The Choson dynasty begins its 518-year reign in Korea. This Choson vase shows the lasting influence of Chinese culture on Korea.

1603
Tokugawa Ieyasu becomes shogun of Japan. The Tokugawa shogunate will rule Japan for more than 250 years.

1200

1450

1700

1300s Kingdom of Benin established in West Africa.

1492 Christopher Columbus voyages from Spain to the Americas.

Two Golden Ages of China

Reading Focus

■ How did Tang and Song rulers ensure Chinese unity and prosperity?

■ How did Chinese society reflect Confucian traditions?

■ What were the literary and artistic achievements of Tang and Song China?

Main Idea The Tang and Song dynasties restored culture and prosperity to China.

Vocabulary

usurp

tributary state

land reform

gentry

pagoda

Taking Notes

On a sheet of paper, copy this Venn diagram. As you read, add information about the Tang and Song. Include information that applies to both dynasties in the intersecting parts of the circles. Part of the diagram has been filled out to help you get started.

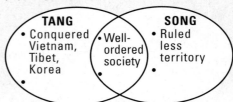

TANG
• Conquered Vietnam, Tibet, Korea

• Well-ordered society

SONG
• Ruled less territory

Setting the Scene Many people in China had reason to distrust Empress Wu Zhao (woo jow). From humble beginnings, she had risen to a position of influence with the emperor. After his death, she had ruthlessly taken power into her own hands, unseating her own sons from the throne. She had even declared herself "Son of Heaven," the age-old title of China's emperors. No other woman had ever dared do such a thing!

Now, rival princes and Confucian scholars were raising the banner of revolt against her. The poet Lo Binwang wrote a declaration condemning the empress as a "vile character" who had usurped, or illegally taken over, the throne. "Rise, rise, all men!" Lo Binwang wrote. "Consider, the orphans of our emperor are left helpless and defenseless while their father's grave is hardly dry!"

When the empress saw the declaration, she demanded to know who wrote it. But, surprisingly, she did not direct her anger at Lo Binwang. Rather, she berated her own ministers for failing to bring such a talented writer into her service! Like other educated Chinese, Wu prized a skilled and brilliant writer, no matter what side he was on.

In the late 600s, Wu Zhao became the only woman to rule China in her own name. Her strong rule helped guide China through one of its most brilliant periods. At a time when Europe was fragmented into many small feudal kingdoms, China remained unified under two powerful dynasties—the Tang and the Song.

The Brilliant Tang

After the Han dynasty collapsed in 220, China remained divided for nearly 400 years. Yet China escaped the decay that disrupted Western Europe after the fall of Rome. Farm production expanded and technology slowly improved. Buddhism spread, while learning and the arts continued. Even Chinese cities survived. Although invaders stormed northern China, they often adopted Chinese civilization rather than demolishing it.

Meanwhile, various dynasties rose and fell in the south. During the brief Sui dynasty (589–618), the emperor Sui Wendi reunited the north and south. But China was not restored to its earlier glory until the emergence of the Tang dynasty in 618.

Building an Empire The first Tang emperor, Li Yuan, was a general under the Sui dynasty. When the Sui began to crumble, his ambitious 16-year-old son, Li Shimin, urged him to lead a revolt. Father and son crushed all rivals and established the Tang dynasty. Eight years later, Li Shimin compelled his aging father to step down and mounted the throne himself, taking the name Tang Taizong. Brilliant general, government reformer, historian, and master of the calligraphy brush, Tang Taizong would become China's most admired emperor.

Later Tang rulers carried empire building to new heights, conquering territories deep into Central Asia. Chinese armies forced the neighboring lands of Vietnam, Tibet, and Korea to become **tributary states.** That is, while these states remained independent, their rulers had to acknowledge Chinese supremacy and send regular tribute to the Tang emperor. At the same time, students from Korea and Japan traveled to the Tang capital to learn about Chinese government, law, and arts.

Government and the Economy Tang rulers, such as Empress Wu Zhao, helped restore the Han system of uniform government throughout China. They rebuilt the bureaucracy and enlarged the civil service system to recruit talented officials trained in Confucian philosophy. They also set up schools to prepare male students for the exams and developed a flexible new law code.

Tang emperors instituted a system of **land reform.** That is, they broke up large agricultural holdings and redistributed the land to peasants. This policy strengthened the central government by weakening the power of large landowners. It also increased government revenues, since the peasants who farmed their own land would be able to pay taxes.

Under the Tang, a system of canals encouraged internal trade and transportation. The Grand Canal linked the Huang He to the Yangzi River. As a result, food grown in the south could be shipped to the capital in the north. At the time, the Grand Canal was the longest waterway ever dug by human labor.

Decline Like earlier dynasties, the Tang eventually weakened. Later Tang emperors lost territories in Central Asia to the Arabs. Corruption, high taxes, drought, famine, and rebellions all contributed to the downward swing of the dynastic cycle. In 907, a rebel general overthrew the last Tang emperor. This time, however, the chaos following the collapse of a dynasty did not last long.

Prosperity Under the Song

In 960, a scholarly general reunited much of China and founded the Song dynasty. The Song ruled 319 years, slightly longer than the Tang; however, the Song controlled less territory than the Tang. In addition, the Song faced the constant threat of invaders in the north. In the early 1100s, the battered Song retreated south of the Huang He. There, the Southern Song continued to rule for another 150 years.

Despite military setbacks, the Song period was a golden age. Chinese wealth and culture dominated East Asia even when its armies did not. Under the Song, the

Technology of Tang and Song China

Mechanical clock, 700s

The Chinese learned of water-powered clocks from Middle Easterners. Mechanical clocks used a complex series of wheels, shafts, and pins, turning at a steady rate, to tell exact time.

Gunpowder, 850

The earliest form of gunpowder was made from a mixture of saltpeter, sulfur, and charcoal, all found in abundance in China. It was first used in fireworks and later in weapons.

Block printing, 700s
Movable type, 1040s

Both printing processes were based on earlier techniques, such as seals (first used in the Middle East). In block printing, a full page of characters was carved onto a wooden block. Movable type was made up of pre-cut characters that were combined to form a page.

Connections to Today

In addition to the advances shown here, the Chinese developed a smallpox vaccine, invented a spinning wheel, and pioneered the use of arches in bridge building. In time, many of these developments traveled westward. Modernized versions of most of these inventions are still widely used today.

Skills Assessment **Chart Explain how one of the inventions shown here could have aided the spread of Chinese civilization to other lands.**

Chinese economy expanded. The center of farming shifted from the wheat fields of the north to the rice paddies of the Yangzi in the south. New strains of rice and improved irrigation methods helped peasants produce two rice crops a year. The rise in productivity created surpluses, allowing more people to pursue commerce, learning, or the arts.

Under both the Tang and Song, foreign trade flourished. Merchants arrived from India, Persia, and Arabia. Chinese merchants carried goods to Southeast Asia in exchange for spices and special woods. Song porcelain has been found as far away as East Africa. To improve trade, the government issued paper money. China's cities, which had been mainly centers of government, now prospered as centers of trade.

Chinese Society

Under the Tang and Song, China was a well-ordered society. At its head was the emperor, whose court was filled with aristocratic families. The court supervised a huge bureaucracy, from which officials fanned out to every part of China. Aside from the court, China's two main social classes were the gentry and the peasantry.

Gentry Most scholar-officials at court came from the gentry, or wealthy landowning class. They alone could afford to spend years studying the Confucian classics in order to pass the grueling civil service exam. When not in government service, the gentry often served in the provinces as allies of the emperor's officials.

The Song scholar-gentry valued learning more than physical labor. They supported a revival of Confucian thought. New schools of Confucian philosophers emphasized social order based on duty, rank, and proper behavior. Although corruption and greed existed among civil servants, the ideal Confucian official was a wise, virtuous scholar who knew how to ensure harmony in society.

Peasants Most Chinese were peasants who worked the land, living on what they produced. Drought and famine were a constant threat, but new tools and crops did improve the lives of many peasants. To add to their income, some families produced handicrafts such as baskets or embroidery. They carried these products to nearby market towns to sell or trade for salt, tea, or iron tools.

Peasants lived in small, largely self-sufficient villages that managed their own affairs. "Heaven is high," noted one Chinese saying, "and the emperor far away." Peasants relied on one another rather than the government. When disputes arose, a village leader and council of elders put pressure on the parties to resolve the problem. Only if such efforts failed did villagers take their disputes to the emperor's county representative.

In China, even peasants could move up in society through education and government service. If a bright peasant boy received an education and passed the civil service examinations, both he and his family rose in status.

Merchants In market towns and cities, some merchants acquired vast wealth. Still, according to Confucian tradition, merchants had an even lower social status than peasants because their riches came from the labor of others. An ambitious merchant therefore might buy land and educate at least one son to enter the ranks of the scholar-gentry.

The Confucian attitude toward merchants affected economic policy. Some rulers favored commerce but sought to control it. They often restricted where foreign merchants could live and even limited the activities of private traders. Still, Chinese trade flourished during Song times.

Status of Women Women had higher status in Tang and early Song times than they did later. Within the home, women were called upon to

Advice for Families in China

During the Tang and Song dynasties, women sometimes enjoyed higher status than they did later. The following excerpt is from a collection of essays offering practical advice to families. A scholar, Yüan Tsai, wrote it in the 1100s, during the Song dynasty. Here, he discusses how to treat daughters and how women want to help family members.

"Without going overboard, people should marry their daughters with dowries appropriate to their family's wealth. Rich families should not consider their daughters outsiders but should give them a share of the property. Sometimes people have incapable sons and so have to entrust their affairs to their daughters' families; even after their deaths, their burials and sacrifices are performed by their daughters. So how can people say that daughters are not as good as sons?

Generally speaking, a woman's heart is very sympathetic. If her parents' family is wealthy and her husband's family is poor, she wants to take her parents' wealth to help her husband's family prosper. If her husband's family is wealthy but her parents' family is poor, then she wants to take from her husband's family to enable her parents to prosper. Her parents and husband should be sympathetic toward her feelings and indulge some of her wishes. When her own sons and daughters are grown and married, if either her son's family or her daughter's family is wealthy while the other is poor, she wishes to take from the wealthy one to give to the poor one. Her sons and daughters should understand her feelings and be somewhat indulgent. But taking from the poor to make the rich richer is unacceptable, and no one should ever go along with it."

—Yüan Tsai, quoted in *Chinese Civilization and Society* (Ebery)

A Tang Woman
This ceramic figurine of a woman kneeling at the imperial court, holding a bamboo flute, dates from the Tang dynasty.

Skills Assessment

1. Yüan would agree that
   A daughters should be allowed to choose their own husbands.
   B sons take better care of their families than daughters.
   C daughters are as good as sons.
   D dowries are not necessary.

2. Yüan suggests that
   E a married daughter should be allowed to help her poor relatives.
   F poor relatives should go to work for rich ones.
   G daughters should have nothing to do with their parents after they are married.
   H sons and daughters should make their own way in the world.

3. **Critical Thinking** **Making Inferences** What responsibility does Yüan imply that family members have toward one another? Explain.

Skills Tip

As you read a historical document, look for statements that the author assumes everyone in the audience will accept without question. Such assumptions can help you understand the accepted beliefs and values of the author's culture.

Song Landscape Painting
Landscapes painted during the
Song dynasty stressed the harmony of nature. In *Travelers
Among Mountains and Streams,*
painter Fan Kuan balances a towering mountain against the rushing
stream below. In the lower right,
a tiny line of travelers on horseback emerges from the woods.

**Theme: Arts and
Literature** Why do you think
the painter made the human
figures so small?

run family affairs. Wives and mothers-in-law had great authority, managing
servants and family finances. Still, families valued boys more highly than
girls. When a young woman married, she completely became a part of her
husband's family. She could not keep her dowry and could never remarry.

Women's subordinate position was reinforced in late Song times when
the custom of footbinding emerged. The custom probably began at the
imperial court but later spread to the lower classes. The feet of young girls
were bound with long strips of cloth, producing a lily-shaped foot about
half the size of a foot that was allowed to grow normally. Tiny feet and a
stilted walk became a symbol of nobility and beauty.

Footbinding was extremely painful. Yet the custom survived and in
time spread to lower classes. Even peasant parents feared that they could
not find a husband for a daughter with large feet.

Not all girls in China had their feet bound. Peasants who needed their
daughters to work in the fields did not accept the practice. Yet most women
did have to submit to footbinding. Women with bound feet often could
not walk without help. Thus, footbinding reinforced the Confucian tradition that women should remain inside the home.

Arts and Literature of the Tang and Song

A prosperous economy supported the rich culture of Tang and Song China.
The splendid palaces of the emperors were long ago destroyed, but many
paintings, statues, temples, and ceramics have survived.

Landscape Painting Along with poetry, painting and calligraphy were
essential skills for the scholar-gentry. In both of these crafts, artists sought
balance and harmony through the mastery of simple strokes and lines. The
Song period saw the triumph of Chinese landscape painting. Steeped in the
Daoist tradition, painters sought to capture the spiritual essence of the natural world. "When you are planning to paint," instructed a Song artist, "you
must always create a harmonious relationship between heaven and earth."

Misty mountains and delicate bamboo forests dominated Chinese landscapes. Yet Chinese painters also produced realistic, vivid portraits of emperors or lively scenes of city life.

Other Arts Buddhist themes dominated sculpture and influenced Chinese architecture. The Indian stupa evolved into the graceful Chinese pagoda, a multistoried temple with eaves that curve up at the corners. Chinese sculptors created striking statues of the Buddha. These statues created such a strong impression that, today, many people picture the Buddha as a Chinese god rather than an Indian holy man.

The Chinese perfected skills in making porcelain, a shiny, hard pottery that was prized as the finest in the world. They developed beautiful glazes to decorate vases, tea services, and other objects that westerners would later call "chinaware." Artists also produced porcelain figures of neighing camels, elegant court ladies playing polo, and bearded foreigners fresh from their travels on the Silk Road.

A Flood of Literature Prose and poetry flowed from the brushes of Tang and Song writers. Scholars produced works on philosophy, religion, and history. Short stories that often blended fantasy, romance, and adventure made their first appearance in Chinese literature.

Still, among the gentry, poetry was the most respected form of Chinese literature. Confucian scholars were expected to master the skills of poetry. We know the names of some 200 major and 400 minor Tang and Song poets. Their works touched on Buddhist and Daoist themes as well as on social issues. Many poems reflected on the shortness of life and the immensity of the universe.

Probably the greatest Tang poet was Li Bo (LEE BOW). A zestful lover of life and freedom, he spent most of his life moving from place to place. He wrote some 2,000 poems celebrating harmony with nature or lamenting the passage of time. A popular legend says that Li Bo drowned when he tried to embrace the reflection of the moon in a lake.

More realistic and less romantic were the poems of Li Bo's friend Du Fu. His verses described the horrors of war or condemned the lavishness of the court. A later poet, Li Qingzhao (LEE CHING jow), described the experience of women left behind when a loved one goes off to war. Her poems reflect a time when invasion threatened to bring the brilliant Song dynasty to an end.

Primary Source

Li Bo: Devoted Father
Separated from his children, Li Bo wrote a poem to them:

"This is the tree I myself put in
When I left you, nearly three
    years past;
A peach tree, level with the eaves,
And I sailing cannot yet turn
    home!

Pretty daughter, P'ing-yang is
    your name,
Breaking blossom, there beside
    my tree,
Breaking blossom, you cannot
    see me
And your tears flow like the
    running stream;

And little son, Po-ch'in you are
    called,
Your big sister's shoulder you
    must reach
When you come there underneath
    my peach,
Oh, to pat and pet you too, my
    child!"

—Li Bo, "Letter to His
Two Small Children"

Skills Assessment

Primary Source How do Li Bo's feelings still relate to our lives?

SECTION 1 Assessment

Recall

1. **Identify: (a)** Sui Wendi, **(b)** Tang Taizong, **(c)** Wu Zhao, **(d)** Grand Canal, **(e)** Li Bo.
2. **Define: (a)** usurp, **(b)** tributary state, **(c)** land reform, **(d)** gentry, **(e)** pagoda.

Comprehension

3. In what ways did the rise of the Tang and Song dynasties benefit China?
4. **(a)** Describe the social structure of China under the Tang and Song dynasties. **(b)** How did the social structure reflect Confucian traditions?

5. **(a)** What ideas and traditions shaped Chinese painting? **(b)** What themes did Chinese poets address?

Critical Thinking and Writing

6. **Connecting to Geography** How might a map of China before the Tang dynasty look different from a map of China afterward? Give two examples.
7. **Applying Information** "Distant water cannot put out a nearby fire." How does this saying reflect the nature of village government under the Tang and Song dynasties?

Activity

Preparing a Museum Guide
Find two illustrations of Chinese porcelain or painting from the Tang or Song periods. (If possible, make copies of them.) Then, for each selection, write an entry that might appear in a guide to a museum exhibit. List the date and artist (if known), and briefly describe what the work shows.

The Mongol and Ming Empires

Reading Focus

- How did the Mongols conquer and rule a huge empire?
- What were the effects of Mongol rule on China?
- How did the Ming restore Chinese rule?
- What policies did the Ming pursue with regard to the outside world?

Taking Notes

On a sheet of paper create a flowchart like this one. Add important events as you read this section. Use the chart to help you focus on key events in the section.

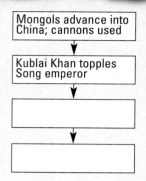

Mongols advance into China; cannons used

↓

Kublai Khan topples Song emperor

↓

[ ]

↓

[ ]

Main Idea Mongol armies conquered China, much of Asia, and part of Europe, but in time, the Ming dynasty regained control in China.

Biography

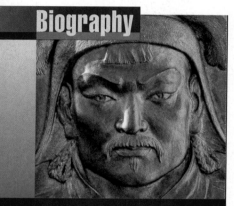

Genghiz Khan 1162–1227

When Temujin—later known as Genghiz Khan—was a boy, his father was poisoned by a rival Mongol clan. Then, at the age of 15, Temujin was taken prisoner. For the rest of his life, he never forgot the humiliation of being locked in a wooden collar and paraded before his enemies.

Though he regained his freedom, Temujin wandered among drifting clans. He grew up with a reputation for courage and leadership. He took revenge on the clan that had imprisoned him and, in time, became supreme ruler of all the Mongols. Once despised, Genghiz Khan would be admired and feared across two continents.

Theme: Impact of the Individual How might Temujin's experiences have motivated him to unite the Mongol clans?

Setting the Scene

The Mongols were tough, skilled warriors who lived in the saddle. They could travel for days at a time on their shaggy ponies, drinking mare's milk and eating only a few handfuls of grain. They were also considered the most skilled horse riders in the world. An observer described Mongol battle tactics:

> "They keep hovering about the enemy, discharging their arrows first from one side and then from the other. . . . Their horses are so well broken-in to quick changes of movement, that upon the signal given, they instantly turn in any direction, and by these rapid maneuvers many victories have been obtained."
>
> —Marco Polo, *A Description of the World*

About 1200, the Mongols burst out of Central Asia to conquer an empire stretching across Asia and Europe. In the process, they overran Song China and imposed Mongol rule on its people.

Building the Mongol Empire

The Mongols were a nomadic people who grazed their horses and sheep on the steppes of Central Asia. Rival Mongol clans spent much of their time warring with one another. In the early 1200s, however, a brilliant Mongol chieftain united these warring tribes. This chieftain took the name Genghiz Khan, meaning "World Emperor." Under his leadership, Mongol forces triumphantly conquered a vast empire that stretched from the Pacific Ocean to Eastern Europe.

Conquests Genghiz Khan imposed strict military discipline and demanded absolute loyalty. His highly trained, mobile armies had some of the most skilled horsemen in the world. Genghiz Khan had a reputation for fierceness. He could order the massacre of an entire city. Yet he also could be generous, rewarding the bravery of a single fighter.

Mongol armies conquered the Asian steppe lands with some ease, but as they turned on China, they faced the problem of attacking walled cities. Chinese and Turkish military experts taught them to use cannons and other new weapons. The Mongols and Chinese launched missiles against each other from metal tubes filled with gunpowder. This use of cannons in warfare would soon spread westward to Europe.

Genghiz Khan did not live to complete the conquest of China. His heirs, however, continued to expand the Mongol empire. For the next 150 years, they dominated much of Asia. Their furious assaults toppled empires and spread destruction from southern Russia through Muslim lands in the Middle East to China. In China, the Mongols devastated the flourishing province of Sichuan (see CHWAHN) and annihilated its great capital city of Chengdu.

Mongol Rule Once conquest was completed, the Mongols were not oppressive rulers. Often, they allowed conquered people to live much as they had before—as long as they regularly paid tribute to the Mongols.

Genghiz Khan had set an example for his successors by ruling conquered lands with toleration and justice. Although the Mongol warrior had no use for city life, he respected scholars, artists, and artisans. He listened to the ideas of Confucians, Buddhists, Christians, Muslims, Jews, and Zoroastrians.

The Mongol Peace In the 1200s and 1300s, the sons and grandsons of Genghiz Khan established peace and order within their domains. Today, many historians refer to this period of order as the *Pax Mongolica*, or Mongol Peace.

Political stability set the stage for economic growth. Under the protection of the Mongols, who now controlled the great Silk Road, trade flourished across Eurasia. According to a contemporary, Mongol rule meant that people "enjoyed such a peace that a man might have journeyed from the land of sunrise to the land of sunset with a golden platter upon his head without suffering the least violence from anyone."

Cultural exchanges increased as foods, tools, inventions, and ideas spread along the protected trade routes. From China, the use of windmills and gunpowder moved westward into Europe. Techniques of papermaking reached the Middle East, and crops and trees from the Middle East were carried into East Asia.

Skills Assessment

Geography At its height, the Mongol empire was the largest in the world up to that time.

1. **Location** *On the map, locate (a) Beijing, (b) Hangzhou, (c) Venice, (d) Tibet, (e) Russia.*
2. **Region** *Describe what happened to the Mongol empire between 1227 and 1294.*
3. **Critical Thinking Linking Past and Present** *Look at the atlas maps in the Reference Section at the end of this book. What countries would Marco Polo pass through if he made his journey today?*

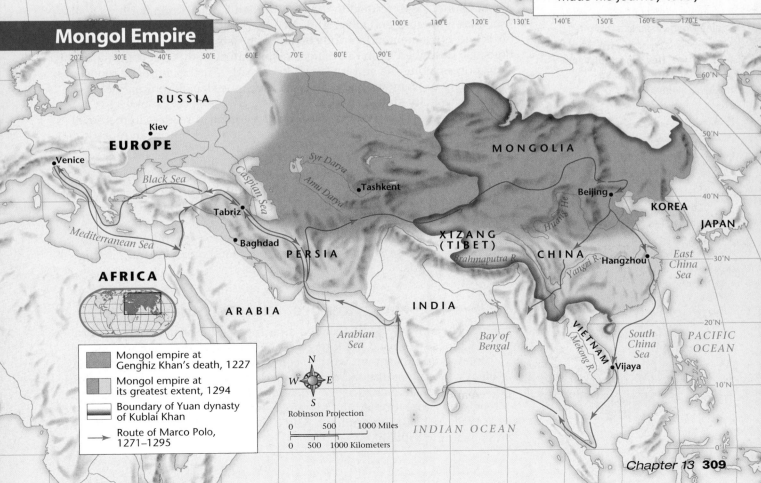

Mongol Empire

Mongol empire at Genghiz Khan's death, 1227

Mongol empire at its greatest extent, 1294

Boundary of Yuan dynasty of Kublai Khan

Route of Marco Polo, 1271–1295

Robinson Projection

0   500   1000 Miles

0   500   1000 Kilometers

China Under Mongol Rule

Although Genghiz Khan had subdued northern China, the Mongols need-ed nearly 70 more years to conquer the south. Genghiz Khan's grandson, Kublai (KOO blī), finally toppled the last Song emperor in 1279. From his capital at Cambulac, present-day Beijing, Kublai Khan ruled all of China as well as Korea, Tibet, and Vietnam.

Government Kublai Khan tried to prevent the Mongols from being ab-sorbed into Chinese civilization as other conquerors of China had been. He decreed that only Mongols could serve in the military. He also reserved the highest government jobs for Mongols or for other non-Chinese officials whom he employed. Still, because there were too few Mongols to control so vast an empire, Kublai allowed Chinese officials to continue to rule in the provinces.

Under Mongol rule, an uneasy mix of Chinese and foreign ways devel-oped. Kublai adopted a Chinese name for his dynasty, the Yuan (yoo AHN), and turned Cambulac into a Chinese walled city. At the same time, he had Arab architects design his palace, and many rooms reflected Mongol steppe dwellings.

Kublai Khan was a capable but demanding emperor. He rebuilt and extended the Grand Canal to his new capital, though at a terrible cost in human lives. He also welcomed many foreigners to his court, including the African Muslim world traveler Ibn Battuta.

A Western Visitor The Italian merchant Marco Polo was one of many visitors to China during the Yuan dynasty. In 1271, Polo left Venice with his father and uncle. He crossed Persia and Central Asia to reach China. During his stay in China, he spent 17 years in Kublai's service. He returned to Venice by sea after visiting Southeast Asia and India.

In his writings, Marco Polo left a vivid account of the wealth and splen-dor of China. He described the royal palace of Kublai Khan, with its walls "covered with gold and silver and decorated with pictures of dragons and birds and horsemen and various breeds of beasts and scenes of battle." Polo also described China's efficient royal mail system, with couriers riding swift ponies along the empire's well-kept roads. Furthermore, he reported that the city of Hangzhou was 10 or 12 times the size of Venice, one of Italy's richest city-states.

As you have read, Marco Polo's book astonished readers in medieval Europe. In the next centuries, Polo's reports sparked European interest in the riches of Asia.

Other Contacts As long as the Mongol empire prospered, con-tacts between Europe and Asia continued. The Mongols tolerat-ed a variety of beliefs. The pope sent Christian priests to Beijing, while Muslims set up their own communities in China. Meanwhile, some Chinese products moved toward Europe. They included gunpowder, porcelain, and playing cards.

The Ming Restore Chinese Rule

The Yuan dynasty declined after the death of Kublai Khan. Most Chinese despised the foreign Mongol rulers. Confucian scholars re-treated into their own world, seeing little to gain from the barbarians. Heavy taxes, corruption, and natural disasters led to frequent uprisings. Finally, Zhu Yuanzhang (DZOO yoo ahn DZUHNG), a peasant leader, forged a rebel army that toppled the Mongols and pushed them back beyond the Great Wall. In 1368, he founded a new Chinese dynasty, which he called the Ming, meaning brilliant.

Ming Porcelain
Ming dynasty artisans created a unique form of blue and white porcelain. Today, collectors have paid over a million dollars for gen-uine Ming vases like this one.

Theme: Continuity and Change How does this vase build on earlier Chinese achievements?

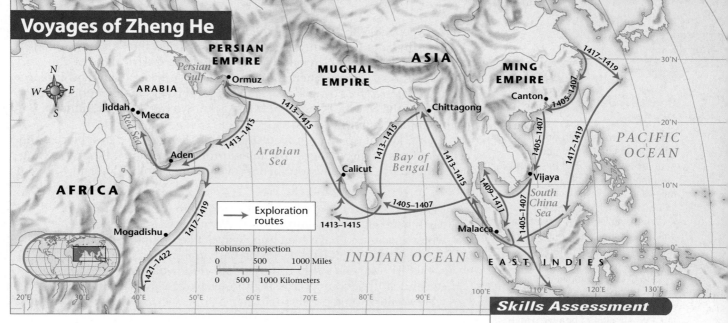

Voyages of Zheng He

(Map labels: PERSIAN EMPIRE, Persian Gulf, Ormuz, ARABIA, Jiddah, Mecca, Red Sea, Aden, AFRICA, Mogadishu, MUGHAL EMPIRE, ASIA, Chittagong, Calicut, Arabian Sea, Bay of Bengal, MING EMPIRE, Canton, Vijaya, PACIFIC OCEAN, South China Sea, Malacca, INDIAN OCEAN, EAST INDIES)

Exploration routes

Robinson Projection
0   500   1000 Miles
0   500   1000 Kilometers

Skills Assessment

Geography Between 1405 and 1433, Chinese explorer Zheng He visited many lands bordering the Indian Ocean.

1. **Location** On the map, locate **(a)** East Indies, **(b)** Calicut, **(c)** Malacca, **(d)** Arabia, **(e)** Mogadishu.
2. **Movement (a)** Where did Zheng He travel from 1405 to 1407? **(b)** When did he reach the Persian Gulf?
3. **Critical Thinking Synthesizing Information** Look at the map of African Kingdoms and Trading States in Section 3 of the previous chapter. Besides Mogadishu, what other East African cities might Zheng He have been able to visit?

Early Ming rulers sought to reassert Chinese greatness after years of foreign rule. The Ming restored the civil service system, and Confucian learning again became the road to success. The civil service exams became more rigorous than ever. A board of censors watched over the bureaucracy, rooting out corruption and disloyalty.

Economic Revival Economically, Ming China was immensely productive. The fertile, well-irrigated plains of eastern China supported a population of more than 100 million. In the Yangzi Valley, peasants produced huge rice crops. Better methods of fertilizing helped to improve farming. In the 1500s, new crops reached China from the Americas, especially corn and sweet potatoes.

Chinese cities were home to many industries, including porcelain, paper, and tools. The Ming repaired the extensive canal system that linked various regions and made trade easier. New technologies increased output in manufacturing. Better methods of printing, for example, led to the production of a flood of books.

Cultural Flowering Ming China also saw a revival of arts and literature. Ming artists developed their own styles of landscape painting and created brilliant blue and white porcelain. Ming vases were among the most valuable and popular Chinese products exported to the West.

Confucian scholars continued to produce classical poetry. At the same time, new forms of popular literature, meant to be enjoyed by the common people, began to emerge. Ming writers composed novels, including *The Water Margin,* about an outlaw gang that tries to end injustice by corrupt officials. Ming writers also produced the world's first detective stories. Performing artists developed a popular tradition of Chinese opera that combined music, dance, and drama.

China and the World

Early Ming rulers proudly sent Chinese fleets into distant waters. The most extraordinary of these overseas ventures were the voyages of the Chinese admiral Zheng He (DZUHNG HEH).

The Voyages of Zheng He In 1405, Zheng He commanded the first of seven expeditions. He departed at the head of a fleet of 62 huge ships and hundreds of smaller ones, carrying a crew of more than 25,000 sailors. The largest ships measured 400 feet long. The goal of each expedition was to promote trade and collect tribute from lesser powers across the "western seas."

Global Connections

Beasts From Across the Sea

Zheng He's voyages from China left a lasting impression on the peoples he visited. But his return to China left an equally powerful —and totally unexpected— impression on the Chinese.

Wherever Zheng He went, he collected animals to bring back to China. Back in China, they were kept in the imperial zoo.

One of these animals was known to the Chinese as a *qilin,* a legendary beast whose appearance was a sign of heaven's favor. People flocked to marvel at this bizarre creature. It stood 15 feet tall, had the body of a deer and the tail of an ox, and was covered with red spots.

Today, we call it the giraffe.

Theme: Global Interaction
Why might Zheng He have collected animals from foreign lands?

Between 1405 and 1433, Zheng He explored the coasts of Southeast Asia and India and the entrances to the Red Sea and the Persian Gulf. He also dropped anchor and visited many ports in East Africa. In the wake of the expeditions, Chinese merchants settled in Southeast Asian and Indian trading centers. The voyages also showed local rulers the power and strength of the Middle Kingdom. Many acknowledged the supremacy of the Chinese empire.

Zheng He set up an engraved stone tablet listing the dates, places, and achievements of his voyages. The tablet proudly proclaimed that the Ming had unified the "seas and continents" even more than the Han and Tang had done:

> "The countries beyond the horizon and from the ends of the earth have all become subjects. . . . We have crossed immense water spaces and have seen huge waves like mountains rising sky-high, and we have set eyes on barbarian regions far away . . . while our sails loftily unfurled like clouds day and night continued their course, crossing those savage waves as if we were walking on a public highway. . . ."
> —Zheng He, quoted in *The True Dates of the Chinese Maritime Expeditions in the Early Fifteenth Century* (Duyvendak)

Turning Inward In 1433, the year Zheng He died, the Ming emperor suddenly banned the building of seagoing ships. Later, ships with more than two masts were forbidden. Zheng He's huge ships were retired and rotted away.

Why did China, with its advanced naval technology, turn its back on overseas exploration? Historians are not sure. However, some speculate that the fleets were costly and did not produce any profits. Also, Confucian scholars at court had little interest in overseas ventures. To them, Chinese civilization was the most successful in the world. They wanted to preserve its ancient traditions, which they saw as the source of stability. In fact, such rigid loyalty to tradition would eventually weaken China and once again leave it prey to foreign domination.

Fewer than 60 years after China halted overseas expeditions, the explorer Christopher Columbus would sail west from Spain in search of a sea route to Asia. As you will see, this voyage made Spain a major power and had a dramatic impact on the entire world. We can only wonder how the course of history might have changed if the Chinese had continued the explorations they had begun under the Ming.

SECTION 2 Assessment

Recall

1. **Identify:** **(a)** Kublai Khan, **(b)** Marco Polo, **(c)** Zheng He.

Comprehension

2. How did the Mongol conquests promote trade and cultural exchanges?
3. How did Kublai Khan organize Mongol rule in China?
4. How did the Ming emperors try to restore Chinese culture?
5. What was the purpose of Zheng He's overseas expeditions?

Critical Thinking and Writing

6. **Making Inferences** What does Marco Polo's awe at the glories of China suggest about the differences between China and Europe at that time?
7. **Recognizing Causes and Effects** Describe one effect of each of the following on China: **(a)** the rise of the Ming dynasty, **(b)** the Mongol invasion, **(c)** the expulsion of the Mongols.

Activity

Organizing a Debate
Organize a debate that might have taken place at the Ming court between Confucian scholars, who want to end overseas voyages, and court officials, who want to finance more expeditions by Zheng He.

Reading Focus

- How did geography affect life in the Korean peninsula?

- How did Korea maintain its unity and independence despite Chinese influence?

- What were the major achievements of the Choson dynasty?

Vocabulary

celadon

hangul

literacy rate

Taking Notes

Begin a concept web like this one. As you read this section, fill in the blank circles with relevant information about Korea. Add more circles as needed.

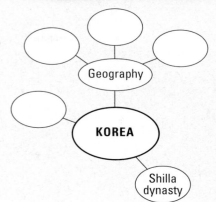

Main Idea Korea's history and culture were linked closely to those of China and Japan.

Setting the Scene

For centuries, Korea survived in the shadow of powerful neighbors, China and Japan. Koreans thus came to see their land as a "shrimp among whales." Yet Korea had another name, "Land of the Morning Calm." Whether tossed in turbulent seas or at rest in a calm land, Koreans had their own identity.

As early as Han times, China extended its influence to Korea. Although Koreans absorbed many Chinese traditions, they maintained a separate and distinct culture.

Geography of the Korean Peninsula

Korea is located on a peninsula that juts south from the Asian mainland with its tip pointing toward Japan. At the northern end of the peninsula, mountains and the Yalu River separate Korea from China.

Mountains and Seas An early visitor once compared Korea's landscape to "a sea in a heavy gale." Low but steep mountains cover nearly 70 percent of the Korean peninsula. The most important range is the T'aebaek (TEH BEHK). It runs from the north to the south along the eastern coast, with smaller chains branching off to form hilly areas. Because farming is difficult on the mountains, most people live along the western coastal plains, Korea's major farming region.

Korea has a 5,400-mile coastline with hundreds of good harbors. In addition, the offshore waters feature thousands of islands. Since earliest times, Koreans have depended upon seafood for most of the protein in their diet. Today, South Korea has the third largest fishing industry in the world.

The Impact of Location Korea's location on China's doorstep has played a key role in its development. From its powerful mainland neighbor, Korea received many cultural and technological influences. At various times in history, China extended political control over the Korean peninsula. Throughout its history, Korea has also served as a cultural bridge linking China and Japan. From early times, Koreans adapted and transformed Chinese traditions before passing them on to the Japanese.

Despite these strong ties, the Korean language is not related to Chinese. The earliest Koreans probably migrated eastward from Siberia and northern Manchuria during the Stone Age. They evolved

Mountains of Korea
"Over the mountains, mountains!" says one Korean proverb. This photograph shows a steep ridge in the T'aebaek Range.

Theme: Geography and History How would mountains affect settlement patterns?

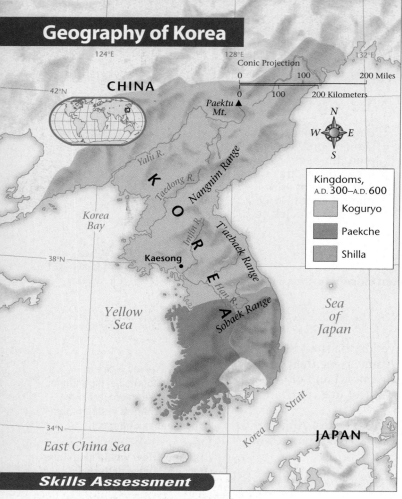

Geography of Korea

CHINA

124°E 128°E 132°E

Conic Projection
0   100   200 Miles
0   100   200 Kilometers

42°N

Paektu ▲
Mt.

Yalu R.

Taedong R.

Nangnim Range

K
O
R
E
A

Imjin R.

T'aebaek Range

Han R.

Sobaek Range

Korea
Bay

38°N

Kaesong •

34°N

Yellow
Sea

East China Sea

Sea
of
Japan

Korea
Strait

JAPAN

Kingdoms,
A.D. 300–A.D. 600

Koguryo

Paekche

Shilla

Skills Assessment

Geography Korea occupies a peninsula that juts south from China toward the islands of Japan.

1. **Location** On the map, locate **(a)** T'aebaek Range, **(b)** Yalu River, **(c)** Korea Strait, **(d)** Koguryo, **(e)** Paekche, **(f)** Shilla.
2. **Region** Why do most Koreans live along the western coastal plain?
3. **Critical Thinking** **Predicting Consequences** In the 1590s, Japan made plans to invade China. What effect might this have had on Korea?

their own ways of life before the first wave of Chinese influence reached the peninsula during the Han dynasty. In 108 B.C., the Han emperor Wudi invaded Korea and set up a military colony there. From this outpost, Confucian traditions and Chinese ideas about government, as well as Chinese writing and farming methods, spread to Korea.

Korea United

Between about A.D. 300 and 600, powerful local rulers forged three separate kingdoms: Koguryo (KOH GUH REE OH) in the north, Paekche (PEHK CHEH) in the southwest, and Shilla (SHIL LAH) in the southeast. Although they shared the same language and cultural background, the three kingdoms often warred with one another or with China. Still, Chinese influences continued to arrive. Missionaries spread Mahayana Buddhism, which took root among the rulers and nobles. Korean monks then traveled to China and India to learn more about Buddhism. They brought home the arts and learning of China.

In 668, with the support of the Tang empress Wu Zhao, the Shilla kingdom united the Korean peninsula. Unlike China, Korea had only three dynasties in its history. The Shilla ruled from 668 to 918, the Koryo (KOR EE OH) ruled from 918 to 1392, and the Choson (CHOH SUHN), or Yi, ruled from 1392 to 1910.

Chinese Influence Under the Shilla dynasty, Korea became a tributary state, acknowledging Chinese overlordship but preserving its independence. Over the centuries, Korea came to see its relationship to China in Confucian terms, as that of a younger brother who owed respect and loyalty to an older brother. Koreans also adopted the Confucian emphasis on the family as the foundation of the state.

Confucian ideas affected the rights of women. Early on, Korean women had the right to inherit property. Some upper-class women held public roles. Over time, as Confucian views took root, women's rights became restricted. Women could no longer inherit property, and a woman's position within the family became more subordinate.

At the same time, Koreans adapted and modified Chinese ideas. For example, they adapted the Chinese civil service examination to reflect their own system of inherited ranks. In China, even a peasant could win political influence by passing the exam. In Korea, only aristocrats were permitted to take the test.

Buddhist Influence During the Koryo age, Buddhism reached its greatest influence in Korea. Korean scholars wrote histories and poems based on Chinese models, and artists created landscape paintings following Chinese principles. The Koryo dynasty built their capital at Kaesong (KEH SUNG) following the plan of the Tang capital at Chang'an.

Koreans used woodblock printing from China to produce a flood of Buddhist texts. Later, Korean inventors made movable metal type to print large numbers of books. Koreans improved on other Chinese inventions. They learned to make porcelain from China, but then perfected techniques of making celadon, a porcelain with an unusual blue-green glaze. Korean celadon vases and jars were prized throughout Asia. In the 1200s, when the Mongols overran Korea and destroyed many industries, the secret of making celadon was lost forever.

Choson: The Longest Dynasty

The Mongols occupied Korea until the 1350s. In 1392, the brilliant Korean general Yi Song-gye (EE SUNG KEH) set up the Choson dynasty. In *Songs of the Flying Dragons,* Korea's leading poets held Yi up as a model of virtue and wisdom for future rulers:

> "When you have men at your beck and call,
> When you punish men and sentence them,
> Remember, my Lord, His mercy and temperance.
> If you are unaware of people's sorrow,
> Heaven will abandon you.
> Remember, my Lord, His labor and love."
> —*Songs of the Flying Dragons*

Yi reduced Buddhist influence and set up a government based upon Confucian principles. Within a few generations, Confucianism had made a deep impact on Korean life.

A Korean Alphabet Despite Chinese influence, Korea preserved its distinct identity. In 1443, Korea's most celebrated ruler, King Sejong (SEH JONG) decided to replace the complex Chinese system of writing. "The language of this land," he noted, "is different from China's." Sejong had experts develop hangul, an alphabet using symbols to represent the sounds of spoken Korean.

Although Confucian scholars rejected hangul at the outset, its use quickly spread. Hangul was easier for Koreans to use than the thousands of characters of written Chinese. Its use led to an extremely high literacy rate, or percentage of people who can read and write.

Japanese Invasions In the 1590s, an ambitious Japanese ruler decided to invade China by way of Korea. Japanese armies landed and for years looted and burned across the peninsula. To stop the invaders at sea, the Korean admiral Yi Sun-shin used metal-plated "turtle boats." After six years, the Japanese armies withdrew from Korea. As they left, however, they carried off many Korean artisans to introduce their skills to Japan.

Connections to Today

A Peninsula Divided

Korean unity lasted almost 1,300 years. But today, the Korean peninsula is again divided into hostile camps.

North Korea is a communist country. South Korea is a democracy. Each nation wants to rule the entire peninsula. Both sides have massed soldiers and equipment along the border in preparation for war.

The United States is South Korea's most powerful ally. North Korea maintains close ties to Communist China. As a result, Korea is one of the world's hot spots. The Korean War (1950–1953) was fought there, and there is a constant fear that the troubled Korean Peninsula may be the site of more bloodshed.

Theme: Continuity and Change How is today's division of Korea different from that created by early kingdoms?

SECTION 3 Assessment

Recall
1. **Identify:** (a) Shilla, (b) Koryo, (c) Choson, (d) Yi Song-gye, (e) Sejong.
2. **Define:** (a) celadon, (b) hangul, (c) literacy rate.

Comprehension
3. How did the relative location of the Korean peninsula influence the development of Korean civilization?
4. Give two examples of how Koreans adapted or modified Chinese ideas under the Shilla or Koryo dynasty.

5. (a) How did Confucianism influence Korea during the Choson dynasty? (b) How did Korea preserve its own identity?

Critical Thinking and Writing
6. **Analyzing Literature** Reread the excerpt from *Songs of the Flying Dragons* in this section. How does this poem reflect Confucian influences?
7. **Analyzing Information** Today, Hangul Day is a holiday in South Korea. Why do you think Koreans celebrate the creation of their alphabet?

Activity

Making a Poster
Draw a poster that expresses the relationship between Korea and China during either the Shilla, Koryo, or Choson dynasty. Use symbols to show the exchange of ideas.

Reading Focus

- What geographic features influenced the early development of Japan?

- How did Chinese civilization influence early Japanese traditions?

- What traditions emerged at the Heian court?

Vocabulary

archipelago

tsunami

selective borrowing

kana

Taking Notes

On a sheet of paper copy this concept web. As you read the section, add circles to the left with more information about the influence of China and circles to the right with more information about Japan's own traditions.

(concept web diagram) Ideas of government · China's influence · **EMERGENCE OF JAPAN** · Japanese traditions · Shinto

Main Idea | **Japan borrowed elements of Chinese civilization but remained free of Chinese control.**

Geography and History

Tsunami: The Killer Wave

Picture an ocean wave seven stories tall—heading right at you. That's what the people on the Japanese island of Honshu faced on June 15, 1896. The huge wave—a tsunami—slammed into 200 miles of Japanese coastline. Whole villages were swept away. Nearly 30,000 people were killed.

Tsunamis begin far out at sea, when an undersea earthquake, landslide, or volcano sets the water in motion. The wave can travel at up to 600 miles per hour. In deep water, the wave is barely noticeable on the surface. But in shallow water, it reaches horrific height, sometimes as much as 100 feet.

Theme: Geography and History How might Japan's geography have increased death tolls from tsunamis?

Setting the Scene Prince Shotoku of Japan's ruling Yamato clan wanted to create an orderly society. In 604, he outlined ideals of behavior for both the royal court and ordinary people. "Harmony should be valued," he wrote, "and quarrels avoided." Shotoku's words reflected a strong Confucian influence about social order. As he stated:

> "Everyone has his biases, and few men are far-sighted. Therefore some disobey their lords and fathers and keep up feuds with their neighbors. But when the superiors are in harmony with each other and inferiors are friendly, then affairs are discussed quietly and the right view of matters prevails."
>
> —Prince Shotoku, *Laws*

Like Korea, Japan felt the powerful influence of Chinese civilization early in its history. At the same time, the Japanese continued to maintain their own distinct culture.

Geography: Japan, a Land Apart

Japan is located on an archipelago (ahr kuh PEHL uh goh), or chain of islands, about 100 miles off the Asian mainland and east of the Korean peninsula. Its four main islands are Hokkaido (hoh KĪ doh), Honshu (hahn SHOO), Kyushu (kee oo SHOO), and Shikoku (shee KOH koo).

Land and Sea Japan is about the size of Montana, but four fifths of its land is too mountainous to farm. As a result, most people settled in narrow river valleys and along the coastal plains. A mild climate and sufficient rainfall, however, helped Japanese farmers make the most of the limited arable land. As in ancient Greece, the mountainous terrain at first was an obstacle to unity.

The surrounding seas have both protected and isolated Japan. It was close enough to the mainland to learn from Korea and China, but too far away for the Chinese to conquer. Japan thus had greater freedom to accept or reject Chinese influences than did other East Asian lands. At times, the Japanese sealed themselves off from foreign influences, choosing to go their own way.

The seas that helped Japan preserve its identity also served as trade routes. The Inland Sea was an especially important link among various

Japanese islands. The seas also offered plentiful food resources. The Japanese, like the Koreans, developed a thriving fishing industry.

Ring of Fire Japan lies in a Pacific region known as the Ring of Fire, which also includes the Philippines, Indonesia, and parts of Australia and South America. This region is subject to frequent earthquakes and volcanoes. Underwater earthquakes can launch killer tidal waves, called tsunami (tsoo NAH mee), that sweep over the land without warning, wiping out everything in their path.

The Japanese came to fear and respect the dramatic forces of nature. Today, as in the past, soaring Mount Fuji, with its snowcapped volcanic crater, is a sacred symbol of the beauty and majesty of nature.

Early Traditions

The people we know today as the Japanese probably migrated from the Asian mainland more than 2,000 years ago. They slowly pushed the earlier inhabitants, the Ainu, onto the northernmost island of Hokkaido.

Yamato Clan Early Japanese society was divided into uji, or clans. Each uji had its own chief and a special god or goddess who was seen as the clan's original ancestor. Some clan leaders were women, suggesting that women enjoyed a respected position in society.

By about A.D. 500, the Yamato clan came to dominate a corner of Honshu, the largest Japanese island. For the next 1,000 years, the Yamato Plain was the heartland of Japanese government. The Yamato set up Japan's first and only dynasty. They claimed direct descent from the sun goddess, Amaterasu, and chose the rising sun as their symbol. Later Japanese emperors were revered as living gods. While this is no longer the case, the current Japanese emperor still traces his roots to the Yamato clan.

Shinto Early Japanese clans honored kami, or nature spirits. This worship of the forces of nature became known as Shinto, meaning "the way of the gods." Shinto never evolved into an international religion like Christianity, Buddhism, or Islam. Still, its traditions have survived to the present day. Hundreds of Shinto shrines dot the Japanese countryside. Though simple in design, they are generally located in beautiful, natural surroundings. Shinto shrines are dedicated to special sites or objects such as mountains or waterfalls, ancient gnarled trees, or even oddly shaped rocks.

The Korean Bridge The Japanese language is distantly related to Korean but completely different from Chinese. From early on, Japan and Korea were in continuous contact with each other. Korean artisans and metalworkers settled in Japan, bringing sophisticated skills and technology. Japanese and Korean warriors crossed the sea in both directions to attack each other's strongholds. Some of the leading families at the Yamato court claimed Korean ancestors.

By about A.D. 500, missionaries from Korea had introduced Buddhism to Japan. With it came knowledge of Chinese writing and culture. This opening sparked a sudden surge of Japanese interest in Chinese civilization.

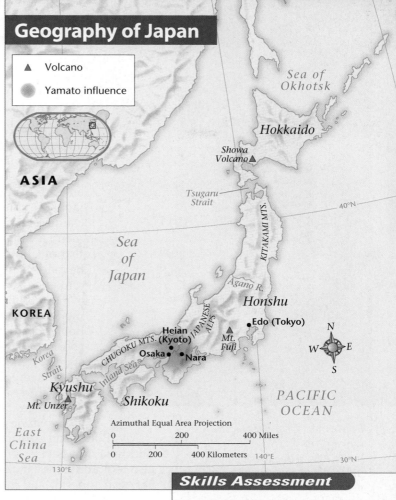

Geography of Japan

▲ Volcano

● Yamato influence

ASIA

Sea of Okhotsk

Hokkaido

Showa Volcano ▲

Tsugaru Strait

40°N

KITAKAMI MTS.

Sea of Japan

Agano R.

Honshu

KOREA

Edo (Tokyo)

Heian (Kyoto)

JAPANESE ALPS

Mt. Fuji ▲

CHUGOKU MTS.

Osaka Nara

N
W   E
S

Korea Strait

Inland Sea

Kyushu

Mt. Unzen ▲

Shikoku

PACIFIC OCEAN

East China Sea

Azimuthal Equal Area Projection

0   200   400 Miles

0   200   400 Kilometers

130°E

140°E

30°N

Skills Assessment

Geography Japan is located on an archipelago. In addition to its four main islands, Japan includes over 3,000 smaller islands.

1. **Location** On the map, locate **(a)** Hokkaido, **(b)** Honshu, **(c)** Kyushu, **(d)** Shikoku, **(e)** Mount Fuji.
2. **Interaction** Explain how two geographic features might have influenced Japanese life.
3. **Critical Thinking Drawing Conclusions** Which city was more likely to feel the influence of the Yamato clan—Osaka or Edo? Why?

Protector of a Buddhist Monastery
In the 700s, a Japanese emperor ordered that pagodas and Buddhist monasteries be built throughout Japan. The warrior god shown here was meant to protect a Buddhist temple from evil spirits.

Theme: Global Interaction
How does this statue show the influence of China on Japan?

Primary Sources and Literature

See "Murasaki Shikibu: The Tale of Genji" in the Reference Section at the back of this book.

Japan Looks to China

In the early 600s, Prince Shotoku of the Yamato clan decided to learn about China directly instead of through Korean sources. He sent young nobles to study in China. Over the next 200 years, many Japanese students, monks, traders, and officials visited the Tang court.

Imported From China Each mission spent a year or more in China—negotiating, trading, but above all studying. They returned to Japan eager to spread Chinese thought, technology, and arts. They also imported Chinese ideas about government. Japanese rulers adopted the title "Heavenly Emperor" and claimed absolute power. They strengthened the central government, set up a bureaucracy, and adopted a law code similar to that of China. Still, the new bureaucracy had little real authority beyond the royal court. Out in the countryside, the old clans remained strong.

In 710, the Japanese emperor built a new capital at Nara, modeled on the Tang capital at Chang'an. There, Japanese nobles spoke Chinese and dressed in Chinese fashion. Their cooks prepared Chinese dishes and served food on Chinese-style pottery. Tea drinking, along with an elaborate tea ceremony, was imported from China. Japanese officials and scholars used Chinese characters to write official histories. Tang music and dances became very popular, as did gardens designed along Chinese lines.

As Buddhism spread, the Japanese adopted pagoda architecture. Buddhist monasteries grew rich and powerful. Confucian ideas and ethics also took root. They included the emphasis on filial piety, the relationships between superior and inferior, and respect for learning.

Selective Borrowing In time, the initial enthusiasm for everything Chinese died down. The Japanese kept some Chinese ways but discarded or modified others. This process is known as selective borrowing. Japan, for example, never accepted the Chinese civil service examination to choose officials based on merit. Instead, they maintained their tradition of inherited status through family position. Officials were the educated sons of nobles.

By the 800s, as Tang China began to decline, the Japanese court turned away from its model. After absorbing all they could from China, the Japanese spent the next 400 years digesting and modifying these cultural acquisitions to produce their own unique civilization. The Japanese asserted their identity by revising the Chinese system of writing and adding kana, or phonetic symbols representing syllables. Japanese artists developed their own styles.

The Heian Period

This blending of cultures took place from 794 to 1185. During this time, the imperial capital was in Heian (hay AHN), present-day Kyoto. There, emperors performed traditional religious ceremonies, while wealthy court families like the Fujiwara wielded real power. The Fujiwara married their daughters to the heirs to the throne, thus ensuring their authority.

An Elegant Court At the Heian court an elegant and sophisticated culture blossomed. Noblewomen and noblemen lived in a fairy-tale atmosphere of beautiful pavilions, gardens, and lotus pools. Elaborate rules of etiquette governed court ceremony. Courtiers dressed with extraordinary care in delicate, multicolored silk. Draping one's sleeve out a carriage window was a fine art.

Although men at court still studied Chinese, women were forbidden to learn the language. Despite these restrictions, it was Heian women who produced the most important works of Japanese literature of the period. Using the new kana, women of the court produced fine diaries, essays, and collections of poetry.

In the 900s, Sei Shonagon, a lady-in-waiting to the empress, wrote *The Pillow Book.* In a witty series of anecdotes and personal observations, she provides vivid details of court manners, amusements, decor, and dress. In one section, Shonagon discusses the importance of keeping up a good appearance at court:

> "Nothing can be worse than allowing the driver of one's ox-carriage to be poorly dressed. It does not matter too much if the other attendants are shabby, since they can remain at the rear of the carriage; but the drivers are bound to be noticed and, if they are badly turned out, it makes a painful impression."
>
> —Sei Shonagon, *The Pillow Book*

Lady Murasaki The best-known Heian writer was Sei Shonagon's rival, Murasaki Shikibu. Her monumental work, *The Tale of Genji,* was the world's first full-length novel.

The Tale of Genji recounts the adventures and loves of the fictional Prince Genji and his son. In one scene, Genji moves with ease through the festivities at an elaborate "Chinese banquet." After dinner, "under the great cherry tree of the Southern court," the entertainment begins. There is music—Genji performs skillfully on the 13-stringed zither and does the Wave Dance. But the main event of the evening is a Chinese poetry contest. Genji and other guests are given a "rhyme word," which they must use to compose a poem in Chinese. Genji's word is "Spring" and his poem is the hit of the banquet.

Elegant though they are, the Heian poems and romances are haunted by a sense of sadness. The writers lament that love does not last and the beauty of the world is soon gone. Perhaps this feeling of melancholy was prophetic. While noble men and women strolled through manicured gardens, outside the walls of the court, clouds of rebellion and civil war were gathering.

Biography

Murasaki Shikibu
978 (?) –1031(?)

"If only you were a boy, how happy I would be!" said Murasaki Shikibu's father. Although he was praising her intelligence, he was also revealing how Japan valued men over women. Growing up, Murasaki studied with her brother. This fact was probably kept secret, because learning by girls was considered improper.

After the death of her husband and child, she went to the imperial court as a lady-in-waiting. There, as Lady Murasaki, she penned the world's first novel, *The Tale of Genji,* which has been celebrated for over a thousand years.

Theme: Impact of the Individual What personal qualities can you infer that Lady Murasaki possessed?

SECTION 4 Assessment

Recall
1. **Identify: (a)** Ring of Fire, **(b)** Yamato clan, **(c)** Amaterasu, **(d)** Shinto, **(e)** Shotoku, **(f)** Sei Shonagon, **(g)** Murasaki Shikibu.
2. **Define: (a)** archipelago, **(b)** tsunami, **(c)** selective borrowing, **(d)** kana.

Comprehension
3. Describe two ways in which geography affected Japanese life and culture.
4. **(a)** What early Japanese traditions were influenced by China? **(b)** How did the Japanese preserve their own identity and culture?

5. How did women influence culture at the Heian court?

Critical Thinking and Writing
6. **Comparing** How was the Japanese development of kana similar to the Korean development of hangul?
7. **Understanding Sequence (a)** Arrange the following events in the order in which they occurred: Emperor builds a new capital at Nara; Shotoku sends nobles to China; the Japanese court turns away from its Chinese model; missionaries introduce Buddhism to Japan. **(b)** Explain why the events occurred in that order.

Activity
Take It to the NET

Use the Internet to view photographs or paintings of Mount Fuji on the Japanese island of Honshu. (If possible, print out two or three of these images.) Then, write a short poem or essay describing your impression of the mountain and its surroundings.

Reading Focus

- How did feudalism develop in Japan?
- What changes took place under the Tokugawa shoguns?
- What cultural and artistic traditions emerged in feudal Japan?

Vocabulary

shogun

daimyo

samurai

bushido

kabuki

bunraku

haiku

Taking Notes

As you read this section, prepare an outline of Japan's feudal age. Use Roman numerals to indicate major headings, capital letters for the subheadings, and numbers for the supporting details. The sample at right has been started for you.

I. Japanese feudalism emerges
   A. The world of warriors
      1. Daimyo
      2. Samurai
   B. Status of noble-women
      1.
      2.

Main Idea During feudal times, military rulers called shoguns dominated Japanese society and eventually created a strong central government.

Setting the Scene The poet Sogi was one of the leading writers of Japan in the 1400s. In verses like this one, he expresses a sense of uncertainty and despair:

> "To live in the world
> Is sad enough without this rain
> Pounding on my shelter."
> —Sogi, *Haiku*

The 1400s, when Sogi lived, were a time of political intrigue, rebellions, and feudal warfare in Japan. Disorder continued through the following century. Yet, despite the turmoil, a new Japanese culture blossomed.

Japanese Feudalism Emerges

While the emperor presided over the splendid court at Heian, rival clans battled for control of the countryside. Local warlords and even Buddhist temples formed armed bands loyal to them rather than to the central government. As these armies struggled for power, Japan evolved a feudal system. As in the feudal world of medieval Europe, a warrior aristocracy dominated Japanese society.

In theory, the emperor stood at the head of Japanese feudal society. In fact, he was a powerless, though revered, figurehead. Real power lay in the hands of the **shogun,** or supreme military commander. Minamoto Yoritomo was appointed shogun in 1192. He set up the Kamakura shogunate, the first of three military dynasties that would rule Japan for almost 700 years.

The World of Warriors Often the shogun controlled only a small part of Japan. He distributed lands to vassal lords who agreed to support him with their armies in time of need. These great warrior lords were later called **daimyo** (DĪ myoh). They, in turn, granted land to lesser warriors called **samurai,** meaning "those who serve." Samurai were the fighting aristocracy of a war-torn land.

Like medieval Christian knights in Europe, samurai were heavily armed and trained in the skills of fighting. They also developed their own code of values. Known as **bushido** (BOO shee doh), or the "way of the warrior," the code emphasized honor, bravery, and absolute loyalty to one's lord.

Connections to Today

The Martial Arts

Nearly 1,500 years ago, warriors in China, Japan, and Korea learned ways to fight without weapons. These techniques, developed originally by Buddhist monks from India and Tibet, were called the martial, or military, arts.

Today, millions of people around the world learn and practice different forms of martial arts. Discipline—both physical and mental—is a key to success. Those who practice the Korean art of tae kwon do agree to be committed to 11 "tenets," or principles. These include showing respect for teachers, parents, and other elders and always finishing what you begin.

Theme: Continuity and Change Why do you think the martial arts are still popular?

The true samurai was supposed to have no fear of death. "If you think of saving your life," it was said, "you had better not go to war at all." Samurai prepared for hardship by going hungry or walking barefoot in the snow. For a samurai, it was said, "when his stomach is empty, it is a disgrace to feel hungry." A samurai who betrayed the code of bushido was expected to commit *seppuku* (seh POO koo), or ritual suicide, rather than live without honor.

Status of Noblewomen   At first, some noblewomen in Japanese feudal society trained in the military arts. A few even became legendary warriors. At times, some noblewomen supervised their family's estates.

As the age of the samurai progressed, however, the position of women declined steadily. When feudal warfare increased, inheritance was limited to sons. Unlike the European ideal of chivalry, the samurai code did not set women on a pedestal. Instead, the wife of a warrior had to accept the same hardships as her husband and owed the same loyalty to his overlord.

Peasants, Artisans, and Merchants   Far below the samurai in the social hierarchy were the peasants, artisans, and merchants. Peasants, who made up 75 percent of the population, formed the backbone of feudal society in Japan. Peasant families cultivated rice and other crops on the estates of samurai. Some peasants also served as foot soldiers in feudal wars. On rare occasions, an able peasant soldier might rise through the ranks to become a samurai himself.

Artisans, such as armorers and swordmakers, provided necessary goods for the samurai class. Merchants had the lowest rank in Japanese feudal society. However, as you will see, their status gradually improved.

Mongol Invasions   During the feudal age, most fighting took place between rival warlords, but the Mongol conquest of China and Korea also threatened Japan. When the Japanese refused to accept Mongol rule, Kublai Khan launched an invasion from Korea in 1274. After a fleet carrying 30,000 troops arrived, a typhoon wrecked many Mongol ships.

In 1281, the Mongols landed an even larger invasion force, but again a typhoon destroyed much of the Mongol fleet. The Japanese credited their miraculous delivery to the *kamikaze* (kah mih KAH zee), or divine winds. The Mongol failure reinforced the Japanese sense that they were a people set apart who enjoyed the special protection of the gods.

Armor for a Warrior
This painting shows Japanese artisans constructing armor and weapons for a samurai warrior. Unlike the solid steel plates worn by European feudal knights, the samurai's armor was made up of thin strips of steel held together by brightly colored silk cords.

Theme: Economics and Technology   What might be the advantages and disadvantages of the type of armor used by a samurai?

A Zen Buddhist Temple
Zen monks were the leading scholars and artists of feudal Japan. This temple was a Zen monastery and a peaceful retreat for visiting shoguns seeking advice.

Theme: Religions and Value Systems How does the setting of this temple reflect Zen values?

Order and Unity Under the Tokugawas

The Kamakura shogunate crumbled in the aftermath of the Mongol invasions. A new dynasty took power in 1338, but the level of warfare increased after 1450. To defend their castles, daimyo armed peasants as well as samurai, which led to even more ruthless fighting. A popular saying of the time declared, "The warrior does not care if he's called a dog or beast. The main thing is winning."

Gradually, several powerful warriors united large parts of Japan. By 1590, the brilliant general Toyotomi Hideyoshi (hee day YOH shee), a commoner by birth, had brought most of Japan under his control. He then tried, but failed, to conquer Korea and China. In 1600, the daimyo Tokugawa Ieyasu (toh kuh GAH wah ee YAY yah soo) defeated his rivals to become master of Japan. Three years later, he was named shogun. The Tokugawa shogunate ruled Japan until 1868.

Centralized Feudalism The Tokugawa shoguns were determined to end feudal warfare. They kept the outward forms of feudal society but imposed central government control on all Japan. For this reason, their system of government is called centralized feudalism.

The Tokugawas created a unified, orderly society. To control the daimyo, they required these great lords to live in the shogun's capital at Edo (present-day Tokyo) every other year. A daimyo's wife and children had to remain in Edo full time, giving the shogun a powerful check on the entire family. The shogun also forbade daimyo to repair their castles or marry without permission.

New laws fixed the old social order rigidly in place and upheld a strict moral code. Only samurai were allowed to serve in the military or hold government jobs. They were expected to follow the traditions of bushido. Peasants had to remain on the land. Lower classes were forbidden to wear luxuries such as silk clothing.

Women, too, faced greater restrictions under the Tokugawas. One government decree, sent to all villages, stated, "However good-looking a wife may be, if she neglects her household duties by drinking tea or sightseeing or rambling on the hillsides, she must be divorced." Women's freedom to move about, or even travel with their husbands, was strictly regulated.

Economic Growth While the shoguns tried to hold back social change, the Japanese economy grew by leaps and bounds. With peace restored to the countryside, agriculture improved and expanded. New seeds, tools, and the use of fertilizer led to greater output of crops.

Food surpluses supported rapid population growth. Towns sprang up on the lands around the castles of daimyo. Edo grew into a booming city, where artisans and merchants flocked to supply the needs of the daimyo and their families.

Trade flourished within Japan. New roads linked castle towns and Edo. Each year, daimyo and their servants traveled to and from the capital, creating a demand for food and services along the route. In the cities, a wealthy merchant class emerged. In accordance with Confucian tradition, merchants had low social status. Still, Japanese merchants gained influence by lending money to daimyo and samurai. Sometimes, merchants further improved their social position by arranging to marry their daughters into the samurai class.

Zen Buddhism and Japanese Culture

During Japan's feudal age, a Buddhist sect from China won widespread acceptance among samurai. Known in Japan as Zen, it emphasized meditation and devotion to duty.

Zen had seemingly contradictory traditions. Zen monks were great scholars, yet they valued the uncluttered mind and stressed the importance of reaching a moment of "non-knowing." Zen stressed compassion for all, yet samurai fought to kill. In Zen monasteries, monks sought to experience absolute freedom, yet rigid rules gave the master complete authority over his students.

Zen beliefs shaped Japanese culture in many ways. At Zen monasteries, upper-class men learned to express devotion to nature in such activities as landscape gardening. Zen Buddhists believed that people could seek enlightenment, not only through meditation, but through the precise performance of everyday tasks. For example, the elaborate rituals of the tea ceremony reflected Zen values of peace, simplicity, and love of beauty. Zen reverence for nature also influenced the development of fine landscape paintings.

Changing Artistic Traditions

Cities such as Edo and Osaka were home to an explosion in the arts and theater. At stylish entertainment quarters, sophisticated nobles mixed with the urban middle class. Urban culture emphasized luxuries and pleasures and differed greatly from the feudal culture that had dominated Japan for centuries.

Theater In the 1300s, feudal culture had produced Nō plays performed on a square, wooden stage without scenery. Men wore elegant carved masks while a chorus chanted important lines to musical accompaniment. The action was slow. Each movement had a special meaning. Many Nō plays presented Zen Buddhist themes, emphasizing the need to renounce selfish desires. Others recounted fairy tales or the struggles between powerful feudal lords.

In the 1600s, towns gave rise to a popular new form of drama, kabuki (kuh BOO kee). Kabuki was influenced by Nō plays, but it was less refined and included comedy or melodrama. Kabuki plays often portrayed family or historical events. Dressed in colorful costumes, actors used lively and

Primary Source

Perfect Serenity
Kenko, a Zen Buddhist priest of feudal Japan, wrote of the fleeting nature of worldly things:

"If we were never to fade away . . . but linger on forever in the world, how things would lose their power to move us! The most precious thing in life is its uncertainty. The May fly waits not for the evening, the summer cicada knows neither spring nor autumn. What a wonderfully unhurried feeling it is to live even a single year in perfect serenity! If that is not enough for you, you might live a thousand years, and still feel it was but a single night's dream. We cannot live forever in this world."

—Kenko, *Essays in Idleness*

Skills Assessment

Primary Source How do Kenko's words reflect what you know about Buddhist beliefs?

Kabuki Theater

For nearly 400 years, audiences in Japan have enjoyed kabuki theater. Kabuki plays combine drama, dance, and music. Dressed in colorful costumes, actors use lively and exaggerated movements. The stories range from thrilling adventures to comedies of family life.

Fast Facts

- In the 1700s, a single kabuki performance might last an entire day.

- Scenery is changed in full view of the audience by stage hands in black costumes.

- Kabuki fans shout the names of their favorite actors during pauses in the action.

The elaborate makeup may take many hours to apply.

Some kabuki plays recount tales of honor and betrayal in feudal Japan. In this modern performance, a samurai must identify the head of his brother, a traitor.

Musicians accompany the drama on traditional instruments such as this samisen.

Kabuki was founded by a woman named Okuni. However, women were soon banned from performing. Here, men play the women's roles, as they still do today.

Portfolio Assessment

INTERNET   Use the Internet or library resources to find out more about Japanese theater. Then, prepare a class presentation. If possible, include visual aids.

exaggerated movements to convey action. Kabuki was originated by an actress and temple dancer named Okuni, who became famous for her performance of warrior roles. However, women were soon banned from performing on stage.

Puppet plays, known as bunraku, were also enormously popular in towns. A narrator told a story while handlers silently manipulated near-life-sized puppets. Bunraku plays catered to popular middle-class tastes.

Literature The feudal age produced stories like the *Tale of the Heike* about a violent conflict between two families. Another important prose work was *Essays in Idleness,* a collection of short essays by Kenko, a Zen Buddhist priest. Many of the essays express Zen values, but others contain witty observations about human nature. "How boring it is," Kenko wrote, "when you meet a man after a long separation and he insists on relating at interminable length everything that has happened to him in the meantime."

Japanese poets adapted Chinese models, creating miniature poems called haiku. In only three lines—totaling 17 syllables in the Japanese language—these tiny word pictures express a feeling, thought, or idea. The poem by Sogi at the beginning of this section is an example of haiku.

Painting and Printmaking Japanese paintings often reflected the influence of Chinese landscape paintings, yet Japanese artists developed their own styles. On magnificent scrolls, painters boldly recreated historical events, such as the Mongol invasions.

In the 1600s, the vigorous urban culture produced a flood of colorful woodblock prints to satisfy middle-class tastes. Some woodblock artists produced humorous prints. Their fresh colors and simple lines give us a strong sense of the pleasures of town life in Japan.

Looking Ahead

The Tokugawa shogunate brought peace and stability to Japan. Trade flourished, merchants prospered, and prosperity contributed to a flowering of culture. Still, the shoguns were extremely conservative. They tried to preserve samurai virtues and ancient beliefs.

In the 1500s, Japan faced a new wave of foreign influence. The shogun at first welcomed the outsiders, then moved to sever foreign ties. In the next unit, you will read about Japan's uneasy relationship with an expanding Europe.

SECTION 5 Assessment

Recall
1. **Identify:** (a) Minamoto Yoritomo, (b) Toyotomi Hideyoshi, (c) Tokugawa Ieyasu, (d) Zen.
2. **Define:** (a) shogun, (b) daimyo, (c) samurai, (d) bushido, (e) kabuki, (f) bunraku, (g) haiku.

Comprehension
3. (a) What groups or individuals held the most power in feudal Japan? (b) What values did bushido emphasize?
4. Describe three results of the centralized feudalism imposed by the Tokugawas.
5. How did the growth of towns influence Japanese arts and literature?

Critical Thinking and Writing
6. **Analyzing Information** Why do you think the Tokugawas wanted to restrict the role of women?
7. **Linking Past and Present** Elaborate rituals such as the tea ceremony reflected Zen values. Are there any activities in our society today that follow a clearly defined ritual? If so, what values do these rituals reflect?

Activity
Take It to the NET

Use the Internet to learn more about the life of the Tokugawa shoguns. Then, write a descriptive essay to share what you learn. Include visuals if you wish.

Creating a Chapter Summary

On a sheet of paper copy the table shown here. Fill in the spaces under each heading to help you review key information about China, Korea, and Japan.

For additional review and enrichment activities, see the interactive version of *World History* available on the Web and on CD-ROM.

	CHINA	KOREA	JAPAN
PERIODS OR DYNASTIES	Tang, Song, Yuan, Ming		
OUTSIDE INFLUENCES			
TYPE OF SOCIETY			
MAIN ACHIEVEMENTS			

Web Site Self-Test
For practice test questions for Chapter 13, see
www.phschool.com.

Building Vocabulary

(a) Classify each of the chapter vocabulary words listed below under *one* of the following themes: Art and Literature, Political and Social Systems, Geography and History.
(b) Choose *one* word in each category and write a sentence explaining how that word relates to the theme.

1. tributary state
2. land reform
3. gentry
4. celadon
5. hangul
6. archipelago
7. tsunami
8. shogun
9. bushido
10. bunraku

Recalling Key Facts

11. Which two dynasties united and ruled China between the 600s and 1200s?
12. What impact did Mongol rule have on Asia?
13. What lands did Zheng He visit?
14. Describe the location of Korea in relation to China and Japan.
15. How has Japan's island status affected its history?
16. How did life in Japan change under the Tokugawas?

Critical Thinking and Writing

17. **Synthesizing Information** Review what you have read about the Mongol empire in this chapter and in earlier chapters. **(a)** How was the Mongol period both destructive and constructive? **(b)** What do you think were the three greatest effects of the Mongol conquests?
18. **Applying Information** Using the information in this chapter and in earlier chapters, construct a time chart of major Chinese dynasties. **(a)** When did each dynasty rise and fall? **(b)** What periods fall between major dynasties? **(c)** Make one generalization about the history of dynasties in China.
19. **Drawing Conclusions** **(a)** Describe the Japanese practice of selective borrowing. **(b)** How have Americans borrowed from other cultures? Give two examples. **(c)** What are some of the benefits and disadvantages of borrowing from other cultures?
20. **Connecting to Geography** **(a)** In what ways are the geographies of Japan and Korea similar? **(b)** What similar effects has geography had on these nations?

The following passage is from a 1315 book of regulations for Chinese students. Read the passage, then answer the questions that follow.

"You should concentrate on your book and keep a dignified appearance. You should count the number of times you read an assigned piece. If, upon completion of the assigned number, you still have not memorized the piece, you should continue until you are able to recite it. On the other hand, if you have memorized the piece quickly, you should still go on to complete the assigned number of readings.

Only after a book has been thoroughly learned should you go on to another. Do not read too many things on a superficial level. Do not attempt to memorize a piece without understanding it. Read only those books which expound virtues. Do not look into useless writings."

—Chieng Tuan-li, *A Schedule for Learning*

21. According to the author, how should a student behave while reading a book?
22. What are two key procedures to follow when reading?
23. **(a)** What kinds of books does the author think a student should read? **(b)** What kinds of books does he advise students to avoid? **(c)** What does this suggest about his view of the goal of education?
24. How does this instruction reflect the new school of Confucian thought that emerged during the Song dynasty?
25. Compare the way a Chinese student of the fourteenth century read a book to the way you read a book.

Use the Internet to research an invention or technological discovery from early China during the time period discussed in this chapter. Then, create and deliver a brief presentation about it. You should tell when the item or technique was invented, how it was discovered or created, and whether it is still used today.

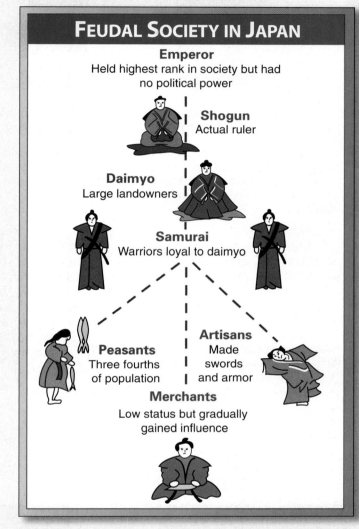

FEUDAL SOCIETY IN JAPAN

Emperor Held highest rank in society but had no political power

Shogun Actual ruler

Daimyo Large landowners

Samurai Warriors loyal to daimyo

Peasants Three fourths of population

Artisans Made swords and armor

Merchants Low status but gradually gained influence

The organization chart above illustrates the social levels of feudal society in Japan. Study the chart and then answer the following questions:

26. **(a)** Who occupied the highest position in Japanese feudal society? **(b)** How does the chart show this?
27. Who occupied the lowest position in Japanese feudal society?
28. What group made up the largest part of the population?
29. Why does the chart show no lines connecting the peasants, artisans, and merchants?

Skills Tip

Organization charts are usually arranged from highest (top) to lowest (bottom). Connecting lines show relationships between groups.

Chapter 8

The Rise of Europe
(A.D. 500–A.D. 1300)

From 500 to 1000, Europe was a fragmented, largely isolated region. Feudalism, the manor economy, and the Roman Catholic Church were dominant forces during the early Middle Ages.

- Between 400 and 700, Germanic invaders carved Europe up into small kingdoms.
- In the 800s, Charlemagne temporarily reunited much of Europe. He revived learning and furthered the blending of German, Roman, and Christian traditions.
- Feudalism, based on mutual obligations among lords and vassals, gave a strict order to medieval society.
- The Church guided the spiritual lives of Christians and was the most powerful political force in medieval Europe.
- By the 1000s, advances in agriculture and commerce spurred economic revival.

Chapter 9

The High Middle Ages
(A.D. 1050–A.D. 1450)

During the High Middle Ages, economic conditions improved, and learning and the arts flourished. At the same time, feudal monarchs moved to centralize their power, building a framework for the modern nation-state.

- In England and France, long-lasting traditions of royal government evolved.
- In the Holy Roman Empire, conflicts erupted between popes and secular rulers.
- European contacts with the Middle East during the Crusades revived interest in trade and exploration.
- Beginning in the 1300s, famine, plague, and war marked the decline of medieval Europe.

Chapter 10

The Byzantine Empire and Russia (A.D. 330–A.D. 1613)

After the fall of Rome, the Greco-Roman heritage survived in the Byzantine empire. Byzantine civilization shaped the developing cultures of Russia and Eastern Europe.

- The Byzantine empire served as a center of world trade and a buffer between Western Europe, and the Arab empire.
- Traders and missionaries carried Byzantine culture and Eastern Orthodox Christianity to Russia, Eastern Europe, and Ethiopia.
- Czars Ivan III and Ivan IV expanded the Russian empire and laid the foundation for extreme absolute power.
- Invasions and migrations created a mix of ethnic and religious groups in Eastern Europe.
- Jews fleeing the Crusades and the Inquisition migrated further into Eastern Europe and the Middle East.

	A.D. 500	A.D. 700	A.D. 900
AFRICA		A.D. **600s** Islam spreads to North Africa	A.D. **800s** Ghana controls gold-salt trade
THE AMERICAS		A.D. **600s** Mayan civilization thrives	A.D. **800s** Mississippian civilization flourishes
ASIA AND OCEANIA	A.D. **500s** Buddhism introduced to Japan	A.D. **622** Muhammad's hijra from Mecca to Medina	
EUROPE	A.D. **500s** Byzantine empire reaches height		A.D. **800** Charlemagne crowned emperor by pope

Chapter 11

The Muslim World
(A.D. 622–A.D. 1629)

The religion of Islam emerged on the Arabian Peninsula in the 600s. Muslim civilization eventually created cultural ties among diverse peoples across three continents.

- Muhammad was the prophet of Islam, a monotheistic religion. Through the Quran, the Five Pillars, and the Sharia, Islam was both a religion and a way of life.
- The Arab empire was ruled by several powerful caliphates. After 850, they were replaced by independent dynasties ruling separate Muslim states.
- Learning, literature, science, medicine, and trade flourished during the golden age of Muslim civilization.
- By the 1500s, the Mughals, Ottomans, and Safavids dominated the Muslim world with powerful empires in India, Eastern Europe, the Middle East, and North Africa.

Chapter 12

Kingdoms and Trading States of Africa (750 B.C.–A.D. 1586)

Despite geographic barriers, many civilizations rose and flourished in Africa. Kingdoms in the west and city-states in the east became important commercial and political centers.

- The Bantu migrations, contacts with Greece and Rome, the spread of Islam, and trade with Asia contributed to Africa's diversity.
- Between 800 and 1600, a succession of powerful West African kingdoms controlled the rich Sahara trade route.
- Indian Ocean trade routes led to the growth of prosperous city-states along the East African coast.
- Art and oral literature fostered common values and a sense of community among the peoples of Africa.

Chapter 13

Spread of Civilizations in East Asia (A.D. 500–A.D. 1650)

After 400 years of fragmentation, China reemerged as a united empire and the most powerful force in East Asia. Although Korea and Japan were heavily influenced by Chinese civilization, each maintained its own identity.

- China expanded and prospered under the powerful Tang and Song dynasties.
- During the 1200s and 1300s, the Mongols ruled much of Asia. After the fall of the Mongols, the Ming restored Chinese culture and later imposed a policy of isolation.
- While maintaining its own identity, Korea served as a cultural bridge linking China and Japan.
- The seas allowed Japan to preserve its unique culture while selectively borrowing religious, political, and artistic traditions from China.
- During the 1100s, Japan created a feudal society that was ruled by powerful military lords.

A.D. 1100   A.D. 1300   A.D. 1500

A.D. 1000
East African trading cities prosper

A.D. 1250
Empire of Mali reaches height

A.D. 1500
Kongo kingdom flourishes

A.D. 1000s
Anasazis build pueblo towns

A.D. 1438 Incan empire founded

A.D. 1500 Aztec empire reaches height

A.D. 960
Song dynasty in China founded

A.D. 1206
Delhi sultanate founded

A.D. 1368
Ming dynasty ends Mongol rule

A.D. 1520
Reign of Suleiman begins

A.D. 1066
Normans conquer Britain

A.D. 1215
English Magna Carta signed

A.D. 1389 Ottomans defeat Serbs at Kosovo

A.D. 1462 Reign of Ivan the Great begins

Early Modern Times

1300–1800

OUTLINE

Themes

As you read about developments that led to the emergence of modern Europe and the first age of global interaction, you will encounter the following unit themes.

Economics and Technology A scientific revolution enabled explorers to travel the world in search of trade and riches. Dramatic economic developments, such as the rise of capitalism, affected all social classes.

Global Interaction Exploration by powerful nations led to increased competition for trade. The spread of cultural beliefs and the exchange of material goods often were accomplished by conquest and by destruction of native cultures.

Political and Social Systems Absolute monarchs forged modern nation-states with strong central governments. The struggle between monarchs and Parliament in England was an important step in the development of modern democracy.

Religions and Value Systems Classical and Christian humanist ideals shaped the Renaissance. While the Protestant Reformation shattered the religious unity of Europe, Christianity continued to spread to new lands.

Unit Theme Activity

For Your Portfolio The chapters in this unit illustrate changes that led to the first era of global interaction. As you read the chapters, prepare a portfolio project highlighting these developments. Your project might take one of the following forms:
- **Chart or other detailed graphic organizer**
- **Debate**
- **Diary**

The Palace of Versailles was designed to glorify the power of France and its monarch, Louis XIV. It served as the capital of France and as the royal residence from 1682 until the French Revolution.

WHY STUDY HISTORY?

Because Problem Solving of the Past Can Provide Insight for Today

How do you lift a million two-ton limestone blocks to build a pyramid? How do you unite a vast empire stretching some 2,000 miles? These were real problems faced by real people—the ancient Egyptians and the Incas of Peru. These pages show how Europeans of the fifteenth century solved a problem in their time. By studying how people solved problems in the past, we can gain new insights about how to solve today's problems.

Fifteenth-century problem: Gaining control of the pepper trade

Pepper plant

The Problem Long ago, in the jungles of India, a woody climbing vine was discovered whose small berries imparted a wonderful flavor to food. Soon, pepper had emerged as the world's most precious spice. During the Middle Ages in Europe, pepper was worth its weight in gold, and taxes and rents were often paid in peppercorns.

Europeans knew they could make much money by trading pepper and other spices. But Arab traders controlled the route across the Mediterranean Sea. And marauding bandits and forbidding geography made it very dangerous to travel overland to Asia.

Possible Solutions There seemed to be two ways to solve the problem. Traders could travel overland to Asia. To do so, though, they would have to seize the trade route from the Arabs, defeat dangerous bandits, and survive the hostile terrain. Or they could try to find a new, ocean route to the East. But this solution would require them to learn new navigation techniques, while overcoming their fear of ocean travel. Many Europeans at the time believed that the oceans were full of sea monsters—terrifying creatures with "horns, flames, and huge eyes 16 or 20 feet across."

Solution: Education

The nation of Portugal led the way in Europe's exploration of the seas. Prince Henry, known as the Navigator (left), spearheaded the drive. At Sagres in southern Portugal, Henry gathered astronomers, cartographers, and other experts. Under his direction, they prepared maps, redesigned ships, and trained captains and crews for long voyages on the open sea. Henry sent out expedition after expedition. At last, in 1434, Captain Gil Eanes rounded Cape Bojador off the coast of West Africa and then returned to Portugal. This journey brought a swift end to the terrifying myths about the "Sea of Darkness" and set the stage for the European Age of Discovery.

Solution: New navigational tools

Early European sailors had no way to determine their location in the open sea. Fearful of getting lost, they hugged the coastline, keeping well in sight of land. Then, in the 1400s, Portuguese mariners learned to trust astronomy and mathematics to guide them safely to and from their destinations. Cartographers produced more accurate maps. Sailors learned to use the astrolabe and the sextant, instruments that helped them to calculate latitude at sea. The magnetic compass enabled them to determine direction. Armed with these new tools, Europeans could now set out across the ocean, traveling for weeks without sighting land.

Astrolabe

Magnetic compass

Sextant

Solution: Improved ships

To meet the challenge of prolonged ocean voyages, Europeans had to design larger and better ships. The Portuguese again led the way with the caravel, a long, shallow ship whose steering rudder and triangular sails allowed it to sail against the wind. The highly maneuverable caravel was the ideal ship for exploring unknown seas.

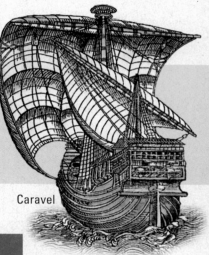

Caravel

Twenty-first-century problem and solution

The problems we face today may be different from those faced by people in the past. But problem-solving techniques remain the same. First, we must identify the problem. Then, we look for solutions. For example, environmental pollution is a serious problem. One way people are working to solve this problem is by learning more about it and by seeking new laws to regulate the sources of pollution.

Earth Day has become an annual opportunity to draw attention to environmental problems. Here, teenagers in Los Angeles are preparing an antipollution petition to present to their city government.

Portfolio Assessment

Connecting to Today Identify a problem in your school or community. Then, list three steps you might take to solve the problem.

The Renaissance and Reformation 1300–1650

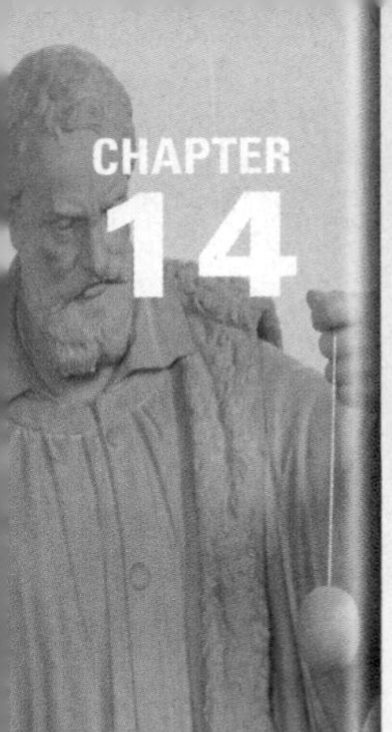

Chapter Preview

1 The Renaissance in Italy
2 The Renaissance Moves North
3 The Protestant Reformation
4 Reformation Ideas Spread
5 The Scientific Revolution

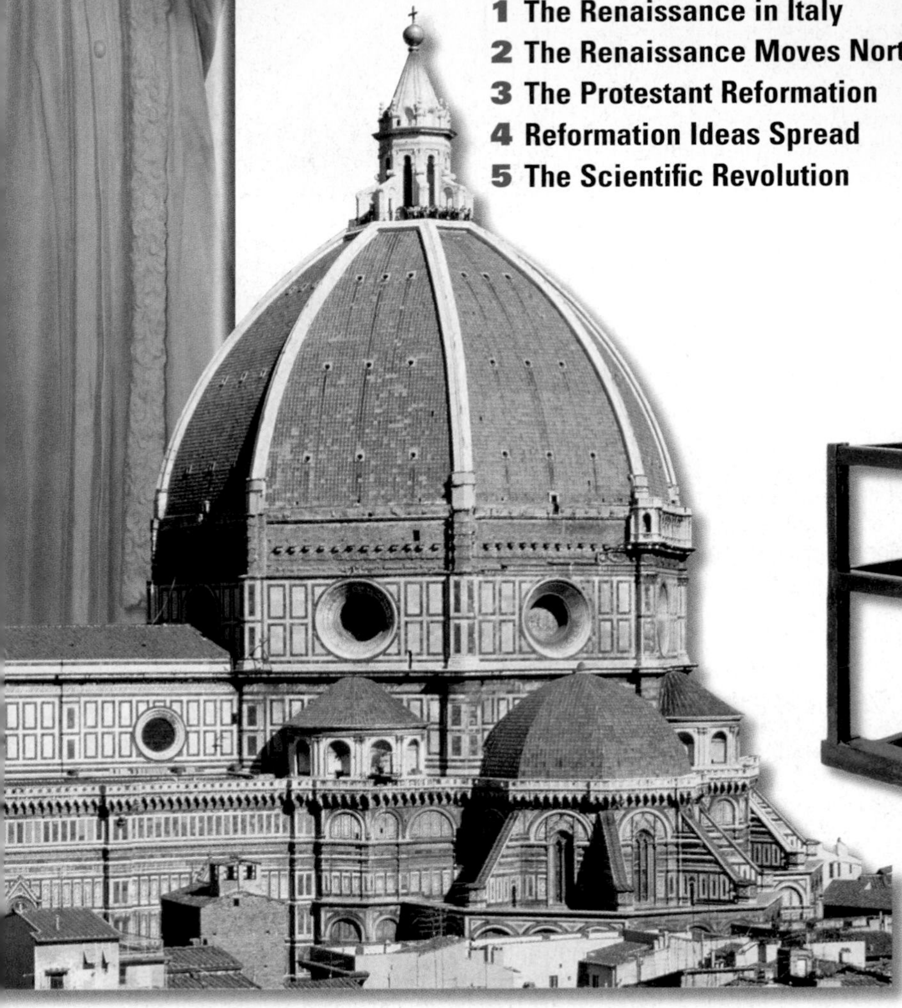

CHAPTER EVENTS

1300s
The Renaissance begins in Italian city-states. The cathedral in Florence, topped by this magnificent dome, reflects the wealth and artistic brilliance of Renaissance Italy.

1434
The Medici family gains control of the government of Florence.

1456
The first Gutenberg Bible is printed. The introduction of the printing press with movable type ushers in a printing revolution in Europe.

1300	1375	1450

GLOBAL EVENTS

1324 Mansa Musa makes hajj.

1368 The Ming dynasty is founded in China.

1453 Constantinople falls to the Ottoman Turks.

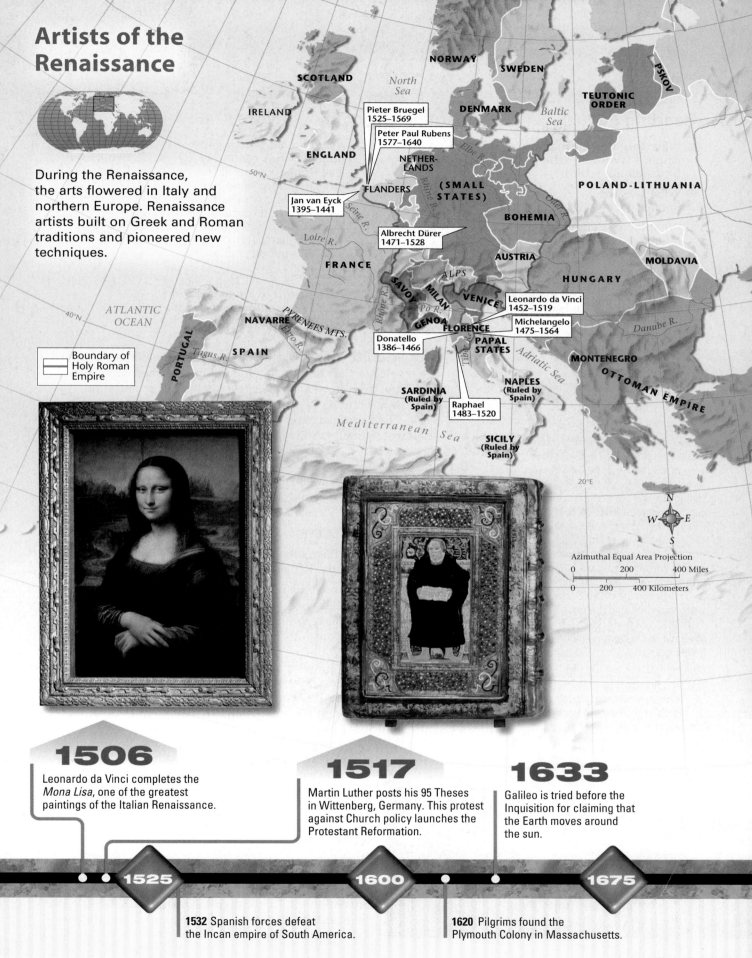

Artists of the Renaissance

During the Renaissance, the arts flowered in Italy and northern Europe. Renaissance artists built on Greek and Roman traditions and pioneered new techniques.

Pieter Bruegel
1525–1569

Peter Paul Rubens
1577–1640

Jan van Eyck
1395–1441

Albrecht Dürer
1471–1528

Leonardo da Vinci
1452–1519

Michelangelo
1475–1564

Donatello
1386–1466

Raphael
1483–1520

Boundary of
Holy Roman
Empire

Azimuthal Equal Area Projection

0   200   400 Miles

0   200   400 Kilometers

1506
Leonardo da Vinci completes the *Mona Lisa*, one of the greatest paintings of the Italian Renaissance.

1517
Martin Luther posts his 95 Theses in Wittenberg, Germany. This protest against Church policy launches the Protestant Reformation.

1633
Galileo is tried before the Inquisition for claiming that the Earth moves around the sun.

1525

1600

1675

1532 Spanish forces defeat the Incan empire of South America.

1620 Pilgrims found the Plymouth Colony in Massachusetts.

The Renaissance in Italy

Reading Focus

- Why were the Italian city-states a favorable setting for a cultural rebirth?

- What was the Renaissance?

- What themes and techniques did Renaissance artists and writers explore?

Vocabulary

patron
humanism
humanities
perspective

Taking Notes

As you read, prepare an outline of this section. Use Roman numerals to indicate major headings, capital letters for the sub-headings, and numbers for the supporting details. The sample at right will help you get started.

I. The Italian city-states
  A. Why Italy?
    1. Remains of Roman heritage
    2. Prosperous city-states
    3.
  B. Florence and the Medicis
    1.
    2.
II.

Main Idea   The Renaissance that began in Italy was characterized by an interest in learning and the arts and a desire to explore the human experience.

Geography and History

The Islands of Venice

One of the world's most remarkable cities was born after the fall of the western Roman empire. As invaders began conquering Italy, refugees fled to the islands in the Adriatic Sea. They drove wooden pilings into the marshy area to make a flat surface so that they could build houses. By Renaissance times, Venetian sailors were bringing back a wealth of trade goods from East and West.

The Grand Canal, an S-shaped waterway, became the main "street." Venetians row from island to island in flat-bottomed boats, called gondolas. Over 150 canals and 400 bridges link the islands into a single, unique city.

Theme: Geography and History How did Venetians adapt to geography?

N W E S

Setting the Scene The philosopher Marsilio Ficino smiled with pleasure as he watched the sun cast a golden glow over his native city of Florence. To Ficino, this glow symbolized the revival of art and thought taking place in Italy. Dipping his pen in ink, he began to write. "This century," he wrote, "like a golden age has restored to light the liberal arts, which were almost extinct: grammar, poetry, rhetoric, painting, sculpture, architecture, music." What a glorious time to be alive, he thought.

As Ficino recognized, a new age had dawned in Western Europe. Europeans called it the Renaissance, meaning "rebirth." It began in the 1300s and reached its peak around 1500.

The Italian City-States

The Renaissance began in Italy, then spread north to the rest of Europe. Italy was the birthplace of the Renaissance for several reasons.

Why Italy? The Renaissance was marked by a new interest in the culture of ancient Rome. Because Italy had been the center of the Roman empire, it was a logical place for this reawakening to begin. Architectural remains, statues, coins, and inscriptions—all were visible reminders of Roman grandeur.

Italy differed from the rest of Europe in other ways. Its cities survived the Middle Ages. In the north, city-states like Florence, Milan, Venice, and Genoa grew into prosperous centers of trade and manufacturing. Rome, in central Italy, and Naples, in the south, along with a number of smaller city-states, also contributed to the Renaissance cultural revival.

A wealthy and powerful merchant class in these city-states further promoted the cultural rebirth. These merchants exerted both political and economic leadership, and their attitudes and interests helped to shape the Italian Renaissance. They stressed education and individual achievement. They also spent lavishly to support the arts.

Florence and the Medicis Florence, perhaps more than any other city, came to symbolize the energy and brilliance of the Italian Renaissance. Like the ancient city of Athens, it produced a dazzling number of gifted poets, artists, architects, scholars, and scientists in a short span of time.

In the 1400s, the Medici (MEH dee chee) family of Florence organized a successful banking business. Before long, the family expanded into wool manufacturing, mining, and other ventures. The Medicis ranked among the richest merchants and bankers in Europe. Money translated into cultural and political power. Cosimo de' Medici gained control of the Florentine government in 1434, and the family continued as uncrowned rulers of the city for many years.

Cosimo's grandson Lorenzo, known as "the Magnificent," represented the Renaissance ideal. A clever politician, he held Florence together in the late 1400s during difficult times. He was also a generous patron, or financial supporter, of the arts. Under Lorenzo, poets and philosophers frequently visited the Medici palace. Artists learned their craft by sketching ancient Roman statues displayed in the Medici gardens.

What Was the Renaissance?

The Renaissance was a time of creativity and change in many areas—political, social, economic, and cultural. Perhaps most important, however, were the changes that took place in the way people viewed themselves and their world.

A New Worldview Spurred by a reawakened interest in the classical learning of Greece and Rome, creative Renaissance minds set out to transform their own age. Their era, they felt, was a time of rebirth after what they saw as the disorder and disunity of the medieval world.

In reality, Renaissance Europe did not break completely with its medieval past. After all, monks and scholars of the Middle Ages had preserved much of the classical heritage. Latin had survived as the language of the Church and of educated people. And the mathematics of Euclid, the astronomy of Ptolemy, and the works of Aristotle were well known to late medieval scholars.

Yet the Renaissance did produce new attitudes toward culture and learning. Unlike medieval scholars, who were more likely to focus on life after death, Renaissance thinkers explored the richness and variety of human experience in the here and now. At the same time, there was a new emphasis on individual achievement. Indeed, the Renaissance ideal was the person with talent in many fields.

A Spirit of Adventure The Renaissance supported a spirit of adventure and a wide-ranging curiosity that led people to explore new worlds. The Italian navigator Christopher Columbus, who sailed to the Americas in 1492, represented that spirit. So did Nicolaus Copernicus, a Polish scientist who revolutionized the way people viewed the universe. Renaissance writers and artists, eager to experiment with new forms, were also products of that adventurous spirit.

Humanism At the heart of the Italian Renaissance was an intellectual movement known as humanism. Based on the study of classical culture, humanism focused on worldly subjects rather than on the religious issues that had occupied medieval thinkers. Most humanist scholars were pious

Renaissance Italy, 1505

Duchy of Milan
Republic of Genoa
Republic of Florence
Papal States
Republic of Venice
Kingdoms under Spanish sovereignty
Other city-states

Skills Assessment

Geography At the time of the Renaissance, Italy was made up of numerous republics, kingdoms, and city-states.

1. **Location** On the map, locate **(a)** Florence, **(b)** Venice, **(c)** Rome, **(d)** Papal States, **(e)** Duchy of Milan.
2. **Place** **(a)** In which state was Pisa an important city? **(b)** Who controlled Corsica and Sicily?
3. **Critical Thinking**
   Making Inferences Based on this map, why was Venice in a good position to trade with the Muslim world?

Christians who hoped to use the wisdom of the ancients to increase their understanding of their own times.

Humanists believed that education should stimulate the individual's creative powers. They returned to the **humanities**, the subjects taught in ancient Greek and Roman schools. The main areas of study were grammar, rhetoric, poetry, and history, based on Greek and Roman texts. Humanists did not accept the classical texts without question, however. Rather, they studied the ancient authorities in light of their own experiences.

Francesco Petrarch (PEE trahrk), a Florentine who lived in the 1300s, was an early Renaissance humanist. In monasteries and churches, he found and assembled a library of Greek and Roman manuscripts. Through his efforts and those of others encouraged by his example, the works of Cicero, Homer, and Virgil again became known to Western Europeans. Petrarch also wrote literature of his own. His *Sonnets to Laura,* love poems inspired by a woman he knew only from a distance, greatly influenced later writers.

A Golden Age in the Arts

The Renaissance attained its most glorious expression in its paintings, sculpture, and architecture. Wealthy patrons played a major role in this artistic flowering. Popes and princes supported the work of hundreds of artists. Wealthy and powerful women such as Isabella d'Este of Mantua were important patrons of the arts as well.

Humanist Concerns Renaissance art reflected humanist concerns. Like artists of the Middle Ages, Renaissance artists portrayed religious figures such as Jesus and Mary. However, they often set these figures against Greek or Roman backgrounds. Painters also produced portraits of well-known figures of the day, reflecting the humanist interest in individual achievement.

Perspective
Renaissance artists used perspective to create an illusion of depth. The diagram below shows how the lines in this painting by Antonello da Messina recede from the viewer toward a single vanishing point.

Theme: Arts and Literature
How does the size of objects in this painting add to the sense of depth?

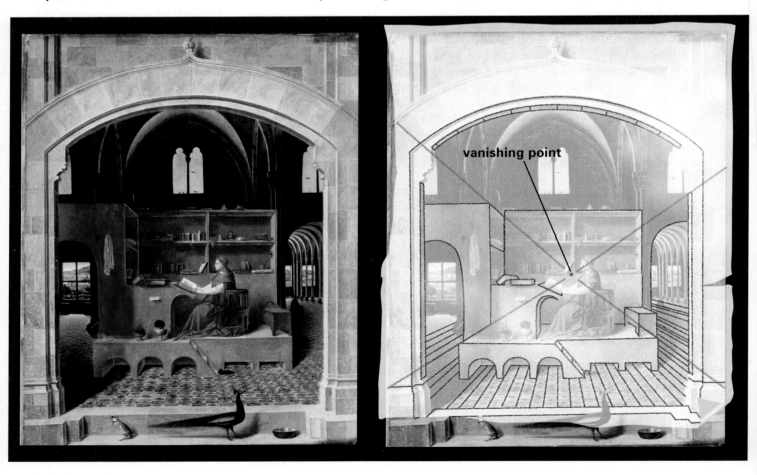

vanishing point

Renaissance artists studied ancient Greek and Roman works and revived many classical forms. The sculptor Donatello, for example, created a life-size statue of a soldier on horseback. It was the first such figure done since ancient times.

New Techniques Roman art had been very realistic, and Renaissance painters developed new techniques for representing both humans and landscapes in a realistic way. Renaissance artists learned the rules of perspective. By making distant objects smaller than those close to the viewer, artists could paint scenes that appeared three-dimensional.

Renaissance painters used shading to make objects look round and real. Painters and sculptors also studied human anatomy and drew from live models. As a result, they were able to portray the human body more accurately than medieval artists had done.

Women Artists Some women overcame the limits on education and training to become professional artists. Sometimes, these women kept their work secret, allowing their husbands to pass it off as their own. Still, a few women artists did gain acceptance. In the 1500s, Sofonisba Anguissola (soh foh NIHZ bah ahn gwee SOH lah), an Italian noblewoman, became court painter to King Philip II of Spain.

Architecture Renaissance architects rejected the Gothic style of the late Middle Ages as cluttered and disorderly. Instead, they adopted the columns, arches, and domes that had been favored by the Greeks and Romans. For the cathedral in Florence, Filippo Brunelleschi (broo nehl LEHS kee) created a majestic dome, which he modeled on the dome of the Pantheon in Rome.

Three Geniuses of Renaissance Art

Renaissance Florence was home to many outstanding painters and sculptors. The three most celebrated Florentine masters were Leonardo da Vinci, Michelangelo, and Raphael.

Leonardo Leonardo da Vinci (dah VIHN chee) was born in 1452. His exploring mind and endless curiosity fed a genius for invention. He made sketches of nature and of models in his studio. He even dissected corpses to learn how bones and muscles work. "Indicate which are the muscles and which the tendons, which become prominent or retreat in the different movements of each limb," he wrote in his notebook.

Today, people admire Leonardo's paintings for their freshness and realism. Most popular is the *Mona Lisa*, a portrait of a woman whose mysterious smile has baffled viewers for centuries. *The Last Supper*, showing Christ and his apostles on the night before the crucifixion, is both a moving religious painting and a masterpiece of perspective. Because Leonardo was experimenting with a new type of paint, much of *The Last Supper* decayed over the years, but it has recently been restored.

Leonardo thought of himself as an artist, but his talents and accomplishments ranged over many areas. His interests extended to botany, anatomy, optics, music, architecture, and engineering. He made sketches for flying machines and undersea boats centuries before the first airplane or submarine was actually built.

Michelangelo Like Leonardo, Michelangelo was a many-sided genius—sculptor, engineer, painter, architect, and poet. As a young man, he shaped marble into masterpieces like the *Pietà*, which captures the sorrow of Mary as she cradles the dead Christ on her knees. Michelangelo's statue of David, the biblical shepherd who killed the giant Goliath, recalls the harmony and grace of ancient Greek tradition.

Primary Source

The Genius of Leonardo
Italian artist and architect Giorgio Vasari is best known for his engaging book of biographies of Italian artists, including Leonardo da Vinci (pictured above):

"Leonardo practiced not one art but all of those that are dependent upon design, and he had great talent for geometry besides being very musical, playing the lute with great ability and being excellent in the art of improvisation. . . . In entertaining, Leonardo was so pleasant that he won everyone's heart. Although he may well be said to have owned nothing and to have worked little, he always kept a servant as well as horses."

—Giorgio Vasari, *Lives of the Most Eminent Italian Painters, Sculptors, and Architects*

Skills Assessment

Primary Source What personal details did Vasari include about Leonardo da Vinci?

Virtual Field Trip

www.phschool.com

Web Museum of Art

To see other details from the ceiling, use the Internet address above to link to the Web Museum of Art.

A Masterpiece by Michelangelo
Michelangelo spent four years painting biblical scenes on the ceiling of the Sistine Chapel. One of the most dramatic images, the *Creation of Adam*, shows God bringing the first man to life with a touch.

Theme: Religions and Value Systems How does Michelangelo suggest the power of God?

One of Michelangelo's greatest projects was painting a huge mural to decorate the ceiling of the Sistine Chapel in Rome. It was an enormous task, depicting the biblical history of the world, from the Creation to the Flood. For four years, the artist lay on his back on a wooden platform suspended just a few inches below the chapel ceiling. In a poem, Michelangelo later described his ordeal:

"My stomach is thrust toward my chin
My beard curls up toward the sky
My head leans right over onto my back . . .
The brush endlessly dripping onto my face."
—Michelangelo, *Poems*

Michelangelo was also a talented architect. His most famous design was for the dome of St. Peter's Cathedral in Rome. It served as a model for many later structures, including the United States Capitol building in Washington, D.C.

Raphael A few years younger than Leonardo and Michelangelo, Raphael (RAF ee uhl) studied the works of those great masters. His paintings blend Christian and classical styles. He is probably best known for his tender portrayals of the madonna, the mother of Jesus.

In *The School of Athens*, Raphael pictures an imaginary gathering of great thinkers and scientists, such as Plato, Aristotle, Socrates, and the Arab philosopher Averroës. With typical Renaissance self-confidence, Raphael included the faces of Michelangelo, Leonardo—and himself.

Italian Renaissance Writers

Poets, artists, and scholars mingled with politicians at the courts of Renaissance rulers. A literature of "how-to" books sprang up to help ambitious men and women who wanted to rise in the Renaissance world.

Castiglione's Ideal Courtier The most widely read of these handbooks was *The Book of the Courtier*. Its author, Baldassare Castiglione (bahl dahs

SAHR ray kahs steel YOHN ay), describes the manners, skills, learning, and virtues that a member of the court should have. Castiglione's ideal courtier was a well-educated, well-mannered aristocrat who mastered many fields, from poetry to music to sports.

Castiglione's ideal differed for men and women. The ideal man, he wrote, is athletic but not overactive. He is good at games, but not a gambler. He plays a musical instrument and knows literature and history but is not arrogant. The ideal woman offers a balance to men. She is graceful and kind, lively but reserved. She is beautiful, "for outer beauty," wrote Castiglione, "is the true sign of inner goodness."

Machiavelli's Successful Prince Niccolò Machiavelli (mahk ee uh VEHL ee) wrote a different kind of handbook. Machiavelli had served Florence as a diplomat and had observed kings and princes in foreign courts. He also had studied ancient Roman history. In *The Prince*, published in 1513, Machiavelli combined his personal experience of politics with his knowledge of the past to offer a guide to rulers on how to gain and maintain power.

Unlike earlier political writers, such as Plato, Machiavelli did not discuss leadership in terms of high ideals. Instead, *The Prince* looked at real rulers, such as the Medicis, in an age of ruthless power politics. Machiavelli stressed that the end justifies the means. He urged rulers to use whatever methods were necessary to achieve their goals. On the issue of honesty in government, for example, he taught that getting results was more important than keeping promises. He wrote:

> "How praiseworthy it is for a prince to keep his word and live with integrity rather than craftiness, everyone understands; yet . . . those princes have accomplished most who paid little heed to keeping their promises, but who knew how craftily to manipulate the minds of men."
> —Niccolò Machiavelli, *The Prince*

Machiavelli saw himself as an enemy of oppression and corruption. But critics attacked his cynical advice. Some even claimed that he was inspired by the devil. (In fact, the term "Machiavellian" came to refer to the use of deceit in politics.) Later students of government, however, argued that Machiavelli provided a realistic look at politics. His work continues to spark debate because it raises important ethical questions about the nature of government and the use of power.

 Primary Sources and Literature

See "Niccolò Machiavelli: Discourses," in the Reference Section at the back of this book.

SECTION 1 Assessment

Recall
1. **Identify:** (a) Lorenzo de' Medici, (b) Francesco Petrarch, (c) Leonardo da Vinci, (d) Michelangelo, (e) Raphael, (f) Baldassare Castiglione, (g) Niccolò Machiavelli.
2. **Define:** (a) patron, (b) humanism, (c) humanities, (d) perspective.

Comprehension
3. What conditions in Italy contributed to the emergence of the Renaissance?
4. Identify the concerns and attitudes emphasized during the Renaissance.

5. How did Renaissance art reflect humanist concerns?

Critical Thinking and Writing
6. **Making Inferences** Why might powerful rulers and wealthy business people choose to become patrons of the arts during the Renaissance?
7. **Linking Past and Present** In *The Prince*, Machiavelli advised rulers that it "is much safer to be feared than loved." (a) What did he mean by that? (b) Do you think a political leader today would be wise to follow that advice? Why or why not?

 Activity
Take It to the NET

Use the Internet to learn more about a major artist of the Italian Renaissance. You may choose one of the artists mentioned in this section or another artist such as Fra Angelico, Benvenuto Cellini, Sandro Botticelli, or Titian. Prepare a report on one artwork. Include a copy of the work.

The Renaissance Moves North

Reading Focus

- Which artists brought the Renaissance to northern Europe?
- What themes did humanist thinkers and other writers explore?
- What impact did the printing revolution have on Europe?

Vocabulary

engraving
vernacular
utopian

Taking Notes

On a sheet of paper begin a table like the one shown here. Add information about the Renaissance under each heading as you read the section.

DUTCH	GERMAN	FLEMISH	ENGLISH	FRENCH	SPANISH
Erasmus	Dürer				

Main Idea The Renaissance slowly spread to northern Europe, where artists and writers experimented with new methods and ideas.

Setting the Scene "Had I not torn myself from Rome, I could never have resolved to leave," wrote Dutch priest Desiderius Erasmus. "There one enjoys sweet liberty, rich libraries, the charming friendship of writers and scholars, and the sight of antique monuments." Inspired by his visit to Italy, Erasmus helped spread the Renaissance to northern Europe.

Unlike Italy, northern Europe recovered slowly from the ravages of the Black Death. Only after 1450 did the north enjoy the economic growth that had earlier supported the Renaissance in Italy.

Artists of the Northern Renaissance

The northern Renaissance began in the prosperous cities of Flanders, a region that included parts of present-day northern France, Belgium, and the Netherlands. Spain, France, Germany, and England enjoyed their great cultural rebirth 100 years later, in the 1500s.

A "German Leonardo" Albrecht Dürer traveled to Italy in 1494 to study the techniques of the Italian masters. Returning home, he employed these methods in paintings and, especially, in engravings. In this form of art, an artist etches a design on a metal plate with acid. The artist then uses the plate to make prints. Many of Dürer's engravings portray the religious upheaval of his age.

Through his art as well as through essays, Dürer helped to spread Italian Renaissance ideas in his homeland. Because of his wide-ranging interests, which extended far beyond art, he is sometimes called the "German Leonardo."

Flemish Painters Among the many artists of Flanders in the 1400s, Jan and Hubert van Eyck (van ĪK) stand out. Their portrayals of townspeople as well as religious scenes abound in rich, realistic details. The van Eycks also developed oil paint. Northern artists used this new medium to produce strong colors and a hard surface that could survive the centuries.

In the 1500s, Pieter Bruegel (PEE tuhr BROY guhl) used vibrant colors to portray lively scenes of peasant life. Bruegel's work influenced later Flemish artists, who painted scenes of daily life rather than religious or classical themes.

In the 1600s, Peter Paul Rubens blended the realistic tradition of Flemish painters like Bruegel with the classical themes and artistic freedom of the Italian Renaissance. Many of his enormous paintings portray pagan figures from the classical past.

Northern Humanists

Like Italian humanists, northern European humanist scholars stressed education and classical learning. At the same time, they emphasized religious themes. They believed that the revival of ancient learning should be used to bring about religious and moral reform.

Erasmus The great Dutch priest and humanist Desiderius Erasmus used his knowledge of classical languages to produce a new Greek edition of the New Testament. He also called for a translation of the Bible into the **vernacular**, or everyday language of ordinary people. He scorned "those who are unwilling that Holy Scripture, translated into the vernacular, be read by the uneducated . . . as if the strength of the Christian religion consisted in the ignorance of it."

To Erasmus, an individual's chief duties were to be open-minded and of good will toward others. As a priest, he was disturbed by corruption in the Church and called for reform. In *The Praise of Folly*, Erasmus uses humor to expose the ignorant and immoral behavior of many people of his day, including the clergy.

More Erasmus's friend, the English humanist Thomas More, also pressed for social reform. In *Utopia*, More describes an ideal society in which men and women live in peace and harmony. No one is idle, all are educated, and justice is used to end crime rather than to eliminate the criminal. Today, the word **utopian** has come to describe any ideal society.

Writers for a New Audience

Scholars like More and Erasmus wrote mostly in Latin. In northern towns and cities, the growing middle class demanded new works in the vernacular. This audience particularly enjoyed dramatic tales and earthy comedies.

Rabelais The French humanist François Rabelais had a varied career as a monk, physician, Greek scholar, and author. In *Gargantua and Pantagruel*, he chronicles the adventures of two gentle giants. On the surface, the novel is

Dürer, the "German Leonardo"
Albrecht Dürer, shown in a self-portrait (below right), helped bring the genius of the Italian Renaissance to northern Europe. Many of his finest works were engravings, such as the portrait of a peasant couple (below left).

Theme: Arts and Literature How do these works reflect the Renaissance interest in the individual?

Shakespeare's World of Drama

"He was not of an age, but for all time," said one of Shakespeare's contemporaries of him. A later poet said, "He was the man who of all modern, and perhaps ancient poets, had the largest and most comprehensive soul." Today, no plays are performed more frequently around the world than those of William Shakespeare.

In *A Midsummer Night's Dream,* a love potion causes confusion among two young couples and makes Titania, the queen of the fairies, fall in love with a man who has the head of a donkey. One character comments:

"Alas, poor Yorick! I knew him, Horatio, a fellow of infinite jest."

Prince Hamlet mourns his father's deceased court jester.

"What fools these mortals be"

"All the world's a stage, / And all the men and women merely players:/ They have their exits and their entrances;/ And one man in his time plays many parts."

—William Shakespeare, *As You Like It*

Portfolio Assessment

INTERNET Use the Internet or library resources to find out more about the dramas of William Shakespeare. Form small groups, and have each group choose a different play. Then, pick out a passage from the play, cast and rehearse it, and perform it for the rest of the class.

a comic tale of travel and war. But Rabelais uses his characters to offer opinions on religion, education, and other serious subjects.

Shakespeare The towering figure of Renaissance literature was the English poet and playwright William Shakespeare. Between 1590 and 1613, he wrote 37 plays that are still performed around the world.

Shakespeare's comedies, such as *Twelfth Night,* laugh at the follies of young people in love. His history plays, such as *Richard III,* depict the power struggles of English kings. His tragedies show people crushed by powerful forces or their own weaknesses. In *Romeo and Juliet,* two teenagers fall victim to an old family feud.

Shakespeare's love of words vastly enriched the English language. More than 1,700 words appeared for the first time in his works, including *bedroom, lonely, generous, gloomy, heartsick, hurry,* and *sneak.*

Cervantes The Renaissance in Spain in the early 1600s also led to the production of great works. Best known is *Don Quixote* (DAHN kee HOH tay), by Miguel de Cervantes (suhr VAN teez), an entertaining tale that mocks romantic notions of medieval chivalry. The novel follows the adventures of Don Quixote, a foolish but idealistic knight, and Sancho Panza, his faithful servant. (You will read more about *Don Quixote* in a later chapter.)

The Printing Revolution

In 1456, Johann Gutenberg of Mainz, Germany, printed the first complete edition of the Bible using the first printing press and printing inks in the West. Within twenty years, the development of movable type made book production even easier. A printing revolution had begun that would transform Europe. By 1500, more than 20 million volumes had been printed.

Gutenberg and his successors built on earlier advances. Methods of making paper had reached Europe from China about 1300. The Chinese and Koreans had been using movable metal type for centuries, although Europeans may have developed their technology independently.

The printing revolution brought immense changes. Printed books were cheaper and easier to produce than hand-copied works. With books more readily available, more people learned to read. Readers gained access to a broad range of knowledge, from medicine and law to astrology and mining. Printed books exposed educated Europeans to new ideas, greatly expanding their horizons. As you will read, the new presses would contribute to the religious turmoil that engulfed Europe in the 1500s.

Connections to Today

A Revolution in Communication

The development of the printing press fostered a communications revolution. Information once available to a small percentage of people could now spread to vast numbers.

Today, thanks to a new communications revolution, information can be spread around the world instantaneously. Writer Marshall McLuhan has described the world as a "global village," one in which we are closely linked by telephone, television, and computer communications. Faxes, instant messaging, and e-mail all speed up our communication process. We can now share knowledge, experiences, and emotions with people around the world. Consequently, the world today may seem no larger than a small village of Renaissance times.

Theme: Economics and Technology How has communications technology made the world smaller?

SECTION 2 Assessment

Recall
1. **Identify: (a)** Albrecht Dürer, **(b)** Jan van Eyck, **(c)** François Rabelais, **(d)** William Shakespeare, **(e)** Miguel de Cervantes, **(f)** Johann Gutenberg.
2. **Define: (a)** engraving, **(b)** vernacular, **(c)** utopian.

Comprehension
3. How did Dürer help bring the Renaissance to northern Europe?
4. What themes did Erasmus and More raise in their writings?

5. What were three effects of the printing revolution?

Critical Thinking and Writing
6. **Recognizing Causes and Effects** Why do you think the cultural flowering of the northern Renaissance did not begin until after economic growth had taken place?
7. **Linking Past and Present** What are some ways in which Shakespeare's plays and sonnets still "live" today?

Activity

Creating Compound Words Shakespeare invented new words by combining two existing words. Examples of these compound words are *eyesore, heartsick, hot-blooded, leapfrog,* and *tongue-tied.* Look up definitions of these words. Then, create five compound words of your own.

Reading Focus

- How did abuses in the Church spark widespread criticism?

- How did Martin Luther challenge Catholic authority and teachings?

- What role did John Calvin play in the Reformation?

Vocabulary

indulgence

recant

predestination

theocracy

Taking Notes

On a sheet of paper draw a flowchart like the one shown here. As you read this section, add important events and ideas that contributed to the Protestant Reformation.

Church involved in worldly affairs
↓
Tetzel sells indulgences to raise money for new cathedral
↓
↓

Main Idea The ideas of Martin Luther and John Calvin led people to separate from the Roman Catholic Church and form new Protestant churches.

Setting the Scene During the Renaissance, the Church increasingly came under fire. Christians at all levels of society accused the clergy of corruption and worldliness. One peasant even compared the clergy to "wicked wolves." He protested, "Instead of saving the souls of the dead and sending them to Heaven, they gorge themselves at banquets after funerals."

During the Middle Ages, the Church had renewed itself from within. In the 1500s, though, new calls for reform unleashed forces that would shatter Christian unity. This movement is known as the Protestant Reformation.

Abuses in the Church

Beginning in the late Middle Ages, the Church had become increasingly caught up in worldly affairs. Popes competed with Italian princes for political power. They fought long wars to protect the Papal States against invasions by secular rulers. They intrigued against powerful monarchs who tried to seize control of the Church within their lands.

Like other Renaissance rulers, popes maintained a lavish lifestyle. Popes were also patrons of the arts. They hired painters and sculptors to beautify churches.

To finance such projects, the Church increased fees for services such as marriages and baptisms. Some clergy also promoted the sale of indulgences. According to Church teaching, an **indulgence** was a lessening of the time a soul would have to spend in purgatory, a place where souls too impure to enter heaven atoned for sins committed during their lifetimes. In the Middle Ages, the Church had granted indulgences only for good deeds, such as going on a crusade. By the late 1400s, however, indulgences could also be obtained in exchange for money gifts to the Church.

Many Christians protested such practices, especially in northern Europe. Christian humanists such as Erasmus urged a return to the simple ways of the early Christian Church. They stressed Bible study and rejected what they saw as the worldliness of the Church.

Luther's Protest

In 1517, protests against Church abuses erupted into a full-scale revolt. The man who triggered the revolt was a German monk and professor of theology named Martin Luther.

As a young man, Luther prayed and fasted and tried to lead a holy life. Still, he believed he was doomed to eternal damnation. He also grew disillusioned with what he saw as Church corruption and worldliness. At last, an incident in the town of Wittenberg prompted him to take action.

The 95 Theses In 1517, a priest named Johann Tetzel set up a pulpit on the outskirts of Wittenberg. He offered indulgences to any Christian who contributed money for the rebuilding of the Cathedral of St. Peter in Rome. Tetzel claimed that purchase of these indulgences would assure entry into heaven not only for the purchasers but for their dead relatives as well. "Don't you hear the voices of your dead parents and other relatives crying out?" he demanded.

To Luther, Tetzel's actions were the final outrage. He drew up 95 theses, or arguments, against indulgences. Among other things, he argued that indulgences had no basis in the Bible, that the pope had no authority to release souls from purgatory, and that Christians could be saved only through faith. In accordance with the custom of the time, he posted his list on the door of Wittenberg's All Saints Church.

Luther Versus the Church Almost overnight, copies of Luther's 95 Theses were printed and distributed across Europe, where they stirred furious debate. The Church called on Luther to **recant**, or give up his views. Luther refused. Instead, he developed even more radical new doctrines. Before long, he was urging Christians to reject the authority of Rome. Because the Church would not reform itself, he wrote, it must be reformed by secular authorities.

In 1521, the pope excommunicated Luther. Later that year, the new Holy Roman emperor, Charles V, summoned Luther to the diet, or assembly of German princes, at Worms. Luther went, expecting to defend his writings. Instead, the emperor simply ordered him to give them up. Luther again refused to recant:

> "Unless I am convicted by Scripture and plain reason—I do not accept the authority of popes and councils, for they have contradicted each other—I am captive to the Word of God. I cannot and will not recant anything, for to go against conscience is neither right nor safe."
> —Martin Luther, Speech Before the Diet of Worms

Charles declared Luther an outlaw, making it a crime for anyone in the empire to give him food or shelter. Still, Luther had many powerful supporters. One prince hid him at a castle in Wartburg. Luther remained in hiding for nearly a year. Throughout Germany, in the meantime, thousands hailed him as a hero. They accepted his teachings and, following his lead, renounced the authority of the pope.

Selling Indulgences
This 1517 cartoon shows Johann Tetzel selling indulgences to the people of Wittenberg. A jingle in the upper left corner said, "As soon as the coin in the coffer rings, a soul from purgatory springs."

Theme: Religions and Value Systems Do you think the artist who drew this picture approved of Tetzel's actions? Why or why not?

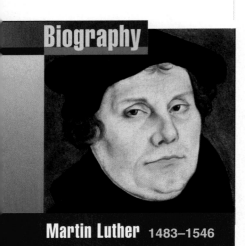

Martin Luther 1483–1546

"I am rough, boisterous, stormy, and altogether warlike," concluded Martin Luther. Luther's strong personality allowed him to take on the powerful Catholic Church. As a monk, Luther closely studied the Bible and came to believe that only its words—and not the pope or the Catholic Church—should dictate a person's actions.

When he appeared at the Diet of Worms, Luther was 37 years old. Though depressed and fearful about the confrontation, he held to his beliefs. According to one report, Luther declared, "Here I stand, I cannot do otherwise." When he refused to retract his statements, an order was given to destroy his books. Yet his influence grew, leading to a division within Christianity and the founding of a new church that took his name.

Theme: Impact of the Individual What inspired Luther's firm stand against the Church?

Luther's Teachings At the heart of Luther's teachings were several beliefs. First, he rejected the Church doctrine that good deeds were necessary for salvation. Instead, Luther argued that salvation was achieved through faith alone.

Second, Luther upheld the Bible as the sole source of religious truth. He denied other authorities, such as Church councils or the pope.

Third, Luther rejected the idea that priests and the Church hierarchy had special powers. Instead, he talked of a "priesthood of all believers." All Christians, he said, had equal access to God through faith and the Bible. Luther translated the Bible into the German vernacular so that ordinary people could study it by themselves. Every town, he said, should have a school so that girls and boys could learn to read the Bible.

Luther wanted to change other church practices. He rejected five of the seven sacraments because the Bible did not mention them. He banned indulgences, confession, pilgrimages, and prayers to saints. He simplified the elaborate ritual of the mass and instead emphasized the sermon. And he permitted the clergy to marry. These and other changes were adopted by the Lutheran churches that were set up by Luther's followers.

Spread of Lutheran Ideas

Luther's ideas found a fertile field in northern Germany and Scandinavia. While the new printing presses spread Luther's writings, fiery preachers denounced Church abuses. By 1530, the Lutherans were using a new name, Protestant, for those who "protested" papal authority.

Widespread Support Why did Lutheranism win widespread support? Many clergy saw Luther's reforms as the answer to Church corruption. A number of German princes, however, embraced Lutheran beliefs for more selfish reasons. Some saw Lutheranism as a way to throw off the rule of both the Church and the Holy Roman emperor. Others welcomed a chance to seize Church property in their territory. Still other Germans supported Luther because of feelings of national loyalty. They were tired of German money going to support churches and clergy in Italy.

The Peasants' Revolt Many peasants also took up Luther's banner. They hoped to gain his support for social and economic change.

In 1524, a Peasants' Revolt erupted across Germany. The rebels called for an end to serfdom and demanded other changes in their harsh lives. Luther, however, strongly favored social order and respect for political authority. As the Peasants' Revolt grew more violent, Luther denounced it. With his support, nobles suppressed the rebellion, killing tens of thousands of people and leaving thousands more homeless.

The Peace of Augsburg During the 1530s and 1540s, Holy Roman emperor Charles V tried to force Lutheran princes back into the Catholic Church, but with little success. Finally, after a number of brief wars, Charles and the princes reached a settlement. The Peace of Augsburg, signed in 1555, allowed each prince to decide which religion—Catholic or Lutheran—would be followed in his lands. Most northern German states chose Lutheranism. The south remained largely Catholic.

John Calvin

Two other reformers, Ulrich Zwingli and John Calvin, presented further challenges to the Catholic Church. Zwingli, a priest and an admirer of Erasmus, lived in the Swiss city of Zurich. Like Luther, he rejected elaborate church rituals and stressed the importance of the Bible. John Calvin had a logical, razor-sharp mind. His ideas had a profound effect on the direction of the Reformation.

What Is the Goal of Education?

Both the Renaissance and the Reformation stressed the importance of education. What is your goal in pursuing an education? Think about the goals of modern-day schools as you compare the following viewpoints.

China 500 B.C.

Chinese philosopher Confucius explained how learning was essential for both the individual and the community:

66 Extension of knowledge comes from the investigation of things. When things are investigated, knowledge is extended. When knowledge is extended, the will becomes sincere. When the will is sincere, the heart can be set right. When the heart is right, the personal life can be cultivated. When the personal life is cultivated, the community can be regulated. When the community is regulated, the government can be made orderly. And when the government is orderly, there will be peace in the world. 99

Germany 1524

Protestant reformer Martin Luther called for German communities to set up and pay for Christian schools:

66 The world has need of educated men and women to the end that men may govern the country properly and women may properly bring up their children, care for their domestics, and direct the affairs of the household. . . . The welfare of the state depends on the intelligence and virtue of its citizens. 99

United States 1990s

This poster was designed for school guidance counselors.

You can branch out into any field you like...

if you have the proper roots in education.

Cuba 1883

José Martí, a poet and political leader, turned away from classical ideas about what should be taught:

66 The schools teach classes in ancient geography, rules of rhetoric, and similar things of long ago, but in their place there should be courses in health; advice on hygiene; practical counseling; clear and simple studies of the human body, its parts, functions, ways of adjusting one to the other, economizing one's strength, and directing it well so that there will be no reason to restore it later. 99

Skills Assessment

1. What goal of education is stressed by both Confucius and Luther?
   - **A** gaining knowledge for its own sake
   - **B** making a good living
   - **C** cultivating the personal life
   - **D** contributing to the community

2. Who would be most likely to favor classes in physical education?
   - **E** Confucius
   - **F** Luther
   - **G** Martí
   - **H** the designer of the poster

3. **Critical Thinking Making Decisions** Identify a future career for yourself. Which educational theory would be most useful in helping you achieve this goal? Why? Explain why more than one type of education would be helpful.

Skills Tip

It is important to recognize that a writer may express his or her point of view as an absolute truth to convince others of its validity.

Teachings Calvin was born in France and trained as a priest and lawyer. In 1536, Calvin published the *Institutes of the Christian Religion.* In this book, which was read by Protestants everywhere, he set forth his religious beliefs. He also provided advice on how to organize and run a Protestant church.

Like Luther, Calvin believed that salvation was gained through faith alone. He, too, regarded the Bible as the only source of religious truth. But Calvin put forth a number of ideas of his own. He preached predestination, the idea that God had long ago determined who would gain salvation. To Calvinists, the world was divided into two kinds of people—saints and sinners. Calvinists tried to live like saints, believing that only those who were saved could live truly Christian lives.

Calvin's Geneva In 1541, Protestants in the city-state of Geneva in Switzerland asked Calvin to lead their community. In keeping with his teachings, Calvin set up a theocracy, or government run by church leaders.

Calvin's followers in Geneva came to see themselves as a new "chosen people" entrusted by God to build a truly Christian society. Calvinists stressed hard work, discipline, thrift, honesty, and morality. Citizens faced fines or other harsher punishments for offenses such as fighting, swearing, laughing in church, or dancing. Calvin closed theaters and frowned on elaborate dress. To many Protestants, this emphasis on strict morality made Calvinist Geneva seem a model community.

Like Luther, Calvin believed in religious education for girls as well as for boys. Women, he felt, should read the Bible—in private. Calvin also allowed women to sing in church, a practice that many church leaders criticized.

Spread of Calvinism Reformers from all over Europe visited Geneva and then returned home to spread Calvin's ideas. By the late 1500s, Calvinism had taken root in Germany, France, the Netherlands, England, and Scotland. This new challenge to the Roman Catholic Church set off bloody wars of religion across Europe.

In Germany, Calvinists faced opposition not only from Catholics, but from Lutherans as well. In France, wars raged between French Calvinists, called Huguenots, and Catholics. Calvinists in the Netherlands organized the Dutch Reformed Church. To avoid persecution, "field preachers" gave sermons in the countryside, away from the eyes of town authorities.

In Scotland, a Calvinist preacher named John Knox led a religious rebellion. Under Knox, Scottish Protestants overthrew their Catholic queen. They then set up the Scottish Presbyterian Church.

Calvin on Greed

John Calvin warns his followers in Geneva and elsewhere against worldly values:

"We have a frenzied desire, an infinite eagerness, to pursue wealth and honor, intrigue for power, accumulate riches, and collect all those frivolities [extras] which seem conducive to luxury and splendor. On the other hand, we have a remarkable dread, a remarkable hatred of poverty, mean birth, and a humble condition, and feel the strongest desire to guard against them. . . . The course which Christian men must follow is this: first, they must not long for, or hope for, or think of any kind of prosperity apart from the blessing of God; on it they must cast themselves, and there safely and confidently recline."

—John Calvin, *On the Christian Life*

Skills Assessment

Primary Source What activities did John Calvin warn against?

SECTION 3 Assessment

Recall

1. **Identify: (a)** Protestant Reformation, **(b)** Martin Luther, **(c)** Peace of Augsburg, **(d)** John Calvin, **(e)** Huguenot, **(f)** John Knox.
2. **Define: (a)** indulgence, **(b)** recant, **(c)** predestination, **(d)** theocracy.

Comprehension

3. Why did many Christians call for Church reform?
4. **(a)** How did Martin Luther's ideas differ from those expressed by the Catholic Church?

(b) Why did Luther gain wide-spread support?
5. Identify five ideas taught by John Calvin.

Critical Thinking and Writing

6. **Synthesizing Information** How did the Reformation reflect humanist ideas?
7. **Analyzing Information** Why do you think Luther's teachings caused a split in the Catholic Church when earlier reform movements did not?

Activity

Writing an Obituary
Read some obituaries, or death notices, in a current newspaper. Then, using the same style of writing, prepare a brief obituary of Martin Luther. The obituary should list key events in Luther's life and explain why he will be remembered. Try to avoid bias.

Reformation Ideas Spread

Reading Focus

- What ideas did radical reformers support?
- Why did England form a new church?
- How did the Catholic Church reform itself?
- Why did some groups face persecution?

Vocabulary

annul

canonize

compromise

scapegoat

ghetto

Taking Notes

On a sheet of paper draw a Venn diagram like the one shown here. As you read the section, add information from the text.

ENGLISH REFORMATION
- King Henry VIII establishes Church of England
- Widespread persecution

CATHOLIC REFORMATION
- Council of Trent

Main Idea Both the Protestant and Catholic reformations brought sweeping changes to Europe.

Setting the Scene

Henry III, the Catholic king of France, was deeply disturbed by Calvinist reformers in Geneva. "It would have been a good thing," he wrote, "if the city of Geneva were long ago reduced to ashes, because of the evil doctrine which has been sown from that city."

Throughout Europe, Catholic monarchs and the Catholic Church fought back against the Protestant challenge. They also took steps to reform the Church and to restore its spiritual leadership of the Christian world. At the same time, Protestant ideas continued to spread.

Radical Reformers

As the Reformation continued, hundreds of new Protestant sects sprang up. These sects often had ideas that were even more radical than those of Luther and Calvin. A number of groups, for example, rejected infant baptism. Infants, they argued, are too young to understand what it means to accept the Christian faith. Only adults, they felt, should receive the sacrament of baptism. They became known as Anabaptists.

A few Anabaptist sects sought radical social change as well. Some wanted to abolish private property. Others sought to speed up the coming of God's day of judgment by violent means. When radical Anabaptists took over the city of Munster in Germany, even Luther advised his supporters to join Catholics in suppressing the threat to the traditional order.

Most Anabaptists were peaceful. They called for religious toleration and separation of church and state. Despite harsh persecution, these groups influenced Protestant thinking in many countries. Today, the Baptists, Quakers, Mennonites, and Amish all trace their ancestry to the Anabaptists.

The English Reformation

In England, religious leaders such as John Wycliffe had called for Church reform as early as the 1300s. By the 1520s, some English clergy were toying with Protestant ideas. The break with the Catholic Church, however, was the work not of religious leaders but of King Henry VIII. For political reasons, Henry wanted to end papal control over the English church.

Seeking an Annulment At first, Henry VIII stood firmly against the Protestant revolt. The pope even awarded him the title "Defender of the Faith" for a pamphlet that he wrote denouncing Luther.

Henry VIII
Henry VIII wrote love songs, played tennis, and married six times. He was also ruthless to his enemies. He had dozens of people beheaded, including his second and fifth wives.

Theme: Impact of the Individual What impression of Henry do you get from this picture?

In 1527, an issue arose that set Henry at odds with the Church. After 18 years of marriage, Henry and his Spanish wife, Catherine of Aragon, had one surviving child, Mary Tudor. Henry felt that England's stability depended on his having a male heir. He wanted to marry Anne Boleyn, hoping that she would bear him a son. Because Catholic law does not permit divorce, he asked the pope to annul, or cancel, his marriage. Popes had annulled royal marriages before. But the current pope refused. He did not want to offend the Holy Roman emperor Charles V, Catherine's nephew.

Break With Rome   Henry was furious. Spurred on by his advisers, many of whom leaned toward Protestant teachings, he decided to take over the English church. Acting through Parliament, he had a series of laws passed. They took the English church from the pope's control and placed it under Henry's rule. In 1534, the Act of Supremacy made Henry "the only supreme head on Earth of the Church of England." Many loyal Catholics refused to accept the Act of Supremacy and were executed for treason. Among them was Sir Thomas More, the great English humanist. More was later canonized, or recognized as a saint, by the Catholic Church.

At the same time, Henry appointed Thomas Cranmer archbishop. Cranmer annulled the king's marriage. Henry then wed Anne Boleyn, who bore him a second daughter, Elizabeth. In the years ahead, Henry married four more times but had only one son, Edward.

The Church of England   Between 1536 and 1540, royal officials investigated English convents and monasteries. Claiming that they were centers of immorality, Henry ordered them closed. He then confiscated, or seized, their lands and wealth. Henry shrewdly granted some of these lands to nobles and other high-ranking citizens. He thus secured their support for the Anglican Church, as the new Church of England was called.

Despite these actions, Henry was not a religious radical. He rejected most Protestant doctrines. Aside from breaking away from Rome and allowing use of the English Bible, he kept most Catholic forms of worship.

Religious Turmoil   When Henry died in 1547, his 10-year-old son, Edward VI, inherited the throne. The young king's advisers were devout Protestants. Under Edward, Parliament passed new laws that brought the Protestant reforms to England. Thomas Cranmer drew up the *Book of Common Prayer*. It imposed a moderate form of Protestant service, while keeping many Catholic doctrines. Even so, the changes sparked uprisings that were harshly suppressed.

When Edward died in his teens, his half-sister, Mary Tudor, became queen. She was determined to return England to the Catholic faith. Under Queen Mary, hundreds of English Protestants were burned at the stake.

The Elizabethan Settlement   On Mary's death in 1558, the throne passed to Elizabeth. For years, Elizabeth had survived court intrigues, including the religious swings under Edward and Mary. As queen, Elizabeth had to determine the future of the Church of England. Moving cautiously at first, she slowly enforced a series of reforms that later were called the Elizabethan settlement.

The queen's policies were a compromise, or acceptable middle ground, between Protestant and Catholic practices. The Church of England preserved much Catholic ceremony and ritual. It kept the hierarchy of bishops and archbishops, but the queen reaffirmed that the monarch was the head of the Anglican Church. At the same time, Elizabeth restored a version of the *Book of Common Prayer*, accepted moderate Protestant doctrine, and allowed English to replace Latin in church services.

During a long reign, Elizabeth used all her skills to restore unity to England. Even while keeping many Catholic traditions, she made England a firmly Protestant nation. After her death, England faced new religious

Biography

Elizabeth I 1533–1603

"She takes great pleasure in dancing and music," noted an English observer of Queen Elizabeth I. "In her youth she danced very well and composed measures and music and had played them herself." The normally thrifty queen employed some 50 singers, 40 musicians, and several songwriters to stage concerts for her.

Elizabeth also loved to see plays. She especially enjoyed the works of William Shakespeare, whom she helped to promote. The queen provided financial support and prestige for major acting groups, which led to a flowering of English theater.

Elizabeth's popular 45-year reign inspired other writers of the day. Poet Edmund Spenser dedicated *The Faerie Queene* to Elizabeth.

Theme: Impact of the Individual How did Queen Elizabeth help promote English arts?

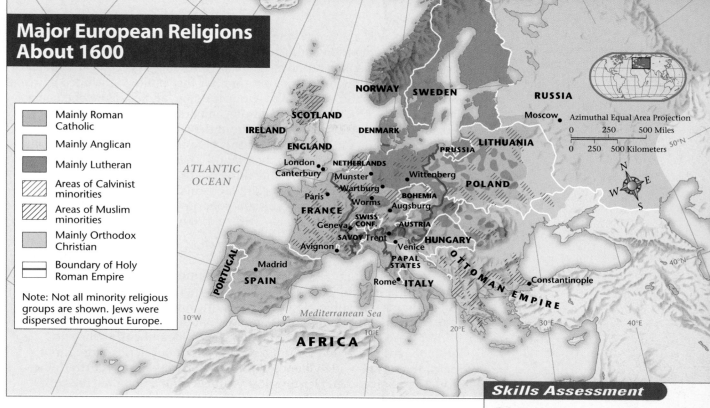

Major European Religions About 1600

Mainly Roman Catholic

Mainly Anglican

Mainly Lutheran

Areas of Calvinist minorities

Areas of Muslim minorities

Mainly Orthodox Christian

Boundary of Holy Roman Empire

Note: Not all minority religious groups are shown. Jews were dispersed throughout Europe.

Azimuthal Equal Area Projection

0 250 500 Miles

0 250 500 Kilometers

storms. But it escaped the endless religious wars that tore apart France and many other European states during the 1500s.

The Catholic Reformation

As the Protestant Reformation swept across northern Europe, a vigorous reform movement took hold within the Catholic Church. The leader of this movement, known as the Catholic Reformation, was Pope Paul III. During the 1530s and 1540s, he set out to revive the moral authority of the Church and roll back the Protestant tide. To end corruption within the papacy itself, he appointed reformers to key posts. They and their successors guided the Catholic Reformation for the rest of the century.

Council of Trent   To establish the direction that reform should take, the pope called the Council of Trent in 1545. It met off and on for almost 20 years. The council reaffirmed traditional Catholic views, which Protestants had challenged. Salvation comes through faith and good works, it declared. The Bible, while a major source of religious truth, is not the only source.

The council also took steps to end abuses in the Church. It provided stiff penalties for worldliness and corruption among the clergy. It also established schools to create a better-educated clergy who could challenge Protestant teachings.

The Inquisition   To deal with the Protestant threat more directly, Pope Paul strengthened the Inquisition. As you have read, the Inquisition was a Church court set up during the Middle Ages. The Inquisition used secret testimony, torture, and execution to root out heresy. It also prepared the Index of Forbidden Books, a list of works considered too immoral or irreligious for Catholics to read. It included books by Luther and Calvin.

Ignatius of Loyola   In 1540, the pope recognized a new religious order, the Society of Jesus, or Jesuits. Founded by Ignatius of Loyola, the Jesuit order was determined to combat heresy and spread the Catholic faith.

Skills Assessment

Geography As a result of the Reformation, Europe was largely divided into Catholic and Protestant lands.

1. **Location**   On the map, locate **(a)** England, **(b)** Scotland, **(c)** Wittenberg, **(d)** Worms, **(e)** Geneva.
2. **Region**   **(a)** What was the majority religion in France? **(b)** Name one country that was mainly Lutheran.
3. **Critical Thinking**
   Predicting Consequences Based on this map, identify two areas where you think religious conflicts would be least likely to break out. Explain.

Ignatius was a Spanish knight raised in the crusading tradition. After his leg was shattered in battle, he found comfort reading about saints who had overcome mental and physical torture. Vowing to become a "soldier of God," Ignatius drew up a strict program for the Jesuits. It included spiritual and moral discipline, rigorous religious training, and absolute obedience to the Church. Led by Ignatius, the Jesuits embarked on a crusade to defend and spread the Catholic faith throughout the world.

To further the Catholic cause, Jesuits became advisers to Catholic rulers, helping them combat heresy in their lands. They set up schools that taught humanist and Catholic beliefs and enforced discipline and obedience. Daring Jesuits slipped into Protestant lands in disguise to minister to the spiritual needs of Catholics. Jesuit missionaries spread their Catholic faith to distant lands, including Asia, Africa, and the Americas.

Teresa of Avila As the Catholic Reformation spread, many Catholics experienced renewed feelings of intense faith. Teresa of Avila symbolized this renewal. Born into a wealthy Spanish family, Teresa entered a convent in her youth. Finding convent routine not strict enough, she set up her own order of nuns. They lived in isolation, eating and sleeping very little and dedicating themselves to prayer and meditation.

Impressed by her spiritual life, her superiors in the Church asked Teresa to reorganize and reform convents and monasteries throughout Spain. Teresa was widely honored for her work, and after her death the Church canonized her. Her mystical writings rank among the most important Christian texts of her time.

Results Did the Catholic Reformation succeed? By 1600, Rome was a far more devout city than it had been 100 years earlier. Across Catholic Europe, piety and charity flourished. The reforms did slow the Protestant tide and even returned some areas to the Catholic Church. Still, Europe remained divided into a Catholic south and a Protestant north.

Widespread Persecution

During this period of heightened religious passion, persecution was widespread. Both Catholics and Protestants fostered intolerance. Catholic mobs attacked and killed Protestants. Protestants killed Catholic priests and wrecked Catholic churches. Both Catholics and Protestants persecuted radical sects like the Anabaptists.

Witch Hunts Almost certainly, the religious fervor of the times contributed to a wave of witch hunting. Those accused of being witches, or agents of the devil, were usually women, although some men faced similar attacks. Between 1450 and 1750, tens of thousands of women and men died as victims of witch hunts.

Scholars have offered various reasons for this persecution. At the time, most people believed in magic and spirits. They saw a close link between magic and heresy. In addition, during times of trouble, people often look for scapegoats on whom they can blame their problems. People accused of witchcraft were often social outcasts—beggars, poor widows, midwives blamed for infant deaths, or herbalists whose potions were seen as gifts from the devil.

Most victims of the witch hunts died in the German states, Switzerland, and France, all centers of religious conflict. When the wars of religion came to an end, the persecution of witches also declined.

Jews and the Reformation The Reformation brought hard times to Europe's Jews. For many Jews in Italy, the early Renaissance had been a time of relative prosperity. Unlike Spain, which had expelled its Jews in 1492, Italy allowed Jews to remain. Some Jews followed the traditional trades they had

Global Connections

Witch Hunt in Salem

Witch hunts were not just a European phenomenon. They also took place across the Atlantic in the English colonies. In 1692, a witch hunt broke out in the town of Salem Village, Massachusetts. The panic began when two girls suffered strange fits. When coaxed to explain their behavior, the girls accused neighbors of casting spells on them. Soon, accusations spread like wildfire throughout the town. Before the witch hunt ended the following year, at least 200 people had been named, and 20 people had been executed as witches.

Theme: Political and Social Systems How did witch hunts disrupt communities during the Renaissance?

been restricted to in medieval times. They were goldsmiths, artists, traders, and moneylenders. Others expanded into medicine, law, government, and business. Still, pressure remained strong on Jews to convert. By 1516, Venice ordered Jews to live in a separate quarter of the city, which became known as a ghetto. Other Italian cities also forced Jews into walled ghettos.

During the Reformation, restrictions on Jews increased. At first, Luther hoped that Jews would be converted to his teachings. However, when they did not convert, he called for them to be expelled from Christian lands and for their synagogues and books to be burned. In time, some German princes did expel Jews. Others confined Jews to ghettos, requiring them to wear a yellow badge if they traveled outside.

In the 1550s, Pope Paul IV placed added restrictions on Jews. Even Emperor Charles V, who supported toleration of Jews in the Holy Roman Empire, banned them from Spanish colonies in the Americas. After 1550, many Jews migrated to Poland-Lithuania and to parts of the Ottoman empire, where they were permitted to prosper. Dutch Calvinists allowed Jewish families who were driven out of Portugal and Spain to settle in the Netherlands.

Looking Ahead

The upheavals of the Catholic and Protestant reformations sparked wars of religion in Europe until the mid-1600s. At that time, issues of religion began to give way to issues of national power. As you will read, Catholic and Protestant rulers often made decisions based on political interests rather than for purely religious reasons.

Cause and Effect

Long-Term Causes	Immediate Causes
• Roman Catholic Church becomes more worldly • Humanists urge a return to simple religion • Strong national monarchs emerge	• Johann Tetzel sells indulgences in Wittenberg • Martin Luther posts 95 Theses • Luther translates the Bible into German • Printing press allows spread of reform ideas • Calvin and other reformers preach against Roman Catholic traditions

Protestant Reformation

Immediate Effects	Long-Term Effects
• Peasants' Revolt • Founding of Lutheran, Calvinist, Anglican, Presbyterian, and other Protestant churches • Weakening of Holy Roman Empire • Luther calls for Jews to be expelled from Christian lands	• Religious wars in Europe • Catholic Reformation • Strengthening of the Inquisition • Jewish migration to Eastern Europe • Increased antisemitism

Connections to Today

• About one fourth of Christians are Protestant
• Religious conflict in Northern Ireland

Skills Assessment **Chart** The Protestant Reformation brought sweeping changes to Western Europe. **Identify one religious and one political effect of the Reformation.**

SECTION 4 **Assessment**

Recall
1. **Identify:** (a) Henry VIII, (b) Elizabeth I, (c) Council of Trent, (d) Inquisition, (e) Jesuits, (f) Teresa of Avila.
2. **Define:** (a) annul, (b) canonize, (c) compromise, (d) scapegoat, (e) ghetto.

Comprehension
3. Why were the Anabaptists considered radical?
4. Describe the steps by which England became a Protestant country.
5. What were the goals of the Catholic Reformation?

6. Why did persecution increase after the Reformation?

Critical Thinking and Writing
7. **Recognizing Causes and Effects** If the Catholic Church had undertaken reform earlier, do you think that the Protestant Reformation would have occurred? Explain.
8. **Recognizing Point of View** The Protestant term for the Catholic Reformation was the Counter-Reformation. (The prefix *counter* means "against.") How do these two terms reflect different points of view?

Activity
Writing a News Report Prepare a script for a TV news program reporting on King Henry VIII and his break with the Catholic Church. You might wish to include visuals and interviews as well.

Reading Focus

- How did astronomers change the way people viewed the universe?

- What was the new scientific method?

- What advances did Newton and other scientists make?

Vocabulary

heliocentric
hypothesis
scientific method
gravity

Taking Notes

On a sheet of paper, begin a concept web like this one. As you read this section, fill in the blank circles with information about the Scientific Revolution. Add as many other circles as you need.

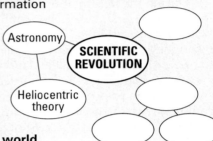

Astronomy · **SCIENTIFIC REVOLUTION** · Heliocentric theory

Main Idea — A new way of thinking, based on experimentation and observation, changed the way Europeans looked at the world.

Galileo

In addition to his work in astronomy, Galileo made important discoveries about the motion of pendulums and falling objects. This statue honors Galileo.

Theme: Impact of the Individual In this statue, what might be the meaning of the object Galileo holds in his hand?

Setting the Scene In 1609, Galileo Galilei trained his new telescope on the night sky. Its specially ground lens allowed him to view amazing sights. He saw mountains on the moon, fiery spots on the sun, and four moons circling the planet Jupiter. "I did discover many particulars in Heaven that had been unseen and unheard of until this our age," he later wrote. Galileo's observations supported a new view of the universe.

Leaders of the Renaissance and the Reformation looked to the past for models. Humanists turned to ancient classical ideas. Religious reformers were inspired by the Bible and early Christian times. By contrast, the profound change that took place in science in the mid-1500s pointed ahead, toward a future shaped by a new way of thinking about the physical universe. We call that historical change the Scientific Revolution.

Changing Views of the Universe

Until the mid-1500s, European scholars accepted the theory of the ancient Greek astronomer Ptolemy. Ptolemy taught that the Earth was the center of the universe. Not only did this view seem to agree with common sense, it also matched the teachings of the Church. In the 1500s and 1600s, some startling discoveries radically changed the way Europeans viewed the physical world.

A Revolutionary Theory In 1543, Polish scholar Nicolaus Copernicus (koh PER nuh kuhs) published *On the Revolutions of the Heavenly Spheres*. In it, he proposed a heliocentric, or sun-centered, model of the universe. The sun, he said, stood at the center of the universe. The Earth was just one of several planets that revolved around the sun.

Most experts rejected this revolutionary theory. In Europe at the time, all scientific knowledge and many religious teachings were based on the arguments developed by classical thinkers. If Ptolemy's reasoning about the planets was wrong, they believed, then the whole system of human knowledge might be called into question. But in the late 1500s, the Danish astronomer Tycho Brahe (TEE koh BRAH uh) provided evidence that supported Copernicus's theory. Brahe set up an astronomical observatory. Every night for years, he carefully observed the sky, accumulating data about the movement of the heavenly bodies.

After Brahe's death, his assistant, the brilliant German astronomer and mathematician Johannes Kepler, used Brahe's data to calculate the orbits of the planets revolving around the sun. His calculations supported Copernicus's heliocentric view. At the same time, however, they showed that each planet did not move in a perfect circle, as both Ptolemy and Copernicus believed, but in an oval-shaped orbit called an ellipse.

Galileo Scientists of many lands built on the foundations laid by Copernicus and Kepler. In Italy, Galileo Galilei assembled an astronomical telescope. As you have read, he observed the four moons of Jupiter moving slowly around that planet—exactly, he realized, the way Copernicus said that the Earth moved around the sun.

Galileo's discoveries caused an uproar. Other scholars attacked him because his observations contradicted ancient views about the world. The Church condemned him because his ideas challenged the Christian teaching that the heavens were fixed, unmoving, and perfect.

In 1633, Galileo was tried before the Inquisition. Threatened with death unless he withdrew his "heresies," Galileo agreed to state publicly that the Earth stood motionless at the center of the universe. "Nevertheless," he is said to have muttered as he left the court, "it does move."

A New Scientific Method

Despite the opposition of religious authorities, by the early 1600s a new approach to science had emerged. Unlike most earlier approaches, it did not rely on authorities like Aristotle or Ptolemy or even the Bible. It depended instead upon observation and experimentation.

A Step-by-Step Process The new approach to science required scientists to collect and accurately measure data. To explain the data, scientists used reasoning to propose a logical hypothesis, or possible explanation. They then tested the hypothesis with further observation or experimentation. Complex mathematical calculations were used to convert the observations and experiments into scientific laws. After reaching a conclusion, scientists repeated their work at least once—and usually many times—to confirm their findings. This step-by-step process of discovery became known as the scientific method.

Bacon and Descartes The new scientific method was really a revolution in thought. Two giants of this revolution were the Englishman Francis Bacon and the Frenchman René Descartes (ruh NAY day KAHRT). Each devoted himself to the problem of knowledge.

Skills Assessment

Chart The scientific method, still used today, was based on careful observation and measurement of objective data. **Why do you think step 7 is important?**

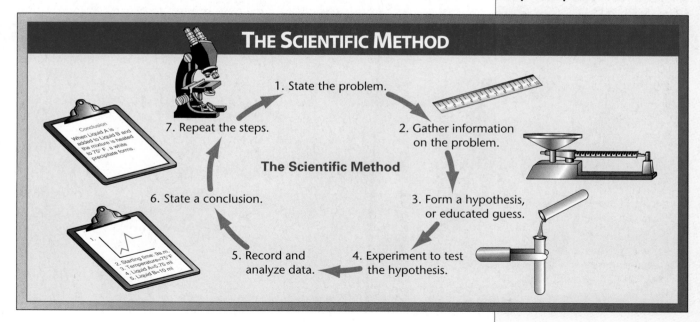

THE SCIENTIFIC METHOD

The Scientific Method

1. State the problem.
2. Gather information on the problem.
3. Form a hypothesis, or educated guess.
4. Experiment to test the hypothesis.
5. Record and analyze data.
6. State a conclusion.
7. Repeat the steps.

Conclusion: When Liquid A is added to Liquid B and the mixture is heated to 75° F, a white precipitate forms.

Both Bacon and Descartes rejected Aristotle's scientific assumptions. They also challenged the scholarly traditions of the medieval universities that sought to make the physical world fit in with the teachings of the Church. Both argued that truth is not known at the beginning of inquiry but at the end, after a long process of investigation.

Bacon and Descartes differed in their methods, however. Bacon stressed experimentation and observation. He wanted science to make life better for people by leading to practical technologies. Descartes emphasized human reasoning as the best road to understanding. In his *Discourse on Method,* he explains how he decided to discard all traditional authorities and search for provable knowledge. Left only with doubt, he concluded that the doubter had to exist and made his famous statement, "I think, therefore I am."

Newton Ties It All Together

As a student in England, Isaac Newton devoured the works of the leading scientists of his day. By age 24, he had formed a brilliant theory to explain why the planets moved as they did. According to one story, Newton saw an apple fall from a tree. He wondered whether the force that pulled that apple to the Earth might not also control the movements of the planets.

In the next 20 years, Newton perfected his theory. Using mathematics, he showed that a single force keeps the planets in their orbits around the sun. He called this force gravity.

In 1687, Newton published *Mathematical Principles of Natural Philosophy,* explaining the law of gravity and other workings of the universe. Nature, argued Newton, follows uniform laws. All motion in the universe can be measured and described mathematically.

To many, Newton's work seemed to link physics and astronomy, to bind the new science as gravity itself held the universe together. An English poet caught the spirit of what would later be called the Newtonian revolution:

"Nature and Nature's Laws lay hid in night,
 God said, Let Newton be! and all was light."
  —Alexander Pope, *Epitaphs*

For over 200 years, Newton's laws held fast. In the early 1900s, startling new theories of the universe called some of Newton's ideas into question.

Exploring Human Anatomy
Leonardo da Vinci dissected more than 30 corpses in order to create precise sketches of the human body (PAST). Today, doctors study anatomy with the aid of advanced computer technology (PRESENT).

Theme: Economics and Technology How were anatomical drawings useful to Leonardo? How is computer imaging useful to doctors today?

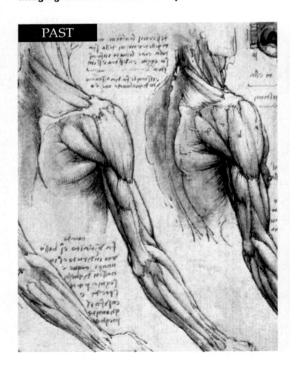

PAST

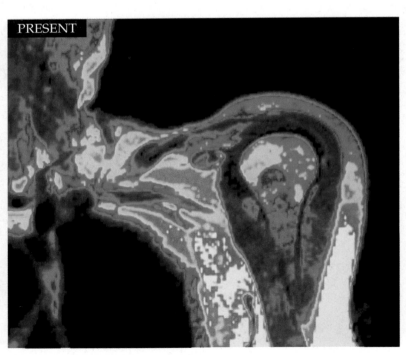

PRESENT

Yet Newton's laws of motion and mechanics continue to have many practical uses. Newton also helped develop an important new branch of mathematics—calculus.

Other Scientific Advances

The 1500s and 1600s saw breakthroughs in many branches of science. Some of the most significant advances occurred in chemistry and medicine.

Chemistry Chemistry slowly freed itself from the magical notions of medieval alchemists, who had believed it was possible to transform ordinary metals into gold. In the 1600s, Robert Boyle distinguished between individual elements and chemical compounds. He also explained the effect of temperature and pressure on gases. Boyle's work opened the way to modern chemical analysis of the composition of matter.

Medicine Medieval physicians relied on the ancient works of Galen. Galen, however, had made many errors, in part because he had limited knowledge of human anatomy. During the Renaissance, artists and physicians made new efforts to study the human body. In 1543, Andreas Vesalius published *On the Structure of the Human Body*, the first accurate and detailed study of human anatomy. A French physician, Ambroise Paré, developed a new and more effective ointment for preventing infection. He also developed a technique for closing wounds with stitches.

In the early 1600s, William Harvey, an English scholar, described the circulation of the blood for the first time. He showed how the heart serves as a pump to force blood through veins and arteries. Later in the century, the Dutch inventor Anthony van Leeuwenhoek perfected the microscope and became the first human to see cells and microorganisms. These pioneering scientists opened the way for further advances.

Looking Ahead

The rapid advance in science and technology that began in the 1500s has continued to this day. Thinkers like Bacon, Descartes, and Newton applied the scientific method to the pursuit of knowledge. Their work encouraged others to search for scientific laws governing the universe. Such ideas opened the way to the Enlightenment of the 1700s and a growing belief in human progress.

SECTION 5 Assessment

Recall

1. **Identify:** (a) Nicolaus Copernicus, (b) Johannes Kepler, (c) Galileo Galilei, (d) Francis Bacon, (e) René Descartes, (f) Isaac Newton, (g) Robert Boyle.
2. **Define:** (a) heliocentric, (b) hypothesis, (c) scientific method, (d) gravity.

Comprehension

3. Why did some people oppose the heliocentric theory of the universe?
4. How did the scientific method differ from earlier approaches?

5. How did Newton try to explain the workings of the universe?

Critical Thinking and Writing

6. **Making Inferences** Newton wrote, "If I have seen further [than others] it is by standing on the shoulders of giants." (a) What do you think he meant? (b) Who might be some of the "giants" to whom Newton was referring?
7. **Applying Information** Identify three ways in which your life today might have been different if the Scientific Revolution had never occurred.

Activity

Take It to the NET

Use the Internet to learn more about the life and work of William Harvey. Then, prepare a brief biographical sketch of Harvey. Include a diagram of the circulatory system that he described.

Creating a Chapter Summary

On a sheet of paper make a table like the one shown here. Use it to summarize major events that you have learned about in this chapter. Some cells have been partly filled in to help you get started.

iTEXT

For additional review and enrichment activities, see the interactive version of *World History* available on the Web and on CD-ROM.

	RENAISSANCE	PROTESTANT REFORMATION	CATHOLIC REFORMATION	SCIENTIFIC REVOLUTION
WHAT IT WAS	• Time of creativity and change			
CAUSES				
IMPORTANT EVENTS		• Luther posts 95 Theses •		
KEY PEOPLE			• Ignatius of Loyola •	

Web Site Self-Test
For practice test questions for Chapter 14, see **www.phschool.com**.

Building Vocabulary

Write sentences using the chapter vocabulary words listed below, leaving blanks where the vocabulary words would go. Then, exchange your sentences with another student, and fill in the blanks in each other's sentences.

1. patron
2. humanism
3. vernacular
4. utopian
5. indulgence
6. predestination
7. annul
8. ghetto
9. heliocentric
10. hypothesis

Recalling Key Facts

11. **(a)** What was the Renaissance? **(b)** When and where did it begin?
12. What three different kinds of plays did William Shakespeare write?
13. Why did Martin Luther post his 95 Theses?
14. How did the English Reformation occur?
15. What is the scientific method?
16. What did Descartes mean by the statement "I think, therefore I am"?

Critical Thinking and Writing

17. **Connecting to Geography** How did artists translate new techniques of the Renaissance to their landscape paintings?

18. **Comparing** **(a)** Compare and contrast the Renaissance in Italy with the Renaissance in northern Europe. **(b)** How would you account for the differences?

19. **Understanding Sequence** An English author wrote, "The preaching of sermons is speaking to a few of mankind, but printing books is talking to the whole world." How does this statement suggest a relationship between two of the key events discussed in this chapter?

20. **Recognizing Causes and Effects** Why did England escape the kinds of religious wars that tore apart other European nations?

21. **Linking Past and Present** Modern scientists refer to the discoveries of Copernicus as the Copernican Revolution. Why do you think they use that term?

The passage below is from the Council of Trent called by Pope Paul III in 1545 to establish the direction of Catholic reform. Read the passage, then answer the questions that follow.

"This holy Council cautions all bishops so to live . . . that they can bring together truth and behavior as a kind of constant example of thrift, modesty, and decency, and especially of that holy humility that so strongly commends men to God. Therefore, following the example set by our fathers at the Council of Carthage, it is ordered that bishops shall content them-selves not only with modest household furniture and simple food, but with regard to the rest of their manner of living and to their whole house, so that nothing appears that is alien to this holy institution of the Church and that does not show simplicity, zeal for God, and contempt for worldly things."

—Canons and Decrees of the
Holy Council of Trent

22. To what group of people is this passage mainly addressed?
23. **(a)** What orders are given in the passage? **(b)** On what authority are these orders given?
24. What does this document imply about the situation in the Church before the Council?
25. How can you tell that the reformers at the Council of Trent looked to the example of the early Christian Church?
26. **(a)** Do you think the reformers at Trent would agree with Protestant reformers about world-liness in the Church? **(b)** Do you think they would agree about the subject of papal authority?

Skills Assessment
Take It to the NET

Use the Internet to research the invention of the printing press and its effects on Renaissance Europe. Then, write an essay in which you try to persuade the reader that the invention of the Internet either will or will not have a similar effect on world civilization in the future.

Michelangelo sculpted this huge statue of the Israelite prophet Moses for the tomb of Pope Julius II. It stands almost eight feet tall and took years to complete. Study the statue, then answer the following questions:

27. How was this choice of subject typical of the Renaissance?
28. How does the sculpture show Renaissance humanism?
29. How does the sculpture show Michelangelo's atten-tion to anatomical detail?
30. Why would an artist like Michelangelo need the support of a powerful patron like the pope?

Skills Tip

When you study a work of art, use what you know about the period in which it was created. In particular, it is important to understand what themes and topics were of con-cern to artists of that period.

The First Global Age: Europe and Asia

1415–1796

Chapter Preview

1 The Search for Spices

2 Diverse Traditions of Southeast Asia

3 European Footholds in Southeast Asia and India

4 Encounters in East Asia

CHAPTER EVENTS

1498

Portuguese explorer Vasco da Gama reaches India after rounding Africa. His voyage sets the stage for the rise of a Portuguese trading empire.

1511

Portugal seizes Malacca.

1522

The *Vittoria* completes the first circumnavigation of the globe. The expedition's original leader, Ferdinand Magellan, and four other ships do not survive the voyage.

1400   1480   1560

GLOBAL EVENTS

1456 The Gutenberg Bible is printed.

1500 The kingdom of Kongo thrives.

1519 Hernan Cortés lands in Mexico.

Trade Between Europe, Africa, and Asia About 1700

Ocean trade routes permitted the development of cultural and economic ties between Europe, Africa, and Asia.

Ports controlled by
- England
- Portugal
- France
- Netherlands
- Spain
- Trade routes

20°W 0°

ENGLAND NETHERLANDS
EUROPE
FRANCE
PORTUGAL SPAIN

40°N

ASIA

JAPAN
Deshima

Canary Islands

PERSIA

CHINA
Macao

PACIFIC OCEAN

ARABIA

INDIA
Bombay
Calcutta

East China Sea

From Mexico 20°N

Cape Verde Islands
Bissau

Arabian Sea

Goa
Madras
Cochin

Manila

AFRICA

Bay of Bengal

South China Sea

PHILIPPINES

Accra

São Tomé

ATLANTIC OCEAN

60°E 80°E

INDIAN OCEAN

Malacca

100°E

From Europe

Mombasa
Zanzibar

0°

Batavia

EAST INDIES

120°E 140°E

Mozambique
Sofala

MADAGASCAR

20°S

Ft. Dauphin

AUSTRALIA

Cape Town

20°E 40°E

40°S

Robinson Projection

0 500 1000 Miles

0 500 1000 Kilometers

N W E S

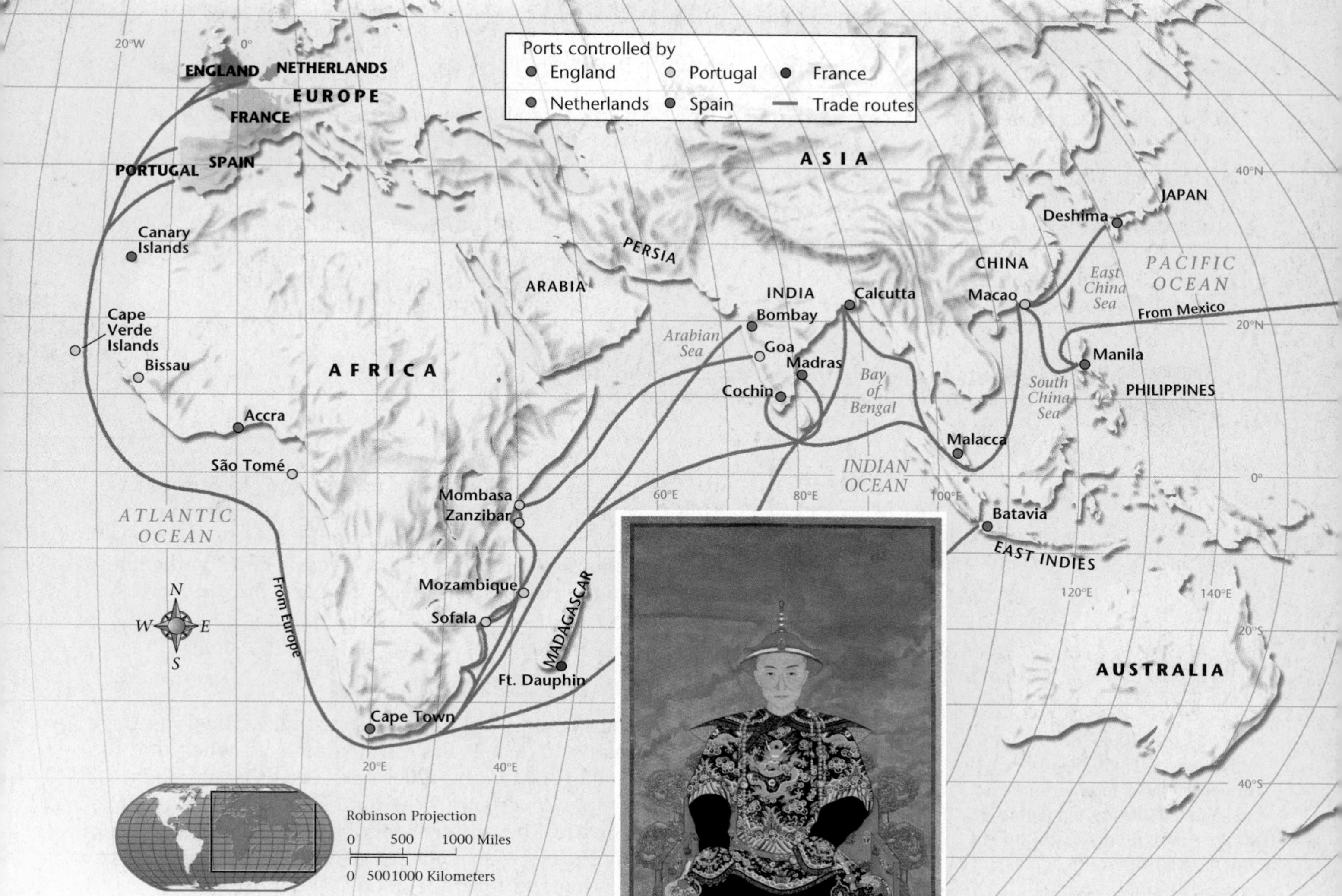

1641
The Dutch seize Malacca from the Portuguese.

1736
China's Emperor Qianlong, shown here, begins a long reign. Qianlong expands China's territory but rejects western efforts to increase trade with China.

1640 1720 1800

1630s Japan bars western merchants.

1642 The English Civil War begins.

1789 The French Revolution begins.

The Search for Spices

Reading Focus

- Why did Europeans cross the seas?
- How did Portugal's eastward explorations lead to the development of a trading empire?
- How did Columbus's voyages affect the search for a passage to the Indies?

Vocabulary

cartographer
astrolabe
caravel
scurvy
circumnavigate

Taking Notes

Copy the table below. As you read the section, add information about the explorations of Portugal and Spain in the 1400s and 1500s.

PORTUGAL	SPAIN
• Henry the Navigator sponsors voyages •	• Columbus sails for India; reaches Caribbean •

Main Idea A desire to share in the rich spice trade of the East spurred Europeans to explore the oceans.

Setting the Scene Today, we take pepper for granted. To Europeans of past ages, though, this spice was as valuable as gold. Ancient Romans paid as much as $125 for 12 ounces of pepper. During the Middle Ages, the pepper in your local supermarket could have paid a year's rent. By the late 1400s, the desire to share in the rich spice trade of the East spurred Europeans to explore the oceans.

Europeans Explore the Seas

Europeans had traded with Asia long before the Renaissance. The Crusades introduced Europeans to many luxury goods from Asia. Later, when the Mongol empire united much of Asia in the 1200s and 1300s, Asian goods flowed to Europe along complex overland trade routes.

The Black Death and the breakup of the Mongol empire disrupted trade. By the 1400s, though, Europe was recovering from the plague. As its population grew, so did the demand for trade goods. The most valued items were spices, such as cinnamon, cloves, nutmeg, and pepper. People used spices in many ways—to preserve food, add flavor to dried and salted meat, and make medicines and perfumes. The chief source of spices was the Moluccas, an island chain in present-day Indonesia, which Europeans then called the Spice Islands.

Motives In the 1400s, Muslim and Italian merchants controlled most trade between Asia and Europe. Muslim traders brought prized goods to eastern Mediterranean ports. Traders from Venice and other Italian cities then carried the precious cargoes to European markets. Europeans, however, wanted to gain direct access to the riches of Asia. To do so, the Atlantic powers—first Portugal, then Spain—sought a route to Asia that bypassed the Mediterranean.

The desire for wealth was not the only motive that lured people to sea. Some voyagers were still fired by the

The Spice Trade
Voyages of exploration were driven by the desire for access to spices. Nutmeg, cinnamon, cloves, and pepper were among the most prized trade items.

Theme: Economics and Technology Why were spices so costly?

centuries-old desire to crusade against the Muslims. The Renaissance spirit of inquiry further fired people's desire to learn more about the lands beyond Europe.

Improved Technology Several improvements in technology helped Europeans conquer the vast oceans of the world. Cartographers, or map-makers, created more accurate maps and sea charts. European sailors also learned to use the astrolabe, an instrument developed by the ancient Greeks and perfected by the Arabs, to determine their latitude at sea.

Along with more reliable navigational tools, Europeans designed larger and better ships. The Portuguese developed the caravel, which combined the square sails of European ships with Arab lateen, or triangular, sails. Caravels also adapted the sternpost rudder and numerous masts of Chinese ships. The new rigging made it easier to sail across or even into the wind. Finally, European ships added more weaponry, including sturdier cannons.

Portugal Sails Eastward

Portugal, a small nation on the western edge of Spain, led the way in exploration. By the 1400s, Portugal was strong enough to expand into Muslim North Africa. In 1415, the Portuguese seized Ceuta (say oo tah) on the North African coast. The victory sparked the imagination of Prince Henry, known to history as Henry the Navigator.

Mapping the African Coast Prince Henry embodied the crusading drive and the new spirit of exploration. He hoped to expand Christianity and find the source of African gold.

At Sagres, in southern Portugal, Henry gathered scientists, cartographers, and other experts. They redesigned ships, prepared maps, and trained captains and crews for long voyages. Henry then sent out ships that slowly worked their way south to explore the western coast of Africa.

Henry died in 1460, but the Portuguese continued their quest. In 1488, Bartholomeu Dias rounded the southern tip of Africa. Despite the turbulent seas, the tip became known as the Cape of Good Hope because it opened the way for a sea route to Asia.

On to India In 1497, Vasco da Gama led four ships around the Cape of Good Hope. After a 10-month voyage, da Gama finally reached the great spice port of Calicut on the west coast of India. The long voyage home took a heavy toll. The Portuguese lost half their ships. Many sailors died of hunger, thirst, and scurvy, a disease caused by a lack of vitamin C in their diets during months at sea. Still, the venture proved highly profitable to the survivors. In India, da Gama had acquired a cargo of spices that he sold at a profit of 3,000 percent.

Da Gama quickly outfitted a new fleet. In 1502, he forced a treaty of friendship on the ruler of Calicut. Da Gama then left Portuguese merchants there to buy spices when prices were low and to store them near the dock until the next fleet could return. Soon, the Portuguese seized key ports around the Indian Ocean to create a vast trading empire.

Columbus Sails to the West

News of Portugal's successes spurred other nations to look for a sea route to Asia. An Italian navigator from the port of Genoa, Christopher Columbus, sought Portuguese backing for his own plan. He wanted to reach the Indies* by sailing west across the Atlantic. Like most educated Europeans, Columbus knew that the Earth was a sphere. A few weeks

---

*The Indies, or East Indies, was the European name for a group of islands in Southeast Asia. Today, they are a part of Indonesia.

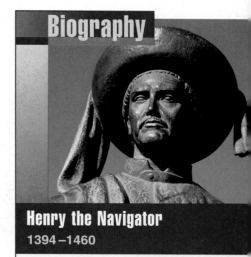

Biography

Henry the Navigator
1394–1460

As a younger son of Portugal's King John I and Queen Philippa, Henry was not destined to rule his nation. This did not stop him, however, from carving out a place in history. During the campaign to conquer Ceuta, in northern Africa, he found his true calling. Inspired by stories of gold beyond the Sahara, he recognized Portugal's need for a sea route to distant lands.

Henry's interest in gaining wealth for Portugal was equaled by his desire to spread Christianity. In 1420, he was made a knight in a religious order. Already the governor of a province in southern Portugal, Henry paid for voyages of exploration with funds provided by the order. Each ship that set out from his court in Sagres bore a red cross on its sails, indicating the dual quest to find new lands and new converts to Christianity.

Theme: Impact of the Individual How might Portugal's history have been different if Henry had been the oldest son?

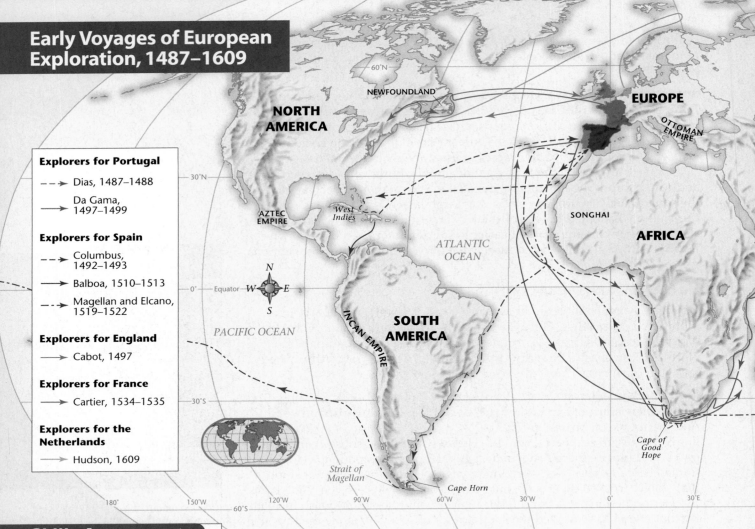

Early Voyages of European Exploration, 1487–1609

60°N

NEWFOUNDLAND

NORTH AMERICA

EUROPE

OTTOMAN EMPIRE

30°N

AZTEC EMPIRE

West Indies

SONGHAI

AFRICA

ATLANTIC OCEAN

Equator 0°

PACIFIC OCEAN

INCAN EMPIRE

SOUTH AMERICA

30°S

Cape of Good Hope

Strait of Magellan

Cape Horn

180°   150°W   120°W   90°W   60°W   30°W   0°   30°E

60°S

Explorers for Portugal
- - -> Dias, 1487–1488
⟶ Da Gama, 1497–1499

Explorers for Spain
- - -> Columbus, 1492–1493
⟶ Balboa, 1510–1513
- · - · Magellan and Elcano, 1519–1522

Explorers for England
⟶ Cabot, 1497

Explorers for France
⟶ Cartier, 1534–1535

Explorers for the Netherlands
⟶ Hudson, 1609

Skills Assessment

Geography Beginning in the later 1400s, European nations sent explorers across the oceans in search of riches. New technology, such as the astrolabe and the caravel, made these voyages possible.

1. **Location** On the map, locate (a) Ottoman empire, (b) West Indies, (c) Strait of Magellan.
2. **Movement** (a) What region seems to have been of the most interest to explorers for England and the Netherlands? (b) What tool would they have used to determine location during their voyage?
3. **Critical Thinking**
   Making Inferences Why do you think explorers tended to take similar routes?

sailing west, he reasoned, would bring a ship to eastern Asia. His plan made sense, but Columbus made two errors. First, he greatly underestimated the size of the Earth. Second, he had no idea that two continents lay in his path.

Voyages of Columbus After Portugal refused to help him, Columbus persuaded Ferdinand and Isabella of Spain to finance his "enterprise of the Indies." In 1492, the Catholic rulers had driven the Muslims from their last stronghold in Spain. To strengthen their power, they sought new sources of wealth. Queen Isabella was also anxious to spread Christianity in Asia.

On August 3, 1492, Columbus sailed west with three small ships, the *Pinta,* the *Niña,* and the *Santa María.* Although the expedition encountered good weather and a favorable wind, no land came into sight. Provisions ran low, and the crew became anxious. Finally, on October 12, a lookout yelled, "Land! Land!"

Columbus then spent several months cruising the islands of the Caribbean. Because he thought he had reached the Indies, he called the people of the region Indians. In 1493, he returned to Spain to a hero's welcome. In three later voyages, Columbus remained convinced he had reached the coast of East Asia. Before long, though, other Europeans realized that Columbus had found a route to continents previously unknown to them.

Line of Demarcation Spain and Portugal pressed rival claims to the lands Columbus explored. In 1493, Pope Alexander VI stepped in to keep the peace. He set a Line of Demarcation dividing the non-European world

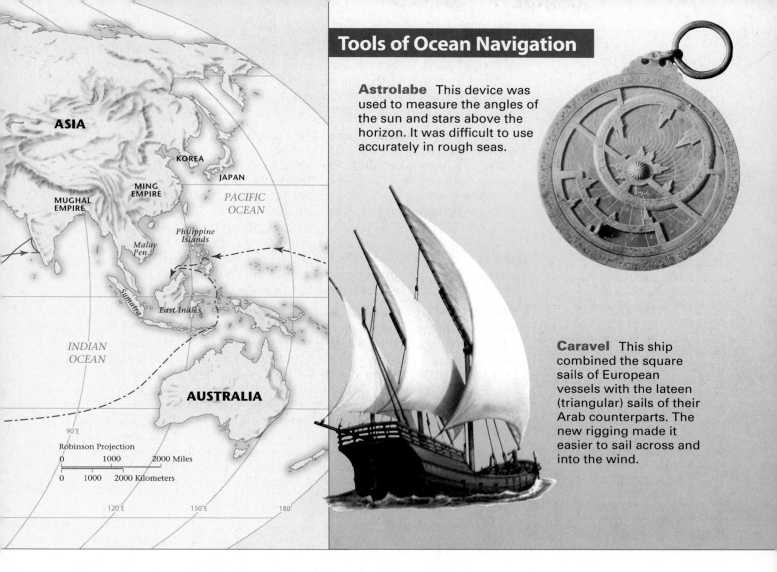

Tools of Ocean Navigation

Astrolabe This device was used to measure the angles of the sun and stars above the horizon. It was difficult to use accurately in rough seas.

Caravel This ship combined the square sails of European vessels with the lateen (triangular) sails of their Arab counterparts. The new rigging made it easier to sail across and into the wind.

Map labels: ASIA, KOREA, JAPAN, MING EMPIRE, MUGHAL EMPIRE, PACIFIC OCEAN, Philippine Islands, Malay Pen., Sumatra, East Indies, INDIAN OCEAN, AUSTRALIA

Robinson Projection
0   1000   2000 Miles
0   1000   2000 Kilometers
90°E   120°E   150°E   180°

---

into two zones. Spain had trading and exploration rights in any lands west of the line. Portugal had the same rights east of the line.

In 1500, the Portuguese captain Pedro Alvarez Cabral was blown off course as he sailed around Africa. Landing in Brazil, which lay east of the Line of Demarcation, he claimed it for Portugal.

Naming the "New World" In 1507, a German cartographer read reports about the "New World" written by an Italian sailor, Amerigo Vespucci. The mapmaker labeled the region America. The islands Columbus had explored in the Caribbean became known as the West Indies.

The Search Continues

Europeans continued to seek new routes around or through the Americas. In 1513, the Spanish adventurer Vasco Núñez de Balboa, with the help of Native Americans, hacked a passage through the tropical forests of Panama. From a ridge on the west coast, he gazed at a huge body of water that he called the South Sea. On September 20, 1519, a minor Portuguese noble named Ferdinand Magellan set out from Spain with five ships. His crew included men from Europe, Africa, and Southeast Asia.

Perils at Sea As the ships sailed south and west, through storms and calms and tropical heat, Magellan had to put down more than one mutiny. At last, the fleet reached the coast of South America. Carefully, they explored each bay, hoping for one that would lead to the Pacific.

In November 1520, Magellan's ships entered a bay at the southern tip of South America. Amid brutal storms, rushing tides, and unpredictable winds, Magellan charted a passage that became known as the Strait of Magellan. The ships emerged from this lashing into Balboa's South Sea, which Magellan renamed the Pacific—peaceful—Ocean.

Circumnavigating the Globe Their mission accomplished, most of the crew wanted to return to Spain the way they had come. Magellan, however, insisted they push on across the Pacific to the East Indies. Three more weeks, he thought, would bring them to the Spice Islands.

Magellan soon found that the Pacific was much wider than he imagined. For nearly four months, the ship plowed across the uncharted ocean. Finally in March 1521, the fleet reached the Philippines. There, Magellan was killed when he got involved in a local conflict. In the end, only one ship and 18 sailors completed the voyage. On September 8, 1522, nearly three years after setting out, the survivors reached Seville. The Spanish hailed them as the first people to circumnavigate, or sail around, the world.

Search for a Northwest Passage "I believe that never more will any man undertake to make such a voyage," predicted Antonio Pigafetta, a survivor of the Magellan voyage. But he was wrong. While Spain and Portugal claimed their zones, English, Dutch, and French explorers searched the coast of North America for a northwest passage to Asia.

In 1497, King Henry VII of England sent a Venetian navigator known as John Cabot to seek a more northerly route than the one Columbus had charted. Cabot found rich fishing grounds off Newfoundland, which he claimed for England. Later the French captain Jacques Cartier explored the St. Lawrence River, while Henry Hudson, sailing for the Dutch, explored the Hudson River. None of them found the hoped-for route to Asia, but the search for a Northwest Passage continued for centuries.

Looking Ahead

The European age of exploration set off a period of growing global interdependence that continues today. Yet the activities of European explorers brought both tragedy and triumph. As trade increased, conflicts between Europe and other civilizations would become more pronounced. These conflicts emerged first in Asia.

SECTION 1 Assessment

Recall
1. **Identify:** **(a)** Henry the Navigator, **(b)** Vasco da Gama, **(c)** Christopher Columbus, **(d)** Vasco Núñez de Balboa, **(e)** Ferdinand Magellan.
2. **Define:** **(a)** cartographer, **(b)** astrolabe, **(c)** caravel, **(d)** scurvy, **(e)** circumnavigate.

Comprehension
3. Why did European nations seek a sea route to Asia?
4. **(a)** Describe the routes taken by explorers for Portugal during the 1400s and early 1500s. **(b)** How did this affect Portugal's trade?

5. **(a)** Why did Columbus decide to sail westward? **(b)** What influence did his voyages have on other explorers?

Critical Thinking and Writing
6. **Making Decisions** What pros and cons would you weigh if you were a sailor trying to decide whether to sign on with da Gama, Columbus, or Magellan?
7. **Comparing** **(a)** In what way were the mistakes that Columbus and Magellan made similar? **(b)** How did their mistakes differ?

Activity
Take It to the NET

Use the Internet to find out about the coat of arms that Christopher Columbus used after his voyages. How did Columbus modify the original plan for his coat of arms? Present your findings and a drawing of the coat of arms to the class.

Diverse Traditions of Southeast Asia

Reading Focus

■ What are the key geographic features of Southeast Asia?

■ What impact did Indian civilization have on new kingdoms and empires?

■ What factors contributed to the growth of Vietnamese culture?

Vocabulary

matrilineal

stupa

padi

Taking Notes

As you read this section, prepare an outline of the contents. Use Roman numerals to indicate major headings. Use capital letters for the subheadings and numbers for the supporting details. The sample at right will help you get started.

I. Geography of Southeast Asia
  A. Location
    1. Mainland set apart by mountains and plateaus
    2.
  B. Trade routes in the southern seas

Main Idea Because of its location, Southeast Asia was affected by the cultures of both China and India.

Setting the Scene
According to the chronicles of early Burma (modern Myanmar), King Anawrata spoke to a Buddhist monk named Thera Arahanta.

> " 'Preach to me somewhat—yea, but a little—of the Law preached by the Lord, the Master.'
> And Arahanta preached the Law, beginning with the things not to be neglected. . . . Then the king's heart was full of faith, steadfast, and immovable. Faith sank into him as oil filtered a hundred times soaks into cotton."
> —*The Glass Palace Chronicle of the Kings of Burma*

Buddhism was one of many exports from India that had a profound effect on the peoples of Southeast Asia. Sandwiched between China and India, the region known today as Southeast Asia was strongly influenced by both of these powerful neighbors. Yet the distinct cultures of Southeast Asia retained their own unique identities.

Geography of Southeast Asia

Southeast Asia is made up of two major regions. The first region, mainland Southeast Asia, includes several peninsulas that jut south between India and China. Today, the mainland is home to Myanmar (MEE uhn mahr), Thailand, Cambodia, Laos, Vietnam, and part of Malaysia. The second region, island Southeast Asia, consists of more than 20,000 islands scattered between the Indian Ocean and the South China Sea. It includes the present-day nations of Indonesia, Singapore, Brunei (bru NĪ), and the Philippines.

Location The mainland is separated from the rest of Asia by mountains and high plateaus. Still, traders and invaders did push overland into the region. Mountains also separate the four main river valleys of Southeast Asia—the Irrawaddy (ihr uh WAHD ee), Chao Phraya, Mekong, and Red. These river valleys were home to early civilizations.

Island Southeast Asia has long been of strategic importance. All seaborne trade between China and India had to pass through either the Malacca or Sunda straits. Whoever commanded the straits controlled rich trade routes.

Trade Routes in the Southern Seas The monsoons, or seasonal winds, shaped trading patterns in the "southern seas." Ships traveled northeast in

Southeast Asia
As the Irrawaddy River reaches the sea, its valley flattens out into a broad delta. The Irrawaddy River valley, like other Southeast Asian river valleys, served as a home to the region's early civilizations.

Theme: Geography and History What are the other major rivers of Southeast Asia?

Virtual Field Trip

www.phschool.com

**Angkor Wat
Cambodia**

To learn more about Angkor Wat, use the Internet address above to link to the Web site for Angkor Wat.

Khmer Temple
Although Angkor Wat lies in ruins today, its intricate carvings suggest the magnificence of the original complex. The central towers represent the peaks of mythical Mount Meru, which was believed to be the home of the gods.

Theme: Religions and Value Systems Why might the builders of Angkor Wat have chosen to represent Mount Meru in their design?

summer and southwest in winter. Between seasons, while waiting for the winds to shift, merchants harbored their vessels in Southeast Asian ports, which became important centers of trade and culture. Soon, an international trade network linked India, Southeast Asia, and China to East Africa and the Middle East.

The key products of Southeast Asia were spices. Only a fraction of the spices traded in the region was destined for markets in Europe. Most cargoes went to East Asia, the Middle East, and East Africa.

Early Traditions The peoples of Southeast Asia developed their own cultures before Indian or Chinese influences shaped the region. At Bang Chiang in Thailand, archaeologists have found jars and bronze bracelets at least 5,000 years old. This evidence is challenging old theories about when civilization began in the region.

Over the centuries, diverse ethnic groups speaking many languages settled in Southeast Asia. Living in isolated villages, they followed their own religious and cultural patterns. Many societies were built around the nuclear family rather than the extended families of India and China.

Women had greater equality in Southeast Asia than elsewhere in Asia. Female merchants took part in the spice trade, gaining fame for their skill in bargaining, finance, and languages. In some port cities, they gained enough wealth and influence to become rulers. Matrilineal descent, or inheritance through the mother, was an accepted custom in Southeast Asia. Women also had some freedom in choosing or divorcing marriage partners. Even after Indian and Chinese influences arrived, women retained their traditional rights.

Impact of India

Indian merchants and Hindu priests filtered into Southeast Asia, slowly spreading their culture. Later, Buddhist monks and scholars introduced Theravada beliefs. Following the path of trade and religion came the influence of writing, law, government, art, architecture, and farming.

Increasing Contacts In the early centuries A.D., Indian traders settled in port cities in growing numbers. They gave presents to local rulers and married into influential families. Trade brought prosperity as merchants exchanged products such as cottons, jewels, and perfume for raw materials such as timber, spices, and gold.

In time, local Indian families exercised considerable power. Also, people from Southeast Asia visited India as pilgrims or students. As these contacts increased, Indian beliefs and ideas won widespread acceptance. Indian influence reached its peak between 500 and 1000.

Islam Long after Hinduism and Buddhism took root in Southeast Asia, Indians carried a third religion, Islam, into the region. By the 1200s, Muslims ruled northern India. From there, traders spread Islamic beliefs and Muslim civilization throughout the islands of Indonesia and as far east as the Philippines.* Arab merchants, too, spread the new faith. The prevalence of Islam in lands surrounding the Indian Ocean contributed to the growth of a stable, thriving trade network.

New Kingdoms and Empires

The blend of Indian influences with local cultures produced a series of kingdoms and empires in Southeast Asia. Some of these states rivaled those of India.

Pagan The kingdom of Pagan (pah GAHN) arose in the fertile rice-growing Irrawaddy Valley in present-day Myanmar. In 1044, King Anawrata (ah nuh RAH tuh) united the region. He is credited with bringing Buddhism to the Burman people. Buddhism had reached nearby cultures long before, but Anawrata made Pagan a major Buddhist center. He filled his capital city with magnificent stupas, or dome-shaped shrines, at about the same time that people in medieval Europe were beginning to build Gothic cathedrals.

Pagan flourished for some 200 years after Anawrata's death, but fell in 1287 to conquering Mongols. When the Burmans finally threw off foreign rule, they looked back with pride to the great days of Pagan.

The Khmer Empire Indian influences also helped shape the Khmer (kuh MEHR) empire, which reached its peak between 800 and 1350. Its greatest rulers controlled much of present-day Cambodia, Thailand, and Malaysia. The Khmer people adapted Indian writing, mathematics, architecture, and art. Khmer rulers became pious Hindus. Like the princes and emperors of India, they saw themselves as god-kings. Most ordinary people, however, preferred Buddhism.

In the 1100s, King Suryavarman II built the great temple complex at Angkor Wat. The ruins that survive today, though overgrown with jungle and pocked by the bullets of recent wars, are among the most impressive in the world. Hundreds of carved figures tell Hindu myths and glorify the king. Although the images of Vishnu, Shiva, and the Buddha reflect strong Indian influence, the style is uniquely Khmer.

Srivijaya The trading empire of Srivijaya (shree vah JĪ yah), in Indonesia, flourished from the 600s to the 1200s. Srivijaya controlled the Strait of

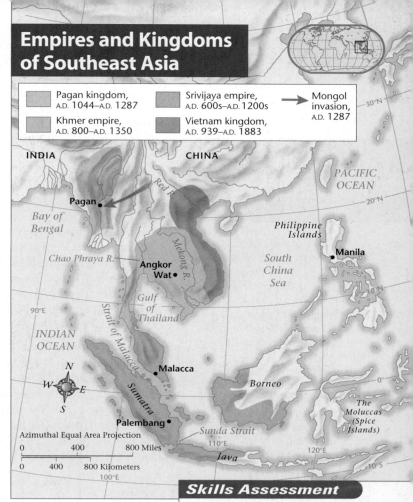

Empires and Kingdoms of Southeast Asia

Pagan kingdom, A.D. 1044–A.D. 1287		Srivijaya empire, A.D. 600s–A.D. 1200s	→ Mongol invasion, A.D. 1287
Khmer empire, A.D. 800–A.D. 1350		Vietnam kingdom, A.D. 939–A.D. 1883	

Skills Assessment

Geography The region we call Southeast Asia consists of both a mainland area and thousands of islands. It was home to numerous ancient and diverse cultures.

1. **Location** On the map, locate **(a)** Pagan kingdom, **(b)** Angkor Wat, **(c)** the Moluccas, **(d)** Sunda Strait.
2. **Movement** From which direction did the Mongol invasion take place?
3. **Critical Thinking Understanding Sequence** During which centuries were these empires and kingdoms most likely to have come into contact with one another?

---

*Today, Indonesia has the largest Muslim population of any nation in the world.

Malacca, which, as you have learned, was vital to shipping. Both Hinduism and Buddhism reached this island empire. As elsewhere in Southeast Asia, however, the local people often blended Indian beliefs into their own forms of worship, based on nature spirits.

Later, Islam spread to Sumatra, Java, and other islands. Local rulers adopted the new religion, which cemented commercial links with other Muslim trading centers around the Indian Ocean.

Vietnam Emerges

In most of Southeast Asia, Indian influence outweighed Chinese influence. Indian traditions spread mostly through trade rather than conquest. China, however, sent military forces to conquer the neighboring state of Annam (now northern Vietnam).

The heart of northern Vietnam was the Red River delta, around present-day Hanoi. There, the river irrigated fertile rice padis, or fields, which provided food for a growing population. The Vietnamese had their own distinct culture. As in other parts of Southeast Asia, women often held positions of authority.

Chinese Domination In 111 B.C., Han armies conquered the region. China remained in control for 1,000 years. During that time, the Vietnamese absorbed Confucian ideas. They adopted the Chinese civil service system and built a government bureaucracy similar to that found in China. Vietnamese nobles learned to speak the Chinese language and read Chinese characters. Unlike the rest of Southeast Asia, where Theravada Buddhism had the strongest impact, Vietnam adopted Mahayana beliefs from China. Daoism also helped shape Vietnamese society.

Resistance Despite these powerful Chinese influences, the Vietnamese preserved a strong sense of their separate identity. In A.D. 39, two noble sisters, Trung Trac and Trung Nhi, led an uprising that briefly drove the Chinese occupiers from the land. They tried to restore a simpler form of government based on ancient Vietnamese traditions. To this day, the Trung sisters are remembered as great martyrs and heroes. Finally in 939, as the Tang dynasty collapsed in China, Vietnam was able to break free from China. The Vietnamese turned back repeated Chinese efforts to reconquer their land, but did remain a tributary state of China.

Biography

Trung Sisters
d. A.D. 42(?)

Although the Chinese conquest of Annam introduced Confucian values, many local traditions continued for centuries. Women remained involved in politics, law, and trade. Still, officials were surprised when sisters Trung Trac and Trung Nhi forged a legacy for themselves as freedom fighters.

The sisters managed to do what no one else could. They forced the conquering Chinese out and established home rule. They did this by recruiting and training over 80,000 men and women to fight. Thirty-six of their generals were women.

After three years, however, the Chinese emperor sent an army against the sisters. According to legend, after a terrible defeat, the Trung sisters drowned themselves to avoid capture.

Theme: Impact of the Individual Why are the Trung sisters still revered in Vietnam today?

SECTION 2 Assessment

Recall
1. **Identify:** (a) Pagan, (b) Anawrata, (c) Khmer, (d) Suryavarman II, (e) Trung sisters.
2. **Define:** (a) matrilineal, (b) stupa, (c) padi.

Comprehension
3. How did geography make Southeast Asia of strategic importance?
4. How did India influence Pagan, the Khmer empire, and Srivijaya?
5. (a) How did China influence Vietnam? (b) How did Vietnam preserve its identity?

Critical Thinking and Writing
6. **Analyzing Information** Women's social status was limited in both India and China. Why do you think Southeast Asian women were able to retain their equality despite strong Indian and Chinese cultural influence?
7. **Comparing** How did the spread of Indian influence through Southeast Asia differ from the spread of Chinese influence through the same region?

Activity

Making a Map
Create a map showing foreign influences in Southeast Asia. First, draw or trace an outline map of the region. Use arrows to show the origins and directions of influences— for example, blue arrows for trade routes, red arrows for invasion routes. Then, show what products or ideas traveled along these routes.

European Footholds in Southeast Asia and India

Reading Focus

■ How did the Portuguese and the Dutch build empires in the East?

■ How did Spain control the Philippines?

■ How did the decline of Mughal India affect European traders?

Vocabulary

outpost

sepoy

Taking Notes

Begin a concept web like this one. As you read this section, fill in the blank circles with information about European influence in Southeast Asia and India. Add more circles as necessary.

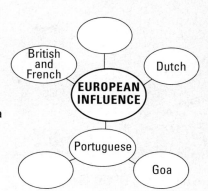

Main Idea   Europeans used military power to build trading empires in Southeast Asia.

Setting the Scene

In 1511, a Portuguese fleet commanded by Afonso de Albuquerque (ahl boo KEHR keh) dropped anchor off Malacca, a rich Muslim trading port that controlled the sea route linking India, Southeast Asia, and China. "Have you come in peace or in war?" asked the sultan. "Peace," replied Albuquerque. The true goal of the Portuguese, however, was not peace, but conquest.

The fleet remained at anchor for several weeks. Then they opened fire. The Portuguese quickly took the city, killing its inhabitants and seizing its wealth. On the ruins of a mosque, Albuquerque built a fort. The sultan had fled, thinking the invaders would loot and leave. But when he heard about the fort, he realized that the Portuguese had come to stay.

Portugal was the first European power to gain a foothold in Asia. The Portuguese ships were small in size and number, but the firepower of their shipboard cannons was unmatched. In time, this superior firepower helped them win control of the rich Indian Ocean spice trade and build a Portuguese trading empire in Asia. Before long, however, other European nations would challenge Portugal.

Portugal's Empire in the East

After Vasco da Gama's voyage, the Portuguese, under Albuquerque's command, burst into the Indian Ocean. In 1510, they seized the island of Goa off the coast of India, making it their major military and commercial base. Albuquerque then moved to end Muslim power and turn the Indian Ocean into a "Portuguese lake."

Trading Outposts   Albuquerque burned coastal towns and crushed Arab fleets at sea. The Portuguese attacked Aden, at the entrance to the Red Sea, and took Ormuz, gateway to the Persian Gulf. In 1511, Albuquerque took Malacca, massacring the city's Muslims and making the Europeans hated and feared.

In less than 50 years, the Portuguese had built a trading empire with military and merchant outposts, or distant areas under their control, rimming the southern seas. They seized cities on the east coast of Africa so they could resupply and repair their ships. For most of the 1500s, Portugal controlled the spice trade between Europe and Asia.

Impact   Despite their sea power, the Portuguese remained on the fringe of Asian trade. They had neither the strength nor the resources to conquer

Primary Source

The Portuguese in India
Afonso de Albuquerque explained to his soldiers why the Portuguese wanted to capture Malacca:

"The king of Portugal has often commanded me to go to the Straits, because . . . this was the best place to intercept the trade which the Moslems . . . carry on in these parts. So it was to do Our Lord's service that we were brought here; by taking Malacca, we would close the Straits so that never again would the Moslems be able to bring their spices by this route. . . . I am very sure that, if this Malacca trade is taken out of their hands, Cairo and Mecca will be completely lost."

—*The Commentaries of the Great Afonso de Albuquerque*

Skills Assessment

Primary Source   Why did Portugal want to control Malacca?

much territory on land. In India and China, where they faced far stronger empires, they merely sought permission to trade.

The intolerance of Portuguese missionaries caused resentment. In Goa, they attacked Muslims, destroyed Hindu temples, and introduced the Inquisition. Portuguese ships even sank Muslim pilgrim ships on their way to Mecca. Some Asian merchants chose to trade with the Portuguese. Others, however, chose to bypass Portuguese-controlled towns and continue their older trade patterns.

Rise of the Dutch

The Dutch were the first Europeans to challenge Portuguese domination in Asia. The land we know today as the Netherlands included a group of provinces and prosperous cities on the North Sea. The region had long been a center of handicrafts and trade. Through royal marriages, it fell under Spanish rule in the early 1500s. Later, the Protestant northern provinces won independence.

Sea Power In 1599, a Dutch fleet returned to Amsterdam from Asia after more than a year's absence. It carried a cargo of pepper, cloves, and other spices. Church bells rang to celebrate this "Happy Return." Those who had invested in the venture received 100 percent profit. The success of this voyage led to a frenzy of overseas activity.

By the late 1500s, Dutch warships and trading vessels put the Netherlands in the forefront of European commerce. They used their sea power to set up colonies and trading posts around the world. At the southwestern tip of Africa, the Dutch built the Cape Town settlement, where they could repair and resupply their ships.

Dutch Dominance In 1602, a group of wealthy Dutch merchants formed the Dutch East India Company. In the next decades, the Dutch strove to make themselves the major European power in the east. In 1641, they captured Malacca from the Portuguese and opened trade with China. Before long, they were able to enforce a monopoly in the Spice Islands, controlling shipments to Europe as well as much of the trade within Southeast Asia.

Like the Portuguese, the Dutch used military force to further their trading goals. At the same time, they forged closer ties with local rulers than the Portuguese had. Many Dutch merchants married Asian women.

Trade brought the Dutch enormous wealth. At home, Dutch merchants built tall mansions along the canals of Amsterdam and hired artists like Rembrandt to paint their portraits. In the 1700s, however, the growing power of England and France contributed to the decline of the Dutch trading empire in the East.

Spain Seizes the Philippines

While the Portuguese and Dutch set up bases on the fringes of Asia, Spain took over the Philippines. Magellan had claimed the archipelago for Spain in 1521. Within about 50 years, Spain had conquered and colonized the islands, renaming them for the Spanish king Philip II. Unlike most other peoples of Southeast Asia, the Filipinos were not united. As a result, they could be conquered more easily.

In the spirit of the Catholic Reformation, Spanish priests set out to convert the Filipino people to Christianity. Later, missionaries from the Philippines tried to spread Catholic teachings in China and Japan.

The Philippines became a key link in Spain's overseas trading empire. The Spanish shipped silver mined in Mexico and Peru across the Pacific to the Philippines. From there, they used the silver to buy goods in China. In this way, large quantities of American silver flowed into the economies of East Asian nations.

Disaster!

CYCLONE RIPS THROUGH CALCUTTA

When the English East India Company chose the location for the port city of Calcutta (Kolkata) in 1696, they did not realize its danger. Calcutta was built on the Hooghly River, part of the Ganges River delta system that flows into the Bay of Bengal. The bay is hit several times a year with devastating tropical storms. On October 11, 1737, the region was hit by one of the most destructive cyclones in history.

The storm surge—walls of water pushed by powerful winds—is the deadliest part of a cyclone. Waves start small, but as the storm approaches the shore, the surge grows. Finally, huge waves crash onto the shore, flooding the land.

Violent winds and rain struck Calcutta. Breaking waves caused a deafening roar. Then, a monstrous 40-foot wave crashed down on the shore. According to some reports, as many as 300,000 people died and 20,000 boats sank.

Desperate sailors were tossed from their ships and drowned. Of the nine British ships anchored in the Ganges before the storm hit, only one remained afloat. After the storm, bits of the shattered ships were found hanging in trees six miles upriver.

Portfolio Assessment

INTERNET   Use the Internet or other research sources to learn about other tropical storms such as a hurricane in the United States. Make a chart listing precautions that people in coastal areas can take to minimize damage and loss of life.

Mughal India and European Traders

Before the 1700s, European traders made very little impression on India, which was enjoying one of its greatest periods of strength and prosperity. In 1526, Babur had founded the Mughal dynasty. European merchants were dazzled by India's splendid court and its many luxury goods. There seemed little of value that Europeans could offer to the sophisticated civilization of Mughal India.

Industry and Commerce Besides producing spices, India was the world leader in textile manufacturing. It exported large quantities of silk and cotton cloth, from sheer muslins to elaborate chintzes. Handicrafts and shipbuilding added to the country's wealth.

The Mughal empire was larger, richer, and more powerful than any kingdom in Europe. When Europeans sought trading rights, Mughal emperors saw no threat in granting such concessions. The Portuguese and later the Dutch, English, and French thus were permitted to build forts and warehouses in coastal towns.

Turmoil and Decline When Akbar's successors ended his policy of religious toleration, conflicts rekindled between Hindu and Muslim princes. Years of civil war drained Mughal resources. Rulers then increased taxes, sparking peasant rebellions. Several weak rulers held the throne in the early 1700s. Corruption became widespread, and the central government eventually collapsed.

British-French Rivalry As Mughal power faltered, French and English traders played off rival Indian princes against one another. Both the English and French East India companies made alliances with local officials and independent rajahs. Each company organized its own army of sepoys, or Indian troops.

By the mid-1700s, the British and the French had become locked in a bitter struggle for global power. In 1756, war between Britain and France erupted in Europe. The fighting soon spread, involving both nations' lands in Asia and the Americas.

In India, Robert Clive, an agent of the British East India Company, used an army of British troops and sepoys to drive the French from their trading posts. The Company then forced the Mughal emperor to recognize its right to collect taxes in Bengal in the northeast. By the late 1700s, the Company had become the real ruler of Bengal, able to use its great wealth to spread its influence into other parts of India.

Prized Imports
Indian artisans created products like this hand-painted cotton wall hanging for European markets. Indian cottons became so popular in England that, to protect the English textile industry, Parliament tried to ban them.

Theme: Global Interaction
How does this wall hanging reflect both Indian and European culture?

SECTION 3 Assessment

Recall
1. **Identify: (a)** Afonso de Albuquerque, **(b)** Robert Clive.
2. **Define: (a)** outpost, **(b)** sepoy.

Comprehension
3. **(a)** How did the Portuguese gain control of the spice trade? **(b)** How were they challenged by the Dutch?
4. **(a)** Why was Spain easily able to conquer the Philippines? **(b)** Why did Spain want to control the islands?

5. **(a)** Why did Mughal power decline? **(b)** What effect did the decline have on France and Britain?

Critical Thinking and Writing
6. **Analyzing Information** How did Europeans build on existing trade networks in the Indian Ocean?
7. **Drawing Conclusions** Some people have argued "to the victors belong the spoils [riches] of the enemy." How do events in this section support this statement?

Activity
Take It to the NET

Use the Internet to learn more about Goa, the Portuguese base in the East. Plan a visit that a modern-day tourist might take to this island. Include historical background that visitors should have, as well as sites that they should see.

Encounters in East Asia

Reading Focus

- How was European trade with China affected by the Manchu conquest?

- What factors led Korea to isolate itself from other nations?

- What attitude did the Tokugawa shoguns have toward foreign traders?

Taking Notes

As you read this section, make a table to show how westerners acted and were received in East Asia. Use this table as a model.

	CHINA	KOREA	JAPAN
WESTERN BEHAVIOR AND ATTITUDES	• Matteo Ricci speaks Chinese • Macartney offends emperor		
RESPONSE TO WESTERNERS	• Restrict trade		

Main Idea China, Korea, and Japan limited contact with western nations.

Setting the Scene

The Europeans who reached Asia in the 1500s often made a poor impression on their hosts. The Italian traveler Niccoló Manucci told how Asians thought that Europeans "have no polite manners, that they are ignorant, wanting in ordered life, and very dirty."

Europeans, by contrast, wrote enthusiastically about China. In 1590, a visitor described Chinese artisans "cleverly making devices out of gold, silver and other metals." He was also impressed with their abilities in handicrafts and gunsmithing, and wrote: "They daily publish huge multitudes of books."

Portuguese ships first reached China by way of the South China Sea during the Ming dynasty. To the Chinese, the Portuguese were "southern barbarians." Like other foreigners, they lacked the civilized ways of the Middle Kingdom.

European Trade With China

The Ming dynasty, you will recall, ended its overseas explorations in the mid-1400s. Confucian officials had little use for foreigners. "Since our empire owns the world," said a Ming document, "there is no country on this or other sides of the seas which does not submit to us."

Strict Limits on Trade Portuguese traders reached China by sea in 1514. To the Chinese, the newcomers had little to offer in exchange for silks and porcelains. European textiles and metalwork were inferior to Chinese products. The Chinese therefore demanded payment in gold or silver.

The Ming eventually allowed the Portuguese a trading post at Macao, near Canton, present-day Guangzhou (gwahng JOH). Later, they let Dutch, English, and other Europeans trade with Chinese merchants, but only under strict limits. Foreigners could trade only at Canton under the supervision of imperial officials. When each year's trading season ended, they had to sail away.

Scholars and Missionaries A few European scholars, like the brilliant Jesuit priest Matteo Ricci, did make a positive impression on Ming China.

China and Foreign Trade
This fan shows the harbor in Canton, with European flags flying over warehouses in the background. Strict limits on foreign trade kept Europeans from gaining a foothold in China.

Theme: Economics and Technology How does the scene on this fan suggest the limitations placed on European merchants?

In the 1580s, Ricci learned to speak Chinese and adopted Chinese dress. Ricci and other priests had little success spreading their religious beliefs, although Chinese rulers welcomed the chance to learn the arts and sciences of Renaissance Europe.

The Manchu Conquest

By the early 1600s, the aging Ming dynasty was decaying. Revolts erupted, and Manchu invaders from the north pushed through the Great Wall. The Manchus ruled a region in the northeast that had long been influenced by Chinese civilization. In 1644, victorious Manchu armies seized Beijing and made it their capital.

Qing Rule The Manchus set up a new dynasty called the Qing (CHIHNG), meaning "pure." To preserve their distinct identity, the Manchus barred intermarriage between Manchus and Chinese. Manchu women were forbidden to follow the traditional Chinese practice of footbinding. Still, the Manchus won the support of the Chinese scholar-officials because they adopted the Confucian system of government. For each top government position, the Qing chose two people, one Manchu and one Chinese. Local government remained in the hands of the Chinese, but Manchu troops stationed across the empire ensured loyalty.

Two rulers oversaw the most brilliant age of the Qing. Kangxi (kahng SHEE), who ruled from 1661 to 1722, was an able administrator and military leader. He extended Chinese power into Central Asia and promoted Chinese culture. Kangxi's grandson Qianlong (chyehn LOHNG) had an equally successful reign from 1736 to 1796. He expanded China's borders to rule the largest area in the nation's history. Qianlong retired after 60 years because he did not want to rule longer than his grandfather had.

Prosperity The Chinese economy expanded under both emperors. New crops from the Americas, such as potatoes and corn, boosted farm output, which in turn contributed to a population boom. China's population rose from 140 million in 1740 to over 300 million by 1800. Peace and prosperity encouraged further growth in handicraft industries, including silk, cotton, and porcelain. Internal trade grew, as did the demand for Chinese goods from all over the world.

Response to Westerners The Qing maintained the Ming policy of restricting foreign traders. Still, Europeans kept pressing to expand trade to cities other than Guangzhou. In 1793, Lord Macartney arrived in China at the head of a British diplomatic mission. He brought samples of British-made goods to show the Chinese the advantages of trade with westerners. The Chinese thought the goods were gifts offered as tribute to the emperor and looked on them as rather crude products.

Further misunderstandings followed. Macartney insisted on an audience with the emperor. The Chinese told Macartney he would have to perform the traditional kowtow, touching his head to the ground to show respect to the emperor. Macartney refused. He also offended the Chinese by speaking of the natural superiority of the English. The negotiations faltered. In the end, Qianlong did receive Macartney, but the meeting accomplished nothing. Later, in a letter to King George III of Britain, Qianlong rejected the request for trading rights.

At the time, Qianlong's attitude seemed justified by China's successes. After all, he already ruled the world's greatest empire. Why should he negotiate with a nation as distant as Britain? In the long run, however, his policy proved disastrous. Even then, there was much the Chinese could have learned from the West. In the 1800s, China would learn about western advances—especially in military technology—the hard way.

Connections to Today

Guangzhou's International Trade

For centuries, the thriving port of Guangzhou has welcomed merchants from many lands. Today, thousands of business people from all over the world attend the twice-yearly Guangzhou Fair. There they buy Chinese products to sell overseas and market their own goods to sell in China.

Many foreign companies have opened branches in Guangzhou. They have done so because of its status as one of 14 "coastal open cities." This special designation allows Guangzhou to extend privileges, including lower taxes, to foreign companies that want to do business there.

Theme: Economics and Technology How has Guangzhou continued to thrive from international trade?

Analyzing Primary Sources

Letter From the Celestial Emperor to the "Barbarian" King

In the following excerpt, Emperor Qianlong denies the request of King George III for greater trading rights in China.

"We have perused [read] the text of your state message and the wording expresses your earnestness. From it your sincere humility and obedience can clearly be seen. It is admirable and we fully approve. . . .

As to what you have requested in your message, O King, namely to be allowed to send one of your subjects to reside in the Celestial Empire to look after your country's trade, this does not conform to the Celestial Empire's ceremonial system, and definitely cannot be done. . . .

Moreover, the territories ruled by the Celestial Empire are vast, and for all the envoys of vassal [inferior] states coming to the capital there are definite regulations. . . . There has never been any precedent for allowing them to suit their own convenience. . . . Furthermore, there are a great many Western Ocean countries altogether, and not merely your one country. If, like you, O King, they all beg to send someone to reside at the capital, how could we grant their request in every case? It would be absolutely impossible for us to do so. How can we go so far as to change the regulations of the Celestial Empire . . . because of the request of one man—of you, O King? . . .

We have never valued ingenious articles, nor do we have the slightest need of your country's manufacturers. . . . You, O King, should simply act in conformity with our wishes by strengthening your loyalty and swearing perpetual obedience so as to ensure that your country may share the blessings of peace."

—Qianlong, letter to George III

Lord Macartney's Mission
Artist William Alexander traveled to China with Lord Macartney. He did not attend the British meeting with the emperor, however, and had to rely on a British officer's firsthand drawings to produce this picture.

Skills Tip

When you analyze a primary source, pay careful attention to the author's point of view. Point of view is the author's beliefs or values that color his or her perceptions.

Skills Assessment

1. Emperor Qianlong seems to treat King George as
   A an equal.
   B an inferior.
   C a superior.
   D a threat.

2. What reason does the emperor not give for denying the king's request?
   E historical precedent
   F current regulations
   G lack of interest in British goods
   H fear of foreign influence

3. **Critical Thinking Recognizing Points of View** **(a)** What words or phrases convey Emperor Qianlong's view of the British king? **(b)** How does the emperor characterize his own nation?

Japanese Screens
Shoguns and daimyo filled their castles with brilliant, multipaneled screen paintings. Many screens depicted the beauties of nature or scenes of everyday life. This screen shows the activities of Japanese and Portuguese seafarers aboard a large ship.

Theme: Art and Literature
How did the artist create a sense of motion?

Korea and Isolation

Like China, Korea restricted outside contacts in the 1500s and 1600s. Earlier, Korean traders had far-ranging contacts across East Asia. A Korean map from the 1300s accurately outlines lands from Japan to the Mediterranean. Koreans probably acquired this knowledge from Arab traders who had visited Korea.

The Choson dynasty, you will recall, firmly embraced Confucian ideas. Like the Chinese, Koreans felt that Confucian learning was the most advanced in the world. The low status of merchants in Confucianism also led Koreans to look down on foreign traders.

Two other events led the Koreans to turn inward. A Japanese invasion in the 1590s devastated the land of Korea. Then in 1636, the Manchus conquered Korea before overrunning Ming China. When the Manchus set up the Qing dynasty in China, Korea became a tributary state, run by its own government but forced to acknowledge China's supremacy. The two invasions left Korea feeling like "a shrimp among whales."

In response, the Koreans chose isolation, excluding all foreigners except the Chinese and a few Japanese. When European sailors were shipwrecked on Korean shores, they were imprisoned or killed. As a result, Korea became known in the West as the "Hermit Kingdom."

Even though Korea had few contacts with the world for about 250 years, this period was a great age for Korean arts and literature. In one satirical tale, author Pak Chi-won describes a poor scholar who breaks with tradition to become a merchant. Here, Master Ho describes doing business in an isolated country:

> "Our country has no trade with other countries, and . . . everything we use is produced and consumed in the same province. . . . With ten thousand yang, you can buy just about all of one particular item produced in the country. You can buy the whole lot, whether you load it on a cart or on a boat."
>
> —Pak Chi-won, "The Story of Ho"

Japan and Foreign Traders

Unlike the Chinese or Koreans, the Japanese at first welcomed western traders. In 1543, the Portuguese reached Japan. Later came the Spanish, Dutch, and English. They arrived at the turbulent time when strong daimyo were struggling for power. The Japanese quickly acquired western firearms and built castles modeled on European designs. In fact, the new weapons may have helped the Tokugawa shoguns centralize power and impose order.

Japan was much more open to European missionaries than China. Jesuits, like the Spanish priest Francis Xavier, found the Japanese curious and eager to learn about Christianity. A growing number of Japanese adopted the new faith.

The Tokugawa shoguns, however, grew increasingly hostile toward foreigners. After learning how Spain had seized the Philippines, they may have seen the newcomers as agents of an invading force. In addition, Japanese officials disliked the intrigues and competition among Christian missionaries. They also suspected that Japanese Christians—who may have numbered as many as 300,000—owed their allegiance to the pope, rather than to Japanese leaders. In response, the Tokugawas expelled foreign missionaries. They brutally persecuted Japanese Christians, killing many thousands of people.

By 1638, the Tokugawas had barred all western merchants and forbidden Japanese to travel abroad. To further their isolation, they outlawed the building of large ships, thereby ending foreign trade. In order to keep informed about world events, they permitted just one or two Dutch ships each year to trade at a small island in Nagasaki harbor. Through this tiny gateway, a few Japanese did learn about some foreign ideas. They studied Dutch medical texts, for example, which they found to be more accurate than Chinese ones.

Looking Ahead

Japan maintained its policy of strict isolation for more than 200 years. Isolation had a profound effect on Japan. Without outside influence, Japanese culture turned inward. Still, art and literature spread beyond the upper classes. Artists found new ways to interpret traditions.

During this time, internal trade boomed. Cities grew in size and importance, and some merchant families gained wealth and status. By the early 1700s, Edo (present-day Tokyo) had a million inhabitants, more than either London or Paris.

In 1853, Japan was forced to reopen contacts with the western world. Renewed relations unleashed an extraordinary period of change that helped Japan emerge as a major world power.

Global Connections

The Jesuits in Asia

Although Jesuit missionaries in Asia failed to win many converts to Christianity, they succeeded in spreading western ideas and technology. In China, Jesuit priest Matteo Ricci introduced an accurate world map and helped manufacture European-style cannons. Later Jesuits served as heads of the bureau that planned China's official calendar. The Jesuits also translated more than 100 books on science, math, and technology into Chinese. In Japan, Jesuits introduced the printing press.

Cultural influences also flowed in the other direction. The Jesuits introduced Europeans to the works of Confucius.

Theme: Religions and Value Systems What western ideas did the Jesuits introduce in Asia?

SECTION 4 Assessment

Recall
1. **Identify:** **(a)** Matteo Ricci, **(b)** Manchus, **(c)** Kangxi, **(d)** Qianlong, **(e)** Hermit Kingdom, **(f)** Francis Xavier.

Comprehension
2. **(a)** How was economic prosperity reflected in Qing China? **(b)** How did the Qing restrict trade with other nations?
3. Why did Korea pursue a policy of isolation?
4. Why did the Japanese policy toward trade and foreigners change over time?

Critical Thinking and Writing
5. **Linking Past and Present** Why do some people in the United States today support limited overseas ties?
6. **Making Generalizations** **(a)** Based on your reading, what generalization might you make about the attitude of European traders to the countries of East Asia? **(b)** What generalization might you make about how East Asians felt toward Europeans? **(c)** What evidence might you give to support each generalization?

Activity

Writing a Dialogue
Write a dialogue between two officials in China, Korea, or Japan. One official should express a willingness to establish relations with European powers. The other should argue in favor of a policy of isolation.

Creating a Chapter Summary

On a sheet of paper make a cause-and-effect diagram like the one shown here. Fill in the causes and effects of European exploration to help you review this chapter. Add more boxes as needed.

For additional review and enrich-ment activities, see the interactive version of *World History* available on the Web and on CD-ROM.

| Demand for Asian goods | | | | |

EUROPEAN EXPLORATION AND FOOTHOLDS IN ASIA

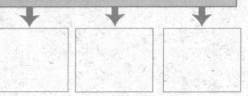

| Portuguese gain Goa, Macao | Dutch East India Company formed | | | |

Web Site Self-Test
For practice test questions for Chapter 15, see **www.phschool.com**.

Building Vocabulary

Review the meaning of the chapter vocabulary words listed below. Then, write a sentence for each word in which you define the word and describe its relation to the first global age.

1. cartographer
2. astrolabe
3. caravel
4. scurvy
5. circumnavigate
6. matrilineal
7. stupa
8. padi
9. outpost
10. sepoy

Recalling Key Facts

11. What different motives led Europeans to explore the oceans?
12. What was the Line of Demarcation?
13. Why was Magellan's voyage of 1519–1522 important?
14. How did Christianity spread to the Philippines?
15. Which two European nations competed for influence in India?
16. What important policy did Japanese leaders follow between 1638 and 1853?

Critical Thinking and Writing

17. **Linking Past and Present** **(a)** Why were spices such valued trading goods in the 1400s? **(b)** What goods and resources play a similar role in the world economy today?
18. **Analyzing Information** How did European encounters with India, China, and Japan link economic, religious, and political activity?
19. **Identifying Alternatives** How might Tokugawa policy have been changed to encourage greater contact with other civilizations?
20. **Recognizing Points of View** Many people admire explorers such as Columbus and da Gama as bold adventurers. Others condemn them as vicious conquerors. **(a)** Who do you think might hold each of these viewpoints? **(b)** What evidence can be given to support each opinion?

21. **Connecting to Geography** How did weather conditions in the "southern seas" contribute to travel in the region and cultural exchange in Southeast Asian ports?

The following diary entry is from the log that Christopher Columbus kept on his first voyage. To dispel the crew's fears of how long the voyage was, Columbus always reckoned "fewer leagues than we actually made" and kept confidential records of the actual distance traveled. Martín Alonso Pinzón was the captain of the *Pinta*. Read the entry, then answer the questions that follow.

> *"Saturday, 6 October 1492*
> *I maintained my course to the west and made 120 miles between day and night, but told the people 99. This evening Martín Alonso Pinzón told me that he thought it would be wise to steer to the SW by west in order to reach the island of Japan, which is marked on the chart that I had shown him. In my opinion it is better to continue directly west until we reach the mainland. Later we can go to the islands on the return voyage to Spain. My decision has not pleased the men, for they continue to murmur and complain. Despite their grumblings I held fast to the west."*
>
> —The Log of Christopher Columbus (Fuson, tr.)

22. Where did Martín Alonso Pinzón think they were?
23. What mainland did Columbus think they were near?
24. **(a)** What problem did Columbus face with the crew? **(b)** How did Columbus respond?
25. How might a captain like Martín Alonso Pinzón be a problem for Columbus?

Use the Internet to research one of the European voyages that began the first global age. If possible, find a primary source from the voyage, such as the letters of Christopher Columbus. Then, write a series of news reports that the voyager might have written if he had been able to send news flashes about his travels back to his home country.

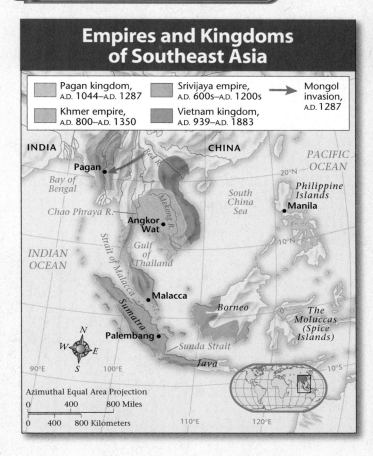

Empires and Kingdoms of Southeast Asia

- Pagan kingdom, A.D. 1044–A.D. 1287
- Khmer empire, A.D. 800–A.D. 1350
- Srivijaya empire, A.D. 600s–A.D. 1200s
- Vietnam kingdom, A.D. 939–A.D. 1883
- → Mongol invasion, A.D. 1287

Azimuthal Equal Area Projection

Use the map to answer the following questions:

26. In which empire was Angkor Wat located?
27. What is the location of the Philippine Islands in relation to China?
28. Why did the location of the city of Malacca make the city important to Southeast Asian trade?
29. **(a)** Is China north or south of the Equator? **(b)** Is Java north or south of the Equator? **(c)** Identify the islands through which the Equator runs.
30. Does the region shown in this map lie in the Eastern Hemisphere or the Western Hemisphere?

Skills Tip

Lines of latitude run horizontally and identify whether an area is north or south of the Equator. Lines of longitude show if an area is in the Eastern or Western Hemisphere.

The First Global Age: Europe, the Americas, and Africa 1492–1750

Chapter Preview

1 Conquest in the Americas
2 Spanish and Portuguese Colonies in the Americas
3 Struggle for North America
4 Turbulent Centuries in Africa
5 Changes in Europe

1492
Columbus lands in the Americas. A global exchange of goods and ideas begins.

1521
Cortés completes conquest of the Aztecs, acquiring for Spain vast stores of gold, including ornaments such as this one.

1607
Jamestown is founded by British colonists.

CHAPTER
EVENTS

1500

1550

1600

GLOBAL
EVENTS

1498 Portuguese explorer da Gama rounds Africa and reaches India.

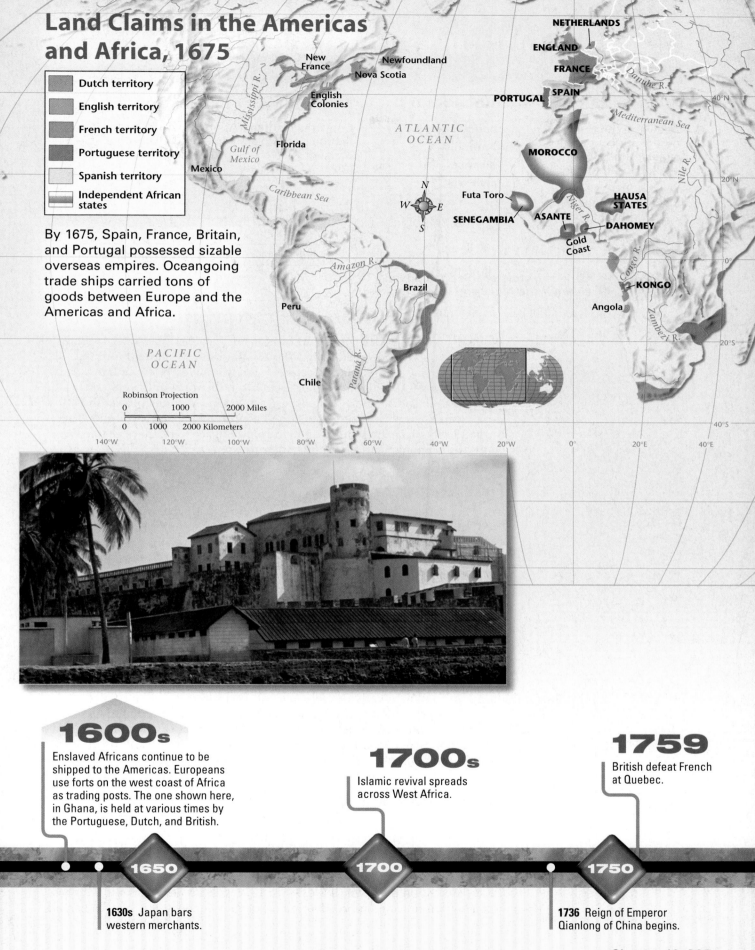

Land Claims in the Americas and Africa, 1675

Legend:
- Dutch territory
- English territory
- French territory
- Portuguese territory
- Spanish territory
- Independent African states

By 1675, Spain, France, Britain, and Portugal possessed sizable overseas empires. Oceangoing trade ships carried tons of goods between Europe and the Americas and Africa.

Robinson Projection

0   1000   2000 Miles

0   1000   2000 Kilometers

Map labels: New France, Newfoundland, Nova Scotia, English Colonies, Florida, Mexico, Gulf of Mexico, Mississippi R., Caribbean Sea, Amazon R., Brazil, Peru, Paraná R., Chile, ATLANTIC OCEAN, PACIFIC OCEAN, NETHERLANDS, ENGLAND, FRANCE, PORTUGAL, SPAIN, Danube R., Mediterranean Sea, 40°N, 20°N, Nile R., MOROCCO, Futa Toro, SENEGAMBIA, Niger R., HAUSA STATES, ASANTE, DAHOMEY, Gold Coast, Congo R., KONGO, Angola, Zambezi R., 0°, 20°S, 40°S

1600s

Enslaved Africans continue to be shipped to the Americas. Europeans use forts on the west coast of Africa as trading posts. The one shown here, in Ghana, is held at various times by the Portuguese, Dutch, and British.

1700s

Islamic revival spreads across West Africa.

1759

British defeat French at Quebec.

1650

1700

1750

1630s Japan bars western merchants.

1736 Reign of Emperor Qianlong of China begins.

Conquest in the Americas

Reading Focus

- What were the results of the first encounters between the Spanish and Native Americans?

- How did Spanish conquistadors conquer the Aztec and Incan empires?

- Why were the Spanish victorious?

Main Idea   Various factors enabled the Spanish to conquer the Aztec and Incan empires.

Vocabulary

conquistador
immunity
alliance
civil war

Taking Notes

Copy this diagram. As you read, add other factors that help to explain why the Spanish were able to conquer Native American empires. Add as many boxes as you need.

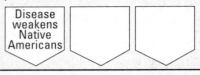

Disease weakens Native Americans

EUROPEANS CONQUER NATIVE AMERICANS

Setting the Scene   Spanish soldiers who reached the Aztec capital of Tenochtitlán in 1519 were amazed by its size and splendor. From the emperor's palace, reported one soldier, "We had a clear view of the . . . [majestic temples] of the nearby cities, built in the form of towers and fortresses, . . . and others . . . all whitewashed, and wonderfully brilliant."

Within a few years, the Spanish had captured and destroyed the Aztec capital. In its place, they built a new capital, Mexico City, that became the heart of the Spanish empire in the Americas.

First Encounters

In 1492, Christopher Columbus landed in the islands that are now called the West Indies, in the Caribbean. There, he encountered the Taíno people. The Taínos lived in villages and grew corn, yams, and cotton, which they wove into cloth. They were friendly and generous toward the Spanish.

Friendly relations soon evaporated, however. Spanish conquistadors (kahn KEES tuh dohrz), or conquerors, followed in the wake of Columbus. They settled on the islands of Hispaniola (now the Dominican Republic and Haiti), Cuba, and Puerto Rico. They seized the gold ornaments worn by the Taínos, then made them pan for more gold. At the same time, the newcomers forced the Taínos to convert to Christianity.

Meanwhile, a deadly but invisible invader was at work—disease. Europeans unknowingly carried diseases such as smallpox, measles, and influenza to which Native Americans had no immunity, or resistance. These diseases spread rapidly and wiped out village after village. As a result, the Native American population of the Caribbean islands declined by as much as 90 percent in the 1500s. This cycle of disease and death was repeated in many other places across the Western Hemisphere.

The Conquistadors

From Cuba, Spanish explorers probed the coasts of the Americas. They spread stories of empires rich in gold. Attracted by the promise of riches as well as by religious zeal, a flood of adventurers soon followed.

Cortés in Mexico   Among the earliest conquistadors was Hernan Cortés. Cortés landed on the coast of Mexico in 1519 with about 600 men, 16 horses, and a few cannons. As he headed inland toward Tenochtitlán, he was helped

Virtual Field Trip

www.phschool.com

**University of Minnesota
Duluth, Minnesota**

For more images and information about the Aztecs and the Spanish conquest, use the Internet address above to link to the department of history at the University of Minnesota.

Conquistadors in Mexico
Pedro de Alvarado was one of the Spanish conquistadors who conquered Mexico. This illustration shows Alvarado and his men facing off against a troop of Aztec soldiers.

Theme: Economics and Technology Based on this picture, identify two technological advantages the Spanish had over the Aztecs.

by Malinche (mah LIHN chay), a young Indian woman who served as his translator and adviser. The Spanish called her Doña Marina. Malinche knew both the Mayan and Aztec languages, and she learned Spanish quickly.

From Malinche, Cortés learned that many conquered peoples hated their Aztec overlords. The Aztecs, you will recall, sacrificed thousands of captives to their gods each year. Malinche helped Cortés arrange **alliances** with these discontented groups. They would help one another fight the Aztecs.

Moctezuma's Dilemma Meanwhile, messengers brought word about the newcomers to the Aztec emperor Moctezuma. He wondered if the leader of the pale-skinned, bearded strangers might be Quetzalcoatl, the god-king who had long ago vowed to return from the east. Moctezuma sent gifts of gold and silver, but urged the strangers not to continue to Tenochtitlán.

Cortés had no intention of turning back. Fighting and negotiating by turns, he led his forces inland toward the capital. At last, they arrived in Tenochtitlán, where they were dazzled by the grandeur of the city.

Fall of Tenochtitlán Moctezuma welcomed Cortés to his capital. However, relations between the Aztecs and Spaniards soon grew strained, and the Aztecs drove the Spanish from the city. Moctezuma was killed in the fighting.

Cortés retreated to plan an assault. In 1521, in a brutal struggle, Cortés and his Indian allies captured and demolished Tenochtitlán. An unknown Aztec lamented, "Broken spears lie in the road; / We have torn our hair with grief. / The houses are roofless now, and their walls are red with blood." On the ruins of Tenochtitlán, the Spanish later built Mexico City.

Pizarro in Peru Cortés's success inspired other adventurers. Among them was Francisco Pizarro. He arrived in Peru in 1532, just after the Incan ruler Atahualpa (ah tah WAHL pah) won the throne from his brother in a bloody **civil war**. A civil war is fought between groups of people in the same nation.

Helped by Indian allies, Pizarro captured Atahualpa after slaughtering thousands of his followers. The Spanish demanded a huge ransom for the ruler. The Incas paid it, but the Spanish killed Atahualpa anyway.

Despite continuing resistance, the invaders overran the Incan heartland. From Peru, Spanish forces surged across Ecuador and Chile. Before long, Spain added much of South America to its growing empire.

 Primary Sources and Literature

See "Bernal Díaz: The True History of the Conquest of New Spain" in the Reference Section at the back of this book.

FACT FINDER

Native American Population of Central Mexico

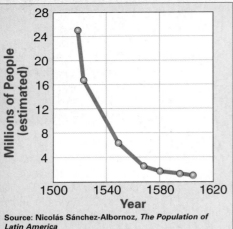

Source: Nicolás Sánchez-Albornoz, *The Population of Latin America*

Skills Assessment

Graph Disease and conquest combined to reduce drastically the Native American population. This graph shows what happened to central Mexico's Native Americans after the arrival of the Spanish in 1519. **How did the Native American population change during the period shown on the graph?**

Reasons for Victory

How could a few hundred European soldiers conquer huge Native American empires with populations in the millions? Several reasons explain the amazing Spanish success.

1. Superior military technology was a key factor. The Spaniards' horses frightened some Indians, who had never seen such animals. Spanish muskets and cannons killed Indian soldiers, while metal helmets and armor protected the Spanish from the Indians' arrows and spears.
2. Division and discontent among the Indians aided the Spanish. The Spanish won allies by playing on old hatreds among rival Indian groups. In fact, Indians provided Cortés and Pizarro with much of their fighting power.
3. Disease brought by the Europeans weakened the Aztecs and Incas. As tens of thousands of Indians died, some of the bewildered and demoralized survivors felt that their gods were less powerful than the god of their conquerors.
4. Many Indians believed that the disasters they suffered marked the world's end. To Aztecs, the destruction of Tenochtitlán signaled the end of the reign of the sun god.

Ongoing Resistance Native Americans continued to resist the invaders, however. For years, Mayas fought Spanish rule. Long after the death of Atahualpa, revolts erupted among the Incas. Throughout the Americas, Indians resisted Europeans by preserving aspects of their own culture, such as language, religious traditions, and clothing.

Looking Ahead

The Spanish seized gold and silver statues and ornaments from the Aztecs and Incas. After depleting these sources, they forced Native Americans to mine silver in Peru and Mexico. In the 1500s and early 1600s, treasure fleets sailed each year to Spain or the Spanish Philippines loaded with gold and silver. As you will read, this flood of wealth created both benefits and problems for the economy of Europe.

SECTION 1 Assessment

Recall

1. **Identify:** (a) Taínos, (b) Hernan Cortés, (c) Malinche, (d) Moctezuma, (e) Francisco Pizarro, (f) Atahualpa.
2. **Define:** (a) conquistador, (b) immunity, (c) alliance, (d) civil war.

Comprehension

3. How were Native Americans of the Caribbean region affected by their early encounters with Europeans?
4. What methods did Pizarro use to conquer the Incan empire?
5. (a) How did divisions within the Aztec and Incan empires help the Spanish? (b) What other reasons explain the rapid success of the Spanish conquistadors over Native Americans?

Critical Thinking and Writing

6. **Comparing** Compare the Spanish conquest of the Americas with the Reconquista or the Crusades. (a) How were they similar? (b) How were they different?
7. **Identifying Main Ideas** Review the three paragraphs under the heading First Encounters. For each paragraph, write a single sentence identifying the main idea of the paragraph.

Activity
Take It to the NET

Use the Internet to research the life of Malinche, whose name means "traitor." Then, write a paragraph explaining why you believe she does or does not deserve this name.

Spanish and Portuguese Colonies in the Americas

Reading Focus

- How did Spain rule its empire in the Americas?
- What were the chief features of colonial society and culture?
- How did Portugal and other European nations challenge Spanish power?

Vocabulary

viceroy
plantation
encomienda
peon
peninsular
creole
mestizo
mulatto
privateer

Taking Notes

Copy this partially completed concept web. As you read, write key facts and ideas about the Spanish empire in the Americas in the appropriate circles. Add as many circles as you need.

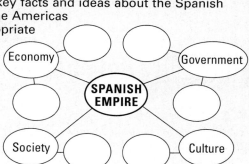

Main Idea Native American, African, and European traditions blended to form new cultures in the Americas.

Setting the Scene Spain was immensely proud of its rich silver mines in the Potosí region of Peru. By the 1540s, tons of Potosí silver filled Spanish treasure ships. Year after year, thousands of Native Americans were forced to extract the rich ore from dangerous shafts deep inside the Andes Mountains. Many Indians died in the terrible conditions, only to be replaced by thousands more.

Scenes such as this were repeated in Mexico, the Caribbean, and other parts of Spain's empire. A flood of Spanish settlers and missionaries followed the conquistadors. Wherever they went, they claimed the land and its people for their king and Church. When there was resistance, the newcomers imposed their will by force. As devout Christians, they thought it was their duty to bring their religion and civilization to the Indians.

From the first, though, Christian Europeans had much to learn from the peoples that they conquered. In the end, a new culture emerged that reflected European, Native American, and African traditions.

Ruling the Spanish Empire

In the 1500s, Spain claimed a vast empire stretching from California to South America. In time, it divided these lands into five provinces. The most important were New Spain (Mexico) and Peru.

Spain was determined to maintain strict control over its empire. To achieve this goal, the king set up the Council of the Indies to pass laws for the colonies. He also appointed viceroys, or representatives who ruled in his name, in each province. Lesser officials and *audiencias,* or advisory councils of Spanish settlers, helped the viceroy rule. The Council of the Indies in Spain closely monitored these colonial officials to make sure they did not assume too much authority.

The Catholic Church To Spain, winning souls for Christianity was as important as gaining land. The Catholic Church played a key role in the colonies, working with the government to convert Native Americans to Christianity. Church leaders often served as royal officials and helped to regulate the activities of Spanish settlers. As Spain's American empire expanded, Church authority expanded along with it.

Franciscan, Jesuit, and other missionaries baptized thousands of Native Americans. In frontier regions, they built mission churches and worked to turn new converts into loyal subjects of the Catholic king of Spain. They forcibly imposed European culture over Native American culture.

They also introduced European clothing, the Spanish language, and new crafts such as carpentry and locksmithing.

The Economy To make the empire profitable, Spain closely controlled its economic activities, especially trade. Colonists could export raw materials only to Spain and could buy only Spanish manufactured goods. Laws forbade colonists from trading with other European nations or even with other Spanish colonies. The most valuable resources shipped from Spanish America to Spain were silver and gold.

Sugar cane was introduced into the West Indies and elsewhere and quickly became a profitable resource. The cane was refined into sugar, molasses, and rum. Sugar cane, however, had to be grown on plantations, large estates run by an owner or the owner's overseer. Finding the large numbers of workers needed to make the plantations profitable was a major problem.

At first, Spanish monarchs granted the conquistadors encomiendas, the right to demand labor or tribute from Native Americans in a particular area. The conquistadors used this system to force Native Americans to work under the most brutal conditions. Those who resisted were hunted down and killed. Disease, starvation, and cruel treatment caused catastrophic declines in the population.

Bartolomé de las Casas A few bold priests, like Bartolomé de las Casas, condemned the evils of the encomienda system. In vivid reports to Spain, Las Casas detailed the horrors that Spanish rule had brought to Native Americans and pleaded with the king to end the abuse.

Prodded by Las Casas, Spain passed the New Laws of the Indies in 1542, forbidding enslavement of Native Americans. The laws were meant to end abuses against Native Americans, but Spain was too far away to enforce them. Many Native Americans were forced to become peons, workers forced to labor for a landlord in order to pay off a debt. Landlords advanced them food, tools, or seeds, creating debts that workers could never pay off in their lifetime.

Bringing Workers From Africa To fill the labor shortage, Las Casas urged colonists to import workers from Africa. Africans were immune to tropical diseases, he said, and had skills in farming, mining, and metalworking. Las Casas later regretted that advice because it furthered the brutal African slave trade. The Spanish began bringing Africans as slave laborers to the Americas by the 1530s.

As demand for sugar products skyrocketed, the settlers imported millions of Africans as slaves. They were forced to work as field hands, miners, or servants in the houses of wealthy landowners. Others became peddlers, skilled artisans, artists, and mechanics.

In time, Africans and their American-born descendants greatly outnumbered European settlers in the West Indies and parts of South America. Often, they resisted slavery by rebelling or running away. In the cities, some enslaved Africans earned enough money to buy their freedom.

Colonial Society and Culture

In Spanish America, the mix of diverse peoples gave rise to a new social structure. The blending of Native American, African, and European peoples and traditions resulted in a new American culture.

Social Structure At the top of colonial society were peninsulares, people born in Spain. (The term *peninsular* referred to the Iberian Peninsula, on which Spain is located.) Peninsulares filled the highest positions in both colonial governments and the Catholic Church. Next came creoles,

American-born descendants of Spanish settlers. Creoles owned most of the plantations, ranches, and mines.

Other social groups reflected the mixing of populations. They included mestizos, people of Native American and European descent, and mulattoes, people of African and European descent. Native Americans and people of African descent formed the lowest social classes.

Cities Spanish settlers preferred to live in towns and cities. The population of Mexico City grew so quickly that by 1550 it was the largest Spanish-speaking city in the world.

Colonial cities were centers of government, commerce, and European culture. Around the central plaza, or square, stood government buildings and a Spanish-style church. Broad avenues and public monuments symbolized European power and wealth. Cities were also centers of intellectual and cultural life. Architecture and painting, as well as poetry and the exchange of ideas, flourished.

Education To meet the Church's need for educated priests, the colonies built universities. The University of Mexico was established as early as 1551. A dozen Spanish American universities were busy educating young men long before Harvard, the first university in the 13 English colonies, was founded in 1636.

Women wishing an education might enter a convent. One such woman was Sor Juana Inés de la Cruz. Refused admission to the University of Mexico because she was a girl, Juana entered a convent at the age of 16. There, she devoted herself to study and the writing of poetry. She earned a reputation as one of the greatest poets ever to write in the Spanish language.

Cultural Blending Although Spanish culture was dominant in the cities, the blending of diverse traditions changed people's lives throughout the Americas. Settlers learned Native American styles of building, ate foods native to the Americas, and traveled in Indian-style canoes. Indian artistic styles influenced the newcomers. At the same time, settlers taught their religion to Native Americans. They also introduced animals, especially the horse, that transformed the lives of many Native Americans.

Africans added to this cultural mix with their farming methods, cooking styles, and crops, including okra and palm oil. African drama, dance, and song heightened Christian services. In Cuba, Haiti, and elsewhere, Africans forged new religions that blended African and Christian beliefs.

The Portuguese Colony in Brazil

A large area of South America remained outside the Spanish empire. By the Treaty of Tordesillas in 1494, Portugal claimed Brazil. (See the map in Section 3.) Portugal issued grants of land to Portuguese nobles, who agreed to develop the land and share profits with the crown. Landowners sent settlers to build towns, plantations, and churches.

The Economy Unlike Spain's American lands, Brazil offered no instant wealth from silver or gold. Early settlers clung to the coast, where they cut and exported brazilwood, used to produce a precious dye. Before long,

A New Society and Culture
The social structure and culture of Spain's American empire reflected its unique blend of people. This portrait depicts a Spanish man, his Mexican wife, and their mestizo daughter.

Theme: Diversity What were the social classes in Spain's American empire?

Southwestern Architecture: A Blending of Cultures

When the Spanish explorers entered what is today the American Southwest, they found Native American buildings that had existed for centuries. The Spanish settlers and the Native Americans influenced each other's building styles and created a unique architecture that survives to this day.

The Pueblo Indians used a mixture of mud and sand, called adobe, to construct the Taos Pueblo in New Mexico (below). Built around 1350, this collection of apartment-style houses has flat roofs formed by long poles, closely grouped rooms, and small windows. For protection, the main entrances were in the rooftops. The front doorways are a modern addition.

Known as "The White Dove of the Desert," San Xavier del Bac (right) was completed in the late 1700s. Spanish priests directed the work of Tohono O'odham Indian laborers to create this outpost of Spanish culture in the desert near Tucson, Arizona.

Built in the 1920s in Santa Fe, New Mexico, the Institute of American Indian Arts Museum, (right) blends Native American and Spanish architecture. The twin towers resemble the bell towers of a Spanish church. The main contours of the building follow the shape of an Indian pueblo.

Portfolio Assessment

INTERNET — Use the Internet or library resources to find out more about the architecture of the American Southwest. Then, prepare a class presentation that identifies Native American and Spanish features of a particular building. If possible, include photographs, drawings, or a model of the building you have selected.

Fast Facts

- Pueblo Indians used "puddled," or poured, adobe before the Spanish arrived. Spanish settlers introduced the use of adobe bricks.

- Both the Pueblos and the Spanish built their communities around a central plaza, or square.

- Taos Pueblo is still inhabited today.

Creativity Is Our Tradition

they turned to plantation agriculture and cattle raising. They forced Indians and Africans to clear land for sugar plantations. As many as five million Africans were sent to Brazil.

The thickly forested Amazon basin remained largely unexplored by settlers. However, ruthless adventurers slowly pushed inland. They attacked and enslaved Native American peoples and claimed for themselves land for immense cattle ranches. Some even discovered gold.

A New Culture As in Spanish America, a new culture emerged in Brazil that blended European, Native American, and African patterns. European culture dominated the upper and middle classes, but Native American and African influences left their mark. Portuguese settlers, for example, eagerly adopted Indian hammocks. A settler expressed his enthusiasm:

> "Would you believe that a man could sleep suspended in a net in the air like a bunch of hanging grapes? Here this is the common thing. . . . I tried it, and will never again be able to sleep in a bed, so comfortable is the rest one gets in the net."
> —quoted in *Latin America: A Concise Interpretive History* (Burns)

Challenging Spanish Power

In the 1500s, the wealth of the Americas helped make Spain the most powerful country in Europe. Its lofty position fueled envy among its European rivals. Many English and Dutch shared the resentment that French king Francis I felt when he declared, "I should like to see Adam's will, wherein he divided the Earth between Spain and Portugal."

European nations challenged Spain's power in various ways. To get around Spain's strict control over colonial trade, smugglers traded illegally with Spanish colonists. In the Caribbean and elsewhere, Dutch, English, and French pirates preyed on Spanish treasure ships. Some pirates, called privateers, even operated with the approval of European governments. England's Queen Elizabeth, for example, knighted Francis Drake for his daring raids on Spanish ships and towns.

Like the Spanish, the Dutch, English, and French hunted for gold empires and for a northwest passage to Asia. As you will read, these nations explored the coasts and planted settlements in North America.

Geography and History

Piracy on the Seas

Of all the privateers who plundered Spanish colonies, none was bolder than the Englishman whom the Spanish called *El Draque* (the Dragon). But Sir Francis Drake was more than just a pirate. He was also a skilled and daring explorer.

Drake led the second expedition ever to sail around the world. After a violent storm, he rounded the tip of South America in 1578 with only his flagship, the *Golden Hind*. But that one ship was enough. Spain's settlements along the Pacific coast were unguarded. After all, no hostile ship had ever made it into these waters before! Drake plundered one Spanish town and captured two treasure ships before continuing on his mission. Thanks to these raids and others, *El Draque* enriched his queen—and won the lasting hatred of the Spanish.

Theme: Geography and History Why was Drake able to surprise the Spanish?

SECTION 2 Assessment

Recall

1. **Identify:** (a) Council of the Indies, (b) Bartolomé de las Casas, (c) New Laws of the Indies, (d) Sor Juana Inés de la Cruz.
2. **Define:** (a) viceroy, (b) plantation, (c) encomienda, (d) peon, (e) peninsular, (f) creole, (g) mestizo, (h) mulatto, (i) privateer.

Comprehension

3. Describe how Spain controlled its American empire.
4. (a) How did the mix of peoples in Spanish America result in a new social structure? (b) Give three examples of cultural blending in Spain's American empire.
5. How did other European nations challenge Spanish power in the Americas?

Critical Thinking and Writing

6. **Comparing** (a) In what ways were the Spanish and Portuguese empires in the Americas similar? (b) In what ways were they different?
7. **Solving Problems** How might the Spanish have solved the problem of finding a dependable labor supply without resorting to the use of slavery?

Activity

Making a Poster
Review what you have read about Spanish treatment of Native Americans. Then, design a poster Bartolomé de las Casas could have used to rouse public opinion in Spain to protect the Indians.

Reading Focus

- What problems did settlers in New France face?
- What traditions of government evolved in the 13 English colonies?
- How did competition for power affect Europeans and Native Americans?

Vocabulary

missionary
revenue
compact

Taking Notes

Copy this partially completed table. As you read, fill in key information on the French and English colonies in North America.

	FRENCH COLONIES	ENGLISH COLONIES
LOCATION		East coast of North America
ECONOMY	Based mostly on fishing and fur trading	
GOVERNMENT		
GROWTH		

Main Idea **France and England set up colonies and competed for dominance in North America.**

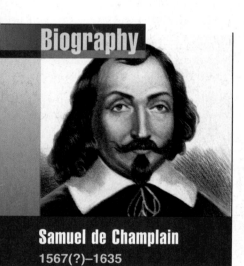

Biography

Samuel de Champlain
1567(?)–1635

Samuel de Champlain was an explorer, geographer, and mapmaker. As founder and first governor of the French colony of Quebec, he is known as the Father of New France, the French colonial empire in North America.

Champlain explored many of the waterways of New France. He especially loved the St. Lawrence River, which he said was "beautiful as the Seine, rapid as the Rhône, and deep as the sea." He helped to make it the main highway for trade through New France and to make himself the force behind the colony's settlement.

Theme: Impact of the Individual Why is Champlain considered the Father of New France?

Setting the Scene

In the 1600s, other European powers moved into the Americas and began building settlements. France, the Netherlands, England, and Sweden joined Spain in claiming parts of North America.

At first, the Europeans were disappointed. North America did not yield vast treasure or offer a water passage to Asia, as they had hoped. Before long, though, the English and French were turning large profits by growing tobacco in Virginia, fishing off the North Atlantic coast, and trading fur from New England to Canada.

By 1700, France and England controlled large parts of North America. As their colonies grew, they developed their own governments, different from each other and from that of Spanish America.

Building New France

By the early 1500s, French fishing ships were crossing the Atlantic each year to harvest rich catches of cod off Newfoundland, Canada. Distracted by wars at home, however, French rulers at first paid little attention to Canada—New France, as they called it. Not until 1608 did Samuel de Champlain build the first permanent French settlement in Quebec. Jesuits and other **missionaries**, hoping to spread Christianity to Native Americans, soon followed. They advanced into the wilderness, trying to convert Native Americans they met.

Slow Growth Helped by Native American allies, French explorers and fur traders traveled inland, claiming vast territory. Soon, France's American empire reached from Quebec to the Great Lakes and down the Mississippi to Louisiana and the Gulf of Mexico.

The population of New France grew slowly. Wealthy landlords owned huge tracts, or areas of land, along the St. Lawrence River. They sought settlers to farm the land, but the harsh Canadian climate attracted few French peasants.

Many who went to New France soon abandoned farming in favor of fur trapping and trading. They faced a hard life in the wilderness, but the soaring European demand for fur ensured good prices. Fishing, too, supported settlers who lived in coastal villages and exported cod and other fish to Europe.

Government Policy In the late 1600s, the French king Louis XIV set out to strengthen royal power and boost **revenues,** or income from taxes, from his overseas empire. He appointed officials to oversee justice and economic activities in New France. He also sent more settlers and soldiers to North America. The Catholic Louis, however, prohibited Protestants from settling in New France.

By the early 1700s, French forts, missions, and trading posts stretched from Quebec to Louisiana. Yet the population of New France remained small compared to that of the 13 English colonies expanding along the Atlantic coast.

The 13 English Colonies

The English built their first permanent colony at Jamestown, Virginia, in 1607. Its early years were filled with disaster. Many settlers died of starvation and disease. The rest survived with the help of friendly Native Americans. The colony finally made headway when the settlers started to grow and export tobacco, a crop they learned about from the Indians.

In 1620, other English settlers, the Pilgrims,* landed at Plymouth, Massachusetts. They were seeking religious freedom, rather than commercial profit. Before coming ashore, they signed the Mayflower Compact, in which they set out guidelines for governing their North American colony. A compact is an agreement among people. Today, we see this document as an important early step toward self-government. It read:

> "We, whose names are underwritten . . . having undertaken for the Glory of God, and Advancement of the Christian Faith . . . a voyage to plant [a] colony in the [Americas] . . . do enact, constitute, and frame, such just and equal Laws . . . as shall be thought most [fitting] and convenient for the general Good of the Colony."
>
> —Mayflower Compact

Many Pilgrims died in the early years of the Plymouth colony. Local Indians, however, taught them to grow corn and helped them survive in the new land. Soon, a new wave of Puritan immigrants arrived to establish the Massachusetts Bay Colony.

Growth In the 1600s and 1700s, the English established 13 colonies. Some, like Virginia and New York, were commercial ventures, organized for profit. Others, like Massachusetts, Pennsylvania, and Maryland, were set up as havens for persecuted religious groups.

Geographic conditions helped shape different ways of life in the New England, middle, and southern colonies. In New England, many settlers were farmers who transferred to North America the village life they had enjoyed in England. In parts of the South, there emerged a plantation economy based on tobacco, rice, and other crops.

Like New Spain, the English colonies needed workers to clear land and raise crops. A growing number of Africans were brought to the colonies and sold as slaves. In several mainland colonies, enslaved Africans and their descendants outnumbered people of European descent.

Government Like the rulers of Spain and France, English monarchs asserted control over their American colonies. They appointed royal governors to oversee colonial affairs and had Parliament pass laws to regulate colonial trade. Yet, compared with settlers in the Spanish and French colonies, English colonists enjoyed a large degree of self-government. Each

Primary Source

Pilgrim Courage
Governor William Bradford of Plymouth Colony wrote a first-hand account of its early days, describing what happened after half the Pilgrims had died:

"[Of the 50 left . . . only six or seven were sound. These six or seven] . . . spared no pains night nor day, but with abundance of toil and hazard of their own health, fetched them wood, made them fires, dressed them meat, made their beds, washed their [filthy] clothes, clothed and unclothed them. . . . All this [was done] willingly and cheerfully, without any grudging in the least, showing herein their true love unto their friends and brethren."

—William Bradford, *Of Plymouth Plantation: 1620–1647*

Skills Assessment

Primary Source Why were the "sound" Pilgrims' actions necessary to the survival of Plymouth Colony?

---

*Pilgrims were a band of English Puritans, a Protestant group, who rejected the practices of the official Church of England.

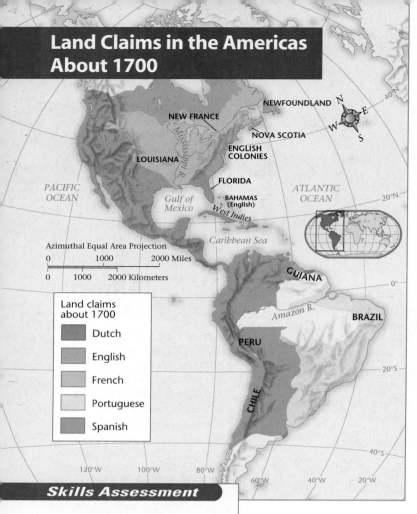

Land Claims in the Americas About 1700

NEWFOUNDLAND

NEW FRANCE

NOVA SCOTIA

ENGLISH COLONIES

LOUISIANA

Mississippi R.

FLORIDA

BAHAMAS (English)

Gulf of Mexico

West Indies

PACIFIC OCEAN

ATLANTIC OCEAN

Caribbean Sea

Azimuthal Equal Area Projection

0   1000   2000 Miles

0   1000   2000 Kilometers

GUIANA

Amazon R.

BRAZIL

PERU

CHILE

Land claims about 1700

- Dutch
- English
- French
- Portuguese
- Spanish

120°W   100°W   80°W   60°W   40°W   20°W

40°N   20°N   0°   20°S   40°S

Skills Assessment

Geography In the 1700s, European nations competed for colonies and trade in the Americas.

1. **Location** On the map, locate (a) New France, (b) Florida, (c) West Indies.
2. **Region** In what regions of North America did England have colonies?
3. **Critical Thinking** **Synthesizing Information** Based on the map and what you have read, why did England and France clash several times during the 1700s?

colony had its own representative assembly elected by propertied men. The assemblies advised the royal governor and made decisions on local issues.

The tradition of consulting representative assemblies grew out of the English experience. Beginning in the 1200s, Parliament had played an increasingly important role in English affairs. Slowly, too, English citizens had gained certain legal and political rights. England's American colonists expected to enjoy the same rights. When colonists later protested British policies in North America, they viewed themselves as "freeborn Englishmen" who were defending their traditional rights.

Competing for Power

By the 1600s, Spain, France, England, and the Netherlands were competing for colonies and trade around the world. All four of these nations had colonies in North America, where they often fought over territory. After several naval wars with the Netherlands, the English seized the Dutch colony of New Netherland in 1664 and renamed it New York. English settlers in Georgia clashed with the Spanish in nearby Florida.

Competition was also fierce in the Caribbean region. Dutch planters developed sugar production in the Caribbean into a big business. The French acquired Haiti, the richest of the sugar colonies, as well as Guadeloupe and Martinique. The English took Barbados and Jamaica. By the 1700s, the French and English Caribbean islands, worked by enslaved Africans, had surpassed the whole of North America in exports to Europe.

British-French Rivalry During the 1700s, Britain and France emerged as bitter rivals for power around the globe. They clashed in Europe, North America, Africa, and Asia. In North America, the French and Indian War raged from 1754 to 1763. A worldwide struggle, known as the Seven Years' War, erupted in Europe in 1756 and spread to India and Africa.

Although France held more territory in North America, the British colonies had more people. Trappers, traders, and farmers from the English colonies were pushing west into the Ohio Valley, a region claimed by France. The French, who had forged alliances with local Indians, fought to oust the intruders.

During the war, British soldiers and colonial troops launched a series of campaigns against the French in Canada and on the Ohio frontier. At first, France won several victories. Then, in 1759, the tide turned in Britain's favor. From ships anchored in the St. Lawrence River, British troops launched an attack on Quebec, the capital of New France. The British scaled steep cliffs along the river and captured the city. Though the war dragged on until 1763, the British had won control of Canada.

The Peace Treaty The 1763 Treaty of Paris officially ended the worldwide war. The treaty ensured British dominance in North America. France ceded Canada and its lands east of the Mississippi River to Britain. As you have read, the British also forced the French out of India. France, however, regained the rich sugar-producing islands in the Caribbean and the slave-trading outposts in Africa that the British had seized during the war.

Impact on Native Americans

As in Spanish America, the arrival of European settlers in North America had a profound impact on Native Americans. Some Native Americans traded or formed alliances with the newcomers. On the Great Plains, as we will see, the arrival of the horse transformed the lifestyle of buffalo-hunting Indians.

War and Disease Frequently, however, clashes erupted. As settlers claimed more land, Native Americans resisted their advance. Bitter fighting resulted. In the end, superior weapons helped the English to victory. Year by year, the flood of new settlers pushed the frontier—and the Indians—slowly westward.

As elsewhere, the Native American population of North America plummeted. Disease weakened or killed large numbers. For example, in 1608, an estimated 30,000 Algonquins lived in Virginia. By 1670, there were only about 2,000 Algonquins remaining.

Native American Legacy While encounters with Europeans often brought disaster to Native American societies, the Indian way of life helped shape the emerging new culture of North America. Settlers adopted Native American technologies. From Indians, they learned to grow corn, beans, squash, and tomatoes and to hunt and trap forest animals. Today's Thanksgiving menu of turkey and pumpkin pie reflects Indian foods.

Trails blazed by Indians became highways for settlers moving west. Across the continent, rivers like the Mississippi, lakes like Okeechobee, and mountains like the Appalachians bear Indian names. Some Europeans came to respect Native American medical knowledge. Today, many people are taking a new look at Indian religious traditions that stress respect for the natural environment.

Impact on Native Americans
In their contest for North America, European nations enlisted Indian allies. This leader of the Iroquois sided with the English.
Theme: Global Interaction How did the flood of European settlers affect the Indians of North America?

SECTION 3 Assessment

Recall
1. **Identify:** (a) Samuel de Champlain, (b) Louis XIV, (c) Jamestown, (d) Pilgrims, (e) Mayflower Compact, (f) French and Indian War, (g) Treaty of Paris.
2. **Define:** (a) missionary, (b) revenue, (c) compact.

Comprehension
3. Why did New France grow slowly?
4. What form of government did the 13 English colonies set up?
5. (a) How did Britain come to dominate North America? (b) What impact did European competition for colonies have on Native Americans?

Critical Thinking and Writing
6. **Connecting to Geography** Study the map in this section and the physical map of North America in the Reference Section of this book. (a) Which waterways were vitally important to French colonies in North America? (b) How might France's rivals take advantage of this geographic dependence?
7. **Comparing** Compare New France and the 13 English colonies in terms of (a) population, (b) government, (c) economy.

Activity

Making a Travel Brochure Suppose you are a minister to Louis XIV of France. To attract people to New France, he has asked you to advertise the benefits of life in the Americas. Make a colorful brochure with maps, illustrations, and persuasive messages.

Turbulent Centuries in Africa

Reading Focus

- How did the arrival of Europeans in Africa lead to the Atlantic slave trade?

- How did the slave trade contribute to the rise of new African states?

- What groups battled for power in southern Africa?

Vocabulary

triangular trade
repeal
monopoly

Taking Notes

Copy this partially completed flowchart. As you read, fill in key events in the development of the Atlantic slave trade. Add as many boxes to the chart as you need.

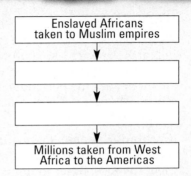

Enslaved Africans taken to Muslim empires

↓

↓

↓

Millions taken from West Africa to the Americas

Main Idea The Atlantic slave trade, the rise of new states, and power struggles created turbulence in Africa.

Setting the Scene "The first object which saluted my eyes when I arrived on the coast was the sea, and a slave ship which was then riding at anchor and waiting for its cargo. These filled me with astonishment, which was soon converted into terror when I was carried on board." So wrote Olaudah Equiano. In the 1750s, when he was 11 years old, Equiano was seized from his Nigerian village by slave traders. He was then transported as human cargo from West Africa to the Americas.

Enslaved Africans like Equiano formed part of an international trade network that arose during the first global age. Encounters between Europeans and Africans had been taking place since the 1400s. By then, as you have read, Africa was home to diverse societies, and Islam had become an important force in some parts of the continent. As Europeans arrived, they would bring their own influences to Africa.

European Outposts in Africa

In the 1400s, Portuguese ships explored the coast of West Africa, looking for a sea route to India. They built small forts along the West African coast to trade for gold, collect food and water, and repair their ships.

The Portuguese lacked the power to push into the African interior. They did, however, attack the coastal cities of East Africa, such as Mombasa and Malindi, which were hubs of international trade. With cannons blazing, they expelled the Arabs who controlled the East African trade network and took over this thriving commerce for themselves.

The Portuguese, however, gained little profit from their victories. Trade between the interior and the coast soon dwindled. By 1600, the once-prosperous East African coastal cities had sunk into poverty.

Other Europeans soon followed the Portuguese into Africa. The Dutch, the English, and the French established forts along the western coast of Africa. Like the Portuguese, they exchanged muskets, tools, and cloth for gold, ivory, hides, and slaves.

The Atlantic Slave Trade

In the 1500s, Europeans began to view slaves as the most important item of African trade. Slavery had existed in Africa, as elsewhere around the world, since ancient times. Egyptians, Greeks, Romans, Persians, Indians, and Aztecs often enslaved defeated foes. Our word *slave* comes from the large number of Slavs taken from southern Russia to work as unpaid laborers in Roman times.

The Arab empire also used slave labor, often captives taken from Africa. In the Middle East, many enslaved Africans worked on farming estates or large-scale irrigation projects. Others became artisans, soldiers, or merchants. Some rose to prominence in the Muslim world even though they were officially slaves.

European and African Slave Traders   The Atlantic slave trade began in the 1500s, to fill the need for labor in Spain's American empire. In the next 300 years, it grew into a huge and profitable business. Each year, traders shipped tens of thousands of enslaved Africans across the Atlantic to work on tobacco and sugar plantations in the Americas.

Europeans seldom went into the interior to take part in slave raids. Instead, they relied on African rulers and traders to seize captives in the interior and bring them to coastal trading posts and fortresses. There, the captives were exchanged for textiles, metalwork, rum, tobacco, weapons, and gunpowder. The slave trade intensified as the demand for slaves increased in the Americas and as the demand for luxury goods increased in Africa.

Triangular Trade   The Atlantic slave trade formed one part of a three-legged trade network known as the triangular trade. On the first leg, merchant ships brought goods to Africa to be traded for slaves. On the second leg, known as the Middle Passage, the slaves were transported to the West Indies. There, the enslaved Africans were exchanged for sugar, molasses, and other products. On the final leg, these products were shipped to Europe or European colonies in the Americas. The prosperity of port cities such as Nantes in France, Bristol in England, and Salem in Massachusetts thus depended in large part on the slave trade.

Horrors of the Middle Passage   For enslaved Africans, the Middle Passage was a horror. Once purchased, Africans were packed below the decks of slave ships. Hundreds of men, women, and children were crammed into a single vessel. Slave ships became "floating coffins" on which up to half the Africans on board died from disease or brutal mistreatment.

The Slave Trade
Merchants from many lands engaged in the slave trade. Arabs, such as those on the ship below, brought human cargoes out of East Africa. Portuguese traders carried slaves to the Americas from West Africa. A Portuguese soldier is depicted in the delicate ivory carving.

Theme: Global Interaction
Why was there a growing demand for slaves in the Americas?

Biography

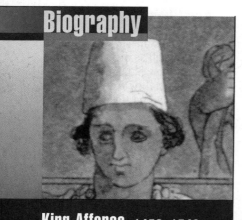

King Affonso 1456–1543

"Most powerful and excellent King of the Kongo, We convey you greetings in that We much love and esteem you." So wrote the king of Portugal to King Affonso in 1512. Affonso (born Nzinga Mbemba) had a long and warm relationship with the Portuguese. However, some years later, in 1526, Affonso wrote in dismay to the king of Portugal: "Merchants are taking every day our natives, sons of the land and sons of our nobles and vassals and our relatives, because the thieves and men of bad conscience . . . grab them and get them to be sold. . . . Our country is being completely depopulated."

In the end, Affonso's ties to Portugal were not strong enough. He sought help to build modern ships, but no Portuguese shipbuilders ever arrived. And his attempts to end the slave trade had no effect.

Theme: Impact of the Individual Why do you think Affonso is admired today, even though his efforts failed?

Primary Sources and Literature

See "King Affonso I: Letter to King John of Portugal" in the Reference Section at the back of this book.

Some enslaved Africans resisted. A few tried to seize control of the ship and return to Africa. Others committed suicide by leaping overboard. One African recalled such an incident during the Middle Passage:

> "One day . . . two of my wearied countrymen who were chained together . . . jumped into the sea; immediately another . . . followed their example. . . . two of the wretches were drowned, but [the ship's crew] got the other, and afterwards flogged him unmercifully for thus attempting to prefer death to slavery."
>
> —Olaudah Equiano, *The Life of Gustavus Vassa*

African Leaders Resist Some African leaders tried to slow down the transatlantic slave trade or even to stop it altogether. They used different forms of resistance. But in the end, the system that supported the trade was simply too strong for them.

An early voice raised against the slave trade was that of Affonso I, ruler of Kongo in west-central Africa. As a young man, Affonso was tutored by Portuguese missionaries. After becoming king in 1505, he called on the Portuguese to help him develop Kongo as a modern Christian state.

Before long, however, Affonso grew alarmed. Each year, more and more Portuguese came to Kongo to buy slaves. They offered high prices, and government officials and local chiefs eagerly entered the trade. Even Christian missionaries began to buy and sell Africans.

Affonso insisted that "it is our will that in these Kingdoms there should not be any trade of slaves nor outlet for them." Kongo, he stated, could benefit from contacts with Europe, but the trade in human lives was evil. His appeal failed, and the slave trade continued.

In the late 1700s, another African ruler, the almamy of Futa Toro in northern Senegal, tried to halt the slave trade in his lands. Since the 1500s, French sea captains had bought slaves from African traders in Futa Toro. The almamy decided to put a stop to this practice. In 1788, he forbade anyone to transport slaves through Futa Toro for sale abroad. The sea captains and local chiefs protested, and called on the almamy to repeal, or cancel, the law. The almamy refused. He returned the presents the captains had sent him in hopes of winning him over to their cause. "All the riches in the world would not make me change my mind," he said.

The almamy's victory was short-lived, however. The inland slave traders simply worked out a new route to the coast. Sailing to this new market, the French captains easily purchased the slaves that the almamy had prevented them from buying in Senegal. There was nothing the almamy could do to stop them.

Impact of the Atlantic Slave Trade Historians are still debating the number of Africans who were affected by the Atlantic slave trade. In the 1500s, they estimate, about 2,000 enslaved Africans were sent to the Americas each year. In the 1780s, when the slave trade was at its peak, that number topped 80,000 a year. By the mid-1800s, when the overseas slave trade was finally stopped, an estimated 11 million enslaved Africans had reached the Americas. Another 2 million probably died under the brutal conditions of the voyage between Africa and the Americas.

The slave trade caused the decline of some African states and the rise of others. In West Africa, the loss of countless numbers of young women and men resulted in some small states disappearing forever. At the same time, there arose new African states whose way of life depended on the slave trade. The rulers of these powerful new states waged war against other Africans so they could gain control of the slave trade in their region and reap the profits.

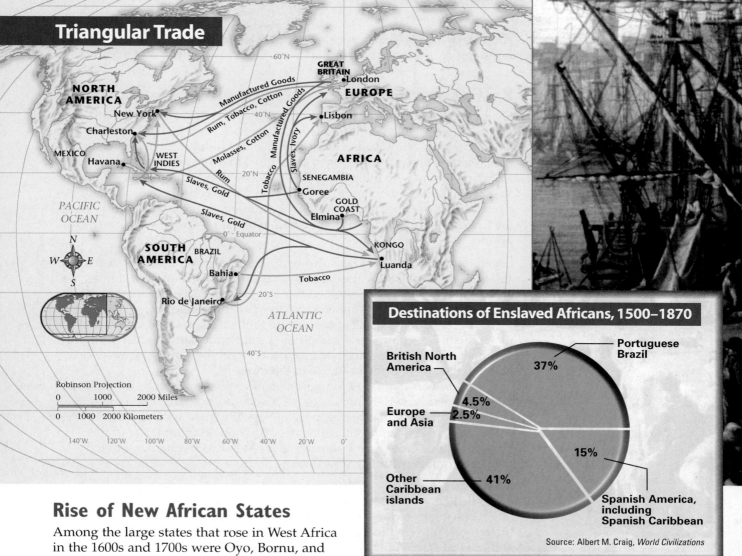

Triangular Trade

Destinations of Enslaved Africans, 1500–1870

- Portuguese Brazil **37%**
- British North America **4.5%**
- Europe and Asia **2.5%**
- Other Caribbean islands **41%**
- Spanish America, including Spanish Caribbean **15%**

Source: Albert M. Craig, *World Civilizations*

Rise of New African States

Among the large states that rose in West Africa in the 1600s and 1700s were Oyo, Bornu, and Dahomey. Another state, the Asante kingdom, emerged in the area occupied by modern Ghana.

The Asante Kingdom In the late 1600s, an able military leader, Osei Tutu, won control of the trading city of Kumasi. From there, he conquered neighboring peoples and organized the Asante kingdom. Osei Tutu claimed that his right to rule came from heaven. Leading chiefs served as a council of advisers but were subject to the royal will.

Officials chosen by merit rather than by birth supervised an efficient bureaucracy. They managed the royal monopolies over gold mining and the slave trade. A monopoly is the exclusive control of a business or industry. The Asante traded with Europeans on the coast, exchanging gold and slaves for firearms. But they shrewdly played off rival Europeans against one another to protect their own interests.

Islamic Crusades In the 1700s and early 1800s, an Islamic revival spread across West Africa. It began among the Fulani people in northern Nigeria. The scholar and preacher Usman dan Fodio denounced the corruption of the local Hausa rulers. He called for social and religious reforms based on the Sharia, or Islamic law. In the early 1800s, Usman inspired Fulani herders and Hausa townspeople to rise up against their rulers.

Usman and his successors set up a powerful Islamic state. Under their rule, literacy increased, local wars quieted, and trade improved. Their success inspired other Muslim reform movements in West Africa. Between

Skills Assessment

Geography The Atlantic slave trade was part of the triangular trade network that linked merchants in Africa, Europe, and the Americas.

1. **Location** On the map, locate **(a)** Africa, **(b)** West Indies, **(c)** New York, **(d)** Charleston.
2. **Movement** What goods were sent to Africa?
3. **Critical Thinking Analyzing Information** Between 1500 and 1870, most enslaved Africans were taken to what two regions of the Americas?

about 1780 and 1880, more than a dozen Islamic leaders rose to power, replacing old rulers or founding new states in the western Sudan.

Battles for Power in Southern Africa

Over many centuries, Bantu-speaking peoples had migrated into southern Africa. In 1652, Dutch immigrants also arrived in the region. They built Cape Town to supply ships sailing to or from the East Indies. Dutch farmers, called Boers, settled around Cape Town. Over time, they ousted or enslaved the Khoisan herders who lived there. The Boers held to a Calvinist belief that they were the elect, or chosen, of God. They looked on Africans as inferiors.

In the 1700s, Boer herders and ivory hunters began to push north from the Cape Colony. As they did, they had to battle several powerful African groups.

Shaka and the Zulus   The Zulus had migrated into southern Africa in the 1500s. In the early 1800s, they emerged as a major force under a ruthless and brilliant leader, Shaka. He built on the successes of earlier leaders who had begun to organize young fighters into permanent regiments.

Between 1818 and 1828, Shaka waged relentless war and conquered many nearby peoples. He absorbed their young men and women into Zulu regiments. By encouraging rival groups to forget their differences, he cemented a growing pride in the Zulu kingdom.

Shaka's wars disrupted life across southern Africa. Groups driven from their homelands by the Zulus adopted Shaka's tactics. They then migrated north, conquering still other peoples and creating their own powerful states.

Later Shaka's half brother took over the Zulu kingdom. About this time, the Zulus faced a new threat, the arrival of well-armed, mounted Boers migrating north from the Cape Colony.

Boers Versus Zulus   In 1815, the Cape Colony passed from the Dutch to the British. Many Boers resented British laws that abolished slavery and otherwise interfered in their way of life. To escape British rule, they loaded their goods into covered wagons and started north. In the late 1830s, several thousand Boer families joined this "Great Trek."

As the migrating Boers came into contact with Zulus, fighting quickly broke out. At first, Zulu regiments held their own. But in the end, Zulu spears could not defeat Boer guns. The struggle for control of the land would rage until the end of the century, as you will read later.

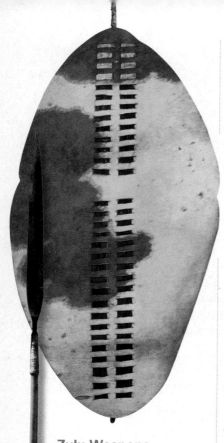

Zulu Weapons
The Zulus developed a new type of stabbing spear with a short shaft and a broad blade. For protection, they used ox-hide shields that were four feet high. Zulu armies won battles against the Boers, the English, and neighboring African peoples.

Theme: Economics and Technology Why were Europeans eventually able to defeat the Zulus?

SECTION 4 Assessment

Recall
1. **Identify: (a)** Middle Passage, **(b)** Asante, **(c)** Usman dan Fodio, **(d)** Boer, **(e)** Shaka, **(f)** Great Trek.
2. **Define: (a)** triangular trade, **(b)** repeal, **(c)** monopoly.

Comprehension
3. **(a)** Describe attempts by Africans to stop the slave trade. **(b)** What was the impact of the slave trade on life in Africa?
4. What steps did the Asante ruler take to ensure his power?
5. How did southern Africa become a battleground for rival groups?

Critical Thinking and Writing
6. **Solving Problems (a)** What kinds of information would a modern historian need to determine the number of Africans involved in the slave trade? **(b)** Why might a historian have trouble finding this information?
7. **Analyzing Information (a)** Why do you think European traders rarely took part directly in slave raids? **(b)** What effect did participation in the slave trade have on West African states?

Activity
Take It to the NET

Use the Internet to research the Zulu leader, Shaka. Then, write a newspaper article that describes his life, his character, and his role in the history of southern Africa.

Changes in Europe

Reading Focus

- How did European explorations lead to a global exchange?
- What impact did the commercial revolution and mercantilism have on European economies?
- How did these changes affect ordinary people?

Vocabulary

inflation
capitalism
entrepreneur
joint stock company
mercantilism
tariff

Taking Notes

Copy this diagram. As you read, fill in ways in which exploration and increased trade affected life in Europe. To help you get started, part of the diagram has been filled in.

EUROPEAN EXPLORATION AND TRADE

New foods from the Americas

Main Idea European exploration and increased trade stimulated a global exchange, a commercial revolution, and other changes in Europe.

Setting the Scene
In 1570, Joseph de Acosta visited the Americas. He wrote in amazement about the many strange forms of life that he saw there. "[There are] a thousand different kinds of birds and beasts of the forest, which have never been known, neither in shape nor name. . . ." To Europeans like Acosta, the Americas seemed like a "new world."

As you have read, European explorations between 1500 and 1700 brought major changes to Asia, Africa, and the Americas. Here, we will look at the impact that these explorations had on Europe itself.

A Global Exchange

When Columbus returned to Spain in March 1493, he brought with him "new" plants and animals that he had found in the Americas. Later that year, Columbus returned to the Americas. With him were some 1,200 settlers and a collection of European animals and plants. In this way, Columbus began a vast global exchange that would have a profound effect on the world. In addition to people, plants, and animals, it included technology and even disease. Because this global exchange began with Columbus, we call it the Columbian Exchange.

New Foods From the Americas, Europeans brought home a variety of foods, including tomatoes, pumpkins, and peppers. Perhaps the most important foods from the Americas, however, were corn and the potato. Easy to grow, the potato helped feed Europe's rapidly growing population. Corn spread all across Europe and to Africa and Asia, as well.

At the same time, Europeans carried a wide variety of plants and animals to the Americas. Foods included wheat and grapes from Europe itself, and bananas and sugar cane from Africa and Asia. Cattle, pigs, goats, and chickens, unknown before the European encounter, added protein to the Native American diet. Horses and donkeys also changed the lives of Native Americans. The horse, for example, gave the nomadic peoples of western North America a new, more effective way to hunt buffalo.

Impact on Population The transfer of food crops from continent to continent took time. By the 1700s, however, corn, potatoes, manioc, beans, and tomatoes were contributing to population growth around the world. While other factors help account for the population explosion that began at this time, new food crops from the Americas were probably a key cause.

Global Connections

Europe's Sweet Tooth

Today, we take sugar for granted. But at one time, it was strictly a luxury item that few European households could afford. Then, in 1493, Columbus brought sugar cane plants to the Caribbean. The new crop thrived. As sugar supplies increased, sugar prices fell, and the former luxury item appeared on more and more European tables. It was also used to sweeten a popular new treat from the Americas—chocolate.

Still, Europe's new "sweet tooth" had a tragic side effect. In just 150 years, close to 4 million Africans were shipped as slaves to the Caribbean and Brazil to work the sugar plantations there.

Theme: Global Interaction
Who was originally responsible for bringing sugar cane to the Americas?

The Columbian Exchange sparked the migration of millions of people. Each year, shiploads of European settlers sailed to the Americas. Europeans also settled on the fringes of Africa and Asia. As you have read, the Atlantic slave trade forcibly brought millions of Africans to the Americas. The Native American population declined drastically.

The vast movement of peoples led to the transfer of ideas and technologies. Language also traveled. Words such as *pajama* (from India) or *hammock* and *canoe* (from the Americas) entered European languages.

A Commercial Revolution

The opening of direct links with Asia, Africa, and the Americas had far-reaching economic consequences for Europeans. Among these consequences were an upsurge in prices, known as the price revolution, and the rise of modern capitalism.

The Price Revolution   In the early modern age, prices began to rise in parts of Europe. The economic cycle that involves a rise in prices linked to a sharp increase in the amount of money available is today called inflation.

European inflation had several causes. As the population grew, the demand for goods and services rose. Because goods were scarce, sellers could raise their prices. Inflation was also fueled by an increased flow of silver and gold. By the mid-1500s, tons of these precious metals were flowing into Europe from the Americas. Rulers used much of the silver and gold to make coins. The increased money in circulation, combined with the scarcity of goods, caused prices to rise.

Growth of Capitalism   Expanded trade and the push for overseas empires spurred the growth of European capitalism, the investment of money to make a profit. Entrepreneurs, or enterprising merchants, organized, managed, and assumed the risks of doing business. They hired workers and paid for raw materials, transport, and other costs of production.

As trade increased, entrepreneurs sought to expand into overseas ventures. Such ventures were risky. Capitalist investors were more willing to take the risks when demand and prices were high. Thus, the price revolution of the early modern age gave a boost to capitalism.

Entrepreneurs and capitalists made up a new business class devoted to the goal of making profits. Together, they helped change the local European economy into an international trading system.

New Business Methods   Early capitalists discovered new ways to create wealth. From the Arabs, they adapted methods of bookkeeping to show profits and losses from their ventures. During the late Middle Ages, as you have read, banks sprang up, allowing wealthy merchants to lend money at interest. The joint stock company, also developed in late medieval times, grew in importance. It allowed people to pool large amounts of capital needed for overseas ventures.

Bypassing the Guilds   The growing demand for goods led merchants to find ways to increase production. Traditionally, guilds controlled the manufacture of goods. But guild masters often ran small-scale businesses without the capital to produce for large markets. They also had strict rules regulating quality, prices, and working conditions.

Enterprising capitalists devised a way to bypass the guilds. The "putting-out" system, as it was called, was first used to produce textiles but later spread to other industries. Under the "putting-out" system, a merchant capitalist distributed raw wool to peasant cottages. Cottagers spun the wool into thread and then wove the thread into cloth. Merchants bought the wool cloth from the peasants and sent it to the city for finishing and dyeing. Finally, the merchants sold the finished product for a profit.

The Commercial Revolution

The Commercial Revolution spurred trade, promoted new business methods, and increased competition for profits among European nations. Use the quotation, picture, and graph to learn about this revolution.

The Port of Marseille, France, 1700s

The Clove Market

In his book published in 1998, journalist Charles Corn described one way the Dutch East India Company maintained its profits in cloves:

"The Dutch East India Company by now had gained the power to restrict production to meet Europe's demand for cloves, thereby maintaining high prices and preventing a glutted market. To achieve this end, the company engaged in a ploy . . . : balancing off the island's supply of spices against what it perceived to be the world's demand for them. Such a scheme introduced the practice of [required] cultivation of spice trees in groves officially authorized and the careful [destruction] of those the company did not approve."
—Charles Corn, *The Scents of Eden*

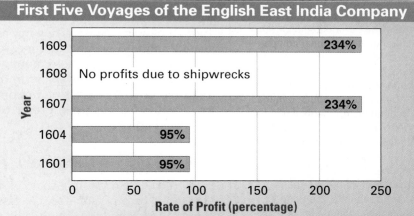

First Five Voyages of the English East India Company

Year	Rate of Profit (percentage)
1609	234%
1608	No profits due to shipwrecks
1607	234%
1604	95%
1601	95%

Source: Sir William Wilson Hunter, *A History of British India*

Skills Assessment

1. The range of profits on the English East India Company's first five voyages was from
   A 95 percent to 234 percent.
   B total loss to 234 percent.
   C 1601 to 1609.
   D $0 to $234.

2. The Dutch East India Company tried to improve its profits on cloves by
   E planting more clove trees.
   F using extra ships to bring cloves to market.
   G keeping production low in relation to demand.
   H increasing the supply of cloves on the market.

3. **Critical Thinking Drawing Conclusions (a)** What evidence here might lead you to conclude that shipping was important to the Commercial Revolution? **(b)** What role did the profit motive play in the Commercial Revolution? Use evidence to support your answer.

Skills Tip

Bar graphs have both a vertical axis and a horizontal axis, with each measuring a different element. Distinguish between the two before turning to the rest of the graph.

"TAKE US TO YOUR LEADER . . .
WE'VE COME TO NEGOTIATE A
FREE TRADE AGREEMENT WITH
EARTH."

Connections to Today

The Banana Wars

Governments have been using tariffs to protect their own industries for years. This practice continues today, as the "Banana Wars" between the United States and Europe demonstrate. American multinational companies produce bananas in countries like Honduras and Ecuador. Former European colonies in the Caribbean also produce bananas. European governments decided to let Caribbean bananas come into their countries more cheaply than the bananas produced by American firms, thus taking market share from the American firms. To retaliate, the United States government placed a 100 percent tariff on certain goods from Europe, making them much more expensive. Some 500 years after they began, tariff wars go on.

Theme: Continuity and Change Why do tariff wars develop?

The "putting-out" system separated capital and labor for the first time. From this system controlled by merchants, the next step would be the capitalist-owned factories of the Industrial Revolution of the 1700s, as you will read.

Mercantilism

European monarchs enjoyed the benefits of the commercial revolution. In the fierce competition for trade and empire, they adopted a new economic policy, known as mercantilism, aimed at strengthening their national economies.

Mercantilists supported several basic ideas. They believed that a nation's real wealth was measured in its gold and silver treasure. To build its supply of gold and silver, they said, a nation must export more goods than it imported.

The Role of Colonies Overseas empires were central to the mercantile system. Colonies, said mercantilists, existed for the benefit of the parent country. They provided resources and raw materials not available in Europe. In turn, they enriched a parent country by serving as a market for its manufactured goods.

To achieve these goals, European powers passed strict laws regulating trade with their colonies. Colonists could not set up their own industries to manufacture goods. They were also forbidden to buy goods from a foreign country. In addition, only ships from the parent country or the colonies themselves could be used to send goods in or out of the colonies.

Increasing National Wealth Mercantilists urged rulers to adopt policies to increase national wealth and government revenues. To boost production, governments exploited mineral and timber resources, built roads, and backed new industries. They imposed a single national currency and established standard weights and measures.

Governments also sold monopolies to large producers in certain industries as well as to big overseas trading companies. Finally, governments imposed tariffs, or taxes on imported goods. Tariffs were designed to protect local industries from foreign competition by increasing the price of imported goods.

The Lives of Ordinary People

How did these economic changes affect Europeans? In general, their impact depended on a person's social class. Merchants who invested in overseas ventures acquired wealth. But the price revolution hurt nobles. Their wealth was in land, and they had trouble raising money to pay higher costs for stylish clothing and other luxuries. Some sold off land, which in turn reduced their income. In towns and cities, the wages of hired workers did not keep up with inflation, creating poverty and discontent.

Most Europeans were still peasants. Europe's growing involvement in the world had little immediate effect on their lives. Changes took generations, even centuries, to be felt. For example, tradition-bound peasants were often reluctant to grow foods brought from the Americas. Only in the later 1700s did German peasants begin to raise potatoes. Even then, many complained that these strange-looking tubers tasted terrible.

Within Europe's growing cities, there were great differences in wealth and power. Successful merchants dominated city life. Guilds, too, remained powerful. And as trade grew, another group—lawyers—gained importance for their skills in writing contracts. Middle-class families enjoyed a comfortable life. Servants cooked, cleaned, and waited on them. Other city residents, such as journeymen and other laborers, were not so lucky. They often lived in crowded quarters on the edge of poverty.

Regardless of social class, European families were patriarchal. As husband and father, a man was responsible for the behavior of his wife and children. Women had almost no property or legal rights. A woman's chief roles were as wife and mother. Society stressed such womanly virtues as modesty, household economy, obedience, and caring for the family. Middle-class women might help their husbands in a family business. Peasant women worked alongside their husbands in the fields.

Looking Ahead

In the 1500s and 1600s, Europe emerged as a powerful new force on the world scene. The voyages of exploration marked the beginning of what would become European domination of the globe. In the centuries ahead, competition for empire would spark wars in Europe and on other continents.

European expansion would spread goods and other changes throughout the world. It would also revolutionize the European economy and transform its society. The concept of "the West" itself emerged as European settlers transplanted their culture to the Americas and, later, to Australia and New Zealand.

For centuries, most Europeans knew little or nothing about other lands. Exposure to different cultures was both unsettling and stimulating. As their horizons broadened, they had to reexamine old beliefs and customs.

Cause *and* Effect

Long-Term Causes	Immediate Causes
• Scientific Revolution • Europeans search for a sea route to Asia	• Columbus and other Europeans arrive in the Americas • Europeans encounter new plants and animals in the Americas

Columbian Exchange

Immediate Effects	Long-Term Effects
• Millions of Native Americans die from diseases • Enslaved Africans sent to the Americas • American foods introduced into Europe	• Exchange of ideas, foods, art, and language between Europe and the Americas • Population migration from Europe to the Americas • Growth of capitalism

Connections to Today

• Multicultural societies in the Americas
• Worldwide reliance on staples such as corn and potatoes

Skills Assessment   **Chart** The arrival of Columbus in the Americas set off a global exchange of people, goods, and ideas. **Based on the chart, name one immediate and one long-term effect of the Columbian Exchange.**

SECTION 5 Assessment

Recall
1. **Identify:** (a) Columbian Exchange, (b) commercial revolution, (c) "putting-out" system.
2. **Define:** (a) inflation, (b) capitalism, (c) entrepreneur, (d) joint stock company, (e) mercantilism, (f) tariff.

Comprehension
3. How did the voyages of Columbus lead to global exchanges of goods and ideas?
4. Explain how each of the following contributed to economic changes in Europe: (a) the price revolution, (b) capitalism, (c) mercantilism.

5. How did the economic changes of the 1500s and 1600s affect the lives of ordinary people?

Critical Thinking and Writing
6. **Linking Past and Present** Global exchanges of goods, ideas, and even diseases continue today. How has modern technology quickened the speed with which global exchanges occur? Provide examples to support your answer.
7. **Inferring** Do you think the European policy of mercantilism was beneficial or harmful for the people of Africa and the Americas? Explain.

Activity

Creating a Map
Create an illustrated map of the world showing the movement of items in the Columbian Exchange. Label Europe, Asia, Africa, and North and South America. Create symbols to stand for products and use arrows to indicate the direction in which they traveled.

Creating a Chapter Summary

Copy this graphic organizer. Complete the organizer by writing in major changes that occurred in Europe, the Americas, and Africa as a result of the first global age from 1492 through the 1700s.

For additional review and enrichment activities, see the interactive version of *World History* available on the Web and on CD-ROM.

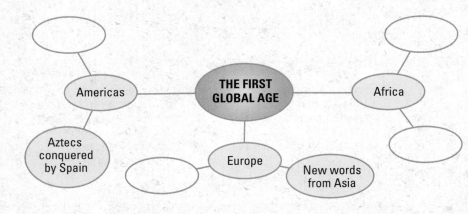

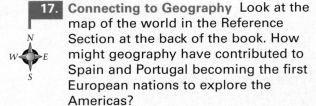

Web Site Self-Test
For practice test questions for Chapter 16, see **www.phschool.com**.

Building Vocabulary

Use the chapter vocabulary words listed to create a crossword puzzle. Exchange your puzzle with a classmate. Complete the puzzle and then check each other's answers.

1. **conquistador**
2. **civil war**
3. **encomienda**
4. **creole**
5. **mestizo**
6. **missionary**
7. **compact**
8. **capitalism**
9. **mercantilism**
10. **tariff**

Recalling Key Facts

11. How did the Spanish conquistadors treat the Native Americans they encountered?
12. Describe three examples of cultural blending in Spain's empire in the Americas.
13. How did Britain gain control of North America from the French?
14. Why were Africans brought to Spanish colonies in the Americas?
15. Why was there conflict in southern Africa in the 1700s and 1800s?
16. What was the Columbian Exchange?

Critical Thinking and Writing

17. **Connecting to Geography** Look at the map of the world in the Reference Section at the back of the book. How might geography have contributed to Spain and Portugal becoming the first European nations to explore the Americas?

18. **Linking Past and Present** How might your life be different if France had defeated England in the Seven Years' War?

19. **Recognizing Points of View** How might each of the following people have viewed European conquests in the 1500s and 1600s: **(a)** a Spaniard, **(b)** a Native American, and **(c)** an African?

20. **Recognizing Causes and Effects (a)** What were three causes of the growth of the Atlantic slave trade? **(b)** What were three immediate effects of the slave trade on Africa? **(c)** What do you think might have been some long-term effects of the slave trade on Africa's later development? Explain.

Read the excerpt below about the Middle Passage. Then, answer the questions that follow.

"I now saw myself deprived of all chances of returning to my native country. . . [and] my present situation. . .was filled with horrors of every kind. . . .The stench of the hold, while we were on the coast was so intolerably loathsome that it was dangerous to remain there for any time. . . .The closeness of the place, and the heat of the climate, added to the number in the ship, which was so crowded that each had scarcely room to turn himself, almost suffocated us. . . .The shrieks of the women, and the groans of the dying, rendered the whole a scene of horror almost inconceivable."

—Olaudah Equiano, *The Life of Gustavus Vassa*

21. **(a)** Who was the author of the excerpt? **(b)** Do you consider him a reliable source of information about the Middle Passage? Why or why not?
22. **(a)** What are some of the descriptive words used by the author about conditions aboard a slave ship? **(b)** What emotions are these words likely to arouse in the reader?
23. How did climate conditions affect the Middle Passage?
24. **(a)** Did the author think that he might one day return to Africa? **(b)** Why do you think he felt this way?
25. Many enslaved Africans died during the Middle Passage. Based on the above account, what were some of the reasons for the high death toll?

Use the Internet to research the exports of Brazil or another European colony in the Americas during the first global age. Then, write a business report describing how that colony helped increase the wealth of the colonizing nation. If possible, compare the colonial exports with the exports that the area produces as an independent nation today.

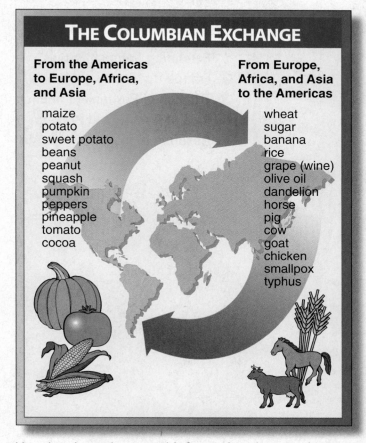

THE COLUMBIAN EXCHANGE

From the Americas to Europe, Africa, and Asia	From Europe, Africa, and Asia to the Americas
maize	wheat
potato	sugar
sweet potato	banana
beans	rice
peanut	grape (wine)
squash	olive oil
pumpkin	dandelion
peppers	horse
pineapple	pig
tomato	cow
cocoa	goat
	chicken
	smallpox
	typhus

Use the chart above and information that you have learned in this chapter to answer the following questions:

26. When and with what event did this global exchange begin?
27. **(a)** Name three food crops that spread from the Americas to Europe, Africa, and Asia. **(b)** Name three domesticated animals that were introduced to the Americas.
28. How did the exchange cause a decline in the Native American population?
29. What effects did the Columbian Exchange have on the European economy?
30. How would life improve for people in both Europe and the Americas as a result of the global exchange?

Skills Tip

A flowchart represents a process in a simplified form. Some show a step-by-step process. Others show a cycle. Look at the arrows to understand the direction of the process.

The Age of Absolutism
1550–1800

Chapter Preview

1 **Extending Spanish Power**
2 **France Under Louis XIV**
3 **Triumph of Parliament in England**
4 **Rise of Austria and Prussia**
5 **Absolute Monarchy in Russia**

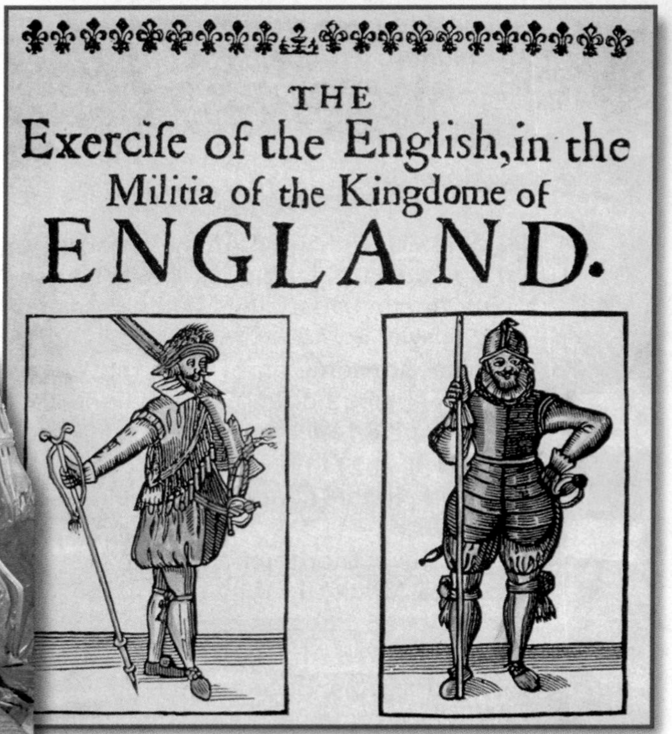

THE
Exercife of the English, in the
Militia of the Kingdome of
ENGLAND.

1642
The English Civil War begins, pitting the king's troops (left) against the armies of Parliament (right).

1556
Philip II (second from right) becomes king of Spain. Under Philip, Spain is the wealthiest and most powerful state in Europe.

1618
Religious conflict between German Protestants and Catholics sparks the Thirty Years' War.

CHAPTER EVENTS

1550   1600   1650

GLOBAL EVENTS

1556 Akbar the Great becomes emperor of India.

1607 British colonists found Jamestown.

European Nation-States, 1700

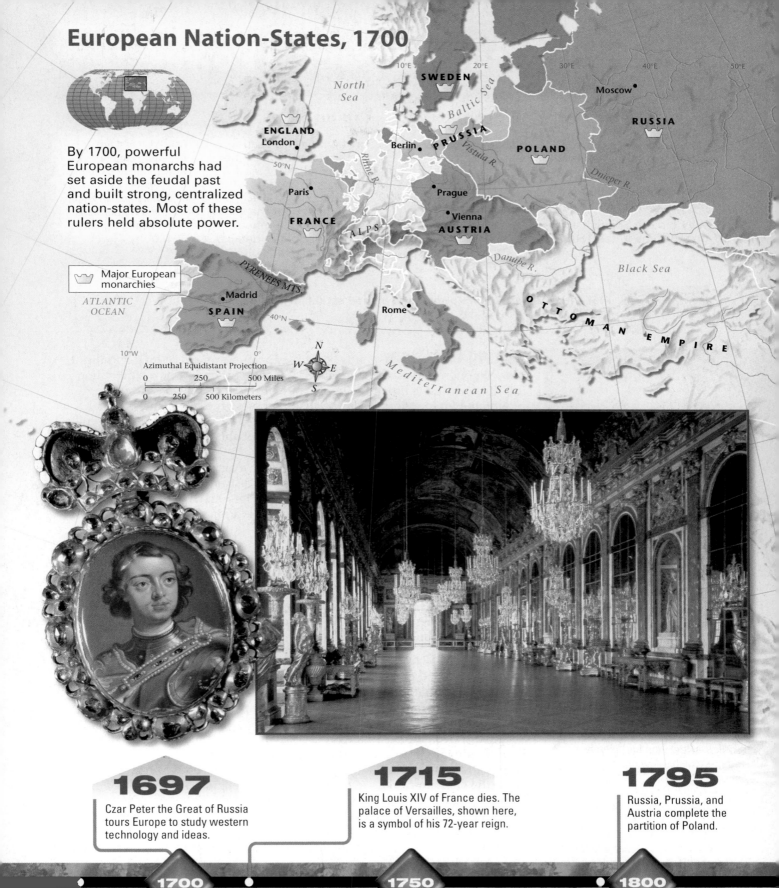

By 1700, powerful European monarchs had set aside the feudal past and built strong, centralized nation-states. Most of these rulers held absolute power.

Major European monarchies

North Sea

SWEDEN

Baltic Sea

Moscow

RUSSIA

ENGLAND
London

Berlin
PRUSSIA

POLAND

Vistula R.

Dnieper R.

Rhine R.

Paris

Prague

FRANCE

Vienna
AUSTRIA

ALPS

Danube R.

Black Sea

OTTOMAN EMPIRE

ATLANTIC OCEAN

Madrid

SPAIN

PYRENEES MTS.

Rome

Mediterranean Sea

Azimuthal Equidistant Projection

0   250   500 Miles
0   250   500 Kilometers

1697

Czar Peter the Great of Russia tours Europe to study western technology and ideas.

1715

King Louis XIV of France dies. The palace of Versailles, shown here, is a symbol of his 72-year reign.

1795

Russia, Prussia, and Austria complete the partition of Poland.

1700

1750

1800

1680s Asante kingdom is organized in West Africa.

1754 The French and Indian War erupts in North America.

1793 The emperor of China rejects British trade.

Extending Spanish Power

Reading Focus

■ How did Spanish power increase under Charles V and Philip II?

■ How did the arts flourish during Spain's golden age?

■ Why did the Spanish economy decline in the 1600s?

Vocabulary

absolute monarch

divine right

armada

Taking Notes

As you read this section, prepare an outline of the contents. Use Roman numerals to indicate major headings. Use capital letters for the sub-headings and numbers for the supporting details. The example will help you get started.

I. Charles V and the Hapsburg Empire
   A. Wearing two crowns
      1. Spain
      2. Holy Roman Empire and Netherlands
   B. An empire divided
      1.
      2.
II.

Main Idea   Philip II extended Spain's power and helped establish a golden age.

Global Connections

Cartloads of Silver and Gold

Old Spanish shipping records tell a tale about amazing wealth: "On 22 March 1595, ships from the Indies . . . began to discharge and deposit with the Chamber of Commerce 332 cartloads of silver, gold, and pearls of great value." This was the haul for *just one day*—and the flow of riches continued for *years!*

A major part of this wealth enriched the royal family. Most of the rest went into the hands of private traders. For Spain, American silver and gold financed a golden age of art, literature—and power.

Theme: Economics and Technology What impact could wealth from the Americas have on the arts in Renaissance Spain?

Setting the Scene

"It is best to keep an eye on everything," Philip II of Spain often said—and he meant it. As king of the most powerful nation in Europe, he gave little time to pleasure. Instead, he plowed through a mountain of paperwork each day, making notes on even the most trivial matters. Once the Spanish ambassador to England wrote about an unfamiliar kind of insect he had seen in London. "Probably fleas," Philip scribbled on the letter.

Philip's determination to "keep an eye on everything" extended far beyond trivia. It helped him build Spain into a strong centralized state. By the late 1500s, he had concentrated all power into his own hands. Over the next 200 years, other European monarchs would pursue similar goals.

Charles V and the Hapsburg Empire

By the 1500s, Spain had shaken off the feudal past and emerged as the first modern European power. Under Queen Isabella and King Ferdinand, Spain had expelled the last Muslim rulers and enforced religious unity. In 1492, Isabella financed Columbus's voyage across the Atlantic, leading to the Spanish conquest of the Americas.

Wearing Two Crowns In 1519, Charles V,* grandson of Ferdinand and Isabella, inherited a huge empire. The new king faced a nearly impossible challenge. He not only inherited the crown of Spain but was also the heir of the Austrian Hapsburgs. The sprawling Hapsburg empire included the Holy Roman Empire and the Netherlands.

Ruling two empires involved Charles in constant warfare. As a devout Catholic, he fought to suppress the Protestant movement in the German states. After years of religious warfare, however, Charles was forced to allow the German princes to choose their own religions.

His greatest foe was the Ottoman empire. Under Suleiman, Ottoman forces advanced across central Europe to the walls of Vienna, Austria. Although Austria held firm, the Ottomans occupied much of Hungary. Ottoman naval forces also challenged Spanish power in the Mediterranean.

An Empire Divided Perhaps the Hapsburg empire was too scattered and diverse for any one person to rule. Exhausted and disillusioned, Charles V gave up his titles and entered a monastery in 1556. He divided his empire,

---

* Within Spain, the king was known as Charles I. However, historians usually refer to him as Charles V, his title as ruler of the Austrian Hapsburg empire.

leaving the Hapsburg lands in central Europe to his brother Ferdinand, who became Holy Roman emperor. He gave Spain, the Netherlands, southern Italy, and Spain's overseas empire to his 29-year-old son Philip.

Philip II and Divine Right

Like his father, King Philip II was hard-working, devout, and ambitious. During his 42-year reign, he sought to expand Spanish influence, strengthen the Catholic Church, and make his own power absolute. Thanks in part to silver from the Americas, he made Spain the foremost power in Europe.

Unlike many other monarchs, Philip devoted much time to government work. He seldom hunted, never jousted, and lived as sparsely as a monk. His isolated, somber palace outside Madrid reflected the King's character. Known as the Escorial (ehs KOHR ee uhl), it served as a church, a residence, and a tomb for members of the royal family.

As did Ferdinand and Isabella, Philip further centralized royal power, making every part of the government responsible to him. He reigned as an **absolute monarch,** a ruler with complete authority over the government and the lives of the people. Like other European rulers, Philip asserted that he ruled by **divine right.** That is, he believed that his authority to rule came directly from God.

Partly as a result of the concept of divine right, Philip saw himself as the guardian of the Roman Catholic Church. The great undertaking of his life was to defend the Catholic Reformation and turn back the rising Protestant tide in Europe. Within his own lands, Philip enforced religious unity. He turned the Inquisition against Protestants and other people thought to be heretics.

The Wars of Philip II

Philip fought many wars as he attempted to advance Spanish Catholic power. At the battle of Lepanto in 1571, Spain and its Italian allies soundly defeated an Ottoman fleet in the Mediterranean. Although Christians hailed this as a great victory, the Ottoman empire remained a major power in the Mediterranean region.

Revolt in the Netherlands During the last half of his reign, Philip battled Protestant rebels in the Netherlands. At the time, the region included 17 provinces that are today Belgium, the Netherlands, and Luxembourg. It was the richest part of Philip's empire. Protestants in the Netherlands resisted Philip's efforts to crush their faith. Protestants and Catholics alike opposed high taxes and autocratic Spanish rule, which threatened local traditions of self-government.

In the 1560s, riots against the Inquisition sparked a general uprising in the Netherlands. Savage fighting raged for decades. In 1581, the northern, largely Protestant provinces declared their independence from Spain and became known as the Dutch Netherlands. They did not gain official recognition, however, until 1648. The southern, mostly Catholic provinces of the Netherlands remained part of the Spanish empire.

Invading England By the 1580s, Philip saw England's Queen Elizabeth I as his chief Protestant enemy. First secretly, then openly, Elizabeth had supported the Dutch against Spain. She even encouraged English captains,

Philip II of Spain
From 1556 to 1598, Philip II ruled the wealthiest, most powerful nation in Europe. Devoted to his family and to the Catholic Church, Philip could also be ruthless toward his enemies.

Theme: Impact of the Individual What impression of Philip II does this painting give you? Explain.

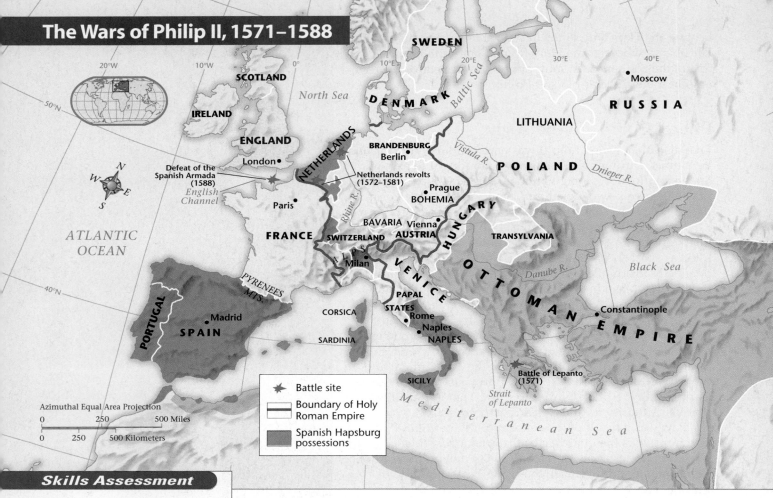

The Wars of Philip II, 1571–1588

SWEDEN

North Sea

SCOTLAND

IRELAND

DENMARK

Baltic Sea

• Moscow

RUSSIA

LITHUANIA

ENGLAND

London •

NETHERLANDS

BRANDENBURG

Berlin •

Vistula R.

POLAND

Dnieper R.

Defeat of the
Spanish Armada
(1588)

English
Channel

Netherlands revolts
(1572–1581)

Prague •
BOHEMIA

Paris •

Rhine R.

BAVARIA

Vienna •

AUSTRIA

HUNGARY

TRANSYLVANIA

ATLANTIC
OCEAN

FRANCE

SWITZERLAND

ALPS

Milan •

VENICE

OTTOMAN

Danube R.

Black Sea

PYRENEES
MTS.

PORTUGAL

CORSICA

PAPAL
STATES

Rome •
Naples •
NAPLES

EMPIRE

• Constantinople

• Madrid

SPAIN

SARDINIA

SICILY

Battle of Lepanto
(1571)

Strait
of Lepanto

Mediterranean Sea

Azimuthal Equal Area Projection

0   250   500 Miles

0   250   500 Kilometers

★ Battle site

▭ Boundary of Holy
Roman Empire

▨ Spanish Hapsburg
possessions

Skills Assessment

Geography To defend Spanish power and Roman Catholicism, Philip II sent Spanish forces across Europe.

1. **Location** On the map, locate (a) Spain, (b) Madrid, (c) Ottoman empire, (d) Strait of Lepanto, (e) Netherlands, (f) English Channel.
2. **Region** Which battles shown on the map took place in a territory ruled directly by Spain?
3. **Critical Thinking Analyzing Information** Why do you think Spain joined Italy in defending the Strait of Lepanto?

known as Sea Dogs, to plunder Spanish treasure ships. Francis Drake, the most daring Sea Dog, looted Spanish cities in the Americas. To Philip's dismay, instead of punishing the pirate, Elizabeth made him a knight.

To end English attacks and subdue the Dutch, Philip prepared a huge armada, or fleet, to carry a Spanish invasion force to England. In 1588, the Armada sailed with more than 130 ships, 20,000 men, and 2,400 pieces of artillery. The Spanish were confident of victory. "When we meet the English," predicted one Spanish commander, "God will surely arrange matters so that we can grapple and board them, either by sending some strange freak of weather or, more likely, just by depriving the English of their wits."

The "strange freak of weather," however, favored the other side. In the English Channel, lumbering Spanish ships took losses from the lighter, faster English ships. Suddenly, a savage storm blew up, scattering the Armada. After further disasters at sea, the tattered remnants limped home in defeat.

While the defeat of the Spanish Armada ended Philip's plan to invade England, it had little short-term effect on his power. In the long term, however, Spain's naval superiority did dwindle. In the 1600s and 1700s, Dutch, English, and French fleets challenged—and surpassed—Spanish power both in Europe and around the world.

Spain's Golden Age

The century from 1550 to 1650 is often called Spain's *siglo de oro*, or "golden century," for the brilliance of its arts and literature. Philip II was a patron of the arts and also founded academies of science and mathematics.

Painters Among the famous painters of this period was El Greco, meaning "the Greek." Born on the Greek island of Crete, El Greco had studied in

Renaissance Italy before settling in Spain. He produced haunting religious pictures, dramatic views of the city of Toledo, and striking portraits of Spanish nobles, done in a dramatically elongated style.

El Greco's use of vibrant colors influenced the work of Diego Velázquez (vuhl LAHS kehs), court painter to King Philip IV. Velázquez is perhaps best known for his vivid portraits of Spanish royalty.

Writers Spain's golden century produced outstanding writers like Lope de Vega. A peasant by birth, he wrote more than 1,500 plays, including witty comedies and action-packed romances. In *The Sheep Well*, Lope de Vega shows King Ferdinand and Queen Isabella saving a village from the hands of a villainous feudal lord.

Miguel de Cervantes wrote *Don Quixote*, the first modern novel in Europe. It pokes fun at medieval tales of chivalry. Dressed in rusty armor, the madman Don Quixote rides out on his broken-down plowhorse in search of adventure. He battles a windmill, which he thinks is a giant, and mistakes two flocks of sheep for opposing armies. He is accompanied by Sancho Panza, a practical-minded peasant.

Don Quixote mocked the traditions of Spain's feudal past. Yet Cervantes admired both the unromantic, earthy realism of Sancho Panza and the foolish but heroic idealism of Don Quixote.

Economic Decline

In the 1600s, Spanish power and prosperity slowly declined. Lack of strong leadership was one reason. The successors of Philip II were far less able rulers than he.

Economic problems were also greatly to blame. Costly overseas wars drained wealth out of Spain almost as fast as it came in. Then, too, treasure from the Americas led Spain to neglect farming and commerce. The government heavily taxed the small middle class, weakening a group that in other European nations supported royal power. The expulsion of Muslims and Jews from Spain deprived the economy of many skilled artisans and merchants. Finally, American gold and silver led to soaring inflation, with prices rising much higher in Spain than elsewhere in Europe.

Even though Spain continued to rule a huge colonial empire, its strength slipped away. By the late 1600s, France had replaced Spain as the most powerful European nation.

Primary Sources and Literature

See "Miguel de Cervantes: Don Quixote" in the Reference Section at the back of this book.

SECTION 1 Assessment

Recall

1. **Identify:** **(a)** Hapsburgs, **(b)** *siglo de oro,* **(c)** El Greco, **(d)** Diego Velázquez, **(e)** Miguel de Cervantes.
2. **Define:** **(a)** absolute monarch, **(b)** divine right, **(c)** armada.

Comprehension

3. **(a)** How did Philip II ensure absolute power? **(b)** How did he try to further Catholicism?
4. Why is the period from 1550 to 1650 considered Spain's golden age?
5. Why did Spanish power and prosperity decline?

Critical Thinking and Writing

6. **Recognizing Points of View** The English referred to the fierce storm that battered the Spanish Armada in 1588 as "the Protestant wind." **(a)** What does this nickname mean? **(b)** What nickname might the Spanish have given to the storm?
7. **Understanding Sequence** Create a time line showing key events in Spain's history between the rise of King Ferdinand and Queen Isabella and the end of its "golden century." Include events from this chapter and earlier chapters.

Activity

Take It to the NET

Use the Internet to learn more about the life and times of Miguel de Cervantes and his famous novel *Don Quixote*. Then, prepare a presentation giving examples of how the author used the characters of Don Quixote and Sancho Panza to satirize society.

France Under Louis XIV

Reading Focus

- How did France rebuild after its wars of religion?
- How did Louis XIV strengthen royal power?
- What successes and failures did Louis XIV experience?

Vocabulary

intendant
levée
balance of power

Taking Notes

Begin a concept web like this one. As you read this section, fill in the blank circles with relevant information about Louis XIV. Add as many circles as you need.

- Sun as symbol
- **LOUIS XIV**
- No meetings of Estates General

Main Idea Under the absolute rule of Louis XIV, France became the leading power of Europe.

Setting the Scene

"I have had an idea that will . . . give much pleasure to the people here," wrote Louis XIV, the young king of France. His plan was to throw a grand party. Each guest would receive a lottery ticket for a prize of jewelry—and every ticket would be a winner. At Louis's bidding, some 600 noble guests flocked to the royal palace for a week of sumptuous feasts, pageants, sports, dances, plays, and music. This extravaganza was the first of many spectacles organized by Louis XIV.

By the late 1600s, Louis was absolute monarch of France and the most powerful ruler in Europe. Yet, just 100 years earlier, France had been torn apart by turbulent wars of religion.

Rebuilding France

From the 1560s to the 1590s, religious wars between Huguenots (French Protestants) and the Catholic majority tore France apart. Leaders on both sides used the strife to further their own ambitions.

The worst incident began on St. Bartholomew's Day, August 24, 1572. As Huguenot and Catholic nobles gathered to celebrate a royal wedding, violence erupted that led to the massacre of 3,000 Huguenots. In the next few days, thousands more were slaughtered. For many, the St. Bartholomew's Day Massacre symbolized the complete breakdown of order in France.

Catholics vs. Huguenots
In the war between French Catholics and Protestants, both sides committed acts of violence. Here, Huguenot rioters destroy and loot a Catholic church.

Theme: Political and Social Systems Why did some French nobles encourage actions like these?

Henry IV In 1589, a Huguenot prince inherited the French throne as Henry IV. Knowing that a Protestant would face severe problems ruling a largely Catholic land, he became Catholic. "Paris is well worth a Mass," he is supposed to have said. To protect Protestants, however, he issued the Edict of Nantes in 1598. It granted the Huguenots religious toleration and let them fortify their own towns and cities.

Henry IV then set out to heal his shattered land. His goal, he said, was not the victory of one sect over another, but "a chicken in every pot"—a good Sunday dinner for every peasant. Under Henry, the government reached into every area of French life. Royal officials administered justice, improved roads, built bridges, and revived agriculture. By building the royal bureaucracy and reducing the influence of nobles, Henry IV laid the foundations for royal absolutism.

Richelieu When Henry IV was killed by an assassin in 1610, his nine-year-old son, Louis XIII, inherited the throne. For a time, nobles reasserted their power. Then, in 1624, Louis appointed Cardinal Armand Richelieu (RIHSH uh loo) as his chief minister. This cunning, capable leader spent the next 18 years strengthening the central government.

Richelieu sought to destroy the power of the Huguenots and nobles, two groups that did not bow to royal authority. He smashed the walled cities of the Huguenots and outlawed their armies, while still allowing them to practice their religion. At the same time, he defeated the private armies of the nobles and destroyed their fortified castles. While reducing their independence, Richelieu tied nobles to the king by giving them high posts at court or in the royal army.

Richelieu handpicked his able successor, Cardinal Jules Mazarin. When five-year-old Louis XIV inherited the throne in 1643, the year after Richelieu's death, Mazarin was in place to serve as chief minister. Like Richelieu, Mazarin worked tirelessly to extend royal power.

Louis XIV, the Sun King

Soon after Louis XIV became king, disorder again swept France. In an uprising called the *Fronde,* nobles, merchants, peasants, and the urban poor rebelled—each group for its own reasons. On one occasion, rioters drove the boy king from his palace. It was an experience Louis would never forget.

When Mazarin died in 1661, Louis resolved to take over the government himself. "I have been pleased to entrust the government of my affairs to the late Cardinal," he declared. "It is now time that I govern them myself."

"I Am the State" Like his great-grandfather Philip II of Spain, Louis XIV firmly believed in divine right. He wrote:

> "God's power is felt in an instant from one end of the world to the other; royal power takes the same time to act throughout the kingdom. It preserves the order of the whole kingdom, as does God with the whole world."
> —Louis XIV, quoted in *From Absolutism to Revolution* (Rowen)

Louis took the sun as the symbol of his absolute power. Just as the sun stands at the center of the solar system, he argued, so the Sun King stands at the center of the nation. Louis is often quoted as saying, *"L'etat, c'est moi"*—"I am the state."

During his reign, Louis did not once call a meeting of the Estates General, the medieval council made up of representatives of all French social classes. In fact, the Estates General did not meet between 1614 and 1789. Thus, unlike the English Parliament, the Estates General played no role in checking royal power.

Biography

Cardinal Armand Richelieu
1585–1642

Armand Richelieu's parents expected great things from him. They even invited the king of France to attend Armand's christening, promising that someday he would be a leader of France.

The young boy also aspired to greatness as he was growing up. At first, he received training to become a disciplined and authoritative military officer. Then, at his family's request, he switched directions. At age 17, he began training to become a bishop in the church. The path was different but the purpose was the same: to become a leader and to serve the king.

Over the next 40 years, Armand Richelieu rose to the top of France in both religious and political circles. He became the true power behind the throne of King Louis XIII.

Theme: Impact of the Individual How did Richelieu's training as both a soldier and a bishop prepare him to be a strong political leader?

Strengthening Royal Power Louis spent many hours each day attending to government affairs. To strengthen the state, he followed the policies of Richelieu. He expanded the bureaucracy and appointed **intendants,** royal officials who collected taxes, recruited soldiers, and carried out his policies in the provinces. The office of intendant and other government jobs often went to wealthy middle-class men. In this way, Louis cemented ties between the middle class and the monarchy.

Under Louis XIV, the French army became the strongest in Europe. The state paid, fed, trained, and supplied up to 300,000 soldiers. Louis used this highly disciplined army to enforce his policies at home and abroad.

Colbert and the Economy Louis's brilliant finance minister, Jean Baptiste Colbert (kohl BEHR), followed mercantilist policies to bolster the economy. Colbert had new lands cleared for farming, encouraged mining and other basic industries, and built up luxury trades such as lacemaking. To protect French manufacturers, he put high tariffs on imported goods. He also encouraged overseas colonies, such as New France in North America, and regulated trade with the colonies to enrich the royal treasury.

Colbert's policies helped make France the wealthiest state in Europe. Yet Louis XIV was often short of cash. Not even the financial genius of Colbert could produce enough income to support the huge costs of Louis's court or pay for his many foreign wars.

Versailles, Symbol of Royal Power

In the countryside near Paris, Louis XIV turned a royal hunting lodge into the immense palace of Versailles (ver sī). He spared no expense to make it the most magnificent building in Europe. Its halls and salons displayed the finest paintings and statues, and glittering chandeliers and mirrors. In the royal gardens, millions of flowers, trees, and fountains were set out in precise geometric patterns.

Versailles became the perfect symbol of the Sun King's wealth and power. As both the king's home and the seat of government, it housed at least 10,000 people, from nobles and officials to servants.

Court Ceremonies Louis XIV perfected elaborate ceremonies that emphasized his own importance. Each day began in the king's bedroom with a major ritual known as the **levée,** or rising. High-ranking nobles competed for the honor of holding the royal wash basin or handing the king his diamond-buckled shoes. At night, the ceremony was repeated in reverse. Wives of nobles vied to attend upon women of the royal family.

Rituals such as the levée served a serious purpose. French nobles were descendants of the feudal lords who held power in medieval times. Left at their estates, these nobles were a threat to the power of the monarchy. By luring nobles to Versailles, Louis turned them into courtiers angling for privileges rather than warriors battling for power. Louis carefully protected their prestige and left them free from paying taxes.

Cultural Flowering The king and his court supported a "splendid century" of the arts. Louis sponsored musical entertainments and commissioned plays by the best writers. The age of Louis XIV was the classical age of French drama. Jean Racine (rah SEEN) wrote tragedies based on ancient Greek myths. The actor-playwright Molière (mohl YAIR) turned out comedies, such as *The Miser*, that poked fun at French society.

In painting, music, architecture, and decorative arts, French styles became the model for all Europe. A new form of dance drama, ballet, gained its first great popularity at the French court. As a leading patron of culture, Louis sponsored the French Academies, which set high standards for both the arts and the sciences.

Did You Know?

A High-Maintenance King

"No expense is too great." Applying this rule certainly helped Louis XIV make sure his every wish was fulfilled. For example:

- As much as $1.5 billion may have been taken from France's treasury to build his lavish palace at Versailles. Tens of thousands of workers spent several decades building the palace.
- One minor item for the Versailles palace was his bathtub, which was carved out of a single piece of priceless Languedoc marble.
- Guards were stationed at every fountain in Versailles's gardens. The guards' job was to whistle whenever the king approached so that the water would be turned on fully.

Theme: Impact of the Individual What does the extravagance of Louis XIV say about the power of the French monarch?

You Are There . . .

Living at Versailles

King Louis XIV has summoned you to live at Versailles. As a French noble, you are both honored and intimidated. After all, life at court can be demanding. Dress, conduct, and events are strictly prescribed. One mistake and you may be ridiculed—or even banished. But the chance is too good to miss!

As you ride through the front gate, under the golden seal, you are stunned by the size of the main palace. It stretches for more than a quarter of a mile and contains 1,300 rooms.

An explosion of color commands your attention as you stroll through the formal gardens of Versailles with other nobles. Flower beds are divided into geometric patterns, and you are amazed at the endless variety of plants, bubbling fountains, and impressive statues.

You find it easy to believe that the king has said, "My dominant passion is certainly love of glory." Everything you have seen at Versailles is extravagant. All this magnificence does not come without a price, however. The kitchen is so far away from your apartments that your food often arrives cold.

Portfolio Assessment

To gain favor with the king, you decide to create a tour brochure of Versailles. You are so taken by the beauty of a particular site within the palace or on the grounds that you focus the guide on that area.

Successes and Failures

Louis XIV ruled France for 72 years, far longer than any other monarch. During his reign, French culture, manners, and customs replaced those of Renaissance Italy as the standard for European taste. In both foreign and domestic affairs, however, many of Louis's policies were costly failures.

Wars of Louis XIV Louis XIV poured vast resources into wars to expand French borders. At first, he did gain some territory. His later wars were disastrous, though, because rival rulers joined forces to check French ambitions. Led by the Dutch or the English, these alliances fought to maintain the balance of power, a distribution of military and economic power that would prevent any one nation from dominating Europe.

In 1700, Louis's grandson Philip V inherited the throne of Spain. Louis declared that France and Spain "must regard themselves as one." But neighboring powers led by England were determined to prevent this union. The War of the Spanish Succession dragged on until 1713, when an exhausted France signed the Treaty of Utrecht. Philip remained on the Spanish throne, but France agreed never to unite the two crowns.

The King as Warrior
Although Louis XIV is best remembered for his extravagant court, he also expanded France's military might. This painting depicts Louis as a gallant warrior.

Theme: Impact of the Individual What symbols does this artist use to glorify Louis XIV?

Persecution of the Huguenots Louis saw France's Protestant minority as a threat to religious and political unity. In 1685, he revoked the Edict of Nantes. More than 100,000 Huguenots fled France.

The persecution of the Huguenots was perhaps the king's most costly blunder. The Huguenots had been among the most hard-working and prosperous of Louis's subjects. Their loss was thus a serious blow to the French economy, just as the expulsion of Muslims and Jews had hurt Spain.

Looking Ahead

Louis XIV outlived his sons and grandsons. When he died in 1715, his five-year-old great-grandson inherited the throne as Louis XV. Although France was then the strongest state in Europe, years of warfare had drained the treasury. The prosperity nurtured by Colbert evaporated under the burden of bad harvests, heavy taxes, and other problems.

Louis XV was too weak a king to deal with such problems. He devoted his days to pleasure, ignoring the growing need for reform. He often quoted an old proverb, "After us, the deluge." As you will read, the deluge came during the reign of the next king.

SECTION 2 Assessment

Recall
1. **Identify: (a)** St. Bartholomew's Day Massacre, **(b)** Edict of Nantes, **(c)** *Fronde,* **(d)** Versailles, **(e)** War of the Spanish Succession.
2. **Define: (a)** intendant, **(b)** levée, **(c)** balance of power.

Comprehension
3. **(a)** What were the effects of the French wars of religion? **(b)** How did Henry IV rebuild French unity?
4. Describe how Louis XIV strengthened the power of the monarchy.

5. How did Louis's persecution of the Huguenots harm France?

Critical Thinking and Writing
6. **Comparing** How were the ideas of Louis XIV about monarchy similar to those of Philip II of Spain?
7. **Applying Information** On his deathbed, Louis XIV told his heir, "I have loved war too well; do not copy me in this, nor in the lavish expenditures I have made." Why do you think Louis gave this advice?

Activity

Designing a Set
Imagine that your school is putting on a play about Louis XIV at Versailles. You have been asked to design the set. Make a list of furniture, paintings, and other items you would want to include in the set.

Triumph of Parliament in England

Reading Focus

- How did the Tudors and Stuarts differ in their relations with Parliament?
- How did the English Civil War lead to the rise of the Commonwealth?
- What were the causes and results of the Glorious Revolution?

Vocabulary

dissenter

habeas corpus

limited monarchy

Taking Notes

Create a flowchart that shows the events in England that ultimately led to the strengthening of Parliament. Use this chart as a model, and add boxes as needed.

Tudors consult with and control Parliament
↓
James asserts claim to absolute power and clashes with Parliament
↓
↓

Main Idea During the 1600s, the British Parliament asserted its rights against royal claims to absolute power.

Setting the Scene

"The most high and absolute power in the realm consists in the Parliament," wrote an English statesman in the 1560s. He was voicing a tradition that had roots in the Middle Ages. But in 1603, a monarch with far different ideas took the throne of England. "Kings are called gods," declared James I, "because they sit upon God's throne on Earth." Before long, James was on a collision course with Parliament.

In the 1600s, while Louis XIV perfected royal absolutism in France, England developed in a different direction. In this section, we will look at why and how Parliament asserted itself against royal power.

The Tudors and Parliament

From 1485 to 1603, England was ruled by the Tudor dynasty. Although the Tudors believed in divine right, they shrewdly recognized the value of good relations with Parliament. As you have read, when Henry VIII broke with the Roman Catholic Church, he turned to Parliament to legalize his actions. Parliament approved the Act of Supremacy, making the monarch head of the Church of England.

A constant need for money also led Henry to consult Parliament frequently. Although he had inherited a bulging treasury, he quickly used up his funds fighting overseas wars. To levy new taxes, the king had to seek the approval of Parliament. Members of Parliament tended to vote as Henry's agents instructed. Still, they became accustomed to being consulted on important matters.

Like her father, Elizabeth I both consulted and controlled Parliament. Her advisers conveyed the queen's wishes to Parliament and forbade discussion of certain subjects, such as foreign policy or the queen's marriage. Her skill in handling Parliament helped make "Good Queen Bess" a popular and successful ruler.

The Early Stuarts

Elizabeth died in 1603 without a direct heir. The throne passed to her relatives the Stuarts, the ruling family of Scotland. The Stuarts were neither as popular as the Tudors nor as skillful in dealing with Parliament. They also inherited problems that Henry and Elizabeth had long suppressed. The result was a "century of revolution" that pitted the Stuart monarchs against Parliament.

The Royal Challenge   The first Stuart monarch, James I, had agreed to rule according to English laws and customs. Soon, however, he was lecturing Parliament about divine right. "I will not be content that my power be disputed upon," he declared. Leaders in the House of Commons fiercely resisted the king's claim to absolute power.

James repeatedly clashed with Parliament over money and foreign policy. He needed funds to finance his lavish court and wage wars. When members wanted to discuss foreign policy before voting funds, James dissolved Parliament and collected taxes on his own.

James also found himself embroiled in disputes with dissenters, Protestants who differed with the Church of England. One group, called Puritans, sought to "purify" the church of Catholic practices. Puritans called for simpler services and a more democratic church without bishops. James rejected their demands, vowing to "harry them out of this land or else do worse."

A positive result of the king's dispute with the Puritans was his call for a new translation of the Bible. The King James version that appeared in 1611 has had a lasting influence on English language and literature.

Parliament Responds   In 1625, Charles I inherited the throne. Like his father, Charles behaved like an absolute monarch. He imprisoned his foes without trial and squeezed the nation for money. By 1628, though, his need to raise taxes forced Charles to summon Parliament. Before voting any funds, Parliament insisted that Charles sign the Petition of Right. It prohibited the king from raising taxes without the consent of Parliament or from imprisoning anyone without just cause.

Charles did sign the petition, but he then dissolved Parliament in 1629. For 11 years, he ignored the petition and ruled the nation without Parliament. During that time, he created bitter enemies, especially among Puritans. His Archbishop of Canterbury, William Laud, tried to force all clergy to follow strict Anglican rules, dismissing or imprisoning dissenters. Many people felt that the archbishop was trying to revive Catholic practices.

In 1637, Charles and Laud tried to impose the Anglican prayer book on Scotland. The Calvinist Scots revolted. To get funds to suppress the Scottish rebellion, Charles finally had to summon Parliament in 1640. When it met, however, Parliament launched its own revolt.

The Long Parliament   The 1640 Parliament became known as the Long Parliament because it lasted on and off until 1653. Its actions triggered the greatest political revolution in English history. In a mounting struggle with the king, Parliament tried and executed his chief ministers, including Archbishop Laud. It further declared that the Parliament could not be dissolved without its own consent and called for the abolition of bishops.

Charles lashed back. In 1642, he led troops into the House of Commons to arrest its most radical leaders. They escaped through a back door and soon raised their own army. The clash now moved to the battlefield.

The English Civil War

The civil war that followed lasted from 1642 to 1649. Like the *Fronde* that occurred about the same time in France, the English Civil War posed a major challenge to absolutism. But while the forces of royal power won in France, in England the forces of revolution triumphed.

Cavaliers and Roundheads   At first, the odds seemed to favor the Cavaliers, or supporters of Charles I. Many Cavaliers were wealthy nobles, proud of their plumed hats and fashionably long hair. Well trained in dueling and warfare, the Cavaliers expected a quick victory. But their foes proved to be tough fighters with the courage of their convictions. The

---

Primary Source

A Voice for Absolutism
In 1651, two years after the English Civil War ended, English political philosopher Thomas Hobbes published Leviathan. *In the book, he explained why he favored an absolute monarch:*

"During the time men live without a common power to keep them all in awe, they are in that condition which is called war.... In such condition, there is no place for industry . . . no arts; no letters; no society; and, which is worst of all, continual fear and danger of violent death. And the life of man [is] solitary, poor, nasty, brutish, and short."

—Thomas Hobbes, *Leviathan*

Skills Assessment

Primary Source   How might people who supported Parliament over the monarch have argued against Hobbes's view?

Virtual Field Trip

www.phschool.com

**Cromwell Museum
Huntington, England**

To see other images relating to the
career of Oliver Cromwell, use the
Internet address above to link to
the Cromwell Museum.

A Victory for Parliament
The Battle of Marston Moor was
a turning point in the English Civil
War. Though wounded in the neck,
Oliver Cromwell (center, on horse)
rallied his troops to defeat the
forces of King Charles I.

**Theme: Continuity and
Change** How would a modern
battle scene differ from this one?

forces of Parliament were composed of country gentry, town-dwelling
manufacturers, and Puritan clergy. They were called Roundheads because
their hair was cut close around their heads.

The Roundheads found a leader of genius in Oliver Cromwell. A
Puritan member of the lesser gentry, Cromwell was a skilled general. He
organized the "New Model Army" for Parliament into a disciplined fighting force. Inspired by Puritan chaplains, Cromwell's army defeated the
Cavaliers in a series of decisive battles. By 1647, the king was in the hands
of parliamentary forces.

Execution of a King Eventually, Parliament set up a court to put the
king on trial. It condemned him to death as "a tyrant, traitor, murderer,
and public enemy." On a cold January day in 1649, Charles I stood on a
scaffold surrounded by his foes. "I am a martyr of the people," he declared.

Showing no fear, the king told the executioner that he himself would
give the sign for him to strike. After a brief prayer, Charles knelt and placed
his neck on the block. On the agreed signal, the executioner severed the
king's head with a single stroke.

The execution sent shock waves throughout Europe. In the past, kings
had occasionally been assassinated or died in battle. But for the first time, a
ruling monarch had been tried and executed by his own people. The parliamentary forces had sent a clear signal that, in England, no ruler could claim
absolute power and ignore the rule of law.

The Commonwealth

After the execution of Charles I, the House of Commons abolished the monarchy, the House of Lords, and the official Church of England. It declared
England a republic, known as the Commonwealth, under the leadership
of Oliver Cromwell.

Challenges to the Commonwealth The new government faced many
threats. Supporters of Charles II, the uncrowned heir to the throne, attacked
England by way of Ireland and Scotland. Cromwell led forces into Ireland
to crush the uprising. He then took harsh measures against the Irish Catholic
majority. In 1652, Parliament passed a law exiling most Catholics to barren

Our Puritan Heritage

Decades before the Puritans gained power in England, a group of settlers tried their hand at building a Puritan society across the Atlantic. Massachusetts Bay was a new colony without any traditions of established churches, strong government, or historic communities. The Puritans knew that to assure survival of their beliefs and culture, they would have to educate their children in their own ways. That was one reason the Puritans built schools, including Harvard College.

Eventually, the colonies became the United States. Over time, the rest of the country adopted the Puritan tradition of establishing public schools to help train children to become good citizens of their community. A literate, well-informed citizenry has continued to be a major aim of American schools to this day.

Theme: Political and Social Systems What other institutions help to train American children to be good citizens?

land in the west of Ireland. Any Catholic found disobeying this order could be killed on sight.

Squabbles also splintered forces within the Commonwealth. One group, called Levellers, thought that poor men should have as much say in government as the gentry, lawyers, and other leading citizens. "The poorest he that is in England hath a life to live as the greatest he," wrote one Leveller. In addition, female Levellers asserted their right to petition Parliament.

These Leveller ideas horrified the gentry who dominated Parliament. Cromwell and his generals suppressed the Levellers, as well as more radical groups who threatened property ownership. As the challenges to order grew, Cromwell took the title Lord Protector in 1653. From then on, he ruled through the army.

Puritan Society Under the Commonwealth, Puritan preachers tried to root out godlessness and impose a "rule of saints." The English Civil War thus ushered in a social revolution as well as a political one.

Parliament enacted a series of laws designed to make sure that Sunday was set aside for religious observance. Anyone over the age of 14 who was caught "profaning the Lord's Day" could be fined. To the Puritans, theaters were "spectacles of pleasure too commonly expressing mirth and levity." So, like John Calvin in Geneva, Cromwell closed all theaters. Puritans also frowned on lewd dancing, taverns, and gambling.

Puritans felt that every Christian, rich and poor, must be able to read the Bible. To spread religious knowledge, they encouraged education for all people. By mid-century, families from all classes were sending their children to school, girls as well as boys.

Puritans pushed for changes in marriage to ensure greater fidelity. In addition to marriages based on business interests, they encouraged marriages based on love. As in the past, women were seen mainly as caretakers of the family, subordinate to men. When some radical Protestant groups allowed women to preach sermons, most Puritans were shocked.

Although Cromwell could not accept open worship by Roman Catholics, he believed in religious freedom for other Protestant groups. He even welcomed Jews back to England, after more than 350 years of exile.

End of the Commonwealth Oliver Cromwell died in 1658. Soon after, the Puritans lost their grip on England. Many people were tired of military rule and strict Puritan ways. In 1660, a newly elected Parliament invited Charles II to return to England from exile.

England's "kingless decade" ended with the restoration of the monarchy. Yet Puritan ideas about morality, equality, government, and education endured. In the following century, these ideas would play an important role in shaping the United States of America.

From Restoration to Glorious Revolution

In late May 1660, cheering crowds welcomed Charles II back to London. One supporter wrote:

"This day came his Majesty, Charles the Second to London, after a sad and long exile . . . with a triumph of above 20,000 horse and [soldiers], brandishing their swords, and shouting with inexpressible joy; the ways strewd with flowers, the bells ringing, the streets hung with tapestry."

—John Evelyn, *Diary*

With his charm and flashing wit, young Charles II was a popular ruler. He reopened theaters and taverns and presided over a lively court in the manner of Louis XIV. Charles restored the official Church of England but tolerated other Protestants such as Presbyterians, Quakers, and Baptists.

The Struggle Between King and Parliament

In England, a battle for power raged between king and Parliament during the 1600s. The monarchy was abolished and then restored. The picture, the source, and the time line depict a few highlights of that struggle.

King Versus Parliament

James I and Divine Right (1603)

"Kings are called gods because they sit upon God's throne on earth."

English Bill of Rights (1689)

"1. That . . . suspending of laws . . . by regal authority, without consent of Parliament is illegal.
4. That levying money for or to the use of the crown . . . without grant of Parliament . . . is illegal."

Restoration: Charles II in Triumph

1603 Stuart rule begins	**1629** Charles I dissolves Parliament	**1649** Parliament orders execution of Charles I; Cromwell rules	**1688** Glorious Revolution	**1689** Parliament passes Bill of Rights

1600   1620   1640   1660   1680   1700

1640
Long Parliament meets

1642
English
Civil War

1660
Parliament restores Stuart rule;
Charles II is crowned

Skills Tip

On a time line, equal intervals of time should be represented by an equal amount of space.

Skills Assessment

1. In which of the following years did Parliament seem to have the most power?
   A 1629
   B 1640
   C 1660
   D 1689

2. The person who painted the picture of Charles II probably
   E favored the monarchy.
   F fought for Cromwell.
   G supported Parliament.
   H disliked the new king.

3. **Critical Thinking Applying Information** (a) What advice would you give to an English monarch in the 1600s who wanted to keep his or her throne? (b) What advice would you give to a member of Parliament in the 1600s who wanted the monarchy to continue?

Although Charles accepted the Petition of Right, he shared his father's faith in absolute monarchy and secretly had Catholic sympathies. Still, he shrewdly avoided his father's mistakes in dealing with Parliament.

A New Clash With Parliament   Charles's brother, James II, inherited the throne in 1685. Unlike Charles, James flaunted his Catholic faith. He further angered his subjects by suspending laws at whim and appointing Catholics to high office. Many English Protestants feared that James would restore the Roman Catholic Church.

In 1688, alarmed parliamentary leaders invited James's Protestant daughter, Mary, and her Dutch Protestant husband, William III of Orange, to become rulers of England. When William and Mary landed with their army late in 1688, James II fled to France. This bloodless overthrow of a king became known as the Glorious Revolution.

English Bill of Rights   Before they could be crowned, William and Mary had to accept several acts passed by Parliament in 1689 that became known as the English Bill of Rights. The Bill of Rights ensured the superiority of Parliament over the monarchy. It required the monarch to summon Parliament regularly and gave the House of Commons the "power of the purse." A king or queen could no longer interfere in Parliamentary debates or suspend laws. The Bill of Rights also barred any Roman Catholic from sitting on the throne.

The Bill of Rights also restated the traditional rights of English citizens, such as trial by jury. It abolished excessive fines and cruel or unjust punishment. It affirmed the principle of habeas corpus. That is, no person could be held in prison without first being charged with a specific crime.

Later, the Toleration Act of 1689 granted limited religious freedom to Puritans, Quakers, and other dissenters, though not yet to Catholics. Still, only members of the Church of England could hold public office.

> ▶ **Primary Sources and Literature**
>
> **See "The English Bill of Rights" in the Reference Section at the back of this book.**

Looking Ahead

The Glorious Revolution did not create democracy, but a type of government called limited monarchy, in which a constitution or legislative body limits the monarch's powers. English rulers still had much power, but they had to obey the law and govern in partnership with Parliament. In the age of absolute monarchy elsewhere in Europe, the limited monarchy in England was radical enough.

SECTION 3 Assessment

Recall
1. **Identify: (a)** James I, **(b)** Charles I, **(c)** Petition of Right, **(d)** Cavalier, **(e)** Roundhead, **(f)** Oliver Cromwell, **(g)** Leveller, **(h)** English Bill of Rights.
2. **Define: (a)** dissenter, **(b)** habeas corpus, **(c)** limited monarchy.

Comprehension
3. **(a)** How did Tudor monarchs handle Parliament? **(b)** Why did the early Stuarts clash with Parliament?
4. **(a)** Explain two causes of the English Civil War. **(b)** Why did

many people welcome the return of the monarchy?
5. Describe two results of the Glorious Revolution.

Critical Thinking and Writing
6. **Analyzing Information   (a)** How might Puritan teachings have led some women to seek greater liberties? **(b)** Why do you think many men were upset by the idea of women speaking in public?
7. **Linking Past and Present**   Which aspects of Commonwealth society are part of American society today? Which are not?

Activity
Drawing a Political Cartoon Draw a political cartoon that might have appeared in England in 1649 about the execution of Charles I. Take the point of view of either a Roundhead or a Cavalier.

Rise of Austria and Prussia

Reading Focus

- What were the causes and results of the Thirty Years' War?

- How did Austria and Prussia emerge as great powers?

- How did European diplomats try to maintain a balance of power?

Vocabulary

elector

mercenary

depopulation

Taking Notes

On a sheet of paper, copy the chart shown at right. As you read this section, add events that occurred before and after the Peace of Westphalia.

PEACE OF WESTPHALIA

Before	After
• Thirty Years' War	• Germany divided into many states
• Frederick becomes Holy Roman emperor	•

Main Idea ▸ Two great empires, Austria and Prussia, rose out of the ashes of the Thirty Years' War.

Setting the Scene

Year after year, war ravaged the German states of central Europe. Bodies of victims littered fields and roads. As the Thirty Years' War dragged on, almost every European power was sucked into the conflict. "We have had blue coats and red coats and now come the yellow coats," cried the citizens of one German town. "God have pity on us!"

Finally, two great German-speaking powers, Austria and Prussia, rose out of the ashes. Like Louis XIV in France, their rulers perfected skills as absolute monarchs.

The Thirty Years' War

The French philosopher Voltaire noted that, by early modern times, the Holy Roman Empire was neither holy, nor Roman, nor an empire. Instead, it was a patchwork of several hundred small, separate states. In theory, these states were under the authority of the Holy Roman emperor, who was chosen by seven leading German princes called **electors.** In practice, the emperor had little power over the many rival princes. Religion further divided the German states. The north was largely Protestant, and the south was Catholic. This power vacuum sparked the Thirty Years' War.

The War Begins The war had both religious and political causes. It began in Bohemia, the present-day Czech Republic. Ferdinand, the Hapsburg king of Bohemia, sought to suppress Protestants and to assert royal power over local nobles. In May 1618, a few rebellious Protestant noblemen tossed two royal officials out of a castle window in Prague. This act sparked a general revolt, which Ferdinand moved to suppress. As both sides sought allies, what began as a local conflict widened into a general European war.

The following year, Ferdinand was elected Holy Roman emperor. With the support of Spain, Poland, and other Catholic states, he tried to roll back the Reformation. In the early stages of the war, he defeated the Bohemians and their Protestant allies. Alarmed, Protestant powers like the Netherlands and Sweden sent troops into Germany.

Before long, political motives outweighed religious issues. Catholic and Protestant rulers shifted alliances to suit their own interests. At one point, Catholic France joined Lutheran Sweden against the Catholic Hapsburgs.

The Thirty Years' War Begins

In an act known as the Defenestration of Prague, rebellious nobles in Bohemia tossed two royal officials out of a castle window. Both men survived, but the defiant act sparked the terrible Thirty Years' War.

Theme: Diversity What opposing groups do the men shown in this picture represent?

Europe After the Thirty Years' War

SWEDEN
NORWAY
RUSSIA
Moscow
Azimuthal Equal Area Projection
0   250   500 Miles
0   250   500 Kilometers

SCOTLAND
North Sea
IRELAND
DENMARK
Baltic Sea
PRUSSIA
POLAND
ENGLAND
DUTCH NETH.
Berlin
London
WESTPHALIA
SPANISH NETH.
SAXONY
SILESIA
Prague
BOHEMIA
Paris
ALSACE
Vienna
TRANSYLVANIA
ATLANTIC OCEAN
LORRAINE
BAVARIA
FRANCE
SWISS FED.
AUSTRIA
HUNGARY
Milan
OTTOMAN
Black Sea
PORTUGAL
Madrid
CORSICA
PAPAL STATES
Rome
Naples
EMPIRE
Constantinople
SPAIN
SARDINIA
Mediterranean Sea
SICILY
CRETE
AFRICA

Legend:
- Controlled by Spanish Hapsburgs
- Controlled by Austrian Hapsburgs
- Italian city-states
- Prussia
- Boundary of Holy Roman Empire

Skills Assessment

Geography After the Thirty Years' War, the Peace of Westphalia redrew the map of Europe.

1. **Location** On the map, locate (a) Poland, (b) Sweden, (c) Spanish Netherlands, (d) Westphalia.
2. **Region** (a) In 1648, who controlled Bohemia? (b) What lands did the Spanish Hapsburgs control?
3. **Critical Thinking Drawing Conclusions** How can you tell from the map that the Holy Roman Empire was not a strong, unified state?

A Brutal Conflict The fighting took a terrible toll. Roving armies of mercenaries, or soldiers for hire, burned villages, destroyed crops, and killed without mercy. A novel of the time describes episodes of nightmare violence, such as the plundering of a village by marauding soldiers:

> "For one of [the peasants] they had taken they thrust into the baking oven and there lit a fire under him, . . . as for another, they put a cord around his head and twisted it so tight with a piece of wood that the blood gushed from his mouth and nose and ears. In a word each had his own device to torture the peasants."
>
> —Jacob von Grimmelshausen, *Simplicissimus*

Murder and torture were followed by famine and disease. Wolves, not seen in settled areas since the Middle Ages, stalked the deserted streets of once-bustling villages. The war led to severe depopulation, or reduction in population. Although exact population statistics do not exist, historians estimate that as many as one third of the people in the German states may have died as a result of the war.

Peace at Last Finally, in 1648, the exhausted combatants accepted a series of treaties, known as the Peace of Westphalia. Because so many powers had been involved in the conflict, the war ended with a general European peace and an attempt to settle other international problems as well.

France emerged a clear winner, gaining territory on both its Spanish and German frontiers. The Hapsburgs were big losers because they had to accept the almost total independence of all the princes of the Holy Roman Empire. The Netherlands and the Swiss Federation (present-day Switzerland) won recognition as independent states.

The Thirty Years' War left Germany divided into more than 360 separate states, "one for every day of the year." These states still formally acknowledged the leadership of the Holy Roman emperor. Yet each state had its own government, coinage, state church, armed forces, and foreign policy. Germany, potentially the most powerful nation in Europe, thus remained fragmented for another 200 years.

Hapsburg Austria

Though weakened by war, the Hapsburgs still wanted to create a strong united state. They kept the title of Holy Roman emperors, but focused their attention on expanding their own lands. To Austria, they added Bohemia, Hungary, and, later, parts of Poland and Italy.

Unity and Diversity   Uniting these lands proved difficult. Divided by geography, they also included diverse peoples and cultures. By the 1700s, the Hapsburg empire included Germans, Magyars, Slavs, and others. In many parts of the empire, people had their own languages, laws, assemblies, and customs.

The Hapsburgs did exert some control over these diverse peoples. They sent German-speaking officials to Bohemia and Hungary and settled Austrians on confiscated lands in these provinces. The Hapsburgs also put down revolts in Bohemia and Hungary. Still, the Hapsburg empire never developed a centralized system like that of France.

Maria Theresa   In the early 1700s, the emperor Charles VI faced a new crisis. He had no son. His daughter, Maria Theresa, was intelligent and capable, but no woman had yet ruled Hapsburg lands in her own name. Charles persuaded other European rulers to recognize his daughter's right to succeed him. When he died, however, many ignored their pledge.

The greatest threat came in 1740, when Frederick II of Prussia seized the rich Hapsburg province of Silesia. Maria Theresa set off for Hungary to appeal for military help from her Hungarian subjects. The Hungarians were ordinarily unfriendly to the Hapsburgs. But she made a dramatic plea before an assembly of Hungarian nobles. According to one account, the nobles rose to their feet and shouted, "Our lives and blood for your Majesty!" She eventually got further help from Britain and Russia.

During the eight-year War of the Austrian Succession, Maria Theresa was not able to force Frederick out of Silesia. Still, she did preserve her empire and win the support of most of her people. Equally important, she strengthened Hapsburg power by reorganizing the bureaucracy and improving tax collection. She even forced nobles and clergy to pay taxes and tried to ease the burden of taxes and labor services on peasants. As you will read, many of her reforms were later extended by her son and successor, Joseph II.

The Rise of Prussia

While Austria was molding a strong Catholic state, Prussia emerged as a new Protestant power. In the 1600s, the Hohenzollern (HOH uhn tsahl ern) family ruled scattered lands across north Germany. After the Peace of Westphalia, ambitious Hohenzollern rulers united their lands by taking over the states between them. Like absolute rulers elsewhere, they set up an efficient central bureaucracy and reduced the independence of their nobles, called Junkers (YOON kerz).

To achieve their goals, Prussian rulers like Frederick William I forged one of the best-trained armies in Europe. Great emphasis was placed on military values. One Prussian military leader boasted, "Prussia is not a state which possesses an army, but an army which possesses a state."

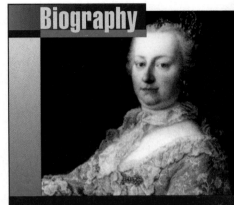

Biography

Maria Theresa 1717–1780

When Maria Theresa became Hapsburg empress at the age of 23, her chances of remaining in power seemed very slim. She later said, "I found myself . . . without money, without credit, without army, without experience and knowledge of my own, and finally without counsel, because each one of them first wanted to wait and see what would happen."

But the determined empress survived. She appointed superb advisers and was able to maintain control of her empire. During her 40-year reign, Vienna became a center for music and the arts.

Maria Theresa had one thing in common with most women of her day—her duties included motherhood. She gave birth to a total of 16 children—11 girls and 5 boys. Among them were future emperors Joseph II and Leopold II and Queen Marie Antoinette of France.

Theme: Impact of the Individual   What traits did Maria Theresa need to stay in power?

Frederick William won the loyalty of the Junkers by giving them positions in the army and government. By 1740, Prussia was strong enough to challenge its rival Austria.

Frederick II Frederick William made sure that, from an early age, his son Frederick was trained in the art of war:

> "His tutor must take the greatest pains to imbue my son with a sincere love for the soldier's profession and to impress upon him that nothing else in the world can confer upon a prince such fame and honor as the sword."
> —Frederick William, quoted in *The Heritage of World Civilizations* (Craig)

In fact, young Frederick preferred playing the flute and writing poetry. Frederick William despised these pursuits and treated the young prince so badly that he tried to flee the country. Discovering these plans, Frederick William put his son in solitary confinement. A friend who had helped Frederick was beheaded while the 18-year-old prince was forced to watch.

Military Successes Frederick's harsh military training did have an effect. After becoming king in 1740, Frederick II lost no time in using his army. As you read, he boldly seized Silesia from Austria, sparking the War of the Austrian Succession. In several later wars, Frederick made brilliant use of his disciplined army, forcing all to accept Prussia as a great power. His exploits earned him the name Frederick the Great.

Keeping the Balance of Power

By 1750, the great powers of Europe included Austria, Prussia, France, England, and Russia. They formed various alliances to maintain the balance of power. Though nations sometimes switched partners, two rivalries persisted. Prussia battled Austria for control of the German states, while Britain and France competed for overseas empire.

On occasion, European rivalries ignited a worldwide conflict. The Seven Years' War, which lasted from 1756 until 1763, was fought on four continents. Prussia, Austria, Russia, France, and Britain battled in Europe. Britain and France also fought in India and Africa. In North America, the French and Indian War also involved Native American nations. The Treaty of Paris ending the wars gave Britain a huge empire.

SECTION 4 Assessment

Recall
1. **Identify:** **(a)** Peace of Westphalia, **(b)** Maria Theresa, **(c)** War of the Austrian Succession, **(d)** Frederick the Great, **(e)** Seven Years' War.
2. **Define:** **(a)** elector, **(b)** mercenary, **(c)** depopulation.

Comprehension
3. What impact did the Thirty Years' War have on the German states?
4. **(a)** What two major powers emerged in Europe at the end of the Thirty Years' War? **(b)** How were the goals of these two nations similar?

5. **(a)** Why did European nations seek a balance of power? **(b)** What methods did they use?

Critical Thinking and Writing
6. **Linking Past and Present** Westphalia was the first modern peace conference. **(a)** Why was such a conference needed? **(b)** How do nations try to settle disputes today?
7. **Making Inferences** "Prussia is not a state which possesses an army, but an army which possesses a state." What values do you think would be emphasized in such a state?

Activity

Mentoring a Monarch
Both Louis XIV and Frederick William wrote instructions for training their sons to rule. With a partner, create a list of eight to ten rules for a successful absolute monarch in the 1600s and 1700s.

Absolute Monarchy in Russia

Reading Focus

- How did Peter the Great try to make Russia into a modern state?

- What steps did Peter take to expand Russia's borders?

- How did Catherine the Great strengthen Russia?

Vocabulary

westernization

boyar

warm-water port

partition

Taking Notes

As you read this section, make a Venn diagram to compare events in the reigns of Peter the Great and Catherine the Great. Use this diagram as a model, and add more information.

PETER
- Visited western countries

Adopted western ideas

CATHERINE
- Established port on the Black Sea

Main Idea Czar Peter the Great and his successor, Catherine the Great, strengthened Russia and expanded Russian territory.

Setting the Scene

Along the Dutch waterfront, curious observers noticed that Peter Mikhailov was no ordinary man. For one thing, he stood almost seven feet tall. He had a booming laugh but also a furious temper. By day, he dressed in shabby clothes and worked as a shipyard carpenter. At night, he was entertained by royalty. For Peter Mikhailov was none other than Peter the Great, czar of Russia. His mission was to learn all he could about the more advanced nations of Western Europe.

In the early 1600s, Russia was still a medieval state, untouched by the Renaissance and Reformation and largely isolated from Western Europe. As you have read, the "Time of Troubles" had plunged the state into a period of disorder and foreign invasions. The reign of the first Romanov czar in 1613 restored a measure of order. Not until 1682, however, did a czar emerge who was strong enough to regain the absolute power of earlier czars. Peter the Great pushed Russia on the road to becoming a great modern power.

Peter the Great

Peter, just 10 years old when he came to the throne, did not take control of the government until 1689. Though he was not well educated, the young czar was immensely curious. He spent hours in the "German quarter," the Moscow suburb where many Dutch, Scottish, English, and other foreign artisans and soldiers lived. There, he heard of the advanced technology that was helping Western European monarchs forge powerful empires.

Journey to the West In 1697, Peter set out to study western technology for himself. He spent hours walking the streets of European cities, noting the manners and homes of the people. He visited factories and art galleries, learned anatomy from a doctor, and even had a dentist teach him how to pull teeth. In England, Peter was impressed by Parliament. "It is good," he said, "to hear subjects speaking truthfully and openly to their king."

Returning to Russia, Peter brought along a group of technical experts, teachers, and soldiers he had recruited in the West. He then embarked on a policy of westernization, that is, the adoption of western ideas, technology, and culture. But persuading fellow Russians to change their way of life proved difficult. To impose his will, Peter became the most autocratic of Europe's absolute monarchs.

Peter Westernizes Russia
As part of his program of westernization, Peter the Great ordered Russian nobles to shave their beards and dress in western style. Those who refused had to pay a special "beard tax."

Theme: Continuity and Change How is the noble in this cartoon reacting to Peter's beard policy?

Expansion of Russia, 1689–1796

Map labels: Bering Sea, ARCTIC OCEAN, Nizhiye Kolymsk, DENMARK, SWEDEN, Berlin, Baltic Sea, PRUSSIA, St. Petersburg, Vienna, Warsaw, Novgorod, AUSTRIA, Moscow, Perm, URAL MTS., SIBERIA, Turukhansk, Yakutsk, Petropavlovsk, Okhotsk, Sea of Okhotsk, RUSSIA, Odessa, Sibir, Yeniseysk, Constantinople, Sevastopol, Azov, Tomsk, Krasnoyarsk, Black Sea, CAUCASUS MTS., Volga R., Ural R., Irkutsk, Amur R., OTTOMAN EMPIRE, Mediterranean Sea, Aral Sea, Caspian Sea, Sea of Japan, Dnieper R., Don R., Danube R., Dniester R., Elbe R., Vistula R.

Legend:
- Russia, 1689
- Land added by Peter the Great by 1725
- Land added by Catherine the Great by 1795
- Land added by 1796
- Austria, 1796
- Prussia, 1796
- Trade routes
- Bering's exploration route, 1725–1729

Azimuthal Equal Area Projection
0 500 1000 Miles
0 500 1000 Kilometers

Skills Assessment

Geography During the 1600s and 1700s, Russia expanded both eastward and westward to become the largest nation in the world.

1. **Location** On the map, locate **(a)** Sweden, **(b)** Baltic Sea, **(c)** St. Petersburg, **(d)** Black Sea, **(e)** Siberia, **(f)** Bering Sea.
2. **Place** Why were ports on the Black Sea more appealing to Russia than those on the Baltic?
3. **Critical Thinking** **Predicting Consequences** How might this map look different if Peter the Great had not modernized Russia?

Autocrat and Reformer At home, Peter pursued several related goals. He wanted to strengthen the military, expand Russian borders, and centralize royal power. To achieve his ends, he brought all Russian institutions under his control, including the Russian Orthodox Church. He forced the haughty boyars, or landowning nobles, to serve the state in civilian or military jobs.

Under Peter, serfdom spread in Russia, long after it had died out in Western Europe. By tying peasants to land given to nobles, he ensured that nobles could serve the state. Further, he forced some serfs to become soldiers or labor on roads, canals, and other government projects.

Using autocratic methods, Peter pushed through social and economic reforms. He imported western technology, improved education, simplified the Russian alphabet, and set up academies for the study of mathematics, science, and engineering. To pay for his sweeping reforms, Peter adopted mercantilist policies, such as encouraging exports. He improved the waterways and canals, developed mining and textile manufacturing, and backed new trading companies.

Some changes had a symbolic meaning. As you read, after returning from the West, Peter insisted that boyars shave their beards. He also forced them to replace their old-fashioned robes with Western European clothes. To end the practice of secluding upper-class women in separate quarters, he held grand parties at which women and men were expected to dance together. Russian nobles resisted this radical mixing of the sexes in public.

Peter had no mercy for any who resisted the new order. When elite palace guards revolted, he had over 1,000 of the rebels tortured and executed. As an example of his power, he left their rotting corpses outside the palace walls for months.

Expansion Under Peter

From his earliest days as czar, Peter worked to build Russian's military power. He created the largest standing army in Europe and set out to extend Russian borders to the west and south.

Search for a Warm-Water Port   Russian seaports, located along the Arctic Ocean, were frozen over in the winter. To increase Russia's ability to trade with the West, Peter desperately wanted a warm-water port—one that would be free of ice all year round.

The nearest warm-water coast was located along the Black Sea. To gain control of this territory, Peter had to push through the powerful Ottoman empire. In the end, Peter was unable to defeat the Ottomans and gain his warm-water port. However, the later Russian monarch Catherine the Great would achieve that goal before the century ended.

War With Sweden   In 1700, Peter began a long war against the kingdom of Sweden. At the time, Sweden dominated the Baltic region. Early on, Russia suffered humiliating defeats. A Swedish force of only 8,000 men defeated a Russian army five times its size. Undaunted, Peter rebuilt his army along western lines. In 1709, he defeated the Swedes and won land along the Baltic Sea.

Peter's City   On land won from Sweden, Peter built a magnificent new capital city, St. Petersburg. Seeking to open a "window on the West," he located the city on the swampy shores of the Neva River near the Baltic coast. He forced tens of thousands of serfs to drain the swamps. Many thousands died, but Peter got his city. He then invited Italian architects and artisans to design great palaces in western style. Peter even planned the city's parks and boulevards himself.

Just as Versailles became a monument to French absolutism, St. Petersburg became the great symbol of Peter's desire to forge a modern Russia. A hundred years later, Russia's best-known poet, Alexander Pushkin, portrayed Peter as a larger-than-life ruler, determined to tame nature no matter what the cost:

> "Here we at Nature's own behest
> Shall break a window to the West,
> Stand planted on the ocean level;
> Here flags of foreign nations all
> By waters new to them will call
> And unencumbered we shall revel."
> —Alexander Pushkin, *The Bronze Horseman*

Toward the Pacific   Russian traders and raiders also crossed the plains and rivers of Siberia, blazing trails to the Pacific. Under Peter, Russia signed a treaty with Qing China, defining their common border in the east. The treaty recognized Russia's right to lands north of Manchuria.

In the early 1700s, Peter hired the Danish navigator Vitus Bering to explore what became known as the Bering Strait between Siberia and Alaska. Russian pioneers crossed into Alaska and migrated as far south as California. Few Russians moved east of the Ural Mountains at this time, but on a map, Russia was already the largest country in the world, as it still is today.

Legacy of Peter the Great

When Peter died in 1725, he left behind a mixed legacy. He had expanded Russian territory, gained ports on the Baltic Sea, and created a mighty army. He had also ended Russia's long period of isolation. From the 1700s on, Russia would be increasingly involved in the affairs of Western Europe. Yet

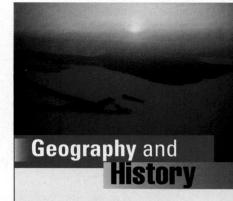

Geography and History

Being "Sent to Siberia"

Russia's absolute monarchs needed a place to exile both criminals and political opponents for long periods of time. What place was better than the arctic region of Siberia to the north? Siberia had an extremely inhospitable climate—temperatures could average –59°F in winter—and it was far away from everything Russian. There was little chance for escape, as it was almost impossible to survive the vast, frozen, sparsely populated region. In fact, approximately 10 to 15 percent of the exiles never made it to Siberia. They died along the way.

Exiles started with a trickle in the early 1600s, but by the early 1800s, the number grew to 2,000 a year. After a revolt in 1825, the czar sent 150,000 people off to their freezing fate. Today, the expression "sent to Siberia" still implies that a person is being punished or has become an outcast.

 Theme: Geography and History   Why was Siberia chosen as a place for exile?

many of Peter's ambitious reforms died with him. Nobles, for example, soon ignored his policy of service to the state.

Like earlier czars, Peter the Great had brandished terror to enforce his absolute power. His policies contributed to the growth of serfdom, which served only to widen the gap between Russia and the West that Peter had sought to narrow.

Catherine the Great

Peter died without naming a successor, setting off power struggles among various Romanovs. Under a series of ineffective rulers, Russian nobles reasserted their independence. Then, a new monarch took the reins of power firmly in hand. She became known to history as Catherine the Great.

A German princess by birth, Catherine had come to Russia at the age of 15 to wed the heir to the Russian throne. She learned Russian, embraced the Russian Orthodox faith, and won the loyalty of the people. In 1762, her mentally unstable husband, Czar Peter III, was murdered by a group of Russian army officers. Whether or not Catherine was involved in the assassination plot, she certainly benefited from it. With the support of the military, she ascended the Russian throne herself.

An Efficient Ruler Catherine proved to be an efficient, energetic empress. She reorganized the provincial government, codified laws, and began state-sponsored education for boys and girls.

Like Peter the Great, she embraced western ideas. At court, she encouraged French language and customs, wrote histories and plays, and organized court performances. As you will read in the next chapter, she was also a serious student of the French thinkers who led the intellectual movement known as the Enlightenment.

A Ruthless Absolute Monarch Like other absolute monarchs, Catherine could be ruthless. She granted a charter to the boyars outlining important

The Wealth of Catherine the Great
Catherine the Great (pictured above) enjoyed the splendor of being an absolute monarch. The ornate horse-drawn carriage was a gift from one of the Russian nobles who had conspired in the murder of her husband.

Theme: Political and Social Systems Compare this picture to pictures of the French court at Versailles in this chapter. Why do you think great displays of wealth were important to absolute monarchs?

rights, such as exemption from taxes. At the same time, she allowed them to increase their stranglehold on the peasants. When peasants rebelled against the harsh burdens of serfdom, Catherine took firm action to repress them. As a result, conditions grew worse for Russian peasants. Under Catherine, even more peasants were forced into serfdom.

Like Peter the Great, Catherine was determined to expand Russia's borders. After a war against the Ottoman empire, she finally achieved Peter's dream of a warm-water port on the Black Sea. She also took steps to seize territory from neighboring Poland.

Partition of Poland As you have read, Poland had once been a great European power. However, Polish rulers were unable to centralize their power or diminish the influence of the Polish nobility. The divided Polish government was ill prepared to stand up to the increasing might of its neighbors Russia, Prussia, and Austria.

In the 1770s, Catherine the Great, Frederick the Great, and Emperor Joseph II of Austria hungrily eyed Poland. To avoid fighting one another, the three monarchs agreed to partition, or divide up, Poland. At the first partition, in 1772, Catherine took part of eastern Poland, where many Russians and Ukrainians lived. Frederick and Joseph nibbled at Polish territory from the west.

Poland was partitioned again in 1793 and a third time in 1795. By the time Austria, Prussia, and Russia had taken their final slices, the independent kingdom of Poland had vanished from the map. Not until 1919 would a free Polish state reappear.

Looking Ahead

By the mid-1700s, absolute monarchs ruled four of the five leading powers in Europe. Britain, with its strong Parliament, was the only exception. As these five nations competed with one another, they often ended up fighting to maintain the balance of power.

At the same time, new ideas were in the air. Radical changes would soon shatter the French monarchy, upset the balance of power, and revolutionize European societies. In the next unit, you will read about how the Enlightenment, the French Revolution, the rise of Napoleon Bonaparte, and the Industrial Revolution would transform Europe.

SECTION 5 Assessment

Recall
1. **Identify:** (a) Peter the Great, (b) St. Petersburg, (c) Vitus Bering, (d) Catherine the Great.
2. **Define:** (a) westernization, (b) boyar, (c) warm-water port, (d) partition.

Comprehension
3. (a) List three goals of Peter the Great. (b) Explain one reform that Peter undertook to achieve each goal.
4. Why did Peter seek to expand Russian territory?
5. Describe how two policies of Catherine the Great strengthened Russia.

Critical Thinking and Writing
6. **Comparing** Compare the goals and policies of Peter the Great to those of *one* of the following monarchs: (a) Louis XIV of France, (b) Frederick II of Prussia, (c) Maria Theresa of Austria.
7. **Drawing Conclusions** Peter the Great said of the English Parliament, "It is good to hear subjects speaking truthfully and openly to their king." Based on what you have read, do you think Peter followed this idea in his own kingdom? Give a reason to support your answer.

Activity
Take It to the NET

Use the Internet to learn about the city of St. Petersburg today. Then, write a commentary that Peter the Great might make on the city if he were to see it today. Tell how he would react to a statue such as *The Bronze Horseman* or to the Hermitage Museum.

Creating a Chapter Summary

On a sheet of paper make a table to compare the nations of Europe during the Age of Absolutism. Use the table shown here as a guide to get started.

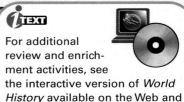

iTEXT

For additional review and enrichment activities, see the interactive version of *World History* available on the Web and on CD-ROM.

	SPAIN	FRANCE	ENGLAND	AUSTRIA/ PRUSSIA	RUSSIA
GOVERNMENT	Philip II; absolute ruler				
WARS	Defeats Ottomans in 1571				
RELIGION	Catholic				
ECONOMY					
OTHER					

Web Site Self-Test
For practice test questions for Chapter 17, see **www.phschool.com**.

Building Vocabulary

Use the chapter vocabulary words listed below to create a crossword puzzle. Exchange puzzles with a classmate. Complete the puzzles and then check each other's answers.

1. **absolute monarch**
2. **divine right**
3. **balance of power**
4. **habeas corpus**
5. **limited monarchy**
6. **mercenary**
7. **depopulation**
8. **westernization**
9. **boyar**
10. **partition**

Recalling Key Facts

11. What was the Spanish Armada?
12. Explain what the statement "I am the state" meant.
13. Describe the results of the English Civil War.
14. How did the Glorious Revolution limit royal power in England?
15. What reforms did Peter the Great carry out?
16. How and when did the kingdom of Poland lose its independence?

Critical Thinking and Writing

17. **Connecting to Geography** (a) How did resources of Spanish colonies in the Americas contribute to the decline of Spain? (b) How did resources from French colonies enrich France?
18. **Analyzing Primary Sources** Bishop Bossuet, a court preacher under Louis XIV, wrote, "Let God take away his hand and the world will fall back into nothingness; let authority fail in the kingdom, and total confusion will result." (a) According to Bossuet, what is the benefit of absolute monarchy? (b) What assumption does he make about the source of royal power? (c) How might the history of France in the late 1500s have influenced Bossuet's viewpoint?
19. **Recognizing Causes and Effects** (a) What were the immediate causes of the English Civil War? (b) What were some of the long-term causes?
20. **Recognizing Points of View** How might each of the following have viewed Peter the Great: (a) a boyar, (b) a serf, (c) Catherine the Great?

This passage is from a letter written to Louis XIV by a tutor to the king's children. Read the excerpt, then answer the questions that follow.

"For nearly thirty years, your principal Ministers have destroyed and reversed all the ancient customs of the state in order to raise your authority to its highest pitch. They no longer speak of the state and its constitution; they only speak of the King and his royal pleasure. They have pushed your revenues and your expenses to unprecedented heights. They have raised you up to the sky in order, they say, to out-shine the grandeur of all your predecessors; that is to say, in order to impoverish the whole of France for the introduction of monstrous luxuries of court. . . .

Meanwhile, your people die of hunger. The cultivation of the soil is almost stagnant, and no longer offers employment to working men. All commerce is destroyed."

—Archbishop François de Fénelon, *Letters*

21. **(a)** What did Fénelon criticize about the rule of Louis XIV? **(b)** Whom did he blame besides the king?
22. Fénelon wrote the letter anonymously, that is, unsigned. Why do you think he sent it this way?
23. What reforms do you think Fénelon would have welcomed?
24. Do you think the letter is a reliable source of information about the reign of Louis XIV? Why or why not?
25. How do you think the king might have responded to the charges made in the letter? Explain.

Use the Internet to research one of the absolute monarchs described in the text. Then, write a brief biography of the monarch. Focus on the characteristics that made this person an example of absolutism, and on how this ruler affected the country he or she ruled. Be sure to list the sources you used in writing your biography.

The maps below, which show Poland in three different years, make it possible to see how the area changed over time. Study the maps, then answer the questions that follow.

Partitions of Poland 1701–1795

1701
Baltic Sea
Moscow
PRUSSIA
RUSSIA
Vistula R.
Elbe R.
Oder R.
Warsaw
POLAND
Kiev
Dnieper R.
Danube R.
Vienna
AUSTRIA
Black Sea

1772
Baltic Sea
Moscow
30°E 35°E
55°N
PRUSSIA
Vistula R.
Elbe R.
Oder R.
Warsaw
POLAND
Kiev
RUSSIA
Dnieper R.
50°N
Danube R.
Vienna
AUSTRIA
20°E 25°E
15°E 45°N
Black Sea

1795
Baltic Sea
PRUSSIA
Vistula R.
Elbe R.
Oder R.
Warsaw
Dnieper R.
RUSSIA
Kiev
Danube R.
Vienna
AUSTRIA
Black Sea

N W E S

Azimuthal Equal Area Projection
0   250   500 Miles
0   250   500 Kilometers

26. What country was divided into two separate territories by Poland in 1701?
27. **(a)** How did the size of Poland's territory change from 1701 to 1772? **(b)** What was the status of Warsaw in 1795?
28. **(a)** What had happened to Poland by 1795? **(b)** What three countries divided the Polish territory?
29. In addition to the partition of Poland, what other territorial change can you see on these maps?
30. What do you think happened to the Polish people after the final partition?

When you compare maps of a place over time, first make sure that you are looking at the same area on each map. Then, note any changes.

Unit-in-Brief
4 Early Modern Times

Chapter 14

The Renaissance and Reformation
(1300–1650)

Between the 1300s and 1500s, Europe experienced a period of cultural rebirth known as the Renaissance. During the same period, the Protestant Reformation and the Scientific Revolution reshaped European civilization.

- Beginning in Italy and later spreading to northern Europe, the Renaissance reached its most glorious expression in painting, sculpture, and architecture.
- The intellectual movement known as humanism stressed the study of classical Greek and Roman cultures and the development of the individual.
- Reformers like Martin Luther and John Calvin challenged church corruption and eventually broke away from the Roman Catholic Church entirely.
- In response to the Protestant Reformation, the Catholic Church undertook its own vigorous reform movement.
- Religious fervor led to widespread intolerance and persecution by both Protestants and Catholics.
- During the Scientific Revolution, startling discoveries by individuals such as Copernicus, Newton, and Galileo changed the way Europeans viewed the physical world.

Chapter 15

The First Global Age: Europe and Asia
(1415–1796)

Beginning in the 1500s, European powers gradually built trading empires in Asia. Thus began a period of increasing global interdependence that has continued to the present day.

- Improvements in technology helped European explorers navigate the vast oceans of the world.
- In his search for a sea route to Asia, Christopher Columbus came upon the Americas, two continents previously unknown to Europeans.
- Although they were strongly influenced by China and India, the nations of Southeast Asia retained their own unique cultural identities.
- The desire for spices led Europeans to seek control of the Indian Ocean trade network.
- By the late 1500s, the Dutch replaced the Portuguese as the major European power in Asia. In the 1700s, England and France vied for dominance.
- During the 1500s and 1600s, China and Korea restricted contact with the outside world.
- The Japanese initially welcomed western traders, but they later adopted a similar policy of isolation.

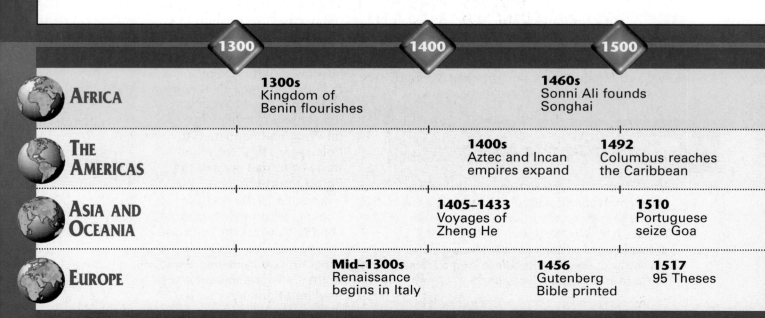

	1300	1400	1500
AFRICA	**1300s** Kingdom of Benin flourishes		**1460s** Sonni Ali founds Songhai
THE AMERICAS		**1400s** Aztec and Incan empires expand	**1492** Columbus reaches the Caribbean
ASIA AND OCEANIA		**1405–1433** Voyages of Zheng He	**1510** Portuguese seize Goa
EUROPE	**Mid–1300s** Renaissance begins in Italy	**1456** Gutenberg Bible printed	**1517** 95 Theses

Chapter 16

The First Global Age: Europe, the Americas, and Africa (1492–1750)

During the age of exploration, European powers built colonial empires in the Americas. New patterns of conquest and global exchange had an enormous impact on the civilization of Africa as well.

- Spanish conquistadors vanquished the Aztec and Incan civilizations and set up a vast empire in the Americas.
- By the 1600s, Spain, France, England, and the Netherlands were competing for trade and colonies.
- The arrival of European settlers in the Americas brought disaster to Native Americans.
- Beginning in the 1400s, Europeans began establishing trading outposts in Africa.
- Millions of slaves were imported from Africa to meet labor needs in American colonies. The slave trade led to the fall of some African states and the rise of others.
- The Columbian Exchange was a vast global interchange of people, animals, culture, ideas, and technology.
- Beginning in the 1500s, Europe experienced a commercial revolution that brought about dramatic economic changes, including the rise of capitalism.

Chapter 17

The Age of Absolutism (1550–1800)

During the 1500s and 1600s, European monarchs struggled to centralize their power. As they vied for the lead in overseas empires, the center of world civilization shifted to Europe.

- During the 1500s, wealth from the Americas helped make Spain the most powerful nation in Europe.
- Following a period of religious and social turmoil, Louis XIV achieved royal absolutism and helped France become the most powerful nation in Europe during the 1600s.
- Despite efforts at absolutism by several English monarchs, Parliament successfully asserted itself against royal power.
- The Thirty Years' War involved most of Europe. After the Peace of Westphalia, Prussia emerged as a new Protestant power.
- The Hapsburgs expanded Austrian territory but were unable to develop a strong centralized system.
- Peter the Great of Russia centralized royal power, embarked on a program of modernization, and sought to expand Russian territory from Europe to the Pacific.

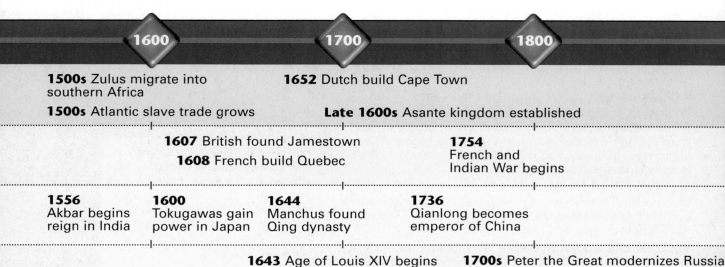

1600   **1700**   **1800**

1500s Zulus migrate into southern Africa

1500s Atlantic slave trade grows

1652 Dutch build Cape Town

Late 1600s Asante kingdom established

1607 British found Jamestown
1608 French build Quebec

1754 French and Indian War begins

1556 Akbar begins reign in India

1600 Tokugawas gain power in Japan

1644 Manchus found Qing dynasty

1736 Qianlong becomes emperor of China

1643 Age of Louis XIV begins   **1700s** Peter the Great modernizes Russia

1558 Elizabeth begins reign

1687 Newton explains theory of gravity

UNIT 5

Enlightenment and Revolution

1707–1850

OUTLINE

Themes

As you read about the revolutionary ideas that brought dramatic changes to western society and government, you will encounter the following themes.

Continuity and Change Enlightenment ideas about society and government stood in sharp contrast to the prevailing standards. Since the 1700s, Enlightenment ideas have spread around the world.

Economics and Technology During the 1700s, advances in farming, transportation, and manufacturing contributed to the Industrial Revolution. Production of goods shifted from the home to the factory. Laissez-faire economists, utilitarians, and socialists offered plans to deal with the consequences of this change.

Impact of the Individual Thinkers such as John Locke, Voltaire, and Jean-Jacques Rousseau and political leaders such as Napoleon Bonaparte and Simón Bolívar encouraged national pride and human rights.

Political and Social Systems Revolutionaries, inspired by the Enlightenment, urged radical changes in government. Early industrialization created a new working class, while merchants and skilled artisans formed a growing new middle class.

Unit Theme Activity

For Your Portfolio The chapters in this unit describe the revolutionary changes in governments and economies that occurred in the 1700s. As you read the chapters, prepare a portfolio project showing the impact of development of factories. Your project might take one of the following forms:
• Diary
• Report
• Illustration

These monuments at the Plaza General San Martin in Buenos Aires, Argentina, display pride in national revolutionary heroes. Most nations in Latin America had won their independence by 1825.

WHY STUDY HISTORY?

Because the Spread of Democracy Requires Informed Citizens

Democracy is hard work. Sure, you enjoy many rights and freedoms. You can speak out against the government if you think it's doing something wrong. You can own property, call a public meeting, practice your religion, travel wherever you wish. The list goes on. But you also have responsibilities. Being a good citizen requires you to obey the laws of the nation, to vote, to practice tolerance. For centuries, people struggled and died to achieve democracy. It is up to you to maintain and protect the unique system they won.

Americans Proclaim the Principles of Democracy

In July 1776, American colonists issued the Declaration of Independence. Besides proclaiming American independence from Great Britain, this document set out the basic principles of democracy—that "all men are created equal," with the right to "life, liberty, and the pursuit of happiness." Governments, it went on, can exist only if they have the "consent of the governed." If the government is unjust, then people have the right to "alter or abolish it." These twin ideals of democratic self-government and individual liberty remain the foundation of our nation today.

Signing of the Declaration of Independence

Democratic Stirrings in France

Stirrings of democracy helped inspire the French Revolution of 1789. People from all levels of French society, such as the Parisian women shown here, fought to overthrow the absolute monarchy that had ruled the nation for centuries. Inspired by the American Declaration of Independence, a new French national assembly adopted the Declaration of the Rights of Man and the Citizen. In it, they asserted the equality of all men, the sovereignty of the people, and the inalienable rights of the individual to liberty, property, and security.

Fighting for Freedom in Latin America

The new democratic ideas soon reached Spain's colonies in Latin America. Most colonists had no say in government, and discontent was widespread. Spurred by the revolutions in France and North America, colonists embarked on a series of wars of independence that continued until they had thrown off European rule. Simón Bolívar, the principal leader in the battle for freedom, is shown here.

What You Can Do: Stay Informed

Our democratic way of life is not guaranteed. We must work to maintain it. And the first step is to keep informed. Two hundred years ago, when our nation was founded, news spread slowly. Today, however, we have a continuous stream of information—radio, TV, newspapers, the Internet. Here, a man reads a newspaper to find out about the events of the day.

Spread of Democracy in the Twentieth Century

The quest for democratic self-government continued in the twentieth century. Here, Indonesians in 1999 vote in their first free elections in over 40 years.

Portfolio Assessment

Connecting to Today List three specific ways in which you keep informed about current affairs. Create a poster encouraging others to keep informed in the same or similar ways.

CHAPTER 18

The Enlightenment and the American Revolution

1707–1800

Chapter Preview

1 Philosophy in the Age of Reason
2 Enlightenment Ideas Spread
3 Britain at Mid-Century
4 Birth of the American Republic

CHAPTER EVENTS

1707
The Act of Union unites England and Scotland. This British flag uses symbols from each country's flag to show unity.

1721
Johann Sebastian Bach publishes his Brandenburg Concertos. Bach composes music for the harpsichord, shown here, and for many other instruments.

1740
Frederick II begins his reign in Prussia.

1700 ● 1720 1740

GLOBAL EVENTS

1736 Qianlong begins a 60-year reign as emperor of China.

North America, 1783

The American Revolution transformed maps of North America as the United States became an independent nation.

Legend:
- United States territory
- British territory
- French territory
- Russian territory
- Spanish territory
- Claimed by U.S. and Great Britain
- Claimed by U.S. and Spain
- Claimed by Russia, Spain, and Great Britain

ALASKA
Yukon R.
Mackenzie R.
Arctic Circle
60°N
Hudson Bay
Saskatchewan R.
CANADA
St. Lawrence R. — Quebec
Halifax
Boston
New York
Philadelphia
40°N
40°W
CALIFORNIA
Snake R.
Colorado R.
Missouri R.
Mississippi R.
Ohio R.
LOUISIANA
UNITED STATES
ATLANTIC OCEAN
Rio Grande
New Orleans
Charleston
NEW SPAIN
FLORIDA
Tropic of Cancer
Gulf of Mexico
BAHAMAS (Br.)
PACIFIC OCEAN
BELIZE
Mexico City
CUBA
HISPANIOLA
PUERTO RICO
MARTINIQUE (Fr.)
20°N
JAMAICA
GUADELOUPE (Fr.)
Caribbean Sea
MOSQUITO COAST
SOUTH AMERICA
140°W   120°W   100°W   80°W   60°W

Azimuthal Equal Area Projection
0   500   1000 Miles
0   500   1000 Kilometers

N W E S

1759
The *philosophe* Voltaire, shown here, publishes *Candide*. The novel mocks French society.

1762
Jean-Jacques Rousseau publishes *The Social Contract.*

1781
The British army surrenders to the Americans after the Battle of Yorktown. This painting shows American and French officers planning the siege.

1760   1780   1800

1763 The Treaty of Paris is signed by France and Great Britain.

1789 Parisians storm the Bastille.

Philosophy in the Age of Reason

Reading Focus

- How did scientific progress promote trust in human reason?
- How did the social contract and separation of powers affect views on government?
- How did new ideas affect society and the economy?

Vocabulary

natural law

social contract

natural right

philosophe

physiocrat

laissez faire

Taking Notes

Make a table like the one here. Add information about each thinker as you read this section.

THINKER	WORKS AND IDEAS
Hobbes	• Wrote *Leviathan* •
Locke	
Montesquieu	
Voltaire	
Diderot	
Rousseau	
Wollstonecraft	
Smith	

Main Idea Enlightenment thinkers tried to apply reason and the laws of nature to human society.

Setting the Scene

By the early 1700s, European thinkers felt that nothing was beyond the reach of the human mind. The following lines by the English poet Alexander Pope celebrated the successes of humans—the "wondrous creature"—in the Scientific Revolution:

> "Go, wondrous creature! mount where Science guides;
>   Go, measure earth, weigh air, and state the tides;
>   Instruct the planets in what orbs to run,
>   Correct old Time, and regulate the sun."
>   —Alexander Pope, *Essay on Man*

Progress and Reason

The Scientific Revolution of the 1500s and 1600s had transformed the way people in Europe looked at the world. In the 1700s, other scientists expanded European knowledge. Joseph Priestley and Antoine Lavoisier (ahn TWAHN lah vwah ZYAY), for example, built the framework for modern chemistry. Edward Jenner developed a vaccine against smallpox, a disease whose path of death spanned the centuries.

Scientific successes convinced educated Europeans of the power of human reason. If people used reason to find laws that governed the physical world, why not use reason to discover natural laws, or laws that govern human nature? Using the methods of the new science, reformers set out to study human behavior and solve the problems of society. Thus, the Scientific Revolution led to another revolution in thinking, known as the Enlightenment. Through the use of reason, insisted Enlightenment thinkers, people and governments could solve every social, political, and economic problem. Heaven could be achieved here on Earth.

Two Views of the Social Contract

In the 1600s, two English thinkers, Thomas Hobbes and John Locke, set forth ideas that were to become key to the Enlightenment. Both men lived through the upheavals of the English Civil War. Yet they came to very different conclusions about human nature and the role of government.

Smallpox Vaccinations
In this painting, Edward Jenner vaccinates a child against smallpox. The smallpox vaccine was one of many scientific developments of the 1700s.

Theme: Art and Literature What elements of the painting suggest that smallpox was a major problem before Jenner developed his vaccine?

Hobbes Thomas Hobbes set out his ideas in a work titled *Leviathan*. In it, he argued that people were naturally cruel, greedy, and selfish. If not strictly controlled, they would fight, rob, and oppress one another. Life in the "state of nature"—without laws or other control—would be "solitary, poor, nasty, brutish, and short."

To escape that "brutish" life, said Hobbes, people entered into a social contract, an agreement by which they gave up the state of nature for an organized society. Hobbes believed that only a powerful government could ensure an orderly society. For him, such a government was an absolute monarchy, which could impose order and compel obedience.

Locke John Locke had a more optimistic view of human nature. People were basically reasonable and moral, he said. Further, they had certain natural rights, or rights that belonged to all humans from birth. These included the right to life, liberty, and property.

In *Two Treatises of Government*, Locke argued that people formed governments to protect their natural rights. The best kind of government, he said, had limited power and was accepted by all citizens. Thus, unlike Hobbes, Locke rejected absolute monarchy.

Locke then set out a radical idea. A government, he said, has an obligation to the people it governs. If a government fails its obligations or violates people's natural rights, the people have the right to overthrow that government. This right to revolution would echo across Europe and around the world in the centuries that followed.

Separation of Powers

In the 1700s, France saw a flowering of Enlightenment thought. An early and influential thinker was the Baron de Montesquieu (MON tehs kyoo). Montesquieu studied the governments of Europe, from Italy to England. He read all he could about ancient and medieval Europe and learned about Chinese and Native American cultures. His sharp criticism of absolute monarchy opened the doors for later debate.

In 1748, Montesquieu published *The Spirit of the Laws*. In it, he discussed governments throughout history and wrote admiringly about Britain's limited monarchy. Montesquieu felt that the British had protected themselves against tyranny by dividing the various functions and powers of government among three separate branches: the legislative, executive, and judicial. (In fact, he had misunderstood the British system, which did not separate powers in this way.) Still, he felt that the separation of powers was the best way to protect liberty. Montesquieu also felt that each branch of government should be able to serve as a check on the other two, an idea that we call checks and balances.

The *Philosophes* and Society

In France, a group of Enlightenment thinkers applied the methods of science to better understand and improve society. They believed that the use of reason could lead to reforms of government, law, and society. These thinkers were called *philosophes*, which means "lovers of wisdom." Their ideas soon spread beyond France and even beyond Europe.

Voltaire Defends Freedom of Thought Probably the most famous of the *philosophes* was François-Marie Arouet, who took the name Voltaire. "My trade," said Voltaire, "is to say what I think," and he did so throughout his long, controversial life. Voltaire used biting wit as a weapon to expose the abuses of his day. He targeted corrupt officials and idle aristocrats. With his pen, he battled inequality, injustice, and superstition. He detested the slave trade and deplored religious prejudice.

Biography

Montesquieu 1689–1755

Born to wealth, Charles Louis de Secondat inherited the title Baron de Montesquieu. Like many other reformers, his privileged status did not keep him from becoming a voice for democracy. His *Persian Letters* ridiculed the French elite. In *The Spirit of the Laws,* he advanced the idea of separation of powers—a foundation of modern democracy.

Montesquieu's belief in democracy did not mean that he considered all people equal. For example, he held a common view of his time that men were superior to women. However, he thought that women would make good government officials. According to Montesquieu, women's "weakness" would make them "gentle" rulers, thus benefiting the people.

Theme: Impact of the Individual What reforms did Montesquieu promote?

Comparing Viewpoints

What Limits Should There Be on Freedom of Speech?

"I do not agree with a word that you say, but I will defend to the death your right to say it." Whether or not Voltaire said these exact words, he passionately believed in this idea. But his idea has not been universally accepted. To consider whether there should be limits on freedom of speech, examine these viewpoints.

England 1643

John Milton, Puritan writer, expressed views about freedom of expression that later influenced Enlightenment thinkers:

❝ Give me liberty to know, to utter, and to argue freely according to conscience, above all liberties. ❞

China 1957

Mao Zedong led a government in China based on the ideals of the communist philosopher Karl Marx:

❝ What should our policy be toward non-Marxist ideas? As far as unmistakable counterrevolutionaries and saboteurs of the socialist cause are concerned, the matter is easy. We simply deprive them of their freedom of speech. ❞

Canada 1985

The criminal code of Canada outlaws public remarks against religious, racial, or ethnic groups:

❝ Everyone who, by communicating statements other than in private conversation, willfully promotes hatred against any identifiable group is guilty of . . . an indictable offense and is liable to imprisonment for a term not exceeding two years. ❞

United States 1942

Uncle Sam silences an American who is careless in his speech during World War II. "Loose talk" could reveal important secrets to the enemy, costing American lives.

QUIET!

LOOSE TALK CAN COST LIVES

Skills Assessment

1. Who seems to support complete freedom of speech, free from all restrictions?
   A John Milton
   B Uncle Sam
   C Mao Zedong
   D Karl Marx

2. According to Canadian law, freedom of speech
   E does not apply to immigrants.
   F is everyone's right.
   G should be limited under certain circumstances.
   H exists only in public situations.

3. Critical Thinking Analyzing Information (a) Study the poster. What does it seem to say about freedom of speech? (b) Should freedom of speech ever be limited? If so, under what conditions?

Skills Tip

Before comparing points of view, you must identify the main idea of each separate point of view. Then, look for ways in which the views are the same or different.

Voltaire's outspoken attacks offended both the French government and the Catholic Church. He was imprisoned and forced into exile. Even as he saw his books outlawed and even burned, he continued to defend the principle of freedom of speech.

The *Encyclopedia* Another *philosophe*, Denis Diderot (dee DROH), labored for some 25 years to produce a 28-volume *Encyclopedia*. As the editor of this huge work, Diderot did more than just gather articles on human knowledge. His purpose was "to change the general way of thinking" by explaining the new ideas on topics such as government, philosophy, and religion. Diderot's *Encyclopedia* included articles by leading thinkers of the day, including Montesquieu and Voltaire.

In their *Encyclopedia* articles, the *philosophes* denounced slavery, praised freedom of expression, and urged education for all. They attacked divine-right theory and traditional religions. Critics raised an outcry. The French government argued that the *Encyclopedia* was an attack on public morals, and the pope threatened to excommunicate Roman Catholics who bought or read the volumes.

Despite these and other efforts to ban the *Encyclopedia*, as many as 20,000 copies were printed between 1751 and 1789. When translated into other languages, it helped spread Enlightenment ideas throughout Europe and across the Atlantic to the Americas.

Rousseau The most controversial *philosophe*, Jean-Jacques Rousseau (ZHAHN ZHAHK roo SOH), was a strange, difficult man. Coming from a poor family, he never felt comfortable in the glittering social world of Enlightenment thinkers.

Rousseau believed that people in their natural state were basically good. This natural innocence, he felt, was corrupted by the evils of society, especially the unequal distribution of property. This view was later adopted by many reformers and revolutionaries.

In 1762, Rousseau set forth his ideas about government and society in *The Social Contract*. Rousseau felt that society placed too many limitations on people's behavior. He believed that some controls were necessary, but that they should be minimal. Additionally, these controls should be imposed only by governments that had been freely elected.

Rousseau put his faith in the "general will," or the best conscience of the people. The good of the community as a whole, he said, should be placed above individual interests. Thus, unlike many Enlightenment thinkers who put the individual first, Rousseau felt that the individual should be subordinate to the community.

Rousseau has influenced political and social thinkers for more than 200 years. Woven through his work is a profound hatred of all forms of political and economic oppression. His bold ideas would help fan the flames of revolt in years to come.

Women and the Enlightenment The Enlightenment slogan "free and equal" did not apply to women. Women did have "natural rights," said the *philosophes*. But unlike the natural rights of men, these rights were limited to the areas of home and family.

By the mid-1700s, a small but growing number of women protested this view. They questioned the notion that women were by nature inferior to men and that men's domination of women was therefore part of "nature's plan." Germaine de Staël in France and Catharine Macaulay and Mary Wollstonecraft in Britain argued that women were being excluded from the social contract itself. Their arguments, however, were ridiculed and often sharply condemned.

Wollstonecraft was a well-known British social critic. She accepted that a woman's first duty was to be a good mother. At the same time, however, she felt that a woman should be able to decide what is in her own interest and should not be completely dependent on her husband. In 1792, Wollstonecraft published *A Vindication of the Rights of Woman*. In it, she called for equal education for girls and boys. Only education, she argued, could give women the tools they needed to participate equally with men in public life.

New Economic Thinking

Other thinkers known as **physiocrats** focused on economic reforms. Like the *philosophes*, physiocrats looked for natural laws to define a rational economic system.

Laissez Faire Physiocrats rejected mercantilism, which required government regulation of the economy to achieve a favorable balance of trade. Instead, they urged a policy of **laissez faire** (LEHS ay FAIR), allowing business to operate with little or no government interference. Unlike mercantilists, who called for acquiring gold and silver wealth through trade, the physiocrats claimed that real wealth came from making the land more productive. Extractive industries, they said, such as agriculture, mining, and logging, produced new wealth. Physiocrats also supported free trade and opposed tariffs, or taxes on trade.

Adam Smith British economist Adam Smith greatly admired the physiocrats. In his influential work, *The Wealth of Nations*, he argued that the free market should be allowed to regulate business activity. Smith tried to show how manufacturing, trade, wages, profits, and economic growth were all linked to the market forces of supply and demand. Wherever there is a demand for goods or services, he said, suppliers will seek to meet it. They do so because of the profits and other economic rewards they can get from fulfilling the demand.

Smith was a strong supporter of laissez faire. He believed that the marketplace was better off without any government regulation. At the same time, however, he argued that government had a duty to protect society, administer justice, and provide public works.

Adam Smith's ideas would gain increasing influence as the Industrial Revolution spread across Europe and beyond. His emphasis on the free market and the law of supply and demand would help to shape immensely productive economies in the 1800s and 1900s.

Germaine de Staël
Madame de Staël argued that women had been excluded from the ideals of the Enlightenment. She wrote a number of books, including an analysis of Rousseau.

Theme: Diversity According to the *philosophes,* how were natural rights different for men and for women?

SECTION 1 Assessment

Recall
1. **Identify: (a)** Thomas Hobbes, **(b)** John Locke, **(c)** Baron de Montesquieu, **(d)** Voltaire, **(e)** Denis Diderot, **(f)** Jean-Jacques Rousseau, **(g)** Mary Wollstonecraft, **(h)** *The Wealth of Nations*.
2. **Define: (a)** natural law, **(b)** social contract, **(c)** natural right, **(d)** *philosophe,* **(e)** physiocrat, **(f)** laissez faire.

Comprehension
3. How did the achievements of the Scientific Revolution contribute to the Enlightenment?

4. Explain the views of Thomas Hobbes, John Locke, and the Baron de Montesquieu.
5. How did the *philosophes* influence ideas on society and the economy?

Critical Thinking and Writing
6. **Defending a Position** Rousseau put the common good over the interest of the individual. Do you agree with that position? Explain.
7. **Predicting Consequences** Suppose that Mary Wollstonecraft encountered another important *philosophe*. What course might their conversation follow?

Activity

Creating a Cartoon
Draw a cartoon to illustrate the ideas of one or more of the *philosophes* you read about in this section. Write a brief caption to accompany your cartoon.

Enlightenment Ideas Spread

Reading Focus

■ What roles did censorship and salons play in the spread of new ideas?

■ How did *philosophes* influence enlightened despots?

■ How did the Enlightenment affect arts and literature?

■ Why were the lives of the majority unaffected?

Vocabulary

censorship

salon

enlightened despot

baroque

rococo

Taking Notes

On a sheet of paper draw a concept web to help you record information from this section. The web at right has been started for you. Add more circles as needed.

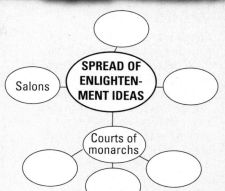

Main Idea Enlightenment ideas spread across Europe and prompted some rulers to make reforms.

Setting the Scene Paris, the heart of the Enlightenment, drew many intellectuals and others eager to debate the new ideas. Reforms proposed one evening became the talk of the town the next day. Even an enemy of the Enlightenment admitted that "an opinion launched in Paris was like a battering ram launched by 30 million men."

From France, Enlightenment ideas flowed across Europe and beyond. Everywhere, thinkers examined traditional beliefs and customs in the light of reason and found them flawed. Even absolute monarchs experimented with Enlightenment ideas, although they drew back when changes threatened the established way of doing things.

The Challenge of New Ideas

The ideas of the Enlightenment spread quickly through many levels of society. Educated people all over Europe eagerly read not only Diderot's *Encyclopedia* but also the small, cheap pamphlets that printers churned out on a broad range of issues. More and more, they saw the need for reform to achieve a just society.

During the Middle Ages, most Europeans had accepted without question a society based on divine-right rule, a strict class system, and a belief in heavenly reward for earthly suffering. In the Age of Reason, such ideas seemed unscientific and irrational. A just society, Enlightenment thinkers taught, should ensure social justice and happiness in this world.

Censorship Government and church authorities felt they had a sacred duty to defend the old order. They believed that the old order had been set up by God. To protect against the attacks of the Enlightenment, they waged a war of censorship, or restricting access to ideas and information. They banned and burned books and imprisoned writers.

Philosophes and writers like Montesquieu and Voltaire sometimes disguised their ideas in works of fiction. In the *Persian Letters*, Montesquieu uses two fictional Persian travelers, named Usbek and Rica, to mock French society. The hero of Voltaire's humorous novel *Candide*, published in 1759, travels across Europe and even to the Americas and the Middle East in search of "the best of all possible worlds." Voltaire slyly uses the tale to expose the corruption and hypocrisy of European society.

Salons The new literature, the arts, science, and philosophy were regular topics of discussion in salons, informal social gatherings at which writers,

Global Connections

An American *Philosophe*

Benjamin Franklin first traveled to Europe when he was just 18. There, he wrote in his *Autobiography*, "... I spent little upon myself except ... in books. I had improved my knowledge, ... though I had by no means improved my fortune. But I had made some very ingenious acquaintance, whose conversation was of great advantage to me, and I had read considerably."

Franklin's activities in Europe gave him firsthand exposure to Enlightenment ideas. He carried this new knowledge back to the American colonies, where he helped to create a country based on those ideas—the United States.

Theme: Global Interaction How was the transmission of ideas across the Atlantic different in Franklin's time than it is today?

Virtual Salons

Salons provided a way for people to gather and share ideas. Today, many people do this without ever meeting—through the Internet.

Every day, millions of people use the Internet to exchange ideas easily. In "chat rooms," people send messages instantly, even if the recipient is on the other side of the world. In "newsgroups," people submit thoughts on a given topic and respond to the comments of others.

Many discussions on the Internet lack the serious-minded tone of a salon conversation. And because participants meet only through computers, there is no way to be sure who is on the other end of the line. But the popularity of the Internet shows that people will find a way to gather and discuss their ideas, even in a "virtual" living room.

Theme: Continuity and Change How does a "virtual" salon compare to the salons of the 1700s?

artists, *philosophes*, and others exchanged ideas. The salon originated in the 1600s, when a group of noblewomen in Paris began inviting a few friends to their homes for poetry readings. By the 1700s, some middle-class women began holding salons. In the drawing rooms of these *salonières* (sah lohn YAIR), middle-class citizens could meet with the nobility on an equal footing to discuss and spread Enlightenment ideas.

One of the most respected salons was run by Madame Geoffrin. In her home on the Rue St. Honoré, she brought together the brightest and most talented people of her day. The young musical genius Wolfgang Amadeus Mozart played for her guests, and Diderot was a regular at her weekly dinners for philosophers and poets.

Enlightened Despots

Discussions of Enlightenment ideas also enlivened the courts of Europe. *Philosophes* tried to persuade European rulers to adopt their ideas. If they could "enlighten" the ruling classes, they thought, they could bring about reform. Some monarchs did accept Enlightenment ideas. They became **enlightened despots,** or absolute rulers who used their power to bring about political and social change.

Frederick the Great As king of Prussia from 1740 to 1786, Frederick II exerted extremely tight control over his subjects. Still, he saw himself as the "first servant of the state," with a duty to work for the common good.

Frederick admired Voltaire's work and lured the *philosophe* to Berlin to develop a Prussian academy of science. When Frederick was not busy fighting wars, he had swamps drained and forced peasants to grow new crops such as the potato. He had seed and tools distributed to peasants who had suffered in Prussia's wars. Frederick also tolerated religious differences, welcoming victims of religious persecution. "In my kingdom," he said, "everyone can go to heaven in his own fashion."

Frederick's reforms were directed mainly at making the Prussian government more efficient. He reorganized the civil service and simplified laws. But a "rationalized" bureaucracy also meant a stronger monarchy—and more power for Frederick himself.

Catherine the Great Catherine II of Russia read the works of the *philosophes* and exchanged letters with Voltaire and Diderot. She praised Voltaire as someone who had "fought the united enemies of humankind: superstition, fanaticism, ignorance, trickery."

Catherine, who became empress in 1762, toyed with Enlightenment ideas. Early in her reign, she made some limited reforms in law and government. She granted nobles a charter of rights and criticized the institution of serfdom. Still, like Frederick in Prussia, Catherine intended to give up no power. In the end, her political contribution to Russia was not reform but an expanded empire.

Joseph II The most radical of the enlightened despots was the Hapsburg emperor Joseph II, son and successor of Maria Theresa. An eager student of the Enlightenment, Joseph traveled in disguise among his subjects to learn of their problems. His efforts to improve their lives won him the nickname the "peasant emperor."

Maria Theresa had begun to modernize Austria's government. Joseph continued her reforms. Despite opposition, he granted toleration to Protestants and Jews in his Catholic empire. He ended censorship and attempted to bring the Catholic Church under royal control. He sold the property of many monasteries and convents and used the proceeds to build hospitals. Joseph even abolished serfdom. Like many of his other reforms, however, this measure was canceled after his death.

Virtual Field Trip

www.phschool.com

**Utah Museum of Fine Arts
Salt Lake City, Utah**

For more information about the
works of Elisabeth Vigée LeBrun,
use the Internet address above to
link to the Web site of the Utah
Museum of Fine Arts.

Enlightenment Painters
During the 1700s, many artists
began painting very personal,
detailed scenes. In *The Marquise
de Peze and the Marquise de
Rouget with Her Two Children*,
French artist Elisabeth Vigée LeBrun
shows the relationships between
mothers and young children.

Theme: Art and Literature
**What elements of this painting
identify its style as rococo rather
than baroque?**

The Arts and Literature

In the 1600s and 1700s, the arts evolved to meet changing tastes. As in
earlier periods, artists and composers had to please their patrons, the men
and women who commissioned works from them or gave them jobs.

Courtly Art In the age of Louis XIV, courtly art and architecture were
either in the Greek and Roman tradition or in a grand, complex style
known as baroque. Baroque paintings were huge, colorful, and full of
excitement. They glorified historic battles or the lives of saints. Such
works matched the grandeur of European courts.

By the mid-1700s, architects and designers developed the rococo style.
Unlike the heavy splendor of the baroque, rococo art was personal, elegant,
and charming. Furniture and tapestries featured delicate shells and flowers.
Portrait painters showed noble subjects in charming rural settings, surrounded by happy servants and pets.

Middle-Class Audiences A new audience, the growing middle class,
emerged with its own requirements. Successful merchants and prosperous
town officials wanted their portraits painted, but without frills. They liked
pictures of family life or realistic town or country scenes. Dutch painters
such as Rembrandt van Rijn (REHM brant van RĪN) conferred great dignity
on merchants and other ordinary, middle-class subjects.

Trends in Music New kinds of musical entertainment evolved during
this era. Ballets and operas—plays set to music—were performed at royal
courts. Before long, opera houses sprang up from Italy to England to amuse
the paying public. The music of the period followed ordered, structured
forms well suited to the Age of Reason.

Among the towering musical figures of the era was Johann Sebastian
Bach. A devout German Lutheran, Bach wrote complex and beautiful religious works for organ and choirs. Another German-born composer, George
Frederick Handel, spent much of his life in England. There, he wrote *Water
Music* and other pieces for King George I, as well as many operas. His most
celebrated work, the *Messiah*, combines instruments and voices. Today, it is
a standard at Christmas and Easter concerts.

The Great Mozart

Wolfgang Amadeus Mozart died when he was just 35 years old. His musical genius, however, has lived for centuries. Today, his work is celebrated around the world.

Mozart wrote the opera *The Magic Flute* during the last year of his life. Here, the high priest is passing judgment on a kidnapper. Mozart's operas are famous for their outstanding arias (solos), recitatives (sung dialogues), and ensembles (group singing).

Mozart was a prolific composer. He wrote operas, symphonies, piano concertos, string quartets, and scores of other works, including church music. In all, he composed more than 600 pieces of music.

Mozart's music is admired throughout the world today. It can be playful, serious, uplifting, or somber. Many of his melodies are instantly recognized. People use his music in everything from car commercials to Internet greeting cards.

Fast Facts

- Mozart was a child prodigy. He played the harpsichord at age 4 and began to compose music at age 5. A year later, he performed for the empress of Austria.

- Mozart's father, Leopold, was an accomplished musician. He took his young son on performing tours throughout Europe. Wolfgang never attended school.

Portfolio Assessment

Listen to a recording of one of Mozart's compositions. Then, write a journal entry in which you tell how the music affected you. What feelings did it evoke? What images did it bring to mind? Explain why you think Mozart's music is held in such high regard.

In 1762, a six-year-old prodigy, Wolfgang Amadeus Mozart, burst onto the European scene to gain instant celebrity as a composer and performer. Over the next three decades, his brilliant operas, graceful symphonies, and moving religious music helped define the new style of composition. Although he died in poverty at age 35, his musical legacy thrives today.

The Novel By the 1700s, literature developed new forms and a wide new audience. Middle-class readers, for example, liked stories about their own times told in straightforward prose. One result was an outpouring of novels, or long works of prose fiction. English novelists created many popular works. Daniel Defoe wrote *Robinson Crusoe*, an exciting tale about a sailor shipwrecked on a tropical island. In *Pamela*, Samuel Richardson used a series of letters to tell a story about a servant girl. This technique was adopted by other authors of the period.

Lives of the Majority

Most Europeans were untouched by either courtly or middle-class culture. They remained what they had always been—peasants living in small rural villages. Their culture, based on centuries-old traditions, changed slowly.

Peasant life varied across Europe. Villages in Western Europe were relatively more prosperous than those in Eastern Europe. In the West, serfdom had largely disappeared. Instead, some peasants worked their own patches of land. Others were tenants of large landowners, paying a yearly rent for the land they farmed. Still others were day laborers who hired themselves out to work on other people's farms.

In central and Eastern Europe, however, serfdom was firmly rooted. In Russia, it spread and deepened in the 1700s. Peasants owed labor services to their lords and could be bought and sold with the land.

Despite advances, some echoes of serfdom survived in Western Europe. In France, peasants still had to provide free labor, repairing roads and bridges after the spring floods just as their ancestors had done. In England, country squires had the right to hunt foxes across their tenants' lands, tearing up plowed and planted fields.

By the late 1700s, radical ideas about equality and social justice seeped into peasant villages. While some peasants eagerly sought to topple the old order, others resisted efforts to bring about change. In the 1800s, war and political upheaval, as well as changing economic conditions, would transform peasant life in Europe.

SECTION 2 Assessment

Recall
1. **Identify:** **(a)** *Candide*, **(b)** Joseph II, **(c)** Johann Sebastian Bach, **(d)** George Frederick Handel, **(e)** Wolfgang Amadeus Mozart, **(f)** Daniel Defoe.
2. **Define:** **(a)** censorship, **(b)** salon, **(c)** enlightened despot, **(d)** baroque, **(e)** rococo.

Comprehension
3. Explain how each of the following affected the spread of new ideas: **(a)** censorship, **(b)** salons.
4. What were the goals of enlightened despots?

5. How did the Enlightenment affect **(a)** arts and literature, **(b)** the lives of the majority?

Critical Thinking and Writing
6. **Analyzing Information** **(a)** What did Frederick II mean when he said, "In my kingdom, everyone can go to heaven in his own fashion"? **(b)** How did his actions reflect that idea?
7. **Making Inferences** How did the Enlightenment bring together ideas of both the Renaissance and the Reformation?

Activity
Take It to the NET

Search the Internet for information about salons in the 1700s. Identify types of people who attended salons in the 1700s, and create a list of people you would invite to a modern salon. Explain your choices.

Reading Focus

■ What influences spurred Britain's rise to global power?

■ How did the growth of constitutional government reflect conditions in politics and society?

■ How did George III reassert royal power?

Vocabulary

constitutional government

cabinet

prime minister

oligarchy

Taking Notes

As you read this section, make an outline of the information. Use Roman numerals for the main headings. Use capital letters for the subheadings, and use numbers for the supporting details. The outline at right has been started for you.

I. Rise to global power
  A. Geography
    1. Location good for trade
    2. From outposts to empire
  B. Success in war
    1. Won Nova Scotia and Newfoundland
    2.

Main Idea   Britain's island location, colonial possessions, and powerful navy contributed to its rise to world power.

A Powerful Navy
By the mid-1700s, Britain controlled territories in North America, South America, Asia, and the Pacific. These scattered holdings required a strong navy, including men-of-war like the one shown here.

Theme: Political and Social Systems   How might a strong navy benefit trade?

Setting the Scene   Supporters of mercantilism found success in England. In the mid-1600s, a mercantilist wrote, "Foreign trade is . . . the honor of the kingdom, the noble profession of the merchant, . . . the means of our treasure, the sinews of our wars, the terror of our enemies."

Over the next century, Britain embraced mercantilism and built a colonial and commercial empire that reached around the world. At the same time, Britain developed a constitutional monarchy, a political system somewhere between the absolute monarchies of Europe and later democracies.

Rise to Global Power

Why did Britain, a small island kingdom on the edge of Europe, rise to global prominence in the 1700s? Here, we can look at a few reasons for the nation's success.

Geography   Location placed England in a position to control trade during the Renaissance. In the 1500s and 1600s, English merchants sent ships across the world's oceans and planted outposts in the West Indies, North America, and India. From these tiny settlements, England would build a global empire.

Success in War   In the 1700s, Britain was generally on the winning side in European conflicts. Each victory brought valuable rewards. With the Treaty of Utrecht, France gave Britain Nova Scotia and Newfoundland in North America. Britain also monopolized the slave trade in Spanish America. The slave trade brought enormous wealth to British merchants, who invested their profits in other ventures. In 1763, the Treaty of Paris ending the French and Indian War and the Seven Years' War brought Britain all of French Canada. The British East India Company also pushed the French out of India.

Unlike its European rivals, Britain had no large standing army. Instead, it built up its fleet. By 1763, Britain had developed a more powerful navy than its greatest rival, France. With superior naval power, it could protect its growing empire and trade.

A Favorable Business Climate   England offered a more favorable climate to business and commerce than did its European rivals. Although England followed mercantilist policies, it put fewer restrictions on trade than France. Also, while British nobles, like most other nobles in Europe, looked down on trade, some did engage in business activities.

Union With Scotland At home, England expanded by merging with its neighbor, Scotland. In 1707, the Act of Union joined the two countries in the United Kingdom of Great Britain. The United Kingdom also included Wales. The union brought economic advantages to both lands. Free trade between the two created a larger market for farmers and manufacturers. Many Scots, however, resented the union. On two occasions, they supported the claims of Stuart princes who sought to regain the British throne. Eventually, though, growing prosperity made the union more acceptable.

Ireland England had controlled Ireland since the 1100s. In the 1600s, English rulers tried to subdue Catholic Ireland by sending Protestants from England and Scotland to settle there. They gave Protestant settlers title to Irish Catholics' lands. The Irish fiercely resisted Protestant rule. Uprisings led to increased repression. Catholics were forbidden to own weapons, marry non-Catholics, or teach.

Growth of Constitutional Government

In the century following the Glorious Revolution, three new political institutions arose in Britain: political parties, the cabinet, and the office of prime minister. The appearance of these institutions was part of the evolution of Britain's **constitutional government**—that is, a government whose power is defined and limited by law. The British constitution is not a single document. Instead, it consists of all acts of Parliament over the centuries. It also includes documents such as the Magna Carta and Bill of Rights, as well as unwritten traditions that protect citizens' rights.

Political Parties Two political parties emerged in England in the late 1600s—Tories and Whigs. Tories were generally landed aristocrats who

Skills Assessment

Geography During the 1600s in Ireland, England gave Irish lands to English and Scottish settlers. In Scotland, failed rebellions in 1715 and 1745–1746 marked the end of armed resistance to English control.

1. **Location** On the map, locate **(a)** Irish Sea, **(b)** Dublin, **(c)** Edinburgh, **(d)** London.
2. **Region** What percentage of land in Ireland was owned by Catholics in 1603? In 1685?
3. **Critical Thinking Drawing Conclusions** How might it benefit England economically to join with its neighbors?

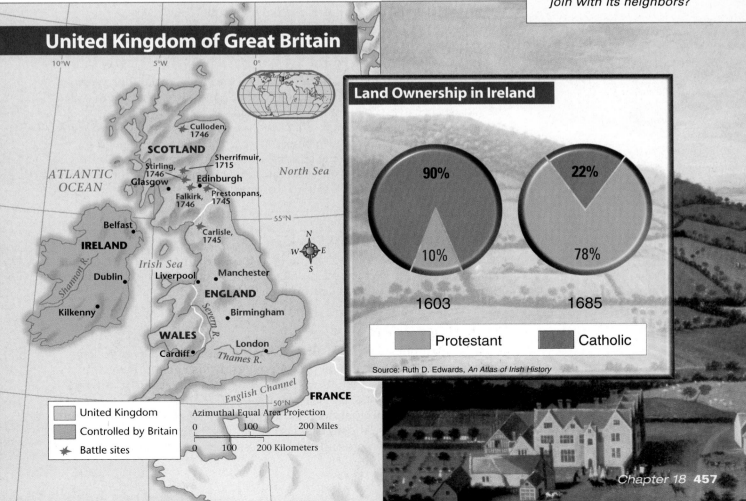

United Kingdom of Great Britain

Land Ownership in Ireland

90%

10%

1603

22%

78%

1685

Protestant   Catholic

Source: Ruth D. Edwards, *An Atlas of Irish History*

United Kingdom

Controlled by Britain

Battle sites

Azimuthal Equal Area Projection

0   100   200 Miles

0   100   200 Kilometers

Political Campaigns
William Hogarth's painting *The Election II—Canvassing for Votes* shows campaigners trying to win votes for their candidates. In England during the 1700s, only men who owned land could vote.

Theme: Political and Social Systems Why might leaders have thought that voting should be limited to landowning men?

sought to preserve older traditions. They supported broad royal powers and a dominant Anglican Church. Whigs backed the policies of the Glorious Revolution. They were more likely to reflect urban business interests, support religious toleration, and favor Parliament over the crown.

These early political parties were unlike the party organizations that we know today. They represented exclusive social circles among rich, powerful men in Parliament. The modern political party, which represents groups of voters and has a distinct platform, did not appear until the 1800s.

The Cabinet System The cabinet, another new feature of government, evolved in the 1700s after the British throne was inherited by a German Protestant prince. George I spoke no English and relied on the leaders in Parliament to help him rule. Under George I and his German-born son George II, a handful of parliamentary advisers set policy. They were called the cabinet because they met in a small room, or "cabinet."

In time, the cabinet gained official status. It was made up of leaders of the majority party in the House of Commons. The cabinet remained in power so long as it enjoyed the support of the Commons. If the Commons voted against a cabinet decision, the cabinet resigned. This cabinet system (also called a parliamentary system) was later adopted by other countries.

The Prime Minister Heading the cabinet was the prime minister. The prime minister was the leader of the majority party in Parliament and in time the chief official of the British government. From 1721 to 1742, the able Whig leader Robert Walpole molded the cabinet into a unified body, requiring all members to agree on major issues. Although the title was not yet used, Walpole is often called Britain's first prime minister.

Politics and Society

The age of Walpole was a time of peace and prosperity. But even as Parliament and the cabinet assumed new powers, British government was far from democratic. Rather, it was an oligarchy—a government in which the ruling power belongs to a few people.

In Britain as on the continent, landowning aristocrats were seen as the "natural" ruling class. The highest nobles held seats in the House of Lords. Other wealthy landowners and rich business leaders in the cities controlled elections to the House of Commons. The right to vote was limited to a relatively few male property owners, and their votes were bought openly.

The lives of most people contrasted sharply with those of the ruling elite. The majority made a meager living from the land. In the 1700s, even that poor existence was threatened. Wealthy land-owners bought up farms and took over common lands, evicting tenant farmers and small landowners. Many landless families drifted into towns, where they faced a harsh existence.

A small but growing middle class included successful merchants and manufacturers. They controlled affairs in the towns and cities. Some improved their social standing by marrying into the landed gentry. The middle class also produced talented inventors and entrepreneurs who helped usher in the Industrial Revolution.

George III Reasserts Royal Power

In 1760, George III began a 60-year reign. Unlike his father and grandfather, the new king was born in England. He spoke English and loved Britain. But George was eager to recover the powers the crown had lost. Following his mother's advice, "George, be a king!" he set out to reassert royal power. He wanted to end Whig domination, choose his own ministers, dissolve the cabinet system, and make Parliament follow his will.

Personal Rule Gradually, George found seats in Parliament for "the king's friends." Then, with their help, he began to assert his leadership. Many of his policies, however, would prove disastrous.

After the Seven Years' War, George and his advisers decided that English colonists in North America must pay the costs of their own defense. When colonists protested, Parliament passed harsh measures to force them to obey. In 1775, these and other conflicts triggered the American Revolution, which ended in a loss for Britain.

Cabinet Rule Restored Britain's loss of its American colonies discredited the king. Increasingly, too, he suffered from bouts of mental illness. In the crisis of leadership that followed, cabinet rule was restored in 1788.

In the decades ahead, revolution engulfed France, and Napoleon Bonaparte's armies stormed across Europe, dragging Britain into long wars. During that time, the cabinet controlled the government. The British came to see the prime minister as their real political leader.

George III
This portrait shows the king just a few years after the start of his reign. One of his priorities was to regain power for the throne.

Theme: Art and Literature
What elements of the painting reflect the king's authority?

SECTION 3 Assessment

Recall
1. **Identify:** **(a)** Act of Union, **(b)** Tories, **(c)** Whigs, **(d)** Robert Walpole, **(e)** George III.
2. **Define:** **(a)** constitutional government, **(b)** cabinet, **(c)** prime minister, **(d)** oligarchy.

Comprehension
3. Explain how each of the following contributed to Britain's rise to global power: **(a)** geography, **(b)** success in war, **(c)** attitudes toward business and commerce.

4. How did the British cabinet and office of prime minister develop?
5. What goals did George III have when he became king?

Critical Thinking and Writing
6. **Analyzing Information** How did the British political party system affect most people in Britain?
7. **Predicting Consequences** How might people in Ireland and the American colonies react to British attempts to increase control over those regions?

Activity

Creating a Diagram
Make a diagram showing the relationship among the English crown, prime minister, cabinet, and Parliament during the reigns of George I and George II.

Reading Focus

- What were the chief characteristics of the 13 English colonies?
- How did growing discontent lead to the American Revolution?
- How did the new constitution reflect the ideas of the Enlightenment?

Vocabulary

popular sovereignty
Loyalist
federal republic

Taking Notes

On a sheet of paper draw a time line to show important dates leading up to the emergence of the United States government. Use the time line shown here to help you get started.

French and Indian War ends	Boston Massacre		
1763	**1770**	**1776**	**1789**

Main Idea Colonial opposition to British trade and tax policies led to independence and the founding of the United States of America.

Setting the Scene Early in 1776, English colonists in North America eagerly read the newly published *Common Sense*. The pamphlet called on them to declare their independence from Britain. Its author, Thomas Paine, a recent immigrant from England, wrote with passion tempered by reason. "In the following pages," he declared, "I offer nothing more than simple facts, plain arguments, and common sense."

In *Common Sense*, Paine echoed the themes of the Enlightenment. He rejected ancient prejudice and tyranny, while appealing to reason, natural laws, and the promise of freedom. He wrote:

> "'Tis repugnant to reason, to the universal order of things, to all examples from former ages, to suppose that this Continent can long remain subject to any external power."
> —Thomas Paine, *Common Sense*

Colonists hotly debated Paine's arguments. As resentment of British policies grew, however, many came to agree with his radical ideas.

The 13 English Colonies

By 1750, a string of 13 prosperous colonies stretched along the eastern coast of North America. They were part of Britain's growing empire. Colonial cities such as Boston, New York, and Philadelphia were busy commercial centers that linked North America to the West Indies, Africa, and Europe. Colonial shipyards produced many vessels used in that global trade.

Britain applied mercantilist policies to its colonies. In the 1600s, Parliament had passed the Navigation Acts to regulate colonial trade and manufacturing. For the most part, these acts were not rigorously enforced. Smuggling was common and was not considered a crime by the colonists. Even prominent colonists might gain part of their wealth from smuggled goods.

By the mid-1700s, too, the colonies were home to diverse religious and ethnic groups. Social distinctions were more blurred than in Europe, although government and society were dominated

Colonial Unity
Benjamin Franklin created this political cartoon at the beginning of the French and Indian War. The segmented snake represents Britain's colonies in North America.

Theme: Political and Social Systems How does this cartoon suggest Franklin's attitude toward colonial involvement in the war?

JOIN, or DIE.

by wealthy landowners and merchants. In politics as in much else, there was a good deal of free discussion. Colonists felt entitled to the rights of English citizens, and their colonial assemblies exercised much control over local affairs.

Although the ways of life between the colonists of New England and those in the south differed, they all shared common values, respect for individual enterprise, and a growing self-confidence. Many also had an increasing sense of their own destiny separate from Britain.

Growing Discontent

After 1763, relations between Britain and the 13 colonies grew strained. The Seven Years' War and the French and Indian War in North America had drained the British treasury. King George III and his advisers thought that the colonists should help pay for the war and for troops still stationed along the frontier. Britain began to enforce the long-neglected laws regulating colonial trade, and Parliament passed new laws to increase the taxes paid by the colonies.

The British measures were not burdensome, but colonists bitterly resented what they saw as an attack on their rights. "No taxation without representation," they protested. Because they had no representatives in Parliament, they believed, Parliament had no right to tax them. Parliament did repeal some of the hated measures, such as a tax on all paper, but in general, it asserted its right to impose taxes on the colonies.

Early Clashes A series of violent clashes intensified the crisis. In March 1770, British soldiers in Boston opened fire on a crowd that was pelting them with stones and snowballs. Colonists called the death of five protesters the "Boston Massacre." In December 1773, a handful of colonists hurled a cargo of recently arrived British tea into the harbor to protest a tax on tea. The incident became known as the Boston Tea Party. When Parliament passed harsh laws to punish Massachusetts for the destruction of the tea, other colonies rallied to oppose the British response.

As tensions increased, fighting spread, representatives from each colony gathered in Philadelphia. There, they met in a Continental Congress to decide what action to take. Members included some extraordinary men. Among the participants were the radical yet fair-minded Massachusetts lawyer John Adams, who had defended at trial the British soldiers involved in the Boston Massacre; Virginia planter and soldier George Washington; and political and social leaders from all 13 colonies.

Declaring Independence The Congress set up a Continental Army, with George Washington in command. In April 1775, the crisis exploded into war. Although many battles ended in British victories, they showed that the Patriots were determined to fight at any cost. In 1776, the Second Continental Congress took a momentous step, voting to declare independence from Britain. Thomas Jefferson of Virginia was the principal author of the Declaration of Independence, a document that clearly reflects the ideas of John Locke.

The Declaration claimed that people had the right "to alter or to abolish" unjust governments—a right to revolt. It also emphasized the principle of popular sovereignty, which states that all government power comes from the people. Jefferson carefully detailed the colonists' grievances against Britain. Because the king had trampled colonists' natural rights, he argued, the colonists had the right to rebel and set up a new government that would protect them. Aware of the risks involved, on July 4, 1776, American leaders adopted the Declaration, pledging "our lives, our fortunes, and our sacred honor" to creating and protecting the new United States of America.

The American Revolution in the East

Quebec
Montreal
St. Lawrence R.
Fort Ticonderoga, 1775, 1777
NH
Saratoga, 1777
To England, 1776
Bunker Hill, 1775
Boston
MA
Lake Huron
Lake Ontario
Lake Erie
NY
Hudson R.
CT
RI
Lexington/Concord, 1775
Delaware R.
PA
NJ • New York
Valley Forge, 1777-78
Trenton, 1776
From England, 1776
Brandywine Creek, 1777
Philadelphia
MD • Baltimore
DE
ATLANTIC OCEAN
Potomac R.
VA
Chesapeake Bay
Yorktown
Yorktown, 1781
French blockade, 1781
King's Mountain, 1780
NC
Moores Creek Bridge, 1776
Camden, 1780
SC
GA
Charleston
Savannah

APPALACHIAN MTS.

N W E S

40°W 50°W 40°N 30°N

Battle sites
Route of American forces
Route of British forces

Albers Equal Area Projection
0   250   500 Miles
0   250   500 Kilometers

Skills Assessment

Geography Battles were fought across the colonies, but toward the end of the war, most took place in the southern colonies.

1. **Location** On the map, locate (a) Saratoga, (b) Valley Forge, (c) Yorktown.
2. **Movement** What route did British troops take after landing at Charleston?
3. **Critical Thinking Making Inferences** How was the arrival of the French fleet important during the Battle of Yorktown?

The American Revolution

At first, the American cause looked bleak. The British had professional soldiers, a huge fleet, and plentiful money. They occupied most major American cities. Also, about one third of the colonists were Loyalists, who supported Britain. Many others refused to fight for either side.

The Continental Congress had few military resources and little money to pay its soldiers. Still, colonists battling for independence had some advantages. They were fighting on their own soil for their farms and towns. Although the British held New York and Philadelphia, rebels controlled the countryside.

To counteract these advantages, the British worked to create alliances within the colonies. A number of Native American groups sided with the British, while others saw potential advantages in supporting the Patriot cause. Additionally, the British offered freedom to any enslaved people who were willing to fight the colonists.

The French Alliance A turning point in the war came in 1777, when the Americans triumphed over the British at the Battle of Saratoga. This victory persuaded France to join the Americans against its old rival, Britain. The alliance brought the Americans desperately needed supplies, trained soldiers, and French warships. Spurred by the French example, the Netherlands and Spain added their support.

Hard times continued, however. In the brutal winter of 1777–1778, Continental troops at Valley Forge suffered from cold, hunger, and disease. Throughout this crisis and others, Washington proved a patient, courageous, and determined leader able to hold the ragged army together.

Treaty of Paris Finally in 1781, with the help of the French fleet, which blockaded the Chesapeake Bay, Washington forced the surrender of a British army at Yorktown, Virginia. With that defeat, the British war effort crumbled. Two years later, American, British, and French diplomats signed the Treaty of Paris ending the war. In that treaty, Britain recognized the independence of the United States of America. It also accepted the new nation's western frontier as the Mississippi River.

A New Constitution

The national government set up by a document that Americans called the Articles of Confederation was too weak to rule the new United States effectively. To address this problem, the nation's leaders gathered once more in Philadelphia. During the hot summer of 1787, they met in secret to hammer out the Constitution of the United States. This framework for a strong yet flexible government has adapted to changing conditions for more than 200 years.

The Impact of Enlightenment Ideas The framers of the Constitution had absorbed the ideas of Locke, Montesquieu, and Rousseau and had studied history. They saw government in terms of a social contract into which "We the People of the United States" entered. They provided not only for an elective legislature but also for an elected president rather than a hereditary monarch. For the first president, voters would choose George Washington, who had led the army during the war.

The Constitution created a **federal republic,** with power divided between the federal, or national, government and the states. A central feature of the new federal government was the separation of powers among the legislative, executive, and judicial branches, an idea borrowed directly from Montesquieu. Within that structure, each branch of government was provided with checks and balances on the other branches.

The Bill of Rights, the first 10 amendments to the Constitution, recognized the idea that people had basic rights that the government must protect. These rights included freedom of religion, speech, and the press, as well as the rights to trial by jury and to private property.

Limited Freedom In 1789, the Constitution became the supreme law of the land. It set up a representative government with an elected legislature to reflect the wishes of the governed.

Yet most Americans at the time did not have the right to vote. Only white men who were able to meet certain property requirements could vote. Women could not cast a ballot, nor could African Americans— enslaved *or* free—or Native Americans. It would take more than a century of struggle before the right to vote and equal protection under the law were extended to all adult Americans.

Looking Ahead

Despite these limitations, the Constitution of the United States created the most progressive government of its day. From the start, the new republic shone as a symbol of freedom to European countries and to reformers in Latin America. Its constitution would be copied or adapted by many lands throughout the world.

The Enlightenment ideals that had inspired American colonists brought changes in Europe, too. In 1789, a revolution in France toppled the monarchy in the name of liberty and equality. Before long, other Europeans took up the cry for freedom. By the mid-1800s, most absolute monarchs across Europe would see their powers greatly reduced.

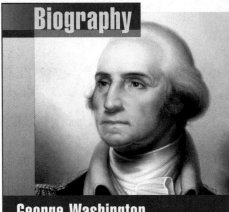

Biography

George Washington
1732–1799

As president, George Washington acted on the Enlightenment ideals given form in the Constitution. Some leaders felt that the president should have a grand title. Instead, Washington chose to be addressed as "Mr. President." He believed that a simple form of address was more appropriate for the leader of a republic.

Toward the end of his second term in office, some hoped that he would run again, becoming a president for life. Again, Washington disagreed. Later presidents followed this example. No president would run for a third term until 1940—nearly 150 years after Washington left office.

Theme: Impact of the Individual How did Washington's presidency reflect the ideas of the Enlightenment?

SECTION 4 Assessment

Recall

1. **Identify:** **(a)** Navigation Acts, **(b)** Continental Congress, **(c)** George Washington, **(d)** Battle of Saratoga, **(e)** Treaty of Paris of 1783, **(f)** Bill of Rights.
2. **Define:** **(a)** popular sovereignty, **(b)** Loyalist, **(c)** federal republic.

Comprehension

3. Describe colonial law, society, and politics in the mid-1700s.
4. Explain why conflict between the colonists and Britain increased after 1763.
5. Give an example of how Enlight-enment ideas were reflected in each of the following: **(a)** the Declaration of Independence, **(b)** the United States Constitution.

Critical Thinking and Writing

6. **Analyzing Information** Describe the idea of separation of powers. Then, give two examples of how your life would be different if the Constitution did not guarantee separation of powers.
7. **Recognizing Point of View** What reasons might a Loyalist have for opposing the American Revolution?

Activity
Take It to the NET

Use the Internet to research the Battle of Saratoga during the American Revolution. Then, write a letter that an American officer might have written home describing the battle and its significance.

18 Review and Assessment

Creating a Chapter Summary

On a sheet of paper, draw a web like the one shown here. Add information to the empty circles to help you recall important ideas of the Enlightenment and important ideas from the Enlightenment that were used in the American Constitution.

For additional review and enrichment activities, see the interactive version of *World History* available on the Web and on CD-ROM.

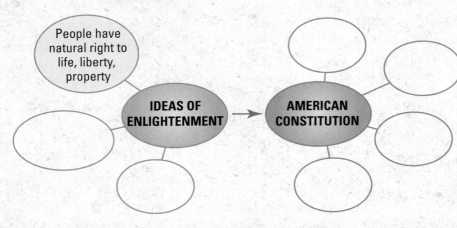

People have natural right to life, liberty, property

IDEAS OF ENLIGHTENMENT

AMERICAN CONSTITUTION

Web Site Self-Test
For practice test questions for Chapter 18, see **www.phschool.com**.

Building Vocabulary

Classify each of the chapter vocabulary words listed below under *one* of the following themes: art and literature; political and social systems; religions and value systems.

1. **natural law**
2. *philosophe*
3. **enlightened despot**
4. **baroque**
5. **rococo**
6. **constitutional government**
7. **cabinet**
8. **prime minister**
9. **Loyalist**
10. **federal republic**

Recalling Key Facts

11. According to John Locke, what should happen if a government violates people's natural rights?
12. According to Adam Smith, how should wages and prices be regulated?
13. How did serfdom differ in Eastern and Western Europe?
14. What areas combined to form the United Kingdom of Great Britain?
15. How did taxation create tensions between the American colonies and the British government?

Critical Thinking and Writing

16. **Linking Past and Present** Today, we talk about human rights rather than natural rights. **(a)** Describe a human rights issue that has been in the news recently. **(b)** Choose one *philosophe* from this chapter and describe how he or she might respond to the issue.
17. **Analyzing Information** **(a)** What ideas about government do you think English settlers brought with them to the Americas? **(b)** How might those ideas have contributed to the outbreak of the American Revolution?
18. **Defending a Position** During the American Revolution, Thomas Paine used the following words to encourage the colonists during a particularly grim time: "What we obtain too cheaply, we esteem too light; it is [costliness] only that gives everything its value."
    (a) What did he mean by this? **(b)** Do you agree or disagree? Give an example to defend your position.
19. **Connecting to Geography** **(a)** During the American Revolution, how did the location of the war help the Americans? **(b)** Why was it a problem for the British?

This passage is from a selection by Voltaire titled "Tolerance." In it, Voltaire describes people who abuse their power. In the first part of the excerpt, he uses the first person, "I," to show how these people think. In the remainder, he uses the third person, "they," to describe the effects of their actions on others. Read the passage, then answer the questions that follow.

"I possess a dignity and power founded on ignorance; I walk on the heads of the men who lie at my feet; if they should rise and look me in the face, I am lost; I must bind them to the ground, therefore, with iron chains. Thus have reasoned the men whom centuries of bigotry have made powerful. They have other powerful men beneath them, and these have still others, who all grow rich with the spoils of the poor, grow fat on their blood, and laugh at their stupidity. They all hate tolerance, as . . . tyrants dread the word liberty."

—Voltaire, *Philosophical Dictionary*

20. Why would people who abuse their power be "lost" if others were to "rise and look me in the face"?

21. What do you think Voltaire meant by the phrase "grow fat on their blood"?

22. What is Voltaire's tone in this passage? How does it suggest Voltaire's own beliefs?

23. Who are some of the intolerant people Voltaire might have had in mind when he wrote this?

24. **(a)** Identify a simile used in this excerpt. **(b)** Identify a metaphor in the excerpt.

Skills Tip

To illustrate a point, authors may use similes and metaphors. A simile is a description that uses "like" or "as" to draw comparisons. A metaphor uses the comparison as the description itself.

Use the Internet to research one of the political thinkers described in the text. Then, write a letter to that person explaining whether you think his or her ideas continue to be relevant in the present day.

SEPARATION OF POWERS

Executive Branch
(President)
Carries out laws
Proposes laws
Can veto laws
Negotiates foreign treaties
Serves as commander in chief of the armed forces
Appoints federal judges, ambassadors, and other high officials
Can grant pardons to federal offenders

Legislative Branch
(Congress)
Passes laws
Can override President's veto
Approves treaties and presidential appointments
Can impeach and remove President and other high officials
Creates lower federal courts
Appropriates money
Prints and coins money
Raises and supports the armed forces
Can declare war
Regulates foreign and interstate trade

Judicial Branch
(Supreme Court and Other Federal Courts)
Interprets laws
Can declare laws unconstitutional
Can declare executive actions unconstitutional

This table shows the powers held by each branch of the United States government. Study the table and answer the following questions:

25. Who heads the executive branch?

26. What is the main role of the legislative branch?

27. In 1748, Montesquieu wrote, "There is no liberty, if the power of judging is not separated from the legislative and executive powers. Were it joined with the legislative, the life and liberty of the subject would be exposed to arbitrary control, for the judge would then be the legislator. Were it joined to the executive power, the judge might behave with all the violence of an oppressor." How does this table relate to Montesquieu's statement?

The French Revolution and Napoleon

1789–1815

Chapter Preview

1 On the Eve of Revolution
2 Creating a New France
3 Radical Days
4 The Age of Napoleon Begins
5 The End of an Era

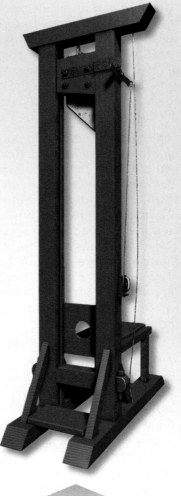

1793

During the Reign of Terror, which begins in 1793, the guillotine is used to execute thousands of French citizens.

1789

After a battle with royal troops, Parisians capture the Bastille on July 14, 1789.

1799

Napoleon overthrows the Directory.

CHAPTER EVENTS

1790   1795   1800

GLOBAL EVENTS

1789 The United States Constitution is ratified.

1793 China rejects British trade offer.

Revolutionary France at War, 1793

Map legend:
- France, 1793
- Allied countries against France
- Boundary of Holy Roman Empire

By 1793, the French Revolution had plunged France into a general European war that would last on and off for more than 20 years and transform Europe.

Map labels:
IRELAND · GREAT BRITAIN · NETHERLANDS · HANOVER · PRUSSIA · KINGDOM OF DENMARK AND NORWAY · SWEDEN · North Sea · Baltic Sea · Vistula R. · POLAND · RUSSIAN EMPIRE · AUSTRIAN NETHERLANDS · PRUSSIA · SAXONY · Oder R. · Elbe R. · PRUSSIA · Rhine R. · Seine R. · Loire R. · ATLANTIC OCEAN · FRANCE · SWISS CONFED. · BAVARIA · AUSTRIA · HUNGARY · ALPS · VENETIAN REPUBLIC · Rhone R. · Po R. · PAPAL STATES · Danube R. · OTTOMAN EMPIRE · Adriatic Sea · PORTUGAL · SPAIN · Ebro R. · Tagus R. · PYRENEES MTS. · KINGDOM OF SARDINIA · Tiber R. · KINGDOM OF NAPLES · Mediterranean Sea

50°N · 40°N · 10°W · 0° · 10°E · 20°E

Azimuthal Equal Area Projection
0 150 300 Miles
0 150 300 Kilometers

1804
In a magnificent ceremony, Napoleon crowns himself emperor of the French.

1812
Napoleon invades Russia.

1815
Napoleon abdicates after British and Prussian forces defeat him at Waterloo. The Duke of Wellington is the victorious British general.

Timeline: 1805 · 1810 · 1815

1804 Haiti declares independence from France.

1812 The United States declares war on Britain.

On the Eve of Revolution

Reading Focus

- What was the social structure of the old regime?
- Why did France face economic troubles in 1789?
- Why did Louis XVI call the Estates General?
- Why did a Paris crowd storm the Bastille?

Vocabulary

bourgeoisie
deficit spending

Taking Notes

As you read this section, create a chart to identify causes of the French Revolution. Use the incomplete chart below as a model. Add more arrows for causes if you need them.

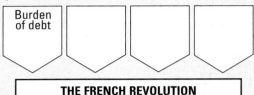

Burden of debt

THE FRENCH REVOLUTION

Main Idea Social unrest, economic troubles, and the desire for political reforms led to the French Revolution.

Setting the Scene On April 28, 1789, unrest exploded at a Paris wallpaper factory. A rumor had spread that the factory owner was planning to cut wages even though bread prices were soaring. Enraged workers vandalized the owner's home. Later, they stopped some nobles returning from an afternoon at the racetrack. They forced the nobles to shout: "Long live the Third Estate [the common people]!"

Riots like these did not worry most nobles. They knew that France faced a severe economic crisis but thought that financial reforms would ease the problem. Then, rioters would be hanged, as they deserved.

The nobles were wrong. The crisis went deeper than government finances. Reform would not be enough. By July, the hungry, unemployed, and poorly paid people of Paris had taken up arms. Their actions would push events further and faster than anyone could have foreseen.

The Old Regime

In 1789, France, like the rest of Europe, still clung to an outdated social system that had emerged in the Middle Ages. Under this *ancien regime*, or old order, everyone in France belonged to one of three classes: the First Estate, made up of the clergy; the Second Estate, made up of the nobility; or the Third Estate, the vast majority of the population.

The Clergy In the Middle Ages, the Church had exerted great influence throughout Christian Europe. In 1789, the French clergy still enjoyed enormous wealth and privilege. The Church owned about 10 percent of the land, collected tithes, and paid no direct taxes to the state. High Church leaders such as bishops and abbots were usually nobles who lived very well. Parish priests, however, often came from humble origins and might be as poor as their peasant congregations.

The First Estate did provide some social services. Nuns, monks, and priests ran schools, hospitals, and orphanages. But during the Enlightenment, *philosophes* targeted the Church for reform. They criticized the idleness of some clergy, Church interference in politics, and its intolerance of dissent. In response, many clergy condemned the Enlightenment for undermining religion and moral order.

The Nobles The Second Estate was the titled nobility of French society. In the Middle Ages, noble knights had defended the land. In the 1600s, Richelieu and Louis XIV had crushed the nobles' military power but given them other rights—under strict royal control. Those rights included top jobs in government, the army, the courts, and the Church.

At Versailles, ambitious nobles competed for royal appointments while idle courtiers enjoyed endless entertainments. Many nobles, however, lived far from the center of power. Though they owned land, they had little money income. As a result, they felt the pinch of trying to maintain their status in a period of rising prices.

Many nobles hated absolutism and resented the royal bureaucracy that employed middle-class men in positions that once had been reserved for the aristocracy. They feared losing their traditional privileges, especially their freedom from paying taxes.

The Third Estate In 1789, the Third Estate numbered about 27 million people, or 98 percent of the population. It was a diverse group. At the top sat the bourgeoisie (boor zhwah ZEE), or middle class. The bourgeoisie included prosperous bankers, merchants, and manufacturers. It also included the officials who staffed the royal bureaucracy, as well as lawyers, doctors, journalists, professors, and skilled artisans.

The bulk of the Third Estate—9 out of 10 people in France—were rural peasants. Some were prosperous landowners who hired laborers to work for them. Others were tenant farmers or day laborers.

The poorest members of the Third Estate were urban workers. They included apprentices, journeymen, and others who worked in industries such as printing or clothmaking. Many women and men earned a meager living as servants, stable hands, porters, construction workers, or street sellers of everything from food to pots and pans. A large number of the urban poor were unemployed. To survive, some turned to begging or crime.

Discontent From rich to poor, members of the Third Estate resented the privileges enjoyed by their social "betters." Wealthy bourgeois families could buy political office and even titles, but the best jobs were still reserved for nobles. Urban workers earned miserable wages. Even the smallest rise in the price of bread, their main food, brought the threat of greater hunger or even starvation.

The Old Regime
In this cartoon, a priest and a noble stand on a stone crushing a peasant. The stone represents burdensome taxes and feudal dues. Taken together, the pie graphs below show inequalities among France's three estates.
Theme: Political and Social Systems Why did the Third Estate consider the distribution of land unfair?

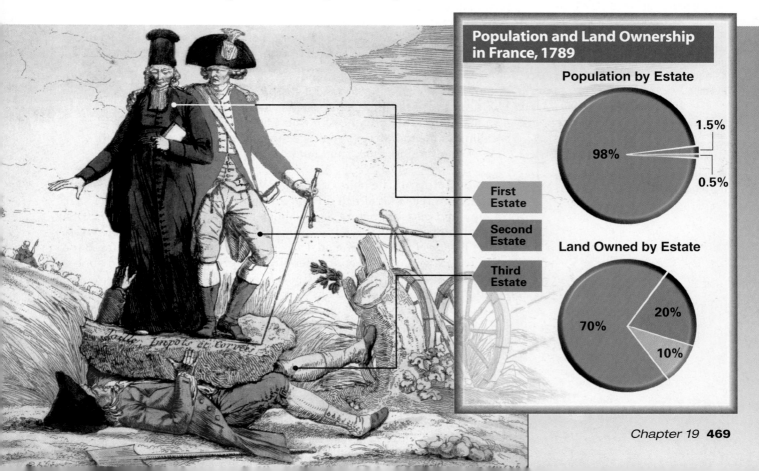

First Estate
Second Estate
Third Estate

Population and Land Ownership in France, 1789

Population by Estate

1.5%
98%
0.5%

Land Owned by Estate

70%
20%
10%

Bread Riots in France
The British embassy in Paris sent regular reports to London. The excerpts below describe the effects of rising bread prices:

"November 27, 1788
The price of bread has again been raised . . . the consequences of which has already been felt in the instance of more than 40 bakers having been obliged to shut up shop. In the provinces these discontents have still risen higher. . . . The public magazines of wheat have been broken open and pillaged.

December 11, 1788
Bread has again been raised. . . . The distress of the poor is already very great as may be conceived, and the unusual severity of the weather is at this moment peculiarly unfortunate for them; nor on this account, is it very surprising that robberies should be frequent, which at present is the case in an alarming degree. It is by no means safe to walk the streets late in the evening."

—O. Browning, *Dispatches from Paris*

Skills Assessment

Primary Source What were the effects of the rising prices?

Peasants were burdened by taxes on everything from land to soap to salt. Though they were technically free, many owed fees and services that dated back to medieval times, such as the corvée (kohr VAY), which was unpaid labor to repair roads and bridges. Peasants were also incensed when nobles, hurt by rising prices, tried to reimpose old manor dues. Also, only nobles had the right to hunt wild game. Peasants were even forbidden to kill rabbits that ate their crops.

In towns and cities, Enlightenment ideas led people to question the inequalities of the old regime. Why, people demanded, should the first two estates have such great privileges at the expense of the majority? It did not meet the test of reason! Throughout France, the Third Estate called for the privileged classes to pay their share.

Economic Troubles

Economic woes added to the social unrest and heightened tensions. One of the causes of the decline was a mushrooming financial crisis that was due in part to years of **deficit spending,** that is, a government's spending more money than it takes in.

The Burden of Debt Louis XIV had left France deeply in debt. Wars like the Seven Years' War and the American Revolution strained the treasury even further. Costs generally had risen in the 1700s, and the lavish court soaked up millions. To bridge the gap between income and expenses, the government borrowed more and more money. By 1789, half its tax income went just to pay interest on this enormous debt.

To solve the financial crisis, the government would have to increase taxes, reduce expenses, or both. However, the nobles and clergy fiercely resisted any attempt to end their exemption from taxes.

Poor Harvests Other economic troubles added to the financial crisis. A general economic decline had begun in the 1770s. Then, in the late 1780s, bad harvests sent food prices soaring and brought hunger to poorer peasants and city dwellers.

Hard times and lack of food inflamed these people. In towns, people rioted, demanding bread. In the countryside, peasants began to attack the manor houses of the nobles. Arthur Young, an English visitor to France, witnessed the violence:

"Everything conspires to render the present period in France critical: the [lack] of bread is terrible; accounts arrive every moment from the provinces of riots and disturbances, and calling in the military, to preserve the peace of the markets."
—Arthur Young, *Travels in France During the Years 1787–1789*

Failure of Reform The heirs of Louis XIV were not the right men to solve the economic crisis that afflicted France. Louis XV, who ruled from 1715 to 1774, pursued pleasure before serious business and ran up more debts. His grandson, Louis XVI, was well-meaning but weak and indecisive. He wisely chose Jacques Necker, a financial wizard, as an adviser. Necker urged the king to reduce extravagant court spending, reform government, and abolish burdensome tariffs on internal trade. When Necker proposed taxing the First and Second estates, however, the nobles and high clergy forced the king to dismiss the would-be reformer.

As the crisis deepened, the pressure for reform mounted. Finally, the wealthy and powerful classes demanded that the king summon the Estates General before making any changes. French kings had not called the Estates General for 175 years, fearing that nobles would use it to recover the feudal powers that they had lost under absolute rule. To reform-minded nobles, the Estates General seemed to offer a chance to carry out changes

Virtual Field Trip

www.phschool.com

**WebMuseum
Paris, France**

To see other David paintings of the French Revolution and Napoleonic era, use the Internet address above to link to the WebMuseum.

The Tennis Court Oath
In this painting, Jacques Louis David captures the moment when delegates at the National Assembly took the Tennis Court Oath.

Theme: Continuity and Change Why did the Third Estate want to change the voting system used in the Estates General?

like those that had come with the Glorious Revolution in England. They hoped that they could bring the absolute monarch under the control of the nobles and guarantee their own privileges.

Louis XVI Calls the Estates General

As 1788 came to a close, France tottered on the verge of bankruptcy. Bread riots were spreading, and nobles, fearful of taxes, were denouncing royal tyranny. A baffled Louis XVI finally summoned the Estates General to meet at Versailles the following year.

The Cahiers In preparation, Louis had all three estates prepare *cahiers* (kah YAY), or notebooks, listing their grievances. Many cahiers called for reforms such as fairer taxes, freedom of the press, or regular meetings of the Estates General. In one town, shoemakers denounced regulations that made leather so expensive they could not afford to make shoes. Some peasants demanded the right to kill animals that were destroying their crops. Servant girls in the city of Toulouse demanded the right to leave service when they wanted and that "after a girl has served her master for many years, she receive some reward for her service."

The cahiers testified to boiling class resentments. One called tax collectors "bloodsuckers of the nation who drink the tears of the unfortunate from goblets of gold." Another one of the cahiers condemned the courts of nobles as "vampires pumping the last drop of blood" from the people. Another complained that "20 million must live on half the wealth of France while the clergy . . . devour the other half."

The Tennis Court Oath Delegates to the Estates General from the Third Estate were elected, though only propertied men could vote. Thus, they were mostly lawyers, middle-class officials, and writers. They were familiar with the writings of Voltaire, Rousseau, and other *philosophes*. They went to Versailles not only to solve the financial crisis but also to insist on reform.

The Estates General convened in May 1789. From the start, the delegates were deadlocked over the issue of voting. Traditionally, each estate had met and voted separately. Each group had one vote. Under this system, the First and Second estates always outvoted the Third Estate two to one.

This time, the Third Estate wanted all three estates to meet in a single body, with votes counted "by head."

After weeks of stalemate, delegates of the Third Estate took a daring step. Claiming to represent the people of France, they declared themselves to be the National Assembly. They then invited delegates from the other estates to help them write a constitution, a document that describes the basic rules and laws of government.

A few days later, the National Assembly found its meeting hall locked and guarded. Fearing that the king planned to dismiss them, the delegates moved to a nearby indoor tennis court. As curious spectators looked on, the delegates took their famous Tennis Court Oath. They swore "never to separate and to meet wherever the circumstances might require until we have established a sound and just constitution."

When reform-minded clergy and nobles joined the Assembly, Louis XVI grudgingly accepted it. But royal troops gathered around Paris, and rumors spread that the king planned to dissolve the Assembly.

Suspicion and rumor continued to poison the atmosphere as the crisis deepened in early July. The king, who had brought back Necker to deal with the financial crisis, again dismissed the popular minister. Food shortages were also getting worse because of the disastrous harvest of 1788.

Storming the Bastille

On July 14, 1789, Paris seized the spotlight from the National Assembly meeting in Versailles. The streets buzzed with rumors that royal troops were going to occupy the capital. More than 800 Parisians assembled outside the Bastille, a grim medieval fortress used as a prison for political and other prisoners. The crowd was demanding weapons and gunpowder believed to be stored there.

The commander of the Bastille refused to open the gates and opened fire on the crowd. In the battle that followed, many people were killed. Finally, the enraged mob broke through the defenses. They killed the commander and five guards and released a handful of prisoners, but found no weapons.

When told of the attack, Louis XVI asked, "Is it a revolt?" "No, sire," replied a noble. "It is a revolution." The storming of the Bastille quickly became a symbol of the French Revolution. Supporters saw it as a blow to tyranny, a step toward freedom. Today, the French still celebrate July 14 as Bastille Day, the French national holiday.

SECTION 1 Assessment

Recall

1. **Identify:** (a) *ancien regime,* (b) Jacques Necker, (c) cahiers, (d) Tennis Court Oath, (e) National Assembly, (f) Bastille.
2. **Define:** (a) bourgeoisie, (b) deficit spending.

Comprehension

3. Why were members of the Third Estate discontented with conditions under the old regime?
4. What economic troubles did France have in 1789?
5. What issues arose when Louis XVI called the Estates General in 1789?

6. What was the significance of the storming of the Bastille?

Critical Thinking and Writing

7. **Understanding Sequence** List key decisions and events of 1788 and 1789 in the order in which they occurred. Briefly explain the significance or effects of each decision and event in your list.
8. **Defending a Position** Suppose that you are Jacques Necker. Write a paragraph or two explaining how your economic reform program will benefit France.

Activity

Writing a Cahier
Imagine that you belong to one of the following groups in 1789 France: nobles, high clergy, parish priests, bourgeoisie, peasants, urban workers. Write a cahier describing who you are and what you think is the chief problem facing the nation.

Creating a New France

Reading Focus

- How did popular revolts contribute to the French Revolution?

- What moderate reforms did the National Assembly enact?

- How did foreign reaction to the revolution help lead to war?

Vocabulary

faction
émigré
republic

Taking Notes

As you read this section, prepare an outline following this model. Use Roman numerals for major headings, capital letters for subheadings, and numbers for supporting details.

    I. Revolts in Paris and the provinces
       A. The Great Fear
          1. Inflamed by famine and rumors
          2.
       B. Paris in arms
    II. Moderate reforms

Main Idea   The National Assembly instituted political and social reforms in the moderate first stage of the revolution.

Setting the Scene   Excitement, wonder, and fear engulfed France as the revolution unfolded at home and spread abroad. Today, historians divide this revolutionary era into four phases. The moderate phase of the National Assembly (1789–1791) turned France into a constitutional monarchy. Then, a phase (1792–1793) of escalating violence led to a Reign of Terror (1793-1794). There followed a period of reaction against extremism, known as the Directory (1795–1799). Finally, the Age of Napoleon (1799–1815) consolidated many revolutionary changes. In this section, you will read about the moderate start of the French Revolution.

Revolts in Paris and the Provinces

The political crisis of 1789 coincided with the worst famine in memory. Starving peasants roamed the countryside or flocked to the towns, where they swelled the ranks of the unemployed. As grain prices soared, even people with jobs had to spend up to 80 percent of their income on bread.

The Great Fear   In such desperate times, rumors ran wild and set off what was later called the "Great Fear." Tales of attacks on villages and towns spread panic. Other rumors asserted that government troops were seizing peasant crops.

Inflamed by famine and fear, peasants unleashed their fury on nobles who were trying to reimpose medieval dues. Defiant peasants attacked the homes of nobles, set fire to old manor records, and stole grain from storehouses. The violent attacks died down after a period of time, but they clearly demonstrated peasant anger with an unjust regime.

Paris in Arms   Paris, too, was in turmoil. As the capital and chief city of France, it was the revolutionary center. A variety of factions, or small groups, competed to gain power. Moderates looked to the Marquis de Lafayette, the aristocratic "hero of two worlds" who had fought alongside George Washington in the American Revolution. Lafayette headed the National Guard, a largely middle-class militia organized in response to the arrival of royal troops in Paris. The Guard was the first group to don the tricolor—a red, white, and blue badge which was eventually adopted as the national flag of France.

Paris in Arms
In this engraving, an angry mob of men and women march through the streets of Paris.
Theme: Geography and History   Why do you think Paris was the center of the French Revolution?

Primary Sources and Literature

See the "Declaration of the Rights of Man and the Citizen" in the Reference Section at the back of this book.

A more radical group, the Paris Commune, replaced the royalist government of the city. It could mobilize whole neighborhoods for protests or violent action to further the revolution. Newspapers and political clubs—many even more radical than the Commune—blossomed everywhere. Some demanded an end to the monarchy and spread scandalous stories about the royal family and members of the court.

Moderate Reforms

Peasant uprisings and the storming of the Bastille stampeded the National Assembly into action. On August 4, in a combative all-night meeting, nobles in the National Assembly voted to end their privileges. They agreed to give up their old manorial dues, exclusive hunting rights, special legal status, and exemption from taxes.

An End to Special Privilege "Feudalism is abolished," announced the proud and weary delegates at 2 A.M. As the president of the Assembly later observed, "We may view this moment as the dawn of a new revolution, when all the burdens weighing on the people were abolished, and France was truly reborn."

Were the votes on the night of August 4 voluntary? Both contemporary observers and modern historians note that the nobles gave up nothing that they had not already lost. In the months ahead, the National Assembly turned the reforms of August 4 into law, meeting a key Enlightenment goal—the equality of all citizens before the law.

Declaration of the Rights of Man In late August, as a first step toward writing a constitution, the Assembly issued the Declaration of the Rights of Man and the Citizen. The document was modeled in part on the American Declaration of Independence, written 13 years earlier. All men, the French declaration announced, were "born and remain free and equal in rights." They enjoyed natural rights to "liberty, property, security, and resistance to oppression." Like the writings of Locke and the *philosophes*, the constitution insisted that governments exist to protect the natural rights of citizens.

The Declaration further proclaimed that all male citizens were equal before the law. Every Frenchman had an equal right to hold public office "with no distinction other than that of their virtues and talents." In addition, the Declaration asserted freedom of religion and called for taxes to be levied according to ability to pay. Its principles were captured in the enduring slogan of the French Revolution, "Liberty, Equality, Fraternity."

Uncertain and hesitant, Louis XVI was slow to accept the reforms of the National Assembly. Parisians grew suspicious as more royal troops arrived. Nobles continued to enjoy gala banquets while people were starving. By autumn, anger again turned to action.

Women March on Versailles On October 5, thousands of women streamed down the road that led from Paris to Versailles. "Bread!" they shouted. They demanded to see the king.

Much of the crowd's anger was directed at the queen, Marie Antoinette. Ever since she had married Louis in 1770, she had come under attack for being frivolous and extravagant. She eventually grew more serious and even advised the king to compromise with moderate reformers. Still, she remained a source of scandal. Early in the revolution, the radical press spread the story that she had answered the cries of hungry people for bread by saying, "Let them eat cake." Though the story was untrue, it helped inflame feelings against the queen.

The women refused to leave Versailles until the king met their most important demand—to return to Paris. Not too happily, the king agreed. The next morning, the crowd, with the king in tow, set out for the city. At the head of the procession rode women perched on the barrels of seized

cannons. They told bewildered spectators that they were bringing Louis XVI, Marie Antoinette, and their son back to Paris. "Now we won't have to go so far when we want to see our king," they sang. Crowds along the way cheered the king, who now wore the tricolor.

In Paris, the royal family moved into the Tuileries (TWEE luh reez) palace. For the next three years, Louis was a virtual prisoner.

The National Assembly Presses Onward

The National Assembly soon followed the king to Paris. Its largely bourgeois members worked to draft a constitution and to solve the continuing financial crisis. To pay off the huge government debt—much of it owed to the bourgeoisie—the Assembly voted to take over and sell Church lands.

Reorganizing the Church In an even more radical move, the National Assembly put the French Catholic Church under state control. Under the Civil Constitution of the Clergy, issued in 1790, bishops and priests became elected, salaried officials. The Civil Constitution ended papal authority over the French Church and dissolved convents and monasteries.

Reaction was swift and angry. Many bishops and priests refused to accept the Civil Constitution. The pope condemned it. Large numbers of French peasants, who were conservative concerning religion, also rejected the changes. When the government punished clergy who refused to support the Civil Constitution, a huge gulf opened between revolutionaries in Paris and the peasantry in the provinces.

Constitution of 1791 The National Assembly completed its main task by producing a constitution. The Constitution of 1791 set up a limited monarchy in place of the absolute monarchy that had ruled France for centuries. A new Legislative Assembly had the power to make laws, collect taxes, and decide on issues of war and peace. Lawmakers would be elected by taxpaying male citizens. Still, only about 50,000 men in a population of more than 27 million could qualify as candidates to run for the Assembly.

To make government more efficient, the constitution replaced the old provinces with 83 departments of roughly equal size. It abolished the old provincial courts, and it reformed laws. The middle-class framers of the constitution protected private property and supported free trade. They compensated nobles for land seized by the peasants, abolished guilds, and forbade urban workers to organize labor unions.

Women March on Versailles
As famine gripped Paris, poor mothers did not have enough food for their children. On October 5, 1789, thousands of women decided to bring Louis XVI to Paris, where he could no longer ignore their suffering.

Theme: Continuity and Change Based on this painting, in what ways do you think the march challenged traditional roles of women?

REFORMS OF THE NATIONAL ASSEMBLY

Political	Social and Economic	Religious
• Proclaimed all male citizens equal before the law • Limited the power of the monarchy • Established the Legislative Assembly to make laws • Granted all tax-paying male citizens the right to elect members of the Legislative Assembly	• Abolished special privileges of the nobility • Announced an end to feudalism • Called for taxes to be levied according to ability to pay • Abolished guilds and forbade labor unions • Compensated nobles for lands seized by peasants	• Declared freedom of religion • Took over and sold Church lands • Placed the French Catholic Church under control of the state • Provided that bishops and priests be elected and receive government salaries

Skills Assessment

Chart The National Assembly produced the Declaration of the Rights of Man and the Citizen, the Civil Constitution of the Clergy, and the Constitution of 1791. These documents brought far-reaching change to France. **Which reforms in the chart were due to the Civil Constitution of the Clergy?**

To moderate reformers, the Constitution of 1791 seemed to complete the revolution. Reflecting Enlightenment goals, it ended Church interference in government and ensured equality before the law for all male citizens. At the same time, it put power in the hands of men with the means and leisure to serve in government.

Louis's Failed Flight Meanwhile, Marie Antoinette and others had been urging the king to escape their humiliating situation. Louis finally gave in. One night in June 1791, a coach rolled north from Paris toward the border. Inside sat the king disguised as a servant, the queen dressed as a governess, and the royal children.

The attempted escape failed. In a town along the way, Louis's disguise was uncovered by someone who held up a piece of currency with the king's face on it. A company of soldiers escorted the royal family back to Paris, as onlooking crowds hurled insults at the king. To many, Louis's dash to the border showed that he was a traitor to the revolution.

Reaction Outside France

Events in France stirred debate all over Europe. Supporters of the Enlightenment applauded the reforms of the National Assembly. They saw the French experiment as the dawn of a new age for justice and equality. European rulers and nobles, however, denounced the French Revolution.

Widespread Fears European rulers increased border patrols to stop the spread of the "French plague." Fueling those fears were the horror stories that were told by émigrés (EHM ih grayz)—nobles, clergy, and others who had fled France and its revolutionary forces. Émigrés reported attacks on their privileges, their property, their religion, and even their lives. "Enlightened" rulers turned against French ideas. Catherine the Great of Russia burned Voltaire's letters and locked up her critics.

In Britain, Edmund Burke, who earlier had defended the American Revolution, bitterly condemned revolutionaries in Paris. He predicted all too accurately that the revolution would become more violent. "Plots and assassinations," he wrote, "will be anticipated by preventive murder and preventive confiscation." Burke warned: "When ancient opinions and rules of life are taken away . . . we have no compass to govern us."

Threats From Abroad The failed escape of Louis XVI brought further hostile rumblings from abroad. In August 1791, the king of Prussia and the emperor of Austria—who was Marie Antoinette's brother—issued the Declaration of Pilnitz. In this document, the two monarchs threatened to intervene to protect the French monarchy. The declaration may have been mostly bluff, but revolutionaries in France took the threat seriously and prepared for war. The revolution was about to enter a new, more radical phase of change and conflict.

War at Home and Abroad

In October 1791, the newly elected Legislative Assembly took office. Faced with crises at home and abroad, it would survive for less than a year. Economic problems fed renewed turmoil. Assignats, the revolutionary currency, dropped in value, which caused prices to rise rapidly. Uncertainty about prices led to hoarding and additional food shortages.

Internal Divisions   In Paris and other cities, working-class men and women, called sans-culottes* (sanz kyoo LAHTZ), pushed the revolution into more radical action. By 1791, many sans-culottes demanded a **republic**, or government ruled not by a monarch, but by elected representatives.

Within the Legislative Assembly, several hostile factions competed for power. The sans-culottes found support among radicals in the Legislative Assembly, especially the Jacobins. A revolutionary political club, the Jacobins were mostly middle-class lawyers or intellectuals. They used pamphleteers and sympathetic newspaper editors to advance the republican cause. Opposing the radicals were moderate reformers and political officials who wanted no more reforms at all.

War on Tyranny   The radicals soon held the upper hand in the Legislative Assembly. In April 1792, the war of words between French revolutionaries and European monarchs moved onto the battlefield. Eager to spread the revolution and destroy tyranny abroad, the Legislative Assembly declared war first on Austria, then on Prussia, Britain, and other states. The great powers expected to win an easy victory against France, a land divided by revolution. In fact, however, the fighting that began in 1792 lasted on and off until 1815.

---

*Sans-culottes means "without culottes," the fancy knee breeches worn by upper-class men. Shopkeepers, artisans, and other working-class men wore trousers, not culottes.

SECTION 2 Assessment

Recall

1. **Identify:** **(a)** Great Fear, **(b)** tricolor, **(c)** Legislative Assembly, **(d)** Declaration of Pilnitz, **(e)** Jacobins.
2. **Define:** **(a)** faction, **(b)** émigré, **(c)** republic.

Comprehension

3. What role did the people of Paris play in the French Revolution?
4. Describe one reform that the National Assembly enacted through each of the following documents: **(a)** the Declaration of the Rights of Man and the Citizen, **(b)** the Civil Constitution of the Clergy, **(c)** the Constitution of 1791.
5. **(a)** Why did some people outside France react negatively to the French Revolution? **(b)** How did these feelings lead to war?

Critical Thinking and Writing

6. **Comparing** Compare the women's march on Versailles to the storming of the Bastille in terms of goals and results.
7. **Defending a Position** The Declaration of the Rights of Man has been called the "death certificate" of the old regime. Do you agree? Why or why not?

Activity
Take It to the NET

Use the Internet to research the life of Marie Antoinette. Then, write a feature article about her as it might appear in a popular magazine of today. Include interesting details about her family, friends, and habits that would appeal to your readers.

Reading Focus

- Why did radicals abolish the monarchy?
- How did the excesses of the Convention lead to the Directory?
- What impact did the revolution have on women and daily life?

Vocabulary

suffrage
nationalism
secular

Taking Notes

On a sheet of paper, make a time line like the one begun here. The time line should extend from August 1792 to July 1794. Add dates and important events as you read this section.

August 1792	September 1792	January 1793	July 1794
Mob invades royal palace	September massacres		

Main Idea A radical phase of the revolution led to the monarchy's downfall and a time of violence known as the Reign of Terror.

Setting the Scene Someone who had left Paris in 1791 and returned in 1793 could have gotten lost. Almost 4,000 streets had new names. Louis XV Square was renamed the Square of the Revolution. King-of-Sicily Street, named for the brother of Louis XVI, had become the Rights of Man Street.

Renaming streets was one way that Jacobins tried to wipe out all traces of the old order. In 1793, the revolution entered a radical phase. For a year, France experienced one of the bloodiest regimes in its long history as determined leaders sought to extend and preserve the revolution.

The Monarchy Abolished

Dismal news about the war heightened tensions. Well-trained Prussian forces were cutting down raw French recruits. Royalist officers deserted the French army, joining émigrés and others hoping to restore the king's power.

Outbreaks of Violence Battle disasters quickly inflamed revolutionaries who thought the king was in league with the invaders. On August 10, 1792, a crowd of Parisians stormed the Tuileries and slaughtered the king's guards. The royal family fled to the Legislative Assembly.

A month later, citizens attacked prisons that held nobles and priests accused of political offenses. These prisoners were killed, along with many ordinary criminals. Historians disagree about the people who carried out the "September massacres." Some call them bloodthirsty mobs. Others describe them as patriots defending France from its enemies. In fact, most were ordinary citizens fired to fury by real and imagined grievances.

The French Republic Backed by Paris crowds, radicals took control of the Assembly. Radicals called for the election of a new legislative body called the National Convention. Suffrage, the right to vote, was to be extended to all male citizens, not just to property owners.

The Convention that met in September 1792 was a more radical body than earlier assemblies. It voted to abolish the monarchy and declare France a republic. Deputies then drew up a new constitution for France. The Jacobins, who controlled the Convention, set out to erase all traces of the old order. They seized lands of nobles and abolished titles of nobility.

Death of the King and Queen During the early months of the Republic, the Convention also put Louis XVI on trial as a traitor to France. The king was convicted by a single vote and sentenced to death. On a foggy morning

Did You **Know?**

The Origin of Madame Tussaud's Wax Museum

In the 1780s, Marie Tussaud ran two wax museums in Paris and was art tutor to the sister of Louis XVI. During the revolution, she was imprisoned as a royalist. Even so, the leaders of the revolution admired her art skills. Tussaud escaped the guillotine by agreeing to make wax models of the revolutionaries and their victims, such as Louis XVI and Marie Antoinette, shown above.

After the revolution, Tussaud took her collection to London. There she established the wax museum that still bears her name. Today, tourists from around the world marvel at the realistic sculptures of the famous and infamous in Madame Tussaud's Wax Museum.

Theme: Art and Literature
How did Tussaud's art skills save her life?

Execution of a King

The following excerpt is from an eyewitness report of the execution of King Louis XVI, January 21, 1793. It was written by Henry Essex Edgeworth de Firmont, a priest who accompanied the king to the scaffold.

The Machine of Terror
The guillotine made it easy to behead large numbers of people quickly. It became a symbol of the Reign of Terror.

"The path leading to the scaffold was extremely rough and difficult to pass; the King was obliged to lean on my arm, and from the slowness with which he proceeded, I feared for a moment that his courage might fail; but what was my astonishment, when arrived at the last step, I felt that he suddenly let go my arm, and I saw him cross with a firm foot the breadth of the whole scaffold; silence, by his look alone, fifteen or twenty drums that were placed opposite to me; and in a voice so loud, that it must have been heard at the Pont Tourant, I heard him pronounce distinctly these memorable words: 'I die innocent of all the crimes laid to my charge; I pardon those who have occasioned my death; and I pray to God that the blood you are going to shed may never be visited on France.'

He was proceeding, when a man on horseback, in the national uniform, and with a ferocious cry, ordered the drums to beat. Many voices were at the same time heard encouraging the executioners. They seemed reanimated themselves, in seizing with violence the most virtuous of Kings, they dragged him under the axe of the guillotine, which with one stroke severed his head from his body. All this passed in a moment. The youngest of the guards, who seemed about eighteen, immediately seized the head, and showed it to the people as he walked around the scaffold; he accompanied this monstrous ceremony with the most atrocious and indecent gestures. At first an awful silence prevailed; at length some cries of 'Vive la République! [Long live the republic!]' were heard. By degrees the voices multiplied, and in less than ten minutes this cry, a thousand times repeated, became the universal shout of the multitude, and every hat was in the air."

—Henry Essex Edgeworth de Firmont, *Report by a Priest of His Majesty's Household*

Skills Assessment

1. Based on this account, how would you describe the king's manner at his execution?
   A frightened and confused
   B cold and unemotional
   C proud and brave
   D angry and violent

2. The man on horseback orders the drums to beat in order to
   E silence the crowd.
   F signal that the execution is about to take place.
   G show respect for the king.
   H announce that the king is dead.

3. **Critical Thinking** **Drawing Conclusions** **(a)** Based on this account, what was Father Firmont's attitude toward the king? Toward the revolutionaries? How can you tell? **(b)** Do you think Firmont's feelings affected his account? Explain.

Skills Tip

Bias is a leaning in favor of or against someone or something. When analyzing an eyewitness account, look for words that indicate the writer's bias.

in January 1793, Louis mounted a scaffold in a public square in Paris. He tried to speak, but his words were drowned out by a roll of drums. Moments later, the king was beheaded.

In October, Marie Antoinette was also executed. The popular press celebrated her death. The queen, however, showed great dignity as she went to her death. Their son, the uncrowned Louis XVII, died of unknown causes in the dungeons of the revolution.

The Convention Defends the Republic

By early 1793, danger threatened France on all sides. The country was at war with much of Europe, including Britain, the Netherlands, Spain, and Prussia. In the Vendée (vahn DAY) region of France, royalists and priests led peasants in rebellion against the government. In Paris, the sans-culottes demanded relief from food shortages and inflation. The Convention itself was bitterly divided between Jacobins and a rival group, the Girondins.

Committee of Public Safety   To deal with the threats to France, the Convention created the Committee of Public Safety. The 12-member committee had almost absolute power as it battled to save the revolution. The Committee prepared France for all-out war, issuing a *levée en masse*, or mass levy that required all citizens to contribute to the war effort:

> "All Frenchmen are in permanent requisition for the service of the armies. The young men shall go to battle; the married men shall forge arms and transport provisions; the women shall make tents and clothing and shall serve in the hospitals; the children shall turn old lint into linen; the aged shall take themselves to the public places in order to arouse the courage of the warriors and preach the hatred of kings and the unity of the Republic."
> —*Proclamation of the National Convention,* August 23, 1793

Spurred by revolutionary fervor, French recruits marched off to defend the republic. Young officers developed effective new tactics to win battles with masses of ill-trained but patriotic forces. Soon, French armies overran the Netherlands. They later invaded Italy. At home, they crushed peasant revolts. European monarchs shuddered as the revolutionaries carried "freedom fever" into conquered lands.

Robespierre   At home, the government battled counterrevolutionaries under the guiding hand of Maximilien Robespierre (ROHBZ pyair). Robespierre, a shrewd lawyer and politician, quickly rose to the leadership of the Committee of Public Safety. Among Jacobins, his selfless dedication to the revolution earned him the nickname "the incorruptible." The enemies of Robespierre called him a tyrant.

Robespierre had embraced Rousseau's idea of the general will as the source of all legitimate law. He promoted religious toleration and wanted to abolish slavery. Though cold and humorless, he was popular with the sans-culottes, who hated the old regime as much as he did. He believed that France could achieve a "republic of virtue" only through the use of terror, which he coolly defined as nothing more than "prompt, severe, inflexible justice." "Liberty cannot be secured," Robespierre cried, "unless criminals lose their heads."

The Reign of Terror   Robespierre was one of the chief architects of the Reign of Terror, which lasted from about July 1793 to July 1794. Revolutionary courts conducted hasty trials. Spectators greeted death sentences with cries of "Hail the Republic!" or "Death to the traitors!"

Perhaps 40,000 people died during the Terror. About 15 percent were nobles and clergy. Another 15 percent were middle-class citizens, often moderates who had supported the revolution in 1789. The rest were peasants and sans-culottes involved in riots or revolts against the Republic. Many were executed, including victims of mistaken identity or false accusations by their neighbors. Many more were packed into hideous prisons, where deaths were common.

The engine of the Terror was the guillotine. Its fast-falling blade extinguished life instantly. A member of the legislature, Dr. Joseph Guillotin (GEE oh tan), had introduced it as a more humane method of beheading than the uncertain ax. But the guillotine quickly became a symbol of horror. In a speech given on February 5, 1794, Robespierre explained why the horror was necessary to achieve the goals of the revolution:

> "It is necessary to stifle the domestic and foreign enemies of the Republic or perish with them. . . . The first maxim of our politics ought to be to lead the people by means of reason and the enemies of the people by terror. . . . If the basis of popular government in time of peace is virtue, the basis of popular government in time of revolution is both virtue and terror."
> —Maximilien Robespierre, quoted in
> *Pageant of Europe* (Stearns)

Within a year, however, the Reign of Terror consumed its own. Weary of bloodshed and fearing for their own lives, members of the Convention turned on the Committee of Public Safety. On the night of July 27, 1794, Robespierre was arrested. The next day he was executed. After the heads of Robespierre and other radicals fell, executions slowed down dramatically.

Reaction and the Directory

In reaction to the Terror, the revolution entered a third stage. Moving away from the excesses of the Convention, moderates produced another constitution, the third since 1789. The Constitution of 1795 set up a five-man Directory and a two-house legislature elected by male citizens of property.

The Reign of Terror
During the Reign of Terror, lists of those to be executed, such as the one below, were posted for all to see. In Paris and other cities, cartloads of the condemned rolled to the guillotine.

Theme: Impact of the Individual Why did Robespierre think the Terror was justified?

The middle-class and professional people of the bourgeoisie were the dominant force during this stage of the French Revolution. The Directory held power from 1795 to 1799.

Weak but dictatorial, the Directory faced growing discontent. Peace was made with Prussia and Spain, but war with Austria and Great Britain continued. Corrupt leaders lined their own pockets but failed to solve pressing problems. When rising bread prices stirred hungry sans-culottes to riot, the Directory quickly suppressed them. Another threat to the Directory was the revival of royalist feeling. Many émigrés were returning to France, and they were being welcomed by devout Catholics, who resented measures that had been taken against the Church. In the election of 1797, supporters of a constitutional monarchy won the majority of seats in the legislature.

As chaos threatened, politicians turned to Napoleon Bonaparte, a popular military hero who had won a series of brilliant victories against the Austrians in Italy. The politicians planned to use him to advance their own goals—a bad miscalculation! Before long, Napoleon would outwit them all to become ruler of France.

Women in the Revolution

As you have seen, women of all classes participated in the revolution from the very beginning. Working-class women protested and fought in street battles. In Paris and elsewhere, women formed their own political clubs. A few women, like Jeanne Roland, were noted leaders. Roland supported the revolution through her writings, her salon, and her influence on her husband, a government minister.

Rights for Women Many women were very disappointed when the Declaration of the Rights of Man did not grant equal citizenship to women. Olympe de Gouges (oh LAMP duh GOOZH), a journalist, demanded equal rights in her *Declaration of the Rights of Woman.* "Woman is born free," she proclaimed, "and her rights are the same as those of man." Therefore, Gouges reasoned, "all citizens, be they men or women, being equal in the state's eyes, must be equally eligible for all public offices, positions, and jobs." After opposing the Terror and accusing certain Jacobins of corruption, Gouges was sent to the guillotine.

Women did gain some rights for a time. The government made divorce easier, a move that was aimed at weakening Church authority. Government officials also allowed women to inherit property, hoping to undermine the tradition of nobles leaving large estates to their oldest sons. These reforms and others did not last long after Napoleon gained power.

Setbacks As the revolution progressed, women's right to express their views in public came under attack. In 1793, a committee of the National Convention declared that women lacked "the moral and physical strength necessary to practice political rights." Women's revolutionary clubs were banned and violators were arrested.

Women were imprisoned and sent to the guillotine. Among the many women who became victims of the Terror were republicans like Gouges and moderates like Roland. As she mounted the steps to the guillotine, Roland cried, "O liberty, what crimes are committed in your name!"

Changes in Daily Life

By 1799, the 10-year-old French Revolution had dramatically changed France. It had dislodged the old social order, overthrown the monarchy, and brought the Church under state control.

New symbols such as the red "liberty caps" and the tricolor confirmed the liberty and equality of all male citizens. The new title "citizen" applied to people of all social classes. Titles were eliminated. Before he was executed, Louis XVI was called Citizen Capet, from the name of the dynasty that had ruled France in the Middle Ages. Elaborate fashions and powdered wigs gave way to the practical clothes and simple haircuts of the sans-culottes. To show their revolutionary spirit, enthusiastic parents gave their children names like Constitution, Republic, or August Tenth.

Nationalism Revolution and war gave the French people a strong sense of national identity. In earlier times, people had felt loyalty to local authorities. As monarchs centralized power, loyalty shifted to the king or queen. Now, the government rallied sons and daughters of the revolution to defend the nation itself.

Nationalism, a strong feeling of pride in and devotion to one's country, spread throughout France. The French people attended civic festivals that celebrated the nation and the revolution. A variety of dances and songs on themes of the revolution became immensely popular.

By 1793, France was a nation in arms. From the port city of Marseilles (mahr SAY), troops marched to a rousing new song. It urged the "children of the fatherland" to march against the "bloody banner of tyranny." This song, "La Marseillaise" (mahr say EHZ), would later become the French national anthem. The second verse and chorus appear at right.

Social Reform Revolutionaries pushed for social reform and religious toleration. They set up state schools to replace religious ones and organized systems to help the poor, old soldiers, and war widows. With a major slave revolt raging in the colony of St. Domingue (Haiti), the government also abolished slavery in their Caribbean colonies.

The Convention tried to de-Christianize France. It created a secular, or nonreligious, calendar with 1793 as the Year I of the new era of freedom. It banned many religious festivals, replacing them with secular celebrations. Huge public ceremonies boosted support for republican and nationalist ideals.

The Arts In the arts, France adopted a grand classical style that echoed the grandeur of ancient Rome. A leading artist of this period was Jacques Louis David (dah VEED). He immortalized on canvas such stirring events as the Tennis Court Oath and, later, Napoleon's coronation. David helped shape the way future generations pictured the French Revolution.

SECTION 3 Assessment

Recall
1. **Identify:** (a) Committee of Public Safety, (b) Maximilien Robespierre, (c) Directory, (d) Olympe de Gouges, (e) "La Marseillaise," (f) Jacques Louis David.
2. **Define:** (a) suffrage, (b) nationalism, (c) secular.

Comprehension
3. Why did radical revolutionaries oppose the monarchy?
4. How did the Reign of Terror cause the National Convention to be replaced by the Directory?

5. Describe one effect of the French Revolution on each of the following: (a) women, (b) daily life.

Critical Thinking and Writing
6. **Analyzing Primary Sources** Robespierre wrote, "Terror is nothing but prompt, severe, inflexible justice." Explain why you agree or disagree with Robespierre.
7. **Predicting Consequences** How do you think French nationalism affected the war between France and the powers of Europe?

Activity

Presenting a Poster
Create a poster that might have been used to support or oppose *one* of the following: the goals of the Jacobins; the abolition of the monarchy; the policies of the Committee of Public Safety; French nationalism; equal rights for women.

The Age of Napoleon Begins

Reading Focus

- How did Napoleon rise to power?
- How were revolutionary reforms changed under Napoleon?
- How did Napoleon build an empire in Europe?

Vocabulary

plebiscite

annex

blockade

Taking Notes

Begin a concept web like this one. As you read, fill in the blank circles with relevant information about Napoleon. Add as many circles as you need.

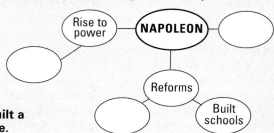

Main Idea Napoleon rose to power in France and built a vast empire that included much of Europe.

Setting the Scene

"He was like an expert chess player, with the human race for an opponent, which he proposed to checkmate." Thus did Madame Germaine de Staël (STAHL), a celebrated writer and intellectual, describe Napoleon Bonaparte. Napoleon himself expressed a more humble view of his rise to power. "Nothing has been simpler than my elevation," he once observed. "It is owing to the peculiarities of the time."

From 1799 to 1815, Napoleon would dominate France and Europe. A hero to some, an evil force to others, he gave his name to the final phase of the revolution—the Age of Napoleon.

Napoleon's Rise to Power

Napoleon Bonaparte was born in Corsica, a French-ruled island in the Mediterranean. His family were minor nobles, but had little money. At age nine, he was sent to France to be trained for a military career. When the revolution broke out, he was an ambitious 20-year-old lieutenant, eager to make a name for himself.

Napoleon favored the Jacobins and republican rule. However, he found the conflicting ideas and personalities of the French Revolution confusing. He wrote to his brother in 1793: "Since one must take sides, one might as well choose the side that is victorious, the side which devastates, loots, and burns."

Early Successes During the turmoil of the revolution, Napoleon rose quickly in the army. In December 1793, he drove British forces out of the French port of Toulon (too LOHN). He then went on to win several dazzling victories against the Austrians, capturing most of northern Italy and forcing the Hapsburg emperor to make peace. Hoping to disrupt British trade with India, he led a colorful expedition to Egypt in 1798. The Egyptian campaign proved to be a disaster, but Napoleon managed to hide stories of the worst losses from his admirers in France.

Success fueled his ambition. By 1799, he moved from victorious general to political leader. That year, he helped overthrow the weak Directory and set up a three-man

FACT FINDER

The Rise of Napoleon

1769	Born on island of Corsica
1785	Becomes officer in French army
1793	Helps capture Toulon from British; promoted to brigadier general
1795	Crushes rebels opposed to the National Convention
1796–1797	Becomes commander in chief of the army of Italy; wins victories against Austria
1798–1799	Loses to the British in Egypt and Syria
1799	Overthrows Directory and becomes First Consul of France
1804	Crowns himself emperor of France

Skills Assessment

Chart Napoleon's successes on the battlefield helped him become emperor. **Where and when did Napoleon experience a military setback? Did that setback affect his rise to power? Explain.**

governing board known as the Consulate. Another constitution was drawn up, but Napoleon soon took the title First Consul. In 1802, he had himself named consul for life.

A Self-made Emperor Two years later, Napoleon had acquired enough power to assume the title Emperor of the French. He invited the pope to preside over his coronation in Paris. During the ceremony, however, Napoleon took the crown from the pope's hands and placed it on his own head. By this action, Napoleon meant to show that he owed his throne to no one but himself.

At each step on his rise to power, Napoleon had held a plebiscite (PLEHB ih sīt), or ballot in which voters say yes or no. Each time, the French strongly supported him. To understand why, we must look at his policies.

France Under Napoleon

During the consulate and empire, Napoleon consolidated his power by strengthening the central government. Order, security, and efficiency replaced liberty, equality, and fraternity as the slogans of the new regime.

Reforms To restore economic prosperity, Napoleon controlled prices, encouraged new industry, and built roads and canals. To ensure well-trained officials and military officers, he set up a system of public schools under strict government control.

At the same time, Napoleon backed off from some of the revolution's social reforms. He made peace with the Catholic Church in the Concordat of 1801. The Concordat kept the Church under state control but recognized religious freedom for Catholics. Revolutionaries who opposed the Church denounced the agreement, but Catholics welcomed it.

Napoleon won support across class lines. He encouraged émigrés to return, provided that they took an oath of loyalty. Peasants were relieved when he recognized their right to lands they had bought from the Church and nobles during the revolution. The middle class, who had benefited most from the revolution, approved Napoleon's economic reforms and the restoration of order after years of chaos. Napoleon also made jobs "open to

The Coronation
David depicted the splendor and power of the new French emperor in the painting *Napoleon Crowning the Empress Josephine.* Years later, Napoleon would divorce Josephine and marry an Austrian princess.

Theme: Impact of the Individual How did Napoleon emphasize his personal power at the coronation ceremony?

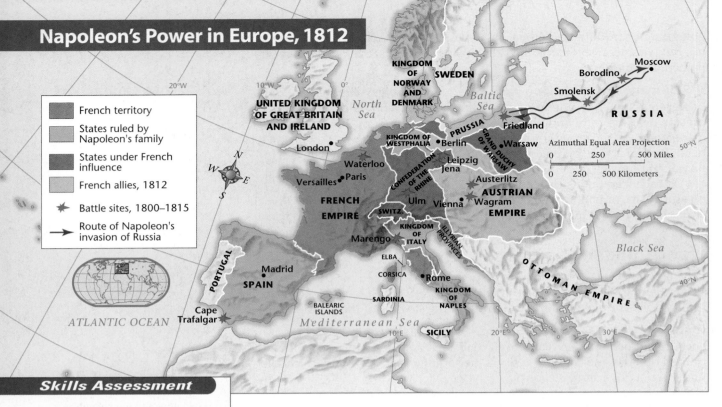

Napoleon's Power in Europe, 1812

Map Legend:
- French territory
- States ruled by Napoleon's family
- States under French influence
- French allies, 1812
- ★ Battle sites, 1800–1815
- → Route of Napoleon's invasion of Russia

Azimuthal Equal Area Projection
0   250   500 Miles
0   250   500 Kilometers

Skills Assessment

Geography Napoleon won a vast empire in Europe. But resistance in Spain and a disastrous invasion of Russia would turn the tide against him.

1. **Location** On the map, locate **(a)** Spain, **(b)** Moscow, **(c)** Waterloo.
2. **Place** What part of the Italian peninsula was French territory?
3. **Critical Thinking** **Drawing Conclusions** Do you think the spread of nationalism would weaken or strengthen Napoleon's power? Explain.

all talent," a popular policy among those who remembered the old aristocratic monopoly of power.

Napoleonic Code Among Napoleon's most lasting reforms was a new law code, popularly called the Napoleonic Code. It embodied Enlightenment principles such as the equality of all citizens before the law, religious toleration, and advancement based on merit.

But the Napoleonic Code undid some reforms of the French Revolution. Women, for example, lost most of their newly gained rights and could not exercise the rights of citizenship. Male heads of households regained complete authority over their wives and children. Again, Napoleon valued order and authority over individual rights.

Building an Empire

From 1804 to 1814, Napoleon furthered his reputation on the battlefield. He successfully faced down the combined forces of the greatest European powers. He took great risks and even suffered huge losses. "I grew up on the field of battle," he once said, "and a man such as I am cares little for the life of a million men." By 1810, his Grand Empire reached its greatest extent.

As a military leader, Napoleon valued rapid movements and made effective use of his large armies. He developed a new plan for each battle, so opposing generals could never anticipate what he would do next. His enemies paid tribute to his leadership. Napoleon's presence on the battlefield, said one, was "worth 40,000 troops."

The Grand Empire As Napoleon created a vast French empire, he redrew the map of Europe. He annexed, or added outright, some areas to France, including the Netherlands, Belgium, and parts of Italy and Germany. He also abolished the tottering Holy Roman Empire and created a 38-member Confederation of the Rhine under French protection. He cut Prussian territory in half, turning part of old Poland into the Grand Duchy of Warsaw.

Napoleon controlled much of Europe through forceful diplomacy. One tactic was to put friends and relatives on the thrones of Europe. For example, after unseating the king of Spain, he placed his own brother, Joseph

Bonaparte, on the throne. He also forced alliances on European powers from Madrid to Moscow. At various times, the rulers of Austria, Prussia, and Russia reluctantly signed treaties with the "Corsican upstart," as his enemies called him.

In France, Napoleon's successes boosted the spirit of nationalism. Great victory parades filled the streets of Paris with cheering crowds. The people celebrated the glory and grandeur that Napoleon had won for France.

France Versus Britain Britain alone remained outside Napoleon's European empire. With only a small army, Britain relied on its sea power to stop Napoleon's drive to rule the continent. In 1805, Napoleon prepared to invade England. But at the Battle of Trafalgar, fought off the southwest coast of Spain, British admiral Horatio Nelson smashed a French fleet.

With an invasion ruled out, Napoleon struck at Britain's lifeblood, its commerce. He waged economic warfare through the Continental System, which closed European ports to British goods. Britain responded with its own blockade of European ports. A blockade involves shutting off ports to keep people or supplies from moving in or out. During their long struggle, both Britain and France seized neutral ships suspected of trading with the other side. British attacks on American ships sparked anger in the United States and eventually triggered the War of 1812.

In the end, Napoleon's Continental System failed to bring Britain to its knees. Although British exports declined, its powerful navy kept open vital trade routes to the Americas and India. Meanwhile, trade restrictions created a scarcity of goods in Europe, sent prices soaring, and intensified resentment against French power.

Cause *and* Effect

Long-Term Causes	Immediate Causes
• Corrupt, inconsistent, and insensitive leadership • Prosperous members of Third Estate resent privileges of First and Second estates • Spread of Enlightenment ideas	• Huge government debt • Poor harvests and rising price of bread • Failure of Louis XVI to accept financial reforms • Formation of National Assembly • Storming of Bastille

The French Revolution

Immediate Effects	Long-Term Effects
• Declaration of the Rights of Man and the Citizen adopted • France adopts its first written constitution • Monarchy abolished • Revolutionary France fights coalition of European powers • Reign of Terror	• Napoleon gains power • Napoleonic Code established • French public schools set up • French conquests spread nationalism • Revolutions occur in Europe and Latin America

Connections to Today

• French law reflects Napoleonic Code
• France is a democratic republic

Skills Assessment **Chart** The French Revolution was a major turning point. Its impact spread far beyond France. **How did Napoleon spread the ideas of the French Revolution?**

SECTION 4 Assessment

Recall
1. **Identify: (a)** Consulate, **(b)** Concordat of 1801, **(c)** Napoleonic Code, **(d)** Confederation of the Rhine, **(e)** Battle of Trafalgar, **(f)** Continental System.
2. **Define: (a)** plebiscite, **(b)** annex, **(c)** blockade.

Comprehension
3. Describe Napoleon Bonaparte's rise to power.
4. **(a)** What revolutionary reforms were undone by Napoleon? **(b)** How did Napoleon preserve some of the principles of the Enlightenment?

5. **(a)** How did Napoleon come to dominate most of Europe? **(b)** Why did his efforts to subdue Britain fail?

Critical Thinking and Writing
6. **Analyzing Information** What opinions do you think each of the following had of Napoleon? **(a)** royalists, **(b)** Catholic priests, **(c)** soldiers, **(d)** republicans.
7. **Making Decisions** Suppose you were a French voter in 1803. How would you have voted on the plebiscite to make Napoleon emperor? Explain your reasons.

Activity
Take It to the NET

Use the Internet to research one of the battles identified on the map in this section. Make a map that shows the terrain of the battle site, and the positions, strengths, and movements of the opposing forces. Write a paragraph or two explaining the outcome.

Reading Focus

- What challenges threatened Napoleon's empire?
- What events led to Napoleon's downfall?
- What were the goals of the Congress of Vienna?

Vocabulary

guerrilla warfare
abdicate
legitimacy

Taking Notes

On a sheet of paper, make a flowchart like the partially completed one at right. As you read this section, add events that led to the downfall of Napoleon. Add as many boxes as you need.

DOWNFALL OF NAPOLEON

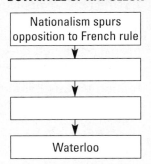

| Nationalism spurs opposition to French rule |
| ↓ |
| |
| ↓ |
| |
| ↓ |
| Waterloo |

Main Idea Napoleon was finally defeated, but revolutionary ideals and the postwar peace settlement affected Europe for many years.

Setting the Scene Napoleon watched the battle for the Russian city of Smolensk from a chair outside his tent. As fires lit up the walled city, he exclaimed:

"It's like Vesuvius erupting. Don't you think this is a beautiful sight?"

"Horrible, Sire," replied an aide.

"Bah!" snorted Napoleon. "Remember, gentlemen, what a Roman emperor said: 'The corpse of an enemy always smells sweet.'"

In 1812, Napoleon pursued his dream of empire by invading Russia. The campaign began a chain of events that eventually led to his downfall. Napoleon's final defeat brought an end to the era of the French Revolution.

Challenges to Napoleon's Empire

Under Napoleon, French armies spread the ideas of the revolution across Europe. They backed liberal reforms in the lands they conquered. In some places, they helped install revolutionary governments that abolished titles of nobility, ended Church privileges, opened careers to men of talent, and ended serfdom and manorial dues. The Napoleonic Code, too, was carried across Europe. French occupation sometimes brought economic benefits as well, by reducing trade barriers and stimulating industry.

Impact of Nationalism Napoleon's successes, however, contained the seeds of defeat. Although nationalism spurred French armies to success, it worked against them, too. Many Europeans who had welcomed the ideas of the French Revolution nevertheless saw Napoleon and his armies as foreign oppressors. They resented the Continental System and Napoleon's effort to impose French culture.

From Rome to Madrid to the Netherlands, nationalism unleashed revolts against France. In the German states, leaders encouraged national loyalty among German-speaking people to counter French influence.

Resistance in Spain Resistance to foreign rule bled French occupying forces in Spain. In 1808, Napoleon replaced the king of Spain with his own brother, Joseph Bonaparte. He also introduced reforms that sought to undermine the Spanish Catholic Church. But many Spaniards remained loyal to their former king and devoted to the Church. When the Spanish resisted the invaders, well-armed French forces responded with brutal repression. Far from crushing resistance, however, the French reaction further inflamed Spanish nationalism. Efforts to drive out the French intensified.

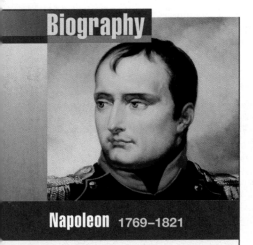

Biography

Napoleon 1769–1821

Perhaps history has seen no greater believer in nepotism than Napoleon. Nepotism is favoritism shown to relatives by a person in high office.

"I am building a family of kings," Napoleon proudly said. In addition to making his brother Joseph king of Spain, he made Louis king of Holland and Jerome king of Westphalia. His sister Caroline became queen of Naples, and Elisa was named Grand Duchess of Tuscany. Then, his mother wanted a title, too! He named her Imperial Highness, Lady, Mother of the Emperor. His final family appointment went to his son, whom he named king of Rome.

Theme: Impact of the Individual How do you think nepotism benefited Napoleon?

Spanish patriots conducted a campaign of **guerrilla warfare,** or hit-and-run raids, against the French. (In Spanish, *guerrilla* means "little war.") Small bands of guerrillas ambushed French supply trains or troops before melting into the countryside. These attacks kept large numbers of French soldiers tied down in Spain, when Napoleon needed them elsewhere. Eventually, the British sent an army under Arthur Wellesley, later the Duke of Wellington, to help the Spanish fight France.

War With Austria Spanish resistance encouraged Austria to resume hostilities against the French. In 1805, at the Battle of Austerlitz, Napoleon had won a crushing victory against an Austro-Russian army of superior numbers. Now, in 1809, the Austrians sought revenge. But once again, Napoleon triumphed—this time at the battle of Wagram. By the peace agreement that followed, Austria surrendered lands populated by more than three million subjects.

The next year, after divorcing his wife Josephine, Napoleon married the Austrian princess Marie Louise. By marrying the daughter of the Hapsburg emperor, he and his heirs could claim kinship with the royalty of Europe.

Defeat in Russia Napoleon's alliance with the Austrian royal family was especially disturbing to Czar Alexander I of Russia. The Russians were also unhappy with the economic effects of Napoleon's Continental System. Yet another cause for concern was that Napoleon had enlarged the Grand Duchy of Warsaw that bordered Russia on the west. These and other issues led the czar to withdraw Russia from the Continental System. Napoleon responded to the czar's action by assembling his Grand Army.

In 1812, more than 400,000 soldiers from France and other countries invaded Russia. To avoid battles with Napoleon, the Russians retreated eastward, burning crops and villages as they went. This "scorched earth" policy left the French hungry and cold as winter came. Napoleon entered Moscow in September. He realized, though, that he

Resistance in Spain
Spanish artist Francisco Goya stressed raw human emotions. Goya's *The Third of May, 1808* shows French soldiers executing Spanish prisoners. His drawing *And They Are Like Wild Beasts* depicts a furious battle between Spanish women and the French.

Theme: Art and Literature How did Goya emphasize nationalism in these artworks?

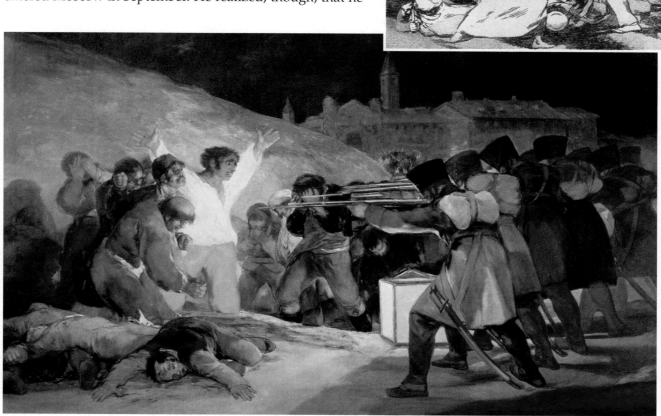

was not able to feed and supply his army through the long Russian winter. In October, he turned homeward.

The 1,000-mile retreat from Moscow turned into a desperate battle for survival. Russian attacks and the brutal Russian winter took a terrible toll. Philippe Paul de Ségur, an aide to Napoleon, described the grim scene as the remnants of the Grand Army returned:

> "In Napoleon's wake [was] a mob of tattered ghosts draped in . . . odd pieces of carpet, or greatcoats burned full of holes, their feet wrapped in all sorts of rags. . . . [We] stared in horror as those skeletons of soldiers went by, their gaunt, gray faces covered with disfiguring beards, without weapons . . . with lowered heads, eyes on the ground, in absolute silence."
> —*Memoirs of Philippe Paul de Ségur*

Only about 10,000 soldiers of the once-proud Grand Army survived. Many died. Others deserted. French general Michel Ney sadly concluded: "General Famine and General Winter, rather than Russian bullets, have conquered the Grand Army." Napoleon rushed to Paris to raise a new force to defend France. His reputation for success had been shattered.

Downfall of Napoleon

The disaster in Russia brought a new alliance of Russia, Britain, Austria, and Prussia against a weakened France. In 1813, they defeated Napoleon in the Battle of the Nations at Leipzig.

Exile and Return The next year, Napoleon abdicated, or stepped down from power. The victors exiled him to Elba, an island in the Mediterranean. They then recognized Louis XVIII, brother of Louis XVI, as king of France.

The restoration of Louis XVIII did not go smoothly. The Bourbon king agreed to accept the Napoleonic Code and honor the land settlements made during the revolution. However, many émigrés rushed back to France bent on revenge. An economic depression and the fear of a return to the old regime helped rekindle loyalty to Napoleon.

As the victorious allies gathered in Vienna for a general peace conference, Napoleon escaped his island exile and returned to France. Soldiers flocked to his banner. As citizens cheered Napoleon's advance, Louis XVIII fled. In March 1815, the emperor of the French entered Paris in triumph.

Battle of Waterloo Napoleon's triumph was short-lived. His star soared for only 100 days, while the allies reassembled their forces. On June 18, 1815, the opposing armies met near the town of Waterloo in Belgium. British forces under the Duke of Wellington and a Prussian army commanded by General Blücher crushed the French in an agonizing day-long battle. Once again, Napoleon was forced to abdicate and to go into exile on St. Helena, a lonely island in the South Atlantic. This time, he would not return.

Legacy of Napoleon Napoleon died in 1821, but his legend lived on in France and around the world. His contemporaries as well as historians have long debated his legacy. Was he "the revolution on horseback," as he claimed? Or was he a traitor to the revolution?

No one, however, questions Napoleon's impact on France and on Europe. The Napoleonic Code consolidated many changes of the revolution. The France of Napoleon was a centralized state with a constitution. Elections were held with expanded, though limited, suffrage. Many more citizens had rights to property and access to education than under the old regime. Still, French citizens lost many rights promised so fervently by republicans during the Convention.

On the world stage, Napoleon's conquests spread the ideas of the revolution. He failed to make Europe into a French empire. Instead, he sparked

Geography and History

The Battle of Waterloo

Waterloo—to this day it symbolizes utter defeat. But on the morning of the battle, Napoleon felt certain of victory. "This whole affair will not be more serious than swallowing one's breakfast," he said.

But both weather and terrain conspired against him. First, he held off his attack until the rain-soaked ground could dry. (Cannonballs just stick in mud; they can do more damage bouncing along dry ground.) These lost hours gave the enemy time to move in more troops. Second, Napoleon ordered a frontal attack against an enemy positioned on an upward slope. The crest of its ridge helped shield the opposition from French artillery barrages. At Waterloo, more than 20,000 French soldiers died, and Napoleon suffered his final defeat.

Theme: Geography and History How did geography help defeat Napoleon at Waterloo?

Napoleon's Retreat From Moscow

"My greatest and most difficult enterprise," said Napoleon in June 1812 as he eagerly took on the challenge of conquering Russia. A few months later, he would see things differently, and so would his troops. After a disheartening defeat, Napoleon had to hurry back to Paris to squelch rumors that he had been killed, leaving his shrinking army to face the long, brutal winter in Russia.

Fast Facts

- Russian soldiers set Moscow ablaze to avoid handing it over intact to Napoleon's army.

- When the Grand Army retreated from Moscow in October, the line of French troops stretched for more than 50 miles.

- French troops experienced temperatures as low as −40º F.

As French troops stumbled their way through blinding snow, they grew desperate for shelter. Soldiers resorted to building huts using the frozen corpses of their fallen comrades, stacking them like logs to create walls.

Russian forces harassed the retreating French army throughout November.

The Grand Army of France was forced to follow the same path retreating from Moscow that it used to get there. As the army passed over an old battlefield, one observer commented, "It was covered with the debris of helmets . . . wheels, weapons, rags of uniforms—and 30,000 corpses half-eaten by wolves."

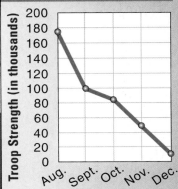

Napoleon's Troops in Russia

Troop Strength (in thousands): 200, 180, 160, 140, 120, 100, 80, 60, 40, 20, 0

Month: Aug., Sept., Oct., Nov., Dec.

Source: Charles Joseph Minard, 1861

Starting with 422,000 troops in June, Napoleon lost almost half of his forces to fighting, desertion, and famine by August. Grand Army troop strength continued to fall drastically from August through December.

Portfolio Assessment

INTERNET Use the Internet or library resources to learn about another disastrous march in history. Some such marches were the Trail of Tears in North America in 1838–1839, the Long March in China in 1934–1935, or the Bataan Death March in the Philippines in 1942. Write a news story in which you include a map of the route and statistics on loss of life.

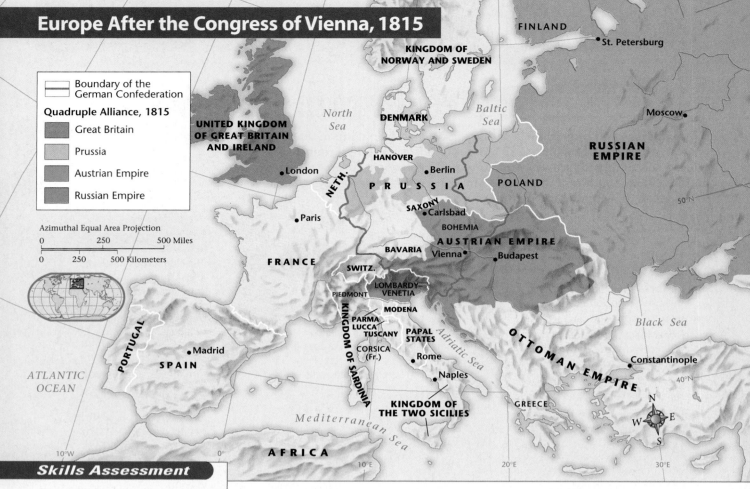

Europe After the Congress of Vienna, 1815

FINLAND

KINGDOM OF NORWAY AND SWEDEN

St. Petersburg

Boundary of the German Confederation

Quadruple Alliance, 1815

Great Britain

Prussia

Austrian Empire

Russian Empire

North Sea

DENMARK

Baltic Sea

Moscow

RUSSIAN EMPIRE

UNITED KINGDOM OF GREAT BRITAIN AND IRELAND

London

HANOVER

Berlin

P R U S S I A

POLAND

50°N

Azimuthal Equal Area Projection

0   250   500 Miles

0   250   500 Kilometers

Paris

SAXONY
Carlsbad

BOHEMIA

AUSTRIAN EMPIRE

FRANCE

BAVARIA

Vienna

Budapest

SWITZ.

LOMBARDY–VENETIA

PIEDMONT

MODENA

KINGDOM OF SARDINIA

PARMA
LUCCA
TUSCANY

PAPAL STATES

CORSICA (Fr.)

Rome

Adriatic Sea

O T T O M A N   E M P I R E

Black Sea

Constantinople

40°N

PORTUGAL

Madrid

SPAIN

ATLANTIC OCEAN

Naples

KINGDOM OF THE TWO SICILIES

GREECE

N W E S

Mediterranean Sea

10°W

0°

AFRICA

10°E

20°E

30°E

nationalist feeling across Europe. The abolition of the Holy Roman Empire would eventually help in creating a new Germany. Napoleon also had a dramatic impact across the Atlantic. In 1803, his decision to sell France's vast Louisiana Territory to the American government doubled the size of the United States and ushered in an age of American expansion.

The Congress of Vienna

After Waterloo, diplomats and heads of state again sat down at the Congress of Vienna. They faced the monumental task of restoring stability and order in Europe after years of revolution and war.

Gathering of Leaders The Congress met for 10 months, from September 1814 to June 1815. It was a brilliant gathering of European leaders. Diplomats and royalty dined and danced, attended concerts and ballets, and enjoyed parties arranged by their host, Emperor Francis I of Austria.

While the entertainment kept thousands of minor players busy, the real work fell to Prince Clemens von Metternich of Austria, Czar Alexander I of Russia, and Lord Robert Castlereagh (KAS uhl ray) of Britain. Defeated France was represented by Prince Charles Maurice de Talleyrand.

Goals of the Congress The chief goal of the Vienna decision makers was to create a lasting peace by establishing a balance of power and protecting the system of monarchy. Each of the leaders also pursued his own goals. Metternich, the dominant figure at the Congress, wanted to restore the *status quo* (Latin for "the way things are") of 1792. Alexander I urged a "holy alliance" of Christian monarchs to suppress future revolutions. Lord Castlereagh was determined to prevent a revival of French military power.

The aged diplomat Talleyrand shrewdly played the other leaders against one another to get defeated France accepted as an equal partner.

Balance of Power The peacemakers also redrew the map of Europe. To contain French ambitions, they ringed France with strong countries. In the north, they added Belgium and Luxembourg to Holland to create the kingdom of the Netherlands. To prevent French expansion eastward, they gave Prussia lands along the Rhine River. They also allowed Austria to reassert control over northern Italy. This policy of containment proved fairly successful in maintaining the peace.

Restoration of Monarchs To turn back the clock to 1792, the architects of the peace promoted the principle of legitimacy, restoring hereditary monarchies that the French Revolution or Napoleon had unseated. Even before the Congress began, they had put Louis XVIII on the French throne. Later, they restored "legitimate" monarchs in Portugal, Spain, and the Italian states.

Problems of the Peace To protect the new order, Austria, Russia, Prussia, and Great Britain extended their wartime alliance into the postwar era. In the Quadruple Alliance, the four nations pledged to act together to maintain the balance of power and to suppress revolutionary uprisings.

The Vienna statesmen achieved their immediate goals, but they failed to foresee how powerful new forces such as nationalism would shake the foundations of Europe. They redrew national boundaries without any concern for national cultures. In Germany, they created a loosely organized German Confederation with Austria as its official head. But many Germans who had battled Napoleon were already dreaming of a strong, united German nation. Their dream would not come true for more than 50 years, but the story of German unification began in this period.

Looking Ahead

Despite clashes and controversies, the Congress created a framework for peace. Its decisions influenced European politics for the next 100 years. Europe would not see war on a Napoleonic scale until 1914.

The ideals of the French Revolution were not destroyed at Vienna. In the next decades, the French Revolution would inspire people in Europe and Latin America to seek equality and liberty. The spirit of nationalism ignited by Napoleon also remained a powerful force.

Biography

Prince Clemens von Metternich 1773–1859

As Austria's foreign minister, Metternich used a variety of means to achieve his goals. In 1809, when Napoleon seemed vulnerable, Metternich favored war against France. In 1810, after France had crushed Austria, he supported alliance with France. When the French army was in desperate retreat from Russia, Metternich became the "prime minister of the coalition" that defeated Napoleon. At the Congress of Vienna, Metternich helped create a new European order and made sure that Austria had a key role in it. He would skillfully defend that new order for more than 30 years.

Theme: Impact of the Individual Why did Metternich's policies toward France change?

SECTION 5 Assessment

Recall

1. **Identify:** (a) Joseph Bonaparte, (b) Duke of Wellington, (c) Marie Louise, (d) scorched earth policy, (e) Waterloo, (f) Clemens von Metternich, (g) Quadruple Alliance.
2. **Define:** (a) guerrilla warfare, (b) abdicate, (c) legitimacy.

Comprehension

3. What challenges did Napoleon face in: (a) Spain, (b) Austria?
4. How did the defeat in Russia lead to Napoleon's downfall?
5. What were the chief goals of the Congress of Vienna?

Critical Thinking and Writing

6. **Linking Past and Present** The powers of Europe used the Quadruple Alliance to protect the postwar order. How do international alliances and organizations help provide order in the world today?
7. **Connecting to Geography** Review the map on the preceding page. (a) What two states were the leading powers in the German Confederation? (b) How do you think this affected future attempts to unify Germany?

Activity

Take It to the NET

Use the Internet to research the Congress of Vienna. Imagine that you have recently returned from attending the Congress and are writing an editorial about its decisions. Explain how the agreements will affect your nation.

Creating a Chapter Summary

On a sheet of paper, make a time line to recall the chief events of the French Revolution and Napoleonic era. Use the model shown here as a guide for getting started.

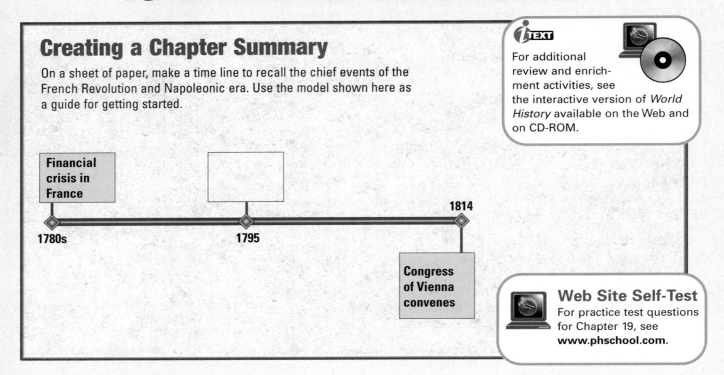

Financial crisis in France

1780s

1795

1814

Congress of Vienna convenes

i TEXT

For additional review and enrichment activities, see the interactive version of *World History* available on the Web and on CD-ROM.

Web Site Self-Test
For practice test questions for Chapter 19, see **www.phschool.com.**

Building Vocabulary

Use these vocabulary words and their definitions to create a matching quiz. Exchange quizzes with another student. Check each other's answers when you are finished.

1. **bourgeoisie**
2. **deficit spending**
3. **émigré**
4. **republic**
5. **suffrage**
6. **nationalism**
7. **plebiscite**
8. **annex**
9. **abdicate**
10. **legitimacy**

Recalling Key Facts

11. Why was there discontent with the old regime in France?
12. Why did a crowd storm the Bastille?
13. What was the slogan of the French Revolution?
14. What was the Reign of Terror?
15. List the reforms that Napoleon made as leader of France.
16. **(a)** How did Napoleon build an empire in Europe? **(b)** What were two reasons for his downfall?
17. How did the Congress of Vienna try to restore the balance of power in Europe?

Critical Thinking and Writing

18. **Synthesizing Information** A French noble wrote this on the causes of the revolution: "The most striking of the country's troubles was the chaos in its finances, the result of years of extravagance. . . . No one could think of any remedy, except to search for fresh funds." **(a)** What did the noble mean by "chaos in its finances"? **(b)** How were fresh funds raised? **(c)** How did this lead to revolution?

19. **Connecting to Geography** **(a)** How did the geography of the Russian empire work against Napoleon's Grand Army? **(b)** Do you think geography can affect the outcome of modern warfare? Explain.

20. **Analyzing Primary Sources** Review the words of "La Marseillaise," which appears in Section 3. How does the song express some of the ideals of the French Revolution?

21. **Comparing** Review the English Civil War. **(a)** How were the English Civil War and the French Revolution similar? **(b)** How were they different?

Read the excerpt below from an eyewitness account of the battle at Waterloo. Then answer the questions that follow.

> "Our division, which had stood upwards of 5000 men at the commencement of the battle, had gradually dwindled down into a solitary line of skirmishers. . . . Presently a cheer which we knew to be British commenced far to the right, and made everyone prick up his ears; it was Lord Wellington's long-wished-for orders to advance. . . . [To] people who had been so many hours enveloped in darkness, in the midst of destruction, and naturally anxious about the result of the day, the scene which now met the eye conveyed a feeling of more exquisite gratification than can be conceived. . . . The French were flying in one confused mass. British lines were seen in close pursuit, and in admirable order, as far as the eye could reach to the right, while the plain to the left was filled with Prussians."

—Captain J. Kincaid,
Adventures in the Rifle Brigade

22. What nationality is the writer?
23. What evidence is given that the French fought fiercely?
24. Why do the soldiers cheer?
25. How does the writer feel about victory?
26. How does this battle differ from the guerrilla warfare fought against the French in Spain?

Use the Internet to research one of the symbols of the French Revolution or the French republic, such as the Bastille, the tricolor, or "La Marseillaise." Then, write a brief historical analysis of the symbol. Explain how it originated, what it represented to French citizens during the revolution, and how it continues to be an important symbol to the French people today.

The Plumb-pudding in danger, or State Epicures taking un Petit Soup
the great Globe itself and all which it went is too small to satisfy such insatiable appetites

In the political cartoon (above), the figure at left represents the British and the figure at right represents Napoleon. Use the cartoon to answer the following questions:

27. What is represented by the meal on the table?
28. Why are the two figures carving the meal?
29. Does the cartoonist portray Napoleon favorably? Explain.
30. How would people of the time have known which nations were represented by the two men in the cartoon?
31. Which of the two sides, if any, does the cartoon favor? Explain.
32. (a) Compose a title for the cartoon. (b) Explain the meaning of the title you created.

Skills Tip

To understand a political cartoon's point of view, first try to figure out the meaning of the cartoon's various figures and symbols.

CHAPTER 20

The Industrial Revolution Begins

1750–1850

Chapter Preview

1 Dawn of the Industrial Age
2 Britain Leads the Way
3 Hardships of Early Industrial Life
4 New Ways of Thinking

1760s

James Watt improves on the steam engine. Watt's engine, shown here, provides a vital source of power.

1800

Robert Owen begins social reforms at New Lanark.

1807

Robert Fulton develops the first successful steamboat, the *Clermont*. Steam power allows the vessel, shown here, to travel against the current without difficulty.

CHAPTER EVENTS

1750   1775   1800

GLOBAL EVENTS

1762 Catherine the Great comes to power in Russia.

1804 Napoleon becomes emperor of France.

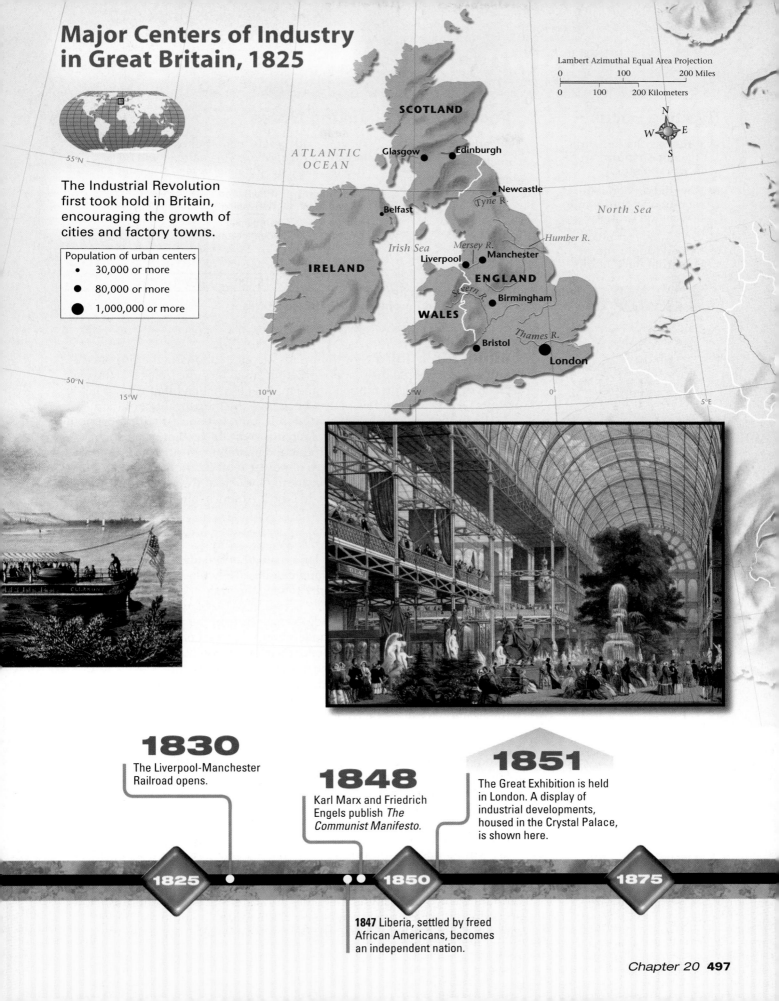

Major Centers of Industry in Great Britain, 1825

Lambert Azimuthal Equal Area Projection

0   100   200 Miles
0   100   200 Kilometers

The Industrial Revolution first took hold in Britain, encouraging the growth of cities and factory towns.

Population of urban centers
- 30,000 or more
- 80,000 or more
- 1,000,000 or more

SCOTLAND

ATLANTIC OCEAN

Glasgow   Edinburgh

Newcastle

Tyne R.

Belfast

North Sea

Irish Sea

Humber R.

Mersey R.

Liverpool   Manchester

IRELAND

ENGLAND

Severn R.   Birmingham

WALES

Bristol

Thames R.

London

55°N
50°N
15°W   10°W   5°W   0°   5°E

1830
The Liverpool-Manchester Railroad opens.

1848
Karl Marx and Friedrich Engels publish *The Communist Manifesto.*

1851
The Great Exhibition is held in London. A display of industrial developments, housed in the Crystal Palace, is shown here.

1825   1850   1875

1847 Liberia, settled by freed African Americans, becomes an independent nation.

Dawn of the Industrial Age

Reading Focus

- Why was the Industrial Revolution a turning point in world history?

- How did an agricultural revolution contribute to population growth?

- What new technologies helped trigger the Industrial Revolution?

Vocabulary

anesthetic

enclosure

smelt

Taking Notes

As you read, create a chart of causes of the Industrial Revolution. This sample will help you get started. Add categories as needed.

Agricultural Revolution	Population Explosion	New Technology	
• Dikes	• Declining death rates	•	
• Fertilizer	•	•	

INDUSTRIAL REVOLUTION

Main Idea The Industrial Revolution had an impact on every aspect of life in Western Europe and the United States.

Setting the Scene For thousands of years following the rise of civilization, most people lived and worked in small farming villages. However, a chain of events set in motion in the mid-1700s changed that way of life for all time. Today, we call this period of change the Industrial Revolution.

The Industrial Revolution started in Britain. In contrast with most political revolutions, it was neither sudden nor swift. Instead, it was a long, slow, uneven process in which production shifted from simple hand tools to complex machines. New sources of power replaced human and animal power. In the 250 years since it began, the Industrial Revolution has spread from Britain to the rest of Europe, to North America, and around the globe.

A Turning Point in History

In 1750, most people worked the land, using handmade tools. They lived in simple cottages lit by firelight and candles. They made their own clothes and grew their own food. In nearby towns, they might exchange goods at a weekly outdoor market.

Like their ancestors, these people knew little of the world that existed beyond their village. The few who left home traveled only as far as their feet or a horse-drawn cart could take them. Those bold adventurers who dared to cross the seas were at the mercy of the winds and tides.

With the beginning of the Industrial Revolution, the rural way of life began to disappear. By the 1850s, many country villages had grown into industrial towns and cities. Their inhabitants bought food and clothing in stores that offered a large variety of machine-made goods. Their homes were crowded, multistory apartment buildings.

Industrial-age travelers moved rapidly between countries and continents by train or steamship. Urgent messages flew along telegraph wires. New inventions and scientific "firsts" poured out each year. Between 1830 and 1855, for example, an American dentist first used an anesthetic, or drug that prevents pain during surgery; an American inventor patented the first sewing machine; a French physicist measured the speed of light; and a Hungarian doctor introduced antiseptic methods to reduce the risk of women dying in childbirth.

Still more stunning changes occurred in the next century, creating our familiar world of skyscraper cities and carefully tended suburbs. How and why did these great changes occur? Historians point to a series of interrelated causes that helped trigger the industrialization of the West.

A New Agricultural Revolution

Oddly enough, the Industrial Revolution was made possible in part by a change in the farming fields of Western Europe. The first agricultural revolution took place some 11,000 years ago, when people learned to farm and domesticate animals. About 300 years ago, a second agricultural revolution took place. It greatly improved the quality and quantity of farm products.

Improved Methods of Farming The Dutch led the way in this new agricultural revolution. They built earthen walls known as dikes to reclaim land from the sea. They combined smaller fields into larger ones to make better use of the land and used fertilizer from livestock to renew the soil.

In the 1700s, British farmers expanded on Dutch experiments. Some farmers mixed different kinds of soils to get higher crop yields. Others tried out new methods of crop rotation. Lord Charles Townshend urged farmers to grow turnips, which restored exhausted soil. Jethro Tull invented a new mechanical device, the seed drill, to aid farmers. It deposited seeds in rows rather than scattering them wastefully over the land.

Educated farmers exchanged news of experiments through farm journals. King George III himself, nicknamed "Farmer George," wrote articles about his model farm near Windsor Castle.

Enclosure Movement Meanwhile, rich landowners pushed ahead with enclosure, the process of taking over and fencing off land formerly shared by peasant farmers. In the 1500s, they had enclosed land to gain pastures for sheep and increased wool output. By the 1700s, they wanted to create larger fields that could be cultivated more efficiently.

As millions of acres were enclosed, farm output rose. Profits also rose because large fields needed fewer workers. But such progress had a human cost. Many farm laborers were thrown out of work, and small farmers were forced off their land because they could not compete with large landholders. Villages shrank as cottagers left in search of work.

In time, jobless farmworkers migrated to towns and cities. There, they formed a growing labor force that would tend the machines of the Industrial Revolution.

Changes in Agriculture
New inventions contributed to an agricultural revolution during the 1600s and 1700s. Today, the development of new sources of fuel encourages even more use of machine power in farming.

Theme: Economics and Technology How might agricultural developments increase farm productivity and efficiency?

PAST

This four Wheel Drill Plow, with a Seed and a Manure Hopper, was first Invented in the Year 1745 and is now in Use with W.ᵐ Ellis at Little Gaddesden near Hempstead in Hertfordshire, where any person may View the same. It is so light that a Man may Draw it, but Generally drawn by a pony or little Horse.

PRESENT

James Watt 1736–1819

How did a clever Scottish engineer become the "Father of the Industrial Revolution"? After repairing a Newcomen steam engine, James Watt had become fascinated with the idea of improving the device. Within a few months, he knew he had a product that would sell.

Still, Watt lacked the money needed to produce and market it. Fortunately, he found a series of partners, including the shrewd Matthew Boulton. Soon, Boulton could boast, "I have at my disposal what the whole world demands, something which will uplift civilization more than ever by relieving man of all undignified drudgery. I have *steam power*."

Theme: Impact of the Individual How might the Industrial Revolution have been different if Watt had not found a business partner?

The Population Explosion

The agricultural revolution contributed to a rapid growth of population that continues today. Precise population statistics for the 1700s are rare, but those that do exist are striking. Britain's population, for example, soared from about 5 million in 1700 to almost 9 million in 1800. The population of Europe as a whole shot up from roughly 120 million to about 190 million during the same period. Such growth had never before been seen.

The population boom of the 1700s was due more to declining death rates than to rising birthrates. The agricultural revolution reduced the risk of famine. Because they ate better, women were healthier and had stronger babies. In the 1800s, better hygiene and sanitation, along with improved medical care, further slowed deaths from disease.

New Technology

A third factor that helped trigger the Industrial Revolution was the development of new technology. New sources of energy, along with new materials, enabled business owners to change the ways work was done.

An Energy Revolution From the beginning of human history, the energy for work was provided mostly by the muscles of humans and animals. In time, water mills and windmills were added to muscle power.

During the 1700s, people began to harness new sources of energy. One vital power source was coal, used to develop the steam engine. In 1712, inventor Thomas Newcomen had developed a steam engine powered by coal to pump water out of mines. About 1769, Scottish engineer James Watt improved on Newcomen's engine. Watt's engines would become a key power source of the Industrial Revolution.

Improved Iron Coal was also a vital source of fuel in the production of iron, a material needed for construction of machines and steam engines. The Darby family of Coalbrookdale pioneered new methods of producing iron. In 1709, Abraham Darby used coal to smelt iron, or separate iron from its ore. When he discovered that coal gave off impurities that damaged the iron, Darby found a way to remove the impurities from coal.

Darby's experiments led him to produce better-quality and less expensive iron, and his son and grandson continued to improve on his methods. In the decades that followed, high-quality iron was used more and more widely, especially after the world turned to building railroads.

SECTION 1 Assessment

Recall
1. **Identify:** (a) Charles Townshend, (b) Jethro Tull, (c) Thomas Newcomen, (d) James Watt, (e) Abraham Darby.
2. **Define:** (a) anesthetic, (b) enclosure, (c) smelt.

Comprehension
3. Describe how the Industrial Revolution changed daily life, becoming a turning point in history.
4. Identify three causes of the population explosion in Europe.

5. Explain the impact of each of the following technologies: (a) steam power, (b) improved iron.

Critical Thinking and Writing
6. **Recognizing Causes and Effects** What were the immediate and long-term effects of the agricultural revolution?
7. **Predicting Consequences** How do you think increased population contributed to the Industrial Revolution?

Activity

Creating a Mechanical Drawing
Suppose that you are trying to develop a way to draw water from a well that is faster than pulling up one bucket of water at a time. Draw a sketch of a machine that would speed up the process and require less human labor.

Britain Leads the Way

Reading Focus

■ Why was Britain the starting point for the Industrial Revolution?

■ What changes transformed the textile industry?

■ What new technologies were part of the revolution in transportation?

Vocabulary

capital
factory
turnpike

Taking Notes

Copy this concept web. As you read, fill in the circles with key factors that helped Britain take an early lead in industry.

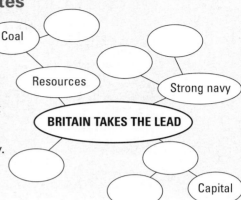

Main Idea The Industrial Revolution originated in Britain.

Setting the Scene Visitors crowded into London's Crystal Palace in 1851. The immense structure housed the Great Exhibition, a display of the "Works of Industry of all Nations." The palace itself was specially built for the occasion. A vast cavern of glass and iron, it symbolized the triumph of the industrial age.

In the century before the exhibition, Britain had been the first nation to industrialize. Its success became the model for other countries, in Europe and around the world.

Why Britain?

Why did the Industrial Revolution begin in Britain? Historians have identified a number of key factors that helped Britain lead the way.

Resources Britain was a small nation in area. However, it had large supplies of coal to power steam engines. It also had plentiful iron to build the new machines. In addition to natural resources, a labor supply was necessary. Large numbers of workers were needed to mine the coal and iron, build the factories, and run the machines. The agricultural revolution of the 1600s and 1700s freed many people in Britain from farm labor and led to a population boom.

New Technology In the 1700s, Britain had plenty of skilled mechanics who were eager to meet the growing demand for new, practical inventions. Technology was an important part of the Industrial Revolution, but it did not cause it. After all, other societies, such as the ancient Greeks or Chinese, had advanced technology for their time but did not move on to industrialization. Only when other necessary conditions existed, including demand and capital, did technology pave the way for industrialization.

Economic Conditions From the mid-1600s to 1700s, trade from a growing overseas empire helped the British economy prosper. Beginning with the slave trade, the business class accumulated capital, or wealth to invest in enterprises such as shipping, mines, railroads, and factories. Many were ready to risk their capital in new ventures.

At home, the population explosion boosted demand for goods. However, a growing population alone would not have resulted in increased production. General economic prosperity also helped make the new consumer goods affordable to members of every social class.

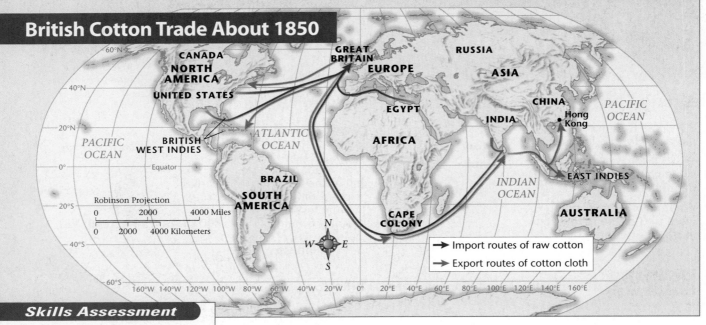

British Cotton Trade About 1850

CANADA
NORTH AMERICA
UNITED STATES
BRITISH WEST INDIES
PACIFIC OCEAN
ATLANTIC OCEAN
Equator
BRAZIL
SOUTH AMERICA
GREAT BRITAIN
EUROPE
RUSSIA
ASIA
EGYPT
AFRICA
CHINA
Hong Kong
INDIA
PACIFIC OCEAN
INDIAN OCEAN
EAST INDIES
CAPE COLONY
AUSTRALIA

Robinson Projection
0   2000   4000 Miles
0   2000   4000 Kilometers

→ Import routes of raw cotton
→ Export routes of cotton cloth

Skills Assessment

Geography As its textile industry grew, Great Britain needed more raw cotton. It also sought out new markets for finished cotton cloth.

1. **Location** On the map, locate **(a)** Great Britain, **(b)** United States, **(c)** British West Indies.
2. **Movement** **(a)** Name two overseas sources that supplied raw cotton to Britain. **(b)** Name two overseas markets to which Britain exported its cotton cloth.
3. **Critical Thinking** **Predicting Consequences** What might have happened to the British cotton industry if Britain had lost control of India?

Political and Social Conditions Britain had a stable government that supported economic growth. It built a strong navy to protect its empire and overseas trade. Although the upper class tended to look down on business people, it did not reject the wealth produced by the new entrepreneurs.

Religious attitudes also played a role. Many entrepreneurs came from religious groups that encouraged thrift and hard work. At the same time, many people focused more on worldly concerns than on the afterlife. Thus, risk takers such as inventors and bankers felt free to devote their energies to material achievements.

Changes in the Textile Industry

The Industrial Revolution first took hold in Britain's largest industry, textiles. In the 1600s, cotton cloth imported from India had become popular. British merchants tried to organize a cotton cloth industry at home. They developed the putting out system, in which raw cotton was distributed to peasant families who spun it into thread and then wove the thread into cloth. Skilled artisans in the towns then finished and dyed the cloth.

Major Inventions Under the "putting-out" system, production was slow. As the demand for cloth grew, inventors came up with a string of remarkable devices that revolutionized the British textile industry. For example, using John Kay's flying shuttle, weavers worked so fast that they soon outpaced spinners. James Hargreaves solved that problem by producing the spinning jenny in 1764, which spun many threads at the same time. A few years later, Richard Arkwright invented the waterframe, which used water power to speed up spinning still further.

The First Factories The new machines doomed the "putting-out" system. They were too large and expensive to be operated at home. Instead, manufacturers built long sheds to house the machines. At first, they located the sheds near rapidly moving streams, which provided water power to run the machines. Later, machines were powered by steam engines.

Spinners and weavers came each day to work in these first factories—places that brought together workers and machines to produce large quantities of goods. Early observers were awed at the size and output of these establishments. One onlooker noted: "The same [amount] of labor is now performed in one of these structures which formerly occupied the industry of an entire district."

Synthesizing Information

Impact of the Railroad

The steam locomotive was one of the key inventions of the Industrial Revolution. The maps, the cartoon, and the graph below all relate to the growth of railroads in Great Britain.

English Cartoon, Early 1800s

Railways in Great Britain

1840

1850

—— Railway lines

Travel Times to London

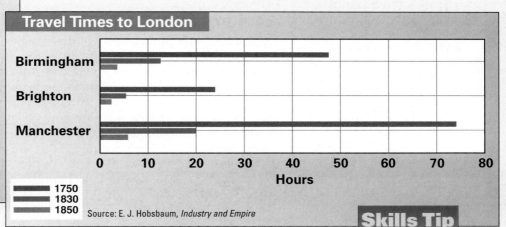

- 1750
- 1830
- 1850

Source: E. J. Hobsbaum, *Industry and Empire*

Skills Assessment

1. Between 1750 and 1830, travel time from Birmingham to London decreased by about
   A 12 hours.
   B 24 hours.
   C 36 hours.
   D 48 hours.

2. Which of the three pieces of evidence above supports the conclusion that railroads reached more places in 1850 than in 1830?
   E the maps only
   F the graph only
   G the maps and the graph
   H the maps and the cartoon

3. **Critical Thinking** **Drawing Conclusions** (a) Based on the evidence provided here, what were some of the benefits and drawbacks of railroads? (b) What other positive or negative effects do you think railroads might have had? Give two examples.

Revolution in Transportation

As production increased, entrepreneurs needed faster and cheaper methods of moving goods from place to place. Some capitalists invested in turnpikes, which were privately built roads that charged a fee to travelers who used them. Others had canals dug to link rivers or connect inland towns with coastal ports. Engineers also built stronger bridges and upgraded harbors to help the expanding overseas trade.

On Land   The great revolution in transportation, however, was the invention of the steam locomotive. It was this invention that made possible the growth of railroads. In the early 1800s, pioneers like George Stephenson developed steam-powered locomotives to pull carriages along iron rails. The railroad did not have to follow the course of a river. This meant that tracks could go places rivers did not, allowing factory owners and merchants to ship goods over land.

The world's first major rail line, from Liverpool to Manchester, opened in England in 1830. In the following decades, railroad travel became faster and railroad building boomed. By 1870, rail lines crisscrossed Britain, Europe, and North America.

On Sea   Other inventors applied steam power to improve shipping. In 1807, an American, Robert Fulton, used Watt's steam engine to power the *Clermont* up the Hudson River in New York. Fulton's steamboat traveled at a record-breaking speed of more than five miles an hour!

Designing steamships for ocean voyages was more difficult. The coal needed for the voyage took up much of the cargo space. But by the late 1800s, steam-powered freighters with iron hulls were carrying 10 to 20 times the cargo of older wooden ships.

Looking Ahead

As the Industrial Revolution got under way, it triggered a chain reaction. In response to growing demand, inventors developed machines that could produce large quantities of goods more efficiently. As the supply of goods increased, prices fell. Lower prices made goods more affordable and thus created more consumers who further fed the demand for goods. The Industrial Revolution affected not only how goods were made but also how people lived. It brought a tidal wave of economic and social changes that swept the industrializing nations of the world.

SECTION 2 Assessment

Recall

1. **Identify:** **(a)** John Kay, **(b)** James Hargreaves, **(c)** Richard Arkwright, **(d)** George Stephenson.
2. **Define:** **(a)** capital, **(b)** factory, **(c)** turnpike.

Comprehension

3. Describe four factors that helped bring about the Industrial Revolution in Britain.
4. How did the Industrial Revolution transform the textile industry?
5. How did transportation improve in the early 1800s? Give three examples.

Critical Thinking and Writing

6. **Analyzing Information** Explain how each of the following helped contribute to demand for consumer goods in Britain: **(a)** population explosion, **(b)** general economic prosperity.
7. **Connecting to Geography** Look at the map of the British cotton trade in this section. **(a)** To what continents did Britain export its cotton cloth? **(b)** Explain how advances in transportation, such as the steamboat, contributed to Britain's global cotton trade.

Activity
Take It to the NET

Research connections between mining and transportation. Write a brief explanation of how canals affected the coal industry.

Reading Focus

- What was life like in the new industrial city?
- How did the factory system change the way people worked?
- What benefits and problems did industrialization bring to the working class and the new middle class?

Vocabulary

urbanization
tenement
labor union

Taking Notes

Copy this table. As you read, list the characteristics of the working class and the middle class. Add more entries as needed.

THE WORKING CLASS	THE MIDDLE CLASS
Factory and mine workers	Merchants, inventors, skilled artisans
Tenement housing	

Main Idea The Industrial Revolution created material benefits as well as social problems.

Setting the Scene The Industrial Revolution brought great riches to most of the entrepreneurs who helped set it in motion. For the millions of workers who crowded into the new factories, however, the industrial age brought poverty and harsh living conditions. One observer commented on the disease-ridden neighborhoods and polluted air:

> "The population . . . is crowded into one dense mass of cottages separated by unpaved and almost pestilential streets. This is an atmosphere loaded with the exhalation of a large manufacturing city."
> —J. P. Kay, quoted in *Mill Life at Styal*

In time, reforms would curb many of the worst abuses of the early industrial age in Europe and the Americas, and people at all levels of society would benefit from industrialization. Until then, working people could look forward only to lives marked by dangerous working conditions; unsafe, unsanitary, and overcrowded housing; and unrelenting poverty.

The New Industrial City

The Industrial Revolution brought rapid **urbanization,** or the movement of people to cities. Changes in farming, soaring population growth, and an ever-increasing demand for workers led masses of people to migrate from farms to cities. Almost overnight, small towns around coal or iron mines mushroomed into cities. Other cities grew up around the factories that entrepreneurs built in once-quiet market towns.

The British market town of Manchester numbered 17,000 people in the 1750s. Within a few years, it exploded into a center of the textile industry. Its population soared to 40,000 by 1780 and 70,000 by 1801. Visitors described the "cloud of coal vapor" that polluted the air, the pounding noise of steam engines, and the filthy stench of its river.

In Manchester, as elsewhere, a gulf divided the urban population. The wealthy and the middle class lived in pleasant neighborhoods. Vast numbers of poor, however, struggled to survive in foul-smelling slums. They packed into tiny rooms in **tenements,** multistory buildings divided into crowded apartments. These buildings had no running water, only community pumps. There was no sewage or sanitation system, and wastes and garbage rotted in the streets. Cholera and other diseases spread rapidly. In time, reformers pushed for laws to improve conditions in city slums.

Primary Sources and Literature

See "Charles Dickens: Hard Times" in the Reference Section at the back of this book.

Virtual Field Trip

www.phschool.com

Dunaskin Open Air Museum Ayrshire, Scotland

To find more information about iron production during the Industrial Revolution, use the Internet address above to link to the Dunaskin Open Air Museum.

Forging the Anchor
This painting by William James Muler shows workers laboring to make an anchor of iron. The image provides a glimpse of the factory system.

Theme: Art and Literature
How would you describe the artist's opinion of factories?

The Factory System

The heart of the new industrial city was the factory. There, the technology of the machine age imposed a harsh new way of life on workers.

Rigid Discipline The factory system differed greatly from farmwork. In rural villages, people worked hard, but their work varied according to the season. In factories, workers faced a rigid schedule set by the factory whistle. "While the engine runs," said an observer, "people must work—men, women, and children are yoked together with iron and steam."

Working hours were long. Shifts lasted from 12 to 16 hours. Exhausted workers suffered accidents from machines that had no safety devices. They might lose a finger, a limb, or even their lives. Workers were exposed to other dangers, as well. Coal dust destroyed the lungs of miners, and textile workers constantly breathed air filled with lint. If workers were sick or injured, they lost their jobs.

Women Workers Employers often preferred to hire women workers rather than men. They thought women could adapt more easily to machines and were easier to manage than men. More important, they were able to pay women less than men, even for the same work.

Factory work created special problems for women. Their new jobs took them out of their homes for 12 hours or more a day. They then returned to crowded slum tenements to feed and clothe their families, clean, and cope with sickness and other problems. Family life had been hard for poor rural cottagers. In industrial towns, it was even grimmer.

Child Labor Factories and mines also hired many boys and girls. Often, nimble-fingered and quick-moving children changed spools in textile mills. Others clambered through narrow mine shafts, pushing coal carts. Because children had helped with farmwork, parents accepted the idea of child labor. And the wages the children earned were needed to keep their families from starving.

Employers often hired orphans, making deals with local officials who were glad to have the children taken off their hands. Overseers beat children accused of idling. A few enlightened factory owners did provide basic education and a decent life for child workers. More often, though, children, like their parents, were slaves to the machines.

Spinning Thread in a Textile Mill

It is your first day at work and you're already exhausted. You wanted to help your family by earning extra money, so you came to Manchester to work with your uncle in a textile mill. You must work on several machines at once, keeping the thread from tangling and breaking. The factory still seems so strange.

The thunder of the spinning mule vibrates through the floor. This machine allows you to make thread faster by yourself than hundreds of people spinning by hand.

It is hard to breathe. Cotton dust flies out of the machines. You hear other workers coughing, their lungs filled with the thick dust.

Children dart in and out, untying knots in the thread. You wince as you see a little boy almost get his hand caught in a machine. The boss gives you a disapproving look, so you try to focus on your own work.

Portfolio Assessment

After a 12-hour day at the mill, you decide to write a letter to your family. In your letter, describe your new job and say whether you want to keep working here in Manchester or go back home to the farm.

Worker Protests
On a hot August day in 1819, workers gathered in St. Peter's Fields in Manchester to hear reformers speak. Suddenly, soldiers attacked the crowd. The incident became known as the Peterloo Massacre.

Theme: Art and Literature
Did the artist who created this cartoon favor the workers or the soldiers? Explain.

In the 1830s and 1840s, British lawmakers looked into abuses in factories and mines. Government commissions heard about children as young as five years old working in factories. Some died; others were stunted in growth or had twisted limbs. Most were uneducated. Slowly, Parliament passed laws to regulate child labor in mines and factories.

The Working Class

In rural villages, farm families had strong ties to a community in which they had lived for generations. When they moved to the new industrial cities, many felt lost and bewildered. In time, though, factory and mine workers developed their own sense of community.

Protests As the Industrial Revolution began, weavers and other skilled artisans resisted the new "labor-saving" machines that were costing them their jobs. Some smashed machines and burned factories. In England, such rioters were called Luddites after a mythical figure, Ned Ludd, who supposedly destroyed machines in the 1780s.

Protests met harsh repression. When workers held a rally in Manchester in 1819, soldiers charged the crowd, killing a dozen and injuring hundreds more. Workers were forbidden to organize in groups to bargain for better pay and working conditions. Strikes were outlawed.

Spread of Methodism Many working-class people found comfort in a new religious movement. In the mid-1700s, John Wesley had founded the Methodist Church. Wesley stressed the need for a personal sense of faith. He urged Christians to improve their lot by adopting sober, moral ways.

Methodist meetings featured hymns and sermons promising forgiveness of sin and a better life to come. Methodist preachers took this message of salvation into the slums. There, they tried to rekindle hope among the working poor. They set up Sunday schools where followers not only studied the Bible but also learned to read and write. Methodists helped channel workers' anger away from revolution and toward social reform.

The New Middle Class

Those who benefited most from the Industrial Revolution were the entrepreneurs who set it in motion. This new middle class came from several sources. Some members were merchants who invested their growing profits in factories. Others were inventors or skilled artisans who developed new technologies. Some rose from "rags to riches," a pattern that the age greatly admired.

Middle-class families lived in solid, well-furnished homes. They dressed and ate well. Middle-class men gained influence in Parliament, where they opposed any effort to improve conditions for workers.

As a sign of their new standard of living, middle-class women were encouraged to become "ladies." They took up "ladylike" activities, such as drawing, embroidery, or playing the piano. A "lady" did not work outside the home or do housework. Instead, the family hired a maid-servant. The family then set about educating its daughters to provide the same type of happy, well-furnished home for their future husbands. Sons gained an education that allowed them to become businessmen.

The new middle class valued hard work and the determination to "get ahead." They had confidence in themselves and often little sympathy for the poor. If they thought of the faceless millions in the factories and mines, they generally supposed the poor to be responsible for their own misery. Some believed the poor were so lazy or ignorant that they could not "work their way up" out of poverty.

Benefits and Problems

Since the 1800s, people have debated whether the Industrial Revolution was a blessing or a curse. The early industrial age brought terrible hardships. Said English writer Thomas Carlyle, "Something [ought] to be done."

In time, "something" would be done. Reformers pressed for laws to improve working conditions. Workers' organizations called labor unions won the right to bargain with employers for better wages, hours, and working conditions. Eventually, working-class men gained the right to vote, which gave them political power.

Despite the social problems created by the Industrial Revolution—low pay, unemployment, dismal living conditions—the industrial age did bring material benefits. As demand for mass-produced goods grew, new factories opened, creating more jobs. Wages rose so that workers had enough left after paying rent and buying food to buy a newspaper or visit a music hall. As the cost of railroad travel fell, people could visit family in other towns. Horizons widened; opportunities increased.

Industrialization has spread around the world today. Often, it begins with great suffering. In the end, however, it produces more material benefits for more people.

SECTION 3 Assessment

Recall
1. **Identify:** (a) Luddite, (b) John Wesley, (c) Methodism.
2. **Define:** (a) urbanization, (b) tenement, (c) labor union.

Comprehension
3. Describe life in the new industrial city.
4. (a) What were the main characteristics of factory work? (b) What special problems did factory work create for women?
5. How did the conditions of the early industrial age improve?

Critical Thinking and Writing
6. **Comparing** Compare the life of a farmworker with that of an early factory worker.
7. **Connecting to Geography** Look at the chapter opener map. What geographic feature do many of the industrial centers share? Why do you think this is so?

Activity
Take It to the NET

Search the Internet for information about working conditions during the Industrial Revolution. Draw a political cartoon that illustrates the life of factory workers. Write a caption for your cartoon.

Reading Focus

- What was laissez-faire economics?
- How did the views of utilitarians differ from those of socialists?
- What were the ideas of "scientific socialism," introduced by Karl Marx?

Vocabulary

utilitarianism
socialism
means of production
communism
proletariat

Taking Notes

As you read this section, prepare an outline of its contents. Use Roman numerals to indicate major headings. Use capital letters for subheadings, and use numbers for the supporting details. The example here will help you get started.

I. Laissez-faire economics
  A. Legacy of Adam Smith
    1. Benefits of free market
    2.
  B. Malthus on population
    1. Population outpaces food supply
    2.

Main Idea The Industrial Revolution fostered new ideas about business and economics.

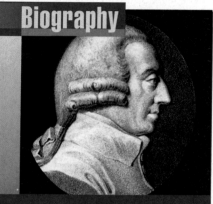

Biography

Adam Smith 1723–1790

If anyone fit the image of the "absent-minded professor," it was Adam Smith. He forgot things, spoke awkwardly, and rambled as he walked. "I am a beau in nothing but my books," Smith once said. Still, he had one of history's keenest minds.

At the age of 14, Smith was a student at a university in his native Scotland. There, and later in Paris, he met many influential thinkers of the Enlightenment. He also met local merchants, gaining practical knowledge about business.

Smith spent 10 years writing *The Wealth of Nations.* Published in 1776, it became an instant bestseller. Readers embraced Smith's ideas about laissez-faire and the benefits of capitalism.

Theme: Impact of the Individual How did Smith's education shape his work?

Setting the Scene Everywhere in Britain, Thomas Malthus saw the effects of the population explosion—crowded slums, hungry families, unemployment, and widespread misery. After careful study, in 1798 he published his "Essay on the Principle of Population." Poverty and misery, he concluded, were unavoidable because the population was increasing faster than the food supply. Malthus wrote: "The power of population is [far] greater than the power of the Earth to produce subsistence for man."

Malthus was one of many thinkers who tried to understand the staggering changes taking place in the early industrial age. As heirs to the Enlightenment, these thinkers looked for natural laws that governed the world of business and economics.

Laissez-Faire Economics

During the Enlightenment, physiocrats argued that natural laws should be allowed to operate without interference. As part of this philosophy, they believed that government should not interfere in the free operation of the economy. In the early 1800s, middle-class business leaders embraced this laissez-faire, or "hands-off," approach.

Legacy of Adam Smith The main prophet of laissez-faire economics was Adam Smith, author of *The Wealth of Nations.* Smith asserted that a free market—the unregulated exchange of goods and services—would come to help everyone, not just the rich.

The free market, Smith said, would produce more goods at lower prices, making them affordable by everyone. A growing economy would also encourage capitalists to reinvest profits in new ventures. Supporters of this free-enterprise capitalism pointed to the successes of the industrial age, in which government had played no part.

Malthus on Population Like Smith's book, Thomas Malthus's writings on population shaped economic thinking for generations. Malthus grimly predicted that population would outpace the food supply. The only checks on population growth, he said, were war, disease, and famine. As long as population kept increasing, he went on, the poor would suffer. He thus urged families to have fewer children.

During the early 1800s, many people accepted Malthus's bleak view. It proved to be too pessimistic, however. Although the population boom did continue, the food supply grew even faster. As the century progressed, living conditions for the western world also slowly improved—and then people began having fewer children. By the 1900s, population growth was no longer a problem in the West, but it did continue to afflict many nations elsewhere.

Ricardo on Wages Another influential British economist, David Ricardo, agreed with Malthus that the poor had too many children. In his "iron law of wages," Ricardo pointed out that when wages were high, families had more children. But more children meant a greater supply of labor, which led to lower wages and higher unemployment. Like Malthus, Ricardo did not hold out hope for the working class to escape poverty. Because of such gloomy predictions, economics became known as the "dismal science."

Neither Malthus nor Ricardo was a cruel man. Yet both opposed any government help for the poor. To these supporters of laissez-faire economics, the best cure for poverty was not government relief but the unrestricted "laws of the free market." They felt that individuals should be left to improve their lot through thrift, hard work, and limiting the size of their families.

The Utilitarians

Others adapted laissez-faire doctrines to justify some government intervention. By 1800, Jeremy Bentham was preaching **utilitarianism,** the idea that the goal of society should be "the greatest happiness for the greatest number" of its citizens. To Bentham, all laws or actions should be judged by their "utility." Did they provide more pleasure (happiness) than pain? He strongly supported individual freedom, which he believed guaranteed happiness. Still, he saw the need for government to become involved under certain circumstances.

Bentham's chief follower, John Stuart Mill, also argued that actions are right if they promote happiness and wrong if they cause pain. He reexamined the idea that unrestricted competition in the free market was always good. Often, he said, it favored the strong over the weak.

Although he believed strongly in individual freedom, Mill wanted the government to step in to improve the hard lives of the working class. "The only purpose for which power can be rightfully exercised over any member of a civilized community, against his will," Mill wrote, "is to prevent harm to others. His own good, either physical or moral, is not a sufficient warrant [cause]." While middle-class business and factory owners were entitled to increase their own happiness, therefore, government should prevent them from doing so in a manner that harmed workers.

Mill further called for giving the vote to workers and women. These groups could then use their political power to win reforms. Utilitarians also worked for reforms in many other areas affecting workers and the poor, from child labor to public health.

Most middle-class people rejected Mill's ideas. Only in the later 1800s were his views slowly accepted. Today's democratic governments, however, have absorbed many ideas from Mill and the other utilitarians.

Emergence of Socialism

While the champions of laissez-faire economics praised individual rights, other thinkers focused on the good of society in general. They condemned the evils of industrial capitalism, which they believed had created a gulf between rich and poor. To end poverty and injustice, they offered a radical solution—**socialism.** Under socialism, the people as a whole rather than private individuals would own and operate the **means of production**—the

Overcrowded Conditions Thomas Malthus warned that population growth could exhaust the food supply, bringing misery to the poor. In *Bishopsgate Street,* artist Gustave Doré captures the squalor and overcrowded conditions of a London slum.

Theme: Political and Social Systems What did Malthus recommend as a solution to the problems of the early industrial age?

farms, factories, railways, and other large businesses that produced and distributed goods.

Socialism grew out of the Enlightenment faith in progress, its belief in the basic goodness of human nature, and its concern for social justice. Socialists wanted to develop a world in which society would operate for the benefit of all members, rather than just for the wealthy. In a socialist society, one reformer predicted:

> "There will be no war, no crime, no administration of justice, as it is called, no government. Besides there will be neither disease, anguish, melancholy, nor resentment. Every man will seek . . . the good of all."
> —William Godwin, "Political Justice"

The Utopians Early socialists tried to build self-sufficient communities in which all work was shared and all property was owned in common. When there was no difference between rich and poor, they felt, fighting between people would disappear. These early socialists were called Utopians, after Thomas More's ideal community. The name implied that they were impractical dreamers. However, the Utopian Robert Owen did set up a model community to put his ideas into practice.

Robert Owen A poor Welsh boy, Owen became a successful mill owner. Unlike most industrialists at the time, he refused to use child labor. He campaigned vigorously for laws that limited child labor and encouraged the organization of labor unions.

Owen insisted that the conditions in which people lived shaped their character. To prove his point, he set up his factory in New Lanark, Scotland, as a model village. He built homes for workers, opened a school for children, and generally treated employees well. He showed that an employer could offer decent living and working conditions and still run a profitable business. By the 1820s, many people were visiting New Lanark to study Owen's reforms.

The "Scientific Socialism" of Karl Marx

In the 1840s, Karl Marx, a German philosopher, condemned the ideas of the Utopians as unrealistic idealism. He put forward a new theory, "scientific socialism," which he claimed was based on a scientific study of history.

As a young man in Germany, Marx agitated for reform. Forced to leave his homeland because of his radical ideas, he lived first in Paris and then settled in London. He teamed up with another German socialist, Friedrich Engels, whose father owned a textile factory in England.

Marx and Engels wrote a pamphlet, *The Communist Manifesto*, which they published in 1848. "A spectre is haunting Europe," it began, "the spectre of communism." Communism is a form of socialism that sees class struggle between employers and employees as unavoidable.

Marxism In *The Communist Manifesto*, Marx theorized that economics was the driving force in history. The entire course of history, he argued, was "the history of class struggles" between the "haves" and the "have-nots." The "haves" have always owned the means of production and thus controlled society and all its wealth. In industrialized Europe, Marx said, the "haves" were the bourgeoisie. The "have-nots" were the proletariat, or working class.

According to Marx, the modern class struggle pitted the bourgeoisie against the proletariat. In the end, he predicted, the proletariat would be triumphant. It would then take control of the means of production and set up a classless, communist society. Such a society would mark the end of the struggles people had endured throughout history, because wealth and power would be equally shared.

Marx despised capitalism. He believed it created prosperity for only a few and poverty for many. He called for an international struggle to bring about its downfall. "Working men of all countries," he urged, "unite!"

Looking Ahead

At first, Marxism gained popularity with many people around the world. Leaders of a number of reform movements adopted the idea that power should be held by workers rather than by business owners. Marx's ideas would never be practiced exactly as he imagined them, however.

Failures   As time passed, the failures of Marxist governments would illustrate the flaws in his arguments. Marx claimed that his ideas were based on scientific laws. However, many of the assumptions on which he based his theories were wrong. He predicted that the misery of the proletariat would touch off a world revolution. Instead, by 1900, the efforts of reformers and governments led to improved conditions for the working class. As a result, Marxism lost some of its appeal in the industrially developed countries of Europe and North America.

Marx also predicted that workers would unite across national borders to wage class warfare. Instead, nationalism won out over working-class loyalty. In general, people felt stronger ties to their own countries than to the international communist movement.

Revolutions   These failures did not doom the movement instantly. In the late 1800s, Russian socialists embraced Marxism, and the Russian Revolution of 1917 set up a communist-inspired government. For much of the 1900s, revolutionaries around the world would adapt Marxist ideas to their own needs. Independence leaders in Asia, Latin America, and Africa would turn to Marxism. By the 1990s, however, nearly every nation would incorporate elements of free-market capitalism. To many people, Adam Smith's ideas seemed to be of more lasting value than those of Karl Marx.

Primary Source

The Working Class
Karl Marx and Friedrich Engels give their view on how the Industrial Revolution affected workers:

"Owing to the extensive use of machinery and to division of labor, the work of the proletarians has lost all individual character, and, consequently, all charm for the workman. He becomes [a limb] of the machine, and it is only the most simple, most monotonous, and most easily acquired knack, that is required of him. Hence, the cost of production of a workman is restricted almost entirely to the means of [survival] that he requires for his maintenance. . . ."

—Karl Marx and Friedrich Engels, *The Communist Manifesto*

Skills Assessment

Primary Source How would Marx expect a worker to feel about his or her job?

SECTION 4 Assessment

Recall
1. **Identify: (a)** Thomas Malthus, **(b)** iron law of wages, **(c)** John Stuart Mill, **(d)** Utopians, **(e)** Karl Marx.
2. **Define: (a)** utilitarianism, **(b)** socialism, **(c)** means of production, **(d)** communism, **(e)** proletariat.

Comprehension
3. Describe the views of laissez-faire economists **(a)** Adam Smith, **(b)** Thomas Malthus, and **(c)** David Ricardo.
4. Contrast the approaches of utilitarians and socialists to solving economic problems.

5. **(a)** Describe Karl Marx's view of history. **(b)** How have events challenged that view?

Critical Thinking and Writing
6. **Linking Past and Present** Choose one economic or political theory discussed in this section. Does that theory seem to apply to the American economy today? Explain.
7. **Applying Information** How might the rise of Methodism and workplace reforms alter Marxist predictions of world revolution?

Activity

Asking Questions
Write five questions you might ask if you were conducting an interview with Robert Owen. Include questions about his goals, how he tried to accomplish them, and whether he succeeded.

Creating a Chapter Summary

Copy this chart on a sheet of paper. Complete the chart by naming the invention or idea developed by each person on the left. One row has been filled in to help you get started.

For additional review and enrichment activities, see the interactive version of *World History* available on the Web and on CD-ROM.

INVENTORS AND THINKERS	INVENTIONS AND IDEAS
Jethro Tull	
Thomas Newcomen	
Richard Arkwright	
George Stephenson	
John Wesley	Methodism
Adam Smith	
David Ricardo	
Jeremy Bentham	
Robert Owen	
Karl Marx	

Web Site Self-Test
For practice test questions for Chapter 20, see **www.phschool.com**.

Building Vocabulary

(a) Classify each of the chapter vocabulary words listed below under *one* of the following themes: Continuity and Change; Political and Social Systems; Economics and Technology. **(b)** Choose one word in each category and write a sentence explaining how that word relates to the theme.

1. **anesthetic**
2. **smelt**
3. **capital**
4. **factory**
5. **urbanization**
6. **labor union**
7. **utilitarianism**
8. **means of production**
9. **proletariat**

Recalling Key Facts

10. How did the enclosure movement affect people?
11. What new source of energy helped trigger the Industrial Revolution?
12. List three reasons why the Industrial Revolution began in Britain.
13. Why did large numbers of people migrate to cities?
14. List the government reforms sought by John Stuart Mill.

Critical Thinking and Writing

15. **Connecting to Geography** Explain the link between Britain's natural resources and its rise as an industrial nation.
16. **Analyzing Political Cartoons** Study the political cartoon in Section 3. **(a)** What is the subject of the cartoon? **(b)** Who are the men on horseback? **(c)** Who are the people under attack? **(d)** What do you think was the artist's purpose in creating the cartoon?
17. **Analyzing Information** Describe how the Industrial Revolution affected each of the following: **(a)** size of population, **(b)** cities, **(c)** working and living conditions, **(d)** women and children.
18. **Linking Past and Present** **(a)** How did thinkers in the 1800s disagree about the role of government in helping the poor? **(b)** Give three examples to show that this debate continues today.
19. **Defending a Position** Do you think that the negative social consequences of the Industrial Revolution could have been avoided? Use material from this chapter to defend your position.

In the excerpt below, a British newspaper correspondent details the daily life of cotton-mill workers in the northern industrial town of Manchester. Read the excerpt, then answer the questions that follow.

"The streets in the neighborhood of the mills are thronged with men and women and children flocking to their labour. . . . The factory bell rings from five minutes before six until the hour strikes. Then—to the moment—the engine starts and the day's work begins. Those who are [late], be it but a moment, are fined twopence, and in many mills, after the expiration of a very short time of grace, the doors are locked, and the laggard, besides the fine, loses his morning work.

. . . I fear that I cannot say much for the cleanliness of the workpeople. They have an essentially greasy look, which makes me sometimes think that water would run off their skins, as it does off a duck's back. In this respect the women are just as bad as the men. . . . The spinners and piecers . . . fling shoes and stockings aside, but I fear it is very seldom that their feet see the interior of a tub, with plenty of hot water and soap."

—from "A Working Day" in *Labour and the Poor in England and Wales, 1849–1851*

20. Who made up the work force at the mill?
21. How were workers punished for being late?
22. How did the correspondent view the workers' personal hygiene habits?
23. Why might the spinners and piecers work barefoot?
24. Based on what you have read, would the correspondent view himself as a member of the proletariat? Explain your answer.

Skills Tip

When you read a primary source, try to determine whether the writer identifies with the people or events being described. Is the writer's viewpoint sympathetic or unsympathetic?

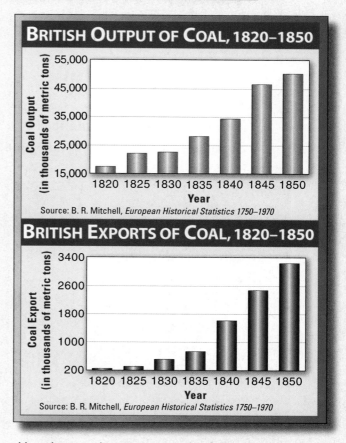

BRITISH OUTPUT OF COAL, 1820–1850

Coal Output (in thousands of metric tons)

Year

Source: B. R. Mitchell, *European Historical Statistics 1750–1970*

BRITISH EXPORTS OF COAL, 1820–1850

Coal Export (in thousands of metric tons)

Year

Source: B. R. Mitchell, *European Historical Statistics 1750–1970*

Use the graphs to answer the following questions:

25. By what year had the coal output of 1820 doubled?
26. **(a)** By about how many metric tons did coal output increase between 1820 and 1840? **(b)** Between 1840 and 1850?
27. Write a sentence that summarizes the information about coal output and exports presented in these graphs.

 Skills Assessment

Take It to the NET

Use the Internet to research primary or secondary sources on the daily life of factory workers during the Industrial Revolution. Then, write a paper explaining why you do or do not think that the benefits of living in an industrialized nation today outweigh some of the social consequences of the Industrial Revolution.

Revolutions in Europe and Latin America

1790–1848

Chapter Preview

1 An Age of Ideologies
2 Revolutions of 1830 and 1848
3 Latin American Wars of Independence

1810
Father Miguel Hidalgo urges Mexicans to fight for independence from Spain.

1804
Haiti declares independence from France.

1819
Simón Bolívar, later known as "The Liberator," seizes Bogota from the Spanish.

**CHAPTER
EVENTS**

1800

1810

1820

**GLOBAL
EVENTS**

1803 United States buys Louisiana from France.

1820 Several thousand British colonists settle in South Africa.

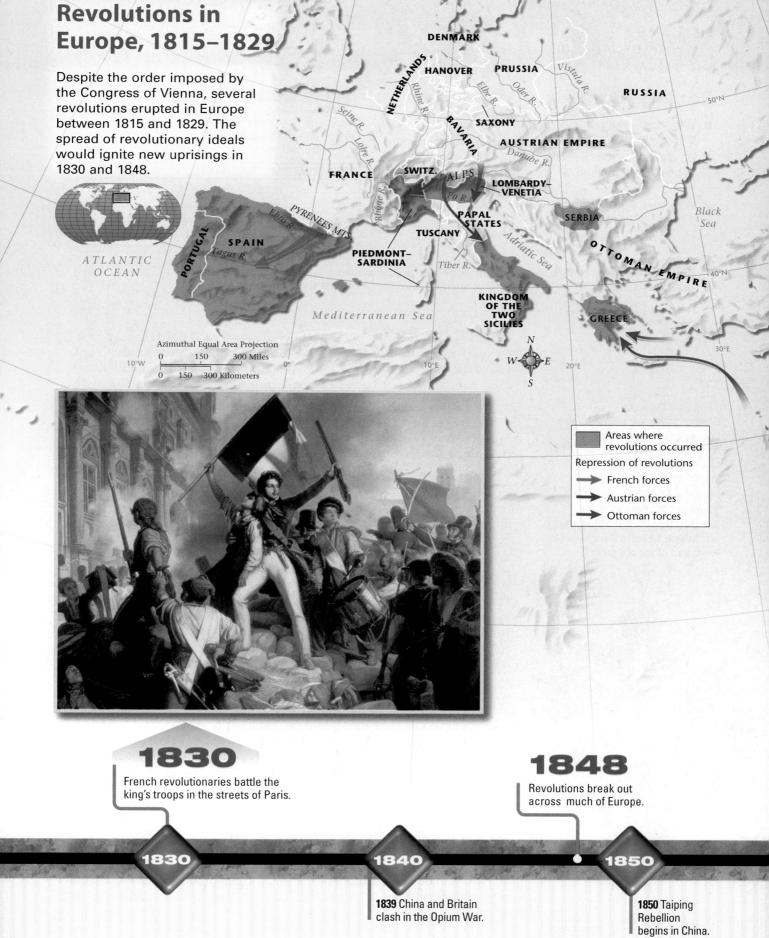

Revolutions in Europe, 1815–1829

Despite the order imposed by the Congress of Vienna, several revolutions erupted in Europe between 1815 and 1829. The spread of revolutionary ideals would ignite new uprisings in 1830 and 1848.

DENMARK

NETHERLANDS HANOVER PRUSSIA

Vistula R.

RUSSIA

50°N

Seine R.

Rhine R.

Elbe R.

Oder R.

SAXONY

BAVARIA

AUSTRIAN EMPIRE

Danube R.

FRANCE

Loire R.

SWITZ.

ALPS

Po R.

LOMBARDY–VENETIA

SERBIA

Black Sea

Rhône R.

PAPAL STATES

TUSCANY

40°N

PORTUGAL

SPAIN

Tagus R.

Ebro R.

PYRENEES MTS.

PIEDMONT–SARDINIA

Tiber R.

Adriatic Sea

OTTOMAN EMPIRE

ATLANTIC OCEAN

Mediterranean Sea

KINGDOM OF THE TWO SICILIES

GREECE

30°E

Azimuthal Equal Area Projection

0   150   300 Miles

0   150   300 Kilometers

10°W   0°   10°E   20°E

N W E S

	Areas where revolutions occurred
Repression of revolutions	
→	French forces
→	Austrian forces
→	Ottoman forces

1830
French revolutionaries battle the king's troops in the streets of Paris.

1848
Revolutions break out across much of Europe.

1830   1840   1850

1839 China and Britain clash in the Opium War.

1850 Taiping Rebellion begins in China.

An Age of Ideologies

Reading Focus

- What were the goals of conservatives?

- How did liberalism and nationalism challenge the old order?

- Why was Europe plagued by revolts after 1815?

Vocabulary

ideology

universal manhood suffrage

autonomy

Taking Notes

Copy this chart. As you read this section, list the ideas of conservatism, liberalism, and nationalism.

CONSERVATISM	LIBERALISM	NATIONALISM

Main Idea After 1815, the clash of people with opposing ideologies plunged Europe into an era of turmoil that lasted more than 30 years.

The Conservative Order
Conservatives were determined to preserve the old order. At the heart of that order was the monarchy, symbolized in the Austrian empire by the Hapsburg coat of arms shown here.

Theme: Political and Social Systems What other institutions besides the monarchy were part of the old order?

Setting the Scene A "revolutionary seed" had been planted in Europe, warned Prince Clemens von Metternich. The ideas spread by the French Revolution and Napoleon Bonaparte, he believed, not only threatened Europe's monarchs but also undermined its basic social values:

> "Passions are let loose . . . to overthrow everything that society respects as the basis of its existence: religion, public morality, laws, customs, rights, and duties, all are attacked, confounded, overthrown, or called in question."
> —*Memoirs of Prince Metternich*

At the Congress of Vienna, the powers of Europe tried to uproot that "revolutionary seed." Other voices, however, kept challenging the order imposed in 1815. The clash of people with opposing ideologies, or systems of thought and belief, plunged Europe into more than 30 years of turmoil.

Conservatives and the Old Order

The Congress of Vienna was a victory for the conservative forces, which included monarchs and their officials, noble landowners, and church leaders. Conservatives supported the political and social order that had existed before the French Revolution. Conservative ideas also appealed to peasants, who wanted to preserve traditional ways.

Conservatives of the early 1800s wanted to turn the clock back to the way things had been before 1789. After all, they had benefited under the old order. They wanted to restore royal families to the thrones they had lost when Napoleon swept across Europe. They supported a social hierarchy in which lower classes were expected to respect and obey their social superiors. Conservatives also backed an established church—Catholic in Austria and southern Europe, Protestant in northern Europe, and Orthodox in eastern Europe.

Conservatives believed that talk about natural rights and constitutional government could lead only to chaos, as it had in France in 1789. If change had to come, they argued, it must come slowly. Conservatives felt that they benefited all people by defending peace and stability. Conservative leaders like Metternich sought to suppress revolutionary ideas. Metternich urged monarchs to oppose freedom of the press, crush protests in their own countries, and send troops to douse the flames of rebellion in neighboring lands.

The Liberal and Nationalist Challenge

Challenging the conservatives at every turn were liberals and nationalists who were inspired by the Enlightenment and the French Revolution. Liberalism and nationalism ignited a number of revolts against established rule.

Liberal Goals Because liberals spoke mostly for the bourgeoisie, or middle class, their ideas are sometimes called "bourgeois liberalism." Liberals included business owners, bankers, and lawyers, as well as politicians, newspaper editors, writers, and others who helped to shape public opinion.

Liberals wanted governments to be based on written constitutions and separation of powers. Liberals spoke out against divine-right monarchy, the old aristocracy, and established churches. They defended the natural rights of individuals to liberty, equality, and property. They called for rulers elected by the people and responsible to them. Thus, most liberals favored a republican form of government over a monarchy, or at least wanted the monarch to be limited by a constitution.

The liberals of the early 1800s saw the role of government as limited to protecting basic rights such as freedom of thought, speech, and religion. They believed that only male property owners or others with a financial stake in society should have the right to vote. Only later in the century did liberals support the principle of universal manhood suffrage, giving all adult men the right to vote.

Liberals strongly supported the laissez-faire economics of Adam Smith and David Ricardo. They saw the free market as an opportunity for capitalist entrepreneurs to succeed. As capitalists and often employers, liberals had different goals from those of workers laboring in factories, mines, and other enterprises of the early Industrial Revolution.

Nationalist Goals For centuries, European rulers had gained or lost lands through wars, marriages, and treaties. They exchanged territories and the people in them like pieces in a game. As a result, by 1815 Europe had several empires that included many nationalities. The Austrian, Russian, and Ottoman empires, for example, each included diverse peoples.

In the 1800s, national groups who shared a common heritage set out to win their own states. Within the diverse Austrian empire, for example, various nationalist leaders tried to unite and win independence for each particular group. Nationalism gave people with a common heritage a sense of identity and the goal of creating their own homeland. At the same time, however, nationalism often bred intolerance and led to persecution of other ethnic or national groups.

Revolts Against the Old Order

Spurred by the ideas of liberalism and nationalism, revolutionaries fought against the old order. During the early 1800s, rebellions erupted in the Balkan Peninsula and elsewhere along the southern fringe of Europe. The Balkans, in southeastern Europe, were inhabited by people of various religions and ethnic groups. These peoples had lived under Ottoman rule for more than 300 years.

The Serb Revolt
In 1804, the Serb leader Karageorge, shown below, led a revolt against Ottoman rule. Ottoman troops crushed this rebellion by 1813, but renewed resistance would eventually lead to Serbian independence.

Theme: Political and Social Systems Why did the Ottoman empire face frequent rebellions in the 1800s?

Independence for Serbia The first Balkan people to revolt were the Serbs. From 1804 to 1813, the Serb leader Karageorge led a guerrilla war against the Ottomans. The bitter struggle was unsuccessful, but it fostered a sense of Serbian identity. A revival of Serbian literature and culture added to the sense of nationhood.

In 1815, Milos Obrenovic led the Serbs in a second, more successful rebellion. One reason for the success was that Obrenovic turned to Russia for assistance. Like the Serbs, the Russian people were Slavic in language and Christian Orthodox in religion. By 1830, Russian support helped the Serbs win autonomy, or self-rule, within the Ottoman empire. The Ottoman sultan later agreed to formal independence. In the future, Russia would continue to defend Serbian interests and affect events in the Balkans.

Independence for Greece In 1821, the Greeks, too, revolted, seeking to end centuries of Ottoman rule. At first, the Greeks were badly divided. But years of suffering in long, bloody wars of independence helped shape a national identity. Leaders of the rebellion justified their struggle as "a national war, a holy war, a war the object of which is to reconquer the rights of individual liberty." They sought help from Western Europeans, who admired ancient Greek civilization.

The Greeks won sympathy in the West. In the late 1820s, Britain, France, and even conservative Russia forced the Ottomans to grant independence to some Greek provinces. By 1830, Greece was independent. The European powers, however, pressured the Greeks to accept a German king, a move meant to show that they did not support revolution. Still, liberals were enthusiastic, and nationalists everywhere saw reasons to hope for a country of their own.

Other Challenges Several other challenges to the Vienna peace settlement erupted in the 1820s. Revolts occurred along the southern fringe of Europe. In Spain, Portugal, and various states in the Italian peninsula, rebels struggled to gain constitutional governments.

Metternich urged conservative rulers to act decisively and crush the dangerous uprisings. In response, a French army marched over the Pyrenees to suppress a revolt in Spain. Austrian forces crossed the Alps to smash rebellious outbreaks in Italy.

Troops dampened the fires of liberalism and nationalism, but could not smother them. In the next decades, sparks would flare anew. Added to liberal and nationalist demands were the goals of the new industrial working class. By the mid-1800s, social reformers and agitators were urging workers to support socialism or other ways of reorganizing property ownership.

SECTION 1 Assessment

Recall
1. **Identify:** (a) conservatives, (b) liberals, (c) nationalists, (d) Karageorge, (e) Milos Obrenovic.
2. **Define:** (a) ideology, (b) universal manhood suffrage, (c) autonomy.

Comprehension
3. What were the goals of conservative leaders?
4. (a) How did the political goals of liberals differ from those of conservatives? (b) How did nationalists threaten the system set up by Metternich?
5. (a) Why did the Serbs and Greeks revolt? (b) Why were there uprisings in Spain, Portugal, and the Italian states?

Critical Thinking and Writing
6. **Applying Information** How did ideologies like liberalism and nationalism contribute to unrest?
7. **Analyzing Information** Why do you think liberals of the early 1800s supported limited voting rights?

Activity
Take It to the NET

On the Internet, find a site that contains some of the writings of Metternich. Print an excerpt that describes one of the key ideas of conservatism. Explain the main idea of the excerpt and explain why Metternich supported this idea.

Reading Focus

- Why did revolutions occur in France in 1830 and 1848?
- How did revolution spread in 1830?
- What were the results of the 1848 revolutions?

Vocabulary

ultraroyalist
recession

Taking Notes

Copy this graphic organizer. As you read, fill in information about conditions before and after the revolutions of 1848.

REVOLUTIONS OF 1848	
Before	**After**
• France is a monarchy	• France is a republic
•	•

Main Idea Revolutions broke out across Europe in 1830 and 1848, but most failed to achieve their goals.

Setting the Scene The quick suppression of liberal and nationalist uprisings in the 1820s did not end Europe's age of revolutions. "We are sleeping on a volcano," warned Alexis de Tocqueville, a liberal French leader who saw widespread discontent. "Do you not see that the Earth trembles anew? A wind of revolution blows, the storm is on the horizon."

In 1830 and 1848, Europeans saw street protests explode into full-scale revolts. As in 1789, the upheavals began in Paris and radiated out across the continent.

The French Revolution of 1830

When the Congress of Vienna restored Louis XVIII to the French throne, he wisely issued a constitution, the Charter of French Liberties. It created a two-house legislature and allowed limited freedom of the press. Still, although Louis was careful to avoid absolutism, the king retained much power.

Sources of Unrest Louis's efforts at compromise satisfied few people. Ultraroyalists, the king's supporters on the far right, despised constitutional government and wanted to restore the old regime. The "ultras" included many high clergy and émigré nobles who had returned to France in the years after the revolution.

The ultras faced bitter opposition from other factions. Liberals wanted to extend suffrage and win a share of power for middle-class citizens like themselves. On the left, radicals yearned for a republic like that of the 1790s. And in working-class slums, men and women wanted what they had wanted in 1789—a decent day's pay and bread they could afford.

The July Revolution When Louis XVIII died in 1824, his younger brother, Charles X, inherited the throne. Charles, a strong believer in absolutism, rejected the very idea of the charter. In July 1830, he suspended the legislature, limited the right to vote, and restricted the press.

Liberals and radicals responded forcefully to the king's challenge. In Paris, angry citizens threw up barricades across the narrow streets. From behind them, they fired on the soldiers and pelted them with stones and roof tiles. Within days, rebels controlled Paris. The revolutionary tricolor flew from the towers of Notre Dame cathedral. A frightened Charles X abdicated and fled to England.

With the king gone, radicals wanted to set up a republic. Moderate liberals, however, insisted on a constitutional monarchy. The Chamber of

Deputies, the lower house of the French legislature, chose Louis Philippe as king. He was a cousin of Charles X and in his youth had supported the revolution of 1789.

The "Citizen King" The French called Louis Philippe the "citizen king" because he owed his throne to the people. Louis got along well with the liberal bourgeoisie. Like them, he dressed in a frock coat and top hat. Sometimes, he strolled the streets, shaking hands with well-wishers. Liberal politicians and professionals filled his government.

Under Louis Philippe, the upper bourgeoisie prospered. Louis extended suffrage, but only to France's wealthier citizens. The vast majority of the people still could not vote. The king's other policies also favored the middle class at the expense of the workers.

The French Revolution of 1848

In the 1840s, discontent grew. Radicals formed secret societies to work for a French republic. Utopian socialists called for an end to private ownership of property. (See the previous chapter.) Even liberals denounced Louis Philippe's government for corruption and called for expanded suffrage.

Near the end of the decade, discontent was heightened by a recession, or period of reduced economic activity. Factories shut down and people lost their jobs. Poor harvests caused bread prices to rise. Newspapers blamed government officials for some of the problems. As in 1789, Paris was ripe for revolution.

"February Days" In February 1848, when the government took steps to silence critics and prevent public meetings, angry crowds took to the streets. During the "February Days," iron railings, overturned carts, paving stones, and toppled trees again blocked the streets of Paris. Church bells rang alarms, while women and men on the barricades sang the revolutionary "La Marseillaise." A number of demonstrators clashed with royal troops and were killed.

As the turmoil spread, Louis Philippe abdicated. A group of liberal, radical, and socialist leaders proclaimed the Second Republic. (The First Republic had lasted from 1792 until 1804, when Napoleon became emperor.)

From the start, deep differences divided the new government. Middle-class liberals wanted moderate political reforms. Socialists wanted far-reaching social and economic change that would help hungry workers. In the early days of the new republic, the socialists forced the government to set up national workshops to provide jobs for the unemployed.

"June Days" By June, however, upper- and middle-class interests had won control of the government. They saw the national workshops as a waste of money, and they shut them down.

Furious, workers took to the streets of Paris, rallying to the cry "Bread or Lead!" This time, however, bourgeois liberals turned violently against the protesters. Peasants, who feared that socialists might take their land, also attacked the rioting workers. At least 1,500 people were killed before the government crushed the rebellion.

The fighting of the "June Days" left a bitter legacy. The middle class both feared and distrusted the left, while the working class nursed a deep hatred for the bourgeoisie.

Louis Napoleon By the end of 1848, the National Assembly, dominated by members who wanted to restore order, issued a constitution for the Second Republic. It created a strong president and a one-house legislature. But it also gave the vote to all adult men, the widest suffrage in the world at the time. Nine million Frenchmen now could vote, compared with only 200,000 who had that right before.

Art and Revolution

Art became more than an expression of beauty and truth in Europe during the mid-1800s. Many European painters, writers, and composers took an active role in the politics of the time. They used their artistic works to fuel the revolutionary spirit.

Les Misérables
THE WORLD'S MOST POPULAR MUSICAL

IMPERIAL THEATRE
249 WEST 45TH STREET

French writer Victor Hugo is still revered as a champion of French democracy. His novel *Les Misérables* offers a bleak view of French society in the years leading up to the revolution of 1848. The above poster was created to promote the modern theatrical version of *Les Misérables.*

This painting (above), called *The Uprising,* captures the passion of the French revolutionaries. The painter Honoré Daumier (1808–1879), who was a revolutionary in his own right, used a paintbrush as others might have used a gun or a sword. As a young man, Daumier was imprisoned for drawing caricatures of Emperor Louis Philippe. Daumier's satirical works helped inspire further protests, and much of his work captured the spirit of the revolution he helped to create.

European composers, such as Richard Wagner of Germany (right), also felt the revolutionary spirit and expressed it through their music. The popular music of the day was marked by a new passion and freedom of expression. It seemed to carry the revolutionary and republican spirit through the air.

Portfolio Assessment

INTERNET

Using the Internet or library resources, create a display of revolutionary art. You may use works of art, including paintings or drawings. You may choose to illustrate the display with excerpts of revolutionary writings, including poetry, song lyrics, or prose.

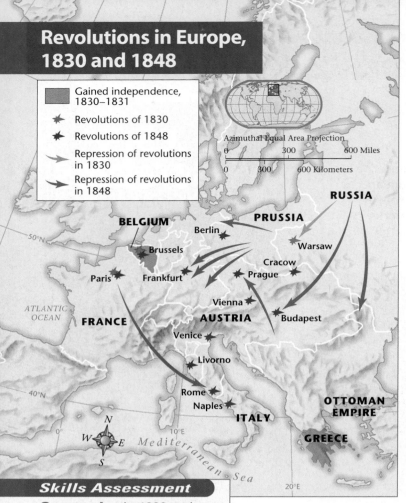

Revolutions in Europe, 1830 and 1848

Gained independence, 1830–1831

✦ Revolutions of 1830

✦ Revolutions of 1848

→ Repression of revolutions in 1830

→ Repression of revolutions in 1848

Azimuthal Equal Area Projection

0   300   600 Miles

0   300   600 Kilometers

RUSSIA

PRUSSIA

BELGIUM

Berlin

Brussels

Warsaw

Cracow

Paris   Frankfurt   Prague

ATLANTIC
OCEAN

FRANCE

Vienna

AUSTRIA   Budapest

Venice

Livorno

Rome

Naples   OTTOMAN
EMPIRE

ITALY

Mediterranean Sea   GREECE

10°E

20°E

N W E S

50°N

40°N

0°

Skills Assessment

Geography In 1830 and again in 1848, revolutions in France sparked uprisings throughout Europe. Although most rebellions were quickly crushed, their ideals survived.

1. **Location** On the map, locate (a) Paris, (b) Warsaw, (c) Budapest.
2. **Place** Which countries gained independence in 1830 and 1831?
3. **Critical Thinking Making Inferences** How can you tell from the map that the revolution in Budapest was unsuccessful?

When elections for president were held, the overwhelming winner was Louis Napoleon, nephew of Napoleon Bonaparte. The "new" Napoleon attracted the working classes by presenting himself as a man who cared about social issues such as poverty. At the same time, his famous name, linked with order and past French glory, helped him with conservatives.

Once in office, Louis Napoleon used his position as a steppingstone to greater power. By 1852, he had proclaimed himself emperor, taking the title Napoleon III. (He was the third Napoleon because the son of Napoleon I had died in his youth without ever ruling France.) Thus ended the short-lived Second Republic.

Like his celebrated uncle, Louis Napoleon used a plebiscite to win public approval for his seizure of power. A stunning 90 percent of voters supported his move to set up the Second Empire. Many thought that a monarchy was more stable than a republic. Millions of French hoped that Napoleon III would restore the glory days of Napoleon Bonaparte.

Napoleon III, like Louis Philippe, ruled at a time of rapid economic growth. For the bourgeoisie, the early days of the Second Empire brought prosperity and contentment. In time, however, Napoleon III would embark on foreign adventures that would bring down his empire and end French leadership in Europe.

The Spread of Revolution

In both 1830 and 1848, the revolts in Paris inspired uprisings to break out elsewhere in Europe. As Metternich said, "When France sneezes, Europe catches cold." Most of the uprisings were suppressed by military force. But here and there, rebels did win changes from conservative governments. Even when they failed, revolutions frightened rulers badly enough to encourage reform later in the century.

Belgium The one notable success for Europe's revolutionaries in 1830 took place in Belgium. In 1815, the Congress of Vienna had united the Austrian Netherlands (present-day Belgium) and the Kingdom of Holland under the Dutch king. The Congress had wanted to create a strong barrier to help prevent French expansion in the future.

The Belgians resented the new arrangement. The Belgians and Dutch had different languages, religions, and economic interests. The Belgians were Catholic, while the Dutch were Protestant. The Belgian economy was based on manufacturing; the Dutch, on trade.

In 1830, news of the Paris uprising that toppled Charles X ignited a revolutionary spark in Belgium. Students and workers threw up barricades in Brussels, the capital. The Dutch king turned to the other European powers for help. Britain and France knew that the Belgians were threatening to disrupt the boundaries set up by the Congress of Vienna, but they believed that they would benefit from the separation of Belgium and Holland. They therefore supported Belgian demands for independence. The conservative powers—Austria, Prussia, and Russia—were too busy putting down revolts of their own to help the Dutch king. As a result, in 1831, Belgium became an independent state with a liberal constitution.

Poland   Nationalists in Poland also staged an uprising in 1830. But, unlike the Belgians, the Poles failed to win independence for their country.

In the late 1700s, Russia, Austria, and Prussia had divided up Poland. Poles had hoped that the Congress of Vienna would restore their homeland in 1815. Instead, the great powers handed most of Poland to Russia.

In 1830, Polish students, army officers, and landowners rose in revolt. The rebels failed to gain widespread support, however, and were brutally crushed by Russian forces. Some survivors fled to Western Europe and the United States, where they kept alive the dream of freedom.

1848: Another Wave of Rebellion

In 1848, revolts in Paris again unleashed a tidal wave of revolution across Europe. For opponents of the old order, it was a time of such hope that they called it the "springtime of the peoples."

Sources of Discontent   Although events in France touched off the revolts, grievances had been piling up for years. Unrest came from many sources. Middle-class liberals wanted a greater share of political power for themselves, as well as protections for the basic rights of all citizens. Workers demanded relief from the miseries of the Industrial Revolution. And nationalists of all classes ached to throw off foreign rule. By 1848, discontent was so widespread that it was only a matter of time before it exploded into full-scale revolution.

Metternich Falls   In the Austrian empire, a revolt broke out in Vienna, taking the government by surprise. Metternich, who had dominated Austrian politics for more than 30 years, tried to silence the students who took to the streets. But when workers supported the students, Metternich resigned and fled in disguise. The Austrian emperor then promised reform.

Revolution quickly spread to other parts of the empire. In Budapest, Hungarian nationalists led by Louis Kossuth demanded an independent government. They also called for an end to serfdom and a written constitution to protect basic rights. In Prague, the Czechs made similar demands. Overwhelmed by events, the Austrian government agreed to the reforms.

The gains were temporary. Austrian troops soon regained control of Vienna and Prague. With Russian help, Austrian forces also smashed the rebels in Budapest. Many were imprisoned, executed, or forced into exile.

Revolution in Italy   Uprisings also erupted in the Italian states. Nationalists wanted to end domination of Italy by the Austrian Hapsburgs. As elsewhere, nationalist goals were linked to demands for liberal reforms such as constitutional government. Workers suffering economic hardships demanded even more radical changes. From Venice in the north to Naples in the south, Italians set up independent republics. Revolutionaries even expelled the pope from Rome and installed a nationalist government.

Before long, however, the forces of reaction surged back here, too. Austrian troops ousted the new governments in northern Italy. A French army restored the pope to power in Rome. In Naples, local rulers canceled the reforms they had reluctantly accepted.

Turmoil in the German States   In the German states, university students passionately demanded national unity and liberal reforms. Economic hard times and a potato famine brought peasants and workers into the struggle. Workers destroyed the machines that threatened their livelihood, while peasants burned the homes of wealthy landowners.

In Prussia, liberals forced King Frederick William IV to agree to a constitution written by an elected assembly. Within a year, though, he dissolved the assembly. Later, he issued his own constitution keeping power in his own hands or those of the upper classes.

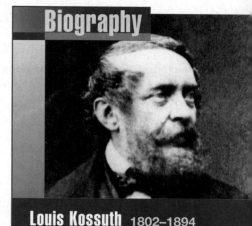

Biography

Louis Kossuth   1802–1894

For two decades, Louis Kossuth had been an activist, writing pamphlets designed to inflame patriotic feelings in the Hungarians. As a result, he was imprisoned by Austrian officials for three years. When he was released, he immediately renewed his activities. He became editor of a nationalistic newspaper and was recognized as the leading voice for Hungarian independence.

Kossuth went on to organize Hungarian revolutionary forces and to declare Hungary's independence in 1848. When Russia intervened, however, Kossuth was forced to flee.

He traveled to the United States, where he spoke before both houses of Congress. His subsequent tour of the country was so well received that a county in Iowa and towns in five states were named in his honor. Tragically, Kossuth would never return to his Hungarian homeland.

Theme: Impact of the Individual   Why was Kossuth unable to win Hungarian independence?

THE GREAT SEA SERPENT OF 1848

An Eventful Year

This English cartoon comments on the revolutions of 1848 and the reaction of European rulers.

Theme: Political and Social Systems Based on the cartoon, (a) What ideal caused the revolutions of 1848? (b) How did the revolutions affect Europe's monarchs?

Frankfurt Assembly Throughout 1848, delegates from German states met in the Frankfurt Assembly. "We are to create a constitution for Germany, for the whole land," declared one leader with great optimism.

Divisions soon emerged. Delegates debated endlessly on such topics as whether the new Germany should be a republic or a monarchy, and whether or not to include Austria in a united German state. Finally, the assembly offered Prussia's Frederick William IV the crown of a united Germany. To their dismay, the conservative king rejected the offer because it came not from the German princes but from the people—"from the gutter," as he described it. By early 1849, the assembly was dissolved, under threat from the Prussian military. Outside the assembly, middle-class reformers and workers with radical demands clashed. Conservative forces rallied, dousing the last flames of revolt. Hundreds of people were killed. Many more went to prison. Thousands of Germans left their homeland. Most traveled to the United States, attracted by the young nation's promise of democratic government and economic opportunity.

Looking Ahead

By 1850, rebellion faded, ending the age of liberal revolution that had begun in 1789. Why did the uprisings fail? The rulers' use of military force was just one reason. In general, revolutionaries did not have mass support. In Poland in 1830, for example, peasants did not take part in the uprising. In 1848, a growing gulf divided workers seeking radical economic change and liberals pursuing moderate political reform.

By mid-century, Metternich was gone from the European scene. Still, his conservative system remained in force. In the decades ahead, liberalism, nationalism, and socialism would win successes not through revolution but through political activity. Ambitious political leaders would unify Germany and Italy. Workers would campaign for reforms through unions and the ballot box, as they increasingly won the right to vote.

SECTION 2 Assessment

Recall

1. **Identify:** (a) Charter of French Liberties, (b) Charles X, (c) Louis Philippe, (d) Louis Napoleon, (e) Louis Kossuth, (f) Frankfurt Assembly, (g) Frederick William IV.
2. **Define:** (a) ultraroyalist, (b) recession.

Comprehension

3. Describe one cause and one effect of (a) the French revolution of 1830, (b) the French revolution of 1848.
4. (a) To what lands did revolution spread in 1830? (b) Were these revolutions successful? Explain.

5. Why did most of the revolutions of 1848 fail to achieve their goals?

Critical Thinking and Writing

6. **Identifying Alternatives** Do you think that European rulers could have prevented nationalist revolts by granting autonomy to some groups of people? Why or why not?
7. **Making Decisions** Suppose you had been a conservative adviser to King Frederick William IV of Prussia. Would you have advised the king to accept the crown offered by the Frankfurt Assembly? Explain the reasons for your decision.

Activity

Take It to the NET

In recent years, various ethnic groups have sought independence, just as national groups did in 1830 and 1848. Use the Internet to find news articles about the people of East Timor, Chechnya, Bosnia, or another land where people have struggled to win an independent nation. Write a brief essay describing their struggle.

Latin American Wars of Independence

Reading Focus

- What caused discontent in Latin America?

- How did Haitians, Mexicans, and people in Central America win independence?

- How did the nations of South America win independence?

Vocabulary

peninsular

creole

mestizo

mulatto

truce

Taking Notes

Copy the partially completed table below. As you read, fill in the left column with the names of leaders who led independence movements in Latin America. Fill in the right column with the name of the country or countries that each leader helped liberate.

LEADERS	COUNTRIES
Iturbide	Mexico
San Martín	Argentina, Chile, Peru

Main Idea In the early 1800s, many new nations emerged in Latin America as independence movements freed people from European rule.

Setting the Scene Like many wealthy Latin Americans,* young Simón Bolívar (boh LEE vahr) was sent to Europe to complete his education. There, he became a strong admirer of the ideals of the Enlightenment and the French Revolution.

One afternoon, Bolívar and his Italian tutor sat talking about freedom and the rights that ordinary people should have. Bolívar's thoughts turned to his homeland, held as a colony by Spain. He fell on his knees and swore a solemn oath: "I swear before God and by my honor never to allow my hands to be idle nor my soul to rest until I have broken the chains that bind us to Spain."

In later years, Bolívar would fulfill his oath, leading the struggle to liberate northern South America from Spain. Elsewhere in Latin America, other leaders organized independence movements. By 1825, most of Latin America had been freed from colonial rule.

Sources of Discontent

By the late 1700s, the revolutionary fever that gripped Western Europe had spread to Latin America. There, discontent was rooted in the social, racial, and political system that had emerged during 300 years of Spanish rule.

Ethnic and Social Hierarchy Spanish-born peninsulares dominated Latin American political and social life. Only they could hold top jobs in government and the Church. Many creoles—the European-descended Latin Americans who owned the haciendas, ranches, and mines—bitterly resented their second-class status. Merchants fretted under mercantilist policies that tied the colonies to Spain.

Meanwhile, a growing population of mestizos, people of Native American and European descent, and mulattoes, people of African and European descent, were angry at being denied the status, wealth, and power that were available to whites. Native Americans suffered economic misery under the Spanish, who had conquered the lands of their ancestors. In the Caribbean region and parts of South America, masses of enslaved Africans who worked on plantations longed for freedom.

The Ruling Class
This is a portrait of Don Tomas Mateo Cervantes, an aristocrat and government official of Cuba in the late 1700s. The portrait was painted by Vincente Escobar, a Cuban of African descent.

Theme: Political and Social Systems How was ethnic background linked to class in Latin America?

---

*Latin America refers to the regions in Middle and South America colonized by Europeans, especially the Spanish, French, and Portuguese, whose languages are rooted in Latin. It includes Spanish-speaking countries from Mexico to Argentina, Portuguese-speaking Brazil, and French-speaking Haiti.

Beyond dissatisfaction with Spanish rule, the different classes had little in common. In fact, they distrusted and feared one another. At times, they worked together against the Spanish. But once independence was achieved, the creoles, who had led the revolts, dominated the governments.

Enlightenment Ideas In the 1700s, educated creoles read the works of Enlightenment thinkers. They watched colonists in North America throw off British rule. Translations of the Declaration of Independence and the Constitution of the United States even circulated among the creole elite.

Women actively participated in the exchange of ideas. In some cities, women hosted and attended salons, called tertulias, where independence and revolution were discussed.

During the French Revolution, young creoles like Simón Bolívar traveled in Europe and were inspired by the ideals of "liberty, equality, and fraternity." Despite their admiration for Enlightenment ideas and revolutions in other lands, most creoles were reluctant to act.

Napoleon Bonaparte The spark that finally ignited widespread rebellion in Latin America was Napoleon's invasion of Spain in 1808. Napoleon ousted the Spanish king and placed his brother Joseph on the Spanish throne. In Latin America, leaders saw Spain's weakness as an opportunity to reject foreign domination and demand independence from colonial rule.

Haiti's Struggle for Independence

Even before Spanish colonists hoisted the flag of freedom, revolution had erupted elsewhere in Latin America, in a French-ruled colony on the island of Hispaniola. Haiti, as it is now called, was France's most valued possession in the 1700s.

In Haiti, French planters owned very profitable sugar plantations worked by nearly a half million enslaved Africans. Sugar plantations were labor intensive. The slaves were overworked and underfed. Haiti also had about 25,000 free mulattoes. Many were wealthy, and some also owned slaves. However, they did not have full equality with the French creoles.

A Slave Revolt In the 1790s, revolutionaries in France were debating ways to abolish slavery in the West Indies. However, debating the issue in Paris did not help enslaved Haitians gain their freedom. Embittered by suffering and inspired by the talk of liberty and equality, Haiti's slaves exploded in revolt in 1791.

The rebels were fortunate to find an intelligent and skillful leader in Toussaint L'Ouverture (too SAN loo vuhr TYOOR), a self-educated former slave. Although untrained, Toussaint was a brilliant general. He was also an inspiring commander. On the eve of one crucial battle, he rallied his troops with these stirring words: "We are fighting so that liberty—the most precious of all earthly possessions—may not perish."

The struggle was long and complex. Toussaint's army of former slaves faced many enemies. Some mulattoes joined French planters against the rebels. France, Spain, and Britain each sent armies to Haiti. The fighting took more lives than any other revolution in the Americas.

By 1798, the rebels had achieved their goal; enslaved Haitians had been freed. And even though Haiti was still a French colony, Toussaint's forces controlled most of the island.

Independence In France, meantime, Napoleon Bonaparte rose to power. In 1802, he sent a large army to reconquer Haiti. Toussaint urged Haitians once again to take up arms, this time to fight for full independence from France. The guerrilla forces were aided by a deadly ally, yellow fever, a disease which took a growing toll on the invaders. In April 1802, the French agreed to a truce, or temporary peace.

Analyzing Primary Sources

Toussaint L'Ouverture on Slavery

In the late 1700s, Toussaint L'Ouverture led a successful revolt in Haiti to eliminate slavery. But Toussaint was haunted by the fear that the French, who still held Haiti as a colony, would try to reestablish slavery. Many French officials, as well as colonists, had already expressed such a desire. Toussaint wrote to the French Directory to oppose any plans to reimpose slavery.

Above, Toussaint L'Ouverture and his army of former slaves battle for independence from France.

"The attempts on . . . liberty which the colonists propose are all the more to be feared because it is with the veil of patriotism that they cover their detestable plans. We know that they seek to impose some of them on [the French government] by illusory and [deceptive] promises, in order to see renewed in this colony its former scenes of horror. . . . My attachment to France, my knowledge of the blacks, make it my duty not to leave you ignorant either of the crimes which they meditate or the oath that we renew, to bury ourselves under the ruins of a country revived by liberty rather than suffer the return of slavery. . . .

Blind as they are! They cannot see how [their] odious conduct . . . can become the signal of new disasters and irreparable misfortunes, and far from making them regain what in their eyes liberty for all has made them lose, they expose themselves to a total ruin and the colony to its inevitable destruction. Do they think that men who have been unable to enjoy the blessing of liberty will calmly see it snatched away? They supported their chains only so long as they did not know any condition of life more happy than that of slavery. But today when they have left it, if they had a thousand lives they would sacrifice them all rather than be forced into slavery again. . . .

But if, to re-establish slavery in [Haiti], this was to be done, then I declare to you it would be to attempt the impossible: we have known how to face dangers to obtain our liberty, we shall know how to brave death to maintain it."

—Toussaint L'Ouverture, quoted in *The Black Jacobins* (James)

Skills Assessment

1. What is the tone of Toussaint's letter?
   - **A** diplomatic
   - **B** peaceful
   - **C** warning
   - **D** friendly

2. What does Toussaint say will happen if the French try to reestablish slavery?
   - **E** The British will take over.
   - **F** The colony will be ruined by war.
   - **G** The blacks will feel resentful.
   - **H** The French will be condemned.

3. **Critical Thinking Making Inferences (a)** Why do you think Toussaint emphasized that one paragraph in his letter? **(b)** What might you infer about Toussaint himself from this letter?

Skills Tip

Italics in excerpts from old documents may represent underlining or some other form of emphasis in the original document.

Independent Nations of Latin America About 1844

Independent nations with date of independence

*United Provinces of Central America had dissolved by 1841

**Gran Colombia had dissolved by 1830

Azimuthal Equal Area Projection

Gulf of Mexico

BAHAMAS (Br.)
HAITI 1804
DOMINICAN REPUBLIC 1844

MEXICO 1821

Mexico City

BELIZE (Br.)

CUBA (Sp.)

JAMAICA (Br.)

PUERTO RICO (Sp.)

UNITED PROVINCES OF CENTRAL AMERICA*

GUATEMALA 1839
EL SALVADOR 1839
HONDURAS 1838
NICARAGUA 1838
COSTA RICA 1838

TRINIDAD (Br.)

BRITISH GUIANA
DUTCH GUIANA
FRENCH GUIANA

Caracas

VENEZUELA 1830**

PANAMA (part of Colombia)

Bogotá

PACIFIC OCEAN

COLOMBIA 1819

Quito

ECUADOR 1822

GRAN COLOMBIA**

Equator 0°

PERU 1824

Lima

BRAZIL 1822

La Paz

BOLIVIA 1825

20°S

PARAGUAY 1811

Asunción

Rio de Janeiro

CHILE 1818

ARGENTINA 1816

URUGUAY 1828

ATLANTIC OCEAN

Santiago

Buenos Aires

Montevideo

PATAGONIA

Cape Horn

FALKLAND ISLANDS (Argentine 1820–1833)

40°S

Latin America About 1790

NEW SPAIN

UNITED STATES

BAHAMAS (Br.)

HISPANIOLA

Mexico City

CUBA

West Indies

GUIANAS

Bogotá

NEW GRANADA

BRAZIL

Lima

PERU

LA PLATA

Rio de Janeiro

Buenos Aires

British

Dutch

French

Portuguese

Spanish

Skills Assessment

Geography In the early 1800s, many Latin American nations won independence from European rule.

1. **Location** On the main map, locate (a) Mexico, (b) Gran Colombia, (c) Haiti.
2. **Place** Which nation of South America was once a Portuguese colony?
3. **Critical Thinking Synthesizing Information** Why did so many nations of Latin America gain independence by 1830?

Shortly after, the French captured Toussaint and carried him in chains to France. Ten months later, he died there in a cold mountain prison. But Haiti's struggle for freedom continued. In 1804, Haitian leaders declared independence. With yellow fever destroying his army, Napoleon abandoned Haiti. In the following years, rival Haitian leaders fought for power. Finally, in 1820, Haiti became a republic.

Independence for Mexico and Central America

The slave revolt in Haiti frightened creoles in Spanish America. Although they wanted power themselves, most had no desire for economic or social changes that might threaten their way of life. In 1810, however, a creole priest in Mexico, Father Miguel Hidalgo (hih DAHL goh), raised a cry for freedom that would echo across the land.

El Grito de Dolores Father Hidalgo presided over the poor rural parish of Dolores. On September 15, 1810, he rang the church bells summoning the people to prayer. When they gathered, he startled them with an urgent appeal. We do not know his exact words, but his message is remembered: "My children, will you be free? Will you make the effort to recover the lands stolen from your forefathers by the hated Spaniards 300 years ago?" Father Hidalgo's speech became known as "el Grito de Dolores"—the cry of Dolores. It called Mexicans to fight for "Independence and Liberty."

A ragged army of poor mestizos and Native Americans rallied to Father Hidalgo and marched to the outskirts of Mexico City. At first, some creoles supported the revolt. However, they soon rejected Hidalgo's call for an end to slavery and his plea for reforms to improve conditions for Native Americans. They felt that these policies would cost them power.

After some early successes, the rebels faced growing opposition. Less than a year after he issued the "Grito," Hidalgo was captured and executed, and his followers scattered.

José Morelos Another priest picked up the banner of revolution. Father José Morelos was a mestizo who called for wide-ranging social and political reform. He wanted to improve conditions for the majority of Mexicans, abolish slavery, and give the vote to all men. For four years, Morelos led rebel forces before he, too, was captured and shot in 1815.

Spanish forces, backed by conservative creoles, hunted down the surviving guerrillas. They had almost succeeded in ending the rebel movement when events in Spain had unexpected effects on Mexico.

Independence Achieved In Spain in 1820, liberals forced the king to issue a constitution. This move alarmed Agustín de Iturbide (ee toor BEE day), a conservative creole in Mexico. He feared that the new Spanish government might impose liberal reforms on the colonies as well.

Iturbide had spent years fighting Mexican revolutionaries. Suddenly in 1821, he reached out to them. Backed by creoles, mestizos, and Native Americans, he overthrew the Spanish viceroy. Mexico was independent at last. Iturbide took the title Emperor Agustín I. Soon, however, liberal Mexicans toppled the would-be monarch and set up the Republic of Mexico.

Although Mexico was free of Spanish rule, the lives of most people changed little. Military leaders dominated the government and ruled by force of arms. The next 100 years would see new struggles to improve conditions for Mexicans.

New Republics in Central America Spanish-ruled lands in Central America declared independence in the early 1820s. Iturbide tried to add these areas to his Mexican empire. After his overthrow, local leaders set up a republic called the United Provinces of Central America. The union was short-lived. It soon fragmented into the separate republics of Guatemala, Nicaragua, Honduras, El Salvador, and Costa Rica. Like Mexico, the new nations faced many social and economic problems.

Independence in South America

In South America, Native Americans had rebelled against Spanish rule as early as the 1700s. These rebellions had limited results, however. It was not until the 1800s that discontent among the creoles sparked a widespread drive for independence.

A Native American Revolt The strongest challenge to Spanish rule by Native Americans was led by Tupac Amaru, who claimed descent from Incan kings. He demanded that the government end the brutal system of forced Indian labor. Spanish officials rejected the demand for reform. In 1780, Tupac Amaru organized a Native American revolt. A large army crushed the rebels and captured and killed their leader. Still, the revolt did have some positive effects. The Spanish king ordered officials to look into the system of forced labor and eventually abolished it.

▶ Primary Sources and Literature

See "Miguel Hidalgo: Decree of Hidalgo" in the Reference Section at the back of this book.

Connections to Today

Mexican Independence Day

Today, the people of Mexico remember Father Hidalgo's speech as "el Grito de Dolores," which means "the cry of Dolores." Every September 15, the anniversary of the speech, the president of Mexico rings a bell—suggestive of the church bell in Dolores. The president then honors the Grito de Dolores by repeating it.

The next day, September 16, marks the anniversary of the beginning of the fight against the Spanish. It is celebrated as Mexican Independence Day, a national holiday. Schools and businesses shut down, and people throw huge parties. Fireworks light the night sky.

The massive celebration is very different from the event at Dolores that it celebrates, but the spirit of independence is the same.

Theme: Continuity and Change Why is the ringing of bells an important custom of Mexican Independence Day?

Virtual Field Trip

www.phschool.com

**The Library of Congress
Washington, D.C.**

To learn more about the Latin
American wars of independence
and the history of Chile, use the
Internet address above to link to
the Library of Congress.

San Martín Crossing the Andes

In this painting, José de San Martín and Bernardo O'Higgins lead their army in a dramatic march over the Andes into Chile. San Martín won independence for Chile when he defeated the Spanish at the battle of Maipú in 1818.

Theme: Geography and History How do you think the successful march across the Andes affected San Martín's army?

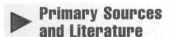

Primary Sources and Literature

See "Simón Bolívar: Address to the Congress of Venezuela" in the Reference Section at the back of this book.

Bolívar In the early 1800s, discontent spread across South America. Educated creoles like Simón Bolívar admired the French and American revolutions. They dreamed of winning their own independence from Spain.

In 1808, when Napoleon Bonaparte occupied Spain, Bolívar and his friends saw it as a signal to act. In 1810, Bolívar led an uprising that established a republic in his native Venezuela. Bolívar's new republic was quickly toppled by conservative forces. For years, civil war raged in Venezuela. The revolutionaries suffered many setbacks. Twice Bolívar was forced into exile on the island of Haiti.

Then, Bolívar conceived a daring plan. He would march his army across the Andes and attack the Spanish at Bogotá, the capital of the viceroyalty of New Granada (present-day Colombia). First, he cemented an alliance with the hard-riding *llaneros*, or Venezuelan cowboys. Then, in a grueling campaign, he led an army through swampy lowlands and over the snowcapped Andes. Finally, in August 1819, he swooped down to take Bogotá from the surprised Spanish.

Other victories followed. By 1821, Bolívar had succeeded in freeing Caracas, Venezuela. "The Liberator," as he was now called, then moved south into Ecuador, Peru, and Bolivia. There, he joined forces with another great South American leader, José de San Martín.

San Martín Like Bolívar, San Martín was a creole. He was born in Argentina but went to Europe for military training. In 1816, this gifted general helped Argentina win freedom from Spain. He then joined the independence struggle in other areas. He, too, led an army across the Andes, from Argentina into Chile. He defeated the Spanish in Chile before moving into Peru to strike further blows against colonial rule.

Bolívar and San Martín tried to work together, but their views were too different. In 1822, San Martín stepped aside, letting Bolívar's forces win the final victories against Spain.

Dreams and Disappointments The wars of independence had ended by 1824. Bolívar now worked tirelessly to unite the lands he had liberated into a single nation, called Gran Colombia. Bitter rivalries, however, made that dream impossible. Before long, Gran Colombia split into three independent countries: Venezuela, Colombia, and Ecuador.

Bolívar faced another disappointment as power struggles among rival leaders triggered destructive civil wars. Spain's former South American colonies faced a long struggle to achieve stable governments—and an even longer one for democracy. Before his death in 1830, a discouraged Bolívar wrote, "We have achieved our independence at the expense of everything else." Contrary to his dreams, no social revolution took place. South America's common people had simply changed one set of masters for another.

Independence for Brazil When Napoleon's armies conquered Portugal, the Portuguese royal family fled to Brazil. During his stay in Brazil, the Portuguese king introduced many reforms, including free trade. He encouraged the development of local industries and allowed Brazilian merchants to trade with nations other than Portugal.

When the king returned to Portugal, he left his son Dom Pedro to rule Brazil. "If Brazil demands independence," the king advised Pedro, "proclaim it yourself and put the crown on your own head."

In 1822, Pedro followed his father's advice. A revolution had brought new leaders to Portugal. They planned to abolish the reforms that had benefited Brazil and they demanded that Dom Pedro return to Portugal. Dom Pedro refused to leave and submit to the Portuguese officials. Instead, he became emperor of an independent Brazil. He accepted a constitution that provided for freedom of the press, freedom of religion, and an elected legislature. Brazil remained a monarchy until 1889, when social and political turmoil led it to become a republic.

Cause and Effect

Independence Movements in Latin America

Long-Term Causes	Immediate Causes
• European domination of Latin America • Spread of Enlightenment ideas • American and French revolutions • Growth of nationalism in Latin America	• People of Latin America resent colonial rule and social injustices • Revolutionary leaders emerge • Napoleon invades Spain and ousts Spanish king

Immediate Effects	Long-Term Effects
• Toussaint L'Ouverture leads slave revolt in Haiti • Bolívar, San Martín, and others lead successful revolts in Latin America • Colonial rule ends in much of Latin America • Attempts made to rebuild economies	• 18 separate republics set up • Continuing efforts to achieve stable democratic governments and to gain economic independence

Connections to Today

• Numerous independent nations in Latin America
• Ongoing efforts to expand prosperity and democracy in Latin America

Skills Assessment **Chart** The French Revolution and the Napoleonic wars had a lasting impact on Latin America. **What difficulties did Latin Americans face after independence?**

SECTION 3 Assessment

Recall
1. **Identify:** (a) Toussaint L'Ouverture, (b) Miguel Hidalgo, (c) el Grito de Dolores, (d) José Morelos, (e) Tupac Amaru, (f) Simón Bolívar, (g) Dom Pedro.
2. **Define:** (a) peninsular, (b) creole, (c) mestizo, (d) mulatto, (e) truce.

Comprehension
3. How did social structure contribute to discontent in Latin America?
4. (a) What was the first step on Haiti's road to independence?

(b) Why did creoles refuse to support Hidalgo or Morelos?
5. How did successful military campaigns lead to the creation of independent nations in South America?

Critical Thinking and Writing
6. **Comparing** Compare the ways in which Mexico and Brazil achieved independence.
7. **Connecting to Geography** Review the subsection Independence in South America and the map in this section. How does the map show that Bolívar failed to achieve one of his dreams?

Activity

Creating a Poster
Imagine that you are an artist in the service of Bolívar or San Martín. You have been hired to create a poster urging people to join the armies fighting against Spain. Your poster should highlight the goals of the revolutionary armies. It should also be eyecatching and convincing.

21 Review and Assessment

Creating a Chapter Summary

Below is a partially completed graphic organizer on the causes of revolution in Europe and Latin America between 1800 and 1848. Copy the organizer and fill in the causes that led to revolutions.

Enlightenment ideas spread

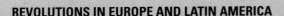

REVOLUTIONS IN EUROPE AND LATIN AMERICA

 For additional review and enrichment activities, see the interactive version of *World History* available on the Web and on CD-ROM.

 Web Site Self-Test
For practice test questions for Chapter 21, see **www.phschool.com**.

Building Vocabulary

For each term below, write a sentence in which you show some connection between the term and the revolutions that occurred between 1800 and 1848.

1. **ideology**
2. **autonomy**
3. **ultraroyalist**
4. **recession**
5. **peninsular**
6. **creole**
7. **mestizo**
8. **mulatto**

Recalling Key Facts

9. In the early 1800s, what were the main goals of **(a)** conservatives, **(b)** liberals, **(c)** nationalists?
10. What were the causes of the French revolution of 1830?
11. Describe the outcomes of the 1848 rebellions in Europe.
12. How did Napoleon spark the revolutions that erupted in Latin America?
13. **(a)** How did Mexico gain independence from Spain? **(b)** How did Mexico's independence change the lives of its people?
14. Why is Simón Bolívar known as "The Liberator"?

Critical Thinking and Writing

15. **Recognizing Causes and Effects** How did the clash of conservatism, liberalism, and nationalism contribute to unrest in Europe in the 1800s?
16. **Recognizing Points of View** In the 1820s, Britain, France, and Russia supported the Greek struggle for independence. **(a)** Why did these European powers support the Greeks? **(b)** Did the European powers usually respond to revolution in this way? Explain.
17. **Analyzing Information** You have read Metternich's comment: "When France sneezes, Europe catches cold." **(a)** What did he mean by those words? **(b)** Was Metternich correct? Explain.
18. **Predicting Consequences** Do you think that the suppression of nationalist revolutions in the mid-1800s put an end to nationalism? Why or why not?
19. **Connecting to Geography** **(a)** How did climatic conditions help Haitians defeat the French? **(b)** Do you think the distance between Europe and Latin America affected the Latin American wars for independence? Explain.

In 1814, after a defeat in Caracas, Venezuela, Simón Bolívar fled to the British colony of Jamaica. There, he wrote a letter stating his principles. Read the excerpt below and answer the questions that follow.

> "There is nothing we have not suffered at the hands of that unnatural stepmother—Spain. . . . Americans, under the existing Spanish system, occupy a position in society no better than that of serfs suitable for labor. . . . And even this status is surrounded with galling restrictions, such as the prohibition against the cultivation of European crops, the existence of royal monopolies, or the ban on factories. . . . To this add the exclusive trading privileges. . . . In short, do you wish to know what our future was?— simply the cultivation of the fields of indigo, grain, coffee, sugar cane, cacao, and cotton; raising cattle on the empty plains, hunting wild game in the wilderness; digging in the earth to mine gold for the insatiable greed of Spain."
>
> —Simón Bolívar, "Letter From Jamaica"

20. Why do you think Bolívar calls Spain an "unnatural stepmother"?

21. According to Bolívar, what position in society did Latin Americans occupy?

22. What restriction was placed on Latin American farmers?

23. Who had monopolies on some industries?

24. Why do you think there was a ban on factories?

25. What does Bolívar say was the ultimate purpose of all Latin American labor?

26. What do you think were the effects of the publication of this letter?

Use the Internet to do an in-depth study of one of the revolutions that you have studied in this chapter. Create an outline that identifies the causes, key events, and results of the revolution. Note the Internet sites that you used by listing their titles, authors, and addresses.

"You have the floor; explain yourself!"

In his satirical cartoons, French artist Honoré Daumier (1808–1879) protested unfair social conditions, legal injustices, and middle-class corruption. He was once imprisoned for drawing an unflattering caricature of the king. Study his cartoon titled "You have the floor; explain yourself!" Then, answer the following questions:

27. In this court scene, (a) who is the speaker? (b) What do his words mean?

28. How well do you think the accused will be able to defend himself?

29. In this cartoon, what do the unbalanced scales of justice symbolize?

30. Based on the cartoon, what was Daumier's view of the French justice system?

31. Do you think Daumier's cartoons helped bring about change? Explain.

Skills Tip

A political cartoon expresses one person's point of view. The cartoon may be fac tually accurate or inaccurate. To amuse the reader, a cartoon's message is often exaggerated.

Chapter 18

The Enlightenment and the American Revolution (1707–1800)

The Enlightenment was a movement in Western Europe and North America that sought to discover natural laws and apply them to social, political, and economic problems. Since the 1700s, Enlightenment ideas have spread around the world, creating upheaval and change as they have challenged established traditions.

- The ideas of thinkers such as Locke, Montesquieu, and Rousseau would justify revolutions and inspire principles of representative government.
- Enlightenment thinkers called *philosophes* applied the methods of science to their efforts to understand and improve society.
- Physiocrats rejected mercantilism in favor of laissez-faire economics.
- Despite a growing middle class, most Europeans remained peasants who lived in small rural villages, untouched by Enlightenment ideas.
- England established a constitutional monarchy and built the most powerful commercial empire in the world.
- After years of growing dissent, Britain's North American colonies won independence in the American Revolution.
- Inspired by Enlightenment ideas, the United States adopted a constitution that would serve as a model for other democratic nations.

Chapter 19

The French Revolution and Napoleon (1789–1815)

Between 1789 and 1815, the French Revolution destroyed an absolute monarchy and disrupted a social system that had existed for over a thousand years. These events ushered in the modern era in European politics.

- France was burdened by an outdated class system, a severe financial crisis, and a monarchy too indecisive to enact reforms.
- In 1789, dissatisfied members of the middle class called for a constitution and other reforms. Meanwhile, hunger and social resentment sparked rioting among peasants and poor city dwellers.
- In the first phase of the French Revolution, moderates attempted to limit the power of the monarchy and guarantee basic rights of the people.
- In 1793, as enemies outside France denounced the revolution, radicals executed the king and queen and began a Reign of Terror.
- From 1799 to 1815, Napoleon Bonaparte consolidated his power within France and subdued the combined forces of the greatest powers of Europe.
- Under Napoleon, French armies spread the ideas of revolution across Europe.
- In 1815, the Congress of Vienna sought to undo the effects of the French Revolution and the Napoleonic era.

1725   **1750**   **1775**

 AFRICA

1700s Islamic revival in Africa

 THE AMERICAS

1763 Britain wins control of Canada

1775 American Revolution begins

 ASIA AND OCEANIA

1756 Seven Years' War affects India

1770 Cook claims Australia for Britain

 **EUROPE**

1751 Diderot publishes *Encyclopedia*

1764 Spinning jenny invented

Chapter 20

The Industrial Revolution Begins
(1750–1850)

During the 1700s, production began to shift from simple hand tools to complex machines, and new sources of energy replaced human and animal power. Known as the Industrial Revolution, this transformation marked a crucial turning point in history and changed the lives of people all over the world.

- An agricultural revolution contributed to a population explosion that, in turn, fed the growing industrial labor force.
- Abundant resources and a favorable business climate allowed Britain to take an early lead in industrialization.
- New sources of energy, such as coal and steam, fueled factories and paved the way for faster means of transporting people and goods.
- A series of remarkable inventions revolutionized the British textile industry and led to the creation of the first factories.
- Rapid urbanization and the rise of the factory system at first created dismal living and working conditions.
- Laissez-faire economists, utilitarians, and socialists put forth their own ideas for solving the problems of industrial society.
- Karl Marx promoted communism, a radical form of socialism that would have a worldwide influence.

Chapter 21

Revolutions in Europe and Latin America
(1790–1848)

With the Congress of Vienna, the great powers sought to return to the political and social order that had existed prior to 1789. However, in the early 1800s, a wave of violent uprisings swept across Western Europe and Latin America, fueled by the political ideas of the French Revolution and the economic problems of the Industrial Revolution.

- Two opposing ideologies emerged in Europe. Liberals embraced Enlightenment ideas of democracy and individual rights, while conservatives sought to preserve the old political and social order.
- Nationalism inspired independence movements among peoples with a shared heritage but also bred intolerance and persecution of minorities.
- In 1830 and 1848, ideological tensions and social inequalities sparked uprisings in France and elsewhere in Europe. Although most of these democratic revolutions were suppressed, they served to hasten reform later in the century.
- In Latin America, discontent with foreign domination led to a series of independence movements that freed most of the region from colonial rule by 1825.

1800   **1825**   **1850**

1788 Futa Toro outlaws slave trade

1830s Boers begin Great Trek

1818 Shaka begins Zulu conquests

1847 Liberia becomes independent

1789 United States Constitution takes effect

1819 Bolívar captures Bogotá

1810 "El Grito de Dolores" in Mexico

1793 Emperor Qianlong rejects British trade

1839 Opium War begins in China

1789 French Revolution begins

1804 Napoleon becomes emperor

1815 Congress of Vienna

1830 First railway opens in Britain

1848 Revolutions sweep Europe; *The Communist Manifesto* published

A Look Ahead: The Modern Era

Industrialism and a New Global Age

Life in the Industrial Age (1800–1914)

From the mid-1800s, industrialism spread rapidly across Europe to North America and beyond. This second Industrial Revolution transformed the economies of the world and solidified patterns of life familiar to us today.

- By the mid-1800s, other western nations—particularly Germany and the United States—were challenging Britain's position as the world's industrial giant.
- Steel, electricity, and advances in communications and transportation marked the second Industrial Revolution.
- By the late 1800s, "big business" came increasingly to dominate industry.
- With the spread of industry, a more complex social structure, dominated by middle-class values, evolved. Although the poor endured harsh conditions, the overall standard of living for workers improved.
- Artistic movements such as romanticism, realism, and expressionism reflected various responses to social and technological changes.

Nationalism Triumphs in Europe (1800–1914)

The 1800s saw an upsurge of nationalism in Europe. Nationalism unified some countries and sparked divisiveness and conflict in others.

- Between 1862 and 1890, Otto von Bismarck molded the German states into a powerful empire. To strengthen the German state, Bismarck promoted economic development, aggressive foreign policy goals, and domestic reforms.
- Although nationalist forces unified Italy in 1870, a long history of fragmentation created a host of problems for the new state.
- Nationalist feelings among diverse ethnic groups in Eastern Europe created widespread unrest and helped hasten the decline of the Ottoman and Hapsburg empires.
- Reluctant to surrender absolute power, Russian czars of the 1800s swung between reform and repression.

Growth of Western Democracies (1815–1914)

In Britain, France, and the United States, reformers struggled for an extension of democratic rights and social change. Although many inequalities persisted, these efforts paved the way for great improvements in the quality of life.

- The British Parliament passed a series of reforms designed to help those whose labor supported the new industrial society. Suffrage was extended to all male citizens, prompting women to seek the vote as well.
- Following its defeat in the Franco-Prussian War and a fierce internal revolt, France established the Third Republic, which instituted a series of important reforms.
- By 1900, the United States had become the world's leading industrial giant, a global power, and a magnet for immigrants seeking freedom and opportunity.

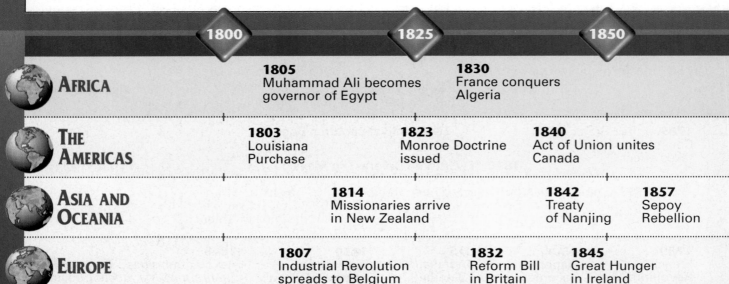

	1800	1825	1850
AFRICA	**1805** Muhammad Ali becomes governor of Egypt	**1830** France conquers Algeria	
THE AMERICAS	**1803** Louisiana Purchase	**1823** Monroe Doctrine issued	**1840** Act of Union unites Canada
ASIA AND OCEANIA	**1814** Missionaries arrive in New Zealand		**1842** Treaty of Nanjing **1857** Sepoy Rebellion
EUROPE	**1807** Industrial Revolution spreads to Belgium	**1832** Reform Bill in Britain	**1845** Great Hunger in Ireland

The New Imperialism
(1800–1914)

During the 1800s, European powers embarked on a period of aggressive expansion known as the Age of Imperialism. Despite fierce resistance, these powers brought much of the world under their control between 1870 and 1914.

- The Industrial Revolution gave western powers both the means and the motives to seek global domination.
- With little regard for traditional patterns of settlement, European powers partitioned almost the entire African continent.
- Taking advantage of the slowly crumbling Ottoman empire, Britain, France, and Russia competed to extend their influence over Algeria, Egypt, and other Ottoman lands.
- Britain set up a profitable system of colonial rule, controlling over 60 percent of India.
- Western powers carved out spheres of influence along the Chinese coast. China tried unsuccessfully to resist foreign influence with belated efforts at modernization and reform.
- By the early 1900s, leaders in many colonized regions were forging their own nationalist movements.

New Global Patterns
(1800–1914)

Imperialism resulted in a global exchange that profited industrial nations but disrupted local economies in Africa, Asia, and Latin America. Radical changes reshaped the lives of both subject peoples and westerners.

- As a defense against western imperialism, Japan transformed itself into a modern industrial power and set out on its own imperialist path.
- By 1900, western powers had claimed most islands in the Pacific and divided up most of Southeast Asia.
- The British colonies of Canada, Australia, and New Zealand won independence relatively quickly.
- Although Latin American nations struggled to set up stable governments and economies, a pattern of military rule and economic dependency emerged.
- The United States created its own sphere of influence in the Western Hemisphere.
- Europeans forced subject peoples to accept western ideas about government, technology, and culture.

1875 **1900** **1925**

1869 Suez Canal opens

1884 Berlin Conference carves up Africa

1896 Ethiopia defeats Italy at battle of Adowa

1876 Diaz gains power in Mexico

1898 Spanish-American War

1914 Panama Canal opens

1868 Meiji restoration begins

1885 Indian National Congress formed

1900 Boxer Uprising in China

1908 Young Turks overthrow sultan

1870 Italy unified

1871 Germany unified

1894 Dreyfus affair begins

1905 Bloody Sunday in Russia

1918 Women win suffrage in Britain

World Wars and Revolutions

World War I and Its Aftermath (1914–1919)

Many forces—including nationalism, militarism, and imperialist rivalries—propelled Europe into World War I. This massive conflict engulfed much of the world for four years and ushered in a new age of modern warfare.

- Two huge alliances emerged in Europe: the Central Powers, dominated by Germany and Austria-Hungary, and the Allies, led by France, Britain, and Russia.
- Although the assassination of Archduke Francis Ferdinand in 1914 ignited World War I, historians agree that all the major powers share blame for the conflict.
- Trench warfare and new weapons contributed to a stalemate on the Western Front.
- In 1917, the United States entered the war, allowing the Allies to achieve victory.
- The Paris Peace Conference imposed heavy penalties on Germany and redrew the map of Eastern Europe.

Revolution in Russia (1917–1939)

Lenin and his successors transformed czarist Russia into the communist Soviet Union. This experiment in single-party politics and a state-run economy would exert a powerful influence over the modern world for almost 75 years.

- In March 1917, political, social, and economic conditions in Russia sparked a revolution that overthrew the czar and paved the way for more radical changes.
- After leading the Bolsheviks to power in November 1917, Lenin hoped to build a communist state based on the ideas of Marx.
- Lenin's successor, Stalin, imposed "five-year plans" to build industry and increase farm output.
- Stalin created a totalitarian state, employing censorship, propaganda, and terror to ensure personal power and push the Soviet Union toward modernization.

Nationalism and Revolution Around the World (1910–1939)

Between 1919 and 1939, the desire for democracy and self-determination contributed to explosive struggles in many regions. New leaders in Africa, Latin America, and Asia built liberation movements that would change the world.

- The Mexican revolution opened the door to social and economic reforms.
- African leaders opposed imperialism and reaffirmed traditional cultures.
- Arab Nationalism led to Pan-Arabism, uniting Arabs against foreign domination.
- In India, Gandhi led a campaign of nonviolent resistance to British rule.
- In China, foreigners extended their spheres of influence. Later, Communists and Nationalists engaged in civil war.
- In the 1920s and 1930s, extreme nationalism and economic upheaval set Japan on a militaristic and expansionist path.

1910   **1920**   **1930**

AFRICA
1912 African National Congress formed in South Africa
1919 First Pan-African Congress held in Paris

THE AMERICAS
1910 Mexican Revolution begins
1919 Red Scare in United States
1929 Stock market crash

ASIA AND OCEANIA
1911 Civil war in China
1923 Atatürk begins modernization of Turkey

EUROPE
1914 World War I begins
1917 Russian Revolution
1922 Mussolini rules Italy
1933 Hitler rules Germany

Crisis of Democracy in the West
(1919–1939)

After World War I, western nations worked to restore prosperity and ensure peace. At the same time, political and economic turmoil in the 1920s and 1930s challenged democratic traditions and led to the rise of dictators.

- The Great Depression of the 1930s created financial turmoil and widespread suffering throughout the industrialized world.
- Scientific discoveries, new trends in literature and the arts, and social changes all contributed to a sense of uncertainty.
- Unrest in Italy helped Mussolini lead his Fascist party to power in the 1920s.
- In Germany, Hitler rose to power by appealing to extreme nationalism, antisemitism, anti-communism, and resentment of the Treaty of Versailles. In the 1930s, he turned the German state into a totalitarian Nazi dictatorship.
- Three systems of government—democracy, communism, and fascism—competed for influence in postwar Europe.

World War II and Its Aftermath
(1931–1955)

Between 1939 and 1945, nations all over the globe fought World War II, the largest and most costly conflict in history. The war shifted the balance of world power from Western Europe to the United States and the Soviet Union.

- The Axis powers—Germany, Italy, and Japan—embarked on a course of aggression in the late 1930s. France and Britain first adopted a policy of appeasement but declared war when Hitler invaded Poland.
- During the Holocaust, the Nazis systematically killed more than six million Jews, as well as millions of other people the Nazis considered undesirable.
- The United States, the Soviet Union, and the Allied Powers joined to defeat Germany.
- To force a Japanese surrender, the United States dropped two atomic bombs.
- The Cold War followed World War II, pitting the western democracies, led by the United States, against the communist bloc, dominated by the Soviet Union.

1940 **1950** **1960**

1935
Italy invades
Ethiopia

1948 South Africa makes apartheid
the law of the land

1941
Bombing of
Pearl Harbor

1947
United States announces
Marshall Plan

1930s
Gandhi leads
anti-British protests
in India

1945
Japan
surrenders and
World War II ends

1949
People's Republic of China
established

1939 World War II begins

1949 NATO formed

1941 Holocaust begins

1955 Warsaw Pact formed

The World Today

The World Since 1945: An Overview (1945–Present)

Since the end of World War II, the world has changed rapidly. Although we cannot yet determine the long-term impact of events of the recent past, we can identify political, social, and economic trends that have shaped the postwar years.

- The collapse of western colonial empires led to the emergence of nearly 100 new countries, mostly in Africa and Asia.
- Nuclear weapons, terrorism, and human rights are enduring issues in an increasingly interdependent world.
- Complex economic ties link the rich nations of the global North and the poor nations of the global South.
- Urbanization, modernization, women's movements, and technology have brought dramatic social changes.
- Technology has revolutionized medicine and agriculture and helped create a global, westernized popular culture.

Europe and North America (1945–Present)

Within a framework of growing regional cooperation, Western Europe enjoyed tremendous economic growth after World War II. At the same time, the Cold War pitted the West, led by the United States, against the Soviet Union and its allies.

- In the postwar era, Western European nations expanded social programs and introduced the welfare state. By the 1980s, an economic slowdown forced cuts in social programs.
- The United States led world opposition to communism, pursued economic prosperity, and extended civil rights.
- Efforts to reform inefficiencies in government and the economy led to the collapse of the Soviet Union.
- After shaking off Soviet domination, nations of Eastern Europe faced economic challenges and ethnic conflicts.

East Asia and Southeast Asia (1945–Present)

China, Japan, and other Asian nations have achieved varying degrees of success in their efforts to modernize. Several of these nations enjoy growing trade and other ties, linking the nations of the Pacific Rim from Asia to the Americas.

- After World War II, Japan introduced democratic reforms and by the 1960s had emerged as an economic superpower.
- Under Communist rule, the People's Republic of China achieved modest economic gains while sacrificing individual political freedoms.
- The "Asian tigers"—Taiwan, Hong Kong, Singapore, and South Korea—vaulted into the class of newly industrialized nations.
- Cold War tensions sparked long, devastating conflicts in Korea, Vietnam, and Cambodia.

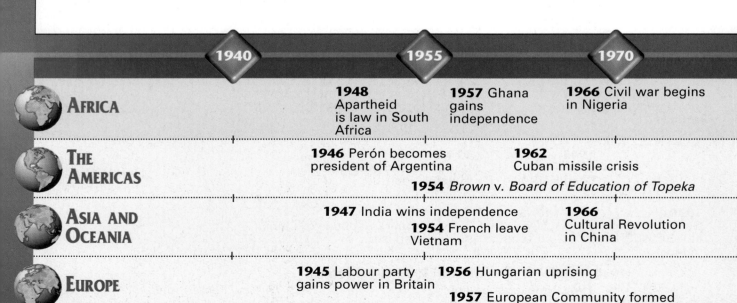

1940 **1955** **1970**

AFRICA

1948 Apartheid is law in South Africa

1957 Ghana gains independence

1966 Civil war begins in Nigeria

THE AMERICAS

1946 Perón becomes president of Argentina

1962 Cuban missile crisis

1954 *Brown* v. *Board of Education of Topeka*

ASIA AND OCEANIA

1947 India wins independence

1954 French leave Vietnam

1966 Cultural Revolution in China

EUROPE

1945 Labour party gains power in Britain

1956 Hungarian uprising

1957 European Community formed

South Asia and the Middle East (1945–Present)

In South Asia and the Middle East, nations cast off western rule and set out to modernize. They have often confronted similar challenges—from religious strife and border conflicts to urbanization and population growth.

- Upon achieving independence, India built on the legacy of British rule to create the world's largest democracy.
- Ethnic and religious rivalries have fueled ongoing conflict among people of South Asia.
- When secular governments in the Middle East did not yield promised improvements, some reformers rejected western models and called for a reaffirmation of Islamic values.
- The long Arab-Israeli struggle and other conflicts have focused world attention on the Middle East.

Africa (1945–Present)

Leaders of new African nations set out to build strong central governments, achieve economic growth, and raise standards of living. They have faced a variety of obstacles, including economic dependency and political instability.

- After independence, a number of new nations experienced military or one-party rule. Many have since introduced multi-party democracy.
- African nations experimented with different economic systems, including socialism and mixed economies.
- After decades of conflict, South Africa abandoned its system of apartheid in the 1990s and made a transition to democratic rule.
- In Africa, as elsewhere, modernization and urbanization have disrupted traditional cultures and ways of life.

Latin America (1945–Present)

Despite setbacks, Latin American nations have tried to sustain economic growth and overcome a legacy of poverty and social inequality. Marxism, military rule, and the Roman Catholic Church have been continuing influences in the region.

- In the postwar period, poverty and uneven distribution of wealth fed social unrest in many nations.
- Latin America was a focus of Cold War politics, especially after a communist revolution in Cuba in 1959.
- Through trade, investment, and military intervention, the United States was a dominant force in Latin America.
- Although Mexico enjoyed economic gains in agriculture and manufacturing, most people remained in poverty.
- Argentina and Brazil experienced economic growth and long periods of military rule.

1985   **2001**   **2015**

1980s Drought causes famine in parts of Africa
1994 Mandela wins first multiracial election in South Africa
2001 Bloody civil war continues in Congo

1993 Canada, United States, and Mexico sign NAFTA
2001 Terrorists attack World Trade Center and Pentagon

1979 Revolution in Iran   **1989** Tiananmen Square massacre in China
1998 India and Pakistan test nuclear weapons
2001 Terrorist camps bombed in Afghanistan

1970s Greece restores civilian rule
1991 Breakup of Soviet Union
1999 NATO air strikes against Serbia result in peace agreement
2002 Most of European Union introduces common currency into circulation

Reference Section

Contents

PRIMARY SOURCES AND LITERATURE

Instruction of Ptah-hotep

Ptah-hotep, who lived around 2450 B.C. in Egypt, was a vizier, or chief minister, to a pharaoh during the Old Kingdom. In the excerpt below, Ptah-hotep describes some practical rules for behavior that he believes will help his son live a successful life.

Vocabulary Before you read the selection, look up the following words in a dictionary: **arrogant, counsel, venture, council.**

> **Main Idea** In this letter, Ptah-hotep describes rules of behavior that he believes will help his son live a successful life.

Be not arrogant because of your knowledge, and be not puffed up because you are a learned man. Take counsel with the ignorant as with the learned, for the limits of art cannot be reached, and no artist is perfect in his skills. . . .

If you are a leader, commanding the conduct of many, seek out every good aim, so that your policy may be without error. A great thing is truth, enduring and surviving; it has not been upset since the time of Osiris. He who departs from its laws is punished. It is the right path for him who knows nothing. Wrongdoing has never brought its venture safe to port. Evil may win riches, but it is the strength of truth that it endures long. . . .

If you want your conduct to be good, free from every evil, then beware of greed. It is an evil and incurable sickness. No man can live with it; it causes divisions between fathers and mothers, and between brothers of the same mother; it parts wife and husband; it is a gathering of every evil, a bag of everything hateful. A man thrives if his conduct is right. He who follows the right course wins wealth thereby. But the greedy man has no tomb. . . .

If you are a worthy man sitting in the council of his lord, confine your attention to excellence. Silence is more valuable than chatter. Speak only when you know you can resolve difficulties. He who gives good counsel is an artist, for speech is more difficult than any craft. . . .

If you listen to my sayings, then all your affairs will go forward. . . . If the son of a man accepts what his father says, no plan of his will fail. . . . Failure follows him who does not listen. . . .

Egyptian tomb painting

Analyzing Primary Sources

1. Which of the following statements best summarizes the main idea of the fourth paragraph?

   A Speak only when you have something helpful to say.

   B Achieve excellence so that you may council the lord.

   C Remain silent while in the council of the lord.

   D Give good counsel in order to gain wealth.

2. The author wishes his son to listen to his advice so that his son will be

   E greedy.

   F sick.

   G successful.

   H arrogant.

3. **Critical Thinking Making Inferences** What do you think Ptah-hotep means by the phrase "the greedy man has no tomb" (third paragraph)?

The Epic of Gilgamesh

The Sumerian *Epic of Gilgamesh* dates from about 2000 B.C. It is a collection of tales about a hero named Gilgamesh. The main themes of the poem are the unpredictability of the gods and the inevitability of death. These themes may be a reflection of life in Sumer, where the flooding of the Tigris and Euphrates rivers was both unpredictable and devastating.

Vocabulary Before you read the selection, look up the following words in a dictionary: **attain, slough, boon.**

> **Main Idea** In this epic poem, Gilgamesh comes to realize that death is the common lot of all people, even fearless heroes.

Utnapishtim says to him, to Gilgamesh. . . .
"About a plant I will tell thee. . . .
Its thorns will prick thy hands just as does the rose.
If thy hands obtain the plant, thou wilt attain [eternal] life."
No sooner had Gilgamesh heard this, . . .
He tied heavy stones to his feet.
They pulled him down into the deep and he saw the plant.
He took the plant, though it pricked his hands.
He cut the heavy stones from his feet.
The sea cast him up upon its shore.
Gilgamesh says to him, to Urshanabi, the boatman:
"Urshanabi, this plant is a plant apart,
Whereby a man may regain his life's breath. . . .
Its name shall be 'Man Becomes Young in Old Age.'
I myself shall eat it
And thus return to the state of my youth."
Gilgamesh saw a well whose water was cool.
He went down into it to bathe in the water.
A serpent snuffed the fragrance of the plant;
It came up from the water and carried off the plant,
Going back to shed its slough.
Thereupon Gilgamesh sits down and weeps.
His tears running down over his face.
He took the hand of Urshanabi, the boatman:
"For whom, Urshanabi, have my hands toiled?
For whom is being spent the blood of my heart?
I have not obtained a boon for myself.
For the serpent have I effected a boon!"

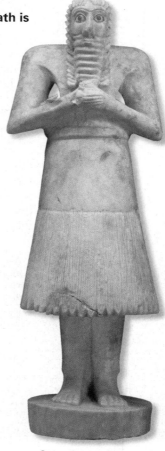

Sumerian sculpture

Analyzing Literature

1. What does Gilgamesh decide to do after hearing Utnapishtim?
   - **A** seek help from a boatman named Urshanabi
   - **B** search for a plant that brings eternal life
   - **C** bathe in a well with cool water
   - **D** battle a serpent who carries away youth

2. At the end of this selection, Gilgamesh weeps because
   - **E** the serpent has shed its skin.
   - **F** he has toiled with his hands for too long.
   - **G** he has failed to find everlasting life and must accept death.
   - **H** he has eaten all of the plant.

3. **Critical Thinking Synthesizing Information** Which physical characteristic of a snake leads the author to choose it as the creature who benefits from the plant?

Psalm 23

The Psalms are a collection of 150 religious hymns. These songs reflect the Israelites' belief in their God as the powerful savior of Israel. Many of the psalms praise the faithfulness of God to each of his people. In this psalm, the speaker describes his faith in God's protection.

Vocabulary Before you read the selection, look up the following words in a dictionary: **righteousness, anoint.**

Main Idea The Twenty-Third Psalm celebrates the Israelites' sense of a special relationship with a loving God.

The LORD is my shepherd, I shall not want;

he makes me lie down in green pastures.
He leads me beside still waters;

he restores my soul.
He leads me in paths of righteousness
for his name's sake.

Even though I walk through the valley of the shadow of death,
I fear no evil;
for thou art with me;
thy rod and thy staff,
they comfort me.

Thou preparest a table before me
in the presence of my enemies;
thou anointest my head with oil,
my cup overflows.

Surely goodness and mercy shall follow me
all the days of my life;
and I shall dwell in the house of the LORD
for ever.

Prayer book in Hebrew

Analyzing Literature

1. The speaker of the Twenty-Third Psalm says that he

   A feels protected by God.

   B feels abandoned by God.

   C fears the anger of God.

   D fears Israel's enemies.

2. According to the speaker, God's strength

   E helps the sheep find water.

   F overcomes the power of death.

   G provides housing and food for the Israelites.

   H builds an army to defeat the enemies of the Israelites.

3. **Critical Thinking Making Generalizations**
   (a) Identify the qualities of God and the Israelites that lead the speaker to compare God to a shepherd. **(b)** How does the Twenty-Third Psalm reflect some of the basic beliefs of Jewish monotheism?

Confucius: *Analects*

The *Analects* are a collection of 497 verses recorded by Confucius' followers long after his death (perhaps in the fourth century B.C.). Confucius' teachings emphasize duty and responsibility as a means of ensuring social order and good government.

Vocabulary Before you read the selection, look up the following words in a dictionary: **homage, bias, induce, piety, incompetent.**

Main Idea | **In these sayings, Confucius emphasizes that education and self-sacrifice are the keys to becoming a superior person.**

The Master said, He who rules by moral force is like the pole-star, which remains in its place while all the lesser stars do homage to it.

The Master said, If out of the three hundred Songs I had to take one phrase to cover all my teaching, I would say 'Let there be no evil in your thoughts.'

Mêng Wu Po asked about the treatment of parents. The Master said, Behave in such a way that your father and mother have no anxiety about you, except concerning your health.

Tzu-kung asked about the true gentleman. The Master said, He does not preach what he practices till he has practiced what he preaches.

The Master said, A gentleman can see a question from all sides without bias. The small man is biased and can see a question only from one side.

The Master said, Yu, shall I teach you what knowledge is? When you know a thing, to recognize that you know it, and when you do not know a thing, to recognize that you do not know it. That is knowledge.

Chi K'ang-tzu asked whether there were any form of encouragement by which he could induce the common people to be respectful and loyal. The Master said, Approach them with dignity, and they will respect you. Show piety towards your parents and kindness towards your children, and they will be loyal to you. Promote those who are worthy, train those who are incompetent; that is the best form of encouragement.

Confucius

Analyzing Primary Sources

1. According to the excerpts, which one saying did Confucius pick to best summarize his teachings?

   A Show piety towards your parents and kindness towards your children.

   B Let there be no evil in your thoughts.

   C He does not preach what he practices till he has practiced what he preaches.

   D A gentleman can see a question from all sides without bias.

2. Confucius says that a gentleman

   E is knowledgeable.

   F is respectful and loyal.

   G can understand more than one point of view on a question or issue.

   H can recognize those who are worthy.

3. **Critical Thinking Identifying Main Ideas** Use your own words to describe Confucius' definition of knowledge.

Thucydides: *History of the Peloponnesian War*

This excerpt from Thucydides' *History of the Peloponnesian War* records a speech made by the Athenian leader Pericles in honor of those who died fighting Sparta in the first year of the war (431 B.C.). In the speech, Pericles describes the superior qualities of Athenian democracy as compared with life in Sparta.

Vocabulary Before you read the selection, look up the following words in a dictionary: **extravagance, vainglory, degradation, absorption, aloof, notwithstanding, attainment.**

> **Main Idea** This speech by the Athenian leader Pericles is one of the most famous defenses of democracy of all time.

For our government is not copied from those of our neighbors: we are an example to them rather than they to us. Our constitution is named a democracy, because it is in the hands not of the few but of the many. But our laws secure equal justice for all in their private disputes, and our public opinion welcomes and honors talent in every branch of achievement, not for any sectional reason but on grounds of excellence alone. And as we give free play to all in our public life, so we carry the same spirit into our daily relations with one another. . . .

We are lovers of beauty without extravagance, and lovers of wisdom without unmanliness. Wealth to us is not mere material for vainglory but an opportunity for achievement; and poverty we think it no disgrace to acknowledge but a real degradation to make no effort to overcome. Our citizens attend both to public and private duties, and do not allow absorption in their own various affairs to interfere with their knowledge of the city's. We differ from other states in regarding the man who holds aloof from public life not as 'quiet' but as useless; we decide or debate, carefully and in person, all matters of policy, holding, not that words and deeds go ill together, but that acts are foredoomed to failure when undertaken undiscussed. For we are noted for being at once adventurous in action and most reflective beforehand. Other men are bold in ignorance, while reflection will stop their onset. But the bravest are surely those who have the clearest vision of what is before them, glory and danger alike, and yet notwithstanding go out to meet it. . . . In a word I claim that our city as a whole is an education to Greece, and that her members yield to none, man by man, for independence of spirit, many-sidedness of attainment, and complete self-reliance in limbs and brain.

The Parthenon in Athens

Analyzing Primary Sources

1. Pericles defines democracy as a system based on

   A equal justice for all in their private disputes.

   B the say of many citizens, not just a few.

   C beauty without extravagance and wisdom without unmanliness.

   D free play in public life.

2. According to Pericles, a good citizen

   E participates fully in public debate.

   F is quiet during public debate.

   G acts boldly without discussion.

   H attends exclusively to his own business.

3. **Critical Thinking Synthesizing Information** What does Pericles mean when he states that Athens is "an education to Greece"?

Aristotle: *The Politics*

The Greek philosopher Aristotle (384 B.C.–322 B.C.) was suspicious of democracy, which he thought could lead to mob rule. Instead, Aristotle favored rule by a single strong and virtuous leader. In this excerpt from *The Politics*, Aristotle outlines the forms of government and discusses the strengths and weaknesses of each form.

Vocabulary Before you read the selection, look up the following words in a dictionary: **treatise, constituted, despotic, generic.**

Main Idea In this selection, Aristotle describes the characteristics of an ideal state as well as practical matters relating to the preservation and improvement of government.

First let us consider what is the purpose of a state and how many forms of government there are by which human society is regulated. We have already said, earlier in this treatise . . . that man is by nature a political animal. And therefore men, even when they do not require one another's help, desire to live together all the same, and are in fact brought together by their common interests. . . . Well-being is certainly the chief end of individuals and of states. . . .

The conclusion is evident: governments which have a regard to the common interest are constituted in accordance with strict principles of justice, and are therefore true forms; but those which regard only the interest of the rulers are all defective and perverted forms. For they are despotic, whereas a state is a community of free men. . . .

We call that form of government in which one rules, and which regards the common interest, kingship or royalty; that in which more than one, but not many, rule, aristocracy. It is so called, either because the rulers are the best men, or because they have at heart the best interest of the state and of the citizens. But when the citizens at large administer the state for the common interest, the government is called by the generic name—constitutional government. . . .

Of the above-mentioned forms, the perversions are as follows: of royalty, tyranny; of aristocracy, oligarchy; of constitutional government, democracy. For tyranny is a kind of monarchy which has in view the interest of the monarch only; oligarchy has in view the interest of the wealthy; democracy, of the needy; none of them the common good of all.

Students at an Athenian school

Analyzing Primary Sources

1. According to Aristotle, the form of government known as constitutional government is one in which

   A one rules, and which regards the common interest.

   B the citizens at large administer the state for the common interest.

   C more than one, but not many, rule.

   D the interests of the needy are placed above all.

2. Which of the following does Aristotle describe as the corrupt form of aristocracy?

   E tyranny

   F oligarchy

   G monarchy

   H democracy

3. **Critical Thinking Identifying Main Ideas** What do you think Aristotle means when he states that "man is by nature a political animal"?

The Mahabharata

An epic of the ancient Aryans, the *Mahabharata* became a major source of Hindu social and religious doctrine. Indian storytellers still recite segments of the 100,000 stanzas to entertain and instruct village audiences. This excerpt tells of the rewards the god Indra bestows upon a dutiful king, Vasu.

Vocabulary Before you read the selection, look up the following words in a dictionary: **accustomed, celestial, crystalline, garland, lotuses, sustain, renowned.**

Main Idea **In this epic, an Indian king is given earthly rule and supernatural gifts as reward for upholding the law of the gods.**

Two Hindu gods

Indra said:

May never on earth, O lord of this earth, the Law be confused! Protect it, for the upheld Law holds up all the world. Guard thee this worldly Law, forever on guard and attentive; if yoked to the Law, you shall win the blessed worlds of eternity. You standing on earth have become the dear friend of me standing in heaven—now possess . . . a country beyond all others, with riches and jewels and all good things—Mother Earth, mother of plenty: live on her in the land of the Cedis, king of the Cedis!

The country people are accustomed to the Law, quite content and upright. No lies are spoken there even in jest, let alone in earnest. Sons are devoted to their elders there; they do not divide off from their fathers. Cows are never yoked to the cart, and even lean cows yield plenty. All the classes abide by their own Law, in this land of the Cedis. . . .

This large celestial crystalline chariot in the sky, which it is the God's privilege to enjoy, this airborne chariot will come to you as my gift. Among all mortals you alone shall stand upon a grand and sky-going chariot, and indeed, you will ride there above, like a God come to flesh! And I give you this garland Vaijayanti, woven of lotuses that never fade, which shall sustain you in battle, never hurt by swords. That shall be your mark of distinction here, sovereign of men—grand, rich, unmatched, and renowned as "India's Garland"!

Analyzing Literature

1. What does Indra say will be Vasu's reward for pleasing the gods?

   A Vasu will be given a place among the gods.

   B Vasu will receive jewels and a herd of cattle.

   C Vasu will ride through the skies on a crystal chariot.

   D Vasu will not be required to obey the Law.

2. According to Indra, Vasu will rule

   E Mother Earth.

   F the heavens.

   G his sons.

   H the afterlife.

3. **Critical Thinking Making Inferences** The heroes of epics frequently embody the values of the cultures that produced them. Describe some of the values that King Vasu represents.

Asoka: *Edicts*

During his rule of Maurya India beginning in 268 B.C., Asoka converted to Buddhism, rejected violence, and resolved to rule by moral example. Asoka had stone pillars set up across India announcing laws, or edicts, and describing the just actions of his government. The following are excerpts from several of the pillars.

Vocabulary Before you read the selection, look up the following words in a dictionary: **righteousness, circumspection, disparages, concord, conformity, exhortation, abstention.**

Main Idea The stone pillars set up across India by Asoka announced laws and promised fair and just government.

This world and the other are hard to gain without great love of Righteousness, great self-examination, great obedience, great circumspection, great effort. Through my instruction respect and love of Righteousness daily increase and will increase. . . . For this is my rule—to govern by Righteousness, to administer by Righteousness, to please my subjects by Righteousness, and to protect them by Righteousness.

Whoever honors his own [religion] and disparages another man's, whether from blind loyalty or with the intention of showing his own [religion] in a favorable light, does his own [religion] the greatest possible harm. Concord is best, with each hearing and respecting the other's teachings. It is the wish of the [king] that members of all [religions] should be learned and should teach virtue.

All the good deeds that I have done have been accepted and followed by the people. And so obedience to mother and father, obedience to teachers, respect for the aged, kindliness . . . to the poor and weak, and to slaves and servants, have increased and will continue to increase. . . . And this progress of Righteousness . . . has taken place in two manners, by enforcing conformity to Righteousness, and by exhortation. I have enforced the law against killing certain animals and many others, but the greatest progress of Righteousness . . . comes from exhortation in favor of noninjury to life and abstention from killing living beings.

I have done this that it may endure . . . as long as the moon and sun, and that my sons and my great-grandsons may support it; for by supporting it they will gain both this world and the next.

Sculpture from one of Asoka's pillars

Analyzing Primary Sources

1. This excerpt from the Edicts provides evidence that Asoka

   A was in favor of performing animal sacrifices.

   B wanted to place Buddhism above all other religions.

   C believed in the power of daily religious rituals.

   D sought to promote tolerance of diverse religions.

2. Based on the passage you can tell that Asoka was probably a

   E vegetarian.

   F monk.

   G dictator.

   H judge.

3. **Critical Thinking Drawing Conclusions**
   Which of his actions does Asoka view as the best promotion of Righteousness? Why do you think this is so?

St. Paul:
First Letter to the Corinthians

Around A.D. 51, Paul founded a Christian community in the thriving commercial city of Corinth. After his departure, he wrote two letters to the newly converted Christians to encourage and guide them in their faith. This excerpt from Paul's First Letter to the Corinthians focuses on the importance of love in a Christian life.

Vocabulary Before you read the selection, look up the following word in a dictionary: **prophetic**.

Main Idea In this letter, Paul declares that, for a Christian, love is more important than any other quality.

If I speak in the tongues of men and of angels, but have not love, I am a noisy gong or a clanging cymbal. And if I have prophetic powers and understand all mysteries and all knowledge, and if I have all faith, so as to remove mountains, but have no love, I am nothing. If I give away all I have, and if I deliver my body to be burned, but have not love, I gain nothing.

Love is patient and kind; love is not jealous or boastful; it is not arrogant or rude. Love does not insist on its own way; it is not irritable or resentful; it does not rejoice at wrong, but rejoices in the right. Love bears all things, believes all things, hopes all things, endures all things.

Love never ends; as for prophecies, they will pass away; as for tongues, they will cease; as for knowledge, it will pass away. For our knowledge is imperfect and our prophecy is imperfect; but when the perfect comes, the imperfect will pass away. When I was a child, I spoke like a child, I thought like a child, I reasoned like a child; when I became a man, I gave up childish ways. For now we see in a mirror dimly, but then face to face. Now I know in part; then I shall understand fully, even as I have been fully understood. So faith, hope, love abide, these three; but the greatest of these is love.

Early Christian symbols

Analyzing Primary Sources

1. In his letter to the Corinthians, Paul states that love

   A can be fully understood by people in this life.

   B is a greater virtue than knowledge or faith.

   C has the power to remove mountains.

   D will pass away with an individual's death.

2. According to Paul, people will be able to achieve perfect knowledge when they

   E reach adulthood.

   F love their neighbors.

   G come face to face with God.

   H have prophetic powers.

3. **Critical Thinking Synthesizing Information** What does Paul mean when he says love "endures all things"?

The Quran

The Quran, the holy scriptures of Islam, contains 114 suras, or verses. Muslims believe that the Quran is the actual word of God as revealed to the prophet Muhammad. This excerpt from the Quran tells the faithful what they should do to be righteous and faithful Muslims.

Vocabulary Before you read the selection, look up the following words in a dictionary: **wayfarers, redemption, alms, perchance.**

Main Idea | **This excerpt from the Quran encourages believers to fast and observe the holy month of Ramadan.**

Righteousness does not consist in whether you face towards the east or the west. The righteous man is he who believes in God and the Last Day, in the angels and the Scriptures and the prophets; who for the love of God gives his wealth to his kinsfolk, to the orphans, to the needy, to the wayfarers and to the beggars, and for the redemption of captives; who attends to his prayers and pays the alms-tax; who is true to his promises and steadfast in trial and adversity and in times of war. Such are the true believers; such are the god fearing. . . .

Believers, fasting is decreed for you as it was decreed for those before you; perchance you will guard yourselves against evil. Fast a certain number of days, but if any one of you is ill or on a journey let him fast a similar number of days later on; and for those that can afford it there is a ransom: the feeding of a poor man. He that does good of his own account shall be rewarded; but to fast is better for you, if you but knew it.

In the month of Ramadan the Quran was revealed, a book of guidance with proofs of guidance distinguishing right from wrong. Therefore whoever of you is present in that month let him fast. But he who is ill or on a journey shall fast a similar number of days later on.

God desires your well-being, not your discomfort. He desires you to fast the whole month so that you may magnify Him and render thanks to Him for giving you his guidance.

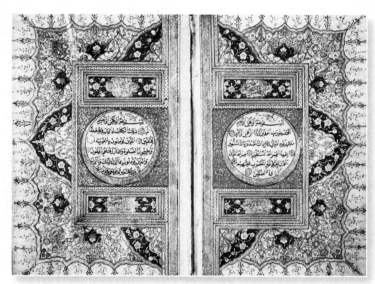

Pages from the Quran

Analyzing Primary Sources

1. According to the excerpt above, what is one goal of the Quran?

   A It helps the faithful distinguish right from wrong.

   B It helps the faithful guard against evil.

   C It helps the faithful question the will of God.

   D It helps the faithful increase their worldly wealth.

2. The "righteous man" does not have to fast during Ramadan if he

   E gives money to the poor.

   F is ill.

   G believes in God.

   H has not committed evil acts.

3. **Critical Thinking Applying Information** How does this passage from the Quran support the five pillars of Islam?

Murasaki Shikibu:
The Tale of Genji

Murasaki Shikibu's *Tale of Genji* **is considered one of the finest works of Japanese literature. The novel provides insight into the court life and mores of tenth-century Japan. In this excerpt, the elaborate rituals associated with Prince Genji's transition from childhood to manhood are described. The passage also reflects the Japanese aristocracy's emphasis on official titles and social ranks.**

Vocabulary Before you read the selection, look up the following words in a dictionary: **initiation, zeal, prescribed, loath, homage, chamberlain, obeisance.**

Main Idea | **This excerpt from the novel describes the royal coming of age ceremony in Heian Japan.**

Though it seemed a shame to put so lovely a child into man's dress, he was now twelve years old and the time for his Initiation was come. The Emperor directed the preparations with tireless zeal and insisted upon a magnificence beyond what was prescribed. . . .

Genji arrived at the hour of the Monkey [3 P.M.]. He looked very handsome with his long childish locks, and the Sponsor, whose duty it had just been to bind them with the purple filet, was sorry to think that all this would soon be changed and even the Clerk of the Treasury seemed loath to sever those lovely tresses with the ritual knife. . . .

Duly crowned, Genji went to his chamber and changing into man's dress went down into the courtyard and performed the Dance of Homage, which he did with such grace that tears stood in every eye. . . .

When the courtiers assembled to drink the Love Cup, Genji came and took his place among the other princes. The Minister of the Left came up and whispered something in his ear; but the boy blushed and could think of no reply. A chamberlain now came over to the Minister and brought him a summons to wait upon His Majesty immediately. . . . Then, when he had made him drink out of the Royal Cup, the Emperor recited a poem in which he prayed that the binding of the purple filet might symbolize the union of their two houses; and the Minister answered him that nothing should sever this union save the fading of the purple band. Then he descended the long stairs and from the courtyard performed the Grand Obeisance. Here too were shown the horses from the Royal Stables and the hawks from the Royal Falconry, that had been decreed as presents for the Genji. At the foot of the stairs, the Princes and the Courtiers were lined up to receive their bounties, and gifts of every kind were showered upon them.

Lady Murasaki Shikibu

Analyzing Literature

1. Genji's initiation into manhood is symbolized by

   A his honored position at the Emperor's banquet.

   B the cutting of his hair and changing of his garments.

   C the lining up of the Princes for their gifts.

   D the Emperor's show of affection for the Prince.

2. The importance of the ceremony is reflected in the

   E social rank of the Minister of the Left.

   F performance of the Dance of Homage.

   G elaborate preparations and emphasis on social rank.

   H binding of the hair.

3. **Critical Thinking Linking Past and Present** What kinds of ceremonies do we have today that recognize the transition from childhood to adulthood?

Geoffrey Chaucer:
The Canterbury Tales

In *The Canterbury Tales*, Geoffrey Chaucer presents a portrait of English society in the 1300s. The story involves 29 men and women who tell stories to one another while on pilgrimage to the tomb of Thomas Becket in Canterbury. The detailed descriptions of each character provide a sharp look at three classes of medieval society: clergy, nobles, and common people. In these passages, Chaucer describes a noble knight, a wealthy merchant, and a humble plowman.

Vocabulary Before you read the selection, look up the following words in a dictionary: **sovereign, heathen, motley, estimable, negotiation**.

Main Idea In this poem, Chaucer describes three characters who represent different classes and occupations of medieval society.

There was a *Knight,* a most distinguished man,
Who from the day on which he first began
To ride abroad had followed chivalry,
Truth, honor, generousness, and courtesy.
He had done nobly in his sovereign's war
And ridden into battle, no man more,
As well in Christian as heathen places,
And ever honored for his noble graces. . . .

There was a Merchant with a forking beard
And motley dress; high on his horse he sat,
Upon his head a Flemish beaver hat
And on his feet daintily buckled boots. . . .
He was expert at currency exchange.
This estimable Merchant so had set
His wits to work, none knew he was in debt,
He was so stately in negotiation,
Loan, bargain, and commercial obligation. . . .

[The Plowman] was an honest worker, good and true,
Living in peace and perfect charity. . . .
For steadily about his work he went
To thrash his corn, to dig or to manure
Or make a ditch; and he would help the poor
For love of Christ and never take a penny
If he could help it, and, as prompt as any,
He paid his tithes in full when they were due. . . .

A medieval town

Analyzing Literature

1. What quality do the Knight and the Plowman have in common?

   A wealth

   B bravery

   C honesty

   D sharp wits

2. What conclusion can you draw from these passages?

   E The Knight fought in the Crusades.

   F The Merchant is successful at business.

   G The Plowman is overworked and desperately poor.

   H The Knight and the Merchant look down on the Plowman.

3. **Critical Thinking Applying Information**
   (a) Which of the three characters described in these excerpts represents a class of people who were powerful in early feudal society? **(b)** Which of these characters represents a class that grew more powerful in the High Middle Ages?

Niccolò Machiavelli: *Discourses*

The Florentine writer Niccolò Machiavelli (1469–1527) is best known for his book *The Prince,* in which he describes how a ruler can get and keep power. However, in his book *Discourses on the First Ten Books of Titus Livy,* Machiavelli concludes that the best-governed state is ruled by the people rather than by a ruthless prince.

Vocabulary Before you read the selection, look up the following words in a dictionary: **populace, subservient, licentious, trepidation**.

Main Idea In his *Discourses,* Machiavelli describes methods for establishing and preserving republics.

In short, to bring this topic to conclusion, I say that, just as princely forms of government have endured for a very long time, so, too, have republican forms of government; and that in both cases it has been essential for them to be regulated by laws. For a prince who does what he likes is a lunatic; and a populace which does what it likes is unwise. If, therefore, it be a question of a prince subservient to the laws and of a populace chained up by laws, more virtue will be found in the populace than in the prince; and if it be a question of either of them loosed from control by the law, there will be found fewer errors in the populace than in the prince, and these of less moment and much easier to put right. For a licentious and turbulent populace, when a good man can obtain a hearing, can easily be brought to behave itself; but there is no one to talk to a bad prince, nor is there any remedy except the sword. . . .

When the populace has thrown off all restraint, it is not the mad things it does that are terrifying, nor is it of present evils that one is afraid, but of what may come of them, for amidst such confusion there may come to be a tyrant. In the case of bad princes it is just the opposite: it is present evils that are terrifying, but for the future there is hope, since men are convinced that the evil ways of a bad prince may make for freedom in the end. . . . The reason why people are prejudiced against the populace is because of the populace anyone may speak ill without fear and openly, even when the populace is ruling. But of princes people speak with the utmost trepidation and the utmost reserve.

Analyzing Primary Sources

1. Machiavelli states that the only way to bring an unruly prince under the law is to

   A obtain a hearing.

   B use physical combat.

   C discuss the people's legal rights.

   D choose a tyrant.

2. Machiavelli concludes that the greatest threat posed by an unlawful populace is the

   E rise of a dictator.

   F violence of the mob.

   G loss of a prince.

   H destruction of property.

3. **Critical Thinking Making Inferences** **(a)** According to Machiavelli, what do princely and republican forms of government have in common? **(b)** Why do you think Machiavelli believes that the populace loosed from control is more subject to criticism than a prince loosed from control?

Bernal Díaz: *The True History of the Conquest of New Spain*

Bernal Díaz del Castillo (c. 1492–1581) accompanied Hernan Cortés on his conquest of the Aztecs in present-day Mexico. Díaz wrote his history many years later to refute what he viewed as inaccurate accounts of the conquest. The following excerpt describes a meeting between Cortés and Moctezuma, the Aztec king, in the Aztec city of Tenochtitlán.

Vocabulary Before you read the selection, look up the following words in a dictionary: **oratory, league.**

Main Idea This memoir provides an account of the Aztec capital of Tenochtitlán at the time of the Spanish conquest.

When we climbed to the top of the great [temple] there was a kind of platform, with huge stones where they put the poor Indians to be sacrificed, and an image like a dragon and other evil figures, with a great deal of blood that had been shed that day. Moctezuma, accompanied by two priests, came out from an oratory dedicated to the worship of his cursed idols. . . .

Then Moctezuma took him [Cortés] by the hand and bade him look at his great city and at all the other cities rising from the water, and the many towns around the lake. . . .

There we stood looking, for that large and evil temple was so high that it towered over everything. From there we could see all three of the causeways that led into Mexico. . . .

We saw the fresh water that came from Chapultepec, which supplied the city, and the bridges on the three causeways, built at certain intervals so the water could go from one part of the lake to another, and a multitude of canoes, some arriving with provisions and others leaving with merchandise. We saw that every house in this great city and in the others built on the water could be reached only by wooden drawbridges or by canoe. We saw temples built like towers and fortresses in these cities, all white-washed; it was a sight to see. . . .

After taking a good look and considering all that we had seen, we looked again at the great square and the throngs of people, some buying and others selling. The buzzing of their voices could be heard more than a league away. There were soldiers among us who had been in many parts of the world, in Constantinople and Rome and all over Italy, who said that they had never before seen a market place so large and so well laid out, and so filled with people.

Aztec gold ornament

Analyzing Primary Sources

1. What scene is Bernal Díaz describing in this excerpt?

   A a view of Tenochtitlán's market and surroundings from the top of a tall temple

   B an indoor temple with many religious statues

   C a view of Tenochtitlán's temple from the market place

   D a view of the markets in Constantinople and Rome

2. Which of the following best describes the author's view of the Aztecs?

   E generous and busy

   F evil and prosperous

   G loving and kind

   H athletic and loud

3. **Critical Thinking Recognizing Points of View** Which words and phrases in the excerpt above reveal the author's opinion of the Aztec's religion?

King Affonso I:
Letter to King John of Portugal

In 1490, the Portuguese converted the son of a Kongo king to Christianity and then helped him to assume his father's throne. The king, born Nzinga Mbemba, was renamed Affonso. King Affonso soon realized that his relationship with Portugal had extremely negative consequences, as can be seen from his letter in 1526 to King John of Portugal.

Vocabulary Before you read the selection, look up the following words in a dictionary: **comply, jurisdiction, depopulated.**

Main Idea In this letter, the king of Kongo asks the king of Portugal to end the slave trade.

African carving of Portuguese soldiers

Sir, Your Highness of Portugal should know how our Kingdom is being lost in so many ways. This is caused by the excessive freedom given by your officials to the men and merchants who are allowed to come to this Kingdom to set up shops with goods and many things which have been prohibited by us. Many of our vassals, whom we had in obedience, do not comply because they have the things in greater abundance than we ourselves. It was with these things that we had them content and subjected under our jurisdiction, so it is doing a great harm not only to the service of God, but to the security and peace of our Kingdoms and State as well.

And we cannot reckon how great the damage is, since the mentioned merchants are taking every day our natives, sons of the land and the sons of our noblemen and vassals and our relatives. The thieves and men of bad conscience grab them wishing to have the things and wares of this Kingdom which they are ambitious of; they grab them and get them to be sold. And so great, Sir, is the corruption and licentiousness that our country is being completely depopulated, and your Highness should not agree with this nor accept it as in your service. And to avoid it we need from those your Kingdoms no more than some priests and a few people to teach in schools, and no other goods except wine and flour for the holy sacrament.

That is why we beg of Your Highness to help and assist us in this matter, commanding your factors that they should not send here either merchants or wares, because *it is our will that in these kingdoms there should not be any trade of slaves nor outlet for them.* Concerning what is referred to above, again we beg of Your Highness to agree with it. . . .

Analyzing Primary Sources

1. Which of the following best describes the author's purpose in writing this letter?

   A to ask the king for money to help in ending the slave trade

   B to inform the king of the abuses taking place and to ask for his help in ending them

   C to inform the king about the extent of trade taking place in the kingdom

   D to ask the king for an explanation for why people are being enslaved

2. What does Affonso request of King John in the last paragraph?

   E that he not send any merchants or wares

   F that he send teachers

   G that he send priests

   H that he pray for Affonso

3. **Critical Thinking Recognizing Causes and Effects** According to King Affonso, how have the Portuguese affected his kingdom and state?

Miguel de Cervantes: *Don Quixote*

In his novel *Don Quixote,* Spanish writer Miguel de Cervantes tells the story of a madman who thinks he is a medieval knight. While Don Quixote's exploits often seem ridiculous, his devotion to the virtues underlying chivalry give his actions dignity. In this famous excerpt, Don Quixote does battle with a group of windmills against the advice of his down-to-earth companion, Sancho Panza.

Vocabulary Before you read the selection, look up the following words in a dictionary: **nigh, leagues, millstone, caitiffs.**

Main Idea In this excerpt, Don Quixote's devotion to knighthood leads him to attack a windmill, which he sees as a menacing giant.

Just then they came in sight of thirty or forty windmills that rise from that plain, and no sooner did Don Quixote see them than he said to his squire: "Fortune is guiding our affairs better than we ourselves could have wished. Do you see over yonder, friend Sancho, thirty or forty hulking giants? I intend to do battle with them and slay them. With the spoils we shall begin to be rich, for this is a righteous war. . . ."

"What giants?" asked Sancho Panza.

"Those you see over there," replied his master, "with the long arms; some of them have them well-nigh two leagues in length."

"Take care, sir," cried Sancho. "Those over there are not giants but windmills, and those things that seem to be armed are their sails, which when they are whirled around by the wind turn the millstone."

"It is clear," replied Don Quixote, "that you are not experienced in adventures. Those are giants, and if you are afraid, turn aside and pray whilst I enter into fierce and unequal battle with them."

Uttering these words, he clapped spurs to Rozinante, his steed, without heeding the cries of his squire, Sancho, who warned him that he was not going to attack giants, but windmills. But so convinced was he that they were giants that he neither heard his squire's shouts nor did he notice what they were, though he was very near them. Instead, he rushed on, shouting in a loud voice: "Fly not, cowards and vile caitiffs; one knight alone attacks you!" At that moment a slight breeze arose and the great sails began to move. . . .

He ran his lance into the sail, but the wind twisted it with such violence that it shivered the lance in pieces and dragged both rider and horse after it, rolling them over and over on the ground, sorely damaged.

Analyzing Literature

1. When Don Quixote attacks the giants, he expects

   A to gain great wealth.

   B to fail because he fights alone.

   C Sancho to join him.

   D to be tossed in the air.

2. Don Quixote believes a knight should

   E attack only after being attacked.

   F act boldly when he finds an enemy.

   G seek help before fighting an unequal battle.

   H enter a battle only to gain material wealth.

3. **Critical Thinking Drawing Conclusions** **(a)** What values of chivalry motivate Don Quixote's attack on the windmills? **(b)** How do you think Cervantes feels about Don Quixote and his ideals? Explain.

The English Bill of Rights

When the Catholic king, James II, was forced from the English throne in 1688, Parliament offered the crown to his Protestant daughter Mary and her husband William of Orange. But Parliament insisted that William and Mary submit to a Bill of Rights. This document, a continuation of the struggle between the crown and Parliament, sums up the powers that Parliament had been seeking since the Petition of Right in 1628.

Vocabulary Before you read the selection, look up the following words in a dictionary: **subvert, extirpate, abdicated, prerogative, redress.**

Main Idea | **This document ensured the superiority of Parliament over the monarchy and spelled out basic rights.**

Whereas, the late King James II . . . did endeavor to subvert and extirpate the Protestant religion and the laws and liberties of this kingdom . . . and whereas the said late King James II having abdicated the government, and the throne being vacant. . . .

    The said lords [Parliament] . . . being now assembled in a full and free representative [body] of this nation . . . do in the first place . . . declare:

1. That the pretended power of suspending of laws or the execution of laws by regal authority without consent of Parliament is illegal. . . .
4. That levying money for or to the use of the crown by pretense of prerogative without grant of Parliament . . . is illegal;
5. That it is the right of the subjects to petition the king, and all commitments and prosecutions for such petitioning are illegal.
6. That . . . raising or keeping a standing army within the kingdom in time of peace, unless it be with consent of Parliament, is against law. . . .
8. That election of members of Parliament ought to be free. . . .
9. That the freedom of speech and debates or proceedings in Parliament ought not to be challenged or questioned in any court or place out of Parliament. . . .
10. That excessive bail ought not to be required, nor excessive fines imposed, nor cruel and unusual punishments inflicted. . . .
13. And that, for redress of all grievances and for the amending, strengthening, and preserving of the laws, Parliaments ought to be held frequently. . . .

English Houses of Parliament (1800s)

Analyzing Primary Sources

1. Which of the following statements best summarizes these excerpts from the Bill of Rights?

   A The king's powers are limited by the Parliament.

   B The Parliament's powers are limited by the monarch.

   C The Parliament's duty is to amend and preserve laws.

   D The king's powers to raise an army are unlimited.

2. This Bill of Rights required the monarch to

   E raise money for paying the members of Parliament.

   F summon Parliament regularly.

   G cancel laws he or she considered unjust.

   H keep a standing army to defend the country.

3. **Critical Thinking Making Inferences** Why do you think the members of Parliament included item 9? Why do you think this item was important?

John Locke: *Two Treatises on Government*

English philosopher John Locke (1632–1704) published *Two Treatises on Government* in 1690. In the writings, Locke holds that all people possess natural rights, including property and personal freedom. Locke also states that governments hold their power only with the consent of the people. Locke's ideas heavily influenced revolutions in America and France.

Vocabulary Before you read the selection, look up the following words in a dictionary: **promulgated, extemporary, inroads, transgress, endeavor, forfeit, devolves.**

Main Idea **In this essay, Locke states that the primary purpose of government is to protect the natural rights of the people.**

But though men, when they enter into society give up the equality, liberty, and executive power they had in the state of Nature into the hands of society . . . the power of the society or legislative constituted by them can never be supposed to extend farther than the common good. . . . Whoever has the legislative or supreme power of any commonwealth, is bound to govern by established standing laws, promulgated and known to the people, and not by extemporary decrees, by [unbiased] and upright judges, who are to decide controversies by those laws; and to employ the force of the community at home only in the execution of such laws, or abroad to prevent or redress foreign injuries and secure the community from inroads and invasion. And all this to be directed to no other end but the peace, safety, and public good of the people. . . .

The reason why men enter into society is the preservation of their property; and the end while they choose and authorize a legislative is that there may be laws made, and rules set, as guards and fences to the properties of all the society, . . .

Whensoever, therefore, the legislative [power] shall transgress this fundamental rule of society, and either by ambition, fear, folly, or corruption, endeavor to grasp themselves, or put into the hands of any other, an absolute power over the lives, liberties, and estates of the people, by this breach of trust they forfeit the power the people had put into their hands for quite contrary ends, and it devolves to the people; who have a right to resume their original liberty, and by the establishment of a new legislative (such as they shall think fit), provide for their own safety and security. . . .

Analyzing Primary Sources

1. Which of the following statements best summarizes the excerpt above?

   A People should give up their fundamental rights in order to establish absolute monarchies.

   B People establish governments in order to set and enforce laws. If a government does not do this, the people may abolish it.

   C Most legislative powers are corrupt.

   D Judges may need to act outside the law.

2. Which of the following groups has the final authority of government in Locke's opinion?

   E the legislature

   F the prince

   G the people

   H the judges

3. **Critical Thinking Making Inferences** According to Locke, what do people give up when they enter into a society? Why do you think people do this?

Jean-Jacques Rousseau:
The Social Contract

In *The Social Contract*, Rousseau (1712–1778) proposes an ideal society formed through a "social contract," and based on the natural will of the people. Rousseau believed that people in their natural state were basically good but were corrupted by the evils of society. The first lines of *The Social Contract*, "Man is born free, but is everywhere in chains," reflect this idea.

Vocabulary Before you read the selection, look up the following words in a dictionary: **indivisible, sovereign**.

Main Idea | **In consenting to form a government, Rousseau says, individuals choose to give up their self-interest in favor of the common good.**

Find a form of association that defends and protects the person and goods of each associate with all the common force, and by means of which each one, uniting with all, nevertheless obeys only himself and remains as free as before. This is the fundamental problem which is solved by the social contract. . . .

[F]irst of all, since each one gives his entire self, the condition is equal for everyone, and since the condition is equal for everyone, no one has an interest in making it burdensome for the others. . . .

If, then, everything that is not the essence of the social compact is set aside, one will find that it can be reduced to the following terms: Each of us puts his person and all his power in common under the supreme direction of the general will; and in a body we receive each member as an indivisible part of the whole.

Instantly, in place of the private person of each contracting party, this act of association produces a moral and collective body, composed of as many members as there are voices in the assembly, which receives from this same act its unity, its common self, its life, and its will. This public person, formed thus by the union of all the others, formerly took the name City, and now takes that of Republic or body politic, which its members call State when it is passive, Sovereign when active, Power when comparing it to similar bodies. As for the associates, they collectively take the name People; and individually are called Citizens as participants in the sovereign authority, and Subjects as subjects to the laws of the State. . . .

Analyzing Primary Sources

1. According to Rousseau, "social contract" provides a solution to the fundamental problem of finding a form of government in which

   A people's differences can be solved peacefully.

   B people remain as free as they were without government.

   C people are not subject to unjust or immoral laws.

   D minorities are protected.

2. The Republic or body politic is defined by Rousseau as the

   E assembly.

   F collective body formed when the social contract is dissolved.

   G collective body formed when private persons enter into the social contract.

   H collective body appointed by the king.

3. **Critical Thinking Drawing Conclusions** Why does Rousseau believe that people are safe putting themselves under the direction of the "general will"?

Declaration of the Rights of Man and the Citizen

The French National Assembly issued this document in 1789 after having overthrown the established government in the early stages of the French Revolution. The document was modeled in part on the English Bill of Rights and on the American Declaration of Independence.

Vocabulary Before you read the selection, look up the following words in a dictionary: **auspices, imprescriptible, indispensable.**

Main Idea This declaration states the natural rights of French citizens and establishes the equality of all citizens before the law.

Therefore the National Assembly recognizes and proclaims, in the presence and under the auspices of the Supreme Being, the following rights of man and of the citizen:

1. Men are born and remain free and equal in rights. Social distinctions may be founded only upon the general good.
2. The aim of all political association is the preservation of the natural and imprescriptible rights of man. These rights are liberty, property, security, and resistance to oppression. . . .
4. Liberty consists in the freedom to do everything which injures no one else. . . .
5. Law can only prohibit such actions as are hurtful to society. . . .
6. Law is the expression of the general will. Every citizen has a right to participate personally, or through his representative, in its formation. It must be the same for all, whether it protects or punishes. All citizens, being equal in the eyes of the law, are equally eligible to all dignities and to all public positions and occupations, according to their abilities, and without distinction except that of their virtues and talents.
7. No person shall be accused, arrested, or imprisoned except in the cases and according to the forms prescribed by law. . . .
9. As all persons are held innocent until they shall have been declared guilty, if arrest shall be deemed indispensable, all harshness not essential to the securing of the prisoner's person shall be severely repressed by law. . . .
11. The free communication of ideas and opinions is one of the most precious of the rights of man. Every citizen may, accordingly, speak, write, and print with freedom. . . .
13. A common contribution is essential for the maintenance of the public [military] forces and for the cost of administration. This should be equitably distributed among all the citizens in proportion to their means.

Paris protesters during the French Revolution

Analyzing Primary Sources

1. Which of the following describes the tax policy set forth in this document?

   A All citizens must pay the same amount of tax.

   B Only citizens in the military must pay taxes.

   C All citizens pay taxes in proportion to their wealth.

   D There should be no taxes imposed on citizens.

2. Which article above specifically protects citizens from police brutality and torture?

   E 5

   F 6

   G 9

   H 11

3. **Critical Thinking Applying Information** Give one real-life example of each of the four natural rights listed under article 2.

Miguel Hidalgo:
Decree of Hidalgo

Father Miguel Hidalgo of Mexico called for freedom from Spanish rule in 1810. The following decree, also issued in 1810 from Guadalajara, Jalisco, was an attempt to gain additional support for the uprising from Native Americans, blacks, and mestizos. In the end, Hidalgo's rebellion failed because creoles feared that more rights for Native Americans and an end to slavery would cost them power. Less than one year after the start of the uprising, Hidalgo was captured and executed, and his followers scattered.

Vocabulary Before you read the selection, look up the following words in a dictionary: **yoke, exactions.**

Main Idea In this decree, Hidalgo calls for an end to slavery and to the heavy taxes imposed on the poor in Mexico.

Miguel Hidalgo

From the happy moment that the valiant American nation took up arms to shake off the heavy yoke that has oppressed it for three centuries, one of the principal objectives has been to extinguish such duties that cannot advance its fortune, especially those which in these critical circumstances do not well serve that end or provide for the real need of the kingdom in meeting the costs of the struggle, so therefore there is now put forward here the most urgent remedy in the following declarations:

1. That all owners of slaves shall give them their freedom before the end of ten days, under penalty of death, which shall be applied to those who violate this article.
2. That from now on the collection of tributes according to [race] shall cease, as shall exactions that are demanded of the Indians.
3. That all legal business, documents, letters and actions can be on common paper, with the requirement of the seal totally abolished.

Analyzing Primary Sources

1. Item 2 of the Decree of Hidalgo calls for an end to
   A slavery.
   B collection of any taxes.
   C collection of taxes based on race.
   D all business transactions with mestizos and Indians.

2. What does "the seal" probably symbolize in item 3 above?
   E approval from Spanish authorities
   F a postage stamp

   G a special type of paper used for legal documents
   H respect for Native American traditions

3. **Critical Thinking Defending a Position** Latin American liberation movements were often based on Enlightenment ideas about natural rights. Describe some of the natural rights Hidalgo could have listed in his decree as explanations for why he wished to abolish slavery, taxes based on race, and the requirement of the seal.

Simón Bolívar: *Address to the Congress of Venezuela*

Encouraged by the revolutions in British North America and France, colonists in Spanish South America soon began to create a force for independence. Simón Bolívar was one of the leaders of this movement. The excerpt below, from Bolívar's Address to the Second National Congress of Venezuela, was given in 1819.

Vocabulary Before you read the selection, look up the following words in a dictionary: **pernicious, inflexible, arduous, erroneous, incentives, succulent.**

Main Idea In this speech, Bolívar offers advice on what type of government to set up in Venezuela.

Subject to the threefold yoke of ignorance, tyranny, and vice, the American people have been unable to acquire knowledge, power, or [civic] virtue. The lessons we received and the models we studied, as pupils of such pernicious teachers, were most destructive. . . .

If a people, perverted by their training, succeed in achieving their liberty, they will soon lose it, for it would be of no avail to endeavor to explain to them that happiness consists in the practice of virtue; that the rule of law is more powerful than the rule of tyrants, because, as the laws are more inflexible, everyone should submit to their beneficent austerity; that proper morals, and not force, are the bases of law; and that to practice justice is to practice liberty. Therefore, Legislators, your work is so much the more arduous, inasmuch as you have to reeducate men who have been corrupted by erroneous illusions and false incentives. Liberty, says Rousseau, is a succulent morsel, but one difficult to digest. . . .

Legislators, meditate well before you choose. Forget not that you are to lay the political foundation for a newly born nation which can rise to the heights of greatness that Nature has marked out for it if you but proportion this foundation in keeping with the high plane that it aspires to attain. Unless your choice is based upon the peculiar . . . experience of Venezuelan people—a factor that should guide you in determining the nature and form of government you are about to adopt for the well-being of the people . . . the result of our reforms will again be slavery.

Simón Bolívar

Analyzing Primary Sources

1. Which statement best summarizes Bolívar's view of the people of Latin America?

   A They have not been well prepared for self-government by their former Spanish rulers.

   B They have been well prepared for self-government by the Spanish.

   C They had been ruled fairly by the Spanish.

   D They have very little desire for self-government.

2. Bolívar states that a government will be most effective if it

   E adheres closely to theories of good government.

   F imitates other successful governments.

   G is molded to fit the character of the nation for which it is built.

   H is based on the rule of law.

3. **Critical Thinking Defending a Position** Would you describe Bolívar as practical or idealistic? Use examples from the excerpt to defend your opinion.

Charles Dickens: *Hard Times*

In *Hard Times*, Charles Dickens protests the dehumanizing conditions of factory life in nineteenth-century England. In this excerpt from the novel, Dickens describes early morning in a fictional factory town named Coketown. (Coke is a form of coal.)

Vocabulary Before you read the selection, look up the following words in a dictionary: **clogs, melancholy, monotony, consign, decomposition, unfathomable, shrouded.**

Main Idea In this excerpt from the novel, Dickens depicts the labor conditions of the early Industrial Revolution.

The Fairy palaces burst into illumination, before pale morning showed the monstrous serpents of smoke trailing themselves over Coketown. A clattering of clogs upon the pavement; a rapid ringing of bells; and all the melancholy mad elephants, polished and oiled up for the day's monotony, were at their heavy exercise again.

Stephen bent over his loom, quiet, watchful, and steady. A special contrast, as every man was in the forest of looms where Stephen worked, to the crashing, smashing, tearing piece of mechanism at which he laboured. Never fear, good people of an anxious turn of mind, that Art will consign Nature to Oblivion. Set anywhere, side by side, the work of God and the work of man; and the former, even though it be a troop of Hands of very small account, will gain in dignity from the comparison.

So many hundred Hands in this Mill; so many hundred horse Steam Power. It is known, to the force of a single pound weight, what the engine will do; but, not all the calculators of the National Debt can tell me the capacity for good or evil, for love or hatred, for patriotism or discontent, for the decomposition of virtue into vice, or the reverse, at any single moment in the soul of one of these its quiet servants, with the composed faces and the regulated actions. There is no mystery in it; there is an unfathomable mystery in the meanest of them, for ever. . . .

The day grew strong, and showed itself outside, even against the flaming lights within. The lights were turned out, and the work went on. The rain fell, and the Smoke-serpents, submissive to the curse of all that tribe, trailed themselves upon the earth. In the waste-yard outside, the steam from the escape pipe, the litter of barrels and old iron, the shining heaps of coals, the ashes everywhere, were shrouded in a veil of mist and rain.

The work went on, until the noon-bell rang. More clattering upon the pavements. The looms, and wheels, and Hands all out of gear for an hour.

A spinning mule

Analyzing Primary Sources

1. What are the "melancholy mad elephants" to which Dickens refers in the excerpt above?

   A factory workers

   B factory owners

   C power looms

   D steam locomotives

2. According to this passage, facts cannot predict

   E the national debt.

   F the potential output of a factory.

   G the amount of work an individual can complete in a day.

   H the capacity of any individual for good or evil.

3. **Critical Thinking Making Inferences**
   (a) Why does Dickens refer to the factory workers as "Hands"? **(b)** What seems to be his attitude toward the workers? **(c)** What seems to be his general attitude toward the Industrial Revolution?

WORLD ATLAS

World Atlas

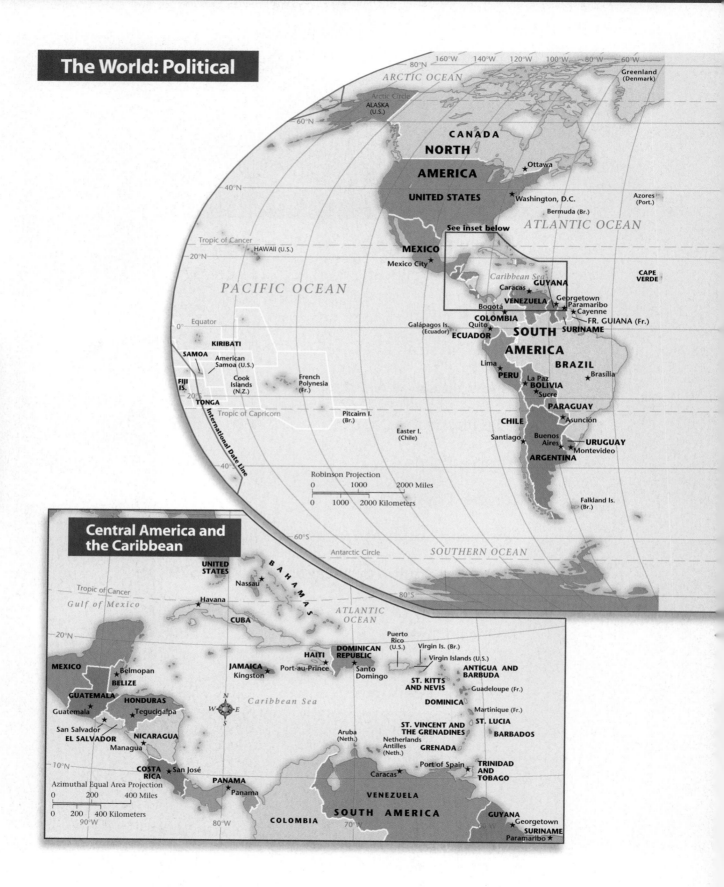

The World: Political

ARCTIC OCEAN
Arctic Circle
ALASKA (U.S.)
Greenland (Denmark)

CANADA
NORTH
AMERICA
Ottawa ★

UNITED STATES
Washington, D.C. ★
Azores (Port.)
Bermuda (Br.)

ATLANTIC OCEAN

Tropic of Cancer
HAWAII (U.S.)
MEXICO
Mexico City ★
See inset below

Caribbean Sea
Caracas ★
GUYANA
CAPE VERDE

VENEZUELA
Georgetown ★
Paramaribo ★
Bogotá ★
COLOMBIA
Cayenne ★
FR. GUIANA (Fr.)

PACIFIC OCEAN

Equator
Galápagos Is. (Ecuador)
Quito ★
ECUADOR
SOUTH
SURINAME
AMERICA

KIRIBATI
SAMOA
American Samoa (U.S.)
Lima ★
BRAZIL
Brasília ★
PERU
La Paz
FIJI IS.
Cook Islands (N.Z.)
French Polynesia (Fr.)
BOLIVIA
Sucre ★
TONGA
Tropic of Capricorn
Pitcairn I. (Br.)
PARAGUAY
Asunción ★
CHILE
Easter I. (Chile)
Santiago ★
Buenos Aires ★
URUGUAY
Montevideo ★
ARGENTINA

International Date Line

Robinson Projection
0   1000   2000 Miles
0   1000   2000 Kilometers

Falkland Is. (Br.)

Antarctic Circle
SOUTHERN OCEAN

Central America and the Caribbean

UNITED STATES
Nassau ★
BAHAMAS

Tropic of Cancer
Gulf of Mexico
Havana ★
ATLANTIC OCEAN

CUBA

Puerto Rico (U.S.)
Virgin Is. (Br.)
DOMINICAN REPUBLIC
Virgin Islands (U.S.)

MEXICO
Belmopan ★
HAITI
JAMAICA
Port-au-Prince ★
Santo Domingo ★
ANTIGUA AND BARBUDA
BELIZE
Kingston ★
ST. KITTS AND NEVIS
Guadeloupe (Fr.)

GUATEMALA
HONDURAS
Caribbean Sea
DOMINICA
Martinique (Fr.)
Guatemala ★
Tegucigalpa ★

San Salvador ★
N
ST. VINCENT AND THE GRENADINES
ST. LUCIA
EL SALVADOR
NICARAGUA
W   E
Aruba (Neth.)
Netherlands Antilles (Neth.)
BARBADOS
Managua ★
S
GRENADA

COSTA RICA
San José ★
Port of Spain ★
TRINIDAD AND TOBAGO
PANAMA
Caracas ★
Azimuthal Equal Area Projection
Panama ★
0   200   400 Miles
VENEZUELA
0   200   400 Kilometers
SOUTH AMERICA
GUYANA
COLOMBIA
Georgetown ★
SURINAME
Paramaribo ★

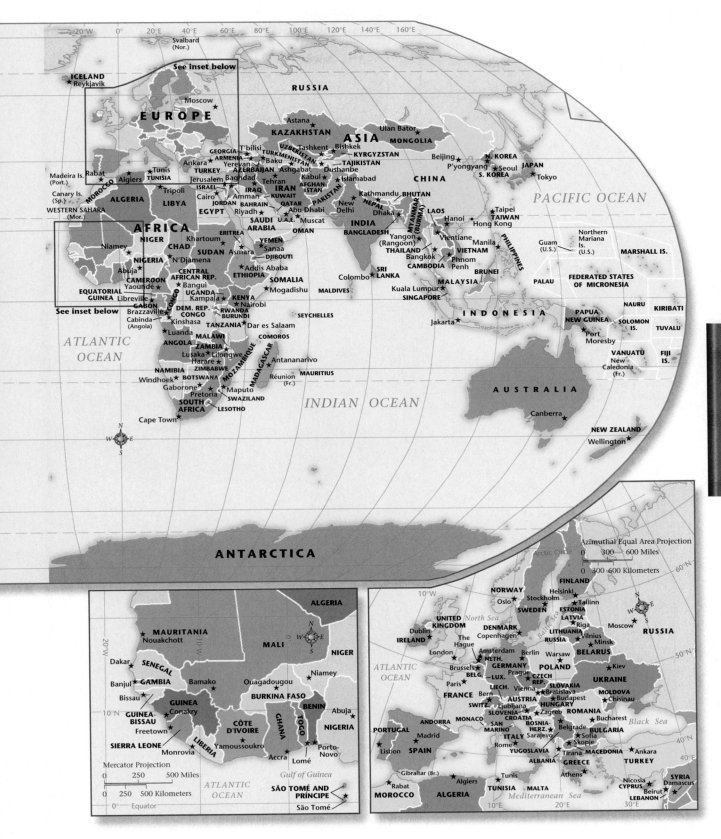

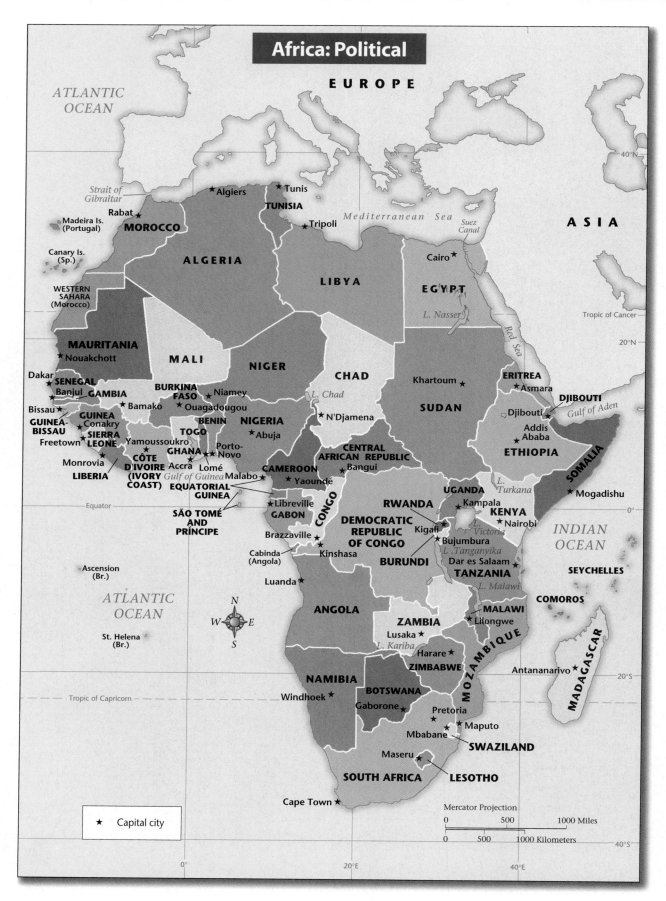

Africa: Political

EUROPE

ATLANTIC OCEAN

ASIA

Mediterranean Sea

Strait of Gibraltar

★Algiers   ★Tunis
            TUNISIA
Rabat★
Madeira Is.   **MOROCCO**   ★Tripoli
(Portugal)

Canary Is.   **ALGERIA**   **LIBYA**   **EGYPT**
(Sp.)   Cairo★

Suez Canal

WESTERN   L. Nasser
SAHARA   Tropic of Cancer
(Morocco)
                                                                20°N
MAURITANIA   Khartoum★   **ERITREA**
★Nouakchott   **MALI**   **NIGER**   ★Asmara
Dakar★   **CHAD**   **DJIBOUTI**
★ **SENEGAL**   L. Chad   **SUDAN**   Djibouti★ Gulf of Aden
Banjul★ **GAMBIA**   **BURKINA** ★Niamey   Addis
Bissau★   **FASO**   N'Djamena★   Ababa★
★ **GUINEA** ★Bamako ★Ouagadougou **NIGERIA**   **ETHIOPIA**   **SOMALIA**
GUINEA- Conakry **BENIN**   **CENTRAL**
BISSAU ★ ★ **SIERRA** **TOGO** ★Abuja **AFRICAN REPUBLIC**   L.
Freetown   **LEONE** Yamoussoukro★ Porto-   ★Bangui   Turkana   ★Mogadishu
        CÔTE **GHANA**★ ★Novo   **UGANDA**
Monrovia★ **D'IVOIRE** Accra★ ★Lomé **CAMEROON** **RWANDA** ★Kampala
LIBERIA **(IVORY** Gulf of Guinea Malabo★ ★Yaoundé   **KENYA**
        COAST) **EQUATORIAL**   Nairobi★
        GUINEA   **CONGO** Kigali★ L.   Equator 0°
SÃO TOMÉ   ★Libreville   **DEMOCRATIC** ★Bujumbura Victoria
AND   **GABON**   **REPUBLIC** **BURUNDI**   **INDIAN**
PRÍNCIPE   **OF CONGO** Dar es Salaam★ **OCEAN**
            Brazzaville★   L. Tanganyika
            Cabinda★   Kinshasa   **TANZANIA**   **SEYCHELLES**
Ascension   (Angola)
(Br.)   ★Luanda   L. Malawi   **COMOROS**
ATLANTIC   **MALAWI**
OCEAN   **ANGOLA**   **ZAMBIA** ★Lilongwe
                                              Lusaka★
St. Helena   L. Kariba
(Br.)   N   Antananarivo★
                    W ✦ E   **ZIMBABWE** Harare★ **MOZAMBIQUE** **MADAGASCAR**
                        S   **NAMIBIA** **BOTSWANA**   20°S
                              Windhoek★ Gaborone★ Pretoria★
Tropic of Capricorn   ★Maputo
                                        Mbabane★ ★ **SWAZILAND**
                                        Maseru★
                              SOUTH AFRICA **LESOTHO**

                              Cape Town★

Mercator Projection
0   500   1000 Miles
0   500   1000 Kilometers
                                                            40°S

★ Capital city

0°   20°E   40°E

World Atlas

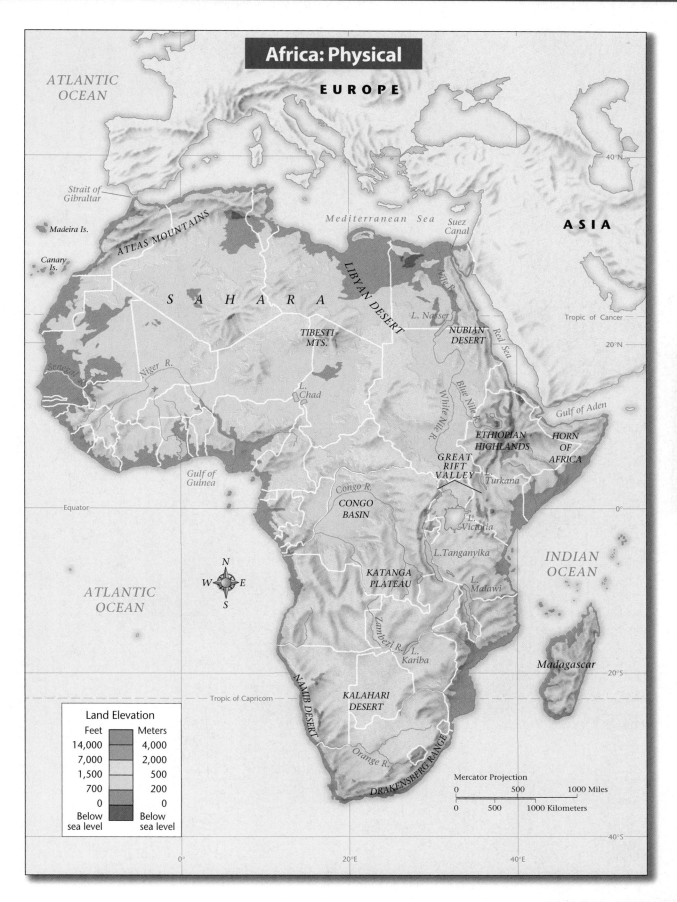

Africa: Physical

EUROPE

ATLANTIC OCEAN

Mediterranean Sea

Suez Canal

ASIA

40°N

Strait of Gibraltar

Madeira Is.

Canary Is.

ATLAS MOUNTAINS

S A H A R A

LIBYAN DESERT

Nile R.

L. Nasser

NUBIAN DESERT

Red Sea

Tropic of Cancer

20°N

TIBESTI MTS.

Senegal R.

Niger R.

L. Chad

White Nile R.

Blue Nile R.

Gulf of Aden

ETHIOPIAN HIGHLANDS

HORN OF AFRICA

Gulf of Guinea

Congo R.

CONGO BASIN

GREAT RIFT VALLEY

L. Turkana

Equator

0°

L. Victoria

L. Tanganyika

INDIAN OCEAN

ATLANTIC OCEAN

KATANGA PLATEAU

L. Malawi

Zambezi R.

L. Kariba

Madagascar

20°S

NAMIB DESERT

KALAHARI DESERT

Tropic of Capricorn

Orange R.

DRAKENSBERG RANGE

40°S

N
W   E
S

Land Elevation

Feet	Meters
14,000	4,000
7,000	2,000
1,500	500
700	200
0	0
Below sea level	Below sea level

Mercator Projection

0	500	1000 Miles
0	500	1000 Kilometers

0°   20°E   40°E

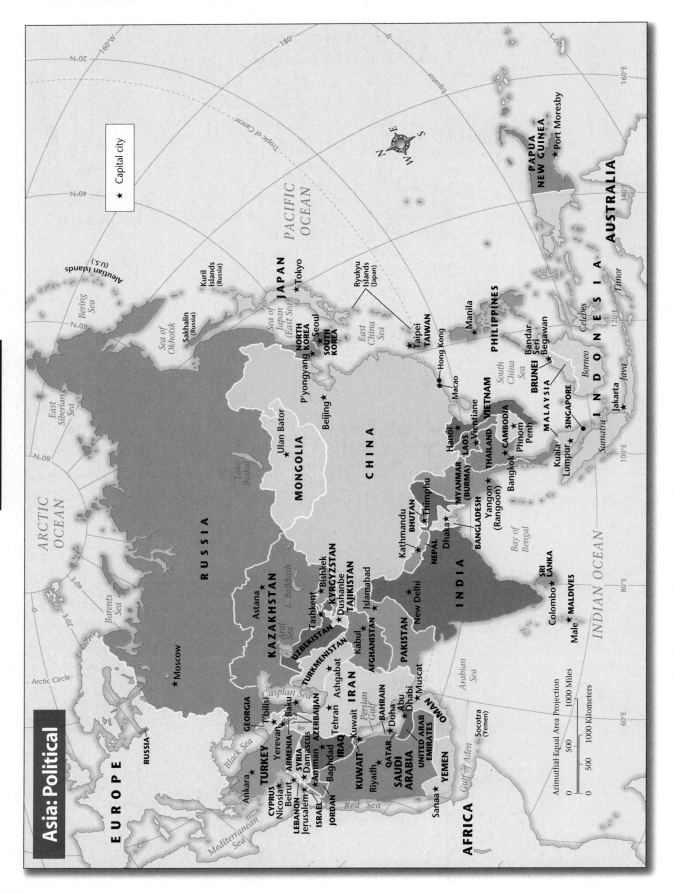

World Atlas

Asia: Political

★ Capital city

EUROPE

RUSSIA

ARCTIC OCEAN

Arctic Circle

Barents Sea

East Siberian Sea

Bering Sea

Aleutian Islands (U.S.)

PACIFIC OCEAN

Tropic of Cancer

Equator

Sea of Okhotsk

Kuril Islands (Russia)

Sakhalin (Russia)

Sea of Japan (East Sea)

JAPAN Tokyo

Ryukyu Islands (Japan)

East China Sea

★ Taipei **TAIWAN**

Manila **PHILIPPINES**

PAPUA NEW GUINEA ★ Port Moresby

AUSTRALIA

Moscow ★

RUSSIA

Black Sea

GEORGIA
Tbilisi ★
ARMENIA Baku ★
Yerevan ★ **AZERBAIJAN**

Caspian Sea

Aral Sea

KAZAKHSTAN
Astana ★

L. Balkhash

MONGOLIA
Ulan Bator ★

Lake Baikal

CHINA

Beijing ★

P'yongyang ★ **NORTH KOREA**

Seoul ★ **SOUTH KOREA**

Hong Kong ●

Macao ●

VIETNAM
Hanoi ★
LAOS
Vientiane ★

South China Sea

BRUNEI
Bandar Seri Begawan ★

Borneo

MALAYSIA
Kuala Lumpur ★
SINGAPORE ●

I N D O N E S I A

Celebes

Jakarta ★

Java

Sumatra

Timor

TURKEY
Ankara ★

CYPRUS
Nicosia ★
LEBANON
Beirut ★
Jerusalem ★
ISRAEL
JORDAN
Amman ★
Damascus ★
SYRIA

Mediterranean Sea

Red Sea

Baghdad ★
IRAQ
Kuwait ★
KUWAIT

Tehran ★
IRAN

Ashgabat ★
TURKMENISTAN

UZBEKISTAN
Tashkent ★
KYRGYZSTAN
Bishkek ★
Dushanbe ★
TAJIKISTAN
Islamabad ★

Kabul ★
AFGHANISTAN

PAKISTAN

New Delhi ★

Kathmandu ★
NEPAL
Thimphu ★
BHUTAN

Dhaka ★
BANGLADESH

MYANMAR (BURMA)
Yangon (Rangoon) ★

THAILAND
Bangkok ★

CAMBODIA
Phnom Penh ★

Bay of Bengal

I N D I A

SRI LANKA
Colombo ★
Male ★ **MALDIVES**

INDIAN OCEAN

BAHRAIN
QATAR
Doha ★
Abu Dhabi ★
UNITED ARAB EMIRATES
Muscat ★
OMAN

Riyadh ★
SAUDI ARABIA

YEMEN
Sanaa ★

Persian Gulf

Arabian Sea

Socotra (Yemen)

Gulf of Aden

AFRICA

Azimuthal Equal Area Projection

1000 Miles

1000 Kilometers

500

500

0

0

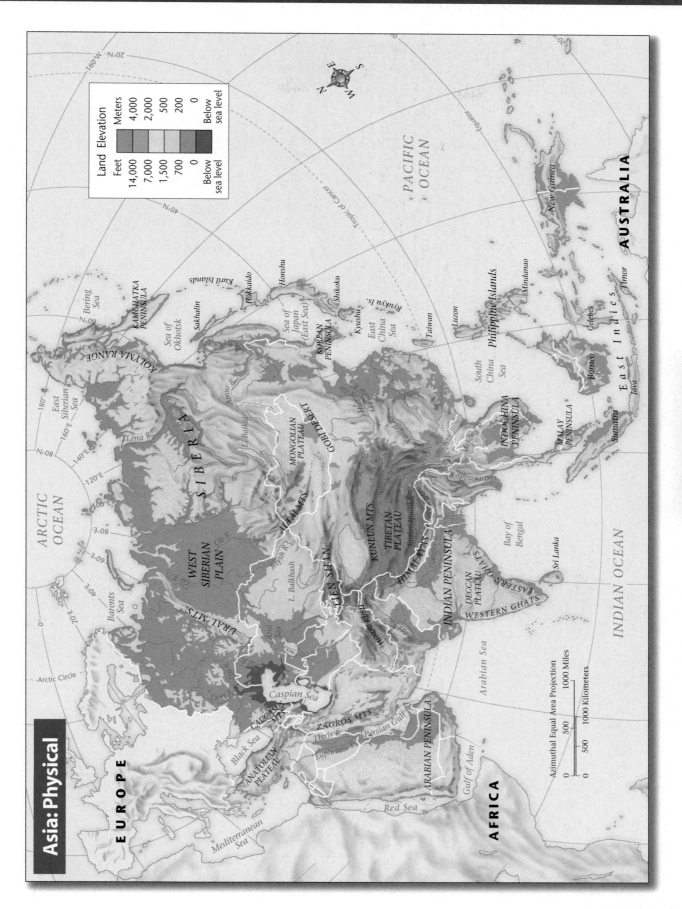

Land Elevation

Feet	Meters
14,000	4,000
7,000	2,000
1,500	500
700	200
0	0
Below sea level	Below sea level

EUROPE

AFRICA

AUSTRALIA

ARCTIC OCEAN

PACIFIC OCEAN

INDIAN OCEAN

Equator

Tropic of Cancer

Arctic Circle

Bering Sea

KAMCHATKA PENINSULA

KOLYMA RANGE

East Siberian Sea

Barents Sea

Lena R.

Yenisei R.

Ob R.

Irtysh R.

SIBERIA

WEST SIBERIAN PLAIN

URAL MTS.

Don R.

Volga R.

Black Sea

Caspian Sea

CAUCASUS MTS.

ANATOLIAN PLATEAU

Mediterranean Sea

ZAGROS MTS.

Tigris R.

Euphrates R.

Persian Gulf

ARABIAN PENINSULA

Gulf of Aden

Red Sea

Arabian Sea

L. Balkhash

Aral Sea

ALTAI MTS.

TIEN SHAN

HINDU KUSH

KUNLUN MTS.

TIBETAN PLATEAU

HIMALAYA

Indus R.

Ganges R.

Brahmaputra R.

INDIAN PENINSULA

DECCAN PLATEAU

WESTERN GHATS

EASTERN GHATS

Bay of Bengal

Sri Lanka

MONGOLIAN PLATEAU

GOBI DESERT

L. Baikal

Amur R.

Huang He

Chang Jiang

Mekong R.

Irrawaddy R.

Sea of Okhotsk

Sakhalin

Kuril Islands

Hokkaido

Sea of Japan (East Sea)

Honshu

Shikoku

Kyushu

Kyūshū Is.

KOREAN PENINSULA

East China Sea

Taiwan

South China Sea

INDOCHINA PENINSULA

MALAY PENINSULA

Sumatra

Java

Borneo

Celebes

E a s t   I n d i e s

Luzon

Mindanao

Philippine Islands

Timor

New Guinea

Azimuthal Equal Area Projection

1000 Miles

1000 Kilometers

500

500

0

0

Europe: Political

ICELAND
★Reykjavik

Barents Sea

Norwegian Sea

Faroe Is.
(Den.)

Shetland Is.
(Br.)

ATLANTIC
OCEAN

FINLAND

Helsinki
●St. Petersburg

NORWAY

SWEDEN

Oslo★

★Stockholm

Tallinn

ESTONIA

RUSSIA

Scotland

North Sea

Riga
LATVIA

Moscow★

N.
Ireland

LITHUANIA

Dublin★

UNITED
KINGDOM

DENMARK
Copenhagen★

Vilnius

RUSSIA

★Minsk

IRELAND

Wales

NETHERLANDS

BELARUS

England

The
Hague

Amsterdam

Berlin

POLAND
Warsaw★

★Kiev

London★

Brussels

Paris★

BELGIUM

GERMANY

Prague
CZECH REP.

UKRAINE

LUXEMBOURG

SLOVAKIA

LIECHTENSTEIN

Vienna ★★Bratislava

MOLDOVA

Bay of
Biscay

FRANCE

Bern

★Budapest

★Chisinau

SWITZ.

AUSTRIA

Ljubljana

HUNGARY

ROMANIA

SLOVENIA

Zagreb

Belgrade

Bucharest★

Black Sea

PORTUGAL

ANDORRA

SAN
MARINO

CROATIA

BOSNIA–
HERZEGOVINA

MONACO

ITALY

Adriatic Sea

Sarajevo

YUGOSLAVIA

BULGARIA

Bosporus

★Lisbon

Corsica
(Fr.)

VATICAN
CITY

Rome

★

Sofia

Madrid

ALBANIA

SKOPJE

Istanbul●

Ankara

SPAIN

Sardinia
(It.)

MACEDONIA

Tirana

TURKEY

Balearic Is.
(Sp.)

Strait of
Gibraltar

Gibraltar
(Br.)

Sicily

MALTA

GREECE

Aegean
Sea

Mediterranean Sea

Athens★

AFRICA

Crete

N
W   E
S

Azimuthal Equal Area Projection

0   250   500 Miles

0   250   500 Kilometers

★ Capital city

● Major city

World Atlas

576 *Reference Section*

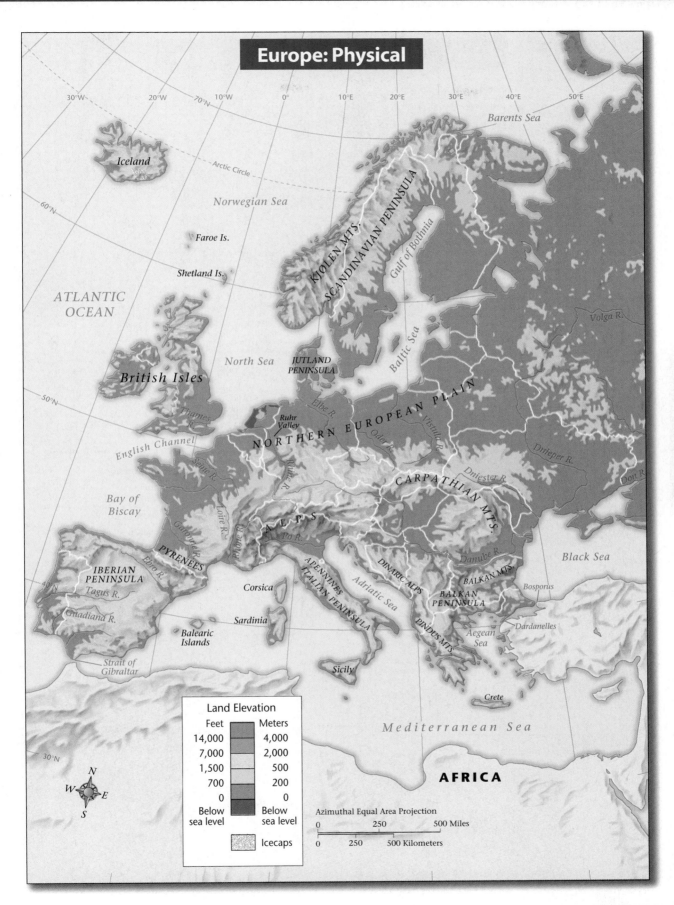

Europe: Physical

30°W 20°W 70°N 10°W 0° 10°E 20°E 30°E 40°E 50°E

Barents Sea

Iceland

Arctic Circle

Norwegian Sea

Faroe Is.

KIØLEN MTS.

SCANDINAVIAN PENINSULA

Gulf of Bothnia

60°N

Shetland Is.

Volga R.

ATLANTIC OCEAN

North Sea

JUTLAND PENINSULA

Baltic Sea

British Isles

50°N

Thames R.

Ruhr Valley

Elbe R.

NORTHERN EUROPEAN PLAIN

Oder R.

Vistula R.

Dnieper R.

English Channel

Seine R.

Rhine R.

Dniester R.

CARPATHIAN MTS.

Don R.

Bay of Biscay

Loire R.

Garonne R.

Rhône R.

A L P S

Po R.

Danube R.

Black Sea

PYRENEES

IBERIAN PENINSULA

Ebro R.

APENNINES

ITALIAN PENINSULA

DINARIC ALPS

Adriatic Sea

BALKAN MTS.

BALKAN PENINSULA

Bosporus

40°N

Tagus R.

Corsica

Guadiana R.

Sardinia

Balearic Islands

Dardanelles

PINDUS MTS.

Aegean Sea

Strait of Gibraltar

Sicily

Crete

Land Elevation

Feet	Meters
14,000	4,000
7,000	2,000
1,500	500
700	200
0	0
Below sea level	Below sea level

Icecaps

Mediterranean Sea

AFRICA

30°N

N
W   E
S

Azimuthal Equal Area Projection

0   250   500 Miles

0   250   500 Kilometers

World Atlas

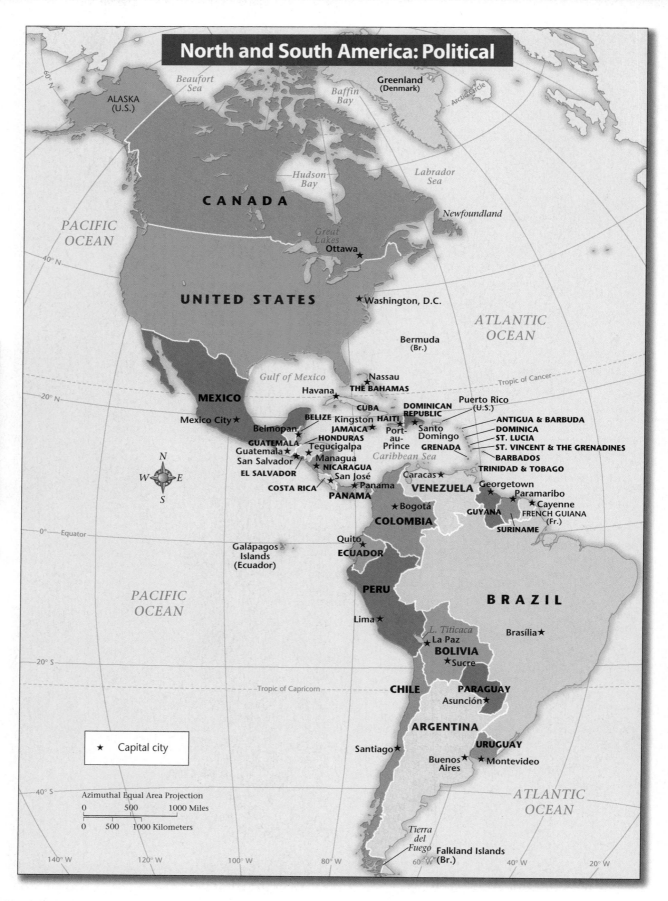

North and South America: Political

Beaufort
Sea

ALASKA
(U.S.)

Greenland
(Denmark)

Arctic Circle

60° N

Baffin
Bay

Hudson
Bay

Labrador
Sea

CANADA

Newfoundland

PACIFIC
OCEAN

Great
Lakes

Ottawa ★

40° N

UNITED STATES

★ Washington, D.C.

ATLANTIC
OCEAN

Bermuda
(Br.)

Gulf of Mexico

★ Nassau

Tropic of Cancer

Havana

THE BAHAMAS

20° N

MEXICO

CUBA

Puerto Rico
(U.S.)

DOMINICAN
REPUBLIC

Mexico City ★

BELIZE

Kingston

HAITI

Santo
Domingo

ANTIGUA & BARBUDA

Belmopan ★

Port-
au-
Prince

DOMINICA

GUATEMALA ★

JAMAICA

ST. LUCIA

HONDURAS

Guatemala ★

Tegucigalpa ★

GRENADA

ST. VINCENT & THE GRENADINES

San Salvador ★

Managua

BARBADOS

EL SALVADOR

★

NICARAGUA

Caribbean Sea

TRINIDAD & TOBAGO

San José

COSTA RICA

★ Panama

Caracas ★

Georgetown
★

Paramaribo

PANAMA

VENEZUELA

★ Cayenne

★ Bogotá

GUYANA

FRENCH GUIANA
(Fr.)

COLOMBIA

SURINAME

0° Equator

Quito

Galápagos
Islands
(Ecuador)

★

ECUADOR

PERU

BRAZIL

PACIFIC
OCEAN

Lima ★

L. Titicaca

Brasília ★

★ La Paz

20° S

BOLIVIA

★ Sucre

Tropic of Capricorn

CHILE

PARAGUAY

Asunción ★

ARGENTINA

URUGUAY

Santiago ★

Buenos
Aires

★ Montevideo

ATLANTIC
OCEAN

40° S

Azimuthal Equal Area Projection

0   500   1000 Miles

0   500   1000 Kilometers

Tierra
del
Fuego

Falkland Islands
(Br.)

★ Capital city

N
W   E
S

140° W   120° W   100° W   80° W   60° W   40° W   20° W

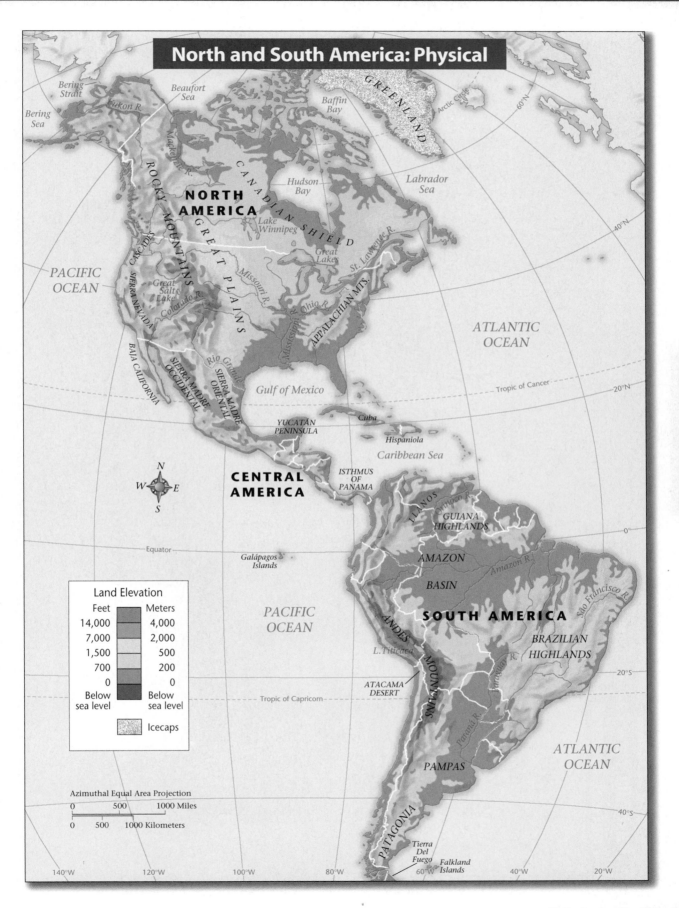

North and South America: Physical

NORTH AMERICA

CENTRAL AMERICA

SOUTH AMERICA

Bering Strait
Bering Sea
Beaufort Sea
GREENLAND
Baffin Bay
Arctic Circle
60°N
Yukon R.
Mackenzie R.
CANADIAN SHIELD
Hudson Bay
Labrador Sea
ROCKY MOUNTAINS
GREAT PLAINS
Lake Winnipeg
Great Lakes
St. Lawrence R.
40°N
CASCADES
PACIFIC OCEAN
SIERRA NEVADA
Great Salt Lake
Colorado R.
Missouri R.
Mississippi R.
Ohio R.
APPALACHIAN MTS.
ATLANTIC OCEAN
BAJA CALIFORNIA
SIERRA MADRE OCCIDENTAL
SIERRA MADRE ORIENTAL
Rio Grande
Gulf of Mexico
Tropic of Cancer
20°N
YUCATÁN PENINSULA
Cuba
Hispaniola
Caribbean Sea
ISTHMUS OF PANAMA
Galápagos Islands
Equator
LLANOS
Orinoco R.
GUIANA HIGHLANDS
AMAZON BASIN
Amazon R.
0°
ANDES
São Francisco R.
L. Titicaca
MOUNTAINS
BRAZILIAN HIGHLANDS
ATACAMA DESERT
Paraguay R.
20°S
Tropic of Capricorn
Paraná R.
PAMPAS
ATLANTIC OCEAN
PATAGONIA
Tierra Del Fuego
Falkland Islands
40°S
PACIFIC OCEAN

Land Elevation

Feet		Meters
14,000		4,000
7,000		2,000
1,500		500
700		200
0		0
Below sea level		Below sea level

Icecaps

Azimuthal Equal Area Projection

0   500   1000 Miles

0   500   1000 Kilometers

140°W   120°W   100°W   80°W   60°W   40°W   20°W

N W E S

World Atlas

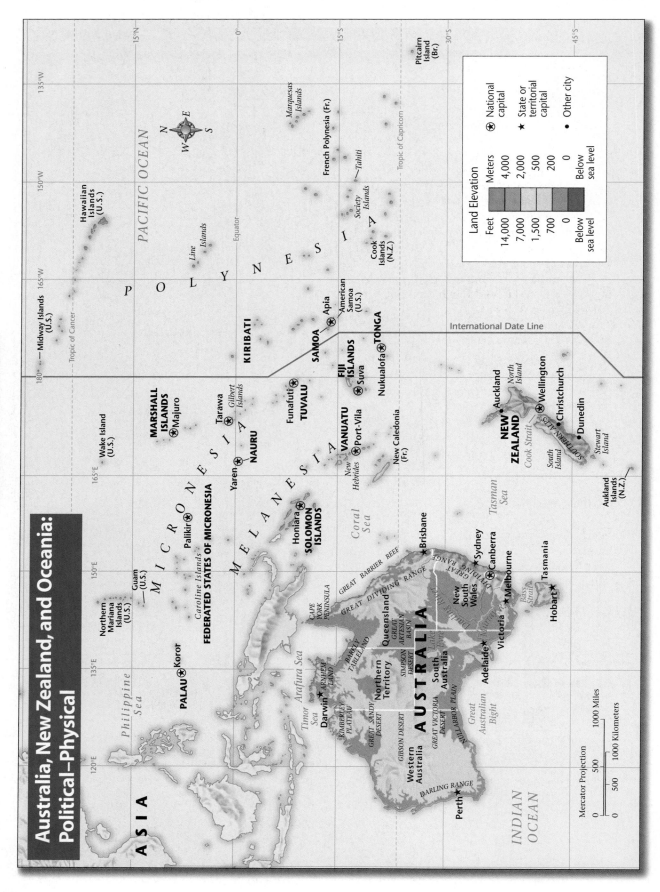

Australia, New Zealand, and Oceania: Political–Physical

World Atlas

ASIA

Philippine Sea

PALAU ✪ Koror

Northern Mariana Islands (U.S.)

Guam (U.S.)

Caroline Islands

FEDERATED STATES OF MICRONESIA

M I C R O N E S I A

Palikir ✪

MARSHALL ISLANDS ✪ Majuro

Wake Island (U.S.)

Tarawa ✪ *Gilbert Islands*

Yaren ✪ **NAURU**

KIRIBATI

Funafuti **TUVALU**

M E L A N E S I A

Honiara ✪ **SOLOMON ISLANDS**

New Hebrides **VANUATU** ✪ Port-Vila

New Caledonia (Fr.)

Coral Sea

Arafura Sea

Timor Sea

Darwin ★ **ARNHEM LAND**

Northern Territory

Western Australia

GIBSON DESERT

GREAT SANDY DESERT

KIMBERLEY PLATEAU

BARKLY TABLELAND

CAPE YORK PENINSULA

GREAT BARRIER REEF

GREAT DIVIDING RANGE

Queensland

GREAT ARTESIAN BASIN

SIMPSON DESERT

GREAT VICTORIA DESERT

South Australia

NULLARBOR PLAIN

Great Australian Bight

A U S T R A L I A

DARLING RANGE

Perth ★

Adelaide ★

New South Wales

★ Canberra

Sydney ●

Victoria Melbourne ★

Bass Strait

Tasmania

Hobart ★

Brisbane ★

GREAT DIVIDING RANGE

Tasman Sea

INDIAN OCEAN

SAMOA ✪ Apia

American Samoa (U.S.)

FIJI ISLANDS ✪ Suva

TONGA Nukualofa

International Date Line

Line Islands

Equator

P O L Y N E S I A

PACIFIC OCEAN

Midway Islands (U.S.)

Tropic of Cancer

Hawaiian Islands (U.S.)

Marquesas Islands

French Polynesia (Fr.)

Tahiti

Society Islands

Cook Islands (N.Z.)

Tropic of Capricorn

Pitcairn Island (Br.)

NEW ZEALAND

Auckland ●

North Island

Wellington ✪

Christchurch ●

Dunedin ●

SOUTHERN ALPS

Cook Strait

South Island

Stewart Island

Aukland Islands (N.Z.)

Land Elevation

Feet	Meters
14,000	4,000
7,000	2,000
1,500	500
700	200
0	0
Below sea level	Below sea level

⊛ National capital

★ State or territorial capital

● Other city

Mercator Projection

0   500   1000 Miles

0   500   1000 Kilometers

Understanding Map Projections

Geographers and historians use globes and maps to represent the Earth. A globe is like a small model of the Earth. It shows major geographic features, representing the land-masses and bodies of water accurately. However, a globe is not always convenient to use. A map, on the other hand, which can be printed on a piece of paper or in a book, is a more convenient way to show the Earth. Unfortunately, no map can be an exact picture of the Earth because all maps are flat and the Earth's surface is curved.

Mapmakers have developed many ways of showing the curved Earth on a flat surface. Each of these ways is called a map projection. The three maps on this page show different types of map projections—each with its advantages and disadvantages.

Robinson Projection The Robinson projection shows correct shapes and sizes of land-masses for most parts of the world. They are commonly used today by geographers. You will find numerous Robinson projections in this book. The locator maps that appear with most of the maps in the book are Robinson projections.

Mercator Projection The Mercator projection, one of the earliest projections developed, accurately shows the directions north, south, east, and west. As you can see, the parallels and meridians are straight lines intersecting each other at right angles. This makes it easy to plot distances on the map. As a result, Mercator projections are useful for showing sailors' routes and ocean currents. Sizes become distorted, however, as you move farther away from the equator.

Interrupted Projection The Interrupted projection shows the sizes and shapes of land-masses accurately. However, the interruptions in the oceans make it difficult to measure distances and judge directions across water.

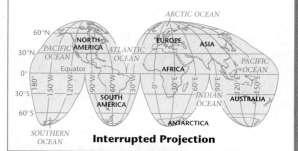

Map Projections

Robinson Projection

Mercator Projection

Interrupted Projection

Skills Assessment

Geography Map projections enable mapmakers to show the curved Earth on a flat page. Each of the projections shown here has its advantages and disadvantages.

1. **Location** On the maps, locate *(a)* North America, *(b)* Africa, *(c)* Australia.
2. **Region** *(a)* On an Interrupted projection, which continent is divided into sections? Why is it divided? *(b)* List three pages in this textbook on which you can find a Robinson projection.
3. **Critical Thinking** **Comparing** Locate Antarctica on the Robinson and Mercator projections. On which map is its size shown more accurately? Explain why this is so.

Glossary

This Glossary defines many important terms and phrases. Some terms are phonetically respelled to aid in pronunciation. See the Pronunciation Key below for an explanation of the respellings. The page number following each definition is the page on which the term or phrase is first discussed in a chapter. All terms that appear in blue type in the text are included in this Glossary.

PRONUNCIATION KEY When difficult terms or names first appear in the text, they are respelled to aid in pronunciation. A syllable in small capital letters receives the most stress. The key below lists the letters used for respelling. It includes examples of words using each sound and shows how they are respelled.

SYMBOL	EXAMPLE	RESPELLING
a	hat	(hat)
ay	pay, late	(pay), (layt)
ah	star, hot	(stahr), (haht)
ai	air, dare	(air), (dair)
aw	law, all	(law), (awl)
eh	met	(meht)
ee	bee, eat	(bee), (eet)
er	learn, sir, fur	(lern), (ser), (fer)
ih	fit	(fiht)
ī	mile	(mīle)
ir	ear	(ir)
oh	no	(noh)
oi	soil, boy	(soil), (boi)
oo	root, rule	(root), (rool)
or	born, door	(born), (dor)
ow	plow, out	(plow), (owt)
u	put, book	(put), (buk)
uh	fun	(fuhn)
yoo	few, use	(fyoo), (yooz)
ch	chill, reach	(chihl), (reech)
g	go, dig	(goh), (dihg)
j	jet, gently, bridge	(jeht), (JEHNT lee), (brihj)
k	kite, cup	(kīt), (kuhp)
ks	mix	(mihks)
kw	quick	(kwihk)
ng	bring	(brihng)
s	say, cent	(say), (sehnt)
sh	she, crash	(shee), (krash)
th	three	(three)
y	yet, onion	(yeht), (UHN yuhn)
z	zip, always	(zihp), (AWL wayz)
zh	treasure	(TREH zher)

A

abdicate give up a high office (p. 490)

absolute monarch ruler with complete authority over the government and lives of the people he or she governs (p. 413)

acropolis (uh KRAHP uh lihs) highest and most fortified point within a Greek city-state (p. 106)

acupuncture medical treatment in which needles are inserted under the skin at specific points to relieve pain or treat various illnesses (p. 96)

ahimsa (uh HIM sah) Hindu belief in nonviolence and a reverence for all life (p. 78)

alliance formal agreement between two or more nations or powers to cooperate and come to one another's defense (pp. 111, 387)

alloy mix or blend one metal with another (p. 167)

alphabet letters that represent spoken sounds (p. 44)

anesthetic drug that prevents pain during surgery (p. 498)

animism belief that spirits and forces may live in animals, objects, or dreams (p. 12)

annex add a territory onto an existing state or country (p. 486)

annul cancel or invalidate (pp. 214, 352)

anthropology study of the origins and development of people and their societies (p. 8)

antisemitism prejudice against Jews (p. 196)

apostle leader or teacher of a new faith or movement (p. 142)

apprentice young person learning a trade from a master (p. 200)

aqueduct in ancient Rome, bridgelike stone structure that carried water from the hills into the cities (p. 138)

arabesque intricate design made up of curved lines that suggest floral shapes, used to decorate rugs, textiles, and glassware (p. 263)

archaeology study of past people and cultures (p. 8)

archipelago (ahr kuh PEHL uh goh) chain of islands (p. 316)

aristocracy government headed by a privileged minority or upper class (p. 106)

armada fleet of ships (p. 414)

artifact object made by human beings (p. 8)

artisan skilled craftworker (p. 16)

assassination murder of a public figure, usually for political reasons (p. 120)

assimilate absorb or adopt another culture (p. 122)

astrolabe instrument used to determine latitude by measuring the position of the stars (p. 365)

atman (AHT muhn) in Hindu belief, a person's essential self (p. 77)

autocrat ruler who has complete authority (p. 236)

autonomy self-rule (p. 520)

B

balance of power distribution of military and economic power that prevents any one nation from becoming too strong (p. 420)

baroque ornate style of art and architecture popular in the 1600s and 1700s (p. 453)

barter economy system in which one set of goods or services is exchanged for another (p. 43)

bill of exchange issued by a banker in one city to a merchant who could exchange it for cash in a distant city, thus freeing him from traveling with gold, which was easily stolen (p. 199)

bishop high-ranking Church official with authority over a local area, or diocese (p. 145)

blockade shutting off of a port to keep people or supplies from moving in or out (p. 487)

bourgeoisie (boor zhwah ZEE) the middle class (p. 469)

boyar landowning noble in Russia under the czars (pp. 242, 432)

brahman according to Aryan belief, the single spiritual power that resides in all things (p. 57)

bunraku Japanese puppet plays (p. 325)

bushido (BOO shee doh) code of conduct for samurai during the feudal period in Japan (p. 320)

C

cabinet parliamentary advisors to the king who originally met in a small room, or "cabinet" (p. 458)

caliph successor to Muhammad as political and religious leader of the Muslims (p. 256)

calligraphy fancy or stylized handwriting (pp. 63, 263)

canon law body of laws of a church (p. 195)

canonize recognize one as a saint (p. 352)

capital money or wealth (pp. 199, 501)

capitalism economic system in which the means of production are privately owned and operated for profit (p. 404)

Glossary

Glossary

caravel improved type of sailing ship in the 1400s (p. 365)

cartographer mapmaker (p. 365)

caste in traditional Indian society, unchangeable social group into which a person is born (pp. 57, 267)

cataract waterfall (p. 25)

celadon porcelain with an unusual blue-green glaze (p. 314)

censorship restriction on access to ideas and information (p. 451)

census population count (p. 135)

charter in the Middle Ages, a written document that set out the rights and privileges of a town (p. 199)

chinampas artificial islands made of earth piled on reed mats anchored to a shallow lake bed (p. 159)

chivalry code of conduct for knights during the Middle Ages (p. 189)

circumnavigate travel all the way around the Earth (p. 368)

city-state political unit made up of a city and the surrounding lands (p. 18)

civil law body of law dealing with private rights of individuals (p. 40)

civilization complex, highly organized social order (p. 15)

civil war war fought between two groups of people in the same nation (p. 387)

clan group of families with a common ancestor (p. 62)

codify arrange and set down in writing (p. 40)

colony territory settled and ruled by people from another land (p. 44)

comedy in ancient Greece, play that mocked people or social customs (p. 119)

commodity valuable product (p. 284)

common law system of law that is the same for all people, based on court decisions that have become accepted legal principles (p. 207)

communism form of socialism advocated by Karl Marx; according to Marx, class struggle was inevitable and would lead to the creation of a classless society in which all wealth and property would be owned by the community as a whole (p. 512)

compact agreement (p. 395)

compromise acceptable middle ground (p. 352)

conquistador (kahn KEES tuh dor) name for the Spanish explorers who claimed lands in the Americas for Spain in the 1500s and 1600s (p. 386)

constitutional government government whose power is defined and limited by law (p. 457)

consul in ancient Rome, official from the patrician class who supervised the government and commanded the armies (p. 129)

covenant binding agreement (p. 46)

creole person in Spain's colonies in the Americas who was an American-born descendant of Spanish settlers (pp. 390, 527)

criminal law branch of law that deals with offenses against others, such as robbery, assault, or murder (p. 40)

crusade holy war (p. 214)

cultural diffusion spread of ideas, customs, and technologies from one people to another (p. 19)

culture way of life of a society that is handed down from one generation to the next by learning and experience (p. 8)

cuneiform (kyoo NEE uh form) wedge-shaped writing of the ancient Sumerians (p. 36)

curriculum formal course of study (p. 185)

czar title of the ruler of the Russian empire (p. 243)

D

daimyo (DĪ myoh) warrior lord directly below the shogun in feudal Japan (p. 320)

decimal system system of numbers based on 10 (p. 83)

decipher decode (p. 32)

deficit spending situation in which a government spends more money than it takes in (p. 470)

delta triangular area of marshland formed by deposits of silt at the mouth of some rivers (p. 25)

democracy government in which the people hold ruling power (p. 107)

demotic system of ancient Egyptian writing, simpler than hieroglyphics, that was developed for everyday use (p. 32)

depopulation reduction in population (p. 428)

desertification process by which fertile or semidesert land becomes desert (p. 281)

dharma (DAHR muh) in Hindu belief, an individual's religious and moral duties (p. 77)

diaspora (dī AS puhr uh) the scattering of people (p. 47)

dictator ruler who has complete control over a government; in ancient Rome, a leader appointed to rule for six months in times of emergency (p. 129)

diet assembly or legislature (p. 247)

diocese district or region under the care of a bishop (p. 145)

direct democracy system of government in which citizens participate directly in the day-to-day affairs of government rather than through elected representatives (p. 112)

dissent different or opposing ideas (p. 81)

dissenter Protestant whose views and opinions differed with those of the Church of England (p. 422)

divine right belief that a ruler's authority comes directly from God (p. 413)

domesticate tame animals and adapt crops for the purpose of cultivation (p. 12)

dowry payment to the bridegroom or his family in an arranged marriage (p. 87)

dynastic cycle rise and fall of Chinese dynasties according to the Mandate of Heaven (p. 64)

dynasty ruling family (p. 25)

E

elector one of seven German princes who would choose the Holy Roman emperor (p. 427)

émigré (EHM ih gray) person who flees his or her country for political reasons (p. 476)

empire group of states or territories controlled by one ruler (p. 18)

enclosure in England in the 1700s, the process of taking over and fencing off public lands (p. 499)

encomienda right the Spanish government granted to its American colonists to demand labor or tribute from Native Americans (p. 390)

engineering application of science and mathematics to develop useful structures and machines (p. 138)

engraving art form in which an artist etches a design on a metal plate with acid and then uses the plate to make multiple prints (p. 342)

enlightened despot absolute ruler who uses his or her power to bring about political and social change (p. 452)

entrepreneur person who assumes financial risks in the hope of making a profit (p. 404)

epic long, narrative poem (p. 222)

epidemic outbreak of a rapidly spreading disease (p. 225)

ethics moral standards of behavior (p. 47)

ethnic group large group of people who share the same language and cultural heritage (p. 245)

exchequer treasury (p. 207)

excommunication exclusion from the Roman Catholic Church as a penalty for refusing to obey Church laws (p. 195)

expansionism policy of increasing the amount of territory a government holds (p. 95)

F

faction small group (p. 473)

factory place in which workers and machines are brought together to produce large quantities of goods (p. 502)

federal republic government in which power is divided between the national, or federal, government and the states (p. 463)

feudal contract exchange of pledges between lords and vassals (p. 186)

feudalism (FYOO duhl ihz uhm) loosely organized system of government in which local lords governed their own lands but owed military service and other support to a greater lord (pp. 64, 186)

fief (FEEF) in the Middle Ages, an estate granted by a lord to a vassal in exchange for service and loyalty (p. 186)

filial piety respect for parents (p. 90)

flying buttress stone support on the outside of a building that allowed builders to construct higher walls and leave space for large stained-glass windows (p. 223)

fresco colorful painting completed on wet plaster (p. 102)

friar monk who traveled throughout Europe's growing towns to preach to the poor (p. 195)

frontier sparsely populated, undeveloped area on the outskirts of civilization (p. 182)

G

gentry wealthy, landowning class (p. 304)

geography study of people, their environments, and their resources (p. 6)

ghetto separate section of a city where members of a minority group are forced to live (p. 355)

glacier thick sheet of ice that covered parts of the Earth during the ice age (p. 12)

global warming worldwide temperature increase (p. 157)

Glossary

glyph pictograph or other symbol carved into a surface (p. 164)

golden age period of great cultural achievement (p. 83)

gravity force that tends to pull one mass or object to another (p. 358)

griot (GREE oh) professional storyteller in early West Africa (p. 297)

guerrilla warfare fighting carried on through hit-and-run raids (p. 489)

guild in the Middle Ages, association of merchants or artisans who cooperated to protect their economic interests (p. 200)

H

habeas corpus principle that a person cannot be held in prison without first being charged with a specific crime (p. 426)

haiku form of Japanese poetry that expresses a feeling, thought, or idea in three lines, or 17 syllables (p. 325)

hajj one of the Five Pillars of Islam, the pilgrimage to Mecca that all Muslims are expected to make at least once in their lifetime (p. 254)

hangul alphabet that uses symbols to represent the sounds of spoken Korean (p. 315)

heliocentric based on the belief that the sun is the center of the universe (pp. 123, 356)

helot member of a class of state-owned slaves in ancient Sparta (p. 106)

heresy religious belief that is contrary to the official teachings of a church (p. 146)

hierarchy (HĪ uhr ahr kee) system of ranking people within a society (p. 35)

hieroglyphics (hi er oh GLIHF ihks) form of picture writing developed by the ancient Egyptians (p. 32)

hijra Muhammad's flight from Mecca to Medina in 622 (p. 253)

historian person who studies how people lived in the past (p. 10)

humanism intellectual movement at the heart of the Italian Renaissance that focused on worldly subjects rather than on religious issues (p. 337)

humanities study of subjects taught in ancient Greece and Rome, such as grammar, rhetoric, poetry, and history (p. 338)

hypothesis possible explanation (p. 357)

I

icon holy image of Christ, the Virgin Mary, or a saint venerated in the Eastern Orthodox Church (p. 237)

ideogram picture that symbolizes an idea or action (p. 32)

ideology system of thought and belief (p. 518)

illumination artistic decoration in books (p. 224)

immunity natural protection (p. 386)

imperialism domination by one country of the political, economic, or cultural life of another country or region (p. 133)

indulgence in the Roman Catholic Church, pardon for sins committed during a person's lifetime (p. 346)

inflation economic cycle that involves a rapid rise in prices linked to a sharp increase in the amount of money available (pp. 148, 226, 404)

intendant official appointed by French king Louis XIV to govern the provinces, collect taxes, and recruit soldiers (p. 418)

interdict in the Roman Catholic Church, excommunication of an entire region, town, or kingdom (p. 195)

J

janizary elite force of the Ottoman army (p. 273)

jihad in Islam, an effort in God's service (p. 254)

joint family family organization in which several generations share a common dwelling (p. 87)

joint stock company private trading company in which shares are sold to investors to finance business ventures (p. 404)

journeyman salaried worker who was employed by a guild master (p. 200)

jury group of people sworn to make a decision in a legal case (pp. 112, 207)

K

kabuki (kuh BOO kee) form of Japanese drama developed in the 1600s (p. 323)

kana in the Japanese writing system, phonetic symbols representing syllables (p. 318)

karma in Hindu belief, all the actions that affect a person's fate in the next life (p. 77)

kiva large underground chamber used by the Anasazi for religious ceremonies (p. 169)

knight noble in Europe who served as a mounted warrior for a lord in the Middle Ages (p. 187)

Glossary

L

labor union workers' organization (p. 509)

laissez faire policy allowing business to operate with little or no government interference (p. 450)

land reform breakup of large agricultural holdings for redistribution among peasants (p. 303)

latifundia huge estates bought up by newly wealthy Roman citizens (p. 133)

latitude distance north or south of the Equator (p. 6)

lay investiture creation of bishops by anyone who is not a member of the clergy (p. 213)

legion basic unit of the ancient Roman army, made up of about 5,000 soldiers (p. 131)

legislature lawmaking body (p. 108)

legitimacy principle by which monarchies that had been unseated by the French Revolution or Napoleon were restored (p. 493)

levée morning ritual during which nobles would wait upon King Louis XIV (p. 418)

levy collect (p. 218)

limited monarchy government in which a constitution or legislative body limits the monarch's powers (p. 426)

lineage group claiming a common ancestor (p. 295)

literacy rate percentage of people who can read and write (p. 315)

loess fine windblown yellow soil (p. 60)

logic rational thinking (p. 115)

longbow six-foot-long bow that could rapidly fire arrows with enough force to pierce most armor (p. 228)

longitude distance east or west of the Prime Meridian (p. 6)

Loyalist colonist who supported Britain during the American Revolution (p. 462)

M

manor during the Middle Ages in Europe, a lord's estate, which included one or more villages and the surrounding lands (p. 189)

mansa title for the king of Mali (p. 285)

martyr person who suffers or dies for his or her beliefs (p. 144)

matrilineal term for a family organization in which kinship ties are traced through the mother (pp. 295, 370)

means of production farms, factories, railways, and other large businesses that produce and distribute goods (p. 511)

medieval referring to the Middle Ages in Europe or the period of history in between ancient and modern times (p. 182)

mercantilism policy by which a nation sought to export more than it imported in order to build its supply of gold and silver (p. 406)

mercenary soldier serving in a foreign army for pay (pp. 149, 428)

messiah savior sent by God (p. 142)

mestizo person in Spain's colonies in the Americas who was of Native American and European descent (pp. 391, 527)

middle class new class of people, including merchants, traders, and artisans—who stood between peasants and nobles (p. 200)

millet in the Ottoman empire, a religious community of non-Muslims (p. 273)

minaret slender tower of a mosque, from which Muslims are called to prayer (p. 259)

missi dominici agents of Emperor Charlemagne who traveled throughout the empire to check the condition of the roads, listen to grievances, and see that justice was done (p. 184)

missionary someone sent on a religious mission (p. 82)

moksha (MAHK shuh) in Hindu belief, the ultimate goal of existence, achieving union with brahman (p. 77)

monarchy government in which a king or queen exercises central power (p. 106)

money economy system by which goods and services are paid for through the exchange of a token of agreed value (p. 43)

monopoly complete control of a product or business by one person or group (pp. 95, 401)

monotheistic believing in one God (pp. 46, 253)

monsoon seasonal wind; in India, the winter monsoon brings hot, dry weather and the summer monsoon brings rain (p. 53)

mosaic picture made from chips of colored stone or glass (p. 138)

mosque Muslim house of worship (p. 254)

muezzin mosque official who climbs to the top of a minaret to call the faithful to prayer (p. 259)

mulatto in Spain's colonies in the Americas, person

Glossary

who was of African and European descent (pp. 391, 527)

mummification (muhm mih fih KAY shuhn) practice of preserving the bodies of the dead (p. 29)

mural large wall painting (p. 85)

mystic person who devotes his or her life to seeking spiritual truths (p. 57)

N

nationalism a strong feeling of pride in and devotion to one's country (p. 483)

natural law rule or law that governs human nature (p. 446)

natural right right that belongs to all humans from birth (p. 447)

nirvana in Buddhism, union with the universe and release from the cycle of rebirth (p. 79)

nomad person who moves from place to place in search of food (p. 11)

nuclear family family unit consisting of parents and children (p. 295)

O

oasis fertile area in a desert, watered by a natural well or spring (p. 252)

oba title for the king of Benin (p. 288)

oligarchy government in which ruling power belongs to a few people (pp. 106, 458)

oracle bone bone used by priests in Shang China to predict the future (p. 63)

ostracism used in ancient Greece to banish or send away a public figure who threatened democracy (p. 112)

outpost distant military station (pp. 283, 373)

P

padi field (p. 372)

pagoda multistoried Buddhist temple with eaves that curve up at the corners (p. 307)

papal supremacy authority of medieval popes over all secular rulers (p. 193)

papyrus (puh PĪ ruhs) plant that grows along the banks of the Nile; used by the ancient Egyptians to make a paperlike material (p. 32)

partition divide (p. 435)

partnership group of merchants who joined together to finance a large-scale venture that would have been too costly for any individual trader (p. 199)

patriarch in the Byzantine empire, highest church official in a major city (pp. 145, 237)

patriarchal describing a family headed by the father, husband, or oldest male (p. 47)

patrician member of the landholding upper class in ancient Rome (p. 129)

patrilineal term for a family organization in which kinship ties are traced through the father (p. 295)

patron person who provides financial support for the arts (p. 337)

peninsular member of the highest class in Spain's colonies in the Americas (pp. 390, 527)

peon worker forced to labor for a landlord in order to pay off a debt (p. 390)

perspective artistic technique used to give drawings and paintings a three-dimensional effect (p. 339)

phalanx in ancient Greece, a massive formation of heavily armed foot soldiers (p. 106)

pharaoh (FAIR oh) title of the rulers of ancient Egypt (p. 25)

philosophe member of a group of Enlightenment thinkers who tried to apply the methods of science to the improvement of society (p. 447)

philosophy system of ideas (p. 89)

physiocrat Enlightenment thinker who searched for natural laws to explain economics (p. 450)

pictogram drawing used to represent a word (p. 17)

plains fertile flatlands (p. 157)

plantation large estate run by an owner or overseer and worked by laborers who live there (p. 390)

plateau raised area of level land (p. 52)

plebeian (plih BEE uhn) member of the lower class in ancient Rome, including farmers, merchants, artisans, and traders (p. 129)

plebiscite ballot in which voters have a direct say on an issue (p. 485)

polis city-state in ancient Greece (p. 106)

polytheistic believing in many gods (p. 16)

pope head of the Roman Catholic Church (p. 146)

potlatch ceremonial giftgiving by wealthy Native Americans of the Northwest Coast (p. 171)

predestination idea that God long ago determined who will gain salvation (p. 350)

prehistory period of time before writing systems were invented (p. 8)

prime minister head of the cabinet in a parliamentary

government; usually the leader of the largest party in the legislature (p. 458)

privateer pirate (p. 393)

proletariat working class (p. 512)

prophet spiritual leader believed to be interpreting God's will (p. 47)

province land outside the city of Rome that was controlled by the Roman government (p. 133)

pueblo Southwestern Native American village (p. 168)

Q

quipu knotted strings used by Incan officials for record keeping (p. 164)

R

rajah elected warrior chief of an Aryan tribe in ancient India; local Hindu ruler in India (pp. 57, 268)

recant give up one's views or beliefs (p. 347)

recession period of reduced economic activity (p. 522)

reincarnation in Hinduism, belief in the rebirth of the soul in another bodily form (p. 77)

religious toleration policy of allowing people to worship as they choose (p. 219)

repeal cancel (p. 400)

republic system of government in which officials are chosen by the people (pp. 129, 477)

revenue money taken in through taxes (p. 394)

rhetoric art of skillful speaking (p. 115)

rococo personal, elegant style of art and architecture made popular during the mid-1700s and featuring fancy design in the shape of leaves, shells, and scrolls (p. 453)

S

sabbath holy day for rest and worship (p. 47)

sacrament sacred ritual of the Roman Catholic Church (p. 191)

salon informal social gathering at which writers, artists, and philosophers exchanged ideas; originated in France in the 1600s (p. 451)

samurai member of the warrior class in Japanese feudal society (p. 320)

satirize make fun of (p. 137)

satrap governor of a province in the Persian empire (p. 42)

savanna grassy plain with irregular patterns of rainfall (p. 280)

scapegoat person, group, or thing forced to take the blame for the crimes or mistakes of others (p. 354)

schism permanent division in a church (p. 216)

scholasticism in medieval Europe, school of thought that used logic and reason to support Christian belief (p. 221)

scientific method painstaking method used to confirm findings and to prove or disprove a hypothesis (p. 357)

scribe in ancient civilizations, specially trained person who knew how to read, write, and keep records (p. 18)

scurvy disease caused by the lack of vitamin C in someone's diet (p. 365)

sect small religious group (p. 80)

secular having to do with worldly, rather than religious, matters (pp. 193, 483)

selective borrowing adopting or adapting some cultural traits but discarding others (p. 318)

sepoy Indian soldier who served in an army set up by the French or English East India company (p. 376)

serf in medieval Europe, peasant bound to the lord's land (p. 189)

shah king (p. 274)

shogun in Japanese feudal society, supreme military commander who held more power than the emperor (p. 320)

shrine altar, chapel, or other place that is sacred (p. 102)

silt rich soil carried by flooding rivers (p. 24)

simony selling of Church offices (p. 195)

slash-and-burn agriculture farming method in which forest and brush are cut down and burned to create planting fields (p. 294)

smelt melt in order to get the pure metal away from its waste matter (p. 500)

social contract agreement by which people give up their freedom to a powerful government in order to avoid chaos (p. 447)

socialism system in which the people as a whole rather than private individuals own all property and operate all businesses (p. 511)

social mobility ability to move up in social class (p. 261)

steppe sparse, dry grassland (pp. 18, 240)

stipend a fixed salary given to public office holders (p. 112)

strait narrow water passage (p. 103)

Glossary

stupa large domelike Buddhist shrine (pp. 83, 371)

subcontinent large landmass that juts out from a continent (p. 52)

suffrage right to vote (p. 478)

sultan Muslim ruler (p. 259)

sultanate land ruled by a sultan (p. 267)

surplus extra or excess (pp. 15, 284)

T

tariff tax on imported goods (p. 406)

technology tools and skills people use to meet their basic needs (p. 8)

tenant farmer someone who would pay rent to a lord in order to farm the land (p. 199)

tenement building multistory building divided into crowded apartments (p. 505)

theocracy government run by religious leaders (p. 350)

tithe payment to a church equal to one tenth of a person's income (p. 192)

tolerance acceptance (p. 42)

tournament mock battle in which knights would compete against one another to show off their fighting skills (p. 187)

tragedy in ancient Greece, a play that focused on human suffering and very often ended in disaster (p. 117)

triangular trade colonial trade route among Europe and its colonies, the West Indies, and Africa in which goods were exchanged for slaves (p. 399)

tribune official in ancient Rome who was elected by the plebeians to protect their interests (p. 129)

tributary state independent state that has to acknowledge the supremacy of another state and pay tribute to its ruler (p. 303)

tribute payment that conquered peoples were forced to make to their conquerors (p. 160)

troubadour wandering poet in Europe in the Middle Ages (p. 189)

truce temporary peace (p. 528)

tsunami very large, damaging wave caused by an earthquake or very strong wind (p. 317)

turnpike privately built road that charges a fee to travelers who use it (p. 504)

tyrant in ancient Greece, ruler who gained power by force (p. 108)

U

ultraroyalist émigré noble or member of the clergy in France who opposed constitutional government and favored the restoration of the old regime (p. 521)

universal manhood suffrage right of all adult men to vote (p. 519)

urbanization movement of people from rural areas to cities (p. 505)

usurp illegally take over a throne (p. 302)

usury (YOO zhuh ree) practice of lending money with interest (p. 200)

utilitarianism idea that the goal of society should be to bring about the greatest happiness for the greatest number of people (p. 511)

utopia ideal society (p. 343)

V

vassal in medieval Europe, a lord who was granted land in exchange for service and loyalty to a greater lord (p. 186)

veneration special regard (p. 54)

vernacular everyday language of ordinary people (pp. 222, 343)

veto power to block a government action (p. 129)

viceroy representative who ruled one of Spain's provinces in the Americas in the king's name; one who governed in India in the name of the British monarch (p. 389)

vizier chief minister who supervised the business of government in ancient Egypt (p. 25)

W

warlord local military ruler (p. 96)

warm-water port port that is free of ice all year (p. 433)

westernization adoption of western ideas, technology, and culture (p. 431)

Z

ziggurat (ZIHG oo rat) pyramid-temple dedicated to the chief god or goddess of an ancient Sumerian city-state (p. 36)

Glossary

A

abdicate/abdicar renunciar a un alto puesto oficial (pág. 490)

absolute monarch/monarca absoluto gobernante que tiene autoridad absoluta sobre la administración y la vida de los que están bajo su mando (pág. 413)

acropolis/acrópolis el punto más alto y fortificado de una ciudad estado griega (pág. 106)

acupuncture/acupuntura tratamiento médico por el que se introducen agujas en la piel en puntos específicos, para aliviar el dolor o como tratamiento de diversas enfermedades (pág. 96)

ahimsa/*ahimsa* creencia hindú en la no violencia y en el respeto a todas las formas de vida (pág. 78)

alliance/alianza acuerdo formal de cooperación y defensa mutua entre dos o más naciones o poderes (págs. 111, 387)

alloy/aleación mezcla o fusión de dos metales (pág. 167)

alphabet/alfabeto letras que representan los sonidos del lenguaje hablado (pág. 44)

anesthetic/anestesia droga que suprime el dolor durante la cirugía (pág. 498)

animism/animismo creencia de que los espíritus y fuerzas pueden vivir en animales, objetos o sueños (pág. 12)

annex/anexar agregar un territorio a un estado o país existente (pág. 486)

annul/anular cancelar o invalidar (págs. 214, 352)

anthropology/antropología estudio del origen y desarrollo de los pueblos y sus sociedades (pág. 8)

antisemitism/antisemitismo prejuicio contra los judíos (pág. 196)

apostle/apóstol líder o maestro de una nueva fe o movimiento (pág. 142)

apprentice/aprendiz joven que aprende un oficio de su maestro (pág. 200)

aqueduct/acueducto en la antigua Roma, estructura parecida a un puente que llevaba agua desde las colinas hasta las ciudades (pág. 138)

arabesque/arabesco diseño intrincado formado por líneas curvas que sugieren formas florales y que se usa para decorar alfombras, tejidos y objetos de vidrio (pág. 263)

archaeology/arqueología estudio de pueblos y culturas antiguas (pág. 8)

archipelago/archipiélago cadena de islas (pág. 316)

aristocracy/aristocracia gobierno encabezado por una minoría privilegiada o de clase alta (pág. 106)

armada/armada flota de barcos (pág. 414)

artifact/artefacto objeto hecho por seres humanos (pág. 8)

artisan/artesano trabajador cualificado que hace objetos a mano (pág. 16)

assassination/asesinato acto de dar muerte a una figura pública, generalmente por razones políticas (pág. 120)

assimilate/asimilar absorber o adoptar otra cultura (pág. 122)

astrolabe/astrolabio instrumento que mide la posición de las estrellas para determinar la latitud (pág. 365)

atman/*atman* según la creencia hindú, el ser esencial de una persona (pág. 77)

autocrat/autócrata gobernante que tiene autoridad total (pág. 236)

autonomy/autonomía autogobierno (pág. 520)

B

balance of power/equilibrio de poder distribución del poder militar y económico que evita que una nación se vuelva demasiado fuerte (pág. 420)

baroque/barroco estilo artístico y arquitectónico elaborado que se dio en los siglos XVII y XVIII (pág. 453)

barter economy/economía de trueque sistema en el que se utiliza el intercambio de mercancías o servicios (pág. 43)

bill of exchange/letra de cambio documento emitido por un banco a un comerciante que podía cambiar por dinero en una ciudad distante, para evitar que viajara con oro, que se podía robarse fácilmente (pág. 199)

bishop/obispo funcionario eclesiástico de alto nivel con autoridad sobre un área local o diócesis (pág. 145)

blockade/bloqueo cierre de un puerto para evitar que las personas o provisiones puedan entrar o salir (pág. 487)

bourgeoisie/burguesía clase media (pág. 469)

boyar/*boyar* noble ruso que poseía tierras en la época de los zares (págs. 242, 432)

brahman/brahmán de acuerdo con la creencia aria, el poder espiritual que reside en todas las cosas (pág. 57)

bunraku/*bunraku* en Japón, funciones teatrales de títeres (pág. 325)

bushido/*bushido* código de conducta de los samuráis durante el período feudal japonés (pág. 320)

Spanish Glossary

C

cabinet/gabinete miembros del parlamento consejeros del rey que originalmente se reunían en un pequeño cuarto o "gabinete" (pág. 458)

caliph/califa sucesor de Mahoma como líder religioso y político de los musulmanes (pág. 256)

calligraphy/caligrafía escritura refinada o estilizada que se realiza a mano (pág. 263)

canon law/derecho canónico conjunto de leyes de una iglesia (pág. 195)

canonize/canonizar reconocer a alguien como santo (pág. 352)

capital/capital dinero o riqueza (págs. 199, 501)

capitalism/capitalismo sistema económico por el que los medios de producción son propiedad privada y se administran para obtener beneficios (pág. 404)

caravel/carabela embarcación rápida y ligera a vela del siglo XV (pág. 365)

cartographer/cartógrafo persona que hace mapas (pág. 365)

caste/casta grupo social en la sociedad tradicional de India, en el que una persona nace y del que no se puede cambiar (págs. 57, 267)

cataract/catarata cascada, caída de agua (pág. 25)

celadon/celadón esmalte poco común de color verde azulado (pág. 314)

censorship/censura restricción en el acceso a ideas o información (pág. 451)

census/censo recuento de la población (pág. 135)

charter/fueros en la Edad Media, documento escrito que establecía los derechos y privilegios de una ciudad (pág. 199)

chinampas/chinampas islas artificiales hechas de tierra apilada sobre bases de juncos en lagos de poca profundidad (pág. 159)

chivalry/caballerosidad código de conducta de los caballeros durante la Edad Media (pág. 189)

circumnavigate/circunnavegar navegar alrededor de la Tierra (pág. 368)

city-state/ciudad estado unidad política compuesta por una ciudad y las tierras que la rodean (pág. 18)

civil law/ley civil cuerpo legal que trata de los derechos privados de los individuos (pág. 40)

civilization/civilización orden social complejo y altamente organizado (pág. 15)

civil war/guerra civil guerra en la que luchan dos grupos de personas de una misma nación (pág. 387)

clan/clan grupo de familias con un antepasados comunes (pág. 62)

codify/codificar organizar y dejar por escrito (pág. 40)

colony/colonia territorio poblado y gobernado por personas de otro lugar (pág. 44)

comedy/comedia en la antigua Grecia, obra de teatro donde se hacía burla de personas o costumbres (pág. 119)

commodity/mercancía producto valioso (pág. 284)

common law/ley común sistema legal igual para todos, basado en las decisiones de las cortes que se han vuelto principios legales aceptados (pág. 207)

communism/comunismo forma de socialismo defendida por Karl Marx; según él la lucha de clases era inevitable, y llevaría a la creación de una sociedad sin clases en la que todas las propiedades pasarían a ser propiedad de la comunidad (pág. 512)

compact/pacto acuerdo (pág. 395)

compromise/acuerdo aceptación de una posición intermedia (pág. 352)

conquistador/conquistador término que se refiere a los exploradores españoles que apropiaron tierras en América para España en los siglos XVI y XVII (pág. 386)

constitutional government/gobierno constitucional gobierno cuyo poder está definido y limitado por la ley (pág. 457)

consul/cónsul funcionario de la clase patricia que en la Roma antigua supervisaba el gobierno y dirigía los ejércitos (pág. 219)

covenant/convenio acuerdo que obliga a las partes (pág. 46)

creole/criollo descendiente de colonos españoles nacido en las colonias españolas de América (págs. 390, 527)

criminal law/ley criminal rama de la ley que se ocupa de las ofensas contra otros, tales como robo, agresión u homicidio (pág. 40)

crusade/cruzada guerra santa (pág. 214)

cultural diffusion/difusión cultural divulgación de ideas, costumbres y tecnología a distintos pueblos o culturas (pág. 19)

culture/cultura forma de vida de una sociedad que se pasa de una generación a la siguiente mediante el aprendizaje y la experiencia (pág. 8)

cuneiform/cuneiforme tipo de escritura de los antiguos sumerios cuyos caracteres tenían forma de cuña (pág. 36)

curriculum/currículo curso formal de estudios (pág. 185)

czar/zar título del regente del imperio ruso (pág. 243)

D

daimyo/daimio señor de la guerra que en el Japón feudal estaba directamente abajo del shogún (pág. 320)

decimal system/sistema decimal sistema numérico basado en el número 10 (pág. 83)

decipher/descifrar decodificar (pág. 32)

deficit spending/gasto deficitario situación en la que un gobierno gasta más de lo que recauda (pág. 470)

delta/delta área triangular de tierra pantanosa que se forma en la boca de algunos ríos con los depósitos de limo (pág. 25)

democracy/democracia gobierno en el que es el pueblo quien tiene el poder de gobernar (pág. 107)

demotic/demótico sistema de escritura del antiguo Egipto, más simple que los jeroglíficos, que se desarrolló para el uso diario (pág. 32)

depopulation/despoblación reducción del número de la población (pág. 428)

desertification/desertización proceso por el que la tierra fértil o semifértil se convierte en desierto (pág. 281)

dharma/*dharma* entre los hindúes, las obligaciones morales y religiosas de un individuo (pág. 77)

diaspora/diáspora diseminación de un pueblo (pág. 47)

dictator/dictador dirigente con control absoluto sobre el gobierno; en la antigua Roma, líder designado para gobernar durante seis meses en casos de emergencia (pág. 129)

diet/asamblea legislatura o asamblea legislativa (pág. 247)

diocese/diócesis distrito o región a cargo de un obispo (pág. 145)

direct democracy/democracia directa sistema de gobierno en el que los ciudadanos participan directamente en lugar de a través de representantes electos en los asuntos del día a día del gobierno (pág. 112)

dissent/desacuerdo ideas diferentes u opuestas (pág. 81)

dissenter/disidente protestante cuyos puntos de vista y opiniones diferían de los de la Iglesia de Inglaterra (pág. 422)

divine right/derecho divino creencia de que la autoridad de un gobernante proviene directamente de Dios (pág. 413)

domesticate/domesticar entrenar o adaptar animales y plantas con el propósito de cultivarlos (pág. 12)

dowry/dote en un matrimonio de conveniencia, pago al futuro esposo o a su familia (pág. 87)

dynastic cycle/ciclo dinástico florecimiento y caída de las dinastías chinas de acuerdo con el Mandato del Cielo (pág. 64)

dynasty/dinastía familia gobernante (pág. 25)

E

elector/elector uno de los siete príncipes germanos que elegían al emperador sagrado de Roma (pág. 427)

émigré/exiliado persona que deja su país por razones políticas (pág. 476)

empire/imperio grupo de estados o territorios controlados por un gobernante (pág. 18)

enclosure/cercamiento en Inglaterra en el siglo XVIII, el proceso de apropiación y cercado de tierras públicas (pág. 499)

encomienda/encomienda derecho a exigir tributo o trabajo a los nativos americanos, que el gobierno español otorgó a sus colonos en América (pág. 390)

engineering/ingeniería aplicación de las ciencias y matemáticas al desarrollo de máquinas y estructuras útiles (pág. 138)

engraving/grabado forma de arte en la que un artista graba un diseño con ácido en una placa de metal y después la usa para producir múltiples impresiones (pág. 342)

enlightened despot/déspota ilustrado gobernante absoluto que usa su poder para precipitar cambios políticos y sociales (pág. 452)

entrepreneur/empresario persona que asume riesgos financieros con la esperanza de obtener beneficios (pág. 404)

epic/poema épico largo poema narrativo (pág. 222)

epidemic/epidemia brote de una enfermedad que se extiende rápidamente (pág. 225)

ethics/ética estándar moral de conducta (pág. 47)

ethnic group/grupo étnico grupo grande de personas que comparten el idioma y la herencia cultural (pág. 245)

Spanish Glossary

exchequer/erario público tesoro de la nación (pág. 207)

excommunication/excomunión exclusión de la Iglesia Católica Romana como castigo por negarse a obedecer las leyes de la iglesia (pág. 195)

expansionism/expansionismo política de aumentar el territorio que posee un gobierno (pág. 95)

F

faction/facción grupo pequeño (pág. 473)

factory/fábrica lugar donde los trabajadores y las máquinas producen grandes cantidades de mercaderías (pág. 502)

federal republic/república federal gobierno en el que el poder se divide entre el gobierno nacional o federal y los estados (pág. 463)

feudal contract/contrato feudal intercambio de promesas entre señores y vasallos (pág. 186)

feudalism/feudalismo vago sistema de gobierno en el que los señores gobernaban sus propias tierras pero debían servicio militar y otras formas de apoyo a un superior (págs. 64, 186)

fief/feudo en la Edad Media, propiedad que el señor daba a un vasallo a cambio de servicios y lealtad (pág. 186)

filial piety/piedad filial respeto hacia los padres (pág. 90)

flying buttress/contrafuerte soporte de piedra en el exterior de un edificio que permitía la construcción de paredes más altas que dejaban espacio para grandes vidrieras (pág. 223)

fresco/fresco pintura colorida realizada sobre una pared de yeso húmedo (pág. 102)

friar/fraile monje que viajaba por las ciudades europeas en desarrollo para predicar a los pobres (pág. 195)

frontier/frontera área poco poblada y subdesarrollada, situada en las afueras de la civilización (pág. 182)

G

gentry/alta burguesía la aristocracia rural (pág. 304)

geography/geografía estudio de las personas, el entorno y los recursos (pág. 6)

ghetto/ghetto área separada de una ciudad donde se fuerza a vivir a los miembros de una minoría (pág. 355)

glacier/glaciar gruesa capa de hielo que cubría parte de la Tierra durante la era glacial (pág. 12)

global warming/calentamiento global aumento de la temperatura del planeta (pág. 157)

glyph/glifo pictografía u otro símbolo tallado en una superficie (pág. 164)

golden age/edad de oro período de grandes logros culturales (pág. 83)

gravity/gravedad fuerza que atrae una masa u objeto hacia otro (pág. 358)

griot/_griot_ antiguo narrador de historias profesional en África Occidental (pág. 297)

guerrilla warfare/guerra de guerrillas lucha que se caracteriza por rápidos ataques y retiradas (pág. 489)

guild/gremio en la Edad Media, asociación de comerciantes o artesanos que cooperaban para proteger sus intereses económicos (pág. 200)

H

habeas corpus/habeas corpus principio por el que no puede encarcelarse a una persona sin haber sido antes condenada formalmente por un crimen específico (pág. 426)

haiku/haiku poema japonés que expresa un sentimiento, pensamiento o idea en tres líneas o 17 sílabas (pág. 325)

hajj/hayyi uno de los Cinco Pilares del Islam, la peregrinación a la Meca que se espera hagan todos los musulmanes por lo menos una vez en la vida (pág. 254)

hangul/_hangul_ alfabeto que usa símbolos para representar gráficamente los sonidos del idioma coreano (pág. 315)

heliocentric/heliocéntrico sistema basado en la creencia de que el sol es el centro del universo (págs. 123, 356)

helot/ilota en la antigua Esparta, miembro de una clase de esclavos que pertenecían al estado (pág. 106)

heresy/herejía creencia religiosa contraria a las enseñanzas oficiales de la iglesia (pág. 146)

hierarchy/jerarquía sistema que clasifica a las personas de una sociedad (pág. 35)

hieroglyphics/jeroglíficos escritura pictográfica desarrollada en el antiguo Egipto (pág. 32)

hijra/héjira trayecto de Mahoma de la Meca a Medina en el año 622 (pág. 253)

historian/historiador persona que estudia el modo de vida de la gente en el pasado (pág. 10)

humanism/humanismo movimiento intelectual en el apogeo del Renacimiento italiano centrado en temas de este mundo en lugar de en temas religiosos (pág. 337)

humanities/humanidades estudio de materias que se enseñaban en la antigua Grecia y Roma, tales como gramática, retórica, poesía e historia (pág. 338)

hypothesis/hipótesis explicación posible (pág. 357)

I

icon/ícono imagen sagrada de Cristo, la Vírgen María o de un santo venerado por la iglesia ortodoxa oriental (pág. 237)

ideogram/ideograma imagen que simboliza una idea o acción (pág. 32)

ideology/ideología sistema de pensamiento y creencias (pág. 518)

illumination/iluminación decoración artística en libros (pág. 224)

immunity/inmunidad protección natural (pág. 386)

imperialism/imperialismo dominio por parte de un país de la vida política, económica o cultural de otro país o región (pág. 133)

indulgence/indulgencia perdón por los pecados cometidos en vida concedido por la Iglesia Católica Romana (pág. 346)

inflation/inflación ciclo económico caracterizado por un rápida subida de los precios ligada a un aumento rápido del dinero disponible (págs. 148, 226, 404)

intendant/intendente oficial nombrado por el rey francés Luis XIV para gobernar las provincias, recaudar impuestos y reclutar soldados (pág. 418)

interdict/interdicto en la Iglesia Católica Romana, excomunión de una región, ciudad o reino (pág. 195)

J

janizary/jenízaro fuerza de élite del ejército otomano (pág. 273)

jihad/yihad en el Islam, un esfuerzo al servicio de Dios (pág. 254)

joint family/familia extendida organización familiar en la que varias generaciones comparten una vivienda (pág. 87)

joint stock company/compañía de capital social compañía comercial privada cuyas acciones se venden a inversores para financiar aventuras empresariales (pág. 404)

journeyman/jornalero trabajador asalariado empleado por un jefe de gremio (pág. 200)

jury/jurado grupo de personas que bajo juramento deben tomar una decisión en un caso legal (págs. 112, 207)

K

kabuki/kabuki género teatral japonés desarrollado en el siglo XVII (pág. 323)

kana/*kana* en el sistema japonés de escritura, símbolos fonéticos que representan sílabas (pág. 318)

karma/karma según la creencia hindú, todas las acciones que afectan el destino de una persona en su próxima vida (pág. 77)

kiva/kiva gran cámara subterránea usada por los anazasi para realizar ceremonias religiosas (pág. 169)

knight/caballero en Europa medieval, noble que servía como guerrero a caballo para un señor (pág. 187)

L

labor union/sindicato organización de trabajadores (pág. 509)

laissez faire/*laissez faire* política que permite que los negocios operen con poca o ninguna intervención del estado (pág. 450)

land reform/reforma agraria división de grandes propiedades dedicadas a la agricultura para distribuirlas entre los campesinos (pág. 303)

latifundia/latifundios grandes propiedades adquiridas por los ciudadanos romanos que se habían vuelto ricos recientemente (pág. 133)

latitude/latitud distancia hacia el norte o sur del ecuador (pág. 6)

lay investiture/investidura laica creación de obispos por parte de alguien que no es clérigo (pág. 213)

legion/legión unidad básica del ejército de la antigua Roma, que consistía de unos 5,000 soldados (pág. 131)

legislature/asamblea legislativa cuerpo encargado de hacer las leyes (pág. 108)

legitimacy/legitimidad principio por el que las monarquías que habían sido derrocadas por la Revolución Francesa o por Napoleón debían restituirse (pág. 493)

levée/recepción matutina ritual de la mañana en el que los nobles atendían al rey Luis XIV (pág. 418)

levy/recaudar cobrar impuestos (pág. 218)

limited monarchy/monarquía limitada gobierno en el que la constitución o el cuerpo legislativo limitan los poderes de la monarquía (pág. 426)

lineage/linaje grupo de antepasados comunes (pág. 295)

Spanish Glossary

literacy rate/tasa de alfabetización porcentaje de personas que pueden leer y escribir (pág. 315)

loess/loes tierra fina y amarilla que se lleva el viento (pág. 60)

logic/lógica pensamiento racional (pág. 115)

longbow/arco largo arco de seis pies de largo que podía lanzar con rapidez flechas con suficiente fuerza como para atravesar casi todos los tipos de armaduras (pág. 228)

longitude/longitud distancia hacia el este o el oeste del Primer Meridiano (pág. 6)

Loyalist/*Loyalist* colono leal a Gran Bretaña durante la Revolución Americana (pág. 462)

M

manor/feudo propiedad de un Señor que incluía uno o más pueblos y las tierras que los rodeaban en la Edad Media en Europa (pág. 189)

mansa/mansa título del rey de Mali (pág. 285)

martyr/mártir persona que sufre o muere por sus creencias (pág. 144)

matrilineal/matrilineal organización familiar en la que los lazos de parentesco se siguen a través de la madre (págs. 295, 370)

means of production/medios de producción granjas, fábricas, ferrocarriles y otros grandes negocios que producen y distribuyen mercancías (pág. 511)

medieval/medieval que se refiere a la Edad Media en Europa o al período histórico situado entre la época antigua y la moderna (pág. 182)

mercantilism/mercantilismo política por la que una nación trataba de exportar más de lo que importaba para aumentar sus reservas de oro y plata (pág. 406)

mercenary/mercenario soldado que sirve en un ejército extranjero a cambio de dinero (págs. 149, 428)

messiah/mesías salvador enviado por Dios (pág. 142)

mestizo/mestizo persona de las colonias españolas de América descendiente de nativos y europeos (págs. 391, 527)

middle class/clase media nueva clase social, situada entre los campesinos y los nobles, que incluye mercaderes, comerciantes y artesanos (pág. 200)

millet/millet comunidad religiosa no musulmana en el impero otomano (pág. 273)

minaret/minarete torre esbelta de una mezquita desde la que se convoca a los musulmanes a la oración (pág. 259)

missi dominici/*missi dominici* agentes del emperador Carlomagno que viajaban por el imperio para comprobar el estado de los caminos, oir quejas, y asegurarse de que se hiciera justicia (pág. 184)

missionary/misionero persona a quien se envía en una misión religiosa (pág. 82)

moksha/moksha según la creencia hindú, el objetivo final de la existencia, llegar a la unión con el brahman (pág. 77)

monarchy/monarquía gobierno en el que el poder reside en el rey o la reina (pág. 106)

money economy/economía de dinero sistema por el que las mercancías y servicios se pagan mediante el intercambio de una moneda con un valor establecido (pág. 43)

monopoly/monopolio control total de un producto o negocio por una persona o grupo (págs. 95, 401)

monotheistic/monoteísta creencia en un solo Dios (págs. 46, 253)

monsoon/monzón viento de temporada; en India, el monzón de invierno trae tiempo seco y caliente, y el de verano trae lluvias (pág. 53)

mosaic/mosaico imagen hecha con pedazos de piedras o vidrio de colores (pág. 138)

mosque/mezquita templo musulmán (pág. 254)

muezzin/muecín musulmán que desde lo alto de un minarete llama a los religiosos a la oración (pág. 259)

mulatto/mulato en las colonias españolas de América, descendiente de africanos y europeos (págs. 391, 527)

mummification/momificación práctica de preservar los cuerpos de los muertos (pág. 29)

mural/mural pintura de gran tamaño sobre una pared (pág. 85)

mystic/místico persona que dedica su vida a buscar verdades espirituales (pág. 57)

N

nationalism/nacionalismo fuerte sentimiento de orgullo y devoción hacia el propio país (pág. 483)

natural law/ley natural reglas o leyes que gobiernan la naturaleza humana (pág. 446)

natural right/derecho natural derechos que todas las personas tienen desde el momento en que nacen (pág. 447)

nirvana/nirvana en el budismo, unión con el universo y liberación del ciclo de la reencarnación (pág. 79)

Spanish Glossary

nomad/nómada persona que se traslada de un lugar a otro en busca de alimentos (pág. 11)

nuclear family/familia nuclear unidad familiar que consiste en los padres y sus hijos (pág. 295)

O

oasis/oasis área fértil de un desierto, regada por aguas subterráneas o por un manantial (pág. 252)

oba/oba título del rey de Benin (pág. 288)

oligarchy/oligarquía gobierno en el que el poder de gobernar está en manos de unas pocas personas (pág. 106, 458)

oracle bone/huesos oraculares huesos usados por los sacerdotes de la China Shang para predecir el futuro (pág. 63)

ostracism/ostracismo en la Grecia antigua, el acto de desterrar o enviar lejos una figura pública que amenazaba la democracia (pág. 112)

outpost/puesto de avanzada estacionamiento militar distante (págs. 283, 373)

P

padi/arrozal campo de arroz (pág. 372)

pagoda/pagoda templo budista de varios pisos con aleros que se curvan en las esquinas (pág. 307)

papal supremacy/supremacía papal en la Edad Media, autoridad de los papas sobre los demás gobernantes (pág. 193)

papyrus/papiro planta que crece a lo largo de los bancos del Nilo; usado por los antiguos egipcios para hacer un material parecido al papel (pág. 32)

partition/partición parte, división (pág. 435)

partnership/sociedad grupo de comerciantes que se unen para financiar un negocio a gran escala que hubiera sido demasiado costoso para un comerciante individual (pág. 199)

patriarch/patriarca en el imperio bizantino, el funcionario de rango más alto en la Iglesia de una ciudad importante (págs. 145, 237)

patriarchal/patriarcal familia regida por el padre, esposo o varón de mayor edad (pág. 47)

patrician/patricio miembro de la clase alta terrateniente en la antigua Roma (pág. 129)

patrilineal/patrilineal organización familiar en la que los lazos de parentesco se siguen a través del padre (pág. 295)

patron/mecenas persona que proporciona apoyo financiero a la cultura y las artes (pág. 337)

peninsular/peninsular miembro de la clase más alta en las colonias españolas de América (págs. 390, 527)

peon/peón trabajador forzado a trabajar para un terrateniente para pagar una deuda (pág. 390)

perspective/perspectiva técnica artística usada para lograr el efecto de tercera dimensión en dibujos y pinturas (pág. 339)

phalanx/falange en la antigua Grecia, formación masiva de soldados de infantería fuertemente armados (pág. 106)

pharaoh/faraón título de los gobernantes del antiguo Egipto (pág. 25)

philosophe/philosophe miembro de un grupo de pensadores de la Ilustración que trataron de aplicar métodos científicos para mejorar la sociedad (pág. 447)

philosophy/filosofía sistema de ideas (pág. 89)

physiocrat/fisiócrata pensador de la Ilustración que buscaba leyes naturales para explicar la economía (pág. 450)

pictogram/pictograma dibujo utilizado para representar una palabra (pág. 17)

plains/planicies tierras planas y fértiles (pág. 157)

plantation/plantación gran propiedad administrada por un dueño o capataz y cultivada por trabajadores que viven en ella (pág. 390)

plateau/meseta área elevada de tierra plana (pág. 52)

plebeian/plebeyo en la antigua Roma, miembro de clase baja, que incluía granjeros, mercaderes, artesanos y comerciantes (pág. 129)

plebiscite/plebiscito votación en la que los votantes expresan su opinión sobre un tema en particular (pág. 485)

polis/ciudad estado ciudad de la antigua Grecia que tenía su propio gobierno (pág. 106)

polytheistic/politeísta creencia en muchos dioses (pág. 16)

pope/papa cabeza de la Iglesia Católica Romana (pág. 146)

potlatch/potlatch entre los americanos nativos de la costa noroeste, entrega ceremonial de presentes (pág. 171)

predestination/predestinación idea de que Dios determinó hace mucho tiempo quién alcanzaría la salvación (pág. 350)

prehistory/prehistoria período de tiempo anterior a la invención de los sistemas de escritura (pág. 8)

Spanish Glossary

prime minister/primer ministro jefe del gabinete en un gobierno parlamentario; generalmente el líder del partido mayoritario de la legislatura (pág. 458)

privateer/bucanero pirata (pág. 393)

proletariat/proletariado clase trabajadora (pág. 512)

prophet/profeta líder espiritual a quien se le atribuye la interpretación de la voluntad de Dios (pág. 47)

province/provincia territorio situado fuera de Roma que estaba controlado por el gobierno romano (pág. 133)

pueblo/pueblo poblado de los nativos americanos del Sudoeste (pág. 168)

Q

quipu/quipo cuerdas con nudos que usaban los aztecas como sistema de registro (pág. 164)

R

rajah/rajá jefe guerrero electo de una tribu aria en la antigua India; gobernante local hindú en India (págs. 57, 268)

recant/retractarse abandonar las propias creencias o puntos de vista (pág. 347)

recession/recesión período de reducción de la actividad económica (pág. 522)

reincarnation/reencarnación en el hinduismo, creencia del renacimiento del alma en otra forma corporal (pág. 77)

religious toleration/tolerancia religiosa política que permite a las personas practicar su religión como quieran (pág. 219)

repeal/revocar cancelar (pág. 400)

republic/república sistema de gobierno en el que los gobernantes son elegidos por el pueblo (págs. 129, 477)

revenue/rentas públicas dinero que se recauda por impuestos (pág. 394)

rhetoric/retórica arte de hablar con habilidad (pág. 115)

rococo/rococó estilo artístico y arquitectónico elegante y personal que se dio a mediados del siglo XVIII y que presentaba sofisticados diseños en forma de hojas, conchas marinas y volutas (pág. 453)

S

sabbath/sabbat día sagrado para descansar y rendir culto (pág. 47)

sacrament/sacramento ritual sagrado de la Iglesia Católica Romana (pág. 191)

salon/salón reunión social informal en la que escritores, artistas y filósofos intercambian ideas; comenzó en Francia en el siglo XVII (pág. 451)

samurai/samurai miembro de la clase guerrera en la sociedad japonesa feudal (pág. 320)

satirize/satirizar burlarse de algo (pág. 137)

satrap/sátrapa gobernador de una provincia del imperio persa (pág. 42)

savanna/sabana planicie con pastizales cuyo régimen de lluvias es irregular (pág. 280)

scapegoat/chivo expiatorio persona, grupo o cosa a quien se culpa por los crímenes o faltas de otros (pág. 354)

schism/cisma división permanente de una iglesia (pág. 216)

scholasticism/escolasticismo en la Europa medieval, escuela de pensamiento que usaba la lógica y la razón para apoyar las creencias cristianas (pág. 221)

scientific method/método científico método concienzudo que se usa para confirmar hallazgos y poner a prueba hipótesis (pág. 357)

scribe/escriba en las civilizaciones antiguas, persona especialmente entrenada que sabía leer, escribir y mantener registros (pág. 18)

scurvy/escorbuto enfermedad causada por la falta de vitamina C en la dieta (pág. 365)

sect/secta pequeño grupo religioso (pág. 80)

secular/secular que tiene que ver más con asuntos mundanos que religiosos (págs. 193, 483)

selective borrowing/préstamo selectivo adoptar o adaptar algunos rasgos culturales y descartar otros (pág. 318)

sepoy/cipayo soldado de India que servía en un ejército inglés o francés de la East India Company (pág. 376)

serf/siervo en la Europa medieval, campesino ligado a la tierra del Señor (pág. 189)

shah/sha rey (pág. 274)

shogun/shogún en la sociedad feudal japonesa, jefe militar supremo con más poder que el emperador (pág. 320)

shrine/altar capilla u otro lugar sagrado (pág. 102)

silt/limo tierra fértil que arrastran las crecidas de los ríos (pág. 24)

simony/simonía venta de objetos religiosos
(pág. 195)

slash and burn agriculture/agricultura de cortar y quemar método de cultivo que consiste en cortar selva o matorrales y quemarlos para crear campos de cultivo (pág. 294)

smelt/fundir fundir mineral para separar el mineral puro del desperdicio (pág. 500)

social contract/contrato social acuerdo por el que las personas entregan su libertad a un gobierno poderoso para evitar el caos (pág. 447)

socialism/socialismo sistema en el que el pueblo como un todo, más que los individuos, son dueños de todas la propiedades y manejan todos los negocios (pág. 511)

social mobility/mobilidad social capacidad para ascender de clase social (pág. 261)

steppe/estepa tierra de pastos escasos y secos (págs. 18, 240)

stipend/estipendio salario fijo de los funcionarios públicos (pág. 112)

strait/estrecho paso angosto de agua (pág. 103)

stupa/*stupa* gran altar budista en forma de cúpula (págs. 83, 371)

subcontinent/subcontinente gran masa de tierra que sobresale de un continente (pág. 52)

suffrage/sufragio derecho al voto (pág. 478)

sultan/sultán gobernante musulmán (pág. 259)

sultanate/sultanía territorio regido por un sultán (pág. 267)

surplus/excedente exceso, extra (págs. 15, 284)

T

tariff/tasa impuesto a mercancías importadas (pág. 406)

technology/tecnología herramientas y conocimiento que usan las personas para satisfacer sus necesidades básicas (pág. 8)

tenant farmer/campesino arrendatario persona que paga una renta a un Señor por trabajar en sus tierras (pág. 199)

tenement building/inquilinato edificio de varios pisos dividido en apartamentos llenos de gente (pág. 505)

theocracy/teocracia gobierno administrado por líderes religiosos (pág. 350)

tithe/diezmo pago a la iglesia, igual a un décimo de los ingresos de una persona (pág. 192)

tolerance/tolerancia aceptación (pág. 42)

tournament/torneo batalla fingida en la que los caballeros competían entre sí para mostrar sus habilidades en la lucha (pág. 187)

tragedy/tragedia en la antigua Grecia, obra teatral que trataba del sufrimiento humano y que acababa en un desastre (pág. 117)

triangular trade/comercio triangular ruta colonial de comercio entre Europa y sus colonias en las Indias Occidentales y África, en donde las mercancías se cambiaban por esclavos (pág. 399)

tribune/tribuno funcionario de la antigua Roma elegido por los plebeyos para proteger sus intereses (pág. 129)

tributary state/estado tributario estado independiente que debe reconocer la supremacía de otro estado y pagar tributo a su gobernante (pág. 303)

tribute/tributo pago obligatorio de los pueblos conquistados a los conquistadores (pág. 160)

troubadour/trobador en la Edad Media, poeta europeo ambulante (pág. 189)

truce/tregua paz temporaria (pág. 528)

tsunami/tsunami ola enorme y destructiva causada por un terremoto o vientos muy fuertes (pág. 317)

turnpike/carretera de peaje camino construido por intereses privados que cobran un peaje a los viajeros que lo usan (pág. 504)

tyrant/tirano en la antigua Grecia, gobernante que llegó al poder por medio de la fuerza (pág. 108)

U

ultraroyalist/ultrarealista en Francia, noble exiliado o miembro de la iglesia que se oponía al régimen constitucional y apoyaba la reinstauración del antiguo régimen (pág. 521)

universal manhood suffrage/sufragio universal masculino derecho de todos los hombres adultos a votar (pág. 519)

urbanization/urbanización movimiento de personas de las áreas rurales a las ciudades (pág. 505)

usurp/usurpar apoderarse ilegalmente de un trono (pág. 302)

usury/usura práctica de prestar dinero con interés (pág. 200)

utilitarianism/utilitarismo idea de que el objetivo de la sociedad debería ser lograr la mayor felicidad posible para el mayor número posible de personas (pág. 511)

utopia/utopía sociedad ideal (pág. 343)

Spanish Glossary

V

vassal/vasallo en la Europa Medieval, señor a quien se le otorgaron tierras a cambio de servicios y lealtad a un señor más poderoso (pág. 186)

veneration/veneración estima especial (pág. 54)

vernacular/vernacular lenguaje diario de las personas comunes (págs. 222, 343)

veto/veto poder de bloquear una acción del gobierno (pág. 129)

viceroy/virrey representante que regía una de las provincias de España en las Américas en nombre del rey; quien gobernaba en India en nombre del monarca británico (pág. 389)

vizier/visir ministro principal que supervisaba los asuntos de gobierno en el antiguo Egipto (pág. 25)

W

warlord/jefe militar cabeza de un ejército local (pág. 96)

warm-water port/puerto de aguas templadas puerto que carece de hielo en todo el año (pág. 433)

westernization/occidentalización adopción de las ideas, tecnología y cultura occidentales (pág. 431)

Z

ziggurat/zigurat templo piramidal dedicado al dios o diosa principal de una antigua ciudad estado sumeria (pág. 36)

Index

Italicized letters after page numbers refer to the following: *c* = chart; *g* = graph; *m* = map; *n* = footnote; *p* = picture; *ps* = primary source.

Index

Index

Index

Index

Index

Index

Index

Index

Index

Index

Index

Index

Poem of the Cid, 222*ps*
Poems (Michelangelo), 340
Poetics (Aristotle), 118*ps*
poetry
　of ancient China, 307
　of ancient Greece, 117
　haiku, 320, 325
　Muslim poetry, 263, 265
Poland
　diet, 247
　Jewish settlements in, 245,
　　246, 355
　partition of, 411, 435
　revolution for independence
　　in, 525
　Roman Catholic Church in,
　　245
polis, 106
"Political Justice" (Godwin),
　512
political parties, 457–458
Polo, Marco, 218, 308, 310
polytheism, 16, 28
Pomos, 170
Pompeii, 138, 139
Pompey, 134
Pope, Alexander, 358, 446
popes
　and early Christian church,
　　146
　papal supremacy, 193
　secular power in Middle
　　Ages, 193, 195
population
　and Industrial Revolution,
　　500, 510
　and land ownership in
　　France 1789, 469
　Native American population
　　decline, 388*g*, 397
porcelain, 307, 310, 378
Portugal
　African colonization, 292,
　　398
　Brazilian colony of, 391, 393,
　　533
　empire in East, 373–374
　explorations of, 332, 365
　Goa seized by, 373
　and Inquisition, 374
　Japan's trade with, 380–381
　and Line of Demarcation,
　　366–367
　and Malacca, 362, 374

plantation economies of, 393
Prince Henry, 332, 365
religious intolerance of
　missionaries from, 374
shipbuilding by, 332, 365
trade with China, 377–378
Poseidon, 131
postal service, 135, 218
potatoes, 378, 403, 452
　and famine, 525
potlatch, 171
Powell, Colin, 179, 179*p*
Prague, 525
Praise of Folly, The (Erasmus),
　343
predestination, 350
prehistory, 8
Prentice Hall world history
　Web site, xxxii
Presbyterians, 424
Priestley, Joseph, 446
priests, duties of, 191
prime minister, 458
Prince Henry, 332, 365
Prince, The (Machiavelli), 341*ps*
princeps, 135
printing, 303, 334, 345, 362
printing press, 345
privateers, 393
Problem Solving and Decision
　Making
　See skills
*Proclamation of the National
　Convention*, 480
Procopius, 239
proletariat, 512–513
prophets, of Judaism, 47
Protestant and Catholic land
　ownership in Ireland,
　xxxvi*g*, 457*g*
Protestant Reformation, and
　Renaissance, 346–348, 350
Protestants
　and American colonies, 395*n*
　and Church of England, 422
　and Edict of Nantes, 417, 420
　and Inquisition, 413
　naming of, 348
　persecution of, 416, 420
　and Thirty Years' War, 410
　See also Luther, Martin;
　　specific denominations
Prussia
　and Junkers, 429–430

and partition of Poland, 411,
　435
and Quadruple Alliance, 493
revolution in, 525–526
rise of, 429–430
See also Germany
Ptah-hotep, 25–26
Ptolemy, 140, 337, 356
public works, civilization
　development and, 17
pueblos, 155, 168–169, 392
Pueblos, 170
Puerto Rico, 386
Punic Wars, 126, 132–133, 283
puppet plays, 325
purgatory, 347
Puritans, 39, 39*p*, 395*n*, 422,
　424, 426
Pushkin, Alexander, 433
"putting-out" system, 404, 406,
　502
Pyrenees, 132
Pythagoras, 122

Q

Qajars, 275
Qianlong, emperor of China,
　363*p*, 378–379, 385, 444
Qin dynasty, 90, 93, 94*m*
Qing dynasty, 378–379, 380
Quadruple Alliance, 493
Quakers, 351, 424, 426
Quebec, 385, 394, 396
Quechua, 164
quipus, 164
Quran, 250*p*, 252*ps*, 253, 254,
　255, 271, 287

R

Rabelais, Francois, 343, 345
Racine, Jean, 418
railroads
　in Great Britain 1840 and
　　1850, 503*m*
　impact of, 503
　Liverpool–Manchester
　　Railroad, 497
rain forests, 163, 288
rajahs, 57, 81, 268
Ramayana, 58, 67*ps*
Ramses II, pharaoh of Egypt,
　2*p*, 27, 31, 33
Raphael, 340
rats, 227

recession, definition of, 533
Recognizing Bias and Propa-
　ganda
　See skills
Reconquista, 205, 218–219
*Record of Buddhist Kingdoms,
　A* (Faxian), 83*ps*, 95*ps*
Red River, 369
Red Sea, 289
Reign of Terror, 466, 473, 479,
　480–481, 481*p*
reincarnation, 77
religion
　and afterlife, 28, 29
　of Anasazi, 169
　and "ancestor worship," 63
　of ancient Egypt, 28–29, 31
　of ancient Greece, 109
　and animal sacrifice, 82
　animism, 12
　of Aryans, 51, 57
　and astrology, 42
　of Aztec empire, 162
　in Babylon, 41, 42
　and baptism, 351
　Buddhism, 78–80
　of China's early civilizations,
　　62–63, 89–92
　Christianity, 43, 47, 135,
　　141–146
　earth-mother goddess
　　worship, 12
　Hinduism, 76–78
　and human sacrifice, 158, 162
　and immortality, 92
　of Incan empire, 167
　of Indus Valley civilization,
　　54
　Judaism, 45–47
　and land ownership in
　　Ireland, 457*g*
　major religions of Eastern
　　Europe, 233*m*
　of Mayas, 158
　Methodist Church, 508
　monotheism, 46, 253
　95 Theses, 335
　and origin of government,
　　16
　and Peace of Augsburg, 348
　persecution of religious
　　groups, 135, 143, 144–145,
　　196, 200, 211, 245, 246, 381,
　　395

Index

Index

Index

Index

Index

Index

Credits

Staff Credits

The people who made up the *World History: Connections to Today* team—representing design services, editorial, editorial services, electronic publishing technology, manufacturing & inventory planning, market research, marketing services, online services & multimedia development, planning & budget, product planning, production services, project office, publishing processes, and rights & permissions—are listed below. Bold type denotes the core team members.

Margaret Antonini, Laura Bird, Lois Brown, Laura Chadwick, Rhett Conklin, Jim Doris, Libby Forsyth, Doreen Galbraith, Joe Galka, Nancy Gilbert, **Holly Gordon,** Katharine Graydon, Lance Hatch, Helen Issackedes, **John Kingston,** Elizabeth Kiszonas, Carol Lavis, Marian Manners, Bill McAllister, Xavier Niz, Robert Prol, **Maureen Raymond,** Amy Reed, Ryan Richards, **Kirsten Richert,** Margie Schulz, Annette Simmons, **Frank Tangredi,** Elizabeth Torjussen

Additional Credits

Greg Abrom, Ernest Albanese, Mary Aldridge, Rob Aleman, Diane Alimena, Penny Baker, Rui Camarinha, Devorah Cohen, Martha Conway, Ed Cordero, Mark Cryan, Paul Delsignore, Mark Elias, Catalina Gavilanes, Robin Giraldo, Evan Holstrom, Joanne Hudson, Marilyn Leitao, Martin Levik, Vickie Menanteaux, Art Mkrtchyan, LaShonda Morris, Robert Siek, Helen Young

Illustration Credits

Maps: Mapping Specialists Limited **Features 61, 286** José Morales, S.I. International; **139** Malcolm McGregor; **227, 507** Ben Stahl, Klimt Represents; **375,** Richard Courtney, S.I. International; **557** Penny Haufe, Klimt Represents

Cover: Eiffel Tower, Strasbourg Statue and Obelisk of Luxor, (Paris, France) 1991, Stephen Simpson/ FPG International Corp. **Cover and title page border:** clockwise from top left: Ife Figure. South-Western Nigeria, c.12-15th centuries A.D., Bronze (Nigeria National Museum, Lagos, Nigeria). Photo: John Picton; Heiroglyphs. Bas-Relief, near White Chapel of Karnak dedicated to Amon-Min, ithyphallic god of fertility, limestone (Egypt). Erich Lessing/Art Resource, NY; Zapotec Urn from Monte Alban (Mexico), Charles & Josette Lenars/CORBIS; Detail of Greek translation of discourse by Emperor Nero on the freedom of Greeks, stone. Museo della Civilta Romana, Rome, Italy/Roger-Viollet, Paris/Bridgeman Art Library, London/NY; Queen Elizabeth I (England) Bedfordshire, Woburn Abbey/A.K.G., Berlin/Superstock; Copy of the Aztec Sun Stone Calender c. 16th, Malachite (Mexico) Ian Mursell/ Mexicolore/Bridgeman Art Library,

London/NY; Terra-cotta warriors from tomb of Qin Shinuang (China), Christopher Arnesen/Tony Stone Images; Mohandas Gandhi, CORBIS/Hulton-Deutsch Collection; Enconium of Darius I, Acheamenid Period, Archaelogical Museum, Teheran, Iran, SEF/Art Resource, NY **Interior: vi** top: Ministere de la Culture et de la Communication. Direction Regionale des affaires Culturelles de Rhone-Alpes. Service Regional de l'Archeologie; bottom: Scala/Art Resource, NY. **vii** top: O. Louis Mazzatenta/NGS Image Collection; middle: C. M. Dixon; bottom: Lee Boltin Picture Library. **viii** top: © University Museum of Cultural Heritage, University of Oslo bottom: Christel Gerstenberg/CORBIS **ix** top: *A Qadi Hears a Case* (detail), Bibliothéque Nationale de France, Paris; middle: © British Museum; bottom: © Copyright 1998 PhotoDisc, Inc. **x** top: Library of Congress; middle: The Science Museum/Science & Society Picture Library; bottom: Hermitage, St. Petersburg, Russia/The Bridgeman Art Library, London/NY **xi** top: SuperStock; middle: The Granger Collection, NY; bottom: Dannielle Hayes/Omni-Photo Communications, Inc. **xii** top: ©Regis Bossu/CORBIS Sygma; bottom: Collection of Whitney Museum of American Art **xiii** top: *Port of Marseille, France, 1754,* Joseph Vernet, The Granger Collection, NY; middle: The Granger Collection, NY; M.&E. Bernheim/Woodfin Camp & Associates **xiv** top: Robert Frerck/Odyssey Productions/Chicago; middle: *La Ferte Loupiere,* © G. Dagli Orti, Paris; bottom: CORBIS **xv** top: *Paso de los Andes,* Vilas y Prades, Museo Historico y Militar de Chile; bottom left: The Granger Collection, NY; bottom right: Korean Cultural Service **xvi** top: James Stanfield/National Geographic Society; middle: George Bernard/Photo Researchers, Inc.; bottom: The Kon-Tiki Museum, Oslo; **xvii** top: A. Ramsey/Stock, Boston; bottom left: The Granger Collection, NY; bottom right: Private Collection/The Bridgeman Art Library, London/NY **xix** top right: The Oriental Institute of the University of Chicago; bottom left: Lee Boltin Picture Library **xx** Topkapi Sarayi Museum, Istanbul/Ergun Cagatay/Tetragon **xxv** top: West Point Museum Collections, United States Military Academy, West Point, NY; bottom: *A Spaniard, his Mexican wife, and their daughter from a series on mixed marriages,* Miguel Cabrera, Museo de America, Madrid/ The Bridgeman Art Library, London/NY **xxvi** top: Library of Congress; left: Palace of Versailles, France/SuperStock **xxvii:** Bibliothéque Nationale de France top: Library of Congress **xxviii** NASA/Science Photo Library /Photo Researchers, Inc. **xxix** top,right: ©Dan Groshong/Corbis Sygma; middle: Ray Ellis/Photo Researchers; middle,right: Collection-Academia Sinica, Taipei; photo: Wan-go Weng; bottom: *The Election II - Canvassing for Votes* by William Hogarth, Sir John Soane Museum,

London/The Bridgeman Art Library, London/NY **xxx** top: Scala/Art Resource, NY; middle: Ford Motor Company; bottom: SEF/Art Resource,NY **xxxi** top: E T Archive; middle,left:CORBIS; middle: Reuters/CORBIS,Bettmann; middle,right: Dannielle Hayes/Omni-Photo Communications, Inc.; bottom,left: Lee Boltin Picture Library; bottom,right: Picasso Museum, Paris, France/Giraudon, Paris / SuperStock © 2001 Estate of Pablo Picaso/Artists Rights Society (ARS), NY; **xxxviii** ©Hulton Getty/ Liaison Agency **xxxix** Mireille Vautier/Woodfin Camp & Associates **xl** Arcadio Cartoonists & Writers Syndicate,cartoonweb.com **xliii** The Granger Collection, NY **xliv** The ScienceMuseum/Science & Society Picture Library **xlv** *A Spaniard, his Mexican Wife, and their daughter from a series on mixed marriages,* Miguel Cabrera, Museo de America, Madrid/The Bridgeman Art Library, London/NY **xlviii** Walker Art Gallery, Liverpool/The Bridgeman Art Library, London/NY **liv–1** Richard Passmore/Tony Stone Images **2** top: Garrett/National Geographic Society; middle: Collection-Academia Sinica, Taipei, photo: Wan-go Weng; bottom: Arvind Garg/Liaison International **3** top, left: Corel Professional Photos CD-ROM™; top, right: Photofest; bottom: John Elk/Tony Stone Images, Inc. **4** left: Lascaux Caves, France/SuperStock; middle: The Granger Collection, NY; right: Ministere de la Culture et de la Communication. Direction Regionale des affaires Culturelles de Rhone-Alpes. Service Regional de l'Archeologie **5** left: SuperStock; middle: Dorling Kindersley Ltd. courtesy of the Museum of London; right–2: © G. Dagli Orti, Paris, France **7** top: © Geoffrey Clifford/Woodfin Camp & Associates; bottom: Novosti Press/The Image Bank **9** top, right: CORBIS; bottom, left: Brett Houk; bottom, right–4: Corel Professional Photos CD-ROM™; background: Arvind Garg/Liaison Agency **11** CORBIS/Bettmann—UPI **12** Lascaux Caves, France/SuperStock **13** left: Illustration by Peter McCarty from FROZEN MAN by David Getz, 1994, by Peter McCarty. Reprinted by permission of Henry Holt and Company, LLC; middle, left: Bernhard Grobruck/Contrast/Liaison Agency; middle: and top, right: CORBIS Sygma **14** bottom: Erich Lessing/Art Resource, NY; top: © George Holton/Photo Researchers, Inc. **17** top: © J. M. Kenoyer/Dept. of Archaeology and Museums, Government of Pakistan; middle: © Jehangir Gazdar/Woodfin Camp & Associates, Inc; bottom: © J. M. Kenoyer/Dept. of Archaeology and Museums, Government of Pakistan **18** The Kon-Tiki Museum, Oslo **21** © Punch-Bill Tidy/Rothco Cartoons **22** top, left: Musée du Louvre, Paris/Giraudon, Paris/SuperStock; left: Courtesy of The Oriental Institute of the University of Chicago; right: Tony Stone Images **23** left: Scala/Art Resource, NY; right: Museum of Israel, Jerusalem—Lauros-Giraudon,

Paris/SuperStock **25** Kenneth Garrett/National Geographic Society **27** The Granger Collection, NY **28** Musée du Louvre, Paris/Giraudon, Paris/SuperStock **29** *Mummified Cat,* The Louvre © Photo Réunion des Musées Nationaux **30** left–2: Scala/Art Resource, NY; top, right: Erich Lessing/Art Resource, NY; bottom, right: © Fred J. Maroon/Photo Researchers, Inc. **32** Gary Cralle/The Image Bank **36** The Granger Collection, NY **39** The Granger Collection, NY **41** top and middle: © Michael Holford; bottom: The Metropolitan Museum of Art, Purchase, H. Dunscombe Colt Gift, 1961 (61.62) **42** top: The Granger Collection, NY; bottom: © Kevin Schafer/Peter Arnold, Inc. **45** Scala/Art Resource, NY **46** top: Rafael Macia/Photo Researchers, Inc.; bottom, left: The Jewish Museum, NY/Art Resource, NY **50** top, left: The Victoria and Albert Museum; left: Paolo Koch/Photo Researchers, Inc.; right: The Granger Collection, NY **51** left: *Dragon Head,* late Zhou dynasty. Courtesy of the Freer Gallery of Art, Smithsonian Institution, Washington, D.C. (32.14); right: CORBIS **54** Hulton Getty/Liaison Agency **57** National Museum of India, New Delhi, India/The Bridgeman Art Library, London/NY **59** SuperStock **62** left: *"Fu" Kuang-Ting, Shang Dynasty,* c. 1700 B.C.–1100 B.C. The Lowe Art Museum, The University of Miami/SuperStock; right: National Museum, Beijing, China/Erich Lessing/Art Resource, NY **63** © Dan Groshong/CORBIS Sygma **67** *The Earliest Cities* by Jean-Michel Coblence/CASTERMAN S.S. **68** left: Ministere de la Culture et de la Communication. Direction Regionale des affaires Culturelles de Rhone-Alpes. Service Regional de l'Archeologie; right: Kenneth Garrett/National Geographic Society **69** *Dragon Head,* late Zhou dynasty. Courtesy of the Freer Gallery of Art, Smithsonian Institution, Washington, D.C. (32.14) **70–71** SuperStock **72** top, left: E T Archive; top, right: © British Museum; bottom, left: Ralph Rainer Steffens/Bildarchiv Steffens, Mainz; bottom, right: Laurie Platt Winfrey, Inc. **73** top, right: © The Stock Market; bottom: SuperStock **72–73** National Museum of Scotland **74** left: The Ashmolean Museum/© Copyright Dorling Kindersley; middle: Archaeological Museum, Sarnath/Robert Harding Picture Library; right: Keren Su/Tony Stone Images **75** left: Christie's Images/The Bridgeman Art Library, London/NY; right: CORBIS/Richard A. Cooke **76** Lauros-Giraudon/Art Resource, NY **77** *Krishna's Combat with Indra,* c. 1585–90, Gouache, (detail) Courtesy of the Trustees of the Victorian & Albert Museum **78** W. Hille/Leo de Wys, Inc. **81** © Viren Desai/Dinodia Picture Agency **84** left: Abdullah Khandwani; right: Dorling Kindersley Ltd. **86** SEF/Art Resource, NY **87** Los Angeles County Museum of Art, From the Nasli and Alice Heeramaneck Collection, Museum Associates Purchase **88** © 1983 Steve McCurry/Magnum Photos **90** Bibliothèque Nationale, Paris, France/The Bridgeman Art Library/London/NY **91** The Ashmolean Museum © Dorling Kindersley **92** Chengde, Hubei Province, China/Kurt Scholz/SuperStock **93** O. Louis Mazzatenta/NGS Image Collection **95** Werner Forman/Art Resource, NY **96** Garry Gay/The Image Bank **100** top, left: © Copyright 1998 PhotoDisc, Inc.; left: SuperStock; right: © Peter Connolly, Spalding, Lincolnshire—Trustees of the National Museum of Scotland, Edinburgh **101** left: Lee Boltin Picture Library; right: Giraudon/Art Resource, NY **103** Knossos, Crete/Kurt Scholz/SuperStock **104** C. M. Dixon **107** Vanni/Art Resource, NY **108** Bildarchiv Preussischer Kulturbesitz **109** Stephen Dunn/Allsport **113** Benito/Liaison Agency **115** Alinari/Art Resource, NY **117** © Copyright 1998 PhotoDisc, Inc. **118** top: Martha Swope © Time Inc.; bottom: (detail), The Art Museum, Princeton University. Museum purchase, Caroline G. Mather Fund. Photographer: Bruce White **120** Erich Lessing/Art Resource, NY **122** Private Collection/The Bridgeman Art Library, London/NY **125** © Michael Holford **126** top, left: Paola Koch/Photo Researchers, Inc.; left: CORBIS/Gianni Dagli Orti; right: CORBIS **127** left: McRae Books Srl; right: E T Archive **128** CORBIS/Gianni Dagli Orti **130** *Lady Playing the Cithara* (detail), The Metropolitan Museum of Art, Rogers Fund, 1903 (03.14.5) Photograph © 1986 The Metropolitan Museum of Art **132** Scala/Art Resource, NY **133** © Stephane Compoint/CORBIS Sygma **135** Direzione Generale Musei Vaticani **136** H. M. Herget/NGS Image Collection **138** Paola Koch/Photo Researchers, Inc. **139** bottom, left: CORBIS **140** © Leonard Von Matt/Photo Researchers, Inc. **142** © André Held **143** Masolino da Panicale/E T Archive **145** top: Byzantine Collection, Dumbarton Oaks, Washington, D.C.; bottom: The Metropolitan Museum of Art, The Cloisters Collection, 1950. (50.4) Photograph © 1978 The Metropolitan Museum of Art, NY **147** McRae Books Srl **149** Walters Art Gallery, Baltimore **150** Illustration by Matthew Frey-Wood Ronsaville Harlin, Inc. **154–155** Michael Holford **154** top, left: M. L. Corvetto/The Image Works; left: Lee Boltin Picture Library **155** right: Trans. no. 3519(2) (Photo by P. Hollembeak/J. Beckett) Courtesy Department of Library Services, American Museum of Natural History **158** top: Otis Imboden © National Geographic Society; bottom: Chris Trotman/Duomo Photography, Inc. **159** top: Lee Boltin Picture Library; bottom: © Justin Kerry **161** top: Museum für Völkerivnde Wien, Foto-Archiv, Foto Nr. 61.240; middle: *La Gran Tenochtitlán*, 1940, (detail) Reproduccion Autorizada Por El Instituto Nacional De Bellas Artes Y Literatura/Banco de Mexico. Photo: Bob Schalkwijk; bottom: National Museum of Anthropology, Mexico City/Werner Forman, Art Resource, NY **163** Museo Nacional de Antropologia y Arqueologia Lima, Peru/Loren McIntyre **164** North

Wind Picture Archives **166** M. L. Corvetto/The Image Works **169** top and middle: CORBIS/Richard A. Cooke; bottom: Ohio State Museum/Werner Forman Archive/Art Resource, NY **170** © British Museum **173** The Bodleian Library, Oxford, UK **174** left: Christie's Images/The Bridgeman Art Library, London/NY; right: Bildarchiv Preussischer Kulturbesit **175** left: Lee Boltin Picture Library **176–177** SuperStock **178** left: The Granger Collection, NY; bottom, left: Photo: Kim Yong-chui/Korean Cultural Service; right: Korean Cultural Service **179** top, left: AP/Wide World Photos; top, right: Hulton Getty/Liaison Agency; middle: NASA; bottom: Lisa Quinones/Black Star **180** left: Pierre Belzeaux/Rapho Agence/Photo Researchers, Inc.; right: Giraudon/Art Resource, NY **181** left: SuperStock; right: Bibliothèque Nationale/Archiv für Kunst und Geschichte, Berlin **185** © University Museum of Cultural Heritage—University of Oslo **187** image © Copyright 1998 PhotoDisc, Inc. **188** left: © British Museum **189** Private Collection/The Bridgeman Art Library, London/NY **190** *February* from the Tres Riches Heures du duc de Berry (book of hours) painted by the Flemish [Limbourg, Limburg] Brothers from 1415, Giraudon/Art Resource, NY **193** *Virgin and Child*, miniature from the Book of Kells, Hiberno-Saxon ms., c. A.D. 800, Folio 7V. The Granger Collection, NY **194** top, right: Archiv Gerstenberg; bottom, right: The Pierpont Morgan Library/Art Resource, NY; bottom, left: The Granger Collection, NY; background: © G. Dagli Orti, Paris; **195** The Granger Collection, NY **196** © Israel Museum, Jerusalem **200** C. M. Dixon **204** top, left: image © Copyright 1998 PhotoDisc, Inc.; left: *The Siege of Antioch (First Crusade) 1098*, William of Tyre, Bibliothèque Nationale, Paris, France/The Bridgeman Art Library, London, NY; right: Christopher Guy/reproduced by the kind permission of the Dean and Chapter of Worcester **205** *The Entrance of Joan of Arc into Orleans*, Jean-Jacques Sherrer, Musée des Beaux-Arts, Orleans, France/Roger Viollet, Paris/The Bridgeman Art Library, London/NY **206** Philip Mould, Historical Portraits Ltd, London, UK/The Bridgeman Art Library, London, NY **207** image © Copyright 1998 PhotoDisc, Inc. **208** The Royal Collection © 2000 Her Majesty Queen Elizabeth II **209** The Granger Collection, NY **212** © Meyer/Kunsthistorisches Museum, Vienna **214** Scala/Art Resource, NY **218** The Granger Collection, NY **220** Giraudon/Art Resource, NY **221** By permission of The British Library (Harley ms 4431) **223** top: © Agence Top, Paris; bottom: SuperStock **224** Sonia Halliday Photography **227** top, left: *La Ferte Loupiere*, © G. Dagli Orti, Paris **228** top: Froissart's Chronicle, Battle of Janera, 1367 (detail), Bibliothèque Nationale, Paris/The Bridgeman Art Library, London/NY; middle: CORBIS; bottom: Courtesy of the Trustees of British Library, Roy.14.E.IV. **232** top,

left: Robert Frerck/Odyssey Productions, Chicago; left: Christel Gerstenberg/CORBIS; right: Bernard Cox/John Bethell PhotoLibrary, St. Albans **233** left, middle: Zamek Krolewski W. Warszawie/Collection of the Royal Castle in Warsaw; right: Hermitage, St. Petersburg, Russia/Bridgeman Art Library, London/NY **235** top, right: Marvin Trachtenberg; bottom: CORBIS/Gianni Dagli Orti; background: Robert Frerck/Odyssey Productions, Chicago **236** Scala/Art Resource, NY **237** Icon of Christ and St. Maenas, Photo Jacqueline Hyde © Réunion des Musées Nationaux **241** © G. Dagli Orti, Paris **243** Archiv für Kunst und Geschichte, Berlin **245** © Artephot/R. Percheron, Paris **250** top, left: Robert Frerck/Odyssey Productions/Chicago; left: Giraudon/Art Resource, NY; right: Private Collection/The Bridgeman Art Library, London/NY **251** left: © D. Banerjeb/Dinodia Picture Agency **251** right: Topkapi Sarayi Museum, Istanbul/Ergun Cagatay/Tetragon **252** Mohamed Lounes/Liaison Agency **253** Courtesy of the Trustees of British Library **254** © M. Reichenthal/The Stock Market **255** *A Qadi Hears a Case*, (detail), Bibliothèque Nationale de France, Paris **257** Robert Frerck/Odyssey Productions/Chicago **259** Historical Pictures/Stock Montage, Inc. **261** British Library/The Bridgeman Art Library, London/NY **262** top: (detail), Topkapi Sarayi Museum, Istanbul/Ergun Cagatay/Tetragon, bottom: Joseph Nettis/Photo Researchers, Inc. **263** The Granger Collection, NY **264** top: The Metropolitan Museum of Art, Harris Brisbane Dick Fund, 1939. (39.20) Photograph © 1982 The Metropolitan Museum of Art, NY; middle: British Museum, London/The Bridgeman Art Library, London/NY; bottom: Scala/Art Resource NY **266** By permission of The British Library [1.0. 1379 (Ethé 2296) Folio 34] **269** (detail) Victoria & Albert Museum/The Bridgeman Art Library, London, NY **270** Donato-Toronto Sun, Canada/Rothco Cartoons **273** © Sonia Halliday Photographs **278** top, left: © British Museum; middle: © British Museum; right: Werner Forman/Art Resource, NY **279** Kal Muller/Woodfin Camp & Associates **280** Martin Dohrn-Science Photo Library/Photo Researchers, Inc. **282** (detail), Museum Expedition. Courtesy, Museum of Fine Arts, Boston, MA **285** Lee Boltin Picture Library **288** © British Museum **292** Georg Gerster/Photo Researchers, Inc. **294** left: Lee Boltin Picture Library; right: Robert Harding Picture Library **296** M. & E. Bernheim/ Woodfin Camp & Associates **297** A. Ramsey/Stock, Boston **299** Jason Laure **300** top, left: E T Archive; left: Michael Holford; right: © Copyright 1998 PhotoDisc, Inc. **301** left: Collection of the National Palace Museum. Taiwan, Republic of China; right: Victoria & Albert Museum, London/Art Resource, NY **303** top: Science Museum/ Michael Holford; middle: © Uniphoto, Inc.; bottom: © Jonathan Wallen/Harry N. Abrams, Inc. **305**

Werner Forman Archive—Idemitsu Museum of Arts, Tokyo/Art Resource, NY **306** *Travelers Among Mountains and Streams* (detail), Fan K'uan, National Palace Museum, Taiwan, Republic of China **308** James Stanfield / National Geographic Society **310** The Metropolitan Museum of Art, Gift of Robert E. Tod, 1937. (37.191.1) **313** Carmen Redondo/CORBIS **315** Flags of North and South Korea © Copyright 1998 PhotoDisc, Inc. **316** Janette Ostier Gallery, Paris, France/Giraudon, Paris/SuperStock **318** Laurie Platt Winfrey, Inc. **319** E T Archive **320** © 1998 PhotoDisc, Inc. **321** left: Werner Forman/Art Resource, NY; right: The Metropolitan Museum of Art, Rogers Fund, 1904. (04.4.2) Photograph by Schecter Lee. Photograph © 1986 The Metropolitan Museum of Art **322** © John Bryson/The Image Bank **324** left: Charles & Josette Lenars/CORBIS; right: Torii Kiyonaga © British Museum; bottom: Stapleton Collection, UK/The Bridgeman Art Library, London/NY **328** left and middle: Giraudon/Art Resource, NY; right: Bernard Cox/John Bethell PhotoLibrary, St. Albans **329** left: Giraudon/Art Resource, NY; middle, left: Robert Harding Picture Library; middle, right: Lee Boltin Picture Library; right: Werner Forman Archive—Idemitsu Museum of Arts, Tokyo/Art Resource, NY **330–331** Werner Forman/Art Resource, NY **332** top and middle: The Granger Collection, NY; bottom: North Wind Picture Archives **333** top, left: The Granger Collection, NY; left: National Maritime Museum/© Dorling Kindersly Ltd.; top, right: © 1994 Larry Kunkel/FPG International Corp.; middle: The Granger Collection, NY; bottom: Mary Kate Denny/PhotoEdit; top, left: Science Museum, London/The Bridgeman Art Library, London/NY; left: Scala/Art Resource, NY; top, right: Dorling Kindersley Ltd. Courtesy of St. Bride Printing; bottom, right: Courtesy of the Trustees of British Library **335** left: *Mona Lisa*, Leonardo da Vinci, Scala/Art Resource NY; right: Private Collection, Great Britain **336** Richard Elliott/Tony Stone Images **338** *St. Jerome in His Study*, Antonello da Messina, The National Gallery, London **339** Library of Congress **340** *The Creation of Adam*, Michelangelo, Scala/Art Resource, NY **343** left: Library of Congress; right: *Self Portrait*, Albrecht Dürer, SuperStock **344** top: Scala/Art Resource, NY; left: Tom Skudra/Stratford Festival Archives; bottom, right: Clive Barda/Performing Arts Library **347** Mansell Collection/Time Inc. **348** The Granger Collection, NY **349** Cambridge Education Corp. **351** Portrait of Henry VIII, Hans Holbein, the Younger, Belvoir Castle, Leicestershire/The Bridgeman Art Library, London/NY **352** Walker Art Gallery, Liverpool/The Bridgeman Art Library, London/NY **356** Science Museum, London / The Bridgeman Art Library, London/NY **358** left: Windsor Castle, Royal Library/Archiv für Kunst und Geschichte, Berlin; right:

ry Pommett **603** Archive Photos **604** *The Balloon,* Pierre Puvis de Chavannes © Photo Réunion des Musées Nationaux **606** CORBIS/Bettmann **610, 611, 612** The Granger Collection, NY **615** Private Collection/The Bridgeman Art Library, London/NY **616** top,left: UIllstein Veroffentlichung nur mit Urhebervermerk; bottom,left: Tony Stone Images; right: The Granger Collection, NY **617** © Jean-Loup Charmet **619** CORBIS/Hulton Deutsch Collection **620** The Granger Collection, NY **621** SuperStock **622** left: image©Copyright 1998 PhotoDisc, Inc.; top,right: Private Collection/The Bridgeman Art Library, London/NY **624** Staatliche Museen zu Berlin - PreuBischer Kulturbesitz Museum für Volkerkunde **625** UIllstein Veroffentlichung nur mit Urhebervermerk **626** Hulton Getty/Liaison Agency **628** *On the Bosphorous, Istanbul,* (detail), Atkinson Art Gallery, Southport, Lancs/The Bridgeman Art Library, London/NY **629** Archive Photos/Popperfoto **630** Paolo Koch/Photo Researchers, Inc. **633** Henry Wilson **635** ET Archive **637** bottom,left: ET Archive **639** Agence France Presse/Archive Photos **641** The Granger Collection, NY **642** left: Museum of New Zealand Te Papa Tongarewa (B19095) **642**; right: ET Archive **642** top,left: ET Archive **643** CORBIS/Bettmann **645** top: Richard Vogel/Liaison Agency; bottom: Reprinted with permission of Iruma City Museum **646** Museum of Fine Arts, Boston/Laurie Platt Winfrey, Inc. **648** Transportation Museum, Tokyo **652** CORBIS **655** The Granger Collection, NY **658** CORBIS/Underwood & Underwood **663** Koninklijk Instituut voor de Tropen, TROPENMUSEUM **664** Rhodes Memorial Museum, USA/The Bridgeman Art Library, London/NY **665** ©Branger-Viollet **666** Musee Picasso, Barcelona, Spain/INDEX/ Bridgeman Art Library, London/NY/ ©2001 Estate of Pablo Picasso/Artists Rights Society(ARS), NY; middle: Werner Forman/Art Resource, NY; right: Picasso Museum, Paris, France/Giraudon, Paris /SuperStock, ©2001 Estate of Pablo Picasso/Artists Rights Society(ARS), NY **670** left: Ford Motor Company; middle: Archiv für Kunst und Geschichte, Berlin; right: The Royal Collection ©2000 Her Majesty Queen Elizabeth II **671** left: Tony Stone Images right: ET Archive **672-673**: US Army Center of Military History **674** top: PECUB, Cartoonists & Writers Syndicate; bottom: Culver Pictures, Inc. **675** top: CORBIS; top inset: Leslie E. Kossoff/AP/Wide World Photos; bottom: Alain Morvan/The Liaison Agency **676** top,left: National Archives; Culver Pictures; right: Imperial War Museum/ Archive Photos **677** left: Library of Congress; right: Collection of Whitney Museum of American Art **679** Courtesy of the Library of Congress **680** L'Illustration Paris **681** Christel Gerstenberg/CORBIS **683** John McCutchson/The Chicago Tribune, 1914. Photo: Ken Karp **684** Bildarchiv Preussischer Kulturhesitz, Berlin **686** background:

CORBIS; bottom,left: Culver Pictures, Inc.; bottom,right: Culver Pictures, Inc.; bottom,right: René Dazy Collection, Paris **688** top: Smithsonian Institution; middle: Bilderdrenst Suddeutscher Verlag, Munich; bottom: © James A. Bryant **690** The Granger Collection, NY **691** CORBIS **692, 694** National Archives **699** The Imperial War Museum, London **700** top,left: Sovfoto/Novosti; left: *The Storming of the Winter Palace, 7th November, 1917,* Novosti/The Bridgeman Art Library, London/NY; right: Sovfoto/Eastfoto **701** left: The Granger Collection, NY; right: David King Collection **703** Archive für Kunst und Geschichte, London **704** *Lenin and a Manifestation,* 1919 (detail), Novosti/The Bridgeman Art Library, London/NY **705** Hulton Getty/Liaison Agency **707** Sovfoto/ Novosti **708** AP/Wide World Photos **710** CORBIS/Scheufler Collection **711** The Bettmann Archive/CORBIS **713** *Gulag Prisoners,* Getman/The Jamestown Foundation, Washington, DC. **714** Sovfoto/Novosti **715** Scala/Art Resource, NY **716** top: Sovfoto/Eastfoto; middle: Archiv für Kunst und Geschichte, London; bottom: ITAR-TASS/ Sovfoto **719** Sovfoto/Eastfoto **720** top, left: Photograph ©The Detroit Institute of Arts, 1995. Palacio Nacional stairway, Mexico City. © Dirk Bakker, photographer, detail; left: The Central Zionist Archives; right: Irene Hubbell/Root Resources **720** top,left: (detail) Photograph ©The Detroit Institute of Arts, 1995. Palacio Nacional stairway, Mexico City. © Dirk Bakker, photographer. **721** CORBIS Sygma **723** The Granger Collection, NY **724** (detail) Photograph ©The Detroit Institute of Arts, 1995. Palacio Nacional stairway, Mexico City. © Dirk Bakker, photographer. **727** Julio Donoso/Contact Press Images/PNI **728** Turkish Culture and Information Office, NYC **731** Culver Pictures, Inc. **732** By permission of The British Library (F839) **733** Popperfoto/Archive Photos **735** Roger Viollet/Liaison Agency **738** AP/Wide World Photos **740** inset: CORBIS/ Bettmann **744** top left: © /Topham/The Image Works; middle: *Compostion No. 4,* 1920, Fernand Leger, Musee Leger, Biot, France/The Bridgeman Art Library, London/NY, Artists Rights Society(ARS), NY; right: CORBIS **745** left: Private Collection/The Bridgeman Art Library, London/NY; right: The Granger Collection, NY **746** © Elke Walford/Hamburger Kunsthalle, Hamburg **747, 748, 749** The Granger Collection, NY **752** Private Collection/The Bridgeman Art Library, London/NY **753** *The Persistence of Memory,* Salvador Dali, The Museum of Modern Art, NY (C) 1996 Demart Pro Arte, Geneva/Artists Rights Society (ARS), NY **755** middle: CORBIS/Frank Driggs; bottom,right: Frank Driggs/Archive Photos; top, left: CORBIS/Bettmann **756** CORBIS **759** left: Italian Government Tourist Board; right:©by Giancarlo Costa/Ferrovie Dello Stato, 1940 **761** CORBIS **762** Bildarchiv Preussischer Kulturbesitz **763** © Keystone/The Image Works **764** © Topham/The Im-

age Works **768** top,left: Brown Brothers; The Granger Collection, NY; right: Movietone News/CORBIS/Bettmann-UPI **769** left: The Granger Collection, NY; right: CORBIS/Bettmann **770** CORBIS/Bettmann **771** CORBIS/Bettmann-UPI **775** The Granger Collection, NY **777** background: Brown Brothers; right: Hulton Getty/Liaison Agency **779** CORBIS **780** Archive Photos **783** left: Culver Pictures, Inc. **783** top,right: CORBIS/Ira Nowinski; bottom,right: CORBIS/Bettmann-UPI **784** top: The Imperial War Museum London; bottom: © Michael Patrick /Folio, Inc. **787** AP/Wide World Photos **788** CORBIS/Bettmann **790** left: Archive Photos; right: AP/Wide World Photos **792** CORBIS/Bettmann **797** The Granger Collection, NY **798** left: Collection of the Whitney Museum of American Art; middle: *Lenin and a Manifestation, 1919* (detail), Novosti/The Bridgeman Art Library, London/NY; right: (detail) Photograph ©The Detroit Institute of Arts, 1995. Palacio Nacional stairway, Mexico City. © Dirk Bakker, photographer. **799** right: *The Persistence of Memory,* Salvador Dali, The Museum of Modern Art, New York (C) 1996 Demart Pro Arte, Geneva/Artists Rights Society (ARS), New York ; right: Archive Photos **800-801** Earth Imaging/Tony Stone Images **802** top,left: Gary Retherford/Photo Researchers, Inc.; top,right: Rogers/Monkmeyer; bottom: Michael Newman/PhotoEdit **803** top: AP/Wide World Photos; middle: SBG; bottom: Agence France Presse/CORBIS **804** top,left: Bob Martin/Sports Illustrated; left: Rudi Von Briel/PhotoEdit; right: NASA/Science Photo Library/Photo Researchers, Inc. **805** left: Marc & Evelyne Bernheim/Woodfin Camp & Associates; right: Hayes Davidson/Nick Wood **807** CORBIS **810** top: Bob Martin/Sports Illustrated; top,left: Carl Yarbrough/Sports Illustrated; bottom,left: Tom Lynn/Sports Illustrated **811** ©Dan Hofoss-Canada/Rothco **813** top: AP/Wide World Photos; bottom: Betty Press/Woodfin Camp & Associates **815** Michael Newman/PhotoEdit **816** TOLES © 1992 The Buffalo News. Reprinted with permission of UNIVERSAL PRESS SYNDICATE. All rights reserved. **817** Yousuf Karsh/Woodfin Camp & Associates **819** top: Betty Press/Woodfin Camp & Associates; bottom: Steve Vidler/SuperStock **821** top: Yagi Studio/SuperStock; middle: CORBIS/Sygma; bottom: Michael Newman/PhotoEdit **822** NASA/LBJ **823** AP/Wide World Photos **825** ABU-The Sunday Observer, Bombay/Rothco Cartoons **826** top,left ©Regis Bossu/CORBIS Sygma; left: Sovfoto/Tass; right: Halstead/Liaison Agency **827** left: CORBIS/Reuters; top,right: 0851 Gamma/Liaison Agency; middle, right: Tony Stone Images; bottom, right: 0851 Gamma/Liaison Agency **828 and 829** ©Hulton Getty/Liaison Agency **830** Georg Gerster/Photo Researchers, Inc. **834** Gamma Presse Images/Liaison Agency **835** Michael Philippot/CORBIS/Sygma

836 ©Thomas Del Braise/The Stock Market **837** left: Lionel Cironneau/ AP/Wide World Photos; right: Regis Bossu/CORBIS Sygma **839** J. Baylor Roberts/National Geographic Society **841** Dan Budnik/Woodfin Camp & Associates **842** top: La Presse/CORBIS Sygma; bottom: ©J.P. Laffont/CORBIS Sygma **843** Carl Mydans/Life Mafgazine ©Time Inc. **845-3** Gerd Ludwig/National Geographic Society **846** Shone/Liaison Agency **847** left: AP/Wide World Photos; right: Swersey/Liaison Agency **849** Dean Conger/CORBIS **850** © Chuck Fishman/Contact Press Images **851** left: Darolle/CORBIS Sygma; right: Vittoriano Rastelli/CORBIS **856** top,left: ©Fallender/Sipa Press; left: (detail) China Stock/Liu Ligun, artist; right: CORBIS **857** Paul Lowe/Magnum Photos, INC. **858** ©Hulton Getty/Liaison Agency **861** ©The Stock Market/Ken Straiton **863** SuperStock **864** Camera Press/Retna, LTD **865** Lee Foster/Bruce Coleman, Inc. **866** left: ©1989 Stuart Franklin/Magnum Photos, Inc.; background: © Fallender/Sipa Press **869** Naomi Duguid/Asia Access **871** ©Hulton-Deutsch Collection /CORBIS **872** Noboru Hashimoto/CORBIS Sygma **875** Alberto Garcia/Saba **876** ©Stuart Isett/CORBIS Sygma **877** ©Robert Fried www.robertfriedphotography.com **880** top,left: Raghu Rai/Magnum Photos; middle,top: Amrit P. Singh; middle,bottom: Alain Evrard/Photo Researchers, Inc.; right: AP/Wide World Photos **881** left: S.Compoint/CORBIS Sygma; right: CORBIS/Reuters **884** Raghu Rai/Magnum Photos **885** Eddie Adams/Liaison Agency **886** © Hillary/Royal Geographic Society **889** ©1997 Richard T. Nowitz **891** Ray Ellis/Photo Researchers **892** Marlene Nelson/Copyright Wasma'a K. Chorbachi **893** Greg English/Sygma **895** Reuters/Kai /Pfaffenbach /Archive Photos **896** Howard Sochurek/Life Magazine ©Time Inc. **897** top: Caputo/Stock, Boston; top,right: Jean-Claude Aunos/Liaison Agency; left: David Turnley/Corbis; bottom,right: Nacerdine Zebar/Liaison Agency; **898** ©1999 Michael Coyne/Black Star **899** D. Wells/Image Works **905** Jagdish Agarwa/Dinodia Picture Agency **906** top,left: Peter Turnley/CORBIS; middle: AP/Wide World Photos; right:. Robert Frerck/Odyssey Productions/Chicago **907** Reuters/CORBIS/Bettmann **909** Courtesy of the Director, National Army Museum **910** CORBIS/ Bettmann-UPI **912** Hulton Getty/Liaison Agency **912** Bas/Rothco Cartoons **913** Reza/Imax/CORBIS Sygma **914** Michael Dwyer/Stock Boston **918** Nik Wheeler /CORBIS **919** ©Marc & Evelyne Bernheim/Woodfin Camp & Associates **920** Bruno Barbey/Magnum **923** AP/Wide World Photos **925** left: Gamma Presse Images/Liaison Agency right: Shahn Kermani/Liaison Agency **926** Joe Traver/Liaison **927** background: Peter Turnley/CORBIS; inset: Noel Quidu/Liaison **928** ©T. Hegenbart/Black Star **932** top,left: Ary Diesendruck /Tony

Stone Images; left: Americas Magazine Oas; right: AP/Wide World Photos **933** left: Alain Mingam/Liaison Agency; middle: Enrique Shore/Woodfin Camp & Associates; right:Antonio Ribeiro/Liaison Agency; **935** Vera Lentz/Black Star **936-937** Courtesy of the artist. **938** ©Daher/Liaison Agency **940** ©P.Robert/CORBIS Sygma **941** COR-BIS **942** Mireille Vautier/Woodfin Camp & Associates **945** AP/Wide World Photos **946** Don Goode/Photo Researchers, Inc. **947** background: ©Ilkka Ulimonen/ CORBIS Sygma; middle: AP/Wide World Photos **948** Mireille Vautier/Woodfin Camp & Associates **949** and **950** AP/Wide World Photos **952** Ary Diesendruck/Tony Stone Images **953** ©Les Stone/CORBIS Sygma **954** Ben Gibson/Katz/Woodfin Camp & Associates **957** AP/Wide World Photos **958** left: NASA/SCIENCE Photo Library/Photo Researchers, Inc.; middle: ©Regis Bossu/Corbis Sygma; right SuperStock **959** left: Marlene Nelson/ Copyright Wasma'a K. Chorbachi; middle: Nik Wheeler/Corbis; right: Mireille Vautier/Woodfin Camp & Associates **960-961** CORBIS/Pablo Corral V **962** Musee du Louvre, Paris/Giraudon, Paris/SuperStock **963** The Oriental Institute Museum **964** The Jewish Museum, NY/Art Resource, NY **965** Bibliotheque Nationale, Paris, France/The Bridgeman Art Library/London/NY **966** ©Copyright 1998 PhotoDisc, Inc. **967** Bildarchiv Preussischer | Kulturbesitz **968** CORBIS **969** Archaeological Museum, Sarnath/Robert Harding Picture Library **970** McRae Books Srl **971** Giraudon/Art Resource, NY **972** E T Archive **973** Bibliotheque Nationale/Archiv für Kunst und Geschichte, Berlin **975** Lee **973** Archaelogical Museum, Sarnath/Robert Harding Picture Library **975** LeeBoltin Picture Library **976** Nationalmuseet, Copenhagen/The Bridgeman Art Library, London **978** British Information Service **981** Private Collection/The Bridgeman Art Library, London/New York **982** Schalkwijk/Art Resource, NY **983** Dannielle Hayes/Omni-Photo Communications, Inc. **984** The Election II-Canvassing for Votes by William Hogarth, Sir John Soane Museum, London/The Bridgeman Art Library, LondonNY **984** The Science Museum/Science & Society Picture Library **985** Museum of Fine Arts, Boston/Laurie Platt Winfrey, Inc. **986** Bildarchiv Preussischer Kulturbesitz, Berlin **987** By permission of The British Library (F839) **988** The Granger Collection, NY **989** Rudi Von Briel/PhotoEdit **990** SuperStock **992** CORBIS/Bettmann-UPI **993** © Chuck Fishman/Contact Press Images **994** Shone/Liaison Agency **996** AP/Wide World Photos **997** ©Stuart Isett/CORBIS Sygma **998** Reuters/CORBIS/Bettmann **999** © Fallender/Sipa Press

Acknowledgements

6 Excerpt from *The Overview Effect* by Frank White. Copyright © 1987, Houghton Mifflin. **55** "The Rig Veda/Hymn to Indra" from *Reading About the World, Volume 1.* Used by permission of Michael Myers, Translator, Washington State University. **65** "The Spirits Are Good" from *The Book of Songs* by Arthur Waley, Translator. Copyright © 1937 by Arthur Waley, Translator. Used by permission of Grove/Atlantic Inc. **67** Excerpt from *The Ramayana*, translated by Kenneth Anderson, aka Krishna Dharma. Copyright © 1998 by Kenneth Anderson, aka Krishna Dharma. Published by Torchlight Publishing, Inc. **80** Excerpt from *The Dhammapada*, edited by Anne Bancroft. Copyright © 1997 Element Books Limited. Used by permission of Element Books Limited and Anne Bancroft, editor. **104** Excerpt from *The Illiad* by Homer; translated by Robert Fitzgerald. Copyright © 1974 by Robert Fitzgerald. Published by Anchor Books/Doubleday. **137** Excerpt from *The Aeneid of Virgil*, translated by C. Day Lewis, reprinted by permission of Oxford University Press, Inc. **191** Excerpt from *The Canterbury Tales* by Geoffrey Chaucer, translated into modern English by Nevill Coghill. Copyright © 1951, 1958, 1960 by Neville Coghill. Reproduced by permission of Penguin Books Ltd. **222** From *The Song of Roland Done into English in the Original Measure*, translated by C. Scott Moncrieff. Copyright © 1919 Chapman & Hall Ltd. Used by permission of the publishers and the executors of the Estate of C. Scott Moncrieff. **287** Excerpt from *Leo Africanus: Description of Timbuktu*, translated by Paul Brians. Copyright © 1998 by Paul Brians, Department of English, Washington State University. **296** Excerpt from *Through African Eyes Volume 1: The Past; the Road to Independence* by Leon E. Clark. Copyright © 1988, 1991 by Leon E. Clark. Published by CITE Books and Distributed by Apex Press. **307** "Letter to His Small Children" from *Li Po and Tu Fu Poems*, translated by Arthur Cooper. Copyright © 1973 by Arthur Cooper. **529** Excerpt from *The Black Jacobins: Toussaint L'Ouverture and the San Domingo Revolution* by C. L. R. James. Copyright © 1963 by Random House, Inc. **579** From "A Foreign Volunteer at the Battle of the Volturno, April 2, 1860" from *Garibaldi: Great Lives Observed*, edited by Denis Mack Smith. Copyright © 1969 by Prentice Hall, Inc. Reprinted by permission of the author. **717** Excerpt from "Requiem," translated by Robin Kemball, Copyright © 1974 by Robin Kemball, from *Selected Poems* by Anna Akhmatova, edited and translated by Walter Arndt. Reprinted by permission of Ardis. **719** From *Assignment in Utopia* by Eugene Lyons. Copyright © 1937, by Harcourt, Brace & World, Inc., and reproduced with their permission. Published in Great Britain by George G. Harrap & Co. Ltd. Reprinted by permission. **723** Excerpt from "Zeferino Diego Ferreira: The Life Story of a Villista," by Laura Cummings. Copyright © 1999 by University of Arizona *Journal of the Southwest*. **737** Excerpt from *Japanese Imperialism and the Massacre in Nanjing*, translated by Robert P. Gray. Copyright © 1996. **765** "Sophie Yaari Tells Her Story" from *To Save A Life: Stories of Jewish Rescue* by Ellen Land-Weber. Copyright © 1984, 1999 to Ellen Land-Weber. **774** Four lines of "In Memory of W. B. Yeats," from *W. H. Auden: Collected Poems* by W. H. Auden. Copyright © 1940 and renewed 1968 by W. H. Auden. Reprinted by permission of Random House, Inc. and Faber and Faber Limited. **786** From "Major Werner Pluskat, aged 32, 352 Artillery Regiment, 352nd Division" from *Nothing Less Than Victory: An Oral History of D-Day* by Russell Miller. Copyright © 1993 by Russell Miller. Reprinted by permission of Peters Fraser & Dunlop Group, Ltd. **825** "No Time" by Nguyen Sa from *A Thousand Years of Vietnamese Poetry* (ed. Nguyen Ngoc Bich). Copyright © 1962, 1967, 1968, 1969, 1970, 1971, 1972, 1974, by Asia Society, Inc. **833** "A Man's Place" from *The New York Times Magazine*, May 16, 1999 by Claudia Goldin in a conversation moderated by Michael Weinstein. Copyright © 1999, The New York Times Company. **847** Quoted by Alexander Solzhenitsyn in *The New York Times*, January 4, 1997. Copyright © 1997, The New York Times Company. **855** "Liberal Leaders Warn Yeltsin to Protect His People," Reuters Limited, October 6, 1999. Copyright © 1999 Reuters Limited. **859** "The Art and Practice of Japanese Management" by John Micklethwait and Adrian Wooldridge. This article is adapted from *The Witch Doctors*. (c) 1996 by Times Books. **879** From "A Modern Rouge et Noir," translated by Deborah Cao and Lawrence Tedesco from *Voices from the Whirlwind: An Oral History of the Chinese Cultural Revolution*, edited by Feng Jicai. Copyright © 1990 by Foreign Language Press, Beijing, China. Reprinted by permission of the publisher. **901** Excerpt adapted from "A Man is Like a Stalk of Wheat" from *The Yellow Wind* by David Grossman. Copyright © 1988 by David Grossman and Koteret Rashit. English translation copyright © 1988 by Haim Watzman. Reprinted by permission of Farrar, Straus & Giroux, Inc. **910** Excerpt from "Negro Nation of Ghana is Born in Africa" by Thomas F. Brady. Copyright © 1957, The New York Times Company. **939** Excerpt from *Revolution Through Peace* by Dom Helder Camara, translated by Amparo McLean. English translation copyright © 1971 by Harper & Row Publishers, Inc. **954** Excerpt from "For Brazil's Street Children, a Happy Path to Take" by James Brooke. Copyright © 1993, The New York Times Company. **968** Excerpt from *The Mahabharata*, translated by J. A. B. van Buitenen. Copyright © 1973 by University of Chicago Press. **971** From *The Koran*, translated by N. J. Dawood. Copyright © 1956, 1959, 1966, 1968, 1974 by N. J. Dawood. Published by Penguin Books, Ltd. **973** "The Prolouge" from *The Canterbury Tales* by Geoffrey Chaucer, translated into modern English by Nevill Coghill. Copyright © 1951, 1958, 1960 by Neville Coghill. Reproduced by permission of Penguin Books Ltd. **975** "The True History of the Conquest of New Spain" from *The Bernal Diaz Chronicles*, translated by Albert Idell. Translation copyright © 1956 by Albert Idell. Used by permission of Doubleday, a division of Bantam Doubleday Dell Publishing Group, Inc. **977** Excerpt from *Don Quixote of La Mancha* by Miguel de Cervantes; translated by Walter Starkie. Copyright © 1957 by Macmillan & Co., Ltd., London. Translation copyright © 1964 by Walter Starkie and published by The New American Library. **985** Excerpt from *The Autobiography of Fukuzawa Yukichi*, by Fukuzawa Yukichi, translated by Eiichi Kiyooka. Translation copyright © 1960 by Eiichi Kiyooka. Copyright © 1966 by Columbia University Press. **986** Excerpt from *All Quiet on the Western Front* by Erich Maria Remarque. Copyright © 1929, 1930 by Little, Brown and Company; copyright © renewed 1957, 1958 by Erich Maria Remarque. **991** Excerpt from *Things Fall Apart* by Chinua Achebe. Copyright © 1959 by Chinua Achebe. Published by Doubleday Dell Publishing Group, Inc. Originally published by Heinemann Educational Books, Ltd. **994, 998, 999** "Perestroika" by Mikhail Gorbechev, "Glory and Hope" by Nelson Mandela, and "The Outlook for China: Human Rights" by Harry Wu from *Vital Speeches Of the Day*. Used by permission of The City News. **995** "New Years Address" from *Uncaptive Minds* by Vaclav Havel. Reprinted by permission of Uncaptive Minds, a publication of the Institute for Democracy in Eastern Europe. **996** "Latin America: the Democracy Option" by Mario Vargas Llosa from *Harper's Magazine*. Copyright © 1987 by Harper's Magazine. Reproduced from the June issue by special permission. **997** From *Freedom From Fear and Other Writings* by Aung San Suu Kyi, forwarded by Vaclav Havel, translated by Michael Aris. Translation copyright © 1991 by Aung San Suu Kyi and Michael Aris. Used by permission of Penguin, a division of Penguin Books USA, Inc.

Note: Every effort has been made to locate the copyright owner of material reprinted in this book. Omissions brought to our attention will be corrected in subsequent printings.